FREE
MARKETS
and
SOCIAL
JUSTICE

☐

FREE MARKETS *and* SOCIAL JUSTICE

☐

CASS R. SUNSTEIN

New York   Oxford
Oxford University Press
1997

Oxford University Press

Oxford   New York

Athens   Auckland   Bangkok   Bogota   Bombay   Buenos Aires
Calcutta   Cape Town   Dar es Salaam   Delhi   Florence   Hong Kong
Istanbul   Karachi   Kuala Lumpur   Madras   Madrid   Melbourne
Mexico City   Nairobi   Paris   Singapore   Taipei   Tokyo   Toronto

and associated companies in
Berlin   Ibadan

Published by Oxford University Press, Inc.
198 Madison Avenue, New York, New York 10016

Oxford is a registered trademark of Oxford University Press

Library of Congress Cataloging-in-Publication Data
Sunstein, Cass R.
Free markets and social justice / Cass R. Sunstein.
p. cm.
Includes index.
ISBN 0-19-510272-X
1. Law—Economic aspects. 2. Free enterprise. 3. Social justice.
I. Title.
K487.E3S86   1997
330.12′2—dc20   96-5503

1 3 5 7 9 8 6 4 2

Printed in the United States of America
on acid-free paper

Acknowledgments

My greatest debt is to those of my colleagues at the University of Chicago who have tried to teach me something about economics, especially Douglas Baird, Gary Becker, Richard Craswell, Richard Epstein, William Landes, Randall Picker, Richard Posner, and Alan Sykes. I am grateful for their patience, good humor, and generosity with an occasionally skeptical and frequently confused pupil. Craswell and Posner offered detailed and exceptionally helpful comments on the manuscript; I know that I have not been able to respond to all of their concerns, but the book is much better because of their assistance. Becker has been extremely helpful on some of the foundational issues and especially generous in discussing his own closely related work in progress. As I was finishing the manuscript, Richard Thaler, a significant influence on this book, joined the University of Chicago, and I benefited from a number of discussions with him. Many other friends and colleagues have provided valuable conversation and comments on aspects of this book. I single out for particular thanks Bruce Ackerman, Jon Elster, Stephen Holmes, Martha Nussbaum, Susan Moller Okin, Richard Stewart, and David Strauss. My editor, Helen McInnis, offered valuable suggestions and much-appreciated encouragement. I am also grateful to Sophie Clark, who provided valuable research assistance, and to Marlene Vellinga, who performed a wide range of secretarial tasks.

The essays in this book were written between 1990 and 1995. They have been significantly revised, partly to minimize repetition, partly to make sure the discussion is as current as possible, and most important because in many places I was able to clarify and improve the argument.

The revised essays first appeared under the following titles and in the following places; I am grateful for permission to reprint them here.

"Preferences and Politics," 20 *Phil. & Pub. Aff.* 3 (1991); "Social Norms and Social Roles," 96 *Colum. L. Rev.* (1996); "Incommensurability and Valuation in Law," 92 *Mich. L. Rev.* 779 (1994); "Well-Being and the State," 107 *Harv. L. Rev.* 1303 (1994); "Reinventing the Regulatory State," 62 *U. Chi. L. Rev.* 1 (1995); "Why Markets Won't Stop Discrimination," 8 *Soc. Phil & Policy* 21

(1991); "The First Amendment in Cyberspace," 104 *Yale L.J.* 1755 (1995); "On Property and Constitutionalism," 14 *Cardozo L. Rev.* 907 (1993); "Political Equality and Unintended Consequences," 94 *Colum. L. Rev.* 1390 (1994); "Paradoxes of the Regulatory State," 57 *U. Chi. L. Rev.* 407 (1990); "Endogenous Preferences, Environmental Law," 22 *J. Legal Stud.* 217 (1993); "Democratizing America Through Law," 25 *Suffolk L. Rev.* 949 (1992); "Health-Health Tradeoffs," 63 *U. Chi. L. Rev.* (1996); "Congress, Constitutional Moments, and the Cost-Benefit State," 48 *Stan. L. Rev.* 247 (1996).

Contents

FREE
MARKETS
and
SOCIAL
JUSTICE

Introduction

We are in the midst of a period of mounting enthusiasm for free markets. This is of course true in many of the former Communist nations. It is true for much of the West as well, prominently including England and the United States.

Free markets are often defended as an engine of economic productivity, and properly so. But they are also said to be required for social justice, and here things become far more complex. Certainly there are connections between free markets and social justice. A system aspiring to social justice aspires to liberty, and a system of free markets seems to promise liberty, because it allows people to trade goods and services as they wish. In fact, a system of free markets seems to promise not merely liberty but equality of an important sort as well, since everyone in a free market is given an equal right to transact and participate in market arrangements. This form of equality should not be trivialized or disparaged. For example, race and sex discrimination has often consisted of exclusions of certain classes of people from the market domain. In both South Africa and the United States, discriminatory practices frequently took the form of incursions on free markets in employment.

An appreciation of the virtues of free markets has been an important part of the economic analysis of law, perhaps the most influential development in legal education in the last quarter-century, and a development with growing effects on public policy in the United States and abroad. As it operates in law schools, economic analysis is concerned above all with the consequences of legal rules. Often its practitioners have asked whether intrusions on free markets have desirable consequences. If the minimum wage is increased, what, exactly, will happen? What are the real-world consequences of bans on discrimination, legal rules for controlling air pollution, and rent control laws? There are limits to how much economic theory can say on such issues; empirical evidence is necessary. But by looking at the effects of law on incentives, economics can point in the right direction. Often it can show that the consequences of intrusions on markets will be unfortunate or even perverse. The economic analysis of law has produced significant advances, many of which are discussed in this book. Much remains to be learned.

This book is not, however, a simple celebration of free markets, and it raises a number of questions about economic analysis of law in its conventional form. Free markets can produce economic inefficiency and (worse) a great deal of injustice. Even well-functioning economic markets should not be identified with freedom itself. Freedom is a complex notion, to say the least, and free markets can sharply limit freedom as that term is usually understood. In fact, free markets depend on a range of coercive legal interventions, including the law of property, which can be a serious intrusion on the freedom of people who lack ownership rights. And it should not be necessary to emphasize that important forms of equality—including race and sex equality—can be undermined, not promoted, by free markets. Race discrimination is often fueled by market forces.

Moreover, economics—at least as it is used in the conventional economic analysis of law—often works with tools that, while illuminating, may be crude or lead to important errors. Consider, for example, descriptive or "positive" economics. The economic analysis of law has been built on a certain conception of human rationality, in which people are seen as "rational profit-maximizers." For some purposes, this is a helpful foundation. Certainly it is true that most people try, most of the time, to find ways of promoting their own ends. But it is not always clear in what sense human beings can be said to be "rational" or "profit-maximizers." The motivational foundations of human behavior have enormous complexity. Sometimes people do not seem at all rational. Sometimes they are ignorant and sometimes they seem to defeat their own goals. People rely on rules of thumb, or heuristic devices, that cause them badly to misunderstand probabilities and facts; this can lead to irrationality for individuals and societies alike. Sometimes people undervalue their own futures, or suffer from weakness of will, or choose what they know, on reflection, they ought not to choose. Sometimes people care not just about social outcomes, but also about the "meaning" of such outcomes, that is, the values expressed in and by the outcomes. This point very much bears on law, in such areas as environmental protection, race and sex equality, and occupational safety and health (chapter 2).

Above all, social norms are an important determinant of behavior, and they have received far too little attention from those interested in free markets, economic analysis of law, and social justice. A number of puzzles and anomalies underlie human decisions. Analysis of law, economic or otherwise, would do well to incorporate an understanding of these puzzles and anomalies (chapters 2 and 4).

Thus far, I have been discussing descriptive or positive economics. If we turn to the evaluative side—to questions about what the law should be or do—economic analysis of law encounters equally serious problems. In its usual form, economics offers an inadequate understanding of social welfare. Often it is concerned with the satisfaction of existing preferences. This is far from an unworthy goal; the frustration of peoples' preferences can lead to misery and injustice. But in any society, existing preferences should not be taken as natural or sacrosanct. They are a function of context. Sometimes they are a product of deprivation, injustice, or excessive limits in available opportunities.

Moreover, the economists' conception of social welfare is too "flat," insofar as it evaluates diverse social goods along the same metric. People care about things not just in terms of amounts, but also in different ways. Some human goods, like cash, are simply for use. But people value things for reasons other than use. They respect other people; sometimes they love each other; they see some things, like a painting or a beach, as objects of awe and wonder (chapter 3). A well-functioning legal system attempts to make space for people's diverse valuation of diverse human goods. This point bears on the uses and the limits of free markets.

More particularly, this book develops seven basic themes:

1. *The myth of laissez-faire.* The notion of "laissez-faire" is a grotesque misdescription of what free markets actually require and entail. Free markets depend for their existence on law. We cannot have a system of private property without legal rules, telling people who owns what, imposing penalties for trespass, and saying who can do what to whom. Without the law of contract, freedom of contract, as we know and live it, would be impossible. (People in Eastern Europe are learning this lesson all too well.) Moreover, the law that underlies free markets is coercive in the sense that in addition to facilitating individual transactions, it stops people from doing many things that they would like to do. This point is not by any means a critique of free markets. But it suggests that markets should be understood as a legal construct, to be evaluated on the basis of whether they promote human interests, rather than as a part of nature and the natural order, or as a simple way of promoting voluntary interactions.

2. *Preference formation and social norms.* It is important not only to know what choices and preferences are, but also to know how they are formed, and whether they are really connected with human well-being. Unjust institutions can breed preferences that produce individual and collective harm. Severe deprivation—including poverty—can be an obstacle to the development of good preferences, choices, and beliefs. For example, a society in which people "prefer" to become drug addicts, or violent criminals, has a serious problem. Such preferences are likely to be an artifact of existing social norms, and those norms may disserve human freedom or well-being.

In this light a society should be concerned not simply and not entirely with satisfying the preferences that people already have, but more broadly with providing freedom in the process of preference-formation. Social practices, including law, will inevitably affect preferences. There is no way for a legal system to remain neutral with respect to preference formation. In these circumstances it is fully legitimate for government and law to try to shape preferences in the right way, not only through education, but also (for example) through laws forbidding racial discrimination, environmental degradation, and sexual harassment, and through efforts to encourage attention to public issues and to diverse points of view.

3. *The contextual character of choice.* Choices are a function of context. If someone takes a job that includes a certain danger, or chooses not to recycle on a Tuesday in March, or discriminates against a certain female job candidate, we cannot infer a great deal about what he "prefers" or "values." All of these choices might be different in a different context. Our discriminator may support a law banning discrimination; people who do not recycle in March may recycle in May or June, and they may well support laws that mandate recycling. Economists and economically oriented analysts of law sometimes think that they can derive, from particular choices, large-scale or acontextual accounts of how much people value various goods. This is a mistake, involving extravagant inferences from modest findings.

4. *The importance of fair distribution.* It is necessary to know not simply whether a society is rich in economic terms, but also how its resources are distributed. Thus a problem with gross domestic product, as a measure of social well-being, is its obliviousness to distributional concerns. Free markets can help fuel economic growth, and economic growth can improve people's lives. But many citizens are not benefited by growth, and at a minimum government should take steps to combat human deprivation and misery in the midst of growth. In any case, it is important to develop standards for measuring social well-being that allow people, in their capacity as citizens and voters, to focus on the issue of distribution.

5. *The diversity of human goods.* I have noted that human beings value things not just in different amounts, but also in different ways. They value a friend in one way; a park in another; a species in another; a spouse in another; an heirloom in another; a large check in another; a pet in still another. The way they value a funny movie is qualitatively different from the way they value a tragedy, a mountain, a beach, or a car. Insofar as economics uses a single metric or scale of value, it flattens qualitative differences. For some purposes the flattening is very useful, but for other purposes it is harmful. Such qualitative differences can be crucial to private life, public life, and social science.

These points help show the inadequacy, in some settings, of social ordering through markets. Some goods should not be sold on markets at all; consider the right to vote or the right to be free from discrimination on the basis of sex. Markets work best when (what we rightly treat as) consumption choices are at issue. In a liberal society, some choices should be understood not to involve consumption choices at all. For example, the choice to vote, and the decision how to vote, are not best understood as involving mere consumption. How a person votes should depend not on anyone's "willingness to pay," but on the reasons offered for and against a certain candidate. The right to vote is debased if it is understood as simply a matter of "buying" something.

This claim bears on a range of issues involving the use of markets for distributing such goods as reproductive capacity, sex, endangered species, and environmental amenities in general. Some goods are best allocated on the basis of an inquiry not into economic value, but into the reasons offered for any particular allocation.

6. *Law can shape preferences*. We have seen that no market can exist without legal rules. Legal rules must also allocate entitlements. In a system of private property, it is necessary to say who owns what, at least in the first instance. It is also necessary to create rules of tort law, saying who can do what to whom, and who must pay for injuries and harms. As a great deal of empirical work has shown, these legal rules, allocating basic entitlements, have effects on choices and preferences. Someone who has been given a legal entitlement —to chocolate bars, clean air, freedom from sexual harassment, environmental goods—may well value the relevant good more than he would if the good had been allocated to someone else in the first instance. The preference-shaping effects of the initial allocation via law raise important questions for the analysis of law and free markets. They suggest that government and law may not be able to leave preferences "as they are."

7. *Puzzles of human rationality*. Are human beings rational? What criteria should we use to answer that question? These questions have become all the more urgent in light of recent work attempting to apply economic models of rationality to race and sex discrimination, family choice, pollution problems, aging, even sexual encounters (and hence to the problem of AIDS). Such work has been highly illuminating, but it is important to know in exactly what sense people might be said to be (or not to be) "rational" when they choose spouses, recycle garbage, reject employees of certain kinds, or engage in sexual or risky activity. Any views on such matters may well depend on a controversial account of what it means to be rational.

I am especially interested in the consequences for law and policy of recent experimental and theoretical work on rationality, social norms, and individual valuations. This work suggests that people's choices and judgments are quite different from what traditional economists predict. People's choices are a function of the distinctive social role in which they find themselves, and we may act irrationally or quasi-rationally. In particular, this work points to the important role of social norms involving fairness, reciprocity, and cooperation in producing individual choice. If we do not uncover the relationship between rationality and social norms, we will make major mistakes in designing policies to accomplish our goals.

This book investigates these points in many different contexts, involving property, protection of nature, race and sex discrimination, broadcasting, occupational safety, and much more. I do not take these points to pose across-the-board challenges to the use of free markets. On the contrary, I argue that in some situations, constitutions themselves should protect free markets (chapter 7), and also that market-oriented policies are far better in the areas of health, safety, and the environment than is generally recognized (chapters 13 and 14). But free markets are a tool, to be used when they promote human purposes, and to be abandoned when they fail to do so. Moreover, economic analysis of law should be based on an understanding of how human beings actually behave. An inquiry into these topics has a substantial empirical direction, and I shall refer to empirical matters—involving smoking, polluting, discriminating, and other issues—at many points. But it is also important to be clear on our underlying judgments about social justice.

The book comes in three basic parts. Part I deals with foundations—with the appropriate role of existing "preferences," the importance of social norms, the question whether human goods are commensurable, and issues of distributional equity. I claim that the term "preference" is highly ambiguous and that people's "preferences," as they are expressed in the market domain, should not be deemed sacrosanct. On the contrary, market "preferences" are sometimes a product of background injustice or of social norms that people do not really like. Acting as citizens, people should be permitted to change those norms. I also argue that human goods are not commensurable; there is no metric by which we can assess such goods as environmental quality, employment, more leisure time, less racial discrimination, and so forth. My discussion of "measuring well-being" is designed to respond to this problem; my general treatment of incommensurability shows how the absence of a unitary metric plays a large role in both law and daily life.

Part II deals with rights. The basic goal is to show that markets have only a partial and instrumental role in the protection of rights. In a claim of special relevance to current disputes in the United States, I argue that free markets are not likely to stop discrimination on the basis of race and sex. On the contrary, markets often promote discrimination. I also claim that in recent years, the free speech *principle* has been wrongly identified with free speech *markets*—as in the striking claim by a recent chairman of the Federal Communications Commission that television "is just another appliance," or "a toaster with pictures." Against this view, I argue that the free speech principle is mostly about democratic deliberation, not about free markets. This idea has a range of consequences for how we think about (for example) radio, the Internet, and cable television. This claim certainly bears on the subject of campaign finance regulation, to which a chapter is devoted.

But Part II shows that markets can play an important role in a regime of rights. Thus I argue that constitutions, at least in Eastern Europe, should attempt to protect private property and market ordering. This argument depends on the claim that constitutions should be "countercultural," in the sense that they should protect against those aspects of a country's culture and traditions that are most likely to produce harm. In Eastern Europe, there is a pressing need to establish the institutions of a civil society, including a degree of market exchange.

Part III deals with regulation, especially in the context of risks to life and health. A common theme is that reliance on "free markets" would be a huge mistake for regulatory policy and that deregulation would often be a foolish solution. On the other hand, many of the problems in federal regulation in the United States stem from Soviet-style command-and-control regulation, which produces billions of dollars in wasted money and laws that are far too ineffectual in improving health and saving lives. American government does not set sensible priorities; it does not use the best regulatory tools; risk regulation sometimes increases risks. Regulation is also an ineffective tool for redistributing wealth. Thus, the essays in Part III try to develop approaches that would promote both economic and democratic goals. A particular theme is the uses and limits of cost-benefit analysis. Balancing of costs and benefits is far better than absolutism. But everything depends on how "costs" and "benefits" are specified. I suggest that many statutes have goals other than economic efficiency, and that such statutes are entirely legitimate. With respect to statutes not based on economic grounds, we should try to promote social commitments in the most cost-effective manner.

I also suggest that it is time to move beyond the increasingly tired and decreasingly helpful question whether we should have "more" or "less" government or "more" or "less" in the way of free markets. These dichotomies are far to crude. As we have seen, markets depend on government. Sometimes government can improve existing markets by creating good incentives for socially desirable behavior. Sometimes markets should be supplemented by government services, like education, job training programs, and health care. There is no inconsistency in urging greater reliance on market instruments in some areas while insisting on a larger role for the public sector in others. In any case, future problems are not usefully approached by asking whether there should be "more" or "less" regulation. The real question is what kinds of regulations (emphatically including those that make markets possible) promote human well-being in different contexts.

In a book of this sort it would be far too ambitious to attempt to announce a theory of justice. But debates that seem intractable at the most abstract levels may admit of solutions when the question is narrowed and sharpened, and hence an inquiry into the relation between markets and justice may be most productive when we draw close attention to the setting in which market remedies are proposed. To the seven points I have listed above we may therefore add one more: Achievement of social justice is a higher value than the protection of free markets; markets are mere instruments to be evaluated by their effects. Whether free markets promote social justice is an impossible question to answer in the abstract. Far more progress can be made by examining the contexts in which markets, adjustments of markets, and alternatives to markets are proposed as solutions.

I

FOUNDATIONAL
ISSUES

Preferences and Politics

The drafting of the U.S. Constitution, it is often said, signaled a rejection of conceptions of politics founded on classical ideals in favor of a quite different modern view. The precise terms of the supposed shift are not altogether clear, but it is possible to identify the most prominent strands. The classical conception assumes a relatively homogeneous people and prizes active participation by the polity's citizenry. In the classical conception, the polity is self-consciously concerned with the character of the citizens; it seeks to inculcate virtue in them and to profit from a commitment to the public good. Plato said that politics is the "art whose business it is to care for souls"; and under the classical conception, civic virtue, not private interest, is the wellspring of political behavior. Whether or not the state imposes a "comprehensive view" on the nation,[1] it relies relatively little on private rights to constrain government. The underlying vision of "republican" politics is one of frequent participation and deliberation in the service of decision, by the citizenry, about the sorts of values according to which the nation will operate.

In the modern account, by contrast, government is above all respectful of the diverse conceptions of the good held by its many constituents. People are taken as they are, not as they might be. Modern government has no concern with souls. It does not try to inculcate virtue. Although electoral processes are ensured, no special premium is placed on citizen participation. Self-interest, not virtue, is understood to be the usual motivating force of political behavior. Politics is typically, if not always, an effort to aggregate private interests. It is surrounded by checks, in the form of rights, protecting private liberty and private property from public intrusion.

In this system, the goal of the polity is quite modest: the creation of the basic ground rules under which people can satisfy their desires and go about their private affairs. Much of this is said to be captured in *The Federalist* No. 10, in which Madison redescribed the so-called republican problem of the corruption of virtue as the so-called liberal problem of the control of factions, which, as Madison had it, were inevitable if freedom was to be preserved.

In fact, the conventional division between the American founders and their classical predecessors is far too crude. The founders attempted to create a deliberative democracy, one in which the institutions of representation, checks and balances, and federalism would ensure a deliberative process among political equals rather than an aggregation of interests.[2] But respect for private preferences, rather than collective deliberation about public values or the good life, does seem to be a distinguishing feature of American constitutionalism. Indeed, the view that government should refuse to evaluate privately held beliefs about individual welfare, which are said to be irreducibly "subjective," links a wide range of views about both governmental structure and individual rights.

I want to explore the question whether a contemporary democracy might not sometimes override the private preferences and beliefs of its citizens, not in spite of its salutary liberalism but because of it. It is one thing to allow for and to affirm competing conceptions of the good; it is quite another to suggest that political outcomes must generally be justified by, or even should always respect, private preferences, especially as these are expressed in the market domain. A large part of my focus here is on the phenomenon of *endogenous preferences*. By this term I mean to indicate that preferences are not fixed, global, and stable, but are instead adaptive to a wide range of factors—including the context in which the preference is expressed, the existing legal rules, social norms, past consumption choices, and culture in general. The phenomenon of endogenous preferences casts doubt on the notion that a democratic government ought to respect private desires and beliefs in all or almost all contexts. It bears on a number of particular problems as well, and I take up many of these problems later in this book.

The argument proceeds in several stages. In section I, I discuss some problems in the whole idea of "preferences" and set forth some fairly conventional ideas about welfare and autonomy in order to argue against the idea that government ought never or rarely to override private preferences. In section II, I contend that in three categories of cases, private preferences, as expressed in consumption choices, should be overridden. The first category involves what I call collective judgments, including considered beliefs, aspirations for social justice, and altruistic goals; the second involves preferences that have adapted to undue limitations in available opportunities or to unjust background conditions; the third category points to intrapersonal collective action problems that, over a lifetime, impair personal welfare or freedom. In all of these cases, I suggest, a democracy should be free and is perhaps obliged to override private preferences.

I. Against Subjective Welfarism

Should a constitutional democracy take preferences as the basis for political choice? In contemporary politics, law, and especially economics, a conventional answer is affirmative. Modern economics, for example, is dominated by a conception of welfare based on the satisfaction of existing preferences, as measured by willingness to pay in the market domain; in politics and law, something called "paternalism" is disfavored in both the public and private realms. But the idea that government ought to take preferences as the basis for political decisions is a quite modern one. This is not to say that the idea is without foundations. Partly a function of the perceived (though greatly overstated) difficulty of making interpersonal comparisons of utility, the idea is also a product of the epistemological difficulties of assessing a person's preferences in terms of their true connection with individual welfare, and, perhaps most of all, the genuine political dangers of allowing government to engage in such inquiries.

The constellation of ideas that emerges from these considerations has been exceptionally influential. It embodies a conception of political justification that might be described as "subjective welfarism." On this view, the government, even or perhaps especially in a democracy, should attend exclusively to conceptions of welfare as subjectively held by its citizens, and these conceptions are best found in the market domain. A wide range of prominent approaches to politics turns out to reflect aspects of subjective welfarism. These include, for example, certain forms of utilitarianism; the view that some version of economic efficiency ought to be treated as the foundational norm for political life; opposition to paternalism in public and private life; approaches to politics modeled on bargaining theory (rational or otherwise); and conceptions of politics that see the democratic process as an effort to aggregate individual preferences.

It is important to understand that subjective welfarism, thus defined, may or may not be accompanied by a broader notion that ethical and moral questions should generally be treated in welfarist or subjectivist terms. It is as a political conception, rather than an ethical one, that subjective welfarism underlies a wide range of approaches to public life, including ideas about institutional arrangements and individual or collective rights. What I want to argue here is that subjective welfarism, even as a political conception, is unsupportable by reference to principles of autonomy or welfare, the very ideas that are said to give rise to it.

Conceptual Puzzles

An initial problem is that the notion of a "preference" is quite ambiguous—perhaps fatally so (see chapter 2 for a more detailed discussion). Suppose someone takes a job as a welder, or recycles newspapers, or buys aspirin rather than chocolate bars on a weekend afternoon. The idea of a "preference" might be understood as simply a choice, as in the idea, influential within economics, of the "revealed preference." It is of course illuminating to catalogue choices. But if this is what we are doing, it is unnecessary and perhaps misleading to use the notion of a "preference." If we are really talking about choices, we can dispense with the idea of "preference" entirely. We will have a list of choices. Perhaps we can work with that list.

But if we are really working just with choices, we will encounter many problems. Choices are inarticulate, and hence unhelpful predictors of behavior, without an account of what lies behind them. Take a simple example. If

Jones prefers X over Y, we might think that he will not prefer Y over X or Z; the introduction of the third alternative, Z, ought not to change Jones's preferences for X over Y. But we can readily imagine cases in which the new alternative does precisely this.[3] Jones might, for example, always select the second largest piece of cake, or might want to be a person of relative moderation. Empirical work has encountered an effect called "extremeness aversion," in which people make choices that avoid the extremes.[4] It is necessary to inquire into motivational issues of this kind in order to draw inferences from choices.

More broadly, choices are a function of prevailing social norms and hence of context, which can activate particular norms. If you are in a certain group, you may well choose a drink of Perrier over a Coca-Cola, or vice-versa, because of local practices. You may purchase an American car, or not, because of existing norms in your community. For this reason, a choice of one good over another may tell us very little about further choices, unless we know about the motivations and context of the choice.

If this is right, it is necessary to explain behavior not only by reference to choices but by reference to some account of what underlies choices, or of what choices are *for,* and in this way to introduce an account of motivation. And if this is right, it is impossible to explain behavior by reference to choices, without using the apparatus that the "revealed preference" idea was intended to eliminate. We should conclude that if preferences are identified with choices, and if choices are used as a basis for making claims about policy or prediction, we will encounter large difficulties.

On the other hand, the notion of a "preference" is often meant to refer not to choices themselves, but to something that lies behind and accounts for choices.[5] But this idea introduces difficulties of its own—indeed, the very difficulties that the "revealed preference" idea was intended to overcome. Jones takes a job; Smith buys aspirin instead of a chocolate bar; Wilson purchases a car equipped with an airbag. If we think of a preference as something that lies behind a choice, what is it exactly? Is it a steady mental state? A physical entity? How can it be identified or described? Internal mental states are extraordinarily complex, and the constellation of motivations that lies behind a choice in one setting may be quite different from the constellation that produces a choice in a different time and place. People's decisions are based on whims, second-order preferences, aspirations, judgments, drives of various kinds, and so forth, each potentially coming to the fore depending on the context.

In this light, it is far from simple to identify a "preference" as an acontextual entity that stands behind choices and explains them. For example, a decision not to recycle is a choice, but the relationship between that choice and an independent entity called a "preference" is often obscure. A choice to drink a glass of Perrier, rather than Coca-Cola, may turn on complex internal desires and judgments that cannot be captured in any simple way. These considerations suggest that it might well be best to work in a more fine-grained way with choices on the one hand and with complex mental states on the other. Those mental states will produce different outcomes in different situations.

Is It Possible for Government Simply to "Respect" Preferences?

Let us put this point to one side, for the moment, and identify preferences with choices as these are expressed in the market domain. The initial objection to the view that government should take preferences, thus understood, "as they are," or as the basis for political outcomes, is one of impossibility. Whether people have a preference for a commodity, a right, or anything else is in part a function of whether the government has allocated it to them in the first instance.[6] There is no way to avoid the task of initially allocating an entitlement (short of anarchy). A system of so-called laissez-faire is not one of "no allocation" or "no regulation"; instead, it requires government to set out a range of initial entitlements as reflected in the law of contract, tort, and property. The decision to grant an entitlement to one person frequently makes that person value that entitlement more than if the right had been allocated to someone else. (It also makes other people value it less than they would otherwise.) Government must not only allocate rights to one person or another; it must also decide whether or not to make the right alienable through markets or otherwise. The initial allocation serves to reflect, to legitimate, and to reinforce social understandings about presumptive rights of ownership. That allocation can have an important causal connection to individual perceptions of the good or right in question.

For example, a decision to give employees a right to organize, farmers a right to be free from water pollution, or women a right not to be subjected to sexual harassment will have an impact on social attitudes toward labor organization, clean water, and sexual harassment. The allocation therefore has an effect on social attitudes toward the relevant rights and on their valuation by both current owners and would-be purchasers. And when preferences are a function of legal rules, the government cannot take preferences as given and work from them. Moreover, the rules cannot be justified by reference to the preferences, which do not predate the rules.

There is also evidence that the initial allocation creates the basic "reference state" from which values and judgments of fairness are subsequently made, and those judgments affect preferences and private willingness to pay.[7] Of course, a decision to make an entitlement alienable or inalienable (consider the right to vote or reproductive capacities) can have preference-shaping effects. Because of the preference-shaping effects of the rules of allocation, it is difficult to see how a government might even attempt to take preferences "as given" or as the basis for decisions in any global sense.

Welfare and Autonomy

To some degree this concern might be put to one side. Surely there is a difference between a government that concerns itself self-consciously and on an ongoing basis with private preferences and a government that sets up the basic rules of property, contract, and tort, and then lets things turn out however they may. If this distinction can be sustained, disagreements about the relationship between politics and preferences turn on competing notions of autonomy (or freedom) on the one hand and welfare on the other. Subjective welfarism is founded on the claim that an approach that treats preferences as sovereign is most likely to promote both individual autonomy, rightly conceived, and individual or social welfare.

It will be useful to begin with welfare. Even if one accepted a purely welfarist view, one might think that the process of promoting welfare should take place not by satisfying current preferences (especially as expressed in the market domain) but by promoting those preferences and satisfying them to such an extent as is consonant with the best or highest conception of human happiness. This view is connected with older (and some current) forms of utilitarianism; it also has roots in Aristotle. Here one does not take existing preferences as given, and one does not put all preferences on the same plane. A criterion of welfare remains the ultimate one, but the system is not focused solely on preference satisfaction, since it insists that welfare and preference satisfaction are entirely different things.

A central point here is that preferences are shifting and endogenous rather than exogenous, and as a result are a function of current information, consumption patterns, social norms, legal rules, and general social pressures. An effort to identify welfare with preference satisfaction might be easier to understand if preferences were rigidly fixed at some early age, or if learning were impossible. If this were so, democratic efforts to reflect on, change, or select preferences would breed only frustration. But because preferences are shifting and endogenous, and because the satisfaction of existing preferences might lead to unhappy or deprived lives, a democracy that treats all preferences as fixed will lose important opportunities for welfare gains.

With respect to welfare, then, the problem posed by the endogeneity of preferences is not the origin of desires but their (more than occasional) malleability. At least if the relevant cases can be confidently identified in advance, and if government action can be justified by reference to particular good reasons, the argument for democratic interference will be quite powerful. Respect for preferences that have resulted from unjust background conditions and that will lead to human deprivation or misery hardly appears the proper course for a liberal democracy.

For example, legal rules prohibiting or discouraging addictive behavior may have significant advantages in terms of welfare. Regulation of heroin or cigarettes (at least if the regulation can be made effective) might well increase aggregate social welfare, by decreasing harmful behavior, removing the secondary effects of those harms, and producing more healthful and satisfying lives. Similarly, governmental action relating to the environment, broadcasting, or culture—encouraging or requiring, for example, protection of beautiful areas, broadcasting about public issues, high-quality programs, or public support of artistic achievement—may in the end generate (or, better, prevent obstacles to the generation of) new preferences, providing increased satisfaction and in the end producing considerable welfare gains. The same may well be true of antidiscrimination measures, which affect the desires and attitudes of discriminators and victims alike. A system that takes existing private preferences as the basis for political choice will sacrifice important opportunities for social improvement on welfarist criteria. This point was a crucial one in the early stages of utilitarian thought; it has been lost more recently with the shift from older forms of welfarism to the idea of "revealed preferences."

Moreover, the satisfaction of private preferences, whatever their content and origins, does not respond to a persuasive conception of autonomy (or freedom). Many preferences are a result of social norms and conditions that make them far from autonomous. The notion of autonomy should refer instead to decisions reached with a full and vivid awareness of available opportunities, with reference to relevant information, and without illegitimate or excessive constraints on the process of preference formation. When these conditions are not met, decisions should be described as unfree or nonautonomous; for this reason, it is most difficult to identify autonomy with preference satisfaction.[8] If preferences are a product of available information, existing consumption patterns, social norms or pressures, and governmental rules, it seems odd to suggest that individual freedom lies exclusively or by definition in preference satisfaction, or that current preferences should, on grounds of autonomy, be treated as the basis for settling political issues. It seems even odder to suggest that all preferences should be treated equally, independently of their basis and consequences, or of the reasons offered in their support.

For purposes of autonomy, then, governmental interference with existing choices or desires may be justified because of problems in the origins of those desires. Welfare-based arguments that invoke endogeneity tend to emphasize the malleability of preferences after they are formed; arguments based on autonomy stress what happens before the preferences have been created, that is, the conditions that gave rise to them. Because of this difference, the two arguments will operate along different tracks; and in some cases autonomy-based arguments will lead to conclusions different from those that would emerge from arguments based on welfare. In many cases, however, considerations of autonomy will argue powerfully against taking preferences as the basis for social choice.

Consider, for example, a decision to purchase dangerous foods, consumer products, or cigarettes by someone unaware of the (serious) health risks; an employer's decision not to hire blacks because of a background of public and private segregation or racial hostility in his community, hostility that he personally deplores; a person who disparages or has no interest in art and literature because the culture in which he has been reared centers mainly around television; a decision of a woman to adopt a traditional gender role because of the social stigma attached to refusing to do so; a decision not to purchase cars equipped with seat belts or not to wear a motorcycle helmet, produced by the social pressures imposed by one's peer group; a lack of interest in environmental diversity resulting from limitation of one's personal experiences to industrialized urban areas; a decision not to employ blacks at a restaurant because of fear of violence from whites.

These examples are different from one another. The source of the problem varies in each. But in all of them, the interest in liberty or autonomy does not call for governmental inaction, even if that were an intelligible category. Indeed, in many or perhaps all of these cases, regulation removes a kind of coercion.

One goal of a democracy, in short, is to ensure autonomy not merely in the satisfaction of preferences, but also, and more fundamentally, in the processes of preference formation. John Stuart Mill himself was emphatic on this point, going so far as to suggest that government itself should be evaluated in large measure by its effects on the character of the citizenry.[9] The view that freedom requires an opportunity to choose among alternatives finds a natural supplement in the view that people should not face unjustifiable constraints on the free development of their preferences and beliefs. It is not altogether clear what such a view would require—a point to which I will return. At the very least, however, it would see a failure of autonomy, and a reason for government response, in beliefs and preferences based on insufficient information or opportunities.

Governmental action might also be justified on grounds of autonomy when the public seeks to implement, through democratic processes culminating in law, widely held social aspirations or collective desires. Individual consumption choices, as expressed in the political domain, often diverge from collective considered judgments: people may seek, through law, to implement a democratic decision about what courses to pursue. If so, it is ordinarily no violation of autonomy to allow those considered judgments to be vindicated by governmental action. Respect for collective aspirations or considered judgments, produced by a process of deliberation on which competing perspectives are brought to bear, reflects a conception of political freedom having deep roots in the American constitutional tradition and considerable independent appeal.[10] On this view, political autonomy can be found in collective self-determination, as citizens decide, not what they "want" as consumers, but instead what their values are as citizens, and what those values require. What they want must be supported by reasons.

To summarize: On the thinnest version of the account offered thus far, the mere fact that preferences, as expressed in the market domain, are what they are is at least sometimes and perhaps generally an insufficient justification for political action. Government decisions need not be and in some cases should not be justified by reference to such preferences alone. More broadly, a democratic government should sometimes take private preferences as an object of deliberation, evaluation, and even control—an inevitable task in light of the need to define initial entitlements—and precisely in the interest of welfare and autonomy. Of course, there are serious risks of overreaching here, and there must be some constraints (usually labeled "rights") on this process. Checks laid down in advance are an indispensable part of constitutional government. Those checks will include, at a minimum, basic guarantees of political liberty and personal security, and such guarantees may not be compromised by processes of collective self-determination. I return to this point later.

II. Democratic Rejection of Revealed Preferences: A Catalogue

In this section, I attempt to particularize the claims made thus far by cataloguing cases in which considerations of autonomy and welfare justify governmental action that subjective welfarism would condemn. In all of these cases, I claim that participants in a liberal government ought to be concerned with whether its citizens are experiencing satisfying lives and that the salutary liberal commitment to divergent conceptions of the good ought not to be taken to disable government from expressing that concern through law. The cases fall into three basic categories.

Collective Judgments and Aspirations

Citizens in a democratic polity might act to embody in law not the preferences that they hold as private consumers, but instead what might be described as collective judgments, including aspirations or considered reflections. Measures of this sort are a product of deliberative processes on the part of citizens and representatives. In that process, people do not simply determine what they "want." The resulting measures cannot be understood as an attempt to aggregate or trade off private preferences.

Politics, Markets, and the Dependence of Preferences on Context

Frequently political choices cannot be easily understood as a process of aggregating prepolitical desires. Some people may, for example, support nonentertainment broadcasting on television, even though their own consumption patterns favor situation comedies; they may seek stringent laws protecting the environment or endangered species, even though they do not use the public parks or derive material benefits from protection of such species; they may approve of laws calling for social security and welfare, even though they do not save or give to the poor; they may support antidiscrimination laws even though their own behavior is hardly race- or gender-neutral. The choices people make as political participants are different from those they make as consumers. As political participants, people are choosing for the collectivity rather than for individuals; they are not choosing the same "thing" as they choose in markets. For this reason, the resulting choice may well be different. Democracy thus calls for an intrusion on markets.

The widespread disjunction between political and consumption choices presents something of a puzzle. Indeed, it sometimes leads to the view that market ordering is undemocratic, and that choices made through the political process are always a preferable basis for social ordering.

A generalization of this sort is far too broad in light of the multiple break-downs of the political process and the advantages of market ordering in many arenas. Respect for private markets is an important way of respecting diver-gent conceptions of the good and is thus properly associated with individual liberty. Respect for markets is also an engine of economic productivity, an important individual and collective goal. But it would be a mistake to suggest, as some do, that markets always reflect individual choice more reliably than politics; or that democratic choices differ from consumption outcomes only because of confusion, as voters fail to realize that they must ultimately bear the costs of the programs they favor; or that voting patterns merely reflect a willingness to seek certain goods so long as other people are footing the bill.

Undoubtedly, consumer behavior sometimes seems a better or more realis-tic reflection of actual preferences than political behavior. But in light of the fact that preferences depend on context, and do not exist in the abstract, the very notion of a "better reflection" of "actual" preferences is a confusing one; there is no such thing as an "actual" (in the sense of unitary or acontexual) preference in these settings. In markets and politics, people are not choosing the same thing. The collective character of politics means that they are making a decision for the group rather than for themselves alone, and this will predict-ably lead to differences in attitudes. Moreover, these differences might be ex-plained by the fact that political behavior reflects a variety of norms or influ-ences that are distinctive to the context of politics, and that can justify according additional weight to what emerges through the political setting.

These influences include four closely related phenomena. First, citizens may seek to implement individual and collective aspirations in political behav-ior but not in private consumption. As citizens, people may seek the aid of the law to bring about a social state that they consider to be in some sense higher than what emerges from market ordering. Second, people, in their capacity as political actors, may attempt to satisfy altruistic or other-regarding desires, which diverge from the self-interested preferences sometimes characteristic of markets. Third, political decisions might vindicate what might be called meta-preferences or second-order preferences. People have wishes about their wishes, and sometimes they try to vindicate those second-order wishes, includ-ing considered judgments about what is best, through law. Fourth, people may precommit themselves, in democratic processes, to a course of action that they consider to be in the general interest. The adoption of a constitution is itself an example of a precommitment strategy.

Three qualifications are necessary here. First, some of these objections might be translated into the terms of subjective welfarism. Some preferences, after all, are most effectively expressed in democratic arenas, and that expres-sion can be supported precisely on the grounds that they are subjectively held and connected to a certain form of individual and collective welfare. My broader point, however, is that political choices can reflect a kind of delibera-tion and reasoning, transforming values and perceptions of interests, that is often inadequately captured in the marketplace. It is this point that amounts to a rejection or at least a reformation of subjective welfarism as a political conception. It is here that democracy becomes something other than an aggregative mechanism, that politics is seen to be irreducible to bargaining, and that prepolitical "preferences" are not taken as the bedrock of political justification.

Second, to point to these various possibilities is not at all to deny that market or private behavior frequently reflects considered judgments, altruism, aspirations, or far more complex attitudes toward diverse goods than are captured in conventional accounts of preference structures. There are countless counterexamples to any such claim. All I mean to suggest is that divergences between market and political behavior will sometimes be attributable to phenomena of the sort I have described.

Third, a democratic system must be built on various safeguards to ensure that its decisions are in fact a reflection of deliberative processes of the kind described here. Often, of course, such processes are distorted by the presence of narrow self-interest on the part of political actors, by the fact that some groups are more organized than others, by disparities in wealth and influence, and by public and private coercion of various kinds. I am assuming here that these problems have been sufficiently overcome to allow for a favorable characterization of the process. No one should deny that politics, in its current form, is subject to numerous distorting factors, and that people attempt to use government power for self-interested or venal reasons.

Explanations

Thus far I have suggested that people may seek, through law, to implement collective desires that diverge from market choices. Is it possible to come up with concrete explanations for the differences? There are a number of possibilities.

First, the collective character of politics, which permits a response to collective action problems, is critical here. People may not want to implement their considered judgments, or to be altruistic, unless there is assurance that others will be bound to do so as well. More simply, people may prefer not to contribute to a collective benefit if donations are made individually, with no guarantee that others will participate; but their most favored system, obtainable only or at best through democratic forms, might be one in which they contribute if (but only if) there is assurance that others will do so as well. Perhaps people feel ashamed if others are contributing and they are not. Perhaps they feel victimized if they are contributing and others are not. In any case, the satisfaction of aspirations or altruistic goals will sometimes have the characteristics of the provision of public goods or the solution of a prisoner's dilemma.

Second, the collective character of politics might overcome the problem, discussed later, of preferences and beliefs that have adapted, at least to some extent, to an unjust status quo or to limits in available opportunities. Without the possibility of collective action, the status quo may seem intractable, and private behavior, and even desires, will adapt accordingly. But if people can act in concert, preferences might take on a quite different form. Consider social movements involving the environment, labor, and race and sex discrimination. The collective action problem thus interacts with aspirations, altruistic desires, second-order preferences, and precommitment strategies. All of these are most likely to be enacted into law if an apparatus such as democratic rule is available to overcome collective action problems.

Third, social and cultural norms might incline people to express aspirational or altruistic goals more often in political behavior than in markets. Such norms may press people, in their capacity as citizens, in the direction of a concern for others or for the public interest.

Fourth, the deliberative aspects of politics, bringing additional information and perspectives to bear, may affect preferences as expressed through governmental processes. A principal function of a democratic system is to ensure that through representative or participatory institutions, new or submerged voices, or novel depictions of where interests lie and what they in fact are, are heard and understood. If representatives or citizens are able to participate in a collective discussion of (for example) broadcasting or levels of risk in the workplace, they might well generate a fuller and richer picture of diverse social goods, and of how they might be served, than can be provided through individual decisions as registered in the market. It should hardly be surprising if preferences, values, and perceptions of both individual and collective welfare are changed as a result of that process.

Fifth, and finally, consumption decisions are a product of the criterion of private willingness to pay, which creates distortions of its own. Willingness to pay is a function of ability to pay, and it is an extremely crude proxy for utility or welfare. Political behavior removes this distortion—which is not to say that it does not introduce distortions of new kinds.

Qualifications

Arguments from collective desires are irresistible if the measure at issue is adopted unanimously. But more serious difficulties are produced if (as is usual) the law imposes on a minority what it regards as a burden rather than a benefit. Suppose, for example, that a majority wants to require high-quality television and to ban violent and dehumanizing shows, but that a significant minority wants to see the latter. (I put the First Amendment questions to one side; they are taken up in chapter 8.) It might be thought that those who perceive a need to bind themselves, or to express an aspiration, should not be permitted to do so if the consequence is to deprive others of an opportunity to satisfy their preferences.

The foreclosure of the preferences of the minority is unfortunate, but in general it is difficult to see what argument there might be for an across-the-board rule against collective action of this sort. If the majority is prohibited from vindicating its considered judgments through legislation, an important arena for democratic self-government will be eliminated. The choice is between the considered judgments of the majority and the preferences (and perhaps judgments as well) of the minority. On the other hand, the foreclosure of the minority should probably be permitted only when less restrictive alternatives, including private arrangements, are unavailable to serve the same end.

Of course, the argument for democratic outcomes embodying collective judgments is not always decisive. It is easy to imagine cases in which that argument is weak. Consider a law forbidding atheism or agnosticism, or barring the expression of unpatriotic political displays. And while I cannot provide in this space a full discussion of the contexts in which the case for democratic outcomes is overcome, it might be useful to describe, in a preliminary way, several categories of cases in which sharp constraints on collective judgments seem especially appropriate.

First, if the particular choice foreclosed has some special characteristic entitling it to protection from collective invasion, and especially if it is a prerequisite for deliberative democracy itself, it is appropriately considered a right, and the majority has no authority to intervene. Political expression and participation are prime examples. The equal political rights of members of the minority, as citizens, should be respected even if a general aspiration, held by the majority, argues for selective exclusions. So, too, other rights fundamental to autonomy or welfare—consider consensual sexual activity—ought generally to be off-limits to government. I offer no account of rights here; I simply mention that rights, defended as such under the appropriate account, may operate as barriers against the outcomes of democratic deliberation.

Second, some collective desires might be objectionable or a product of unjust background conditions. A collective judgment that racial intermarriage is intolerable could not plausibly be justified even if it is said to reflect a collective social aspiration. To explain why, it is of course necessary to offer an argument challenging that judgment and invoking principles of justice. Such an argument might itself involve notions of autonomy or welfare. However that may be, the example suggests that the collective judgment must not be objectionable on moral grounds.

Third, some collective desires might reflect a special weakness on the part of the majority: consider a curfew law, a ban on high-salt products, or perhaps prohibition. In such circumstances, a legal remedy might remove desirable incentives for private self-control, have unintended side effects resulting from the "bottling-up" of desires, or prove unnecessary in light of the existence of alternative remedies.

Fourth, there would be a problem if the majority's decision were objectionable on distributional grounds. If, for example, it came down especially hard on poor people, there might well be a requirement of compensation. When any one of these concerns arises, the case for protection of collective judgments is less plausible. But in many contexts, these concerns are absent, and democratic controls initiated on these grounds are justified.

Excessive Limitations in Opportunities or Unjust Background Conditions

Citizens in a democracy might override existing preferences in order to foster and promote diverse experiences, with a view to providing broad opportunities for the formation of preferences and beliefs and for critical scrutiny of current desires. This goal usually supports private ordering and freedom of contract as well. But it calls for collective safeguards when those forces push toward homogeneity and uniformity, as they often do in industrialized nations. Here the argument for governmental controls finds a perhaps ironic origin in Mill. Such controls are necessary to cultivate divergent conceptions of the good and to ensure a degree of reflection on those conceptions.

A system that took this goal seriously could start from a range of different foundations. It might find its roots in the principles that underlie a deliberative democracy itself. Here the notions of autonomy and welfare would be defined by reference to the idea of free and equal persons acting as citizens in setting up the terms of democratic life. That idea will impose constraints on the sorts of preferences and beliefs that a political system would be permitted to inculcate. Perhaps more controversially, the system could be regarded as embodying a mild form of liberal perfectionism. Such a system would seek to encourage autonomy. It would try to allow people to become, in more ways than they now are, the masters of the narratives of their own lives. It could prize the inculcation of critical and disparate attitudes toward prevailing conceptions of the good. Liberal education is of course the principal locus of these concerns, but the principles embodied in liberal education need not be confined to the school system. Still another foundation would be Aristotelian. Here the governing goal would be to ensure that individual capabilities are promoted and not thwarted by governmental arrangements.[11] And this set of ideas, a different kind of perfectionism, is not so dramatically different from Mill's version of utilitarianism.

If government can properly respond to preferences that are based on limitations in available opportunities, it might well undertake aggressive initiatives with respect to the arts and broadcasting: subsidizing public broadcasting, ensuring a range of disparate programming, or calling for high-quality programming not sufficiently provided by the marketplace. Indeed, the need to provide diverse opportunities for preference formation suggests reasons to be quite skeptical of unrestricted markets in communication and broadcasting. In view of the inevitable effects of programming on character, beliefs, and even conduct, it is hardly clear that governmental "inaction"—understood as free markets in programming—is always appropriate in a constitutional democracy. Indeed, the contrary seems true. (I take up this issue in more detail in chapter 8.)

As expressed in the market domain, people's preferences are sometimes based on an effort to reduce cognitive dissonance by adjusting to undue limitations in current practices and opportunities. When this is so, respect for preferences seems unjustified on grounds of autonomy and, under certain conditions, welfare as well. Preferences might be regarded as nonautonomous insofar as they are an outgrowth of unjust background conditions, and collective responses to such preferences might yield welfare gains. This point has significant implications. For example, workers may well underestimate the risks of hazardous activity partly in order to reduce the dissonance that would be produced by an accurate understanding of the dangers of the workplace. Democratic controls might produce gains in terms of both welfare and autonomy.

Similar ideas help account for principles of antidiscrimination. In general, the beliefs of both beneficiaries and victims of existing injustice are affected by dissonance-reducing strategies. The phenomenon of blaming the victim has distinct motivational foundations: the strategy of blaming the victim, or assuming that an injury or an inequality was deserved or inevitable, permits nonvictims or members of advantaged groups to reduce dissonance by enabling them to maintain that the world is just—a pervasively, insistently, and sometimes irrationally held belief.[12] There are many empirical questions here. But it is clear that reduction of cognitive dissonance is a powerful motivational force, and it can operate as a significant obstacle to the recognition of social injustice or irrationality.

Victims also participate in dissonance-reducing strategies, including the lowering of their own self-esteem to accommodate both the fact of victimization and the belief that the world is essentially just. Sometimes it is easier to assume that one's suffering is warranted than that it has been imposed cruelly or by chance. Consider here the astonishing fact that after a draft lottery, participants decided that the results of the purely random process, whether favorable or not, were deserved.[13] The phenomenon of blaming the victim also reflects the "hindsight effect," through which people unjustifiably perceive events as having been more predictable than they in fact were, and therefore suggest that victims or disadvantaged groups should have been able to prevent the negative outcome. All of these phenomena make reliance on existing or revealed preferences highly problematic in certain contexts.

There is suggestive evidence to this effect in psychological literature in this area. Some studies reveal that people who engage in cruel behavior begin to devalue the objects of their cruelty; observers tend to do the same.[14] Such evidence bears on antidiscrimination law in general. Certain aspects of American labor and race discrimination law can be understood as a response to the basic problem of distorted beliefs and preferences. For example, the Supreme Court has emphatically rejected freedom-of-choice plans as a remedy for school segregation.[15] Such plans would simply permit whites and blacks to send their children to whichever school they wished. The Court's rejection of such plans might well be puzzling, but the outcome becomes more reasonable if it is seen as based in part on the fact that, in this area, preferences and beliefs have conspicuously grown up around and adapted to the segregative status quo. Under these circumstances, freedom of choice is no solution at all; indeed, in view of the background and context the term seems an oxymoron.

In labor law as well, American law rejects freedom of contract and freedom of choice in order to protect collective bargaining. Some of this legislation must stand on a belief that private preferences have been adaptive to a status quo skewed against unionization. Special steps are therefore necessary in order to encourage collective bargaining, which also, of course, overcomes the prisoner's dilemma faced by individual workers, and therefore facilitates collective deliberation on the conditions of the workplace.

Poverty itself is perhaps the most severe obstacle to the free development of preferences and beliefs. Programs that attempt to respond to the deprivations faced by poor people—most obviously by eliminating poverty, but also through broad public education and regulatory efforts designed to make cultural resources generally available regardless of wealth—are fully justified in this light. They should hardly be seen as objectionable paternalism or as unsupportable redistribution. Indeed, antipoverty efforts are tightly linked with traditional efforts to promote security and independence in the interest of creating the conditions for full and equal citizenship.

Sometimes, of course, preferences are only imperfectly adapted. At some level there is a perception of injury, but a fear of social sanctions or a belief that the cause is intractable prevents people from seeking redress. Here the collective character of politics, permitting the organization of numerous people, can be exceedingly helpful.

By itself, the fact that preferences are shifting and endogenous is hardly a sufficient reason for the imposition of democratic controls. Almost all preferences are to some degree dependent on existing law and current opportunities, and that fact cannot be a reason for governmental action without creating a license for tyranny. The argument for democratic controls in the face of endogenous preferences must rely on a belief that welfare or autonomy will thereby be promoted. Usually self-conscious governmental interference should be avoided. But far too often, the salutary belief in respect for divergent conceptions of the good is transformed into an unwillingness to protect people from either unjust background conditions or a sheer lack of options.

The actual content of democratic controls here will be controversial, and it probably should begin and usually end with efforts to provide information and to increase opportunities. Thus, for example, governmentally required disclosure of risks in the workplace is a highly laudable strategy. In a few cases, however, these milder initiatives are inadequate, and other measures are necessary. A moderately intrusive strategy could involve economic incentives, which might take the form of tax advantages or cash payments. For example, the government might give financial inducements to day-care centers as a way of relieving child-care burdens. Such a system might well be preferable to direct transfers of money to families, a policy that will predictably lead many more women to stay at home. In view of the sources and consequences of the differential distribution of child-care burdens, it is fully legitimate for the government to take steps in the direction of equalization. The most intrusive option, to be used rarely, is direct coercion, as in the case of governmentally mandated use of safety equipment.

The category of democratic responses to endogenous preferences of this sort overlaps with that of measures that attempt to protect collective aspirations. Frequently, aspirations form the basis for laws that attempt to influence processes of preference formation.

Intrapersonal Collective Action Problems

There is also an argument for democratic controls on existing choices when they are a function of past acts of consumption and when such acts alter desires or beliefs in such a way as to cause long-term harm. In such cases, the two key facts are that preferences are endogenous to past consumption decisions and that the effect of those decisions on current preferences is pernicious. For government to act in this context, it is important that it be confident of its conclusions; in the face of uncertainty, freedom of choice is appropriate here. An absence of information on the part of the private actors is usually a necessary condition for collective controls.

Regulations of addictive substances, myopic behavior, and habits are familiar examples. In the case of an addiction, the problem is that the costs of nonconsumption increase dramatically over time as the benefits of consumption remain constant or fall sharply. The result is that the aggregate costs, over time or over a life, of consumption can much exceed the aggregate benefits, even though the initial consumption choice provides benefits that exceed costs. Individual behavior that is rational for each individual consumption choice ultimately leads people into severely inferior social states. In such cases, people, if fully informed, would in all likelihood not want to choose the good in the first place. Governmental action is a possible response.

Menahem Yaari offers the example of a group of traders attempting to induce alcoholism in an Indian tribe.[16] At the outset, alcoholic beverages are not extremely valuable to consumers. The consumers are willing to buy only for a low price, which the traders accept. But as a result of consumption, the value of the beverages to the consumers steadily increases to the point where they are willing to pay enormous sums to obtain them. Thus, the traders are able

> to manoevre the Indian into a position where rationality conflicts with Pareto-efficiency, i.e., into a position where to be efficient is to be irrational and to be rational is to be inefficient. . . . [T]he disadvantage, for an economic unit, of having endogenously changing tastes is that, even with perfect information and perfect foresight, the unit may find itself forced to follow an action which, by the unit's own standards, is Pareto-dominated.[17]

Because of the effect over time of consumption on preferences, someone who is addicted to heroin is much worse off than he would have been had he never started, even though the original decision to consume was not irrational in terms of immediate costs and benefits. Statutes that regulate addictive substances respond to a social belief, grounded on this consideration, that the relevant preferences should not be formed in the first place.

We might describe this situation as involving an intrapersonal collective action problem, in which the costs and benefits, for a particular person, of engaging in an activity change dramatically over time. A central point here is that consumption patterns induce a significant change in preferences, and in a way that makes people worse off in the long run. In the case of addictions, there will also be interconnections between intrapersonal collective action problems and preferences and beliefs that are adaptive to unjust background conditions, at least as a general rule. (Yaari's own example, involving whites trading alcohol with Native Americans, is a prime example.) The problem of drug addiction is hardly distributed evenly throughout the population, and the process of addiction is in large part a response to social institutions that severely limit and condition the range of options.

While addiction is the most obvious case, it is part of a far broader category. Consider, for example, myopic behavior, defined as a refusal, because the short-term costs exceed the short-term benefits, to engage in activity having long-term benefits that dwarf long-term costs. Another kind of intrapersonal collective action problem is produced by habits, in which people engage in behavior because of the subjectively high short-term costs of changing their behavior, regardless of the fact that the long-term benefits exceed the long-term costs. *Akrasia,* or weakness of the will, has a related structure, and some laws respond to its individual or collective forms.

For the most part, problems of this sort are best addressed at the individual level or through private associations, which minimize coercion; but social regulation is a possible response. Statutes that subsidize the arts or public broadcasting, or that discourage the formation of some habits and encourage the formation of others, are illustrations. There are similar arguments for incentive-based or even compulsory recycling programs (the costs of participation decrease substantially over time, and often turn into benefits) and for democratic restrictions on smoking cigarettes.

The problem with collective controls in this context is that they are unlikely to be fine tuned. They will often sweep up so many people and circumstances as to create serious risks of error and abuse. Moreover, there are many questions of practical implementation, in addition to issues of basic principle. Regulatory controls may not work in practice. In some settings, however, citizens will be able to say with confidence that the effect of consumption on preferences will lead to severe harms to human welfare or autonomy, and that regulatory alternatives will make things better. In such cases democratic controls are justified.

IV. Conclusion

A constitutional democracy should not be self-consciously concerned, in a general and comprehensive way, with the souls of its citizens. Under modern conditions, liberal constraints on the operation of the public sphere, and general respect for divergent conceptions of the good, are indispensable. At the same time, it would be a grave mistake to characterize liberal democracy as a system that requires existing preferences, as expressed in the market domain, to be taken as the basis for governmental decisions. Liberalism does not forbid citizens, operating through democratic channels, from enacting their considered judgments into law, or from counteracting, through the provision of opportunities and information, preferences and beliefs that have adjusted to an unjust status quo. Ironically, a system that forecloses these routes—and that claims to do so in the name of liberalism or democracy—will defeat many of the aspirations that gave both liberalism and democracy their original appeal, and that continue to fuel them in so many parts of the world.

Notes

1. See John Rawls, *Political Liberalism* (New York: Columbia University Press, 1993).

2. See Joseph Bessette, *The Mild Voice of Reason: Deliberative Democracy and American National Government* (Chicago: University of Chicago Press, 1994); Cass R. Sunstein, *The Partial Constitution* (Cambridge: Harvard University Press, 1993), ch. 1.

3. See Amartya Sen, "Internal Consistency of Choice," 61 *Econometrica* 495 (1993); Elliot Aronson, *The Social Animal*, 7th ed. (New York: W. H. Freeman, 1995), pp. 124–25.

4. See Amos Tversky and Itamar Simonson, "Context-Dependent Preferences," 39 *Mgmt. Sci.* 1179 (1993).

5. See George Stigler and Gary Becker, "De Gustibus Non Est Disputandum," 67 *Am. Econ. Rev.* 76 (1977).

6. This is an empirical claim with a good deal of empirical support, taken up in detail and with many citations in chapter 8. A good overview is Richard Thaler, *Quasi-Rational Economics* (New York: Russell Sage Foundation, 1991).

7. See Daniel Kahneman, Jack Knetsch, and Richard Thaler, "Fairness and the Assumptions of Economics," in *Rational Choice: The Choice Between Economics and Psychology*, Robin Hogarth and Melvin Reder, eds. (Chicago: University of Chicago Press, 1987), pp. 101–16, esp. 113–14.

8. See Joseph Raz, *The Morality of Freedom* (New York: Oxford University Press, 1986), ch. 16.

9. See John Stuart Mill, *Considerations on Representative Government* (1861; reprint, Buffalo: Prometheus Books, 1991).

10. See Amartya Sen, "Rationality and Social Choice," 85 *Am. Econ. Rev.* 1 (1995).

11. See Amartya Sen, *Inequality Reexamined* (Cambridge: Harvard University Press, 1993) and *Commodities and Capabilities* (New York: North-Holland, 1985).

12. See Melvin J. Lerner, *The Belief in a Just World* (New York: Plenum Press, 1980).

13. Samuel Rubin and John Peplau, "Belief in a Just World and Reaction to Another's Lot," 29 *J. of Soc. Issues* 73 (1973).

14. See Aronson, *supra* note 3.

15. Green v. County School Bd., 391 U.S. 430 (1968).

16. See Menahem Yaari, "Endogenous Changes in Tastes: A Philosophical Discussion," in *Decision Theory and Social Ethics*, Hans Gottinger and Werner Leinfellner, eds. (Boston: D. Reidel, 1978), pp. 59–98.

17. *Id.* at 82.

Social Norms
and Social Roles

I. Tales of Rationality and Choice

Ultimatums and Fairness

Economists have invented a game: the ultimatum game.[1] The people who run the game give some money, on a provisional basis, to two players. The first player is instructed to offer some part of the money to the second player. If the second player accepts that amount, he can keep what is offered, and the first player gets to keep the rest. But if the second player rejects the offer, neither player gets anything. No bargaining is allowed. Both players are informed that these are the rules. Using standard assumptions about rationality, self-interest, and choice, economists predict that the first player should offer a penny and the second player should accept.

This is not what happens. Offers usually average between 30 percent and 40 percent of the total. Offers of less than 20 percent are often rejected. Often there is a 50–50 division. These results cut across the level of the stakes and also across diverse cultures.

Littering

Why do people litter? Why do they throw things out instead? Social psychologist Robert Cialdini tried to find out.[2] He placed flyers under the windshield wipers of cars and waited to see what drivers would do with them. Cialdini made arrangements so that before reaching their cars, some people would see someone (a Cialdini associate) walk past them, pick up from the street a bag from a fast-food restaurant, and throw it in the trashcan. Of the group who saw both the responsible behavior and noticed the flyers, *almost none* threw them on the street. In the control experiment, with no one showing responsible behavior, over one-third of the drivers threw the flyers on the street.

Would it make sense to say that nearly all of the first set of drivers "had a preference for" throwing garbage in the trashcan, whereas merely two-thirds of the second set "had that preference"? This would not exactly be false, but it would not be very illuminating. Whether people put things in a trashcan, or litter instead, is partly a function of social norms and the observed behavior of other people.

Smoking, Rationality, and Race

About 400,000 Americans die each year from smoking-related causes. Government has tried to reduce smoking through educational campaigns designed to inform people and especially teenagers of the risks. Despite this fact, about one million Americans begin smoking each year, many of them teenagers, and people worry that educational campaigns will succeed, if at all, only with well-educated families.

But consider this. Nationally, 22.9 percent of white teenagers smoked in 1993, a number that has been basically unchanged in the last decade. But in the same year, only about 4.4 percent of African-American teenagers smoked, a number that is *four times smaller* than the number a decade before. What accounts for this difference? Part of the explanation appears to lie in differing understandings of what is fashionable. And part of that difference may lie in a private antismoking campaign in the African-American community, symbolized most dramatically by posters in Harlem subways showing a skeleton resembling the Marlboro man lighting a cigarette for a black child. The caption reads: "They used to make us pick it. Now they want us to smoke it."

Recycling in the Hamptons

In East Hampton, New York— part of the famous and wealthy "Hamptons"— what used to be called the East Hampton Dump is now the East Hampton Recycling and Disposal Center. At the East Hampton Recycling and Disposal Center, there are separate bins for green glass, clear glass, newspapers, tin cans, paper other than newspaper, and more.

Almost every day in August, people at the Center can be found patiently separating their garbage for placement in the relevant bins. Sometimes this takes a long time. The people at the Center tend to own expensive cars— Mercedes Benz, BMWs—that are parked near the bins. As they separate their garbage, they look happy.

John Jones

John Jones lives in California. Here is a description of some aspects of his behavior.

1. He buys smoke alarms and installs them in three rooms in his house.
2. He loves chocolate and ice cream, and eats a lot of both. He also eats a fair amount of frozen foods; he makes sure that they are "lean" whenever he has a choice. According to his doctor, he is slightly over his ideal weight.

3. On warm days, he likes to ride his bicycle to and from work, and he enjoys riding his bicycle on busy city streets, even though he has heard about a number of collisions there.
4. He is happily married. He tries to share the work around the house, but he doesn't much like domestic labor. He does less than his share. He acknowledges that this is both true and unfair, and he supports many policies that are conventionally described as "feminist."
5. He buckles his seatbelt whenever he is in a car. His own car is a Volvo, and he bought it partly because it is said to be an especially safe car.
6. He is not worried about the risk of an earthquake in California. On some days, he says that he doesn't think that an earthquake is very likely; on other days, he claims to be "fatalistic about earthquakes."
7. He does not recycle. He considers recycling a personal "irritation." He is mildly embarrassed about this, but he has not changed his behavior.
8. He considers himself an environmentalist; his votes reflect his enthusiasm for environmentalism. He supports aggressive regulation designed to protect people from risks to their life and health. In fact, he is in favor of mandatory recycling, notwithstanding his own failure to recycle.
9. In his own mind, his resources fall in various mental "compartments." Some money is reserved for retirement; some money is saved for charitable donations. Some money is kept for vacation. Some money is for monthly bills. His forms of mental accounting are very diverse. He is fully aware of this.

Is Jones inconsistent? Is Jones risk-averse or risk-inclined? What is Jones's dollar valuation of a human life, or his own life?

My goal in this chapter is to challenge some widely held understandings of rationality, choice, and freedom, and to use that challenge to develop some conclusions about human behavior and also the appropriate domain and uses of law. I urge that behavior is pervasively a function of social norms; that changes in norms might be the best way to improve individual and social well-being; and that government deserves to have, and in any case inevitably does have, a large role in "norm management." Far too little attention has been given to the place of norms in human behavior, to the relationship between norms and law, and to the control of norms as an instrument of legal policy.

Part of my motivation is practical. Consider table 2.1. What is notable is that these risks of death could be much reduced with different social norms. With respect to smoking, diet/activity, alcohol, firearms, sexual behavior, motor vehicles, and illicit drugs, current norms are a major problem in the sense that new norms could save lives. A regulatory policy that targets social norms

Table 2.1. Preventable Risks of Death in the U.S.

Risk	Percent of Total Deaths	Range	Total Deaths/Year
Tobacco	19	14–19	400,000
Diet/activity	14	14–27	300,000
Alcohol	5	3–10	100,000
Microbial	4	—	90,000
Toxic agents	3	3–6	60,000
Firearms	2	—	35,000
Sexual behavior	1	—	30,000
Motor vehicles	1	—	25,000
Illicit drugs	<1	—	20,000

Source: J. M. McGinnis and W. H. Foege, "Actual Causes of Death in the U.S.," 270 *JAMA* 2207 (1993). Reprinted by permission.

may well be the most effective possible strategy. Social norms are also part and parcel of systems of race and sex equality; if norms would change, existing inequalities would be greatly reduced. It is thus transparently important to see whether changes in social norms, brought about through law, might operate to save lives and otherwise improve human well-being.

But part of my motivation is theoretical; it involves a conceptual puzzle. In the last decade there has been an active debate about whether and to what extent law should respect "preferences."[3] But the term "preferences" is highly ambiguous, and it is not clear what the participants in this debate are actually talking about when they say that "preferences" should or should not be respected by law. When the term is clarified, it becomes clear that the term "preference" can be understood in several different ways, and these differences are too often collapsed. When the idea of a "preference" is explored, it becomes clear that it may well be too ambiguous and too coarse-grained to be a foundation for normative or positive work.

More particularly, I aim to make a set of conceptual or descriptive points:

1. For many purposes, it would be best to dispense with the idea of "preferences," despite the pervasiveness of that idea in positive social science and in arguments about the appropriate domains of law and the state. In normative work, the idea elides important distinctions among the mental states of human agents. In positive work, the idea tends to disregard contextual factors that produce diverse choices in diverse settings.

2. Many important and well-known anomalies in behavior are best explained by reference to social norms and to the fact that people feel shame when they violate those norms. In fact, money itself is not fungible, and this is because of social norms.[4]

3. There is no simple contrast between "rationality" and social norms. Individual rationality is a function of social norms. Many efforts to drive a wedge between the two rest on obscure "state of nature"

thinking—that is, on efforts to discern what people would like or prefer if social norms did not exist. Those efforts are doomed to failure.[5]

4. Social states are often more fragile than might be supposed, because they depend on social norms to which—and this is the key point—people may not have much allegiance. What I will call *norm entrepreneurs*—people interested in changing social norms—can exploit this fact; if successful, they produce what I will call *norm bandwagons* and *norm cascades*. Successful law and policy try to take advantage of learning about norms and norm change.

I also aim to make two claims about the appropriate domain of law. These claims have a great deal to do with law's *expressive function*—that is, the function of law in expressing social values and commitments.

1. Individual choices are a function of social norms, social meanings, and social roles, which individual agents may deplore, and over which individual agents have little or no control. Collective action—in the form of information campaigns, persuasion, economic incentives, or legal coercion—might be necessary to enable people to change norms that they do not like.

2. Some norms are obstacles to human autonomy and well-being. It is appropriate for law to alter norms if they diminish autonomy by, for example, discouraging people from becoming educated or exposed to diverse conceptions of the good. It is appropriate for law to alter norms if they diminish well-being by, for example, encouraging people to risk their lives by driving very fast, using firearms, or taking dangerous drugs.

An Insufficiently Charted Domain

Libertarians, some economic analysts of law, and many liberals[6] give inadequate attention to the pervasive functions of social norms, social meanings, and social roles. Often it is said that in a free society, governments should respect both choices and preferences. But the case for respecting these things depends partly on their genesis, and as I have indicated the determinants of choices, indeed the meaning of the term "preference," remain most obscure. We should agree that social norms play a part in determining choices; that people's choices are a function of their particular social role; and that the social or expressive meaning of acts is an ingredient in choice.[7] We should try to see whether social norms, social roles, and social meanings can be obstacles to human well-being, and whether something might be done to change them, even if people are making "choices," even if there is neither force nor fraud, and whether or not there is "harm to others."

One of my central points here is that individual agents have little control over social norms, social meanings, and social roles, even when they wish these to be very different from what they are.[8] This is not an argument against norms, meanings, and roles. Human beings can live, and human liberty can exist, only within a system of norms, meanings, and roles; but in any particular form, these things can impose severe restrictions on well-being and autonomy. Agents who seek to make changes face a collective action problem. In fact, there are many reasons why a legal system might seek to alter norms, meanings, and roles. The most important reason is that the resulting reforms might enhance autonomy. They might also help overcome caste-like features of current society; they certainly fall within the legitimate expressive function of law.

For example, it is impossible for an individual to say whether the act of smoking seems daring, or the act of recycling seems exotic, or the act of rejecting sexual harassment seems extreme and humorless. This is so even though the relevant norms greatly influence behavior. If, for example, smokers seem like pitiful dupes rather than exciting daredevils, the incidence of smoking will go down. If people who fail to recycle are seen as oddballs, more people will recycle. If the role of secretary does not include susceptibility to unwanted sexual attention, there will be less unwanted sexual attention. The point very much bears on current public disputes. If single parenthood is stigmatized, and if lesbian couples are treated just as "couples," social practices will change accordingly. Thus, government might try to inculcate or to remove *shame*, fear of which can be a powerful deterrent to behavior.

Government cannot avoid affecting social norms. Any system of government and law will predictably influence norms. A market economy will, for example, have predictable effects on norms, and historically it has been justified on just this ground, as a way of softening social divisions by allowing people to interact with one another on a mutually beneficial basis. A good deal of governmental action is designed to change norms, meanings, or roles, and in that way to increase the individual benefits or decrease the individual costs associated with certain acts. In fact, social norms can operate as *taxes* on or as *subsidies* to behavior. There is a thin line between education and provision of information on the one hand and attempted norm-change on the other.

More particularly, I hope to draw attention to the fact that people's conception of appropriate action and even of their "interest" is very much a function of the particular social role in which they find themselves. This is true of judges, lawyers, doctors, parents, children, waiters, wives, husbands, colleagues, friends, and law school deans. Attention to the place of social role shows that for many purposes, the contrast between "rationality" and social norms[9] is unhelpful. What is rational for an agent is a function of, and mediated by, social roles and associated norms. And when social norms appear not to be present, it is only because they are so taken for granted that they seem invisible.

At the same time, norms and roles create a division between the judgments and desires that are displayed publicly and the judgments and desires that would be displayed without current norms and roles.[10] People's private judgments and desires diverge greatly from public appearances. For this reason, current social states can be far more fragile than is generally thought—as small shocks to publicly endorsed norms and roles decrease the cost of displaying deviant norms and rapidly bring about large-scale changes in publicly displayed judgments and desires. Hence societies experience *norm bandwagons* and *norm cascades*. Norm bandwagons occur when the lowered cost of expressing new norms encourages an ever-increasing number of people to reject previously popular norms, to a "tipping point" where it is adherence to the old norms that produces social disapproval. Norm cascades occur when societies are presented with rapid shifts toward new norms.[11] Something of this kind happened with the attack on apartheid in South Africa, the fall of Communism, the election of Ronald Reagan, the rise of the feminist movement, and the current assault on affirmative action.

To spell out the most general point emerging from the discussion: The notion of "a preference" can be deeply confusing and in many of its uses, it impairs both positive and normative analysis of law. In its standard form, a preference is supposed to be something that lies behind choices and that is more abstract and general than choices are.[12] What lies behind choices is not a thing but an unruly amalgam of things—aspirations, tastes, physical states, responses to existing roles and norms, values, judgments, emotions, drives, beliefs, whims—and the interaction of these forces will produce outcomes of a particular sort in accordance with the particular context. Hence we might say that *preferences are constructed, rather than elicited, by social situations,*[13] in the sense that they are very much a function of the setting and the prevailing norms.

I will be emphasizing the highly contextual nature of choice and hence the fine-grained nature of anything capable of being described as a person's "preferences." Some people think that the notion of "preference" can be identified with "rational self-interest" in a way that abstracts from social roles and norms. As the examples cited suggest, the attempt at abstraction makes positive work treacherous; social norms are very much a part of what underlies choice. If preferences are understood to be bound up with social norms—with the wellsprings of shame and pride—positive analysis will be more accurate; but we will have to disaggregate the various wellsprings of choice. This point bears on the appropriate content of law and on the vexing question of paternalism; it also shows that important collective action problems, calling for a legal response, can appear in some unusual settings.

II. Definitions and Concepts

Norms

The term "social norms" might be understood in many different ways. For present purposes, we might, very roughly, understand "norms" to be social attitudes of approval and disapproval, specifying what ought to be done and what ought not to be done. There are social norms about littering, dating, smoking, singing, when to stand, when to sit, when to show anger, when, how, and with whom to express affection, when to talk, when to listen, when to discuss personal matters, when to use contractions. In fact, there are social norms about nearly every aspect of human behavior.

"It isn't done" is a frequent reaction to certain conduct—even though the relevant "it" is indeed done. The attitudes that embody themselves in social norms span an exceptionally wide range. They may or may not begin or maintain themselves as a result of reflective judgments. Social norms may or may not promote liberty and well-being; they may or may not be easily malleable or go very deep into one's self-understanding. Some norms set good manners, for example, how to hold one's fork; others reflect morally abhorrent views, as in the taboo on interracial relations; others reflect hard-won moral commitments, as in the taboo on racial epithets. Sometimes norms are codified in law. A social norm can count as such whether or not people have thought deeply about whether it makes sense.

Social norms are enforced through social sanctions; these sanctions create a range of unpleasant (but sometimes pleasant) emotional states in the minds of people who have violated them. If someone behaves inconsistently with social norms, public disapproval may produce shame and a desire to hide. Sometimes the unpleasant feelings brought about by violations of social norms are intense, and the social consequences of having or anticipating these feelings can be substantial. For example, lack of education, or an enormous amount of education, can produce a good deal of shame in certain communities; so too with the decision to be promiscuous, to get pregnant, or to use, or not to use, alcohol, cigarettes, or unlawful drugs.

From these points we might conclude that choice among options is a function not only of (a) the intrinsic value of the option—a book, a job, a drink—but also of (b) the reputational benefit or cost of the choice and also of (c) the effects of the choice on one's self-conception. Someone may watch a television show on public broadcasting not only because it is enjoyable, but because there are reputational advantages from doing so and advantages as well from the standpoint of promoting one's self-conception. Social norms are a key determinant in reputational benefit or cost. They can also affect self-conception. Hence, changes in social norms can affect choices if intrinsic value is held constant, by altering the effects of reputational incentives and consequences for self-conception. The three-part division is a bit crude, since perceptions of intrinsic value will be a function of social norms; those perceptions do not exist in a vacuum. I return to these thoughts later.

In a way, social norms reduce freedom, understood very broadly as the power to do whatever one would like to do. Certainly norms stop people from doing things that (if the norms were different) they would like to do, and certainly people would sometimes like the norms to change. As I have indicated, norms can drive a wedge between people's public actions and statements and their private judgments or desires. Some people very much want norms to be other than what they are, and they regret the fact (if they recognize it) that they have no power to change them. But it would be quite ludicrous to deplore social norms, to see them only as constraints on freedom, or to wish them to disappear. In fact, norms make freedom possible. Social life is not feasible—not even imaginable—without them. In the absence of social norms, we would be unable to understand one another. Norms establish conventions about the meanings of actions. Social norms are thus facilitative as well as constraining. If everyone knows the norms concerning a raised voice, or wearing bluejeans, then people can raise their voices, or wear bluejeans, without having to decide what these actions mean.

There is a further and, for present purposes, an especially important point. Good social norms solve collective action problems, by encouraging people to do useful things that they would not do without the relevant norms.[14] Consider voting, behaving courteously, keeping promises, cleaning up after one's dog, writing tenure letters, and doing one's share of administrative work. Without social norms, coercion or economic incentives—perhaps with large financial investments—would be required to ensure that collective action problems are solved. And when norms are inadequate, or start to disintegrate, society can encounter large difficulties and even collapse.

On the other hand, some people *like* to incur the disapproval that follows from norm-violation, and hence some people like to "flout convention" by rejecting prevailing norms—for example, by dating someone of another race, smoking, playing loud music in public, or wearing bizarre clothes. Of course, people who violate generally held social norms might be behaving consistently with particular norms in a relevant subculture. This is true when people in a certain group wear clothing of a certain kind, or when people who smoke cigarettes receive peer group approval simply by virtue of the fact that they are violating more broadly held norms. (Those who reject generally held norms may be the most committed of conformists.)

The fact that some people like to reject social norms is highly relevant to law. For example, a serious problem with legal efforts to inculcate social norms is that the source of the effort may be disqualifying. If Nancy Reagan tells teenagers to "Just Say No" to drugs, many teenagers may think that it is good to say "yes." It is said that propaganda efforts in the former Soviet Union failed simply because the source of the propaganda was not trusted; hence the government's effort to inculcate norms of its choosing fell on deaf ears. These points bear on the regulation of risk, particularly in the areas of teenage smoking and potentially dangerous sexual activity. Efforts by private or public authorities to stigmatize certain acts may have the opposite effect.

The fact that norms are socially contested can lead to the creation of many diverse *norm communities*. People who are dissatisfied with prevailing norms can vote with their feet, using the power of "exit" to become members of groups built on especially congenial norms. Many American high schools reflect this phenomenon, as students find groups that are defined in a supportive and relatively crisp way, and as groups intermingle only on occasion. On the other hand, the existence of norm communities is not a full solution to the problems posed by some social norms. It can be very costly to exit from the norm community in which one finds oneself, and the fact that one has been raised in that community may make other options seem unthinkable or horrific even though they might be much better. And apparently free or dissident communities may be based on norms that are highly reactive to and even defined by reference to more generally held norms; it might be better if the community as a whole could do something about those norms. As we will see, these points bear on the legitimate role of government.

Strange as it may seem, social norms mean that money itself is not fungible.[15] The uses of money, and the place for different "kinds" of money, are pervasively affected by social norms. People put money in different mental compartments and act accordingly. Some money is specially reserved for the support of children. Some money is for gifts; some is for one's own special fun. Some money is to be given to charities. Some money is for summer vacation. Some money is for a rainy day. Some money is for celebrations. If you receive a fee for a lecture, or a small amount from the lottery, you may use it for a special dinner.

Social norms make for qualitative differences among human goods, and these qualitative differences are matched by ingenious mental operations involving qualitative differences among different "kinds" of money. Thus a study of practices in Orange County, California, reports that residents keep "a variety of domestic 'cash stashes'—'generally one in the billfold of each adult, children's allowances and piggy banks, a petty cash fund in a teapot-equivalent, a dish of change for parking meters or laundry'—or 'banked stashes of money,' including Christmas club savings and accounts designated for special expenditures as property or other taxes, vacations, or home and car insurance payments."[16]

In short, there are complex procedures of "mental accounting" in which money that falls in certain compartments is assessed only in terms of its particular intended uses and not compared with money that has been placed in different mental compartments.[17] We cannot understand the uses of money itself without understanding the role of social norms. Social theorists have often feared that the use of money would "flatten" social life, above all by erasing qualitative distinctions; but it would be more accurate to report that social life, pervaded as it is by social norms, has "unflattened" money, by insisting on and enforcing qualitative distinctions.[18] "There is no single, uniform, generalized money, but multiple monies: people earmark different currencies for many or perhaps all types of social interactions . . . [a]nd people will in fact respond with anger, shock, or ridicule to the 'misuse' of monies for the wrong circumstances or social relations."[19] Thus norms and law barring the use of money in certain contexts are complemented by norms barring the use of certain money (say, retirement money) for certain purposes (say, gambling or vacation).

Roles

In General

Many norms are intensely *role-specific*. Consider the following social roles: doctor, employee, waiter, book-buyer, law school dean, wife, friend, pet-owner, colleague, student. Each of these roles is accompanied by a remarkably complex network of appropriate norms. The network is not easily reduced to rules, but people know, often very well, what they are. If you are a waiter, and treat your restaurant's patrons the way you treat your friends, you will probably not be a waiter very long (except perhaps in California). If you are a student, and treat a teacher as if he were your employee at the local factory, you will be perceived as misbehaving very badly. If you treat a colleague in the way you treat your doctor, you will undoubtedly seem quite odd. If you treat a friend the way doctors treat patients, or lawyers treat clients, you probably won't have many friends. People rapidly internalize social norms about what their roles entail. Violations of role-specific norms can seem jarring and produce prompt social punishment (or reward).

Roles are accompanied by a wide range of included and excluded reasons for action. In your capacity as a lawyer, you can act only on the basis of certain reasons. For example, you may reveal something told to you in confidence only to prevent a crime; you cannot breach a confidence on the ground that it would be profitable to do so. In your capacity as a teacher of English, you are not supposed to rank students on the basis of family connections, looks, or athletic ability. In your capacity as a judge, you may look only at a restricted set of considerations, a set far more restricted than those you may examine if you are a legislator. In your capacity as a friend, you are not permitted to violate a confidence on the ground that it would be fun to gossip about the problem revealed by what you have been told. Confusion of one's role—Is X speaking as a friend or as a colleague? Is the judge a closet legislator? What exactly is my relationship to my employer?—can cause uncertainty, awkwardness, or much worse.

Roles and Freedom

Are social roles an obstacle to freedom? In a way the answer is yes, since people would often like to do things that their role forbids and would often like to change the nature of their roles. But this would be a far too simple conclusion. Without roles, life would be very hard to negotiate. Like social norms, social roles are facilitating as well as constraining. The existence of a clear role makes communication much easier. By sharply constraining the domain of permissible actions, roles simplify things and in that sense increase personal freedom.

Of course, some of the norms associated with certain roles are silly or even oppressive, and some people deplore them for this reason. What can they do? Large-scale changes in social roles normally require collective action, whether private or public—a point with considerable importance for those interested in the appropriate domain of law. But sometimes individual people act in ways inconsistent with their roles precisely in order to draw attention to their silly or oppressive character. Thus, a slave in the pre-Civil War South might decide not to act deferentially; a student might raise his voice against an abusive teacher; a woman in an unequal society might insist that domestic labor should be shared; a homosexual man might "flaunt it"; a teacher in business school might wear bluejeans. In fact, attacks on norms associated with particular roles often have a great deal to do with perceptions of injustice.

There are many possible reasons for rejecting prevailing norms with respect to role. Some people depart from the prevailing norm because of their *reflective judgments*. Such people think, on reflection, that the norm is too silly or too unworthy to affect behavior, or that relevant roles diminish autonomy or well-being. Marrying someone of a different race may reflect this judgment; sharing domestic labor on an equal basis almost certainly does.[20] In other cases, the departure simply *expresses defiance*, and the real desire is to flout convention, whatever the norm is. Many apparently odd practices involving dress and manners are rooted in this phenomenon; some people find defiance an intrinsic good, and what they are defying is more or less incidental. In still other cases, the departure is the expression of an individual *desire or taste*, which the person would pursue whether or not it is inconsistent with social roles and accompanying norms. Consider the view that Coca-Cola is actually better than all other drinks, a view that might be reflected in unconventional drink selections in many imaginable places.

We might stress here that people's behavior is a function of, among other things, the *intrinsic value*, to them, of the particular good in question; the *reputational effects* of having or failing to have that good; and the *consequences for self-conception* of having or failing to have that good.[21] Social norms influence reputational effects and consequences for self-conception. In this way, the intrinsic value of some good—a watch, an item of clothing, a job, a meal—might not be enough to determine choice. Things with little intrinsic value might be chosen because of their reputational effects (consider the huge numbers of people who purchase certain best-selling high-brow books that they are unlikely to read); things with considerable intrinsic value might be rejected because of their consequences for self-conception (consider a romance novel). Norms are critical to both phenomena.

Roles and Law

Prevailing roles and norms can be fortified by legal requirements; they may even owe their existence to law. Law is frequently an effort to prescribe roles. There are many specific legal provisions for people occupying different roles—parents, spouses, employers, employees, homeowners, nuclear power plant operators, animal owners, doctors, stockbrokers, landlords, automobile sellers, and others. By prescribing appropriate behavior, law can help constitute the relevant social roles. Much of the law relating to families, employer-employee relations, and professional obligations has this feature. In fact, many roles are so deeply internalized that they seem "natural," even though they owe their origin to social and even legal conventions.

Often law tries to redefine roles. In recent years, this has happened with respect to the roles of employee, husband, father, disabled person, and judge. Thus, for example, modern law has said that husbands may not rape their wives; that absent fathers owe duties of support to their children; that disabled people have certain rights of access to the workplace. All of these measures can be seen as attempts to create new or better norms to define the relevant roles.

Law's pervasive attention to roles shows the poverty of the familiar idea that "efficiency" and "distribution" exhaust the concerns of law and the state. Sometimes society and law revisit a currently conceived role for reasons that have nothing to do with either efficiency or distribution. People occupying a certain role may, for example, not be treated with appropriate respect; they may not receive love and affection; or they may not be targets of (deserved) shame. There are limits to the law's power to redefine roles. But law may certainly be able to move things in particular directions.

Citizens and Consumers

Of course each of us occupies many different roles, and there is much to be said about the constraints imposed by these diverse roles. But for present purposes, an especially important and pervasive difference involves the relationship between *citizen* and *consumer*.

Let us return to John Jones in the fifth tale in section I. The example shows that in your capacity as a citizen, you might urge a result—with respect to, say, the duties of polluters or commercial broadcasters—that is quite different from what you seek through your market behavior in your capacity as a consumer. Acting as citizens, many people try to change social practices, and they often try to do this by altering social norms associated with a particular role. Sometimes these efforts are a function of the role of citizen and associated norms. In their private capacity—as consumers, employers, or family members—people may do what they know, on balance, to be unjust, and as citizens, they may support measures that better reflect their convictions. Sometimes efforts to change norms and roles reflect an understanding that human beings are selfish or have weakness of will, and that some measures should be taken to ensure behavior that, on reflection, we would like to follow.

In addition, citizens do or say things just because of existing social norms, which impose sanctions on publicly expressed dissident behavior or judgments; in their private capacity, people may be freer to do or say as they (in a sense, and subject to the prevailing norms) wish. In all cases, the difference is connected to the fact that a citizen is helping to make a judgment not simply for himself but for a collectivity. In this sense, there are important contextual differences between market behavior and voting behavior. The former does not affect the collectivity in the same way, and hence those concerned, for example, to protect the environment may believe that their own behavior is largely irrelevant, whereas laws can make a great deal of difference. Partly, for this reason, the role of citizen is accompanied by norms that can discourage selfishness and encourage attention to the public good.[22] "The very idea that I treat the prevention of environmental damage just like buying a private good is itself quite absurd. The amount I am ready to pay for my toothpaste is typically not affected by the amount you pay for yours. But it would be amazing if the payment I am ready to make to save nature is totally independent of what others are ready to pay for it, since it is specifially a social concern. The 'lone ranger' model of environmental evaluation confounds the nature of the problem at hand."[23]

In fact, many efforts to change law are at least partly an outgrowth of the difference between citizens and consumers (chapter 1). Consider laws outlawing sexual harassment, providing incentives to share domestic labor,[24] or granting workers a right to unionize. It should be clear that in such cases, there is no simple relationship among choices, preferences, norms, and roles. There may be conflict or tension between two or more of these.

Meaning

By "meaning," I refer to the expressive dimension of conduct (not excluding speech) in the relevant community.[25] The expressive dimension involves the *attitudes and commitments that the conduct signals*. A complex body of First Amendment doctrine deals with the problem of "expressive conduct," that is, acts that carry an expressive purpose and effect, such as flag-burning, draftcard-burning, sleeping in parks. But most conduct has an expressive function—not in the sense that the actor necessarily intends to communicate a message, but in the sense that people will take the conduct to be expressing certain attitudes and commitments.

Consider some examples. If I light up a cigarette, I will, in certain parts of the United States, be signaling something relatively precise and very bad about myself, my self-conception, and my concern for others. In other parts of the United States, the signals are very different. In France, a smoker gives still different signals. If you fail to attend church—or if you do attend church, and tell everyone about it—your act will have particular meanings, and these have everything to do with the community in which you find yourself. If I decide not to get married, or not to have children, my act will convey a restricted range of possible meanings, and I will not have much control over those meanings. (If I were a woman, my decisions to this effect would have a quite different set of meanings. The meaning of a woman's not marrying or having children is quite different from a man's.)

Language also has social meanings, extending far beyond the words themselves and reflected in the attitudes and commitments signaled by how people talk. Context determines those meanings. The words, "You look great today," can have many different possible social meanings: consider their use from a mother to a fifteen-year-old daughter, from a male employer to a female employee, from a doctor to a convalescent patient, from a homosexual male student to a male classmate. If you refer to women as "girls," you are also making (whatever your intentions) a certain set of statements about yourself and about your views on gender issues. A description of certain Americans as "blacks" will have a different meaning in 1996 (after the adoption of the term "African-American") from what it was in, say, 1976.

As with social norms and social roles, the social meanings of acts are something about which individuals can do relatively little (most of the time).[26] If a lawyer drives a Harley-Davidson motorcycle to Wall Street, his own attitude toward his act will have little relation to what other people take his act to mean. If a nonsmoker asks someone not to smoke, the social meaning of the act will be quite different in New York in 1996 from what it was in the same city in 1966, and different as well from what it is in Germany in 1996. This is a pervasive characteristic of social meanings. If you buckle your seat belt in Boston, you will communicate no insult to the driver; but things would have been very different twenty years ago, and within certain subgroups the buckling of a seat belt still connotes cowardice or accusation.

On the other hand, there are contexts in which a person or a small group of people may make inroads on social meanings. In a household, a woman may be able to alter, a little or a lot, the social meaning to her family of her refusal to do dishes or to make dinner, or her decision to go out with colleagues at night. In a company, a single person or a small group may be able to alter the social meaning of discourteous or aggressive behavior formerly taken as natural or normative, or even as definitive of membership in a certain group. But the most entrenched social meanings are—by definition—not movable without concerted action on the part of many people. Hence private groups often attempt to bring about changes in meanings and the norms that produce them. Religious organizations, feminist groups, animal rights' activists, groups challenging "political correctness," are prominent recent examples. Often they have been highly successful; sometimes they produce norm cascades.

The expressive dimension of action has everything to do with the actor's particular social role—with the way in which acts conform to or violate expectations associated with the role. Because of the social meaning of action, a lawyer, acting as a lawyer, may not make jokes that would be perfectly acceptable with her family or friends. If a law school dean wears shorts to teach contracts, or calls students by their first name, he will be signaling something important and a bit radical; at a small college, the signals would be altogether different.

Many roles are ascriptive and not chosen, even in postfeudal societies. We cannot fully control the roles in which we find ourselves. To be sure, people have power to assume or not to assume some roles. You can decide whether to be a spouse, a parent, a teacher, a dean, and so forth. And within limits, you can decide what it means to be any of these things; people can certainly alter the roles associated with parent, wife, and husband, even if they cannot do a great deal about the meanings associated with their choices. But many roles are assigned rather than voluntarily assumed—child, man, African-American, old person, short person, and more. A role that is assigned might be described as a *status*, a distinctive kind of role that, if surrounded by objectionable norms, raises special problems (see the discussion of caste in section

VI). And many roles cannot be easily rejected in most societies—driver, employee, student, citizen, family member.

Beliefs About Facts

Choices, meaning, role, and norms are commonly based on beliefs about relevant facts. In fact, beliefs about facts help generate all of these things. Someone may believe, for example, that cigarette smoking is not dangerous, and he may smoke partly for that reason. If he really believed that smoking was dangerous, perhaps he would not smoke. Choices are pervasively a function of beliefs. The same is true for social norms. Consider the dramatic recent shifts with respect to social norms governing cigarette smoking. Such norms have a great deal with prevailing beliefs about whether smoking causes harm to nonsmokers. When the belief shifts, the norm shifts as well.

Norms about behavior are interpenetrated with beliefs about harm and risk. Thus, many religiously grounded norms about personal cleanliness and hygiene often owe their origins to beliefs about what is healthy; but the norms often outstrip the beliefs and receive a moral grounding that is not simply reducible to an instrumental judgment about likely risks. When someone violates a norm relating to hygiene, people's reaction is different—more stern and more deeply moralized— than it would be if the reaction were based solely on the incremental increase in risk.

There are complex interactions between understandings of facts and social roles. Certainly beliefs about facts help generate roles. Beliefs about natural differences between men and women, or blacks and whites, affect social understandings about the appropriate roles of men and women or blacks and whites. When people see that apparent differences between social groups are not grounded in fact, the roles associated with group members may shift accordingly. Attacks on claimed natural differences have affected perceptions of appropriate role.

But the converse is also true: Understandings of facts may be a function of roles and accompanying norms. There is a complex scientific literature on the differences between men and women; much of the relevant work, even in its most scientific forms, rests palpably on conceptions of roles and of surrounding norms. When the social role of a certain group is to be laborers, or wives, it may be hard for most people to believe that all people are (in some relevant sense) equal.

Judgments about fact are similarly entangled with social norms. When most people smoke, it is hard for most people to believe that smoking is dangerous. The norm affects the belief, just as the belief affects the norm. In fact, norms and judgments about risk are hard to separate.

Divisions in the Self and Norm Bandwagons

I have noted that social norms can make people act and talk publicly in ways that are different from how they actually think, or from how they act and talk privately. People comply with norms that they wish were otherwise or even despise. Under the apartheid regime in South Africa, public criticism of apartheid—at least within South Africa—much understated private opposition to apartheid. The same is truth for Communist regimes.[27] Even in democracies, the deterrent effect of social norms on acts and beliefs creates a sharp disjunction between public acts (including speech) and private thought. Hence a state of affairs may persist even though there is widespread opposition to it. And eventually the norms may affect private thought itself.

Political actors might be able to exploit this disjunction in order to bring about large-scale social change. In fact, many political participants can be described as *norm entrepreneurs*; consider Martin Luther King, Jr., William Bennett, Louis Farrakhan, Catharine MacKinnon, Ronald Reagan, and Jerry Falwell. Individuals who are in favor of changes in norms face a free-rider problem. Political actors, whether public or private, can exploit current dissatisfaction with existing norms by (a) signaling their own commitment to change, (b) creating coalitions, (c) making defiance of the norms seem or be less costly, and (d) making compliance with new norms seem or be more beneficial. We might say that the intrinsic value of some option may be held constant, but the reputational and self-conception values may shift dramatically. There can be a "tipping point" when norms start to push in new directions.

When the free-rider problem begins to be solved, through reducing the cost of acting inconsistently with prevailing norms, private thoughts will be stated publicly, and things can shift very quickly. Something of this sort happened in both South Africa and Eastern Europe, producing more rapid and more peaceful changes than anyone anticipated. Part of the reason is that hostility to the regimes was widespread and intense—but inconsistent with existing social norms and hence mostly invisible and thus much underestimated. When the norms began to collapse, the regimes collapsed too.

This point bears on norm bandwagons. People may publicly support an existing norm not because they are genuinely committed to it, but because they fear social sanctions. As I have said, there is a bandwagon effect when those sanctions diminish or disappear, as many people join the group opposing the existing norm and urging a new one. The result can be astonishingly rapid change.[28] An effect of this kind occurred with two opposing and recent movements—the feminist movement and the recent opposition to "political correctness" in the university. In many circles, it occurred as well with respect to both smoking and recycling.

III. Choices and Preferences

If we attend to the functions of norms, meanings, and roles, how will we understand the relationship between choices and preferences? An initial problem is that the notion of a "preference" is quite ambiguous. When we say that someone "prefers" to do as he chooses, what exactly do we mean? There are two major possibilities. I have briefly discussed them in chapter 1; we are now in a position to see how attention to the place of norms, meanings, and roles complicates both of them.

Preferences as Choices

The idea of a "preference" might be understood as simply a choice, as in the idea, influential within economics, of the "revealed preference." On this view, preferences *are* choices. But choices are imperfect predictors of behavior without an account of what lies behind them.[29] From the bare fact of (particular) choices, it is not always possible to make robust claims about future choices. Because of the function of norms, meanings, and roles, even the weakest axioms of revealed preference theory can fail. John Jones, in the fifth tale in section I, presents an illustration; his particular choices do not allow observers to offer general predictions. But for the present let us take a simpler example. If Jones prefers X over Y, we might think that he will not prefer Y over X or Z; the introduction of the third alternative, Z, ought not to change Jones's preferences for X over Y. After all, Jones prefers X to Y, and he would have to be an odd person to prefer Y to X simply because of the introduction of Z.

But we can readily imagine cases in which the new alternative Z has precisely this effect. Jones might, for example, always select the second largest piece of cake, or he might want to be a person of relative moderation. Empirical work has encountered an effect called "extremeness aversion," in which people make choices that avoid the extremes.[30] Extremeness aversion is a product of social norms. People are generally taught to avoid extremes, and people who make extreme choices seem like malcontents, oddballs, or (never a word of praise) extremists. There are many examples. A voter might, for example, choose a Republican candidate over a Democratic candidate; but the introduction of some third candidate, say Ross Perot, may change the underlying choice, because it makes some new characteristic salient to voters,[31] or because it shifts the outcome produced by the decision, making it moderate where it would otherwise be extreme.

More broadly, choices are a function of prevailing social meanings and roles, which can bring into effect a wide range of relevant norms. If you are in a certain social group, you may well choose a drink of brandy or wine over Coca-Cola simply because of local practices. The choice of Coca-Cola may signal excessive informality, an unwillingness to unwind and enjoy oneself, or even disrespect. In a different group, your choice may be different (regardless of what you would choose if you were in your house alone). You may purchase an American car, or display the flag on July 4, because of existing norms in your community. Perhaps your purchase of a non-American car would signal a lack of patriotism; perhaps your failure to display the flag would be taken as a political protest, whether or not you meant it that way. If you run a local television station, your decision whether to allow violent programming is very much a function of prevailing norms, even if such programming would attract a large audience.

To take a science fiction example: If you lived in a society of vegetarians, the act of eating meat—at, let us suppose, specially designated animal flesh restaurants—would be very different from what it is in a society of meat-eaters. And if you lived in a society of vegetarians, you might well choose not to eat meat. The meanings of actions are set by forces that are emphatically human but that are largely outside of the control of the individual agent.

These points suggest that to explain or predict behavior, it is important not only to know about choices but also to have some account of what underlies choices, or of what choices are *for*, and in this way to introduce an account of motivation. Here social norms, meanings, and roles will be crucial. And if this is right, it is impossible to explain behavior by reference to choices, without using the very apparatus that the "revealed preference" idea was intended to eliminate. Normative arguments on the basis of choices alone will also run into serious trouble. Choices do not suggest acontextual valuation of social goods, and thus even if we want to respect people's valuations, we will have to look not at but behind choices.

Preferences Behind Choices

Let us turn, then, to another and more promising conception of a "preference." The term is often meant to refer not to choices themselves, but to something that lies behind and accounts for choices.[32] This idea has obvious advantages. It seeks to provide the motivational story on which choices are by themselves inarticulate, and if the motivational story is uncovered, positive work should be possible. And if we can identify what lies behind choices, perhaps we can get a sense of people's own conception of what promotes their well-being, and this is surely relevant for purposes of both ethics and politics.

But this idea introduces difficulties of its own—indeed, the difficulties that the "revealed preference" notion was intended to overcome. Recall John Jones, the protagonist of the fifth tale earlier. Can we provide an account of Jones's motivation or "preferences"? Perhaps we can; but no simple answer would make sense. Several possibilities do present themselves. From the fact that Jones pays a certain premium for automobile safety, we might judge that he is risk-averse—someone who prefers to avoid danger—and we might even attempt to generate numbers capturing his own conception of the value of his life. But when it comes to bicycle-riding, Jones is somewhat reckless. And in his capacity as voter, Jones's valuations appear still more complex. To get an account of his motivation, we need to know many details—something like a personality profile.

The point raises some larger issues. If we think of a preference as something that lies behind choice, what is it exactly? Plainly it is a disposition or a mental state of some kind. And plainly people do have dispositions of various sorts. But internal mental states can be extraordinarily complex. I have already referred to the place of intrinsic value, reputational effects, and consequences for self-conception. People's decisions can be based on whims, responses to norms, second-order preferences, aspirations, judgments, emotions, drives of various kinds, conceptions of role, and more, with all these producing particular results depending on the context. What lies behind a choice in one setting may be quite different from what lies behind a choice in a different time and place.

In this light, it can be hard to make predictions about individuals or groups without knowing a great deal. Of course, the value of positive work lies in its predictive value and in what the evidence shows. If good predictions can be made by positing "preferences," then there is nothing wrong with positing preferences. Of course, there are regularities in people's behavior, and these regularities can be connected to people's dispositions. But general dispositions of various kinds—to avoid extremes, to comply with norms, to drink beer rather than wine—manifest themselves in particular choices only in accordance with context. No simple thing called a "preference" accounts for choice. Preferences are not the building-blocks for a theory of decision; whatever we call a "preference" needs to be further unpacked.

Some of the most intriguing work in modern economics—especially by Gary Becker and Timur Kuran—attempts to include, as part of people's "preferences," responses to social norms and pressures, effects of past decisions on current ones, and desires that anticipate and emerge from habits and addictions.[33] I believe that this recent work will eventually be seen as an important step in the direction of dividing "preferences" into further subcategories. For many purposes, it might well be best to dispense altogether with the idea of preference and to work instead with choices on the one hand and with complex and somewhat unruly mental states on the other—or to relate choices to more concrete influences, such as norms, price changes, increases in leisure time, roles, and so forth. I believe that this point gives us reason to doubt the elaborate edifice of social science based on notions of "preference" or "metapreference" (though much of the edifice can remain if reconstructed on different foundations).

Shifting from positive to normative, we can see that the complexity of mental states also makes it hard for governments to know how to respond to people's choices. Choices depend on norms that people may not endorse on reflection; hence, it is not clear how government should handle smoking, drug use, single parenthood, risky sexual activity, recycling, and much more. Collective efforts to discourage damaging or risky behavior, or to encourage norms that promote well-being or solve collective action problems, might well be consistent with people's underlying aspirations and judgments.

The next task is to separate positive, descriptive, and normative inquiries more sharply, and in the process to try to untangle relevant mental states and their influences. Of course, it may be the case that once we understand a person, or a group, very well, we will understand those mental states and their relation to external forces, and we may be able to make a wide range of predictions about how different forces will affect behavior.

IV. Anomalies

Willingness to Pay versus Willingness to Accept: The Place of Shame

Recent empirical work suggests that many claims in economics (including the Coase theorem) rest on an intriguingly false assumption, one that suggests that it may sometimes be impossible for government to take preferences "as they are."[34] The basic finding is this: The initial grant of an entitlement of some good X to some person A can make A value X far more than he would if X had been initially allocated to B. (It also makes B value it less than he otherwise would.) The initial allocation—the legal rule saying who owns what, before people begin to contract with one another—serves to create, to legitimate, and to reinforce social understandings about presumptive rights of ownership. The effect of the initial allocation of a commodity or an entitlement is commonly described as the "endowment effect."[35]

This point has received considerable empirical confirmation, often in the context of environmental amenities. One study found that people would demand about five times as much to allow destruction of trees in a park as they would pay to prevent the destruction of those same trees.[36] When hunters were questioned about the potential destruction of a duck habitat, they said that they would be willing to pay an average of $247 to prevent the loss—but would demand no less than $1044 to accept it.[37] In another study, participants required payments to accept degradation of visibility ranging from 5 to more than 16 times higher than their valuations based on how much they were willing to pay to prevent the same degradation.[38] A related experiment tried to ascertain the "existence value" of a houseplant that grows like a pine tree. The subjects were told that any trees not sold or kept would be killed at the end of the experiment. The mean willingness to pay (WTP) to avoid the "kill" option was $7.81. The mean willingness to accept (WTA) payment to allow a tree to be killed was $18.43.[39]

In general, the range of the disparity appears to vary from slight amounts to a ratio of more than four to one, with WTA usually doubling WTP. In field studies, environmental goods tend to reflect a disparity of factors from two to over ten.[40] In some environmental experiments involving trees, the WTA/WTP ratio is extraordinarily high, ranging between 60/1 and 90/1.[41]

What explains this phenomenon? There are many possibilities, and none is likely to be entirely satisfactory (chapter 10). My suggestion is that some of the difference between WTP and WTA has to do with social norms and social meaning. If someone says that she is willing to accept $X to allow the expiration of a species, the meaning of her action is altogether different from what it is if she says that she is willing to pay $X (and no more) to prevent the extinction. Under prevailing social norms, one ought not to accept even a great deal of money to allow destruction of an environmental amenity—partly because the good at issue is collectively owned, partly because its loss may be irreversible, and partly because it is not thought to be commensurable with its cash equivalent (in the sense that it is not valued in the same way or along a single metric).

In these circumstances, people who announce their willingness to accept cash for the loss of a pond or a species feel *shame*. They believe that they are assuming responsibility for the destruction of something intrinsically valuable, not replaceable, and owned by many people. Because of the risk of shame, people will demand a great deal, and they may even refuse any amount that is offered.[42] By contrast, those who refuse to pay an enormous or infinite amount to *save* an environmental amenity do not feel the same degree of shame (if they feel shame at all). They are confronted with a different set of social norms.

Take an analogy. If someone is asked how much she would be willing to accept to allow her dog's life to be shortened by six months—or how much she would be willing to accept to allow her dog to suffer severe pain for, say, one week—she might well say: "No amount is sufficient." The question is very different if a veterinarian is asking someone whether unusual and expensive medical procedures should be used to prolong a dog's life or reduce its pain. Here the answer need not be: "No amount is too high."

Some intriguing work suggests that the disparity between WTA and WTP is connected with the assignment of moral responsibility for the destruction of environmental assets, which are perceived as intrinsic goods. The WTA measure assigns responsibility to the individual whereas the WTP measure does so more ambiguously. These findings are consistent with the norm-based explanation I am offering here. People want to avoid or to minimize the feeling that they have been morally culpable for producing the loss of an environmental amenity.[43] Feelings of moral culpability are tightly connected with prevailing social norms.

Shame, Altruism, and Free-Riding

Our point relates to the first tale in section I; we are now in a position to explain the apparent anomaly. When two people are supposed to divide an amount given to them under the stated conditions, the offeror in the ultimatum game feels shame—because he is demonstrating that he is a greedy and even horrible person—if he offers a penny or a dollar from a total of (say) $200. If a sum is given to two people under the conditions of the game, good people share; they do not try to keep almost all of the money for themselves. For his part, the offeree feels mistreated—treated in a contemptuous way—if a small or token amount is suggested. The social meaning of the statement "How about five cents for you?" is contempt; the social meaning of responding "Great!" is a willingness to be dishonored.

Experimental work shows that people contribute to a shared good, and refuse to free ride, far more often than economists predict.[44] It also shows that agents are especially willing to cooperate, and hence to solve collective action problems without coercion, if most other people are seen as cooperators. In such circumstances, the social norm is to cooperate and the social meaning of noncooperation is greed or selfishness. By contrast, it emerges that when a number of people free ride, and are seen to free ride, cooperation breaks down. In these circumstances, no social norms call for cooperation and hence the social meaning of cooperation is a willingness to be a "dupe" or a "sucker." The desire to contribute to a collective good is palpably a function of social norms. If social norms do not lead most people to contribute, contributions decrease steadily and dramatically. The first tale about ultimatums and fairness should therefore be taken as a metaphor for many social outcomes.

My suggestion, then, is that apparent puzzles of rationality are often a product of social norms and the moral judgments that are intertwined with those norms. Of course, a full explanation would have to include an account of how norms emerge as well, and we should not allow the term "social norms" to become our stock response to any apparently anomalous social behavior. But once prevailing norms are specified, we may be able to make robust predictions about behavior and its transformation and also to test the role of norms by asking whether the anomalous behavior continues when it is not observed publicly.

These points suggest that it may well be impossible to distinguish between what is entailed by "rationality" and what is entailed by social norms. For the individual agent, rationality is a function of social norms. A norm-free conception of rationality would have to depend on a conception of what people's rational "interests" are in a social vacuum. Since people never act in a social vacuum, such a conception would not be intelligible. Some economists appear to think it natural to suppose that it is in people's interest not to pick up their garbage (see the second tale in section I); they write as if social norms against littering add a kind of new or artificial factor to the individual calculus. But if we make this supposition, we are saying something about the individual's calculus without the antilittering norm; and what is the basis for any particular conception of how that calculus will come out? No such conception will be free of an understanding of people's *ends,* which are seen as such partly because of social influences, including social norms. Why, for example, is picking up garbage a cost rather than a benefit?

An implicit (but undefended and obscure) state of nature theory seems to lie at the heart of many distinctions between social norms and rationality, or rational self-interest. Thus, it is sometimes suggested that rational self-interest can be defined by seeing what people would do or would like in the "state of nature." But this is an unhelpful line of thought. Any state of nature will include social norms, and to know what it is rational for people to do, it is necessary to identify prevailing norms. The only way toward an account of individual rationality, or rational self-interest, that is separate from social norms is through an inquiry that is frankly normative and defended as such. Such an account must include an understanding of what people's ends *should be.* But to offer an account of this kind, it would be necessary to offer an understanding of what ends it is good for people to have, and such an understanding would take us far afield from positive economics or social science.

V. Government Action: On Autonomy and Tools

Sometimes it is desirable to change choices. Government might attempt to change choices by changing social norms, social meaning, and social roles. In fact, changes in norms may be the cheapest and most effective way to make things better, whatever are our criteria for assessing that matter. The relation between behavior and norms has yet to receive sustained attention; when we attend to that relation, we see that government has a policy instrument of great potential value.

To be sure, the fact that private people have the power to create norm communities may make government action less necessary or less desirable. Often the best step is to allow those communities to be formed and to see how they work out. But sometimes it is too costly for individuals to create or join those communities, and sometimes the generally held norm is too damaging to human well-being. These issues cannot be solved in the abstract; the judgment depends on the details. But it is clear that existing norms can create problems of various sorts and that collective action may be required.

Norms and Paternalism

Common objections to "paternalism" or "perfectionism" are not easy to sustain in such contexts. Recall that people usually do not choose norms, meaning, and roless; all of these are (within limits) imposed. As I have said, it would be ludicrous to deplore norms, meaning, and roles; they make life possible and they facilitate social engagement. They provide the context within which free interaction is possible. Nonetheless, some of them operate as severe limits on autonomy or well-being, and certainly they should not be treated as fixed or as given regardless of their content or consequences.

Private groups can test or even change norms. Indeed, the testing of current norms, meaning, and roles is a crucial function of groups intermediate between citizens and the state. Religious groups can in this sense be norm entrepreneurs; the same is true for environmental and civil rights organizations. But sometimes private groups are unable to produce desirable change on their own. This is a point missed by the idea that the sole basis for government action is to avoid force, fraud, and "harm to others." Obstacles to autonomy and to good lives can also come from bad roles, norms, and meaning.

Changes in norms and meaning can promote human well-being. Often all or most people would, on reflection, like to see a change in a particular norm, but they cannot bring about the change on their own, because in his individual capacity, each person has limited power to alter meaning, norms, or role. The case of mandatory helmets for hockey players is a familiar example.[45] Hockey players may prefer not to wear helmets if the meaning of helmet-wearing is cowardice; but their preferred solution, available only through a mandate, is a system in which all are required to wear helmets, and hence players wear helmets without signaling cowardice. Of course, shifts in norms, meaning, and roles are pervasive. Consider, for example, changing norms with respect to smoking, littering, drug use, polluting, racial discrimination, sexual relations outside of marriage, the role of women and men, and interracial relationships.

In fact, it is often hard to know what people would "like" or prefer, because their judgments and desires are entangled with norms, meaning, and role, and because once one or more of these is changed, they may be better off either objectively or subjectively. If government changes the social meaning of smoking (see the third tale in section I), has it acted illegitimately? What if most people, or most smokers, would, on reflection, want smoking to have a different meaning? Or suppose that government tries to change an aspect of a certain social role, like that of unwed fathers, high school teachers, homosexuals, or workers. Or suppose that government provision of information has effects on norms. Surely, the consequences of the change matter; surely, it matters if the change is supported by (most or all) unwed fathers, high school teachers, homosexuals, or workers, and if members of each group face a collective action problem.

Tools

Suppose that government is concerned about changing norms, meaning, or roles. It has many different tools for doing so; some of these are only mildly intrusive, whereas others foreclose choice. A good government should have a presumption in favor of the least intrusive means, moving up in the hierarchy when necessity dictates.

Most modestly, government may restrict itself to *education*, understood as simple statements of fact. We have seen that norms, meaning, and role can be a function of beliefs, and beliefs are mutable. Perhaps prevailing beliefs are false and warrant correction. People may think that AIDS is a disease limited to homosexuals, that smoking does not harm nonsmokers, or that there is no relation between cholesterol and heart disease or between diet and cancer. Provision of information may change prevailing norms with respect to, say, sexuality and diet. Changing norms with respect to smoking are almost certainly a result of information from government about health risk. In principle, there should be no objection to governmental efforts to correct false beliefs, even if the correction affects norms, meaning, and role. In fact, the change along this dimension may be the most important consequence of education, which may, for example, remove certain kinds of shame.

Government may also attempt to engage in *persuasion*, understood as a self-conscious effort to alter attitudes and choices rather than simply to offer information. Consider the third tale in section I; assume that some such advertisement had been issued by state officials. Perhaps it would have been effective (though its social meaning would have been altogether different if issued by officials rather than by members of the private African-American community). The "Just Say No" policy for drugs falls in the category of attempted persuasion; so too with efforts to control AIDS by strongly encouraging abstinence from sex or the use of condoms. Here government does not restrict itself to the provision of information, but instead uses rhetoric and vivid images to change norms, meaning, or role, and in this way to persuade people to choose a certain course.

Some people think that although the provision of information can be justified, government may rarely or never attempt to persuade. But if norms, roles, and meanings are beyond individual control, and sometimes bad, this thought is hard to sustain, at least if government is subject to democratic controls.

Consider in this connection the problem of smoking and the lessons of the third tale. Among blacks between 18 and 24, the rate has fallen from 37.1 percent in 1965, to 31.8 percent in 1979, to 20.4 percent in 1987, to 11.8 percent in 1991.[46] Among whites in the same age group, the rate fell from 38.4 percent in 1965 to 27.8 percent in 1987—but it has remained more or less constant since that time.[47] The change among black teenagers is universally described as a "public health success story," but one that government officials cannot explain. Though no one has a full account of this phenomenon, changing social norms appear to be playing a substantial role. Smoking does not have the same cachet in the African-American community that it has among whites. If government could bring about a general change in social norms governing smoking among teenagers—through, for example, attempts at persuasion—it is hardly clear that there would be a good objection to its behavior.

Government might also use economic instruments to *tax* or *subsidize* choices. Of course, education is assisted publicly, as are day care, museums, and public broadcasting (at least as of this writing). Alcoholic drinks, tobacco products, generation of waste, and some polluting activities are met with taxes (though some of these are subsidized too). We can understand economic incentives as efforts in part to counteract social meaning, social norms, or social roles with financial benefits or penalties designed to produce a good "equilibrium." A social meaning that is perceived to be bad might be "matched" with a financial incentive. Some such incentives may amount to efforts to change social norms or social meaning.

Government might also impose *time, place, and manner restrictions*. It might ban smoking in public places. It might say that television shows containing violence may be shown only in certain time slots. It might require government itself to choose low-polluting motor vehicles. It might ban affirmative action in the public sector but allow it in the private sector. Strategies of this kind might affect the social meaning of the relevant activity very generally. But they do not entirely foreclose choice; they channel it instead.

The most intrusive kind of government action is of course *straightforward coercion*. Thus, government might prohibit the use of certain drugs; require everyone to recycle or buckle their seat belts; or make education mandatory for people under a certain age.

VI. Government Action: Four Grounds

In this section I discuss several grounds for governmental efforts to change norms, meanings, and roles. The unifying theme is *the expressive function of law*—a term that I use to identify the function of law in expressing social values and in encouraging social norms to move in particular directions.

My discussion will not by any means exhaust law's expressive uses, and I do not discuss any of these grounds in much detail; I offer instead a brief and far from definitive sketch of some possibilities. An account of legitimate grounds for changes in norms will overlap a great deal with—and may even be reducible to—an account of the legitimate bases for governmental action. My purpose here is hardly to offer such an account, but instead to see how some fairly standard ideas might be brought to bear on the particular subjects under discussion. In none of these cases do I urge that social norms should be free from scrutiny on the merits by individual citizens. Government ought not to inculcate norms that cannot be supported and evaluated publicly, and on the basis of reasons. Like rules, norms will typically have a degree of crudeness and rigidity, and it is entirely appropriate for citizens to conclude that there are contexts in which even good norms make no sense.

Nor do I urge that the mere fact that behavior is a function of norms provides some warrant for governmental action. To defend governmental action, some claim has to be offered about how such action will make things better. A reference to norms helps undermine the view that government should restrict itself to the satisfaction of "preferences." We have seen that this term is highly ambiguous and that norms can often undermine human well-being. But to defend a change, the idea of well-being has to be specified, and it has to be shown that the change would improve matters under the relevant criteria.

To introduce the analysis, we might make a few initial distinctions.

- In some cases, all or almost all people will support an effort to change a norm, a meaning, or a role. In the case of hockey helmets, for example, there may be near-unanimous agreement that things would be better if the meaning of helmet-wearing were not coward-ice. In the case of cleaning up after one's dog, almost everyone may agree that things would be better if there was a norm in favor of cleaning up. Of course any such agreement may depend on norms that should themselves be brought into question. We might say that the agreement can be "impeached" by showing that people do not, on reflection, endorse the norms that produce agreement, or that there are problems with those norms.
- In some cases, all or almost all people will agree that behavior is a function not of intrinsic value, and not of effects on people's (well-considered) judgments about their self-conception, but instead of the reputational consequences of choice; and they will agree too that it would be better if the reputational consequences were different. All or almost all people might agree, for example, that use of drugs in a certain community stems from the reputational benefits of using drugs and the reputational costs of refusing to do so. They might also agree that things would be better if using drugs produced reputational harm rather than benefit; they might act accordingly via law (with education, attempted persuasion, economic incentives, or coercion). In this kind of case, there is also a possibility of "impeachment" of the agreement along lines suggested above.
- In some cases, existing norms may be part and parcel of a caste system. They may turn a morally irrelevant characteristic—race and gender are the most obvious examples—into a signaling device with

respect to social role and associated norms. If a caste system is unjust, it is appropriate to alter norms, roles, and meanings that perpetuate it.

- In some cases, existing norms undermine people's autonomy, by discouraging them from being exposed to diverse conceptions of the good and from giving critical scrutiny to their own conceptions, in such a way as to make it impossible for them to be, in any sense, masters of the narratives of their own lives.

These are brief notations on some highly controversial subjects. Needless to say, I cannot attempt here to defend an account of the appropriate role of the state; my purpose is more modestly to connect the project of norm management with some familiar ideas about what the state legitimately does. Notably, there are cases in which it is unnecessary to choose among two or more of the general grounds for government action; people with varying theoretical commitments might believe that a particular action makes sense. Hence political participants might achieve an *incompletely theorized agreement* on a particular outcome—an agreement on what steps make best sense, unaccompanied by a shared understanding of why, exactly, they make best sense. Those interested in possible changes in norms would do well to take advantage of such agreements.

Norms and Some Unusual Collective Action Problems

Standard Formulations and Conventional Accounts

In a standard formulation, many social practices would be inefficient if not for certain social norms; the norms solve a collective action problem. They do the work of law. They may provide conventions on which everyone voluntarily settles; table manners are an example. Or they may solve prisoner's dilemmas through social sanctions imposed on deviants; this is true of the idea that people should clean up after their dogs. And because of the absence of good norms, some existing practices are highly inefficient. Take the standard case of littering, captured in the second tale in section I. Under conventional assumptions, each person may well litter—if the costs of throwing things in the garbage are wholly internalized, whereas the benefits of doing so are spread across a wide range of people. In the conventional account, "rational" individuals, acting in their "self-interest," will produce a great deal of litter, and perhaps so much that legal regulation is ultimately required. This idea helps explain legal responses to environmental degradation, as in the cases of mandatory recycling, taxes on or fees for polluting activity, and command and control regulation.

Puzzles

But many questions might be raised about the standard formulation and the conventional account. The relevant changes do not bring about Pareto improvements. Some people are losers; in fact, many people may be losers, for example, those who dislike helmets and seat belts no matter how many people wear them. We should distinguish the simplest cases—in which all or nearly all people favor a change in norms—from cases in which there are mere majorities. If everyone would favor a situation in which people pick up after their dogs, but this result cannot be brought about without government action, the case is easy: Government action should be initiated. But if 65 percent of people would favor the change, and 35 percent like the status quo, we have a harder case. Perhaps the change would be favored under the Kaldor-Hicks criterion (Do the winners win more than the losers lose?); but that criterion is highly controversial. When a mere majority favors a change, any decision about whether government action is appropriate must depend on answers to a large question in political theory.

Even more fundamentally, the words "rational" and "self-interest" obscure a great deal, since they take so much for granted. As we have seen, there is no sharp dichotomy between rationality and social norms or between self-interest and social norms; what is rational and what is in an agent's self-interest are functions of social norms. Return to our second tale and suppose that there is a social norm to the effect that everyone should pick up litter. If the norm is in place, people who act in their rational self-interest will not litter. In the second tale, were the nonlitterers or the control group acting in their rational self-interest? What is rational, and what promotes self-interest, depends on many exogenous factors, including existing norms.

There is a further point. Suppose that there is no norm against littering; that people think that there is too much litter; and that they would like to create a new, antilittering norm. Would it be right to say that this is a case in which a collective action problem would be best solved with the aid of social norms? The statement would not be false but it would be misleading and incomplete. *What creates the collective action problem is an array of individual judgments and desires that are themselves (in all likelihood) in part a function of social norms.* If people "want" a new norm, their desire probably stems from many other norms—such as norms favoring clean rather than dirty parks, norms in favor of shared rather than maldistributed burdens, norms in favor of solutions through norms rather than coercion or fines.

In short, when a situation is supposed to create a prisoner's dilemma that would be satisfied by some norm Z, the situation presupposes a range of norms A through Y that are being held constant and not being put in contention. Then the question becomes: Why is it that norm Z (say, the norm with respect to littering) is put into question, rather than some other norm (say, the norm favoring clean parks)? This question has yet to be addressed in existing work on collective action and social norms. An answer might be found in one of two ways. We might put in question—as the source of the collective action problem—those norms that are most weakly held or not part of the agents' deepest convictions and understandings. Typically, changes in the norms sought to solve collective action problems seem to be a form of "tinkering," encouraging conduct that preserves what people believe most deeply, have thought through most carefully, or most take for granted. On this economistic view, we are asking which norms can be changed most cheaply, looking at subjective convictions.

Alternatively, we might look not to agents' subjective convictions but venture instead an objective account of human needs and human interests. With such an approach, a collective action problem exists because if agents could agree on the norm in question—say, one that favors littering—things would be better rather than worse. It is not clear, however, that an objective approach of this kind can coexist with ordinary understandings of collective action problems, since the ordinary understandings are rooted in subjective desires. A possible conclusion of what I have said thus far is that in the context of norms, the ordinary understandings face a conceptual problem.

Legal Responses

However rationality and self-interest are defined, a well-functioning society needs many norms that make it rational for people, acting in their self-interest, to solve collective action problems. When such problems exist, it is often because of the prevailing social norms that make rational self-interest take a certain form. A large task is therefore to try to inculcate superior norms. Effective responses promote efficiency and simultaneously enhance a form of freedom, by producing outcomes that citizens reflectively judge best but cannot obtain on their own.

Much legal regulation has this goal. Such regulation might even consist of direct coercion, designed to generate good norms and to pick up the slack in their absence. There are laws designed to ensure that everyone picks up after their dog; that people do not litter; that people do not smoke in certain places. These laws are rarely if ever enforced through criminal prosecutions. But they have an effect in shaping social norms and social meaning. They help to inculate both shame and pride; they help define the appropriate sources of these things. They readjust the personal calculation, making what is rational, and what is in one's self-interest, different from what they were before.

The key point is that such a change may be supported by the reflective judgments of all or most people. When it is, there should generally be no objection in principle. The point very much bears on the phenomenon of norm bandwagons. People may actually reject existing norms but fail to state their opposition publicly, and once public opposition becomes less costly, new norms may rapidly come into place. Government can be a help in this endeavor by engaging in educational campaigns or by enacting laws that lead to good norms.

Autonomy and Well-Being

Thus far, I have tried to avoid the most controversial quesions and to build from common understandings. Let us venture now into more complicated territory, connected with the idea of autonomy. Of course, a liberal society might want to ensure that all of its citizens are autonomous. For the moment, let us understand the notion in a way that leaves open many questions but that will be helpful for our limited purposes here. A citizen can be understood as autonomous insofar as she is able to choose among a set of reasonably good options and is reflective and deliberative about her choice. A society can be understood as self-governing, and as politically autonomous, to the extent that its citizens face a range of reasonably good options and exercise capacities of reflection and deliberation about their choices.

It should be clear that social norms, meanings, and roles may undermine individual autonomy. Above all, this is because norms can compromise autonomy itself, by stigmatizing it. People may believe, on reflection, that the act of being well-educated should not be a source of shame; but in some communities, a good deal of education may be inconsistent with prevailing social norms. Or exposure to diverse options, and reflection about which is best, may seem inconsistent with existing norms. In such cases, autonomy cannot exist without collective assistance; people are able to produce the norms, meanings, and roles that they reflectively endorse only with governmental involvement. Something must be done collectively if the situation is to be changed.

To promote autonomy, a society might seek to ensure that everyone has a minimal degree of education, a certain level of exposure to diverse conceptions of the good, and what might be considered the material bases of autonomy: food, shelter, and freedom from criminal violence. In modest forms, this project is fully compatible with political liberalism; perfectionalist liberals might insist on a good deal in this vein in order to allow people to be (more or less) masters of the narratives of their own lives. In either case, social norms can undermine the liberal project, and government might try to alter them in order to promote autonomy. Prevailing norms and meanings may be adaptive to limits in existing opportunities; but they are nonetheless an obstacle to autonomy.

A government that seeks to promote autonomy might well work against efforts by subcommunities to require conformity to a single defining creed. In fact, conflicts between antidiscrimination principles and religious liberty have everything to do with perceived limits on governmental ability to change norms, meanings, and roles in subgroups that deny autonomy. These conflicts are generally resolved in favor of the latter, especially in the area of sex equality. But if we attend to the autonomy-denying effects of norms and meaning, it might well make sense to resolve the conflicts against subgroups, even religious ones.

Outside of the domain of autonomy, we might think that there are obstacles to well-being in norms that encourage people to take high risks, simply because the failure to do so signals—in light of those norms—cowardice or worse. Norms that encourage people to carry guns, use dangerous drugs, drive well over the speed limit, and so forth may properly be an object of governmental attack because of their potentially pernicious effects on people's lives. The key point is that behavior persists because of reputational incentives. Perhaps information and persuasion are the best tools for government to use. But in some cases economic incentives or coercion may be justified.

Caste

Many problems of discrimination actually raise issues of caste. We might say that we have a system with caste-like features when a highly visible and morally irrelevant factor is turned, by social and legal practices, into a systematic source of social disadvantage.[48] An important and disastrous feature of this situation is the *signaling effect* of the characteristic that is shared by lower caste members. That characteristic promotes a certain social role for caste members, since it is associated with a range of undesirable or otherwise stigmatizing traits. Often an attack on a caste system amounts to an attack on that social role and its associated social norms—especially as a result of behavioral norms shared, or thought to be shared, by members of the lower caste. For lower caste members, the problem is that the shared characteristic carries with it a meaning—stupidity, helplessness, tendency to violence, passivity, venality—that cannot be controlled by individual agents.

Suppose, for example, that it is thought important to alter social norms about gender relations. The social role of "being a woman" is associated with a wide range of social norms and social meanings, encompassing many examples from the present and recent past. Thus, it may be that women do the majority of domestic labor. In these circumstances, a man who does most of the domestic labor might seem odd, or in some way woman-ish, and a woman who asks for something like equality in domestic labor might seem odd, selfish, or in some way man-ish. A woman in her fifties might be seen in a way fundamentally different from a man in his fifties, because of social norms associated with gender. Or a single woman might be stigmatized, or inquired about, in ways fundamentally different from what happens to a similarly situated man. Or a woman who complains about apparently mild forms of sexual harassment might seem to be a radical, a troublemaker, or someone without a sense of humor.

A wide range of "choices" might emerge from the underlying social norms. These choices might reflect adaptation by lower caste members to existing injustice; they might be a product of the social opprobrium attached to violation of social norms by lower caste members. The choices might even be called "preferences"; certainly desires can be affected. But many women believe, on reflection, that the social meaning of being a woman is bad for them and that it should be changed. These women face a collective action problem that may be best solved with government action. In any case, a caste system tends to deny autonomy to lower caste members.

This is simply a stylized discussion of the problems faced by people who live within a caste system, and who might seek to enlist the law to make things better. Such people face a free-rider problem that pervasively undermines reform efforts.

Expressive Action

Many laws have an expressive function. They "make a statement" about how much, and how, a good or bad should be valued. They are an effort to constitute and to affect social meanings, social norms, and social roles.

Of course, human goods are valued in different ways; people have a wide variety of evaluative stances toward relationships and goods (chapters 3 and 5). Laws with expressive functions are often designed to promote a certain way of valuing certain goods. Many such laws are intended to say that specified goods *should be valued in a way that deters thinking of them as mere objects for use*. Laws forbidding the purchase and sale of certain goods can be so understood. A ban on the sale of children is designed (among other things) to say that children should be valued in a way that forbids the acceptance of cash as a reason for taking them out of parental care. A ban on vote-selling can be viewed similarly. We might understand such a law as an effort to make a certain statement about the pricelessness—not the infinite value—of the right to vote. In the environmental area, debates over market valuation are partly debates over this question (chapter 3). Some people think that environmental amenities, like beaches or species, should be seen with awe and wonder and ought not to be taken as objects for human consumption. In their view, market valuation should therefore be viewed with suspicion; it threatens to affect social norms and social meanings in undesirable ways.

Laws with expressive justifications may or may not be designed to have social consequences. Some such laws might be defended on the ground that they will affect social norms and move them in appropriate directions. At this stage there are empirical questions: Do laws affect social norms and social meanings? Under what conditions? But laws with expressive justifications might be defended for the statement they make, quite independently of consequences. Certainly this is true for individual behavior. People may avoid a certain course of action because of the meaning of that course, apart from consequences.

VII. Blocked Grounds

What I have suggested here should unsettle some common understandings about government "paternalism" and "meddling." If private choices are a function of roles, norms, and meanings over which private people have no sovereignty, many imaginable initiatives from government are consistent with individual autonomy, rightly conceived. But this conclusion ought not to suggest that government should be licensed to do however it wishes.

Often government action should be rejected on simple pragmatic grounds—because, for example, it is likely to be futile or counterproductive. The "Just Say No" campaign with respect to drug use probably falls in this category. Or perhaps government has mistakenly concluded that there is a collective action problem calling for governmental response. Perhaps most people are happy that littering is not stigmatized; perhaps efforts to stigmatize teenage smoking will backfire and make smoking seem bold or glamorous. If government action would be ineffective or counterproductive, it should not go forward.

It is also true that government interference with norms, role, or meaning might be confused or otherwise wrong. Government might compound a collective action problem, respond to well-organized private groups promoting unjust goals, or aggravate a caste-like situation. Imagine an effort to *promote* the use of cigarettes, alcohol, or drugs, or to *discourage* the buckling of seat belts, or to increase the opprobrium associated with the role of being a homosexual. Nothing I have said suggests that government is not properly criticized when it engages in activity of this sort. But any such criticism should be on the merits, not on the ground that government may not interfere with private preferences or choices.

There is a final point. A liberal society limits the permissible bases for governmental action. It might well describe the limits as "rights." A full account of these limits would be far too ambitious for my purposes here; but a few notes will be helpful.

Some government action designed to change norms, meaning, and role might be based on religious grounds. These should be banned as reasons for public action. At least in the American constitutional system, for example, it is unacceptable for government to attempt to legislate on the ground that the divinity of Jesus Christ requires a certain state of affairs. So, too, it would be unacceptable to base government action on grounds that deny the basic equality of human beings—as in efforts to encourage norms that treat members of racial minorities as second-class citizens. In a similar vein, many efforts to change norms would impair autonomy rather than promote it.

In any case, some human interests are properly denominated rights, and efforts to change norms, meanings, and role should not be allowed to invade rights. A wide range of imaginable efforts ought to be rejected because of this risk. Consider, for example, a suggestion that the meaning of refusing government officials into your home is now "personal courage and independence"— accompanied by the not implausible thought that things would be better if the meaning were "unpatriotic unwillingness to cooperate with the crime-fighting effort," culminating in a proposal that everyone should be required to open their homes to the government. There is a collective action here. But if it is believed that people should have a right to keep government officials from their homes, this proposal should be rejected.

Political liberals go further and urge rejection of any ground for action that is based on a "comprehensive view."[49] Of course, there are many complexities in this claim. What is important for present purposes is that on any sound view of liberalism, there is no *general* basis, in principle, for objection to proposals of the sort I have suggested. Political liberals ought to acknowledge, for example, that social roles and social meanings may undermine the equality and liberty of citizens and that changes require collective action. The constraints imposed by political liberalism impose no bans on those changes.

Conclusion

Many claims about the appropriate limits of law are insufficiently attentive to the pervasive effects of social norms, social meanings, and social roles. In fact, these effects have yet to receive much attention. But the behavioral effects of law are an important matter for lawmakers to understand, and those effects have everything to do with social norms. An understanding of norms will therefore bear a great deal on effective regulatory policy. Many of the most dramatic gains in health and safety regulation are a product of changes in norms, meanings, and roles.

Norms relate to some broader issues as well. Often it is said that the common law, and a liberal regime dedicated to freedom, take "preferences" as they are and do not seek to change them. But the term "preferences" is highly ambiguous. If the term is meant to refer to "choices," it should be understood that choices are very much a function of context, including governing norms, meanings, and roles. Certainly the particular choices made by people in markets—in their capacity as consumers or laborers—do not suggest global or acontextual valuations of relevant goods. If the term "preferences" is meant to refer not to choices but to the mental states behind choices, it is important to recognize that those mental states include assessments of social norms, the expressive meaning of acts, and the expectations associated with a dazzling variety of social roles. Norms and roles affect both public action and public talk, in ways that can much disguise how people think privately. This point has large implications. In particular, norms can be far more fragile than they appear; "norm entrepreneurs" can help solve collective action problems, and "norm bandwagons" are common.

While social life would be impossible without norms, meanings, and roles, individual people have little control over these things. The result can be severe limits on human well-being. Certainly there is a problem with existing norms when all or almost all people would seek a change and when existing norms deny people the preconditions for autonomy. In fact, lives are shortened and unjustified inequalities are perpetuated by the existence of many current norms. People need collective help if they want to change norms, meaning, or roles. Collective help may be futile or counterproductive; it may be illegitimately motivated. But these matters require an inquiry into context. The issue should not be foreclosed by resort to confusing claims about the need to respect private choice.

Notes

1. See Colin Camerer and Richard Thaler, "Ultimatums, Dictators, and Manners," 9 *J. Econ. Persp.* 209 (1995); John Kagel and Alvin Roth, eds., *Handbook of Experimental Economics* (Princeton: Princeton University Press, 1995), pp. 270, 274-75 282-88, 296-302.

2. Robert Cialdini, et al. "Low-Ball Procedure for Producing Compliance: Commitment Then Cost," 36 *J. Personality Soc. Psychol.* 463 (1978).

3. See, e.g., Richard Epstein, *Simple Rules for a Complex World* (Cambridge: Harvard University Press, 1995).

4. See Viviana Zelizer, *The Social Meaning of Money* (New York: Basic Books, 1994).

5. A qualification is necessary if the definition of rationality is normative and defended as such. In that case, it would be possible to say that a certain norm is irrational because (for example) it makes lives worse.

6. The liberal tradition is very complex on this count, and I will not try to sort out its various strands here. I believe that all of the arguments made here fit well within central strands of that tradition.

7. See the especially instructive discussion in Laurence Lessig, "The Regulation of Social Meaning," 62 *U. Chi. L. Rev.* 993 (1995); though I have referred to this paper at various points, my presentation here owes a general debt to Lessig's argument and in particular to his emphasis on the collective action presented by social meanings.

8. See *id.*

9. See Jon Elster, *The Cement of Society: A Study of Social Order* (Cambridge: Cambridge University Press, 1989). It might be possible to define rationality in a way that abstracts from social norms (see Elster, "Norms of Revenge," 100 *Ethics* 862 [1990], but it would be hard to make robust predictions on the basis of any such definition. The problem lies in a norm-free specification of the "ends" that rational actors pursue. If we understand rationality in purely instrumental terms, we will be unable to make any predictions at all; if we understand it in economic terms, we will find much social irrationality and hence make bad predictions, and in any case the pursuit of wealth will inevitably have some relation to social norms. (Elster sees revenge behavior as inconsistent with rationality, but individuals who seek revenge get hedonic benefit from getting revenge. Hence, Elster's consistent of rationality is normatively invested in a way that seems plausible but needs defense, and that in any case is designed for normative rather than positive purposes.)

10. See Timur Kuran, *Private Truths, Public Lies* (Cambridge: Harvard University Press, 1995), on which I draw throughout this chapter.

11. Cf. Sushil Bikchandani, David Hirshleifer, and Iv. Welch, "A Theory of Fads, Fashions, Custom, and Cultural Changes as Informational Cascades," 100 *J. Polit. Econ.* 992 (1992); Viviana A. Zelizer, *Pricing the Priceless Child: The Changing Social Value of Children* (New York: Basic Books, 1985).

12. This is the idea behind much of Gary Becker's work. See, e.g., G. Becker, *A Treatise on the Family*, 2d ed. (Cambridge: Harvard University Press, 1993). For Becker's most recent statement, see *Accounting for Tastes* (Cambridge: Harvard University Press, 1996).

13. Cf. Paul Slovic, "The Construction of Preference," 50 *Am. Psych.* 364 (1995). I mean to use the idea of construction somewhat more broadly than does Slovic. Note in this connection the striking study by Ross and Samuels, showing that people cooperate when a certain game is denominated "Cooperation," but not when the same game is denominated "Wall Street." See Lee Ross and & Frank Samuels, "The Predictive Power of Personal Reputation" (unpublished manuscript, 1993).

14. See the classic discussion in Edna Ullmann-Margalit, *The Emergence of Norms* (Oxford: Oxford University Press, 1977). Robert Ellickson, *Order Without Law: How neighbors Settle Disputes* (Cambridge: Harvard University Press, 1993) is an important discussion of how norms produce social order and solve collective action problems, in the absence of legal constraints. But norm changes do not produce Pareto improvements; there are losers as well as winners. Moreover, there is a crucial question about

which norms are taken as given, and which are put up for grabs, in the sort of analysis that celebrates certain norms as solving collective action problems.

15. See Zelizer, *supra* note 4.

16. *Id.* at 5, quoting Jean Lave, *Cognition in Practice: Mind, Mathematic, and Culture* (New York: Cambridge University Press, 1988), pp. 132–33.

17. See Richard Thaler, "Mental Accounting Matters" (unpublished manuscript, University of Chicago Business School, 1995).

18. See *id.* for an impressive argument to this effect.

19. Zelizer, *supra* note 4, at 18–19.

20. See Susan Okin, *Justice, Gender, and the Family* (New York: Basic Books, 1989).

21. Cf. Kuran, *supra* note 10.

22. I am describing a possibility, not a certainty. Political behavior is very often selfish.

23. Amartya Sen, "Internal Consistency of Choice," 61 *Econometrica* 495 (1993).

24. See Okin, *supra* note 20, at 134–69.

25. See Lessig, *supra* note 7.

26. See *id.* for discussion of the collective action problem.

27. See Kuran, *supra* note 10, on which I draw for the discussion in this paragraph.

28. *Id.* at 288. ("A specific law, regulation, policy, norm, or custom can be abruptly abandoned when people who have helped sustain it suddenly discover a common desire for change.")

29. See Sen, *supra* note 23; Elliot Aronson, *The Social Animal*, 7th ed. (New York: W. H. Freeman, 1995); Amos Tversky and Itamar Simonson, "Context-Dependent Preferences," 39 *Mgmt. Sci.* 1179 (1993).

30. See Tversky and Simonson, *supra* note 29.

31. Cf. David Leland, "Generalized Similarity Judgments: An Alternative Explanation for Choice Anomalies," 9 *J. Risk and Uncertainty* 151 (1994). See also Itamar Simonson and Amos Tversky, "Choice in Context," 29 *J. Mkt. Res.* 281 (1992).

32. See Becker, *Accounting for Tastes, supra* note 12; George Stigler and Gary Becker, "De Gustibus Non Est Disputandum," 67 *Am. Econ. Rev.* 76 (1977).

33. See Becker, *supra* note 12; Kuran, *supra* note 10; see also ch. 10 of this book.

34. See Richard Thaler, *Quasi-Rational Economics* (New York: Russell Sage Foundation, 1991); see also Dubourg et al., "Imprecise Preferences and the WTP-WTA Disparity," 9 *J. Risk and Uncertainty* 115 (1994).

35. It was first so-called in Richard Thaler, "Toward a Positive Theory of Consumer Choice," 1 *J. Econ. Behavior and Org.* 39 (1980). This essay, along with others of similar interest, can be found in Thaler, *supra* note 34.

36. David S. Brookshire and Don L. Coursey, "Measuring the Value of a Public Good: An Empirical Comparison of Elictation Procedures," 77 *Am. Econ. Rev.* 554 (1987).

37. Judd Hammock and G. M. Brown, *Waterfowl and Wetlands: Toward Bioeconomic Analysis* (Washington, D.C.: Resources for the Future, 1974); Robert Rowe et al., "An Experiment on the Economic Value of Visibility," 7 *J. Env. Econ. and Management* 1 (1980).

38. Thaler, *supra* note 35. A good overview is Elizabeth Hoffman and Matthew L. Spitzer, "The Divergence Between Willingness-to-Pay and Willingness-to-Accept Measures of Value," 71 *Wash. U. L. Q.* 59(1993).

39. See Rebecca Boyce et al., "An Experimental Examination of Intrinsic Values as a Source of the WTA-WTP Disparity," 82 *Am. Econ. Rev.* 1366 (1992).

40. See *id.* at 1366.

41. Brookshire and Coursey, *supra* note 36.

42. Thus, in surveys, nearly 50 percent of people sometimes refuse to name any amount.

43. See Rebecca Boyce et al., *supra* note 39.

44. See Shelley Orbell et al., "Explaining Discussion-Induced Cooperation," 54 *J. Personality and Social Psychol.* 811 (1988); *Handbook of Experimental Economics, supra* note 1, at 26–28, 141–69, 409–11. Note also that cooperation increases when people can talk with one another; discussion significantly raises contribution rates, perhaps because it increases empathy and the shame associated with noncooperation.

45. See Lessig, *supra* note 7.

46. *Statistical Abstract of the United States* (Washington, D.C.: Bureau of the Census, 1993), p. 143.

47. *Id.*

48. See Cass R. Sunstein, *The Partial Constitution* (Cambridge: Harvard University Press, 1993), ch. 10.

49. See John Rawls, *Political Liberalism* (New York: Columbia University Press, 1993).

Incommensurability
and Valuation in Law

In this chapter I make two claims and discuss their implications for law. The first claim is that human values are plural and diverse. By this I mean that we value things, events, and relationships in ways that are not reducible to some larger and more encompassing value. The second claim is that human goods are not commensurable. By this I mean that such goods are not assessed along a single metric. For reasons to be explored, the two claims, though related, are importantly different.

These claims are emphatically not meant to deny the existence of grounds for evaluating private and public choices, both among kinds of valuation and among incommensurable goods. But efforts to insist on a single kind of valuation and to make goods commensurable, while designed to aid in human reasoning, may actually make such reasoning inferior to what it is when it is working well.

For the moment, these claims must remain obscure; I will devote considerable space in an effort to make them more clear. If they are plausible, views of this sort are likely to have important implications for law. To be sure, endorsement of the two claims need not lead to any particular view about legal problems. To say that law ought to value something in a certain way, we need to make a substantive claim about some issue of the good or the right, and a mere reference to the diversity of values does not supply that claim. Nonetheless, I hope to show that debates over ways of valuing things, and over issues of commensurability, help to reveal what is at stake in many areas of the law. A unifying claim involves the expressive function of law—the law's role in reflecting and communicating particular ways of valuing human goods. Many legal debates actually involve the appropriateness of different kinds of valuation in different areas of law.

For example, a liberal society containing diverse social spheres—families, markets, politics, religious organizations—makes space for different kinds of valuation. With an understanding of these diverse kinds, we will be able to see why voluntary exchanges should usually be protected, and also why they should sometimes be blocked. Some otherwise puzzling anomalies in the theory of environmental protection will take on new aspects. An understanding of diverse kinds of valuation helps shed light on certain claims about the nature of sex discrimination. In fact, a Kantian norm, having to do with appropriate ways of valuing human beings, accounts for widespread views about abortion, the distribution of labor within marriage, sexual harassment, prostitution, pornography, surrogacy, and much else. With an understanding of this sort, it will be possible as well to understand some features of practical reason in law, especially in the old area of analogical thinking, but also in the new areas involving the theory and practice of the regulatory state.

In pressing claims about incommensurability and diverse kinds of valuation, I have both a general target and a positive goal. The target consists of monistic theories of value, particularly as these appear in the study of law. Monistic theories are pervasive; they have a strong philosophical pedigree; and, in various guises, they come up in many discussions of particular legal issues. To be sure, it may seem that few people really subscribe to such theories. Most people do not deny that human values are plural. But there is a distinguished tradition of thought, found in such diverse thinkers as Plato and Bentham, that insists that values should be seen as unitary and that human goods should be seen as commensurable. In their most austere forms, these ideas are rarely endorsed explicitly in law; but more modest versions play a large role in the legal context—not simply in economic analysis, but also in some aspects of rights-based thinking insofar as it takes a unitary value as the basis for evaluating law. In any case, problems of commensurability have yet to receive sustained attention in law, and it is important to see exactly how goods are diverse, and in what ways goods are incommensurable, even if some version of these claims might turn out, on reflection, to be widely shared.

I particularly want to show some distinctive ways in which economic analysis of law, and some forms of utilitarianism as well, miss important commitments of a well-functioning legal system. I hope also to establish that a surprisingly wide range of legal disputes can be illuminated by an understanding of incommensurability and diverse kinds of valuation. The value of this enterprise consists not in dictating particular conclusions, which depend on the details, but in enabling us to see an important basis for widespread concerns and convictions. I emphasize that to see values as incommensurable, and to say that people are really disputing appropriate kinds (not levels) of valuation, is not by itself to resolve legal disputes. It is necessary to say something about the right kind—to offer a substantive theory—and to investigate the particulars in great detail in order to make progress in hard cases in law. But an understanding of problems of incommensurability will make it easier to see what is at stake.

This chapter is organized into six sections. The first three sections explore some foundational issues. Section I describes diverse kinds of valuation and responds to the claim that we value different things in the same way. Section II offers a working definition of incommensurability. Section III discusses an important challenge to the claims in sections I and II. It also offers some notes on the stakes, attempting to show why these issues matter.

Section IV makes general remarks about law, with particular emphasis on law's expressive function. The fifth and most detailed section surveys areas in which an understanding of kinds of valuation and of incommensurability may affect our understanding of law. In this section, I discuss a wide range of issues, including social differentiation, the Establishment Clause, political equality, cost-benefit analysis, contract remedies, environmental regulation, and feminism. The sixth section ventures some preliminary remarks on the important issue of choice—choice among different kinds of valuation and choice among incommensurable goods. In the sixth section, I also offer a few notes on the importance of the sense of tragedy in law.

I. Kinds of Valuation

Definitions and Examples

Human beings value goods, things, relationships, and states of affairs in diverse ways.[1] Begin with the distinction between instrumental and intrinsic goods. We value some things purely or principally for use; consider (most) hammers, forks, or money. But we value other things at least in part for their own sake; consider knowledge or friendship. Because it is so pertinent to law, the distinction between instrumental and intrinsic value will play an important role here. But that distinction captures only part of the picture. Intrinsically valued things produce a range of diverse responses. Some bring about wonder and awe; consider a mountain or certain artistic works. Toward some people, we feel respect; toward others, affection; toward others, love. People worship their deity. Some events produce gratitude; others produce joy; others are thrilling; others make us feel content; others bring about delight. Some things are valued if they meet certain standards, like a musical or athletic performance or perhaps a joke.

Negative valuations are similarly diverse. To lose money is to lose an instrumental good—though one that might be used for intrinsic goods, like the preservation of human life. To lose a friend is a different matter. So, too, our responses to intrinsic bads are diverse. We might be horrified by an act of cruelty, disgusted by an ugly scene, shocked by a betrayal of friendship or love, made indignant by a failure of respect, frightened by the prospect of loss, angered by the infliction of a wound, saddened by an undeserved hardship, or frustrated by the failure of our plans. These various terms themselves include a variety of experiences that embody diverse ideas about evaluation. Not all forms of sadness—very much an umbrella term—are the same; so, too, with disgust—compare reactions to cruelty and reactions to ugliness—and so on.

There are, then, different kinds of goods, and human beings experience their lives in ways that reflect a wide variety of kinds of valuation. The term is meant to draw attention to our diverse stances toward relationships or prospects and to the disparate accounts of value through which we conceive and evaluate relationships, events, or prospects. Every kind of valuation embodies a qualitatively distinctive judgment or response. People react to events, to things, and to one another in accordance with the nature and clarity of distinctions among possible kinds of valuation. Someone who does not make appropriate distinctions might be labeled odd or even weird. Someone who does not make enough distinctions might seem thick or obtuse.

We could categorize kinds of valuation in many different ways. For purposes of law, it might make sense to focus on such things as love, affection, respect, wonder, worship, and use;[2] these notions come up in many places of legal dispute. But each of these terms captures a range of qualitatively distinct kinds of valuation. Love for a parent is different from love for a child, which is in turn different from love for a friend, a spouse, a pet, or a house. We might feel wonder toward an act of selfless courage and also toward a musical performance or a beautiful beach. We might feel awe toward an athletic performance and also toward a mountain. How, and how finely, we should categorize kinds of valuation depends on the uses to which the categories will be put. For law and politics, the number of useful categories is undoubtedly smaller than it is for literature or poetry, which may be especially concerned to offer fine-grained accounts.

Distinctions among kinds of valuation are highly sensitive to the particular setting in which they operate. People do not value goods acontextually. In one setting—say, the workplace—the prevailing kinds of valuation might be quite different from what they are elsewhere—say, the home or the ballot box. Moreover, particular goods typically do not admit of a single kind of valuation. The prevailing kind has everything to do with the context and the relationship among the various actors. Thus, a cat might be valued in a certain way by its owner, but in a different way by a landlord, and in still a different way by a government agency. Much of social differentiation stems from this perception. So, too, several kinds of valuation might be directed toward a single object. A person might, for example, both love and respect a friend or a lover.

Different kinds of valuation cannot, without significant loss, be reduced to a single "superconcept," like happiness, utility, or pleasure. Any such reduction produces significant loss because it yields an inadequate description of our actual valuations when things are going well. The inadequate description may work for prediction; but it may also impair predictive accounts of behavior. It will also impair normative judgments about ethics, law, and politics. In making this latter point, I mean to reject relativist or purely conventionalist accounts of kinds of valuation and to suggest that some kinds are more appropriate than others. Judgments about what is appropriate depend of course on theories of the good or the right; from the bare fact that kinds of valuation are diverse, we have no basis for evaluating any legal or social practice. But it is important to have diverse kinds of valuation—indeed we could not make sense of our lives without them—and no matter what current conventions may be, some kinds are poorly suited to some contexts because they produce inferior lives.

Conflicts Among Kinds of Valuation, with Special Reference to Uses of Money

Conflicts among diverse kinds of valuation permeate private and public choice. Suppose Smith has arranged to have lunch with a friend today, but that he has become very busy and perhaps would like to cancel. Suppose Smith thinks in this way: If he cancels, his friend will be disappointed, because he would like Smith's company, and also a bit insulted, because it is cavalier and disrespectful to cancel lunch at the last minute. Maybe Smith should make it up to him, or provide compensation, by offering a nontrivial cash payment. This would be a hopelessly inadequate response. A cash payment would be inconsistent with the way that someone values a friend. Even if the friend would prefer $1, or $10, or $100, or $1000 to lunch with Smith—even though at some point the payment would in some sense be worth far more than the lunch and be readily accepted as an alternative—the offer of cash would be perceived as an insult rather than as compensation. In this context, the difference in kinds of valuation means that a financial exchange would be inappropriate. The kind of valuation of a friend blocks the use of otherwise acceptable grounds for action.[3] As we will see, the law is pervaded by principles of this kind—principles that forbid resort to reasons for action that are acceptable in other contexts.

This case is not exotic. Similar issues permeate the exceptionally complex cluster of social norms regulating the appropriate use of money as an incentive for action. For example, if an employer tells you that, as an employee performing a certain job, you must spend a month away from your home and family, you might well agree. But if someone tells you that he will pay you a monthly salary in order to persuade you to spend a month away from home and family, you will probably feel insulted and degraded, and you may well turn him down.[4] This second offer reflects an inappropriate valuation of you and your family—it suggests that your relationship with your family is simply up for sale. The employer's offer treats you as an object of contempt and perhaps ridicule. In the first case, the same cannot be said. Even though in the first case the relationship might be thought to have been "traded for" cash, the absence from family is a by-product of employment, rather than something brought about as an end in itself, desired for its own sake by one's boss. To see the two cases as the same—as instances of trade-offs between family and income—is to overlook an important distinction in the meanings of the two offers.

Or suppose that we feel awe toward something. If we do, we will not believe that it should be valued in the same way as its cash equivalent. A simple or flat judgment that a mountain is "really worth" $10 million is inconsistent with the way that we (or most of us) value the mountain. This is because the mountain is valued in a different way from the $10 million; the former produces awe and wonder, whereas the latter is for human use—though admittedly $10 million may produce a (different) sort of awe and wonder as well. These points hold even if many people might be indifferent between $10 million and the mountain in the sense that they do not know which they would choose if both were offered; even if $10 million is in some sense the right amount to invest in protection of the mountain from degradation; and even if, as seems clear, infinite valuation of the mountain would be an irrational allocation of scarce social resources. The point certainly does not suggest that pristine areas cannot be degraded. But it does have a range of important and sometimes overlooked consequences for how people involved in the legal system might think about environmental protection.

The point also suggests that indifference curves have quite limited purposes and that they may be misleading on some important matters. It may even suggest that we should question the whole notion of indifference curves. Some people may not be "indifferent" between two goods, even though they do not think that one is better than another.

Attention to diverse kinds of valuation casts general light on the phenomenon of exchanges that are blocked by social norms. If someone offers to pay an adult neighbor to mow his lawn, the neighbor will often regard the request as an insult, because it reflects an inappropriate valuation of the neighbor. The request embodies an improper conception of what the relationship is, or of the attitude with which neighbors render services for each other. The impropriety remains even if the offeree ordinarily would regard the offered wage as a fair price for an hour of mowing services. In an extreme case, if someone asks an attractive person (or a spouse) for sexual relations in return for cash, the same would be said even more vehemently. Because of the existence of diverse kinds of valuation, we may not be able to generalize acontextual preferences from particular decisions.

There is often a connection between blocked exchanges and ideas about equal citizenship. The exchange may be barred by social norms or law because of a perception that, while there may be disparities in social wealth, the spheres in which people are very unequal ought not to invade realms of social life in which equality is a social goal. Often this idea comes from the existence of a kind of valuation based on equal respect. The legal prohibition on vote trading is an example. So, too, with certain complex social bans on the use of wealth to buy services or goods from other people, such as a shoveled walk or a body part. An intricate web of norms covers the exchange of money among both friends and strangers. Some of these norms are connected with the principle of civic equality. Monetary exchange would reflect forms of inequality that are not legitimate in certain spheres. In making these points, I am disregarding many complexities, and I have not tried to justify any particular set of outcomes. I want to suggest only a general point: The refusal to allow economic exchanges is often based on familiar notions of equality that such exchanges would compromise.

There is a further point. We should distinguish between cases in which a monetary offer is entirely inappropriate—say, a large check offered in exchange for an academic article endorsing the offeror's position—and cases in which the monetary sum, while appropriately offered, does not reflect a full or fully accurate valuation of the item in question. Artists, actors, and teachers might well believe that dollar sums cannot truly reflect the social value of what they produce—certainly in the sense that money is not valued in the same way as art or education—without believing that monetary compensation itself is inappropriate. It is a pervasive and intriguing feature of markets that financial compensation is challenged as too low, rather than as inappropriate, or indeed willingly accepted, even in contexts in which the transaction involves a good that is not valued in the same way as money. But it is equally intriguing to note the occasional presence of norms and law that block exchanges on the grounds of an inappropriate kind of valuation.

An understanding of the diverse kinds of valuation thus helps explain the view that some things ought not to be traded on markets and that market exchanges should therefore be prohibited.[5] The objection to commodification should be seen as a special case of the general problem of diverse kinds of valuation. The claim is that we ought not to trade (for example) sexuality or reproductive capacities on markets because economic valuation of these "things" is inconsistent with and may even undermine their appropriate kind (not level) of valuation. The objection is not that markets value sexuality "too much" or "too little"; it is that markets value these activities in the wrong way. Judge Posner's well-known writings on the value of creating some kind of "baby market"[6] do not quite address this particular objection. A judgment about the appropriate way of valuing babies must itself be defended on some basis, and such a judgment does not automatically lead to a particular view about legal rules for adoption or the sale of young children. But the question of appropriate kinds of valuation plays a major role in these debates.

Thus far I have dealt with cases that involve objections to the kind of valuation expressed through cash payments. But we can think of many cases not involving the issue of monetary equivalence. Imagine, for example, that John treats a beautiful diamond in the same way that most people treat friends, or that Jane values a plant in the same way that most people value their children, or that Sandy values her car like most people value art or literature. All of us know people with occasional tendencies of this sort. Indeed, all of us *are* people with occasional tendencies of this sort. But sometimes an improper kind of valuation seems odd, or disrespectful, or even pathological—and all these in part because it makes it impossible to sustain certain sorts of desirable social relationships. Disputes over law and social norms, which are related and sometimes mutually enforcing behavioral influences, often reflect disagreements over proper kinds of valuation, with adjectives of this sort moving to the fore.

Consider, for example, the animal rights movement. Some people think that animals should be treated with dignity and respect, and not as if they exist solely for human consumption and use. This view need not entail the further claim that animal life is infinitely valuable. It is best taken as a recommendation of a shift in the kind of valuation of animals, accompanied by a judgment that the new kind will have consequences for what human beings do. The recommendation may be based on the view that if we see animals (and nature) in this way, we will solve collective action problems faced by human beings in preserving animal life that is important for human lives; it may be based on a noninstrumental effort to extend ideals of basic dignity to all living things. I reiterate that substantive judgments of this sort must be defended; by itself, the reference to diverse kinds of valuation gets us nowhere. The important point is that such judgments are a frequent, though often overlooked, part of social and legal discussion.

The existence of diverse kinds of valuation explains a good deal of private behavior. Norms governing address provide a familiar example. By using some part of a name—last name preceded by "Professor," "Doctor," "Mr.," "Ms.," "Mrs.," "Miss"; last name by itself; first name; nickname or diminutive; some term of endearment—a good deal of signaling takes place about prevailing kinds of valuation. Some of these signals connote respect and admiration; others show contempt; others show affection or love. Of course, different cultures vary greatly on this score, and of course, individual relationships change over time from one kind to another. Note in this regard that the Constitution forbids both the federal government and the states from conferring any "title of nobility." In this way, it commits itself to a certain view of equality among human beings. Though the provision may seem like a historical curiosity to current observers, to the Framers it crucially exemplified this view; as we will see, it is the forerunner of the Equal Protection Clause, with a close connection to judgments about appropriate kinds of valuation.

Strange as it may seem, money itself is not fungible. People put money in different mental compartments and act accordingly. Some money is dedicated to support of children. Some money is for gifts; some is for one's own special fun. Some money is to be given to charities. Some money is for summer vacation. Some money is for a rainy day. Some money is for celebrations. The qualitative differences among human goods are matched by ingenious mental operations involving qualitative differences among different "kinds" of money. There are complex procedures of "mental accounting" in which money that falls in certain compartments is assessed only in terms of its particular intended uses and not compared with money that has been placed in different mental compartments. Much remains to be done on this important question.[7]

Clarifications and Cautionary Notes

Three major clarifications are necessary here. First, my claim about diverse kinds of valuation has largely been a claim about widespread current attitudes. I do believe that those attitudes go very deep and that it would be quite impossible to make sense of our experience without reference to diverse kinds of valuation. But I am speaking about how we value, not about nature or about valuation of goods apart from human attitudes.

Nor are existing kinds of valuation fixed and immutable. Norms change, and prevailing social conceptions about kinds of valuation change as well. Shifts from one kind of valuation to another are perfectly commonplace, at both the individual and social level. Respect can turn into love; love can turn into use; use can become love; love can become respect; love may or may not be accompanied by respect; respect can become affection; so, too, for love. Within societies, kinds of valuation change over time. The shift from feudalism to capitalism can hardly be described in a sentence, but one of its features involved changes in kinds of valuation of work and workers, and this was a prime area of contestation. Marriage may once have involved more use, and less love and affection, than it now does. The abolition of slavery represented a shift from use to a certain measure of respect; so, too, with the attack on racial hierarchy in the aftermath of the attack on school segregation. Much of the change in race relations in the South involved a shift from connections built on deference and what was believed to be a sort of affection to principles of civic equality and respect.

Debates over environmental protection raise similar issues. It is not adequate to say that environmentalists value pristine areas "more" than economists. But it is important to say that environmentalists value pristine areas in a different way. Whereas economists tend to think of the environment as something for human use, environmentalists tend to claim that we should view the environment with awe and wonder or value it for its own sake rather than as an instrumental good. Of course, it is unclear how these different kinds of valuation will or should affect environmental policy, a point to which I will return.

Second, the existence of diverse kinds of valuation does not by itself have any clear implications for law, policy, or even social attitudes. There is a difference between how people should value and how law should value. I do not claim that, because people now value relationships, events, objects, or each other in certain ways, it follows that law should adopt those diverse kinds of valuation. We need not be conventionalists. If a particular kind of valuation were really superior with respect to what is appropriately valued in public or private life, the law might well adopt that kind of valuation, notwithstanding its inconsistency with prevailing social norms. A good deal of constitutional law can be taken as an effort to constrain prevailing kinds of valuation; this is true both for principles of religious liberty and for antidiscrimination norms. Or law might embody a certain kind of valuation precisely because it is law; we might think that cost-benefit analysis is appropriate for law, even if we think that it is inappropriate for spouses or parents. If we are to draw conclusions about appropriate law, policy, and norms, it is because our best account of the good or the right supports a particular constellation of kinds of valuation and because we are able to show that a particular constellation makes sense for law.

Third, those who believe that goods are valued in different ways need not reject the possibility of rational choice or even some form of trade-off among them. On the contrary, believers in diverse kinds of valuation would do well to insist that choices occur and that they might well be judged rational or not. People choose among differently valued goods all the time, and these choices are not immune from evaluation on rational grounds. My affection for my dog and my desire for more cash reflect different kinds of valuation, but it would be quite irrational for me to allow my dog to be sold for fifty dollars. (If I were desperately poor, and if my family were ill and suffering, it could also be irrational for me to refuse to trade my dog for one million dollars, notwithstanding the presence of distinct kinds of valuation.) Someone might well sell for a price the products of her capacity to play Mozart—musical performances—or to write poetry, notwithstanding the fact that she values her capacity as something other than an income-producing asset. In some circumstances, it would surely be irrational for a musician to refuse to perform for a fee. Sometimes the use between differently valued goods depends on judgments about intrinsic value; sometimes extrinsic values become important. These claims about rationality need to be explained in some detail, but they should be sufficient to show that there may indeed be a point to deliberating about cases that involve goods that are valued in different ways.

Social Science, Economics, and Diverse
Kinds of Valuation

Is it useful to note that kinds of valuation are diverse and plural? Perhaps it is not. Perhaps we can make good predictions about social life simply by assuming that there is a single kind of valuation. On this view, a claim about diverse kinds of valuation may usefully describe people's internal lives; it may have deeper psychological truth; it may better account for how lives and choices are actually experienced. But it is fully dispensable for social scientists and lawyers, who can work with an assumption of "as if unitariness"—that is, who can assume that people act as if they value all things in the same way, and who can make accurate predictions with that assumption. So long as we can model choices—so long as ordinal rankings are possible—social scientists need not worry about what I have said here.

This conclusion seems partly right. If we assume that people want to maximize one thing—utility, value, welfare, well-being—we might well be able to make good predictions of various sorts. We might be able to say what sorts of legislation will be enacted in what circumstances. People do make judgments among goods, and if so, we need not decide whether they value these goods in the same way. Much of social science proceeds through simplifying assumptions, even with respect to nonmarket transactions. To the extent that we can make accurate predictions by assuming unitariness, we can indeed dispense with claims about diverse kinds of valuation.

But I believe that, with the assumption of a unitary kind of valuation, we will sometimes offer inadequate predictions, explanations, and recommendations for law. The idea of "revealed preferences" is a predictive failure; to make predictions from choices, we need to offer an account of what lies behind choices (chapter 2), and that account must take into consideration what I am discussing here. Behavior is often a product of judgments about what kinds of valuation are appropriate under what circumstances. As we will see, some of the "demand" for environmental regulation is best understood as a response to claims about the need to value things in different ways. Much of individual conduct is best understood in similar terms.

In this light, we can also make sense out of a familiar debate within the legal culture. In some subjects—contracts, torts, property—people often propose that something important—like a risk to life or health—is in some deep sense equivalent to a certain amount of cash. At this point, some participant in the conversation (perhaps a student) rejects the proposal, whereupon the original speaker suggests that the resistance must depend on a claim of infinite valuation, at which point it is clear that the original proposal was correct. But perhaps the resistance rests on a claim about appropriate kinds, not levels, of valuation. If so, the participant who is making this claim has a lot to explain. She has to explain how to make choices among goods that are valued in different ways. But at least we will be able to understand what she is saying.

We might also begin to see why it might be jarring to conceive of the various harms imposed by law as simple "costs." This formulation begs important questions and ignores qualitative distinctions. It does so by assuming a unitary kind of valuation. In that way, this formulation loads the dice—that is, it prejudices analysis by pointing it in certain controversial directions. As we will see, the point bears on the question of commensurability.

II. Incommensurability

A Provisional Definition

The subject of incommensurability raises many complexities, and I want to bracket at least some of the philosophical debate here, concentrating instead on what is particularly relevant to law.[8] I begin with a rough working definition, designed especially for the legal context: Incommensurability occurs when the relevant goods cannot be aligned along a single metric without doing violence to our considered judgments about how these goods are best characterized. Let me briefly describe the four major elements of this definition. First, by "our considered judgments," I mean our reflective assessments of how certain relationships and events should be understood, evaluated, and experienced. Such reflection involves identifying the nature and depth of various goods in our lives.

Second, the notion of a "single metric" should be understood quite literally. By this I mean a standard of valuation that (1) operates at a workable level of specificity; (2) involves no qualitative distinctions; and (3) allows comparison of different goods along the same dimension. One example of a real-world metric—indeed the most important for present purposes—is money. Ten dollars and $100 can be confidently measured by such a standard, so that $10 is simply a small quantity of the same thing of which $100 is a substantial amount. If two goods are fungible, they are also commensurable. Other metrics include feet, yards, pounds, and of course meters. The difference between lengths of ten yards and 100 yards, or between 1000 pounds and 400 pounds, involves no qualitative distinctions.

An important and contested utilitarian claim is that "utility" furnishes a single metric along which goods can be evaluated. Some utilitarians believe that a single metric is indeed available for ordering valuations. The great utilitarian John Stuart Mill, of course, was unwilling to commit himself fully to this view. I use the term "metric" largely because of the special importance of the metric of dollars to law. As we will see, the use of a single metric is often unhelpful for law, and this point has a wide range of consequences for particular legal disputes. Under this general definition of metric, many possible standards—excellence, well-being, affective allegiance—count as criteria, but not as metrics. Kinds of valuation—love, respect, wonder, worship—embody no metric at all.

Third, with the phrase "doing violence," I mean to suggest that the use of a single metric is inconsistent with the way certain goods are actually experienced, or tend to be experienced when people's lives are going well. The phrase is intended to show that a single metric, nominally descriptive of experience, would actually transform it, in a way that would make a great deal of difference. It would make a great deal of difference because it would elide certain qualitative differences that are important in both life and law. We might label many choices involving commensurable goods *investment decisions*. The decision how to invest so as to maximize expected return does indeed involve commensurable goods. Some people write as if all or most decisions have this form—as if all or most decisions are investment decisions. Some people talk as if life is full of investment decisions, so that a decision made in one context will show a global, acontextual judgment about valuation. It is these points that I am rejecting here. If we saw all human decisions as investment decisions, we would make human experience barely recognizable. There is an additional point. Particular choices reflect the context in which they are made, and those choices rarely reveal a general statement, reflecting an acontextual considered judgment about valuation.

Fourth, by "doing violence to our considered judgments," I mean disrupting our reflective assessments of how certain relationships and events should be understood, evaluated, and experienced. To see dating, for example, as "participation in the marriage market" may be inconsistent with prevailing convictions about what dating behavior entails.

Incommensurability in this very thin sense is a familiar phenomenon. Indeed, it seems that it is closer to the rule than the exception. A decision whether to vacation at the beach in the Indiana Dunes or in Florence entails no single metric. So, too, with the decision whether to see a movie about dinosaurs or instead about Wittgenstein. Or with a decision whether to reduce permissible exposure levels to benzene in the workplace to one part per million.

We might also believe that goods are comparable without believing that they are commensurable—that is, we might think that choices can be made among incommensurable goods, and that such choices are subject to reasoned evaluation, without believing that the relevant goods can be aligned along a single metric. Incommensurability need not entail incomparability. But incommensurability is still an important part of practical reason in life and law. For example, some people do not believe that any unitary metric can capture their diverse valuations of music, friendship, and work. It also seems possible that different forms of music, or different kinds of work and friendship, cannot be made commensurable in this way. To be sure, we can imagine a life or a world in which valuation along a single metric would not be experientially false.

Certainly, we can imagine social changes in which some incommensurable things become commensurable, and vice versa. Some such changes have undoubtedly occurred, and indeed are occurring all the time. But a fully commensurable life or world would be the stuff of science fiction. It would change experience, not "just" words. An argument on its behalf would call for a large-scale revision of current experience.

Valuation and Commensurability

What is the relationship between kinds of valuation and commensurability? It may be tempting to think that there is incommensurability if and only if diverse kinds of valuation are at work. There is an association between these two ideas, but they are not the same. Two points are relevant here. First, and most important, cases of incommensurability can occur even within the same kind of valuation. A parent may value one child in the same way that she values another child, but the two may be incommensurably valued in the sense that they are not valued along the same metric. The valuation of one cannot be understood as simply some fraction of the valuation of another. There is nothing like fungibility. There are important qualitative distinctions.

Consider in this regard the mother's dilemma in *Sophie's Choice:* Which of her two children should be handed over to the Nazi officer? The dilemma is tragic partly because the two lives are not fungible. The mother is forced to assume personal responsibility for the loss of a life for which there is no substitute. This is a common though usually less excruciating phenomenon in the presence of multiple intrinsic goods, when we might have a single kind of valuation, or a few such kinds, without a metric for decisions. Indeed, we might think that commensurability in the sense used here can occur only in the case of instrumental goods having many possible uses.

Second, some people might think that goods are commensurable even if they are valued in different ways. Consider the suggestion that a single metric is available with which to align our different kinds of valuation. For example, Mozart may be valued in a different way from Bob Dylan, but there may be a metric by which to value different composers; and, along that metric, Mozart may be superior to Dylan. (I believe that any such metric would be false to our experience of music, and hence, I do not think that this sort of approach will work; but I am trying here to show how the two claims might be separated.) In any case, some people think that there are diverse values—pleasure from a warm sun, gratitude from unexpected kindness, and so forth—while also believing that these can all be reduced to a general concept like utility, happiness, or pleasure. Utilitarians should not and need not deny the diversity of human goods, or that pleasures and pains come in different forms.[9]

The claim of incommensurability is that no unitary metric accounts for how we actually think and that the effort to introduce one misdescribes experience. There is a further claim (of course, requiring an independent defense) that the misdescription can yield both inaccurate predictions and bad recommendations for ethics and politics.[10] It would do so even if human beings should also decide, free from metrics but equipped with reasons, in favor of some relationships and events instead of others, and even in favor of Mozart over Dylan, if some such judgment becomes useful. Recall that incommensurability, as I have defined it, does not entail incomparability. It may be, for example, that there are describable and workable criteria for finding a composer to be good, and that these criteria, while hardly algorithmic, make it possible to say that some composers are better than others. Indeed, it seems clear that this is the case. We can make similar arguments about hard cases in law, a point taken up in more detail later.

Excluding Reasons for Action

Some of the most intriguing instances of incommensurability arise when the relevant kind of valuation not only prevents use of a single metric, but also excludes certain reasons for action altogether.[11] We need to introduce here the important notion, originated by Joseph Raz, of *exclusionary reasons*. Sometimes social custom or law invokes a second-order reason that excludes certain first-order reasons for action, even if those reasons are perfectly legitimate in some settings. In such cases, the basic goal of the custom or law is to prohibit people from making choices on the basis of certain identifiable considerations. Those considerations are ruled off limits; they are not merely found insufficiently weighty.

Someone may, for example, value loyalty to a lover or spouse in a way that absolutely precludes the acceptance of favors, or cash, as a reason for infidelity. The kind of valuation of the person and relationship rules out a set of reasons that would be perfectly legitimate bases for action in other contexts. The particular kind of valuation is inconsistent with allowing the admission of certain otherwise conventional reasons for behaving in a certain way. The same idea permeates the legal system. Thus, for example, a jury in a tort case is not ordinarily permitted to take into account a defendant's wealth; in interpreting a statute, a judge is usually not supposed to consider what she thinks a good statute would say. Companies may not invoke the need to increase employment—ordinarily an important social goal—as a ground to engage in price fixing. In the law of free speech, offense at the content of ideas is not a legitimate reason to regulate speech, even if the offense is very widespread and intense.

Sometimes the very admission of the relevant reasons is entirely off limits. Sometimes the reasons, though usually barred, may be introduced, but only if they are extraordinarily strong in the specific case. This is a characteristic structure of legal protection of constitutional rights under judge-made doctrine. I want to claim that, in both instances, we have a form of incommensurability as I understand it here.

There is a further and closely related point. Many problems of incommensurability arise because of a conviction that an event, a person, or a relationship is intrinsically good, or an end in itself, rather than something properly treated as a means to some other generalized end, such as wealth, utility, or maximized value. It is easy to use a single metric when all human events are seen as instrumental to improvements along a unitary dimension. If we thought, for example, that all acts were attempts to increase social utility—defined, say, as aggregate human happiness—then it would be utility that would be of intrinsic value, and all else would be instrumental to it. Analysis might therefore be greatly simplified. The same is true of some understandings of maximized wealth. Often issues of incommensurability arise because of the presence of a range of intrinsic goods that are not seen as a means to some other end, particularly in law.

An example may help. Of course, a society cannot spend an infinite amount of resources to improve workplace safety and hence must make complex trade-offs. But many people find it jarring to hear that, in light of actual occupational choices, a worker values his life at (say) $8 million, or that the protection of a life is "worth" $8 million. These claims are jarring not because we believe infinite social resources should be devoted to occupational safety. The claims are jarring because of the widespread perception that a life is not instrumental to some aggregate social goal, but worthy in itself—a belief in conflict with applying the language of prices to human life. This is a plausible concern even if one ultimately concludes that (say) an $8 million expenditure is fully appropriate in cases of lives at risk. Certainly, intrinsic goods do not have infinite value for purposes of law and policy. But even though they do not, the fact that we find it jarring to hear that a life is "worth" a specified amount of money is socially desirable and not a product of simple confusion.

In sum, the recognition of an intrinsic good may entail an evaluative attitude that is incompatible with the use of certain reasons to compromise it. For example, the intrinsic—rather than instrumental—values at stake in a parent-child relationship generally preclude compromising that relationship for cash, unless, perhaps, the cash can be used for other important intrinsic goods. The same may well be true of equal liberty or of much of what falls within the category of rights. Commensurability will not obtain in a world of multiple intrinsic goods, which is emphatically not to say that we do not choose among intrinsic goods, or that rationality does not help in selecting various courses of action.

Incommensurability and Freedom

It might be tempting to think that incommensurability works as a barrier to certain forms of freedom—to the use of a single metric, to certain sorts of exchange, to certain reasons for action. This is true; we have seen cases in which a recognition of incommensurability stops people from doing things. But it is also plausible to see incommensurability as constitutive of some valuable forms of freedom that are not easily dispensable. The presence of incommensurability helps make possible certain relationships, attachments, and attitudes that would otherwise be unavailable.

If friendship and cash were commensurable, or if a park and $100,000 were valued in the same way, we could not have certain attitudes toward friendship and toward parks. Indeed, if parks and $100,000 could be aligned along the same metric, parks would not be parks as we now understand them. If speech were valued in the same way as forks, we could not understand political freedom in the way that we now do. Incommensurability operates as an obstacle to certain sorts of behavior; but it constitutes others and makes them an option for us. For this reason, social norms might be grounded on the insistence that incommensurability of various sorts is desirable as a means of maintaining attitudes and relationships that are parts of good lives.

Choices

We are left at this stage with an obvious question: Does the fact of choice show that options are commensurable after all? I do not think that it does, for choice can occur among incommensurable goods. We should not identify the actuality of choice with a claim of commensurability. It is odd and unnecessary to say that commensurability necessarily "lies behind" or "justifies" all rational or irrational choices. We choose whether to take an exciting job in a new city, when the move would unsettle our family; we decide hard tort cases; we choose between work and leisure; we decide how much to spend to promote worker safety or energy conservation. These choices are based on reasons and evaluated by reference to them. Commensurability is not required for choice.

A claim of *radical incommensurability* would deny this possibility. On this view, choices among incommensurable options are impossible on rational grounds, or relevant goods are so radically incommensurate that there is no process by which human beings can reasonably choose among them. Reasons run out. I think that it is very rare for this form of incommensurability to occur in the intrapersonal case. People often face incommensurability without being at all paralyzed about what to do, and while thinking, rightly, that their judgments are based on reasons. But the interpersonal case is different, and this point is important for law. In some contexts, people who sharply disagree do seem to be close to the unhappy state of radical incommensurability. This is so in the sense that they appear to belong to different cultures, and the difference makes it hard for them to reason together. If two people value something in entirely different ways—a religious object, an act of apparent discrimination, a form of liberty, the free market—they may be unable to talk to one another. Indeed, we may say that one of the marks of a genuine cultural difference is sharp or unbridgeable distinctions in kinds of valuation.

Most of the time, however, radical incommensurability is not present. Both people and societies do make choices among incommensurable goods, and they do so on the basis of reasons. Indeed, this is a principal task for practical reason, especially in law. It follows that we should not identify the existence of good reasons for action with the existence of a unitary metric. Some choices among incommensurable goods are rational, and others are not, because of the connection between any particular choice and the achievement of good lives or good societies (these are of course vague ideas, on which I will say a bit more in section III). A decision to work through lunch is incommensurable with the option to have lunch with a good friend in town just for the day, but it may well be irrational, in these circumstances, to work through lunch. Economic growth is incommensurable with the reduction of race discrimination, but it may well be irrational to refuse to outlaw race discrimination even if that step involves some loss in social wealth. A resistance to these claims about rationality would be based on a highly sectarian conception of what rationality is—that is, a conception that begs the question on the commensurability issue by assuming that there cannot be rationality without commensurability.

If grounds exist for evaluating choices among incommensurable goods, it is reasonable to think that a second-order desire or goal—to be a good person, to have a fair society, to hear an excellent composer—provides a framework for evaluating seemingly diverse and plural goods. If described at a low or intermediate level of abstraction, however, our higher-order goals are themselves plural and incommensurable, even though there is still choice and even reasonable choice. Nevertheless, it is certainly plausible to say that, if the second-order goal operates at a high level of abstraction, we can generate criteria for private and public choice that do help in the assessment of diverse and plural goods. This is a promising strategy; but the relevant criteria cannot be fairly characterized as a metric.

III. Challenges and Stakes

Some people may find claims about incommensurability, and distinctions among kinds of valuation, to be abstruse or of no practical use. Perhaps we are dealing here with a linguistic or rhetorical debate, one that has no consequences for law, ethics, economics. or politics. Or perhaps it is possible to translate relevant descriptions into different terms without losing anything important.

Let us begin with the question whether claims of incommensurability are right as a description of how people perceive certain situations of choice. The law professor and philosopher Donald Regan, for example, says that when someone refuses to specify the monetary value of friendship, "I think what such a person is most likely to mean is that friendship is more valuable than any amount of money, or in other words, that the value of friendship is incomparably greater."[12] With respect to social disapproval of a parent's "purchasing" children, Regan thinks that "it is closer to the truth to say that we regard the value of parenthood as incomparably greater than the value of money, than to say that we regard these values as incommensurable." Regan also thinks that the fact that people deliberate hard and long about choices among incommensurable values weakens the claim of incommensurability, since "[t]he decision process would necessarily be arbitrary. So what is the point?"

Regan's challenge to incommensurability, as a description of what people mean, what they experience, and how they really think, seems to me unsuccessful. Let us take the example of friendship. We can certainly imagine someone who thinks that the value of friendship, or the value of a particular friendship, is just greater than the value of any sum of money. But many people do not think in this way. Some people—perhaps greedy people, perhaps especially desperately poor people—might be willing to sacrifice a friendship in return for a great deal of money. In such cases, friendship does not appear "more" valuable than money. In purely quantitative terms, the friendship appears "less" valuable than the sum of money involved. Yet even those who accept the trade might nonetheless find it disturbing—because, I think, the friendship is not more valuable or less valuable, but differently valuable, and we do violence to the way that it is valuable if we trade it for money straight-up. Friendship involves companionship, and it is in the very nature of companionship to be beyond purchase. Recall that some incommensurabilities are freedom-producing, because they allow certain relationships and attachments that would otherwise be impossible. As the philosopher Robert Nozick is said to have asked, "How much would you have to pay me to like me for who I am?"

Or take the issue of parenthood. A parent who is asked to trade a child for some money might well react with outrage and shock and regard the request as insulting. This reaction is not that of someone asked to sell something very valuable at a discount—of someone asked to sell an expensive suit for a dollar. The recipient of the offer objects not because the amount offered is unconscionably low, but because the kind of valuation is grotesquely unsuitable. The experience of parenthood is inconsistent with having an evaluative attitude that would permit consideration of dollar compensation for its sacrifice. The experience of parenthood rules that alternative off limits. It is this important point of the subject that Regan's challenge misses.

I do not suggest that Regan describes a conceptually impossible attitude toward things. We could imagine someone who believes simply that friendship and parenthood are especially valuable versions of the same thing of which money is just another instance. But this view would not simply describe existing attitudes. It would call for their renovation, and in an extremely dramatic way. If people really valued friendship, parenthood, and money in the same way, they would be fundamentally different from what they now are. In some guises, this would be the stuff of science fiction or horror. In some areas of life or law, the renovation may be justified, all things considered. But it would be a renovation nonetheless.

A tempting response is that the stakes here are purely linguistic—a matter of rhetoric, not substance. Perhaps people who disagree about kinds of valuation, and about commensurability, are just disagreeing about how to talk. Certainly, recognizable emotions and sentiments underlie these disagreements. But perhaps substantive analysis can ultimately proceed in the same way however we decide these matters. Even if legal and policy arguments based on commensurability meet a good deal of verbal resistance at the outset, perhaps rational argument can overcome the resistance.

For example, economic analysis of nonmarket relations often runs into difficulty because of such initially jarring terms as "investment" in one's children, the notion that education is a way of improving "human capital," and the idea of a "marriage market."[13] The terms seem to suggest that intrinsic goods are only of instrumental value. But once we think about these issues, we can see that these terms are simply a means of describing real-world phenomena, and of doing so in a way that makes complex, seemingly intractable problems more manageable.

But we can acknowledge all this while also insisting that certain redescriptions of human phenomena—redescriptions that push in the direction of commensurability—are far from unimportant. The redescriptions are important both because they describe in inadequate ways and because they do not merely redescribe.[14] They also have an important constitutive dimension—that is, they may help transform how (but not necessarily how much) we value or experience various events and relationships. Thus, for example, one might happily endorse economic incentives in the environmental area while also insisting that environmental amenities ought to be valued in a distinctive way, and that there is no metric along which to align our diverse valuations of the various goods at stake—higher gross national product, lower employment, cleaner air, and so forth—in stringent environmental proposals. An insistence on these points should lead to better thought about the relevant values, and it will likely lead to better outcomes as well.

Let us return to some familiar economic redescriptions of human endeavors. If someone really thought about dating and romance as participation in "a marriage market," he would be a strange creature indeed (and unlikely, perhaps, to fare especially well in the relevant practices). If someone thought that she was "selling" an idea, she would have an odd conception of intellectual life and perhaps be unable fully to participate in it, because she would be rejecting its own foundational norms. If a parent thought that, through the provision of love and education, he was simply "investing" in his children, he would have an odd and barely recognizable understanding of the parental role. No one should deny what seems obvious—that people often learn at least partly because of the economic benefits of learning. But if someone really thought that learning was solely a matter of "investing in human capital," she would have a thin and even debased conception of the purpose of learning. She would be thinking of her own capacities and hopes as a sort of commodity, like a bit of silver or gold, or perhaps as a simple source of commodities, like a tractor or an oil well. It is difficult even to imagine the self-conception entailed by this view. To think and talk in these terms may have unfortunate consequences for both thought and action. At the same time, certain values—parenthood, education, and so forth—may be adequately realized only if people refuse to contemplate certain choices or attitudes. It is in this sense that incommensurability is constitutive of our values and not easily dispensable.

It is sometimes said that trade-offs of the relevant sort are happening "implicitly" all the time. People may not trade dollars for lunch engagements with friends, but they do trade off a range of variables in deciding when and with whom to have lunch, and some of these variables are financial. Indeed, it would not be odd for a busy lawyer to cancel lunch with a friend, with a promise to buy lunch next time. People may not think that they are "investing" in their children, but they do allocate limited resources among, for example, leisure, consumer goods, vacation, and education for their offspring. But much depends on what the ambiguous word "implicitly" means. The fact that the trade-off is not made explicitly is hardly a matter of indifference. When the trade-off is made only "implicitly," it is not well described as an ordinary trade-off at all. The actor may be showing a commitment to a certain set of judgments about how relationships and prospects should be valued, and if the trade-offs were made explicitly, that commitment would be undermined or even violated. The explicit trade is not equivalent to the implicit one; the absence of explicitness maintains certain social norms. In an analogous context, Holmes wrote, "[e]ven a dog distinguishes between being stumbled over and being kicked";[15] the difference between a trip and a kick—identical in effect but conveying very different attitudes—is related to the difference between an implicit and an explicit trade. In these circumstances, it is hopelessly underdescriptive to claim that someone "implicitly" trades off (say) cash and friendship in making lunch decisions, even though this way of seeing things might be quite helpful for predictive purposes.

Economic or utilitarian descriptions of human behavior are unlikely by themselves to alter social norms or law in any significant way.[16] But social norms are in a constant process of evaluation and flux, and the description of kinds of valuation is one method by which norms are created and altered. The making of law reflects this process of description and valuation; law can have effects on kinds of valuation as well. Indeed, many of the sharpest disputes in law relate to the appropriate kinds of valuation to bring to bear on disputed problems. Here the pervasive question is what sorts of valuations the law ought to encourage or extinguish.

If kinds of valuation matter to human life, judgments about such kinds will matter a great deal to law as well. And in many areas of law, the question of commensurability occupies a surprisingly important place.

IV. Law in General

Preliminaries

These diverse kinds of valuation do not fit neatly into legal categories. We cannot say that, because people value different events in different ways, it follows that law should have a particular content. Nor can we draw lessons for law from the bare fact of incommensurability in any of the senses discussed here. This is so for several reasons.

First, we need an account of which kinds of valuation are appropriate in order to make recommendations for law. We are not and should not be agnostics or skeptics about appropriate kinds of valuation; they can be evaluated on the basis of reasons. Nor should we think that, because people value a certain thing in a certain way, the law ought to do so as well. Of course, democracy has its claims; but there may be good reason to challenge any particular popularly endorsed judgment on kinds of valuation. Indeed, some aspects of constitutional law represent an effort to discipline democratic discussion by limiting possible kinds of valuation, on the ground that they are too sectarian or inconsistent with principles of civic equality. When there are no constitutional barriers, the democratic process is formally unconstrained, but an important part of democratic debate consists of challenges to the kinds of valuation that prevail among the democratic majority.

Any judgments about appropriate kinds of valuation are of course a complex matter. This is so not least because, in a heterogeneous society, the state ought to allow a wide range of diverse valuations. The regulation of valuations can be a stifling matter. At least as a presumption, the state ought to allow people to value in the way that they see best. These considerations, however, do not imply that the state should or can remain agnostic about proper kinds of valuation. Incommensurabilities—even of the form that block certain reasons for action—are not merely freedom-reducing, but constitutive of certain sorts of freedom, for they make possible certain valuable relationships and commitments. Moreover, a state will have a hard time if it seeks to be entirely neutral about valuations. Global neutrality is impossible. The state has to make decisions about how to allocate rights and entitlements; it has to decide what can be traded on markets and what will be subject to politics, and these decisions inevitably will take some sort of stand on appropriate valuations.

Second, a judgment about the appropriate kind of valuation, even if it can be reached and persuasively defended, need not entail a particular conclusion for law. For example, it might be shown that prostitution entails an improper valuation of human sexuality, but this need not mean that prostitution should be outlawed. To justify outlawing prostitution, we must make an additional set of arguments about both the likely effectiveness of the ban and the principle that supports use of the coercive power of the state. Or we might think that the best human life involves a certain way of valuing the environment, without thereby rejecting, for example, tradable emissions permits as a regulatory tool. Perhaps tradable permits do not affect valuations of the environment; perhaps any such effects are minimal and well justified by the various gains. Or we might believe that animals deserve consideration and therefore ought not to be eaten, but also believe that the law should not require vegetarianism. State-compelled vegetarianism might well be ineffectual and inconsistent with individual liberty, rightly conceived. These examples show that any general claim about the right kind of valuation needs a great deal of supplementation to result in concrete recommendations for law and policy. There are also recurring questions about the feasibility of various legal strategies.

More generally, we can defend one kind of valuation for law and government and other kinds for family, church, and civil society. The law might, for example, insist on calculating the value of human life through conventional economic measures. The calculation might be acceptable if there is an "acoustic separation"[17] between legal measures and private life. At least if the measures do not affect prevailing kinds of valuation and can operate autonomously in their own sphere, the law may be acceptable, even if it does not reflect an appropriate kind of valuation for other contexts.

Third, the legal system has crude remedial tools. Usually it must use monetary remedies. In view of this limitation, the fact that these remedies are not commensurable with some harms is often merely an interesting theoretical point. When someone has lost an arm, or when a river has been polluted, the legal system has to work with money. The tools of the legal system lack sufficient refinement fully to take account of diverse kinds of valuation. What can be said about personal valuations cannot be said about legal institutions. It may follow that public policy ought to operate on the assumption of commensurability even if human beings should not; or it may follow that the legal system must often put problems of incommensurability to one side, leaving those problems for ethics rather than for law.

These disclaimers are important. Nonetheless, the fact of incommensurability, and the existence of diverse kinds of valuation, do help illuminate a wide range of disputes about the substance of law, about legal institutions, and about legal reasoning. In the next section, I offer several examples of pertinent legal debates.

The Expressive Function of Law

A unifying theme for the discussion is *the expressive function of law*. When evaluating a legal rule, we might ask whether the rule expresses an appropriate valuation of an event, person, group, or practice. The point matters for two reasons. The first and most important is based on a prediction about the facts: An incorrect valuation may influence social norms and push them in the wrong direction. For example, if the law wrongly treats something—say, reproductive capacities—as a commodity, the social kind of valuation may be adversely affected. If the law mandates recycling, subsidizes national service, or requires mandatory pro bono work, it may have healthy effects on social valuations of the relevant activities. It is appropriate to evaluate the law on this ground.

We can go further. Some people seem to think that it is possible to assess law solely on the basis of consequences—that an open-ended inquiry into consequences is a feasible way of evaluating legal rules. But this is not actually possible. The effects of any legal rule can be described in an infinite number of ways. Any particular characterization or accounting of consequences will rest not on some specification of the brute facts; instead, it will be mediated by a set of (often tacit) norms determining how to describe or conceive of consequences. Part of the expressive function of law consists in the identification of what consequences count and how they should be described. Because any conception of consequences is interpretive and thus evaluative in character, "pure" or unmediated consequentialism is not a feasible project for law.

A description of the effects of some legal rule is a product of expressive norms that give consequences identifiable social meanings, including norms that deny legal significance to certain consequences. We can therefore see the expressive function both in the effects of law on social attitudes and in the use of law to decide what sorts of consequences matter for legal purposes. When it seems as if we can talk about consequences alone, it is only because the mediating expressive norms are so widely shared that there is no controversy about them.

I have emphasized the possibility that the kinds of valuation reflected in law will affect social valuations in general. Sometimes this claim is right; valuations, like preferences and beliefs, are not a presocial given, but a product of a complex set of social forces, including law. But sometimes law will have little or no effect on valuations. Society is filled with legal provisions for market exchanges of goods and services—like pets and babysitting, for example—that are valued for reasons other than use. Market exchange need not affect social valuations; certainly, intrinsic goods are purchased and sold. The question therefore remains whether the claimed effect on social norms will occur. It is fully plausible, for example, to say that, although a law that permits prostitution reflects an inappropriate valuation of sexuality, any adverse effect of the law on social norms is so small as to be an implausible basis for objection.

But there is a second ground for endorsing the expressive function of law, and this ground does not concern social effects in the same sense. The ground is connected with the individual interest in integrity. Following the brief but suggestive discussion by Bernard Williams,[18] we might say that personal behavior is not concerned solely with producing states of affairs, and that, if it were, we would have a hard time in making sense of important aspects of our lives. There are also issues involving personal integrity, commitment, and the narrative continuity of a life. Williams offers several examples. Someone might refuse to kill an innocent person at the request of a terrorist, even if the consequence of the refusal is that many more people will be killed. Or a pacifist might refuse to take a job in a munitions factory, even if the refusal will have no salutary effects.

Our responses to these cases are not adequately captured in purely consequentialist terms.[19] Now it is possible that, for example, the refusal to kill an innocent person is consequentially justified on balance, for people who refuse to commit bad acts may cultivate attitudes that lead to value-maximizing behavior. But this is a complex matter. My point is only that consequentialist accounts do not fully describe our evaluative attitudes toward such acts.

Moreover, the expression of the appropriate evaluative attitude should be understood as a human good, constitutive of desirable characteristics. By making certain choices and not others, people express various conceptions both of themselves and of others. This is an independently important matter. We should agree on this point even if we also believe that consequences count (mediated as they are by expressive norms), and that people ought not to be fanatical.

There is a rough analog at the social and legal levels. A society might identify the kind of valuation to which it is committed and insist on that kind, even if the consequences of the insistence are obscure or unknown. A society might, for example, insist on an antidiscrimination law for expressive reasons, even if it does not know whether the law actually helps members of minority groups. A society might protect endangered species partly because it believes that the protection makes best sense of its self-understanding, by expressing an appropriate valuation of what it means for one species to eliminate another. A society might endorse or reject capital punishment because it wants to express a certain understanding of the appropriate course of action after one person has taken the life of another.

This point bears on the cultural role of adjudication and especially of Supreme Court decisions. The empirical effects of those decisions are highly disputed. When the Supreme Court says that capital punishment is unconstitutional, that segregation is unlawful, that certain restrictions on hate speech violate the First Amendment, or that students cannot be asked to pray in school, the real-world consequences may be much smaller than we think. But the close attention American society pays to the Court's pronouncements may well be connected with their expressive or symbolic character. When the Court makes a decision, it is often taken to be speaking on behalf of the nation's basic principles and commitments. This is a matter of importance quite apart from consequences, conventionally understood. It is customary and helpful to point to the Court's educative effect. But perhaps its expressive effect, or its expressive character, better captures what is often at stake.

I do not claim that the expressive effects of law, thus understood, are decisive or that they cannot be countered by a demonstration of more conventional bad consequences. As noted earlier—and it is important here—we might insist on a sort of acoustic separation between the domain of law and other spheres, hoping and believing that the kind of valuation appropriate to government will not affect the generally prevailing kind. If OSHA engages in cost-benefit analysis, surely people will not begin to think of their spouses as commodities. But I do suggest that the expressive function is a part of political and legal debate. Without understanding the expressive function of law, we will have a hard time in getting an adequate handle on public views with respect to civil rights, prostitution, the environment, endangered species, capital punishment, and abortion.

V. Law in Particular

I now discuss a number of areas of law in which kinds of valuation are at stake. In some of these areas, issues of commensurability also move to the fore. Of course, there are important differences among these areas, each of which raises distinctive issues of its own. Some of the issues are connected to problems of individual or social choices amid scarcity; others are not. But I believe that it is impossible to obtain a full understanding of these areas of law without reference to ideas of a general sort. In this sense, these very diverse areas share a common subject. They are united by the presence of important questions about appropriate kinds of valuation and about commensurability.

Social Differentiation

A liberal society allows a high degree of social differentiation. It includes the political sphere, the family, markets, intermediate organizations—especially religious organizations—and much more. Michael Walzer's influential book[20] offers an instructive discussion of these different "spheres." It would be especially valuable to be able to understand the social function or purpose of this sort of differentiation. Why might it be a good thing to carve up life in this way? And what exactly is the role of law in this endeavor?

The liberal commitment to social differentiation can be understood as an effort to make appropriate spaces for different kinds of valuation. Without accepting naive conceptions of the public-private distinction, we can see the family as the characteristic liberal sphere for the expression of love. At its best, politics embodies the forms of respect entailed by processes of reason-giving. In many intermediate organizations, people express affection and admiration. In religious organizations, the prevailing kind of valuation is usually one of worship and reverence. The market is typically the sphere for use. Things bought and sold on markets are typically valued in the way associated with pure commodities, although it is important and also true that many things sold on markets—music, vacations in beautiful places, art, childcare—are valued for reasons other than simple use.

Law plays an important and often overlooked role in the construction and maintenance of these various spheres, which are anything but natural. We know far too little to say that, in the state of nature, there is any such division. Markets are of course a function of the law of property, contract, and tort, without which voluntary agreements would not be possible. It is law that decides what can be traded on markets, and how trades can occur. Undoubtedly, families of various sorts would arise in the state of nature, but the particular families we have are emphatically a function of law. The law helps to create an independent familial sphere; it also determines who may be entitled to its protections and disabilities.

The state also insulates the public sphere from civil society, through, for example, the rule of one person, one vote and limitations on expenditures on campaigns. Intermediate organizations, like religious groups and labor unions, also receive various protections, insulations, and disabilities by laws designed to recognize independent social spheres. The creation of diverse social spheres, understood as a mechanism for allowing diverse kinds of valuation, is also an important social good, providing a form of liberty that is indispensable in modern society.

It would be foolish to idealize current practices. Institutional practice often deviates from institutional aspiration. Politics is often a realm for use; it has important marketlike features. It is hardly a simple process of exchanging reasons. The family is not only a place for the expression of love. Women and children have often been used without their consent, sometimes like commodities or objects (consider domestic abuse). People who believe in different kinds of valuation do not deny the gap between current practice and current aspiration. Much social criticism consists of an insistence on that gap, and of a claim for reform in the interest of producing conformity to the aspiration.

Religion, Civic Equality, and Political Liberalism

Our system is one of liberal republicanism. As such, it is committed to a principle of political equality and to a certain view about the relationship between political life and religious conviction. We can make some progress on these abstractions by observing that a liberal republic attempts to exclude certain kinds of valuation from public life. Those kinds of valuation may be too sectarian, or they may be inconsistent with the premise of political equality. A liberal republic thus bans particular "inputs" into politics either because they express a kind of valuation that is suited only to private life, or because they deny political equality, a commitment that entails certain evaluative attitudes toward fellow citizens. What I want to emphasize is that we can get a distinctive purchase on certain constitutional issues in this light.

Under the Constitution, the Establishment Clause is the key example of the ban on certain kinds of valuation. The Constitution rules out valuations that assume certain conceptions of what is sacred, at least those that invoke religious commitments. For example, a law making Easter a national holiday may not rest on the ground that it reflects the sanctity of Jesus Christ. The Establishment Clause generally rules sectarian justifications for statutes out of bounds, even if other, neutral factors could support the same laws. Political liberalism is constituted in part through the idea that certain kinds of valuation are too contentious to be a legitimate part of public life, even if they are a fully legitimate part of private citizenship.

A liberal republic also excludes certain kinds of valuation of human beings as inconsistent with constitutionally prescribed norms of political equality. I have referred to the prohibition on "titles of nobility," a key to the American tradition in this regard. The Equal Protection Clause is now understood very much in these terms. Thus, for example, a law cannot be premised on the ground that blacks are inferior to whites, or women inferior to men.[21] This idea may help make sense of the controversial claim that discriminatory intent is a necessary and sufficient condition for invalidating legislation.

Rights

In an influential if extreme formulation, fomer Judge Robert Bork asks how the Court can protect the right to sexual privacy if it does not protect the right to pollute. On Bork's view, both rights amount to "gratifications," and there is no essential difference between them.[22] A less extreme version of this view is the concern whether the Court can consistently protect sexual privacy without protecting property interests; who is to say that the former is more important than the latter?

We might be able to handle this question better if we insist on qualitative rather than merely quantitative differences among rights. It is not necessarily true that someone will value sexual privacy "more" than continued employment for longer hours at better wages, but it is possible to have a distinct concern about government regulation of the former, and it may be because of the way that sexual privacy is valued that constitutional protection is appropriate. Once claims for constitutional protection are not aligned along a single scale and assessed in purely quantitative terms, it becomes easier to make progress in thinking about fundamental rights.

This general understanding may cast light on some familiar and somewhat mysterious notions in legal and social theory. Consider, for example, Ronald Dworkin's account of rights as "trumps,"[23] or John Rawls's claim that, under the appropriate theory of justice, the principle calling for equal basic liberty is lexically prior to better economic arrangements.[24] If we treat rights as "trumps," we may be taken to be saying not that they are infinitely or even extraordinarily valuable when viewed solely in terms of aggregate levels, but that they are valued in a distinctive way—a way quite different from, and qualitatively higher than, the way we value the competing interests. Because of the distinctive way that rights are valued, it is necessary that the competing interests be (a) of a certain qualitative sort and (b) extraordinary in amount or level, in order to count as reasons for abridgment.

Similarly, in speaking of the lexical priority of equal liberty, we may mean that a just society values this interest in a way that precludes its violation for social and economic advantages. The lexical priority of liberty thus represents an effort to restate Kantian ideals about the priority of equal dignity and respect. We can imagine cases in which this judgment could be fanatical. But it seems clear that, in some cases, a belief in lexical priority may well reflect claims about incommensurability. We might treat equal liberty as a reflection of the foundational commitment to equal dignity and respect and believe that we do violence to the way we value that commitment if we allow it to be compromised for the sake of greater social and economic advantages. On this view, the lexical priority of equal liberty is structurally akin to the refusal to allow a child to be traded for cash, or a promise to be breached as a result of mildly changed circumstances. It reflects a judgment that the prevalent kind of valuation forbids compromising the good for certain reasons, even though those reasons are legitimate bases for action in other contexts.

Blocked Exchanges

An understanding of diverse kinds of valuation helps explain why liberal regimes generally respect voluntary agreements. If people value things in different ways, the state should allow them to sort things out as they choose. If values were commensurable, perhaps we could seek to block certain voluntary exchanges simply because we had better information about relevant costs and benefits than the parties themselves. In the face of diverse kinds of valuation, it is best to permit people to value as they like.[25]

But even a system that generally respects freedom of contract may block exchanges on several grounds. Typically, such grounds involve some form of market failure: A party may lack relevant information, a collective action problem may exist, third parties may be affected, a party may be myopic. But an additional and distinct reason is that some exchanges involve and encourage improper kinds of valuation.

I think that more common arguments stressing distributive considerations or unequal bargaining power often depend, on reflection, on an unarticulated claim about inappropriate valuation. The claim is that to allow purchase and sale of a good will mean that the good will be wrongly valued in a qualitative sense. Consider, for example, the right to vote. Vote trading is objectionable in part because it would allow inappropriate concentration of political power in the hands of a few. The prohibition therefore overcomes a collective action problem. But perhaps the ban on vote-trading also stems from a concern about kinds of valuation. If votes were freely tradable, we would have a different conception of what voting is for—about the values that it embodies—and this changed conception would have corrosive effects on politics.

Some reactions to Judge Richard Posner's argument on behalf of a form of "baby selling" stem from a similar concern. Judge Posner contends that a market for babies would serve most of the relevant policies better than does the current system. In some ways his argument is persuasive. Certainly the desire of infertile couples for children would be better satisfied through a market system. But part of the objection to free markets in babies is not quite engaged by Judge Posner. Instead, the objection is that a system of purchase and sale would value children in the wrong way. This system would treat human beings as commodities, a view that is itself wrong, and a practice with possible harmful consequences for social valuation in general. At most, this is a summary of a complex argument, based partly on uncertain empirical judgments, and it is hardly by itself decisive. But we cannot get an adequate grasp on the problem without seing this concern.

Or consider a possible application of the widely held view that market incentives are preferable to command-and-control regulation (a view endorsed in chapter 13). Might it not be preferable, for example, to allocate tradable racial discrimination rights, so that discriminators, or people who refuse to act affirmatively, can purchase rights from people who do not discriminate or who engage in affirmative action?[26] Suppose it could be shown that an approach of this sort would be more efficient than the approach in the current civil rights laws, and also that it would produce equal or better outcomes in terms of aggregate hiring of minority group members. Even if this were so, it might be thought unacceptable to permit employers to discriminate for a fee, because the way that we do or should value nondiscrimination is inconsistent with granting that permission. This argument might be educative: If discriminators could buy the right to discriminate, perhaps discrimination would not be stigmatized in the way we want. Or it might be expressive: Perhaps society would like to condemn discrimination quite apart from consequential arguments.

In coming to terms with the issue of blocked exchanges, some further points are important. As noted, the recognition of diverse kinds of valuation might well be made part of a conception of law that places a high premium on individual liberty and choice. At least as a general rule, the state should not say that one kind of valuation will be required. Within broad outlines, people ought to be permitted to value as they wish, though we should recognize that any kind of valuation will inevitably be affected by social norms and by law.

Moreover, there is an important difference between urging changes in social norms and urging changes in law. There may be a justified norm against asking a neighbor to mow one's lawn without a law to that effect. Similarly, one might speak on behalf of a powerful norm against certain attitudes toward animals without also recommending laws that, for example, forbid people to eat meat. It is possible to urge people to value animals in a certain way without thinking that the law should require that kind of valuation.

We might understand the distinction between norms and laws in two different ways. First, the distinction might be largely pragmatic. A law imposed on people who do not share the relevant norm may breed frustration and resentment. It may be counterproductive or futile. Second, the difference might be rooted in a principle of liberty, one that calls for a strong presumption in favor of governmental respect for diverse kinds of valuation. A legal mandate may be simply too sectarian or intrusive for a heterogeneous society. Both pragmatism and principle seem to argue in favor of a sharp distinction between norms and law.

There is a final point. Markets are filled with agreements to transfer goods that are not valued simply for use. People purchase music, even if they regard the performances as deserving awe and wonder. They buy human care for their children. They trade the right to see beautiful areas. They purchase pets for whom they feel affection or even love, and whom they hardly regard as solely for human exploitation and use. The objection to the use of markets in certain areas must depend on the view that markets will have adverse effects on existing kinds of valuation, and it is not a simple matter to show when and why this will be the case. For all these reasons, opposition to commensurability, and insistence on diverse kinds of valuation, do not by themselves amount to opposition to market exchange, which is pervaded by choice among goods that participants value in diverse ways.

Legal Reasoning

A belief in diverse kinds of valuation has consequences for current debates about the actual and appropriate nature of legal reasoning. If it can be shown that a well-functioning system of law is alert to these diverse kinds of valuation, theories of legislation, administration, and adjudication may be affected.

Consider, for example, economic analysis of law. It is clear that this form of analysis has produced enormous gains in the positive and normative study of law. The approach has been criticized on many grounds, most familiarly that it is insufficiently attuned to distributive arguments. But perhaps the resistance to economic analysis stems from something quite different and less noticed. In its normative form, economic analysis depends on too thin, flat, and sectarian a conception of value, captured in the notion that legal rules should be designed so as to maximize wealth. The problem with this idea is that the word "wealth" elides qualitative distinctions among the different goods typically at stake in legal disputes. Instead of maximizing wealth, it is desirable to have a highly disaggregated picture of the consequences of legal rules, a picture that enables the judge to see the various goods at stake. This is true not only of the law of free speech and religious liberty, but also of the law of contract and tort. At least under ideal circumstances, it would be good to have a full sense of the qualitatively distinct interests at stake before reaching a decision.

We still lack a full account of practical reason in law. But what I have said here offers some considerations in support of analogical reasoning, the conventional method of Anglo-American law. Analogical reasoning, unlike economic analysis, need not insist on assessing plural and diverse social goods according to a single metric. The analogical thinker may be alert to the manifold dimensions of social situations and to the many relevant similarities and differences. In picking out relevant similarities, the analogizer does not engage in an act of deduction. Instead, she identifies common features in a way that helps constitute both legal and cultural categories, rather than being constrained by some particular theory of value given in advance. Unequipped with or unburdened by a unitary theory of the good or the right, she is in a position to see clearly and for herself the diverse and plural goods that are involved and to make choices among them without reducing them to a single metric. This is one description of the characteristic style of Anglo-American law in its idealized form.

A distinctive feature of analogical thinking is that it is a "bottom-up" approach, building principles of a low or intermediate level of generality from engagement with particular cases. In this respect, it is quite different from "top-down" theories, which test particular judgments by reference to general theory.[27] Because analogy works from particular judgments, it is likely to reflect the plural and diverse goods that people really value. Of course, there are nonanalogical approaches that insist on the plurality of goods, and those approaches also have a "top-down" character.

This approach has disadvantages as well. The use of a single metric makes things simple and orderly where they would otherwise be chaotic. In certain areas of the law, this may be a decisive advantage, all things considered. Certainly, it has been taken as an important advantage in many areas of contemporary law, in which the displacement of common law courts by legislation has been designed to promote rule-of-law virtues inaccessible to ordinary adjudication.

VI. Choices Again

I have not yet dealt with two major questions. The first involves the choice among different kinds of valuation and, more particularly, the decision whether or not to make things commensurable. The second involves the issue of how to make choices among incommensurable goods. The two questions are obviously related. They are also large and complex. To answer them, we would need to answer many of the major questions in ethical and political theory. As I have emphasized, most answers must be developed in the context of particular problems. I offer only a few notations here.

Which Kinds of Valuation?

To come to terms with the question of appropriate kinds of valuation, we should begin by asking whether diversity in kinds is desirable at all. Perhaps we should adopt a unitary kind of valuation, or seek to obtain some sort of commensurability. In many ways, this project unites such diverse thinkers as Plato, Bentham, and, in law, Richard Posner. It seems clear that this approach would have many advantages. It would simplify and order decisions by placing the various goods along a single metric. Often there is indeed pragmatic value in this enterprise (see chapter 12). According to one familiar conception of rationality, this step would increase rationality. Would it not be a large improvement if commensurability could be obtained?

Let us put law to one side for the moment and think about claims for unitariness and commensurability in human life generally. It seems obvious that an answer to this question should turn on what leads to a better conception of the human good. We might make some progress by considering what the world would be like if kinds of valuation really were unitary or if commensurability really did obtain. In such a world, for example, a loss of friendship or the death of a parent would really be like a loss of money, though undoubtedly a lot of it. An achievement in something that one prizes—like art or music—would be valued in the same way as an increase in net worth, or the birth of a new child, or falling in love, or the relief of human suffering, or the victory of a favorite sports team. Offers of cash exchange would really be evaluated solely on the basis of their amount. The distinction between instrumental and intrinsic goods would collapse, in the sense that many intrinsic goods would become both fungible and instrumental.

A great deal would be lost in such a world. A life with genuine commensurability would be flat and dehumanized. It would be inconsistent with an appropriately diversified approach to a good human life. It would eliminate desirable relationships and attitudes. In fact, it would be barely recognizable.

On the other hand, nothing in this brief account is fatal to the view that law and public policy sometimes ought to rest on unitary kinds of valuation or on assumptions of commensurability. It is possible to think that under ideal conditions, the best system of valuation is diverse and plural, but that in light of the weaknesses of human institutions and the constant prospect of bias, confusion, and arbitrariness, public choices should assume a single kind or a unitary metric as the best way of promoting all of the relevant goods. This question cannot be answered a priori or in the abstract. But those who favor legal approaches based on unitary kinds of valuation and commensurability should understand that their approach is best defended as a means of overcoming certain institutional obstacles, and not as reflecting a fully adequate understanding of the relevant problems. I have suggested as well that even if, say, government officials align the diverse effects of regulation along a single metric, they should also provide a disaggregated picture, so that citizens can be aware of qualitative differences and of the various goods at stake.

All this leaves much uncertainty. But it does suggest that, institutional issues aside, we should approve of a large degree of diversity in kinds of valuation. From this it does not follow that any particular kind of valuation is appropriate for any particular sphere. To evaluate kinds of valuation, we also have to think very concretely about what kinds in what places are parts of a good life or a good political system.

Choices Among Incommensurable Goods

How are choices made among incommensurable goods? How can those choices be assessed? The first point is that there is no algorithm or formula by which to answer this question. If we are looking for a certain sort of answer—the sort characteristic of some believers in commensurability—we will be unable to find it. Relatively little can be said in the abstract. Instead, we need to offer detailed descriptions of how such choices are made, and how to tell whether such choices turn out well. Here there are many possible criteria for public and private action, and a mere reference to the existence of incommensurabilities will be unhelpful standing by itself.

In law and politics, a diverse set of standards—liberty, equality, prosperity, excellence, all of these umbrella terms—will be brought to bear on hard cases. A particular goal is to find solutions that will minimally damage the relevant goods. Perhaps an approach that promotes a recognizable form of liberty will only modestly compromise a recognizable conception of equality. Here, too, there is no escape from close examination of particular cases.

Consider, for example, the issue of surrogacy. It would be plausible to conclude that the legal system ought not to criminalize surrogacy but also ought not to require surrogate mothers to hand over their children to the purchasing parents, at least during a brief period after birth. Criminalization would entail difficult enforcement problems and might also discourage arrangements that do much good and little harm. We can understand why surrogacy arrangements might be thought to be connected with sex inequality, but the contribution to discrimination is probably too attenuated to justify criminalization. On the other hand, it may be damaging to the birth mother to force her to hand over a child against her will, especially because before the fact it may be quite difficult for her to know exactly what this action entails. The failure of the legal system to order specific performance is unlikely to have serious adverse consequences on prospective participants in such arrangements. This is, of course, an inadequate treatment of a complex problem. All I mean to do is to suggest some of the lines along which the inquiry might occur. (Compare an approach that would insist on commensurability. Such an approach would be laughably inadequate; it would prevent us from seeing what is really at stake.)

Much of the relevant work here is done in two ways: through analogies and through understanding consequences, mediated as these are through expressive norms. When incommensurable goods are at stake, it is typically asked: What was the resolution of a previous case with similar features? Through this process, people seek to produce vertical and horizontal consistency among their various judgments. This system of testing is designed not to line up goods along a single metric, but to produce the sort of consistency and rigor that characterizes the successful operation of practical reason. The inquiry into consequences avoids monism while still examining the real-world effects of different courses of action. How, for example, will a particular result compromise or promote the relevant goods? This is a characteristic part of practical reasoning in law.

In the context of emissions trading in environmental law, for example, it seems hard to support the empirical claim that the shift from command-and-control government to financial incentives will have serious adverse effects on people's thinking about pollution. Many claims about the educative function of law are actually claims about real-world consequences, understood through expressive norms on which there is no dispute. It is possible to think well about those consequences, and sometimes we can see that the feared effects will not materialize. In this way, it is possible to explore whether there will be damage to some of the goods that are allegedly threatened by certain initiatives. Of course, it is true that, on some issues, we will lack relevant data.

A Note on Tragedy

There is a final point. A recognition of incommensurability is necessary to keep alive the sense of tragedy, and in certain ways this is an individual and collective good, perhaps especially in law. Recognition that all outcomes "impose costs" is not quite the same thing as a sense of tragedy.[28] Though I can hardly discuss this complex matter here, the very notion of tragedy seems to embody a commitment to an understanding of the uniqueness of certain goods, or the irreversibility and irreplaceability of certain losses. If tragedy were understood to mean instead high costs, or the existence of losses that accompany benefits (Kaldor-Hicks rather than Pareto improvements, for example), the sense of tragedy would be dramatically changed. Here, too, we would not have a simple redescription of the problem.

A sense of tragedy is an individual good because it accompanies and makes possible certain relationships and attitudes that are an important part of a good life. It is a collective good for this reason and also because it focuses attention on the fact that, even when the law is doing the right thing, all things considered, much may be lost as well. This is valuable, for example, in current thinking about the environment and occupational safety. In the presence of tragedy, there is a large incentive to create social arrangements so that people do not face that prospect.

At its best, the Anglo-American legal system is alert to the fact that diverse goods are at stake in many disputes. Judges know that not all of these goods can be simultaneously preserved. This awareness is itself desirable because of the pressure that it tends to exert on judges and legislators as well. A redescription of tragedy in terms that assume a monistic theory of value would not create the same sort of pressure.

Conclusion

Human beings value goods, events, and relationships in diverse and plural ways. Sometimes money itself is not fungible. Often we face serious problems of commensurability. This problem does not entail paralysis, indeterminacy, or arbitrariness. Decisions are made all the time among incommensurable goods, at the personal, social, and legal levels, and these decisions may well be rational or irrational. It might even be possible to convert our kinds of valuation for use on a unitary metric, or to make goods, events, and relationships commensurable. But if what I have said here is correct, this would be a sort of tragedy, not least because it would make the very fact of tragedy puzzling or even incomprehensible.

The fact of diverse kinds of valuation, and the existence of incommensurable goods, have not yet played a major role in legal and economic theory. But these issues underlie a surprisingly wide range of legal disputes. No unitary "top-down" theory can account for the complexities of most controversies in law. Perhaps most dramatically, the liberal insistence on social differentiation—markets, families, religious groups, politics, and more—is best justified as an attempt to make a space for distinct kinds of valuation and to give each of them its appropriate place in human life. The Establishment and Equal Protection Clauses are centrally concerned with regulating kinds of valuation. In environmental law, the major issue of contestation is frequently the appropriate kind of valuation of environmental amenities; if beaches, species, and mountains were valued solely for their use, we would not be able to understand them in the way that we now do.

The same issue arises in the law of contract, especially in the award of specific performance remedies. It also plays a role in thinking about the point of damage remedies in tort. In both settings, it is wrong to ignore the highly contextual nature of choice and to act as if a particular decision—not to take out insurance for a certain danger, to accept a job at a certain risk premium—reflects some global judgment simply adaptable for policy use. No global judgment need underlie particular choices. Many blocked exchanges, moreover, attest to social resistance to commensurability. We might also think that attention to these issues shows that cost-benefit analysis is obtuse, because it aligns qualitatively distinct goods along a single metric. In addition to cost-benefit analysis—which might of course be helpful in our at most second-best world—what is desirable is a disaggregated picture of the effects of different courses of action, so that officials and citizens can see those effects for themselves.

In disputes over free speech, large questions are whether speech ought to be valued in the same way as commodities traded on markets, and whether free speech values are unitary or plural. We might think that we ought not to treat free speech as an ordinary commodity and that we should recognize the diverse ends it embodies. Various arguments for revision of existing understandings—market thinking for families and politics, extension of the metaphor of the family, the view that reason-giving ought to occupy all social spheres—might be seen as attempts to renovate current forms of valuation in favor of a new or even unitary kind.

An especially large task for legal theory is to offer an adequate description of how, in legal contexts, choices should be made among incommensurable goods and among different possible kinds of valuation. I have at best started to undertake that task here. There are limits to how much can be said in the abstract; a close inspection of particular contexts will be indispensable to this endeavor. But I conclude with two suggestions. An insistence on incommensurability and on diverse kinds of valuation is one of the most important conclusions emerging from the study of Anglo-American legal practice, and an appreciation of those diverse kinds will yield major gains to those seeking to understand and to evaluate both public and private law.

Notes

1. I owe much help in the discussion here to Elizabeth Anderson, *Value in Ethics and Economics* (Cambridge: Harvard University Press, 1993). Anderson uses the term "modes of valuation" to refer to the same basic idea. I should emphasize that I am discussing our best self-understandings, and that more parsimonious assumptions may be best for predictive purposes (see chapter 12).

2. For an especially instructive discussion of this point, see *id.* at 8–11.

3. Note in this regard the social norm requiring that, in some circumstances, gifts should not take the form of cash, which is regarded as excessively impersonal. As compared with a gift of (say) $30, a gift of (say) a tie costing $30 establishes a distinctive and often preferable relationship between the recipient and the giver—even if in some contexts $30 in cash would be worth more to the recipient than the $30 tie, and even if in some contexts a gift of $30 would be less costly, to the giver, than the gift of a $30 tie. This point is interestingly missed in Joel Waldfogel, "The Deadweight Loss of Christmas," 83 *Am. Econ. Rev.* 1328, 1336 (1993), which finds $4 billion in annual deadweight losses from noncash gifts and which assumes that cash gifts are always more efficient and therefore generally preferable.

4. The example comes from Joseph Raz, *The Morality of Freedom* (New York: Oxford University Press, 1986), pp. 348–49. I am generally indebted to Raz's discussion of incommensurability and especially constitutive incommensurabilities.

5. See Steven Kelman, *What Price Incentives?: Economics and the Environment* (Boston: Auburn House, 1981), pp. 54–83; Margaret J. Radin, "Market-Inalienability," 100 *Harv. L. Rev.* 1849 (1987).

6. See Richard A. Posner, *Sex and Reason* (Cambridge: Harvard University Press, 1992), pp. 409–17; Elisabeth M. Landes and Richard A. Posner, "The Economics of the Baby Shortage," 7 *J. Legal Stud.* 323 (1978); Richard A. Posner, "The Regulation of the Market in Adoptions," 67 *B. U. L.Rev.* 59 (1987).

7. See Viviana A. Zelizer, *The Social Meaning of Money* (New York: Basic Books, 1994); Steven Croley and John Hanson, "The Nonpecuniary Costs of Acccidents," 108 *Harv. L. Rev.* 1785 (1995); Richard Thaler, "Mental Accounting Matters" (unpublished manuscript, 1995).

8. For discussions of commensurability, see Anderson, *supra* note 1, at 44–73; James Griffin, *Well-Being: Its Meaning, Measurement and Moral Importance* (Oxford: Clarendon Press, 1986), pp. 75–92; Martha C. Nussbaum, *The Fragility of Goodness* (Cambridge: Cambridge University Press, 1986), pp 106–24; Raz, *supra* note 4, at 321–66; Michael Stocker, *Plural and Conflicting Values* (Oxford: Oxford University Press), pp. 130–207; Charles Taylor, "The Diversity of Goods," in *Philosophy and the Human Sciences* (Cambridge: Cambridge University Press, 1985), pp. 230, 243; Elizabeth Anderson, "Values, Risks, and Markets Norms," 17 *Phil. & Pub. Aff.* 54, 57–59 (1987); Richard Pildes & Elizabeth Anderson, "Slinging Arrows at Democarcy," 90 *Colum. L. Rev.* 2121, 2145–46 (1990); Amartya Sen, "Plural Utility," in 81 *Proc. of the Aristotelian Socy.* 193, 197–99 (1981); Richard Warner, "Incommensurability as a Jurisprudential Puzzle," 68 *Chi.-Kent L. Rev.* 147 (1992); Richard H. Pildes, "Conceptions of Value in Legal Thought," 90 *Mich. L. Rev.* 1520 (1992) (book review). Compare the discussion of an "integrated personality" in Frank Hahn, "Benevolence," in *Thoughtful Economic Man: Essays On Rationality, Moral Rules and Benevolence*, J. Gay Tulip Meeks, ed. (Cambridge: Cambridge University Press, 1991), pp. 7, 8 (asserting intrapersonal comparability of options grounded in self- and other- regarding motives), with the response in Amartya Sen, "Beneconfusion," in *Thoughtful Economic Man, supra,* at 12, 12–14 (denying this thesis).

See John Stuart Mill, *Utilitarianism*, Oskar Priest, ed. (Indianapolis: Bobbs Merrill, 1957).

> It is quite compatible with the principle of utility to recognize the fact that some kinds of pleasure are more desirable and more valuable than others. It would be absurd that, while in estimating all other things quality is considered as well as quantity, the estimation of pleasure should be supposed to depend on quantity alone.

Id. at 12. See also Mill's criticism of Bentham:

> Nothing is more curious than the absence of recognition in any of his writings of the existence of conscience, as a thing distinct from philanthropy, from affection for God or man, and from self-interest in this world or in the next. . . .
>
> Nor is it only the moral part of man's nature . . . that he overlooks; he but faintly recognises, as a fact in human nature, the pursuit of any other ideal end for its own sake. The sense of honour, and personal dignity . . . the love of beauty, the passion of the artist; the love of order . . . the love of power . . . the love of action . . . the love of ease:—None of these powerful constituents of human nature are thought worthy of a place among the "Springs of Action."

Id. at 66–68.

9. Hence Mill:

> The ingredients of happiness are very various, and each of them is desirable in itself, and not merely when considered as swelling an aggregate. The principle of utility does not mean that any given pleasure, as music, for instance, or any given exemption from pain, as for example health, are to be looked upon as means to a collective something termed happiness, and to be desired on that account. They are desired and desirable in and for themselves; besides being means, they are a part of the end.

Mill, *supra* note 8, at 179. J. J. C. Smart, more cautious on this point, simply states: "[T]he more complex pleasures are incomparably more fecund than the less complex ones; not only are they enjoyable in themselves but they are a means to further enjoyment." J. J. C. Smart, "An Outline of a System of Utilitarian Ethics," in *Utilitarianism: For And Against* J. J. C. Smart and Bernard Williams, eds. (Cambridge: Cambridge University Press, 1973). In light of these descriptions, we might not see "utility" as a metric at all.

10. Sometimes, however, it may be pragmatically valuable to construct a metric consisting of heterogeneous items. The "human development index" used by the United Nations to measure well-being by amalgamating literacy, longevity, and per capita income, provides a useful example. See chapter 4. Similarly, the National Football League measures quarterback proficiency with an index based on heterogeneous qualities, including completion percentage, average gain per attempt, touchdown percentage, and interception percentage. See Dan Pierson, "Harbaugh Passes the Ratings Test," *Chi.Trib.*, Nov. 4, 1990, at C9. The risk with both indices is that the aggregate numbers may deflect attention from important qualitative differences.

11. See Joseph Raz, *Practical Reason and Norms* (London: Hutchinson, 1975), pp. 35–48.

12. See Donald Regan, "Authority and Value," 62 *So. Cal. L. Rev.* 995, 1058 (1989).

13. Consider, for example, Becker's characterization of the "marriage market":

[A]n efficient marriage market assigns imputed income or "prices" to all participants that attract them to suitable polygamous or monogamous marriages. Imputed prices are also used to match men and women of different qualities: some participants . . . choose to be matched with "inferior" persons because they feel "superior" persons are too expensive. . . .

. . .[A]n efficient marriage market usually has positive assortative mating, where high-quality men are matched with high-quality women and low-quality men with low-quality women, although negative assortative mating is sometimes important.

Gary Becker, *A Treatise on the Family* (Cambridge: Harvard University Press, 1991), p. 108.

14. See, e.g., id. at 24 (characterizing "children, prestige and health, altruism, envy and pleasures of the senses" as "commodities"); Richard A. Posner, *Economic Analysis of Law*, 4th ed. (Boston: Little Brown, 1992).

15. Oliver Wendell Holmes, *The Common Law* (Boston: Little Brown, 1881), p. 3.

16. Note, however, the fact that students in economics appear to engage in altruistic behavior less frequently than others, and thus fail to adhere to social norms that solve collective action problems. See Robert H. Frank, et al., "Does Studying Economics Inhibit Cooperation?" *J. Econ. Persp.*, (Spring 1993) at 159 (answering title question in the affirmative).

17. Cf. Meir Dan-Cohen, "Decision Rules and Conduct Rules: On Acoustic Separation in Criminal Law," 97 *Harv. L. Rev.* 625, 625–34 (1984) (distinguishing between decision rules addressed to officials and conduct rules addressed to the public).

18. See Bernard Williams, "A Critique of Utilitarianism," in *Utilitarianism: For and Against, supra* note 9.

19. Consider these remarks by a participant in civil rights demonstrations:

If I had known that not a single lunch counter would open as a result of my action I could not have done differently than I did. If I had known violence would result, I could not have done differently than I did. I am thankful for the sit-ins if for no other reason than that they provided me with an opportunity for making a slogan into reality, by turning a decision into an action. It seems to me that this is what life is all about.

James Miller, *Democracy is in the Streets: From Port Huron to the Siege of Chicago* (New York: Simon and Schuster, 1987), p. 52. Compare Herbert Simon's concern that the 1960s student movement was "plagued by Expressionism":

We are all Expressionists part of the time. Sometimes we just want to scream loudly at injustice, or to stand up and be counted. These are noble motives, but any serious revolutionist must often deprive himself of the pleasures of self-expression. He must judge his actions by their ultimate effects on institutions.

Herbert Simon, *Models of My Life* (New York: Basic Books, 1991), p. 281.

20. Michael Walzer, *Spheres of Justice: A Defense of Pluralism* (New York: Basic Books, 1983).

21. See, e.g., Washington v. Davis, 426 U.S. 229 (1976); Personnel Adm. v. Feeney, 442 U.S. 256 (1979).

22. See Robert H. Bork, *The Tempting of America: The Political Seduction of the Law* (New York: Free Press, 1990), pp. 257–59.

23. See Ronald Dworkin, *Taking Rights Seriously* (Cambridge: Harvard University Press, 1977), pp. xi–xii, 184–205.

24. John Rawls, *A Theory of Justice* (Cambridge: Belknap Press of Harvard University Press, 1971), p. 61 ("[A] departure from the institutions of equal liberty . . . cannot be justified by, or compensated for, by greater social and economic advantages."). Note also Rawls's at least implicit recognition of incommensurability as I understand it here:

If someone denies that liberty of conscience is a basic liberty and maintains that all human interests are commensurable, and that between any two there always exists some rate of exchange in terms of which it is rational to balance the protection of one against the protection of the other, then we have reached an impasse.

John Rawls, *Political Liberalism* (New York: Columbia University Press, 1993), p. 312.

25. This is a large part of the argument in Friedrich A. Hayek, *The Road to Serfdom* (London: G. Routledge, 1944), pp. 57–59:

The welfare and the happiness of millions cannot be measured on a single scale of less and more. The welfare of people . . . cannot be adequately expressed as a single end . . . . [N]othing but partial scales of value exist—scales which are inevitably different and often inconsistent with each other. From this the individualist concludes that the individuals should be allowed, within defined limits, to follow their own values and preferences rather than somebody else's.

26. See Robert Cooter, "Market Affirmative Action," 31 *San Diego L.Rev.* 614. The idea is proposed as satire in Derrick Bell, *Faces at the Bottom of the Well: The Permanence of Racism* (New York: Basic Books, 1992), ch. 5.

27. See Cass R. Sunstein, *Legal Reasoning and Political Conflict* (New York: Oxford University Press, 1996), ch. 3.

28. For discussion, see Nussbaum, *supra* note 8, at 23–84.

Measuring Well-Being

Some people think that there is a deep opposition between "government intervention" and "free markets." But the opposition is too simple. No one is really opposed to "government intervention." Markets depend for their existence on law, which is necessary to establish property rights and to set out the rules governing contracts and tort. Short of anarchy, a system of legal entitlements, set by the state, is inevitable. If we are asking whether the state is an important part of the solution to current social problems, there can be only one answer: It had better be. But what is the relationship between the state and social well-being?

This question assumes special significance in light of the original aspiration of the American founders—to create a deliberative democracy. Public officials would be accountable to the citizenry at large, but they were also supposed to engage in deliberative tasks and to profit from and encourage deliberation among the people as a whole. Both the structure of the national government and the system of individual rights were intended to encourage public deliberation.

Things have not worked out as the Framers envisioned. One of the most serious problems is the public emphasis on issues and events that have little relevance to most people's lives. People lack accurate information about what is most important. In elections, for example, "soundbite politics" often replaces discussion about public issues. The problem affects day-to-day governance too. Instead of focusing on, for example, education and its improvement, public attention is often directed to sensational anecdotes, crude oversimplifications of issues, or scandals about public officials' private lives. In these circumstances, we are likely to end up with misdirected policies or worse—a form of government by faction, the evil most feared by the American founders. A high priority for those thinking about the role of the state should be to develop methods for focusing attention on things that matter to people's lives.

An important part of this task is to establish criteria by which to measure governmental performance. If broadly debated and well-publicized, such criteria should promote democratic discussion and at the same time help to counteract the very problems to which they draw attention. To develop criteria of this kind, we need a theory of social well-being. To be helpful, the theory must be not only substantively plausible but also practical to apply. This constraint is a demanding one. The best substantive theory might well be abandoned because it is not administrable—that is, the underlying data cannot be compiled without great cost, the theory does not allow comparisons among regions or over time, or it is too unruly and complex.

In the United States, there are many measures of economic performance. But here and abroad, gross domestic product (GDP) is the most influential indicator of social well-being. When GDP is growing, it is often thought that a number of good things will happen—employment will increase, poverty will go down, and people will be able to obtain a wide range of valuable things. Concentration on GDP has important political effects. It focuses media, public, and governmental attention in a distinctive way.

Part of my goal here is to show what most economists do not deny: that GDP is an inadequate measure of social well-being, and that we lack an adequate alternative. GDP is too crudely connected to things that people should care about. To overcome the limits of GDP, I offer a simple proposal: Democratic governments should produce an annual "quality of life report," designed to measure their performance in producing good lives for their citizens. This report should be highly publicized and broadly disseminated. I also propose that the ingredients in the report are plural and diverse and not commensurable. Both the fact of incommensurability and the general attack on GDP have some important consequences for law.

I suggest as well that it is important to attend to the relationship between legal provisions and the various ingredients of individual and social well-being. Per capita GDP, for example, becomes more important if money is both necessary and sufficient for the acquisition of valuable things. We might ultimately be able to evaluate legal provisions by exploring their relationship to the various components of individual and social well-being. A quality of life report would help in initiating this project.

In the course of the discussion, I offer a great deal of data about social and economic trends within the United States. The failure to identify the empirical dimensions of legal disputes is a continuing weakness in the legal culture. While the facts identified by a quality of life report will not dispose of strictly legal debates, they do have implications for many legal controversies, especially those involving the criminal justice system, race and sex equality, and government regulation.

I. Gross Domestic Product

In General

One of the simplest measures of social and economic well-being, used internationally and by many nations, is GDP. It refers to the total quantity of goods and services produced, weighted by their respective prices. Goods and services that are not paid for are not included. GDP is highly influential in international comparisons. It also plays a large role in the domestic sphere. To take a crude illustration, consider the astonishing fact that the words "gross national product" appeared in over 20,000 major news stories in the last two years— and that the words "gross domestic product" appeared in over 40,000 stories. It would be an absurd exaggeration to say that ordinary people frequently talk about GDP or GNP. But the numbers for GDP affect legislative deliberations, presidential judgments, media reports on the state of the economy, professional recommendations, and much more. A different measure would focus attention on different things.

Criticisms

Certainly GDP is a useful figure, since it bears a relationship to important social goals. If we think of income as an all-purpose means—as something that people want regardless of what else they want—we might well attend to GDP. There are, however, a number of problems with relying on GDP as a measure of well-being. Some of these problems suggest that GDP is imperfect as a measure of purely economic goals. Some of them suggest that important social, rather than purely economic, variables are not reflected in GDP, though of course it is somewhat artificial to distinguish between the economic and the social.

GDP and Economic Well-Being

GDP's ability to measure economic well-being is doubtful for a number of reasons.

Distributional Issues   If income is unequally distributed, a high GDP may disguise the fact that many people are living bad or even desperate lives. For example, the United States has the highest per capita real GDP in the world. But it also has a higher rate of children living in poverty—one in five—than does any other wealthy country in the world. The rate of children living in poverty is double that of the industrialized nations taken as a whole and four times that of Western Europe. Nearly half of all black children in the United States live in poverty. This crucial economic fact is undisclosed by GDP.

Excluded Goods and Services   GDP does not include goods and services that are free, including some that are closely connected with economic well-being. For example, unpaid domestic labor is not a part of GDP. Many environmental amenities, such as clean air and water, are not reflected in GDP. The GDP figure thus fails adequately to measure either the benefits of a healthy environment or the costs of its degradation.[1] There are other gaps in what GDP measures. It does not, for example, reflect changes in leisure time; but it is clear that any increase in leisure is a gain even in economic terms, since leisure is something for which people are willing to pay, sometimes a great deal.[2] Generally, a serious problem with GDP is that the figure excludes all social costs and benefits that do not have prices.

Unclear Correlations with Other Important Economic Indicators   GDP sometimes seems to be a general placeholder for a number of diverse indicators of economic well-being. But in fact, it may not be closely correlated with some important indicators. Consider two major social goals: reduction of poverty and reduction of unemployment. Of course, GDP growth can be an important factor in counteracting both unemployment and poverty, and nothing I say here is inconsistent with this proposition. But it is also possible for GDP increases to be accompanied by increases in unemployment and hence poverty (which is closely correlated with unemployment); indeed, this has often happened.

Economic growth is a function of productivity growth and employment growth, where productivity is understood as GDP divided by total employment. Increases in productivity can contribute to an increase in GDP, possibly without increasing employment levels at all. For example, converting a plant to use industrial robots may raise production levels and also eliminate the jobs of hundreds of assembly workers. Increases in GDP may therefore fail to produce increases in employment levels. Because poverty is well correlated with unemployment, it follows, too, that when GDP goes up, poverty may not go down.

Table 4.1 shows changes in GDP, unemployment, and poverty from 1970 to the present. GDP growth rates are generally correlated with changes in unemployment rates, particularly in especially high and especially low GDP growth years. There are, however, several years in which the two figures are not correlated. For present purposes, a key point is that GDP rates are far from identical to unemployment and poverty rates. If we know what happens to GDP, we do not necessarily know what happens to unemployment and poverty.

GDP and Social Well-Being

Even if GDP has some virtues as an indicator of economic welfare, it fails to capture important aspects of what we might roughly describe as social well-being.

Uncertain Relation to Valuable Things   It is often thought that GDP serves as a good proxy for valuable things. But the relationship between GDP and important social goals is far from clear.

Consider, for example, the likelihood of subjection to violent crime. Physical security is surely an important ingredient in well-being, but it is at best indirectly reflected in GDP. Consider also the fact that there is no inevitable connection between GDP and life expectancy. Some countries have a relatively low GDP but long life expectancy and low rates of infant mortality.[3] Many countries have a high GDP but do poorly in promoting longevity.[4] Education is an important part of a good life, whether or not educated people accumulate wealth; but the association between education and GDP, while real, is extremely crude. Certainly we can speculate, with some plausibility, that wealthy people are less likely to commit crimes and better able to pay for education,

Table 4.1. GDP Growth Compared with Levels of
Unemployment and Poverty

Year	GDP Growth (%)	Unemployment (%)	Poverty (%)
1970	0.0	4.9	12.6
1971	2.9	5.9	12.5
1972	5.1	5.6	11.9
1973	5.2	4.9	11.1
1974	−0.6	5.6	11.2
1975	−0.8	8.5	12.3
1976	4.9	7.7	11.8
1977	4.5	7.1	11.6
1978	4.8	6.1	11.4
1979	2.5	5.8	11.7
1980	−0.5	7.1	13.0
1981	1.8	7.6	14.0
1982	−2.2	9.7	15.0
1983	3.9	9.6	15.2
1984	6.2	7.5	14.4
1985	3.2	7.2	14.0
1986	2.9	7.0	13.6
1987	3.1	6.2	13.4
1988	3.9	5.5	13.0
1989	2.5	5.3	12.8
1990	0.8	5.5	13.5
1991	−1.2	6.7	14.2
1992	2.1	7.4	14.5

Source: See *Economic Report of the President 1994* (Washington, D.C.: United States Government Printing Office, 1994), p. 304 (Poverty 1992); *Economic Report of the President 1993* (Washington, D.C.: United States Government Printing Office, 1993), p. 351 (GDP 1970–91), 382 (Unemployment 1970–92), 380 (Poverty 1970–91); *Statistical Abstract of the United States 1993* (Washington, D.C.: Bureau of the Census, 1993), p. 444 (GDP 1992).

and that high social wealth can and will be devoted to improving criminal law enforcement, life expectancy, and public health. But these are only speculations. What has been said thus far should show that the connection between GDP and these other goods is extremely unclear.

Dependence on Legal and Social Practices   The value of money depends on social and legal practices that determine what money can be used to buy. If certain exchanges are blocked—if money cannot be used to purchase valuable things— per capita GDP becomes less important. Wealth is less valuable when money cannot be used to buy votes or political power, education, marriage, or goods connected with self-respect. Similarly, the value of money is reduced to the extent that it is unnecessary for someone to have money to obtain important goods. If education, health care, political power, and clean air are free, money is less valuable. (Of course, there may be harmful social effects from prohibiting the use of money as a basis for exchange or from providing goods for free. Both of these decisions may mean that there is less wealth on which to draw.)

In short, the value of money is largely a function of the legal regime. To understand the relationship between GDP and valuable things, it is necessary to understand the set of legal entitlements through which people are enabled to get, or are disabled from getting, things of importance to their lives. It might then be possible to "map" legal provisions onto the various ingredients of well-being.[5]

Commensurability GDP is of course an aggregative measure, and it is aggregative in a distinctive sense.[6] GDP is not simply an index of different values, created to allow ease of understanding and comparison. Instead, it measures diverse items through the same basic dimension of "value," defined in monetary terms.

This approach assumes commensurability in the sense that it acts as if diverse goods can be assessed according to the same metric. This form of valuation is troublesome because it ignores qualitative differences among diverse social goods (chapter 3). Some things (like education and health) have intrinsic as well as instrumental value; other things (like cash) are simply for use. Intrinsically valuable things are themselves valued in different ways. Because GDP is aggregative, it effaces qualitative differences, and for this reason it is a crude indicator of social welfare and an unpromising foundation for democratic deliberation. Suppose, for example, we are told that if the Occupational Safety and Health Administration issues a certain occupational safety regulation, GDP will be reduced by 0.001 percent. To make a sensible evaluation, we need to know a great deal more. To what does this number refer? Does it include greater unemployment, higher inflation, and the scaled-back production of important goods? Does it mean more poverty? At least in principle, it would be much better to have a highly disaggregated system for assessing the qualitatively different goods at stake. People should be informed about the diverse potential effects and make judgments on the basis of an understanding of the qualitative differences. If all the relevant goods are aligned along a single metric, they become less visible, or perhaps invisible.[7]

II. Existing Measures of Well-Being

Current American Approaches

GDP is hardly the only indicator of social welfare. In the United States, over fifty indicators are now in use. The United Nations offers many more.[8] A major problem with the current American approach is that the measures— offered in an endless and barely intelligible succession—lack organization and clarity. In this section, I describe some of the most important indicators.

The unemployment rate, announced every month, includes the number of people sixteen years of age or older who are actively seeking employment. It therefore excludes people who are not seeking work, even if they say that they would like a job and that they are not seeking work because they do not believe that jobs are available for them. Tables 4.2 and 4.3 show differences in

Table 4.2. Civilian Unemployment Rate by Demographic Characteristic
(percent; monthly data seasonally adjusted)

			White					
			Males			Females		
Year	All Civilian Workers	Total	Total	16–19 Years	20 Years and Over	Total	16–19 Years	20 Years and Over
1975	8.5	7.8	7.2	18.3	6.2	8.6	17.4	7.5
1976	7.7	7.0	6.4	17.3	5.4	7.9	16.4	6.8
1977	7.1	6.2	5.5	15.0	4.7	7.3	15.9	6.2
1978	6.1	5.2	4.6	13.5	3.7	6.2	14.4	5.2
1979	5.8	5.1	4.5	13.9	3.6	5.9	14.0	5.0
1980	7.1	6.3	6.1	16.2	5.3	6.5	14.8	5.6
1981	7.6	6.7	6.5	17.9	5.6	6.9	16.6	5.9
1982	9.7	8.6	8.8	21.7	7.8	8.3	19.0	7.3
1983	9.6	8.4	8.8	20.2	7.9	7.9	18.3	6.9
1984	7.5	6.5	6.4	16.8	5.7	6.5	15.2	5.8
1985	7.2	6.2	6.1	16.5	5.4	6.4	14.8	5.7
1986	7.0	6.0	6.0	16.3	5.3	6.1	14.9	5.4
1987	6.2	5.3	5.4	15.5	4.8	5.2	13.4	4.6
1988	5.5	4.7	4.7	13.9	4.1	4.7	12.3	4.1
1989	5.3	4.5	4.5	13.7	3.9	4.5	11.5	4.0
1990	5.5	4.7	4.8	14.2	4.3	4.6	12.6	4.1
1991	6.7	6.0	6.4	17.5	5.7	5.5	15.2	4.9
1992	7.4	6.5	6.9	18.4	6.3	6.0	15.7	5.4

Source: *Economic Report of the President 1993* (Washington, D.C.: United States Government Printing Office, 1993), p. 391.

employment along lines of race and sex; this is significant because although overall unemployment may be low, it is good to know whether members of identifiable social groups are disproportionately out of work.

The poverty level emerged from the 1961 plan of the Department of Agriculture. Like judgments about unemployment, the judgment about who is poor is far from a simple matter of fact. The 1961 estimate measured how much money was necessary to meet nutritional requirements, and this amount was multiplied by three to determine the total income necessary to meet all living expenses. Poverty thresholds have been updated every year by taking into account the consumer price index. Hence, the annual threshold for a family of four was $3169 in 1964, $11,611 in 1987, and $13,924 in 1991. The official measure of poverty does not include noncash income; it therefore excludes food stamps, Medicare and Medicaid, school lunches, and subsidized rental housing. See Table 4.4.

Of course, there are large disparities in terms of race and sex in the percentage of persons and families living in poverty. The percentage of blacks living in poverty is nearly triple that of whites, and the percentage of black female householders in poverty is nearly double that of white female-headed householders.

Table 4.3. Civilian Unemployment Rate by Demographic Characteristic (percent; monthly data seasonally adjusted)

| | | Black and Other or Black | | | | | |
| | | Males | | | Females | | |
Year	Total	Total	16–19 Years	20 Years and Over	Total	16–19 Years	20 Years and Over
1975	14.8	14.8	38.1	12.5	14.8	41.0	12.2
1976	14.0	13.7	37.5	11.4	14.3	41.6	11.7
1977	14.0	13.3	39.2	10.7	14.9	43.4	12.3
1978	12.8	11.8	36.7	9.3	13.8	40.8	11.2
1979	12.3	11.4	34.2	9.3	13.3	39.1	10.9
1980	14.3	14.5	37.5	12.4	14.0	39.8	11.9
1981	15.6	15.7	40.7	13.5	15.6	42.2	13.4
1982	18.9	20.1	48.9	17.8	17.6	47.1	15.4
1983	19.5	20.3	48.8	18.1	18.6	48.2	16.5
1984	15.9	16.4	42.7	14.3	15.4	42.6	13.5
1985	15.1	15.3	41.0	13.2	14.9	39.2	13.1
1986	14.5	14.8	39.3	12.9	14.2	39.2	12.4
1987	13.0	12.7	34.4	11.1	13.2	34.9	11.6
1988	11.7	11.7	32.7	10.1	11.7	32.0	10.4
1989	11.4	11.5	31.9	10.0	11.4	33.0	9.8
1990	11.3	11.8	32.1	10.4	10.8	30.0	9.6
1991	12.4	12.9	36.5	11.5	11.9	36.1	10.5
1992	14.1	15.2	42.0	13.4	13.0	37.2	11.7

Source: *Economic Report of the President 1993* (Washington, D.C.: United States Government Printing Office, 1993), p. 391.

Table 4.4. Persons and Families Below the Poverty Income Level

| | Families Below Poverty Level | | Persons Below Poverty Level | |
Year	Number (millions)	Percent of Population	Number (millions)	Percent of Population
1975	5.5	9.7	25.9	12.3
1977	5.3	9.3	24.7	11.6
1978	5.3	9.1	24.5	11.4
1979	5.5	9.2	26.1	11.7
1980	6.2	10.3	29.3	13.0
1981	6.9	11.2	31.8	14.0
1982	7.5	12.2	34.4	15.0
1983	7.6	12.3	35.3	15.2
1984	7.3	11.6	33.7	14.4
1985	7.2	11.4	33.1	14.0
1986	7.0	10.9	32.4	13.6
1987	7.0	10.7	32.2	13.4
1988	6.9	10.4	31.7	13.0
1989	6.8	10.3	31.5	12.8
1990	7.1	10.7	33.6	13.5
1991	7.7	11.5	35.7	14.2

Source: *Economic Report of the President 1993* (Washington, D.C.: United States Government Printing Office, 1993), p. 380, tbl. B-28.

The consumer price index, the most important indicator of the rate of inflation, is designed to reflect price changes for a set of goods, including housing, clothing, food and drink, medical care, entertainment, education, and tobacco products. Annual percentage changes indicate striking disparities over time, as shown in Table 4.5.

The average weekly earnings of workers in private nonagricultural industries, calculated monthly by the Bureau of Labor Statistics, are provided in current dollars and in constant 1982 dollars, as shown in Table 4.6.

Income distribution is measured in terms of quintiles. Income taxes have little effect on income distribution. Table 4.7 shows changes over time with respect to income, before and after tax, in the United States.

No official government statistics reveal the costs and benefits of government regulation. Some private estimates suggest that economic regulation costs

Table 4.5.   Consumer Price Index (annual percentage change)

	CPI-U[a]			CPI-W[a]
Year	All Items	All Items Excluding Energy	All Items Excluding Food and Energy	All Items
1975	9.1	8.9	9.1	9.1
1976	5.8	5.6	6.5	5.7
1977	6.5	6.4	6.3	6.5
1978	7.6	7.8	7.4	7.7
1979	11.3	10.0	9.8	11.4
1980	13.5	11.6	12.4	13.4
1981	10.3	10.0	10.4	10.3
1982	6.2	6.7	7.4	6.0
1983	3.2	3.6	4.0	3.0
1984	4.3	4.7	5.0	3.5
1985	3.6	3.9	4.3	3.5
1986	1.9	3.9	4.0	1.6
1987	3.6	4.1	4.1	3.6
1988	4.1	4.4	4.4	4.0
1989	4.8	4.7	4.5	4.8
1990	5.4	5.2	5.0	5.2
1991	4.2	4.6	4.9	4.1
1992	3.0	3.2	3.7	2.9

[a]CPI-U is the consumer price index (CPI) for all urban consumers; CPI-W is the CPI for urban wage earners and clerical workers.

Source: The information in this table was compiled from several sources. The CPI-U figures for all items were drawn from the *Statistical Abstract of the United States, 1993* (Washington, D.C.: Bureau of the Census, 1993), p. 482, tbl. 756; *Consumer Price Index Detailed Report* (Washington, D.C.: United States Department of Labor, Bureau of Labor Statistics, 1993), March 1993, at 166, tbl. 6A; and *Consumer Price Index Detailed Report*, March 1992, at 167, tbl. 6A. The CPI-U figures up to 1990 for all items excluding energy and all items excluding food and energy, are from *Economic Report of the President 1993* (Washington, D.C.: U.S. Government Printing Office, 1993), p. 414, tbl. B-58. The CPI-U figures for 1991 and 1992 are from *Economic Report of the President 1994* (Washington, D.C.: U.S. Government Printing Office, 1994), p. 339, tbl. B-62. In 1980, the CPI-U represented 80 percent of the noninstitutional population, and the CPI-W, 32 percent. See Norman Frumkin, *Guide to Economic Indicators* (Armonk: M. E. Sharpe, 1990), p. 63.

Table 4.6. Average Weekly Earnings

Year	Level		Percent Change from Preceding Year	
	Current Dollars	1982 Dollars	Current Dollars	1982 Dollars
1975	163.53	293.06	5.7	−3.0
1976	175.45	297.37	7.3	1.5
1977	189.00	300.96	7.7	1.2
1978	203.70	300.89	7.8	0.0
1979	219.91	291.66	8.0	−3.1
1980	235.10	274.65	6.9	−5.8
1981	255.20	270.63	8.5	−1.5
1982	267.26	267.26	4.7	−1.2
1983	280.70	272.52	5.0	2.0
1984	292.86	274.73	4.3	0.8
1985	299.09	271.16	2.1	−1.3
1986	304.85	271.94	1.9	0.3
1987	312.50	269.16	2.5	−1.0
1988	322.02	266.79	3.0	−0.9
1989	334.04	264.22	3.8	−1.0
1990	345.35	259.47	3.3	−1.8
1991	353.98	255.40	2.5	−1.6
1992	363.95	255.22	2.8	−0.1

Source: *Economic Report of the President 1994* (Washington, D.C.: U.S. Government Printing Office, 1994), p. 320, tbl. B-45; *Economic Report of the President 1993*, p. 396, tbl. B-42.

Table 4.7. Distribution of Income: Households' Shares (percent)

Income Before Taxes	1991	1990	1986	1985	1984	1983	1982	1981	1980	1974
Lowest fifth	3.8	3.9	3.8	3.9	4.0	3.9	4.0	4.0	4.1	4.2
Second fifth	9.5	9.6	9.7	9.7	9.8	9.9	9.9	10.0	10.2	10.6
Third fifth	16.0	16.0	16.4	16.3	16.4	16.4	16.5	16.7	16.8	17.1
Fourth fifth	24.1	24.1	24.0	24.4	24.6	24.6	24.6	24.8	24.8	24.6
Highest fifth	46.5	46.4	46.1	45.7	45.3	45.2	45.0	44.4	44.2	43.5

Income After Taxes	1991	1990	1986	1985	1984	1983	1982	1981	1980	1974
Lowest fifth	4.5	4.6	4.2	4.6	4.7	4.7	4.7	4.9	4.9	4.9
Second fifth	11.0	10.9	10.4	11.0	11.0	11.1	11.3	11.5	11.6	11.7
Third fifth	16.7	16.6	16.1	17.2	17.2	17.4	17.5	17.8	17.9	17.8
Fourth fifth	24.3	24.0	23.2	24.7	24.8	24.8	24.8	25.0	25.1	24.7
Highest fifth	43.6	43.9	46.1	42.6	42.3	42.1	41.8	40.9	40.6	41.0

Source: The 1986–91 figures are derived from the *Statistical Abstract of the United States* (Washington, D.C.: Bureau of the Census, various years), which uses a slightly different definition of "after-tax" income than Norman Frumkin's *Guide to Economic Indicators* (Armonk, N.Y.: M. E. Sharpe, 1990), p. 75, tbl. 15 (presenting the income before and after taxes for 1974–85); *Statistical Abstract 1993*, p. 463, tbl. 722; *Statistical Abstract 1992* (presenting the figures for income before and after taxes in 1991), p. 462, tbl. 731; *Statistical Abstract 1991* (presenting the figures for income before and after taxes in 1990); *Statistical Abstract 1990*, p. 449, tbl. 724 (110th ed. 1990) (describing income before and after taxes for 1986).

the economy about $46 billion annually, and that social regulation (principally environmental controls) costs between $78 and $107 billion; other estimates range as high as $400 billion.[9] The benefits of economic regulation appear low, but the benefits of social regulation range between $42 and $200 billion. No one has fully explored the effects of regulation on GDP. A 1990 study suggested that between 1973 and 1985, the GDP growth rate fell by 0.19 percentage points as a result of environmental controls.[10] This study does not, however, include the health benefits of such controls, which probably led to productivity gains. There are significant disparities in regulatory policy, especially with respect to expenditures per life saved (Table 5.4 in chapter 5).[11]

The Federal Bureau of Investigation compiles statistics showing subjection to violent crime. Table 4.8 reflects changes over time.

Here, then, are some of the most important indicators of social and economic well-being. It should be clear that the system for reporting and disseminating this information is quite ad hoc. There has been no democratic judgment about the ingredients of such key measures as GDP, poverty, and unemployment. There is no effort to put some or many of the indicators into a composite figure, to provide an indication of general changes over time. Nor does the government furnish reports offering a clearly accessible survey of social and economic indicators.

International Measures

The United Nations makes what is probably the most influential international effort to measure well-being, though there have been illuminating efforts elsewhere. I summarize several methods here. A key point is that alternative accounts often place a premium on health and education as well as per capita income.

Human Development Index

The United Nations publishes an annual Human Development Report in order to facilitate comparative assessments of government performance.[12]

Description The report ranks 173 countries and contains comparative information on many things, including access to health services and safe water; numbers of radios, telephones, and televisions; levels of child immunization and malnutrition; public expenditures on education; male-female wage gaps; levels of homicide, rape, and drug crimes; population per doctor; numbers of new AIDS cases; population growth; energy consumption; pollution levels; and much more.

The United Nations approach places particular emphasis on a "human development index" (HDI). This figure is calculated on the basis of longevity, knowledge, and income. "Longevity" is determined on the basis of life expectancy at birth. "Knowledge" is calculated by a formula based on adult literacy and mean years of schooling, with literacy weighted twice as heavily as mean

Table 4.8. Subjection to Violent Crime (rate per 100,000 inhabitants)

Year	Violent Crime	Murder and Non-negligent Homicide	Forcible Rape	Aggravated Assault
1975	487.8	9.6	26.3	231.1
1976	467.8	8.8	26.6	233.2
1977	475.9	8.8	29.4	247.0
1978	497.8	9.0	31.0	262.1
1979	548.9	9.7	34.7	286.0
1980	596.6	10.2	36.8	298.5
1981	594.3	9.8	36.0	289.7
1982	571.1	9.1	34.0	289.2
1983	537.7	8.3	33.7	279.2
1984	539.2	7.9	35.7	290.2
1985	556.6	7.9	37.1	302.9
1986	617.7	8.6	37.9	346.1
1987	609.7	8.3	37.4	351.3
1988	637.2	8.4	37.6	370.2
1989	663.1	8.7	38.1	383.4
1990	731.8	9.4	41.2	424.1
1991	758.1	9.8	42.3	433.3

Source: Federal Bureau of Investigation, U.S. Department of Justice, *Uniform Crime Reports for the United States 1992* (Washington, D.C.: U.S. Department of Justice, 1992), p. 58, tbl. 1 (1992).

years of schooling. To take account of the diminishing value of income, the "income" ingredient is based on an adjustment of per capita GDP, understood as standard of living. The UN measurement weighs the three variables equally. Tables 4.9 and 4.10 show the ranking of the first twelve countries in the 1993 and 1995 reports.

The HDI compiles much valuable information and presents it in a revealing way. For instance, the United States ranks first in both per capita GDP and adjusted real GDP; it also ranks first in mean years of schooling and in overall educational attainment. But it has never ranked first overall. Its sixth ranking in 1993 stems from the fact that life expectancy at birth stood at 75.9 years, for a ranking along that dimension of sixteenth.

The UN report demonstrates that there is no necessary connection between GDP and employment levels. For example, Canada had an unemployment rate in 1990–91 of 10.2 percent, despite a high per capita GNP. Notwithstanding its considerably lower per capita GNP, Japan's unemployment rate was 2.1 percent. Switzerland's unemployment rate of 1.3 percent is the lowest among industrialized nations, but its per capita GNP is slightly below that of the United States, which had a 6.6 percent unemployment rate. Moreover, the performance of some countries appears to be quite variable over time. Notably, the literacy rate in the United States increased from a comparatively low 96 percent in 1985 to a very high 99 percent in 1990.

An intriguing question concerns the precise relationship among the HDI's three variables of longevity, knowledge, and income. Some countries with rela-

Table 4.9.   Human Development Index, 1993 Report

Rank	Life Expectancy at Birth (years) 1990	Adult Literacy Rate (%) 1990	Mean Years of Schooling 1990	Educational Attainment 1990	Real GDP per Capita (PPP$) 1990	Adjusted Real GDP per Capita	HDI 1990
1. Japan	78.6	99.0	10.7	2.87	17,616	5049	0.983
2. Canada	77.0	99.0	12.1	2.98	19,232	5052	0.982
3. Norway	77.1	99.0	11.6	2.95	16,028	5044	0.979
4. Switzerland	77.4	99.0	11.1	2.90	20,874	5074	0.978
5. Sweden	77.4	99.0	11.1	2.90	17,014	5047	0.977
6. USA	75.9	99.0	12.3	3.00	21,449	5075	0.976
7. Australia	76.5	99.0	11.5	2.94	16,051	5044	0.972
8. France	76.4	99.0	11.6	2.94	17,405	5048	0.971
9. Netherlands	77.2	99.0	10.6	2.86	15,695	5042	0.970
10. United Kingdom	75.7	99.0	11.5	2.94	15,804	5043	0.964
11. Iceland	77.8	99.0	8.9	2.72	16,496	5045	0.960
12. Germany	75.2	99.0	11.1	2.90	18,213	5050	0.957

Source: United Nations Development Programme, *Human Development Report 1993* (New York: Oxford University Press, 1993), pp. 11–13.

tively high income ranks (including Algeria, Namibia, and South Africa) have relatively low HDI ranks. Other countries have HDI ranks that are well above their income ranks (including China, Colombia, and Uruguay).

A key issue is whether significant variations exist among groups within each country. In the United States in 1993, for example, whites, standing alone, ranked above Japan in HDI; if American whites lived alone in their own country, it would rank first in the world. By contrast, in 1993 African-Americans ranked thirty-first, and Hispanics thirty-fifth. And despite enormous gains in longevity for women over the last twenty years (an increase in developing countries of nine years, 20 percent more than the increase for men) and over two-thirds increases in female literacy and school enrollment, no nation's HDI improves after being adjusted for sex inequalities. This demonstrates that no nation provides as good lives for women as it does for men. But there are important and revealing variations. For example, women's wages are 88 percent of men's in France and 85 percent in Norway, but only 51 percent in Japan and 59 percent in the United States. The 1995 Human Development Report, dedicated to describing gender inequality, shows a "gender-related development index," which reveals that there are enormous disparities between the well-being of men and women.[13] Many other questions involve comparative data not directly reflected in the HDI's three principal variables. Between 1980 and 1986, for example, there were only 31 drug crimes per 100,000 people per year in Japan, 25 in Israel, and 38 in the Netherlands, compared with 225 in Canada, 234 in the United States, and 403 in Australia.[14] The reported rape rate in the United States is by far the highest in the world—118 per 100,000 women between 15 and 59. In Japan, the rate is only 5 per

Table 4.10. Human Development Index, 1995 Report

Rank	Life Expectancy at Birth (years) 1992	Adult Literacy Rate (%) 1992	Combined First-, Second-, and Third-Level Gross Enrollment Ratio (%) 1992	Real GDP per Capita (PPP$) 1992	Adjusted Real GDP per Capita	Life Expectancy Index	Education Index	GDP Index	Human Development Index 1992	Real GDP per Capita (PPP$) Rank Minus HDI Rank
High Human Development										
1. Canada	72.9	95.8	76	13,605	—	—	—	—	0.888	—
2. USA	77.4	99.0	100	20,520	5,359	0.87	0.99	0.98	0.950	7
3. Japan	76.0	99.0	95	23,760	5,374	0.85	0.98	0.99	0.937	−1
4. Netherlands	79.5	99.0	77	20,520	5,359	0.91	0.92	0.98	0.937	5
5. Finland	77.4	99.0	88	17,780	5,343	0.87	0.95	0.98	0.936	16
6. Iceland	75.7	99.0	96	16,270	5,337	0.85	0.98	0.98	0.934	19
7. Norway	78.2	99.0	81	17,660	5,343	0.89	0.93	0.98	0.933	15
8. France	76.9	99.0	88	18,580	5,345	0.87	0.95	0.98	0.932	8
9. Spain	76.9	99.0	86	19,510	5,347	0.87	0.95	0.98	0.930	3
10. Sweden	77.6	98.0	86	13,400	5,307	0.88	0.94	0.97	0.930	20
11. Australia	78.2	99.0	78	18,320	5,344	0.89	0.92	0.98	0.929	7
12. Belgium	77.6	99.0	79	18,220	5,344	0.88	0.92	0.98	0.927	7
	76.4	99.0	84	18,630	5,345	0.86	0.94	0.98	0.926	2

Source: United Nations Development Programme, *Human Development Report 1995* (New York: Oxford University Press, 1995), p. 155.

100,000, and in many countries it is somewhere between 18 and 35. The United States also has the highest homicide rate, at 8 per 100,000, compared with 1.5 for Japan and Sweden and somewhere between 2 and 3 for Canada, Switzerland, Australia, Finland, Austria, and New Zealand. It should not be surprising that the United States has the highest rate of prisoners, 426 per 100,000, compared with 94 in Canada, 54 in Switzerland, and 77 in the United Kingdom and in Germany.

Difficulties   The HDI approach has important limitations. Any "index" will be controversial, and the equal weighting of the three variables seems somewhat arbitrary. In any case, the three variables are interrelated. Income can "buy" good educational attainment and also longevity; people who are poor tend to live shorter lives. So, too, people who are in good health and who are well-educated have a better chance to make money. The use of the three variables is controversial partly because of these complex interrelations. In addition, there is a degree of crudeness in the choice of the three indicators. It might make sense to include poverty level, access to food, employment figures, and so on. Moreover, educational attainment is not adequately measured by mean years of schooling. Literacy is a form of educational attainment, but it sets a low floor, and in any case it is far from clear that, in assessing educational attainment, we should count literacy for two and mean years for one in some aggregate figure. Perhaps a composite figure could be developed on the basis of a more precise inquiry into relevant factors.

The HDI is also insensitive to ethnic, racial, sex, and regional differences. If, for example, there are important differences between men and women, people should know about this fact. It is also possible for a country with a high HDI score to have a number of people concentrated toward the bottom of the economic ladder and facing desperate conditions; this is also important for people to know.

Alternatives

Other nations, especially those in Scandinavia, have implemented interesting alternatives to HDI. The Swedish assessment of "standard of living" is more disaggregated and less mathematical than the UN approach. The assessment takes account of health and access to health care; education and skills; housing; security of life and property (including freedom from crime); availability of recreation and cultural resources; employment; income and wealth; and political participation.[15] Of special interest is the Swedish rejection of unitary measures of well-being, and the insistence that well-being is not to be measured in purely subjective terms. A key point here is that people may adjust their expectations in light of a status quo characterized by deprivation and injustice, and for this reason it is important to see what people can have or become, not merely what they think about their situation.

Another interesting alternative is a comparative survey of Scandinavian countries, initiated by the University of Helsinki.[16] In addition to the Swedish factors, the Finnish approach emphasizes the quality of the biological and physical environment, including air and water pollution; the nature of relations with other people in the local community, in the family, and within the workplace; and opportunities to enjoy nature. The comparative survey is intended to include both objective and subjective indicators of welfare.

In the same vein, UNICEF lists a wide range of basic indicators, without attempting to aggregate them. These include male and female adult literacy rates; life expectancy at birth; income shares of the lowest 40 percent and the highest 20 percent of the population; GDP per capita; and infant mortality.[17] The Netherlands identifies sixteen variables involving quality of life: three each involving housing, health, spending power, leisure, and employment, combined with a single variable for education.[18] There is also an effort to combine these statistics into an aggregate number showing changes over time for different groups in the population. An organization in Washington, D.C. attempts to measure human suffering through a scale that takes account of income, inflation, infant mortality, nutrition, access to clean water, literacy, and personal freedom. Similar aggregative and separate statistics might be offered for human rights violations.[19]

III. Politics, Well-Being, and Quality of Life

All this has implications for law and policy. A high priority for both domestic and international agencies should be to compile accurate information about quality of life, to allow comparisons across time and space, and to ensure that the relevant reports are widely disseminated.

The American government should compile and distribute an annual "quality of life" report, including, among other things, per capita income, poverty, housing, unemployment, average weekly earnings, inflation, child mortality, longevity, subjection to violent crime, literacy, and educational attainment. The report should also specify minimum standards for such things as income, education, health, and housing and allow for comparison across regions, between men and women, and among different racial and ethnic groups.

These comparisons may spur healthy competition to do well along dimensions that count. If a state knows that it ranks forty-second in, say, unemployment, there will be both local and national pressure to make things better. If a state has an especially high level of violent crime, perhaps priorities can be changed to redress the problem. And if women are doing much worse than men, or blacks much worse than whites, the public can see this fact and perhaps take corrective action.

The quality of life report should be widely disseminated to the public and, in particular, to the news media. Strong evidence indicates that the media can play a large role in counteracting social problems by focusing public and private attention and by giving government incentives to respond.[20] Instead of attending to anecdotes and sensational scandals—or offering statements about supposed trends—the news media should focus on the quality of life report and thus allow debate to be based on actual evidence. The report may well have an especially important role during elections, but it could affect deliberation and policymaking more broadly as well.

A quality of life report of the kind I am proposing could produce two distinct benefits. First, the report may well have desirable social consequences by facilitating priority-setting, imposing appropriate incentives on government officials, and fueling public interest in redressing serious problems. Accurate and widely disseminated information can be an important check on government failure to redress such problems. Consider the striking fact that in modern times, no country with an active, free, and democratic press appears to have suffered from famine.[21]

Second, the very process of compiling a quality of life report would have advantages. We have seen that any conception of what matters is a product of judgments that may be controversial. Human needs have a great deal to do with facts—Do people have jobs? Do they have food or housing?—but they are not simply facts. Any conception of needs is a product of human judgment about what matters. Consider, for example, the very definitions of poverty and unemployment, or the decision whether to include comparative data about groups defined in racial, ethnic, and religious terms. The public understanding of social problems should itself be a product, at least in part, of a good process of social deliberation about how needs are best characterized. By using GDP as the central indicator of social welfare while publishing a wide array of unorganized and somewhat random indicators, the current system offers no such educational benefits.

To say all this is not to suggest that such a report would be simple. But most of the information is now compiled and available somewhere; its systematic presentation and dissemination should not be costly. There is of course a risk of error and bias, especially in view of the fact that the fortunes of an incumbent administration may depend on what emerges. Government manipulation of official statistics is hardly foreign to American experience. At the same time, many government agencies have established a reputation for objectivity, and there is no reason to believe that (for example) the statistics relating to literacy, infant mortality, and poverty levels reflect substantial bias.

To be sure, people have limited information-processing capacities, and these can lead to systematic errors through the use of bad heuristics. Some release of information can actually make things worse. But to some extent, the confusion is a result of what has been made public, and careful presentation of the data should help overcome some of the faulty heuristics. One of the most common heuristics, for example, is that of "availability" (chapter 5). People seem to think that events are more probable if an occurrence can easily be brought to mind. Some of this effect might be counteracted by a report that catalogues a range of events, that allows comparisons, and that shows changes over time. The very need to compile the data would also give desirable incentives to government officials.

I have suggested that both personal and social well-being are in important respects a product of law; that is, they are a function of the things to which the law gives people access. The law can give such access in many ways. It may provide guarantees of certain goods (such as housing, food, medical care); it may allow people to sell their labor; it may permit people to own certain things that they produce or inherit; and it may say that people can freely exchange some, but not all, of what they own. People's entitlements are a function of law, and it is their entitlements that enable them to obtain much of what provides for their well-being. But we lack a systematic account of the relationship between legal entitlements and the components of well-being.

These points have general implications. A homeless person, for example, is deprived of shelter in important part through the law; if he tries to sleep in a place with a roof, the law will call him a trespasser and subject him to civil and criminal penalties. Whether someone has access to medical care depends on the bundle of legal rights that have been conferred. Property rights as we know them are not brute or natural facts, but a product of laws granting and conditioning entitlements of different kinds. It should ultimately be possible to link various components of well-being to different legal permissions and requirements. We could begin to connect deprivations and benefits of various sorts with a range of legal provisions. A quality of life report would help initiate this endeavor.

Of course, no report can substitute for actual reform. What matters is what is done, not what is said. But in some contexts, what is done is a function of what is said. In the area of risk regulation, for example, there is evidence that disclosure of information can be an important regulatory tool, prompting corrective action by employers, employees, and governments generally.[22] In any case, both citizens and public officials are unlikely to know what to do unless they have good information about existing problems and trends. These points have general and complex consequences for the study of law, but I end with a simple claim: Democratic governments could take few more important steps than to initiate a process by which the components of well-being would become a substantial part of political debate.

Notes

1. GDP might thus be modified to account for:

> any depreciation of natural capital stocks, in the same way that net national income is equal to gross national income less estimated depreciation on man-made capital . . . [and] any damage losses accruing to human wellbeing from the extraction, processing and disposal of materials and energy to the receiving environments.

David W. Pearce, *Economic Values and the Natural World* (Cambridge, Mass.: MIT Press, 1993).

2. In 1952, Kuznets attempted to redefine GNP to take leisure into account. See Simon Kuznets, "Long-Term Changes in the National Income of the United States of America Since 1870," in *Income and Wealth of the United States: Trends and Structure*, Simon Kuznets, ed. (Baltimore: Johns Hopkins, 1952), pp. 63–69. Note also that a

1968 study showed a spectacular gain in leisure over the last century. See A. W. Sametz, "Production of Goods and Services: The Measurement of Economic Growth," in *Indicators of Social Change: Concepts and Measurements,* Eleanor Harriet Sheldon, ed. (New York: Russell Sage Foundation, 1968), pp. 77, 83.

The best work on the general subject has been done by Amartya Sen, and I am indebted to Sen's work throughout. See, e.g., Jean Dreze and Amartya Sen, *India: Economic Development and Social Opportunity* (Oxford: Oxford University Press, 1996).

3. See United Nations Development Programme, *Human Development Report 1990* (New York: Oxford University Press, 1990), p. 9, tbl. I.I [hereinafter *Human Development Report 1990*] (presenting information on Sri Lanka, Jamaica, and Costa Rica). The level of childhood immunizations puts the United States twenty-first in the world, tied with Pakistan and below India, Bulgaria, North Korea, Indonesia, and Botswana.

4. See *Human Development Report 1990, supra note 3,* at 9, tbl. I.I.

5. This is a generalization of the "entitlement approach" suggested in Amartya Sen, *Poverty and Famines: An Essay on Entitlement and Deprivation* (New York: Oxford University Press, 1981), pp. 45–51.

6. Economists and others critical of GNP have proposed a number of alternative measures. William Nordhaus and James Tobin, two early critics, suggested that it would be better to attempt to generate a "measure of economic welfare" (MEW). See William D. Nordhaus and James Tobin, "Is Growth Obsolete?" in *The Measurement of Economic and Social Performance,* Milton Moss, ed. (New York: National Bureau of Economic Research: Columbia University Press, 1973), pp. 509, 512–13.

A more recent measure is the Daly and Cobb "index of sustainable economic welfare" (ISEW). See Herman E. Daly and John B. Cobb, *For the Common Good: Redirecting the Economy Toward Community, the Environment, and a Sustainable Future* (Boston: Beacon Press, 1989), pp. 401–55.

7. The use of GDP creates other difficulties, but because these seem less fundamental and in some ways more complex, I simply identify them here.

(a) GDP depends on willingness to pay and thus on existing preferences for various social goods. One could do much worse than to make assessments on the basis of existing preferences; people's well-being is certainly connected with satisfaction of consumption choices. Existing preferences are not, however, an adequate guide to social well-being, because they may depend on unjust background conditions or on simple ignorance. See Amartya Sen, *Commodities and Capabilities* (Professor Dr. P. Hennipman Lectures in Economics, Vol. 7) (New York: North-Holland, 1985).

(b) As noted, GDP is an important method for making cross-national comparisons. But per capita GDP is an inadequate comparative guide if there are large differences in conditions and hence in needs. If distinctive needs are a product of local circumstances, GDP per capita will be an inadequate proxy for well-being.

(c) The existence of positional goods poses a problem for GDP. Positional goods are those that are valuable because only a few people have them. Status symbols of various sorts, including luxury automobiles, are examples. See Richard H. McAdams, "Relative Preferences," 102 *Yale L. J.* 1, 18–19 (1992). If GDP is growing partly because it includes a large number of positional goods, it is not clear that welfare is growing as well.

8. See Norman Frumkin, *Guide to Economic Indicators* (Armonk, N.Y.: M. E. Sharpe, 1990), p. xiii; see *Human Development Report 1993* (New York: Oxford University Press, 1993), pp. 129–34.

9. See Robert W. Hahn and John A. Hird, "The Costs and Benefits of Regulation: Review and Synthesis," 8 *Yale J. on Reg.* 233, 249, 253 (1991).

10. See Dale W. Jorgensen and Peter J. Wilcoxen, "Environmental Regulation and U.S. Economic Growth," 21 *Rand J. Econ.* 314, 315 (1990).

11. Stephen G. Breyer. *Breaking the Vicious Circle: Toward Effective Risk Regulation* (Cambridge: Harvard University Press), pp. 24–27, tbl. 5.

12. See, e.g., *Human Development Report 1990, supra* note 3, at 9.

13. See *Human Development Report 1995* (New York: Oxford University Press, 1995), pp. 76–77. Some of the other data in this paragraph can be found in *Human Development Report 1993, supra* note 8, at 135, tbl. 1.

14. See *id.* at 18, 192, tbl. 30.

15. See Robert Erikson, "Descriptions of Inequality: The Swedish Approach to Welfare Research," in *The Quality of Life*, Martha C. Nussbaum and Amartya Sen, eds. (New York: Oxford University Press, 1993), p. 67, tbl. 1. Cf. Partha Dasgupta, *An Inquiry Into Well-Being and Destitution* (New York: Oxford University Press, 1993), pp. 77–78 (noting the absence of attention to civil and political liberties in conventional measures of well-being, such as the HDI).

16. See Erik Allardt, "Having, Loving, Being: An Alternative to the Swedish Model of Welfare Research," in *The Quality of Life, supra* note 15, at 88–89.

17. See, e.g., United Nations Children's Fund, *The State of the World's Children* (New York: Oxford University Press for UNICEF, 1987), pp. 128–29, tbl. 1.

18. See Ian Miles, "Social Indicators for Real-Life Economics," in *Real-Life Economics* 283, 287–88, Paul Ekins and Manfred Max-Neef, eds. (New York: Routledge, 1992).

19. See Robert V. Horn, *Statistical Indicators for the Economic and Social Sciences* (Cambridge: Cambridge University Press, 1993), pp. 142–44. Note especially the attempt to integrate liberties and economic variables in *Dasqupto, supra* note 15, at 108–16. Two efforts at tabulating human rights records in numerical form are Raymond D. Gastin. *Freedom in the World* (New York: Freedom House, 1992), pp. 572–75, 578–79; and Charles Humana, *World Human Rights Guide* 3rd ed. (New York: Oxford University Press, 1992).

20. See Amartya Sen, *Resources, Values and Development* (Cambridge: Harvard University Press, 1984), pp. 500–03 (discussing the important role of news media in combating famines).

21. See *id.* at 34.

22. See Wesley A. Magat and W. Kip Viscusi, *Informational Approaches to Regulation* (Cambridge, Mass.: MIT Press, 1992), pp. 186–88; Cass R. Sunstein, "Informing America: Risk, Disclosure, and the First Amendment," 20 *Fla. St. U. L. Rev.* 653, 662 (1993); W. Kip Viscusi, Wesley A. Magat, and Joel Huber, Informational Regulation of Consumer Health Risks: An Empirical Evaluation of Hazard Warnings," 17 *Rand J. Econ.* 351, 362 (1986) (concluding, based on empirical study, that warning labels affect consumer behavior).

Experts, Economists, and Democrats

with Richard Pildes

Should government decisions be based on cost-benefit analysis (CBA)? This is one of the most important issues in contemporary law and policy. It raises questions about the nature of individual and collective rationality and also about possible reforms of governmental institutions.

Less familiar, but increasingly important, is the emerging role of comparative risk assessment (CRA). CBA explores whether a particular policy is justified on balance. CRA has the more confined role of ensuring better priority setting by ranking risks in terms of their seriousness. CRA is concerned with ensuring that the most serious risks are addressed first.

A major question raised by both CBA and CRA is that of valuation: How do we compare risks? What would enable us to decide that it is "too costly" to take a certain course of action? In public policy circles, there are two principal answers to such questions. The first is offered by experts, who attempt to rank risks by reference to technocratic considerations. The second is offered by economists, who try to rank risks by seeing how much people are "willing to pay" to eliminate them (or "willing to accept" to face them).

The goal of this chapter is to challenge both the expert and economic approaches and to urge a democratic alternative. The problem with expert approaches is that they ignore some distinctive features of citizen evaluations of risks that are far from irrational. The problem with the economic approach is that private willingness to pay is an inadequate way to evaluate risks or to compare the costs and benefits of proposed policies. Of course, the abstract word "democratic" points to no panacea for handling these problems; but it does suggest some general directions for reform.

I. Conceptions of Rationality and Value

Common Critiques

At first glance, the case for CBA seems altogether compelling. Who could object to the idea that government should compare the costs and benefits of proposed initiatives? But everything depends on how costs and benefits are measured and valued, and on this count there are many legitimate questions. Sometimes CBA is incompletely specified; sometimes it depends on a doubtful theory of value.

A common complaint is that CBA is biased against the benefits of regulation, since these tend to be "soft variables" that are not easily quantified. To the extent that this is a criticism of the way CBA tends to operate in practice, it is a useful cautionary note, but it does not indict the basic theory of CBA. To this criticism the proper response is that CBA ought to be undertaken in a way that is alert to problems of quantification and that is sophisticated about methods for valuing variables that are hard to quantify. Several different techniques are now available for assigning some value to regulatory benefits, such as cleaner air, safer drinking water, or less-hazardous work environments. Many of these techniques, such as contingent valuation, are quite advanced. As we will see, they still face considerable problems. But even if it is hard to value regulatory benefits, CBA seems extremely attractive as a way of comparing proposed solutions with regulatory problems. In the face of a better alternative, the difficulty of valuing "soft variables" is far from a decisive objection.

A second criticism is that CBA fails to address distributional issues or that it is biased against the poor. There is some force to this objection. Actual "willingness to pay" in real market settings—the typical criterion for calculating costs and benefits—depends on ability to pay, and in this sense it can incorporate a kind of bias against the poor, who may not be able to pay much, even for goods they very much want. And to the extent that regulation is designed to promote distributive goals, CBA is unlikely to be helpful. But this point should not count strongly against CBA. Regulators will inevitably have to find some means to assess the trade-offs among employment, health, environmental quality, and cost in choosing among different regulatory standards. CBA can assist regulators with this endeavor, even if we insist that any relevant distributional considerations should also be kept in mind. More specifically, it may well be possible to adjust the analysis for any distributional biases, by reassessing certain variables when they are first assigned or by undertaking a separate distributional assessment. Regulators might first undertake CBA in the ordinary fashion, and then take distributional goals into account by giving them a certain weight at an independent stage of inquiry.

A third objection to CBA is that scientific uncertainty makes it impossible to say anything concrete or quantitative about the benefits and costs of much regulation. Often government agencies do not know exactly how potent a carcinogen is, or the magnitude of risks associated with a certain pollution problem. At most, there is a range of possibilities. The assignment of a number for "benefits" will be based on a great deal of guesswork and perhaps on tacit, unarticulated judgments of value. It will hardly be a purely scientific enterprise, for a range of policy judgments will be involved as well. Judgments about costs may be more tractable, but there are many problems here too. Ex ante estimates will usually depend on industry projections which, as past practice has shown, are likely to be self-serving and hence much inflated.[1] In any case, technological change makes projecting costs a hazardous enterprise.

Often new devices will develop to provide controls at greatly reduced expense.

In light of the difficulty of specifying costs and benefits, CBA often has a spuriously objective and scientific cast. Often the numbers are a matter of guesswork. But this problem is not a sufficient reason to abandon the attempt. Sometimes CBA can be undertaken because the uncertainties are relatively small. Sometimes it is possible to project a range of estimates. When this is not possible, it is useful to do the best we can with those variables that can be identified. Perhaps it will not be feasible to do a full CBA, but government can move in that direction by identifying the range of known costs, known benefits, and factual uncertainties, and by making its own assumptions clear.

Expert and Lay Judgments

The deepest questions about CBA lie elsewhere; they have to do with appropriate valuation. We can get a sense of those objections by attending to a pervasive phenomenon: a sharp conflict between expert and lay judgments about risks. Consider the comparison in Table 5.1.

Table 5.1.   Rating Health Risks

Public	EPA Experts
1. Hazardous waste sites	Medium-to-low
2. Exposure to worksite chemicals	High
3. Industrial pollution of waterways	Low
4. Nuclear accident radiation	Not ranked
5. Radioactive waste	Not ranked
6. Chemical leaks from underground storage tanks	Medium-to-low
7. Pesticides	High
8. Pollution from industrial accidents	Medium-to-low
9. Water pollution from farm runoff	Medium
10. Tap water contamination	High
11. Industrial air pollution	High
12. Ozone layer destruction	High
13. Coastal water contamination	Low
14. Sewage-plant water pollution	Medium-to-low
15. Vehicle exhaust	High
16. Oil spills	Medium-to-low
17. Acid rain	High
18. Water pollution from urban runoff	Medium
19. Damaged wetlands	Low
20. Genetic alteration	Low
21. Nonhazardous waste sites	Medium-to-low
22. Greenhouse effect	Low
23. Indoor air pollution	High
24. X-ray radiation	Not ranked
25. Indoor radon	High
26. Microwave oven radiation	Not ranked

Source: Stephen G. Breyer, *Breaking the Vicious Circle: Toward Effective Risk Regulation* (Cambridge: Harvard University Press, 1993), p. 21. Reprinted by permission.

What accounts for these dramatic disparities? Some of them reflect differences in assessments of facts; others reflect differences in underlying values. For example, public concern over microwave oven radiation may well be based on a simple misperception of facts. There is a "fact" about the level of radiation that microwave ovens emit. On the other hand, evaluations of ozone layer destruction are not based only on facts; there may well be no "fact" that experts can identify, but instead a range of possibilities. In these circumstances, evaluations are partly an outgrowth of value-laden judgments about how to proceed in circumstances of uncertainty in which future generations are at risk. Consider more generally Table 5.2, showing disparities between public and expert perceptions of risk.

From these disparities we might conclude that experts tend to endorse a particular conception of rationality when using CBA (or CRA) to decide among policy choices. Ordinary citizens use a radically different and much more complex and unruly approach in making such decisions. What, more particularly, accounts for this difference?

Expert Perspectives on Risk, Rationality, and Policy

Experts attempt to seek consistency across diverse risks—an admirable goal. But any such effort may well incorporate contentious assumptions about what it would mean for policy choices to be consistent. In particular, an attempt to produce consistency may require regulators to create a single metric along which diverse policies might be compared. In the hands of many people, the preferred approach uses probabilistic, quantitative techniques that treat risk in aggregate terms—as the expected number of injuries, deaths, or other adverse consequences over a given time. This approach thus emphasizes the end states that policies produce, not the processes by which harms are imposed or through which policy is made.

Through these techniques, information such as that in Table 5.3 is generated. To many, this information is startling and disconcerting; it suggests that federal regulation is pervasively arbitrary and chaotic.

Certainly these differences provide good reason to examine whether something has gone wrong. They suggest what should not be denied: Poor priority setting is an unmistakable fact of modern bureaucratic life, and better priority setting is a crucial task for modern government. And in view of the enormous disparities in the seeming cost-effectiveness of programs for reducing risk, who could object to the idea that we should systematize costs and benefits and compare them in order to make more rational policy choices?

This is the foundation of the experts' case for CBA. "Soft" benefits must be properly valued, and distributional considerations must be taken into account where appropriate, but on the experts' view these are marginal refinements to the basic approach. On that view, CBA should be used in order to enable us to make more consistent regulatory policy, to set priorities more effectively, to discipline analysis, and to constrain what would otherwise be ill-informed decisions or power struggles over the direction of policy.

Table 5.2.   Ordering of Perceived Risk for Thirty Activities and Technologies

Activity or Technology	League of Women Voters	College Students	Active Club Members	Experts
Nuclear power	1	1	8	20
Motor vehicles	2	5	3	1
Handguns	3	2	1	4
Smoking	4	3	4	2
Motorcycles	5	6	2	6
Alcoholic beverages	6	7	5	3
General (private) aviation	7	15	11	12
Police work	8	8	7	17
Pesticides	9	4	15	8
Surgery	10	11	9	5
Firefighting	11	10	6	18
Large construction	12	14	13	13
Hunting	13	18	10	23
Spray cans	14	13	23	26
Mountain climbing	15	22	12	29
Bicycles	16	24	14	15
Commercial aviation	17	16	18	16
Electric power (non-nuclear)	18	19	19	9
Swimming	19	30	17	10
Contraceptives	20	9	22	11
Skiing	21	25	16	30
X-rays	22	17	24	7
High school and college football	23	26	21	27
Railroads	24	23	29	19
Food preservatives	25	12	28	14
Food coloring	26	20	30	21
Power mowers	27	28	25	28
Prescription antibiotics	28	21	26	24
Home appliances	29	27	27	22
Vaccinations	30	29	29	25

Source: Paul Slovic, "Perception of Risk," 236 *Science* 280, 281 (April 17, 1987). Reprinted by permission.

Lay Perspectives on Risk, Rationality, and Policy

As we have seen, there is a strikingly consistent finding in risk studies: Ordinary people assess risk in ways that sharply diverge from those of experts. Ordinary citizens do not look only or even primarily to expected annual mortality; they look as well at a number of factors that make risks acceptable or unacceptable in different contexts. These factors cannot be said to generate a "hard" model of risk assessment, but they do represent something like an articulable framework for making judgments about risk levels.

Of course, ordinary citizens disagree sharply among each other, just as experts do. Notably, there are national and international variations in judgments about risk. In a careful study in Canada, women systematically perceived risks as being worse than men perceived them; for every one of the thirty-three items studied, women believed that risks were equal to or higher than what men believed.[2] In the same study, perceptions of both risk and benefit were correlated with age, education, and region of residence.[3] Nearly two dozen studies have shown that women perceive nuclear power as more risky than men do.[4] In a comparative study of American and Hungarian students, the latter perceived risks as lower for eighty-four of ninety activities.[5]

Notwithstanding these differences among citizens, there is a pervasive and sharp distinction between lay and expert perspectives. It is important to be clear about where this difference lies. Some of the difference stems from simple confusion on the part of ordinary citizens or from the use, by citizens, of heuristics that produce systematic errors.[6] But in many cases, the difference does not result from misinformation or from cognitive distortions about risk analysis. For example, when ordinary people are asked to order well-known hazards in the expected value terms that experts use, such as the number of deaths and injuries they cause every year, people often do quite well.[7] Yet if they are then asked to rank these hazards in terms of risk, the orderings of experts and laypeople begin to diverge dramatically.[8] The difference, then, is not only one of information or factual knowledge.

These different understandings of value mean that judgments about risk frequently depend on context. For laypeople, many contextual features are relevant: (1) the catastrophic nature of the risk; (2) whether the risk is uncontrollable; (3) whether the risk involves irretrievable or permanent losses; (4) the social conditions under which a particular risk is generated and managed, a point that connects to issues of consent, voluntariness, and democratic control; (5) how equitably distributed the danger is or how concentrated on identifiable, innocent, or traditionally disadvantaged victims, which ties to both notions of community and moral ideals; (6) how well understood the risk process in question is, a point that bears on the psychological disturbance produced by different risks; (7) whether the risk would be faced by future generations; and (8) how familiar the risk is.[9] Citizens care in particular about how "dreaded" and how "observable" particular risks are. And "[c]itizens' responses to technological risks . . . are far more likely to be dictated by their perceptions of whether they can exercise personal control in the event of an accident than by the careful weighing of the worths of uncertain outcomes."[10]

People systematically assign a high valuation to risks that are perceived to be involuntarily run; compare public reactions to risks from eating sugar with public reactions to risks from nuclear power accidents. About 400,000 people die each year from smoking-related causes, as compared with no apparent deaths from nuclear power accidents; yet enormous resources are invested in preventing the latter, and until recently, few resources were invested in preventing the former. (It is notable that recent regulatory efforts with respect to smoking have followed and produced important changes in social norms.) Qualitative differences of this kind are not included within ordinary cost-benefit techniques to the extent that the latter concentrate only on end states.

It is fully rational to attend to contextual differences of this sort. Indeed, approaches that attend to such differences seem more rational than approaches

Table 5.3. Cost-Effectiveness of Selected Regulations (from the budget for fiscal year 1992, Table C-2, Part 2, p. 370).

Regulation	Agency	Cost Per Premature Death Averted ($ millions 1990)
Unvented Space Heater Ban	CPSC	0.1
Aircraft Cabin Fire Protection Standard	FAA	0.1
Auto Passive Restraint/Seat Belt Standards	NHTSA	0.1
Steering Column Protection Standard	NHTSA	0.1
Underground Construction Standards	OSHA-S	0.1
Trihalomethane Drinking Water Standards	EPA	0.2
Aircraft Seat Cushion Flammability Standard	FAA	0.4
Alcohol and Drug Control Standards	FRA	0.4
Auto Fuel-System Integrity Standard	NHTSA	0.4
Standards for Servicing Auto Wheel Rims	OSHA-S	0.4
Aircraft Floor Emergency Lighting Standard	FAA	0.6
Concrete and Masonry Construction Standards	OSHA-S	0.6
Crane Suspended Personnel Platform Standard	OSHA-S	0.7
Passive Restraints for Trucks & Buses (proposed)	NHTSA	0.7
Side-Impact Standards for Autos (dynamic)	NHTSA	0.8
Children's Sleepwear Flammability Ban	CPSC	0.8
Auto Side Door Support Standards	NHTSA	0.8
Low Altitude Windshear Equipment & Training Standards	FAA	1.3
Electrical Equipment Standards (metal mines)	MSHA	1.4
Trenching and Excavation Standards	OSHA-S	1.5
Traffic Alert and Collision Avoidance (TCAS) Systems	FAA	1.5
Hazard Communication Standard	OSHA-S	1.6
Side-Impact Standards for Trucks, Buses, and MPVs (proposed)	NHTSA	2.2
Grain Dust Explosion Prevention Standards	OSHA-S	2.8
Rear Lap/Shoulder Belts for Autos	NHTSA	3.2
Standards for Radionuclides in Uranium Mines	EPA	3.4
Benzine NESHAP (original: Fugitive Emissions)	EPA	3.4
Ethylene Dibromide Drinking Water Standard	EPA	5.7
Benzene NESHAP (revised: Coke Byproducts)	EPA	6.1
Asbestos Occupational Exposure Limit	OSHA-H	8.3
Benzene Occupational Exposure Limit	OSHA-H	8.9
Electrical Equipment Standards (coal mines)	MSHA	9.2
Arsenic Emission Standards for Glass Plants	EPA	13.5
Ethylene Oxide Occupational Exposure Limit	OSHA-H	20.5
Arsenic/Copper NESHAP	EPA	23.0
Hazardous Waste Listing for Petroleum Refining Sludge	EPA	27.6
Cover/Move Uranium Mill Tailings (inactive sites)	EPA	31.7
Benzene NESHAP (revised: Transfer Operations)	EPA	32.9
Cover/Move Uranium Mill Tailings (active sites)	EPA	45.0
Acrylonitrile Occupational Exposure Limit	OSHA-H	51.5
Coke Ovens Occupational Exposure Limit	OSHA-H	63.5
Lockout/Tagout	OSHA-S	70.9
Asbestos Occupational Exposure Limit	OSHA-H	74.0
Arsenic Occupational Exposure Limit	OSHA-H	106.9
Asbestos Ban	EPA	110.7

Diethylstilbestrol (DES) Cattlefeed Ban	FDA	124.8
Benzene NESHAP (revised: Waste Operations)	EPA	168.2
1,2 Dichloropropane Drinking Water Standard	EPA	653.0
Hazardous Waste Land Disposal Ban (1st, 3rd)	EPA	4,190.4
Municipal Solid Waste Landfill Standards (proposed)	EPA	19,107.0
Formaldehyde Occupational Exposure Limit	OSHA-H	86,201.8
Atrazine/Alachlor Drinking Water Standard	EPA	92,069.7
Hazardous Waste Listing for Wood-Preserving Chemicals	EPA	5,700,000

Source: Stephen G. Breyer, *Breaking the Vicious Circle: Toward Effective Risk Regulation* (Cambridge: Harvard University Press, 1993), pp. 24–27. Reprinted by permission.

that concentrate only on end states. It makes sense to say that expenditures per life saved ought to vary in accordance with (for example) the voluntariness of the risk or its catastrophic quality. Such beliefs are widespread. Interviews with workers, for instance, reveal that their valuations of workplace risks depend on such contextual features as the overall structure of workplace relations, how much say workers have in how the risks are managed, and the nature of the particular jobs performed.[11]

Consider also the fact that the quantitatively identical level of exposure to certain chemicals is viewed as more acceptable by research scientists, exposed during the course of carrying out basic research, than by laboratory assistants, who clean up the hazards after an experiment is finished.[12] For the scientist, the meaning of the risk, and the appropriate level of social resources to be spent to eliminate it, depend on the fact that it is tied up with professional work that is highly valued socially, personally rewarding, voluntarily assumed, and associated with traditions of scientific inquiry. If people do value risks differently depending on these sorts of contextual features, and if these valuations are reasonable, then democratic policy should recognize the relevant contextual differences.

All this is no reason to be complacent about the dramatic disparities shown in Table 5.3. These disparities might well reflect little more than interest-group pressures, confusion, lack of appreciation for trade-offs, or reflexive responses to sensationalist anecdotes. Moreover, policymakers should not defer to citizen assessments of risks in all circumstances. Ours is a republic, not a pure democracy, and a high premium is placed on deliberation rather than on snapshots of public opinion. It is therefore appropriate to ensure that citizens' judgments result from an appropriately structured deliberative process.

As noted previously, citizen valuations are hardly uniform; ordinary people disagree with each other, just as experts do. Sometimes citizens misunderstand the problem. No simple rule can answer the question of how policy should respond in situations of conflict between expert and lay assessments of risk. Nonetheless, it is possible to offer some basic distinctions.

At one pole, citizen assessments of risk sometimes rest on certain heuristics, or rules of thumb for processing information, that are inappropriate bases for making public policy. These heuristics include psychological devices that lead to risk assessments that policymakers should treat as factually erroneous.

For example, cognitive psychologists have uncovered the central role of the "availability" heuristic in ordinary decision making.[13] "Availability" means that people's assessment of one risk depends, at times, on how readily similar events come to their minds. When this effect is at work, people will overestimate the probability that an event will occur if the occurrence of similar events comes easily to mind, but will underestimate the probability otherwise.

Whether similar events do come to mind can depend on how recently they occurred or how dramatically they were presented when they did occur. Lay estimates of how high the risk is from hazardous landfills, for example, may depend on how readily people recall Love Canal or similar episodes. But the "facts" about a certain risk do not differ when someone happens to remember a particularly salient recent event. The gap here between objective and perceived levels of risk is not a function of different values, but of what can properly be viewed as cognitive errors based on false beliefs about the actual probabilities of certain events.

At the other pole are the cases emphasized here: Those in which experts and ordinary citizens value differently the "same" risk (understood in terms, say, of aggregate lives at stake) as a result of features of the context that expert techniques obscure. This is why people might demand, for example, that fewer social resources be devoted to "the same level" of risk reduction, when the risks are viewed as voluntarily assumed rather than when they are viewed as involuntarily imposed, or when the risks occur in social conditions that seem legitimate rather than illegitimate.

Between these poles are situations in which it is unclear whether expert and lay differences stem from factual errors or from different values. For example, experts are often troubled by the public's refusal to view risks in linear terms; laypeople sometimes express greater concern over a low-probability event with large potential tragic costs than probability theory would consider rational. This difference might reflect the well-known cognitive difficulties people manifest in dealing with low- and high-probability events. Alternatively, it might reflect the view that catastrophic events entail costs considerably beyond deaths, injuries, and other material cost, such as the destruction of social stability.

For example, the "Buffalo Creek Syndrome" has been documented several times in the aftermath of major disasters. Nearly two years after the collapse of a dam that left 120 dead and 4,000 homeless, psychiatric researchers continued to find significant psychological and sociological changes; survivors were "characterized by a loss of direction and energy," other "disabling character changes," and a "loss of communality."[14] One evaluator attributed this loss of direction specifically to "the loss of traditional bonds of kinship and neighborliness."[15] The nonlinearity of lay evaluations of risk in the context of potential disasters may thus reflect a high premium on avoiding the distinctive kinds of losses associated with disasters. If so, differences between lay and expert assessments rest on genuine value differences (four times as many deaths may be much more than four times as bad) rather than on factual errors in cognitive processes of ordinary people.

II. Rationality and Reform

Are experts rational or irrational? There are complex theoretical issues in the background here. Sometimes the term "rational" is understood to refer simply to instrumental judgments having to do with the best way to achieve given ends. To the extent that expert and lay judgments diverge because of different judgments about appropriate ends—rather than different instrumental judgment—this understanding of rationality will hardly permit us to choose between them. Sometimes the term "rational" is meant to allow assessments not just of means-ends connections, but of ends themselves. We might, for example, examine how ends have been formed, and when distorting influences appear—like A's judgment that X *is* true because A *wants* X to be true—we might find irrationality. We might find irrationality when people discount risks because they do not want those risks to be large. Irrationality might also be found when ends conflict with one another.

In fact, there is no fully specified understanding of the values that underlie either expert or lay judgments. Experts appear to discount harms by their probability or work from annual aggregate deaths;[16] ordinary people reject this approach in the ways described above. The expert model relies on a one-dimensional scale in which the common metric is how many annual deaths or injuries are likely to occur from a given risk. It is not simple, however, to show how that approach might be defended as "rational." If we are trying to decide which risks to regulate, why would it make sense to take only the total harm and to discount it by its probability, while ignoring all other relevant factors? Voluntarily incurred risks should not be treated the same as involuntarily incurred risks. Risks that involve especially gruesome deaths, such as those from AIDS-related illnesses, should be and are thought different from other risks. It is possible to defend, with reasons, the idea that (for example) catastrophic or irreversible risks deserve priority over noncatastrophic and reversible risks (other things being equal or nearly so), and very hard to defend the opposite idea. Widespread cultural understandings of this sort have a democratic pedigree, and they make a lot of sense.

With these considerations in mind, some seeming anomalies in risk regulation dissolve. What appear to be "special" expenditures to control the risk of AIDS might be justified in light of the nature of death from AIDS, the distinctive fear produced by the AIDS crisis, and the nature of the groups at risk from AIDS. Or a society might rationally reject the ill-fated ignition interlock, which would have prevented cars from starting unless the seat belt is buckled, and approve of other regulations that do not interfere so pervasively with individual choice, even if they do worse from the standpoint of cost per life saved. For this reason, citizen understandings are not merely a competing conception of rationality, but can be richer and more rational than the expert alternatives.

To the extent that CBA promises a disciplined analytic tool for assisting regulatory choices, it is appealing. In light of its substantive appeal and promise of administrability, it may well be a useful approach for regulators to follow. But when it is founded on a conception of value that experts favor but that is often at odds with more widely shared and also-respectable conceptions, it becomes much harder to defend.

CBA should not be abandoned in light of the problems identified here. This is true from both a theoretical and a pragmatic perspective. Even in theory, CBA can help discipline and systematize important aspects of the policy-making process. Above all, it forces more focused and precise thinking about the potential consequences of policy. From the pragmatic point of view, there is even more to be said for retaining some role for CBA. Perhaps this way of proceeding offers a less than full description of what is really at stake; but there are ways of making CBA work relatively well, and if the alternative is a totally intuitive, ad hoc process, the rough tools of CBA seem more than good enough. A completely open-textured and undisciplined regulatory process would be an invitation to allow interest-group power and sensationalist anecdotes, rather than deliberation, to determine regulatory priorities and approaches. In this light, CBA should continue to be a part of the regulatory process, but a part whose relation to the whole is understood in a particular way.

CBA should be undertaken in such a way as to allow disclosure of and publicity for disaggregated cost and benefit data; it is important to know what underlies the numbers, not just the numbers themselves. Moreover, policymakers should view CBA as a tool to inform thoughtful decision making, not as some uniquely scientific method of analysis that dictates what must be done. There is nothing exotic about this suggestion. Few people suppose that CBA can tell us whether to devote limited research funds to AIDS, global climate change, heart disease, or breast cancer. Where expert and lay assessments appear at odds, lay perspectives should be identified and explored to the extent feasible. If lay assessments rest on factual misinformation, or on cognitive distortions in the way inferences are drawn from the known facts, they need not be credited. But to the extent that they reflect different valuations of risk, they should be taken seriously.

To capture the benefits of CBA while recognizing its limitations, several different approaches would be reasonable. First, regulators could use recent work on the contingent valuation or quality of life years (the "QUALY" approach, discussed later) to take account of qualitative distinctions among diverse risks. Most promisingly, such work would make it possible to obtain quantitative measures of qualitative distinctions, as in (for example) the fact that people seem willing to spend three times as much to prevent a cancer death as to prevent an immediate death.[17] If such measures are to be used, it would of course be necessary to ensure that such judgments are reflective (as polls for willingness to pay may not be).

Second, it may make sense to experiment with more formalized efforts to include within CBA many of the factors discussed here. Officials might make explicit the relevant value judgments and the weights assigned to them in the process of ranking. For example, irretrievable losses or involuntarily run risks might be treated distinctively by receiving a specified weight in the assessment of relevant values. Some agencies would do well to experiment with efforts of this kind.

A third possible approach would be an explicitly two-stage decision process. The first stage should consist of a cost-benefit analysis, limited to the kinds of costs and benefits that can reasonably be quantified. In a second stage, officials should explicitly address and articulate the other values, if any are relevant, that CBA does not take into account. Through this two-stage process, both the benefits of CBA and its limitations can be recognized. Efforts to deliberate in this way will also produce clearer understandings of just what trade-offs are involved in the choice among alternatives.

A fourth possible approach would involve the creation of participatory mechanisms to enable citizens to express their judgments about different risks in different contexts. Citizen panels and discussion groups might be convened to this end. There are obvious difficulties in selecting participants and in deciding how to present information about risks. But both nations and states have expressed interest in experimenting with approaches of this sort, and it is hard to evaluate them until we have seen how they work in practice.

III. Economic Approaches: Willingness to Pay or QUALYs as Solutions?

Thus far the discussion has focused on the contrast between expert and lay conceptions of value and rationality. But some defenders of CBA might reject expert conceptions of value; they would insist that the economic tools of CBA are particularly well suited to taking citizen valuations into account. They would argue that turning to economics enables ordinary understandings of risk to be incorporated into policy-making through economic assessments of the costs and benefits—to individuals—of various policy choices. There are two general techniques by which economists seek to make these assessments.

Revealed Preferences and Willingness to Pay

In its most traditional form, CBA attempts to assess all regulatory benefits, including "soft" variables, through measures of private willingness to pay for these benefits. On this view, people reveal the values they attach to various goods through their actual behavior in market or market-like settings. If we attend to the choices people actually make, we will be able to infer from them the valuations they assign to various goods. This process will then appropriately reflect people's understandings of costs and benefits. If, for example, citizens truly fear exposure to nuclear power, their conduct should reveal a willingness to pay a great deal to avoid such exposure—no matter what experts say about the risk. If citizens distinguish between voluntarily incurred risks and involuntarily imposed ones, the willingness-to-pay criterion will reflect the distinction. Diversely valued risks will generate diverse valuations. Properly applied, CBA need not and does not incorporate expert judgments at the expense of citizen judgments. Instead, it relies on the latter.

Some imaginative and provocative approaches attempt to determine the "value of life" by assessing willingness to pay for risk reductions.[18] And to be sure, risks are traded on markets in the sense that "expenditures on seatbelts, airbags, airline safety, safety caps on medicine, preventive check-ups, suntan lotion, and a multitude of other factors represent market expenditures on risk reduction."[19] The Office of Management and Budget has explicitly supported the willingness-to-pay criterion on the ground that "the amount that people are willing to pay for a good or service is the best measure of its value to them."[20] This approach appears to be a prevalent one in the agencies, using a number between $1 million and $4 million per life saved.[21]

But there are several problems with willingness-to-pay approaches based on actual market transactions. First is the considerable difficulty of identifying the actual "risk premium" from market choices. Some people take risks because they like the consumption package and its attendant risks, or because they do not dislike those risks very much; the job of firefighter, police officer, or professional athlete may reflect an employment package in which the costs of the risk are not readily separable from the benefits of the job, taken as a whole. In these circumstances, there is a severe practical problem in trying to measure risk valuation from market choices. The choices may be too "noisy" to make it possible to infer such valuations.

Second, market behavior may reflect not some actual valuation by people who choose, but instead a lack of information about risks or motivational influences that lead to inaccurate judgments about the facts. To be sure, workers are sometimes informed of risk levels and they can demand a risk premium; but to say the least, full information about workplace risks is rare, especially in light of the fact that some risks depend on complex causal mechanisms and take many years to come to fruition. The various heuristics described earlier may distort people's judgments about the facts. There are possible motivational distortions as well. Wishful thinking and the desire to reduce cognitive dissonance—by thinking that you are not, in your daily work, exposing yourself to some cancer risk—may lead people to see risks as lower than they really are.[22]

Third, market behavior should not be taken to reveal acontextual "preferences," if that contentious term is intended to refer to something that lies behind behavior and explains it. We cannot get a good sense of what people value in general simply from people's particular labor market and consumption choices (chapters 1 and 2). Particular choices are a function of context and they are inarticulate—poor predictors of future behavior—without an account of what lies behind them.[23] We cannot rank individual preferences on the basis of choices alone, and without some account of what values underlie choices.

Actual market choices are, of course, heavily dependent on the distribution of income and wealth. Workers who appear willing to accept a certain "wage premium" to work in a more risky environment do not thereby proclaim how much they value their own health. Instead, they may reveal far more narrowly how much they value additional income, in the context of a particular choice and given the amount they now have. Perhaps this valuation should be used by government; but this is far from clear and it certainly does not follow from the mere fact of choice. Any preference arguably revealed through actual behavior is often based on the particular context and may reveal little that is global. Smoke alarm purchases, safety cap expenditures, and the use of suntan lotion cannot plausibly be said to reflect general judgments about the value of life. Such consumption behavior is highly geared to context. In any case, a willingness to spend $X to eliminate a 1/10,000 risk of death does not necessarily entail a willingness to pay $10X to eliminate a 1/1,000 risk of death, a willingness to pay $100X to eliminate a 1/100 risk of death, or a willingness to pay $1,000X to eliminate a 1/10 risk of death. Or a willingness to spend $Y to eliminate a risk in a context when the risk is under the purchaser's control, voluntarily incurred, and limited to just one individual does not reveal how much that person would be willing to pay to avoid the same risk when it is out of her control, involuntarily inflicted, and affects many people. Although willingness to pay purports to be grounded in actual choice patterns, its use in public policy frequently requires purported valuations to be abstracted from the contexts in which they arise. This makes the approach insensitive to highly relevant contextual differences. A related problem for those who seek to rely on market behavior is the sharp disparity between willingness to pay and willingness to accept (chapters 1 and 8); it is not clear that willingness to pay should be the relevant measure, and willingness to accept is likely to be a good deal higher.

Fourth, willingness-to-pay measures ignore the distinction between the valuations people express in private, market transactions and those that they express in democratic arenas. What people are prepared to pay as private consumers is often, and appropriately, different from what they think society (and they, as members of society) ought to pay to avoid certain risks.[24] Much empirical evidence confirms this point; for example, "[p]eople were, in fact, found on average to bid more for an improvement for everyone in the United States than for just themselves."[25] Judgments made in the context of democratic choice are designed to elicit different motivations and different considerations from those made in market transactions. Through exchange of different perspectives, collective decision making, and social-regarding reasoning, democratic arenas produce distinctive valuations. Partly this is a product of social norms; partly it is a product of the fact that in the democratic setting, people are aware of the fact that whatever they are doing, they are doing it together.

Contingent Valuation

In response to these and other problems, public health professionals and economists have developed alternatives that seek to mimic market transactions, but do not rely on them. These are called contingent valuation methods. Rather than looking at actual choices, these methods ask people hypothetical questions about how much they would be willing to pay to avoid certain harms or conditions. The most advanced methods involve lengthy interview sessions designed to provide information, give a sense of context, and allow discussion in a way that fosters deliberative results.[26]

Some economists view contingent valuation not as a different form of willingness to pay, but as fundamentally inconsistent with willingness to pay. The virtue of willingess to pay—indeed, its entire point, on this view—is that it focuses on actual behavior. Because contingent valuation does not, it is unreliable.[27] It does not include an adequate budget constraint; it enables people to behave strategically because they need not validate their preferences through actual choices; it may reflect an absence of adequate information or motivational distortions far worse than those at work in market arenas.

Yet contingent valuation also seems to improve on some of the features of actual willingness to pay. It can be made highly sensitive to context. There is no need to abstract and generalize from context-based choices, because no actual choices are involved. Hypothetical questions can be designed for virtually any context. In addition, distributional problems can be minimized by asking the questions of an appropriately representative pool. Investigators can then average responses to generate an average, hypothetical willingness to pay to avoid various conditions.

Much recent work with contingent valuation techniques has sought to elicit values for different states of health. The results do reflect qualitative differences among what lay people appear to consider diverse risks. In such studies, for example, people purport to be willing to pay a much greater amount to avert cancer deaths (from $1.5 million to $9.5 million) compared with unforeseen instant deaths (from $1 million to $5 million).[28] More generally, this work generates tables similar to Table 5.4. Similarly, these survey techniques purport to show that people value days of illness—from coughing spells, headaches, nausea, sinus congestion, and so forth—in diverse amounts.[29]

Nonetheless, contingent valuation methods have serious limitations as a means of incorporating citizen valuations into public policy. For one thing, it is difficult to believe that people answering hypothetical questions can assign meaningful dollar values to various possible health or other risks. The more context sensitive the method attempts to become, the more its hypothetical nature becomes problematic, bordering on the fantastic. The leading practitioners of contingent valuation purport to discover that people are willing to pay $90 to have a day of relief from angina if they have had it for only one day, but $288 for ten days of relief if they have had angina for twenty days.[30] It is hard to take these figures seriously. (Ask yourself how much you would be willing to pay to avoid a day of angina, two days of coughing spells, or a week of nausea.) In economic terms, people have a difficult time assigning hypothetical dollar values to categories of commodities they virtually never confront in everyday experience. Problems of lack of information are severe and hard to overcome.

Moreover, the results of contingent valuation studies suggest that the answers do not show actual valuation of relevant commodities. They may be based on strategic behavior, as, for example, when a respondent offers a low number, or a high number, not to reflect his valuation, but in order to discourage or encourage certain government behavior. A special problem is that of

Table 5.4. Mortality Values by Cause of Death

Category (per statistical life)	Value Estimates (in million $)		
	Low	Medium	High
Unforeseen instant death	1.0	2.0	5.0
Asthma/bronchitis	1.3	2.5	5.5
Heart disease	1.25	2.75	6.0
Emphysema	1.4	3.5	9.0
Lung cancer	1.5	4.0	9.5

Source: George Tolley, Donald Kenkel, and Robert Fabian, eds., *Valuing Health for Policy: An Economic Approach* (Chicago: University of Chicago Press, 1994), p. 342. Reprinted by permission.

"indifference to quantity," reflected in the astonishing and devastating fact that people will give the same dollar number to save 2000, 20,000, and 200,000 birds—or the same number to save one, two, or three wilderness areas.[31] Relatedly, the valuation of a resource is much affected by whether it is offered alone or with other goods. Willingness to pay for spotted owls drops significantly when the spotted owl is asked to be valued with and in comparison to other species. This evidence suggests that people may be purchasing moral satisfaction rather than stating their real valuation. It is pertinent in this connection that the order and number of questions seem crucial in determining valuation. When asked for their willingness to pay to preserve visibility in the Grand Canyon, people offer a number five times higher when this is the first question than when it is the third question.[32] And some answers are implausibly high. Consider the fact that there is an asserted willingness to pay $32 billion per year to save the whooping crane, an amount that is over ten times what was given to all nonprofit environmental organizations in 1991.[33]

Finally, contingent valuation methods suffers from the private/public valuation distinction and from the use of the inadequate analogy between market behavior and political behavior.[34] What people would be willing to pay to eliminate certain conditions for themselves, and how they think public resources should be allocated in a situation of democratic choice, remain distinct questions. The latter often implicate principles beyond pain reduction, such as moral notions about responsiblity, desert, fairness, and the like, not at issue in the hypothetical private resource decision. Public policy should incorporate citizen valuations to a greater extent than it now does; but what matters are citizen valuations about public choices, not those about self-regarding, private choices.

Alternative Individual Valuation Measures: QUALYs

Efforts to ground collective risk-regulation decisions on citizen valuations, rather than expert ones, need not take the form of willingness to pay or its surrogates. In fact, these valuations need not be made commensurate with dollars in order to be useful for public policy. For those hoping to ground policy in individual valuations, but seeking to formalize the process in ways beyond what is traditionally characteristic of democratic deliberation, other alternatives exist. In the health field, much attention has focused on evaluating preferences for healthy conditions (or aversion to unhealthy ones) in terms of what are called quality-adjusted life years ("QUALYs").[35]

A QUALY is a measure of health based on people's attitudes toward various conditions. It rejects the concept of monetary evaluation of health; instead, it focuses on how people value various health states. It seeks to generate a means of comparing various states of health through a single metric, so that comparisons and trade-offs can be made for public policy purposes. The measure attempts to take into account both quantitative benefits of health improvement, such as increase in life expectancy, and more qualitative improvements, such as quality-of-life benefits.

Like contingent valuation methods, the QUALY approach works by asking people through interview techniques to express their strength of preference for various health states. The most advanced methods disaggregate the process by asking people to describe how they would value a health improvement along several dimensions: mobility, physical activity, social activity, and the kinds of symptom effects involved.[36] The answers to these questions are combined into a single scale, ranked 0.0 (for death) to 1.0 (for optimum functioning). The result is an index of utility for health states measured on an interval (or cardinal) scale. By independently determining the cost of various treatments and their likely outcomes, reseachers can suggest a cost per QUALY of various public programs. Alternative programs can be ranked in what is essentially a utility-based cost-effectiveness scale.

An important advantage of the QUALY method is that it eliminates the distribution-of-income problems of other methods. The QUALY approach rests on a strict egalitarian premise; the value of various states of health should be independent of the economic status of the particular people in those states. Willingness to pay and contingent valuation treat health like any other market commodity, while QUALY approaches view health as a distinct good that should be distributed according to a nonmarket logic. Costs are still relevant, of course, but they are not brought in at the level of individual decisions.

In addition, it seems plausible to think that answers to hypothetical questions are more likely to be meaningful when people are choosing states of health than when people are purporting to assign dollar values to those states. Because the former draws more directly on people's actual experiences with their health and the health of others, it is likely to be more credible. Moreover, the divergence between the valuations people attach to various health states as individuals and as participants in collective decision making seems unlikely to be severe. Indeed, individual rankings of QUALYs appear quite close to actual democratic decision making and in some ways an improvement. There is no collective deliberative process—and this is a real problem for advocates of the QUALY approach—but individual deliberation might be enhanced by considering each health state carefully in a setting not characterized by the compression of issues, interest-group pressures, and time constraints typical of legislative settings.

Of course, the QUALY approach must justify itself against several skeptical objections. Whether people can make the fine-grained distinctions required in what remain hypothetical settings remains an open question. But among public policy methods for evaluating health and risk issues that seek to incorporate individual valuations in a systemtatic and more formal way, the QUALY approach has much to commend it.

IV. An Expert Cadre? Justice Breyer's Proposal

It is appropriate to conclude by offering some thoughts on Justice Stephen Breyer's provocative and influential proposal for an elite core of well-trained and experienced public servants, charged with the task of rationalizing risk regulation and establishing a sensible system of regulatory priorities.[37] Justice Breyer proposes a new career path that would enable a select group of government employees to rotate through executive, legislative, and administrative offices that address health and environmental issues. These employees would be part of a small, centralized administrative group with a broad agenda for rationalizing risk-regulation policy. Their mission would include creating regulatory priorities within as well as across agencies; comparing programs to determine how resources could best be allocated to reduce risks; and, most generally, "building an improved, coherent risk-regulating system, adaptable for use in several different risk-related programs."[38] To realize these goals, Justice Breyer argues that this elite core would require interagency jurisdiction as well as substantial political independence and, perhaps paradoxically, substantial political power.

As an effort to improve priority-setting, this proposal is extremely promising (see the discussion of problems of poor priority setting in chapter 14). But the basic idea places too much stress on the technocratic side of risk regulation and too little on the democratic side. By centralizing so many aspects of risk regulation in a small cadre of experts, this approach provides insufficient space for a deliberative process among competing perspectives about regulation, and too little basis for incorporating reflective public understandings about qualitative differences among diverse risks.

More particularly, any cadre of risk managers should be attentive not simply to numbers of lives saved overall, or per dollar spent, but also to public judgments about the contexts in which risks are incurred, and hence to the full range of factors that make risks tolerable or intolerable. There is truth to the contention that the public wants to save more lives rather than fewer; but the contention is too simple. The public is willing to spend a great deal more to prevent a death from cancer than to prevent an instant death; as we have seen in Table 5.4, it may well be willing to spend three times as much to do so. The public is legitimately interested not only in end-states and quantities—in how many lives are saved—but also in processes and in the contextual factors that determine whether risks are acceptable or not. Risk managers should build into their decisions a careful awareness of qualitative differences among different kinds of risks and should attempt to expose their evaluative judgments to public scrutiny and review.

This conclusion has practical implications, but its implications bear on broader questions about individual and collective rationality. It suggests that a democratic conception of rationality should be built on the aspiration to reason-giving in the public domain. In their current form, expert and economic approaches are insufficiently appreciative of this fact. As we will see in Part III, it is possible to imagine new institutional arrangements that would take advantage of scientific knowledge and an understanding of trade-offs and costs, while also making a large place for reflective democratic judgments about risks.

Notes

1. See, for example, W. Kip Viscusi, *Fatal Tradeoffs: Public and Private Responsibilities for Risk* (New York: Oxford University Press, 1992), pp. 170–73.

2. Paul Slovic, "Perception of Risk" 236 *Science* 129 (April 17, 1987).

3. *Id.*

4. *Id.*

5. *Id.*

6. See generally Daniel Kahneman and Amos Tversky, "Prospect Theory: An Analysis of Decision Under Risk," 47 *Econometrica* 263 (1979). For a clear, nontechnical catalogue, see also Massimo Piattelli-Palmarini, Inevitable Illusions: How Mistakes of Reason Rule Our Minds (New York: Wiley & Sons, 1994).

7. M. Granger Morgan, "Risk Analysis and Management," *Scientific Am.* 32, 35 (July 1993).

8. *Id.* See also Stuart Hill, *Democratic Values and Technological Choices* (Stanford: Stanford University Press, 1992), pp. 55–89, for an optimistic account of citizens' capacities to assess risks.

9. Some of these are discussed in Slovic, *supra* note 2, at 120–25; Carnegie Commission on Science, Technology and Government, *Risk and the Environment: Improving Regulatory Decision Making* (New York: Carnegie Commission, 1993), pp. 88–89; William W. Lowrance, *Of Acceptable Risk: Science and the Determination of Safety* (Los Altos: W. Kaufmann, 1976), pp. 86–94; Stephen G. Breyer, *Breaking the Vicious Circle: Toward Effective Risk Regulation* (Cambridge: Harvard University Press, 1993). It has even been suggested that perceptions of social control over one's environment have a bearing on health and longevity, independent of the level of relevant risks. See S. Leonard Syme, "The Social Animal and Health," *Daedalus* 79, 84–85 (Fall 1994).

10. See Hill, *supra* note 8, at 21.

11. See generally Richard H. Pildes, "The Unintended Cultural Consequences of Public Policy: A Comment on the Symposium," 89 *Mich. L. Rev.* 936, 958–59 (1991).

12. Elizabeth Anderson, "Values, Risks, and Market Norms," 17 *Phil. & Pub. Aff.* 54, 61 (1988). See also Amartya Sen, "Freedoms and Needs: An Argument for the Primacy of Political Rights," *New Republic* 31, 32–33 (Jan 11, 1993) ("There are deep and fundamental and intuitively understood grounds for rejecting the view that confines itself merely to checking the parity of outcomes, the view that matches death for death, happiness for happiness, fulfillment for fulfillment, irrespective of how all this death, happiness, and fulfilment comes about.").

13. Roger Noll and James Krier, "Some Implications of Cognitive Psychology for Risk Regulation," 19 *J. Legal Stud.* 747 (1990).

14. Daniel Fiorino, "Technical and Democratic Values in Risk Analysis," 9 *Risk Analysis* 293, 295 (1989).

15. *Id.* citing J. D. Robinson, M. D. Higgins, and P. K. Bolyard, "Assessing Environmental Impacts on Health: A Role for Behavioral Science," 4 *Envir. Impact Assessment Rev.* 41 (1983).

16. See K. S. Shrader-Frechette, *Risk and Rationality: Philosophical Foundations for Popular Reforms* (Berkeley: University of California Press, 1991); Slovic, *supra* note 2, at 283 ("When experts judge risk, their responses correlate highly with technical estimates of annual fatalities."); Slovic, *supra* note 2, at 121 ("[e]xperts appear to see riskiness as synonymous with expected annual mortality.").

17. George Tolley, Donald Kenkel, and Robert Fabian, eds., *Valuing Health for Policy: An Economic Approach.* (Chicago: University of Chicago Press, 1994), p. 318.

18. See Viscusi, *supra* note 1.

19. Food and Drug Administration, "Regulatory Impact Analysis of the Final Rules to Amend the Food Labeling Regulations," 58 *Fed. Reg.* 2927, 2939 (1993).

20. See Office of Management and Budget, *Regulatory Program of the United States, 1990–1991.* (Washington, D.C.: Executive Office of the President, 1992), pp. 487. The Administrative Conference reached a similar conclusion, though more cautiously. See "Recommendations of the Administrative Conference Regarding Administrative Practice and Procedure and Correction, Recommendation No. 88–7," 53 *Fed. Reg.* 39585, 39586–87 (1988).

21. See Ted R. Miller, "Willingness to Pay Comes of Age: Will the System Survive?," 83 *Nw. U. L. Rev.* 876, 886–89 (1989).

22. See Elliott Aronson, *The Social Animal,* 7th ed. (New York: W. H. Freeman, 1995).

23. See Amartya Sen, "Internal Consistency of Choice," 61 *Econometrica* 495 (1993). For empirical evidence, see Aronson, *supra* note 22, at 298; Itamar Simonson and Amos Tversky, "Choice in Context: Contrast and Extremeness Aversion," 29 *J. Marketing Res.* 281 (1992).

24. See Amartya Sen, "Environmental Evaluation and Social Choice: Contingent Valuation and the Market Analogy," 46 *Japanese Eco. Rev.* 23 (1995).

25. *Valuing Health for Policy, supra* note 17, at 318. For a detailed examination of the difference between individual and social perspectives on health problems, see the recent study of the external costs of smoking and drinking in Willard G. Manning, et al., *The Costs of Poor Health Habits* (Cambridge: Harvard University Press, 1991; Willard G. Manning, et al., "The Taxes of Sin: Do Smokers and Drinkers Pay Their Way?" 261 *JAMA* 1604 (1989).

26. See Valuing Health for Policy, *supra* note 17, at 290–94; Symposium, "Contingent Valuation," J. Econ. Persp. 3 (Fall 1994).

27. Valuing Health for Policy, *supra* note 17, at 187-89; Peter A. Diamond and Jerry A. Hausman, "Contingent Valuation: Is Some Number Better than No Number?" *J. Econ. Persp.* 45, 49–54 (Fall 1994).

28. *Valuing Health for Policy, supra* note 17, at 341–42.

29. *Id.* at 99.

30. *Id.* at 89. The dollar figures are mean bid values, and relief means a "mild day."

31. See Diamond and Hausman, *supra* note 27, at 45; Daniel Kahneman and Sam-

uel Ritov, "Determinants of Stated Willingness to Pay," 9 *J. Risk & Uncertainty* 5 (1994).

32. See Kahneman and Ritov, *supra* note 31.

33. See Richard Stewart, Liability For Natural Resource Injury, in *Analyzing Superfund*, Richard Revesz and Richard B. Stewart, eds. (Washington, D.C.: Resources for the Future, 1995), pp. 236–37.

34. See Sen, *supra* note 24.

35. The measure was first described in Richard Zeckhauser and Donald Shepard, "Where Now for Saving Lives?" 40 *L. & Contemp. Probs.* 5 (1976).

36. An important work in the development of these multidimensional measures is Robert M. Kaplan and James W. Bush, "Health-Related Quality for Life Measurement of Evaluation Research and Policy Analysis," 1 *Health Psych.* 61 (1982). For a general survey of QUALY approaches, see George W. Torrance, "Measurement of Health State Utilities for Economic Appraisal: A Review," 5 *J. Health Econ.* 1 (1986). For a recent general discussion, see *Valuing Health for Policy supra* note 17, at 118–36.

37. Breyer, *supra* note 9, at 59–63.

38. *Id.* at 60.

II

RIGHTS

6

Why Markets Don't Stop Discrimination

Markets, it is sometimes said, are hard on discrimination.[1] An employer who finds himself refusing to hire qualified blacks and women will, in the long run, lose out to those who are willing to draw from a broader labor pool. Employer discrimination amounts to a self-destructive "taste"—self-destructive because employers who indulge that taste add to the costs of doing business. Added costs can only hurt. To put it simply, bigots are weak competitors. The market will drive them out.

On this account, the persistence of employment discrimination on the basis of race and sex presents something of a puzzle. And if markets are an ally of equality and a foe of employment discrimination, perhaps discrimination persists because of something other than markets. Perhaps labor unions are to blame; perhaps the real culprit is the extensive federal regulation of the employment market, including minimum-wage and maximum-hour laws and unemployment compensation. If competitive markets drive out discrimination, the problem for current federal policy lies not in the absence of aggressive antidiscrimination law, but instead in the absence of truly competitive markets.

If this account is correct, the prescription for the future of antidiscrimination law is to seek ways to free up employers from the wide range of governmental disabilities—including, in fact, antidiscrimination law itself. The argument seems to be bolstered by the fact that some groups subject to past and present prejudice—most notably, Jews and Asian Americans—have made substantial progress in employment, at least in part because of the operation of competitive markets.

In this chapter, however, I argue that under plausible assumptions and in many settings, markets will not stop discrimination and that reliance on competitive pressures would be a grave mistake for a government intending to eliminate discriminatory practices. Indeed, markets are often the problem rather than the solution. They guarantee that discrimination will persist. Enthusiasm for markets as an anti-discrimination policy is at best wishful thinking.

I. Why Markets Produce Discrimination:
Standard Accounts

As a provisional matter, let us define discrimination as a decision by a market actor to treat one person differently from another because that person is black or female. It is irrelevant for present purposes whether the differential treatment is based on hostility, fear, taste, unconscious devaluation, selective empathy and indifference, employer self-interest, unwarranted generalizations, or an accurate perception of facts about group members. This definition has a degree of vagueness, and it is certainly disputable whether government should ban all of the conduct that it identifies. But the definition has the advantage of tracking both current law and some ordinary intuitions about the problem.

On one view, the notion that competitive markets act against discrimination, so defined, might seem odd or even idiosyncratic. In the history of the United States as well as other nations, markets and discrimination have accompanied one another at numerous points and in numerous places. Surely, governmentally imposed discrimination, because of its centralized character, has especially egregious effects; but to point to the comparative strength of collective controls is not to say that decentralized markets work in the opposite direction. Indeed, there is good empirical evidence that government programs have succeeded in reducing discrimination produced by the market. The enactment of civil rights legislation appears to have led to increases in black and female employment in various sectors. At least in general, the disputed question has to do not with the direction of change but with the degree of the improvement.[2]

Moreover, study after study has shown that the market often devalues the products and enterprises of both blacks and women.[3] This should not be surprising. In a system with a significant amount of race and sex prejudice, covert and overt, conscious and unconscious, the "willingness to pay" criterion—as it is reflected in the purchasing and selling decisions of employers, employees, consumers, and others—will ensure that those subject to discriminatory attitudes will be at a comparative disadvantage in the market. At least this is so when the participation of disfavored groups is highly visible, as indeed it often is. In this context, the most natural initial judgment is that if discrimination is the problem, markets are hardly the solution.

But the judgment, as stated, seems too crude. Suppose a set of companies in a competitive industry—call them "D companies"—decides not to sell to or employ an identifiable segment of the community; suppose too that the D companies must compete with nondiscriminators engaged in the same line of work ("ND companies"). In the long run, the D companies should be at a significant disadvantage. They will be unable to draw on as large a pool of workers; they will be unable to sell to as large a group of purchasers. In practice, their discriminatory behavior will place a tax on their operations. To say the least, businesses that impose on themselves a tax not faced by their competitors are unlikely to fare well.

As patrons and prospective employees drift to ND companies, the D companies will be driven out. Eventually, the consequences should be nothing short of disastrous for discrimination in general. It is this understanding that accounts for the plausible claim that an effective antidiscrimination policy consists of reliance on decentralized markets.

Notwithstanding its plausibility (and even, in some settings, its accuracy),[4] I want in this section to make three arguments against this claim. In setting out these arguments, I make no claim to special originality. All of them can be found, at least in some form, in standard economic discussions of the problem.

Third Parties

An influential approach to the problem of discrimination, captured in the account just offered, attributes the phenomenon to employers' "taste" for discrimination.[5] On this view, employers discriminate because they do not like to associate with blacks, women, or others. The engine that drives discrimination is employer preferences—not economic self-interest, narrowly defined. Indeed, economic self-interest is in conflict with employers' taste for discrimination. This idea has a degree of truth to it; certainly, it explains many practices by employers. But sometimes discrimination is caused by employer practices that result precisely from economic self-interest, rather than from the employer's noneconomic goals. The reason is that third parties are frequently in a position to impose financial punishments on nondiscriminatory employers.[6] Suppose, for example, that purchasers or fellow employees refuse to buy from or work for a company that does not discriminate. Third parties can pressure employers in the direction of discrimination, even if employers would, other things being equal, choose not to discriminate or have no particular view about whether to discriminate or not. Ironically, it is the failure to discriminate that operates as a tax on the employer's business, rather than vice versa. And when this is so, reliance on competitive pressures will force employers to behave in a discriminatory manner if they wish to survive.

The phenomenon is hardly unusual. Consider, for example, a shopkeeper whose customers do not like dealing with blacks or women; a commercial airline whose patrons react unfavorably to female pilots; a university whose students and alumni prefer a primarily male or white faculty; a law firm whose clients prefer not to have black lawyers; or a hospital whose patients are uncomfortable with female doctors or black nurses. The persistence of private segregation in major league baseball is a familiar example of this phenomenon.

In all of these cases, market pressures create rather than prevent discrimination. An employer who wants to act nondiscriminatorily will be punished, not rewarded. Indeed, an employer who wants not to be a discriminator will be engaging in what is, from his point of view, a form of affirmative action. From his point of view, discrimination is in fact neutral, in the sense that it is a quite ordinary form of profit-maximization through catering to consumer demand. From his point of view, a refusal to discriminate is also economically harmful to him; if he is a nondiscriminator, it is not for the sake of profits, but in order to promote the long-range goal of race and sex equality. If discrimination is to be eliminated, it may well be as a result of legal rules forbidding discrimination from continuing.

Ideas of precisely this sort played a role in the passage of the Civil Rights Act of 1964. Many restaurants and hotels sought regulation constraining their own behavior by outlawing discrimination. Their goal was to obtain the force of the law to overcome the effects of private racism (in the form of violence as well as competitive sanctions). They sought to overcome, through law, the discrimination-producing consequences of market pressures. They sought to "hide behind the law" to do what, in a sense, they wanted to do: to behave nondiscriminatorily. Without the force of law, they would encounter third-party pressures, including social norms (chapter 2), that would push them in the direction of discrimination.

On this account, it remains necessary to explain why third parties are not themselves hurt by their "taste." At least part of the reason lies in the fact that third parties often are not market actors in the ordinary sense—that is, they will not suffer competitive injury in markets if they indulge their discriminatory preferences. Consider, for example, ordinary people who prefer not to fly in airplanes piloted by blacks or women (or having black or male stewards). At least in many cases, the harm suffered by people who indulge their prejudice—perhaps higher prices of some form or another—will not drive them out of any "market," but instead, and more simply, will make them somewhat poorer. For a customer, a racist or sexist taste operates like any other taste, such as the taste for high-sugar cereals, luxury cars, or fancy computers; the taste may increase prices, but market pressures need not make the taste disappear.

In a competitive market that contains private racism and sexism, then, the existence of third-party pressures can create significant spheres of discrimination. To be sure, sometimes the participation of blacks or women (or the handicapped) is invisible; in any case, racism and sexism are currently not so widespread as to make it costly for all employers to act in a nondiscriminatory fashion. Because of their decentralized character, markets are usually far less effective than governmental controls in perpetuating discrimination, as the experience in South Africa has (at least sometimes) showed. Moreover, third-party effects will probably produce a degree of occupational segregation instead of, or as well as, discrimination. But discriminatory practices in many areas are likely to persist over time precisely because of the market, which by its very nature registers consumer preferences, including discriminatory ones.

There is an additional problem here.[7] Suppose that society includes a number of traders who want to interact with blacks or women as well as a number of traders who do not. Suppose, too, that it is difficult for traders who are themselves indifferent to race and sex distinctions to tell which traders are discriminators (a frequent phenomenon in competitive markets). If these conditions are met, discrimination is likely to be a rational strategy for traders. New companies will do poorly if they refuse to discriminate. All this suggests that markets will frequently have great difficulty in breaking down discrimination, if discriminatory tastes are even somewhat widespread.

Statistical or Economically Rational Discrimination

I have referred to the common-sense understanding that employers treat blacks and women differently because of hostility or prejudice on their part—an idea that often accompanies the claim that markets are an enemy of discrimination. This form of hostility or prejudice is frequently described as "irrational." But the category of irrational prejudice is an ambiguous one. Perhaps we can understand it to include (a) a belief that members of a group have certain characteristics when in fact they do not, (b) a belief that many or most members of a group have certain characteristics when in fact only a few do, and (c) reliance on fairly accurate group-based generalizations when more accurate classifying devices are relatively inexpensive and available. In all of these cases, it is possible to say that someone is acting on the basis of irrational prejudice.

Suppose instead, however, that discriminatory behavior is a response to generalizations or stereotypes that, although quite overbroad and from one point of view invidious, provide an economically rational basis for employment decisions.[8] Such stereotypes may be economically rational in the sense that it is cheaper to use them than it is to rely on more fine-grained approaches, which can be expensive to administer. Stereotypes and generalizations, of course, are a common ingredient of day-to-day market decisions. There are information costs in making distinctions within categories, and sometimes people make the category do the work of a more individualized and often far more costly examination of the merits of the particular employee.

Such categorical judgments are not only pervasive; they are entirely legitimate in most settings. We all depend on them every day. Employers rely on "proxies" of many sorts, even though those proxies are overbroad generalizations and far from entirely accurate. For example, test scores, employment records, level of education, and prestige of college attended are all part of rational employment decisions. Emphasis on these factors is a common form of stereotyping; at least in ordinary circumstances, it would be odd to say that such factors reflect hostility or prejudice of the sort that the law should ban. People may use stereotypes not because they are very accurate, but because they are less costly to use than any more individualized inquiry.

There can be no question that at least in some contexts, race and sex operate as similar proxies. In various ways, blacks differ from whites and women differ from men; there are "real differences" between the two groups (see chapter 4 for some details). Indeed, in light of past and present discrimination against blacks and women, it would be shocking if group-based differences were not present. Women, for example, are more likely than men to be the primary caretakers of children and more likely to leave the employment market because of that role. Along every indicator of social welfare—poverty, education, employment, vulnerability to private (or public) violence, participation in violent crime—blacks are less well-off than whites. And in light of those differences, it is fully possible that in certain settings, race- and sex-based generalizations are economically rational as proxies for relevant characteristics. Indeed, it is fully possible that race or sex is, in some contexts, every bit as accurate a signaling device as, say, test score, education, and previous employment. (Notably, the use of those proxies may itself have discriminatory consequences and indeed might be counted as a form of discrimination. But I put this point to one side for now.)

If race or sex can be a good signaling device, an employer might discriminate not because he hates or devalues blacks or women, or has a general desire not to associate with them, or is "prejudiced" in the ordinary sense, but because he believes (on the basis either of plausible assumptions or actual experience) that the relevant stereotypes have sufficient truth to be a basis for employment decisions. For example, an employer might believe that women are more likely to leave a high-pressure job than men, or that they are less suited for physically demanding employment; he might think that blacks are less likely to have the necessary training. With respect to the handicapped, the same scenario is of course readily predictable: "Real differences" call for differential treatment. As I understand it here, statistical discrimination occurs when the employer does not harbor irrational hatred or discriminatory feelings, but instead acts according to stereotypes of the sort that are typically relied on by market actors, and that are no less false than ordinary stereotypes.

It is important to be careful with this point. I do not mean to deny that ordinary, irrational prejudice accounts for a significant amount of discrimination, or even that it is hard both in practice and in principle to distinguish between ordinary prejudice and economically rational stereotyping. Sometimes employers who refuse to follow a stereotype will find employees who will move them far ahead in the marketplace. Moreover, the decision about *what kinds* of economically rational stereotypes should be adopted might itself reflect prejudice. Sometimes people refuse such stereotypes because they perceive them to be unfair. People are highly selective in their creation and selection of the very categories with which they view people—as college graduates? as children of successful parents? as nonreligious? as white males? as tall? as good-looking? People are also selective in their decisions about which categories ought to count in various sectors of social and economic life. Thus, for example, the use of sex as a proxy for flexibility with respect to overtime work may be fully rational; but other proxies may be nearly as good or better. Selectivity in the choice of the proxy may be a product of prejudice. People also tend to notice events that are consistent with previously held stereotypes and to disregard events that are inconsistent with them.[9] This is a built-in obstacle to changes in social norms and social "knowledge," even when the governing norms increasingly fail to mirror reality.

One might agree with all this and still acknowledge what seems undoubtedly true: Discrimination sometimes persists because it is economically rational to rely on a race- or sex-based generalization. And if this is so—if discrimination of this sort is a significant part of modern practice—then markets will be the furthest thing from a corrective. If discrimination is rational, then discriminatory behavior is rewarded in the marketplace. Efforts to view people through more finely tuned (and hence more expensive) devices than stereotypes will be punished.

Moreover, if discrimination is rooted in economically rational stereotypes, it remains necessary to ask what is wrong with it. The (apparent) social consensus that prejudice is irrational tends to downplay the difficulty of finding firm moral foundations for antidiscrimination law. Contemporary American law consistently condemns discrimination even if it is fully rational—that is, if it is as accurate as other generalizations typically used in the labor market. It is no defense to a claim of race or sex discrimination that the practice under attack is reasonable stereotyping. And because contemporary law singles out one kind of rational stereotyping and bans it, the distinction between affirmative action and antidiscrimination norms is extremely thin and perhaps invisible in principle.[10] This is because in some settings, an antidiscrimination norm itself operates to bar economically rational behavior in the interest of long-term social goals. It does so selectively; in the interest of producing a racially improved future, the law forbids rational racial stereotyping when it allows stereotyping of most other kinds. An antidiscrimination norm even requires innocent victims—for example, customers who must pay higher prices—to be sacrificed in the interest of that goal.

Indeed, the distinction between affirmative action and antidiscrimination is crisp only to those who see discrimination as always grounded in hostility and irrationality, which it clearly is not. To say this is hardly to say that there are no differences between affirmative action and an antidiscrimination principle that forbids economically rational behavior. But it is to say that a great failure of the assault on affirmative action is its failure to account for the ways in which a requirement of nondiscrimination involves very much the same considerations.

However we may think about this more adventurous claim, the central point remains. Markets will not drive out discrimination precisely to the extent that discrimination consists of economically rational stereotyping.

The Effects of Discrimination on Human Capital

Suppose that there is widespread discrimination for any number of reasons: employers have a taste for discrimination; third parties impose pressures in discriminatory directions; race or sex is used as a proxy for productivity (whether or not productivity includes the losses produced by the reactions of third parties). If any of these things is so, markets will perpetuate discrimination for yet another reason, one having to do with harmful effects on investment in human capital.[11]

The central point here is that the productivity of blacks or whites and women or men is endogenous to, or a product of, the existence of discrimination in the labor market. Since this is so, it is a mistake to see productivity within any social group as static or independent of decisions by employers.

Such decisions will have important dynamic effects on the choice of blacks and whites or women and men to invest in human capital. Decisions about education, training, drug use, trade-offs between work and leisure, and employment programs will be affected by existing patterns of discrimination. In a market that contains such discrimination, blacks and women will invest relatively less in such programs. Indeed, lower investments on their part are perfectly rational. As market actors, women should invest less than men in training to be (say) pilots, economists, politicians, or lawyers if these professions discriminate against women and thus reward their investment less than that of men.

The result can be a vicious circle or even spiral. Because of existing discrimination, the relevant groups will probably invest less in human capital; because of this lower investment, the discrimination will persist or perhaps increase because its statistical rationality itself increases; because of this effect, investments will decrease still further; and so on. Markets are the problem, not the solution.

Undoubtedly, this picture is too bleak in many settings. Proxies not rooted in sex and race have frequently evolved and employers have used them; such proxies are ordinarily far more accurate, and employers who use them sometimes prosper. More generally, the extraordinary persistence of blacks and women in attempting to enter professions dominated by whites and men is one of the most striking phenomena of the post-World War II period. Blacks and women frequently appear to invest huge amounts of human capital even in sectors that treat them inhospitably. In fact, some people respond to discrimination by increasing rather than decreasing their investments in human capital. In Western history, some racial and ethnic groups have prospered as a result of such investments, notwithstanding discriminatory tastes on the part of employers, customers, and fellow employees. But there can be little question that discrimination does have a large effect on human capital in many contexts, and that the discouraging reception, known to be accorded to blacks and women, perpetuates the exclusion of both groups from certain sectors of the economy. And when this is so, reliance on markets as an antidiscrimination policy is badly misconceived.

In General: Reinforcing Effects

The three arguments thus far—coupled with the existence of race- and sex-based hostility or devaluation on the part of employers—build on standard economic accounts of discrimination. It is notable that none of the various effects unambiguously reflects a market failure in the conventional sense. The incorporation of racist or sexist preferences is efficient, if the efficiency criterion is based on private willingness to pay;[12] so, too, with profit-maximizing reactions to the desires of third parties and with statistical discrimination. In all of these cases, governmental interference will probably produce an efficiency loss, at least in the short term.[13]

The only possible exception is the effect of discrimination on human capital.[14] In that case, it is possible to conceive of discrimination as producing a serious externality, in the form of harmful effects on outsiders—prospective labor market entrants—with corresponding efficiency losses. But it is important to note that there is an optimal level of investment in human capital, and it is not entirely clear why and to what extent existing investments that are adaptive to employer behavior in the labor market should be seen as suboptimal. In fact any generalization that is used in the labor market will have a signaling effect that will shift investments in human capital, and it is not easy to develop a model revealing which signals produce suboptimal investments. In general, then, markets will perpetuate discrimination for reasons that are unrelated to the market failures that provide traditional economic grounds for legal intervention.

Moreover, and crucially, each of these effects reinforces the others in potentially powerful ways. If there is ordinary prejudice, it will interact with statistical discrimination so as to produce more of both. People tend to notice events consistent with their prejudice and disregard events that are inconsistent with them, and the result will be more in the way of both prejudice and statistical discrimination. If third parties attempt to promote discrimination, they will increase the existence of both prejudice and statistical discrimination. Employers will hire fewer blacks and women, who in turn will appear less frequently in desirable positions, with consequent reinforcing effects on both prejudice and statistical discrimination.

In addition, if there is prejudice and statistical discrimination, and if third parties promote discrimination, victims of discrimination will decrease their investments in human capital. Such decreased investments will be a perfectly reasonable response to the real world. And if there are decreased investments in human capital, then prejudice, statistical discrimination, and third-party effects will also increase. Statistical discrimination will become all the more rational; prejudice will hardly be broken down but, on the contrary, strengthened; consumers and employers will be more likely to be discriminators.

Of course, it would be necessary to compile detailed factual evidence to assess the magnitude of the relevant effects. In the abstract, it is hard to know how large they will be. But we know enough to realize that the various effects can be mutually reinforcing and might present a disaster for victims of discrimination and for society as a whole.

By this point the fact that markets often perpetuate discrimination should present no puzzle at all. Markets can be an ally of discrimination. To be sure, the precise relationship between markets and discrimination will depend on the particular circumstances. The likelihood that markets will promote discrimination should increase if third-party prejudice is widespread, if stereotypes or generalizations are accurate, and if ordinary racism and sexism are pervasive. But what may be surprising is not that markets produce discrimination, but that discrimination has decreased as much as it has. And all this follows from quite conventional economic approaches to the problem.

II. Markets and Discrimination: Noneconomic Accounts

In this section, I provide two additional arguments against the view that markets will prevent discrimination. Neither of them is standard within economics, but both of them have considerable explanatory power.

Preference and Belief Formation

In economic theory, preferences and beliefs are usually taken as given—an approach that is often helpful in building models for understanding social life. But in the context of discrimination, and elsewhere as well, this approach will cause both descriptive and normative problems. The central point here is that preferences are endogenous to current laws, norms, and practices (chapters 1 and 2). Once those laws, norms, and practices are entrenched, there are special obstacles to bringing about change through market ordering.

In the setting at hand, the problem is that private preferences, on the part of both discriminators and their victims, tend to adapt to the status quo, and to do so in a way that makes significant change hard to achieve. The reduction of cognitive dissonance is a powerful motivating force: People attempt to bring their beliefs and perceptions in line with existing practice.[15] The victims of inequality may well try to reduce dissonance by adapting their preferences to the available opportunities. Consider the story of the fox who concludes that he does not want unavailable grapes because he considers them sour; the reason that he considers them sour is that they are unavailable.[16] Or people may adapt their aspirations to the persistent and often irrationally held belief that the world is just.[17] The beneficiaries of the status quo tend to do the same, concluding that the fate of the victims is deserved, is something for which victims are responsible, or is part of an intractable, given, or natural order. All of these claims have played an enormous role in the history of discrimination on the basis of race and sex.

There is of course extremely powerful evidence in the psychological literature for the thesis that human beings try to reduce dissonance.[18] Some work here reveals that people who engage in cruel behavior change their attitudes toward the objects of their cruelty and thus devalue them. Observers tend to do the same. The phenomenon of blaming the victim has clear motivational foundations. The notion that the world is just, and that existing inequalities are deserved or desired, plays a large role in the formation of preferences and beliefs. The reduction of cognitive dissonance thus operates as a significant obstacle to the recognition that discrimination is a problem, or even that it exists. Adaptation of beliefs to a social status quo can also affect social norms. The social norms governing women's work may be quite hard to change; the social meaning of being female, or being black, may be nearly intractable (chapter 2).

This problem can be tied quite tightly to the operation of a market economy, whose participants are self-consciously involved in catering to existing tastes and in perpetuating and reinforcing them. Markets, partly because of this effect, are an engine of productivity and respect for individual autonomy in most circumstances; but in this setting, they sometimes perpetuate inequality. This is especially true in the context of sex discrimination, where advertising and consumption powerfully reinforce existing stereotypes, with consequences for the development of preferences and beliefs. Consider, for example, the multiple ways in which the beauty industry, broadly understood, attempts to define and to commodify femininity, in efforts to reach men and women alike. Women as well as men have often adapted their preferences and beliefs to a system of sex inequality.

The inevitable effect of a discriminatory status quo on preferences and beliefs is related to the phenomenon, noted previously, of decreased investment in human capital. In both cases, the response to discrimination is endogenous rather than exogenous and has the consequence of perpetuating existing inequalities. But with respect to preferences and beliefs, the effect is especially pernicious. Here the consequence is not merely to shift investments in self-development but, instead, to make people believe that the existing regime, including discrimination, presents no problem at all.

Once preferences and beliefs are affected, the likelihood of social change through markets diminishes dramatically. Here, as well, there is a mutually reinforcing effect among the various sources of market discrimination. The effect of discrimination on preferences and beliefs fortifies existing prejudice, produces a decrease in investment in human capital, leads to more in the way of statistical discrimination, and increases the unwillingness of third parties to deal with blacks and women.

Baselines and Discrimination Law

Almost by definition, markets incorporate the norms and practices of advantaged groups. Conspicuous examples include the many ways in which employment settings, requirements, and expectations are structured for the able-bodied and for traditional male career patterns. Here the market, dependent as it is on the criterion of private willingness to pay, is extremely unlikely to eliminate discrimination (understood as such by reference to widespead intuitions). To say that the refusal to provide flexible time, child care, or building access for the disabled does not count as "discrimination" is to rely on an exceptionally narrow conception of what discrimination is—a conception that is repudiated in much of current American law, that is inconsistent with an approach that is alert to discriminatory purposes or effects, and that in any case will do very little about existing inequalities.

In these circumstances, a legal system committed to an antidiscrimination principle might in some cases restructure market arrangements so as to put members of disadvantaged groups on a plane of greater equality—not by allowing them to be "like" members of advantaged groups, but by changing the criteria themselves, at least when those criteria do not have a firm independent justification. Consider the conventional test of American discrimination law: Is the member of the disadvantaged group "similarly situated" to the member of the advantaged group? That is: Have women, who are otherwise the same as men, or disabled people, who are otherwise the same as the able-bodied, been treated differently from men or the able-bodied? The problem with this test is that it itself reflects inequality, since it takes the norms and practices of the advantaged groups as the baseline against which to measure equality. And here market ordering, dependent as it is on the criterion of private willingness to pay, will inevitably present a problem.

Ideas of this sort underlie recent efforts to ban discrimination on the basis of pregnancy and disability. As in the case of statistical discrimination, these forms of discrimination are perfectly rational from the standpoint of employers and others. The argument for legal controls is that, in these settings, the criteria used in private markets are hardly prepolitical or natural, have neither good moral status nor powerful independent justification, and at the least should be overridden when their predictable consequences are exclusion or second-class citizenship for certain social groups.

In the case of disability, for example, the handicapped face a wide range of obstacles to participation in both public and private spheres. These obstacles are not a function of "handicap" itself (a most ambiguous concept; what would handicap mean in an entirely different world?) but instead are the inevitable consequence of humanly created barriers, including stairs, doors, and standards in general made by and for the able-bodied. The market in these circumstances is wholly nonresponsive. In light of the humanly created barriers, the market itself may not much value the contributions of handicapped people, which are by hypothesis relatively low if measured by normal productivity standards, understood as these are through the lens of willingness to pay. Discrimination of this sort may well require a legal remedy. And though the specification of the content of that remedy is a difficult question, markets will not respond, even in the long run.

The point, then, is that the valuation of the market will be a reflection of prevailing norms and practices, and those norms and practices sometimes are what an antidiscrimination principle is designed to eliminate or reduce. When this is so, reliance on markets will be unsuccessful. The rationale for antidiscrimination laws in these cases becomes more controversial, complex, and difficult. Certainly the cost of change is highly relevant; an effort to restructure the world would not be worthwhile if it impoverished most or many people. But my basic point remains: Private markets will not stop discrimination.

III. What's Wrong with Discrimination

Thus far, the discussion has been entirely descriptive and explanatory. I have sought to show why markets are unlikely to eliminate discrimination on the basis of race, sex, and disability. But it will not have escaped notice that I have only provisionally defined discrimination—a highly protean concept, in light of the foregoing remarks—or said what is wrong with it. Indeed, one of the largest gaps in present civil rights theory consists of the absence of a full-fledged explanation of just what discrimination is and why we should eliminate it. In this highly tentative section, I want to say something about the appropriate characterization of the claim of discrimination and about how that claim should be treated.

Discrimination should, I suggest, be understood to include any decision that treats an otherwise similarly qualified black, woman, or handicapped person less favorably than a white, male, or able-bodied person, whether the reason for the decision lies in malice, taste, selective empathy and indifference, economic self-interest, or rational stereotyping. This understanding of discrimination picks up not merely overt unequal treatment, but also requirements that are neutral "on their face" but would not have been adopted if the burdened and benefited groups had been reversed.[19] It does not pick up measures merely having discriminatory effects, unless those effects are, in the sense indicated, tied up with racial, sexual, or other bias.

It follows that the claim of discrimination, best understood, is not for prevention of certain irrational acts, or of "prejudice," but instead for the elimination, in places large and small, of something in the nature of a caste system. Hence the antidiscrimination principle is best conceived as an anticaste principle. The concept of caste is hard to define, and I will have to be tentative and somewhat vague about it.[20] I do not mean at all to suggest that the caste-like features of current practices are precisely the same, in nature or extent, as those features of genuine caste societies. I do mean to say that the similarities are what make the current practices a reason for collective concern.

The motivating idea behind an anticaste principle is that without very good reason, legal and social structures should not turn differences that are irrelevant from the moral point of view into social disadvantages. They certainly should not be permitted to do so if the disadvantage is systemic. A systemic disadvantage is one that operates along standard and predictable lines in multiple important spheres of life and that applies in realms—such as education, freedom from private and public violence, wealth, political representation, and political influence—that are deeply implicated in basic participation as a citizen in a democratic society.

In the areas of race and sex discrimination, and of disability as well, the problem is precisely this sort of systemic disadvantage. A social or biological difference has the effect of systematically subordinating the relevant group and of doing so in multiple spheres and along multiple indices of social welfare: poverty, education, political power, employment, susceptibility to violence and crime, and so forth. That is the caste system to which the legal system is attempting to respond.

Differences are usually invoked as the justification for disadvantage. The question is not, however, whether there is a difference—often there certainly is—but whether the legal and social treatment of that difference can be adequately justified. Differences need not imply inequality, and only some differences have that implication. When differences do have that implication, it is a result of legal and social practices, and these might be altered. The problems faced by the handicapped, for example, are not a function of handicap "alone" (as I have noted, an almost impenetrable idea), but instead of the interaction between physical or mental capacities on the one hand and a set of human obstacles made by and for the able-bodied on the other. It is those obstacles, rather than the capacities taken as brute facts, that create a large part of what it means to be handicapped. This understanding, I suggest, provides the principal impetus behind antidiscrimination efforts.

A few disclaimers are necessary here. The anticaste principle, if taken seriously, would call for significant restructuring of social practices. This principle is better set out and implemented by legislative and executive bodies, with their superior democratic pedigree and fact-finding capacities, than by constitutional courts. Moreover, it is important to acknowledge that a wide range of differences among human beings are morally arbitrary, and in a market economy those differences are quite frequently and for fully legitimate reasons translated into social disadvantages. Consider educational background, intelligence, strength, existing supply and demand curves for various products and services, height, and perhaps even willingness to work hard, which can of course be affected by such morally irrelevant factors as family background.

An anticaste principle that would attempt, through law, to counteract all of these factors would indeed be difficult to sustain. In general, the recognition of such factors is inseparable from the operation of a market economy, and a market economy is an important source of freedom, prosperity, and respect for different conceptions of the good. The use of such factors is at least sometimes in the interest of the less or even least well-off, and when this is so, an anticaste principle that would bar their use seems perverse. Moreover, an anticaste principle that would override all morally irrelevant factors would impose extraordinary costs on society, both in its implementation and administrative expense and in its infliction of losses on a wide range of people. Those costs are high enough to make such a global principle immensely unappealing.

The principle therefore has greatest weight in discrete contexts, most notably including race, sex, and disability, in which gains from current practice to the least well-off are hard to imagine; in which second-class citizenship is systemic and occurs in multiple spheres and along easily identifiable and sharply defined lines; in which there will be no global threat to a market economy; and in which the costs of implementation are not terribly high.

IV. Conclusion

Except in limited contexts and under limited conditions, competitive markets will not prevent discrimination. Sometimes discrimination is an economically rational response to the desires of third parties; sometimes it reflects rational stereotyping; sometimes it fuels limited investments in human capital, which create a cycle of discrimination. All of these cases are standard. They account for much of the territory of race and sex discrimination in the United States and elsewhere and explain why, in many contexts, reliance on markets will ensure that discrimination will continue.

I have also offered some less conventional explanations of why markets perpetuate discrimination. A discriminatory status quo has effects on people's beliefs and aspirations, and markets embody the norms and practices of advantaged groups—norms and practices that perpetuate the second-class citizenship of the disadvantaged. These accounts interact with those offered above. Taken together, they provide an explanation for the phenomenon, puzzling to some people, of simultaneous market ordering and discrimination extending over long periods and in many places.

In order to evaluate these conclusions—offered as simple explanations—one needs a theory of what discrimination is and why it ought to be eliminated. It is here that the theory of civil rights remains in a surprisingly primitive state. Discrimination is a protean concept. It covers hatred or devaluation, selective empathy and indifference, false or excessive generalization, rational responses to the desires of third parties, the use of plausible stereotypes, the adoption of criteria that would not be used if the burdened and benefited groups were reversed, and other forms of behavior as well. I have suggested that the problem with discrimination is that it turns a morally irrelevant characteristic into a pervasive source of social disadvantage. Thus understood, an antidiscrimination principle turns into an anticaste principle. And if it is so understood, the distinction between antidiscrimination and affirmative action is thin in practice and perhaps nonexistent in principle.

These points are of course controversial. But if my argument is persuasive, one point should not be: Markets will not cure discrimination. And it is on that point, above all, that I am insisting here.

Notes

1. See generally Clint Bolick, *Changing Course: Civil Rights at the Crossroads* (New Brunswick: Transaction, 1988). At the moment I will not define the protean term "discrimination" precisely; instead, I will rely on common-sense intuitions to the effect that the term prohibits differential treatment of one person because of his or her group membership. I deal here with discrimination, thus understood, on the basis of race, sex, and disability. Other bases for discrimination—age, sexual orientation, religious belief—raise overlapping questions, but they also call up considerations that would complicate the analysis here if they were to be discussed in detail.

2. See, e.g., James Heckman and John Paynor, "The Impact of Federal Antidiscrimination Policy on the Economic Status of Blacks A Study of South Carolina," 79 *Am. Econ. Rev.*, 138 (1989); Richard B. Freeman, "Black Economic Progress After 1964: Who Has Gained and Why?" in *Studies in Labor Markets*, Sherwin Rosen, ed. (Chicago: University of Chicago Press, 1981). But see Richard Posner, "An Economic Analysis of Sex Discrimination Laws," 56 *U. Chi. L. Rev.* 1311 (1989).

3. See, e.g., Martha Dipboye, et al., "Sex and Physical Attractiveness of Raters and Applicants as Determinants of Resume Evaluations," 62 *J. Applied Psychol.* 288 (1977). The reasons for this may range from hostility to statistical discrimination, discussed below.

4. See Fishback, "Can Competition Among Employers Reduce Governmental Discrimination?" 32 *J. Law Econ.* 311 (1989).

5. This view finds its origins in Gary Becker, *The Economics of Discrimination* (Chicago: University of Chicago Press, 1957).

6. Here I follow George Akerlof, "The Economics of Caste and of the Rat Race and Other Woeful Tales," 94 *Q. J. Econ.* 599 (1978).

7. The point is discussed in George Akerlof, "Discriminatory, Status-Based Wages Among Tradition-Oriented, Stochastically Trading Coconut Producers," 93 *J. P. Economy* 265 (1985).

8. See Edmund Phelps, "The Statistical Theory of Racism and Sexism," 62 *Am. Econ. Rev.* 659 (1972); in law, see David Strauss, "The Myth of Colorblindness," in *The Supreme Court Review*, Philip Kurland, et. al., eds. (Chicago: University of Chicago Press, 1986), p. 99.

9. See Elliot Aronson, *The Social Animal*, 7th ed. (Cambridge: Cambridge University Press, 1995).

10. The points made in this paragraph can be found in Strauss, *supra* note 8.

11. Kenneth Arrow, "Models of Job Discrimination," in *Racial Discrimination in Economic Life*, Anthony H. Pascal, ed. (Lexington: Lexington Books, 1972); Shelley Lundberg and William Startz, "Private Discrimination and Social Intervention in Competitive Labor Markets," 73 Am. Econ. Rev., 340 (1983).

12. But compare John Donohue, "Is Title VII Efficient?" 134 *U. Penn. L. Rev.* 1411 (1986), who appears to be relying on a conception of "efficiency" not based on this criterion, but instead based on a notion of social output or production. The same criterion can be found in Stuart Schwab, "Is Statistical Discrimination Efficient?", 76 *Am. Econ. Rev.* 228 (1980).

13. But see Schwab, *supra* note 12; Donohue, *supra* note 12.

14. See Lundberg and Startz, *supra* note 11.

15. See Leon Festinger, *A Theory of Cognitive Dissonance* (Stanford: Stanford University Press, 1957); in the particular context, see the notation in Arrow, *supra* note 11, at 26. In general, see Jon Elster, *Sour Grapes: Studies in the Subversion of Rationality* (Cambridge: Cambridge University Press, 1983).

16. See Elster, *supra* note 15.

17. See *id.*; Melvin J. Lerner, *The Belief in a Just World: A Fundamental Delusion* (New York: Plenum Press, 1980).

18. See, e.g., Aronson, *supra* note 9, at 175–246.

19. See Strauss, "Discriminatory Intent, and the Taming of *Brown*" 56 U. Chi. L. Rev. 935 (1985).

20. I discuss the issue in more detail in Cass R. Sunstein, "The Anticaste Principle," 92 *Mich. L. Rev.* 2410 (1994), and Cass R. Sunstein, *The Partial Constitution* (Cambridge: Harvard University Press, 1993), ch. 10.

The First Amendment
in Cyberspace

I go on this great republican principle, that the people will have virtue and intelligence to select men of virtue and wisdom. Is there no virtue among us? If there be not, we are in a wretched situation. No theoretical checks, no form of government, can render us secure. To suppose that any form of government will secure liberty or happiness without any virtue in the people, is a chimerical idea. If there be sufficient virtue and intelligence in the community, it will be exercised in the selection of these men; so that we do not depend on their virtue, or put confidence in our rulers, but in the people who are to choose them.

James Madison

[T]he right of electing the members of the Government constitutes more particularly the essence of a free and responsible government. The value and efficacy of this right depends on the knowledge of the comparative merits and demerits of the candidates for public trust, and on the equal freedom, consequently, of examining and discussing these merits and demerits of the candidates respectively.

James Madison

[T]elevision is just another appliance. It's a toaster with pictures.

Mark Fowler
former chairman of FCC

I. The Future

Imagine you had a device that combined a telephone, a TV, a camcorder, and a personal computer. No matter where you went or what time it was, your child could see you and talk to you, you could watch a replay of your team's last game, you could browse the latest additions to the library, or you could find the best prices in town on groceries, furniture, clothes—whatever you needed.

Imagine further the dramatic changes in your life if:

- The best schools, teachers, and courses were available to all students, without regard to geography, distance, resources, or disability;
- The vast resources of art, literature, and science were available ev-

erywhere, not just in large institutions or big-city libraries and museums;

- Services that improve America's health care system and respond to other important social needs were available on-line, without waiting in line, when and where you needed them;
- You could live in many places without foregoing opportunities for useful and fulfilling employment, by "telecommuting" to your office through an electronic highway . . . ;

. . . .

- You could see the latest movies, play the hottest video games, or bank and shop from the comfort of your home whenever you chose;
- You could obtain government information directly or through local organizations like libraries, apply for and receive government benefits electronically, and get in touch with government officials easily.[1]

Thus wrote the Department of Commerce on September 15, 1993, when the federal government announced an "Agenda for Action" with respect to "the National Information Infrastructure." The statement may seem weirdly futuristic, but the nation is not at all far from what it prophesies, and in ways that have already altered social and legal relations and categories.

Consider the extraordinarily rapid development of the institution of electronic mail, which lies somewhere between ordinary conversation ("voice mail") and ordinary written communication ("snail mail" or "hard mail"), or which perhaps should be described as something else altogether. E-mail has its own characteristic norms and constraints which are an important part of the informal, unwritten law of cyberspace. These norms and constraints are a form of customary law, determining how and when people communicate with one another. Perhaps there will be a formal codification movement before too long; certainly, the norms and constraints are codified in the sense that, without government assistance, they are easily accessible by people who want to know what they are.

The Commerce Department's claims about location have started to come true. What it meant to "live in California" became altogether different, after the invention of the airplane, from what it meant in (say) 1910. With the advent of new communications technologies, the meaning of the statement, "I live in California" has changed at least as dramatically. If people can have instant access to all libraries and all movies, and if they can communicate with a wide range of public officials, pharmacists, educators, doctors, and lawyers by touching a few buttons, they may as well (for many purposes) live anywhere.

In any case, the existence of technological change promises to test the system of free expression in dramatic ways. What should be expected with respect to the First Amendment?

II. The Present: Markets and Madison

There have been in the United States two models of the First Amendment, corresponding to two free speech traditions.[2] The first emphasizes well-functioning speech markets. It can be traced to Justice Holmes's great *Abrams* dissent,[3] where the notion of a "market in ideas" received its preeminent exposition. The market model emerges as well from *Miami Herald Publishing Co. v. Tornillo*,[4] invalidating a "right of reply" law as applied to candidates for elected office. It finds its most recent defining statement not in judicial decisions, but in an FCC opinion rejecting the fairness doctrine.[5]

The second tradition, and the second model, focuses on public deliberation. The second model can be traced from its origins in the work of James Madison,[6] with his attack on the idea of seditious libel, to Justice Louis Brandeis, with his suggestion that "the greatest menace to freedom is an inert people,"[7] through the work of Alexander Meiklejohn, who associated the free speech principle not with laissez-faire economics but with ideals of democratic deliberation.[8] The Madisonian tradition culminated in *New York Times v. Sullivan*[9] and the reaffirmation of the fairness doctrine in the *Red Lion* case,[10] with the Supreme Court's suggestion that governmental efforts to encourage diverse views and attention to public issues are compatible with the free speech principle—even if they result in regulatory controls on the owners of speech sources.

Under the marketplace metaphor, the First Amendment requires—at least as a presumption—a system of unrestricted economic markets in speech. Government must respect the forces of supply and demand. At the very least, it may not regulate the content of speech so as to push the speech market in its preferred directions. Certainly it must be neutral with respect to viewpoint. A key point for marketplace advocates is that great distrust of government is especially appropriate when speech is at issue. Illicit motives are far too likely to underlie regulatory initiatives. The FCC has at times come close to endorsing the market model, above all in its decision abandoning the fairness doctrine.[11] When the FCC did this, it referred to the operation of the forces of supply and demand and suggested that those forces would produce an optimal mix of entertainment options. Hence former FCC Chair Mark Fowler described television as "just another appliance. It's a toaster with pictures."[12] Undoubtedly, the rise of new communications technologies will be taken to fortify this claim.

Those who endorse the marketplace model do not claim that government may not do anything at all. Of course, government may set up the basic rules of property and contract; it is these rules that make markets feasible. Government is also permitted to protect against market failures, especially by preventing monopolies and monopolistic practices. Structural regulation is acceptable so long as it is a content-neutral attempt to ensure competition. It is therefore important to note that advocates of marketplaces and democracy might work together in seeking to curtail monopoly. Of course, the prevention of monopoly is a precondition for well-functioning information markets.

Government has a final authority, though this authority does not easily fall within the marketplace model itself. Most people who accept the marketplace model acknowledge that government is permitted to regulate the various well-defined categories of controllable speech, such as obscenity, false or misleading commercial speech, and libel. This acknowledgment will have large and not yet explored consequences for government controls on new information technologies. Perhaps the government's power to control obscene, threatening, or libelous speech will justify special rules for cyberspace. But with these qualifications, the commitment to free economic markets is the basic constitutional creed.

Many people think that there is now nothing distinctive about the electronic media or about modern communications technologies that justifies an additional governmental role. If such a role was ever justified, they would argue, it was because of problems of scarcity. When only three television networks exhausted the available options, a market failure may have called for regulation designed to ensure that significant numbers of people were not left without their preferred programming. But this is no longer a problem. With so dramatic a proliferation of stations, most people can obtain the programming they want, or will be able to soon. With cyberspace, people will be able to make or to participate in their own preferred programming in their own preferred "locations" on the Internet. With new technologies, perhaps there are no real problems calling for governmental controls, except for those designed to establish the basic framework.

The second model, receiving its most sustained attention in the writings of Alexander Meiklejohn,[13] emphasizes that our constitutional system is one of deliberative democracy. This system prizes both political (not economic) equality and a shared civic culture. It seeks to promote, as a central democratic goal, reflective and deliberative debate about possible courses of action. The Madisonian model sees the right of free expression as a key part of the system of public deliberation.

On this view, even a well-functioning information market is not immune from government controls. Government is certainly not permitted to regulate speech however it wants; it may not restrict speech on the basis of viewpoint. But it may regulate the electronic media or even cyberspace to promote, in a sufficiently neutral way, a well-functioning democratic regime. It may attempt to promote attention to public issues. It may try to ensure diversity of view. It may promote political speech at the expense of other forms of speech. In particular, educational and public-affairs programming, on the Madisonian view, has a special place.

I cannot attempt in this space to defend fully the proposition that the Madisonian conception is superior to the marketplace alternative as a matter of constitutional law.[14] A few brief notes will have to suffice. The argument for the Madisonian conception is partly historical; the American free speech tradition owes much of its origin and shape to a conception of democratic self-government. The marketplace conception is a creation of the twentieth century, not of the eighteenth. As a matter of history, it confuses modern notions of consumer sovereignty in the marketplace with democratic understandings of political sovereignty, symbolized by the transfer of sovereignty from the King to "We the People." The American free speech tradition finds its origin in that conception of sovereignty, which, in Madison's view, doomed the Sedition Act on constitutional grounds.

But the argument for Madisonianism does not rest only on history. We are unlikely to be able to make sense of our considered judgments about free speech problems without insisting that the free speech principle is centrally (though certainly not exclusively) connected with democratic goals, and without acknowledging that marketplace thinking is inadequately connected with the point and function of a system of free expression. A well-functioning democracy requires a degree of citizen participation, which requires a degree of information; and large disparities in political (as opposed to economic) equality are damaging to democratic aspirations. To the extent that the Madisonian view prizes education, democratic deliberation, and political equality, it is connected, as the marketplace conception is not, with the highest ideals of American constitutionalism.

Some people think that the distinction between marketplace and Madisonian models is now an anachronism. Perhaps the two models conflicted at an earlier stage in history; but in one view, Madison has no place in an era of limitless broadcasting options and cyberspace. Perhaps new technologies now mean that Madisonian goals can best be satisfied in a system of free markets. Now that so many channels, e-mail options, and discussion "places" are available, cannot everyone read or see what they wish? If people want to spend their time on public issues, are there not countless available opportunities? Is this not especially true with the emergence of the Internet? Is it not hopelessly paternalistic, or anachronistic, for government to regulate for Madisonian reasons?

I do not believe that these questions are rhetorical. We know enough to know that even in a period of limitless options, our communications system may fail to promote an educated citizenry and political equality. Madisonian goals may be severely compromised even under technologically extraordinary conditions. There is no logical or *a priori* connection between a well-functioning system of free expression and limitless broadcasting or Internet options. We could well imagine a science fiction story in which a wide range of options coexisted with little or no high-quality fare for children, with widespread political apathy or ignorance, and with social balkanization in which most people's consumption choices simply reinforced their own prejudices and platitudes, or even worse.

Quite outside of science fiction, it is foreseeable that free markets in communications will be a mixed blessing. They could create a kind of accelerating "race to the bottom," in which many or most people see low-quality programming involving trumped-up scandals or sensationalistic anecdotes calling for little in terms of quality or quantity of attention. It is easily imaginable that well-functioning markets in communications will bring about a situation in which many of those interested in politics merely fortify their own unreflective judgments and are exposed to little or nothing in the way of competing views. It is easily imaginable that the content of the most widely viewed programming will be affected by the desires of advertisers, in such a way as to produce shows that represent a bland, watered-down version of conventional morality and that do not engage serious issues in a serious way for fear of offending some group in the audience. From the standpoint of the present, it is easily imaginable that the television—or the personal computer carrying out communications functions—will indeed become "just another appliance . . . a toaster with pictures," and that the educative or aspirational goals of the First Amendment will be lost or even forgotten.

I shall say more about these points later. For now it is safe to say that the law of free speech will ultimately have to make some hard choices about the marketplace and democratic models. It is also safe to say that the changing nature of the information market will test the two models in new ways. My principal purpose here is to discuss the role of the First Amendment and Madisonianism in cyberspace—or, more simply, the nature of constitutional constraints on government regulation of electronic broadcasting. In so doing, I will cover a good deal of ground, and a number of issues of law and policy, in a relatively short space. I do, however, offer a simple point to help organize the discussion. Madisonian conceptions of free speech make a good deal of sense even in a period in which scarcity is no longer a serious problem. I will stress the risks of sensationalism, ignorance, failure of deliberation, and balkanization—risks that are in some ways heightened by new developments. In the process, I discuss some of the questions that are likely to arise in the next generation of free speech law.

I have two other goals as well. I attempt to identify an intriguing model of the First Amendment and to ask whether that model—what I will call the *Turner* model, growing out of a Supreme Court decision of that name—is well adapted to the future of the speech market. A relatively detailed and somewhat technical discussion of *Turner* should prove useful, because the case raises the larger issues in a concrete setting.

I also urge that, for the most part, the emerging technologies do not raise new questions about basic principle but instead produce new areas for applying or perhaps testing old principles. The existing analogies are often very good, and this means that the new law can begin by building fairly comfortably on the old. The principal problem with the old law is not so much that it is poorly adapted for current issues—though in some cases it may be— but that it does not depend on a clear sense of the purpose or point of the system of free expression. In building law for an age of cyberspace, government officials—within the judiciary and elsewhere—should be particularly careful not to treat doctrinal categories as ends in themselves. Much less should they act as if the First Amendment is a purposeless abstraction unconnected to ascertainable social goals. Instead, they should keep in mind that the free speech principle has a point, or a set of points. Among its points is the commitment to democratic self-government.

III. Turner: A New Departure?

The *Turner* case is by far the most important judicial discussion of new media technologies, and it has a range of implications for the future. It is important, however, to say that *Turner* involved two highly distinctive problems: (a) the peculiar "bottleneck" produced by the current system of cable television, in which cable owners can control access to programming; and (b) the possible risk to free television programming created by the rise of pay television. These problems turned out to be central to the outcome in the case. For this reason, *Turner* is quite different from imaginable future cases involving new information technologies, including the Internet, which includes no bottleneck problem. Significantly, the Internet is owned by no one and controlled by no organization. But, at least potentially, the principles in *Turner* will extend quite broadly. This is especially true insofar as the Court adopted ingredients of an entirely new model of the First Amendment and insofar as the Court set out principles governing content discrimination, viewer access, speaker access, and regulation of owners of speech sources.

The Background

In the last decade, it has become clear that cable television will be in competition with free broadcasting. In 1992, motivated in large part by concerns about this form of competition, Congress enacted the Cable Television Consumer Protection and Competition Act (the Act). The Act contains a range of provisions designed to protect broadcasting and local producers, and also at least nominally designed to protect certain consumers from practices by the cable industry. The relevant provisions include rate regulations for cable operators, a prohibition on exclusive franchise agreements between cable operators and municipalities, and restrictions on affiliations between cable programmers and cable operators.

A major part of the Act was motivated by the fear that cable television's success could damage broadcast television. If cable flourishes, perhaps broadcasters will fail? The scenario seems at least plausible in light of important differences in relevant technologies. Broadcast television comes from transmitting antennae. It is available for free, though in its current form, it cannot provide more than a few stations. By contrast, cable systems make use of a physical connection between television sets and a transmission facility, and through this route cable operators can provide a large number of stations. Cable operators are of course in a position to decide which stations, and which station owners, will be available on cable television; cable operators could thus refuse to carry local broadcasters. To be sure, cable operators must respond to forces of supply and demand, and perhaps they would do poorly if they failed to carry local broadcasters. But because they have "bottleneck control" over the stations that they will carry, they are in one sense monopolists, or at least so Congress appears to have thought.

For purposes of policy making, an important consideration is that about

40 percent of Americans lack a cable connection and must therefore rely on broadcast stations. (This is a point of general importance in light of the possibility that access to communications technology will in the future be unequally distributed.) In the Act, the potential conflict between cable and broadcast television led Congress to set out two crucial, hotly disputed provisions. Both provisions required cable operators to carry the signals of local broadcast television stations. These "must-carry" rules were the focus of the *Turner* case.

The first provision, section 4, imposes must-carry rules for "local commercial television stations." Under the Act, cable systems with more than twelve active channels and more than three hundred available channels must set aside as many as one-third of their channels for commercial broadcast stations requesting carriage. These stations are defined to include all full-power television broadcasters, except those that qualify as "noncommercial educational" stations.

Section 5 adds a different requirement. It governs "noncommercial educational television stations," defined to include (a) stations that are owned and operated by a municipality and that transmit "predominantly noncommercial programs for educational purposes" or (b) stations that are licensed by the FCC as such stations and that are eligible to receive grants from the Corporation for Public Broadcasting. Section 5 imposes separate must-carry rules on noncommercial educational stations. A cable system with more than thirty-six channels must carry each local public broadcast station requesting carriage; a station having between thirteen and thirty-six must carry between one and three; and a station with twelve or fewer channels must carry at least one.

What was the purpose of the must-carry rules? This is a complex matter. A skeptic, or perhaps a realist, might well say that the rules were simply a product of the political power of the broadcasting industry. Perhaps the broadcasting industry was trying to protect its economic interests at the expense of cable. Here there is a large lesson for the future. New regulations, ostensibly defended as public-interested or as helping viewers and consumers, will often be a product of private self-interest and not good for the public at all. It is undoubtedly true that industries will often seek government help against the marketplace, invoking public-spirited justifications for self-interested ends.

On the other hand, some people might reasonably think that the must-carry rules were a good-faith effort to protect local broadcasters, not because of their political power, but because their speech is valuable. Their speech is valuable because it ensures that viewers will be able to see discussion of local political issues. Perhaps the must-carry rules—especially section 5, but perhaps section 4 as well—had powerful Madisonian justifications insofar as cable operators might choose stations that failed to offer adequate discussion of issues of public concern, especially to the local community. Other observers might invoke a different justification, also with Madisonian overtones. Perhaps the effort to protect broadcasters was a legitimate effort to safeguard the broadcasting industry, not because of the political power of the broadcasters, and not because of the content of broadcast service, but because millions of Americans must rely on broadcasters for their programming. Perhaps Congress wanted to ensure universal viewer access to the television market. Let us put these possibilities to one side and take up the constitutional issue. In *Turner,* the cable operators challenged sections 4 and 5 as inconsistent with the First Amendment, because those sections interfered with the operation of the speech market.

The Genesis of the Turner Model

In its response, the Court created something very much like a new model for understanding the relationship among new technologies, the speech market, and the First Amendment. This model is a competitor to the marketplace and Madisonian alternatives. And while it is somewhat unruly, it is not difficult to describe. It comes from the five basic components of the Court's response to the cable operators' challenge.

First, the Court held that cable television would not be subject to the more lenient free speech limitations applied to broadcasters. On the Court's view, the key to the old broadcast cases was scarcity, and scarcity is not a problem for cable stations. To be sure, there are possible "market dysfunctions" for cable television; as noted, cable operators may in a sense be a monopoly by virtue of their "bottleneck control." But this structural fact did not, in the Court's view, dictate a more lenient approach in the cable context. In the Court's view, the key point in the past cases had to do with scarcity.

This is an especially significant holding. It suggests that new technologies will generally be subject to ordinary free speech standards, not to the more lenient standards applied to broadcasters. Scarcity is rarely a problem for new technologies.

Second, the Court said that the Act was content-neutral, and therefore subject to the more lenient standards governing content-neutral restrictions on speech. For the Court, the central point is that "the must-carry rules, on their face, impose burdens and confer benefits without reference to the content of speech."[15] This is because "the extent of the interference does not depend upon the content of the cable operators' programming." In the Court's view, the regulations are certainly *speaker-based,* since we have to know who the speaker is to know whether the regulations apply; but they are not content-based, since they do not punish or require speech of a particular content.

This holding is also quite important. It means that Congress will be permitted to regulate particular technologies in particular ways, so long as the regulation is not transparently a subterfuge for a legislative desire to promote particular points of view. It means that Congress can give special benefits to special sources or impose special burdens on disfavored industries.

Third, the Court said that there was insufficient reason to believe that a content-based "purpose" underlay the content-neutral must-carry law. Hence the content neutrality of the law could not be impeached by an investigation of the factors that led to its enactment. The legislative findings suggested that the cable operators have an economic incentive not to carry local signals. This fact led to the important problem supporting the Act: Without the must-carry provision, Congress concluded, there would be a threat to the continued availability of free local broadcast television. The elimination of broadcast television would in turn be undesirable not because broadcasters deserve protection as such—they do not—but because (a) broadcast television is free and (b) there is a substantial government interest in assuring access to free programming, especially for people who cannot afford to pay for television. As Congress had it, the must-carry rules would ensure that the broadcast stations would stay in business.

Fourth, the Court said that strict judicial scrutiny was not required by the fact that the provisions (a) compel speech by cable operators, (b) favor broadcast programmers over cable programmers, and (c) single out certain members of the press for disfavored treatment. The fact that speech was mandated was irrelevant because the mandate was content-neutral and because cable operators would not be forced to alter their own messages to respond to the broadcast signals. So, too, the Court said that a speaker-based regulation would not face special judicial hostility so long as it was content-neutral. It was important in this regard that the regulation of this particular industry was based on the special characteristics of that industry—in short, "the bottleneck monopoly power exercised by cable operators and the dangers this power poses to the viability of broadcast television."[16] In such a case, the Court concluded, legislative selectivity would be acceptable.

Fifth, the Court explored the question whether the must-carry rules would be acceptable as content-neutral regulations of speech. Content-neutral regulations may well be invalid if they fail a kind of balancing test. The Court concluded that "intermediate scrutiny" would be applied. The Court said the appropriate test would involve an exploration whether the regulation furthers an important or substantial government interest, and whether the restriction on First Amendment freedoms is no greater than necessary to promote that government interest. The Court had no difficulty in finding three substantial interests: (a) preserving free local television, (b) promoting the widespread dissemination of information from a multiplicity of sources, and (c) promoting fair competition in the market for television programming. On the Court's view, each of these interests was both important and legitimate.

What is of particular note is the fact that interests (a) and (b) are connected with Madisonian aspirations. Thus, in an especially significant step, the Court suggested that a content-neutral effort to promote diversity may well be justified. In its most straightforward endorsement of the Madisonian view, the Court said that "assuring that the public has access to a multiplicity of information sources is a governmental purpose of the highest order, for it promotes values central to the First Amendment."[17] The Court expressed special concern, in a perhaps self-conscious echo of *Red Lion*, over the cable operator's "gatekeeper control over most (if not all) of the television programming that is channeled into the subscriber's home."[18] The Court also emphasized "[t]he potential for abuse of this private power over a central avenue of communication." It stressed that the First Amendment "does not disable the government from taking steps to ensure that private interests not restrict, through physical control of a critical pathway of communication, the free flow of information and ideas."

On the other hand, the Court thought that it was impossible to decide the case without a better factual record than had been developed thus far. As it stood, the record was insufficient to show whether the must-carry rules would serve these legitimate interests. Would local broadcasters actually be jeopardized without the must-carry rules? Here we should return to the possibility, of which the Court was surely aware, that the rules were really an effort to favor the broadcasting industry, not to help viewers.

The Court suggested that courts should maintain a basic posture of deference to Congress's predictive judgments. On the other hand, Congress's judgments would face a form of independent judicial review, designed to ensure that Congress had made "reasonable inferences based on substantial evidence."[19] The Court therefore remanded the case to the lower court for factual findings on (a) the question whether cable operators would refuse significant numbers of broadcast stations without the must-carry rules and (b) the question whether broadcast stations, if denied carriage, would deteriorate to a substantial degree or fail altogether.

Justice O'Connor's dissenting opinion, joined by three other Justices, also deserves some discussion, since the opinion may have considerable future importance in view of the obvious internal fragmentation of the Court on these questions. Justice O'Connor insisted above all that the must-carry rules were based on content. To reach this conclusion, she investigated the Act and its history to show that the nominally neutral measures were in fact designed to promote local programming. In her view, the existence of content discrimination was not decisive against the must-carry rules. It was still necessary to see whether the government could bring forward a strong interest and show that the regulation promoted that interest. But Justice O'Connor found that the government could not meet its burden.

In Justice O'Connor's view, the interest in "localism" was insufficient justification. In words that have considerable bearing on what government may do with any information superhighway:

> It is for private speakers and listeners, not for the government, to decide what fraction of their news and entertainment ought to be of a local character and what fraction ought to be of a national (or international) one. And the same is true of the interest in diversity of viewpoints: While the government may subsidize speakers that it thinks provide novel points of view, it may not restrict other speakers on the theory that what they say is more conventional.[20]

Justice O'Connor referred independently to the interests in public-affairs programming and educational programming, finding that these interests are "somewhat weightier" than the interest in localism. But in her view, "it is a difficult question whether they are compelling enough to justify restricting other sorts of speech."[21] Because of the difficulty of that question, Justice O'Connor did not say whether "the Government could set some channels aside for educational or news programming."

In her view, the Act was too crudely tailored to be justified as an educational or public-affairs measure. The Act did not neutrally favor educational or public-affairs programming, since it burdened equally "CNN, C-Span, the Discovery Channel, the New Inspirational Network, and other channels with as much claim as PBS to being educational or related to public affairs."[22] Whether or not a neutral law favoring educational and public-affairs programming could survive constitutional scrutiny, this Act could not, for it was insufficiently neutral.

IV. The Turner Model

Description

I have noted that there have been two free speech traditions and two principal models of free speech. The marketplace model eschews content regulation; it is animated by the notion of consumer sovereignty. The Madisonian model may permit and even welcome content regulation; it is rooted in an understanding of political sovereignty. There is now a third model—the *Turner* model—of what government may do. An interesting question, not fully resolved by *Turner* itself, has to do with the extent to which the *Turner* model will incorporate features of its predecessors.

The new model has four simple components. Under *Turner*, (a) government may regulate (not merely subsidize) new speech sources so as to ensure *access for viewers* who would otherwise be without free programming, *and* (b) government may require owners of speech sources to provide access to *speakers*, at least if the owners are not conventional speakers too; *but* (c) government must do all this on a content-neutral basis (at least as a general rule); *but* (d) government may support its regulation not only by reference to the provision of "access to free television programming," but also by invoking such democratic goals as the need to ensure "an outlet for exchange on matters of local concern" and "access to a multiplicity of information sources."

Remarkably, every Justice on the Court appeared to accept (a), (b), and (c) and parts of (d) (with minor qualifications). Perhaps the most notable feature of the Court's opinion is its emphasis on the legitimacy and the importance of ensuring general public (viewer) access to free programming. In this way, the Court accepted at least a modest aspect of the Madisonian ideal, connected with both political equality and broad dissemination of information. This opinion is likely to have continuing importance in governmental efforts to control the information superhighway so as to ensure viewer and listener access. The Court enthusiastically accepted this claim. It said that "to preserve access to free television programming for the 40 percent of Americans without cable" was a legitimate interest. This holding suggests that the government may provide access not only through subsidies, but also through regulation.

On the other hand, the Court's quite odd refusal to distinguish between sections 4 and 5 and its use of the presumption against content discrimination seem to support the marketplace model. Certainly, the Court did not say that it would be receptive to content discrimination if the discrimination were an effort to promote attention to public affairs and exposure to diverse sources. The Court did not claim or in any way imply that educational and public-affairs programming could be required consistently with the First Amendment. On the contrary, it suggested that it would view any content discrimination, including content discrimination having these goals, with considerable skepticism. The result is a large degree of confusion with respect to whether and how government may promote Madisonian aspirations. I will return to this point.

A Problem: Commerce versus Public Affairs

From the standpoint of traditional free speech argument, there is an obvious problem with the analysis offered by the *Turner* Court. Section 4 and section 5 are quite different; they appear to have different justifications. In any case, different carriage requirements in the two sections, targeted to two different kinds of broadcasting, plainly reveal content discrimination. The two sections explicitly define their correlative obligations in terms of the nature, or content, of the programming. This is proof of content discrimination.

How should that discrimination be handled? Under the Madisonian view, there is all the difference in the world between section 4 and section 5. As I have noted, section 5 imposes certain carriage requirements for educational and public-affairs stations, whereas section 4 imposes different carriage requirements for commercial stations. For Madisonians, section 5 stands on far firmer ground, since it is apparently an effort to ensure education and attention to public issues. It seems to serve straightforward democratic functions. This does not mean that it is necessarily legitimate. Perhaps Justice O'Connor's response—to the effect that section 5 does not adequately promote that goal—is decisive against a Madisonian defense of section 5. But section 4 stands on far weaker ground from the Madisonian standpoint. Thus, Madisonians would distinguish between the two provisions and would be far more hospitable toward section 5.

In fact, the Court should have analyzed the two sections differently. The validity of section 4 turned on whether the factual record could support the idea that the section was necessary to ensure the continued availability of free public television. On this score, the Court's basic solution—a remand—was quite reasonable, even if the statute was treated as content-based. On remand, the question would be whether content regulation of this sort was sufficiently justified as a means of saving free public television.

The analysis for section 5 should be quite different. The provision of educational and public-affairs programming is entirely legitimate, certainly if there is no substantial intrusion on speakers who want to provide another kind of programming. The validity of section 5 thus should have turned on whether it was sufficiently tailored to the provision of educational and public-affairs programming. In short, both provisions are content-based, but this phrase should not be used as a talisman. The question was whether the content-based restrictions were sufficiently connected with legitimate goals.

On the other hand, within the marketplace model, the very existence of two separate sections is problematic. Why should the government concern itself with whether stations are commercial or noncommercial? Marketplace advocates would find the Act objectionable simply by virtue of the fact that it distinguishes between commercial and noncommercial stations. To them, the fact that two different sections impose different carriage requirements shows that there is content discrimination in the Act.

Under the two prevailing free speech models, then, it would make sense either to treat section 5 along a different track from section 4 (the better approach), or to question them both as content-discriminatory on their face. Both of these approaches would have been quite plausible. Remarkably, however, no Justice in *Turner* took either approach. Indeed, no Justice drew any distinction at all between section 4 and section 5, and no Justice urged that the existence of two different sections showed that there was content discrimination.

A Paradox and a Provisional Solution: Madisonians and Marketeers versus Turner?

Now let us proceed to a larger matter. As I have noted, the *Turner* Court did not accept a Madisonian model of free speech. The distinction between content-based and content-neutral restrictions was crucial to the opinion, and that distinction hardly emerges from a Madisonian model, which would carve up the free speech universe in a different way. But the Court certainly did not accept the marketplace model in its entirety. In addition to emphasizing the legitimacy of ensuring access to free programming—and of doing so through regulation rather than subsidy—the Court stressed more or less democratic justifications for the must-carry rules, including broad exposure to programming on public issues and to a multiplicity of sources of information.

The Paradox

An especially distinctive feature of the Court's opinion is its ambivalence about the legitimacy of governmental efforts to promote diversity. There is ambivalence on this score because while the Court invoked diversity as a goal, it also made its skepticism about content based regulation quite clear, and many imaginable efforts to promote diversity are content based. Consider the fairness doctrine as well as many European initiatives to promote diversity in the media. The Court found it necessary to insist that Congress was not trying, through the must-carry rules, to ensure exposure to local news sources.

On the other hand, the Court suggested that a content-neutral effort to promote diversity may well be justified. Hence the Court offered a number of justifications for regulation of cable technology. As we have seen, the Court expressed concern over the cable operator's "gatekeeper control over most (if not all) of the television programming that is channeled into the subscriber's home."[23] The Court emphasized "[t]he potential for abuse of this private power over a central avenue of communication." The Court stressed that the First Amendment "does not disable the government from taking steps to ensure that private interests not restrict, through physical control of a critical pathway of communication, the free flow of information and ideas." And thus the Court emphasized "the importance of local broadcasting units" in promoting attention to public issues.

There is therefore an important paradox at the heart of the *Turner* model. The paradox emerges from (a) the presumptive invalidity of content-based restrictions, accompanied by (b) the insistence by the Court on the legitimacy of the goals of providing access to a multiplicity of sources and outlets for exchanges on issues of local concern. This is a paradox because if these goals are legitimate, content-based regulation designed to promote them might well be thought legitimate too. If government may engage in content-neutral restrictions designed self-consciously to provide access to many sources, why may it not favor certain speech directly? The most natural way to provide certain kinds of programming is through content-based regulation.

Substantive Doctrine and Institutional Constraints

Despite appearances, there is good reason for the *Turner* Court's skepticism toward content-based regulation, and the reason operates by reference to institutional considerations involving the distinctive characteristics of judge-made doctrine. Those considerations have everything to do with the potential superiority of (not entirely accurate) rules of law over highly individuated, case-by-case judgments. This defense of *Turner* does not say that the case reflects the best understanding of the substantive content of the free speech principle, but that it may be the best way for the Supreme Court to police that principle in light of its institutional limits.

In brief: In light of the nature of the current electronic media, in which scarcity is a decreasing problem, a presumptive requirement of content neutrality may well be the best way for judges to police objectionable governmental purposes, especially in the form of viewpoint discrimination. If government favors speech of certain kinds through content regulation, there is always a risk that it is actually trying to favor certain views. For example, a regulatory requirement of discussion of abortion, race relations, or feminism would raise serious fears to the effect that government is seeking to promote certain positions. Through insisting on content neutrality—again, at least as a presumption—courts can minimize the risk of impermissibly motivated legislation, and they can do so while limiting the institutional burden faced by judges making more individualized judgments. The presumption in favor of content neutrality has the fortunate consequence of making it unnecessary for courts to answer hard case-by-case questions about the legitimacy of diverse initiatives, many of which will, predictably, be based on illegitimate motivations.

We might thus offer a cautious defense of the *Turner* model over the Madisonian model. The defense would depend on the view that the *Turner* model may well best combine the virtues of (a) judicial administrability (a real problem for Madisonians), (b) appreciation of the risk of viewpoint discrimination (a real problem for Madisonians too), and (c) an understanding of the hazards of relying on markets alone (addressed by *Turner*, insofar as the Court allows Congress considerable room to maneuver). For this reason, the *Turner* model may well be better, at least in broad outline, than the Madisonian and marketplace alternatives.

Countervailing Considerations

There are important countervailing considerations. As indicated previously, the application of the *Turner* model to technologies other than cable raises serious problems, for cable presents the special question of "bottleneck control." Many of the other new technologies raise questions not involving anything like "bottleneck control," which was central to the resolution in *Turner*. In general, regulation of the Internet raises no such problem. In *Turner*, moreover, the principal access issue was the right to hear; in other cases, the central issue, also one of access, will involve the right to speak. Sometimes the principal question will be whether certain speakers can have access to certain audiences. In other contexts, regulatory efforts may involve straightforward educational goals, as in guarantees of free media time to candidates or in provisions to ensure public-affairs programming or programming for children.

As I have argued, moreover, speech should not be treated as a simple commodity, especially in a period dominated by attention to sensationalistic scandals and low-quality fare. In light of the cultural consequences of broadcasting—through, for example, its effects on democratic processes and children's education—we should not think of electronic media as "just . . . appliance[s]," or as "toaster[s] with pictures." At least part of the First Amendment inquiry should turn on the relationship between what broadcasters provide and what a well-functioning democracy requires. If we have any sympathy for Brandeis's judgment—shared by Madison—that "the greatest menace to freedom is an inert people," we will acknowledge that the marketplace model may not perform an adequate educative role, and that a system of free markets may well disserve democratic ideals.

Of course, there are hard issues about which bodies are authorized to decide what programming ought to be offered. But the *Turner* model is vulnerable insofar as it brackets the deeper issues and addresses Madisonian concerns with the useful but crude doctrinal categories "content-based" and "content-neutral." Those categories are crude because they are not tightly connected with any plausible conception of the basic point or points of a system of free speech.

Some qualifications of the *Turner* model, pointing in Madisonian directions, are therefore desirable. The majority does not foreclose such qualifications, and Justice O'Connor's dissenting opinion actually makes some space for arguments of this sort. I will suggest some important qualifications that are nonetheless consistent with the general spirit of *Turner* itself.

V. Speech, Emerging Media, and Cyberspace

New Possibilities and New Problems: Referenda in Cyberspace and Related Issues

It should be unnecessary to emphasize that the explosion of new technologies opens up extraordinary new possibilities. As the Department of Commerce's predictions suggest, ordinary people are starting to be able to participate in a communications network in which hundreds of millions of people, or more, can communicate with each other and indeed with all sorts of service providers—libraries, doctors, accountants, lawyers, legislators, shopkeepers, pharmacies, grocery stores, museums, Internal Revenue Service employees, restaurants, and more. If you need an answer to a medical question, you may be able to push a few buttons and receive a reliable answer. If you want to order food for delivery, you may be able to do so in a matter of seconds. If you have a question about sports, music, or clothing, or about the eighteenth century, you can get an instant answer. People can now purchase many goods on their credit cards without leaving home. It may now be possible to receive a college education without leaving home.

As I have suggested, the very notions of "location" and "home" will change in extraordinary ways. Many of the relevant changes have already occurred. Consider the fact that in 1989, there were about 47.5 million cable television subscribers, accounting for 52.5 percent of television households, whereas by 1995, there were 59 million subscribers, accounting for 61.8 percent of television households.[24] (See Table 7.1) The number of subscribers to major online services is also increasing rapidly, with 6.3 million American subscribers. (See Table 7.2).

Economics and Democracy

Technological developments enjoyed by so many people bring with them extraordinary promise and opportunities from the standpoints of both Madisonianism and the marketplace. From nearly any point of view, nostalgia for pre-existing speech markets makes little sense.

The economic point is obvious, for the costs of transacting—of obtaining information and entering into mutually beneficial deals—will decrease enormously, and hence it will be much easier for consumers to get what they want, whatever it is that they want. To say the least, a shopping trip—for groceries, books, medicines, housing, trial transcripts, clothing—will be much simpler than it now is; it may well be significantly simpler now than it was when this chapter was first written.

At the same time, and equally important, there are potential democratic gains, since communication among citizens and between citizens and their representatives will be far easier. Citizens may be able to express their views to public officials and to receive answers more effectively. To state a view or ask a question on the issue of the day, no town meeting need be arranged. High-quality, substantive discussions may well be possible among large numbers of

Table 7.1. Cable Use

Year	Millions of TV Households	Millions of Homes Passed by Cable	Homes Passed as a Percentage of TV Homes	Millions of Cable Households	Cable Subscribers as a Percentage of Homes Passed	Cable Penetration of TV Households (%)
1989	90.4	80.0	88.5	47.5	59.4	52.5
1990	92.1	84.4	91.6	50.5	59.8	54.8
1991	93.1	87.2	93.7	52.6	60.3	56.5
1992	92.1	88.9	96.5	54.3	61.1	59.0
1993	93.1	90.1	96.8	56.2	62.4	60.4
1994	94.2	91.3	96.9	57.2	62.7	60.7
1995	95.4	92.5	97.0	59.0	63.8	61.8

Source: "NRTC Executive: DirecTv a Big Hit," *Multichannel News*, Dec. 15, 1994, at 32.

people; town meetings that are genuinely deliberative may become common-place. Voting may occur through the Internet. It will also be possible to obtain a great deal of information about candidates and their positions.

In fact, much of this has already occurred. The practice of journalism has changed in the sense that reporters communicate regularly with readers. Before the 1994 elections, public library computers delivered considerable information about the candidates via the World Wide Web of the Internet. The Web also allows people to see photographs of candidates and to have access to dozens of pages of information about them and their positions. An enormous number of elected officials—in the White House, the Senate, and the House—now have e-mail addresses and communicate with their constituents in cyberspace. In Minnesota, five candidates for governor and three candidates for the Senate participated in debates on electronic mail. In 1993, President Clinton established connections with millions of e-mail users, putting his

Table 7.2. Internet Use

Technology	Number of Users
Internet	30–40 million
CompuServe	2,700,000
America Online	2,300,000
Prodigy	2,000,000
The WELL	11,000
Women's Wire	1300

Source: This table was compiled on the basis of data in John Flinn, "The Line on On-Line Services," *S.F. Examiner*, March 1, 1995, at B1, and Philip Elmer-DeWitt, "Welcome to Cyberspace," *Time*, Spring 1995 (Special Issue), at 9. In some countries the number of Internet users has grown more than 1000 percent in the past three years. *Id.*

address into their system and inviting them to give reactions on public issues. Candidates generally are obtaining and publicizing e-mail addresses. The Madisonian framework was based partly on the assumption that large-scale substantive discussions would not be practicable. Technology may well render that assumption anachronistic.

The result may be of particular benefit for people of moderate or low income. People without substantial means may nonetheless make their views heard. So, too, relatively poor candidates may be able to communicate more cheaply. In this way, the new communications technologies may relieve some of the pressure for campaign finance restrictions by promoting the Madisonian goal of political equality. In the midst of economic inequality, perhaps technological advances can make political equality a more realistic goal.

Moreover, education about public issues will be much simpler and cheaper. The government, and relevant interest groups, will be able to state their cases far more easily. And after touching a few buttons, people will be able to have access to substantial information about policy dilemmas—possible wars, environmental risks and regulations, legal developments, trials, medical reform, and a good deal more. Consider simply one example, the astonishing service LEXIS Counsel Connect. With this service, a lawyer can have access to essentially all proposed laws. A lawyer can also join substantive "discussion groups," dealing with, for instance, recent tax developments, risk regulation, securities arbitration, affirmative action, LEXIS Counsel Connect, cyberspace, the First Amendment in cyberspace, and much more. The proliferation of law-related discussion groups on law-related topics is one tiny illustration of a remarkable cultural development. Thus, the Usenet includes more than 10,000 discussion groups, dealing with particle physics, ring-tailed lemurs, and Rush Limbaugh, among countless others.

Dangers

At least from the standpoint of the founding era, and from the standpoint of democratic theory, the new technology also carries with it significant risks. There are two major problems. The first is an absence of deliberation. The second is an increase in social balkanization.

Absence of Deliberation   The Madisonian view of course places a high premium on public deliberation, and it disfavors immediate and inadequately considered government reactions to pressures from the citizenry. The American polity is a republic, not a direct democracy, and for legitimate reasons; direct democracy is unlikely to provide successful governance, for it is too likely to be free from deliberation and unduly subject to short-time reactions and sheer manipulation. From the inception of the American system, a large goal of the system of republicanism has been to "refine and enlarge the public view" through the system of representation.

This process of refinement and enlargement is endangered by decreased costs of communication. As I have noted, discussions in cyberspace may well be both substantive and deliberative; electronic mail and the Internet in particular hold out considerable promise on this score. But communications between citizens and their representatives may also be reactive to short-term impulses and may consist of simple referenda results insufficiently filtered by reflection and discussion.

In the current period, there is thus a serious risk that low-cost or costless communication will increase government's responsiveness to myopic or poorly considered public outcries, or to sensationalistic or sentimental anecdotes that are a poor basis for governance. Although the apparent presence of diverse public voices is often celebrated, electoral campaigns and treatment of public issues already suffer from myopia and sensationalism, and in a way that compromises founding ideals. On this count, it is hardly clear that new technologies will improve matters. They may even make things worse. The phenomenon of "talk radio" has achieved considerable attention in this regard. It is surely desirable to provide forums in which citizens can speak with one another, especially on public issues. But it is not desirable if government officials are responding to immediate reactions to misleading or sensationalistic presentations of issues.

Ross Perot's conception of an "electronic town meeting" is hardly consistent with founding aspirations, at least if the meeting has the power to make decisions all by itself. Democracy by soundbite is hardly a perfect ideal. New technologies may make democracy by soundbite far more likely. Everything depends on how those technologies are deployed in communicating to public officials.

We can make these points more vivid with a thought experiment. Imagine that through the new technologies, the communications options were truly limitless. Each person could design her own communications universe. Each person could see those things that she wanted to see, and only those things. Insulation from unwelcome material would be costless. Choice of particular subjects and points of view would be costless too. Would such a system be a communications utopia? Would it fulfill First Amendment aspirations?

The answer is by no means simple. Of course a system of this kind would have advantages. It might well overcome some of the problems produced by extremes of wealth and poverty, at least insofar as poor people could both speak and hear far more cheaply. But the aspiration to an informed citizenry may not be well served. Under the hypothesized system, perhaps most people would be rarely or poorly informed. Perhaps their consumption choices would disserve democratic ideals. If the system of free expression is designed to ensure against an "inert people," we cannot know, *a priori*, whether a system of well-functioning free markets would be desirable.

Balkanization and Self-Insulation   The hypothesized system would have another problem: It would allow people to screen out ideas, facts, or accounts of facts that they find disturbing. In the current system, people are often confronted with ideas and facts that they find uncongenial. This is an important democratic good; it promotes education and discussion. A well-functioning system of free expression is one in which people are exposed to ideas that compete with their own, so that they can test their own views and understand other perspectives even when they disagree. This process can produce a capacity for empathy and understanding, so that other people are not dehumanized even across sharp differences in judgment and perspective. Important forms of commonality and respect might emerge simply by virtue of presenting the perspectives of others from others' points of view.

A system of individually designed communications options could, by contrast, result in a high degree of balkanization, in which people are not presented with new or contrary perspectives. Such a nation could not easily satisfy democratic and deliberative goals. In such a nation, communication among people with different perspectives might be far more difficult than it now is; mutual intelligibility may become difficult or even impossible. In such a nation, there may be little commonality among people with diverse commitments, as one group caricatures another or understands it by means of simple slogans that debase reality and eliminate mutual understanding.

These suggestions are far from hypothetical. They capture a significant part of the reality of current communications in America. They create serious risks.

A Caution About Responses

It is far from clear how government can or should overcome these various problems. Certainly government should not be permitted to censor citizen efforts to communicate with representatives, even if such communications carry risks to deliberative ideals. It does seem clear, however, that government should be cautious about spurring on its own the use of new technologies to promote immediate, massive public reactions to popular issues. Government by referendum is at best a mixed blessing, with possible unfortunate consequences wherever it is tried. The electronic media should not be used to create a form of government by referendum. Regulatory efforts to facilitate communication need not be transformed into an effort to abandon republican goals.

Rather than spurring referenda in cyberspace, or referenda by soundbite, government should seek to promote deliberation and reflection as part of the process of eliciting popular opinion.[25] Any such efforts might well be made part of a general strategy for turning new communications technologies to constitutional ends. As we have seen, electronic mail has considerable promise on this score.

Some Policy Dilemmas

A large question for both constitutional law and public policy has yet to receive a full democratic or judicial answer: To what extent, if any, do Madisonian ideals have a place in the world of new technologies or in cyberspace? Some people think that the absence of scarcity eliminates the argument for governmental regulation, at least if it is designed to promote attention to public issues, to increase diversity, or to raise the quality of public debate. If outlets are unlimited, why is regulation of any value? In the future, people will be able to listen to whatever they want, perhaps to speak to whomever they choose. Ought this not to be a constitutional ideal?

The question is meant to answer itself, but perhaps enough has been said to show that it hardly does that. Recall first that structural regulation, assigning property rights and making agreements possible, is a precondition for well-functioning markets. Laissez-faire is a hopeless misdescription of free markets. A large government role, with coercive features, is required to maintain markets. Part of the role also requires steps to prevent monopoly and monopolistic practices.

Moreover, Madisonian goals need not be thought anachronistic in a period of infinite outlets. In a system of infinite outlets, the goal of consumer sovereignty may well be adequately promoted. That goal has a distinguished place in both law and public policy, but it should not be identified with the Constitution's free speech guarantee. The Constitution does not require consumer sovereignty; for the most part, the decision whether to qualify or replace that goal with Madisonian aspirations should be made democratically rather than judicially. A democratic citizenry armed with a constitutional guarantee of free speech need not see consumer sovereignty as its fundamental aspiration. Certainly it may choose consumer sovereignty if it likes. But instead it may seek to ensure high-quality fare for children, even if this approach departs from consumer satisfaction. It may seek more generally to promote educational and public-affairs programming.

The choice between these alternatives should be made through the political branches rather than as a matter of constitutional law. I now try to support this basic conclusion and to do so in a way that is attuned to many of the pathologies of "command-and-control" regulation. The goal for the future is to incorporate Madisonian aspirations in a regulatory framework that is alert to the difficulty of anticipating future tastes and developments, that sees that incentives are better than commands, and that attempts to structure future change rather than to dictate its content.

Advertising

It is commonly thought that viewers and listeners purchase a communications product, and that their purchase decisions should be respected; but this picture is not altogether right. The decisions of viewers and listeners are different from most consumption decisions, in the sense that viewers and listeners often pay nothing for programming, and often they are, in a sense, the product that is being sold. For much commercial programming, a key source of revenues is advertisers, and programmers deliver viewers to advertisers in return for money. For this reason, the broadcasting market is not a conventional one in which people purchase their preferred products. Our viewing and listening time is bought and sold.

There is an important consequence for the substantive content of broadcasting: What is provided in a communications market is not the same as what viewers would like to see. Advertisers have some power over the content of communication, for they may withdraw their support from disfavored programming. They may withdraw their support not simply because the programming does not attract viewers, but also because (a) the programming is critical of the particular advertisers, (b) it is critical of commerce is general, (c) it stirs up a controversial reaction from some part of the audience, or (d) it is "depressing" or creates "an unfavorable buying atmosphere." There is a great deal of evidence that advertiser control does affect the content of programming.[26] Controversial programs have been punished; presentations of contested issues, such as abortion, have been affected by advertisers' goals.

In an era of numerous options, the influence of advertising over programming content should be less troublesome, since controversial points of view should find an outlet. Certainly there is no such problem on the Internet. But there will nonetheless continue to be a structural problem in broadcasting markets, since viewers' demand for programs will not be fully responsible for the programs that are actually provided. Many imaginable proposals could help counter this problem. Such proposals should not be found unconstitutional, even if consumer sovereignty is the overriding policy goal.

"Choice" and Culture

If we put the questions raised by advertisers to one side, we might urge that there is a decisive argument in favor of the marketplace model and against Madisonianism. The marketplace ideal values "choice," whereas the Madisonian alternative can be seen to reflect a form of dangerous paternalism or disrespect for people's diverse judgments about entertainment options. Perhaps Madisonianism is illiberal insofar as it does not respect the widely divergent conceptions of the good that are reflected in consumption choices.

The argument is certainly plausible. In most arenas, consumers are allowed to choose as they wish, and governmental interference requires special justification. But in this context, at least, the argument from choice is quite unconvincing, for it wrongly takes people's consumption choices as definitive or exhaustive of choice. In fact, the notion of "choice" is a complex one that admits of no such simple understanding (chapters 1 and 2). In a democratic society, people make choices as citizens too. They make choices in democratic arenas as well as in stores and before their computers. What those choices are depends on the context in which they are made.

For this reason, the insistence on respect for choice, as a defense of the marketplace model, sets up the legal problem in a question-begging way. People do make choices as consumers, and these choices should perhaps be respected. But those choices are heavily geared to the particular setting in which they are made—programming consumption. They do not represent some acontextual entity called "choice." In fact, there is no such acontextual entity.

The question is not whether or not to respect choice, but what sorts of choices to respect. More particularly, the question is whether to allow democratic choices to make inroads on consumption choices. In a free society, consumption choices should usually be respected. But the Constitution does not require this result, and in many settings, democratic judgments contrary to consumption choices are legitimate. For example, a requirement that broadcasters provide free media time for candidates might well receive broad public support, even if viewers would, at the relevant time, opt for commercial programming. There should be no constitutional barrier to such a requirement.

The central point is that in their capacity as citizens assessing the speech market, people may well make choices, or offer considered judgments, that diverge from their choices as consumers. Acting through their elected representatives, the public may well seek to promote (for example) educational programming, attention to public issues, and diverse views. Perhaps the public— or a majority acting in its democratic capacity—believes that education and discussion of public issues are both individual and collective goods. Any system of expression has cultural consequences; it helps create and sustain a certain kind of culture. Perhaps the public wants to ensure a culture of a certain sort, notwithstanding its consumption choices. Perhaps it seeks to protect children and adolescents and sees regulation of broadcasting as a way of accomplishing that goal. Perhaps people believe that their own consumption choices are less than ideal, and that for justice-regarding or altruistic reasons, or because of their basic commitments and judgments, regulations should force broadcasters or cable operators to improve on existing low-quality fare.

Perhaps people seek and hence choose to ensure something like a political community, not in the sense of a place where everyone believes the same thing, but in the sense of a polity in which people are generally aware of the issues that are important to the future of the nation. Perhaps people think that the broadcasting media should have a degree of continuity with the educational system, in the sense that broad dissemination of knowledge and exposure to different views are part of what citizens in a democratic polity deserve. Perhaps people believe that many citizens do not value certain high-quality programming partly because they have not been exposed to it, and perhaps experiments are designed to see if tastes for such programming can be fueled through exposure.

Would measures stimulated by such thoughts be objectionable, illegitimate, or even unconstitutional? I do not believe so. Surely any such efforts should be policed so as to ensure that government is not discriminating against or in favor of certain viewpoints. The mere fact that the democratic majority seeks to overcome consumption choices is not legitimating by itself; the democratic judgment may be unacceptable if it involves viewpoint discrimination or content discrimination suggestive of viewpoint bias. But rightly conceived, our constitutional heritage does not disable the public, acting through the constitutional channels, from improving the operation of the speech market in the ways that I have suggested. Whether it should do so is a question to be answered democratically rather than judicially.

Analogies

An important issue for the future involves the use of old analogies in novel settings. The new technologies will greatly increase the opportunities for intrusive, fraudulent, harassing, threatening, libelous, or obscene speech. With a few brief touches of a finger, a speaker is now be able to communicate to thousands or even millions of people—or to pinpoint a message, perhaps a commercial, harassing, threatening, invasive message, to a particular person. A libelous message, or grotesque invasions of privacy, can be sent almost cost-lessly. Perhaps reputations and lives will be easily ruined or at least damaged. There are difficult questions about the extent to which an owner of a computer service might be held liable for what appears on that service.

At this stage, it remains unclear whether the conventional legal standards should be altered to meet such problems. For the most part, those standards seem an adequate start and must simply be adapted to new settings. For pur-poses of assessing cyberspace, there are often apt analogies on which to draw. In fact, the legal culture has no way to think about the new problems except via analogies. The analogies are built into our very language: e-mail, electronic bulletin boards, cyberspace, cyberspaces, and much more.

Thus, for example, ordinary mail provides a promising foundation on which to build the assessment of legal issues associated with electronic mail. It is far from clear that the standards for libelous or fraudulent communication must shift with the new technologies. To be sure, there will be new and some-what vexing occasions for evaluating the old standards. Judges may not under-stand the novel situations, especially those involving the Internet. In particu-lar, the low cost of sending and receiving electronic mail, and of sending it to thousands or millions of people, may produce some new developments and put high pressure on old categories. But it is by no means clear that the basic principles will themselves have to be much changed.

Access

I have noted that the government has said that "universal access" is one of its goals for the information superhighway. The question of access has several dimensions. To some extent, it is designed to ensure access to broadcasting options for viewers and listeners. Here a particular concern is that poor people should not be deprived of access to a valuable good. Currently, the expense of Internet connections is prohibitively high for many families. This may entail a form of disenfranchisement. There is an additional problem of ensuring access for certain speakers who want to reach part of the viewing or listening public. In cyberspace, of course, people are both listeners and speakers.

Perhaps the goal of universal viewer or listener access should be viewed with skepticism. The government does not guarantee universal access to cars, housing, food, or even health care. It may seem puzzling to suggest that uni-versal access to information technologies is an important social goal. But the suggestion is less puzzling than it appears. Suppose, for example, that a certain technology becomes a principal means by which people communicate with their elected representatives; suppose that such communications become a principal part of public deliberation and in that way ancillary to the right to vote. Suppose too that relevant companies engage in a form of "electronic redlining," in which they bypass poorer areas, both rural and in the inner city.

We know that a poll tax is unconstitutional because of its harmful effects on political equality.[27] On a broadly similar principle, universal access to the network might be thought desirable. To be sure, such access would be most unlikely to be constitutionally mandated, since the right to vote is technically not involved. But universal access could be seen to be part of the goal of political equality. More generally, universal access might be necessary if the network is to serve its intended function of promoting broad discussion between citizens and representatives. It is notable that at least 7 million Americans, most of whom are poor, lack telephones, and hence are without basic access.

There is another point. For any particular speaker, part of the advantage of having access to a certain means of communication is that everyone or almost everyone, or a wide range of people, can be reached. The Postal Service, for example, is justified in part on the ground that a national system of mail is necessary or at least helpful for those who send mail; we can be assured that any letter can reach everyone. The argument is controversial. But perhaps a requirement of universal access can be justified not as an inefficient effort to subsidize people who would be without service, but on the quite different ground that universal service is a way of promoting the communicative interests of those who already have service. The interests of the latter group may well be promoted by ensuring that they can reach everyone or nearly everyone. Arguments of this kind have been used throughout the history of telecommunications regulation. For most of the twentieth century, there have been cross-subsidies, as local companies with local monopolies have charged high prices to certain customers (usually businesses) with which they subsidized less profitable services. Perhaps a similar model would make sense for modern technologies.

There are, however, significant inefficiencies in this model of cross-subsidization,[28] and a system of open-ended competition may well be better than one based on universal access. Open-ended competition may provide universal access, in any case, or something very close to it. Or it may be that open-ended competition, combined with selective subsidies, would be better than the regulatory approach. This question cannot be easily answered in the abstract. Certainly, debate over universal access should not be resolved by constitutional fiat. This is an area for public debate and a large degree of experimentation.

Incentives Rather than Command-and-Control

In general, any regulatory controls should take the form of flexible incentives rather than rigid commands. Command-and-control systems are usually ineffective in achieving their own goals; they tend to promote interest-group power, in which well-organized private groups are able to use governmental authority to redistribute wealth or opportunities in their favor; they also tend to be inefficient (chapter 13).

I cannot discuss this issue in detail here, but the explosion of new technologies reinforces the point. It is predictable that owners of some services will attempt to obtain governmental aid to disadvantage actual or potential competitors. Especially in an era of rapid and only partly foreseeable technological change, the government's basic duty is to provide a framework for competitive development, rather than specification of end-states. Any such specifications will likely prove counterproductive in light of developments that cannot now be predicted.

This is not to say that government regulation has no place, or even that government should restrict itself to the task of ensuring well-functioning markets. But even good Madisonians should insist that rigid dictates ought to be avoided. Regulation will do far better if it takes the form of incentives rather than mandates. Consider, as possible forerunners of future approaches, the FCC's use of auction systems, accompanied by the grant of "points" toward licensing,[29] for preferred licensees. Consider too the use of government subsidies to public broadcasting or to certain high-quality programs, or the transfer of resources from commercial broadcasters for the benefit of noncommercial, educational, or public-affairs programming. Initiatives of this sort would not mandate particular results but instead would create pressures to improve the speech market.

Law

The ultimate shape of constitutional constraints on regulation of the electronic media cannot be foreseen. Too many new possibilities will come into view. Too many distinctions will become relevant. Consider, for example, the fact that for many dozens of years, there has been a clear difference between two different kinds of communication. The first is ordinary broadcasting or publishing, in which an owner makes available a certain range of communications; offers that range of communications as an indivisible package for hundreds, thousands, or millions of subscribers; and sells advertising time for commercial interests. The second involves the mail, in which one person typically sends a message to another, or in which one person might send a message to a group of people; in any case, mail involves highly differentiated, rather than indivisible, communication, in the sense that no single "package" is made available to wide ranges of people. Moreover, no advertisers need be involved. Many of the complexities in free speech law have arisen from this distinction, though the implications of the distinction are of course sharply contested.

New technologies weaken or even undo the distinction between these two categories. In the long-term future, the mail analogy may become the more apposite one, as it becomes simpler and cheaper for a person to send communications to any particular person, or to a large group of people, on such terms as he chooses. Communications may decreasingly come in an indivisible package and increasingly take the particular form that the particular actors choose. In the future, "broadcasting" will increasingly have this characteristic. Often the purchaser of the relevant information will pay for it without the intermediation of advertisers. In such a future, the constitutional issues will take on different dimensions. A key question will be the extent to which the owner or manager of the "mail" may be held liable for injuries that occur as a result of the use of some service. It will be plausible to say that just as the United States and Federal Express are not liable for harms caused by packages they carry, so, too, the owner of an electronic service ought not to pay damages for harms that owners cannot reasonably be expected to prevent or control. But it is far too soon to offer particular judgments on the issues that will arise.

It is nonetheless possible to describe certain categories of regulation and to set out some general guidelines about how they might be approached. I have suggested that existing law provides principles and analogies on which it makes sense to draw. An exploration of new problems confirms this suggestion. It shows that current categories can be invoked fairly straightforwardly to make sense of likely future dilemmas.

A large lesson emerges from the discussion. Often participants in legal disputes, and especially in constitutional disputes, disagree sharply with respect to high-level, abstract issues; the debate between Madisonians and marketplace advocates is an obvious illustration. But sometimes such disputants can converge, or narrow their disagreement a great deal, by grappling with highly particular problems. In other words, debate over abstractions may conceal a potential for productive discussion and even agreement over particulars.[30] This is a strategy through which we might make much progress in the next generation of free speech law.

Requiring Competition

Many actual and imaginable legislative efforts are designed to ensure competition in the new communications markets. There is no constitutional problem with such efforts. The only qualification is that some such efforts might be seen as subterfuge for content regulation, disguised by a claimed need to promote monopoly; but this should be a relatively rare event. If government is genuinely attempting to prevent monopolistic practices, and to offer a structure in which competition can take place, there is no basis for constitutional complaint. Here First Amendment theorists of widely divergent views might be brought into agreement.

Subsidizing New Media

It is predictable that government might seek to assist certain technologies that offer great promise for the future. Such efforts may in fact be a result of interest-group pressure. But in general, there is no constitutional obstacle to government efforts to subsidize preferred communications sources. Perhaps the government believes that some technological innovations are especially likely to do well, or that they could produce particularly valuable benefits with national assistance. So long as there is no reason to believe that government is favoring speech of a certain content, efforts of this kind are unobjectionable as a matter of law.[31] They may be objectionable as a matter of policy, since government may make bad judgments reflecting confusion or factional influence; but that is a different issue.

Subsidizing Particular Programming or
Particular Broadcasters

In her dissenting opinion in *Turner*, Justice O'Connor suggested that the appropriate response to government desire for programming of a certain content is not regulation but instead subsidization.[32] This idea fits well with the basic model for campaign finance regulation, set out in *Buckley v. Valeo*.[33] It also fits with the idea, found in *Rust v. Sullivan*,[34] that the government is unconstrained in its power to subsidize such speech as it prefers. Hence there should be no constitutional objection to government efforts to fund public broadcasting, to pay for high-quality fare for children, or to support programming that deals with public affairs.[35] Perhaps government might do this for certain uses of the Internet.

To be sure, it is doubtful that *Rust* would be taken to its logical extreme. Could the government fund the Democratic Convention but not the Republican Convention? Could the government announce that it would fund only those public-affairs programs that spoke approvingly of current government policy? If we take the First Amendment to ban viewpoint discrimination, funding of this kind should be held to be improperly motivated. On the other hand, government subsidies of educational and public-affairs programming need not raise serious risks of viewpoint discrimination. It therefore seems unexceptionable for government, short of viewpoint discrimination, to subsidize those broadcasters whose programming it prefers, even if any such preference embodies content discrimination. So, too, government might promote "conversations" or fora on e-mail that involve issues of public importance, or that attempt to promote educational goals for children or even adults.

Leaving Admittedly "Open" Channels Available to
Others Who Would Not Otherwise Get Carriage

Suppose that a particular communications carrier has room for five hundred channels; suppose that four hundred channels are filled, but that one hundred are left open. Would it be legitimate for government to say that the one hundred channels must be filled by stations that would otherwise be unable be pay for carriage? Let us suppose that the stations would be chosen through a content-neutral system, such as a lottery. From the First Amendment point of view, this approach seems acceptable. The government would be attempting to ensure access for speakers who would otherwise be unable to reach the audience. It is possible that as a matter of policy, government should have to provide some payment to the carrier in return for the access requirement. But there does not seem to be a First Amendment problem.

Requiring Carriers to Be Common Carriers for a Certain Number of
Stations, Filling Vacancies with a Lottery System or Timesharing

In her dissenting opinion in *Turner*, Justice O'Connor suggested the possibility that carriers could be required to set aside certain channels to be filled by a random method. The advantage of this approach is that it would promote access for people who would otherwise be denied carriage, but without involving government in decisions about preferred content. This approach should raise no First Amendment difficulties.

Imposing Structural Regulation Designed Not to Prevent a Conventional Market Failure, but to Ensure Universal or Near-Universal Consumer Access to Networks

The protection of broadcasters in *Turner* was specifically designed to ensure continued viewer access to free programming. Notably, the Court permitted government to achieve this goal through regulation rather than through subsidy. Of course, subsidy is the simpler and ordinarily more efficient route. If government wants to make sure that all consumers have access to communications networks, why should government not be required to pay to allow such access, as in the food stamp program? The ordinary response to a problem of access is not to fix prices but instead to subsidize people who would otherwise be without access. The *Turner* Court apparently believed that it is constitutionally acceptable for the government to ensure that industry (and subscribers), rather than taxpayers, provide the funding for those who would otherwise lack access.

The precise implications of this holding remain to be seen. It is impossible to foresee the range of structural regulations that might be proposed in an effort to ensure that all or almost all citizens have access to free programming or to some communications network, including any parts of the "informational superhighway." Some regulations might in fact be based on other, more invidious motives, such as favoritism toward a particular set of suppliers; as we have seen, this may well be true of the measure in *Turner* itself. The *Turner* decision means that courts should review with some care any governmental claim that regulation is actually based on an effort to promote free access. But the key point here is that if the claim can be made on the facts, structural regulation should be found acceptable.

Protecting Against Obscene, Libelous, Violent, Commercial, or Harassing Broadcasting or Messages

New technologies have greatly expanded the opportunity to communicate obscene, libelous, violent, or harassing messages—perhaps to general groups via stations on (for example) cable television, perhaps to particular people via electronic mail. Invasions of privacy are far more likely. The Internet poses special problems on these counts. As a general rule, any restrictions should be treated like those governing ordinary speech, with ordinary mail providing the best analogy. If restrictions are narrowly tailored and supported by a sufficiently strong record, they should be upheld.

Consider in this regard a highly publicized case involving "cyberporn" at the University of Michigan. A student is alleged to have distributed a fictional story involving a fellow student, explicitly named, who was, in the story, raped, tortured, and finally killed. The first question raised here is whether state or federal law provides a cause of action for conduct of this sort. Perhaps the story amounts to a threat, or a form of libel, or perhaps the most plausible state law claim would be based on intentional infliction of emotional distress. The next question is whether, if a state law claim is available, the award of damages would violate the First Amendment. At first glance, it seems that the question should be resolved in the same way as any case in which a writer uses a real person's name in fiction of this sort. And it certainly does not seem clear that the First Amendment should prohibit states from awarding damages for conduct of this kind, so long as no political issue is involved.[36] Perhaps the ease of massive distribution of such materials, which can be sent to much of the world with the touch of a button, argues in favor of loosening the constitutional constraints on compensatory damages.

What of a regulatory regime designed to prevent invasion of privacy, libel, unwanted commercial messages, obscenity, harassment, or infliction of emotional distress? Some such regulatory regime will ultimately make a great deal of sense. The principal obstacles are that the regulations should be both clear and narrow. It is easy to imagine a broad or vague regulation, one that would seize on the sexually explicit or violent nature of communication to justify regulation that is far broader than necessary. Moreover, it is possible to imagine a situation in which liability was extended to any owner or operator who could have no knowledge of the particular materials being sent. The underlying question, having to do with efficient risk allocation, involves the extent to which a carrier might be expected to find and to stop unlawful messages; that question depends on the relevant technology.

Consider, more particularly, possible efforts to control the distribution of sexually explicit materials on the Internet. Insofar as the government seeks to ban materials that are technically obscene and imposes civil or criminal liability on someone with specific intent to distribute such materials, there should be no constitutional problem. By hypothesis, these materials lack constitutional protection, and materials lacking constitutional protection can be banned in cyberspace as everywhere else. On the other hand, many actual and imaginable bills would extend beyond the technically obscene, to include (for example) materials that are "indecent," "lewd," or "filthy." Terms of this sort create a serious risk of unconstitutional vagueness or overbreadth. At least at first glance, they appear unconstitutional for that reason.

The best justification for expansive terms of this kind would be to protect children from harmful materials. It is true that the Internet contains pornography accessible to children, some of it coming from adults explicitly seeking sexual relations with children. There is in fact material on the Internet containing requests to children for their home addresses. Solicitations to engage in unlawful activity are unprotected by the First Amendment, whether they occur on the Internet or anywhere else. For this reason, regulation designed to prevent these sorts of requests should not be held unconstitutional.

But when government goes beyond solicitation and bans "indecent" or "filthy" material in general, the question is quite different. Here a central issue is whether the government has chosen the least restrictive means of preventing the relevant harms to children. In a case involving "dial-a-porn," for example, the Court struck down a ban on "indecent" materials on the ground that children could be protected in other ways.[37] On the Madisonian view, this outcome is questionable, since dial-a-porn ranks low on the First Amendment hierarchy. But under existing law, it seems clear that in order to support an extension beyond obscenity, Congress would have to show that less restrictive alternatives would be ineffectual. The question then becomes a factual one: What sorts of technological options exist by which parents or others can provide the relevant protection? To answer this question, it would be necessary to explore the possibility of creating "locks" within the Internet, for use by parents, or perhaps for use by those who write certain sorts of materials.

Different questions would be raised by the imposition of civil or criminal liability, not on the distributors having specific intent to distribute, but on carriers who have no knowledge of the specific materials at issue and could not obtain such knowledge without considerable difficulty and expense. It might be thought that the carrier should be treated like a publisher, and a publisher can of course be held liable for obscene or libelous materials, even if the publisher has no specific knowledge of the offending material. But in light of the relatively low costs of search in the world of magazine and book publishing, it is reasonable to think that a publisher should be charged with having control over the content of its publications. Perhaps the same cannot be said for the owner of an electronic mail service. Here the proper analogy might instead be the carriage of mail, in which owners of services are not held criminally or civilly liable for obscene or libelous materials. The underlying theory is that it would be unreasonable to expect such owners to inspect all the materials they transport, and the imposition of criminal liability, at least, would have an unacceptably harmful effect on a desirable service involving the distribution of a great deal of protected speech. If carriers were held liable for distributing unprotected speech, there would inevitably be an adverse effect on the dissemination of protected speech too. In other words, the problem with carrier liability in this context is that it would interfere with protected as well as unprotected speech.

How do these points bear on the First Amendment issue with respect to the Internet? Some of the services that provide access to the Internet should not themselves be treated as speakers; they are providers of speech, but their own speech is not at issue. This point is closely related to the debate in *Turner* about the speech status of cable carriers. But whether or not a carrier or provider is a speaker, a harmful effect on speech would raise First Amendment issues. We can see this point with an analogy. Certainly it would not be constitutional to say that truck owners will be criminally liable for carrying newspapers containing articles critical of the president. Such a measure would be unconstitutional in its purposes and in its effects, even if the truck owners are not speakers. From this we can see that a criminal penalty on carriers of material that is independently protected by the First Amendment should be unconstitutional. Thus, a criminal penalty could not be imposed for providing "filthy" speech, at least if filthy speech is otherwise protected.

But a penalty imposed on otherwise unprotected materials raises a different question. Suppose that the government imposes criminal liability on carriers or providers of admittedly obscene material on the Internet. The adverse effect on unprotected speech should not by itself be found to offend the Constitution, even if there would be a harmful economic effect, and even unfairness, for the provider of the service. Instead, the constitutional question should turn on the extent of the adverse effects on the dissemination of materials that are protected by the Constitution. If, for example, the imposition of criminal liability for the distribution of unprotected speech had serious harmful effects for the distribution of protected speech, the First Amendment problem would be quite severe. But that question cannot be answered in the abstract; it depends on what the relevant record shows with respect to any such adverse effects.

To answer that question, we need to know whether carrier liability, for unprotected speech, has a significant adverse effect on protected speech as well. We need to know, in short, whether the proper analogy is to a publisher or instead to a carrier of mail. It is therefore important to know whether a carrier could, at relatively low expense, filter out constitutionally unprotected material, or whether, on the contrary, the imposition of criminal liability for unprotected material would drive legitimate carriers out of business or force them to try to undertake impossible or unrealistically expensive "searches." The answer to this question will depend in large part on the state of technology.

Imposing Content-Based Regulation Designed to Ensure Public-Affairs and Educational Programming

It can readily be imagined that Congress might seek to promote education or might try to ensure attention to public affairs via regulation or subsidy of new media. Suppose, for example, that Congress sets aside a number of channels for public-affairs and educational programming, on the theory that the marketplace provides too much commercial programming. This notion has been under active consideration in Congress. A recent bill would have required all telecommunications carriers to provide access at preferential rates to educational and health care institutions, state and local governments, public broadcast stations, libraries and other public entities, community newspapers, and broadcasters in the smallest markets.

Turner certainly does not stand for the proposition that such efforts are constitutional. By hypothesis, any such regulation would be content-based and would therefore meet with a high level of judicial skepticism. On the other hand, *Turner* does not authoritatively suggest that such efforts are unconstitutional. The Court did not itself say whether it would accept content discrimination designed to promote Madisonian goals. Certainly the opinion suggests that the government's burden would be a significant one, but it does not resolve the question.

It is notable that Justice O'Connor's opinion appears quite sensible on this point, and she leaves the issue open. As I have noted, her principal argument is that the "must-carry" rules are too crude. Crudely tailored measures give reason to believe that interest-group pressures, rather than a legitimate effort to improve educational and public-affairs programming, are at work. But if the relevant measures actually promote Madisonian goals, they should be upheld. There is of course reason to fear that any such measures have less legitimate purposes and functions, and hence a degree of judicial skepticism is appropriate. But narrow measures, actually promoting those purposes, are constitutionally valid.

VI. Madison in Cyberspace?

Do Madisonian ideals have an enduring role in American thought about freedom of speech? The Supreme Court has not said for certain; its signals are quite mixed; and the existence of new technologies makes the question different and far more complex than it once was. It is conceivable that in a world of newly emerging and countless options, the market will prove literally unstoppable, as novel possibilities outstrip even well-motivated government controls.

If so, this result should not be entirely lamented. A world in which consumers can select from limitless choices has many advantages, not least from the Madisonian point of view. If choices are limitless, people interested in politics can see and listen to politics; perhaps they can even participate in politics and in ways that were impossible just a decade ago. But that world would be far from perfect. It may increase social balkanization. It may not promote deliberation, but foster instead a series of referenda in cyberspace that betray constitutional goals.

My central point here has been that the system of free expression is not an aimless abstraction. Far from being an outgrowth of neoclassical economics, the First Amendment has independent and identifiable purposes. Rooted in a remarkable conception of political sovereignty, the goals of the First Amendment are closely connected with the founding commitment to a particular kind of polity: a deliberative democracy among informed citizens who are political equals. It follows that instead of allowing new technologies to use democratic processes for their own purposes, constitutional law should be concerned with harnessing those technologies for democratic ends—including the founding aspirations to public deliberation, citizenship, political equality, and even a certain kind of virtue. If the new technologies offer risks on these scores, they hold out enormous promise as well. I have argued here that whether that promise will be realized depends in significant part on judgments of law, including judgments about the point of the First Amendment.

Notes

1. Administration Policy Statement, 58 *Fed. Reg.* 49,026 (1993).

2. The distinction is elided in the best general treatment, Harry Kalven, Jr., *A Worthy Tradition: Freedom of Speech in America* (New York: Harper and Row, 1988).

3. Abrams v. United States, 250 U.S. 616, 624 (1919) (Holmes, J., dissenting).

4. 418 U.S. 241 (1974).

5. Syracuse Peace Council v. Television Station WTVH, 2 F.C.C.R. 5043, 5054–55 (1987).

6. See Cass R. Sunstein, *Democracy and the Problem of Free Speech* (New York: The Free Press, 1993), pp. xvi–xvii.

7. Whitney v. California, 274 U.S. 357, 375 (1927) (Brandeis, J., concurring).

8. Alexander Meiklejohn, *Free Speech and Its Relation to Self-Government* (New York: Harper, 1948).

9. 376 U.S. 254 (1964).

10. Red Lion Broadcasting Co. v. FCC, 395 U.S. 367 (1969).

11. *See* Syracuse Peace Council v. Television Station WTVH, 2 F.C.C.R. 5043, 5055 (1987).

12. Bernard Nossiter, "Lincenses to Coin Money," 240 *Nation* 402 (1985).

13. See Meiklejohn, *supra* note 8.

14. I try to do this in Sunstein, *supra* note 6.

15. Turner Broadcasting Sys., Inc. v. FCC, 114 S. Ct. 2460 (1994).

16. *Id.* at 2468.

17. *Id.* at 2470.

18. *Id.* at 2466.

19. *Id.* at 2471.

20. *Id.*

21. *Id.*

22. *Id.*

23. *Id.* at 2445, 2466.

24. See "DirecTv a Big Hit," *Multichannel News*, Dec. 15, 1994, at 32.

25. See the discussion of the deliberative opinion poll in James S. Fishkin, *Democracy and Deliberation: New Directions for Democratic Reform* (New Haven: Yale University Press, 1991), pp. 1–2, 84.

26. See the extensive discussion in Baker, at 44–70; *see also* Sunstein, at 62–66.

27. See Harper v. Virginia Bd. of Elections, 383 U.S. 663, 666 (1966).

28. See Stephen G. Breyer, *Regulation and Its Reform* (Cambridge: Harvard University Press, 1982).

29. I refer here to the FCC's quite promising auction system, in which points are granted to minority and women applicants. *See* John McMillan, "Selling Spectrum Rights," *J. Econ. Persp.*, Summer 1994, at 145.

30. See Cass R. Sunstein, *Legal Reasoning and Political Conflict* (New York: Oxford University Press, 1996).

31. This follows from Rust v. Sullivan, 500 U.S. 173 (1991).

32. Turner Broadcasting Sys., Inc. v. FCC, 114 S. Ct. 2445, 2478 (1994) (O'Connor, J., dissenting).

33. 424 U.S. 1 (1976).

34. 500 U.S. 173 (1991).

35. There is a question of policy in the background, made highly visible by controversy over government funding of the Corporation for Public Broadcasting and the

National Endowment for the Humanities. In principle, such funding is justified in light of the "public good" features of the relevant products and in light of the possibility that the funded sources can increase opportunities for preference formation by providing greater exposure to high-quality material. But the ultimate value of funding depends on a range of more practical and empirical issues that cannot be decided *a priori*, including the actual products that result, the opportunities to provide private funding instead, and the alternative use of government money.

36. See Hustler v. Falwell, 485 U.S. 46, 51–52 (1988).

37. *Sable Communications*, 492 U.S. at 128–31.

8

On Property and Constitutionalism

It is often said that the abandonment of communism in Eastern Europe has led to a large-scale transition. It is important, however, to distinguish among the quite different features of the current changes. The new reform movements actually involve three distinct movements. The first is a movement from a system of one-party domination to (some form of) democracy. The second is a movement from a command economy to one based, at least to some degree, on markets. The third is a movement from a system in which government is unconstrained by laws laid down in advance to one of constitutionalism and the rule of law.

Although important work has been taking place on all these fronts, participants in current debates generally assume that the three movements are not closely connected. At present, and for the foreseeable future, it seems clear that the transition to markets, understood as a controversial part of the general effort to promote economic development, will be foremost in the minds of the reformers. Democratization also appears on the agenda, but it usually takes a secondary role. In the meantime, the movement for constitutional reform generally draws less public attention, and indeed has been dwarfed by other matters. In many circles, the drafting and the interpretation of the constitution are thought to involve symbolic or even irrelevant matters having no real connection to the hard pragmatic work of economic and political reform.

I believe that the separation of the three movements, and the devaluation of the writing and interpretation of constitutions, are unfortunate and potentially dangerous mistakes. In fact, the current movements in Eastern Europe are closely related. The right kind of constitution could play an important role in fueling economic development and democratic reform; indeed, under current conditions, it may be indispensable to them. The wrong kind of constitution—or no constitution at all—could be devastating to progress in both of these areas.

To offer only one example: Firm constitutional protection of property rights, combined with an independent judiciary, is an excellent way of encouraging international investment in one's nation. Such devices should spur domestic investment and initiative as well. Without constitutional protection, there will be a serious obstacle to the necessary economic activity sought from international and domestic enterprises. Anyone who engages in economic activities in these nations will do so with knowledge that the state may take their property or abrogate their contracts. To say the very least, this will be an obstacle to economic development. Constitutional protection could be part of a set of mechanisms designed to establish a commitment to protection of private enterprise.

In Eastern Europe, there is a more pressing need for constitutional protection of economic and democratic liberties than there has been in the United States or the West. In the United States, for example, the process of constitution-making was simplified by the fact that well before that process began, private property, the common law, and civil society were firmly in place. The constitution-makers could build on, and attempt to protect, existing achievements. The market and the institutions of civil society antedated the Constitution; these institutions included private intermediate associations operating between the individual and the state, such as religious organizations, charitable trusts, local community groups, and business enterprises.

The task of constitution-building in Eastern Europe is both more critical and more daunting, precisely because of the absence of well-established institutions protecting market ordering and civil society. The emergent constitutions must not only create the basic governmental structures and protect the conventional catalog of liberal rights, but also concern themselves with the creation of safeguards for the transition to (some version of) market ordering. If they fail to do so, a large amount of the important work will be done on the legislative front, where there may be unique barriers to success. A particular problem is that democratic politics may make it difficult to create real markets, which will produce such transitional problems as inflation and unemployment. Even more fundamentally, the process of constitution-making and constitution-building could become irrelevant to many of the fundamental issues now facing Eastern Europe. There is a serious current danger that the moment of constitutional opportunity will be irretrievably lost; and if it is, both prosperity and democratization will be at risk.

This chapter comes in two sections. Section I briefly discusses the relationships among property, democracy, and economic growth. My principal goal is to show that property should be seen as a political right, one that reduces dependence on the state and creates the kind of security that is indispensable to genuine citizenship in a democracy. Property rights need not conflict with democracy; in a variety of ways, they help provide the preconditions for self-governance. The creation of private property also serves a number of functions indispensable to economic development.

Section II speculates about the contents of a constitution that is self-consciously designed, as Western constitutions have not been, to create a market economy and to promote the institutions of civil society. My particular goal here is to argue that constitutionalism can play a crucial role in protecting both economic development and democratic self-government. A well-drafted constitution can guard against a system in which ownership rights are effectively subject to continuous political revision; such a system reintroduces all of the problems, both economic and democratic, introduced by common ownership of property. Through cataloguing constitutional provisions, I discuss the possibility of developing a set of economic liberties specifically designed for constitution-making in Eastern Europe. Such a development might ultimately count as one of a range of contributions of the recent events to the theory and practice of constitutionalism—and to the long-overdue integration of economics and constitutionalism.

I. Property, Prosperity, Democracy

Let us begin by distinguishing between two sorts of constitutions. Westerners often think that the constitutions of Eastern European countries, before the abandonment of communism, are not constitutions at all. In fact, however, they do embody a distinct concept of constitutionalism, one that has three basic features.

- Crucially, such constitutions do not distinguish between public and private spheres. They apply their prohibitions and permissions to everyone. The government and the "private" sphere—anyone engaged in business or other activity—are equally subject to the constitution.
- Such constitutions contain duties as well as rights, and the creation of duties is a central constitutional goal. They do not merely grant privileges to citizens, but also impose obligations on them.
- Perhaps most important of all, the central provisions of these constitutions set out very general social aspirations or commitments, including a wide range of social and economic guarantees. Many provisions are designed to state those aspirations, not to create concrete entitlements that citizens can actually vindicate, through an independent judiciary, against government officials. Many "positive" rights, understood as entitlements to protection of social and economic wellbeing, are included. It is understood that these entitlements—like all other rights—are social commitments; but it is not understood that those commitments can actually be invoked against public officials.

Thus, for example, the old Soviet Constitution included the right to work, the right to rest and leisure, the right to health protection, and the right to maintenance in old age, sickness, and disability. It imposed on citizens the duty to preserve and protect socialist property and to enhance the power and prestige of the Soviet State. The Polish Constitution included the right to work, the right to rest and leisure, and the right to health protection. The current Romanian Constitution follows this model; it now includes the right to leisure, the right to work, the right to equal pay for equal work, and measures for the protection and safety of workers. The Bulgarian Constitution similarly offers the right to a holiday, the right to work, the right to labor safety, the right to social security, and the right to free medical care.

Along each of these dimensions, Western constitutions are quite different. The provisions of such constitutions generally apply only to the government and not to private actors. They do not impose duties on citizens, except to the extent that duties are implied by rights. Most important, they aim to create solid individual rights, ones that can actually be invoked by individual citizens in an independent tribunal authorized to bar governmental action. Western constitutions generally do not include broad aspirations. Social and economic guarantees are the exception, and when they exist, they are usually not subject to judicial enforcement. Although many international human rights documents recognize social and economic guarantees, few constitutions allow courts to enforce such guarantees at the behest of individual citizens.

The individual rights protected by Western constitutions are not, of course, limited to private property and economic liberties. They include other political and civil liberties and rights as well. These are indispensable safeguards (chapter 9). My principal goal here, however, is to explain how constitutionalism might work simultaneously to promote the transition to economic markets and to democracy, and for this reason it will be valuable to focus on the right to private property. In this section, I briefly outline some of the functions served by that right. The basic story should be familiar; I recount it here because it seems especially important to keep the concept of private property in mind while exploring the recent wave of constitution-making in Eastern Europe, and because the story very much bears on the project of constitutionalism, to which it is too infrequently related.

Private Property and Economic Prosperity

It is generally understood that a system of private property helps to bring about economic prosperity. There are at least four reasons for this conclusion.[1]

First, the institution of private property creates and takes advantage of the powerful human inclination to bring goods and services to oneself and to people one cares about. This claim need not depend on a proposition about the inevitability or naturalness of human selfishness. The desire to acquire goods might be deeply altruistic, in the sense that people may want to give their goods to others, including the most vulnerable members of society.

In a system of private property, the gains from the use and cultivation of ownership rights accrue to a designated owner. A system without private property stifles incentives and thus can induce both sloth and waste.[2] These points, too, need not depend on especially cynical accounts of human nature. It is necessary only to glance briefly at history, past and present, and to acknowledge that human beings will frequently attempt to accumulate resources for their own purposes—whatever the content of those purposes. Social institutions that appeal to this inclination will increase social productivity.

Second, a system of private property performs a crucial coordinating function. It ensures that the multiple desires of hundreds, thousands, or millions of consumers will be reflected in market outcomes. In this way, it protects against the perverse forms of scarcity produced by a command economy. Public officials cannot possibly know what and how much people will want in advance. Official decisions will thus create both too much and too little production. By contrast, a system of ownership rights, and generally of free alienability, signals people to devote their productive activity to areas in which that activity is most valued. A command-and-control economy is far inferior in this regard. Nearly every citizen of Eastern Europe has seen multiple illustrations of this tendency (on command-and-control, American-style, see chapters 13 and 14).

Third, the institution of private property solves, all at once, a serious collective action problem faced by people in any system without that institution. When property is unowned, no one has a sufficient incentive to use it to its full advantage or to protect it against exploitation. The creation of private property overcomes this problem.

The point can be made more vivid by a glance at the problem of environmental degradation. In recent years, it has been increasingly recognized that that problem—especially severe in Eastern Europe but of critical importance in the West as well—is in significant part a product of the collective action problem produced by the fact that the air and water are public goods, that is, collectively rather than privately owned. The consequence is that the environmental costs of polluting activity are widely diffused among the public and not "internalized," or taken into account, by polluters. Because they do not bear the direct cost, polluters lack an incentive to limit their polluting activity. This system creates a built-in tendency toward excessive pollution levels.

A system without private property can be understood as a massive version of this unfortunate state of affairs. If property is unowned, everyone has an incentive to exploit it, and no one has an incentive to use it to its full advantage. Activity levels will have no relationship to their actual social costs and benefits. Ownership rights help overcome this difficulty. They operate like a well-functioning system of environmental law; they ensure that people have incentives to take account of both the benefits and the harms of what they do. This is an exceedingly important task for a constitutional democracy.

Fourth, a system of private property creates the kind of stability and protection of expectations that are preconditions for investment and initiative, both from international and domestic sources. A company deciding whether to invest in a country will have a greater incentive to do so if it knows that its investment will be protected, and that government confiscation is prohibited by the nation's highest law. A citizen who is seeking to begin a business will be far more likely to do so if he can operate against a secure and stable background, protected against the vicissitudes of government policy. In this way, too, economic development can be facilitated by property rights.

Property and Democracy

The connection between property and prosperity may be reasonably well understood, but the right to private property has not always been considered a precondition for democracy. On the contrary, private property has frequently

been thought to present an obstacle to democracy. For this reason, it is sometimes deemed highly objectionable, or perhaps at best an institution necessary
for economic growth and therefore to be reluctantly accepted despite its corrosive effects on the democratic process.

There is indeed some tension between a system of property rights and a
system of democracy. If property rights are secure, there is a firm limit on
what the democratic process is entitled to do. In this sense, the tension is a
real and enduring one. Moreover, large accumulations of wealth, in the hands
of a few, may be harmful to political equality, a central democratic goal (chapter 7). Notably, a new market economy will likely impose conspicuous short-
term costs—unemployment and inflation—and in the emerging Eastern European democracies, there will probably be a continuous temptation to slow the
transition to markets, or perhaps to reject it altogether. For this reason, the
simultaneous transition to democracy and to economic markets—without the
protection of constitutionalism—will be exceptionally difficult.

In important respects, however, it is quite plausible to think that the right
to a stable system of property rights is actually necessary to democracy and
not opposed to it at all. At least this is so if we define a system of property as
requiring the state to create ownership rights with which it will interfere only
occasionally or in a limited way, with a provision for compensation.

The most fundamental point is that a right to own private property has an
important and salutary effect on the citizens' relationship with the state and—
equally important—on their understanding of that relationship. Because of this
effect, it can be seen as a necessary precondition for the status of citizenship.
Personal security and personal independence from the government are guaranteed in a system in which rights of ownership are protected through public institutions.

This theme has played a large role in classical republican thought. In the
republican view, the status of the citizen implies a measure of independence
from government power. This view was often associated with exclusionary or
discriminatory practices—as, for example, in the notion that people without
property should not be allowed to vote. But it is possible to deplore the exclusion without rejecting the proposition that a democratic state should attempt
to give citizens a sense of independence from the state itself. In fact, the republican tradition, read in light of modern understandings, argues not for an
abolition of private property, but instead for a system that attempts to ensure
that everyone has some. There is certainly a problem with a system in which
many citizens are without private property. But this is a challenge to existing
distributions of property, and not a challenge to the notion of private property itself.

In fact, the ownership of private property is closely associated with the
rule of law. Both of these create a realm of private autonomy in which the
citizenry can operate without fear of public intrusion. That realm is indispensable to a well-functioning public sphere. Only people with a degree of security
from the state are able to participate without fear, and with independence, in
democratic deliberations. In this sense, a sharp, legally produced distinction

between the private and the public spheres can usefully serve the public sphere. Contrary to a conventional understanding, it need not harm it at all.

Even more fundamentally, an appreciation of the functions of private property helps us make some sense of the very controversial division between "private" and "public" spheres. This division is hard to defend or even to understand if it is treated as a metaphysical one—as one that transcends human judgments and decisions—or as a denial of what is clearly true, that public power lies behind the existence and even the operation of the private sphere. A private sphere cannot easily operate without state assistance; private property is certainly a creation of the state. But if we understand the public/private division as a political one, to be justified politically and in terms of its consequences, the division between private and public becomes both intelligible and indispensable. The (social and legal) creation of a private sphere, undertaken by the state, is a key element of the process of creating civil society and market ordering. If civil society and market ordering can be justified, the existence of the private sphere itself becomes unproblematic, at least in the abstract. Of course, its particular content can always be criticized and is frequently subject to democratic redefinition.

The creation of private property can also be connected with the traditional liberal proscription against punishment under vague laws or punishment without laws at all. That proscription is designed to provide the citizenry with a wall of personal security, creating zones of freedom in which people can operate without fear. A system of private property performs these closely related functions.

The central point here is that when private property does not exist, citizens are dependent on the good will of government officials, almost on a daily basis. Whatever citizens have is a privilege and not a right. They come to the state as supplicants or beggars rather than as rightholders. Any challenge to the state may be stifled or driven underground by virtue of the fact that serious challenges could result in the withdrawal of the goods that give people basic security. A right to private property, free from government interference, is in this sense a necessary or at least helpful foundation for a democracy.

In American law, the "unconstitutional conditions doctrine"[3] operates as a response to this concern in the context of government funding, licensing, and employment. Under the unconstitutional conditions doctrine, the government may not use its power to grant (say) welfare benefits as a way to pressure the exercise of free speech rights; thus it may not say that welfare beneficiaries must agree not to criticize the president. In fact, the creation of property rights should be seen as an unconstitutional conditions doctrine written very large. The idea is that government may not use its power over property to pressure rights in general. The existence of property rights generates a strong barrier against this form of pressure, just as the unconstitutional conditions doctrine provides a degree of insulation in narrower settings.

There is a more particular sense in which private property helps to promote independence from government. If government owns the presses, or the means of distribution, freedom of speech cannot easily exist. Indeed, if government owns the newspaper itself, or distributes it in its discretion, there will be serious problems for the system of free expression. More generally, private ownership facilitates the kind of security on which diversity and pluralism depend. Political censorship may be altogether unnecessary if it is understood that current holdings are vulnerable to state control.

The final point is that one of the best ways to destroy a democratic system is to ensure that the distribution of wealth and resources is unstable and constantly vulnerable to reevaluation by the political process. A high degree of stability is necessary to allow people to plan their affairs, to reduce the effects of factional or interest group power in government, to promote investment, and to prevent the political process from breaking down by attempting to resolve enormous, emotionally laden issues about who is entitled to what. Stability and security—a sense of context—are important individual and collective goods.[4] A system in which property rights are open to continuous readjustment will produce serious harm.

In addition, government control of property—through constant readjustment of property rights—simply reintroduces the collective action problem originally solved by property rights. Public choice theory can be seen in part as a generalization of this simple insight.

Like freedom of religious conscience, the right to property helps create a flourishing civil society, an intermediate level between the government and the individual. The development of a civil society can in turn be understood as a mechanism for both creating economic prosperity and for promoting democratic self-governance. A constitutional system that respects private property should be regarded not as an effort to oppose liberal rights to collective self-government, but instead as a way of fortifying democratic processes.

I have not dealt with the question of redistribution. May a state committed to private property try to redistribute resources from some groups to others? In the West, enthusiasm for property rights is often thought to entail a reluctance to allow redistribution of wealth or (worse) complete indifference to the poor. For two reasons, however, respect for private property should not have this consequence. First, property rights help create wealth, and greater wealth will often benefit the most vulnerable as well. Time and again it has been shown that economic growth can often do more than welfare and employment programs to benefit the disadvantaged. Of course, growth does not do everything, and it must be supplemented (chapter 4). The second point, then, is that public education, literacy programs, welfare assistance, employment programs, and the like are a necessary part of any system of property rights. Such rights are best defended in self-consciously instrumental terms, because of the good things that they do. When they do not accomplish good, or enough good, they must be accompanied by other social strategies. As I have said, it is important to try to ensure not merely that everyone has a right to private property, but also that everyone actually has private property. Property rights without property ownership involve a degree of dependence that is debilitating to citizenship.

Properly understood, the defense of property rights is a defense of programs of redistribution as well. These programs should not designed to produce economic equality—a truly disastrous goal—but instead to bring about decent opportunities for all and, equally important, freedom from desperate conditions, or from circumstances that impede basic human functioning.[5]

II. Property and Constitution-Making

I have said that the task of economic development cannot be rigidly separated from the tasks of constitution-making and constitutional interpretation. Without constitutional protection of property rights, there will be continuous pressure to adjust distributions of property on an ad hoc basis. When a group of people acquires a good deal of money, it will be tempting to tax them heavily. When another group verges on bankruptcy, there will be a temptation to subsidize them. After the fact, these steps may seem fair or even necessary. But if everyone knows that government might respond in this way, there will be a powerful obstacle to the development of a market economy. No citizen—and no international or domestic investor—can be secure of his immunity from the state.

A pervasive risk is that governmental control over property rights will undo the decision, made in the basic system creating such rights, to solve a collective action problem faced by public ownership. If property rights are insecure—if they are subject to continuous governmental examination—the system will approach equivalence to one in which there are no such rights at all. This will introduce all of the problems to which a system of property rights is supposed to respond. Above all, it will create individual vulnerability to government and at the same time produce both too little and too much use of existing resources. It will deter economic development and impair the movement toward democracy as well.

In General

I have claimed that a constitution can accomplish a great deal in easing the transition to economic markets and private property. In order for it to do so, constitutional protections must be judicially enforceable. Thus, an independent court must be available to vindicate any rights that the constitution creates. Ordinary citizens must have a general right to raise constitutional objections before a tribunal authorized to provide redress against other public officials. Without judicial review, constitutions tend to be worth little more than the paper on which they are written. They become mere words, or public relations documents, rather than instruments that confer genuine rights.

While the efficacy of courts in carrying out social reform might be disputed,[6] there can be little doubt that judicially enforceable constitutions can have a significant effect on both real-world results and on legal and social culture in general. To be sure, some nations in the West have prospered with little or nothing in the way of judicial enforcement of constitutions. But these nations benefited from the background of a civil society, market economies, and well-defined property rights. For them, constitutional protections were far less important than they are for Eastern Europe.

For Eastern European nations, the drafting and interpretation of a constitution appears to pose two especially distinctive challenges. The first is to begin the process of creating a legal culture with firm judicial protection of individual rights. By individual rights I mean, first and foremost, traditional "negative" rights against government, prominent among them property ownership and freedom of contract. It is, of course, misleading to think of these as genuinely negative rights. They depend for their existence on governmental institutions willing to recognize, create, and protect them. But the defense of traditional rights need not depend on the false claim that they are negative.

The second challenge is to facilitate the creation of a market economy and a civil society—that is, a realm of private action containing institutions (churches, markets, corporations, labor unions, women's organizations, and so forth) that are independent of the state and minimally constrained by it. Through meeting these challenges, a constitution could simultaneously promote democratic goals and help bring about economic prosperity.

To carry out this task, makers and interpreters of constitutions in Eastern Europe should avoid three strategies that contain serious risks: creating unenforceable aspirations; imposing duties as well as rights; and failing to distinguish between the public and private spheres. All of these strategies are characteristic features of communist constitutionalism. Unfortunately, all of them appear to be influencing current debates in the postcommunist era. The new constitutions tend to replicate the errors of the communist constitutions themselves.

The Albanian Constitution is a typical model. It includes the right to work, the right to remuneration in cases of work stoppage, the right to a paid holiday, the right to recreation, the right to social security, guaranteed free medical service, and paid maternity leave. The Hungarian document includes the right to equal pay for equal work and—astonishingly—the right to an income conforming with the quantity and quality of work performed (a provision that, if taken seriously, will coexist most awkwardly with the notion of free markets in labor). The Slovak Constitution includes the right to work, the right to safe working conditions, the right to recreation after work and to a paid holiday, and the right to social security. It also provides rights to education and training for the disabled. The Czech Constitution includes in addition to these the right to a sound and worthy environment—a right found in the new Hungarian Constitution and in the Slovak and Romanian constitutions as well. The Bulgarian Constitution contains many similar rights. The Lithuanian Constitution protects the right to an adequate living standard and to adequate and safe working conditions, as well as the general right to "adequate payment." The Romanian Constitution requires a minimum wage, unemployment insurance, recreation after work, a right to a paid holiday, social assistance, and medical care.

In these various ways, social and economic guarantees are a prominent part of constitutions in postcommunist Eastern Europe. Let us turn, then, to risky strategies in constitution-making for that region.

Aspirations

The first risky strategy is to use a constitution as a place for setting out very general social aspirations or for imposing positive duties on government to furnish social and economic guarantees (including the provision of a social welfare state with entitlements such as equitable remuneration, leisure time, social security, and occupational safety and health). There are three reasons why this would be a dangerous strategy, at least under current conditions for Eastern Europe.

First, to state aspirations and impose positive duties—prominent of course in the Soviet Constitution—runs the risk of turning a constitution into something other than a legal document with real-world consequences. For Eastern Europe, a key current task is to make constitutions into legally binding documents. It is important to remember that if it is to create rights realistically enforceable in the world, a constitution should not list all things to which a country aspires. It should limit itself, for the most part, to rights that it is genuinely able to enforce. It is not impossible for social and welfare guarantees to be taken seriously by courts. But this is not likely, because these rights are vaguely defined, cost a great deal of money perhaps unavailable in poor nations, simultaneously involve the interdependent interests of numerous people, and depend for their existence on active management of government institutions—a task for which judges are ill-suited. The existence of unenforceable rights could in turn tend to destroy the more classical rights—freedom of speech, freedom of religion, and so forth—that might otherwise be genuine ones. If some rights are shown to be unenforceable, it is possible that others will be unenforceable as well. Thus social and economic guarantees may impair the project of producing a culture of constitutionalism and of genuine individual rights.

The second problem with social and economic guarantees is that they could work against the general current efforts to diminish the sense of entitlement to state protection and to encourage individual initiative and self-reliance. Both markets and democracy tend to develop these highly salutary characteristics. Sometimes liberal constitutionalism is praised because it responds accurately to "human nature" and does not try to tinker with it. There is undoubtedly something to this idea; efforts fundamentally to revise human character are usually doomed to failure. But liberal constitutionalism might be defended precisely on the ground that it has healthy effects on human character. When things are going well, markets and democracy tend to create certain types, with many valuable characteristics, including a strong sense of personal responsibility and initiative.

To say this is emphatically not to say that in the postreform era, nations in Eastern Europe should eliminate social welfare protections and leave their citizens to the vicissitudes of the market. Such a route would be a recipe for cruelty and disaster, since it would allow for mass suffering of the kind that is unacceptable in any nation. But these protections should be created at the level of ordinary legislation, and subject to the usual forms of democratic discussion, rather than placed in the foundational document. A serious difficulty with emergent constitutionalism in Eastern Europe is that no clear distinction is being drawn between constitutional law and ordinary law.

The third problem with social and economic guarantees is that they establish government interference with markets as a constitutional duty. The current trend is to limit such interference and to establish the preconditions for private markets, free trade, and free contract. To impose a constitutional duty of interference is to move in precisely the wrong direction.

A possible response to these points would be, first, that no constitution lacking social and economic guarantees was or is likely to be ratifiable in Eastern Europe, and, second, that constitutions should be understood not merely as a place for setting forth legal rights but also as a place for the identification of national ideals. The identification of ideals might serve educational and other functions; it might provide goals to which citizens and officials can aspire; it might inform the interpretation of statutes. There is some truth to this idea. James Madison himself understood constitutional rights in these terms.[7] Americans may well be too focused on the functions of constitutions in courts and insufficiently attentive to the cultural consequences of constitutional guarantees. This point suggests that aspirations and positive rights may perhaps belong at least in Western constitutions, to encourage political attention to fundamental matters (such as shelter, subsistence, medical care, and environmental quality) and to ensure that statutes are interpreted in the light of a full range of appropriate social commitments. Ambiguities in statutes might therefore be resolved favorably in, for example, the area of environmental protection.

In Eastern Europe, however, these ideas are less appealing in view of the unfortunate legacy of communism and the large cultural shift now underway. But perhaps a section outlining social and economic goals, and saying that they are not for judicial enforcement, could enhance the chances of ratification, play a beneficial role in public debate, and accomplish this without compromising the effort to produce genuinely enforceable rights. At most, then, I suggest that any "positive" rights and aspirations should be understood to be unenforceable. This strategy is at work in the constitution of India; it is receiving considerable attention in Poland as well.

Duties

Another strategy, posing similar risks, is to use the constitution as a place for creating "duties" as well as rights. Such duties are not likely to be enforceable through courts. Their statement in a constitution tends to weaken the understanding that the document creates protected rights, with real meaning, against the state. Moreover, countries in Eastern Europe are attempting to eliminate the effects of the notion that the state imposes duties on citizens, rather than giving them rights. It may be that in the West, more emphasis on rights has harmed social deliberation, especially in the United States, where duties should be taken more seriously. But this is the point from which Eastern Europe ought to be emerging.

There is a conceptual point in the background here: Rights and duties are reciprocal. Rights generally impose duties, and duties tend to create rights. If you have a right to freedom of speech, the state is under a duty not to restrict your right to free speech. If you have a right to be free from torture, officials are under a duty not to torture you. What I am suggesting here is that any duties should be imposed on the state, not on the citizen, and should be derivative of citizens' rights.

No Distinction Between Public and Private Spheres

Yet another risky strategy—at least for Eastern Europe—is to make constitutional provisions binding against private people and private organizations as well as against the state. In almost all Western systems, the constitution applies mostly to the government, not to the people in general. This is extremely important, because it recognizes and helps create a private sphere—a civil society that operates independently of the state. It also frees up private organizations—employers, religious organizations, unions, and so forth—to act as they choose.

If people want to apply particular constitutional provisions to particular private organizations, of course they can do so, through ordinary legislation. Often, they should do just that; bans on race and sex discrimination, for example, are an important part of statutory law in the United States. But it might well be a mistake to apply such provisions through the constitution itself, at least in Eastern Europe. Above all, this strategy works to erase the distinction between the private and public spheres, in a way that would tend to defeat current aspirations in Eastern Europe. As noted, that distinction should be enthusiastically embraced on substantive political grounds.

Ironically, these dangers are more serious for the East than for the West. In the United States, for example, the institutions of private property and civil society have been firmly in place for a long time, and social injustice frequently occurs precisely because of the absence of protections against the power of private institutions. The case for a firm right to some forms of social assistance is at least plausible in America. Such a right would not seriously jeopardize existing legal and social institutions; it could not possibly threaten the general belief in markets, solid property rights, and civil society.

Things are very different for systems that are seeking to establish free markets and civil society for the first time, and that already have a strong public commitment to a social welfare state. In such systems, the governing considerations point in the opposite direction. A legal and cultural shift, creating a belief in private property and a respect for markets, is indispensable. It therefore emerges that the case for a constitution protective of market arrangements is powerful in Eastern Europe, even if it is ambiguous in the West.

Constitutionalism and Culture

We might draw a more general conclusion from this discussion. It is often said that constitutions, as a form of higher law, must be compatible with the culture and mores of those whom they regulate. In one sense, however, the opposite is true. Constitutional provisions should be designed to work against precisely those aspects of a country's culture and tradition that are likely to produce harm through that country's ordinary political processes. There is a large difference between the risks of harm faced by a nation committed by culture and history to free markets, and the corresponding risks in a nation committed by culture and history to social security and general state protection against harms produced by markets.

In short: Constitutions should work against the particular nation's most threatening tendencies. This point explains why extremely powerful safeguards against sex discrimination and ethnic and religious oppression are necessary in Eastern Europe (a point that would take me well beyond the scope of this chapter). It is for this reason, above all, that constitutions designed for one nation are ill-adapted for use by others.

Particular Provisions

In the next generation, it would be useful to develop a set of provisions for inclusion in an "economic freedoms" section of proposed constitutions. Indeed, this section could serve as one of the many possible new contributions of current constitution-makers to the general theory and practice of constitutionalism. There is no such section in Western constitutions. Its design should be understood not as an effort to export Western ideas to Eastern Europe, but instead as an exercise in constitution-drafting intended specifically for problems in that part of the world.

I provide in this section a preliminary outline of constitutional provisions that might be adopted in the interest of creating a well-functioning system of property rights and economic markets. The outline amounts to little more than a list; it is intended only to provide a starting point for discussion.

The Rule of Law

In order to comply with the rule of law, a government must ensure that action may not be taken against citizens unless it has laid down, in advance, a pertinent law. The rule of law requires that any such restriction be clear rather than vague and publicly available rather than secret. It must also operate in the world more or less as it does on the books.

A guarantee of the rule of law is both an economic and a democratic right. It creates a wall of protection around citizens, giving insurance that they may engage in productive activity without fear of the state. And by creating this wall of protection, the guarantee creates the kind of security and independence that are prerequisites for the role of a citizen in a democracy.

Protection of Property Against Takings
Without Compensation

Many constitutions contain protections of this kind. The American Constitution embodies this idea in the Fifth Amendment, which says in part, "nor shall private property be taken for public use, without just compensation." A provision of this general sort is important on both economic and democratic grounds. Without such a provision, there is not, in fact or in law, a fully functioning system of private property.

Protection of Property Against Takings
Without Due Process

This is a procedural rather than substantive protection of property. It means that citizens will be provided with a hearing before government may interfere with their holdings. A provision of this sort accomplishes two different tasks. First, it promotes accurate fact-finding. A hearing before an independent tribunal ensures that property will not be taken capriciously or on the basis of whim, or for discriminatory or irrelevant reasons. In the hearing, it is necessary to show the facts that would justify a deprivation of property as a matter of law. Second, the right to a hearing carries out an important dignitary and participatory function. To say that people cannot be deprived of property without a hearing is to say that before it acts against them, the government must listen to what they have to say. This constraint improves governmental legitimacy as well. There is considerable evidence that people feel more secure and trustful if government affords them an opportunity to be heard before it undertakes action harmful to their interests.

Protection of Contracts

Many constitutions protect contractual liberty from governmental invasion— as in, for example, the American constitutional provision to the effect that government shall not pass any "Law impairing the Obligations of Contracts." Constitutional protection of contracts ensures that when citizens engage in economic arrangements, they can do so free from the spectre of governmental intervention. Without this right, there will be a serious deterrent to productive activity.

For those countries that choose this route, there are two central questions. The first is whether the protection applies prospectively or only retroactively. It is reasonable to think that the state should be free to create the background against which people enter into agreements, and that therefore there should be no limit on the state's power to set out, in advance, limits on the terms on which people may contract. This is the approach taken in American law, which allows the government to affect contractual ordering however it wishes, so long as it does so in advance.

The second and related question is the extent to which the "police power"—the reserved authority of government—may limit contractual freedom. It is obvious that the state can forbid contracts for murder and assault. It will probably be agreed that the state may forbid contracts to work for less than a certain monthly wage, or for more than a certain number of hours per week. But does this mean that a state can impair a contract retroactively simply because it believes that the outcome is unfair to one side? If so, freedom of contract becomes a dead letter.

There is an important issue in the background here, involving the use of government power to protect people from bargains that seem unfair. Sometimes people think that the appropriate remedy for an unfair bargain is to disallow the bargain. But it is not at all clear that this purported remedy will help the weaker side. Usually someone in bad circumstances will be presented with a range of unfavorable alternatives and will choose the least unfavorable of them. Efforts to close off that alternative may well be an ineffectual response to the situation. It will do nothing about the background conditions that make for bad alternatives; it is unlikely to be an effective way of redistributing resources or power.

General Ban on Wage and Price Controls   Limits on wages and prices—in the form of floors or ceilings—are of course a standard method for interfering with free markets. There is for this reason a plausible argument that Eastern European countries should commit themselves, in advance, to a decision not to take this course, which is often appealing in the short run but extremely destructive for the future.

A particular problem here is that well-organized private groups will frequently seek government assistance, in the form of regulatory laws enabling them to function as a cartel. This strategy might at first glance have a public interest justification, but it can ultimately be disastrous. For example, a system that creates minimum prices for milk may help some milk producers, but it will also create scarcity in an important commodity and also overcharge consumers, many of them likely to be poor. Maximum prices can in turn produce scarcity, often of important commodities. A system in which government sets minimum and maximum prices will eventually produce many of the economic and democratic problems that Eastern European nations are attempting to solve. The United States has witnessed this very problem with regulation of energy prices. Such regulation helped produce the disastrous energy crisis of the 1970s.

On the other hand, it is also plausible to think that controls on wages and prices will sometimes be desirable during and after the transition to a market economy. Even in such an economy, legal controls on wages and prices sometimes have at least plausible justifications. The category is not limited to the minimum wage; it includes price supports of various kinds as well. A ban on wage and price controls may be excessively strong medicine for the problem at hand. Perhaps a general ban with an explicit or implicit "compelling public interest" exception would make best sense.

Occupational Liberty

Protection of Free Entry into Occupations, Trades, and Business   A provision of this sort can be found in the German Constitution. This is a salutary protection against governmental restrictions on an important form of liberty, one that is part and parcel of free labor markets.

It does, however, contain an ambiguity, similar to that arising under the protection of freedom of contract. It seems clear that government can impose certain statutory limits, requiring that jobs be performed by people who are trained to do them. It can, for example, ensure that doctors actually know something about medicine, or that lawyers are trained in the law. If this is so, it will be necessary to distinguish between legitimate and illegitimate interferences with free entry into occupations, rather than simply say that the government has no role to play in this regard. This issue is probably best resolved through legislative and judicial interpretation, not in the text itself.

The Right to Choose One's Occupation   A provision of this general sort can also be found in the German Constitution. It overlaps a good deal with protection of free entry into trades and has similar virtues. It raises a similar interpretive difficulty, involving the legitimacy of provisions designed to ensure that people are genuinely qualified for jobs.

Prohibition on Forced Labor   This provision seems indispensable to the emerging Eastern European democracies. It nicely complements the right to choose one's occupation by saying that government cannot require people to engage in work that it prefers them to undertake. It also tends to guarantee free labor markets. Such a provision also carries forward, in a particularly crisp way, the traditional liberal prohibition on slavery, embodied in the general idea that "we were [not] made for one another's uses."[8]

Prohibition on Government Monopolies (de jure)

If the goal is to create a market economy, the constitution should say that government may not give itself a legal monopoly over any sector of the economy. A right of exclusive management of agriculture or telecommunications is a sure way to stifle competition and impair economic productivity. The government should be banned from embarking on this course. Under certain narrow conditions, an exception might be permitted—as, for example, where government cannot efficiently perform a certain function unless it creates a monopoly, and where competition is impossible. This is an extremely rare circumstance, however, and a strong burden should be imposed on government to show that it is present in any particular case.

It would probably be a mistake to create a constitutional prohibition on government monopolies that exist in fact but that are not created through law. In the transition from communism, some de facto monopolies are likely, and it is hard to see how a constitutional court can prevent them. Here we encounter one of the limits of constitutionalism: the narrow remedial power of the judiciary.

Nondiscrimination Against Private Enterprises

It probably follows from what has been said thus far that government should be constrained from imposing special disabilities on private enterprises, that is, from taxing, regulating, or otherwise discouraging private entities from operating on equal terms with official organs. Government might well seek to create such disabilities as a way of insulating itself from competition or of protecting its own instrumentalities. If it does so, it will create severe harms to civil society and to economic markets. A prohibition could accomplish considerable good. Of course, there will be some hard interpretive questions here. To see whether there is discrimination, one will have to explore whether private and public enterprises are similarly situated. This will not always be an easy question to answer.

The Right to Travel Within the Nation and to and from the Nation

Protection of the right to travel serves both economic and democratic functions. Especially in a system with some degree of jurisdictional decentralization, the right to travel is a safeguard against oppressive regulation. If citizens can leave, there is a powerful deterrent to such regulation; people are able to "vote with their feet." It is fully plausible to think that in the United States, the right to travel has been one of the greatest safeguards against legislation that is harmful to economic development. The right to travel internally creates a built-in check on tyranny, at least in a federal system. The right to leave one's nation serves the same function. In this sense, the right is simultaneously an economic and a political one.

The Fiscal Constitution

It might be appropriate to introduce a series of provisions amounting to a "fiscal constitution," that is, a document designed to regulate institutions dealing with the relationship between government and the economy. Of course, such provisions would overlap with those discussed previously. I offer a few examples here. I do not discuss monetary arrangements and institutions because they would call for lengthy discussion, but certainly provisions bearing on those issues will warrant consideration.

Ban on Tariffs and Duties It has probably been established, through both theory and practice, that tariffs and duties are on balance harmful to the citizens of a nation. Despite this fact, there is constant political pressure for these measures from the usually narrow groups and interests that would benefit from them. Because tariffs and duties would create aggregate harms but short-term and narrow gains, it might be sensible to enact, in advance, a constitutional prohibition against them. The problem with this strategy is that it is at least reasonable to think that tariffs and duties are necessary under some conditions, and perhaps their availability is an important device for government to have while it is negotiating with other nations.

Balanced Budget In the United States, there has been great interest in a constitutional amendment that would require "balanced budgets." The case for such an amendment is not obscure. For legislators or governments with short-term electoral and domestic problems, it may well make sense to spend more than the nation receives. The dangers of such a course are felt by future generations. A constitutional provision might be directed against this form of myopia.

On reflection, however, it would probably be a mistake to include such a provision in a constitution. A decision not to balance the budget might be the right one in any particular year. The consequences of unbalanced budgets are sharply disputed among economists. It is hardly clear that they are seriously harmful. Moreover, a provision to this effect would not readily be subject to judicial enforcement.

Restrictions on the Taxing Power A fiscal constitution might also impose restrictions on the power of taxation. Most plausible here would be a ban on retroactive taxation. If government may tax resources accumulated in a period in which they could not be taxed, it should not, consistently with the rule of law, be permitted to introduce a tax that will be imposed retroactively.

Ban on Controls on Export or Import of Currency It might well make sense to accompany a right to travel with a prohibition on legal controls on the export or import of currency. Such a prohibition could serve similar functions in guarding against protectionism.

Conclusion

The three transitions now taking place in Eastern Europe should be brought more closely together. Above all, the task of constitution-making can help facilitate the movements toward economic markets and democratic self-government. To this end, I have outlined some possible constitutional provisions designed to protect the basic institutions of private property, free markets, and civil society. A similar analysis might be applied to provisions not directly concerned with the protection of markets—including rights to associational liberty; freedom from discrimination on the basis of sex, race, religion, and ethnicity; and rights of political and religious liberty.

The most general point is that with strong constitutional protection of private property and economic markets, nations in Eastern Europe can take an important step on the way to both economic growth and democratic self-government. The connection between private property and prosperity is well understood; the experience of Eastern Europe confirms a less obvious point, involving the contributions of such rights to the security indispensable to citizenship. In this light, such rights can be defended not on the ground that they conform to "human nature," but on the contrary as part of a system having salutary rather than destructive effects on human character. Both markets and democracy are most plausibly defended in these terms.

To say this is hardly to challenge programs that redistribute resources, training, or opportunities to the poor or that otherwise protect the vulnerable. The instrumental arguments that justify private property call for efforts to ensure that everyone can have some of it. These arguments powerfully support government programs supplementing market arrangements.

Without strong constitutional provisions on behalf of property rights, civil society, and markets, there will probably be a substantial temptation to intrude on all of these institutions, and by so doing, to recreate the very problems that such institutions are supposed to solve. In Eastern Europe, the task of constitution-making is more difficult, and far more pressing, than it was in the West, in which a well-established backdrop of rights and institutions was already in place. The ironic conclusion is that the case for firm constitutional protection of economic freedoms, and for creation and protection of property rights and free markets, is very strong in Eastern Europe; this is so even if the corresponding case in Western countries is quite ambiguous.

Notes

1. See Jeremy Waldron, *The Right to Private Property* (New York: Oxford University Press, 1988). Note that many possible systems can recognize private property in the way I am understanding that idea here. Market socialism, for example, raises many questions, but it is clearly an effort to create something very much like private property so as to generate good incentives.

2. This is a claim about likely facts, not a necessary truth. Social norms may help to overcome some of the problems I am discussing. See Edna Ullmann-Margalit, *The Emergence of Norms* (Oxford: Clarendon Press, 1977).

3. See, generally, Kathleen Sullivan, "Unconstitutional Conditions," 102 *Harv. L. Rev.* 1413 (1989).

4. For this reason, the embrace of "context-smashing" in Roberto Unger, *Politics* (Cambridge: Cambridge University Press, 1987), seems most puzzling.

5. See Amartya Sen, *Commodities and Capabilities* (*Professor Dr. P. Hennipman Lectures in Economics Vol. 7, 1985*) (New York: North-Holland, 1985).

6. See Gerald N. Rosenberg, *The Hollow Hope: Can Courts Bring About Social Change?* (Chicago: University of Chicago Press, 1991).

7. See Cass R. Sunstein, *The Partial Constitution* (Cambridge: Harvard University Press, 1993).

8. John Locke, *Two Treatises on Government*, Peter Laslett, ed. (New York: New American Library, 1960), p. 311.

9

Political Equality and Unintended Consequences

It is a familiar point that government regulation that is amply justified in principle may go very wrong in practice. Minimum wage laws, for example, may reduce employment.[1] Stringent regulation of new sources of air pollution may aggravate pollution problems, by perpetuating the life of old, especially dirty sources. If government closely monitors the release of information, there may be less information. Unintended consequences of this kind can make regulation futile or even self-defeating. By futile regulation, I mean measures that do not bring about the desired consequences. By self-defeating regulation, I mean measures that actually make things worse from the standpoint of their strongest and most public-spirited advocates. We do not lack examples of both of these phenomena. It is unfortunate but true that current campaign finance laws may well provide more illustrations.

Some campaign finance regulation is amply justified in principle. As we will see, there is no good reason to allow disparities in wealth to be translated into disparities in political power. A well-functioning democracy distinguishes between market processes of purchase and sale on the one hand and political processes of voting and reason-giving on the other. Government has a legitimate interest in ensuring not only that political liberties exist as a formal and technical matter, but also that those liberties have real value to the people who have them.[2] The achievement of political equality is an important constitutional goal. Nonetheless, many imaginable campaign finance restrictions would be futile or self-defeating. To take a familiar example, it is now well-known that restrictions on individual expenditures—designed to reduce influence-peddling—can help fuel the use of political action committees (PACs), and thus increase the phenomenon of influence-peddling. This is merely one of a number of possible illustrations.

I can venture no exhaustive account here, and I attempt to describe possibilities rather than certainties. But one of my principal goals is to outline some of the harmful but unintended consequences of campaign finance restrictions. I conclude with some brief notes on what strategies might be most likely to avoid the risk of unintended (or intended but unarticulated) bad consequences. My basic claim here is that we might attempt to avoid rigid command-and-

223

control strategies for restricting expenditures and experiment with more flexible, incentive-based approaches. In this way, the regulation of campaign expenditures might be brought in line with recent innovations in regulatory practice generally.

I. Campaign Finance Reform: Justifications and the Judicial Response

Arguments for Campaign Finance Reform

In principle, the case for campaign finance regulation is very strong. We can identify at least four central grounds for such regulation. First and most obvious, perhaps, is the need to protect the electoral process from both the appearance and the reality of "quid pro quo" exchanges between contributors and candidates. Such exchanges occur whenever contributors offer dollars in return for political favors. The purchase of votes or of political favors is a form of corruption—a large issue in recent campaigns. Corruption is inconsistent with the widely accepted view that public officials should act on the basis of the merits of proposals, and not on the basis of their personal economic interest, or even the interest in increasing their campaign finances. Of course, consideration of the merits will often involve people's preferences, and of course, a willingness to pay cash may reflect preferences. But the link between particular cash payments and any responsible judgment about the merits is extremely weak. Laws should not be purchased and sold; the spectre of quid pro quo exchanges violates this principle.

The second interest involves ensuring that enormous sums of money are devoted to something other than political advertising, thus preventing the waste that results when millions upon millions of dollars are spent on elections. The word "waste" is justified on the plausible assumption that many candidates would prefer to spend less than they must to be elected in an unregulated system; but in such a system each candidate must compete with others. Without regulation, candidates face a prisoner's dilemma in which each must decide whether or not to advertise without knowing what the others will do. A regulatory regime could ensure against this unfortunate state of affairs. To say this is not at all to say that there is no social interest in political advertising. A good deal of advertising provides valuable information. What I am suggesting is that in America, excessive sums are now being spent from any reasonable point of view.

The third interest, independent of corruption, involves political equality. This is a time-honored goal in American constitutional thought. People who are able to organize themselves in such a way as to spend large amounts of cash should not be able to influence politics more than people who are not similarly able. Certainly, economic equality is not required in a democracy; but it is most troublesome if people with a good deal of money are allowed to translate their wealth into political influence. It is equally troublesome if the electoral process translates poverty into an absence of political influence. Of course, economic inequalities cannot be made altogether irrelevant for politics. But the link can be diminished between wealth or poverty on the one hand and political influence on the other. The "one person–one vote" rule exemplifies the commitment to political equality. Limits on campaign expenditures are continuous with that rule.

The fourth interest is in some ways a generalization of the first two. Campaign finance laws might promote the goals of ensuring political deliberation and reason-giving. Politics should not simply register existing preferences and their intensities, especially as these are measured by private willingness to pay. In the American constitutional tradition, politics has an important deliberative function. The constitutional system aspires to a form of "government by discussion." Grants of cash to candidates might compromise that goal by, for example, encouraging legislatures to vote in accordance with private interest rather than reasons.

The goals of political equality and political deliberation are related to the project of distinguishing between the appropriate spheres of economic markets and politics (chapter 3). In democratic politics, a norm of equality is important: Disparities in wealth ought not lead to disparities in power over government. Similarly, democracy requires adherence to the norm of reason-giving. Political outcomes should not be based only on intensities of preferences, as these are reflected in the criterion of private willingness to pay. Taken together, the notions of equality and reason-giving embody a distinctive conception of political respect. Markets operate on the basis of quite different understandings. People can purchase things because they want them, and they need not offer or even have reasons for their wants. Thus markets embody their own conception of equality, insofar as they entail a principle of "one dollar–one vote"; but this is not the conception of equality appropriate to the political sphere.

To distinguish between economic markets and politics is not to deny that an expenditure of money on behalf of a candidate or a cause qualifies as "speech" for First Amendment purposes. Such an expenditure might well be intended and received as a contribution to political and social deliberation. Many people give money in order to promote discussion of a position they favor. Indeed, we might see the ability to accumulate large sums of money as at least a rough indicator that large numbers of people are intensely interested in a candidate's success. If a candidate can accumulate a lot of money, it is probable that many people like what she has to say, or that even if the number of supporters is not so great, their level of enthusiasm is high indeed. In this way, we might take the ability to attract a large amount of money to reveal something important in a deliberative democracy. If and because political dissenters are able to attract funds, they might be able to do especially well in the political "marketplace." This possibility should hardly be disparaged; it is part of democratic self-government.

In this regard, it is perhaps insufficiently appreciated that a system without limits on financial contributions favors people who can attract money without, however, simply favoring the rich over the poor. In theory (if very rarely in practice), some poor people may be able to attract a lot of money when their political commitments find broad support—from, say, a lot of relatively poor people, or from a smaller but intensely interested number of rich ones. Of course, it is hardly unusual for a rich candidate to find it impossible to obtain sufficient funds, because other people are not at all interested in providing support. Many candidates with large personal fortunes have proved dismal failures for just this reason.

These points are not decisive in favor of a system of laissez-faire for political expenditures and contributions. They do not suggest that campaign finance laws make no sense. The correlation between public enthusiasm and the capacity to attract money is crude; it would be foolish to say that a candidate who attracts a lot of money is, for that reason alone, very popular. For one thing, the ability to attract money depends on the initial accumulation of money. For another thing, there can be a large disparity between donations and intensity of interest in a candidate. Candidate A, for example, might, attract large sums of money from wealthy people; but A's supporters may be less intensely interested in her success than are Candidate B's poorer supporters in B's success, even though B's supporters donate less money. The reason that B has attracted less money is that her supporters are poorer, not that they are less enthusiastic about her. Moreover, as I have emphasized, a democracy is concerned with much more than numbers and intensities of preferences. It is interested in reason-giving and deliberation, and a campaign based on resources may compromise those goals.

At the very least, however, an expenditure of money is an important means by which people communicate ideas, and the First Amendment requires a strong justification for any government regulation of an important means of communication. We should think of campaign finance laws as viewpoint-neutral and even content-neutral restrictions on political speech.[3] At least if the laws are fair, the particular content of the speech—the message that is being urged—is irrelevant to whether the campaign finance restriction attaches. This area is especially difficult because while these restrictions can be severe, the government can point to strong reasons on their behalf.

The Law

By far the most important campaign finance case is *Buckley v. Valeo*,[4] which must now be counted as one of the most vilified Supreme Court decisions of the post-World War II era. In *Buckley*, the Court invalidated most restrictions on campaign expenditures. According to the Court, such restrictions are a kind of First Amendment "taking" from some speakers, perhaps rich ones, for the benefit of others, perhaps poor ones. In the key sentence, the Court declared that "the concept that government may restrict the speech of some elements of our society in order to enhance the relative voice of others is wholly foreign to the First Amendment."[5] If the purpose of such laws were to increase political equality, they would be constitutionally unacceptable. The goal of political equality could not be invoked to stop people from spending money on themselves or on candidates of their choice. According to the Court, redistributive arguments for campaign finance laws are therefore impermissible; they amount to a silencing of some for the benefit of others.

The Court did not say that the First Amendment would forbid all campaign finance laws. Limits on campaign contributions are acceptable. Those limits could be justified not on the objectionable ground of promoting political equality (restricting the speech of some to enhance the relative voice of others), but as an entirely legitimate attempt to combat both the appearance and reality of corruption in the form of political favors in return for cash. It is for this reason that government may restrict the amount of money that people can give to candidates for elective office.

By contrast, limits on campaign expenditures are indeed impermissible, since those limits are not easily justified by the anticorruption rationale. The central point is that someone who is spending money on her own campaign, or advertising explicitly on her own for a candidate, is not giving money to a candidate. The reality and appearance of corruption are therefore minimized. According to the Court, limits on expenditures are really an effort to prevent spending by people having or able to attract a substantial amount of money. Since corruption is not at issue, these limits are illegitimate.

In addition, limits on expenditures are far more intrusive than limits on contributions, since expenditure limits do not leave people free to express their views through other means. The *Buckley* Court rejected the view that limits on expenditures were necessary to prevent evasion of the limits on contributions. It did not believe that people would form tacit but mutually understood arrangements with candidates to spend money in excess of allowable contributions.

So much for *Buckley,* which sets out the broad contours of constitutional law. But the decision leaves many uncertainties. The post-*Buckley* cases reveal that there are enormous complexities in holding the line between regulation of contributions and regulation of expenditures.[6] First, it is not clear that this distinction is relevant, since expenditures on behalf of a candidate can create some of the dangers of contributions. Candidates often know who spends money on their behalf. For this reason, an expenditure may in some contexts give rise to the same reality and appearance of corruption. A limit on expenditures may be necessary to prevent evasion of the limit on contributions. Second, the distinction is not crisp even if it is relevant. Suppose that Jones purchases an advertisement in the newspaper for candidate Smith. Might this not be thought a contribution? The slipperiness of the distinction has increased in light of the dramatic rise of political action committees (PACs), a development that, as we will soon see, was stimulated by *Buckley* itself.

PACs are created precisely in order to exert political influence via financial contributions. This raises an obvious question: Is a grant of money to a PAC a contribution or is it an expenditure? It might be thought to be an expenditure, if it does not involve the award of money to a particular, identified candidate; many PACs are devoted to numerous candidates and to general causes. The grant of money to a PAC may thus not involve the risk of "corruption," in the simple sense of an exchange of money for political favors. On the other hand, the PAC could spend a great deal of money on behalf of one candidate; it could be organized by a close friend or ally of the candidate; it could be closely identified with one or a few candidates. Indeed, in practice, a PAC could be nearly indistinguishable from the candidate herself. It is easy for candidates to find out who has given money to PACs and to reward contributors accordingly. In addition, PACs often have unusual access to candidates. If we are concerned about disproportionate access and political influence based on financial contributions, we might well be concerned about PACs. In this light, concern about corruption, as well as political equality and political deliberation, would support treating grants of money to PACs as contributions.

Moreover, people usually know that contributions to PACs will go to certain candidates and not to others, and there is thus some risk of corruption here as well. A limit on contributions to PACs is far less intrusive than a limit on all expenditures; it does leave the individual with the option of making ordinary expenditures on one's own. Finally, PACs are often said to have unusual political influence and for this reason to be a distinctive threat to political equality and political deliberation—basic constitutional goals in a Madisonian system. For all these reasons, a limit on contributions to PACs should probably be thought very different from a limit on an expenditure by a candidate on her own behalf, or by an ordinary citizen purchasing an advertisement on her own behalf to help someone she likes. Related issues are of course raised by limits on contributions by PACs.

The Supreme Court has not clearly resolved the resulting conundrums. In the two key cases, it gave conflicting signals. First, it invalidated a $1000 limit on the amount of money that a PAC can give to promote the election of a candidate.[7] In the Court's view, the PAC expenditure is core political speech, and because the money does not go directly to the candidate, the risk and reality of corruption are not at stake. After all, PAC expenditures are not coordinated with the campaign and are in that sense independent.

On the other hand, in the second case, the Court upheld a $5000 limit on the amount of money an individual or group can give to any PAC.[8] The Court said that this limit does not affect a wide range of other possible expenditures designed to advocate political views, and that Congress could reasonably decide that the limit was necessary to prevent evasion of the limits on direct contributions. The two cases are in obvious tension, and it is therefore unclear whether and how Congress may constitutionally limit contributions to or by PACs. This is an especially important question in light of the large and sometimes corrosive effects of PACs on the political process.

Lochner, Redistribution, and Buckley

Let us put these various complexities to one side and return to the basic issue of political equality. In rejecting the claim that controls on financial expenditures could be justified as a means of promoting political equality, *Buckley* seems highly reminiscent of the pre-New Deal period. Indeed, *Buckley* might well be seen as the modern-day analogue of the infamous and discredited case of *Lochner v. New York*,[9] in which the Court invalidated maximum hour laws.

A principal problem with the pre-New Deal Court was that it treated existing distributions of resources as if they were prepolitical and just, and therefore invalidated democratic efforts at reform.[10] In a key *Lochner* era case, *Adkins v. Children's Hospital*, for example, the Court invalidated minimum wage legislation.[11] In so doing, it said: "To the extent that the sum fixed by the minimum wage statute exceeds the fair value of the services rendered, it amounts to a compulsory exaction from the employer for the support of a partially indigent person, for whose condition there rests upon him no peculiar responsibility, and therefore, in effect, arbitrarily shifts to his shoulders a burden which, if it belongs to anybody, belongs to society as a whole." The language of compulsory subsidy—of taking from some for the benefit of others— was central in the *Lochner* period. Regulatory adjustment of market arrangements was seen as interference with an otherwise law-free and unobjectionable status quo. It was a state-mandated transfer of funds from one group for another, and this kind of mandatory transfer was constitutionally illegitimate.

To compress a long and complex story: This whole approach became unsustainable in 1937, when the legal culture came to think that existing distributions were a product of law, were not sacrosanct, and could legitimately be subject to governmental correction. Throughout the legal system, it was urged that property rights were a function of law rather than nature and ought not to be immunized from legal change. Such changes would not be banned in principle, but would be evaluated on the basis of the particular reasons brought forward on their behalf. In President Roosevelt's words: "We must lay hold of the fact that economic laws are not made by nature. They are made by human beings."[12] And the Supreme Court, overruling *Lochner* itself, offered an uncanny reversal of the *Adkins* dictum, arguing that "the community is not bound to provide what is in effect a subsidy for unconscionable employers."[13]

In its essential premises, *Buckley* is quite similar to the pre-1937 cases. Recall that the Court announced that "the concept that government may restrict the speech of some elements of our society in order to enhance the relative voice of others is wholly foreign to the First Amendment." It added that the "First Amendment's protection against governmental abridgement of free expression cannot properly be made to depend on a person's financial ability to engage in public discussion." The *Buckley* Court therefore saw campaign expenditure limits as a kind of "taking," or compulsory exaction, from some for the benefit of others. The limits were unconstitutional for this very reason. Just as the due process clause once forbade government "interference" with the outcomes of the economic marketplace, so, too, the First Amendment now bans government "interference" with the political marketplace, with the term "marketplace" understood quite literally. In this way, *Buckley* replicates *Lochner*.

On the view reflected in both *Buckley* and *Lochner*, reliance on free markets is government neutrality and government inaction. But in the New Deal period, it became clear that reliance on markets simply entailed another—if in many ways good—regulatory system, made possible and constituted through law. We cannot have a system of market ordering without an elaborate body of law. For all their beneficial qualities, markets are legitimately subject to democratic restructuring—at least within certain limits—if the restructuring promises to deliver sufficient benefits. This is a constitutional truism in the post-New Deal era. What is perhaps not sufficiently appreciated, but what is equally true, is that elections based on existing distributions of wealth and entitlements also embody a regulatory system, made possible and constituted through law. Here, as elsewhere, law defines property interests; it specifies who owns what, and who may do what with what is owned. The regulatory system that we now have for elections is not obviously neutral or just. On the contrary, it seems to be neither, insofar as it permits high levels of political influence to follow from large accumulations of wealth.

Because it involves speech, *Buckley* is in one sense even more striking than *Lochner*. As I have noted, the goal of political equality is time-honored in the American constitutional tradition, whereas the goal of economic equality is not. Efforts to redress economic inequalities, or to ensure that they are not turned into political inequalities, should not be seen as impermissible redistribution, or as the introduction of government regulation into a place where it did not exist before. A system of unlimited campaign expenditures should be seen as a regulatory decision to allow disparities in resources to be turned into disparities in political influence. That may be the best decision, all things considered. But why is it unconstitutional for government to attempt to replace this system with an alternative? The Court offered no answer; its analysis was startlingly cavalier. Campaign finance laws should be evaluated not through axioms, but pragmatically in terms of their consequences for the system of free expression.

II. The Problem of Unintended Consequences

In principle, then, there are good arguments for campaign finance restrictions. Insofar as *Buckley* rejects political equality as a legitimate constitutional goal, it should be overruled. Indeed, the decision probably ranks among the strongest candidates for overruling of the post-World War II period. But there are real limits on how much we can learn from abstract principles alone. Many of the key questions are insistently ones of policy and fact. Was the system at issue in *Buckley* well-designed? How might it be improved? What will be the real-world consequences of different plans? Will they fulfill their intended purposes? Will they be self-defeating? Might they impair democratic processes under the guise of promoting them?

My goal here is to offer a brief catalogue of ways in which campaign finance legislation may prove unhelpful or counterproductive. My particular interest lies in the possibility that campaign finance legislation may have perverse or unintended consequences. The catalogue bears directly on a number of proposals that have been receiving attention in Congress and in the executive branch. Of course, it would be necessary to look at the details in order to make a final assessment. I am describing possibilities, not certainties, and a good deal of empirical work would be necessary to come to terms with any of them.

A general point runs throughout the discussion. Although I have criticized what the Court said in *Buckley*, considerable judicial suspicion of campaign finance limits is justified by a simple point: Congressional support for such limits is especially likely to reflect congressional self-dealing. Any system of campaign finance limits raises the special spectre of governmental efforts to promote the interests of existing legislators. Indeed, it is hard to imagine other kinds of legislation posing similarly severe risks. In these circumstances, we might try to avoid rigid, command-and-control regulation, which poses special dangers, and move instead toward more flexible, incentive-based strategies.

Unintended Consequences in Particular

Campaign Finance Limits May Entrench Incumbents

Operating under the rubric of democratic equality, campaign finance measures may make it hard for challengers to overcome the effects of incumbency. The problem is all the more severe in a period in which it can be extremely difficult for challengers to unseat incumbents. (See Tables 9.1 and 9.2.) The risk of incumbent self-dealing becomes even more troublesome in light of the fact that dissidents or challengers may be able to overcome the advantages of incumbency only by amassing enormous sums of money, either from their own pockets or from numerous or wealthy supporters.

Consider in this regard the presidential candidacy of Ross Perot. The Perot campaign raised many questions, but it is at least notable that large sums of money proved an indispensable mechanism for enabling an outsider to challenge the mainstream candidates. One lesson seems clear. Campaign finance limits threaten to eliminate one of the few means by which incumbents can be seriously challenged.

Whether campaign finance limits, in general, do entrench incumbents is an empirical question. There is also some evidence to the contrary. Usually the largest amounts are spent by incumbents themselves; usually incumbents have an advantage in accumulating enormous sums, often from people who think that they have something to gain from a financial relationship with an officeholder. In these circumstances, one of the particular problems for challengers is that they face special financial barriers by virtue of the ability of incumbents to raise large sums of money. In this light, the fairest generalization is that campaign finance limits, in general, do not entrench incumbents, but that there are important individual cases in which such limits prevent challengers from mounting serious efforts. In any case, any campaign finance reforms should be designed so as to promote more electoral competition.

Table 9.1. Reelection Rates
Senate Incumbents: Reelected, Defeated, or Retired

Year	Retired	Total Seeking Reelection	Defeated in Primaries	Defeated in General Election	Total Reelected	Reelected as Percentage of Those Seeking Reelection
1946	9	30	6	7	17	56.7
1948	8	25	2	8	15	60.0
1950	4	32	5	5	22	68.8
1952	4	31	2	9	20	64.5
1954	6	32	2	6	24	75.0
1956	6	39	0	4	25	86.2
1958	6	28	0	10	18	64.3
1960	5	29	0	1	28	96.6
1962	4	35	1	5	29	82.9
1964	2	33	1	4	28	84.8
1966	3	32	3	1	28	87.5
1968	6	28	4	4	20	71.4
1970	4	31	1	6	24	77.4
1972	6	27	2	5	20	74.1
1974	7	27	2	2	23	85.2
1976	8	25	0	9	16	64.0
1978	10	25	3	7	15	60.0
1980	5	29	4	9	16	55.2
1982	3	30	0	2	28	93.3
1984	4	29	0	3	26	89.7
1986	6	28	0	7	21	75.0
1988	6	27	0	4	23	85.2
1990		32	0	1	31	96.9
1992		28	1	4	23	82.1

Source: Norman J. Orenstein, Thomas E. Mann, and Michael J. Malbin, eds., *Vital Statistics on Congress* (Washington, D.C.: Congressional Quarterly, 1989–90), p. 57 (source for years 1946–88); *Statistical Abstract of the United States 1993* (Washington, D.C.: Bureau of the Census, 1993), p. 277 (source for years 1990–92).

Limits on Individual Contributions Will Produce More (and More Influential) PACs

The early regulation of individual contributions had an important unintended consequence: It led directly to the rise of the political action committee. When individuals were banned from contributing to campaigns, there was tremendous pressure to provide a mechanism for aggregating individual contributions. The modern PAC is the result. See Tables 9.3 and 9.4.

The post-*Buckley* rise of PACs has a general implication. If individual contributions are controlled while PACs face little or no effective regulation, there could be a large shift of resources in the direction of PACs. Of course, a combination of PAC limits and individual contribution limits could counteract this problem. But limits of this kind create difficulties of their own.

Table 9.2. Reelection Rates
House Incumbents: Reelected, Defeated, or Retired

Year	Retired	Total Seeking Reelection	Defeated in Primaries	Defeated in General Election	Total Reelected	Reelected as Percentage of Those Seeking Reelection	Reelected as Percentage of House Membership
1948	29	400	15	68	317	79.3	72.9
1950	29	400	6	32	362	90.5	83.2
1952	42	389	9	26	354	91.0	81.4
1954	24	407	6	22	379	93.1	87.1
1956	21	411	6	16	389	94.6	89.4
1958	33	396	3	37	356	89.9	81.8
1960	26	405	5	25	375	92.6	86.2
1962	24	402	12	22	368	91.5	84.6
1964	33	397	8	45	344	86.6	79.1
1966	22	411	8	41	362	88.1	83.2
1968	23	409	4	9	396	96.8	91.0
1970	29	401	10	12	379	94.5	87.1
1972	40	390	12	13	365	93.6	83.9
1974	43	391	8	40	343	87.7	78.9
1976	47	384	3	13	368	95.8	84.6
1978	49	382	5	19	358	93.7	82.3
1980	34	398	6	31	361	90.7	83.0
1982	40	393	10	29	354	90.1	81.4
1984	22	409	3	16	390	95.4	89.7
1986	38	393	2	6	385	98.0	88.5
1988	23	409	1	6	402	98.3	92.4
1990		407	1	15	391	96.1	89.9
1992		367	19	24	324	88.3	74.5

Source: Norman J. Orenstein, Thomas E. Mann, and Michael J. Malbin, eds., *Vital Statistics on Congress* (Washington, D.C.: Congressional Quarterly, 1989–90), p. 56 (source for years 1946–88); *Statistical Abstract of the United States 1993* (Washington, D.C.: Bureau of the Census, 1993), p. 277 (source for years 1990–92).

Limits on "Hard Money" Encourage a Shift to "Soft Money"

In the 1980s, the tightening of individual contribution limits—"hard money"—helped increase the amount of "soft money," consisting of gifts not to particular candidates but to political parties. It should not be surprising to see that in recent years there has been an enormous increase in fund-raising by political parties, which dispense contributions to various candidates. In 1980, the two parties raised and spent about $19 million; in 1984, the amount rose to $19.6 million; in 1988, it increased to $45 million. Consider Table 9.5.

In some ways the shift from hard to soft money has been a salutary development. It is more difficult for soft money contributors to target particular beneficiaries, and perhaps this reduces the risk of the quid pro quo donation. Reasonable people could believe that soft money poses lower risks to the integrity of the political process while also exemplifying a legitimate form of freedom of speech and association. But the substitution, if it occurs, means that

Table 9.3. PAC Activity: Average PAC Contribution by Year, Committee Type, and Candidate Type

Year	Committee Type	Senate Candidate Type						Total Senate Contribution	House Candidate Type						Total House Contribution
		DI	RI	DC	RC	DO	RO		DI	RI	DC	RC	DO	RO	
1978	Corporate	646	754	613	726	591	707	3,616,388	335	328	366	442	428	413	6,158,069
	Labor	2,367	1,576	2,308	1,500	2,184	1,748	2,831,336	848	708	1,099	596	1,174	938	7,462,424
1980	Corporate	871	666	587	972	654	875	7,731,966	446	401	421	529	461	495	12,743,186
	Labor	2,680	2,245	2,164	1,294	2,501	1,508	4,192,159	1,078	751	1,199	727	1,472	507	9,714,307
1984	Corporate	1,122	1,300	793	952	1,127	1,511	14,260,807	626	573	443	626	546	662	24,004,408
	Labor	2,582	2,175	3,253	735	4,069	4,333	5,580,536	1,622	1,319	1,672	1,073	2,012	1,849	20,289,631
1986	Corporate	1,382	1,603	1,306	1,588	1,347	1,834	21,721,324	728	669	606	600	650	718	27,829,833
	Labor	2,949	2,488	4,269	1,194	4,599	2,683	7,908,118	1,759	1,613	2,315	1,211	2,477	1,365	23,104,302
1988	Corporate	1,638	1,753	1,305	1,617	1,535	1,795	21,928,118	861	771	566	730	722	729	32,404,982
	Labor	3,570	2,743	4,469	1,905	3,948	3,165	7,686,772	2,122	1,685	2,667	1,247	3,022	1,994	27,197,181
1990	Corporate	1,764	1,822	1,211	2,256	794	2,034	21,934,718	1,012	885	709	870	943	922	36,153,692
	Labor	3,799	2,671	4,115	1,424	3,632	3,360	6,746,738	2,342	1,714	2,541	1,437	3,180	3,231	27,952,722

D = Democrat, R = Republican, I = Incumbent, C = Challenger, O = Open seat.

Source: 1 *FEC Reports on Financial Activity, Final Report, Party and Non-Party Political Committees* (Washington, D.C.: Federal Election Commission, 1990).

Table 9.4.   Number of Political Action Committees, by Committee Type: 1980 to 1991 (as of December 31, 1992)

Committee Type	1980	1985	1986	1987	1988	1989	1990	1991
Total	2,551	3,992	4,157	4,165	4,268	4,178	4,172	4,094
Corporate	1,206	1,710	1,744	1,775	1,816	1,796	1,795	1,738
Labor	297	388	384	364	354	349	346	338
Trade/membership/health	576	695	745	865	786	777	774	742
Nonconnected	374	1,003	1,077	957	1,115	1,060	1,062	1,083
Cooperative	42	54	56	59	59	59	59	57
Corporation without stock	56	142	151	145	138	137	136	136

Source: *Statistical Abstract of the United States 1993* (Washington, D.C.: Bureau of the Census, 1993), p. 287.

any contribution limits are easily evaded. Candidates know, moreover, the identity of the large contributors to the party, and for this reason soft money can produce risks of corruption as well.

Limits on PACs Lead to an Increase in Individual Expenditures

Congress has occasionally discussed the possibility of imposing limits on PACs or even eliminating them altogether. If it did so, there would be pressure for more in the way of both individual contributions and individual expenditures. Limits or bans on PAC expenditures will increase the forms of financial help that Congress's original efforts in 1971 were specifically designed to limit. It is ironic but true that new legislation designed to counteract PACs will spur the very activity which Congress initially sought to curtail.

For reasons suggested earlier, this development, even if ironic, may improve things overall. There is a good argument that PAC contributions are especially harmful to democratic processes, because they are particularly likely to be given with the specific purpose of influencing lawmakers. It is also the case that candidates who receive individual contributions are often unaware of the particular reason for the money, whereas PAC beneficiaries know exactly what reasons underlie any donation. For all these reasons, a shift from PACs to individual expenditures may be desirable.

On the other hand, PACs have some distinctive benefits as well. They provide a method by which individuals may band together in order to exercise political influence. Sometimes they offer a helpful aggregative mechanism of the kind that is plausibly salutary in a democracy. A shift from PACs to individual expenditures may be unfortunate insofar as it diminishes the power of politically concerned people to organize and pool their resources on behalf of their favored causes.

On balance, individual expenditures do seem preferable to PACs, because the most severe threats to the quid pro quo and public deliberation come from PAC money. Restrictions on PACs that move people in the direction of individual expenditures and contributions are therefore desirable. My point is only that there is a trade-off between the two.

Table 9.5. Contributions to Congressional Campaigns by Political Action Committees, by Committee Type: 1979 to 1990 (In millions of dollars. Covers amounts given to candidates in primary, general, run-off, and special elections during the two-year calendar period indicated.)

Type of Committee	House of Representatives						Senate					
	Total	Demo-crats	Repub-licans	Incum-bents	Chal-lengers	Open Seats[a]	Total	Demo-crats	Repub-licans	Incum-bents	Chal-lengers	Open Seats[a]
1979–80	37.9	20.5	17.2	24.9	7.9	5.1	17.3	8.4	9.0	8.6	6.6	2.1
1981–82	61.1	34.2	26.8	40.8	10.9	9.4	22.6	11.2	11.4	14.3	5.2	3.0
1983–84, total[b]	75.7	46.3	29.3	57.2	11.3	7.2	29.7	14.0	15.6	17.9	6.3	5.4
Corporate	23.4	10.4	13.1	18.8	2.6	2.0	12.0	3.2	8.8	8.8	1.1	2.2
Trade association[c]	20.4	10.5	9.9	16.5	2.1	1.7	6.3	2.7	3.7	4.5	0.9	1.0
Labor	19.8	18.8	1.0	14.3	3.5	2.0	5.0	4.7	0.3	1.6	2.3	1.2
Nonconnected[d]	9.1	4.7	4.4	4.9	2.9	1.3	5.4	3.0	2.4	2.4	2.0	1.0
1986–86, total[b]	87.4	54.7	32.6	65.9	9.1	12.4	45.3	20.2	25.1	23.7	10.2	11.4
Corporate	26.9	12.9	14.0	22.9	1.0	3.0	19.2	4.8	14.4	11.7	2.7	4.9
Trade association[c]	23.4	12.3	11.2	19.3	1.3	2.8	9.5	3.8	5.7	5.7	1.6	2.1
Labor	22.6	21.1	1.6	14.7	4.3	3.6	7.2	6.6	0.6	2.2	3.2	1.9
Nonconnected[d]	11.1	6.6	4.5	6.1	2.4	2.6	7.7	4.2	3.4	3.1	2.4	2.2
1987–88, total[b]	102.2	67.4	34.7	82.2	10.0	10.0	45.7	24.2	21.5	28.7	8.0	9.0
Corporate	31.6	16.3	15.4	28.6	1.1	1.9	18.8	7.2	11.6	12.7	2.4	3.7
Trade association[c]	28.6	16.5	12.0	24.6	1.5	2.5	10.4	4.8	5.6	7.1	1.3	2.0
Labor	26.8	24.8	2.0	18.3	5.1	3.3	7.1	6.5	0.5	3.6	2.2	1.3
Nonconnected[d]	11.4	7.4	3.9	7.3	2.2	1.9	7.8	4.8	3.0	4.2	2.0	1.6
1989–90, total[b]	108.5	72.2	36.2	87.5	7.3	13.6	41.2	20.2	21.0	29.5	8.2	3.5
Corporate	35.4	18.7	16.7	30.8	1.4	3.2	18.0	6.1	11.9	13.0	3.5	1.5
Trade association[c]	32.5	19.3	13.3	27.5	1.4	3.6	10.0	4.2	5.8	7.2	1.8	0.9
Labor	27.6	25.8	1.8	19.8	3.2	4.5	6.0	5.6	0.4	3.9	1.7	0.4
Nonconnected[d]	8.5	5.5	2.9	5.5	1.1	1.8	5.7	3.5	2.2	4.2	1.1	0.5

[a] Elections in which an incumbent did not seek reelection. [b] Includes other types of political action committees not shown separately. [c] Includes membership organizations and health organizations. [d] Represents "ideological" groups as well as other issue groups not necessarily ideological in nature.

Source: *Statistical Abstract of the United States 1993* (Washington, D.C.: Bureau of the Census, 1993), p. 288.

Limits on PACs Can Hurt Organized Labor and Minority Candidates

Sometimes minority candidates can succeed only with the help of PACs specifically organized for their particular benefit. For this reason, PAC limits will in some circumstances diminish the power of minority candidates. The Congressional Black Caucus has expressed concerns over campaign finance regulation on this ground. Similar results are possible for PACs organized to benefit women. PAC restrictions may also hurt organized labor. Currently, labor PACs spend most of their money on individual candidates, especially incumbent Democrats. By contrast, corporate PACs contribute about equally to Democrats and Republicans and give substantial sums to the parties rather than to individual candidates. A ban on PACs may therefore diminish the influence of labor unions without materially affecting corporate PACs. Perhaps these effects are good or justified on balance. But many people who favor campaign finance regulation might be disturbed to see this effect.

Limits on PACs May Increase Secret Gifts

Many current interest groups appear unconcerned about the possibility of legislatively imposed PAC limits, even though their interests would seem to be jeopardized by the proposed limits. Perhaps it will be easy for them to evade any such limits, especially by offering "soft money" and also by assembling large amounts as a result of contributions from unidentifiable sources. We lack detailed evidence on this issue, but there is reason to think that the concern is legitimate. It is possible that limits on PACs will make it harder to identify sources of money without materially decreasing special interest funding. The current proposals do not respond to this risk.

Limits on Both PACs and Contributions Could Hinder Campaign Activity

Most of my discussion thus far has been based on the assumption that campaign finance reform proposals would limit either PACs or individual contributions. In either case, limitations on one could lead to increased spending through the other. A third option might be to limit both PACs and individual contributions. But this option could quite possibly lead to a number of negative effects. If the limits were successful, campaign activity might be sharply limited as a whole. Any such limit would raise First Amendment problems and perhaps compromise democratic government. Alternatively, resources could be funneled into campaigns through soft money, secret gifts, or other loopholes in the reforms.

Possible Strategies

What I have said thus far suggests considerable reason for caution about campaign finance proposals. It also suggests that those who design such proposals should be attentive to the risks of futile or self-defeating reform. I do not attempt here to describe a fully adequate regulatory system for campaign financing. But I will outline two possibilities that appear especially promising. Both of them respond to the largely unfortunate American experience with command-and-control regulation in the last generation. Such regulation—consisting of rigid mandates and flat bans—is peculiarly likely to be futile or self-defeating (chapter 13). Mandates and bans invite efforts at circumvention. Because of their rigidity, they tend to have unintended adverse consequences; creative members of regulated classes are likely to come up with substitutes posing equal or greater risks. To say this is not to say that mandates and bans are necessarily inferior to alternatives. But it is to say that we ought to explore approaches that make self-interested adaptation less likely.

Incentives Rather Than Bans

The *Buckley* Court was unwilling to accept a flat ban on expenditures. But it was quite hospitable to federal financing accompanied by viewpoint–neutral conditions on what recipients may do. Most notably, the Court upheld the requirement that candidates must promise not to accept private money as a condition for receiving federal dollars. This model of *incentives rather than bans* has a number of attractions. For one, it survives even the rigid constitutional scrutiny of *Buckley* itself. For another, a system of incentives—in the form of federal financing accompanied by a promise not to accept private money—responds to the deepest concerns of people who are skeptical of flat bans. Some people argue that the acquisition of private sums can be at least a crude way to register public enthusiasm for a candidate, and to enable dissidents and outsiders to overcome the advantages of incumbency. But a system of incentives leaves the private remedy intact. At the same time, such a system can help counteract the distortions built into exclusive reliance on private contributions. It does so by allowing electoral competition from people who are not well-financed.

To be sure, some people think that full federal funding of campaigns, with a prohibition on private financing, is the best route for the future. But a system of incentives, promoting rather than requiring public financing, is far more likely to be constitutional. To the extent that full federal funding would foreclose private expenditures, it would violate *Buckley*. By contrast, a system of incentives does not eliminate private expenditures. Such a system allows the private check to continue to exist, a strategy that poses certain risks, but that has benefits as well. Finally, a system of incentives accomplishes many (if not all) of the goals of full public funding. It does this by encouraging candidates not to rely on private funds and by ensuring that people unable to attract money are not placed at a special disadvantage.

A system of incentives could take various forms. Adapting the model upheld in *Buckley*, the government might adopt a system of optional public financing, accompanied by (1) a promise not to accept or to use private money as a condition for receiving public funds, and (2) a regime in which public subsidies are provided to help candidates match all or a stated percentage of the expenditures of their privately financed opponents. Under (2), a candidate could elect to use private resources, but the government would ensure that her opponent would not be at a substantial disadvantage. Of course, any such system would raise many questions. We would, for example, have to decide which candidates would qualify for support, and there is a risk that some people would be unfairly excluded. We would also have to decide what sorts of disparities would be tolerable between candidates raising substantial private funds and candidates relying on government. I suggest only that it is worthwhile to explore a system in which candidates are encouraged but not required to accept only public funds, on the theory that such a system would be less vulnerable to the various risks that I have described in this chapter.

Vouchers

An alternative approach has been suggested by Bruce Ackerman.[14] Ackerman argues for an innovative voucher system, in which voters would be given a special card—citizen vouchers in the form of red, white, and blue money—to be used to finance political campaigns. Under this system, regular money could not be used at all. Candidates could attract citizen vouchers, but they could not use cash. The goal would be to split the political and economic spheres sharply, so as to ensure that resources accumulated in the economic sphere could not be used for political advantage. Ackerman's approach is therefore closely connected to the goal of preventing economic inequalities— fully acceptable in the American tradition—from becoming political in nature.

Obviously, a system of this kind could not be implemented simply, but it might have many advantages. Like any voucher system, such an approach would reduce some of the problems posed by centralized, bureaucratic control of finances and elections. The requirement that candidates use a special kind of "money" could much simplify administration and to some extent make it self-implementing. At the same time, the system would be well-suited to promoting political equality, and it could do this without threatening to diminish aggregate levels of political discussion. Compared with the approach in *Buckley*, a voucher system would leave candidates and citizens quite free to take and give as they choose; but what would be taken and given would not be ordinary money and would be understood to have limited functions.

This system would be quite unruly, and it would undoubtedly be hard for people to get used to it. There would be a risk of evasion here as well. It would not be simple to police the boundary between vouchers and ordinary money. Moreover, the line between campaign expenditures and usual political speech—which would be unaffected by the proposal—is not crisp and simple. The flat ban on the use of ordinary money could raise constitutional and policy objections. Perhaps the ban would run afoul of *Buckley*, though I do not think that it should. A voucher system could also create distinctive implementation problems. A bureaucratic apparatus would still be necessary to provide the vouchers, to decide on their aggregate amount, and to dispense them in the first instance. A voucher system might not sufficiently promote the goal of political deliberation, for candidates would be highly dependent on private support. A voucher system would not be perfect, but a voucher system would so sharply separate the economic and political spheres and allow intensities of interest to be reflected in campaigns, it warrants serious consideration.

Conclusion

In principle, there are strong arguments for campaign finance limits, especially if these are taken as part of a general effort to renew the old aspiration of deliberative democracy. In some respects, the Supreme Court's decision in *Buckley* is the modern analogue to the discredited case of *Lochner v. New York*, offering an adventurous interpretation of the Constitution so as to invalidate a redistributive measure having and deserving broad democratic support. The special problem with *Buckley* is that it permits economic inequalities to be translated into political inequalities, and this is hardly a goal of the constitutional structure. Properly designed campaign finance measures ought to be seen as fully compatible with the system of free expression insofar as those measures promote the goal of ensuring a deliberative democracy among political (though not economic) equals.

There is, however, good reason for the Court and for citizens in general to distrust any campaign finance system actually enacted by Congress, whose institutional self-interest makes this an especially worrisome area for national legislation. Moreover, the argument from principle does not suggest that any particular system will make things better rather than worse. A number of imaginable systems would be futile or self-defeating, largely because of unintended (or perhaps intended) bad consequences. In this chapter, I have tried to identify some of the most important risks.

My general conclusion is that dissatisfaction with *Buckley*, and enthusiasm for the goals of political equality and political deliberation, ought not to deflect attention from some insistently empirical questions about the real-world effects of campaign finance legislation. Any policy reforms will have unanticipated consequences, some of them counterproductive. Private adaptation to public-spirited reform is inevitable. In this context, our task is not merely to debate the theoretical issues, but also to identify the practical risks as systematically as possible and to favor initiatives that seem most likely to promote salutary goals.

Notes

1. See Finis Welch, *Minimum Wages: Issues and Evidence* (Washington, D.C.: American Enterprise Institute for Public Policy Research, 1978), pp. 34, 38. But see David Card and Alan B. Krueger, *Myth and Measurement: The New Economics of the Minimum Wage* (Princeton: Princeton University Press, 1995) (disputing this claim); Stephen Machin and Alan Manning, "The Effects of Minimum Wages on Wage Dispersion and Employment: Evidence from the U.K. Wages Councils," 47 *Indus. & Lab. Rel. Rev.* 319 (1994) (concluding that the minimum wage has either no effect or a positive effect on employment).

2. See, e.g., John Rawls, *Political Liberalism* (New York: Columbia University Press, 1993), pp. 324, 31 ("The first principle of justice should include the guarantee . . . that the worth of the political liberties to all citizens, whatever their social or economic position, is approximately equal.").

3. The restrictions are not entirely content-neutral, because political speech relating to campaigns is being singled out for special treatment. But this should not affect the analysis. Content-based regulations—like a ban on advertising on buses—are disfavored in part because we rightly suspect that illegitimate motivations lie behind them. See Cass R. Sunstein, *Democracy and the Problem of Free Speech* (Cambridge: Harvard University Press, 1993), pp. 168, 77. The content discrimination in campaign finance laws—singling out campaign-related speech—is not similarly a basis for suspicion. On the other hand, the institutional interest of incumbent legislators does justify a large measure of judicial and public skepticism about any reforms that legislators favor.

4. 424 U.S. 1 (1976).

5. *Id.* at 48–49.

6. Compare Austin v. Michigan Chamber of Commerce, 110 S. Ct. 1391, 1395 (1990) (holding that a ban on independent expenditures by corporations using general treasury funds was constitutional as applied to nonprofit Chamber of Commerce) with FEC v. Massachusetts Citizens for Life, 479 U.S. 238, 241 (1986) (holding that a federal ban on general treasury expenditures was unconstitutional as applied to a nonprofit corporation formed to advance a prolife position).

7. See FEC v. National Conservative Political Action Comm., 470 U.S. 480, 482, 483 (1985).

8. See California Medical Ass'n v. FEC, 453 U.S. 182, 184, 185 (1981).

9. 198 U.S. 45 (1905).

10. This point is discussed in more detail in Cass R. Sunstein, *The Partial Constitution* (Cambridge: Harvard University Press, 1993), pp. 40, 67.

11. See Adkins v. Children's Hosp., 261 U.S. 525, 560, 562 (1923).

12. Franklin Delano Roosevelt, *The Public Papers and Addresses of Franklin Delano Roosevelt*, vol 1. (New York: Random House, 1938), p. 657.

13. West Coast Hotel Co. v. Parrish, 300 U.S. 379, 399 (1937).

14. See Bruce A. Ackerman, "Crediting the Voters: A New Beginning for Campaign Finance," *Am. Prospect.*, Spring 1993, at 71.

REGULATION

Endogenous Preferences, Environmental Law

How can we explain the rise of environmental law? By what criteria should we evaluate regulation of pollution? Why do some cities require recycling? Should we tax waste disposal instead? Should we subsidize mass transit in order to reduce automobile pollution, or should we regulate cars? Why do we do one rather than another?

In the last generation, considerable progress has been made on all of these questions. Most of the progress results from the application of varieties or offshoots of welfare economics—expected utility theory, social and public choice theory, and game theory—to environmental problems. If we assume, for example, that participants in the political process are trying to maximize their utility, we can help explain many oddities of American environmental law. We can see why some statutes seem to benefit regional interests.[1] We can understand why old pollution sources are regulated more severely than new ones.[2] We can see why Congress enacts measures that are expensive and only moderately helpful to the environment, but that promise to deliver large benefits to well-organized groups.[3] Perhaps most important, we can understand the omnipresence of largely symbolic environmental legislation—measures that appear on their face to promise vigorous and even draconian regulation, but that in the enforcement process amount to little more than mere words. The pervasive paradox of rigid but underenforced environmental legislation may well match the electoral self-interest of legislators.

With similar tools, we can also think about how best to protect the environment. Many people do want a cleaner environment—to protect life, health, recreational opportunities, endangered species, and so forth. Many people want other things as well, including lower prices, less poverty, and greater employment. In light of the plurality of goods at stake, it is familiarly suggested that we might try to achieve the optimal level of environmental protection, understanding the notion of optimality by reference to people's real desires. This approach might claim a salutary neutrality among diverse goods and among different conceptions of the good, since it takes people and preferences simply as they are.

Approaches of this general sort have provided illuminating work on the genesis of state and federal environmental law. No predictive tool has similar power, and if we want to understand the structure of environmental regulation, much progress remains to be made through use of the same analytic strategies. On the normative side, things are more complex. But at least it seems fair to say that we now lack an alternative framework for normative thinking in the environmental area that can claim to combine the virtues of real-world administrability and substantive plausibility. The extraordinary influence of welfare economics in the regulatory sector of the federal government is undoubtedly at least in part attributable to this fact.

At the same time, the last decade has witnessed a number of intriguing qualifications, refinements, or criticisms of rational actor models, coming mostly from economists, but also from philosophers, political scientists, and psychologists.[4] Some of the work involves "anomalies" of various sorts. The institutional implications of these qualifications and refinements are only beginning to receive sustained elaboration.[5] My principal goal in this chapter is to identify some of those implications in the distinctive context of environmental regulation. Some of the apparently normative challenges to rational actor models turn out to have important positive implications. The challenges point to facts about human behavior and motivation that help explain some of American environmental law, and indeed do so in a way that might add much to the descriptive and predictive work of existing approaches. My particular interest is in the endogeneity of preferences and the social "demand" for regulation, which turns out to have peculiar dimensions.

Throughout the chapter, I will attempt to show how qualifications of rational actor models generate testable hypotheses, and to explore whether such qualifications offer plausible ways to understand the odd shape of current environmental policies. In many cases, however, our current tools do not enable us to sort out the role of plausible but competing explanations for regulatory phenomena. An important task for the future, both conceptual and empirical, is to develop better strategies for assessing causal explanations that, although strikingly different, would produce similar outcomes. Moreover, some challenges to preference satisfaction as a normative ideal have unusual characteristics in the environmental area. It is worth elaborating on those characteristics.

This chapter is organized into four sections. Borrowing from chapter 1, the first suggests that there is sometimes no such thing as a fully acontextual "preference," and that preferences are endogenous to existing legal policy, including the setting of the legal entitlement. This point helps both to explain legislative outcomes and to unsettle some common views about environmental protection on the predictive and normative sides.

The second section claims that private preferences for environmental goods may be adaptive to existing environmental options, and that this can sometimes help explain the social demand for regulation and also "impeach" the preferences that serve as inputs into environmental decisions. The second section also briefly describes the role of the availability heuristic, intrapersonal collective action problems, and the phenomenon of social cascades.

The third section argues that there may be a disparity between private consumption choices and collective judgments, as these are expressed in politics. Partly because of some unusual free-rider problems in the environmental area, preferences for environmental quality may be endogenous to the setting in which they are expressed, and in a way that casts additional doubt on the assumption that preferences can be taken as acontextual.

The fourth and most speculative section argues that people may not always think that there is commensurability between environmental quality and the things against which this good must be "traded off." The social resistance to commensurability helps explain some apparent oddities in the demand for legislation and in public thinking about environmental problems. I also suggest that despite its apparent oddity, the resistance to commensurability is plausible as a normative matter. The assumption that environmental and other goods can be assessed along the same metric does violence to some of our considered judgments about how (not how much) to value pristine areas, species, and other environmental amenities.

I. The Endowment Effect and Status Quo Bias

At the outset it will be useful to offer a catalogue of how law might deal, or fail to deal, with environmental issues. (1) It may fail to resolve collective action problems, conventionally defined. This is a usual understanding of the state of affairs under the common law. (2) It may actually solve collective action problems, conventionally defined. This is part of the optimistic, "public interest" account of environmental legislation. (3) It may reflect the political power of well-organized private groups, redistributing wealth in their favor while failing to improve and perhaps even impairing social welfare. This view is prominent in public choice theory. (4) It may be relatively chaotic and arbitrary, reflecting the order in which issues arise rather than aggregating preferences in an accurate way or embodying any coherent social judgment about the public good. This possibility, discussed in political science and economic writing following Arrow's impossibility theorem,[6] has been infrequently explored in the regulatory and environmental setting. (5) It may be a product of a process of deliberation among citizens and representatives in which private preferences for environmental amenities are transformed and shaped through exposure to new information and new perspectives.

In practice, it may not be easy to distinguish among some of these different possibilities. For example, (3) and (5) are especially hard to separate; we cannot easily test whether some measure claimed to be (5) is in fact (3). But it is useful to keep these possibilities in mind while thinking about both the positive and normative issues.

In this section, I argue that sometimes there are no acontextual preferences with which to do normative or positive work. Preferences can be a function of the initial allocation of the legal entitlement. Evaluation of environmental goods is sometimes an artifact of law. When this is so, policy makers cannot simply identify preferences and try to satisfy them, since the preferences are influenced by law, and since there is no way to identify the preferences that would exist in the absence of law.

The Coase Theorem and the Endowment Effect

With respect to environmental issues, it is natural to begin with the Coase theorem.[7] Notably, the theorem was originally developed in the context of an environmental problem arising in the law of tort. Coase's conclusion was of course that in the absence of transaction costs, the initial assignment of a legal entitlement will be irrelevant to (a) the ultimate use of property or (b) the level of the relevant activities. The theorem suggests, for example, that where transaction costs are zero, it "does not matter" whether an entitlement is given to breathers or to polluters, to railroads or to farmers. The two will in any case bargain to a result that is both efficient and (more striking) the same.

It should be plain that the Coase theorem (like most illuminating work in economics) takes preferences as both static and given. This is a key feature of the claim that the ultimate use of property, and ultimate activity levels, are unaffected by the allocation of the entitlement.

But insofar as the Coase theorem says that the result will be the same independently of the legal rule, it rests on an intriguingly false assumption, one that suggests that it may sometimes be impossible for government to take preferences "as they are." As we saw in chapters 1 and 2, preferences are a function of context; a complex set of mental forces underlie choices, and the notion of "preference," as a shorthand for those forces, can lead in misleading and unprofitable directions. Imagine, for example, a decision to use energy conservation techniques in one's business, to recycle, or to shift to solar energy or natural gas. Any such decision will be based on a range of factors—social norms and pressures, one's reaction to prevailing norms and pressures, economic cost, the importance of cost, one's self-image, inertia, resistance to inertia, judgments about the good, altruism, habit, and much more. These various factors may well shift within the person or across social groups over time.

For present purposes, a particular problem is that whether people have a preference for a good, a right, or anything else is often in part a function of whether the government, or the law, has allocated it to them in the first instance. There is simply no way to avoid the task of initially allocating a legal entitlement, at least short of anarchy (the only system without initial allocations). What people "have" is a product of what the law protects. And with respect to environmental amenities, what people have can be, simply as a matter of fact, a creation of legally conferred rights.[8]

The key point is that the decision to grant an environmentally relevant entitlement to A rather than B can affect the valuations of that entitlement by both A and B. More specifically, the initial grant of the entitlement to A frequently makes A value that entitlement more than he would if the right had been allocated to B. (It also makes B value it less than he otherwise would.) The initial allocation—the legal rule saying who owns what, before people begin to contract with one another—serves to create, to legitimate, and to reinforce social understandings about presumptive rights of ownership. That allocation can help produce individual perceptions about the entitlement in question.[9] It should be clear that if this is so, the demand for environmental regulation will be importantly affected by the initial allocation.

The effect on preferences of the initial allocation of a commodity or an entitlement is commonly described as the "endowment effect."[10] The endowment effect suggests that any initial allocation of an entitlement—and government cannot refuse to make an initial allocation—may well have effects on preferences.

Survey Evidence and Experimental Results

This point has received considerable empirical confirmation, often in the context of environmental amenities. One study found that people would demand about five times as much to allow destruction of trees in a park as they would pay to prevent the destruction of those same trees.[11] When hunters were questioned about the potential destruction of a duck habitat, they said that they would be willing to pay an average of $247 to prevent the loss—but would demand no less than $1044 to accept it.[12] In another study, participants required payments to accept degradation of visibility ranging from five to more than sixteen times higher than their valuations based on how much they were willing to pay to prevent the same degradation.[13] According to yet another study, the compensation demanded for accepting a new risk of immediate death of .001 percent was one or two orders of magnitude higher than the amount of willingness to pay to eliminate an existing risk of the same magnitude.

A related survey showed similarly large status quo biases in willingness to pay for changes in risks. Thus, only 39 percent of respondents would accept $700 to have their chance of a serious accident increased by 0.5 percent (from 0.5 to 1.0 percent); the substantial majority of 61 percent would refuse the trade. By contrast, only 27 percent would trade an identical decrease in accident risk (from 1 to 0.5 percent) for $700; here an even larger majority of 73 percent would refuse to do. In another study, people were willing to pay $3.78 on average to decrease the risk from an insecticide, but 77 percent refused to buy the product at any price, however reduced, if the risk level would increase by an equivalent amount.[14]

Another experiment found a significant disparity between willingness to accept (WTA) and willingness to pay (WTP) in the especially interesting context of irreversible choices about preserving species and other environmental amenities. In one experiment, the authors tried to ascertain the "existence value" of a houseplant that grows like a pine tree. The subjects were told that any trees not sold or kept would be killed at the end of the experiment. The mean willingness to pay to avoid the "kill" option was $7.81. The mean willingness to accept payment to allow a tree to be killed was $18.43.[15] In short: A powerful status quo bias affects reactions to environmental risks or losses.[16]

There are of course notorious problems with survey evidence, which may not be a reliable guide to real-world judgments and behavior. But experimental studies reveal similar effects. For example, a study showed that people who were given certain objects—pens, coffee mugs, and binoculars—placed a much higher valuation on those objects than did those who were required to purchase them. People initially given such things required a relatively high price from would-be purchasers; people not initially given such things would offer a relatively low price to would-be sellers.[17] No such effects were observed for money tokens in otherwise identical experiments.

A similar study gave some participants a mug and others a chocolate bar, and told members of both groups they could exchange one for the other. Participants in a third group, not given either, were told that they could select one or the other; 56 percent of these selected the candy bar. By contrast, 89 percent of those initially given the mug refused to trade it for the candy bar, and only 10 percent of those initially given the candy were willing to trade it for the mug.[18] The different evaluations apparently could not be explained by reference to anything other than the initial endowment.

In some studies, the disparity between WTA and WTP—the extent of the endowment effect—appears to diminish with repeated participation in a market. But it rarely disappears entirely, and many studies show that the disparity persists.[19] The range of the disparity appears to vary from slight amounts to a ratio of more than four to one, with WTA usually doubling WTP. In field studies, environmental goods tend to reflect a disparity of factors from two to over ten.[20] In some environmental experiments involving trees, the WTA/WTP ratio is extraordinarily high, ranging between 60/1 and 90/1.[21]

Explanations

In many settings, then, it has been shown that people place a higher value on rights or goods that they currently hold than they place on the same goods when in the hands of others. The disparity is puzzling; but there are many possible explanations.

Some studies suggest that that assignment creates the basic "reference state" from which judgments of fairness are subsequently made, and those judgments affect preferences and private willingness to pay.[22] On this account, people perceive things as fair if they stay close to the status quo, and judgments of fairness connect to preferences. An especially influential approach to the endowment effect stresses "loss aversion," which refers to the fact that a negative change from the status quo is usually seen as more harmful than a positive change is seen as beneficial. Here too there is a status quo bias.

Perhaps, too, people prefer what they have to what they might have because of psychological attachments to existing allocations. Endowment effects may thus reflect an effort to reduce cognitive dissonance. High valuation of what one owns, and low valuation of what one does not, is a means of reducing dissonance, and in some respects it is highly adaptive. It may well be welfare-promoting.[23] Perhaps the initial allocation has an important legitimating effect. It may suggest that the entitlement "naturally" belongs where it has been placed, and therefore puts a social burden on even voluntary changes. In some cases, the divergence between willingness to pay and willingness to accept is probably a product of the change in social attitudes brought about by the change in the allocation of the entitlement. With respect to sexual harassment, for example, the mere shift in the entitlement appears to have had significant attitudinal effects. The example may be generalizable. As we saw in chapter 2, the allocation of the entitlement may reflect and affect social norms, and social norms can affect people's sense of shame about their behavior. When people are asked to allow environmental amenities to be eliminated, shame may be a powerful barrier to action.

There are other possibilities. Endowment effects may come from experience; people who use a product or have an entitlement may learn to appreciate its value. They may also be a product of strategic considerations. Someone may be unwilling to give up a right because the concession would reveal weakness in bargaining. Sometimes apparent endowment effects might be produced by the wealth effect of the initial allocation of the entitlement. Different allocations produce differences in wealth—someone with more entitlements is to that extent richer—and perhaps some allocations have wealth effects sufficiently large to affect the point at which people will bargain.

Alternately, such effects might derive from what we might call "anticipated ex post regret."[24] People who trade one good for another may fear that in the event of disappointment, they will be left not only with a good of uncertain value, but also with a feeling of personal responsibility and thus intense regret for having brought about that very fact. In the environmental context, the explanation may be connected with the fact that substitutes do not exist for some public goods.[25] It has been suggested—in an account overlapping with that based on shame—that the disparity is connected with intrinsic moral values, involving the assignment of moral responsibility for the destruction of environmental assets. The WTA measure assigns responsibility to the individual. The WTP measure does so more ambiguously.[26] Perhaps some of the disparity can be attributed to the desire to avoid or to minimize the feeling that one has been morally culpable for producing the loss of an environmental amenity.[27]

Notably, some of these explanations do not depend on real preference change at all. They account for endowment effects while holding preferences constant. But these sorts of explanations do not appear sufficient.

For present purposes, it is enough to say that the initial allocation often shapes preferences, and that no legal system can operate without an initial allocation. When this is so, there is no acontextual "preference" with which to do legal or political work. A government deciding on environmental issues cannot be neutral among preferences when—and this is the key point—it does not know what preferences are until it has acted, and when there is no sense in which it can refuse to act (again, short of anarchy).

It is tempting to respond that government might indeed refuse to act—as, for example, by failing to create liability at all. A railroad might be freely permitted to emit air pollution, for instance. Is this not a case of inaction?

Might not a system of this sort turn out to be neutral, in the sense that it simply allows people to do what they want in light of their (prelegal) preferences?

The answer is that such a system would not be neutral, that it would not involve inaction, and that it would not simply allow people to do what they want. A decision to permit railroads to emit pollution is a grant, by law, of a legal entitlement. It allocates the relevant right to the railroads. It is not helpful to point to what would happen in anarchy or in the state of nature. In anarchy or nature, the state does not enforce entitlements at all. In anarchy or nature, the state does not prohibit people from taking corrective action (of whatever sort) when they perceive themselves to be injured. In any legal system, by contrast, a right to pollute is indeed backed by the force of law. It is accompanied by state-enforced prohibitions on certain sorts of corrective action by victims, including physical violence, or the attempted taking, by victims, of relevant property interests. It is in this sense that the state, so long as it exists, inevitably allocates entitlements.

Now let us return to the Coase theorem. In light of the endowment effect, the theorem appears at least sometimes to be inaccurate insofar as it predicts that the allocation of the entitlement will not affect ultimate outcomes. (The theorem remains true insofar as it shows that the result will be efficient regardless of the initial allocation. There is no problem with the theorem to the extent that it says that under ideal conditions, private and social costs are equal.) The difficulty for this prediction is that it overlooks the effects of the initial allocation on preferences. The endowment effect means that contrary to the Coase theorem, the entitlement will tend to stay where it has initially been allocated. People to whom the entitlement has initially been allocated will value it most, and precisely because of the initial allocation. For example, a grant of the initial entitlement to breathers will probably make them value clean air more than they would otherwise.

Status Quo Bias

The endowment effect can be understood as a special instance of a much more general phenomenon: status quo bias. In many settings, people appear to give more weight to the status quo than would be predicted by conventional models of rational choice. The phenomenon appears to occur in many places.

Samuelson and Zeckhauser have shown that the affinity for the status quo appears to affect such diverse forms of behavior as brand allegiance, choice of insurance plans, changing public policies, marketing techniques, and investment decisions.[28] This affinity may be fully rational and it may well reflect the high costs of any transition. It may be that the goods people own become integrated into daily life, so that a form of relocation cost is incurred whenever currently owned goods are lost. Or status quo bias may reflect search costs. Whether or not rational, the phenomenon of status quo bias probably has some of the same roots as the narrower phenomenon of endowment effects. Loss aversion is plausibly at work here; so, too, with the effort to reduce cognition dissonance, the desire to avoid anticipated ex post regret, and the concern about one's moral responsibility for introducing changes in the status quo. In any case, there is evidence that people are more strongly biased toward the status quo than would be predicted by usual theory about decision making under uncertainty.

Positive Implications

If all this is correct, large consequences follow. We can predict that much governmental behavior in the environmental context will be a product of endowment effects. Private and public reactions to risks should reflect a status quo bias. Both supply and demand will be affected. Government regulation of new risks will predictably be more stringent than government regulation of (equivalent) old risks. This is so precisely because the public demand for regulation will be a product of status quo bias.

This is in fact what we observe. It is a defining characteristic of the current system of environmental controls.[29] New risks are regulated far more stringently than old ones, even though this strategy sometimes creates extremely perverse results, by perpetuating the life of the especially severe old risks and thus damaging public health and safety. New stationary sources of air pollution must meet technological requirements not imposed on old sources; new cars are regulated far more heavily than old ones.[30]

The disparity is sometimes explained on the ground that old industries seek to use regulation to stop new entry.[31] This is a plausible explanation. But without a lot of evidence, we cannot be sure that it is true. The disparity may well result in part from status quo bias. It would be useful to attempt to test the competing hypotheses, perhaps by seeing whether more stringent controls on new sources result when the producers of old pollution sources are better organized.

More generally, political participants should be able to exploit endowment effects by attempting to describe the regulatory status quo in a way that takes advantage of the phenomenon of loss aversion. Politicians are frequently successful when they are able to identify and control the perception of the status quo. One example is provided by constant political efforts to lower expectations by describing the status quo as systemically worse than in fact it is, so that the citizenry will rarely perceive deviations as losses but instead only as gains.

There are many examples in the area of environmental regulation. Consider, for example, the controversial and probably irrational Prevention of Significant Deterioration (PSD) program. The PSD program says roughly that states that met national ambient air quality standards in 1977 cannot suffer a deterioration in air quality, even if the air would remain very clean, and even if there are good reasons for allowing new development. The use of the 1977 benchmark seems puzzling and even senseless. There is no clear reason to conclude that the air cannot become dirtier than it happened to be in 1977, so long as it is consistent with the other national standards in the Clean Air Act.

How, then, can we explain the existence of the PSD program, which seems hard to justify on public interest grounds? Certainly part of the explanation comes from public choice theory. Representatives in "clear air" states disproportionately opposed the program, and those in "dirty air" states disproportionately supported it, no doubt in order to prevent the exodus of revenue-producing, polluting companies to "clean air" states.[32] But the apparently broad appeal of the PSD program may owe a good deal as well to the endowment effect. The perception that air quality ought at least to stay where it is— that the government should prevent deterioration from the status quo—seems to have widespread appeal. This is so despite the fact that other things being equal, regulatory efforts to make the air cleaner than it now is often face strong political roadblocks. The asymmetry cannot be fully explained on public interest grounds, for prevention of deterioration can be far worse than actual improvements. It probably has a good deal to do with status quo bias and with the initial endowment reflected in air quality at the time the legislation was under consideration.

Or consider one of the most-criticized features of the Clean Air and Clean Water Acts, the pervasive requirement that companies adopt the "best available technology" (BAT).[33] This strategy has been challenged on the ground that there is at best an incidental relationship between cost-effective environmental policy and adoption of BAT. In principle, it seems unreasonable to require everyone to adopt the best available technology. Instead, government should allow companies a high degree of flexibility in achieving air quality goals. Some companies should switch to clean energy sources, rather than put expensive technology on dirty energy sources; some companies should go out of business because once they pay the environmental costs, their activity is not worthwhile; some companies should not use BAT at all, since they do business in regions in which adoption of expensive technology is not sensible in light of the variables at stake.

An interest-group explanation is not entirely implausible for BAT requirements. But perhaps the requirements can also be understood as an outgrowth of status quo bias. If the technological status quo is thought to be an appropriate benchmark for legal requirements, its use in environmental law may not be so puzzling. There may be general agreement that the technological status quo is the best and fairest foundation for environmental law, even if this view will not survive critical scrutiny.

It is notable too that it appears very dificult (though not impossible) to bring about even rational environmental regulation through tax increases—on, for example, polluting vehicles or gasoline. "Green taxes" are supported by strong justifications; but they are an almost invisible part of our national environmental policy. Perhaps the difficulty can be attributed to the influence of the automobile industry; but some of the spokesmen for the industry have actually favored gasoline taxes. The difficulty may well be understood in terms of the endowment effect, as that effect operates to define the public demand for regulation. The existing price of gasoline marks the status quo from which departures are measured. Government efforts to raise the price therefore meet strong resistance. Hence the public is generally quite hostile to any effort to increase the price of gasoline.

By contrast, there are many popular regulatory requirements that ultimately raise the cost of energy and automobiles, but that do so mostly by affecting new sources. By almost any measure of social welfare, the direct tax approach would be preferable to the regulatory approach.[34] I do not deny that there are many possible explanations for currently dysfunctional environmental policy. But a contributing factor may be that a tax or fee imposes highly visible losses as compared with the status quo, whereas the regulatory approach does no such thing.

Or consider the fact that subsidies to mass transit might well be an especially sensible and inexpensive environmental strategy. If automobiles are a major contributor to air pollution, an important goal is to reduce vehicle miles traveled, as well as (or instead of) improving pollution control devices on cars. This much seems clear from the fact that regulatory requirements have not succeeded in reducing aggregate automobile pollution levels, because the decrease in air pollution per mile traveled has been more than offset by increases in total car use.[35] It follows that an imperative for environmental policy is to create incentives that will decrease the use of the underlying polluting activity (chapters 13 and 14). But this idea has played a relatively little role in policy, especially in the area in which it makes most sense: Government expenditures devoted to mass transit and highways.

Here, too, the political influence of the automobile industry is a plausible contributing factor. But status quo bias may play a large role as well. Because Americans have adapted their behavior to frequent use of the automobile, it is especially difficult to change their behavior in the direction of mass transit. This explanation helps to account for the remarkable comparative popularity in Europe of environmental strategies that do deter automobile use and promote mass transit.[36] In Europe, people have not so deeply adapted their practices and preferences to automobile use. Social norms are thus a culprit here, and they are taken as given when they might be more changeable and fluid than we think (chapter 2).

The point is very general. Public policy often takes the status quo—including, very prominently, the existence of particular firms—as if it were a given. Laws that endanger current institutions are subject to special social scrutiny. To some extent, this is fully rational in light of the real costs of transition. But I hypothesize that a large part of the phenomenon is attributable to a bias in favor of the status quo that is far stronger than traditional theory would predict.

Normative Implications

Thus far, we have seen that many puzzles in current environmental policy might be an outgrowth of the endowment effect and status quo bias. What about on the normative side?

The most general point is that the preference-shaping effects of legal rules cast doubt on the idea that environmental regulation should attempt to satisfy or follow some aggregation of private preferences. If legal rules have inevitable effects on preferences, it is hard to see how a government might even attempt to take preferences "as given" in any global sense. When preferences are a function of legal rules, the rules cannot be justified by reference to the preferences. Social rules and practices cannot be justified by practices that they have produced. Sometimes there is no such thing as a prelegal or prepolitical "preference" that can be used as the basis for decision.

The point has normative implications for environmental policy. One would expect that a decision to give farmers a right to be free from water pollution will have an impact on social attitudes toward clean water. The allocation may well affect the valuation of the rights by both current owners and would-be purchasers. In this sense—again speaking globally—neutrality as among preferences cannot be achieved through legal rules, because the preferences will sometimes be a function, or a creation, of legal rules. In setting policy, it may therefore be important to make some choice about the sorts of preferences that ought to be encouraged, rather than to act as if preferences can be kept constant.

None of this suggests that it is generally impossible for those interested in environmental law to work from existing preferences. Sometimes the endowment effect is small, and in any case we may well be able to generate a relatively narrow range of prices from which to make policy choices. But in valuation of natural resources, the endowment effect can create a significant problem, one that is impairing efforts to make contingent valuation of resources not traded on markets (chapter 4). It follows that some ground should ultimately be identified for choosing between the different outcomes that would be produced by preference-shaping legal rules.

II. Adaptive Preferences, Intrapersonal Collective Action Problems, Cascades, and Heuristics

Private preferences are endogenous to current practices, current opportunities, and past consumption. This conclusion is related to the endowment effect. In this section, I generalize the point.

Adaptive Preferences

People may well adapt their conduct and even their desires to what has been available. Consider here the story of the fox and the sour grapes. The fox does not want the grapes because he considers them to be sour; but his belief to this effect is based on the fact that the grapes are unavailable. It is therefore hard to justify their unavailability by reference to his preferences.[37] In the environmental context, it might be hypothesized that the preference for environmental quality will be especially weak among people who have not been exposed to pristine areas, clean water, and clean air. If the point is right, it has important implications for positive and normative work.[38]

To be sure, it will be hard to test this hypothesis in any authoritative way. There is an overlap between a lack of information on the one hand and an adaptation of preferences to what is available on the other. People unexposed to beautiful areas may be uninterested in them not because of an adaptation, but because they lack relevant information. Moreover, people whose preferences are said to have adapted to the absence of environmental quality are likely to be deprived in a general way. If so, it may be best not to say that their preferences have adapted, but that they are choosing rationally and as best they can among a limited set of opportunities. Both of these phenomena— lack of environmental information and apparent devaluation of environmental quality under conditions of deprivation, because of the need to trade it off against other goods—undoubtedly explain a good deal of private and public behavior. They help account for the fact that poor people seem comparatively uninterested in many forms of environmental protection. There is, however, a third possibility, sometimes realized in the world, in which people's preference for environmental quality is low because of an adaptation to what is available.

If this is so, we should be able to explain both private and public behavior accordingly. Akerlof and Dickens have argued that workers are unwilling to confront the real magnitude of environmental risks faced in the workplace, because it is too distressing for them to do so.[39] On this view, workers, having adapted their preferences and beliefs to a relatively risky status quo, attempt to reduce cognitive dissonance by concluding that the dangers are trivial. The claim is speculative and the relevant evidence is largely anecdotal. But there is some empirical support for the general view. Consider the fact that after the Three Mile Island nuclear power plant accident, it was the people who lived on Three Mile Island who, of all those polled, believed that the relevant risks were lowest.[40]

If the general claim is right, it would follow that the demand for environmental legislation might be relatively low among people deprived of exposure to environmental quality, and the phenomenon would be attributable to adaptation of preferences to what is available. It is extremely difficult to test this hypothesis against more conventional alternatives stressing learning and rational choice under conditions of deprivation. We might, however, begin to investigate the demand for environmental protection across regions and across nations. It would be especially valuable to see how the demand for environmental quality changes over time, perhaps with exposure to pristine areas, perhaps with a social belief that the degradation of environmental amenities is not inevitable, perhaps with the rise of organizations solving collective action problems of various sorts (see next section).

As a normative matter, it might also follow that existing preferences, as expressed in consumption choices, are an uncertain basis for environmental policy, since we cannot without circularity justify environmental outcomes by reference to preferences that those outcomes have generated. Of course, it is right to insist that government should usually respect private choices, partly because of the frustration and resentment that are produced by efforts to bring about change, and partly because of the constant risk of ignorance and bias on the government's part. But if what I have said here is true, it will be necessary to rethink the underanalyzed and vexing issue of paternalism, in environmental law and elsewhere.

Intrapersonal Collective Action Problems

A closely related problem arises when environmental preferences, as expressed in consumption choices, are a function of past acts of consumption and when such acts alter people's desires or beliefs in such a way as to cause long-term (subjective or objective) harm to them. In such cases, the two key facts are (a) that choices are endogenous to past consumption decisions and (b) that the effect of those decisions on current choices is pernicious. The effect is pernicious when the aggregate costs of consumption, over time, exceed the aggregate benefits. The phenomenon is a general one, but it is especially important in the context of environmental protection, where it is often said that it is necessary to alter social or individual habits by inducing people to engage in a different kind of behavior. A pervasive and difficult question involves the cost, especially the transition cost, of the attempted alteration. If choices are endogenous to past consumption behavior, we might hypothesize that the cost will often be lower than anticipated, and precisely because of the change in preference that is brought about by new behavior.

Consider the extreme case of an addiction. Here the problem is that the costs of not consuming the addictive substance increase dramatically over time, as the benefits of consumption remain constant or fall sharply.[41] A possible result is that the aggregate costs, over time or over a life, of consumption exceed the aggregate benefits, even though the initial consumption choice provides benefits that exceed costs. As a result, people can be made much worse off even by their own lights. In such cases, people, if fully informed, might well not want to become involved with the good in the first place. This situation might be described as involving an intrapersonal collective action problem,[42] in which the costs and benefits, within a particular person, of engaging in the same activity change dramatically over time. The key point is that consumption patterns bring about a significant change in preferences and in a way that makes people worse off in the long-run.[43]

While addiction is the most obvious case, it is part of a broad category, including a wide range of environmental examples. Consider, for example, myopic behavior, defined as a refusal—because the short-term costs exceed the short-term benefits—to engage in activity having long-term benefits that dwarf long-term costs. We can see this at both the social and individual levels. *Akrasia,* or weakness of the will, has a related structure (though it may also reflect a problem of incommensurability). Another kind of intrapersonal collective action problem, with particular importance for regulatory policy, is produced by habits, in which people engage in behavior because of the subjectively high short-term costs of change, notwithstanding the fact that the long-term benefits exceed the short-term benefits.

Habits that pose intrapersonal collective action problems are a prominent target of environmental regulation. Consider, for example, the issue of compulsory recycling. It may be that the costs of recycling are initially quite high, simply because the change of behavior is unsettling. The costs may include transition costs and the costs produced by private annoyance and irritation. But once people are in the habit of recycling, some of these costs decrease (perhaps because of learning, perhaps because of preference change), and for many people these costs may even turn into benefits. As a possible analogy, consider the habit of brushing one's teeth in the morning. Even for those who dislike brushing most, a failure to brush may still be more costly than brushing, simply because one is in the habit, and because the habit brings about internalized norms.

It may even be that people in the habit of recycling develop certain social norms and hence desires that help turn the hedonic costs of environmental protection into hedonic benefits and thus help solve the collective action problems pervasively at stake in environmental regulation. If so, there is much more to be said on behalf of recycling, as a policy alternative to a disposal tax, than at first appears. The legally induced change of preferences may well have salutary long-term consequences, though before proceeding, it is important for government to be certain of this fact.

The same considerations bear on the creation of incentives to use mass transit rather than automobiles. It may be that expenditures on mass transit, accompanied by gasoline taxes, will seem futile or be firmly resisted at first. Indeed, the relevant incentives will have to be very strong in order to encourage people to change their behavior, adaptive as this has been to cheap automobile transportation. Here is a case in which preferences are highly adaptive to existing social norms and past consumption choices, a fact that helps account for the high premium placed on automobile transportation in the United States as compared with (for example) Germany and Sweden. But once behavior begins to change, norms and hence preferences may change as well, and the subjective costs of using mass transit may well decrease. It is even possible to imagine a kind of bandwagon effect, as we have in fact seen in the context of recycling behavior.

This is a speculative hypothesis, and it would be good to test it. Some evidence could be produced from examining experience with compulsory seat belt usage. I hypothesize that after seat belt use has been compelled, the costs of buckling up decrease and may even turn into benefits, in the sense that an unbuckled belt will produce discomfort and annoyance. It would follow that states that have enacted and then repealed seat belt laws should see a large short-term increase in seat belt use even after a highly publicized repeal.

Cascades

Habits and customs can be vulnerable to large-scale shifts on the basis of relatively mild government interventions. Sometimes the practice of many people is dependent on what other people do. Once some people change their practices, a wide range of others change as well. Thus, it has been shown that "mass behavior is often fragile in the sense that small shocks can frequently lead to large shifts in behavior."[44]

This is so especially in view of the fact that the modest changes sometimes have a large signaling effect for other people. The signaling effect may suggest what is convenient to do or what is right to do (chapter 2). This point has implications for the positive and normative theory of environmental protection. Compulsory behavior—or disclosure of information—may produce a large-scale cascade in a certain direction as a result of new social norms. Something of this kind may have happened with respect to recycling and "green marketing." As a result, the effects of government policy may be quite different from what would be expected if it were assumed that preferences were rigid and fixed. The costs of regulatory change may therefore turn out to be lower than expected.

If this idea is to be used for policy purposes, it would be valuable to come up with precise predictions about the circumstances in which such cascades will occur. But we already have sufficient reason to believe that current tastes and habits are sometimes vulnerable to large-scale shifts.

The Availability Heuristic

A final problem is that perceptions of the world are endogenous to what events are psychologically "available," in the sense that they come readily to mind.[45] This problem should be grouped with the others in this section, for here, too, we are dealing with preferences and beliefs that are adaptive to context, and in a way that might have positive implications and also impeach their reliability for policy purposes.

If pervasive, the availability heuristic will produce systematic errors. Assessments of risk will be pervasively biased, in the sense that people will think that some risks (a nuclear accident, for example) are high, whereas others (a stroke) are relatively low. One would predict that the availability heuristic would help create a kind of crazy-quilt pattern in regulation, with some events calling for stringent regulation and others calling for little or no regulation at all. The regulation would not be closely associated with actual risk levels. This is the pattern we observe, as studies of American government show extraordinary disparities in expenditures per life saved; see Table 5.4 in chapter 5.

The disparities are plausibly attributed, at least in part, to the availability heuristic. The dramatic difference between expert and public assessments of risk levels (see chapter 5) has something to do with this heuristic, and the difference maps closely onto actual differences in expenditures per life saved. The public demand for regulation therefore appears to be a product of the availability heuristic, which is itself endogenous to the nature and levels of public and private publicity.

Thus, for example, there are enormous expenditures designed to counteract cancers in the workplace, and relatively low expenditures designed to prevent injuries in automobile accidents. The comparative overregulation of certain environmental risks may well be a product of the fact that those risks, when they come to fruition, are highly publicized. Through this route too we might be able to explain the other inexplicably severe controls on nuclear power. We might also be able to explain the extraordinary safety of air travel as compared with other means of transportation.[46]

The availability heuristic also has normative implications. It produces serious biases, and it is important to ensure that these are reduced or eliminated. A comprehensive system of uniform warnings about risk levels might well make public assessments less dependent on sensationalistic anecdotes, which very much affect the operation of the availability heuristic. Government information policies might bring public and expert judgments more closely into line. If this proves difficult, institutional changes, discussed in chapters 5 and 12 might be introduced so as to counteract the distorting features of the public demand for regulation.

III. Collective Judgments and Some Unusual Free-Rider Problems

Environmental measures might reflect the use of law to embody not the preferences that people hold as private consumers, but instead what might be described as "collective judgments," which sometimes solve collective action problems with unusual characteristics. In chapter 1, we saw that in political processes, people's "preferences"—or what backs their choices—are quite different from what they are in market arrangements. These preferences are subject to different norms and different constraints. They are endogenous to the setting in which they appear. It should hardly be surprising that they yield different outcomes.[47]

It is relevant in this connection that some people seek stringent laws protecting the environment or endangered species, even though they do not use the public parks or derive material benefits from protection of species—and even though in their private behavior, they are unwilling to do much to protect environmental amenities. The mere existence of certain environmental goods seems to be highly valued by political participants, even if they are not willing to back up the valuation with dollars in private markets. Of course, many people are so willing, and many people give to organizations that will do so. But it seems clear that the choices people make as political participants are different from those they make as consumers. It is in part for this reason that democratic outcomes are distinct from those that emerge from markets.

IV. Diverse Goods, Context, and Commensurability

The last point is the most speculative and complex, and its implications for positive and normative work are far from clear. The point starts with the fact that most positive theories assess environmental issues by reference to "preferences" for environmental quality viewed abstractly, through a unitary scale, along the same metric—that of utility or of willingness to pay. This approach is perfectly reasonable in light of the fact that people must make choices under conditions of scarcity, and it therefore seems sensible to say that people behave as if they make things commensurable, even if they do not do so knowingly or willingly.

The puzzle stems from the fact that ordinary people appear to resist the use of a unitary scale and the claim of commensurability along a single metric. Borrowing from the discussion in chapter 3, I claim that two goods are incommensurable if they are not valued in the same way, and if their assessment along a single metric therefore does violence to our considered judgments about how (not how much) these goods should be valued. This section attempts to see if it is possible to use this fact to make sense out of some otherwise puzzling phenomena relating to the public's environmental judgments. Through this route it may be possible to understand some features of the apparent demand for regulation, and this is so even if we ultimately conclude that the demand is built on confusion or irrationality. Consider a few examples.

1. Some people feel extremely insulted when asked how much they would accept for a specified level of environmental deterioration, treating the question as outrageous or a form of bribery, as if they had been asked to sell a child, a friendship, or a part of their body. "Studies using WTA questions have consistently received a large number of protest answers, such as 'I refuse to sell' or 'I want an extremely large or infinite amount of compensation for agreeing to this,' and have frequently experienced protest rates of 50 percent or more."[48]

2. Some people say that environmental goods have an infinite value or that the effort to achieve a clean environment should not be "traded off" against other important values. In opinion polls, people sometimes say that we should achieve a clean environment "regardless of cost."

3. Some apparently popular statutes reflect a kind of environmental absolutism. The Endangered Species Act forbids balancing except in the rarest of circumstances. Some statutes, including the Delaney Clause, forbid any entry of carcinogenic substances onto the market, banning trade-offs of any kind.

4. As noted, there are extraordinary disparities in federal expenditures per life saved. In some environmental programs, risks are prevented at enormous cost; the government is willing to spend relatively little to stop other risks. All current efforts to produce uniformity in expenditures have failed.

Phenomena of these sorts may in the end reflect irrationality, confusion, interest-group power, or sheer chance. But it would be useful to explore whether there might not be some other kind of explanation. When people are thinking in these various ways, exactly what are they doing?

We might hypothesize that people's apparently irrational valuation of environmental goods comes partly from an insistence that diverse social goods should not be assessed according to the same metric. Some people think that these diverse goods should be valued in qualitatively different ways. This is not to deny that people make trade-offs among incommensurable goods. But with this hypothesis, some apparent anomalies dissolve or become more readily explicable. Some people, for example, rebel against the idea that we should see all of the following, environmentally related consequences as "costs": unemployment, higher prices, greater poverty, dirtier air, more cancer, respiratory problems, the loss of species. It is tempting to say that this is simply an irrational thought. In a way, of course, all of these things are indeed costs; they are harmful things that society should, other things being equal, attempt to reduce. Moreover, the effort to render them commensurable by assimilating them to a unitary category—costs—is more than plausible. That effort is motivated by the view that through such assimilation, we will render tractable certain social decisions that otherwise become amorphous and unmanageable. If we have six, seven, or a thousand desiderata—if we have plural utility functions—and we assume that these are qualitatively distinct, we may not know what to say or do. A choice among them will be rendered too chaotic, and predictions will become impossible.

But it is also possible to understand the resistance to commensurability, captured in the insistence on qualitative distinctions, on diverse modes of valuation, and on the plurality of social goods. The resistance, with roots in John Stuart Mill, stems from the view that if we make diverse goods commensurable in this way, we will do violence to our considered judgments about how all these should be characterized, experienced, and understood. Some people think that those considered judgments are not embarrassing, but instead are part of what it means to think well. If all these things are understood as "costs," to be assessed via the same metric, important qualitative distinctions may become lost. Simply as a positive matter, it might be hypothesized that when people refuse to trade off environmental quality and other goods, they are making a claim about the diversity of goods and about incommensurability. They are claiming that one set of goods is superior to another, not in the sense that it is infinitely valuable, or in the sense that a small amount of it is more valuable than a large amount of something else, but in the sense that it is important to see that it is to be valued in a distinctive way and that it therefore stands higher in a hierarchy.[49]

This point leaves many ambiguities, and I will not be able to address them all here. But let us consider, as relevant to the proper conception of "trade-offs," the issue of environmental risks in the workplace. It is clear that people take jobs that expose them to certain risks to health and safety. From this, it is tempting to say that a risk of level A is really worth a dollar amount X, or that people value their lives at a certain dollar amount.[50] In a way, this makes obvious sense. But suppose that people firmly resist (as is predictable) the conclusion that the view to them, risk A, or their life, is really worth X.

Suppose they claim that this is not in fact their view. To the evidence of their behavior, suppose they respond that they did indeed take the job, but they adamantly resist any broader inference about their trade-offs between risk and dollars. Suppose that they adamantly resist the view that their particular decisions should play a part in regulatory choices by government. Is it clear that they are not making sense?

Even if they are indeed not making sense, we might be able to use their responses to understand some otherwise peculiar features of the social demand for environmental regulation. And it is even possible that they are making sense. If so, it is because their valuation is not an acontextual one or a global judgment, but instead is highly dependent on and geared only to the particular setting in which the choice is made. When a worker accepts a risky job for cash, it may be wrong to say that he "really" thinks that the risk is equivalent to that amount of cash—if the word "really" is intended to capture an abstract, acontextual judgment. Instead, he has simply taken the job, and this decision, in its context, may mean nothing more general.

Through this route, it might be possible to help account for phenomena (1) through (4) noted earlier. For example, the risk charts might reflect qualitative distinctions among different sorts of hazards. As we saw in chapter 5, people are interested not only in cost per life saved, but also in whether the risk was voluntarily assumed; whether the exposed person, the employer, or the employee knows the facts; whether the underlying activity produces valuable goods; whether the hazard is common; whether the exposure is essential to productive activity; whether the risk is encountered occupationally or elsewhere; whether the people subjected to risk were able to participate in making relevant decisions. With such questions, it may emerge that people's valuations of different risks will vary a good deal with context. Hence the varying valuations may reflect not irrationality or interest-group pressure, but diverse judgments about qualitatively diverse risks.

I do not claim that the actual disparities can be justified in this way. In view of their obvious irrationality, that conclusion would be extravagant. But it may well be rational to allow widely varying expenditures in light of the diverse factors just outlined, and at least some of the current variations might have some such foundation.

It might also be possible to understand some of the reactions to opinion polls and perhaps environmental legislation as well. Let us begin with an exotic example. If a pet owner were asked how much he would accept to allow his pet cat or dog to be used for laboratory experiments, he could be insulted and might well respond very much like the people in (1). This is so even though economic valuation of pets, in terms of purchase price, sale price, and medical expenditures, is perfectly common. This response stems from the fact that the pet owner's ordinary attitude toward his pet is incompatible with the idea that that pet is solely for human experimentation—though that attitude is not incompatible with imposing budgetary limits on sale price and on medical expenditures. In these circumstances, the problem is not that the offered price is too low, or that the pet is infinitely valuable, but that the very idea of sale for the purpose of experimentation seems inappropriate. Some people think of freedom from certain environmental risks, and the protection of pristine areas, in just this way. They value the relevant goods not for their use but for their beauty. The emphasis on "use value" inadequately captures the way they value the relevant goods. We might conclude that much public discussion about the environment is about the appropriate mode (not only the appropriate level) of valuation for diverse human goods.

If something of this kind is right, it may be that people think that the loss through human action of an endangered species is incommensurably (not infinitely) bad, and that this thought should be expressed through regulatory proscriptions. To say the least, this view raises many complexities. All I mean to suggest is that it is a common idea.

In some cases, the claim of incommensurability is understandably but wrongly converted into a claim of infinite value or of incomparability. It is wrongly so converted because people do and must make choices under conditions of scarcity. We might think that (say) a loss of a species cannot really be made commensurable with the loss of jobs, but that neither of these is of infinite value, and that it is appropriate, even if tragic, to sacrifice one incommensurable good for another. The hard questions, not yet fully elaborated in the philosophical literature, remain: How does one make choices when noncommensurable social goods are at stake, and when some of these must be sacrificed? When noncommensurable goods are at stake, how can choices be assessed as reasonable or not? I cannot attempt to answer these questions here. But attention to valuation of the diverse goods at stake in environmental regulation may well provide relevant information on this subject.

Conclusion

Recent refinements and qualifications of rational choice theory have important implications for the study of government regulation. Above all, the endogeneity of preferences offers a large area for positive work. Some environmental outcomes can be explained by status quo bias and the endowment effect. In particular, these phenomena help account for the asymmetry between old and new risks and the public antipathy toward strategies that create incentives to decrease use of automobiles.

Both private and public behavior in the environmental context are an outgrowth of the fact that environmental preferences are endogenous to available opportunities, to shifting social norms, and to past acts of consumption. Some environmental outcomes may well be a reflection of the asymmetry between political and consumption choices, an asymmetry sometimes attributable to the peculiar features of political deliberation. It is incorrect to say that the consumption choice accurately reflects a preference, whereas a political choice does not. The preference is itself endogenous to the setting in which it is expressed. Finally, I suggest that environmental absolutism sometimes results from a resistance to claims of commensurability between environmental and other goods. From these admittedly speculative claims, there is obviously large room for empirical testing.

I have made some normative suggestions as well. Private preferences are an inadequate basis for environmental policy, insofar as these are adaptive to an environmentally inadequate status quo. At least under ideal conditions (met rarely in the real world), democratic choices about the environment are probably to be preferred over private consumption choices, even if free-rider and informational problems could be solved. Finally, claims of incommensurability among diverse environmental goods are at least plausible so long as they are not confused with claims of infinite valuation. Much remains to be done on this important and difficult subject.

In the end, I believe, these sorts of suggestions will point to the need to question whether private preferences should be the exclusive touchstone of environmental policy. We might venture as well an account of what human beings need for good lives [51] and try to set up conditions under which democratic decisions about environmental matters can be most fully informed, so as to ensure appropriate valuation of diverse environmental assets. [52] To undertake such endeavors would be to recover important aspects of the old discipline of political economy. But an account of these abstract and complex claims would take me well beyond the present discussion.

Notes

1. The Prevention of Significant Deterioration program is a conspicuous example. See 42 U.S.C. 7470 et seq. See B. Peter Pashigian, "Environmental Regulation: Whose Self-Interests Are Being Served?" in *Chicago Studies in Political Economy*, George J. Stigler, ed. (Chicago: University of Chicago Press, 1988).

2. This approach is pervasive in environmental law. See, e.g., 42 U.S.C. 7475; 42 U.S.C. 7411; 33 U.S.C. 301.

3. Examples include the emphasis on "scrubbing" coal, see Bruce A. Ackerman and William T. Hassler, *Clean Coal/Dirty Air: or How the Clean Air Act Became a Multibillion Dollar Bail-Out for High Sulfur Coal Producers and What Can be Done About It.* (New Haven: Yale University Press, 1981), and more recently, the clean fuels provisions of the 1990 Clean Air Act, see Jonathan Adler, "Clean Fuels, Dirty Air," in *Environmental Politics*, eds. (New York: Praeger, Michael Greve and Fred Smith, 1991), p. 19.

4. The relevant work is extremely diverse. See, e.g., Richard Thaler, *Quasi-Rational Economics* (New York: Russell Sage Foundation, 1991); Richard Thaler, *The Winner's Curse: Paradoxes and Anomalies of Economic Life* (New York: Free Press, 1992); Thomas Schelling, *Choice and Consequence* (Cambridge: Harvard University Press, 1984); George Ainslie, *Picoeconomics: The Interaction of Successive Motivational States Within the Individual* (Cambridge: Cambridge University Press, 1992); Jon Elster, *Sour Grapes: Studies in the Subversion of Rationality* (Cambridge: Cambridge University Press, 1983); Gary Becker and Kevin Murphy, "A Theory of Rational Addiction," 94 *J. Pol. Econ.* 675 (1988); Amartya Sen, *Inequality Reexamined* (Cambridge: Harvard University Press, 1992); W. Kip Viscusi, *Fatal Tradeoffs: Public and Private*

Responsibilities for Risk (New York: Oxford University Press, 1992), chapters 6, 7, and 8; Jon Elster, *Ulysses and the Sirens: Studies in Rationality and Irrationality* (Cambridge: Cambridge University Press, 1979); Daniel Kahneman and Amos Tversky, "Prospect Theory: An Analysis of Decision under Risk," 47 *Econometrica* 263 (1979); C. C. von Weiszacker, "Notes on Endogenous Change of Tastes," 3 *J. Econ. Theory* 345 (1971); Gary Becker, "The Economic Way of Looking At Life," Law & Economics Working Paper No. 12, University of Chicago, (1993), pp. 15–19. A helpful collection is *Rationality in Action*, Paul Moser, ed. (Cambridge: Cambridge University Press, 1990), especially Part IB.

5. A leading essay is Roger Noll and James Krier, "Some Implications of Cognitive Psychology for Risk Regulation," 19 *J. Legal Stud.* 747 (1990). See, generally, Herbert Hovenkamp, "Legal Policy and the Endowment Effect," 20 *J. Legal Stud.* 225 (1991); Elizabeth Hoffman and Matthew Spitzer, "The Divergence Between Willingness-to-Pay and Willingness-to-Accept Measures of Value," 71 *Wash. U. L. Q.* J9 (1993); Elizabeth Anderson, "Some Problems in the Normative Theory of Rational Choice, With Consequences for Empirical Research" (Univ. of Michigan, Dept. of Philosophy, unpublished manuscript). See also Becker, *supra* note 4, at 19: "An important step in extending the traditional analysis of individual rational choice is to incorporate into the theory a much richer class of attitudes, preferences, and calculations."

6. See Kenneth Arrow, *Social Choice and Individual Values*, 2d ed. (New Haven: Yale University Press, 1963). For a critique, see Richard Pildes and Elizabeth Anderson, "Slinging Arrows at Democracy: Social Choice Theory, Value Pluralism, and Democratic Politics," 90 *Colum. L. Rev.* 2121 (1990)

7. See Ronald Coase, "The Problem of Social Cost," 3 *J. Law & Econ.* 1 (1960).

8. I am not speaking here of wealth effects, to which Coase does refer. See Ronald Coase, *The Firm, the Market, and the Law* (Chicago: University of Chicago Press, 1988), pp. 170–74. Wealth effects consist of the consequences for social demand of shifts in wealth brought about by the allocation of the entitlement. In most real-world cases, it has been persuasively argued that wealth effects are likely to be small. See R. D. Willig, "Consumer's Surplus Without Apology," 66 *Am. Econ. Rev.* 589 (1976), though the point is controversial. The empirical work on endowment effects has shown consequences for willingness to pay that do not depend on material changes in wealth. There is thus an important difference between wealth effects and endowment effects. They are not equivalent phenomena.

9. I do not claim that private preferences are always an artifact of law. In some cases, people order their affairs on the basis of social norms that operate independently of law, and the preferences that undergird those norms are not legally constructed. See Robert Ellickson, *Order Without Law: How Neighbors Settle Disputes* (Cambridge: Harvard University Press, 1991).

10. It was first so-called in Richard Thaler, "Toward a Positive Theory of Consumer Choice," 1 *J. Econ. Behavior and Org.* 39 (1980). This essay, along with others of similar interest, can be found in Thaler, *Quasi-Rational Economics*, *supra* note 4.

11. David S. Brookshire and Don Coursey, "Measuring the Value of a Public Good: An Empirical Comparison of Elicitation Procedures," 77 *Am. Econ. Rev.* 554 (1987).

12. Judd Hammock and G. M. Brown, *Waterfowl and Wetlands: Toward Bioeconomic Analysis* (Washington, D.C.: Resources for the Future [distr. Johns Hopkins University Press, Baltimore], 1974); Robert Rowe et al., "An Experiment on the Economic Value of Visibility," 7 *J. Env. Econ. and Management* 1 (1980).

13. Richard Thaler, "Toward a Positive Theory of Consumer Choice," 1 *J. Econ. Behavior and Org.* 39 (1980). A good overview is Hoffman and Spitzer, *supra* note 5.

14. W. Kip Viscusi, Wesley Magat, and Peter Huber, "An Investigation of the Rationality of Consumer Valuations of Multiple Health Risks," 18 *RAND J. Econ.* 465 (1987).

15. See Rebecca Boyce, et al., "An Experimental Examination of Intrinsic Values as a Source of the WTA-WTP Disparity," 82 *Am. Econ. Rev.* 1366 (1992).

16. See, generally, William Samuelson and Richard Zeckhauser, "Status Quo Bias in Decision Making," 1 *J. Risk and Uncertainty* 7 (1988).

17. Daniel Kahneman, Jack Knetsch, and Richard Thaler, "Experimental Tests of the Endowment Effect and the Coase Theorem," 98 *J. Pol. Econ.* 1325 (1990). See also Jack Knetsch, "The Endowment Effect and Evidence of Nonreversible Indifference Curves," 79 *Am. Econ. Rev.* 1277 (1989); Jack Knetsch and Harry Sinden, "Willingness to Pay and Compensation Demanded: Experimental Evidence of an Unexpected Disparity in Measures of Value," 86 *Q. J. Econ.* 507 (1984).

18. Knetsch, *supra* note 17.

19. See the overview in Hoffman and Spitzer, *supra* note 5.

20. See Boyce et al., *supra* note 15, at 1366.

21. Brookshire and Coursey, *supra* note 11.

22. See Daniel Kahneman, Jack Knetsch, and Richard Thaler, "Fairness and the Assumptions of Economics," in *Rational Choice: The Contrast Between Economics and Psychology.* Robin M. Hogarth and Melvin W. Reder, eds. (Chicago: University of Chicago Press, 1987), pp. 101, 113–14. See also Edward Zajac, *Political Economy of Fairness* (Cambridge: MIT Press, 1995).

23. See Shelley E. Taylor, *Positive Illusions: Creative Self-Deception and the Healthy Mind* (New York: Basic Books, 1989).

24. Cf. Graham Loomes and Robert Sugden, "Regret Theory: An Alternative Theory of Rational Choice Under Uncertainty," 92 *Econ. J.* 805 (1982); Graham Loomes and Robert Sugden, "Disappointment and Dynamic Consistency in Choice Under Uncertainty," 53 *Rev. Econ. Stud.* 271 (1986); David Harless, "Actions Versus Prospects: The Effect of Problem Representation on Regret," 82 *Am. Econ. Rev.* 634 (1992); Chris Starmer and Robert Sugden, "Probability and Juxtaposition Effects: An Experimental Investigation of the Common Ratio Effect," 2 *J. Risk and Uncertainty* 159 (1989); Graham Loomes, "Further Evidence of the Impact of Regret and Disappointment in Choice Under Uncertainty," 55 *Econometrica* 47 (1988).

25. See Michael Hanemann, "Willingness to Pay and Willingness to Accept: How Much Can They Differ?" 81 *Am. Econ. Rev.* 635 ((1991).

26. This is an apparently pervasive social judgment about responsibility, but it must of course be defended; it is not self-evident.

27. See Boyce et al., *supra* note 15.

28. William Samuelson and Richard Zeckhauser, "Status Quo Bias in Decision Making," 1 *J. Risk and Uncertainty* 7 (1988).

29. See Peter Huber, "The Old/New Division in Risk Regulation," 64 *Va. L. Rev.* 613 (1984).

30. See Cass R. Sunstein, *After the Rights Revolution: Reconceiving the Regulatory State* (Cambridge: Harvard University Press, 1990).

31. See *Chicago Studies in Political Economy*, George J. Stigler, ed. (Chicago: University of Chicago Press, 1988).

32. Pashigian, *supra* note 1.

33. 42 U.S.C. 7475; 42 U.S.C. 7411; 33 U.S.C. 301.

34. See Robert W. Crandall, "Policy Watch: Corporate Average Fuel Economy Standards," 6 *J. Econ. Persp.* 171 (1992).

35. Robert W. Crandall, et al., *Regulating the Automobile* (Washington D. C.: Brookings Institution, 1986).

36. See Marcia Lowe, "Shaping Cities," in *State of the World, 1992: A Worldwatch Institute Report on Progress Toward a Sustainable Society*, Lester Brown, ed.(London: Earthscan, 1992).

37. Jon Elster, *supra* note 4.

38. Amartya Sen has insisted on this general point in many places. See Amartya Sen, *Commodities and Capabilities* (New York: North-Holland, 1985); Sen, *Inequality Reexamined, supra* note 4.

39. See George Akerlof and Robert Dickens, "The Economic Consequences of Cognitive Dissonance," 72 *Am. Econ. Rev.* 307 (1982).

40. See Elliott Aronson, *The Social Animal*, 4th ed. (New York: W. H. Freeman, 1984). It is possible, of course, that the people who lived in this area were better informed.

41. But see Alan Schwartz, "Views of Addiction and the Duty to Warn," 75 *Va. L. Rev.* 509 (1989); W. Kip Viscusi, *Smoking: Making the Risky Decision* (New York: Oxford University Press, 1992).

42. Thomas Schelling, "Egonomics, or the Art of Self-Management," 68 *Am. Econ. Rev.* 290 (Papers and Proceedings) (1978); Jon Elster, "Weakness of Will and the Free-Rider Problem," 1 *Econ. & Philos.* 231 (1985). See also Ainslie, *Picoeconomics, supra* note 4; Jon Elster, ed., *The Multiple Self* (Cambridge: Cambridge University Press, 1988).

43. Of course, all consumption has an effect on preferences. For example, exposure to classical music usually increases appreciation. But the pattern under discussion is a rare one; it is that pattern, producing miserable lives, to which a democracy might respond. To be sure, in practice, the response might make things worse rather than better.

44. See Sushil Bikchandani, David Hirshleifer, and Ivo Welch, "A Theory of Fads, Fashions, Custom, and Cultural Change as Informational Cascades," 100 *J. Polit. Econ.* 992 (1992). See also Douglas Baird, *Strategic Behavior and the Law: The Role of Game Theory and Information Economics in Legal Analysis* (Chicago: University of Chicago Program in Law and Economics, 1993), ch. 6.

45. See Noll and Krier, *supra* note 5; Kahneman and Tversky, *supra* note 4; Viscusi, *Fatal Tradeoffs, supra* note 4.

46. See Nancy L. Rose, "Fear of Flying? Economic Analyses of Airline Safety," 6 *J. Econ. Persp.* 75 (1992).

47. Cf. the discussion of "dual utility functions" in Howard Margolis, *Selfishness, Altruism, and Rationality: A Theory of Social Choice* (Cambridge: Cambridge University Press, 1982); see also Mark Sagoff, *The Economy of the Earth : Philosophy, Law and the Environment* (Cambridge: Cambridge University Press, 1988).

48. Robert Cameron Mitchell and Richard T. Carlson, *Using Surveys to Value Public Goods* (Washington, D.C.: Resources for the Future, 1989), p. 34: "These extreme responses reflect the feelings of outrage often seen when communities are faced with the prospect of accepting a new risk such as a nuclear power plant or waste disposal facility." Daniel Kahneman, Jack Knetsch, and Richard Thaler, "The Endowment Effect, Loss Aversion, and Status Quo Bias," 5 *J. Econ. Persp.* 193, 203 (1991).

49. See the discussion of hierarchical incommensurability in Pildes and Anderson, *supra* note 6. One should not make too much of this claim, even if it is descriptively

accurate and normatively plausible. It may still be most parsimonious to study behavior as if people believed in commensurability, even if they do not or believe that they do not. Moreover, the fact that people make choices among diverse goods may be all we need to engage the assumption of commensurability.

50. See W. Kip Viscusi, *Risk by Choice: Regulating Health and Safety in the Marketplace* (Cambridge: Harvard University Press, 1983); Viscusi, *Fatal Tradeoffs*, supra note 4.

51. This is the direction suggested in Sen, *Inequality Reexamined*, *supra* note 4, and Sen, *Commodities and Capabilities*, *supra* note 38.

52. This is the direction suggested in Elizabeth Anderson, *supra* note 5.

Paradoxes of the Regulatory State

By "paradoxes of the regulatory state," I mean self-defeating regulatory strategies—strategies that achieve an end precisely opposite to the one intended, or to the only public-regarding justification that can be brought forward in their support. An example of a regulatory paradox would be a Clean Air Act that actually made the air dirtier, or a civil rights law that increased the incidence of racial discrimination. This definition excludes a number of pathologies of the regulatory state that are clearly related to the phenomenon of regulatory paradoxes, such as strategies whose costs exceed their benefits, or that have unintended adverse consequences. I am interested only in self-defeating regulatory strategies here.

A large literature, inspired by public choice theory and welfare economics, has grown up around the theory that purportedly public-interested regulation is almost always an effort to create a cartel or to serve some private interest at the public expense. Although I shall be drawing on much of that literature here, I do not conclude, as some of that literature appears to, that the appropriate response to regulatory paradoxes is to abandon modern regulation altogether and rest content with the operation of private markets. In many cases, the market itself produces harmful or even disastrous results, measured in terms of efficiency or justice. The appropriate response to the paradoxes of regulation is not to return to a system of "laissez faire," but to learn from past failures. To this end, I outline the lessons, for legislators, judges, and administrators, that are to be drawn from the omnipresence of regulatory paradoxes. My general goal is to describe some reforms by which to restructure regulatory institutions so as to achieve their often salutary purposes, while at the same time incorporating the flexibility, respect for individual autonomy and initiative, and productive potential of economic markets.

I. The Performance of the Regulatory State:
A Prefatory Note

Empirical assessments of the consequences of regulation remain in a primitive state; but it is possible to draw several general conclusions. I outline some of them here.

In many ways things are getting better, not worse. The average American's life expectancy at birth was 47 years in 1900; it rose to 78 in 1990, partly because the death rate from infectious diseases is less than 5 percent, down from 20 percent in 1900. Consider the data in Table 11.1.

Undoubtedly many of these improvements come from social changes having nothing to do with regulation. But the view that regulation has generally proved unsuccessful is far too crude. Some of the progress comes from more and better immunizations, better nutrition, and improved water and sanitation systems, some of which is a result of governmental activity and regulatory controls. In fact, environmental protection has produced enormous gains.[1] Regulatory controls have helped to produce substantial decreases in both the levels and emissions of major pollutants, including sulfur dioxide, carbon monoxide, lead, and nitrogen dioxide. Lead is an especially dangerous substance, and ambient concentrations of lead have decreased especially dramatically, declining 96 percent since 1975; transportation emissions of lead decreased from 122.6 million metric tons in 1975 to 3.5 in 1986. The EPA's phase-down of lead in gasoline was firmly supported by cost-benefit analysis. So, too, carbon monoxide levels fell 57 percent from 1975 to 1991; nixtrous oxide levels fell about 24 percent; and particulate levels fell 26 percent. Most important, the vast majority of counties in the United States are now in compliance with air quality goals. In 1982, about 100 million people lived in nonattainment areas; in 1994, the number was about 54 million.

Water pollution control has shown significant successes as well. Perhaps most important, all sewage in the nation is treated before it is discharged, and the treatment ordinarily brings water to a level safe for swimming. There are many successes with respect to particular water bodies. The Great Lakes are much cleaner than they were in 1965. Phosphorus loading is, for example, substantially down, somewhere between 40 and 70 percent less than in peak years. Levels of PCBs in the Great Lakes are almost 90 percent lower than they were in 1973.

In addition, a number of harmful nutrients have been reduced by nearly 50 percent in national rivers. In 1970, about 25 percent of U.S. river miles were safe for fishing and swimming; the number is now about 56 percent. Industrial pollutants in Chesapeake Bay fell by 53 percent in the brief period from 1988 to 1992. Governmentally required lead and nitrate reductions have produced huge improvements in water quality. Ocean dumping of sludge is now substantially eliminated in the United States. All in all, both air and water are substantially cleaner than they would have been without regulatory controls, and despite a wide range of errors, the American experience serves in some respects as a model for the rest of the world. People continue to be very much concerned about toxic waste sites. But it is notable that since the enactment of the Solid Waste Disposal Act, nearly all toxic byproducts are disposed of in safe ways, and new toxic waste "dumps" are almost entirely a thing of the past.

The risk of a fatal accident in the workplace was reduced by 50 percent between 1970 and 1990, partly because of workers' compensation, occupa-

Table 11.1.   Principal Death Risk Trends

Years	Annual Rate of Increase in Death Rates		
	Work (per 100,000 population)	Home (per 100,000 population)	Motor Vehicle (per 100,000 population)
1930–40	− 1.8	− 0.2	− 3.3
1940–50	− 2.3	− 2.2	− 4.0
1950–60	− 2.8	− 2.1	− 3.5
1960–70	− 1.2	− 1.7	− 0.8
1970–80	− 1.6	− 2.7	− 3.4
1980–90	− 3.2	− 2.4	− 4.3

Source: W. Kip Viscusi, *Fatal Tradeoffs: Public and Private Responsibilities for Risk* (New York: Oxford University Press, 1992), p. 285. Reprinted by permission.

tional safety and health, and other programs. Similarly, automobile safety regulation has significantly reduced deaths and serious injuries.[2] Automobiles are much safer for occupants, and many of the safety-improving features of automobiles are a product of regulatory controls supported by cost-benefit balancing. For example, the requirement that all cars have center-high mounted stop lamps was shown to be highly effective in reducing rear-end collisions. More generally, highway fatalities would have been about 40 percent higher in 1981 if not for governmental controls.[3] Between 1966 and 1974, the lives of about 34,000 passenger car occupants were saved as a result of occupant safety standards. The annual benefits from regulation exceed ten billion dollars. For automobile regulation, in general, the ratio of benefits to costs is extremely high. Indeed, some of the regulations pay for themselves in terms of health and related savings, and the large number of deaths actually prevented is of course a bonus.

More broadly, studies of the costs and benefits of regulatory initiatives show that a number of other measures have produced health and other benefits at especially low costs. Of course, it would be foolish to suggest that government regulation in its current form passes a global cost-benefit test. There is much indeterminacy in the data, and certainly many regulatory efforts have been futile, self-defeating, counterproductive, or much worse. But every detailed study shows a number of regulations that have saved lives at comparatively low cost.

Consider, for example, W. Kip Viscusi's influential discussion, which shows that thirteen of the most important federal regulations pass a cost-benefit test.[4] These include OSHA's hazard communication regulation, saving 200 lives per year; the Consumer Product Safety Commission's unvented space heaters regulation, saving over 60 lives per year; the Federal Aviation Administration's seat cushion flammability regulation, saving 37 lives per year; OSHA's oil and gas well service regulation, saving 50 lives per year; and the National Highway Traffic Safety Administration's (NHTSA) passive restraints/belts regulation, saving no fewer than 1,850 lives per year. OSHA's regulation of asbestos prevents an estimated 396 deaths per year, and it does so at relatively low expense. EPA's regulation of trihalomethanes saves a life at only $300,000 per year; the National Highway Traffic Safety Administration's fuel system integrity controls, also $300,000; the Consumer Product Safety Commission's (CPSC) mandatory smoke detector rule, between $0 and $85,000; NHTSA's roadside hazard removal rule, $0. Consider in this regard the good results shown in Table 11.2.

Finally, regulatory successes are not limited to the areas of safety and health. The most important civil rights initiative—the Voting Rights Act of 1965—appears to have broken up the white monopoly on electoral processes in a number of states. Only two years after passage of the Act, the number of registered blacks in the eleven southern states increased from 1.5 million to 2.8 million—an increase of nearly 90 percent. This is an impressive illustration of regulatory success.

Now turn away from voting rights and toward discrimination in general. Though the evidence is more disputed, the better view is that the Civil Rights Act of 1964 has also had important beneficial consequences. The most careful and impressive study shows that this Act had major effects on the manufacturing sector in South Carolina. "Suddenly in 1965 the black share in employment begins to improve when Title VII legislation becomes effective and the Equal Employment Opportunity Commission begins to press textile firms to employ blacks and when Executive Order 11246 forbids discrimination by government contractors at the risk of forfeit of government business."[5] Many other studies reach a broadly similar conclusion: The federal effort to redress race discrimination has had many favorable consequences. There have been gains in the area of sex discrimination as well.

Finally, the Endangered Species Act has saved a number of species from extinction and endangerment.[6] Thus the American bald eagle was, in 1963, thought to be on the verge of extinction; it is now doing much better, and in 1995 its status was shifted from "endangered" to merely "threatened." The number of gray wolves in Minnesota has grown from 500 to 1750 in a relatively short time; there are now about 10,000 adult peregrine falcons in the United States, compared with very few in the early 1970s; sea lions had declined to a population of 30,000 in 1972 and are now up to 180,000; California gray whales recovered to a population of 21,000 in 1994, when they were removed from the list under the Endangered Species Act. In fact, of the 71 species initially listed under the Act in 1973, only seven are gone, and 44 are stable or improving.

On the other hand, regulation has frequently failed. Sometimes it has imposed enormously high costs for speculative benefits; sometimes it has accomplished little or nothing; sometimes it has aggravated the very problem it was designed to solve. For example, the United States spent no less than $632 billion for pollution control between 1972 and 1985, and some studies suggest that alternative strategies could have achieved the same gains at less than one-fifth the cost. There is no doubt that environmental and safety regulation have taken an unnecessarily high toll on the productivity of the American economy.

Table 11.2.   Cost-Effective Regulations

Regulation	Agency	Cost Per Premature Death Averted ($ millions 1990)
Unvented Space Heater Ban	CPSC	0.1
Aircraft Cabin Fire Protection Standard	FAA	0.1
Auto Passive Restraint/Seat Belt Standards	NHTSA	0.1
Steering Column Protection Standard	NHTSA	0.1
Underground Construction Standards	OSHA-S	0.1
Trihalomethane Drinking Water Standards	EPA	0.2
Aircraft Seat Cushion Flammability Standard	FAA	0.4
Alcohol and Drug Control Standards	FRA	0.4
Auto Fuel-System Integrity Standard	NHTSA	0.4
Standards for Servicing Auto Wheel Rims	OSHA-S	0.4
Aircraft Floor Emergency Lighting Standard	FAA	0.6
Concrete and Masonry Construction Standards	OSHA-S	0.6
Crane Suspended Personnel Platform Standard	OSHA-S	0.7
Passive Restraints for Trucks and Buses (proposed)	NHTSA	0.7
Side-Impact Standards for Autos (dynamic)	NHTSA	0.8
Children's Sleepwear Flammability Ban	CPSC	0.8
Auto Side Door Support Standards	NHTSA	0.8
Low Altitude Windshear Equipment and Training Standards	FAA	1.3
Electrical Equipment Standards (metal mines)	MSHA	1.4
Trenching and Excavation Standards	OSHA-S	1.5
Traffic Alert and Collision Avoidance (TCAS) Systems	FAA	1.5
Hazard Communication Standard	OSHA-S	1.6
Side-Impact Standards for Trucks, Buses, and MPVs (proposed)	NHTSA	2.2
Grain Dust Explosion Prevention Standards	OSHA-S	2.8
Rear Lap/Shoulder Belts for Autos	NHTSA	3.2
Standards for Radionuclides in Uranium Mines	EPA	3.4
Benzene NESHAP (original: Fugitive Emissions)	EPA	3.4

Source: Stephen G. Breyer, *Breaking the Vicious Circle: Toward Effective Risk Regulation* (Cambridge: Harvard University Press, 1993), pp. 24–27. Reprinted by permission.

Studies show reduced output in the economy as a whole as 2.5 percent, with a cumulative impact through 1986 of 11.4 percent from the level that would have been achieved without OSHA and EPA regulation.[7]

The fuel economy standards for new cars appear to have produced no substantial independent gains in fuel economy; consumer demands for fuel efficient cars, in response to gas shortages and high gas prices, were leading in the same direction. Worse, the fuel economy standards have led manufacturers to produce smaller, more dangerous cars; an estimated 2200–3900 mortalities were expected over a ten-year period as a result of regulatory changes in 1989 alone.[8] There is little question that the administration of the Natural Gas Act helped produce the energy crisis of the late 1970s—with huge attendant costs to investment and employment—by artificially restraining the price of gas.[9]

Some of OSHA's carcinogen regulations impose enormous costs for uncertain gains. Indeed, the pattern of OSHA regulation of carcinogens is a crazy quilt; regulations costing up to $40 million per life saved exist in some areas, with no regulations at all in others (Table 5.4). By delaying the entry of beneficial drugs into the market, the Food and Drug Administration has, in many settings, dramatically increased risks to life and health.[10]

Ironically, a large source of regulatory failure in the United States is the use of Soviet-style command-and-control regulation, which dictates, at the national level, technologies and control strategies for hundreds, thousands, or millions of companies and individuals in a nation that is exceptionally diverse in terms of geography, costs and benefits of regulatory controls, attitudes, and mores. A valuable perspective on this problem can be obtained by examining the paradoxes of regulation, which pose a particular dilemma for the administrative state. A government that eliminated self-defeating regulatory strategies would eliminate a significant source of regulatory failure. And although the paradoxes are numerous, six of them have been of major importance in the last generation.

II. The Paradoxes

I have defined a regulatory paradox as a self-defeating regulatory strategy; but whether a strategy is self-defeating depends on how its purposes are described. Any statute that fails to produce a net benefit to society can be described as self-defeating if its purpose is described as the net improvement of the world. But if the statute's purpose is to benefit a particular group or segment of society, and that purpose is achieved, then the statute is not self-defeating at all. For example, a statute benefiting the agricultural industry at the expense of the public will not be self-defeating if its purpose is described as helping farmers. Throughout this discussion I describe the relevant statutory purposes as public-regarding rather than as benefiting special interest groups.

Moreover, I mean to assess whether a statute is self-defeating by comparing the result it has produced with the likely state of affairs had Congress either enacted a different and better statute or enacted no statute at all. Measured against either of these benchmarks, regulation has produced a wide range of paradoxes.

Importantly, nearly all of the paradoxes are a product of the government's failure to understand how the relevant actors—administrators and regulated entities—will adapt to regulatory programs. The world cannot be held constant after regulations have been issued. Strategic responses, the creation of perverse incentives for administrators and regulated entities, unanticipated changes in product mix and private choice—these are the hallmarks of the paradoxes of the regulatory state. The adoption of strategies that take account of these phenomena would produce enormous savings in both compliance costs and safety and health gains.

Paradox 1: Overregulation Produces
Underregulation

The first paradox is that especially aggressive statutory controls frequently produce too little regulation of the private market. This surprising outcome arises when Congress mandates overly stringent controls, so that administrators will not issue regulations at all or will refuse to enforce whatever regulations they or Congress have issued.

The imposition of extremely stringent controls on regulated industries is a common strategy in Congress. Such controls typically ban cost-benefit balancing or indeed trade-offs of any sort. The expectation is that these controls will bring about safety in the workplace, or clean air and water, even if both the agency and industry are reluctant to act, and even if the costs of regulation are high. This strategy was especially popular during the dramatic growth of regulation in the 1960s and 1970s. It both fueled and was fueled by the notion that a safe workplace, or clean air and water, should be treated as involving a right to be vindicated rather than a risk to be managed. Consider President Nixon's proclamation: "Clean air, clean water, open spaces—these should again be the birthright for every American." [11] This form of rights-based thinking was also inspired by evidence that recalcitrant agencies, suffering from inertia or immobilized by the power of well-organized private groups, frequently refused to enforce regulatory controls.

The strategy of imposing stringent regulatory controls or banning cost-benefit balancing is not impossible to understand. It might seem natural to think that if air pollution is a severe problem, the correct response is to reduce it as much as possible; and this idea quickly translates into a command to the EPA to reduce dangerous substances in the atmosphere to a level that will not adversely affect human health. Certainly this seems like a natural thought if health or safety is conceived as a right. Similarly, an obvious method for controlling toxic substances in the workplace is to tell OSHA to eliminate these substances "to the extent feasible." Such strategies might produce too much regulation, but this might be thought a small price to pay for (finally) reducing pollution in the air or deaths in the workplace. In addition, a prohibition on "balancing" might be thought desirable by those fearful that any effort to balance would be distorted by the enforcement agency's undervaluation of life and health, especially in the context of seemingly permanent political divisions between the executive and the legislative branches of government.

But consider the record of both the EPA and OSHA in these settings. Of the several hundred toxic substances plausibly posing significant risks to human health, the EPA had for a long period regulated only seven—five as a result of court orders. The Clean Air Act's severe provisions for listed pollutants, operating in rule-like fashion, led the Environmental Protection Agency to stop listing pollutants at all. Thus, the Act's strict duties of response to danger prompted officials not to recognize the dangers in the first instance. Of the many toxic substances in the workplace, OSHA had for a long time controlled only ten. Stunningly, this is so even though the private organization that once performed some of OSHA's functions had recommended lower exposure limits for hundreds of chemicals.[12] To be sure, those substances that EPA and OSHA regulate are stringently controlled. The regulatory pattern, however, includes not only substantial overregulation of the substances that are subject to federal standards, but also, and possibly more serious, substantial underregulation of dangerous substances, such as chromium, perchloroethylene, and trichloroethylene.

Despite the stringency of statutory standards, many activities in the United States are entirely free from regulatory controls. There is no evidence that the United States generally does a better job than England in protecting workers and citizens from occupational and environmental hazards, even though the English system consciously allows balancing in most contexts and the American system consciously rejects it.[13] Compare in this regard the pattern under rigid criminal statutes, including the "three strikes and you're out policy" for felons and mandatory minimum sentences. These have often produced underregulation by encouraging prosecutors to indict for lesser charges or by leading prosecutors not to enforce at all.

Statutes containing stringent regulatory requirements have thus yielded no protection at all in many settings. What is responsible for this astonishing outcome? It might be tempting to find answers in the power of regulated industries or in the intransigence and deregulatory zeal of government officials. But the pattern of underregulation can be found in the Carter Administration as well as the Reagan Administration, even though President Carter's appointees, drawn in large number from the consumer and environmental movements, were hardly eager to prevent the government from curbing the proliferation of toxic substances. Elaborate and costly procedural requirements for the promulgation of federal regulations undoubtedly provide some explanation, since the process, including judicial review, has built into it enormous delays and perverse incentives. These requirements surely slow down and deter rule making. Industry has every opportunity and every incentive to fend off regulation by making plausible claims that additional information is necessary before regulation can be undertaken. Here we have a subparadox that might explain the overregulation–underregulation paradox: Procedural protections designed to improve agency rule making may lead to little or no agency rulemaking. This explanation is not in itself adequate, however, because organized interests have not prevented agencies from being far more aggressive in other settings.

A large part of the explanation lies in the stringency of the regulatory standard itself. A stringent standard—one that forbids balancing or calls for regulation to or beyond the point of "feasibility"—makes regulators reluctant to act. If, as is customary, regulators have discretion not to promulgate regulations at all, a stringent standard will provide them with a powerful incentive for inaction. Their inaction is not caused by venality or confusion. Instead, it reflects their quite plausible belief that the statute often requires them to regulate to an absurd point. If regulators were to issue controls under the statute, government and private resources would be less available to control other toxic substances; domestic industry costs would increase; ultimately, industries competing in world markets would face a serious risk of shutdown. Under these circumstances, a stringent standard will mobilize political opposition to regulation from within and without government. It will also increase the likelihood of judicial invalidation. Finally, it will require agencies to obtain greater supporting information to survive political and judicial scrutiny, while at the same time making it less likely that such information will be forthcoming from regulated class members. All the incentives are therefore in the direction of issuing fewer regulations.

It is thus unsurprising that a draconian standard produces underregulation as well as overregulation. A crazy quilt pattern of severe controls in some areas and none in others is the predictable consequence of a statute that forbids balancing and trade-offs (Table 5.3 in chapter 5).

The problem goes deeper still. Even if the resistance of the agency has been overcome, and some or many regulations have been issued under a statute calling for stringent regulatory controls, the risk of underregulation does not disappear. Levels of enforcement—inspections and fines—will reflect the agency's reluctance. This has in fact been the pattern with OSHA's safety and health regulations, some of which have been effectively unenforced by Democratic as well as Republican administrations. This, then, is the first paradox of the regulatory state: Stringent regulatory standards produce underregulation.

Paradox 2: Stringent Regulation of New Risks Can Increase Aggregate Risk Levels

Congress is often presented with a risk or problem that can be found in both existing entities and in potential new entrants. For example, automobiles produce carbon monoxide; modern electricity plants emit sulfur dioxide; many existing buildings are inaccessible to the handicapped; and drugs currently on the market pose health hazards to consumers. In such situations, a common strategy has been to impose especially severe limitations on new sources but to exempt old ones. Indeed, such exemptions might be a political prerequisite for enactment of the regulation, since existing companies might otherwise fight very hard against enactment. Congress might require that new automobiles be equipped with pollution control devices, that new plants emitting pollution meet stringent regulatory controls, that new buildings be accessible to the handicapped, and that new drugs survive special safety requirements.

This strategy is a pervasive one in current regulatory law, and it has obvious advantages.[14] Retroactive application of regulatory requirements can be extremely costly; the expense of altering existing practices is often high. Requiring the specified approach only prospectively can achieve significant savings. In addition, it may seem unfair to impose costs on people who would have ordered their affairs quite differently had they been informed beforehand of the regulatory regime.

As a control technique, however, the strategy of imposing costs exclusively on new sources or entrants can be self-defeating. Most important, it will discourage the addition of new sources and encourage the perpetuation of old ones. The problem is not merely that old risks will continue, but that precisely because of regulatory programs, those risks will become more common and last longer—perhaps much longer—than they otherwise would.

Two different phenomena underlie the old risk–new risk paradox. First, those who plan regulatory programs often assume that the programs will not influence private choices. Private choices are, however, a function of current supply and demand. If the program raises the price of new products, it will shift choices in the direction of old risks. Second, a focus on new risks reduces the likely entry of potentially superior sources or technologies and thus perpetuates old ones. Regulatory controls eliminate possibilities that might have turned out to be substantially safer than currently available options. The result is to increase the life of those options.

Examples are not difficult to find. The EPA's program requiring the installation of antipollution technology in new automobiles belongs in the first category. This program has prolonged the use of old, dirty vehicles, retarding the ordinary, salutary retirement of major sources of environmental degradation. Command-and-control regulation of new pollution sources creates incentives to use existing facilities longer, with harmful consequences for the environment. Imposition of high, safety-related costs on new airplanes may well encourage airlines to retain (and repair) old, risky planes.

We might put the EPA's requirement of costly "scrubbing'" strategies for new sources of sulfur dioxide in the second category. This rule has perpetuated the existence of old sources of sulfur dioxide, thus aggravating in many parts of the country the very problem it was designed to solve.[15] So too, the imposition of stringent barriers to nuclear power plants has perpetuated the risks produced by coal, a significantly more dangerous power source. And perhaps worst of all, the FDA's stringent regulatory standards for approving new drugs have forced consumers to resort to old drugs, which are frequently more dangerous, more costly, or less beneficial than the new drugs being kept off the market.

A final example of the old risk–new risk paradox is the Delaney Clause, which prohibits manufacturers from using food additives containing carcinogens. Ironically, this provision has probably increased safety and health risks. The Clause forces manufacturers to use noncarcinogenic, but sometimes more dangerous, substances. In addition, it makes consumers resort to substances already on the market that often pose greater risks than new entrants would. Since the newest and best detection equipment is used on proposed new additives, the statutorily prohibited additive may well pose fewer risks to consumers than substances already on the market that were tested with cruder technology. The Delaney Clause defeats its own purpose.[16]

The phenomenon of careful regulation of new risks and lenient or no regulation of old ones may not simply reflect legislative myopia or confusion. Public choice theory provides a plausible explanation for the phenomenon. A system of regulation that imposes controls solely on new products or facilities should have considerable appeal for those in possession of old ones. If new sources will face regulatory costs, the system of government controls will immunize existing producers from fresh competition. Indeed, the regulatory statute will create a partial cartel, establishing a common interest among current producers and giving them a significant competitive advantage over potential new entrants. The victims of the old-new division, however, often do not yet exist. They are usually hard to identify, do not perceive themselves as victims, and are not politically organized.

It may be for this reason that the careful regulation of new risks is such a popular strategy. It is apt to be favored both by existing industry and by many of those who seek to impose controls in the first instance. The potential victims—consumers and new entrants—often have insufficient political strength to counter the proposals. When this phenomenon is combined with the apparently sensible but sometimes self-defeating idea that a phase-in strategy is better than one that requires conversions of existing producers, it is no surprise that the old risk–new risk division remains so popular. It is a perverse strategy, but it is likely to continue, at least so long as there is no shift from command-and-control regulation to economic incentives.

Paradox 3: To Require the Best Available Technology
Is to Retard Technological Development

Industry frequently fails to adopt the best technology for controlling environmental or other harms. The technology exists or can be developed relatively cheaply, but polluters simply refuse to use it. Congress and the EPA have often responded by requiring that all industries use the best available technology (BAT). The BAT strategy is pervasive in federal environmental law and may indeed be its most distinctive characteristic.

The BAT strategy is motivated by a desire to produce technological innovation, and here it has a surface plausibility. As discussed previously, recent years have witnessed large decreases in air and water pollution, and these decreases are partly attributable to the use of emission control technologies. requiring the adoption of the best available control technology seems a sensible way to ensure that all industries are doing their utmost to prevent pollution. This strategy also appears inexpensive to enforce. The government simply decides on the best technology and then requires all industries to comply.

The BAT approach, however, can defeat its own purposes and thus produce a regulatory paradox. It is an extremely clumsy strategy for protecting the environment. To be sure, the approach is a plausible one if the goal is to ensure that all firms use currently established technology. But a large goal of regulation should be to promote technological innovation in pollution control. Regulation should increase rather than decrease incentives to innovate. Government is rarely in a good position to know what sorts of innovations are likely to be forthcoming; industry will have a huge comparative advantage here. Perversely, requiring adoption of the BAT eliminates the incentive to innovate at all, and indeed creates disincentives for innovation by imposing an economic punishment on innovators. Under the BAT approach, polluting industries have no financial interest in the development of better pollution control technology that imposes higher production costs. Indeed, the opposite is true. The BAT approach encourages industry to seek any means to delay and deter new regulation. Industry will have the information as well as the incentive to persuade administrators, courts, and other authorities that a suggested technology is not "feasible" and should not be required.

If government requires whatever technology is available, then, industry has no economic incentive to develop new mechanisms for decreasing safety and health risks. Moreover, the BAT approach, applicable as it is only to new sources, raises the cost of retiring old facilities, which delays capital turnover and in that way aggravates environmental degradation. The paradox, in a nutshell, is this: Designed to promote good control technology, the BAT strategy actually discourages innovation. It is therefore self-defeating.

Paradox 4: Redistributive Regulation Harms Those at the Bottom of the Socioeconomic Ladder

A common justification for regulation is redistribution. The legislature imposes controls on the market to prevent what it sees as exploitation or unfair dealing by those with a competitive advantage. In principle, the claim for redistribution is often a powerful one. People often enter into harsh deals, simply because their options are so few. In fact, market wages and prices depend on a wide range of factors that are morally irrelevant: supply and demand curves at any particular point; variations in family structure and opportunities for education and employment; existing tastes; and perhaps even differences in initial endowments, including talents, intelligence, or physical strength (chapter 6). So long as the regulation can be made effective and does not produce high ancillary costs (an important qualification), government should not always take these factors as "natural," or let them be turned into social disadvantages.

The inspiration for minimum wage legislation, for example, is easy to identify. Such legislation prevents workers from having to settle for market wages that do not even approach the poverty level and thus offer minimal incentives to work. So, too, occupational safety statutes protect workers against extremely hazardous workplaces; rent control legislation prevents tenants from being subject to unanticipated price increases and perhaps thrown into significantly inferior housing; and implied warranties of habitability protect tenants from living in disgraceful and indeed dangerous apartments.

In all these cases, however, regulation is a poor mechanism for redistributing resources, precisely because it is often self-defeating. The problem is that if everything else is held constant, the market will frequently adjust to the imposition of regulation in a way that will harm the least well off. It is a mistake to assume that regulation will directly transfer resources or create only ex-post winners and losers—an idea exemplified by the assumption that the only effect of the minimum wage is to raise wages for those currently working. An important consequence of the minimum wage is to increase unemployment by raising the price of marginal labor; and those at the bottom of the ladder—the most vulnerable members of society—are the victims.[17] In the same vein, rent control legislation and implied warranties of habitability create incentives for producers (landlords) to leave and disincentives to enter the housing market, with perverse redistributive consequences and especially harsh results for the poor, who may be left without housing at all.[18] It should not be surprising to find that Cambridge, Massachusetts has experienced a dramatic growth in new housing since rent control has been eliminated by state referendum.

Laws forbidding discrimination or requiring affirmative action will to some extent have the same perverse effect, since they will make it more expensive to hire blacks, women, and older people by increasing the likelihood that employers will be subject to a lawsuit in the event of a discharge.[19] Similarly, occupational safety and health regulation does not unambiguously promote the interests of workers. By raising costs, it may depress wages and increase unemployment, thus harming the least well off. In each of these cases, the group that is harmed is likely to be poorly organized and incapable of expressing itself through the political process.

In sum, redistributive regulation will have complex distributive consequences, and the group particularly disadvantaged by the regulation will typically consist of those who are already most disadvantaged. Efforts to redistribute resources through regulation can therefore have serious perverse results.

Three qualifications are necessary here. First, the redistributive regulation, though in some ways perverse, might be part of a system of redistribution that is effective overall. A minimum wage law might be justified as a means of protecting the working poor, if it is accompanied by a welfare system to take care of those who cannot work at all. For this reason, plausible arguments can be made for the minimum wage. It has been argued, for example, that an increase in the minimum wage is necessary to guarantee that work will be sufficiently remunerative to keep people out of poverty and to send a signal about the importance and value of work, thereby increasing the supply of and demand for labor. These effects might outweigh any unemployment effect.

A second qualification of the redistribution paradox relates to the fact that preferences are not static. Preferences are usually taken as exogenous to and independent of the legal rule, but sometimes this is a mistake (chapter 1). If the statute in question transforms preferences and beliefs, the self-defeating effect just described will not occur. For example, laws forbidding sexual harassment aim to alter the desires and beliefs of would-be harassers; and if the laws succeed in this goal, any perverse side effects may be minimal or nonexistent. The same argument may apply to antidiscrimination laws generally. If such laws change attitudes, they may not on balance harm the least well off. There is, however, little empirical evidence on the effects of law in changing preferences and beliefs, and, in any case, this is not likely to result from such redistributive regulation as minimum wage legislation.

The third qualification is that laws that seem to be justified on redistributive grounds are best understood as a response to inadequate information. Occupational safety and health legislation does not transfer resources from employers to employees; but it may be justified as a response to the fact that workers lack information about workplace risks. In the face of inadequate information, a regulatory response may well make sense. In fact, a well-tailored response will make workers better off. But this point leads directly to our fifth paradox.

Paradox 5: Disclosure Requirements May Make People Less Informed

Sometimes markets fail because people are deceived or lack information. Regulatory agencies commonly respond by requiring correction or full disclosure. Congress and agencies have imposed disclosure regulations in many areas, ranging from occupational and environmental risks to potentially deceptive advertising (chapter 13). Here the rationale is straightforward. Whether or not ignorance is bliss, it is an obstacle to informed choice. Surely, it might be asked, regulation cannot be condemned for increasing information?

Disclosure strategies are indeed valuable in many circumstances. But for two reasons, they can be self-defeating. The first is that people sometimes process information poorly. After being given certain data, they actually "know" less than they did beforehand. In particular, when people receive information about probabilities, especially low ones, they frequently rely on heuristics that lead to systematic errors (chapter 10). Thus, for example, people assess probabilities by asking if the event was a recent one, by seeing if an example comes readily to mind, and by misunderstanding the phenomenon of regression to the mean. In addition, disclosure or corrective language can help straighten out one form of false belief but at the same time increase the level of other kinds of false beliefs.[20] Finally, there is a risk of information overload, causing consumers to treat a large amount of information as equivalent to no information at all.[21] All this suggests that with respect to information, less may be more. Additional information can breed confusion and a weaker understanding of the situation at hand.

The second problem is that a requirement of perfect accuracy will sometimes lead producers or other regulated entities to furnish no information whatsoever. For example, if producers are prohibited from advertising, unless they eliminate all potential deception or offer strong substantiation for their claims, they might not advertise at all. The result will be the removal from the market of information that is useful overall.[22] If advertisers must conduct extensive tests before they are permitted to make claims, they will be given a strong incentive to avoid making claims at all. More generally, almost all substantive advertisements will deceive at least some people in light of the exceptional heterogeneity of listeners and viewers. If this is so, efforts to eliminate deception will significantly reduce advertising with substantive content.

These various difficulties suggest that the recent enthusiasm for disclosure requirements is at least in some settings a mistake, for the simple reason that such requirements may defeat their own purpose. Disclosure requirements sometimes ensure that people are less informed; a good deal of thought needs to be given to their content (chapter 13).

Paradox 6: Independent Agencies Are Not Independent

The distinctive institutional legacy of the New Deal period is the "independent" regulatory agency. An agency is independent if Congress has provided that its members can be discharged by the president only for specified causes. If Congress has so provided, it is ordinarily understood that the president cannot discharge independent commissioners simply because he disagrees with their views, and that his supervisory authority is sharply limited. Independent agencies, some of them antedating the New Deal, include the Federal Trade Commission, the Federal Communications Commission, the Interstate Commerce Commission, and the National Labor Relations Board. The paradox at issue here is one of institutional design rather than substantive regulatory policy.

The argument for the independent agency stems largely from a belief in the need for expert, apolitical, and technically sophisticated administration of the laws. Even if independent agencies achieved this end, we should question the goal itself. Independent agencies often must make important judgments of value and principle, and on those judgments expertise is never decisive. Consider, for example, the decisions of the National Labor Relations Board defining what constitutes an unfair labor practice; the judgment of the FCC about whether licensees are obliged to present programming on public issues, or whether diversity on the basis of race or sex counts in favor of an applicant for a license; and the safety requirements of the Nuclear Regulatory Commission. None of these policies is based solely on technocratic judgments, and so may properly belong—at least in part—in the political rather than the regulatory sphere.

But even if we accept the premise that political independence is necessary, the fact is that independent agencies are not independent at all. Indeed, such agencies are responsive to shifts in political opinion and even to the views of the president.[23] But the problem is even worse than that. The independent agencies have generally been highly susceptible to the political pressure of well-organized private groups—perhaps even more susceptible, on balance, than executive agencies.[24]

Many of the most egregious illustrations of agency vulnerability to pressure groups can be found in precisely this area. Thus, the Interstate Commerce Commission created and enforced cartels in the transportation industry; the Federal Trade Commission has sometimes behaved in an anticompetitive manner, capitulating to losers in the marketplace; and the FCC has been dominated by the communications industry.[25] Far from acting as disinterested experts, independent administrators often are, in practice, subject to parochial interests.

Why would agencies independent of the president be so susceptible to factional power? The phenomenon might be explained at least in part by the fact that executive agencies, precisely because they are subject to presidential control, are able to withstand the parochial pressures imposed on "independent" agencies that lack the buffer of presidential oversight. The absence of this presidential buffer leaves agencies vulnerable both to individual members and committees of Congress, which sometimes represent narrow factions and well-organized private groups with significant stakes in the outcome of regulatory decisions. Executive agencies are at least sometimes immunized from those pressures precisely because of the protective, insulating wing of the president. Ironically, independence from the president often appears to be a mechanism for increasing susceptibility to factionalism.

The susceptibility of the independent agencies to factionalism does not of course imply that executive agencies are invulnerable to similar forces. The notion that independent agencies are systemically more susceptible to factions than their counterparts within the executive branch seems much too broad. But if Congress wants to ensure independence in the execution of its laws, the independent agency device is a most unlikely way to achieve that goal.

Other Paradoxes, in Brief

I have described some prominent regulatory paradoxes, but there are others as well. For example, it has been argued that the pursuit of the "best interests of the child'" in custody determinations in fact disserves the best interests of children, because of the enormous time spent in resolving the complicated factual question.[26] Protectionist legislation is sometimes justified on the theory that it will help domestic industries develop into potent competitive forces, but in fact, protectionism may induce flabbiness and in the end defeat the goal of promoting international competitiveness. As we have seen, extensive procedural protections, designed to improve agency rule making, may lead to little or no agency rule making. And restrictions on the availability of abortion, defended as a means of protecting human life, appear to have resulted in the death of many women per year and at the same time not to have protected a large percentage of fetuses from the practice of abortion.[27]

Many more paradoxes can be found. There is evidence that mandatory prescriptions for drugs have increased health risks by limiting the availability and raising the cost of prescription drugs; this in turn has decreased self-treatment and encouraged people to use possibly less effective over-the-counter drugs.[28] Product safety regulation may have a "lulling effect" on consumers, leading them to take fewer precautions and to miscalculate risks.[29] Health regulation can increase health risks, if agencies focus on one kind of risk and ignore others that can be aggravated by regulation itself (chapter 12). The government prohibition on cigarette advertising on television, designed to decrease smoking, may have increased smoking because it (1) reduced competition among firms, thus cartelizing the industry over the advertising issue; (2) eliminated the application of the fairness doctrine to cigarettes, which would have ensured a vigorous anticigarette campaign; and (3) saved the industry substantial sums of money.[30]

A final paradox can be found in the law of sex discrimination, where principles of "formal equality" have been invoked to forbid consideration of sex in custody, alimony, and divorce disputes. It is quite possible that equality principles, understood as prohibitions on any form of sex differentiation in law, have in some contexts produced less rather than more in the way of real equality between men and women.[31] When two groups are differently situated, a legal requirement that they be treated the same seems a perverse method of promoting equality between them. Here too, then, legal controls have been self-defeating.

III. Two Questions: What We Don't Know

Causation

It is tempting to react to the regulatory paradoxes by suggesting that the relevant strategies are not self-defeating at all. On the contrary, they might represent a conscious governmental choice and even, on one view, regulatory success. Public choice theory suggests that legislative outcomes are frequently a product of pressure applied by well-organized private groups. It is not difficult to find "cartels in the closet" to account for many or all of the paradoxes and to make them seem far less mysterious.

For example, the apparently perverse effects of redistributive regulation may be actively sought by the benefited groups. On this account, the purpose of minimum wage legislation might not be to help the poor, but rather to immunize union members from competition by people who are willing to work for low wages by limiting entry into the labor market. Far from being unintended consequences, the harmful effects on those at the bottom of the economic ladder may be actively sought. Looked at from this perspective, minimum wage legislation creates a cartel among those not threatened by unemployment, benefiting them at the expense of new entrants into the labor market.

So, too, independent agencies might be created at the behest of groups that know they will have particularly strong influence over public officials not subject to presidential oversight; or Congress might create an independent agency not to ensure technocracy or neutrality, but to increase the power of its members and committees over agency decisions. Similarly, existing industry, in a bid to reduce competition, might acquiesce in or actively seek regulations distinguishing between old and new risks. It is hardly unusual for companies to enlist regulatory law in the service of cartelization.

The overregulation–underregulation phenomenon has a similar explanation. By adopting a draconian standard, legislators can claim to support the total elimination of workplace hazards or dirty air; but legislators and regulated industries know that administrators will shrink from enforcing the law. A "deal" in the form of a stringent, unenforceable standard benefits the politically powerful actors. Hence, the political economy of overregulation is similar to that of open-ended delegations of administrative authority: In both cases, legislative incentives incline Congress toward broad and appealing statutes that will not in practice harm politically powerful groups. The public is the only real loser.

Explained in this manner, the paradoxes of the regulatory state are not mysterious at all. On the contrary, they are perfectly predictable responses to electoral self-interest and to disparities in political influence.

While explanations of this sort have power in some settings, clear evidence on their behalf is often unavailable. It is of course possible that the seemingly paradoxical effects of regulatory programs actually account for their enactment. But this is only a possibility. To explain a phenomenon by reference to its consequences is bad social science, even though it is pervasive in such widely diverse disciplines as neoclassical economics, Marxism, and sociobiology.[32] In the context of the regulatory state, whether public choice explanations are good ones, rather than merely plausible stories, depends not just on the consequences of regulation, but also on a careful investigation into the actual forces that lead to regulation. In the regulatory sphere, such investigations are infrequent.

The most we can say is that the regulatory paradoxes might reflect the influence of well-organized private groups, and that in some settings there is direct or indirect evidence to support that conclusion. At least thus far, any more global conclusion is not supported by what we know about the facts.

Magnitude

Whether the regulatory paradoxes should cause major concern depends on their magnitude. Here too, much of the relevant information remains to be developed. For example, a decision to focus on new sources of pollution would be understandable if that decision would have only a minor effect in perpetuating old sources. But if the effect is substantial, the regulatory policy would almost certainly be ill-considered. Everything depends on the question: How large is the relevant effect? Similarly, the minimum wage might well be justified if its effect is the unemployment of only a few additional people. The relevant question is the elasticity of the demand for labor. Even if some people are misled by compulsory disclosure of risks, perhaps there will be sufficient gains through reducing others' ignorance to justify the regulation. And even if some producers refuse to advertise at all in the face of a substantiation requirement, perhaps the overall level of information will increase.

Critics of regulation sometimes treat the existence of unintended side effects or partly self-defeating strategies as a reason to abandon regulatory controls altogether. But in order to justify that conclusion, it is necessary to gather detailed evidence on the magnitude of the relevant effects in particular regulated markets and overall. In some contexts, regulation having some self-defeating results will on the whole make things better rather than worse. The

American regulatory state, though pervaded by paradoxes, has had a number of substantial successes.

From both theory and experience, it is possible to conclude that the regulatory paradoxes will arise frequently and thus to prescribe efforts to avoid them. Certainly we have far too little information to say, as a general matter, that regulatory programs embodying the paradoxes are by virtue of that fact a bad idea on balance, at least when compared with the preregulatory status quo. Total elimination of such regulatory programs is hardly warranted. Nevertheless, a system that avoided the paradoxes would bring about major improvements.

IV. Lessons

Congress

The paradoxes of regulation provide a number of concrete lessons for Congress. At the most general level, they suggest that legislators should be attentive to the incentive effects of regulatory statutes and the possibility of strategic or self-interested adaptation by administrative agencies and members of regulated classes. Statutes embodying an assumption that the preregulatory world can be held constant—that existing prices, wages, choices, and so forth will endure—are particularly likely to be confounded when implemented.

More specifically, the paradoxes suggest that the legislature should generally avoid best available technology strategies; be concerned with old risks as well as new ones; decline to attempt to redistribute resources through regulation; be attentive to the possibility that disclosure requirements will simply confuse people or chill information in the first instance; create incentives for regulation when regulation is desired; as a rule, place agencies under the control of the president; and call for some form of balancing between the costs and benefits of regulation. Ideas of this sort have direct implications for modern regulatory reform (chapters 12 and 13).

Judges and Administrators

The regulatory paradoxes provide important lessons for judges and administrators as well as legislators. These officials are of course bound by legislative enactments, and to the extent that regulatory statutes unambiguously call for self-defeating strategies, officials have no choice but to honor them. But frequently the interpretation of a statute, or the filling of statutory gaps, is based on an understanding of the real-world consequences of the alternative possibilities. Administrators exercise considerable discretion in giving content to ambiguous laws, and the legal judgment about whether an agency's decision is "arbitrary" within the meaning of the Administrative Procedure Act should be informed by an accurate understanding of the paradoxes of the regulatory state. Attention to the often unanticipated systemic effects of regulatory controls is an imperative for administrators and judges as well as for legislators. I offer three examples here of how these officials can use the knowledge of regulatory paradoxes to inform their actions.

The Overregulation–Underregulation Paradox

In two important cases, the Supreme Court was asked to interpret the provisions of the Occupational Safety and Health Act that regulate exposure to toxic substances. The pertinent language directs the secretary of labor to promulgate the standard that "most adequately assures, to the extent feasible . . . that no employee will suffer material impairment of health or functional capacity even if such employee has regular exposure to the hazard . . . for the period of his working life." The statute also defines "occupational safety and health standard[s]" as measures that require "conditions . . . reasonably necessary or appropriate to provide safe or healthful employment and places of employment."

In *Industrial Union Department, AFL-CIO v. American Petroleum Institute*, [33] the Supreme Court was confronted with an OSHA regulation of benzene. Though the consequences of the regulation were sharply contested, there was reason to believe that the regulation would impose enormous costs for small or speculative gains. A plurality of the Court concluded that the secretary of labor must establish that a toxic substance posed a "significant risk" to health before she could regulate it. There was little direct support for the plurality's conclusion in the language or history of the Act. Unable to point to a solid textual basis for its "significant risk" requirement, the plurality invoked a clear statement principle:

> In the absence of a clear mandate in the Act, it is unreasonable to assume that Congress intended to give the Secretary the unprecedented power over American industry that would result from the Government's view. . . . Expert testimony that a substance is probably a human carcinogen . . . would justify the conclusion that the substance poses some risk of serious harm no matter how minute the exposure and no matter how many experts testified that they regarded the risk as insignificant. That conclusion would in turn justify pervasive regulation limited only by the constraint of feasibility. . . . [T]he Government's theory would give OSHA power to impose enormous costs that might produce little, if any, discernible benefit.[34]

The plurality went on to suggest that the government's interpretation would give the secretary of labor "open-ended" policy-making authority that might amount to an unconstitutional delegation of legislative power. In a concurring opinion advocating an interpretation of the Act that would permit cost-benefit balancing, Justice Powell suggested that "a standard-setting process that ignored economic considerations would result in a serious misallocation of resources and a lower effective level of safety than could be achieved under standards set with reference to the comparative benefits available at a lower cost."

The "significant risk" requirement cannot be found explicitly in the statute; indeed, the text of the relevant provisions suggests that no such requirement was imposed on the secretary of labor. But the plurality's conclusion was nonetheless sound. Realistically speaking, the language of the statute need not be considered dispositive. It is simply a myth to suggest that the Congress that enacted OSHA even considered the question whether regulation could require enormous expenditures to redress minimal risks. Despite the broad language of the toxic substances provision, Congress never focused on that problem. It is a legitimate interpretive strategy to understand broad words not to require an outcome that Congress could not plausibly have contemplated.

In the context of *American Petroleum*, the plurality was therefore correct in considering itself free to read an implicit "significant risk" requirement into the statute. In light of the overregulation–underregulation paradox, it would make little sense to interpret the statute so as to allow—indeed, require—the secretary to regulate to the point of "feasibility" merely because one or a few employees might suffer "material health impairment" as a result of a lifetime of exposure. Such an interpretation would make the Department of Labor reluctant to embark on a course of regulation at all, and as we have seen, would result in less, not more, protection of workers. It would ensure that there would be less regulation of carcinogens or less enforcement of those regulations that were promulgated—or, most likely, both.

In *American Textile Manufacturers Institute v. Donovan*,[35] the Supreme Court decided a question left open in *American Petroleum:* Whether the Occupational Safety and Health Act required cost-benefit analysis. In arguing that it did, the industry contended that the word "feasible" meant that the secretary must show not only a significant risk, but also that the benefits of regulation justified the costs. "Feasibility," in the industry's view, contemplated a balancing of costs and benefits. The government contended that once OSHA had shown a significant risk, it could regulate to the point where the survival of the regulated industry would be endangered by additional controls. For the government, the term "feasibility" connoted not cost-benefit balancing, but instead regulation to the maximum extent "possible."

In accepting the government's argument, the Court relied on the dictionary definition of "feasible," concluding that the term meant "capable of being done, executed, or effected," rather than justified after balancing costs and benefits. This approach to statutory interpretation was not entirely unreasonable. But the same principles that support the plurality view in *American Petroleum* cast doubt on *American Textile Manufacturers.*

First, notwithstanding the statute's language, it is probably unrealistic to believe that Congress actually focused on, and resolved, the question whether the government's approach was to be favored over some kind of balancing of costs and benefits. That question never arose during the debates. Second, a system requiring the secretary to identify a significant risk, but prohibiting her from undertaking cost-benefit analysis, seems utterly irrational. Whether a risk is "significant" depends not only on its magnitude, but also on the costs of eliminating it. A risk that is relatively small might call for regulation if the costs are also small, whereas a large risk might well be best left unregulated if the costs of regulation are enormous. A rational system of regulation looks not at the magnitude of the risk alone, but assesses the risk in comparison to the costs. Finally, a law requiring the secretary to regulate all significant risks to the point of endangering the industry would be a recipe for both overregulation and underregulation.

These considerations could not have controlled the Court's decision if the statute dictated a contrary result, but the word "feasible" was probably capacious enough to accommodate a kind of proportionality requirement. To be sure, the case was a difficult one. But by its reading of the statute, the Supreme Court contributed to the irrationality of the Occupational Safety and Health Act—irrationality that has harmed workers, employers, consumers, and the public at large. An understanding of the overregulation–underregulation paradox might have prevented this result.

The Old Risk–New Risk Paradox

A number of judicial decisions might have been different if courts had been attuned to the old risk–new risk paradox. Consider, for example, one district court's creation, in the face of an ambiguous text, of the "prevention of significant deterioration" (PSD) program in *Sierra Club v. Ruckelshaus*. [36] In that case, the court ruled that state implementation plans under the Clean Air Act must include provisions not merely complying with national air quality standards, but also designed to prevent the degradation of air currently cleaner than those standards require. The consequence of the PSD program is to ensure that especially clean areas remain especially clean. They are not permitted to become dirtier, even if they would continue to provide a safe and healthful environment.

One of the court's goals was to ensure that federal environmental policy protected beauty and visibility in currently pristine areas. While the PSD program has to some degree promoted that goal, it has also had perverse side-effects. For example, it has delayed the salutary substitution of clean, low-sulfur western coal for dirty, high-sulfur eastern coal; at the same time, it has protected dirty existing plants in the East against replacement with cleaner new ones in the West. [37] To protect the atmosphere in Aspen from degradation is, almost inevitably, to perpetuate the existence of old, particularly dirty producers in New York. The foreclosure of new risks has thus increased the magnitude of old ones. It is far from clear that the environment is better off as a whole.

Indeed, it should come as no surprise that the PSD program has become a primary means of protecting eastern industry and eastern states against western interests. States in the West seeking to attract industry have found, perversely, that an environmental program can be used to create a cartel against new entry. A PSD program based on an understanding of the adverse effects of that cartel for the prevention of environmental degradation would take a quite different form.

The court that decided the *Sierra Club* case was unaware of these effects. Because the statutory basis for the decision was quite thin, an understanding of the environmental and nonenvironmental costs associated with the PSD program might well have led to a contrary result.

The Independent Agency Paradox

The precise constitutional status of the independent agency remains an uncertain question. In *Humphrey's Executor v. United States*,[38] the Supreme Court, affirming the constitutional validity of the independent agency, held that Congress could constitutionally prevent the president from removing a member of the Federal Trade Commission simply because it pleased him to do so. Recent decisions have reaffirmed the authority of *Humphrey's Executor* insofar as it recognizes that some degree of independence from the President is permissible.[39] But suppose that members of the Nuclear Regulatory Commission or the Federal Trade Commission act in ways that consistently reject the president's views about public policy. May the president discharge the relevant commissioners? It is frequently assumed that he may not. But neither *Humphrey's Executor* nor any other case explains what "independence" precisely means, or whether it extends to such situations.

The problem might be solved through statutory interpretation that takes account of the independent agency paradox. The relevant provisions allow the president to discharge a commissioner "for cause," defined as "inefficiency, neglect of duty, or malfeasance in office." Although ambiguous, these words do not entirely immunize commissioners from the control of the president; instead, they allow him to remove officials under certain circumstances. For those attuned to the independent agency paradox, it might seem that the words are best read to grant the president something in the way of supervisory and removal power—allowing him, for example, to discharge as inefficient or neglectful of duty those commissioners who have frequently or on important occasions acted in ways inconsistent with his policy wishes.

This result might seem counterintuitive in light of the frequent understanding that independent agencies are to be immunized from presidential policy making. But there is a plausible precedent for precisely this conclusion in a recent Supreme Court decision, *Bowsher v. Synar*.[40] In that case, the Court held that Congress could not delegate power to administer the Gramm–Rudman statute to the comptroller general, because the comptroller was subject to congressional will. In the Court's view, those who execute the law must not be subject to the policy-making authority of Congress, except insofar as legislative instructions are embodied in substantive law. The relevant statute allowed Congress to discharge the comptroller for "inefficiency, . . . neglect of duty, . . . [or] malfeasance." The Court said that these words conferred on Congress "very broad" removal power and would authorize Congress to remove the comptroller for "any number of actual or perceived transgressions of the legislative will."

Thus, the words governing congressional power over the comptroller general and presidential power over independent agencies are essentially identical. If those words have the same meaning in these admittedly different contexts, the president has "very broad" removal power over the commissioners of the independent agencies, with correlative powers of supervision and guidance. It would follow, then, that the independent agencies are in fact subject to a considerable degree of presidential control. They are not, as a matter of statutory law, "independent" of him at all. In view of the independent agency paradox, courts would do well to invoke a clear statement principle that grants the president broad supervisory power over independent agencies unless Congress has expressly stated its will to the contrary. Such an approach would minimize the risks inherent in the independent agency form and promote coordination and accountability in government. It would require Congress to speak unambiguously if it wants to compromise those goals.

V. Conclusion

There are multiple breakdowns in private markets, and government regulation is sometimes an effective response. The administrative state has not been a universal failure; we have seen a wide range of successes. But regulatory programs have not always done what they should, and the paradoxes of the regulatory state have been a pervasive source of its problems. Self-defeating regulatory strategies take many forms. I have discussed six such paradoxes and referred to several others; still others undoubtedly exist.

In proposing reforms for the regulatory state, little can be gained from generalities that point to the frequent problems created by either government regulation or private markets (which are themselves of course a form of regulation). These problems are too particular and too dependent on the context to allow for global prescriptions. It is far more helpful to rely on particularized understandings of how both markets and regulation tend to break down—in short, to learn from the past. The experience of the regulatory state includes many self-defeating regulatory strategies. But enough information is in place to help legislators, administrators, and judges to minimize their adverse effects, and even to prevent their occurrence. The result would be a small but firm step in the direction of an American-style perestroika—a system that is entirely unembarrassed by the use of government to reflect democratic aspirations, to promote economic welfare, and to foster distributional equity, while at the same time insisting on strategies that embody the flexibility, adaptability, productive potential, and decentralization characteristic of private markets.

Notes

1. See John Graham and Jonathan Wiener, eds., Risk *versus* Risk, pp. 8–11 (Cambridge: Harvard University Press, 1995); Gregg Easterbrook, *A Moment on the Earth* (New York: Viking, 1995). Air and water pollution data can be found in *id.*; CEQ, 24th Annual Report, Environmental Quality (1993).

2. See Robert W. Crandall, et al., Regulating the Automobile (Washington, D.C.: Brookings Institution, 1986), pp. 44–74.

3. *Id.* at 75.

4. W. Kip Viscusi. *Fatal Tradeoffs: Public and Private Responsibilities for Risk* (New York: Oxford University Press, 1992).

5. See Heckman and Paynor.

6. See Easterbrook, *supra* note 1; Steven Lewis Yaffee., *Prohibitive Policy: Implementing the Federal Endangered Species Act.* (Cambridge, Mass.: MIT Press, 1982).

7. On productivity losses, see James Robinson, "The Impact of Environmental and Occupational Health Regulation on Producivity Growth in U.S. Manufacturing," 12 *Yale J. on Reg.* 387, 416–17 (1995); on cheaper control strategies, see Thomas H. Tietenberg, Emissions Trading: An Exercise in Reforming Pollution Policy (Washington, D.C.: Resources for the Future, 1985), pp. 41–45.

8. See Crandall et al., *supra* note 2, at 157–58 Robert W. Crandall and John D. Graham, "The Effect of Fuel Economy Standards on Automobile Safety," 32 J. L. & Econ. 97, 115 (1989).

9. See Stephen G. Breyer. Regulation and Its Reform (Cambridge: Harvard University Press, 1982), p. 244.

10. See Henry G. Grabowski and John M. Vernon, The Regulation of Pharmaceuticals: Balancing the Benefits and Risks (Washington D.C.: American Enterprise Institute for Public Policy Research, 1983), pp. 10–13, 46–47.

11. Richard M. Nixon, "State of the Union Address," in *Public Papers of the Presidents of the United States:* GPO, 1970, p. 13.

12. See John M. Mendeloff, *The Dilemma of Toxic Substance Regulation: How Overregulation Causes Underregulation at OSHA* (Cambridge, Mass.: MIT Press, 1988), pp. 2, 82.

13. See David Vogel, *National Styles of Regulation: Environmental Policy in Great Britain and the United States* (Ithaca: Cornell University Press, 1986), p. 163.

14. See Peter Huber, "The Old-New Division in Risk Regulation," 69 *Va. L. Rev.* 1025 (1983). See also Michael T. Maloney and Gordon L. Brady, "Capital Turnover and Marketable Pollution Rights," 31 *J. L. & Econ.* 203, 214–26, 224 (1988) (finding a 27 percent increase in sulfur dioxide emissions as a result of capital turnover deterrence in certain states). Compare W. Kip Viscusi, "Consumer Behavior and the Safety Effects of Product Safety Regulation," 28 *J. L. & Econ.* 527, 552 (1985); Sam Peltzman, "The Health Effects of Mandatory Prescriptions," 30 *J. L. & Econ.* 207, 234–36 (1987).

15. See Bruce A. Ackerman and William T. Hassler, *Clean Coal/Dirty Air: Or How the Clean Air Act Became a Multibillion Dollar Bail-Out for High Sulfur Coal Producers and What Can be Done About It* (New Haven: Yale University Press, 1981), pp. 2, 11–12.

16. See Richard A. Merrill, "FDA's Implementation of the Delaney Clause: Repudiation of Congressional Choice or Reasoned Adaptation to Scientific Progress?," 5 *Yale J. Reg.* 1 (1988). See also Peter W. Huber, *Liability: The Legal Revolution and Its Consequences* (New York: Basic Books, 1988).

17. See Finis Welsh, *Minimum Wages: Issues and Evidence* (Washington, D.C.: American Enterprise Institute for Public Policy Research, 1978). But see David Card and Alan B. Krueger, *Myth and Measurement: The New Economics of the Minimum Wage* (Princeton: Princeton University Press, 1995).

18. See Werner Z. Hirsch, Joel G. Hirsch, and Stephen Margolis, "Regression Analysis of the Effects of Habitability Laws upon Rent: An Empirical Observation on the Ackerman-Komesar Debate," 63 *Cal. L. Rev.* 1098, 1139 (1975).

19. See Richard Posner, "An Economic Anology of Spy Discrimination Laws," 56 *U. Chi. L. Rev.* 1311, 1326, 1331, 1333.

20. See Jacob Jacoby, Margaret C. Nelson, and Wayne D. Hoyer, "Corrective Advertising and Affirmative Disclosure Statements: Their Potential for Confusing and Misleading the Consumer," 46 *J. Mktg.* 61, 70 (Winter 1982); Philip G. Kuehl and Robert F. Dyer, "Applications of the 'Normative Belief' Technique for Measuring the Effectiveness of Deceptive and Corrective Advertisements," 4 *Advances in Cons. Res.* 204, 209 (1976); and Michael B. Mazis and Janice E. Atkinson, "An Experimental Evaluation of a Proposed Corrective Advertising Remedy," 13 *J. Mktg. Res.* 178, 181–83 (1976).

21. See Richard Craswell, "Interpreting Deceptive Advertising" 65 *B. U. L. Rev.* 657, 690–91. (1985)

22. See Howard Beales, Richard Craswell, and Steven C. Salop, "The Efficient Regulation of Consumer Information," 24 *J. L. & Econ.* 491, 520 (1981); and Robert Pitofsky, "Beyond Nader: Consumer Protection and the Regulation of Advertising," 90 *Harv. L. Rev.* 661, 682–83 (1977).

23. See Terry Moe, "Regulatory Performance and Presidential Administration," 26 *Am. J. Pol. Sci.* 197 (1982).

24. See Marvin H. Bernstein, *Regulating Business by Independent Commission* (Princeton: Princeton University Press, 1955), p. 170; and Richard A. Harris and Sidney M. Milkis, *The Politics of Regulatory Change: A Tale of Two Agencies* (New York: Oxford University Press, 1989).

25. See Lucas A. Powe, Jr., *American Broadcasting and the First Amendment* (Berkeley: University of California Press, 1987).

26. See Jon Elster, *Solomonic Judgments: Studies in the Limitations of Rationality* (Cambridge: Cambridge University Press, 1989).

27. Hyman Rodman, Betty Sarvis, and Joy Walker Bonar, *The Abortion Question* (New York: Columbia University Press, 1987), p. 285.

28. See Peltzman, *supra* note 14, at 210–12. A similar study of automobile safety regulation found that such regulation had no effect or perverse effect on safety because it increased risks to pedestrians; see Sam Peltzman, "The Effects of Automobile Safety Regulation," 83 *J. Pol. Econ.* 677 (1975). This study is based on highly questionable assumptions, see Mark Kelman, "Symposium on the Theory of Public Choice: On Democracy-Bashing: A Skeptical Look at the Theoretical and 'Empirical' Practice of the Public Choice Movement," 74 *Va. L. Rev.* 199, 239–45 (1988), and it has been disproved by experience. Indeed, automobile safety regulation is an example of regulatory success. See Crandall et al., *supra* note 2); Jerry L. Mashaw and David L. Harfst, *The Struggle for Auto Safety* (Cambridge: Harvard University Press, 1990).

29. Viscusi, *supra* note 14, at 539, 544, 546.

30. FN32 See Gideon Doron, "How Smoking Increased When TV Advertising of Cigarettes Was Banned," 3 *Regulation* 49 (March/April 1979).

31. See Lenore J. Weitzman, The Divorce Revolution: *The Unexpected Social and Economic Consequences for Women and Children in America* (New York: Free Press, 1985), pp. 323, 357–58; and Mary E. Becker, "Prince Charming: Abstract Equality," 1987 *S. Ct. Rev.* 201, 214–24.

32. The best discussions here are by Jon Elster. See his various criticisms of functional explanations in *Explaining Technical Change: A Case Study in the Philosophy of Science* (Cambridge: Cambridge University Press, 1983); *The Cement of Society: A Study of Social Order* (Cambridge: Cambridge University Press, 1989); and *Nuts and Bolts for the Social Sciences* (Cambridge: Cambridge University Press, 1989).

33. 448 U.S. 607 (1980).

34. *Id.* at 645.

35. 452 U.S. 490 (1981).

36. 344 F. Supp. 253 (D D.C. 1972).

37. R. Shep Melnick, *Regulation and the Courts: The Case of the Clean Air Act* (Washington D.C.: Brookings Institution, 1983), pp. 80–83. See also Ackerman and Hassler, *supra* note 15, at 44–48; and B. Peter Pashigian, *Environmental Regulation: Whose Self-Interests Are Being Served?* in *Chicago Studies in Political Economy*, George J. Stigler, ed. (Chicago: Unversity of Chicago Press, 1988), p. 498.

38. 295 U.S. 602 (1935).

39. See Morrison v. Olson, 487 U.S. 654 (1988); Mistretta v. United States, 109 S. Ct. 647 (1989).

40. 478 U.S. 714 (1986).

Health-Health Trade-Offs

There are deep and fundamental and intuitively understood grounds for rejecting the view that confines itself merely to checking the parity of outcomes,
the view that matches death for death, happiness for happiness, fulfilment
for fulfilment, irrespective of how all this death, happiness, and fulfilment
comes about.

Amartya Sen

I. The Problem

There is a pervasive problem in the regulation of risk, one that is only now
receiving public attention.[1] The problem occurs *when the diminution of one
health risk simultaneously increases another health risk*. Thus, for example, if government bans the manufacture and use of asbestos, it may lead companies to
use more dangerous substitutes.[2] Regulation of nuclear power may make nuclear power safer; but by increasing the cost of nuclear power, such regulation
will ensure reliance on other energy sources, such as coal-fired power plants,
which carry risks of their own. When government requires reformulated gasoline as a substitute for ordinary gasoline, it may produce new pollution problems. When government regulates air pollution, it may encourage industry
to increase the volume of solid waste, and in that sense aggravate another
environmental problem. Fuel economy standards, designed partly to reduce
environmental risks, may make automobiles less safe, and in that way increase
risks to life and health. Regulations designed to control the spread of AIDS
and hepatitis among health care providers may increase the costs of health
care, and thus make health care less widely available, and thus cost lives.[3]

The general problem is ubiquitous. It stems from the fact that government
officials, like individual citizens and the public as a whole, suffer from selective
attention. A large priority for modern government is to develop mechanisms
that overcome the problems posed by the fact that people—both citizens and
regulators—tend to focus on problems that are parts of complex wholes. But
lives are not fungible, and any such mechanism should take account of Sen's
point in the epigraph to this essay. Risks to life and health are qualitatively
diverse, and because of their nature and origins, some risks warrant greater
attention than others.

My goal here is to explore how the law might deal with health-health
trade-offs, in an effort to find ways to make public judgments on this topic
both more democratic and more deliberative. The exploration bears a good

deal on issues of individual and collective rationality and also on questions of appropriate institutional design in light of human selectivity and limitations of foresight. I develop a simple framework for deciding how regulatory agencies should approach such trade-offs. I suggest that this framework is complicated by reference to some peculiar features of rationality in risk assessment.

I also deal with the respective roles of courts, Congress, and the president in managing health-health trade-offs. I urge that agencies often ought to have legal authority to make such trade-offs, and that they ought to exercise that authority much more than they now do. I also argue for a modest but far from trivial judicial role in requiring agencies to consider aggregate rather than isolated risks. Thus, I claim that agency decisions that increase aggregate risk levels should be found arbitrary or capricious under the Administrative Procedure Act.

More generally, I urge that Congress should amend the Administrative Procedure Act (APA) to require agencies to consider ancillary risks and to minimize net risks. I also argue that the Office of Information and Regulatory Affairs (OIRA) should see the reduction of overall risk as one of its principal missions. Much more than it now does, OIRA should undertake a coordinating function so as to ensure that this mission is carried out. In these ways, I hope to connect the question of deliberative outcomes with the subject of institutional structure.

This chapter is organized as follows. In section I, I offer a conceptual map, designed to make some relevant distinctions. In section II, I propose a first approximation of an approach to health-health trade-offs; the first approximation is a simple effort to limit aggregate risks understood in "expected value" terms. I then suggest that this first approximation must be qualified by reference to some complexities in ordinary citizen judgments about risk. People care not only about expected value, but also about whether risks are involuntarily incurred, especially dreaded, inequitably distributed, potentially catastrophic, faced by future generations, and so forth. Reflective judgments of this sort diverge from both expert and economic valuations, though in interestingly different ways. Those reflective judgments bear a great deal on how we think about the "rationality" of risk regulation.

Section III deals with existing law, urging agencies to undertake more health-health trade-offs than they now do and explaining how a judicial role could encourage this to happen. Section IV deals with how Congress and the president might approach health-health trade-offs.

I. A Conceptual Map

Regulated and Ancillary Risks

To get a handle on the problem of health-health trade-offs, we need to make some distinctions. We will call the risks that government is trying to control the *regulated risks* and the risks that are increased by regulation the *ancillary risks*.

Ancillary risks take many different forms, depending on their relationship to the regulated risk. We might say that the increase in acid deposition is not *within the same domain* as the risks prevented by regulation of nuclear power plants. This is true in two different ways: legal and factual. Most important, the law does not consider it in the same domain, for the agency that regulates one of these risks, the Environmental Protection Agency, has no legal authority to regulate the other, which is governed by the Nuclear Regulatory Commission. A pervasive problem in handling health-health trade-offs stems from organization charts that allocate authority to diverse agencies, in a way that makes coordinated responses difficult or impossible. It is also the case that the risk of acid deposition (mostly from coal-fired power plants), simply as a matter of fact, has a different source from the risk from nuclear power plants. This point is important because it suggests that health-healths trade-offs will often require agencies to compile extensive information, possibly in a way that will dwarf existing capacities. Compare a situation in which the regulation of sulfur dioxide emissions increases emissions of carbon monoxide. If this happens, we are dealing in any event with air pollution, indeed air pollution from largely the same technologies, and the EPA has the statutory authority to regulate both sources.

It is therefore possible to imagine a complex continuum of relationships between regulated risks and ancillary risks. Of course, there are differences of degree as well as differences of kind, especially in the factual domain, where relevant inquiries often overlap. And of course we might describe the domain of the regulated risk in many different ways. Usually, the best way to define the risk domain is through the relevant law, which, as we will see, sets constraints on the kinds of risk that agencies might consider.

A well-functioning administrative state would seek a measure of coordination among agencies, so that an agency operating in one domain does not inadvertently or unnecessarily increase risks in other domains. Certainly agencies should coordinate their efforts so as to reduce net or overall risks. But a special problem for coordinated responses is that agencies have quite different standards for deciding when risks require regulation.[4] The International Commission on Radiological Protection, for example, recommends that environmental factors should not cause an incremental cancer risk, for those exposed over a lifetime, of about 3 in 1000. But American agencies do not follow this recommendation, and their own practices are wildly variable. The Nuclear Regulatory Commission sees 1 in 1000 as acceptable; the EPA's acceptable range varies from 1 in 10,000 to 1 in 1,000,000. The FDA has tried to use a standard of 1 in 1 million, but under the Delaney Clause, courts have required a standard of essentially 0. OSHA's understanding of the "significant risk" requirement found in its governing statute means a risk of 1 in 1000; labor groups have sought an increase to 1 in 1 million.

These varying standards make health-health trade-offs quite complex. If one agency is using a standard of 1 in 1000 for risk A, and doing so lawfully, how should it deal with an increase in risk B, when that risk is regulated by a different agency operating lawfully under a different standard? Matters become even more difficult when risks from cancer are being compared with other sorts of risk; qualitative differences—between, for example, a cancer death and a sudden unanticipated death—can justify different responses. I return to this issue later.

There are many different mechanisms by which risk regulation may increase aggregate risks.[5] All of these mechanisms have a degree of complexity, and hence collective judgments that respond to them may well misfire.

- A regulatory ban may result in independent health risks coming from ancillary "replacement" risks. If we ban substance A, the replacement substance B may be dangerous too. If a carcinogenic substance is regulated, perhaps people will use a product that is not carcinogenic but that causes serious risks of heart disease. It is important for government to be aware of this possibility.
- Regulation may produce an offsetting risk that is qualitatively similar to or indistinguishable from the target risk. Perhaps regulation of some substances that threaten to destroy the ozone layer will produce greater use of other substances that also threaten the ozone layer.
- Regulation may force society to lose or forego "opportunity benefits." For example, careful screening procedures that keep out drugs and services may deprive people of certain health benefits at the same time that they protect people from certain health risks. This problem has received recent attention with respect to the Food and Drug Administration, especially with its efforts to control the spread of AIDS.[6]
- Regulated substances may have health benefits as well as health risks, and by eliminating those health benefits, regulation may therefore create health dangers on balance.
- Regulation of one risk may protect a certain group of people while imposing a new risk on another group. This may happen if, for example, a ban on a certain pesticide protects consumers, plants, and animals but increases risks to farmers.
- Most generally, the economic costs imposed by regulation may create health risks as well, as we shall soon see.

The distributional incidence of the ancillary risk may matter a great deal. Sometimes the ancillary risk falls on the same class of people as the regulated risk; sometimes the ancillary risk burdens an entirely different group. And sometimes the group that is newly burdened is politically weak or generally disadvantaged. This may matter a great deal for policy purposes because it suggests that *risk redistribution*, rather than risk reduction, is a possible outcome of regulation. Powerful interest groups may well try to exploit this possibility. Hence it should be expected that odd coalitions will develop to reduce risks of a certain kind, when the result is to shift risks (and control costs) from some groups to others. If poor or minority populations are the victims, there is special reason for social concern. In fact, the distributive incidence of a risk is an important part of risk evaluation.

"Richer Is Safer"

Thus far, we have been discussing cases in which the act of regulating one risk produces ancillary risks through a certain causal chain; but there is a particularly controversial version of this possibility, one that has been receiving much recent attention. Regulations cost money—sometimes a great deal of money—and private expenditures on regulatory compliance may produce less employment and more poverty. People who are unemployed or poor tend to be in worse health and to live shorter lives.[7] If wealthy people face diminished threats to life and health, and if poor people face greater threats, might not costly regulation increase risks simply by virtue of reducing wealth?

This possibility has been reflected in legal opinions, perhaps most prominently in Judge Easterbrook's suggestion that a fetal protection policy might "reduce risk attributable to lead at the cost of increasing other hazards," including the hazards stemming from less income, since "there is also a powerful link between the parents' income and infants' health."[8] The more general question is this: Would it be possible to connect governmentally required expenditures on risk-reduction with shifts in unemployment and poverty?

An incipient literature attempts to do precisely this. A 1990 study attempted to develop a model to quantify the view that "richer is safer."[9] According to Kenney, a single fatality might result from a compulsory expenditure of from $3 million to $7.5 million. In a concurring opinion in a 1991 case involving occupational safety and health regulation, Judge Williams invoked this evidence to suggest that OSHA's refusal to engage in cost-benefit analysis might not be beneficial for workers.[10] Judge Williams reasoned in the following way. If a fatality results from an expenditure of $7.5 million, some regulations might produce more fatalities than they prevent. Many regulations of course cost more than $7.5 million per life saved. In Judge Williams's view, an agency that fails to measure costs against benefits might be failing to measure mortality gains against losses.

The claimed relationship between wealth reductions and mortality is controversial.[11] But a number of studies find such a relationship. Consider the summary in Table 12.1.

This points leads to a broader one with considerable implications for law. Even if agencies are sometimes prevented, by law, from measuring costs against benefits, perhaps they could compare health losses with health gains and conclude that some regulations are not worthwhile because they cost lives on net. In fact, it can be shown that some regulations fail "health-health analysis" (HHA), whether or not they pass benefit-cost analysis (CBA). Consider Table 12.2.

The idea that "richer is safer" has started to affect public deliberations about risk. In a now-celebrated letter written in 1992, James McRae, the act-

Table 12.1. Richer Is Safer

Study	Data	Implicit Income Gains Necessary to Avert One Death (millions)	Comments
Keeney (1990)	Used income and mortality correlations from Kitagawa and Hauser (1960) data, and others	$12.3	Cited in *UAW v. OSHA*, as $7.25 1980 dollars. Represents an upperbound
Joint Economic Committee (1984)	Aggregate U.S. income, employment, mortality and morbidity, 1950–80	$1.8 to $2.7	Reflects income loss from recession of 1974–75
Anderson and Burkhauser (1985)	4878 male workers, over ten years, 1969–79	$1.9 (wages) $4.3 (other income)	Older workers aged 58–63. Measured effects of wages and value of one's home on mortality
Duleep (1986)	9618 white married male workers aged 35–64, over six years, 1973–78	$2.6	Controls for prior disability and educational attainment
Duleep (1989)	13,954 white married male workers aged 25–64, over six years, 1973–78	$6.5	Finds income effects at all income levels
Duleep (1991)	9618 white married male workers aged 35–64, over six years, 1973–78	$3.9	Controls for prior disability, educational attainment, and exposure to occupational hazards
Wolfson (1992)	500,000 Canadian workers, over ten to twenty years	$6.0	Investigates longevity rather than mortality. Finds income effects at highest quintiles of income
National Institutes of Health (1992)	1,300,000 Americans, all ages, 1979–85	$12.4	Estimate reflects effect of income changes on family mortality. Study does not use multiple regression, does not control for prior health status or education
Chirikos and Nestel (1991)	5020 men, aged 50–64, studied during 1971–83	$3.3	Uses two measures of health endowments
Chapman and Hariharan (1993)	5836 older men, over ten years	$12.2	Uses four distinct controls for prior health conditions
Graham, Hung-Chang, and Evans (1992)	Thirty-eight years of age-adjusted mortality and income data for the United States	$4.0	Distinguishes effects of permanent income from those of transitional income

Source: Randall Lutter and John Morrall, "Health-Health Analysis," 8 *Journal of Risk and Uncertainty* 43, 49 (1994). Reprinted by permission.

Table 12.2. Regulations Passing HHA vs. CBA Tests

Budgeted Regulations	Year	Agency	Cost Per Life Saved ($ millions 1992)
1. Steering column protection	1967	NHTSA	0.1
2. Unvented space heaters	1980	CPSC	0.1
3. Cabin fire protection	1985	FAA	0.3
4. Passive restraints/belts	1984	NHTSA	0.4
5. Fuel system integrity	1975	NHTSA	0.4
6. Trihalomethanes	1979	EPA	0.4
7. Underground construction	1989	OSHA-S	0.4
8. Alcohol and drug control	1985	FRA	0.7
9. Servicing wheel rims	1984	OSHA-S	0.7
10. Seat cushion flammability	1984	FAA	0.8
11. Floor emergency lighting	1984	FAA	0.9
12. Crane suspended personnel platform	1988	OSHA-S	1.2
13. Children's sleepware flammability	1973	CPSC	1.8
14. Side doors	1979	NHTSA	1.8
15. Concrete and masonry construction	1988	OSHA-S	1.9
16. Hazard communication	1983	OSHA-S	2.4
17. Asbestos	1986	OSHA-H	2.8
18. Benzene/fugitive emission	1984	EPA	3.8

Regulations failing CBA test

19. Grain dust	1987	OSHA-S	8.8
20. Radionuclides/uranium mines	1984	EPA	9.3

Regulations failing HHA (and CBA) test

21. Benzene	1987	OSHA-H	23.1
22. Ethylene oxide	1984	OSHA-H	34.6
23. Uranium mill tailings/inactive	1983	EPA	37.3
24. Acrylonitrile	1978	OSHA-H	50.8
25. Uranium mill tailings/active	1983	EPA	71.6
26. Asbestos	1989	EPA	72.9
27. Coke ovens	1976	OSHA-H	83.4
28. Arsenic	1978	OSHA-H	125.0
29. DES (cattlefeed)	1979	FDA	178.0
30. Arsenic/glass manufacture	1986	EPA	192.0
31. Benzene/storage	1984	EPA	273.0
32. Radionuclides/DOE facility	1984	EPA	284.0
33. Radionuclides/elim. phos.	1984	EPA	365.0
34. Acrylonitrile	1978	OSHA-H	416.0
35. Benzene/ethylbenz./styr.	1984	EPA	652.0
36. Benzene/maleic anhydride	1984	EPA	1,107.0
37. Formaldehyde	1987	OSHA-H	119,000.0

Source: Randall Lutter and John Morrall, "Health-Health Analysis," 8 *Journal of Risk and Uncertainty* 59 (1994). Reprinted by permission.

ing administrator of OIRA, wrote to the Department of Labor, questioning a proposed OSHA regulation involving air contaminants in the workplace.[12] OSHA had estimated a savings of between eight and thirteen lives per year, at an annual cost of $163 million. McRae suggested that there was a significant gap in OSHA's analysis: If a statistical fatality is produced by an expenditure of $7.5 million, the regulation could actually cause twenty-two additional deaths. McRae asked OSHA to investigate the relation between health, wealth, and safety. OSHA responded that existing data to the effect that richer is safer seemed highly speculative, but it did call for more comments from the public.

Eventually, a public outcry forced OIRA to retreat. Senator Glenn in particular complained of OIRA's "Alice-in-Wonderland type claim that health and safety regulations cause harm to workers" and objected that the richer is safer view "seems to stand logic on its head—to say that controlling a dangerous substance in the workplace makes an increased health hazard to the worker." Despite the public outcry, increasing research on the issue suggests that lives can indeed be lost through required regulatory expenditures, and that, at a minimum, there is reason for government to take the problem seriously.

Why Does It Matter?

We have now seen enough to know that an impressive body of work attempts to measure health gains from regulation against health risks from regulation. But why should we focus on this particular question? Why would it not be better to attend to the overall gains from regulation and to the overall losses from regulation? Cost-benefit analysis is receiving considerable attention from both agencies and Congress, and cost-benefit analysis, properly conceived, takes account of all of the health-related effects of regulation. What is special about health-health trade-offs?

Part of the answer lies in existing public judgments, taken as simple brute facts. People seem to think that regulation is bad if it causes more deaths than it saves; a demonstration to this effect counts strongly against regulation. But people do not always know how to compare health gains (15 lives gained, for example) with monetary losses (an expenditure of $15 million, for example). This uncertainty stems partly from the fact that lives and dollars are not easily made commensurable, and partly from the fact that the appropriate amount to spend on protection of a (statistical) life depends on context. A deliberative judgment on net health trade-offs is easier to reach than a deliberative judgment on other sorts of trade-offs. It may thus be impossible to obtain an incompletely theorized agreement[13] that a net mortality loss is bad—incompletely theorized in the sense that people from diverse theoretical perspectives can agree on that proposition. Incompletely theorized agreements on particular results are an important part of democratic deliberation; they are a distinctive solution to the problems of social pluralism and disagreement.

It would, however, be inadequate for present purposes to rest with existing public judgments, which may be irrational or confused. Perhaps public uncertainty about cost-benefit judgments depends on an obstinate and counterproductive unwillingness to acknowledge that even (risk to) life has its price. But part of the answer lies in attending more closely to problems of incommensurability. As we saw in chapter 3, we might understand incommensurability to arise when no single metric is available by which to assess variables at stake in a social decision. In the area of risk regulation, a single metric is troublesome simply because it elides qualitative distinctions. Cost-benefit analysis attempts to provide such a metric. And if all effects are reduced to the metric of dollars, it may be possible to make simple assessments, in the sense that comparisons and hence trade-offs can become easier. But reduction of mortality and morbidity effects to dollars can erase pertinent qualitative distinctions. It is important for officials to have a sense of these distinctions when they make decisions.

It is in the face of qualitative distinctions—distinctions in *how*, not simply *how much*, things are valued—that participants in democratic deliberation often resist a metric of dollars. To say this is not at all to deny that trade-offs have to be made among qualitatively diverse goods. But perhaps people can make choices more easily when the trade-offs involve qualitatively indistinguishable things, like lives, rather than qualitatively diverse things, like lives and dollars. When it is hard to trade off lives against dollars, the burdens of judgment might be eased when we are trading off lives against lives. A judgment of this kind undoubtedly underlies the interest in "health-health analysis."

There is considerable truth to this suggestion, but it is a bit too crude. As we shall see, lives themselves are not commensurable, in the sense that a single metric—"lives saved"—is itself too flat to account for considered democratic judgments. It matters a great deal which lives and which deaths, and whose lives and whose deaths. A life of a young person may warrant more resources than a life of an old person, because more years can be saved; a life that can be fully lived and enjoyed may be worth more as a greater investment than another sort of life. Problems of incommensurability cannot be eliminated so easily, since they play a large role in health-health comparisons too. On the other hand, it would be possible to reduce problems of commensurability by exploring the number of years, or decently liveable years, that could be saved by different regulatory strategies (see the discussion of quality-adjusted life years in chapter 5). This approach would not eliminate qualitative distinctions among different strategies, but it is a useful way of getting a pragmatic handle on issues of comparison.

II. Incorporating Health-Health Comparisons

First Approximation

Let us try, in a simple, intuitive way, to identify the factors that should enter into deliberative judgments about health-health trade-offs. Begin with a simple case in which the costs of information and inquiry are zero. If this is so, all agencies should investigate all risks potentially at stake. Agencies should always take account of ancillary risks and always try to limit overall or aggregate risks.

Of course, the costs of investigation and inquiry are never zero; in fact, they are often very high. We can readily imagine that agencies could spend all their time investigating ancillary risks and never do anything else. (This is a potential problem with cost-benefit analysis: Cost-benefit analysis may itself fail cost-benefit analysis. Perhaps the costs of undertaking cost-benefit analysis are high and the benefits low.) When the costs of inquiry are not zero, the obligation to inquire into ancillary risks might be a function of several factors. *First* is the costs of delay, understood as the cost of not regulating the regulated risk until more information has been compiled. To figure out this cost, it is necessary to explore the seriousness of the regulated risk and the length of time necessary to investigate the ancillary risk. *Second* is the cost of investigating the ancillary risk, where this cost is understood as a product of the cost of compiling and evaluating the relevant information. *Third* is the benefit of investigating the ancillary risk, with the benefit understood as the likelihood of uncovering information that might help to produce a different and better result.

Under this view, it is of course important to know something about the possible extent of the ancillary risk and the costs of discovering it. Hence it is is impossible to know whether to undertake health-health analysis without making some initial judgments about the ancillary risk, a risk that, by hypothesis, has not yet been explored. Before the actual investigation has occurred, there will be a good deal of intuition and guesswork here; the full facts cannot be known until inquiries have been completed, and the real question is whether it is worthwhile to complete the inquiries or even to embark on them. But even at an early stage, it is possible to know that some ancillary risks are likely to be high, while others are trivial or low. Moreover, some ancillary risks can be investigated relatively inexpensively, whereas others depend on scientific and predictive judgments that require an enormous investment of resources. Of course, an agency might be reluctant to inquire into ancillary risks on the theory that if it does so, it will be unable to regulate the risk at issue before it is too late. It seems clear that the extent and nature of the regulated risk are crucial factors for those deciding whether to explore ancillary risks.

On this simple, intuitive view, we might think in the following way: If it would be enormously expensive to investigate whether fuel economy standards would really produce smaller and more dangerous cars, if the fuel economy standards would themselves do a lot of good, and if the likelihood of a high ancillary risk seems small, then it makes sense to proceed with the fuel economy standards without investigating the ancillary risks. On the other hand, it is easy to imagine a scenario in which investigation of ancillary risks is reasonable, or when failure to investigate would be irrational. Thus, the National Highway Transportation Safety Administration's (NHTSA) actual position with respect to fuel economy standards and safety is that the ancillary risk is worth investigating.

Compare the question how to handle ancillary risks created by a prohibition on the manufacture of asbestos. One ancillary risk arises from the fact that asbestos appears to be the best product for use in brake linings; existing substitutes are far worse. Whether this is true, and how serious the ancillary risk is, can be investigated at the present time. But other ancillary risks involve substitutes for asbestos in products for which no substitutes are now available. On the view of the Environmental Protection Agency, the ban on asbestos will force technological innovation, producing new substances that do the work now done by asbestos.[14] This may be a reasonable view. If so, the government has reason to regulate asbestos now and to wait before evaluating any substitute risks.

Existing Law and Its Rationale

How should we understand existing law in light of this first approximation? Congress has forbidden health-health analysis in many settings, by directing agencies to focus on certain health problems and not to inquire into others. Questions therefore arise about what understanding, if any, accounts for the prohibition.

Some of the relevant statutes might be seen to reflect *categorical, rule-bound judgments* about calculations of the kind just discussed. Congress might think, for example, that the Nuclear Regulatory Commission (NRC) should not ask whether regulation of nuclear power will cause a shift to coal-fired power plants and thus aggravate the problem of acid deposition, because the problem of unsafe nuclear power is an especially serious one, because nuclear power regulation by itself is unlikely to produce significant increases in acid deposition, and because it is very hard for the NRC, given its limited budget and expertise, to make the necessary extrapolations. In light of these considerations, the NRC might plausibly be exempted from the duty of exploring ancillary risks, or even banned from doing so.

Alternatively, the problems posed by ancillary risks might be solved by *division of labor*. Any effects on automobile safety that come from air pollution regulation, causing smaller cars to be produced, might be controlled by the NHTSA. Perhaps NHTSA has the authority to make sure that the ancillary risk does not come to fruition. Any adverse effects of EPA regulation could be prevented by NHTSA. Perhaps the two agencies will coordinate their efforts to ensure that aggregate risks are minimized. Or consider the health risks from regulation inducing unemployment and poverty. It might be thought that the disemployment effects of regulation are or should be addressed by other governmental institutions, including those entrusted with the power to reduce unemployment and poverty.

Of course, there are serious problems with the division of labor strategy. Coordination of risk regulation is difficult to achieve, and in modern government, it has not been pursued in any systematic way. In any case, it would be surprising if a sensible division of labor accounted for existing practice, for there is no evidence that agencies systematically respond to increases in ancillary risk created by regulation.

Another explanation for existing authority to consider some risks but not others would point to the important role of *interest groups* in the regulatory process. On this view, the disparities in regulatory strategies are attributable to the fact that well-organized groups are able to obtain legislation in their interest or to fend off harmful regulation. It should be unsurprising that the statute regulating agricultural practices allows for a form of open-ended balancing; the agricultural groups are in a good position to fend off draconian legislation. But sometimes environmental groups are able to obtain severe restrictions on carcinogenic substances. In fact, interest groups might work together so as to redistribute risks, and the resulting coalitions might well ban agencies from engaging in health-health analysis, for fear that the result will be a failure of the hoped-for redistribution. If, for example, corn producers attempt to obtain an ethanol requirement for gasoline, they will not be disturbed to find that ethanol itself imposes environmental risks. Or if it happens that electric cars produce environmental hazards because of waste disposal problems, the redistribution of the risk may not be bothersome to those who favor electric cars on self-interested grounds. It would even be possible to imagine cases in which the redistributed risk was affirmatively sought, if, for example, those who face the new risk are competitors. Undoubtedly, an investigation of the political economy of risk regulation would reveal many diverse cases in which interest groups pursue their own interests rather than overall risk reduction.

Other explanations would point to *myopia, selective attention, poorly functioning heuristics, sensationalism, credit-claiming, and random agenda selection* as important forces in the production of risk regulation. Some statutes stem from sensationalistic events, like the Love Canal scare, that encourage legislators to hold hearings and claim credit for fixing problems that are not large or that are just part of a complex whole. Such statutes are likely to reflect myopia or selective attention. The result may well be a form of random agenda selection that bans health-health trade-offs, does not adequately reduce risks, or even increases some risks.[15]

Finally, some statutes might reflect public judgments about how to conduct health-health trade-offs. Perhaps the public believes that an increase in a certain risk is not a relevant factor in the assessment of another risk. This could be a product of simple confusion, as in the well-established refusal, on the part of some of the public some of the time, to acknowledge any need for trade-offs. Such judgments should not be given any weight in law; but Congress, responsive to the electorate, appears to disagree with this proposition. Or public judgments might be based on heuristics of certain kinds, productive of errors (chapter 5), connected with gripping anecdotes that make draconian regulation of a certain risk seem quite sensible. In these ways, relevant judgments could be confused, and we might seek a form of expert judgment that would produce more in the way of regulatory rationality. Some such judgments might, however, result from something other than confusion. They might depend on judgments about sensible regulatory priorities and about qualitative differences among risks. I take up this point later.

Incorporating Complexities

Our first approximation has suggested that all risks should be aligned along a single metric—expected annual deaths, aggregate benefits and costs—and hence measured against one another. Both expert and economic approaches attempt to do this, though in interestingly different ways. Experts tend to look at expected annual deaths and to assess risks accordingly. But ordinary people base their judgments on something other than this. As we saw in chapter 5, they look, for example, at whether the risk is faced voluntarily or involuntarily; whether it is equitably distributed; whether it is faced by future generations; whether it is potentially catastrophic; whether it involves a death that is especially dreaded; and whether it is new and poorly understood. Consider the summary in Table 12.3.

If aggravating and mitigating factors are taken into account, it might well be the case that people would find, say, 300 cases of cancer more acceptable than 350 cases of heart disease, given certain assumptions about what causes each. In contingent valuation studies, people purport to be willing to pay far more to prevent cancer deaths (from $1.5 million to $9.5 million) than they would to prevent unforeseen instant deaths (from $1 million to $5 million).[16] It is similarly possible that people might therefore accept a regulated risk involving 100 annual fatalities, even if the ancillary risk involves 110 annual fatalities; perhaps the ancillary risk is less severe because it is voluntarily incurred, not especially dreaded, and well understood. The democratic decision to look at something other than quantity is easy to defend. It is also fully rational.

We come, then, to a complication for the initial approximation: Risks should be evaluated in accordance with the various qualitative factors deemed relevant by ordinary people who are evaluating risk. Of course, it would be possible to assign numbers to these factors if this step aided analysis.

Economic approaches promise to avoid some of the problems of expert valuations. Most important, private willingness to pay should incorporate some or even all of the factors that underlie ordinary lay judgments. It might be possible to ascertain private willingness to pay from studies of actual market behavior and from contingent valuation studies. And from these results it is possible to elicit diverse valuations of diverse social risks. Consider Table 12.4.

There are, however, enormous difficulties in the idea that officials can get, from private willingness to pay, an adequate sense of how to order the risks at stake in regulation. As we saw in chapter 5, health-health trade-offs cannot easily be based on surrogates for market valuation. Actual choices are closely geared to the context in which they are made; it is not clear that one can infer from actual choices in one context people's valuations about other choices in a different context. Contingent valuation studies can build in a sense of context, but the answers may not be reliable. They may depend on questions that seem fantastical or on some effort to show moral commitment rather than to reveal actual trade-offs in a realistic setting. In any case, democratic choices should reflect a process of reason-giving, in which it is asked what policies are best to

Table 12.3

Risk Characteristic	Aggravating Factor	Mitigating Factor
Nature of risk	Dreaded	Acceptable
Permanence	Irreversible/uncontrollable	Reversible/controllable
Duration	Faced by future generations	Faced by those now living
Equity	Unfairly distributed	Fairly distributed
Source of risk	Man-made	Found in nature
Freedom	Voluntarily incurred	Forced exposure
Existing understanding	Known to science	Unknown
Relation to status quo	New	Old
Quantity and quality of remaining life	Long; good or decent	Short; extremely difficult

pursue, rather than a process of preference-satisfaction, in which each person is asked how much he is willing to pay for a certain result. Deliberative outcomes should not be confused with aggregated willingness to pay.

There is no simple way to translate these theoretical points into concrete policies. Real-world democratic institutions are not a simple process of reason-giving; interest groups play a large role and information may be hard to come by. In these circumstances, government officials must proceed nondogmatically and pragmatically, perhaps by taking aggregate numbers based on willingness to pay or expert judgments as a starting point and adjusting them with the supplemental considerations, involving democratic convictions, that I have described here (see chapter 5 for some details).

III. Courts and Existing Law

I now turn to existing law. If an agency takes account of ancillary risks, has it behaved unlawfully? If an agency refuses to consider such risks, should courts require it to do so?

Table 12.4.   Mortality Values by Cause of Death

Category (per statistical life)	Value Estimates (in million $)		
	Low	Medium	High
Unforeseen instant death	1.0	2.0	5.0
Asthma/bronchitis	1.3	2.5	5.5
Heart disease	1.25	2.75	6.0
Emphysema	1.4	3.5	9.0
Lung cancer	1.5	4.0	9.5

Source: George Tolley, Donald Kenkel, and Robert Fabian, eds., *Valuing Health for Policy: An Economic Approach* (Chicago: University of Chicago Press, 1994), p. 342. Reprinted by permission.

Consideration of Ancillary Risks

Suppose first that an agency actually considers health-health trade-offs. Is it permitted to do so under existing law? Agencies have considerable flexibility here, since under current doctrine agencies have a good deal of discretion to interpret ambiguous statutes as they see fit.[17]

Sometimes, however, statutes are unambiguous on this point, and ancillary risks are excluded as reasons for regulatory action or inaction. Under the Delaney Clause, for example, the FDA is almost certainly banned from considering the possibility that the exclusion of foods with carcinogens will increase risks from (say) heart disease. The FDA is prohibited from considering this or any other ancillary risk. A similar problem arises under the toxic substances provision of the Occupational Safety and Health Act, which probably bans OSHA from asking whether richer is safer, or even from balancing workplace risks against ancillary risks created by regulation.

But sometimes agencies are given sufficiently broad authority, and they may, if they choose, consider ancillary risks. Federal law provides that agencies must ask whether pesticides produce "unreasonable adverse effects on the environment," and this term requires the agency to take "into account the economic, social, and environmental costs and benefits of the use of any pesticide."[18] This statute certainly authorizes EPA to consider the possibility that any regulation would create aggregate harms. The Toxic Substances Control Act reads in similar terms. The Clean Air Act and the Federal Water Pollution Control Act allow government to consider a broad range of good and bad environmental effects in requiring technologies to reduce air and water pollution. Outside of the context of toxic substances, the Occupational Safety and Health Act defines occupational safety and health standards as those "reasonably necessary or appropriate" to the goal of ensuring "safe or healthful employment and places of employment." OSHA may reasonably decide that a standard is not "reasonably necessary or appropriate" if the effect of the regulation is to lose aggregate lives. It is almost certainly permitted to consider the effects of regulation in causing risks to life and health through poverty and unemployment.

Refusal to Consider Ancillary Risks

Now suppose that an agency refuses to consider, or to make decisive, the fact that its decision to reduce one risk increases another risk. Perhaps a new regulatory initiative from the Nuclear Regulatory Commission would increase the risks from coal-fired power plants. Is the NRC's refusal to consider such risks unlawful? The first question is whether the statute requires consideration of ancillary risks. The second question is whether, if the statute does not do so, the agency's decision is arbitrary or capricious.

As we have seen, many statutes do not require agencies to consider ancillary risks. In any case, courts defer to reasonable agency interpretations of statutes, so in many instances the agency will have the authority to decide whether to consider ancillary risks. If the agency has the statutory authority not to consider ancillary risks, it is unlikely, under current law, to be found that its decision not to do so was arbitrary. The judgment about arbitrariness should and probably would be based on a framework like that set out in section II. In an extreme case, failure to consider risks that are likely to be large, and that are not terribly costly to investigate, might be seen as arbitrary within the meaning of the APA. Indeed, I believe—for reasons to be elaborated shortly—that courts should be less reluctant than they are now to find agency action arbitrary on this ground.

A great deal of course turns on existing information. When the data about ancillary risks are speculative or unreliable, agencies are probably not required to consider such risks. OSHA could lawfully conclude—as it has in fact concluded—that the evidence that "richer is safer" is too speculative to be used at this time. Its decision to this effect ought not to be found arbitrary or capricious, unless it can be shown that the evidence is in fact solid and that the costs of incorporating it are reasonable. The relevant provision of the statute—the "reasonably necessary or appropriate" language—gives OSHA discretion to do with this evidence as it chooses. Under other statutes, by contrast, an agency that fails to consider ancillary risks would probably be violating the law, at least if the ancillary risks are real and the costs of investigation are not excessive.

Consider in this regard the principal case involving the issue of health-health trade-offs, *Competitive Enterprise Institute (CEI) v. NHTSA*.[19] NHTSA establishes fuel economy standards; in doing so, NHTSA is required to consider the issue of "feasibility." In deciding the question of feasibility, NHTSA has taken account of passenger safety, including risks created by regulation, and while there is a possible statutory issue here, everyone in *CEI* accepted NHTSA's views on this point. The question in the case was whether NHTSA had acted lawfully in refusing to relax its fuel economy standards for certain model years. Automobile companies urged that relaxation was required in order to save lives—because the existing standards would lead to "downsizing" and hence to smaller and more dangerous vehicles—and they presented strong evidence to this effect.

The agency responded that this evidence was unconvincing and that "domestic manufacturers should be able to improve their fuel economy in the future by . . . technological means, without outsourcing their larger cars, without further downsizing or mix shifts toward smaller cars, and without sacrificing acceleration or performance." The court held that this explanation was inadequate. The agency failed to claim or show that in fact, manufacturers would fail to downsize their cars. In any case, downsizing would be costly, and that "cost would translate into higher prices for large cars (as well as small), thereby pressuring consumers to retain their old cars and make the associated sacrifice in safety. The result would be effectively the same harm that concerns petitioners and that the agency fails to negate or justify." The court therefore remanded to the agency for a better explanation or a change in policy.

On remand, the agency offered a somewhat better explanation. NHTSA pointed to what it saw as the absence of clear indications that fuel economy standards had caused any manufacturer to price consumers out of the market for larger, safer cars. NHTSA referred as well to an absence of manufacturer claims about the specific design modifications that would result from the fuel economy standards. The court found this explanation sufficient.[20] In doing so, it applied a highly deferential form of review.

In light of the record, however, and the predictable pressures on an agency like NHTSA, the result in the case might well be questioned. NHTSA may well suffer from a form of "tunnel vision," especially in dealing with fuel economy standards, for which there is a powerful constituency. The interests that call for attention to ancillary safety risks are typically poorly organized, and when the claims come from the automobile manufacturers, NHTSA may be too ready to distrust them. To say this is not to say that NHTSA should be required to relax its fuel economy standards. But it is to say that a demonstration of the sort made by the automobile manufacturers might well serve as a kind of warning signal to the court, requiring a solid response from the agency. In *CEI*, the agency's response could not qualify as solid, as the court itself, while affirming the agency, seemed to suggest. A promising model for the future is provided by an important court of appeals decision holding that under a statute that required open-ended balancing of relevant factors, an agency was required to ask whether the regulatory ban on asbestos would lead to even greater risks.[21]

The point I am making here might well be generalized. Agencies generally ought to be required to show that they are doing more good than harm. Courts should not second-guess reasonable agency judgments; but they should take a "hard look" at agency decisions failing to undertake health-health comparisons.

IV. New Institutions

Congress

In its present form, Congress is ill-equipped to consider the problem of health-health trade-offs. Its committee structure ensures a high degree of fragmentation and does not allow for deliberation on such trade-offs. On the contrary, that structure makes ancillary risks difficult to evaluate or, much worse, even to see. Often ancillary risks are thought to be subject to the jurisdiction of another committee, which means, in practice, that coordination is extremely difficult. In these circumstances, I offer two simple suggestions for legislative reform.

The first is that Congress should create a new legislative committee entrusted specifically with the power to assess aggregate risk levels, to compare risks, and to initiate revision of statutes that increase net risks. This committee should have the power to introduce corrective legislation when a statute, or agency action under a statute, has been shown to increase aggregate risks.

My second suggestion is that Congress should address the problem of health-health trade-offs through a new directive in the Administrative Procedure Act. Notably, recent initiatives designed to require cost-benefit balancing say almost nothing about this problem. The principal exception is a House bill introduced in 1995, which contains a subsection entitled "substitution risks." This subsection says that "each significant risk assessment or risk characterization document shall include a statement of any substitution risks to human health, where information on such risks has been provided to the agency."

This is a strikingly cautious initiative. It does not require agencies to investigate ancillary risks on their own. Nor does it say that agencies may not proceed unless the regulation yields net benefits. I suggest instead a proposed amendment to the Administrative Procedure Act: "*Agencies shall ensure, to the extent feasible, that regulations do not create countervailing risks that are greater than those of the regulated risk.*" (The words "to the extent feasible" are necessary because some investigations are too costly and speculative to be worthwhile.) A modest forerunner of this idea can be found in the "clean fuels" provision of the Clean Air Act, which says that the administrator of the EPA may not prohibit the use of a fuel or fuel addictive "unless he finds . . . that in his judgment such prohibition will not cause the use of any other fuel or fuel additive which will produce emissions which will endanger the public health or welfare to the same or greater degree than the use of the fuel or fuel additive proposed to be prohibited."[22] This idea should be generalized.

Executive Branch

The Office of Information and Regulatory Affairs (OIRA) has been entrusted with the power to coordinate regulatory policy and to ensure reasonable priority-setting. In the Clinton Administration, OIRA appears to have become an advisory body, more limited in its power than it was in the Bush and Reagan administrations. In view of the absence of good priority-setting, and the enormous room for savings costs and increasing regulatory benefits, this is highly unfortunate.

OIRA should see, as one of its central assignments, the task of overcoming governmental myopia and tunnel vision, by ensuring that aggregate risks are reduced and that agency focus on particular risks does not mean that ancillary risks are ignored or increased. This is a more modest and particularized version of Justice Breyer's larger suggestion that officials should have power to set priorities by diverting resources from smaller problems to larger ones (chapter 5). No body in government is now entrusted with the authority to ensure that risk regulation is managed so as to ensure global rationality and coherence. OIRA is well situated to take on that role, at least by attending to the possibility that regulation of some risks may make risk levels higher on balance. An Executive Order should therefore be issued to require OIRA to ensure that health-health comparisons are undertaken to the extent permitted by law. This step would ensure a new degree of coordination in government and overcome the problems of selective attention that now undermine regulatory efforts.

Of course, any such role should be undertaken with an understanding that lives are not fungible and that context matters a great deal. The task is not to maximize life years saved—though that is not a bad starting point—but instead to ensure that democratic judgments are made by reference to the range of variables that people legitimately see as relevant to risk regulation. As we have seen, these variables include the nature and context of the relevant risk.

Conclusion

It would be far too simple to say that the administrative state has been a failure. In many ways, it has been a substantial success; risks to safety and health are much lower than they have been in the past, partly because of regulatory safeguards (see the overview in chapter 11). But regulatory programs are far more costly, and far less effective, than they should be. The various problems of modern regulation usually stem from inadequate attention to incentives and to side-effects. Among the principal side-effects, nowhere addressed in current law, is the increased health risks produced by risk regulation.

This is a significant problem, and through some simple steps, something can be done about it. Trade-offs among risks ought not to be based on a unitary metric, for reasons of both law and basic principle; but trade-offs must nonetheless be made. Incommensurability should not be confused with incomparability. Public institutions should be redesigned so as to ensure that the relevant trade-offs can be undertaken in a manner that entails more in the way of democratic deliberation. Above all, institutions should be designed to ensure that risk reduction is pursued more frequently than risk redistribution. To accomplish this task, it is necessary to take steps to limit interest-group influence over regulatory outcomes.

I have suggested several possible steps. Under existing law, agencies should often be understood to have the authority to engage in health-health trade-offs, and they should exercise that authority far more often than they now do. Courts should play a modest but catalytic role in encouraging agencies to increase aggregate risk reduction. Congress should add to existing legislation a general requirement that agencies consider a range of risks to life and health, including substitute risks, to the extent that this is feasible. Finally, OIRA should undertake the process of scrutinizing risk regulation to show that agency action does not suffer from the kind of tunnel vision exemplified by so much of modern risk regulation.

Problems of selective attention, interest-group power, and myopia have created a range of irrationalities and injustices in modern government. Steps of the kind proposed here would help overcome these problems, not by producing an algorithm for decision, but by increasing the role of democratic deliberation in the regulatory process.

Notes

1. See John Graham and Jonathan Weiner, *Risk versus Risk* (Cambridge: Harvard University Press, 1995), for the best general discussion; I owe a general debt to Graham and Weiner throughout.

2. See Corrosion Proof Fittings v. EPA, 947 F.2d 1201 (5th Cir. 1991).

3. See ADA v. Martin, 984 F.2d 823, 826 (7th Cir. 1993): "OSHA also exaggerated the number of lives likely to be saved by the rule by ignoring lives likely to be lost by it. Since the increased cost of medical care, to the extent passed on to consumers, will reduce the demand for medical care, and some people may lose their lives as a result."

4. See March Sadowitz and John Graham, "A Survey of Permitted Residual Cancer Risks," 6 *RISK* 17 (1995).

5. See Graham and Wiener, *supra* note 1, at 23–25; Aaron Wildavsky, *Searching for Safety* (New Brunswick: Transaction Press, 1988).

6. A general description can be found in Bill Clinton and Al Gore, Reinventing Regulation of Drugs and Medical Devices (1995).

7. See Symposium, "Risk-Risk Analysis," 8 *J. Risk and Uncertainty* 5 (1994); Wildavsky, *supra* note 5.

8. Intl. Union v. Johnson Controls, 886 F.2d 871, 908 (7th Cir., 1989) (Easterbrook, J., dissenting), reversed, 499 U.S. 187 (1991).

9. R. L. Kenney, "Mortality Risks Induced by Economic Expenditures," 10 *Risk Analysis* 147 (1990). See also R. L. Kenney, "Mortality Risks Induced by the Costs of Regulations," 8 *J. Risk and Uncertainty* 95 (1994).

10. UAW v. OSHA, 938 F.2d 1310 (D.C. Cir. 1991). See also Building & Constr. Trades Dept. v. Brock, 838 F.2d 1258 (D.C. Cir. 1988), suggesting that "leaning toward safety may sometimes have the perverse effect of increasing rather than decreasing risk." *Id.* at 1267. See also New York State v. Brown, 854 F.2d 1379, 1395 n.1 (D.C. Cir., 1988) (Williams, J., concurring): "extravagant expenditures on health may in some instances affect health adversely, by foreclosing expenditures on items—higher quality food, shelter, recreation, etc.—that would have contributed more to the individual's health than the direct expenditures thereon."

11. See Paul Portney and Robert Stavins, "Regulatory Review of Environmental Policy," 8 *J. of Risk and Uncertainty* 111 (1995).

12. J. B. MacRae, Statement before the Senate Committee on Governmental Affairs, March 19, 1992.

13. See Cass R. Sunstein, "Incompletely Theorized Agreements," 108 *Harv. L. Rev.* 1733 (1995).

14. *Id.* at 1756.

15. See Stephen Breyer, *Breaking the Vicious Circle: Toward Effective Risk Regulation* (Cambridge: Harvard University Press, 1993).

16. See George Tolley, Donald Kenkel, and Robert Fabian, eds., *Valuing Health for Policy: An Economic Approach* (Chicago: University of Chicago Press, 1994). pp. 341–42.

17. See Chevron USA v. NRDC, 467 US 837 (1984).

18. 7 U.S.C. 136(bb).

19. 956 F.2d 321 (D.C. Cir. 1992).

20. CEI v. NHTSA, 1995 WL 39252 (D.C. Cir. 1995).

21. Corrosion Proof Fittings v. EPA, 947 F.2d 1201 (5th Cir. 1991).

22. 42 U.S.C. 7545(c)(2)(C).

Democratizing
America Through Law

American government should be more effective, more efficient, and more democratic. Recent institutions are the source of these problems. Legal reforms could dramatically improve these institutions without great difficulty.

I propose three such reforms. First, government should rely much more than it now does on the provision of information, on disclosure, and on education. Second, economic incentives should replace much of the command-and-control regulation that has become so characteristic of our administrative institutions. Third, the law should promote more decentralization in the private and public spheres, allowing greater flexibility for states and localities, for employers, and for workers.

In recent decades, prescriptions of this general sort have been set out by economists with considerable care and clarity. There can be no doubt that legal initiatives in these directions would increase the efficiency of contemporary government; they would also help guarantee that regulation is effective in accomplishing its goals. These would be large improvements, especially in a period in which American industries must compete in increasingly international markets. I will therefore devote considerable attention to explaining how efficiency and efficacy might be increased by legal reforms.

It is important to emphasize, however, that the late twentieth century has been a period in which much of the world has been embarking on the task of democratization. In such a period, it would be odd to concentrate regulatory efforts on efficiency and efficacy alone. This is particularly so in light of the fact that from the standpoint of democratic theory, the contemporary American system of public law is nothing to celebrate. Democratic deliberation on the central issues is discouragingly rare. Powerful interest groups—on the left, right, and center—exert excessive influence over regulatory policy. Sensationalistic anecdotes often dominate public debate. Real participation in the public and private spheres is at best episodic. In this light, few matters deserve higher priority than institutional changes designed to increase the democratic character of the modern state.

The three general reforms would promote not only efficacy and efficiency, but democracy as well. Strategies of disclosure and education are the preconditions for a well-functioning democratic process. Without information, people cannot carry out their roles as citizens. Economic incentives also have the fortunate consequence of requiring participants in the democratic process to focus on the key question: How much reduction in (say) environmental risk do we want and at what price? By contrast, existing approaches tend to distract attention from that question and to direct it toward other issues that are at once less relevant and less intelligible. Decentralization is, under current conditions, an indispensable part of any strategy for general democratization. The national government is simply too remote for general citizen control.

The reforms designed to promote economic efficiency therefore go hand-in-hand with reforms for democratization. To be sure, we will at some stage have to make some difficult choices between efficiency and democracy, two values that sometimes point toward different solutions. But for the next generation, these three fundamental changes will bring about powerful movements in both directions.

In this chapter, I will be painting with an extremely broad brush, dealing with complex questions in general terms. My aim is to set out the broad contours of reform strategies. In order to do this, the discussion of particular questions will have to be greatly compressed. In the near future, of course, the particulars will deserve much greater detail. I sacrifice attention to specifics with the understanding that in thinking about reform of American public law, the general defects of the system have been lost too often, in favor of discussion of unnecessarily incremental changes. (The 104th Congress was an exception; see chapter 14.)

In section I, I discuss the rise of the modern regulatory state, with particular reference to the New Deal period. Here I explore how the New Deal attempted simultaneously to increase economic efficiency and to promote democratization—and how it failed, in important respects, on both counts. In section II, I explore the current state of regulatory government. I attempt to show its multiple inefficiencies and to explore the consequences of those inefficiencies for the economy. I also explain why the current system of public law fails from the democratic point of view. In section III, I outline remedies for the current situation, arguing that across a broad range, the goals of economic efficiency and democratization are entirely compatible. Section IV offers some qualifications to this general claim.

I. The New Deal

President Franklin Roosevelt's New Deal, undertaken in the 1930s, represented a fundamental restructuring of the American legal system. Some people think that it amounted to a kind of constitutional amendment.[1] We need not go so far in order to recognize its foundational status in modern American government. I summarize a long story here.

The New Deal operated against a well-defined constitutional backdrop. That backdrop included the three basic cornerstones of the American legal system: checks and balances; federalism; and individual rights. The New

Dealers viewed all these in the context of the Great Depression, which left huge numbers of Americans out of work. In that context, the New Dealers thought that the preexisting system of individual rights protected both too little and too much. That system consisted largely of the common law catalogue of rights "against" government, including most notably private property and freedom of contract.

For the New Dealers, this catalogue protected far too much, since it immunized existing holdings of property from democratic control. Not everything that people had, under the common law, was genuinely entitled to legal protection. The preexisting system of rights also protected too little, since it furnished no safeguards against the various hazards of the market economy, including unemployment, lack of education, homelessness, disability, and disease.

The emerging conception of rights called for redistribution of various kinds and also for recognition of a novel category of protected interests. The ultimate result was President Roosevelt's second Bill of Rights, including "the right to a useful and remunerative job," "the right to earn enough to provide adequate food and clothing and recreation," "the right of every family to a decent home," "the right to adequate medical care and the opportunity to achieve and enjoy good health," "the right to adequate protection from the economic fears of old age, sickness, accident, and unemployment," and "the right to a good education."[2]

Institutional changes followed from these ideas. Against the backdrop of the new conception of rights, the original system of checks and balances seemed anachronistic. Far from a precious safeguard of liberty against government, it appeared an unnecessary constraint on democratic action designed to promote economic productivity and to protect the disadvantaged. The most radical attacks on checks and balances—including *The Coming American Fascism,* intended not as a warning but on the contrary as an optimistic statement of the wonderful things to come[3]—were rejected. But the attack on checks and balances did have two enduring legacies. It helped produce a concentration of judicial and law-making power in the presidency, which was no longer restricted to execution of the laws, narrowly understood.[4] It also contributed to the New Deal enthusiasm for "independent" regulatory agencies, such as the Federal Trade Commission, the Interstate Commerce Commission, and the Federal Communications Commission. These novel entities combined traditionally separated functions, and they were immunized from direct control by any of the constitutionally specified branches.

Under the New Deal reformation, the system of federalism fared little better. Those who produced the original framework envisioned states as an obstacle to national action, and also as an arena for democratic self-determination. For the New Dealers, however, the states were not a guarantor of freedom, but, on the contrary, a barrier to necessary social change. The right of "exit," so prized in the eighteenth century as a safeguard against state oppression, was now seen as a mechanism by which corporations could discourage states from protecting workers and poor people from the vicissitudes of the market. Far from being a place for genuine self-government, states seemed a vehicle for government by faction. A redirection of authority from the states to the national government was thus indispensable if public officials were to carry out their new tasks. Greatly expanded national power, mostly under the commerce clause, was the result.

Once authority was thus redirected, there was no doubt that the presidency would be a principal beneficiary. In a single bold stroke, President Roosevelt united the Hamiltonian belief in an energetic executive with the Jeffersonian belief in collective self-determination. The presidency became the focal point for democratic self-governance.

In the New Deal period, the belief in economic productivity and the belief in democracy were thoroughly merged. New institutions were necessary above all to improve the operation of the economy—increasing business confidence, providing the preconditions for well-functioning stock markets, ensuring people of the stability of the banks, managing the business cycle, protecting farmers against economic fluctuations. Eventually spurred by Keynesian economics, the New Deal understanding of the role of the state was centered on the goal of economic prosperity. Roosevelt's program is often associated with protection of the disadvantaged, and this idea was indeed central to him. But government assurance of the successful performance of the economy was the principal goal of the New Deal reforms.

On the New Deal view, this idea was in no tension with democratic ideals. On the contrary, the market system that preceded the New Deal was subject to sustained challenge in the New Deal period and precisely on democratic grounds. Before the rise of modern regulatory institutions, the basic system of governance had been created by common law courts, which were hardly accountable to the people. Thus the law of property, tort, and contract was a crucial regulatory system that had been created by the unelected judiciary. Understood as such, it was not an arena for democratic self-government.

In the early part of the century, courts went so far as to interpret the Constitution as embodying common law principles.[5] In this way they immunized the common law from democratric control, striking down minimum wage and maximum hour laws as unjustified intrusion into the economy. By contrast to courts, the new entities created by the New Deal were intended to be popularly accountable. Indeed, those entities would be supervised by the people in ways that would lead to large gains in democratic self-governance. Thus it was that the belief in economic prosperity and democratic government marched hand-in-hand.

In the United States, contemporary governmental structures are an outgrowth of the New Deal reformation. Our current system is not, of course, by any means identical with what emerged from the New Deal period. There have been occasional bursts of governmental activity and retrenchment, and these have been quite important.[6] Above all, the "rights revolution" of the late 1960s and early 1970s witnessed an extraordinary growth of new regulatory entities, rivaling the New Deal itself in scope and importance. Of particular interest was the creation of institutions designed to reduce risks in consumer products, the workplace, and the natural environment. Here the rhetoric of "rights" and "redistribution" accompanied the claims of democracy and efficiency. The new entities were supposed to protect a right to safety in the workplace, in the atmosphere, and in the water—and also to shift resources from (among others) employers to employees. But economic and democratic goals were important here as well. The new institutions were intended to remove a substantial drain on the economy and also to reflect democratic judgments about risk reduction. These institutions had distinct economic goals; they were designed in part to overcome market failures, in particular those stemming from absence of information.

Much the same can be said about the new attack, prominent since the 1960s, on discrimination on the basis of race, sex, and disability. Discrimination has been challenged as a barrier to economic productivity and to the political equality so crucial to democratic principles. In the area of civil rights, economic and democratic aspirations played a central and complementary role.

At least since the election of President Reagan in 1980, the nation has been in a period of large-scale rethinking, in which New Deal reforms have often been rethought in the interest of renewed attention to the capacities of private markets. The enforcement practices of federal agencies have been significantly changed as a result, but there has been no fundamental revision of current institutions. The changes have been largely incremental. At least in general, reform efforts have been quite unimaginative (see chapter 14 for discussion and details).

II. The Status Quo

How has the American system of public law actually performed? Has it promoted economic prosperity and democratic governance? We now have considerable evidence on both scores. There have been many successes, and it would be a mistake to think that regulation has entirely failed in achieving its purposes (chapter 11). But much of the overall story is dismaying.

Inefficiency

The current system is extraordinarily inefficient. The annual net cost of regulation has been estimated at between $400 and $500 billion.[7] There is no question that we need not spend this amount for the gains we actually receive. A 1995 study suggests that better allocations of existing expenditures could save an additional 60,000 lives at no increased cost, and that with better allocations, we could save the same number of lives we now save with $31 billion in annual savings.[8]

So-called economic regulation—calling for price and entry controls in various sectors of the economy—produced unnecessary and exorbitant costs for American consumers. Thus, it is estimated that airline deregulation yielded gains to airlines and travelers of about $15 billion annually.[9] The corresponding numbers for trucking deregulation and railroad deregulation were $30 billion and $15 billion.[10] The Natural Gas Act, which allowed government control of gasoline prices, certainly contributed to the dangerous gas shortages of the 1970s.[11] The resulting inefficiencies led to decreases in industrial production, losses of hundreds of thousands of jobs, and reductions in the supply of gas for millions of Americans.[12]

Nor are inefficiencies limited to the area of economic regulation. The Food and Drug Administration has delayed the entry of beneficial foods and drugs onto the market, significantly increasing risks to safety and health. The "drug lag" has been a serious problem for Americans.[13] The EPA's fuel economy standards appear to have produced uncertain gains in light of the fact that manufacturers were in any case moving to smaller and more efficient cars; but fuel economy standards did lead to significant losses in lives as a result of producing more dangerous, lighter vehicles.[14] The United States spent over a trillion dollars for pollution control between 1972 and 1995. Some studies suggest that alternative strategies could have achieved the same gains at less than one-quarter of the cost (see chapter 11 for more details).[15]

What is the cause of existing problems? A pervasive source of regulatory inefficiency in the United States is the use of rigid, highly bureaucratized "command-and-control" regulation, which dictates, at the national level, control strategies for hundreds, thousands, or millions of companies and individuals in an exceptionally diverse nation. Command-and-control regulation is a dominant part of American government in such areas as environmental protection and occupational safety and health regulation. In the environmental context, command-and-control approaches usually take the form of regulatory requirements of the "best available technology" (BAT), which are almost always imposed only on new pollution sources. BAT strategies are pervasive in federal law. Indeed, they are a defining characteristic of regulation of the air, the water, and conditions in the workplace.

One of the many problems with BAT strategies is that they ignore the enormous differences among plants and industries and geographical areas. In view of these differences, it is wildly inefficient to impose nationally uniform technological requirements. It does not seem sensible to impose the same technology on industries in diverse areas—regardless of whether they are polluted or clean, populated or empty, or expensive or cheap to clean up.

There are other sources of inefficiency as well. BAT strategies require all new industries to adopt costly technology and allow more lenient standards to be imposed on existing plants and industries. Through this route, BAT strategies actually penalize new products, thus discouraging investment and perpetuating old, dirty technology. The result is inefficiency in investment strategies, in innovation, and even in environmental protection.

Such strategies also fail to encourage new pollution control technology and indeed serve to discourage it by requiring its adoption for no financial gain. Under the BAT approach, a company that innovates in this area will simply have to invest more in pollution control. It will be punished rather than rewarded for the development of new control technology. BAT strategies are also extremely expensive to enforce, imposing on the EPA and OSHA an extraordinary monitoring burden. Additional inefficiency stems from the fact that BAT approaches are focused on the technology at the end of the pipe. This is merely a way of aiming at symptoms rather than underlying causes of pollution. For example, sulfur dioxide emissions (the major source of acid rain) are controlled by forcing coal-fired power plants to adopt costly "scrubbing" strategies. A much cheaper method of control is to encourage companies to switch to cleaner coal,[16] or better yet, to provide incentives to use energy sources other than fossil fuels.

In general, governmental specification of the "means" of achieving desired ends is a good way of producing inefficiency. Instead of permitting industry and consumers to choose the means—and thus to impose a form of market discipline on that question—government often selects the means in advance. The governmentally prescribed means is often the inefficient one.

Other inefficiences in existing law stem from inadequate attention to the question of incentives. Consider, for example, the Superfund statute, which was created to deal with the problem of abandoned toxic waste dumps. Congress's basic strategy was to impose joint and several liability on everyone with a connection with the dump in question—managers or owners of the site, generators of the waste, transporters. At first glance, the strategy seems both fair and efficient: fair, because it imposes clean-up duties on everyone; efficient, because it is likely to deter everyone from contributing to the problem of abandoned waste sites. But a predictable consequence of this strategy is to produce incentives, not to clean up, but instead to have protracted litigation on the question who is liable to whom. If everyone is liable, it is almost as bad as if no one is. The liability of each person is effectively "decreased" by virtue of the sheer numbers of people who are liable as well. For each person, contemplating possible courses of action, liability must be understood in the context of a situation in which many other people will be liable too. And if hundreds of people are subject to suit, one can be sure that there will be endless litigation on the liability question. This was predictable, and it is exactly what has happened. Thus, it is that on average, seven years and at least $4 million in transactions costs have been necessary before final clean-up even begins.[17]

More generally, studies of the costs and benefits of regulatory programs show a crazy-quilt pattern, including both too much and too little regulation. Consider, for example, expenditures per life saved (table 5.3 in chapter 5). Some programs pay for themselves in terms of health and related savings. The lives saved are purely a bonus, in the sense that they come for free. Other programs cost between $100,000 and $300,000 per life saved—surely an amount well worth spending. But still other programs cost $89 million per life saved, $92 million per life saved, even $132 million per life saved. To be sure, some disparities, even significant ones, might well be expected in a democracy. But it is difficult to believe that these differences reflect anything but interest-group power and irrationality of various sorts.

This brief summary should be sufficient to suggest that from the standpoint of efficiency, most of modern government is ill directed. There is no real effort at setting priorities. Some programs are not beneficial at all; others have unnecessary and costly side-effects. We could obtain the same benefits much more cheaply.

Sometimes inefficiency in government, particularly when described by economists, seems a dry and technical matter. But the consequences of the status quo are anything but merely technical. They include a range of adverse effects on real human beings: excessively high prices, greater unemployment, lower benefits in terms of safety and health, greater mortality and morbidity, more poverty, and increased difficulty for American companies and workers attempting to compete in an increasingly international market.

Democracy

The New Deal aspired not only to greater efficiency but also to more in the way of democracy. The New Dealers hoped for a system in which citizens and representatives, operating through responsive but expert organs, would make deliberative decisions about the basic system of public law. In place of the undemocratic systems of common law ordering and judge-made constitutionalism, new regulatory institutions would be subject to political will and carry out public instructions. The new regime was to combine a high degree of accountability with a high degree of deliberation.

In practice, this democratic aspiration has often been defeated. People rarely have enough information to participate at all, or at all well, in the processes of government. The extraordinary concentration of regulation in Washington has hampered democratic deliberation both in localities and in the private sphere. The technical complexity of underlying issues has contributed to the power of well-organized interest groups over the regulatory process. Thus the New Deal has helped bring about a kind of Madisonian nightmare of government by faction.[18]

Democratic failures are widespread. The BAT approach, for example, is severely deficient from the standpoint of a well-functioning political process. That approach ensures that citizens and representatives will be focusing their attention not on what levels of reduction are appropriate, but instead on the largely incidental and nearly impenetrable question of what technologies are now available. Because of its sheer complexity, this issue is not easily subject to democratic resolution and is not the relevant one for democratic politics, which is the appropriate degree and nature of environmental protection—an issue to which the BAT question is only incidental.

The focus on the question of "means" also tends to increase the power of well-organized private groups, by allowing them to press environmental and regulatory law in the service of their own parochial ends. These ends include, for example, the promotion of ethanol, which is helpful to corn farmers though not necessarily to environmental protection; other fuels might well be preferable on environmental grounds. Ends favored by parochial interests also include governmentally compelled use of coal scrubbers, which is helpful to eastern coal though not necessarily to air quality. The use of already-clean coal might well be better.[19]

In this respect, the BAT strategy is emblematic of a far more general problem in current regulation. Centralization at the national level diminishes opportunities for citizen participation. It promotes intense and unproductive struggles among well-organized factions. Education of citizens about the key issues—risk levels and risk comparisons—is at best episodic. In their capacity as consumers, citizens, workers, or users of the air and water, people are inadequately informed of the risks that they face. Public attention tends to be focused on particular incidents, which are gripping and sensationalistic but often misleading.

In these circumstances, it is difficult indeed to ensure that citizens and representatives will be involved in deliberating about different strategies for achieving social goals, or (what is more important) in identifying those goals in the first place. By directing attention to means, the current system also creates powerful incentives for interest groups to ensure that they are favored in the legislature or the bureaucracy. Thus current institutions cannot carry out Roosevelt's goal of linking the Hamiltonian commitment to an energetic executive with the Jeffersonian belief in self-government. The democratic aspirations of the New Deal have failed.

III. Remedies

It would be most fortunate if the inefficiencies in current regulation could be remedied through reforms that simultaneously promote democratic government. In this section, I argue that the same remedies that would increase efficiency would promote democracy as well. I deal with three principal reforms: disclosure and education; economic incentives; and decentralization.

Disclosure and Education

Many Americans are unaware of the risks that they face in day-to-day life. Often workers do not know about toxic substances in the workplace or about the risks that such substances cause. Consumers of ordinary foods are usually unable to evaluate the dangers posed by fats, calcium, sugar, and salt. People in small communities do not know that toxic waste dumping has occurred, or if they know the facts, they do not know the risks.

Scenarios of this sort are especially likely in light of the fact that ordinary people have a difficult time in obtaining information about risk. Causation is extremely complex here, and accurate inferences are extremely difficult to draw. Often risks take many years to materialize. Individual susceptibility varies, and changing technology makes learning from the past a hazardous enterprise. It would be reasonable to say that in cases of this sort, the interest in freedom or autonomy—quite apart from efficiency and democracy—requires a governmental remedy. Knowledgeable choices are a precondition for liberty. Claims from efficiency and democracy tend to argue in the same direction. Disclosure by the government itself, or by others at the government's behest, will often promote both efficiency and democracy.

Efficiency

When information is lacking, there may well be a conventional case of market failure under economic criteria. To be sure, information—like other goods— is a scarce commodity. Perhaps the market has produced the optimal level of information. The optimal level is not complete information. If so, there is no market failure, even if there might be a problem under noneconomic criteria. But there are several reasons why the market for information may indeed fail.

First, information is sometimes a public good. Once it is available at all, or to anyone, it is available to everyone or to many people. People can thus capture the benefits of information without having to pay for its production. Once created, a report discussing the risks posed by carcinogens in the workplace may well benefit employees a great deal—but no individual employee has the right incentives to pay his proportional share for the report. Each employee has the incentive to "free ride" on the efforts of others. The result is that too little information will be forthcoming. This point applies to information about shared risks in general. Indeed, the point applies to information about all matters of shared importance. It suggests that there may be a strong case, on economic grounds, for governmental interference in the information market.

Second, manufacturers sometimes have poor incentives to provide information about hazardous products. Competition over the extent of danger may decrease total purchases of the product rather than help any particular manufacturer to obtain greater sales. The phenomenon has sometimes played a role in discouraging competition over safety among manufacturers of tobacco products. At least in principle, the phenomenon may occur frequently, though there are certainly many counterexamples.

Information asymmetries may produce a "lemons" problem, in which dangerous products drive safe ones out of the market.[20] Imagine, for example, that producers know which products are safe, but that consumers cannot tell. Sellers of safe products may not be able to compete if such products sell for no higher price than dangerous ones, if safe products are more expensive to produce, and if consumers are unable to tell the difference. In that case, the fact that sellers have information, whereas buyers do not, will ensure that lemons—here dangerous products—will dominate the market. Regulation designed to provide information is the proper remedy.

All this suggests that there may be a market failure in the provision of information. At least as a presumptive matter, government remedies are an appropriate response. These remedies might take the form of governmentally provided information, education campaigns, or disclosure requirements. Such remedies may cost more than they are worth. But if they work, and if they are not too expensive, they should be favored on economic grounds. They may fortify the operation of the marketplace. They may also be a precondition for free choice, the background assumption of free markets.

We now have a good deal of empirical information about disclosure of risks. In general, studies suggest that disclosure can be a helpful and cost-effective strategy.[21] Workers do indeed respond to new information about risks, quitting or demanding higher salaries. Consumers often react well to the disclosure about danger levels. In general, there is every reason to think that governmentally mandated disclosure, if suitably designed, is an effective mechanism for promoting economic efficiency.

Democracy

Suppose that we wanted to increase the democratic character of contemporary government, by promoting citizen participation in and control over governmental processes. A good initial step would be for government to provide enough information so that people can make knowledgeable judgments.

Government might itself supply information or require disclosure by private citizens and companies. Let us return, for example, to the matter of expenditures per life saved. There is now considerable data on the amount of money spent to save lives in various government programs. As we have seen, what emerges is a crazy quilt. At the very least, the American public should be informed of these disparities so that it can evaluate them. Provision of information about the content and expense of regulatory programs should be high on the governmental agenda.

Or consider the question of risk regulation in general, on which people are poorly informed (chapter 5). For example, they appear not to know that the risks of nuclear power are substantially smaller than the risks posed by other energy sources. They appear not to have a clear sense of the relationships among different risks that are confronted in everyday life. Smoking, for example, produces about 400,000 deaths per year, an annual risk of 3.0 in 10^3; all occupations produce between 11,000 and 200,000 annual deaths, an annual risk of 1.1 to 20 in 10^4; and boxing produces only three deaths a year, an annual risk of 5.4 in 10^4. Information of this sort ought to be widely understood. The fact that it is not creates a significant failure in government regulation. At least equally important, it presents a large obstacle to citizenship. The problem appears in the private sector, in local government, and at the state and national levels. Workers uninformed of risks are unable to participate usefully in the process of deciding among different possible levels of workplace safety. Local communities, seeking to decide whether to allow toxic waste sites or plants that produce sulfur dioxide, need to be in a position to make informed choices. Instead, they tend to react to sensationalistic anecdotes or to scare tactics.

A large virtue of a federal system is that it permits different states, having different values, to make different choices about social arrangements. In the context at hand, many decisions about the relations among industrial development, employment, pollution, and risk must be made at the state level. An absence of information is a severe obstacle to this process. The same is true at the national level, where sensational anecdotes displace reasoned analysis of the alternatives.

The most general way to put the point is to note that on the framers' view, America was supposed to be a deliberative democracy, in which representatives, accountable to the people, would make decisions through a process of deliberation uncontrolled by private factions. Without better information, neither deliberation nor democracy is possible. Legal reforms designed to remedy the situation are a precondition for democratic politics.

Current Steps

The national government has taken a number of steps in the right direction. Mandatory messages about risks from cigarette smoking, first set out in 1965 and modified in 1969 and 1984, are of course the most familiar example. The FDA has long maintained a policy of requiring risk labels for pharmaceutical products. The EPA has done the same for pesticides and asbestos. Congress requires warnings on products with saccharin, and there are numerous other illustrations. Indeed, the effort to provide information counts as one of the most striking, if incipient, developments in modern regulatory law. Three recent initiatives are especially striking.

In 1983, the Occupational Safety and Health Administration issued a Hazard Communication Standard (HCS), applicable to the manufacturing sector. In 1986, the HCS was made generally applicable. Under the HCS, chemical producers and importers must evaluate the hazards of the chemicals they produce or import; develop technical hazard information for materials safety data sheets and labels for hazardous substances; and, most important, transmit this information to users of the relevant substances. All employers must adopt a hazard communication program—including individual training—and inform workers of the relevant risks. There is considerable empirical work suggesting that the HCS is bringing about good results.[22]

In 1986, Congress enacted an ambitious new statute, the Emergency Planning and Community Right to Know Act (EPCRA).[23] Under this statute, firms and individuals must report, to state and local government, the quantities of potentially hazardous chemicals that have been sorted or released into the environment. Users of such chemicals must report to their local fire departments about the location, types, and quantities of stored chemicals. They must also give information about potential adverse health effects. A detailed report suggests that EPCRA has had important beneficial results, spurring innovative, cost-effective programs from the EPA and from state and local government.[24] In fact, this requirement of disclosure has been one of the few unambiguous success stories in modern environmental law.

The Food and Drug Administration has also adopted informational strategies. In its most ambitious set of proposals, the FDA has (a) compelled nutritional labeling on nearly all processed foods, including information relating to cholesterol, saturated fat, calories from fat, and fiber; (b) required compliance with government specified serving sizes; (c) compelled companies to conform to government definitions of standardized terms, including "reduced," "fresh," "free," and "low"; and (d) allowed health claims only if these (1) are supported by scientific evidence and (2) communciate clear and complete information about such matters as fat and heart disease, fat and cancer, sodium and high blood pressure, and calcium and osteoporosis.[25]

These initiatives are simply a beginning. Broader and more ambitious programs, coordinating the general communication of social risks, are very much in order. It has been suggested that government might eventually develop a "national warnings system" containing a systematized terminology for warnings.[26] Such a system could apply to all contexts and risks and give a uniform sense of risk levels. The existence of a uniform language would make it possible to assess risks across a wide range of social spheres. Most important of all, such a system would perform a vital educative function, one that could complement the functioning of markets and provide a necessary precondition for democratic choice. We should ultimately aspire to go far beyond risk regulation and introduce information bearing on democratic affairs in general (chapter 4).

Economic Incentives

By economic incentives, I include three ideas: financial penalties imposed on harm-producing behavior; financial subsidies for benefit-conferring behavior; and trading systems by which people who pollute or cause certain kinds of harm may trade their "rights" to do so. Such incentives should supplement and even displace command-and-control regulation.

Efficiency

It is inefficient for government to prescribe the means for achieving social objectives. Ordinarily it would be far better, on economic grounds, for government (a) to create incentives to engage in socially desirable conduct and (b) to permit the market to decide how companies respond to those incentives.

At least as a general rule, it is especially inefficient for government to dictate technology. A far better approach is to impose a tax on harmful behavior, and to let market forces determine the response to the increased cost. Government should generally impose fees on those who put pollutants into the atmosphere, instead of (for example) mandating costly "scrubbing" technology for sulfur dioxide. Consumption of the harm-producing good will decline. Producers will shift to less harmful methods of production. They might, for example, substitute clean for dirty coal.

More generally, government might adopt a simple, two-step reform policy in the area of social risks and social harms.[27] First, those who impose harm must pay for it—by purchasing permission to do so, perhaps through a licensing procedure. Second, those who obtain the resulting permission should be able to trade their "licenses" with other people. In the pollution context, this would mean that producers who reduce their pollution below a specified level could trade their "pollution rights" for cash. In one stroke, such a system would create market-based disincentives to pollute and market-based incentives for pollution control. Such a system would also reward rather than punish technological innovation in pollution control and do so with the aid of private markets. Very generally, and quite outside the environmental area, it makes sense to think about programs of this sort for regulation of harmful behavior.

An idea of this kind might be made part and parcel of a system of "green taxes." With such a system, nations might impose taxes on people who impose harms on others—users of dirty automobiles, farmers who employ pesticides, coal-fired power plants, gasoline that produces air pollution, products that contribute to destruction of the ozone layer or the greenhouse effect. Tax levies of various sorts are used by many nations already, though they have been slow in coming to the United States.

These levies have had, or are projected to have, excellent results. Thus a higher tax on leaded gasoline in Great Britain increased the market share of unleaded gas from 4 to 30 percent within less than a year.[28] It is estimated that a doubling of pesticide prices would cut pesticide use in half.[29] It is also estimated that a fee of $110 per ton on carbon would decrease carbon dioxide emissions by 20 percent by 2005.[30] An important advantage of such levies is that they would dramatically increase government revenues. This is an especially worthwhile goal in a period of large deficits. The suggested carbon tax would generate over $130 billion.[31] Other such taxes on polluting activity could produce billions of additional dollars in revenue.[32] Of course, taxes of this kind—if meant to raise revenue—have to be designed so that they are not so high as to eliminate the revenue source.

Economic incentives could be applied in other areas as well. Workers' compensation plans, for example, operate as effective guarantees of workplace safety. According to a careful study, "If the safety incentives of workers' compensation were removed, fatality rates in the United States economy would increase by almost 30 percent. Over 1200 more workers would die from job injuries every year in the absence of the safety incentives provided by workers' compensation."[33] This contrasts with a mere 2–4 percent reduction in injuries from OSHA, an amount that links up well with the fact that annual workers' compensation premiums are more than 1000 times as large as total annual OSHA penalties. The tax system could be used to provide better incentives to employers who furnish dangerous workplaces. The Consumer Product Safety Commission might experiment with a system in which producers of harm-producing products must pay a fee into the federal treasury. Ultimately, we might hope for a coordinated system of risk regulation, one that imposed specified fees for harm-producing activities.

Democracy

Thus far, we have seen that a shift to economic incentives would be efficient and effective. What consequences would such a shift have for democratic government?

The answer is that it would have significant consequences, and that these would be extremely beneficial. The current system puts public attention in the wrong places. Imagine, for example, that Congress and the citizenry—following the contemporary model—are focusing on the question whether ethanol, or some other gasoline substitute, should be required in new cars. It is perfectly predictable that in answering this question, well-organized groups with a significant stake in the outcome will bring their influence to bear. It is also predictable that ethanol producers may seek and actually obtain regulatory benefits, for reasons bearing absolutely no relationship to environmental protection.

At the same time, the underlying substantive question—whether ethanol is actually an environmentally superior product—will have to be resolved on the basis of technological complexities not easily addressed by the public or its representatives. If this is the issue on which the political process focuses, we are therefore likely to have a series of laws that represent, not public-spirited deliberation with a measure of broad accountability, but instead trade-offs among well-organized private groups, or, in Madisonian terms, government by faction. By directing attention to means, this system creates strong incentives for interest groups to ensure that they are favored in the legislature or the bureaucracy.

Compare a system of economic incentives. Here the issue is not one of means, but the amount of sulfur dioxide that will be allowed into the atmosphere—an issue to be resolved in the process of deciding how many licenses are to be given out and for how much pollution. A large advantage of this shift is that it would ensure that citizens and representatives would be focusing on how much pollution reduction there should be and at what cost. The right question would be put squarely before the electorate. No longer would it be possible to pretend that environmental protection is costless. No longer would the central issue be displaced by the largely incidental question of means.

Moreover, a system of financial penalties allows far less room for interest-group maneuvering. The large question—how much environmental protection at what cost—does not easily permit legislators to favor a well-organized, narrow group, such as the agricultural lobby or the coal lobby. Special favors cannot readily be provided through a system of economic incentives. The very generality of the question will work against narrow favoritism. To be sure, the ultimate question of pollution reduction may be answered in a way that reflects sustained political pressure rather than democratic deliberation. But the risks are minimized, certainly as compared with the existing system.

There are other democratic advantages. Economic incentives should simultaneously promote coordination and rationality in regulation, by giving government an incentive to attend closely, and for the first time, to how other risks are treated. This should bring a salutary measure of structure and sense to risk regulation in general. As an important by-product, the new system should create a powerful incentive to obtain information about the actual effects of pollution and pollution control. If members of Congress are deciding on the level of risk reduction, they will not want to do so in a vacuum, especially in light of the significant costs of large reductions. Affected groups will therefore be encouraged to engage in research about real-world consequences.

Information about consequences frequently remains in its most preliminary stages. The new premium placed on information should be a particularly important gain. There is every reason to design regulatory strategy that puts a premium on greater research, so that when a nation acts, it knows what it is getting and at what price.

All these considerations suggest that economic incentives—favored so firmly on economic grounds—have as one of their principal justifications a series of democracy-reinforcing, faction-limiting characteristics.

Recent Initiatives

The movement toward economic incentives is preliminary but real. Thus far, it has occurred mostly in the environmental area. An important series of administrative initiatives have brought about "emissions trading," especially under the Clean Air Act.[34] Under the EPA's policy, a firm that reduces its emissions below legal requirements may obtain "credits" that can be used against higher emissions elsewhere.

Through the "offset" policy, which is formally codified in the Clean Air Act, a company may locate in an area not in compliance with national air quality standards if and only if it can offset the new emissions by reducing existing emissions, either from its own sources or from other firms. Through the "banking" policy, firms are permitted to store emission credits for their own future use. Companies may also engage in "netting," by which a firm modifies a source, but avoids the most stringent emissions limits that would otherwise be applied to the modification by reducing emissions from another source within the same plant. And through "bubbles," existing sources may place an imaginary bubble over their plants, allowing different emissions levels by each emitting device so long as the total emissions level is in compliance with aggregate requirements.

We now have a good deal of evidence about the emissions trading program. For various reasons, the use of the program has been quite limited.[35] A study in 1989 showed 42 federal bubbles; 90 state bubbles; 2000 federal offsets; between 5000 and 12,000 acts of netting; and 100 acts of banking.[36] Despite this limited activity, there is considerable evidence that this policy has been successful. Overall, the program has produced savings of between $525 million and $12 billion.[37] By any measure, this is an enormous gain.

On balance, moreover, the environmental consequences have been beneficial. Offsets must, by definition, produce environmental gains. The preliminary evidence shows favorable effects from bubbles as well. There may be modest beneficial effects from banking and modest adverse effects from netting. The overall environmental effect is therefore good, cost entirely to one side.

As part of the process for eliminating lead from gasoline—a decision that was, not incidentally, strongly supported by a cost-benefit study—the EPA also permitted emissions trading. Under this policy, a refinery that produced gasoline with lower than required lead levels could earn credits. These could be traded with other refineries or banked for future use. Until the termination of the program in 1987, when the phasedown of lead ended, emissions credits for lead were widely traded. EPA concluded that there had been a cost savings of about 20 percent over alternative systems, marking total savings in the hundreds of millions of dollars. There have been similar efforts with water pollution and ozone depletion.[38]

Perhaps the most dramatic program of economic incentives can be found in the 1990 amendments to the Clean Air Act. The Act now explicitly creates an emissions trading system for the control of acid deposition. In these amendments, Congress has made an explicit decision about an aggregate emissions level for a pollutant. Whether the particular decision is the correct one may be disputed. But surely there are large democratic benefits from ensuring that public attention is focused on that issue.

There are other beneficial features to the acid deposition provisions. Congress has said that polluters may obtain allowances for emissions avoided through energy conservation and renewable energy. In this way, avoidance of this kind is turned into dollars, in the form of an increased permission to pollute. This provision creates an incentive to shift to conservation and renewable sources, without providing further environmental degradation. Polluters are explicitly permitted to trade their allowances; this is a first in national legislation. In this way, people who are able to reduce their pollution below the specified level receive economic benefits. Again incentives are created for environmentally beneficial behavior. An especially intriguing provision allows spot and advance sales of sulfur dioxide allowances, to be purchasable at $1500 per ton. Through this route, polluters must—for the first time—pay a fee for their pollution. Even more intriguing is a provision calling for auction sales of specified numbers of sulfur dioxide allowances. Here the market is permitted to set the price for polluting activity.

For the most part, however, the Clean Air Act does not require polluters to pay for their "licenses." Instead, government continues to permit them to pollute for free. This is a large obstacle to a sensible system of regulation. We may hope that in the future, Congress will build on the acid deposition model, requiring payments by polluters and others who inflict social harm.

Decentralization

Efficiency

Under current law, national standards are set both for the environment and for workplace safety and health. But as we have seen, the costs and benefits of regulatory activity are widely variable across both time and space. Consider, for example, the issue of clean air. To require the same level of ambient air quality in Los Angeles and Wyoming makes little sense in light of the fact that the costs of achieving that level vary so dramatically. Uniform controls seem implausible if Wyoming has already attained a level of X and if Los Angeles could not do so without suffering profound economic dislocations—including, for instance, ceasing use of the automobile. Such controls would be grotesquely inefficient.

Or return to the area of workplace safety. It is sometimes said that the current system of collective bargaining should be replaced by nationally mandated minimum standards. In fact, the Occupational Safety and Health Administration now imposes a wide range of national requirements for both safety and health. But surely American workers do not agree about the appropriate trade-offs among health, wages, medical benefits, and jobs. Some employees are willing to subject themselves to somewhat greater risks in return for greater benefits. Others seek low-level risks and are willing to take lower salaries in return. Just as consumers make diverse safety-related trade-offs in the purchase of (say) cars, so workers differ in the employment market.

In these circumstances, nationally mandated standards are inefficient because they are ill matched to the extraordinary diversity of worker preferences and judgments. It would be far better to allow a degree of workplace differences, matching that diversity. Decentralization (subject to national minimums for risks that reasonable people would not run) would accomplish this goal.

Democracy

If a central goal is increased democratization, it is indispensable to promote more decentralization. In the area of workplace safety, for example, democratic solutions cannot be achieved at the national level. The market mechanism of "exit"—permitting dissatisfied workers to leave—might well be accompanied by the political mechanism of "voice," by which workers participate in workplace governance. In order for that latter mechanism to operate, it is crucial that workplace conditions be decided on at the local level. Opportunities for greater decentralization are thus part and parcel of the process of democratizing the employment market. The labor union movement is now very weak and in some ways discredited; but it may eventually be possible to develop alternatives, such as workers' councils, that increase worker participation in managerial decisions. Markets are already producing this result, as many companies find it best if workers share managerial roles.

In the area of environmental protection, it is also possible to strengthen state and local options, and precisely in the interest of democratization. Congress might, for example, permit larger variations with respect to air and water quality, accompanied by national "floors" designed to take account of interstate effects. Federal laws should be written so as to minimize preemption of different state solutions. Judge-made preemption doctrines should be designed so as to require a clear congressional statement before allowing such preemption. States should be permitted to avoid federal specifications if they can find a better and cheaper way to meet federal goals (compare the discussion of environmental contracting in chapter 14).

Moreover, the national government might encourage or require the provision of information to states and localities, so as to allow them to decide how to deal with such problems as release of toxic wastes. In this connection, the Toxic Release Inventory compiled under the Superfund statute has been a great success. The existence of the inventory has spurred state and local action. Through all these routes, the democratic process at the local level might be strengthened, thus promoting what is, as a practical matter, the only way to ensure more citizen engagement with governmental affairs.

Current Initiatives

Here too a number of initial steps have been taken in the right direction. The "New Federalism" of the 1970s and 1980s contributed to a reinvigoration of state authority.[39] We have seen a dramatic growth in promising regulatory activity at the state level. Recycling programs are now common. Sometimes fees are required for disposal of solid waste, in an application of the basic principle that "polluters pay." A number of states maintain programs for the reduction of sources of solid waste. California has been especially inventive, adopting programs for reduction of toxic substances[40] and, perhaps most dramatic, for reduction of air pollution in the badly polluted Los Angeles area. The latter program will require conversion of all cars to electric power or other "clean" fuels by 2007; other provisions will encourage public transportation and limit the use of automobiles. North Carolina has adopted a "pollution prevention program" designed to prevent pollution before it occurs, rather than to impose technology at the ends of the pipe. These are simply a few of the many recent initiatives that have begun to implement the time-honored constitutional aspiration that the states might serve as "laboratories," experimenting with different systems for attaining social goals. Of course, some of these initiatives may not make sense; what is important is that they are occurring in a process of experimentation at the state and local levels.

Nor has the national government been inactive in this area. Under the Superfund statute, discussed previously, information about toxic chemical emissions must be provided to the states. The resulting information has been used as the foundation for a wide range of laws at the state level. Oregon now requires pollution reduction goals, as does Massachusetts. States have used the inventory as a basis for enforcement activity. Other national initiatives might similarly act as a spur for state and local decisions.

In fact there is an incipient trend toward more cooperative, information-purveying, norm-based strategies that attempt to use moral suasion. Thus the EPA has inaugurated a "Green Lights" program that tells companies about the advantages from energy-savings light bulbs and light fixtures. This approach saves a great deal of money; it also cuts pollution substantially. The EPA's "33/50" program challenges companies to cut toxic emissions by 33 percent within a short period and 50 percent within a somewhat longer period. The initial results are excellent. OSHA has started a "Star Program" that enables companies with strong safety records and good self-policing mechanisms to avoid annual inspections. These programs appear to embody a trend toward more voluntary and cooperative measures that rely on a combination of information and moral pressure.

IV. Qualifications

There are some important qualifications to the arguments I have made thus far. Informational strategies, economic incentives, and decentralization have genuine limitations.

The Limits of Information

There are two problems with informational strategies. First, the provision of information is expensive. Second, the provision of information is sometimes ineffectual or even counterproductive.

Consider, for example, the fact that the government estimates the cost of the FDA disclosure rules at no less than $1.7 billion over twenty years. The president of the National Food Processors Association claims that the first-year costs alone will exceed $2 billion.[41] In either case, the cost is significant. OSHA's hazard communication policy is estimated to save 200 lives per year—a lot—but at an annual cost of $360 million.[42] The expenditure per life saved is therefore $1.8 million. This is far better than a large number of regulations and an amount well worth spending; but it is more than many agencies spend for life-saving regulations. It is therefore not the case that the OSHA rule stands out as a means of saving lives especially cheaply.

When informational strategies are costly, there are two possible responses from government. The first is to do nothing. If the savings—in terms of health, life, informed choice—are relatively low, costly strategies, even informational ones, make little sense. There will therefore be circumstances in which a government remedy for an absence of information is unwarranted.

The second possibility is to impose a regulatory strategy rather than to require disclosure. By a regulatory strategy, I mean a mandatory outcome, such as a flat ban on the materials in question, or governmental specification of a particular outcome, as in a mandated maximum level of carcinogens in the workplace. Sometimes the regulatory strategy will be cheaper, because the price of disclosing information—changing packaging and so forth—is so high. This is likely to be the right response when most or all people would respond to the information in the same way. In that case, it is unnecessary to provide information, and better simply to dictate an outcome that, by hypothesis, is generally or almost universally preferred. For an especially dangerous substance, one that reasonable people would not choose to encounter, a flat ban is appropriate.

Even when informational strategies are not prohibitively expensive, they may be ineffectual and thus have low benefits. This is so for various reasons.

1. *Information-processing.* People have limited ability to process information (chapter 5). They have a notoriously difficult time in thinking about low-probability events. Sometimes they discount such events to zero; sometimes they treat them as much more dangerous than they actually are. If people are told, for example, that a certain substance causes cancer, they may think that it is far more dangerous than in fact it is. But some carcinogenic substances pose little risk.

For example, California's Proposition 65, an initiative designed to promote citizen awareness of risk levels, requires warnings for exposure to carcinogens. At first glance, the requirement seems unexceptionable, indeed an important advance. But it has in some cases been counterproductive. Consumers appear to think that twelve of every 100 users of a product with the required warning will die from cancer. This estimate exceeds reality by a factor of 1000 or more.[43] With respect to information, less may be more. If information is not provided in a clear and usable form, it may actually make people less knowledgeable than they were before.

2. *Heuristics.* The problem is aggravated by the fact that people tend to use heuristic devices that produce systemic errors. A particular problem here is the "availability heuristic," in accordance with which people tend to think an event is probable if they can readily bring to mind memories of its occurrence. Thus, for example, an airplane disaster will be thought relatively probable, whereas a death from diabetes will not be. There is a good deal of evidence that people overestimate risks from highly visible or sensational causes, but underestimate risks from less dramatic ones.[44]

3. *Motivational distortions.* People often believe themselves to be immune from risks that they acknowledge are significant and real with respect to others. In one study, for example, 97 percent of those surveyed ranked themselves as average or above average in their ability to avoid both bicycle and power mower accidents.[45] Disclosure of information may be an unhelpful tool when people do not internalize the new data.

4. *Dissonance reduction.* The desire to reduce cognitive dissonance may prevent people from recognizing that risks are real even when information is provided (chapters 1 and 5).

5. *Frustration from uncertainty.* Often people feel frustrated and frightened by probabilistic information and greatly prefer a certain answer. This fact can undermine efforts to provide risk information when the truth is that people must inevitably operate under conditions of uncertainty.

6. *Overload.* People face a pervasive risk of information overload, causing consumers to treat a large amount of information as equivalent to no information at all.[46] Certainly this is true when disclosure campaigns are filled with details that cannot be easily processed.

7. *Tenacity of initial beliefs.* Initially held beliefs are not easy to modify. This is so even when new information, undermining those beliefs, has been presented.[47]

8. *Strategic responses.* Companies may respond to disclosure requirements by refusing to provide information at all (if this is an available option). The result will be the removal from the market of information that is useful overall. If industry responds to a requirement of evidentiary support for scientific claims with mere "puffing," consumers may have less information than they did to begin with. If advertisers must conduct extensive tests before they are permitted to make claims, they will be given a strong incentive to avoid making claims at all.[48]

9. *Public good issues.* Information may be an inadequate strategy when greater safety is a public good.[49] Imagine, for example, that the replacement of carcinogen X with safe product Y would benefit all workers simultaneously, because all of them would simultaneously be exposed to Y rather than X. Imagine too that each worker is bargaining separately with the employer. In

that case, no individual employee may have a sufficient incentive to decrease his demand for wages and other benefits to obtain increased safety. Because the benefits of the new substance are provided to everyone, no individual employee will "pay" enough to obtain them, preferring instead to take a free ride on the efforts of others. The result will be too little safety under conventional economic criteria. Here a regulatory response is appropriate.

10. *Disclosure and the disadvantaged.* Disclosure strategies may also have disproportionately little effect on people who are undereducated, elderly, or poor. If this is so, the risks that such strategies are aimed to counteract may continue to be faced by the disadvantaged.[50]

These points suggest that there are real limitations to informational strategies. But the limitations do not bear fundamentally on reform efforts. They should be taken seriously but used productively, providing helpful guidance to those seeking to design effective information requirements.

In this regard, the first and most important point is that some of these very limitations can be overcome through more and better information. Public awareness of the distorting effects of current heuristics can help overcome those effects; general publicity about those effects might therefore supply a corrective. In addition, well-tailored programs would minimize the relevant risks by putting the information in its most understandable form. Instead of labeling a substance a "carcinogen," a uniform system of risk regulation could provide better awareness of risk levels. While informational strategies are no panacea, they would accomplish considerable good, at least if the possible obstacles are kept firmly in mind.[51]

More Effective Communication of Risk Information

These considerations suggest that the form and content of the information disclosed must be such that citizens find it understandable and trustworthy.[52] Systematic study of risk communication strategies only began in the mid-1980s.[53] These studies have shown that much conventional wisdom, on which prior regulatory strategies have been based, is wrong. Information becomes relevant to people through their specific background assumptions, knowledge, and systems of value. Precisely because experts and lay people often differ (chapter 5), the kind of information each requires often differs as well. On efficiency grounds, risk-communication strategies should be tailored to the needs of ordinary people, in order to ensure better decisions. On democratic grounds, the right kind of information should be disclosed so that participation builds trust in both the process and outcome.

A first problem with many government-sponsored risk communications is that they take the form of highly generalized and often inscrutable recommendations, rather than providing information that enables citizens to make evaluations. A second and more important problem is that people filter and process information through their existing frameworks of belief. Effective information disclosure requires knowledge of the beliefs on which citizens are likely to draw. If these background frameworks are incomplete or error-filled, factually accurate information may well be ignored or misunderstood. More information might even make people less informed. Thus, disclosure of the information that an expert decision analyst would use—the exposure-effect relationship of a risk, the cost and efficiency of alternative remediation approaches—may not promote informed choice at all.

Risk-communication experts have developed a general approach to discovering the most effective forms of information disclosure.[54] The appropriate approach can be broken down into three steps. First, policy makers should elicit the background beliefs that average citizens will actually bring to the relevant risk issue. Perhaps those background beliefs are already understood. If they are not, interviews can be helpful, but structured questionnaires might be used where the former are not feasible. Second, initial material should be designed to provide the relevant information in a way that responds to those background beliefs. To the extent that the elicitation process reveals gaps and errors in these beliefs, the material should address them. Rather than providing bare information, the material should provide it in a form directed to taking action. Third, the initial material should be empirically tested with potential users. Iterations of this process yield the most effective forms of information disclosure.

Applying this approach in 1987, experts were able to generate a highly effective brochure for addressing the recent radon scare, a brochure that was far more effective than the widely distributed EPA brochure on that topic. The elicitation process revealed that, in addition to holding many accurate beliefs about radon exposure, people also held many inaccurate beliefs: that radon contamination of surfaces is permanent (39 percent); that radon affects plants (58 percent); that it contaminates blood (38 percent); that it causes breast cancer (29 percent). Few people understood that radon decays quickly (13 percent).[55] The combination of some of these beliefs would make the radon problem seem severe and unsolvable; consider the lack of knowledge of the fact that radon decays quickly.

On the basis of this information, brochures were designed that specifically addressed the flaws and gaps in people's background beliefs. The unsuccessful EPA brochure had been prepared through traditional methods: Scientific experts were asked what information was relevant and it was then packaged attractively. The initial version of the EPA's "Citizen's Guide to Radon," for example, did not discuss whether radon contamination is permanent. When empirically tested, this EPA brochure performed significantly worse than the brochures prepared through the alternative method. When people were asked to recall simple facts, they did equally well with all the brochures. But when faced with tasks requiring inference, the new brochures dramatically outperformed the EPA material. For example, when asked what a homeowner could do to reduce high radon levels in the house, 43 percent of EPA readers answered "don't know" and 9 percent said "there is no way to fix the problem." In contrast, 100 percent of the readers of the brochure designed on the basis of risk-communication studies, and 96 percent of another, answered "hire a contractor to fix the problem."[56]

Informational remedies should also respond to various heuristics and anomalies that affect how people "hear" warnings. For example, it matters a great deal whether a health effect is framed as a loss or a gain. People are more willing to forego gains than to accept losses. Real-world experiments show that pamphlets describing the positive effects of breast self-examination (women who undertake such examinations have a greater chance of finding a tumor at a treatable stage) are ineffective, but that there are significant changes in behavior from pamphlets that stress the negative consequences of a refusal to undertake self-examinations (women who fail to perform such examinations have a decreased chance of finding a tumor at a treatable stage).[57] Similar results were found for efforts to inform people of the advantages of energy insulation: An emphasis on the gains from insulation produced far less change than an emphasis on the losses from noninsulation.[58]

Vivid and personal information can also be more effective than statistical evidence. So, too, people sometimes try to reduce cognitive dissonance by discounting certain risks (chapters 1 and 10), and hence information can be ignored. Efforts to convey information about AIDS, for example, appear to be adversely affected by people's tendency to assume that the risk does not apply to them.[59] It has been suggested that people concerned about the spread of AIDS should attempt to convey information not merely by stating the facts, but also by doing so in a way that is intentionally targeted at the negative (and by no means inevitable) social image of condom use.

Effective regulatory emphasis on information disclosure should learn from these risk–communication investigations. To provide meaningful information about risk, regulators must first learn what people already know and assume, as well as what they need to know. Appropriate information must then be developed, tested, and refined until empirical investigation demonstrates that the intended information is, in fact, being conveyed.[60] The next step in information and education-based regulatory strategies is to incorporate these insights.

When Economic Incentives Fail

There are several possible problems with the use of economic incentives. The clearest cases arise when the appropriate response to a harm-producing activity is a fiat ban. With an especially dangerous pollutant, an increased price is inadequate. The pollutant should be eliminated from the market, at least if (a) its social benefits do not outweigh the relevant danger and (b) less dangerous substitutes are available.

Another problem is that economic incentives might be thought to operate as a regressive tax, in the sense that they raise prices in general, and the increase will come down especially hard on the poor. An increase in the price of gasoline, or in the cost of high-polluting vehicles, will make things more difficult for poor people in particular. Indeed, any effort to require manufacturers and sellers to "internalize" the costs of their production might seem objectionable insofar as it increases prices in a way especially hard on the indigent.

In general, I do not believe that this objection is persuasive. Any regulatory solution will increase prices; economic incentives are not distinctive in this regard. And if the solution is otherwise sensible, it ought not to be treated as a "regressive tax," any more than the price system itself is a regressive tax. In any case, a refusal to require enterprises to bear the social costs of their activities is hardly an effective way of benefiting the poor. The class of people burdened by this refusal includes a variety of people, many of them not poor at all; and the refusal burdens a variety of people, many of them quite poor. It is certainly sensible, however, to worry about the consequences of price increases, produced by market forces or by government, for poor people. The point suggests that the taxes or fines produced by economic incentives might be accompanied by subsidies or transfer payments to people who are needy. Some of these subsidies might be funded out of the very revenues produced by the program itself.

It is also possible to argue, against economic incentives, that they improperly "commodify" certain interests. Perhaps some such interests—the right to bodily integrity, the right to freedom from pollution—ought not to be traded on markets at all. Perhaps such trading debases and diminishes the interests in question, with harmful consequences for social attitudes. In some settings the objection seems persuasive (chapter 3). Thus there is reason to question a decision to allow trading of body parts or of gestational capacities. But in the general context of regulatory law, it is doubtful that the argument takes one very far. It seems implausible to suggest that social attitudes would be materially changed by a system in which polluters and others who cause harm must pay. Indeed, a shift of the entitlement from the polluter to the pollutee might have desirable effects on social attitudes, by establishing the correct starting point. In any case, it seems far better to require people who cause harm to pay, rather than to allow them to do so for free.

Any incentive-based system must confront a range of practical problems. In the environmental context, for example, there is a risk that polluters will cluster in a particular area, thus subjecting people in that area to unacceptably high danger. Determination of the amount of any tax or fine is not a simple scientific exercise. It entails a democratic judgment about appropriate risk levels, and that decision will pose great difficulties. But these sorts of questions should be treated as matters of detail. They do not bear fundamentally on the shift to economic incentives.

National Commitments

Decentralization is not a preferred approach in at least three categories of cases. The first involves national moral commitments that cut across local boundaries. The most obvious candidate is the prohibition of discrimination on the basis of race or sex. Here decentralized solutions are inadequate. The whole point of the national commitment is to ensure adherence to a principle that transcends state boundaries. The Civil War, establishing a prohibition on slavery and a requirement of racial equality, is a core example.

The second category involves interstate spillovers, of which air pollution is the most conspicuous example. Because air pollution in California will affect Nevada, it is not feasible to rely entirely on intrastate controls. There are inadequate political safeguards in one state against the imposition of harms faced by another. In such cases, national intervention is necessary. Even here, however, such intervention should take the form of "floors"—minimum standards—rather than nationally dictated outcomes.

The third category is the most interesting. In a federal system, states compete with each other for revenue-attracting business and industry. This competition creates an important "race to the bottom" with respect to regulatory controls. In many respects this is entirely healthy. The right of exit is a critical check against oppressive law. Indeed, the right of exit is probably a more important constraint on oppressive legislation than the Supreme Court's decisions under the dormant commerce clause, even if all these are taken together. But the race can have unfortunate consequences as well. Suppose, for example, that state A wishes to impose occupational safety and health controls—or even disclosure requirements—on industries within its borders. Suppose that such industries are free to leave. It may well be that in such circumstances, no state will impose the relevant controls, even though all states, if agreement were possible, would choose to do so. President Roosevelt made precisely this argument in supporting child labor legislation at the national level.

In some cases, then, the race to the bottom will put states in a prisoners' dilemma, requiring a cooperative solution in the form of a binding agreement through the national government. Through legislation at the national level, states can prevent the mutually destructive competition to attract business and industry. This argument does not prove as much as might appear. Sometimes national legislation will not be in the interests of the states' own people, since it will drive down profits in a way that will have adverse effects on (among other things) poverty, employment, and the general availability of goods and services. But national legislation will sometimes be justified on this ground. Here, too, specific answers depend on the details.

Democracy and Markets: Potential for Conflict

In this chapter, I have argued that economic and democratic goals can march hand-in-hand. Across a wide range, we can attempt precisely the same reform efforts to bring about both of these goals. For this reason, there is no need to choose between efficiency and democracy, at least for most of our efforts in the next generation. It would be a mistake, however, to pretend that there is no potential for conflict here. An exploration of that potential of course raises extremely large and complex issues. I make a few brief observations.

The most important point is that efficiency is a function of aggregated private willingness to pay, a criterion that is, to say the least, problematic from the democratic point of view. A system is efficient if entitlements have been allocated so as to "maximize value," with reference to private willingness to pay. For believers in a democratic system, however, this criterion is inadequate in two different ways. First, a democracy system operates on the principle of one person, one vote. By contrast, a market allocates "votes" in accordance with how much people are willing to pay for things. Since willingness to pay is a function of ability to pay, wealthy people will be willing to pay far more than poor ones. Indeed, the indigent will be able to pay nothing at all. The principle of political equality, so central to democratic theory, is violated by the efficiency criterion.

Second, a democratic system, at least in America, is not supposed to represent an effort to aggregate private preferences at all (chapter 1). Instead, the process is a deliberative one, in which different information and perspectives are brought to bear. In that deliberative process, preferences are supported by reasons, to be transformed into values and judgments. Markets need not have this reason-giving feature or this deliberative function.

The notion of aggregating private willingness to pay accurately captures the economic ideal of "consumer sovereignty." Despite its value in many contexts, this is a caricature of the American conception of sovereignty. That conception aspires not to aggregated consumption choices, but instead to a transfer of the power of governance from the king to "We the People." Insofar as markets accurately capture private willingness to pay, they are a powerful tool of prosperity, and on a certain, not implausible view, of liberty as well. But this salutary function is not the same as democratic self-governance. The considered judgments of the citizenry may well diverge from aggregated consumption choices. And when there is such a divergence, the former should generally prevail.

These objections to the willingness to pay criterion, invoking democratic principles, are hardly irrelevant to the reform of American public law. They suggest that exclusive use of the principle of cost-benefit analysis is highly objectionable, at least if costs and benefits are defined by reference to willingness to pay (chapter 5), and that there will indeed be conflicts between democratic aspirations and the goal of economic efficiency. But if what I have said is persuasive, a great deal can be done before reaching those conflicts.

Conclusion

Throughout its history, American government has benefited from its democratic features and from structural characteristics that promote both effectiveness and efficiency. The benefits are especially impressive when viewed in comparison to other systems of government. But in its current incarnation, American government suffers from significant failures. The modern regulatory state is often ineffective; it has not been efficient; it is hardly a model of democratic self-governance. In a period in which nations all over the world are seeking to promote both efficiency and democracy, it would be unfortunate indeed if we did not subject our own institutions to skeptical scrutiny.

I have suggested three reforms in democratizing contemporary public law. Information strategies, increasing disclosure and education, should supplement or sometimes even replace regulatory systems. Economic incentives, including taxes and fines, should usually be substituted for command-and-control regulation. Decentralization, allowing bargaining and participation in the private and public spheres, should in many contexts be substituted for centralized dictates from Washington. All of these proposals would respond simultaneously to inefficiencies in modern government and to severe problems from the democratic point of view—most notably factional influence and absence of opportunities for the exercise of political influence.

Reforms of this sort would not accomplish all that is now required from the standpoint of either efficiency or democracy. There are limits to all three strategies. At some point, moreover, it will be necessary to reconcile some serious conflicts between efficiency and democracy. But we now have both the information and the tools by which to accomplish an enormous amount of reform. We need not rest content with the paradoxes and failures of existing institutions.

Notes

1. See Bruce A. Ackerman, *We The People* (Cambridge: Harvard University Press, 1991).

2. Franklin D. Roosevelt, "Message to the Congress on the State of the Union" (Jan. 11, 1944), in Franklin Delano Roosevelt, *The Public Papers and Addresses of Franklin D. Roosevelt*, vol. 13 (New York: Russell and Russell, 1969), p. 41.

3. See L. Dennis, *The Coming American Fascism* (New York: Harper, 1936).

4. See Theodore J. Lowi, *The Personal President: Power Invested, Promise Unfulfilled* (Ithaca: Cornell University Press, 1985).

5. See, e.g., Lochner v. New York, 198 U.S. 45 (1905).

6. See Cass R. Sunstein, *After the Rights Revolution: Reconceiving the Regulatory State* (Cambridge: Harvard University Press, 1990).

7. See Robert Hahn and John Hird, "The Costs and Benefits of Regulation," 8 *Yale J. Reg.* 233 (1990), contains an estimate of $44 billion; for references to other studies, and a suggestion that this is far too low, see "The Total Cost of Regulation?," in *Regulation* 22–25 (Summer 1991). The Office of Management and Budget makes an estimate of between $50 and $150 billion, see Office of Management and Budget, *Regulatory Program of the United States, April 1, 1987–March 31, 1988*, (Washington, D.C.: Executive Office of the President, 1989). p. xii. Thomas D. Hopkins, "The Costs of Federal Regulation," 2 *J. Reg. and Social Costs* 5, 25 (1992), offers an estimate of $400 billion annually.

8. Tammy Tengs et al., "Five Hundred Life-Saving Interventions and Their Cost-Effectiveness," 15 *Risk Analysis*, 369 (1995).

9. Office of Management and Budget, *Regulatory Program of the United States, April 1, 1989–March 31, 1990* (Washington, D.C.: Executive Office of the President, 1991), p. 6, and citations therein.

10. *Id.*

11. See Stephen G. Breyer, *Regulation and Its Reform* (Cambridge: Harvard University Press, 1982).

12. *Id.*

13. See, e.g., Henry G. Grabowski and John M. Vernon, *The Regulation of Pharmaceuticals: Balancing the Benefits and Risks* (Washington, D.C.: American Enterprise Institute for Public Policy Research, 1983).

14. See Robert W. Crandall, et al., *Regulating the Automobile* (Washington, D.C.: Brookings Institution, 1986).

15. See Thomas H. Tietenberg, *Emissions Trading: An Exercise in Reforming Pollution Policy* (Washington, D.C.: Resources for the Future, 1985), pp. 41–45.

16. See Bruce A. Ackerman and William T. Hassler, *Clean Coal/Dirty Air: Or How the Clean Air Act Became a Multibillion Dollar Bail-Out for High-Sulfur Coal Producers and What to Do About it* (New Haven: Yale University Press, 1981).

17. See E. Donald Elliott, "Superfund: EPA Success, National Debacle?," 12 *Natural Resources and Environment,* 233 (1992).

18. See Richard Stewart, "Madison's Nightmare," 56 *U. Chi. L. Rev.* 335 (1990).

19. See Ackerman and Hassler, *supra,* note 16.

20. See George Akerlof, "The Market for 'Lemons': Quality Uncertainty and the Market Mechanism," 84 *Q. J. Econ.* 488 (1970).

21. See W. Kip Viscusi and Wesley A. Magat, with Joel Huber et al., *Learning About Risk: Consumer and Worker Response to Hazard Information* (Cambridge: Harvard University Press, 1987), and Joel Huber, "Informational Regulation of Consumer Health Risks," 17 *Rand J. Econ.* 351 (1986); W. Kip Viscusi and C. O'Connor, "Adaptive Responses to Chemical Labelling," 74 *Am. Econ. Rev.* 942 (1984). The empirical work also shows the need for care in designing disclosure requirements.

22. See *supra* note 21.

23. 42 U.S.C. 9601 et seq.

24. See GAO, *Toxic Chemicals,* Report to the Congress (1991).

25. 58 *Fed. Reg.* 2927 (1992).

26. See W. Kip Viscusi on *Fatal Trade-offs* (Oxford: Oxford Unversity Press, 1992), p. 155.

27. Here I generalize from the helpful discussion in Bruce Ackerman and Richard Stewart, "Reforming Environmental Law," 13 *Colum. J. Env. L.* 171 (1988).

28. *Id.*

29. *Id.* at 146.

30. *Id.* at 148.

31. *Id.* at 145.

32. *Id.*

33. W. Kip. Viscusi, *Reforming Products Liability* (Cambridge: Harvard University Press, 1991), p. 178.

34. See EPA, "Emissions Trading Policy Statement: General Principles for Creation, Banking, and Use of Emission Reduction Credits," 51 *Fed. Reg.* 43,814 (1986).

35. See David Dudek and Martin Palmisano, "Emissions Trading: Why Is This Thoroughbred Hobbled?," 13 *Colum. J. Env. L.* 217 (1988).

36. Robert Hahn and John Hester, "Marketable Permits: Lessons for Theory and Practice," 16 *Ecol. L.Q.* 361, 374 tbl. 2 (1989).

37. *Id.*

38. On ozone depletion, see 53 *Fed. Reg.* 30,566 (Aug 11, 1988); on water pollution, see Robert Hahn and Robert Stavins, "Incentive-Based Environmental Regulation: A New Era From An Old Idea," 18 *Ecology L.Q.* 1, 18–19 (1991).

39. See generally Advisory Commission on Intergovernmental Relations, *Regula-*

tory Federalism: Policy, Process, Impact and Reform (Washington, D.C.: Advisory Commission on Intergovernmental Relations,1984).

40. See the discussion and criticism in W. Kip Viscusi, "Predicting the Effects of Food Cancer Risk Warnings on Consumers," 43 *Food Drug Cosmetic L. J.* 283 (1988).

41. *The Chicago Tribune,* Nov. 7, 1991, p. 2.

42. The figures come from W. Kip Viscusi, supra, note 26, at 264.

43. See Viscusi, *supra* note 40.

44. See Paul Slovic et al "Informing the Public About the Risks from Ionizing Radiation," in *Judgment and Decision Making,* Hal. R. Arkes and Kenneth R. Hammond, eds. (Cambridge: Cambridge University Press, 1986).

45. *Id.* at 116.

46. See Stanley Jacoby, et al., "Corrective Advertising and Affirmative Disclosure Statements," 46 *J. Mktg.* 61, 70 (Winter 1982).

47. *Id.* at 118; Robert C. Ellickson, *Order Without Law: How Neighbors Settle Disputes* (Cambridge: Harvard University Press, 1991).

48. See Richard Craswell, "Interpreting Deceptive Advertising," 65 *B. U. L. Rev.* 657 (1985).

49. This argument depends for its plausibility on transactions cost barrier to free mobility of labor. If labor were completely mobile, the problem should disappear.

50. See George Schucker et al., "The Impact of the Saccharin Warning Label," 2 *J. Pub. Policy & Marketing* 46 (1983).

51. See Wesley A. Magat and W. Kip Viscusi, *Informational Approaches to Regulation* (Cambridge: MIT Press, 1991).

52. This section was originally coauthored with Richard Pildes and appeared in Richard Pildes and Cass R. Sunstein, "Reinventing the Regulatory State," 62 *U. Chi. L. Rev.* 1 (1995).

53. Paul Slovic, "Perception of Risk," in *Social Theories of Risk,* Sheldon Krimsky and Dominic Golding, eds. (Westport, Conn.: Praeger, 1992).

54. The discussion that follows is based on William Morgan, et al., "Communicating Risks to the Public," 26 *Environ. Sci. Technol.* 2048 (1992).

55. *Id.*

56. William Morgan, et. al., *supra,* note 54, at 2054.

57. See Beth Meyerowitz and Shelly Chaiken, "The Effect of Message Framing on Breast Self-Examination," 52 *J. Personality & Soc. Psych.* 500 (1987).

58. Marti Galzales, Elliot Aronson, and Mark Costanzo, "Using Social Cognition and Persuasion to Promote Energy Conservation," 18 *J. Applied Soc. Psych.* 1049 (1988).

59. See Elliot Aronson, *The Social Animal,* 7th ed. (New York: W. H. Freeman, 1995), pp. 91–92.

60. Compare the discussion of the confusion induced by California's toxic substance referendum, in Viscusi, *supra* note 40.

Congress, Constitutional Moments, and the Cost-Benefit State

A Stalled Constitutional Moment?

Spurred by widespread popular dissatisfaction with government and the *Contract with America*, the 104th Congress promised to change the national government in America in fundamental ways. The House of Representatives attempted to rethink government more deeply than at any time since the New Deal; in fact, the New Deal was a central target of the process of rethinking. America may now be experiencing a constitutional moment in which foundational issues are answered in novel ways.[1]

Whether or not this is so, it is safe to say that with the election of the 104th Congress, America has now become a genuinely post-New Deal regulatory state, and for this reason what happened in that Congress is of more than passing interest. What will emerge for the nation remains in a process of development; but it may be described as a *cost-benefit state*, one whose performance will be assessed, both in particular and in general, by comparing the costs of government action against the benefits of government action. This idea requires a good deal of specification, but it unites developments not only in the national legislature, but in the executive branch, the judiciary, and state government as well.

My purpose here is to evaluate legislative efforts to create a new constitutional moment, with particular reference to the modern regulatory state. There was undoubtedly a high level of ambition in the 104th Congress. A large part of the basic agenda of that Congress came under the heading of "rethinking the regulatory state." The *Contract with America* promised to address quite basic issues. Large-scale hearings addressed problems of overregulation and the prospects for cost-benefit balancing. The House passed and the Senate debated measures that, if enacted, would have represented the largest changes to the Administrative Procedure Act (APA) since its enactment in 1946.

Even if we are in the midst of a constitutional moment, it is notable that relatively little happened in the two-year period after election of the 104th Congress. All in all, there was a great deal of noise and bluster, but with a few important exceptions, there was relatively little in the way of concrete results. There is a simple reason for this outcome: The American people had not (yet) committed themselves to large-scale change in the way that American institutions require. The apparently ambitious proposals contained some good features. But many of their provisions were crude, unimaginative, and far more procedural than advertised. Those provisions represented an effort to clog the regulatory process with paperwork requirements, rather than to engage in new and better thinking about the substance of regulation. In tribute to the nation's ambivalence, Congress's institutional weaknesses, and the system of checks and balances—including above all bicameralism and the possibility of presidential veto—fundamental change takes a good deal of time. This point very much bears on the possibility of constitutional moments in the context of the modern state.

Lessons

In fact, both institutional and substantive lessons will emerge from the discussion. On the institutional side, we can see that Congress is quite ill-equipped to produce sensible, constitution-like reform, at least if it tries to offer details. With respect to regulation, a group of generalist representatives—all with many issues to address, few with particular expertise in regulatory law, and many beholden to special interests—is not in a position to produce desirable reforms, unless it restricts itself to a few generalities. Such a group will face sharp internal divisions that are not subject to reasonable mediation without a good deal of specialization in regulation. Indeed, the task of producing constitution-like change in the modern state is far more difficult than it was in the New Deal era. It is easier to create a regulatory state than it is to dismantle one, especially in an era in which America, like every other industrialized nation, is committed to controlling the operation of the marketplace.

These skeptical claims about Congress's institutional capacities are reinforced by recent experience. As we will see, the 104th Congress was split between two different sets of interests: technocratic forces seeking to discipline agency decisions with better policy analysis; and forces of reaction seeking to stop agency action, even when social well-being would be improved by it. Hence there is an interesting contrast between the performance of Congress and that of the executive branch. Even those who reject President Clinton's approach to regulation ought to recognize that his administration has shown far more sophistication and creativity than Congress did.[2] (The same is true for the administrations of President Reagan and Bush.) The executive branch has been highly attuned to the need to compare costs and benefits, to attend to results rather than processes, and to seek to enlist the private sector in least-cost solutions. This fact tends to support the view that improvements in regulatory performance are more likely to come from the executive branch than from Congress, and that Congress ought to leave a substantial amount of discretion to administrators, at least in designing appropriate regulatory tools and perhaps in setting priorities as well. Indeed, many of the current problems are created by statutes that produce poor incentives or forbid more imaginative, cheaper, and more effective solutions—or that ban cost-benefit balancing itself.

On the substantive side, a cost-benefit state may well be better than what we now have: a system containing both economic and democratic failures, where priorities are not set carefully and where factions have excessive power over government. Certainly it is important to provide methods for assessing regulatory performance. At least in principle, some form of cost-benefit analysis could simultaneously promote political accountability and regulatory efficiency. But any movement in this direction should be accompanied by an understanding of the important place of public judgments in regulatory law, the limits of the criterion of private willingness to pay, and the need to create market mechanisms that do not place excessive informational demands on government.

More specifically, I suggest that a general requirement of cost-benefit analysis would indeed be a constitution-like amendment, and a highly undesirable one, if it is understood in the most ambitious possible way: as an effort to ensure that all regulatory statutes are implemented by reference to the criterion of economic efficiency as understood through the criterion of private willingness to pay. Regulatory measures have diverse foundations—including aspirational and redistributive goals—and many legitimate statutes are not rooted in the efficiency criterion at all.

If cost-benefit analysis is understood more modestly as an effort to require balancing rather than absolutism, it is a good idea, and indeed it should generally be required. But so understood, cost-benefit analysis can be specified in many different ways, and it is important to ensure that Congress gives appropriate guidance and that agencies make reasonable rather than unreasonable specifications. I offer some suggestions about how these tasks might be accomplished; to this end I emphasize qualitative as well as quantitative factors, public judgments about risk, and the highly diverse foundations of regulatory enactments.

I. The Attack on the New Deal

The New Deal as Constitutional Revision— and Its Aftermath

The New Deal was of course a substantial reformation of the original constitutional structure.[3] It qualifies as a substantial reformation above all because it refashioned the three basic cornerstones of that structure: federalism; checks and balances; and individual rights.

To compress a long story: In the 1930s the powers of the national government were expanded in an extraordinary way, to the point where the nation exercised something close to general authority to accomplish whatever tasks it thought important. The original understanding of a sharply constrained central government was therefore repudiated by the nation. There were simple grounds for this repudiation. State autonomy seemed an obstacle to democratic self-government, not a crucial part of it—especially in the midst of the Depression, when states were generally perceived as ineffectual entities buffeted about by private factions. As a result of the New Deal, state autonomy was very different in 1940 from what it had been in 1920.

The system of checks and balances also came under sharp criticism. To many observers, especially during the Depression, that system seemed anachronistic and outmoded. Good businesses do not operate through checks and balances; why should good governments paralyze themselves in this way? Responding to such questions, Congress delegated enormous policymaking power to the President and also created a large number of powerful executive and independent agencies. Crucially, Congress attempted to design these agencies so as to limit the consequences of the system of checks and balances by allowing a high degree of administrative autonomy. Thus the new agencies had a large degree of discretionary authority under open-ended statutory standards. They also combined traditionally separated powers of adjudication, execution, and legislation.

These institutional shifts resulted from a crucial national judgment made during the Depression: that individual rights, properly conceived, included not merely the common law catalogue of private interests but also governmental protection against many of the harms and risks of a market economy. These harms and risks included unemployment, poverty, lack of adequate nutrition, homelessness, lack of education, lack of access to medical care, and more. Indeed the common law catalogue seemed overprotective as well as underprotective, for it was unduly solicitous of private property. The common law was a regulatory system enjoying no special status. It should be evaluated pragmatically in terms of its consequences for the human beings subject to it. Here it often seemed to fail. Hence the national government was authorized to engage in a wide range of redistributive policies.

If the New Deal qualifies as a constitutional moment, it is because of its substantial effects on fundamental constitutional commitments.[4] In this connection, an astonishing feature of the New Deal was its relative rapidity. Many of the changes came in the brief period from 1932 through 1936. Rapid change was possible partly because it is a relatively simple step for a legislature to create a range of new bureaucratic institutions, at least if the legislature does not specify their duties in advance. The New Deal entities in fact operated pursuant to little statutory guidance; Congress usually contented itself with open-ended delegations of authority. As we shall see, the relative simplicity of the New Dealers' task makes a dramatic contrast with the complexity of jobs faced by the modern Congress.

The New Deal reformation was the foundation for the basic orientation of the national government until the election of President Ronald Reagan, and possibly since then. One development has been of special importance: the "rights revolution" of the 1960s and 1970s. During that period, many New

Deal tendencies were largely reinforced through the creation of a remarkable array of new agencies. These agencies were designed mostly to protect against threats to life, health, and safety from consumer products, workplaces, and above all the environment in general.[5] This period saw the creation of the Environmental Protection Agency, the Occupational Safety and Health Administration, the Consumer Product Safety Commission, the Council on Environmental Quality, and so on.

It is notable that during both the New Deal and the rights revolution, no mechanism was created to evaluate regulatory performance. There was no system to assess whether agencies were making things better or worse. In the New Deal, any such system might have seemed peculiar in light of the widespread national enthusiasm for the president and for the perceived possibilities of benign administration. Of course, cost-benefit thinking was quite foreign to political actors, and hence cost-benefit analysis played little or no role in the public debate.

One of the most striking features of the period since 1980 is that the New Deal reformation has been subject to sustained national criticism, often under the rubric of cost-benefit analysis. This criticism may well be signaling the first genuinely foundational challenge to American government since the New Deal itself. It is worthwhile to pause over the constitution-like character of recent challenges to the current government structure. Sometimes it is suggested that the national government has far exceeded the appropriate limits of its authority, and that a return to the original structure would make a great deal of sense. Many people are arguing that a devolution of power to the states would promote both democratic and economic goals; consider the Unfunded Mandates Reform Act and Congress's recent interest in "block grants" for states to use basically as they wish.

In this way, there is a wholesale attack on the existing allocation of authority between the national government and the states. But "horizontal" issues of government structure are receiving similar attention. Many people have expressed concern about the extent of policy-making discretion given to regulatory agencies. In their view, Congress should reassert its constitutional prerogatives by narrowing administrative discretion. Hence it is urged that the New Deal's enthusiasm for independent bureaucracy, and for a large law-making role by executive agencies, should be revisited, and that Congress should make the fundamental choices of policy.

Finally, and perhaps most fundamental, pre-New Deal principles of private rights have enjoyed a rebirth with the suggestion that modern regulatory programs violate liberty, rightly conceived. These principles are playing a significant part in current debates, with arguments in favor of removing constraints from the marketplace and of imposing new compensation obligations on government.[6] The movement for deregulation has become far more sweeping than it was in the Reagan period itself. The takings clause has become a rallying cry for a new enthusiasm for the protection of private property—a rallying cry that has been brought by way of challenge to such well-established federal programs as the Endangered Species Act and the Federal Water Pollution Control Act's protection of wetlands.

Some of the criticisms of regulatory performance have been far more pragmatic in character, and it is here that cost-benefit balancing, accompanied by risk analysis, has played a special role. As I have noted, the New Deal period was accompanied by no mechanism for monitoring regulatory performance. But it is now suggested that national government has failed adequately to perform the tasks assigned to it and that it has often made things worse. In this view, there is no suggestion that markets are ideal; but often markets work better than the regulatory programs designed as solutions. In sum, the question is whether the benefits justify the costs. Hence assessment of regulatory performance has increasingly taken the form of the criterion of cost-benefit analysis.

If we are indeed in the midst of a constitutional moment, its initial stage was set with the election of President Ronald Reagan, and it was spurred by the dramatic and largely unanticipated shift in the direction and composition of the Congress in the 1994 elections. The *Contract with America* presented the electorate with a set of promises for fundamental reform. The importance of the Contract should not be understated, for it helped to organize a formerly unruly House of Representatives and also provided public benchmarks against which the House would be measured. I will shortly say a few words about the difficulty of constitution-like revision in the present circumstances. But it is clear that in the 104th Congress, the House of Representatives acted in a remarkably rapid and sweeping fashion, offering the Senate a chance to make the most significant changes in the national government since the New Deal. As we have seen, the Senate declined the opportunity, and if the nation follows the Senate's course in the future, the effort at constitutional revision will have failed. But any predictions on this count would be premature. Let us turn, then, away from theory and toward more pragmatic issues involving the performance of the regulatory state.

Post-New Deal Learning About Regulation

In the last decade, something very close to a consensus has emerged on some of the most important problems in existing government regulation. If government were to act on this consensus, it would introduce important changes. Those changes need not amount to anything like a constitutional moment; we are not speaking here of the most basic constitutional commitments. But the changes would be far from a mere matter of tinkering. The consensus has the following features.

Government Should Engage in Better
Priority-Setting

There can be no doubt that resources for risk reduction are badly allocated. As much as $500 billion may be spent each year on regulation,[7] and of this amount, more than $130 billion is spend on environmental protection.[8] A recent study suggests that better allocations of existing health expenditures could save an additional 60,000 lives at no increased cost—and that with better allocations, we could save the same number of lives we now save with $31 billion in annual savings.[9] There are also serious and apparently unjustified asymmetries in life-saving expenditures. For transportation, there is a median per life year saved of $56,000; for occupational regulation, the number is $346,000; for environmental regulation, it is $4,207,000. There are enormous variations within each group as well. Of course, calculations of costs and benefits are somewhat speculative, and these numbers are of uncertain reliability. Of course, the context in which risks are imposed matter; lives are not fungible with lives (chapter 5). But with better allocations and more deliberative judgments, much could be done to make things better.

The goal of achieving sensible priority-setting is undermined by the fact that agencies have quite different standards for deciding when risks are large enough to require any regulation at all.[10] The International Commission on Radiological Protection recommends that environmental factors should not be allowed to cause an incremental cancer risk, for those exposed over a lifetime, of about 3 in 1000. American agencies do not follow this recommendation, and their own practices are highly variable. The Nuclear Regulatory Commission sees 1 in 1000 as acceptable; the EPA's acceptable range varies from 1 in 10,000 to 1 in 1,000,000. The FDA has tried to use a standard of 1 in 1 million, but under the Delaney Clause, courts have required a standard of essentially 0. OSHA's understanding of the "significant risk" requirement found in its governing statute means a risk of 1 in 1000; labor groups have sought an increase to 1 in 1 million. In view of differences in the contexts in which people face risks, some differences may well make sense. But with the current variations, good priority-setting is unlikely.

Government Should Have a Presumption in Favor of Flexible, Market-Based Incentives Rather Than Rigid Commands

Too often government has chosen to regulate through rigid commands that forbid more flexible and cost-effective means for achieving the same goal. In air and water pollution control, serious problems are caused by the "best available technology" approach, which mandates control technologies for hundreds or even thousands of firms in an exceptionally diverse nation. Through incentive-based systems, billions of dollars might be saved (chapter 13). Existing efforts at seeking better regulatory tools are hobbled by the statutory status quo, which sometimes forbids such tools, and which sometimes requires that they be engrafted on a bureaucratically complex system. Thus a 1989 study suggested that the EPA's emissions trading program had saved between $525 million and $12 billion per year.[11] Thus the Clinton Administration calculates that its market-oriented proposals for amending the Clean Water Act could save between $1 and $12 billion over alternative approaches. Studies show that incentive-based mechanisms for controlling air pollution could have accomplished the same amount at one-quarter the cost.[12]

An especially valuable incentive-based approach consists of disclosure of information. If companies offer information about risk, consumer and worker behavior will probably be affected.[13] The national government has offered many initiatives in this direction. In particular, the Toxic Release Inventory of the Superfund amendments has been highly successful, spurring voluntary reductions at relatively low costs and without requiring governmental mandates. A great deal of work remains to be done in designing informational approaches to risk.

Government Should Be Aware of and Attempt to Counteract Harmful Unintended Consequences

Many regulatory initiatives have unintended harmful consequences, and under existing institutions, there is no systematic way to ensure that those consequences receive attention. Regulation tends to be based on partial perspectives, emerging from close attention to mere pieces of complex problems. Sometimes regulation increases costs and in this sense prices, unemployment, and poverty. Sometimes it has harmful effects on particular sectors of the economy. A special problem arises from "health-health" trade-offs, which arise when regulation of one health risk increases another health risk (chapter 12). Needless to say, it is important to ensure that risk regulation does not actually increase risks on balance. Mechanisms should be created to enable officials to have an understanding of harmful unintended consequences; cost-benefit analysis might be seen as a step in this direction.

Government Needs More Information, and It Should Create Better Incentives to Compile and Provide Accurate Information

Often government lacks information about the harms that regulation is designed to counteract. Often it must act, or fail to act, in a context of considerable scientific uncertainty. It follows that any exercise of quantification can be illusory, or at least give the impression of far more knowledge than people actually have. In these circumstances, government should put a high premium on acquiring as much accurate information as possible. Much of the relevant information can be found in the private sector, which is in the best position to know about the costs of controlling risks and about actual emissions levels. The current regulatory structure does not create good incentives for compiling accurate information on these counts; indeed, it creates incentives to distort the facts. Hence industry faces incentives to report that the costs will be far higher than they will actually be.

Technocratic, Economic, and Democratic Judgments All Have Their Appropriate Place

It seems clear that government should respond to reasonable judgments about risk; but whose judgments should be counted as reasonable? Countless studies have shown that there are systematic differences between expert and citizen judgments about risk (chapter 5).

What is the reason for these differences? Some of them are attributable to citizens' ignorance of the facts. The ignorance has many sources, including sensationalistic media reports and heuristics that produce systematic biases. Thus, the "availability" heuristic suggests that what people think will be partly an artifact of what the media emphasize. Notably, the media tends to emphasize unusual and provocative events rather than chronic risks.[14] The result is substantial distortions in policy, reflected in the "pollutant of the month" syndrome that characterizes regulatory responses.

When citizens are ignorant, government should not respond to them. Citizen judgments that are based on mistaken beliefs should be corrected through education. And when they are mistaken, government should try to act on the basis of reality rather than fiction. But this is only part of the story. Some of the differences between citizens and experts have nothing to do with a misunderstanding of the facts; they involve values instead. Experts focus principally on aggregate lives at stake. By contrast, ordinary citizens care about a range of other variables: whether risks are equitably distributed, faced by future generations, especially dreaded, potentially catastrophic, poorly understood, and voluntarily incurred (chapter 5). Citizen judgments on these points are entirely reasonable. They deserve respect, at least in a democracy.

Government Should Concentrate on Basic Ends Rather Than on Means

A pervasive problem in federal regulation arises when regulatory policy becomes an arena for interest-group struggle. This happened most famously with efforts in 1977 to use the Clean Air Act to promote the interests of eastern coal[15] and, in 1990, with interest-group lobbying on behalf of ethanol and other parochial interests. Interest-group maneuvering is an omnipresent issue in federal regulation.

It is possible to limit interest-group power—and at the same time to reduce cost—through legislative attention to ends rather than to the means of achieving those ends. Thus "performance standards" are generally better than "design standards." What matters is whether the level of emissions is low or high, not whether the relevant company has installed scrubbers. In general, Congress should let administrators decide on the appropriate means for reaching legislatively decreed ends, and administrators should, to the extent feasible, be permitted to rely on market forces to choose those means. If an industry can comply with a sulfur dioxide emission standard with clean coal, or with energy conservation methods, government should be entirely satisfied.

These, then, are the principal lessons of the last generation of experience with regulation. If we keep them in mind, we might think that it is time to enact an Administrative Substance Act. The point of such an act would be to capture new learning with respect to regulatory successes and failures.

II. The 104th Congress: What Happened

Substantive regulatory issues are hardly a new issue for Congress.[16] Recent sessions of Congress devoted a good deal of attention to substantive regulatory reform, usually on a statute-by-statute basis. In 1990, Congress enacted a set of major changes to the Clean Air Act. Changes to the (disastrous) Superfund statute have received considerable attention in recent years.[17] Bills have been introduced to change the Federal Water Pollution Control Act as well.

But the 104th Congress sought something different—far more fundamental and less piecemeal change. The more fundamental change included the welfare system, taxation, federalism, and much more. And after the 1993 elections, it was clear that regulatory reform would be an important legislative priority. Perhaps it would take the form—as many urged that in fact it did—of a basic assault on the regulatory state and indeed on the New Deal reformation of American public law.

It is notable, however, that the 104th Congress faced a far more difficult and complex task than did the New Dealers. This is not only because the nation was palpably ambivalent about such fundamental change. It is also because there is a difference between the elaborate project of reforming existing programs and the relatively simple creation of new bureaucracies acting with vague statutory guidance. Under current conditions, the task of fundamental reform calls for far more numerous and far harder judgments, especially at the legislative level.

Understanding this fact, members of the 104th Congress introduced a truly remarkable array of proposed legislation. In the regulatory arena, much of the debate took place under the general heading of "cost-benefit balancing." As we shall see, the notion of cost-benefit assessment is quite open ended; everything depends on the relevant theory of valuation. But there is an unmistakable and quite general trend in the direction of evaluating governmental performance in cost-benefit terms. This development may ultimately help organize and incorporate much of recent learning about regulatory performance.

Before discussing the details, it is important to say that there were two overarching strands in the reform efforts. The first strand was "technocratic." Here the reformers' goal was to bring to bear the best in the way of sophisticated policy analysis, so as to ensure better priority-setting and attention to consequences. Some of the provisions governing risk analysis, cost-benefit balancing, and use of market-based tools reflected the technocratic strand. Those enthusiastic about many forms of regulation should endorse these provisions. Indeed, the introduction into Congress of sophisticated learning about risk regulation was the most impressive feature of the debate.

The second and much less attractive strand is best described as "reactionary." Here the goal was to stall or eliminate regulation whatever its content—largely with procedural requirements so extensive as to prevent agencies from doing much at all. The reactionary strand can be found in moratorium provisions, provisions calling for many possible rounds of judicial review, and above all "look back" provisions allowing judicial review of agency failure to revise existing rules. A special irony can be found in the combination of proposals for extensive and costly procedural and analytic requirements with proposals for dramatic decreases in appropriations, which would make it far more difficult for agencies to comply with new requirements. The reactionary strand is also ill considered insofar as efforts to slow down or stop regulations will prevent agencies from engaging in many current efforts to ease regulatory burdens through new, more flexible initiatives.

Of course, the technocratic and reactionary strands could make some alliances. Good technocrats believe that overregulation is indeed a problem, and good reactionaries understand that technical tools can limit unjustified regulatory interventions. But the alliance was bound to produce difficulty, since those interested in technical improvements are unlikely to support measures that would drown agencies in paperwork requirements or increase their vulnerability to special interests.

For its part, the opposition to the reform efforts also contained two contrasting approaches. To paint with a broad brush: Moderate forces, enthusiastic about policy analysis, attempted to counter or eliminate the reactionary elements in reform proposals while endorsing the technocratic elements. By contrast, those we might describe as "status quo defenders" treated existing statutes as if they actually made a great deal of sense and were working well; their goal was to protect as much as possible of the existing administrative state. As we shall see, the Clinton Administration mostly belonged in the former camp, at least in its public pronouncements.

The Contract and Two Kinds of Supermandate

The *Contract with America* expressly referred to the issue of government regulation, and it promised prompt action. In an especially good paragraph, one that deserves bipartisan endorsement, the Contract said: "Congress is never forced to ensure that the benefits of regulation, better health and productivity, outweigh the costs, lost jobs, and lower wages. Nor does Congress pursue integrated health and safety goals. Instead, Congress and federal regulators often attack whatever health risk has caught the public's attention, even if its regulatory solution exacerbates other health risks."[18]

The Contract promised several concrete steps, including the following requirements: (a) risk assessment for expensive regulations; (b) a statement of the costs accompanying regulatory initiatives; (c) a comparison of costs and benefits to accompany regulations; (d) an independent peer review panel to certify the risk assessment; and (e) an annual report describing a "regulatory budget," to be followed by a cap below the current level. The cap would be designed to require agencies to find more cost-effective mechanisms and to identify policies whose benefits exceed their costs. Taken together, these steps may or may not qualify as constitutional in character; but they would amount to a large-scale revision of current practice.

We might distinguish at this point between two different possible *supermandates*—requirements that cut across all regulatory statutes and that, in this sense, operate as something like constitutional amendments to existing law. A *substantive supermandate* is a provision that enacts new decisional criteria that agencies must henceforth follow. A general requirement of cost-benefit balancing would fall within this category, especially if cost-benefit balancing is given a degree of specification. So, too, with a general ban on regulation of insignificant risks. A *procedural supermandate* is a provision that requires all agencies to follow new procedures, going beyond the APA and organic statutes. The Contract emphasized procedural supermandates; but its call for cost-benefit comparison moved in the direction of substance.

The Contract was of course the focus of sustained legislative attention, especially in the House. In the Congress as a whole, there was a great deal of debate about the unnecessarily high costs of regulation, the need for better regulatory tools, and the value of balancing rather than absolutism.

Particulars

Unfunded Mandates

The basic goal of the Unfunded Mandates Act is to ban Congress from requiring states to do things for which federal resources have not been appropriated. But the Act also contains several provisions of direct relevance to the subject of regulatory reform. Surprisingly, these "sleeper" provisions received almost no public attention. Moreover, they were not mentioned during the legislative debates over the basic regulatory reform bills—a fact that says a great deal about the possibility of legislative coordination of statutory reforms.

The Unfunded Mandates Act containts two notable provisions. First, significant regulatory actions must be accompanied by a statement that includes "a qualititative and quantitative assessment of the anticipated costs and benefits of the Federal mandate." This statement must also include a statement of future compliance costs; a description of any disproprotionate budgetary effects on particular regions or segments of the private sector; and estimates of the effect of its action "on the national economy, such as the effect on productivity, economic growth, full employment, creation of productive jobs, and international competitiveness of the United States goods and services, if and to the extent that the agency in its sole discretion determines that accurate estimates are reasonably feasible and that such effect is relevant and material."

This provision is largely procedural. It probably will not make much of a difference.

The second noteworthy provision is more important. All agencies must "identify and consider a reasonable number of regulatory alternatives and from those alternatives select the least costly, most cost-effective, or least burdensome alternative that achieves the objectives of the rule." There is an exception if these steps are inconsistent with law or if the agency explains why it has not chosen that least burdensome alternative. This provision could have significant consequences. In many cases, it is questionable whether an agency has chosen the cheapest means of accomplishing regulatory goals. As we have seen, economic incentives may well be able to achieve those goals at much less expense than command-and-control alternatives. It follows that the Unfunded Mandates Act provides the opportunity for a good deal of litigation—about whether existing statutes forbid the approach suggested by the Act—and a good deal of rethinking of existing tools. Agencies may well be required to use economic incentives where they now use technological requirements.

To the extent that the Act encourages agencies to choose cheaper ways of achieving regulatory goals, it is all to the good, and in this way it may be a modest improvement on the current situation. With these two provisions, the Unfunded Mandates Act offers two cautious steps in the direction of general requirements of cost-benefit balancing and the more general regulatory reform measures that were subject to so much debate in Congress.

Moratorium and Legislative Review

H.R. 450 would have imposed a moratorium on all federal regulations. Its key provision created a moratorium period banning federal regulatory rule making (with certain exemptions). The moratorium period was to begin on November 20, 1995, and to end at the earlier of two dates: December 31, 1995; or the day on which a general regulatory reform bill was enacted. On February 24, 1995, H.R. 450 was passed by a vote of 276 to 146.

From the beginning, the prospects for H.R. 450 were poor in the Senate, and for good reason. Though popular in recent years, a general moratorium on federal regulation is a singularly crude, lazy, and largely political response to current problems. Its blunderbuss quality ensures that it will stop measures that are otherwise required by law, or that would do a lot of good, as well as measures that warrant reconsideration (which a moratorium by itself fails to provide). A moratorium fails to make distinctions that public officials ought to make. Thus the moratorium idea never received sustained attention in the Senate.

But on March 30, 1995, the Senate passed what it self-consciously considered an alternative: S. 219, which would require submission of all rules to Congress, with an opportunity for a "veto" of the rule through the normal process of law making. On April 7, President Clinton said that he would veto the House bill but specifically voiced his enthusiastic approval of the Senate bill. On May 17, 1995, the House passed S. 219 by voice vote. But no bill emerged from conference committee or was submitted to the president.

Generic Reform, Supermandates, and APA Amendments: The House

By far the most important, and the most sharply contested, of the regulatory reform proposals involved so-called generic proposals. These proposals would have represented the most important changes to the APA since its enactment in 1946—a modest constitutional moment unto themselves. The principal theme in public debate involved the need for cost-benefit balancing; but procedural supermandates played an enormous role.

The most important generic reform bills in the House contained a wide range of requirements. The principal provisions would have imposed:

1. a requirement of careful risk assessment to accompany regulations;
2. a system of peer review for risk assessments, with a specific provision allowing "peers" with a potential financial stake to participate on peer review panels;

3. a codification of President Reagan's Executive Order on federal regulation, including requirements of cost-effectiveness and least restrictive alternatives;
4. a general requirement of cost-benefit balancing, perhaps amending all statutes that do not require or permit cost-benefit balancing and thus constituting a "supermandate";
5. protection of property rights through a compensation requirement for any government action that reduced the value of property by more than 10 percent; and
6. a regulatory budget.

This was a remarkably ambitious piece of legislation, with many ambiguities and many provisions that warranted and continue to warrant sustained discussion. A general requirement of cost-benefit balancing would amend many substantive statutes; it is in this sense that it would amount to a "supermandate" cutting across multiple federal programs. Certainly, it would be good to have a sense of what these statutes are, and of what the precise consequences of the amendment would be. As we will see, the issue became a central subject of dispute in the Senate.

A compensation requirement for any reduction in property values of 10 percent or more raises even more complex issues. Such a requirement would be unprecedented, and its consequences are far from clear. The major problem with such a requirement is that it may deter valuable projects from going forward. The government does not extract a benefit whenever its regulations cause an increase in property values, and in view of the expense of administering a "10 percent or more" compensation requirement—a requirement that government compensate the relevant losers—might create incentives to fail to introduce desirable regulations. To know whether the compensation requirement makes sense, it is necessary to develop a concrete understanding of its actual effects. To how many regulations would it apply? What effects would it have on the treasury? Would it deter government a good deal, and if it would, would the deterrence be optimal or excessive?

Remarkably, the House held no hearings on these and other questions. And even more remarkably, on February 28—just five days after its reference to committees—a reform bill was passed, by the overwhelming vote of 286 to 141. On April 7, President Clinton said that he would veto the compensation requirement.

Generic Reform and APA Amendments: The Senate

The House bill was never introduced in the Senate. Instead, two principal generic reform bills, overlapping with the House measure, were originally in competition. Senator Roth introduced a comparatively modest bill, S. 291, with two principal sets of provisions. The first would require detailed risk assessment, in ways comparable to the House bill. The second would require agencies to choose economic incentives rather than commands.

The Roth proposal should be compared with the bill that received far more attention and that became the focal point for legislative debate: Senator

Dole's more ambitious and complex proposal, S. 343. In its original form, it included a complex provision making cost-benefit analysis the basis for decision, unless "the text" of another statute "expressly" requires otherwise. The meaning and desirability of this version of the "supermandate" became a key issue in the Senate. Along similar lines, the bill would have precluded agencies from regulating "insignificant" risks (a term that was also undefined). In this way, it would have repealed the well-known and highly controversial Delaney Clause, which forbids the use of carcinogens in food additives. The repeal of the Delaney Clause turned out to be central to the debate over the Dole bill.

The Dole bill would also impose several layers of review, including a process for peer review; here, too, the fact that "peers" had a potential financial interest would not be disqualifying. The Dole bill also contained a system in which people could petition for review of existing rules under the new statutory criteria, and seek judicial review of the denial of any such petition. The Dole bill called for judicial review of both risk-assessment and cost-benefit analysis. It also provided for congressional review of major regulations, in the form of formal submission to the legislature with an opportunity to veto. As we have seen, this provision was also proposed separately.

After complex negotiations within the Senate, a new version of S. 343 emerged, now called the Dole-Johnston bill. In this form, the bill did not expressly amend existing statutes to call for cost-benefit analysis (hence it appeared to delete the so-called supermandate). In a somewhat ambiguous formulation, it proposed certain decisional criteria that would "supplement" and not "supersede" existing legislation. These criteria included requirements that benefits justify costs and that agencies choose least-cost alternatives. The Dole-Johnston version also maintained the provisions requiring agencies to review existing rules and to test them for conformity to the new criteria. To enforce this requirement, it maintained provisions permitting industries to petition for review of existing rules under the new criteria—and included provisions for judicial review of an agency's failure to respond to or to grant a petition for review. Moreover, rules that were not promptly reviewed would expire automatically. Apparently at the behest of lobbyists, a new provision was added to alter the requirements for the Toxic Substances Inventory under the Superfund statute. Under current law, all toxic chemical releases must be disclosed to the public. Under the proposed provision, disclosure would be required only if the EPA found reasonable basis to believe that the toxic release created a risk to human health. This provision turned out to be crucial to Senate debates.

On June 29, Senator Glenn introduced S. 1001, the Democratic alternative. Senator Glenn's bill was endorsed by President Clinton. Senator Glenn self-consciously built on Senator Roth's bill, which had received enthusiastic bipartisan support in the Governmental Affairs Committee. In fact, S. 1001 was different from S. 291 in only a few particulars. Like Senator Roth's bill, S. 1001 was not meant to override the substantive requirements of existing laws; there was no ambiguity on this point. S. 1001 contained far more limited judicial review. It allowed agencies to review existing rules, but it would not call for expiration of those rules that were not reviewed, and it did not provide a petition process for those dissatisfied with existing rules. The Glenn bill would not have required agencies to show that a risk is "significant"; in this way, it would not have repealed the Delaney Clause.

On behalf of his proposal, Senator Glenn emphasized five central points. First, his proposal would contain more limited judicial review of cost-benefit analysis and risk assessment. Second, his proposal would be procedural rather than substantive; it would not affect the Delaney Clause, the Toxic Release Inventory, or the Superfund statute. Third, it would not include a petition process. Fourth, it would include no supermandate and hence would not affect existing statutory requirements. Fifth, it would offer a "sunshine" provision designed to ensure public disclosure of communications between agencies and OMB, and of information relating to the status of regulatory review.

A vigorous debate took place in Congress from June 30 through July 20, 1995. The principal issues were those stressed by Senator Glenn. Particular emphasis was placed on extensive judicial review and the petition process; the supermandate issue; amending the Delaney Clause; and the Toxic Release Inventory. Consider the following much-disputed language from a late draft of the Dole bill:

> (a) The requirements of this section shall supplement, and not supersede, any other decisional criteria otherwise provided by law.
> (b) [N]o final major rule . . . shall be promulgated unless the agency head publishes in the Federal Register a finding that—
> (1) the benefits from the rule justify the costs of the rule;
> (2) the rule employs to the extent practicable flexible reasonable alternatives [that is, economic incentives] . . . ;
> (3) (A) the rule adopts the least cost alternative . . .
> (B) if scientific, technical, or economic uncertainties or nonquantifiable benefits . . .make a more costly alternative . . . appropriate and in the public interest and the agency head provides an explanation of those considerations, the rule adopts the least cost alternative of the reasonable alternatives necessary to take into account such uncertainties or benefits; and
> (4) if a risk assessment is required . . .
> (A) the rule is likely to significantly reduce the human health, safety, and environmental risks to be addressed; or
> (B) if scientific, technical, or economic uncertainties or nonquantiable benefits . . . preclude making the finding of subparagraph (A), promulgating the final rule is nevertheless justified for reasons stated in writing accompanying the rule. . . .

On July 18, the Senate came very close to voting for the Glenn bill, which was defeated by a small margin of 52 to 48. A short time thereafter, the Senate failed to support closure on the Dole bill by a vote of 53 to 47. On July 20, the Dole-Johnston forces fell just two votes short of closure; by a vote of 58 to 40, the Senate failed to close further debate. At this stage the bill was effectively killed, and the prospects for regulatory reform dimmed—despite the fact that a strong majority of the members were in favor of it.

Specific Statutes

Congress also discussed a number of statute-specific proposals. No fewer than twenty-five bills were introduced in an effort to prompt substantive regulatory reform. Among the most prominent of these were proposed amendments to the Endangered Species Act and the Clean Water Act; dramatic revisions were proposed for each. The Clean Water Act amendments were passed in the House by a vote of 240 to 185 on May 16. But the prospects for substantial change were essentially eliminated when President Clinton announced that he would veto the House bill.

Of particular importance was an appropriations bill with no fewer than seventeen provisions designed to limit the power of the EPA. The prospects for these provisions were dim in the Senate. Moreover, it was clear that President Clinton would veto the appropriations bill whether or not it included these provisions. In November 1995, moderate Republicans combined with Democrats to delete the provision from the House bill.

The House of Representatives also inaugurated a new tradition: A "Corrections Day" to be held on the second and fourth Tuesday of each month, in which it would debate bills to repeal or modify regulations from agencies or statutes enacted by Congress. The House adopted the rules for Corrections Day on June 20, 1995, by a vote of 271 to 146. The idea was proposed by Speaker of the House Gingrich.

Evaluation

What are we to make of this complex set of events? It is hard to approve of the performance of the House of Representatives. H.R. 1022 was not a good bill. It contained a number of promising ideas, and in some ways it might well have made things better than they now are. But it was also very much a mess: sloppy, confusing, and filled with provisions that had not been thought through. It was far too rushed and ill considered.

The best that might be said for the House's actions is that prompt passage of H.R. 1022 spurred a debate in the Senate and indeed the nation that was certainly overdue and that might not have otherwise occurred. On this view, H.R. 1022 was not really a proposed law, but instead an action-forcing mechanism designed to prompt a more deliberative effort in the Senate. In fact, this was a general pattern in the 104th Congress. It justifies George Washington's observations about bicameralism, to the effect that the Senate operates like a saucer "cooling" the hot coffee that emerges from the House. Perhaps the goal of the House was to set proposals before the Senate in the hope that seeing the general direction in which the nation should move, the Senate would enact more responsible and careful proposals.

What about the Senate side? A charitable observer could find much ground for enthusiasm. Balancing is better than absolutism, and all of the relevant proposals incorporated an understanding of this fact. Despite its symbolic value, the Delaney Clause is hard to defend; indeed, it is far from clear that the Clause promotes human health, since it prevents very low-risk items from coming on the market.[19] An exemption of de minimis risks would help in the process of good priority-setting. In a number of proposed provisions, Congress showed considerable enthusiasm for market incentives and least-cost solutions. Moreover, the Senate proceeded in a more or less deliberative manner. It held extensive hearings; its members engaged in extensive and sometimes productive debates. Perhaps the 104th Congress can be seen as a transitional one in which a great deal of learning occurred.

But an account of this sort would probably be too enthusiastic. Much of the debate was mired in the question of whether we should have "more" rather than "less" regulation. Most of the debate seemed to be centered on the unhelpful question of whether the Dole bill "went too far" and whether the Glenn bill "did too little." Many of the relevant initiatives were procedural and attempted to discipline the administrative state through paperwork requirements. In the next section, I spell out these criticisms and suggest some possible improvements. But for the moment, a more general conclusion is appropriate. The task of fundamentally reforming the modern regulatory state is complex and unwieldy; the 104th faced (and future Congresses will face) a job far more difficult than anything facing New Deal Congresses—and this notwithstanding the fact that the nation is in far better shape than it was during the Depression. We might even conclude, at least provisionally, that Congress is institutionally ill equipped to attempt major reform of regulation, at least if it does a great deal at the "micro" level. The House was able to act quickly, but only because of the discipline produced by the Contract and Speaker Newt Gingrich, and the resulting product was nothing to celebrate. The Senate was not similarly unified, and the process of deliberation produced nothing at all. I will return to these issues later; for the moment, let us consider how Congress might have done better.

III. Toward New Initiatives

Procedure and Paperwork: Less Is More

Part of Congress's attempt at regulatory reform involved not substantive criteria but paper-producing requirements designed to slow down regulations and to make it harder for agencies to issue them. This strategy is compatible with the "moratorium" idea—not an effort to design good regulations and to prevent bad ones, but instead a blunderbuss strategy whose purpose is to stultify agencies. A particular problem in the relevant bills is the addition of new layers of review—from courts, peers, and Congress itself. In this context, Congress should have followed a strategy of addition by subtraction. Future congresses might build on the current proposals by making them leaner—more in the way of substance, less in the way of paperwork.

Existing Rules and Judicial Review

Much of the debate in the Senate stemmed from the fact that the Dole bill contained complex provisions compelling agencies to undertake reviews of existing rules. These provisions are certainly understandable. They are an effort to ensure that agencies do not maintain rules that cost much and accomplish little or no good. Moreover, regulations can become obsolete, and a mechanism for ensuring periodic review makes good sense.

On balance, however, a mandatory petition process for review of existing rules is not easy to defend. Such a process could increase interest-group power, prevent agencies from devoting their limited resources to the most important matters, increase uncertainty, and allow people in the private sector to divert taxpayer resources for what may well be insufficient gain. Review of existing rules requires substantial resources, and if agencies are required to devote their resources to revisiting current rules, the petition process could create the very kind of rigidity that good regulatory reform is designed to prevent. And in many areas, the petition process is quite unnecessary. Under Presidents Reagan, Bush, and Clinton, many agencies have already done some kind of cost-benefit analysis. For this reason, it is doubtful that the petition process would do much good.

A particular difficulty is raised by the prospect of judicial review. If courts can review denial of petitions to review existing rules, there will be high litigation costs. This is especially true since the petition process would require an agency to decide whether "reasonable questions exist" about the CBA judgment, with judicial review of agency decisions on this point. In many cases, "reasonable questions" do "exist," and hence judicial involvement and management might well be common. If a requirement to review existing rules is to be enacted, it should probably not be judicially enforceable, except in the most extreme cases, and the executive branch should be given the authority to set priorities by reevaluating existing rules in accordance with its own assessment of whether they impose excessive costs. Of course, Congress might well enact new legislation to correct old statutes, or old regulations, that fail cost-benefit analysis.

"Peer Review"

The House and Senate bills show enthusiasm for "peer review." In particular, the Dole bill would require the director of the Office of Science and Technology to develop a "systematic program for the peer review" of risk assessments. This provision moves in a sensible direction: A greater role for the Office of Science and Technology in generating uniform risk assessment guidelines and in ranking risks and establishing priorities for Congress, agencies, and the public.[20] No institution in government is currently charged with this important task.

In its current form, however, a requirement of peer review for risk assessment is premature. Risk assessment is still in developmental stages, and any "systematic program for peer review" could prove enormously expensive. It could also produce unnecessary delay. Of course, no "peers" are entirely objective; judgments about risk necessarily depend on assumptions, and those assumptions will likely be founded on judgments of value. Any "peers" may well have their own agendas, and hence, the process of peer review could aggravate the problems raised by interest-group power over regulation. At this stage, Congress should not mandate peer review, but instead should authorize experimentation with peer review processes and ban those with an actual or potential financial interest from participating on review panels.

Joint Resolution of Disapproval

Both Houses of Congress passed legislation requiring certain regulations to be submitted to Congress for potential veto. Thus, under the Dole bill, major regulations would be submitted to Congress before they could take effect, and Congress could enact a "joint resolution of disapproval" to stop regulations from becoming law. The idea has obvious virtues. It would appear to enhance political accountability insofar as it provides a formal mechanism by which elected representatives may oversee, and eliminate, proposed regulations. It is also possible that the process of congressional review will deter or reduce the number of regulations that are hard to defend in public-interested terms. Perhaps agencies will not submit ill-considered or faction-driven regulations to Congress.

It is unclear, however, how much this provision would add, since Congress can already enact legislation to prevent any and all regulations from becoming law. There are risks as well. A serious problem with congressional review is that it might, in practice, give well-organized interest groups a chance to bring pressure to bear on hundreds or even thousands of regulations. In this way, it might increase rather than decrease the problem of factional influence. Such a provision would also require Congress to spend its limited time in reviewing a wide range of agency rules, many of which should be uncontroversial. The competing considerations do not lead to any obvious conclusion. But it would certainly be plausible to say that this provision should be deleted on the ground that if it is to be written in an acceptable manner, it would not add anything to Congress's existing authority.

Modest Changes

How might the proposals have been improved? I begin with some modest changes, designed to accomplish Congress's apparent goals in a more effective manner.

Valuing Benefits: Some Theoretical Issues

If a substantive supermandate is to operate as a quasi-constitutional amendment to the regulatory state, it makes sense to try to understand what cost-benefit balancing actually entails. Much of the national debate in the last year involved the value of cost-benefit analysis—with proponents seeing CBA as a method for disciplining administrative power by calling for salutary balancing, and adversaries fearing that CBA is a cold-hearted way of sacrificing human health and life for the sake of mere dollars. But this is at best a caricature. By itself, the notion of CBA is very close to empty; everything depends on how costs and benefits are characterized and on how underlying issues of valuation are resolved.

In fact, there are two sorts of criticisms that might be made of a proposed framework (or "supermandate") for evaluating governmental performance.

One sort of criticism is that the framework is wrong—that it ignores certain important variables, or that it is founded on an indefensible theory of value. Another sort of criticism is that it is *incompletely specified*—that its meaning depends on further subsidiary judgments that have yet to be offered. If a framework is incompletely specified, it might be criticized as indeterminate and empty.

CBA is properly subject to the first kind of criticism to the extent that it purports to align values along the single metric of aggregated private willingness to pay, and to evaluate regulation by reference to that criterion. Regulation might well be founded on citizen judgments that have no clear parallel in aggregated willingness to pay. Or it may be rooted in distributive rather than allocative goals; consider the antidiscrimination laws as possible examples. To the extent that CBA is rooted in the technical economists' understanding, it has a great deal to offer, but it cannot capture many appropriate goals of regulation.

As a political creed, however, the principal problem with CBA is that it is incompletely specified. Its meaning depends on how costs and benefits are characterized and on how issues of valuation are resolved. Are equitable concerns a part of CBA? Suppose, for example, that a certain environmental risk is concentrated among African-Americans. Can a good CBA take this into account? Or suppose that some of the benefits of regulation are aesthetic. How will these benefits be valued? Of course, there is an extensive literature on valuation of human life.[21] By itself, CBA does not take a stand on the associated controversies; but regulators asked to operate under CBA must take some such stand.

Cost-Benefit Analysis as a Quasi-Constitutional Amendment   With these points in mind we can ask the general question: Would a general requirement of cost-benefit analysis be a sensible supermandate for the regulatory state? Would such a requirement be a quasi-constitutional amendment, or would it be a modest way of disciplining agency discretion?

The most basic point here is that the modern state includes a diverse array of regulatory statutes, with diverse legitimate purposes, including but not at all limited to economic efficiency. Consider the following:

- Many important regulatory statutes are of course plausibly understood in terms of economic efficiency; they can be seen as efforts to counteract market failures. The Federal Insecticide, Fungicide, and Rodenticide Act and the Toxic Substances Control Act are examples. Such statutes may be designed to overcome an absence of sufficient information on the part of consumers, harms to third parties, or collective action problems of various sorts.
- Some statutes are designed to eliminate illegitimate discrimination or what might be understood as caste-like features in modern society.[22] Though some people think that such statutes can be defended on efficiency grounds, their animating impulse has little to do with economic efficiency.

- Some statutes are designed to protect cultural aspirations. Examples include measures safeguarding pristine areas or the national parks, encouraging high-quality or educational programming, and protecting endangered species.
- Some statutes are designed to redistribute resources to the poor or to others understood as having a good claim to public help. This is a goal of regulation even though regulation is usually a poor tool for this purpose,[23] and even though redistribution may really be benefiting well-organized interest groups with little claim to public assistance. The Social Security Act is an obvious example of redistributive law; the Agricultural Adjustment Act can be understood in this way, with appropriate qualifications for its conspicuous interest-group dimensions.

Doubtless other possibilities could be mentioned.[24] The point is that the highly diverse grounds for federal regulation raise many questions about cost-benefit analysis as a basis for regulation.

If it is intended as a quasi-constitutional amendment to the regulatory state, a cost-benefit supermandate could be understood in many different ways. In its most ambitious form, it would amount to an endorsement of the principle of economic efficiency as the exclusive basis—the "decisional criterion"—for interpretation and application of all statutes. This would be a fundamental change both because it would understand cost-benefit analysis in a particular way—as a shorthand for the criterion of economic efficiency—and because it would amend statutes that, when enacted, seemed motivated by something other than the efficiency criterion.

If this were the understanding of the supermandate, all of the statutes to which the supermandate applies would henceforth be understood in efficiency terms. To say the least, this would be a dramatic shift in national understandings. It would indeed represent a kind of constitutional amendment of the administrative state, rebuilding regulatory efforts on a new foundation. Probably the most ambitious reformers in the Senate and the House came close to this view, though they did not endorse it explicitly.

Another, less ambitious possibility is that the cost-benefit criteria would be understood in efficiency terms, but only for those statutes that were designed to promote economic efficiency. Under this approach, the supermandate would not alter the basic understandings that underlie existing statutes. It would instead have a more modest but nonetheless important goal: imposing a particular understanding of technocratic rationality on statutes formerly understood and implemented in a less precise, more ad hoc, and more intuitive way. As we will see, there is much to be said in favor of this basic approach, though it should be qualified with a recognition that even for "market failure" statutes, goals other than those rooted in economic efficiency may legitimately bear on the decision.

A third and least ambitious possibility is that cost-benefit criteria would be understood in a less technical and more common-sensical way, as an invitation to balance a range of variables under statutes that had formerly been thought to be absolutist and hence to forbid balancing. On this view, a super-mandate would not be so ambitious as to call for use of purely economic criteria. Its more modest goal would be to ask administrators to look at costs, or adverse effects, as well as at benefits. This was probably the goal of the majority of those members of Congress who were in favor of a substantive super-mandate. And if the supermandate is understood in these terms, it makes a great deal of sense. As we will see, the principal objection to such a superman-date is that it is too open ended; Congress can and should take steps to make it clearer, though—I emphasize—without mandating the efficiency criterion outside of the context of "market failure" statutes.

Theory and Practice

In the House and Senate bills, almost no guidance was offered for characterizing costs and benefits, and no guidance at all was offered on the crucial issue of how to value costs and benefits. For this reason, the provisions look highly substantive but are in fact largely procedural. Without guidance to constrain valuation, a requirement of CBA is quite open ended. It is certainly not meaningless, since it sends agencies a signal about the need for balancing a range of considerations, and any such procedural requirement will affect outcomes. Moreover, courts may invalidate outcomes that, by general understandings, seem out of line with existing practice or too absolutist.[25] Certainly, there is a difference between agency behavior under balancing statutes, and agency behavior under statutes that forbid balancing.

It would be possible to conclude that Congress should restrict itself to a call for CBA and leave the details to agencies. Perhaps Congress lacks the detailed understanding that would enable it to answer the more specific questions. But those concerned about administrative discretion would urge some greater guidance from the national legislature. In any case, the generic bills would be much improved if they offered more direction. I offer two suggestions here.

Qualitative Factors As we saw in section I: People care not simply about aggregate amount of lives lived, but also about a range of factors involving the nature of the particular risk. For most people, among the most salient contextual features are (1) the catastrophic nature of the risk; (2) whether the risk is uncontrollable; (3) whether the risk involves irretrievable or permanent losses; (4) whether the risk is voluntarily incurred; (5) how equitably distributed the danger is or how concentrated on identifiable, innocent, or traditionally disadvantaged victims; (6) how well understood the risk in question is; (7) whether the risk would be faced by future generations; and (8) how familiar the risk is.

Any required CBA for diverse regulatory agencies should reflect these points. Certainly it should recognize the limits of understanding everything in quantitative or monetary terms. Any CBA should, moreover, be accompanied by a more disaggregated and more qualitative description of the consequences of government action, so that Congress and the public can obtain a fuller picture than the crude and misleadingly precise "bottom line" of the CBA. This is not at all to deny that it is important to be precise and quantitative when agencies can be precise and quantitative. It is only to say that any bottom line about how to characterize and assess costs and benefits will involve judgments about values, not about science, and Congress and the public should see what those judgments are.

I have suggested that regulatory statutes have legitimate and diverse functions, and that some of those functions do not involve economic efficiency. It is therefore best for Congress to understand costs and benefits in economic terms only for statutes that are designed to overcome market failures. And even here, there is room for qualifying the economic analysis—when, for example, the risk at issue is inequitably distributed, and when political actors believe that it deserves special attention for that reason. When the statute does not involve market failure, Congress should still require cost-benefit balancing as the general background rule; but it should understand the definition of costs and benefits to be sufficiently wide open as to allow administrators to depart from purely economic criteria. Judicial review should be available to police administrative decisions for reasonableness and consistency. In the long run, it might be hoped, a common law of regulatory practice might emerge to create rationality and reasonableness where there is now a high degree of arbitrariness.

The issues I have discussed—the diverse grounds for regulatory statutes, problems of incommensurability, qualitative distinctions—are probably too subtle and complex to justify anything like legislative codification. Instead, they suggest that Congress should (1) enact a general background requirement of cost-benefit balancing, with a relatively open-ended understanding of both costs and benefits; (2) permit agencies to understand cost-benefit analysis in the way that best fits with the particular statutory scheme; (3) impose a cost-effectiveness or "least cost" requirement as part of the supermandate; and (4) require more technical cost-benefit balancing on a statute-by-statute basis, when there is a considered legislative judgment that the statute is a response to a market failure, economically defined. Congress should, however, attempt to impose some constraints on agency valuations and tools, as I now discuss.

Floors and Ceilings   It is of course troublesome to assign dollar values for life, partly for the reasons I have sketched; but since trade-offs of multiple kinds are inevitable, it may be best for Congress to set out some guidelines—floors and ceilings governing expenditures—without pretending to say how much a life is "really worth." In light of the diversity of regulated risks, no single number would make sense for valuing life. It may well make sense to set *benchmark standards* of, say, $10 million per life saved as the maximum amount and $3 million as the minimum. These benchmarks might be accompanied by explicit permission for agencies to select a lower or higher number, if the agency can explain that special circumstances call for that higher number.

There is crudeness, however, in the very notion of "dollars per life saved." A well-functioning regulatory state is not interested in how many lives are saved, but in how many statistical years, or how many decently liveable statistical years, are added by regulation.[26] An agency would do better to save forty statistical years than it would to save three, even though, through both steps, it might be taken to have "saved a life." Where resources are limited, it makes sense to devote resources to saving people who have the most good years ahead. This judgment may appear controversial, but it is supported by economic criteria, and it seems to receive widespread social support and thus to be democratically vindicated. Congress should probably set floors and ceilings not for lives saved but for life-years saved, with permission to depart on the basis of justifications that are articulated publicly and reasonable on the merits. For life-years, a presumptive ceiling of $500,000 might be a reasonable place to start. Of course, any floors and ceilings should be accompanied with adjustments for inflation.

There are problems with approaches of this kind. Certainly Congress is not likely to want to subject itself to the political risks associated with identifying a dollar figure, and any such number will have a degree of arbitrariness. But without a figure per life or life-year saved, agencies effectively have discretion to weight costs and benefits however they wish; this is a good reason for Congress to offer some guidelines. At a minimum, Congress should require agencies to be explicit about their valuations, so that what they do will be subject to legislative and public oversight and review.

Substitute Risks

We have seen that there is a pervasive problem in risk regulation, one that is only now receiving public attention, and one that was not squarely addressed in the proposals before the 104th Congress. The problem occurs *when the diminution of one risk simultaneously increases another risk*. As I have noted, no provision in the current proposals deals squarely and directly with this problem. It would be good for Congress to consider a new provision to this effect:

(1) Agencies shall ensure, to the extent feasible, that regulations do not create countervailing risks that are greater than those of regulated risks.

(2) This section shall not apply if it is inconsistent with the provisions of the enabling statute pursuant to which the agency is acting.

Ambitious Thinking

Thus far, I have offered some modest suggestions. Three more ambitious strategies would accomplish a great deal more.

1. *Rank risks and reallocate resources to more severe problems.* As Justice Breyer has suggested, a statute might well give the president some degree of authority to divert public and private resources from small environmental problems to large ones, so as to ensure greater cost-effectiveness in government and better priority-setting.[27] There are some dangers with this proposal; a small group of bureaucrats should not have the authority to decide on basic social priorities. But a greater degree of presidential priority-setting setting would make sense. Justice Breyer's approach should be qualified by keeping in mind the fact that people are legitimately concerned with the various con-

textual factors discussed earlier—the voluntariness of the risk, its potentially catastrophic character, whether it is especially dreaded, whether it is equitably distributed, and so forth (chapter 5).

2. *Allow plans from private sector that show greater (but cheaper) reductions.* Often the problem with federal regulation is that the government lacks knowledge of the least expensive means of producing the preferred regulatory end. If the private sector were permitted to select the means, it could do so far more cheaply. This point has been recognized in Europe and Japan, under the general rubric of "environmental contracting."[28] In the Netherlands, for example, government has experimented with comprehensive, multimedia environmental targets for pollution reduction, accompanied by agreements from industry groups to achieve overall targets. In return for these agreements, government agrees to eliminate otherwise applicable pollutant-by-pollutant regulations, and to reduce any changes in requirements during the length of the contract period.

In the United States, the EPA has taken modest steps in the same direction. Thus, EPA and Amoco concluded that a plantwide approach would do better in decreasing chemical releases than does the existing command-and-control system. Under the 1990 Clean Air Act, companies can, in essence, "contract out" of technology-based controls for five years, if they achieve a 90 percent reduction in toxic pollutants before EPA promulgates relevant regulations. Under most federal statutes, however, EPA cannot approve private plans as substitutes for public mandates, even if the plans promise better results for less money. Congress should move in the direction of allowing private substitutes, so long as government monitoring is maintained.

3. *Regulate with incentives.* We have seen that command-and-control regulation can waste enormous sums of money. Some statutes forbid agencies from choosing incentive-based strategies, even if agencies know that such strategies would work better. Congress might enact a particular provision to solve this problem. It might say, for example, "Notwithstanding any other provision of law, an agency shall be permitted to regulate with economic incentives, if it can show that these methods will produce the same benefits in a more cost-effective manner."[29] Of course, such a provision would involve risks. It could create further litigation, perhaps initiated by self-interested private groups seeking to stall desirable regulation. It could allow agencies unenthustiastic about regulatory mandates to proceed with less effective means of achieving compliance. But the problems with existing processes—excessive costs, insufficient regulatory benefits—are enough to make it worthwhile to move in this direction.

IV. Possible Futures

In the area of regulatory reform, and particularly in the context of health, safety, and the environment, a number of creative ideas are percolating throughout the nation. These ideas have already had effects on legislation; they will have increasingly significant consequences in the coming years. In this section, I organize those ideas into four general frameworks and make some brief comments on each of them. Table 14.1 is a summary.

Table 14.1. Five Approaches to Regulatory Reform

	1970s Environmentalism	Cost-Benefit Analysis	Pollution Prevention	Free Market Environmentalism	Democratic Environmentalism
Perceived Problems	excessive pollution; power of industry	refusal to balance; absolutism	technological fixes; end of the pipe controls; power of industry	absence of well-defined property rights; environmentalism as a form of socialism; factionalism	command-and-control; poor priority-setting; absence of public deliberation; interest group power
Approved Measures	national ambient air quality standards; technological requirements	Toxic Substances Control Act; FIFRA	elimination of lead (CAA); asbestos rule (TSCA)	common law; the takings approach to environmental regulation; cf. wetlands protection and endangered species act reform	Emergency Planning and Consumer Right to Know Act; National Environmental Policy Act; acid deposition provisions of CBA
Disapproved Measures	common law	Delaney Clause; national ambient air quality standards; technology-based regulation	tinkering with current cars; technological fixes for water pollution	Clean Air Act, especially unholy coalitions	best available technology in CAA and CWA; Superfund; common law
Preferred Solutions	command-and-control; best available technology; technology forcing	balancing requirements	solar energy; electric cars; clean fuels; eliminating "root cause"	create property rights; watch the market work	economic incentives in the form of "polluters pay" and emissions trading
Attitude Toward CBA	hostility	of course favorable	suspicion, since CBA need not produce pollution prevention	better than status quo, but worse than real markets; threatens to be government dictation of outcomes based on inadequate information	potentially favorable, but emphasizes that analysis should be based on judgments not just aggregated willingness to pay; points to differences between lay and expert judgments
Attitude Toward Economic Incentives	hostility	favorable insofar as they minimize costs	suspicion	favorable, but many questions, since there is a large government role in setting prices and/or quantities; understands "economic" incentives as creation of real markets	favorable insofar as they limit factional power, focus democracy on right questions, and put a premium on acquiring information

Table 14.1.   Five Approaches to Regulatory Reform (continued)

	1970s Environ-mentalism	Cost-Benefit Analysis	Pollution Prevention	Free Market Environmentalism	Democratic Environmentalism
Normative Ideal	strict enforcement of statutory mandates	good balancing of relevant variables; maximizing social welfare	clean pollution-free technologies, with "deep" ecology and spiritual values as possible animating ideals; nature as a source of value	consumer sovereignty, based on maximizing welfare through aggregating private preferences for environmental and other goods	well-informed public judgments based on people's ideals and convictions

Cost-Benefit Balancing

One possibility, captured in many of the current proposals, is to shift in the direction of cost-benefit balancing for all statutes. Thus, the various statutes that are defined in terms of health or technology might be amended to allow for CBA. As we have seen, this shift—in the direction of a cost-benefit state—may well make things better. A number of statutes forbid balancing and call for absolutism, and such approaches are not easy to justify. Moreover, it is important to offer some criteria by which to monitor regulatory performance, and CBA is probably the best available technique for embarking on a form of "national performance review" in the regulatory context.

By itself, however, a shift in the direction of CBA would be only a modest improvement over the status quo. We have seen that as an abstraction, CBA lacks a theory of value. If this defect is remedied in the economist's fashion, and if CBA is rooted in the economic criterion of private willingness to pay, it becomes quite controversial and indeed hard to defend as a global approach. Environmental amenities are not best valued by aggregating private willingness to pay.

Apart from the question of valuation, engrafting a cost-benefit requirement onto current law is only a modest shift, and it represents no sufficient fundamental change from the system of command-and-control regulation. If agencies are supposed to undertake the required inquiries on their own, such a system will impose large informational burdens on government, which is by hypothesis required to calculate both costs and benefits. A requirement of CBA allows legislators to take credit for "getting the regulators under control" without forcing them to make hard choices, which are left to agencies and the president. This credit-claiming device can hardly substitute for reinvented government.

Imagine—to take a rough analogy—if the Soviet Union had decided (in, say, 1986) to replace an "absolutist" five-year plan for producing wheat with another five-year plan, one that better recognized the need for balancing competing variables. This step might well have been an improvement; but a five-year plan based on governmental balancing is no less a five-year plan than one based on governmental absolutism. Governmental dictation of outcomes based on CBA is better than governmental dictation based on absolutism, but neither is ideal. A system in which agencies decide what is to be done, after considering all costs and benefits, is likely to be time consuming and will inevitably produce large-scale errors. Such a system imposes enormous data collection requirements on agencies and also forces them to make difficult, and hardly scientific, judgments about basic values. This approach may well be attractive to members of Congress seeking reelection, but it is not a great deal better than the status quo.

In fact, it would be easy to imagine a generation of dreary cycles with respect to regulatory reform. In those cycles, conservatives might require more balancing, more procedures, and fewer deadlines for administrators; liberals might then argue against CBA and for health-based or technology-based standards, fewer procedures, citizen suits for regulatory beneficiaries, and stricter deadlines; a few years later, conservatives seek greater procedural requirements and more attention to costs; liberals respond with their familiar litany; and so on until, say, 2050.

This kind of scenario is not a bad description of regulatory debates since 1980. But its continuation would represent an enormous failure of imagination and creativity. It would fix American policy in outmoded debates of the early 1970s, before the outpouring of learning that makes the "more" or "less" debate seem so unhelpful. A cost-benefit state ought not to content itself with governmental specification of outcomes after governmental cost-benefit judgments. It ought instead to create incentives for nongovernmental actors to generate information and to produce outcomes on the basis of incentives produced by democratic judgments.

Pollution Prevention

In the last decade, many people have expressed enthusiasm for "pollution prevention" as the regulatory strategy of choice.[30] On this view, government should eliminate pollutants from the market rather than require pretreatment or impose technological requirements. Consider, as prominent examples of pollution prevention, the elimination of lead from gasoline; the phaseout of CFCs; government bans on DDT, PCBs, and asbestos; the shift from high-polluting fossil fuels to clean, renewable energy sources; restrictions on mercury pollution in the Greak Lakes and phosphate pollution in local rivers.

Why is pollution prevention so attractive to so many people? Enthusiasts contend that by preventing the production or use of certain pollutants, government can make much more progress than it can by imposing technological controls or fixes. The proper analogy, it is said, is the contrast between prevention and cure. We know that cures tend to be both more expensive and less effective than preventive measures. American government has focused on cures; it should now shift to prevention. On this view, the basic cause of environmental degradation is current technology, above all fossil fuels and current cars; and the capacity of technology to diminish its own environmental damage is rapidly becoming exhausted. Instead of imposing decreasingly effective technological fixes, would it not be better to take steps to ensure that environmentally harmful substances are not produced at all?

Often the answer is affirmative; often pollution prevention is feasible and appropriate. But as a global approach, pollution prevention is inadequate. In some cases, pollution prevention would impose extremely high costs—sometimes including environmental costs—for little in the way of environmental or other gain. Recall here the fact that a court of appeals invalidated one of the most ambitious of recent pollution prevention strategies—the ban on the manufacture and use of asbestos—on the grounds that (a) the benefits of the ban could not, in many sectors, be shown to justify the costs and (b) the ban on asbestos could itself produce a variety of environmental and health-related problems, stemming from the use of environmentally inferior substitutes.[31]

The example can be duplicated in many other contexts. Indeed, the goal of pollution prevention, if taken literally, would be a social disaster. For example, an immediate and wholesale shift to electric cars might appear to be the best way to prevent air pollution from motor vehicles. But electric cars are now extremely expensive, and the costs, for workers and consumers, of a ban on contemporary automobiles would plainly be excessive. In fact, electric cars produce environmental harms of their own—a potential problem for many pollution prevention strategies.

In these circumstances, pollution prevention is sometimes worse than CBA or economic incentives. By imposing a cost on polluting activity, incentives can identify the circumstances in which prevention or instead cure makes best sense. A fee imposed on the production of sulfur dioxide may lead some companies to eliminate sulfur dioxide; in any case, the judgment would be left to (appropriately constrained) market forces. Moreover, cost-benefit analysis may show that pollution prevention is not worthwhile. The appropriate conclusion is that pollution prevention is often a good regulatory strategy, but that it cannot be adopted in all or even most contexts. Whether it is best depends on the pollutant in question, the available substitutes, and the actual effects of the preventive approach.

Free Market Environmentalism

A great deal of creative thought has been put into using "free markets" as a mechanism for promoting environmental and other goals. On this view, the problem of environmental degradation stems from a simple fact: the absence of secure property rights.[32] The environmental problem results from the fact that environmental amenities are unowned. If property rights could be allocated and made secure, environmental problems would be far less severe.

There is much truth to this suggestion, and there is considerable promise to the resulting proposals. If environmental assets can be owned, so that owners face the full costs of excessive development, it is likely that excessive pollution can be prevented. In many settings, free market environmentalism points in promising directions. Consider, for example, possible amendments to the Endangered Species Act, related to proposals introduced in the 104th Congress. In its current form, the Act creates severe problems for any landowner who discovers that his land contains critical habitat for an endangered or threatened species. The reason is that the discovery will subject the property to a range of limitations. Hence a landowner faces an incentive to lie about the facts or to proceed with development as rapidly as possible for fear of facing constraints under the Endangered Species Act. It would be far better to use market approaches so that landowners are rewarded rather than punished by a discovery that threatened or endangered species need their land.

For two reasons, however, free market environmentalism is an incomplete solution. The first reason is practical. In some contexts, it is difficult or even impossible to assign ownership rights. Consider, for example, the problems posed by acid deposition, the greenhouse effect, and destruction of the ozone layer. Economic incentives, based on a form of market thinking, may be preferable to command and control; but it is not easy to imagine a system in which private ownership rights are fully allocated.

The second reason is more theoretical. Free market environmentalism depends on the view that the market paradigm should be deemed normative for purposes of environmental practice. On this view, the key question is how much people would pay for environmental amenities in their capacity as consumers. The answer to that question is taken to define people's "choices" and "values." Indeed, for free market environmentalists it is hard to imagine how choices and values might otherwise be understood. But it is wrong to take private choices, expressed in the market domain, as definitional of choice. Private willingness to pay in the market domain reflects a particular setting, and it does not reflect acontextual or global choices and valuations. The choices people make are a function of the particular role in which they find themselves. As consumers, people make choices that diverge from the choices they make as citizens. The appropriate kind and degree of environmental protection raises issues to be discussed by citizens offering reasons for one or another view. This democratic conception of environmental protection competes with the market-oriented view. Of course, a democratic approach to environmental law will use market incentives in many contexts, partly because of the advantages of market incentives on simple democratic grounds.

Private willingness to pay is undergirded by social norms and existing habits, and these might well be changed; indeed, in the environmental context they had better be. Consider, for example, the issues posed by littering and recycling (chapter 2). Social norms with respect to these issues have shifted dramatically in the last generation. Thus, the act of recycling is in many communities taken for granted, whereas a decade ago, that same act would have been perceived as odd or fanatical. Or consider the issue of smoking. A principal issue here is whether smoking is promoted or undermined by social norms. Large reductions in smoking among African-American teenagers appear to have been brought about by changes in norms. A prime purpose of environmental law is to shift norms and habits, and free market environmentalism puts this issue off the agenda. This is its central weakness.

Democratic Environmentalism

A final approach attempts to found regulatory law on people's reflective judgments, as citizens, about their basic goals. On this view, the most significant problems in the current system consist of interest-group power, myopic responses to sensationalistic anecdotes, and inadequate information. A market-oriented understanding of the regulation is inadequate because it makes no space for public deliberation. A purely technocratic conception is inadequate because it devalues the need to rely on people's reflective judgments. It would do this partly because it would fail to reflect the various qualitative factors discussed earlier—whether a risk is voluntarily incurred, equitably distributed, potentially catastrophic, especially dreaded, and so forth. There is nothing irrational about emphasizing those factors. And as we have seen, there is a difference between the judgments people make as citizens and those they make as consumers; in principle, the former are the relevant judgments with respect to public policy.

A good model here is the Emergency Planning and Community Involvement Right to Know Act, which requires the creation and publication of a list of release levels for each of more than 300 toxic chemicals that exceed threshold quantities. Hence there is, for the first time, annual reporting of toxic chemical releases. The result is a Toxic Release Inventory, in which EPA summarizes the relevant information. By itself, the publicity had two desirable consequences. First, many states and localities had information with which to decide whether to act at the governmental level. The result of the Toxic Release Inventory was to spur decentralized political action. Second, many companies pledged to make voluntary reductions. Thus, the Monsanto Corporation pledged a 90 percent cut within four years; AT&T established a goal of eliminating all toxic air emissions by the turn of the century; many companies have produced new waste reduction initiatives.[33]

For democratic environmentalists, much of the promise of economic incentives lies in the fact that they promise to reduce interest-group power, by removing attention from the question of means, which is so clearly a recipe for interest-group struggle. Economic incentives also have the advantage of focusing democratic attention on the right question. Hence the acid deposition provisions of the 1990 Clean Air Act are a model for the future, insofar as they reflect a democratic judgment about outcomes. The much-criticized (and internationally much-imitated) National Environmental Policy Act is also a model from the democratic point of view, insofar as it requires disclosure of environmental conseqences before government acts, and in that sense spurs political (but not judicial) safeguards.

Of course these are stylized discussions of abstractions that must be brought to bear on complex policy initiatives. It is best to approach particular problems in a pragmatic and experimental manner. All four approaches have something to offer, and they might be combined in many different ways. In some cases involving dangerous substances with good substitutes, the argument for pollution prevention is overwhelming. Where private ownership is possible, free market environmentalism may well be preferable to the alternatives notwithstanding the theoretical objections just offered. In some areas, cost-benefit balancing at the government level is unavoidable. We may believe that for reasons associated with democratic environmentalism, a strong commitment to the protection of endangered species makes a good deal of sense. But even if this is so, it may be best to use market-like instruments to accomplish democratic goals, as through, for example, "habitat credits" that reward rather than punish landowners for finding that their land is important for the continued existence of an endangered species.

Some of the most inventive and promising modern initiatives are rooted in democratic judgments but attempt at the same time to harness private initiative and market forces in the interest of those very judgments. In this way it may be possible to provide space for both free market and democratic environmentalism, nominally opposed foundations that could result in creative accommodations. These are directions in which the most productive reforms might lead. They would produce a kind of cost-benefit state, but one that is neither purely technocratic nor founded on the willingness to pay criterion. In such a state, regulatory outcomes are founded on judgments of value that are reflective, defended with reasons, and developed democratically. An approach of this kind would synthesize emerging enthusiasm for technocratic tools with the basic American commitment to deliberative democracy.

Conclusion: Of Supermandates and Democratic Values

The election of the 104th Congress, together with the *Contract with America*, made it very clear that the United States may be in the midst of a constitutional moment. At the very least, it can be said that in the period between 1990 and 1995, political movements have raised more fundamental questions about the national government than at any time since the New Deal. But the public has not authoritatively committed itself to such fundamental change, and hence the constitutional moment may fail.

Whether or not the last decade of the twentieth century qualifies as part of a constitutional moment, the nation is embarking increasingly on the project of assessing governmental performance by asking whether the benefits justify the costs. The regulatory state is becoming something like a cost-benefit state; this is an unmistakable feature of public life in many institutions of American government. In light of the chaotic and uncoordinated character of modern regulation, this is in many ways a salutary development. But it is only a start, because the abstract ideas of "cost" and "benefit" need above all to be specified by some theory of value. Congress's efforts to come to terms with this problem have been confused and unhelpful.

We might draw a general lesson from this phenomenon. At least since 1980, the executive branch has attempted to embrace a form of cost-benefit analysis for specific purposes—to promote better priority-setting, to move toward market-oriented tools, to exempt insignificant risks, to attend to informed public judgments, to foster voluntary and least-cost compliance, and to focus on ultimate results rather than methods and processes. To be sure, there is much to criticize in the efforts of the executive branch.[34] But all in all, they are quite promising—certainly more so than the various bills that attracted such attention in the 104th Congress.

As we have seen, balancing is far better than absolutism. The point is especially important in light of the fact that with respect to protection of human health, absolutism may actually be counterproductive and hence far from what it seems. But cost-benefit balancing is an abstract idea that needs a great deal of specification, and it is hardly sufficient to engraft a supermandate of "balancing" on top of a structure of command-and-control regulation. Future congressional debate over the regulatory state should not remain frozen in a discussion of whether the regulation imposes excessively high costs (it surely does), and whether more should be done to protect people from a range of harms, including risks to life and health (it surely should).

Because Congress is ill-equipped to redesign the regulatory state, it may be best for Congress to give general signals about what is wrong and to allow the executive branch, within limits, to provide solutions. Statutes that permit or require economic incentives, and that call for suitably constrained balancing, may be the best that Congress can do. But there is a substantive lesson as well. If there is to be an Administrative Substance Act, it should be built on the foundations laid by recent learning about regulatory performance. In the process, it would be possible not only to save billions of dollars unnecessarily wasted on current programs, but also to save many thousands of lives.

A cost-benefit state will have many questions to answer, especially on underlying questions of valuation. I have suggested that a general background requirement of cost-benefit balancing—a substantive supermandate—should be enacted. I have also suggested that this background rule can and should be rejected through clearly expressed legislative judgments in particular statutes, and also that in describing costs and benefits, Congress should allow room for a diverse array of values, and not limit agencies to the criterion of private willingness to pay. Many statutes require or permit agencies to promote goals independent of economic efficiency, and such statutes are entirely legitimate.

An Administrative Substance Act, amending the regulatory state, should include the background requirement I have described and also require agencies to act in a cost-effective fashion. Congress should move as well in the direction of requiring economic criteria where the underlying statute is best understood as remedying a market failure, economically defined. A cost-benefit state, conceived in these terms, could make large improvements without embarking on foundational reform and without answering the hardest questions, by offering initiatives that make sense under any reasonable theory of value.

Notes

1. On the idea of constitutional moments, see Bruce A. Ackerman, *We the People*, vol 1 (Cambridge: Harvard University Press, 1991).

2. See the various "reinventing government" materials, especially Environmental Protection Agency, *Reinventing Environmental Regulation* (March 16, 1995). This report emphasizes greater use of emissions trading, reduced paperwork requirements, multi-

media permitting, lowest-cost approaches, performance-based approaches, and avoidance of maldistributed environmental risks. See also Executive Order 12866, reprinted in 5 U.S.C. note (Supp. 1993); Memorandum of April 24, 1995, by President Clinton to Various Federal Agencies (directing agencies to waive penalties in certain cases and to reduce frequency of required reports); Memorandum of March 4, 1995, by President Clinton for Heads of Departments and Agencies, on "Regulatory Reinvention Initiative" (calling for attention to results rather than red tape and for cutting obsolete regulations); Memorandum of March 23, 1995, by President Clinton for Heads of Executive Departments and Agencies on "Improving Customer Service"; Environmental Protection Agency, *Bridge to a Sustainable Future* (1995); *The New OSHA: Reinventing Worker Safety and Health* (May 16, 1995) (arguing for shift from command and control and better priority-setting). The EPA initiative will simplify reporting burdens; allow grace periods for small business violations; increase the use of emissions trading; consolidate air pollution rules; and create a faster self-certification program for minor changes to pesticides.

3. See Ackerman, *supra* note 1 (discussing New Deal as creation of third American constitutional regime); Cass R. Sunstein, "Constitutionalism After the New Deal," 101 *Harv. L. Rev.* 421 (1987) (discussing substantial effects of New Deal on previous constitutional understandings). I summarize some of the discussion from the latter essay here.

4. I do not intend here to engage the debate over whether the New Deal actually qualifies as a constitutional amendment. In my view, the New Deal should not be so understood. See Cass R. Sunstein, "New Deals," *The New Republic*, Jan 20, 1992, at 32. The idea of a "constitutional moment" should, I think, be seen as a metaphor, connoting large-scale change, rather than as pointing to a technical constitutional amendment. But I do not intend to specify the criteria for deciding whether the nation has experienced a constitutional moment. If the term is seen as a metaphor, rather than a legal term of art, it is sufficient to work from more abstract and intuitive ideas of the sort described in the text.

5. See Cass R. Sunstein, *After the Rights Revolution* (Cambridge: Harvard University Press, 1990).

6. Foundations for these arguments can be found in Richard Epstein, *Takings* (Cambridge: Harvard University Press, 1985); Richard Epstein, *Simple Rules for a Complex World* (Cambridge: Harvard University Press, 1995). See especially the emphasis on property rights and compensation requirements in current bills, discussed below.

7. See Thomas D. Hopkins, "The Costs of Federal Regulation," 2 *J. Reg. & Social Costs* 5, 25 table 2 (1992) (estimate of $400 million).

8. See Paul Portney and Robert Stavins, "Regulatory Review of Environmental Policy," 8 *J. Risk and Uncertainty* 111, 119 n. 1 (1995).

9. Tammy Tengs et al., "Five Hundred Life-Saving Interventions and Their Cost-Effectiveness," 15 *Risk Analysis* 369, 771 table 1 (1995).

10. See March Sadowitz and John Graham, "A Survey of Permitted Residual Cancer Risks," 6 *RISK* 17 (1995).

11. Robert Hahn and John Hester, "Marketable Permits," 16 *Ecol. L. Q.* 361, 374 tbl. 2 (1989).

12. See Thomas H. Tietenberg, *Emissions Trading* (Washington, D.C.: Resources for the Future, 1985).

13. See V. Kerry Smith, William Desvousges, and John Payne, "Do Risk Information Programs Promote Mitigating Behavior," 10 *J. Risk and Uncertainty* 203 (1995);

Wesley Magat, W. Kip Viscusi, and Peter Huber, "Consumer Processing of Hazard Warning Information," 1 *J. Risk and Uncertainty* 201 (1988).

14. See Greenberg et al., "Network Evening News Coverage of Environmental Risk," 9 *Risk Analysis* 119 (1989).

15. See Bruce A. Ackerman and William T. Hassler, *Clean Coal/Dirty Air* (New Haven: Yale University Press, 1981).

16. This account of 104th Congress is based on the following sources: official government documents, including the Congressional Record; newspaper accounts; my own participation as a witness before the Senate Judiciary Committee and the Senate Committee on Environment and Public Works; and informal, off-the-record conversations with people involved in the legislative process. I have provided documentation wherever possible.

17. This is an unmistakable lesson of *Analyzing Superfund* (Richard Revesz and Richard B. Stewart, eds. [Washington, D.C.: Resources for the Future, 1995]).

18. *Contract with America* (New York Times Books, 1995), p. 131.

19. See Richard Merrill, "The FDA's Implementation of the Delaney Clause," 5 *Yale J. on Reg.* 1 (1988).

20. See *Harvard Group on Risk Management Reform, Reform of Risk Regulation* (1995).

21. See, e.g., W. Kip Viscusi, *Fatal Tradeoffs* (Oxford: Oxford University Press, 1992).

22. Consider civil rights laws, laws prohibiting discriminating on the basis of pregnancy, laws protecting the disabled. See Cass R. Sunstein, "The Anticaste Principle," 92 *Mich. L. Rev.* 2410 (1994).

23. See Steven Shavell, "A Note on Efficiency vs. Distributional Equity in Legal Rulemaking," 71 *Am. Econ. Rev.* 414 (1981). Sometimes the expressive function of regulatory statutes is confused with the redistributive function; helpful clarifications emerge from Elizabeth Anderson, *Value in Ethics and Economics* (Cambridge: Harvard University Press, 1993).

24. See Richard Stewart, "Regulation in a Liberal State," 92 *Yale L. J.* 1537 (1983).

25. Corrosion Proof Fittings v. EPA, 947 F.2d 1201 (5th Cir. 1991).

26. See the discussion of quality-adjusted life years in Richard Zeckhauser and Donald Shepard, "Where Now for Saving Lives," 40 *L. & Contemp. Probs.* 5 (1976).

27. This is basically the approach suggested in. Stephen G. Breyer, *Breaking the Vicious Circle* (Cambridge: Harvard University Press, 1993).

28. See Peter Mennell and Richard Stewart, *Environmental Law and Policy* (Boston: Little Brown, 1995). pp. 420–22.

29. Statement of Jonathan Wiener Before the Committee on Governmental Affairs, Federal News Service, Federal Information Systems Corporation, March 8, 1995.

30. See Barry Commoner, *Making Peace With the Planet* (New York: Pantheon, 1990); Commoner, "Failure of the Environmental Effort," 18 *Env. L. Rep.* 10195 (1988).

31. Corrosion Proof Fittings v. EPA, 947 F.2d 1201 (5th Cir. 1991).

32. See Symposium, "Free Market Environmentalism," 15 *Harv. J. of Law and Pub. Policy* 297 (1992).

33. Robert Percival et al., *Environmental Law and Policy* (New York: Foundation Press 1993), pp. 625–26.

34. A good discussion is Thomas McGarity, *Reinventing Rationality* (Oxford: Oxford University Press, 1987).

Afterword

What, then, is the relationship between free markets and social justice? In answering that question, we should recognize that markets, free or otherwise, are not a product of nature. On the contrary, markets are legally constructed instruments, created by human beings hoping to produce a successful system of social ordering. As I have emphasized throughout, there is no opposition between "markets" and "government intervention." Markets are (a particular form of) government intervention. Hence the interactions promoted by markets include coercion as well as voluntary choice. Markets should hardly be identified with freedom. The law of property, for example, coerces people who want access to things that they do not own. And like all instruments, markets should be evaluated by asking whether they promote our social and economic goals.

Often markets do promote the basic goals of a well-functioning social order, and a social order that aspires to be well functioning will not dispense with markets. In the area of free speech, markets are very important, since they facilitate the exchange and the production of information—scientific, political, medical, and much more (chapter 7). In constitutional law generally, property rights and market ordering can diminish unwarranted political interference with the production of social wealth (chapter 8). Environmental protection in the United States has abandoned markets too readily; it should take far more advantage of market thinking than it now does. In the area of risk regulation, economic incentives can promote environmental and safety goals in a cost-effective way. They can do this by channeling private behavior in the right directions (chapters 13 and 14).

For all these reasons, American and indeed Western governments should enlist markets more regularly than they now do. In the aftermath of the New Deal, American government has been much too willing to use rigid, bureaucratized solutions to economic and social problems. It should turn instead to flexible incentives, allowing private adaptation for the sake of public goals. Indeed, this step ranks among the most promising routes for reforms in the twenty-first century. Many creative possibilities can be imagined.

These are important points; but they are not really points about justice. We have seen that markets typically reward people on the basis of factors that are irrelevant from the moral point of view. These morally irrelevant factors include not simply race and gender, which can play a large role in markets, but many other factors that account for market success. Achievements within markets come from the innumerable accidents that allow people to develop the characteristics that markets reward—or that prevent people from developing those characteristics.

These accidents are pervasive. If, for example, you are born to an average family on 57th Street and Dorchester Avenue in Chicago, your life prospects will be very good, and altogether different from what they will be if you are born to most families ten blocks south. If you are born into some families, you will be unlikely to be healthy, strong, well mannered, hard working, or well educated, and these are the characteristics that you may need in order to do well in markets. People from a diverse range of theoretical positions ought to agree that markets will not promote justice unless they are made part of a system that offers minimally decent opportunities to all. In existing societies that use markets, the ideal of equal or even decent opportunities is violated on a daily basis.

Markets are also accompanied by a large network of social norms, and existing norms—involving self-destructive or uncooperative behavior, discrimination, pollution—may produce inefficiency or injustice (chapter 2). Much of our conduct is a product of norms, for which we are not responsible and which we may wish, on reflection, to change. Collective and even governmental action may be necessary to improve norms or generate new ones. Far too little attention has been given to the harmful effects of social norms on individual freedom and well-being. This point bears very much on the role of government. Democratic efforts to promote well-being by improving norms—and changing choices—are fully legitimate. Of course, rights should operate as constraints on this process, and institutions must be developed to reduce the risk of abuse of government power.

As I have emphasized throughout this book, a just society should be closely attentive to the background conditions against which markets proceed. Existing distributions and preferences should not be taken as inevitable or as given. Extreme deprivation is unjust in large part because it denies people the opportunity to form preferences and beliefs that lead to good lives. It is thus important to attend to existing distributions of entitlements—distributions that are a function not of nature but of law—and to the effects of those distributions on the development of people's life prospects and even their desires and beliefs. Many of the chapters in this book challenge market thinking on the ground that it is insufficiently attuned to the harmful effects of unjust background conditions. This is true not only in the context of extreme poverty and deprivation, but also in the area of discrimination on the basis of race and sex (chapter 6), where people's preferences can be formed by background injustice, and even in the area of environmental protection (chapter 10).

To say this is not to say that societies that reject or try to reject markets are just. Usually they are especially unjust, because they use especially unfair mechanisms—various forms of political favoritism—for producing social rewards. But we need not enter into deep philosophical territory in order to recognize that much of the time, markets help or hurt people for reasons that are unfair, in the sense that they are ill connected with any plausible conception of justice.

Identification of injustice does not, of course, lead to any particular set of proposals for change. Disruption of markets may be futile or counterproductive. Markets, rearrangements of markets, and alternatives to markets should be assessed pragmatically and in terms of their actual consequences for those who live with them. We have seen many areas in which the effects of markets are good. We have seen other areas in which government interferences with market ordering, especially through command-and-control regulation, make things worse rather than better. Here there is enormous room for more empirical work and for substantive reforms. It is possible to imagine a wide range of programs that would improve human lives—in part simply by lengthening them—and do so largely through attending to public uses of market incentives. Thus a government attentive to the existence of background injustice should refuse to take existing practices, norms, and distributions as given; but it might well invoke market incentives in the support of social aspirations.

Through this possibility we may begin to see the place of market ordering in a system committed to social justice. Such a system is likely to favor a particular conception of democratic deliberation, one that embodies a belief in political equality and in reason-giving in the public domain. If that system is also committed to social justice, it will see free markets as instrumental goods to be evaluated by their effects. This is hardly a reason to abandon markets. But it is a reason to insist on the priority of democratic goals, including social justice, to market ordering—while enlisting, much of the time, the latter in the service of the former.

Index

MARK JEFFERSON: GEOGRAPHER

BY GEOFFREY J. MARTIN

TO CARL R. ANDERSON

FOREWORD

Mark Jefferson was one of the unusual personalities of American geography. His influence on the development of this professional field in the first half of the present century was critical. Yet it is not easy to fit Jefferson into a category. He was a school-master, devoted to his students and highly effective in stimulating them to their best efforts; but at the same time he was a major contributor of research studies. Between 1909 and 1941 he published 31 professional articles in the *Geographical Review* and its predecessor, the *Bulletin of the American Geographical Society*—more articles than were published by any other geographer in these periodicals during that period. These were the most prestigious of the professional journals, and Jefferson's record is not made up of trivial pieces of writing. Each article was fresh and exciting, filled with new ideas and new ways of looking at old ones.

In his classes at Ypsilanti, Jefferson attracted the bright students, leaving the dull ones to take courses elsewhere. His mathematical precision and his insistence on strict logic transformed geography into an exciting intellectual challenge. The list of outstanding American geographers who were first turned toward a career in geography by Mark Jefferson is amazing.

When I went to the University of Michigan as a new instructor in 1923, Jefferson, in nearby Ypsilanti, was already a legend. He was known to every graduate student as a result of his many important articles. His service as chief cartographer on the American Peace Commission in Paris in 1919 placed him in a select group of leading geographers of that time. The members of the Michigan department—all under 28 years of age—paid Jefferson a visit. He gave us a whole afternoon discussing geography and listening to our still half-formed notions, and the advice he gave us about how to build a new department was invaluable.

Geoffrey Martin has captured the spirit of this remarkable man. He has made skillful use of the many letters and other documents made available to him by the Jefferson family. He has traced the career of one of the most influential of the members of the profession. For any one who would understand the source of many of the currents of geographic thought in America this book is indispensable.

Preston E. James
Syracuse University

PREFACE

Born into a United States torn by civil strife and into a world which had recently witnessed the publication of Darwin's *Origin of Species,* Jefferson lived at a time when the gathering forces of the scientific spirit were being unleashed. The age of the geographer as cosmologist, explorer, traveller was soon to be replaced by a world in which geography was rapidly to win for itself respect as a discipline. In the U.S.A. geography enjoyed the successive traditions of thought merging from Davisian physiography, to military geographic thought predicated by the Second World War. Jefferson lived through all these developments. System builders graced collections of geographic fact with form, others made detailed microcosmic studies of a climate, a region, a country. Jefferson studied what interested him and built with the strength, viability, and largeness of his contribution both spoken and written.

How geography came to arrive at its present position is surely a matter of interest and significance to geographers. The study of the life and works of Mark Jefferson, one of the most scholarly geographers ever to grace the U.S. scene, is an attempt to fill, in part, the void in the literature of geographers' lives and thoughts and contribute to an understanding of the geography of American geographers. The study has been motivated in part by a belief that geographers incur a responsibility to piece together the past and see how a given geography has been produced. The work constitutes an examination of all the archival sources available and relevant to Jefferson, the man and his work. Faults there are many. The work was undertaken with the responsibility in mind not to write up the man so that his life is presented merely as an extension of the idealized moments of his existence, rather has an honest attempt been made to recapture the earth and salt of his life, the very complexion of his human thought. Much of the life of the man has been lost to record. Intellectual honesty necessitates adherence to recorded fact—letters, archives, personal effects, and carefully considered testimony of those who knew him. Strict adherence necessitates omission: honest omission is better than that which a writer in biographical vein thinks may or should have happened.

It has been a pleasure to investigate a vigorous mind, reading, thinking, writing, and talking frankly. No effortless superiority belonged to

Jefferson. He was a quiet achiever rather than a stylish failure. The book constitutes a study of the forces that shaped Jefferson and his thinking—a seeing of the way in which scholarship negotiates life, taking from it what it will, living the rest of time as a necessity, but ever awake to necessity offering chance . . . chance to grow academically, to piece together something new and acquire understanding. The work demonstrates that it is the patient and slow accumulation of a man's work over a lifetime that energizes the discipline with a nonspectacular part of its warp and woof, and that constant teaching over a period of time teaches the teacher and breeds its own essential extension. Some ideas announce their arrival to the academic world with a Caesar-like entry, but others creep in quietly, leaving people largely unaware of their presence until later times. Incidentally revealed is an age when higher education was singularly devoid of procrastination and an academic who derived his vitality and life's sustenance from study. His enjoyment of learning coupled with a sense of what was responsible behaviour led him to a total dedication of self. No promotions were extended to encourage Jefferson to perform well, nor were they needed.

As professor of geography at the Michigan State Normal College (1901-39), he schooled future generations of teachers in the subject matter of geography, influenced geographic thinking by his numerous writings and oral presentations, and helped win respect in the U.S. for his subject as a discipline. As savant he ably represented that which was fine in the U.S. normal school tradition. He was the dedicated scholar and the concerned pedagogue. As scholar he corresponded with an international community, published books and articles noted for their originality of viewpoint, and won corresponding memberships and gold medals from geographical societies. As pedagogue he gave twenty hours weekly to classroom teaching, made his course, "Teachers Geography," an institution, found time to visit Michigan schools and advise on the matter of geography and the curriculum, composed much needed textbooks at a time when the subject was only just beginning to establish itself in the U.S. university, and encouraged numerous students to make of geography a successful life's work. The form and content of the Jefferson legacy is sought in the pages that follow.

The author wishes to express his thanks to all the people and institutions who have made his study a possibility:

To the Jefferson family; to Clara Jefferson, late widow of Mark Jefferson who made available to the author the personal effects and correspondence of Mark Jefferson; to Sally Robinson (née Jefferson) who has extended this privilege without qualification and who has given much of her time to recall; to Phoebe Jefferson who loaned her father's invaluable correspondence of the Paris Peace Conference months; to Barbara Eastman (née Jefferson) who revealed numerous archives and artifacts and corresponded with the author, becoming his most thorough informant; to Geoffrey, Hilary, and Mary Jefferson (now Seaman) who have either spoken with the author or provided archival material.

To the contemporaries of Jefferson who lived with the man in the context of his times and who spoke of him so: Professor Margaret Sill, one-time student of Jefferson, later (1921), faculty colleague of the man until his retirement, and who continues with the geography department of the one-time Michigan State Normal College, has given unremittingly of her time in recollection and recall. Charles C. Colby, also a Jefferson student, has helped in interview and via correspondence. Richard Mahard, another Jefferson student, loaned extensive notes taken from Jefferson's courses in 1935. S. S. Visher has provided information and made numerous valuable suggestions, both in person, and via correspondence. His published obituaries of Mark Jefferson were genesis to this study. Helpful and informative conversations were enjoyed with Raye R. Platt, Gladys Wrigley, Pierre Delvert, and Madame M. Jean-Brunhes Delamarre (Paris). Informative and noteworthy correspondence was enjoyed with Marcel Aurousseau, Charles Seymour, and Griffith Taylor.

To the individuals and institutions who have been of assistance: The American Geographical Society made available its fine archives and resources, otherwise helping with inquiries; Kimball C. Elkins of the Harvard University Library archives; Yale University for access to the Charles Seymour Peace Collection; the National Archives, Washington, D.C., and to senior archivist Herman Friis; the Stratton archives of Wisconsin State University, River Falls, Wisconsin; Robert Bowman who granted the author access to the personal papers of his father at Lincoln, Nebraska; the National Council for Geographic Education who provided some funds for travel in connection with this study. My thanks are due to Sheila Bareham for numerous assistances including the typing of correspondence and manuscript; to Linda Miller (née Berns) for help with archival organization and typing; and to my wife, Norma, who has been living the life of an author's wife!

Finally my thanks are due to the library staff of Eastern Michigan University; to Egbert Isbell, historian and authority on the history of the Michigan State Normal School; to Eugene Elliott (President E.M.U. 1948-1965) who demonstrated faith in the worth of the study; to Carl R. Anderson (historian and Vice-President of Eastern Michigan University), without whose personal encouragement and assistance the completion of the manuscript would not have been possible, this book is dedicated. President Harold E. Sponberg (1965-   ) established the Eastern Michigan University Press in 1967.

The very kind J. K. Wright (Lyme, New Hampshire) lent his exemplary scholarship to a reading of the manuscript during April-May, 1965, gave the author freely of his time in discussing revision, and otherwise made numerous valuable suggestions for manuscript improvement. It is pleasurably appropriate that Preston James (Syracuse University)—personal friend and enthusiast of the work of Mark Jefferson —should write the foreword.

GEOFFREY J. MARTIN
Southern Connecticut State College
New Haven, Connecticut

CONTENTS

MARK JEFFERSON: GEOGRAPHER

Mark Jefferson

CHAPTER ONE

NEW ENGLAND AND SOUTH AMERICA

Daniel Jefferson, born in England 1821, had found early employment in John Chapman's bookstore in London's Strand. Handsome, wealthy, recently graduated from Cambridge, Chapman yet knew nothing of the books. Chapman hired bibliophile Daniel to supply the missing knowledge at a daily wage of four shillings. Above Chapman's bookstore were maintained furnished rooms where literary clients often came to read, among them Miss Evans (George Eliot), Thackeray, Carlyle, Dickens, Field and Emerson. Personal intercourse with a pro-American colleague named Dolf together with continual encouragement from Emerson to visit the States persuaded Daniel Jefferson to leave the shores of a cholera and chartist ravaged Britain, April 7, 1849, on board a frail 700-ton wooden craft.[1] New York was sighted on May 6; on the journey father, mother, and infant had been sick, and father had injured his leg. The child did not recover from the rough crossing and was refused burial in a church cemetery in Baltimore, a town where father had taken the family in search of work. Mother accepted the decision as the will of God. Father, man of letters, was embittered by the incident, which enabled him to tolerate the liberal leaning of his several children as they grew to adulthood. Daniel joined the Company of Wiley and Putnam where he soon distinguished himself by compiling the first edition of *Best Reading of 1856*. Later, he received employment with the Little, Brown & Company in Boston, where his fine critical knowledge of literature was well employed. Daniel Jefferson, too, was a true lover of nature, a good husband and well-meaning father. Mary Jefferson, modest, retiring, and obedient, epitomized mid-nineteenth century New England virtue.

On March 1, 1863 Mark Jefferson became the seventh child born to Daniel and Mary Jefferson at 27 Pine Street, Melrose, Massachusetts. The physical environment embodied much that nature could offer. Nature had been bountiful in her supply of invigorating air, prolific soils, abundant flora and fauna. The Jefferson home graciously distant from the delightfully unkempt roadway, sprawled leisurely to assure the household the scene of much happiness. Elms rose magnificently heavenward, shielding the house in winter from nature's harshness, and affording pleasurable shade during the heat of summer months. This was the scene of Jefferson's birth. In his earliest years Jefferson roamed the nearby woods identifying bird nests, and the more common trees and plants with the aid of Gray's Botany, "playing with too few mates, reading too many good books."

Of the seven children born to Daniel and Mary, it was the seventh, Mark, who displayed noticeable interest in reading. Jefferson's early schooling was derived in a community which insisted on the validity of the Bible's every line, and where by the stuttering will of society, a questioner of the existing order would be regarded as something worse than a liberal or radical. Daniel Jefferson himself was a strong Unitarian and a steady church-goer, a man of God, judging from the eulogies bestowed on him at death in 1896. But there was the inner self of Daniel Jefferson, not held fast in the fetters of a religion that was not open to question, who saw religion as a philosophy, and who bestowed a toleration, generous of its age, upon his children. Mark read and thought freely, was quite influenced by his father. In his early years he acquired the habit of the diarist, writing letters and notes to himself, probably a habit derived from his father. One such letter written by young Mark at the age of 12 years illustrates this habit:[2]

Saturday, September 18th, '75.

I went to school last week and Clarence was discussing with me the fun we should have in Miss Bisbee's school, when Miss Porter called our attention by telling us the seven scholars who had the highest averages would pass up into Mr. Woodman's school, and read the names which were Josie Lovejoy, Emma Atwood, Mark Jefferson, Josie Vinton, Bette Paul, Willie Arthur, Joe Gibbons. In my first two spelling lessons that were recorded I had 100%, in History 100%, in Arithmetic 100%, in Grammar 94%. Mr. Woodman gives us an oral lesson in osteology, and the Physiology and Hygene of the bones. Bones are compounded from mineral and animal substances, the mineral consisting principally of lime and the animal of gristle, this can be proved by burning a bone after which the lime only remains, if the bone be submerged in a weak solution of muriatic acid the gristle alone will remain. The bones in the upper extremities are the collar bone or Clavicle, the shoulder blade or Scapula, the long bone of the arm or Humerous, the two lower bones of the arm Radius and Ulna, the eight small bones in the wrist or Carpus bones, bound together with a band of silvery whiteness called ligaments, the five smaller bones on the back of the hand called Metacarpus bones, the fourteen small bones of the fingers called Philanges. At that point where the bones come in contact with each other they are covered with a thin coating of cartilage which is like India rubber, very yielding, this is a specimen of what he tells us. Last night Mr. Woodman kept us all after school until ten minutes of five o'clock, he tried to get us to recite our grammar but every scholar said, "I don't know", and sat down. I like him pretty well, but he keeps us after school too much.

Mark Jefferson

Soon father's collection of English Classics and the Melrose and Boston Public Libraries virtually came to form Jefferson's environment. Reading voraciously, he soon consumed much of Dickens, Thackeray, Dumas, Scott, Spenser, Jane Austen, the Brontes, Carlyle, Trollope, Emerson, Kipling, Lamb, Kingsley, Chaucer, Longfellow and Shakespeare—Shakespeare especially during college years when Edwin Booth played *Hamlet* in Boston for a week. Jefferson reports attending as near everynight as the 25 cents admission to the gallery allowed. Jefferson also read the boys books by Oliver Optic, Maynard Reid, and R. M. Ballantyne though much preferring Max Muller's *Science of Language,* Ellis' *Early English Pronunciation,* and Kelland and Tait's Quaternions.[3]

Jefferson became a member of the eleven-man class of '84 at Boston University—"a tiny university in a great city." He studied for three years, becoming proficient in Latin, Greek, French, German, Italian, and Spanish. The languages he learned by eye were grammatically correct, extensive of vocabulary, but weak of pronunciation. Jefferson also keenly studied mathematics, astronomy, and philosophy and edited the college "Beacon."[4]

One teacher, Borden P. Bowne, inspired Jefferson. Bowne wrote his own books and insisted his philosophy derived from Lotze. "He was an excellent teacher," reports Jefferson, "a kind and a learned gentleman who humbled me profoundly but not publicly. 1 was eagerly sought by my classmates when they needed help but I was not popular. My self appreciation was too evident."[5]

Into Jefferson's astronomy class one day in November 1883 came Dr. Benjamin Gould, Director and astronomer from the National Observatory of the Argentine Republic at Cordoba. He was seeking an assistant. Jefferson wanted to see the world he had read so much about, to hear languages actually spoken, to be an astronomer, and to wear a black skullcap like Ormsby MacKnight Mitchell in the frontispiece of "the Boy Astronomer." The pay was thrice the amount of a regular schoolteacher's salary. Jefferson had become intensely fond of Theodora Bohnstedt, class of '86, but found Theodora's mother did not approve of him.[6] This was Jefferson's first love, and the manner of his rejection undoubtedly encouraged his departure.

Jefferson accepted the position. He had experienced all the mathematics Boston University could offer, two years of Spanish by eye, and a class in astronomy based on Newcomb and Holden's book *Astronomy*. Jefferson had his sister, Ida, make him the skull cap at once.

The class of '84 was sorry to see Jefferson depart. They expressed their appreciation of his scholarly endeavors in the following letter:[7]

> *The class of '84, realizing the great loss they are to sustain in the breaking of the relations they have held with you for the past three years, take this opportunity of expressing their regrets.*
>
> *We cannot rate too highly your superior scholarship and intellectual ability which should make you a strong power for good, whatever your associations. While we feel that for us the vacant place can never be filled, yet we would forget our own loss in wishing you the best of success in your new field of labor, and assure you that there is left here in College a class who will always be pleased to hear of the future fate of one who has been so honored a member of '84.*
>
>

Yours with best wishes,
Carrie Stone
E. Dawe
O. Powers
For the class.
>

In that same November, 1883, Jefferson sailed for Cordoba on the 3,000 ton *Dolphin,* built by John Roach for Presidential dispatch and rejected for failing to meet naval speed tests. Roach had re-christened her Finance, and with two sisterships, the *Advance* and *Reliance,* tried to operate a mail line to Brazil, the customary route being via Europe. The line later failed. The thirty-day journey to Rio delighted Jefferson, who, away from Boston and Melrose for the first time, experienced the wonderful colors of the trade wind oceans under bright blue skies, the balmy sub-tropical clime, "a more delicious climate than I ever knew before,"[8] a comfortable boat, an invigorating sea air and flying fish— "the silvery flying fish as they leaped forth and spun glittering away over the wave tops, till you could no longer follow them . . .."[9] Jefferson later wrote in the *Journal of Geography:*[10]

Flying fish have always interested me very much. I have known them since an early voyage to Brazil on the Finance in 1883. I remember how we used to dispute about their manner of flight, whether they soared on rigid wings, airplane like, or flew with fins flapping. The "Finance" was not one of the big steamers of those days . . . At her fo'c'sle head, where I loved to perch to watch the flyers, one was not more than fifteen feet above the water, and the fish came up, as they will in the West Indies and tropical Atlantic waters, in schools.

A one day stop at St. Thomas in the Caribbean allowed Jefferson to indulge in a guided tour of the town and harbor by one, "Champagne Charley," and to throw silver coins into the translucent waters, which West Indian boys would retrieve instantly. He was quite shocked at the poverty of these same inhabitants . . . "while the gorgeous rags and turbans of these creatures were not without an element of the picturesque, I never saw anything like the wretchedness and degradation of their condition."[11] Jefferson heard Spanish and Portuguese come to life on each of the one-day stops at Para, Ceara, Pernambuco, and Bahia. And as the little boat swept smoothly south, with sails spread, Jefferson studied mathematics in the morning, Spanish in the afternoon, and beheld the glories of the sunset at eventide. He was aware that the brilliant sunsets were no ordinary occurrence; their particular beauty was attributable to the explosion of Krakatoa on August 27, that same year, which cast dust into the upper atmosphere, creating bright red sunsets even in Europe.

One morning Jefferson awakened to see the looming of the magnificent peaks at Rio's entrance from out of the morning fog. "Rio is grand . . . the scenery is the most splendid that could possibly be imagined, a grand array of bare rock mountains shooting up almost into needle points and clothed at their feet with luxuriant vegetation."[12] In Rio the captain of the *Advance,* sistership to the *Finance,* invited him to dinner after his long voyage and introduced him to black Brazilian coffee. Jefferson consumed it for the rest of his life, though he would mask non-Brazilian coffee in later years by the addition of cream, when Brazilian coffee was not available. The next three days Jefferson spent close to the bay on Mount Tijuca, to escape the yellow fever always prevalent in the city, a vexatious wait for a young man in a hurry, but Jefferson notes in his diary.[13]

Tijuca, high up in a pass between the summits, two hours ride from the city. A clear bracing air, fine mountain scenery, and the rich vegetation of the tropics—all contribute to make Tijuca one of those places where you feel it a positive luxury to be alive.

Five days travel south on a German boat, brought the *Petropolis,* "with its barbarous German cooking . . to anchor in the roads, some ten miles from Buenos Aires on the opposite shore of the La Plata, in another nasty muddy sea, perfectly yellow, like the Amazon."[14] Here in distant sight of Buenos Aires, a three day quarantine period was observed at which time Jefferson insists, "We could do nothing but fish for river monsters."[15] As the *Petropolis* could not pull closer than a league to shore in these shallow waters, row boats and horse drawn carts were employed to carry ashore the passengers. On landing Jefferson at once made his way to the Hotel Provence where Mr. W. G. Davis of the Observatory arranged for the both of them to leave Buenos Aires by train of the next afternoon, January 5th.[16]

> *At seven o'clock we took the river boat at Campana for Rosario, where we arrived Sunday morning. . . . At four o'clock in the afternoon we took the train for Cordoba. After a long ride over immense unbroken plains, on a line so straight that it falls away below the horizon without a change of direction, we arrived at Villa Morea at about midnight, and taking with us from here Mr. Stevens the lively man at the Observatory, came into Cordoba at six o'clock in the morning, January 7th.*

The house, which was to be Jefferson's home for the next three years, boasted eight rooms, a patio itself "a compromise between North and South American styles of building with its little open court, high wall and heavy doors around," and a broad verandah to the front of the house overlooking two benches, "the meeting place of the assistants after meals," and a hallway that accommodated a half-barrel size water jar "constructed of porous clay so that the water oozing through is always evaporating and keeping the water cool."[17] Immediately to the rear of the house two dogs, India and Rover, mutually coexisted with a domesticated ostrich. Soon India gave birth to puppies which Observatory personnel promptly named Alpha, Beta, Gamma, Delta, and Epsilon Leonis. The constellation Leo was on the meridian when they were born. In this one storey house that lay within Observatory grounds, Jefferson was given a large, airy, and handsomely appointed room, the whole facing the Cordilleras to the West, and to the East, an immense Pampa, hundreds of leagues in extent, "so level that our horizon is as even as that seen at sea."[18]

Jefferson was entranced with the immediate prospects of life at the Observatory:[19]

> *Everyone is interested in the work of the Observatory and requires no orders, but they all arrange among themselves; we live in splendid style, get up when we wake, work in our own rooms and whenever we please; except that my meteorological instruments must be read at*

fixed times, four in the afternoon and eleven at night, rain or shine. Also the comet observing wherein I am recording and counting seconds for Mr. Davis demands punctuality . . .[20] *My pleasantest times are the Wednesday and Saturday nights with Davis in the circle room.*

The next three years Jefferson worked at the Argentine National Observatory at Cordoba in the capacity of assistant, later third and then second astronomer. As assistant at the Observatory Jefferson outlined his typical work day program:[21]

Half way between our house and the Observatory is a shed with a series of wet and dry bulb thermometers that I have just been out to read and set for the night (10 p.m.). I rise (now) at 6:30 a.m. and go out: set the thermometers for the day on my way to the Observatory and meantime measure the rainfall at an instrument opposite. Then I go to the Observatory, entering always the north door in daytime; enter room read barometer (11 a.m) and wet and dry bulb thermometer (12 noon) and record them with percentage and species of clouds in the sky, force and direction of wind, and rainfall at a book nearby (12 noon). Next or usually before this I go out through the south dome and read and set the vane (1 p.m.) and return home to take a cup of coffee and go to work, first helping Mr. Davis read last nights chronograph sheets and then reducing stars to true and mean places from the apparent. This work I carry on in my own room of course. At 11:30 breakfast—till 12:30 or 1, then I go over to the Observatory, wind the small chronometers in the N.W. corner and Sundays and Thursdays the clock (2 p.m), which is of course mounted on a pier separate from the building as are all the instrument piers, and deeply founded. Then I go to sleep, read or write—as inclination takes me— till 3:00 p.m. At 4 o'clock I go out again to set thermometers and wind vane and work till 5 when I put on my best bib and tucker and go down into the town for a walk till dinner at 6:35 or 7:00 p.m. according to circumstances. Immediately after dinner we open up the West dome, set the equatorial roughly on the comet, and I with lamp and chronometer go into the next room to count seconds and record time of transits while Mr. Davis observes. This takes 5 minutes to an hour according to the comets distance in time from the reference star of the evening. Then I go into the circle room with whomever has his turn for the evening, for I do not yet work wholly alone here—and work till the programme stars have all passed the meridian with an intermission at 10 p.m. to read standard barometer in the meteorological office—which on Sundays I also read at 8:00 a.m. and 4:00 p.m. Then at 11 or 12 we all assemble in the comedor for an iced drink, and then go to bed for another day.

Under Southern Heavens, Cordoba, Argentina, 1885.

Jefferson quickly distinguished himself by his various abilities: swift and accurate mathematics, a working knowledge of six languages, enthusiasm and promise as an astronomer, neatness of appearance and goodly bearing. Pleasantly enough, within days of his arrival, he was promoted to the position of third astronomer to the Observatory, and his salary was increased from $1200 to $1800 a year.

Jefferson experienced his first earthquake at Cordoba on February 15, 1884, an earthquake that was followed next morning by violent thunderstorms. At six o'clock, Chalmers Stevens, the second astronomer of the Observatory was taking morning coffee with Jefferson when lightning struck the pair. On coming out of a daze Jefferson inquired of Stevens whether he thought there was any relation between the storm and the earthquake, but second astronomer Stevens lay still in his chair. The lightning had travelled down a heavy metal chain which suspended an oil lamp over the table. Stevens was dead.[22] Jefferson was appointed second astronomer and accorded a considerably greater measure of responsibility in the affairs of the Observatory than hitherto, for which he was grateful:[23]

> We are very busy now, Dr. Gould having suddenly given us the revision of several clusters of stars. They follow so closely one after another, often with less than ten seconds between them that it takes three of us—one to observe in the chair and call out "tips," or time of stars crossing the middle thread in the telescope, when he cries "tip"— magnitude, color and so forth of star, with threads lost, which must be known to understand the record that the chronograph is all the while making of the transits. This also the observer must do by pressing a key everytime the star crosses a thread and naming those threads where he loses a transit. Then another assistant is busy with the four microscopes that must be used to obtain the reading of four different parts of the divided circle every time the instrument is set, cries these out one after another, asks for the next setting, at which he then places the instrument by turning the guide circle. Meanwhile a third is busy taking down all the miscellaneous cries that fairly fill the air, recording them in the proper place, demanding verifications of suspicious values, taking from the dial the instant when the observer cries tip and all the while keeping the observer informed, from the former observations, of the probable time, magnitude, and position in the cluster of the star on which the instrument is set that the observer may know which of the innumerable points of light he is to follow. And the while the chronograph is busily writing down the transits in the corner and beating noisily but rhythmically. Fortunately the largest group does not take more than fifteen or twenty minutes as we should give out, especially

the unfortunate at the microscopes. After that the pair who have the evening, go on taking circumpolar and timestars to determine the clock-rate for the evening.

During these years the National Observatory of the Argentine at Cordoba was engaged in four main works:[24]

Firstly, the Uranometria Argentina—maps and a catalogue of all Southern lucid (naked eye) stars. Secondly, the Argentine Zones containing about 75,000 Southern stars, probably three-fourths of those between the first and ninth magnitudes (observations fairly sharp). Thirdly, the Argentine catalogue containing above 30,000 stars determined sharply with several observations in several years. Fourthly, the Argentine Durchmusterung, an approximate list of all southern stars between the first and tenth magnitudes.

It was with this latter work that Jefferson was primarily concerned. The Observatory itself had been engaged since 1870 in compiling this catalogue of the Southern Heavens, a work not previously undertaken. Jefferson's labors were to constitute a part of this handbook and he took his work very seriously, reading much, especially volumes of Greenwich and Washington observations. Jefferson was able to report to his father in Boston on September 16, 1885:

The other night I made my best record—forty-nine stars in an average time of 4½ minutes per star, meaning eleven transits in Right Ascension and four Circle microscopes in Declination for each star. At Washington they expect to observe fifty stars per night, but have many observers and all are old astronomers of a certain eminence.

Jefferson's carriage, together with his long hours, accuracy, and persistence, eventually won for him, May 8, 1886, a permission to make his first comet observations—Comet Fabry—on the great equatorial telescope. For Jefferson observations of telescopic comets were interestingly different from circle work since "the observations are at once published with the observer's name in the *Astronomische Nachrichten* where also appear the final orbits and discussions of value of individual observations."[25] Other of Jefferson's observations were sent by the newly appointed Director Thome to the German astronomer Auwers. Jefferson wrote:[26]

They are to enable him to determine accurately the revolution value of a heliometer screw he used I think for the last transit of Venus. At any rate a good many observatories have been at work on them and my observations come out very nicely so far. Thome thinks they will make a good showing and I hope so.

Continued and intensive observations bothered Jefferson's health and especially his eyes, so that Sundays he was encouraged to pack cocktails, beer, oranges, cheese, tongue, Cordoban rolls, mount his "saible" and accompanied by observers Tucker and Thome, enjoy a hunt in the "camp."[27] Jefferson purchased a two-barrel Maynard French shotgun, 16 bore for $70 paper money, and reports shooting partridges and iguana in delightfully different flat land and noble sierra, which being clothed in purple-blue heliotrope or plentifully sprinkled with verbenas, geraniums, daisies, cactus blossoms, and passion flowers, surpassed in beauty anything he had experienced in North America. Other of Jefferson's travels through these years, 1883 to 1886, were encouraged by his severe eye fatigue. In the closing months of the year 1886, Jefferson suffered continual affliction from his health. This debility coincided with a period of melancholy at the Observatory where a lingering sadness pervaded in the weeks following the death of Mrs. Gould, wife of the head man. Jefferson wanted to live with a native family in the city, to become familiar with the habit of the people, but this was forbidden. He could no longer practice his clarinet, was requested to refrain from remembering Mediterranean music by renditions of "Hymn to Apollo and the Muse" in Greek, even association with town people was discouraged. Jefferson began to feel very much alone. The salaries were fixed by the government and Jefferson considered the Observatory no place for a young man looking for advancement, although salary adequacy was beyond dispute.[28] Perhaps Jefferson desired to pioneer, to try something new and financially more rewarding in an Argentine that was undergoing a period of phenomenal economic expansion. Whatever the reason, and perhaps Jefferson was motivated by a combination of some or all of the foregoing, he packed his bags, and left the Observatory.

Jefferson had bidden farewell to practical astronomy, yet he was never to forget this wonderful schooling. Sixty years later, in 1947, Jefferson was to reminisce of his Cordoba days:[29]

> *I like astronomy. Day-times I was set at the reduction of the mean places of the Southern circumpolar stars from all data extant, by the method of the least squares which I had never heard of before. I liked the technique of star observation . . . Is it not one of man's greatest mental accomplishments that we can in 1946 buy a Nautical Almanac that tells us the hour and minute of every eclipse in 1948 or even later and the place in the world where it can be seen? They are God's eclipses. Astronomers have learned to think some of God's thoughts after him. What other science can match this?*

These three years in Cordoba had provided Jefferson with what he termed an "advanced schooling for the life struggle." This schooling was later to exert such a profound effect on Jefferson's career that it warrants further attention. Jefferson's linguistic ability was enhanced enormously. Between the years 1880 and 1890 Europe was disgorging annually 100,000 emigrants into the Argentine, which became a veritable language laboratory. Living in a land where Spanish was the working language, he was able to strengthen his conversational Spanish, complementing well the grammatical and phonological studies he had made at Boston University between 1880-1883. Soon Jefferson was "hunting up some native of Castille to give me the niceties."[30] Constant intercourse with his bookseller friend, Portabella, was rewarding . . . "He tells me all the Spanish customs and sayings he knows, gets books for me without charging any commission."[31] While living at the Observatory Jefferson had hired a Parisian for three hours a week to talk French with him in his Observatory room.

Thirteen visits to the Italian Opera Company were a major source of pleasure and recreation to Jefferson who, with a reserved seat near the stage, acquired many tips from clarinetist Bonet, on how best to play that instrument. Jefferson enjoyed his perambulation from the hill-top observatory to the town center, though finding it necessary to tote a leaded cane for protection. He was able to increase his circle of acquaintances in Cordoban society, and with much additional study of Italian, especially on cloudy nights when observations were rendered impossible at the Observatory, gave himself a working knowledge of that language.

A Foreigners Club, eighty members strong, had opened a house in Cordoba in 1885, where men from forty different countries were constantly engrossed in their mutual awareness and appreciation of difference. In all of his spare moments Jefferson was at this club talking with its members—"German professors from the university, Englishmen from the railway, Italians and Spaniards from Europe's south"—and reading from the very considerable collection of newspapers always present there.[32] Eighteen months conversation in languages other than English obliged Jefferson to write in August 1885, "Don't be surprised at any deviation from custom in my spelling of English. We follow the sound so closely in Spanish that when I write my own tongue I have to consult the Dictionary at every turn."[33] The study of languages for some years had been Jefferson's prime concern, indeed, it seems likely that the linquistic possibilities of the Argentine were the chief reason for his initial departure from New England. In the Argentine, his plans for the future began to assume form:[34]

> My plans, in their present form, subject for date of execution to the premium on gold here, run somewhat as follows—At least a year of strictest economy and study in Italy and France to round up my knowledge of the principal Latin languages, a return to the States with

funds enough to supply possible difficulties while I look up something temporary in the way of educational employment. I shall take even a very modest school mastership if attainable to begin and trust to make myself known as a candidate for some university position by original work in the modern languages, a professorship in which is my aim and object. If while in Europe I can obtain some employment as here that will permit me to make profounder studies in the customs and languages while covering my outlays so much the better, but I should look on that as a piece of good fortune and count on the probable case of having to stand my own bills.

Jefferson's German friends from the Foreigners Club, numbering among them a professor of philology at the *Colegio Nacional,* urged him to continue his studies at the University of Berlin. Relations with Berlin University were friendly in Cordoba where Dr. Kurtz, the Cordoban botanist, was a companion of the very professor in Berlin under whom Jefferson wished to study. The expenses of such a venture would have been very considerable, especially since both the times and the European tradition mitigated against a student maintaining a part-time job. Jefferson was not unmindful of difficulties ahead:[35]

To enter a German university, the foreigner needs a certificate of good previous schooling: here was my difficulty—had I finished my last year in Boston there would be no trouble as the diploma is sufficient. But things being as they are, arises the question would the Boston University faculty feel justified in giving me the required certificate.

Jefferson alluded to the fact that he had not yet graduated from Boston, for he left the University at the end of his third year of schooling. Funds and possibly a lack of certification were fundamental obstacles that would have to be negotiated before he could study at Berlin.

In Cordoba Jefferson had employed his facility in language to good purpose, devouring all the literature he could obtain in many different tongues. This reading was for Jefferson both vindication of his language studies and fulfillment. He insisted that study of a language in isolation from the study of its people, institutions, mores, and writings was most sterile. More especially did Jefferson read at this time in languages other than English, works on astronomy, travel, meteorology, earth measurement, literature, the state of nature, and European history. He wrote essays, amassed notes, and collected references on subjects which included collimation, Spanish pronunciation in Cordoba, the evolution of European language, Beowulf verbs, Spanish love poetry, situations he wished to recapture because he found them difficult of expression, aneroid measurements of the Andes West of Cordoba and calculations of the earth's size from the dip of the horizon.[36] The latter fascinated Jefferson who read, annotated, and reworked the measurement formulae suggested by E. G. Cassini in *De la Grandeur et de la Figure de la Terre* 1751, and Peter Muller in *Kosmischer Physik* (Braunschweig, 1804).[37]

Of more particular merit among Jefferson's unpublished work at this time are the essays "The name Argentine," "Final and Medial English Sonants," and "The Correlation of Ideas."[38] Both Portabella, his Spanish bookseller friend, and his father in Boston, helped satisfy Jefferson's literary needs, causing expenditures which at this time accounted for no mean part of his living costs. Invariably having read a book Jefferson would précis the work, adopting the tongue of the author, in this manner assuring himself practice both in the reading and writing of these languages.[39] He continued phonological study, commenced in his undergraduate days at Boston University, by placing a mirror before him while seated at his dressing table in the Observatory house and thrusting a knitting needle down his throat until he produced "the right cadence and flex of grunt." In 1885 Jefferson was elected a member of the Argentine Geographical Society, which gave him ready access to men undertaking scientific exploration in South America.

Jefferson never lost contact with the outside world while he was in Cordoba. A continuous interchange of correspondence between him and his parents in Boston, his class of 1884 now scattered, and numerous European travellers whom he had met in the Argentine, kept him informed of life beyond South American lands and occasioned him the opportunity of self-expression. Jefferson's letters were invariably written in a neat, compact hand, beautifully composed, usually containing between two thousand and five thousand words. These letters were sent from the Argentine once every fourteen days either on a forty day journey to Europe or a fifty day journey to the United States. Their content includes contemporary accounts of political problems in the Argentine, the economic opportunities offered by the Pampa, Jefferson's views of man's destiny, the education of his nephew, the wonder of a four season climate, Cleveland and the United States Presidency, Bismark and the German Empire, General Gordon and the Sudan, the inevitability of homesickness. A constant thread winding through Jefferson's South American correspondence is his restlessness, his yearning to devote himself more completely to the study of language. This specific yearning to continue philological studies was fostered and nurtured by correspondence from Bernhard Berenson, one of Jefferson's classmates of 1884 at Boston University, who dwelled constantly upon the then present forces of philistinism prevalent everywhere except at "the sweet retreats" of the European University, those isolated islands of refuge as Oxford, Berlin, or Heidelberg.[40]

But in 1887 Jefferson decided to stay in the Argentine a little longer. He was mightily attracted by opportunities which would later enable him to roam the universities of Europe without care as to means . . . "you know Schliemann's history—how he acquired a fortune in business to apply it in later life to his favorite studies,"[41] and Jefferson was getting to know the people, a circumstance he valued highly.

A Pampean Creole society which did not customarily accept foreigners, extended its sympathy to the young North American who had so narrowly escaped death after Chalmers Stevens had been struck by lightning in the Observatory. An invitation to stay a week-end at the La Paz country place of Don Felix Funes and his sister-in-law, Madame Roca, wife of the Argentine President, was indication enough that "Don Marcos" was to be made welcome in the Argentine. This quite unusual invitation was an experience that Jefferson later came to cherish dearly. He was introduced to the gracious living of the Republic and wrote of its elegant simplicity:[42]

> I made my first two leagues on horseback—all on the estate, rowed in the pond, made use of the bath—a magnificent tank of running water some fifteen by eight feet where you could swim about—admired the ostriches, the horses, the cattle and the peach trees and above all the mountains and the very respectable woods that abound here; for round about Cordoba every tree must have a ditch to bring it water or it dies and the land is level as the sea, except for the barrancas that look for all the world like so many great cracks made by the earthquakes. The service of the house is performed by a swarm of Negro women with the greatest care and promptness, everything in the way of comfort, from the great fan of ostrich feathers over the table to the viands and the wines, is provided.

This kindness was henceforth extended Jefferson throughout Cordoba. Creole society taught Jefferson to ride a horse, a necessary accomplishment in an area where horses outnumbered humans seven to one. After Jefferson's breaking in he was never without a horse in the Argentine, eventually travelling several hundred miles in this fashion. He delighted the Creoles by taking photographs of groups of Creole friends at their country houses, with the camera and equipment left by Stevens, which later he was to put to excellent use. "I have now Stevens old photographic camera and am practicing that art with a view to our Sierra and my future travels. As yet the chief result has been to make an apothecary's shop of my room."[43] Jefferson observed that the Creoles preferred Europeans to North Americans because the latter were oblivious to the merits of Creole life . . .[44]

> *They buy in Europe, they travel in Europe, they affect European manners and mode of life. Their aspiration is to be rich enough to possess English blooded stock and horses. They want to join the Jockey club and use two English phrases in their Spanish—four o'clock, meaning afternoon tea, and high leefe (high life) for fashionable. They like French furniture and want it.*

Jefferson left the Observatory on April 1, 1887 and assumed residence with two native friends in a Cordoban house. The house was comfortable and meant small expense for Jefferson who lost no time in advertising his services locally as a teacher of languages. Teaching English to natives and Spanish to immigrants, Jefferson managed to earn $80 a month, certainly enough to support him until he found a more substantial employment, and in any case he was enjoying a well earned rest. Work abounded at this time in the Argentine and positions for Spanish speaking people were readily available. During one June week alone Jefferson was offered five jobs—"Professor of English in the *Colegio Nacional,* Bookkeeper at $200 a month, assistant on the Brazilian-Argentine boundary commission, Assistant in the La Plata Observatory and a position with Mr. E. A. Hudson, land surveyor." But not one of these did he accept.

In 1887 there occurred the revolution of Tucuman, a province some 350 miles to the north and west of Cordoba. Among the revolutionaries was Justinians Claria, founder and manager of La Providencia Sugar Estate. Claria was one of the first men to die in the struggle, and the estate needed a man clear of mind and with managerial talents to replace him.[45] Some of Jefferson's Creole friends who had travelled north in the Argentine and helped establish La Providencia sugar estate remembered the young-looking North American who could tell the time from the stars, take photographs, who spoke many languages and who, by his personal qualities, had won for himself a position in Creole and Cordoban society. This information did not escape the notice of Don Doroteo, one of the directors and shareholders of La Providencia sugar estate ingenio, who lived in Cordoba. Quite by coincidence D. Doroteo knew Jefferson well—for Jefferson crossed his threshold weekly to teach both his daughters the English language! The combined office of sub-manager and treasurer at La Providencia was offered to Jefferson who accepted the position for one year and held it for three years.

Jefferson arrived at La Providencia sugar estate, thirty miles distant from Tucuman, on June 20, 1887. The Observatory at Cordoba provided him with a collection of meteorological instruments in order that he might establish a station in Tucuman. Jefferson wrote of his intentions . . .[46] "My abode before the end of the month will be one of the most important meteorological stations in the country. I mean to make a special study of all storms and have already begun work on the subject though some important instruments remain unmounted."

He was most impressed with the grandeur of physical plant. Claria, the founder of the factory had been a man of lavish idea but ignorant of the mechanics of an ingenio. Yet his early efforts in 1882 had met with great financial success, for at that time an estate of two hundred thousand dollars value paid for itself in a year. This encouraged Claria to build a plant that nestled congruously among the peach blossoms, orange scents, and varied hues of a near tropic environment. He attempted to capture fragments of the outdoors within the estates dwellings so as to introduce there something of the serenity of nature. "A brick building was put up for the factory of the most luxurious construction. We utilize about a fifth part—every sort of useless luxury is to hand."[47] In this same period of extravagance a residence for the management had been constructed five-eighths of a mile from the factory. It failed to house the overseers who needed to be on hand night and day in the factory; consequently, management found itself obliged to appropriate an ugly brick building built for storehouse space close by the factory, which caused Jefferson to comment, "We are greatly troubled for house room and though my quarters are comfortable enough, as far as South American quarters go, I am yet living in my trunks and my books in boxes or a few in a chair."[48] Peons were housed close by to supply the regular labor for the estate. The whole was kept in good repair by the more skilled of these peons, who used black walnut as the usual wood for door frames, rafters, posts, and other woodwork. "It would surprise you to see our roof; it is one network of black walnut beams and only lacks polish to grace any cathedral for its form and material."[49] Jefferson's inquiring mind wished to know something of the history, extent, and future possibilities of the estate whereon he worked. Consultation of estate archives was revealing:[50]

> It is part of a property granted by a Spanish king in 1717. We possess the original grant to Sargento Mayor Don Andries Artasor y Aquilera, and since that date the successive deeds of sale and bequest are extant in an unbroken chain that inspires much respect for the legal exactness of the early Spaniards, taking into consideration that twenty years ago Tucuman was a wilderness three or four months journey from Buenos Aires across the Salt deserts and the Pampa infested with hostile indi-

ans and has more revolutions in its history than Athens or Rome. The property is most curious too in its external form being a narrow ribbon on the North bank of the Rio Seco from fixed boundaries in the plain where access is easy "to the eternal snows on the hills", its southern boundary, the Rio Seco and its northern and imaginary line always distant from the Rio 1200 yards in a North and South line. On account of the denseness of the forest the surveys have never attained more than five or six leagues from here and the snow remains another ten or fifteen beyond. In the extreme East of this property lie the factory and canefields.

Initially Jefferson's lot as treasurer and sub-manager was an unenviable one:[51]

Some circumstances of my living arrangements have been such as would soon be insufferable under other conditions but when one passes six or seven hours at most out of the twenty-four in his room the only commodity he is apt to think of is his bed and he is not apt to be very particular about that. For more than a week at a time I have had to sleep dressed to save time in the morning when I had work to do early.

[52]When I first came on the 20 June 1887, it was fearfully cold and the manager had me called every morning at 4 or 5 not to do much of anything for I didn't even know what was to be done. That of course was my trial and I succeeded in sticking it out satisfactorily.

Life at La Providencia estate was entirely concerned with sugar. In the summer months of December, January, February, and March the young cane would grow emerald green, under abundant Tucuman rains, sway in the wind, while suckled by the hot, humid, Tucuman climate. This was the off season, the wet season, the time of chills and fevers in Tucuman Province, when activity on the estate was minimal:[53]

In the rainy season . . . all is decidedly wet and then the sun comes out and raises an unwholesome steam. The pools of rain water in the road, stagnating, pass from green to yellow . . . but already my rubber coat and boots have won general respect though at first inclining to merriment.

Jefferson's tasks included the supervision of labor, gauging the market for changes in the price of sugar and for adequate substitutes, caring for the manufacture of fine spirits, keeping the estate's accounts, and coordinating all activity at harvest time. Undoubtedly harvest time and preparation for it taxed Jefferson most fully, at which time he proclaimed that he "ruled the wilderness as a Russian CZAR."

The harvest at La Providencia was not only a time when the estate was most productive, it was also a time of beauty. Enormous fields replete with the sway of emerald cane presented themselves on all sides of the factory in an estate that boasted a twenty mile length and a mile and a half width. The golds, ochres, yellows, and purples, a veritable jazz of cut cane color, merged imperceptibly into a hazy blue foothill zone of the lofty snow-covered Sierra to the West.[54]

> *The period of cultivation is past, everyone braces for the ensuing months. One day a sufficient amount of cane is declared fit for grinding and harvest begins. Gangs are formed, running gear oiled, at last the fires are lighted, those fires that must be maintained to the end. On the day announced the cane begins to arrive in every imaginable sort of vehicle from the indigenous "Aipa" whose wheels are simply cross sections of a huge log, to the modern narrow gauge horse railway that serves our largest plantation.*

At the factory the slow but powerfully revolving cylinders of the conductor began to toil incessantly as though conscious of the quarter million tons of cane before them. More cane-loaded wood carts creaked to the scales as the Santiago men sang "tristes" in the knowledge of the exhausting harvest to come. "The gauchos and Indians did to Spanish words all that Homer had done to Greek words," and the incessant throbbing of the air pumps beneath the evaporating apparatus supplied the rhythm to a continuous process that lasted one hundred days. Each activity and sound, every color, came to mingle in the voice of harvest at the sugar factory. Throughout the 100 day sugar making period between the ripening of cane in May or June and frost in September, the estate employed some 200 Indians from the nearby province Santiago del Estero. They spoke Spanish, had Spanish names, and promised the Virgin rewards if She would heal them when they were sick. The Indians provided labor when the sugar estate required it, but this variety of labor also brought in its wake attendant problems. These Indians were hired each season with an advance of money on a contract signed before the local chief of police, and in addition to cigarette and clothing money which was paid them twice a month during season, they managed to take with them between 50 and 100 dollars at the season's close. Only a few women and boys were brought to the estate—the women to cook and the boys to drag the *bagazo* (crushed cane) from the drying fields to the furnaces where it was burned. The labor was not of the most reliable nature. Men would abscond and cause concern to Jefferson, whose duty it was to look after the entire well-being of La Providencia. In Jefferson's first year at the estate one man escaped, was returned by the police, usually aided by professional trackers, and publicly whipped in order to deter other laborers from breaking their contracts. Within a year, public whipping was forbidden by law. Stocks were then used, which in turn were forbidden, and the strong room was the only punishment management could mete out.

Jefferson was largely responsible for effectively organizing and assigning this labor force to the various tasks that had to be performed on the estate. One section of this force cut the ripe cane; a second section maintained the wood pile, by drying out *bagazo* and by cutting sebil and lance from the virgin forests some six or seven miles to the west of the factory; a third section manned the factory; a fourth section transported the finished product from the storeplace of the estate to the provincial railroad, which, in 1885, was extended from Buenos Aires to pass within one mile of La Providencia. Jefferson's work was efficient. After one year of his management, the estate began to regain the vitality it had enjoyed prior to the Tucuman revolution, and indeed a one month pay was granted to all hands as a bonus with the completion of the harvest in 1888. Jefferson was seeing the world, was broadening his set of experiences rapidly, was preparing himself, albeit unconsciously, for his life's work, for at this time he had no thought of ever teaching geography.

La Providencia unlike Cordoba had no society, not even a village. The nearest doctor was thirty miles distant in Tucuman. Jefferson lived close by the factory with the Director's family, and to his delight no one spoke English! The mechanics, the sugar maker, and the distiller were French, and the blacksmith was Italian; the labor force was Spanish speaking. Living close by the factory with the Director's family, Jefferson was happy with his work making sugar, running a factory, exploiting a wilderness, enjoying pleasant relations with estate personnel. Don Doroteo, part owner and director of La Providencia who had been largely instrumental in securing Jefferson his present appointment, possessed a fine Phillipe-Patek watch which Jefferson could always praise by insisting upon its accuracy. Relations between the two of them were good and Jefferson never went in need of a letter of introduction in the Argentine.

Jefferson's range of interest was very considerable, and already he was beginning to display an ability to withdraw from too much personal involvement with others in order to study subjects of immediate concern. He had already displayed his power of concentration, was already beginning to ask himself of every phenomenon, how . . . why? During his years in South America, Jefferson had evidently gathered a functioning knowledge of Swedish and Danish, for his language study at Boston University, encompassing Latin, Greek, German, French, Italian, and Spanish, had not included Danish or Swedish.[55] References in more than one letter suggest that he had begun to learn the Scandinavian languages in the period, 1884-1888.[56]

During his stay in the Argentine, and especially in the off season at La Providencia, Jefferson seized every opportunity to travel and observe. On January 27, 1886 while still employed at the Observatory, Jefferson had journeyed from Cordoba to Oroya in Peru, returning to Tucuman by April 1st.[57] Every day on his way to and from Oroya whether on horseback, in railroad carriage, or on boat, Jefferson would ask questions—of himself, fellow travellers, indigenous inhabitants. The answers, observations, and conjecture were written into his diary. The first two weeks of April 1887 saw Jefferson travel west from Cordoba through the Sierra de Cordoba on horseback to further rest his eyes. The riding skill that he had acquired from the Creoles was now proving most valuable. But the more Jefferson travelled, the more he wondered at the nature of things entire. Not unnaturally he sought books on the subject of the Argentine and South America, in order that he might understand through the written word what he could not understand in nature, and yet no satisfactory book could he find until he discovered Darwin. Charles Darwin, a young man of twenty-two and already a most competent natural scientist, had visited the Argentine in 1831 and 1832 as part of his five year journey around the world as a guest of Captain Fitz Roy on *HMS Beagle* in a surveying voyage. Six years later and some fifty years prior to Jefferson's residence in the Argentine, Darwin wrote a book, his *Journal of Researches,* originally written with the help of a grant from the Royal Society. Jefferson read the book:[58]

> *I have read and reread it till the volume needs rebinding. I note that my* Origin of Species *is in excellent condition and has pencilled comments in the margins of the first 16 pages only . . . I suspect the famous, bearded old man whose portrait John Murray used to illustrate my 1889 edition of the Researches—could not have written the book.*

The *Journal of Researches* was the book that opened Jefferson's eyes, that showed him the world he was looking at but did not know how to see. Jefferson was deeply impressed with Darwin's work:[59]

> *The discovery of Darwin meant more humiliation for me. There were so many things I didn't quite get. I knew nothing of nature, nothing thorough. Quartz and felspar were just words. How did you tell them apart? How did Darwin know that those long screes of greenish rock on the slopes of the valley leading to the Mendoza pass over the Andes were Cambrian?*
>
> [60]*After reading young Darwin, I looked again at the country and its people and saw them. But I could not follow Darwin with satisfaction for lack of training in natural science. There was beginning to rise in me a consciousness of great lack.*

The immediate inspiration for reading Darwin possibly came from a book, *Excursions of an Evolutionist* by John Fiske,[61] an 1885 Christmas present from Jefferson's father. In thanking his father for the book Jefferson wrote:[62]

> For your own present, you could not have made me one more after my own heart had you been a millionaire bent on getting rid of a year's income. In John Fiske's book I find for the first time set forth what seems to me the only reasonable aspect of the universe in our days. It is needless to say that I admire the book immensely. There is not one word in the whole thing that does not seem to me just the best thing to say in its place. The satisfaction of at last finding one author, and that a man of no mean intelligence, who clearly puts forth the views and arguments that have been forcing themselves on me for the last few years is something considerable. You will readily perceive how much a ready understanding of Fiske's views must have been aided by a good deal of thinking over the same ground especially where I had been wont to use the same bases of argument.
>
> The chief thing that was new and came like a burst of light to me was his references to the full scope of natural selection. It is something I have read too little of, and seems to me the precise thing to fill the demand of the ritualistic theologians that philosophy shall build up as well as destroy.

Jefferson found himself defending his position at the sugar estate to both his parents and his friends. "It is not you will say an intellectual life. I do not know—but it is an active one and near to Nature's heart."[63] Jefferson insisted that life in the great outdoors was good for the body, but his firmest defense of life in Tucuman reads:[64]

> My present chief who is very sparse of compliments or even expressions of favorable opinion assured me that my education was worth more than a fortune to me because it assured me a comfortable livelihood wherever I chanced to fall. I find something true in this point of view—what is false is the notion that therein lies the value of a good education.
>
> A man should be well educated—taught to think rightly and instructed in the elements of now known historic and scientific phenomena—because his intelligence is the mainspring of his life, and as such must be well secured and evenly applied to all his volitions would he fulfil the possibilities of his nature.
>
> With such an education, the livelihood is a secondary consideration and simple. I am certain there are so few well educated men in the world that one can find his place in any occupation of life and with credit. Partly a desire to demonstrate this belief and partly Carlisle's unpracticed preaching that a man should devote what culture he has to work rather than talk and manuscript have moved me to look for and finally accept my present position.

But again that long standing desire to study in Europe swept through him, this time irresistibly. First he would go to Boston University, complete his bachelors degree, then sail for Europe. With thoughts of Boston University and a completed diploma in mind, Jefferson asked for a leave of absence from La Providencia to commence in December, 1888 and to last several months:[65]

> *I have asked leave of absence for some months dating from December to go home and take my degree thus bridging the difficulty I had anticipated in Germany once and for all . . . I shall take the swiftest steamer either Lamport and Holts the only ones that sail direct for New York, or the Italian steamers that make best time and will land me in Genoa 18 days after leaving Buenos Aires. I shall prepare myself as well as possible before and during the journey for taking a speedy examination and trust to Providence as one says that the Boston University Faculty may show disposition to facilitate the execution of my plan.*

The Directorate of La Providencia estate granted Jefferson leave of absence, whereupon he returned to Boston by January 13, 1889, via Cordoba, Buenos Aires, Rio, San Vicente (Cape Verdes), Lisbon, Bordeaux, Paris, London, Liverpool and New York—the quickest and cheapest route in those days. The next five weeks Jefferson passed with his parents, while he busied himself in meeting the requirements set by the Boston University faculty. Jefferson's work for the Bachelors degree was now complete except for a thesis on a subject later to be decided by a Dr. Huntington of the Boston faculty. During the same five weeks Jefferson had found the time to visit Theodora with whom at one time he had kept company at Boston University. Theodora had remained at Boston University, received the Isaac Rich Scholarship in 1885, and had graduated in 1886 on completion of a thesis entitled "The Theory of the Evolution of Animals from Aristotle's Time to the Present." Her mother had died in 1887, and Theodora was living with her Aunt in Horne House, Gilmanton, New Hampshire. Jefferson re-commenced a courtship of Theodora which was to result in marriage in August, 1891. Jefferson hurried back to La Providencia, again via Europe, just in time to supervise the harvest—the official manager, La Torre, being sick with fever. The harvest three weeks old, Jefferson received a suggestion from the Boston faculty that his thesis should be entitled "The Uranography of the Southern Hemisphere."[66] At harvest time Jefferson was busy from "five in the morning until late at night, separating groups of brawling men, heavy with drink," yet he seemed to have an inexhaustible constitution which could work without respite. Jefferson casually observes:[67]

> *It would have been very simple then to select a subject and write it up*

on the long outward journey whereas now I am put to it in full swing of the Harvest and five hundred miles from the needed Astronomical maps and catalogues. However, I have gone so far and certainly shall not turn back for so slight a cause. The essay shall be forthcoming at the earliest possible notice.

He completed the thesis[68] and his degree, was seeing La Providencia safely through another harvest, had accumulated funds enough to fulfill his ambition—language study in Europe. But during his absence in Boston and his total concern for the harvest, Jefferson had not appreciated that inflation was beginning to sweep the Argentine. His plans for Europe were now very much hurried by the price of gold. Jefferson's savings had been decimated, but he had not despaired entirely of university study in Europe.[69]

The old College Year Books claimed "corresponding Faculties" with Athenian and Roman Universities, asserting if I remember rightly, that Boston University graduates may attend the lectures at Rome without further fees. I have written to ask him (Dean Huntington) the significance of the "correspondence". But please ask also, in case it is as I remember. I would like him to send the necessary justifications, as I mean to attend the Roman University if possible.

CHAPTER TWO

THE RETURN TO NEW ENGLAND:

HIGH SCHOOL, HARVARD,

AND W. M. DAVIS.

On October 12, 1889, Jefferson bade a sorrowful farewell to the Argentine. He had arrived there six years previously at the age of twenty years and had bettered his knowledge of languages in what was then a philological laboratory. He had earned a good wage throughout those six years, saved a not inconsiderable amount of money, only to be deprived of much of his savings by inflation. But he had enjoyed the privilege of knowing Spanish life and had revelled in a climate that was wholly lacking in the harshness and austerity of the Boston winter season.

Undoubtedly Jefferson was unhappy to leave the Argentine when he did. A variety of circumstances had combined to drive him from the Argentine and to Europe for a brief stay, then home. Of immediate import was the inflation:[1]

> I sail for Genoa and Rome on the 12th instant my plans having been hurried by the rise of gold. This has already reached 242% and sanguine people think it may be brought to par in about five years if the proper measures be adopted. In that I have no particle of faith. The Government is undoubtedly afflicted at present as it is difficult to chant the usual hymn of progress and good government in face of such a state of finances. But the necessary reforms are so wholly at variance with the notions of the present generation that I have no hopes. What the republic needs is economy in public and private life, not as they understand the word in France either, but rather a certain moderation

in their extravagance . . . There is nothing to be done here now working on a salary which is paid in paper while you must pay gold rates for everything you consume.

Jefferson's departure from the Argentine was also encouraged by the scourge of yellow fever, the dreaded "chu chu" of South America. In mid 1889 the "chu chu" struck the Argentine as it had done only four years previously. Many thousands of people died from this malady for which there was no known cure at that time. Possibly, knowledge that Theodora's father (a Chickering piano salesman) had died of yellow fever in Texas, 1859, brought the reality of danger closer to him, and possibly the numerous exhortations of his father's correspondence encouraged him to put distance between himself and the yellow fever. Jefferson was certainly cognizant of the dangers of yellow fever for he collected newspaper items and reports from many countries on the yellow fever outbreak of the late 1880's.

Another factor that encouraged Jefferson to sail for Europe and home was concern for his family. Both his father and mother were aged by this time and had lost four of their nine children. A fifth was troubled with a severe nervous condition. Mark was the youngest of their children, and his six year's absence from home had made his parents eager for his homecoming. Frequently in correspondence his father indicated to Mark that there was always a place for him at home if he chose to return, that both he and his mother missed him greatly. Undoubtedly Jefferson began to feel the call of home, his place, where he had grown up, where he had a circle of friends, where indeed he had passed his youth hiding, book in hand. Jefferson began to regard his South American years as a "self-imposed exile," and an experience with the world in which we live. Furthermore, his brother Harry had been taken seriously ill on the occasion of his first return to Massachusetts in 1889. Indeed, Harry might well have died at that time, had not Jefferson, a combination of despair and initiative, applied oxygen immediately.

Jefferson fervently desired to make of language study a career. His saving in the Argentine was predicated by his desire to reside in Europe for several months to study languages at French, German, and Italian universities. He had been given letters of introduction to Heidelberg University by Dr. Kurtz, the German botanist at the University in Cordoba; and from Portabella, his Spanish bookseller friend from Cordoba, a letter of introduction to people in Paris, that his study at the Sorbonne might be facilitated. The Argentine inflation deprived Jefferson of the means to finance this plan, abbreviating his intended European residence, hastening his return to Massachusetts.

Finally his affection for Theodora must be reckoned of account. The two had first met at Boston University in 1882. At that time Jefferson had coached her in Greek, taken her to lectures, skated with her on local ponds, and kept company with Theodora on Boston Common. Resenting the hostility of Theodora's mother, Jefferson had taken himself to South America. During his Argentine years, however, Theodora had regularly sent him letters of affection. Jefferson largely ignored these letters, for he was not able to see a place for a woman in the plans he had set for himself. However, on his return to Massachusetts early in 1889, he had met Theodora, and in a very few weeks his early love for her had returned. They walked the country lanes together, enjoyed surrey rides, and kept company the length of his leave. On his return voyage from Melrose, Massachusetts, to Tucuman in the Argentine, he posted her letters of affection on every conceivable occasion. There is little doubt that he had Theodora in his blood when he left the Argentine that October. Later Jefferson wrote:[2]

> *Every act of our lives has a thousand determining causes but only one ground. You are the only ground of my returning to this country and Argentine finances and La Torre and the chu-chu etc. only so many determining causes that made it sooner or later, or this way or that, but would never have brought me here. That is the best I can do towards interpreting the last years page out of my life.*

Perhaps Jefferson's departure from the Argentine was a product of all of the above forces. The fact is, he sailed on the *Aquila* from Buenos Aires, October 12, 1889, bound for Genoa, Italy. The books that Jefferson had collected over the past six years were packaged and sent to Melrose, Massachusetts, aboard a friend's yacht—Mr. Roberts' *Annie Lewis*. The collection was very considerable, and though Jefferson wished to take it to Europe with him, the expense would have proved prohibitive. The journey over the waves, the schools of whales, flying fish, the ship community, Cape Verdes, Mediterranean and Africanist influences all conjoined to render this the most delightful voyage that he ever experienced. Perhaps the voyage was rendered more happy to Jefferson in the knowledge that he was eventually returning to an harbor he could call home. Six years of vagabonding in exile was fatiguing, Jefferson wrote in his old age.[3] The journey is worthy of record as explained by the wanderer's own pen:[4]

> *My winter in Tucuman had been a sick one. But the sea voyage has set me right again and I have determined to come here at once, after some months of French I shall go back to the States to pitch my tent, and this time permanently. As it turns out the idea of sailing for Italy was a happy one as the Italian brought me to Genova at half the*

expense of the French and English lines, while the fare across the Alps is insignificant and the journey is delightful. November 1st we sighted Cape Spartero on the African coast at 1 a.m. fairly abreast of the "Aquila". Presently the lights of Trafalgar point on the Spanish side became visible though we could not distinguish the coast in the starlight unlike the African shore which we passed at a distance of only three miles or so. The Strait was as calm as a lake, the sky perfectly clear and the sea full of phosphorescence. Good fortune sent us a breeze from astern almost equal to the steamer's march so that we could promenade about the decks without noticing the slightest motion of the air. Far astern stretched the great wake of the Aquila a stream of liquid fire. Numbers of dolphins met us and clearly outlined in the phosphorescence swam for miles before us so near that their tails seemed to touch the Aquila's cutwater.

Fifteen minutes later we sighted the bright red light of Taija to the Northeast. From here onward the strait narrows continuously until at Monkey Mount a few miles west of Ceuta a mere passage of twelve miles separates Africa from Europe. Even in the starlight we plainly distinguished both coasts. The lights in the town of Ceuta follow and an instant later those of Gibraltar which we passed at 3:30 a.m.

Of the famous rock only the dark silhouette was visible against the sky. Of course I need not say we regretted not passing the famous fortress by day. We saw what was visible and turned in until daylight. From that daybreak onward our voyage was a series of the most beautiful panoramas imaginable. The African coast now loomed faint and blue in the distance but close to the north the Spanish coast displayed all its marvels. It is useless to attempt the description of so much beauty. One must see it to form any idea.

Inland towers the snow-capped range of the Sierra Nevada de Granada. From the water's edge rises the shore range crowned on every headland by ancient moorish beacon towers, clothed with vines and olives, among which are descried white villages clustering along some shelf on the mountain. Sea and air were truly Mediterranean for their blueness. All day the field glasses were passing from hand to hand the passengers grouping about those who knew the coast, every face bright with the knowledge of speedy arrival. The second day we passed the shores of Ibiza and Mallorca the Balearic islands. After a night of fearful plunging in the Gulf of Lions the 3rd dawned clear and calm before Toulon and then began the fitting conclusion of our delightful journey.

We passed so near the Riviera that we could follow for hours the course of the train from Marseilles bound like the Aquila for Genova.

All the mountains in France the Maritime Alps and in Italy the Apennines are richly wooded with olives and densely strewn with hotels, villages and the famous cities of the Riviera, Niza, Montecarlo, San Remo (we passed so near that an Italian pointed out to me the palace where the late German Emperor passed most of his last illness), Ventimiglia and finally Genova outspread in an amphitheatre of mountains. I only stayed in Genova one day, enough to form some idea of its picturesqueness derived from its immense variety of levels. I came here via Turin, Mont Cenis and Dijon. My first view of the Alps was at Modane on the French side of the Mont Cenis tunnel where we were subject to custom house inspection. I had been asleep passing the tunnel, it was raining on the Italian side and nothing could be seen, moreover it was past midnight. But noticing the extreme cold on getting out of the coach I glanced up and saw the finest display I ever beheld. The night was clear with moonlight and straight above us towered the snow peaks of the Alps. I have seen a good deal of higher mountain ranges than these in South America, but nowhere anything as majestic. All through the Alps I noticed the same appearance of immense height due simply to surprising differences of level. The cliffs tower up so sheer that it is often impossible to descry the sky from the car windows.

Jefferson did not attend the University of Rome as anticipated since he had not received word from Boston University that lecture fees would not be charged him. This, together with the knowledge that he could receive free accommodation in a suite of Parisian rooms with his Argentine friend, Garcia, encouraged him to travel immediately to Paris, his faithful poncho slung in cavalier style about him.

In Paris the 1889 exhibition was being enjoyed by an international clientele. A revivalist spirit of the days of 1789 was in the air, a banquet was held for all the mayors of France, a great exhibition attracted to the capital of France many thousand visitors anxious to view the mistress of Europe and the Western world. Boulevards, sidewalk cafes, the Arch of Triumph, efficient enbridgement of the Seine, were all phenomena which men of culture felt obliged to visit and appreciate. The Eiffel Tower was on display and made eager the people to appreciate the spirit of the New France. Recovery from her brutal beating during the Franco-Prussian War was complete. Parisian morale was high. France had recently recovered from several internal crises, was indulging a colonial venture of breathtaking proportions, and De Lesseps of Suez Canal success was already planning a Panama Canal. Jefferson enjoyed the sophistication and maturity of the European scene after six years of life on an economic frontier that encroached upon the wilderness. In Paris he was able to forget the strain that a strictly regimented life of responsibility on the sugar plantation entailed. He rowed with his Spanish friend Garcia on the Seine and Marne, in a shell, often patronized the sidewalk cafes, attended the theatre, took many energetic promenades in the first city of France, and visited the Sorbonne:[5]

> I attended the first of Gaston Paris' lectures on Old French the other day at the Sorbonne and was rather disappointed. He has nothing to say but what he, Diez and Brachet, Litre etc. have already said and the course is so thinly spread out that I prefer to study in books while earning something. I shall return to the States in December and try to turn my knowledge to account there. My health is greatly improved since leaving South America and now only occasionally reminds me of Tucuman. Here I should be content to stay until next fall if I had occupation but otherwise find it a loss of time.

Other lectures, too, he attended and derived an appreciation of France and French language. On the months of October and November Jefferson commented:[6]

> The weather is by no means agreeable. Paris seems enveloped at this season in perpetual haze. Not fog but a haziness that just suffices to deprive us of the sunlight. The winter will probably be severe as we are already obliged to make a fire in the afternoon though both of us from southern experience are long suffering in the matter of temperatures. The poor will have a hard time in Paris this winter as the affluence of visitors to the Exposition has put up the prices of provisions generally and brought crowds to town from the surrounding country to perform the increased hotel and restaurant service.

Jefferson suffered a severe head cold at this time which contributed to his wretchedness. He had not heard from Theodora and feared that she had ignored his letters. Unknown to Jefferson, Theodora was at that time staying in Paris on her way to visit relatives in Dresden, Germany. Not hearing from Theodora, however, he was encouraged to sail for Massachusetts to learn the circumstances himself. Jefferson did spend three days in London en route, inquiring for his relatives. He found a cousin, Mr. Wigg, in London, who tried in vain to persuade Jefferson that he should return to South America and become an agent of the Wigg Furniture Company. Jefferson crossed the English Channel once again, secured passage on the *Normandie,* departed Havre, November 30, and arrived in New York, December 10, 1889. A swift visit to New Hampshire revealed that Theodora was still in Europe. Jefferson returned to his parents' home in Massachusetts . . . and waited. Weeks later Theodora did return from Germany and was promptly visited by an impatient Jefferson. He found her confined to bed with rheumatic fever. From her bed of sickness she insisted that Jefferson must become a "respectable body" before she could marry him. (Almost certainly the influence of Aunt Mary Horne was at work.) To prove respectability, Jefferson submitted to one year's work as schoolmaster in Massachusetts, during which time he was required not to travel.

From the summer of 1890 to the spring of 1891, Jefferson taught at the Mitchell Boys School, Billerica. In his first week at the school he wrote:[7]

> The school and grounds are the finest I ever saw and Billerica is simply lovely. It lies on a hill overlooking a broad valley clad with trees, and adorned on its further slope with the city of Lowell. Beyond is a blue background of low mountains. There is a river handy, of name to me unknown, and rowing will be possible.

The school building was of wood, pleasingly situated and not overcrowded. Mr. Mitchell, the principal, advertised his boarding school with brochures that had attracted fifty pupils to him by 1890. Jefferson swiftly accommodated himself to a small room he was given on the premises. The floor was of rock maple, neat blackboards surrounded the walls, on whose upper moldings maps on spring rollers soon appeared. A double gas jet provided light from the center of the room, while an iron cot offered him respite from his daily turmoil. A generous row of chairs around the wall, a desk, and a broad window-sill which served as a book shelf, contributed to a spartan room appearance.[8]

> I am here out of a necessity and still I find it rather better than I had imagined and Mr. Mitchell a much more sympathetic man than I had fancied. There are moments of strain, however, when it seems impossible to complete the year. Such a thought is as dangerous as a downwards glance to him who scales a great height, just exactly: it endangers all caretaking and precautions. Occasionally I have fits of talking Spanish with Elliott that nearly make me frantic. At other times I think tearfully of the personal charms of a young lady up in New Hampshire who is to me as the sour grapes of the fable. Five minutes later I may be playing ball with the boys, or telling a select circle of voyages and foreign lands. Then I get disgusted with all sorts of trifles, as always on returning from home where I have my own bed and Mother's good linen, to come here into this little affair that I have to double up to get into and has linen, well, not very reputable. Bah. I am as happy as can be expected under the circumstances.

And of the boys, Jefferson wrote:[9]

> With one or two exceptions the motive for their presence here is stupidity, laziness, or mischievousness. Else other schools would have

enjoyed the light of their presence. In short, this is a sort of Hospital for incurables, a last resort and to Mr. Mitchell's credit be it spoken that he has a considerable degree of success.

From the expansive and expanding Argentine, where refrigeration, speedier shipping, English capital, the railway, wire fences, and initiative were transforming a wilderness into an economic empire, Jefferson was obliged to consort with school boarders, the day long, in a little wooden school house in Billerica. Absent was the largeness of his South American undertakings; his vision of language study at a European university had been crushed by the Argentine inflation which decimated his South American savings; gone were the days of the warmth of Spanish life and the Latin graciousness of manner which so appealed to him; gone was his responsibility for running an entire sugar plantation. He was now slave to a love; a love that he could not live without, and yet a love that was not fulfilled. The woman of his dreams was living with her aunt at Gilmanton, New Hampshire, while he labored in a school house at Billerica, Massachusetts. He lived for a long weekend when he might visit her, for a vacation that they might share time together, for a letter from her, for the time when she would consent to engagement.

Jefferson tolerated this situation by creating his own amusements, driving himself always into work, play, or leisure with a fierce energy that quite infected the boys and made them wonder at him. The two other masters of the school, considerably older than the youthful Jefferson, were too stern and unbending to break faculty-student distance. When he collected stamps, the boys of the school collected stamps, writing to their friends and relatives in many parts of the world for the little adhesives. When the baseball season arrived Jefferson organized a team, managed it, and played pitcher against all comers. He pole vaulted, to keep his body a hard 132 pounds—the boys pole vaulted. He visited his family at Melrose for the weekend, playing whist with the group and talking books with his father—the boys fretted. He organized snowball fights, making sure that the rules of the game were observed. He would go for a walk and allow as many boys to go with him as chose, but few ever completed a Jefferson Saturday walk that might take him many miles on foot. He would row at a furious pace down the little river by the school house, and the boys would try to keep apace of him for a few yards. He would conduct searches for flint arrowheads, enjoy the extravagance of his Parisian-made bow ties, and sling hash for ten boys at his table, and yet find time to mark out a tennis court and teach the boys how to play with improvised bats. Jefferson was so intense, so empathetic under a seemingly gruff exterior, that the boys came to regard him with a fatherly affection. They would crowd into his bedroom-study at night and beg him to tell them more about his South American days. These experiences thrilled the boys so much, that he published "The Adventures of Don Marcos in South America," in the School weekly *Echo*. Within a very few weeks principal Mitchell had appointed Jefferson business manager, editor, and reporter for the school paper. In a fashion the boys became part of a family to Jefferson, and the school a form of home. As the months passed, he wrestled on the mat with the boys in their physical education classes, showed them how to tap maple trees, explained to them how he tried to combat a receding hairline by the application first of Jamaica rum, then of kerosene rubbed deep into the roots of the scalp, and finally by alternate hot and cold water massages. Regularly on Sunday he took twenty of them in line to church. After the service they would retire to Jefferson's room and make maps of the places mentioned in church. He won their respect, encountered no classroom discipline problem as did the second master, Mr. Parmenter, neither did Jefferson refer to force as the supreme arbiter as did principal Mitchell. In his spare moments he frequently indulged a deep and solitary study that obliged him to comment, "There is an amount of enjoyment in solitary study that can hardly be imagined by the uninitiated, yet it certainly tends to unfit a man to live among his kind which makes it dangerous."[10] His pedagogics would occasionally find their way into the letters he would write to Theodora from his bedroom, or prison chamber as he chose to call it:[11]

Really a teacher should become quite encyclopaedic! I wonder why they don't? Probably the best teachers are those who are most positive of character and such persons naturally are slow to learn. That may seem like a paradox yet I firmly believe it—that he who is slowest to learn may be best fitted to teach . . . For this week's English I am proposing to read to the boys one of Dickens' Christmas stories and make the boys retell as much of the story from memory as they can.

Numerous evidences suggest that Jefferson was appreciating the role of pedagogue and that he was beginning to realize he could never teach if the future meritorious works of his pupils were to be his sole reward, other than a modest salary. From 1901-1939 he was to spend thirty-nine years at the Michigan State Normal College training teachers, but he never did teach solely. At this later date he shared his thoughts with his students, discovering and relating his discoveries, making available to them what was believed and thought in the academic world.

While at the Mitchell Boys School Jefferson taught mathematics,

At the Mitchell Boys School, Billerica, Massachusetts.

English, Latin, Spanish, French, enough history to make the languages meaningful, and geography. It is interesting and instructive to trace the growth of a geographic interest on his part:

Notably in geography there exists such an ignorance that I invited my students to my room after dinner. I had prepared everything for map making. I set them to work, and it pleased them so much that they did not want to leave. If this continues I can have them learn to draw all the continents from memory. By this they will learn something, which seems to me a good point of departure for the geographer. Speaking of such matters, have I already told you that I was made active member of the Geographic Institute of the Republic of Argentina in 1887?[12]

Last night I spent in drawing a map of Europe. What a handy thing it is sometimes to teach a particular subject! I am immensely fond of geography and of some regions, notably South America, have some knowledge. But this class work is benefitting me immensely in such regions as the U.S. where I am very ignorant. I certainly doubt if the boys learn as much as I. My method is to draw an outline map on the blackboard without any names or divisions of countries. Then I point out seas, rivers, mountains and cities and demand the names.[13]

Now joined to certain facts suggested by yourself time since, and the remark of a distinguished townswoman of mine, Mrs. Farwell, that I might give "Illustrated Talks on S.A." before the Melrose clubs—all this sets me wondering whether I could interest average American audiences in a modest way in South American things, life, and ways, if aided by proper pictorial accessories.

I always have interested people about those lands, even without picture, witness the select companies that used to assemble nightly in the Cushing House, Hingham.[14]

The singing master sang the boys a song about the Bay o' Biscay this morning and made me think how I last saw it with the sun glancing across the rough crests and up against the black rock cliffs of Spain hanging rainbows through the spray that fell back after each thunderous crash on Finisterre. To think that same sun that shines so brightly in Billerica today may still be sending its slanting evening rays across those black seas to the lofty shore. Shall we ever gaze on those scenes together? The whole coast of Spain, North, East, South, and West, the Atlantic islands, the Riviera, the Pacific coast of South America, Brazil about Rio and the West Indian islands are all shores of towering rock, as different to gaze on from the sea, from Atlantic U.S. and northern Europe as can be. Low shores, like the American and northern French, make me feel as if the world was Sea, and Land the exception and insignificant. Mountain shores make me think less of the ocean and more of the significance of the land. There I realize that the Ocean is but the Highway of the Nations, the notion I remember having from books until the disillusion of my first voyage, which took me along our wretched flat coast as far as Virginia and gave me a poor idea of my country. I should so like to have you see such scenes as the Spanish and Mediterranean coast afford![15]

I spent a good deal of time yesterday drawing my map of Massachusetts on the board. I am quite proud of it. It is about a yard long with blue coast line and rivers, red cities and brown mountains. I am going to teach this state very elaborately, the subject is one I am very fond of and I incline to be as luxurious in the purchase of maps as `of books.[16]

I have . . . drawn a Mercator's projection map of the world, as far as the outline is concerned. I have yet to strengthen the lines and rub out some construction squares. Mr. Mitchell stopped before the boys the other day to congratulate me on my Geographical classes; said he never saw so much interest displayed in the study in his school as now. It is very fascinating to me and always has been, although it is not so easy to keep the boys attentive to the subject in hand.[17]

To one of my geography classes I gave as a reward of good work a 15 minute talk on how mountains came into existence which I had been holding over their heads for some time. Of course I didn't pretend to be deep: only tried to give them a simple, general notion of the way the earth came to wrinkle up in cooling. They seemed to like it.[18]

As the weeks passed a burning resentment of the high school situation consumed him. He was not conditioned to the cramping influence of the schoolhouse, was not used to accepting orders on matters of trivia from higher up, was bored with supervising a class of boys the day long and then shunting them off to bed. Letters from his South American friends continually turned his thoughts away from Billerica and southward toward the Spanish life. After receiving a letter from Kentuckian Alexander, a companion during Cordoban days, he wrote of his feeling in a letter to Theodora:[19]

What did I thrill to on reading Alexander's letter? Why the pleasurable excitement of an adventure loving young man who imagines a friend passing through such scenes as those of the Northern Argentine and Bolivia while I have been leading the slothful enervated life of an American school teacher. Imagine mule trains winding in sinuous course along the margin of torrential streams between fields of cane, tobacco and rice interspersed with groves of lemons and oranges. Further on, behind the plantation the tropical forest rears its deep green tangled mat, clothing the lower swell of hills that pile themselves, five

Mt. Washingtons high in the clear air to hide their snow crests in the clouds.

Presently the road leaves the lower reaches, plunges into the forests. A week later the party is winding up long slopes of grass and heather, soon to pass through the Andine portals to the sterile uplands of Bolivia and toil across barren stretches of sand and rock relieved mostly by patches of sage bush, on by the shores of Titicaca, across the nitrous plain of Atacama, till the defile of Antofagasta frames their first vision of a Pacific sunset! This is the vision filled in with a thousand details from Alexander's character as I read his lines. He says little about the journey, save that he made it. But it is as clear to me as if I had accompanied him. As I love such journies and am fond of his company on them, I thrill to think of them.

Under these circumstances, Jefferson proclaimed:[20]

I hate the Mitchell School, and I am tired of the boys. What a state of affairs! I am tired of it. What would be nice would be to take passage to Mexico in the first boat . . . I certainly gain daily the conviction that I cannot teach school permanently anywhere. Life under such circumstances is not worth living.

Theodora, anxious to have Jefferson please her aunt with whom she lived, requested that he stop smoking—which he did on September 20, 1890. But obedience without reason, brought only conformity without conviction, which led Jefferson to essay numerous brilliant, provocative, and passionate declarations against the indifference of New England conformity. He lived the year at the Mitchell Boys School in love: a shell of a man performed at the High School. His totality was a constellation, an hierarchy of aching assent to Theodora's every wish. It was a beautiful, total love. He spent much of his time, as do men in love, meditating, making notes on scraps of paper, ranging in subject from Greek speculation to the contemporary inadequacy of the Church, but spending most of his time writing letters to Theodora. These letters, sent thrice weekly, averaged not less than 5,000 words each. They were beautifully scribed, indeed works of art quite unlike Jefferson's later inimitable style handed down to the geographic world—terse, concise, without embellishment. It was a poetry that not only won the hand of Theodora from another suitor, a Mr. Curtis Page, but also provided Jefferson with a period of introspection. He was able to use his languages, frequently writing to Theodora in German, French, and occasionally Greek. In the August of 1891, after serving one year in the Billerica Boarding School, he married Theodora and consummated a romance commenced at Boston University some nine years previously.

In the fall of 1891 Jefferson accepted a position as principal of the

Turners Falls High School. He had resigned his position at the Mitchell Boys School, but had not at that time, been able to find another position, especially as he desired $1200 a year instead of the more usually offered $1000 a year. In seeking a position, Jefferson had a rather embittering experience. He obtained interviews for several positions through a "five-percent teachers' agency," only to be rejected once for smoking, a habit recently regained, once for not going to church regularly, once for drinking, and once for travelling far too much, which showed naturally, that he was not a settled body.

At the Turner Falls school Jefferson was requested to teach a class in physical geography. Not having studied physical geography, he refused to teach the subject, and substituted a course in French. The students learned to speak the French language while solving geometrical problems from Bos' *Géométrie Elémentaire*. Jefferson wrote:[21]

> *This book gave us vocabulary and theorems to demonstrate and the familiarity of the subject matter made a sort of conversation possible. The first thing they knew, they were talking a little in French, or something like it. From then on, progress was automatic.*

Jefferson wanted to teach the requested course in physical geography at Turners Falls High School and so, in the summer of 1892, he took an intensive six-week summer course at Harvard University in earth science. It delighted a Jefferson who now began to understand a physical landscape that previously he had but looked upon.[22]

> *That summer I met Professor Shaler, spent a week with him making photographs of Cape Cod for the State Road Commission. But I soon found William Morris Davis who was making a revolution in physical geography at Harvard. Shaler, head of the Lawrence Scientific School, pulled hundreds of students into the Department of Geology by a freshman course of lectures (geology 4) which was immensely popular. He gave them poetic aspects of earth science. From the start in two summer courses I found the work exactly what I wanted.*

He kept diaries of his summer's work, thought the "one R at a time" a great scheme, wore out two pairs of boots tramping the New England countryside six days a week. This training enabled Jefferson to understand Darwin's comprehension of South America. He wanted to pursue such study. Of the following year at Turners Falls High School Jefferson wrote in notes to himself, "This was a marvellous revelation of a world unknown. Now Jefferson must study natural sciences. This year a wonderful class in physical geography among Turners Falls' marvellous Triassic trap and sandstone ridges."

It was not long before word of his ability as a school teacher began to travel. A lawyer and member of the Lexington board of trustees, came to hear him conducting his class. Jefferson was offered a position as both teacher and superintendent of Lexington schools, and at a considerably higher pay than previously. Jefferson accepted the position and in the same year commenced a family which was to include five children by the turn of the century. Possessed of a great measure of efficiency and initiative, Jefferson was not willing merely to execute policy pronounced by the School Board of Education. And there lay a trouble. Soon the Board and Jefferson were opposed on matters which included the time at which school should open, the number of spelling classes to be held each week, what bible instruction should be given, who should read the Lord's Prayer, how Latin should be taught, the amount of woodwork instruction which should be granted each week. Recognizing Jefferson as administratively competent and able of intellect, they were reluctant to release him from his duties. The Board encouraged him to take a vacation, since they felt that his terseness of manner stemmed from overwork. In the February and early March of 1895 he took his wife and first born son, Geoffrey, on a month's cruise through the Windward Islands of the Caribbean Sea, stopping at St. Thomas, St. Kitts, Montserrat, Antigua, Nevis, Guadeloupe, St. Lucia, Martinique, Dominica, St. Vincent, Barbados, and Trinidad. They escaped the coldness of winter, a season that Jefferson shunned till the end of his days. The geographer of the family took many photographs, and spent much of his time trying to convince his wife that the year-round warmth was good for her rheumatism and that life under the Southern Heavens would hold a happy future for them and their family. But Theodora did not wish to leave the New England she knew so well, and Jefferson refrained from pressing her further. On his return from the Caribbean, Jefferson continued as superintendent of the Lexington School, but was hardly happy in the position. Early in 1896, his wife's aunt, Mary Horne, died. By the terms of her will, money had been made available to Jefferson for the purpose of furthering his education. He resigned his post at the Lexington School and enrolled as student in Harvard University.

From the September of 1896 to the July of 1898 Jefferson studied geography and geology at Harvard. He planned to study all the natural science that had enabled Darwin to comprehend the Argentine as evidenced by the *Journal of Researches*. Jefferson selected all the elementary courses possible:[23]

When the Director of the Graduate School found in 1896 that I was electing so many elementary courses and already had an A.B. degree, he suggested that I might be able to get a Ph.D. in the two years I meant to spend if I would select advanced courses following some of the work I had already done. He did not realize that he was cutting the ground from under my feet. I wanted those elementary courses. They were what brought me to Harvard. His suggestion fell on stony ground. I took elementary everything in Natural Science and all the geology and geography I could get.

In his first year at Harvard (1896-1897) Jefferson was awarded an A.B. degree, and in his second year (1897-1898) he was awarded an A.M. degree. More important to Jefferson than the acquisition of these degrees was the discovery of William Morris Davis. Davis had occupied the same post in the Argentine National Observatory at Cordoba in 1873, as had Jefferson in 1883. On his return to Harvard in 1873 Davis was made instructor under Shaler in the Department of Geology. From 1885-1889 Davis enjoyed first an assistant professorship and then a professorship of physical geography. From 1899 until his retirement from Harvard in 1912, Davis held the Sturgis Hooper professorship of geology. Notwithstanding President Eliot's suggestion in a letter of January 1882 that he seek opportunity elsewhere, Davis retained his employ, emerged with his concept of the cycle of erosion, and inspired students (five of them starred in *American Men of Science*) including Bowman, Dodge, Goldthwaite, Huntington, Jefferson, Johnson, Keith, Marbut, and Tarr. It was in 1907 that Huntington dedicated *The Pulse of Asia*, "To William Morris Davis First of Modern Geographers." In the preface to his book Huntington proclaimed "To him [Davis] half the geographers of America, myself among number, owe their instruction in the new science . . ."

When Jefferson enrolled at Harvard in 1896 he met a confident, well-read, much thinking, much published 46-year-old Davis who was finding a place for physical geography as a worthy discipline. Listening to Davis intently, seeing virtue in every idea, hungrily consuming Davis' every spoken and written word, travelling many a field mile with the man, and believing in the value of earth science was a perceptive, intelligent, and well-travelled Jefferson. Davis had an educated audience in the 33-year-old Jefferson: Jefferson had a teacher. Davis and Jefferson were drawn closely together in an enduring relationship which extended from 1896 to the time of Davis' death in 1934. Years later, in autobiographical notes, Jefferson was to write:[24]

When Davis commenced teaching at Harvard, his subject was physical geography, in those days the foundling orphan of the natural sciences. But Davis had made his subject respected on both sides of the Atlan-

tic: in 1899, ten years after he developed the peneplain concept, Davis was given ovations in London, Cambridge and Oxford, where Professor Sollas introduced him as Professor Peneplain Davis. Later the universities of Paris and Berlin called him to give courses, which he did in French and German.

The more you checked his teaching against the out-of-doors, the sounder you found it. Surely Davis read God's thoughts about the surface of the earth . . . As a geographer he (Davis) was entirely new to me: his teaching the best of considerable good teaching. But he was not always easy to take. His was a school of intellectual hard knocks.

We had a would-be student from the Sorbonne with us for some days, but presently he departed with actual tears in his eyes. Professor Davis' teaching was the most interesting thing I ever met. Confronted with the world of out-of-doors his formulae proved up. I took all his courses at Harvard, a summer school with him and two other students in the Rocky Mountains in 1910, a trip in 1911 across Wales, England, France, Switzerland and Italy as far as Milan by train, carriage and on foot, with three Germans, a Norwegian and Czech and Jap, and locally guided and accompanied by native geographers all the way, among them the cream of European geography. Invited to an international geographical Congress at Rome, we were stopped at Milan by a request from Italian royalty to come no further. Italy and Turkey were at war.

One year later Jefferson was appointed first marshall of the Davis-American Geographical Society Transcontinental Excursion (U.S.A.).

He [Davis] put me in personal touch with the geographers of the world. He gave me his books and papers and asked for mine. I was privileged to know his charming home in Cambridge and was in correspondence with him to the end of his life. What a teacher![25]

The courses that Jefferson studied at Harvard in the Geography and Geology Department included:

Shaler, Woodworth, and Woodman—Elementary Geology (Lectures with collateral reading, 2 hours)

Davis—Physiography (Lectures, written exercises, laboratory and field work, 4 hours and additional laboratory and field work)

Ward—Meteorology (Lectures, written exercises, observations, and laboratory work, 4 hours and additional laboratory work)

Davis and Ward—Physiography and Meteorology (Lectures, 2 hours)

Jaggar—Experimental and Dynamical Geology (Lectures [2 hours], laboratory work, and occasional field work)

Ward—Climatology (Lectures, library work, and reports, 3 hours)

Shaler and Jackson—General Palaeontology (Lectures and thesis, 2 hours)

Jackson—Invertebrate Palaeontology (Lectures (2 hours) and laboratory work)

Davis—Physiography (advanced course), (Conferences, reports, and thesis, 1 hour)

Davis—Research Course

Jaggar, in cooperation with Shaler, Davis, Wolff, Smyth, and Woodworth—Advanced Geological Field Work (Field and Library work, with reports, conference of 1 hour, and additional laboratory hours)

Shaler and Jackson—Advanced Palaeontology (Laboratory work and thesis)

This was the only formal education Jefferson ever received in geography. It was sufficient to inspire him to the end of his days.

During Jefferson's years at Harvard, the University boasted 4,000 students, over 400 faculty and research fellows, half a million bound volumes, and was under the sound and imaginative leadership of Charles Eliot. Davis and Shaler were already names recognized wherever geography and geology were read and spoken. Harvard University constituted a fine galaxy of minds which included, among many more, James, Royce, Santayana, Münsterberg, Wright, Greenough, and Copeland. The Harvard Yard was a meeting place of intellect, and Jefferson treasured the privilege those two years afforded him.

In 1897 Davis suggested to Jefferson that he write a thesis concerning the geography of tides. Although Jefferson did not like the suggestion, "saw nothing in it," he undertook the study. Davis approved the paper, wanted to see it in print, but cautioned that it was rather long for magazine publication. Davis arranged for his pupil to read part of the paper to a student-faculty club at Harvard, encouraged him to revise and rearrange the study, then to send an extract to the *National Geographic Magazine*. Editor John Hyde accepted Jefferson's "Atlantic Estuarine Tides" enthusiastically:[26]

> It has . . . been arranged for the National Geographic Society to have a session at the meeting of the American Association for the Advancement of Science at Boston, on August the 25th, and it occurs to me that your paper might with great advantage be read at that meeting, and published in the September number of the Magazine.

The paper was read and W J McGee[27] was one of a number who listened attentively. A little later he wrote to Jefferson inquiring if the secretaryship of the National Geographic Society would be "a temptation" to him.[28] Jefferson replied that the offer was gratifying but $1500 a year in Washington, D.C. would not feed the family. Parts of Jefferson's thesis on tides were printed in three subsequent issues of the *National Geographic Magazine* under the titles "Atlantic Estuarine Tides,"[29] "What is the Tide of the Open Atlantic,"[30] and "Atlantic Coast Tides,"[31] From Cannes, France, December 17, 1898, Davis sent a postcard to Jefferson:[32]

Your article on Tide of Open Atlantic is very interesting and instructive. I am very glad to have so many important points brought together so concisely—The historical is very nicely presented. Keep it up, if you have the time. I have to differ from your closing speculation. Would not the mid-ocean be swept clean and deepened if its form depended on tides alone? The mid-ocean bottom must be the place of strongest back and forth horizontal currents while mid-ocean surface is stationary at the node. Try it in a basin and see where the sediment will collect. Perhaps you have done so already—and your experiment may show my objection to be wrong. I am glad to hear from Ginn and Co. that my everlasting book will soon be published.

Davis continually encouraged Jefferson by taking a personal interest in him and his work. Later Jefferson wrote:[33]

During a ten days' confinement to my bed in the spring of 1898, I reread Caesar's commentaries, partly to pass the time and partly to find out whether Caesar's campaigns were more intelligible in the light of Professor Davis' lectures on French geography, which I had recently heard. Judge of my delight when I found that the origin and course of the Gallic wars were closely bound up with a very prominent feature in the physical geography of France: namely the Central Plateau.

While Jefferson had been confined to bed with pneumonia, Davis visited him and noticed Allen and Greenough's *Caesar* on his bed of sickness. He was interested to find the paper that Jefferson had recently completed, and sent it to Professor Greenough. The latter invited Jefferson to his house where "a pleasant half hour resulted." He was given an autographed copy of Greenough's latest *Caesar,* and "Allen and Greenough" meant two genial gentlemen to Jefferson rather than the Latin Grammar and an edition of the commentaries with which he had been familiar for twenty-two years. "Caesar and the Central Plateau of France" was published in the *Journal of School Geography,* 1899, with a footnote:[34] "I am indebted to Professors W. M. Davis and J. B. Greenough of Harvard University for a careful reading of this paper and valuable suggestions as to the manner of presentation."

Davis had shown Jefferson that Harvard was not merely a collection of books, faculty, and buildings—that it was the hearthplace of an academic way of life.[35]

> *I was learning that the great University in a little city has both students and faculty in residence, to its very great advantage. Has it not always been so? Can the University of London ever mean to England what Cambridge and Oxford have meant?*
>
> *If I had wanted to draw some comparisons between Xenophon and Arrian in my great city university (Boston), how could the instructor help pulling out his watch? Did he not live thirty miles away with a train leaving in a few minutes? At Harvard I knew the dining rooms of several of my instructors . . . Geography was indicated for my life's work by Davis.*

In the summer of 1898 Jefferson taught geography at Harvard University as assistant to W. M. Davis. In the fall of the same year, Jefferson was appointed sub-master of six hundred students at the Brockton High School, and was required to teach "too many subjects": Greek, Latin, bookkeeping, geology, and astronomy. Jefferson asked to add a voluntary course in field work, "the geology of Brockton." Students who took this voluntary work were obliged to come out of school hours, either before eight in the morning or after one o'clock when school closed for the day. Many students accompanied Jefferson on these trips which encouraged other schools to adopt classes in field studies. This encouraged the School Board to print Jefferson's twenty-four page account of "The Fields of Brockton,"[36] which was then adopted as a field text by several schools in the area. Attention was brought to these field trips in *The Brockton Enterprise,* November 13, 1899:

> *The session (Conference of Educators in Springfield) began at 11 a.m. at the High Schoolhouse. Mr. Perry of Worcester introducing the subject of field excursions in connection with High School work in geology . . . No other town is doing so much systematic work in this direction, as Brockton. Attention was called in the discussion to the Brockton plan of weekly excursions . . .*
>
> *Mr. Jefferson followed with an account of work with the weather map in the Brockton school, pointing out the devices employed to make the work practicable, and the way in which the map is actually handled by the pupils until it is familiarly understood.*

At this time inference strongly suggests that Jefferson was corresponding with Britain's A. J. Herbertson who was then engaged in preparing a rainfall map of the world,[37] and this fascinated Jefferson who passed what information he had on to his students.

The following year Jefferson taught Greek and four sections of physical geography which included field work. A number of talks he gave in the community further advertised physiography and geography. *The Brockton Enterprise* occasionally reported Jefferson's talks as "The Physiography of Brockton," November 6, 1889, and "The Geography of Melrose," November 15, 1900. He submitted brief articles to the *Enterprise* on a variety of subjects which included: erratic weather behavior, geographic interpretation of local art, photographic exhibits, or recently published postage stamps, and the geography of current events.

Davis did not forget his pupil teaching at Brockton some twenty miles removed from Harvard. Occasionally Davis would visit Jefferson, talk to his pupils, or address a gathering of teachers from nearby schools which Jefferson might have arranged. He recognized Jefferson as a well-educated mind, and, in March 1899, he wrote:[38]

> *If you have time, I wish you would mark in your copy of my Physical Geography the paragraphs that should be retained, compressed, expanded, and omitted, in reducing the book to* Grammar *grade. I will then exchange your copy for a new one! Two pamphlets go to you by mail today.*

Later in the same year Davis suggested Jefferson's name to President Eliot as the man to teach geography to the Cubans in the forthcoming Harvard Summer School. From the summer of 1898 until Davis' death in 1934, the two men corresponded. They exchanged published papers, ideas and observations relating largely to physiography, and news of their families. Davis' appreciation of Jefferson was fortunate for the latter, who did not find it easy to win people to his side.

In the years 1899-1901, Jefferson lived at Elmwood, an attractive village three miles from Brockton. Founded originally to make cotton gins for sale in the South, the Elmwood community now found its main business accommodating railway commuters from the Brockton shoe factories. W. L. Douglas of the Brockton bank, well known for a "Three Dollar Shoe," offered Jefferson a house at Elmwood possessed by the bank after the financial collapse of the builder. The accommodation was good. The house had its own lighting and sewage system, "an admirable polished oak interior," and was surrounded by fruit trees set in spacious grounds. Jefferson paid twenty dollars a month rental to Douglas, who was anxious to have the dwelling inhabited.

The Jefferson family was happy and content. In 1901 both Mark and Theodora passed their thirty-eighth birthday and had a family of five children. Jefferson was beginning to wonder if he would find a university position, or whether he would settle in Elmwood.

CHAPTER THREE

THE CUBAN SUMMER SCHOOL, HARVARD
UNIVERSITY, 1900

The Spanish-American conflict of the year 1898 had passed. The Battle of Santiago, the Blockade, and the episode of the Rough Riders were history. The post-war Cuba was poverty-ridden, war-torn, and desolate. Educational facilities on the Island were minimal. School attendance was not compulsory, neither were the attendees compulsive in their attendance. President McKinley of the U.S.A., in concert with existing Cuban authority, appointed Alexis E. Frye and Leonard Wood to supervise, improve, and if necessary, remodel Cuban education. Frye gave his services to the cause without salary, and Wood had at that time recently rejected a position of substance with private enterprise in the U.S.A.

Employing foresight, initiative, and hard work, the Cuban Department of Education was able to announce in January, 1900, that 80,000 children were studying in the public schools of Cuba. Four months later, in May, 1900, this figure had risen to 130,000. In that month Mr. Frye announced that 3,379 public schools were flourishing, 3,500 teachers were employed, and 3,500 tons of school equipment and furniture were in use. Frye, earnest in his attempt at educational reform, braved a stormy unrest of those indigenes who visualized a *Cuba libre*. In the face of criticism he reorganized the school curriculum. Under the old system children embroidered dresses, shirts, blouses for the larger part of the day; this work was then sold and the resultant monies were given to the teacher for salary. Frye changed that. He realized the value of a well planned curriculum, the value of teacher self-improvement, and so proposed three Normal schools for the Island.

The establishment of these schools, however, would require time, whereas the educational problems demanded immediate attention. Fortunately, Mr. Frye was not the only American who saw the need for educational facilities and opportunities for the Cuban people. A Mr. Ernest Lee Conant proposed to Frye that during the summer of 1900 some ten or twenty Cuban teachers be sent to Harvard University for an educational experience which would benefit them and, on their return, the Island of Cuba.[1] Mr. Frye could find no encouragement or enthusiasm for this venture, but by enlarging the scheme and proposing that approximately one-third of the teachers of Cuba be given schooling at Harvard University in the summer of 1900, he was able to at once secure support for the venture. The parochial suggestion had failed, the plan for a national movement was to succeed.[2]

Late in June, five army transports—the *Sedgwick, Crook, McPherson, McClellan,* and *Burnside*—jointly collected some thirteen hundred Cuban school teachers from fourteen ports. Two-thirds of these thirteen hundred teachers were women. Some mothers acted as chaperones in the traditional Spanish pattern. Then began the seven-day journey north to Cambridge. Meanwhile President McKinley had sanctioned the plan, Secretary of War, Mr. Root, had provided free transport for the Cubans between their homeland and Cambridge on the Charles River, families in the environs of Harvard had extended their hospitalities to the Caribs, and President Eliot had, by private subscription around Boston, raised $70,000 to defray the expenses of the summer program at Harvard. The Cubans, who had undergone physical examinations before leaving their isle, brought with them physicians conversant with their problems to tend them at times when the passage became rough. By June 30th, the first of the teachers were landed at the Navy Yard at Charlestown. Mr. Mann, who was manager at Harvard for the undertaking, was assisted by sixty younger men, many of whom wore badges, indicating proficiency in the Spanish language. Numerous other officials were present at the landing, at which time each of the ladies was presented with a bouquet of flowers at the Navy Yard. The Cuban women wore brightly colored clothing such as was rarely seen in New England. This was an invasion of Cambridge by people of another culture, but the Cambridge of 1900 was equal to an accommodation of the Caribs. President Eliot of Harvard received protests from local groups concerning painted Cuban women who smoked and drank, but he remained firm in the belief that there should be no encroachment upon their way of life. The visitors, aged from 14 to 60, a majority probably in their twenties, made Cambridge their home for the next six weeks. A beautiful Cuban flag dominated Harvard's University Hall while brilliant U.S. trimmings abounded.

In addition to the regular Harvard summer school, a special program was established for the Cubans.[3] This included regular courses in English, in the history of the United States, in Spanish American colonies, and in physical geography. W. M. Davis recommended Jefferson strongly to President Eliot for the geographer's post, since his one-time pupil was not only thoroughly versed in geography but also because he had lived in Spanish speaking South America for six years. In April, 1900, Jefferson received a letter from President Eliot suggesting that they discuss the possibility of his teaching physical geography to some 1,300 Cuban schoolteachers for the summer session.[4]

> *Dear Sir,*
>
> *May I see you at my office, no. 5, University Hall, Cambridge, within a day or two about teaching Cuban teachers this summer? I expect to be in my office every day this week between twelve and one, and between five and six.*
>
> *Very truly yours,*
> *Charles W. Eliot*

Jefferson accepted the job which the Harvard President offered him and at once began making outlines of his intended 18 lectures and 12 field excursions. The eighteen lectures were entitled:

I.	*Weathering & Soils*
II.	*Transportation*
III.	*Deposition*
IV.	*Limestones*
V.	*Elevation & Depression*
VI.	*Elevation & Depression (continued)*
VII.	*Sculpture*
VIII.	*Crystallines*
IX.	*Rivers & Valleys*
X.	*Rivers & Valleys (continued)*
XI.	*Plains*
XII.	*Mountains*
XIII.	*Mountains (continued)*
XIV.	*Shorelines*
XV.	*Winds*
XVI.	*Climate*
XVII.	*Man on the Earth*
XVIII.	*Man on the Earth (continued)*

The excursions Jefferson planned were essentially to local areas:

I.   Medford (soil and rock weathering)
II.   Beaver Brook (transportation)
III.   Cambridge Clays (deposition)
IV.   Atlantic (marine deposition)
V.   Cambridge Slates (consolidation-elevation)
VI.   Hobbs Brook (valley carving)
VII.   Neponset Marshes (river deposition)
VIII. Riverside Terrace
IX.   Nantasket (shore lines)
X.   Clifton (ocean erosion)
XI.   Arlington Heights (general review)
XII.   Melrose (differential erosion-review)

Summaries of these lectures and excursions were published bilingually in English and Spanish in two little booklets.[5] Each lecture warranted a program summary of approximately 150 words, necessarily planned and written at short notice. For a while Jefferson was taking preparatory wheel trips with his assistants and making final arrangements at Harvard; he was still teaching, examining, and helping with class graduation at the Brockton High School.

After the summer school had commenced, the *Educational Review* noted:[6]

> Great things were expected of the course in geography in the way of arousing and stimulating the interest of the teachers and to effect this purpose the course was divided into two parts, the first to consist of lectures by Mr. Mark S. Jefferson, assistant principal of the Brockton High School, and the second of excursions and tours afield. The work of the course was really that of an elementary geological class, resembling closely the course known as Geology 4, which Professor Shaler gives at Harvard. It consisted chiefly of a rapid study of common land formations, and in order that the work might be carried out successfully, great stress was placed upon the field excursions. It was these field excursions, however, which proved one of the great stumbling blocks in the path of the teachers.
>
> The Cubans, especially the women, are but little used to long car rides and protracted tramps afoot, and to be dragged forth from Cambridge three times a week, carried out into the country, and there, after a tiresome walk, to be lectured upon "sand plains" and relics of the glacial period was almost more than they could endure. Many of them were prostrated with fatigue, and even as the season advanced and they

became more accustomed to the expeditions and felt the strain of a life under new conditions somewhat less, they seemed to take but little interest in the real purpose of the trips.

Jefferson himself wrote an article for *The Enterprise*, Saturday, August 18, 1900, which was entitled "Summer School for Cubans and the work it has done."[7] The newspaper article gives one of the most thorough printed insights into the Cuban Summer School:

Mr. Frye, acting on a chance suggestion of Ernest Lee Conant, sought to select the fittest of Cuban teachers and infuse them with new zeal and inspiration by a summer at Harvard University. Every summer hundreds of eager American teachers flock to Cambridge for advanced instruction at their own expense. Besides knowledge, they obtain there personal contact with foremost American scientists, scholars and men of letters, and our other great universities see similar gatherings each year. Perhaps there is no single agency operative today for the uplifting of our best schools from the dangers of routine and dullness so powerful as this.

A great effort was made to secure those most fit to receive impressions and communicate them to those who must remain behind. The maximum number was at once fixed at 1440, the total seating capacity of Sanders Theatre, where instruction was to be given them in form of lectures. This meant about a third of Mr. Frye's teachers and it was hoped to obtain a selection of the cream of all.

But many things contributed to make this difficult. In fact, many newspapers in Cuba antagonized the movement. Assuming the motive back of the whole thing was self-interest, it was widely asserted that the United States sought to make missionaries of the teachers for the cause of annexation. To teach the children, we were supposed to reason, was cheaper than conquer the adults. In some circles in Cuba it is possible that such sentiments made it imprudent for a teacher to join the party. Again, many Cuban teachers are women, and Creole women would inevitably be astonished if not shocked at the proposition to separate themselves from the protection of their homes even in company with members of their countrywomen. This cause again doubtless contributed to deter many suitable persons from making the venture. From these and other motives it happened that only 1285 Cubans have presented themselves at Harvard of the 1440 for whom preparation was made, and some of these were not those for whom the work was really planned.

The best were teachers of experience, who came with zeal and positive thirst for knowledge and singular absence of animus to defend their methods in the presence of more modern ones proposed. They carry with them to Cuba all that those earnest American teachers who throng the summer schools take back to their school rooms—knowledge, enthusiasm and hope for better things. The proposition that these teachers do extra work was met by a response from more than 90 per cent. They saw good schools and modern apparatus, they who had never known a schoolhouse other than as a room in the teacher's dwelling. They went back wanting things, and some of those things they will obtain.

Others who accompanied them were not filled with their high ambitions. They were teachers of routinary mood seeking an outing; teachers of a few months' or, in some cases, no experience, carried away by the prospect of a bit of travel without expense. Some even may have hoped to remain in the American promised land, once they reach it, and hailed with joy the prospect of so good an introduction to its language. Upon these I am inclined to think the effects of the sojourn in Cambridge has been most surprising and most hopeful, for the influence that none could escape has been the influence of foreign travel and contact with a strange people with a closeness and intimacy never before attained in so short a period. For what Cuban hitherto visiting this region has not in six weeks, but in six months, or even six years, seen so much of New England institutions, business culture, home life and good society, as has been generously bestowed upon these schoolteachers?

Ignorance regards the foreigner with undisguised contempt, and travel is an excellent eye opener. I remember hearing a Portuguese teacher in a little school on one of the Cape Verde Islands hold up the Americans and English as monstrosities because their children fought with their hands until their faces bled, and thought of it again later when a teacher in Concord, Mass., portrayed the Spanish as brutal for their love of bull fighting. Could those two women have traveled they would have learned to be less sweeping in their judgments, and have come nearer the conception of the existence of vice and virtue in all lands.

I think the best elements in New England character for the contemplation of Spanish Americans is our putting our hands to the plough, and our respect for the law. Personal labor is still regarded as degrading in Spanish-American countries and regions rich with nature's bounty show little of man's work after centuries of occupation. Our respect for property everywhere seemed to impress the Cuban visitors deeply, even where to an American it did not seem pronounced.

The Cubans, too, have cultivated certain character elements more than we, and the best of these I think are manners and joyousness.

President Eliot, in his opening address in Sanders Theatre, called it "a unique experiment in mutual service. We are going", he said, "to see how much we can enlarge each other's minds and sympathies, and strengthen each other's sense of brotherhood."

Of this a good deal has been realized. The Americans who have been thrown in contact with the Cubans at Harvard have gained in manners and cheerfulness. It is to be regretted on the American side that there was not more and more intimate contact with the visitors. I have observed with especial interest their conduct under those little privations incident to a sojourn in a foreign land. Coming from a country where all the food has the high Spanish seasoning, where the coffee is high roasted, as in all coffee raising countries, where wine is in universal use at every meal, their six weeks on American food in prohibition Cambridge, with thin American coffee, must have tended to try their patience. Things of this sort are harder to bear than more serious evils, as touching our daily habits. Yet there was no sign. They admitted freely that they missed the home table when asked, but that was all. Almost universal recognition prevailed that they were recipients of unprecedented courtesies. Good literature for a Cuban must still cover much Spanish literature, and Spanish opinions still pervade Spanish-American thought. Thus it is likely that the Spanish conception of the reign of commercialism among us is widely held in Cuba.

One result of this visit will be a complete destruction of any such idea in Cuba henceforth. They have come remembering their traditions of Yankee rudeness, and they go persuaded of the culture of New England and our reliance on education to preserve the institutions of our fathers.

For the summer Jefferson took a room at 41 Matthews Hall, Cambridge: "The room is admirable up one flight, corner on the Quadrangle, and looking out on Harvard Square; sitting room 15' x 12', bedroom and closets." From this vantage point he could see the Cuban teachers walking and talking, frequently in pairs, frequently in groups. Not anxious to be known as one of the teaching faculty of the summer school, he also refused a badge indicating that he could translate. In this way he could enjoy their chatter in the early days of the summer and escape unrecognized:[8]

The Cubans are about, and though the morning is delightful, they evidently have a prejudice against air, as two go by with their handkerchiefs to their noses, and a third with mouth and nose enveloped in a scarf. It reminds me of letting out of Opera at Cordoba in winter when everyone protected mouth and nose with a handkerchief.

He was initially a little apprehensive of his fluency in Spanish, for he

had not spoken the language regularly since his Tucuman sugar plantation days terminated in 1889, though he had maintained a steady correspondence with his South American friends and some Spanish-speaking
boys from his days at the Mitchell Boys School, Billerica. Additionally
he had travelled Cuba in March, 1895, with his wife and first-born. He
wrote to his wife just before summer school commenced:[9]

> I am beginning to feel now that the great thing is to get the first
> lecture off. I have more time from day to day than I have now in
> school for my lessons, and if I am to put in twenty slides every time, it
> cannot be so much to make a forty-five minute talk, even in Spanish.
> Really a good deal depends on what is President Eliot's appreciation,
> which is of value in the long run.

Jefferson need not to have worried. Very soon he wrote to his wife:[10]

> You would love to see me start out on the Sanders platform at 9:30
> a.m. and the hissing start, which is the South American way of making
> conversation stop . . .

> [11] The fatal day is past, the lecture was middling, the slides fine, the
> principles sought brought out well enough and I made myself heard
> with President Eliot stalking about and telling me once from behind to
> speak louder.

> Excursions superb—they worked finely but I am too tired and to-
> morrow must go better than today though the excursions cannot. Frye
> complimented me on the lecture and Dr. Eliot well implied that it was
> no failure.

And again[12]

> . . . The second lecture was a great success—some few did not hear
> everything and when explaining the pictures sometimes I spoke care-
> lessly and was not heard. But I got out in the open, away from my
> notes and fired away and held the attention of all. I spoke easily,
> rapidly enough and came out only 7 minutes late which I thought was
> pretty near. President Eliot has declared himself not badly impressed
> yesterday. Others have spoken very well indeed of it . . .

> I suppose I told you that the excursions yesterday were great, all
> agreed that they had never had a class so diligent and in every way so
> attentive. But thirsty—we are to organize a water supply for the future
> . . . I gave you too bad an impression of the Cubans. The first ship
> was from Santiago, very rustic naturally. The people from the Habana
> region are better. Still they do walk on the grass and throw cigar butts
> around.

The Cubans attended Jefferson's classes well, found the geography to
their liking and requested that he have the series of lectures published
in Spanish in order that they might be able to use them in Cuba.

Jefferson prepared the lectures and offered them to Ginn and Company, but Ginn declined: they had already published *Frye's Grammar School Geography* in 1895 and 1899 and had undertaken a third revision which was published in 1902. The Cubans frequently sought Jefferson, that he might take them to the museum and offer explanations. Some Cubans wanted him to tutor them in the English language, others wished to talk of Caribbean and Cuban problems, others wished simply to chat with him. He enjoyed these moments, although the acceptance on one such occasion of a Cuban cigarette, whose leaf was unseasoned, poisoned his lips rather severely. Frequently he took meals with them. Soon he was receiving photographs of Cuba from the teachers and being showered with invitations to visit them in Cuba. He did visit them three years later in Cuba at which time his students of Sanders Theatre escorted him the length and breadth of the Island, showing him that nothing was too great an inconvenience for them in his behalf.

While lecturing in the Cuban Summer School, Jefferson renewed his acquaintance with the Harvard Geography staff, and more especially W. M. Davis, N. Shaler, and R. DeCourcy Ward. Jefferson borrowed some slides for his lectures from the Harvard departmental collection, while other slides he took from his own collection. He persuaded Davis to undertake several of his excursions to see how they might be improved; he also had the aid of six bilingual assistants equipped with bicycles. The excursions had been carefully planned. Several of the trips were local Harvard field course trips, while others had been especially planned for the occasion by Jefferson who was familiar with that part of the country. Opinions varied as to the success of the excursions.

The *Educational Review* wrote:[13]

> The remarks of the lecturer on the peculiarities of the phenomena which they had been brought out (in the field) to observe received but little attention from the majority of them, and a stray baby by the wayside was enough to completely demoralize a whole party, while an oddity in the way of fence construction has been known to absorb attention entirely to the exclusion of the lecturer. This lack of interest and total inability to concentrate the attention which the Cubans exhibited was more in evidence on these trips than anywhere else but in reality it was everywhere through-out the school: it pervaded the atmosphere, and it soon became easy to see that in spite of certain more or less unavoidable defects in the school, what the Cuban teachers lacked was not the appliances to work with, but the inclination to work. The trip was regarded by them as a gigantic picnic with a little study thrown in, but only a little.

The *Lynn Newspaper* noted:[14]

A very interesting excursion was to Squantum. The teachers on this excursion were the men who are school directors. Of about 40 names called out, 36 were present when we boarded the car at Harvard square, Monday, July 30. We left the square at 1:30 p.m. and went by special car to City Point, and from there to Squantum by a small steamer. On the way down from City Point the teachers were requested to make sketches of the coast line of Thompson's Island and show the slope of the land. They were also told to note the inclination of a grove of pine trees located near the water. This inclination of the trees is caused by the creeping of the earth. As the bases or roots, incline, the top straightens. From the boat there did not appear to be a tree not affected by this creeping of the earth.

Upon arrival at Squantum a few minutes were spent, while on the boat in explanation of the shoreline. The party then landed and remained for about an hour and a half, using the time in the study of the sea cliffs. The explanation was on the stratification of the rock, its cause, and the action of the sea upon the same. On the south side of the point there is a deposit of rock that is slaty in appearance. At this place the teachers were instructed to make sketches showing the inclination of the strata and their sections. In some instances the teachers made very good sketches. These were not intended to be pictorial. After the explanation, the lecturer, Prof. M. S. W. Jefferson, asked the teachers what they had learned from his explanation. The answers came from the older members of the party. The discussion was interesting and the answers indicated close observation on the part of the one answering.

The teachers saw the Myles Standish monument erected to the Indian Chief Squantum. Here, as in other places, the teachers copied the inscription on the monument, and not being satisfied with that they questioned Prof. Jefferson about the reason of the monument being erected. Their questions were answered briefly and to the point, and notes were made of the general appearance of the monument, and the explanation given of its history.

A new feature has been introduced in the lecture work of the excursions. The teachers are now required to write what they think is the cause of the geographical features which are to be explained to them. By this course the instructors are enabled to check the tendency on the part of some of the teachers to know more about the subject than the instructor knows.

The interest in the lecture at Squantum, referred to above, was maintained throughout. This was due to the lecture being delivered without the aid of an interpreter. The lecturer, Prof. Jefferson is the gentleman who has delivered the lectures on physical geography and he has entire charge of all geographical excursions; he is ably assisted by six young men of Harvard. Prof. Jefferson is the only lecturer thus far who has been able to hold the attention of the teachers when assembled in Sanders Theatre. His words have been clear and have gone to all parts of the theatre.

And in a letter to Theodora, Jefferson wrote:[15]

Yesterday was a remarkable day—I offered an extra excursion to Hobbs Brook under my personal supervision to make up one lost by rain. 89 were in my party. Some photographing was going on and the party that started 10 minutes later, from the same spot was found to be 260 strong for a membership of 211 and usual attendance of 120-180!

Jefferson was very happy with the results of the excursions, and so it seems were the Cuban teachers. He was later to remember one incident in some autobiographical notes written just prior to his death in 1949. One of the young lady Cuban schoolteachers wrote a letter which was published in the Cuban *Discussion of Habana*. The letter criticized Jefferson's spoken Spanish, contrary to previous newspaper accounts and to other recorded testimony . . . "The Geography lecture in Horrible Spanish by American professor. He talked of erosion of rocks but quite eroded our patience before he got through." Her report concerning the field excursions was almost as trying. Extracts of the letter published in Cuba were published in the New York *Post* and in the Boston *Herald*. The Cubans were disgusted with their fellow letter-writer and took every opportunity to persuade Jefferson of their true feeling. They showered the unfortunate Jefferson with long unrestrained outpourings of feeling, with elaborately phrased expressions of sorrow and grief, and with protestations of anger against their own complainant. The disturbed teachers stopped Jefferson on the sidewalks, approached him in cafes, groups even ventured to his room of an evening.

Jefferson's geography lectures and excursions became a testing ground for the success of the Cuban Summer School. His performance was vindicated at the close of his last lecture in Harvard's Sanders Theatre when the Cuban schoolteachers simultaneously rose and gave him "an encore"! President Eliot, who had been watching over the summer school with special interest, wrote to Jefferson:[16]

Dear Mr. Jefferson,

Your work as teacher of geography to the Cubans has been so thoroughly done, and the undertaking has proved so serious, that I feel that the compensation which I agreed to give you is insufficient. Will you please suggest a sum which would seem to you a suitable compen-

sation? I do not promise to adopt your suggestion; but I shall consider it carefully. Shall you be able to go on any of the remaining excursions; or are you proposing to leave Cambridge at once?

The following day Jefferson received a check for $500 from President Eliot. The earlier agreed salary had been $250.

Later President Eliot wrote to Jefferson:[17]

I have written to E. O. Fisk & Co., as you requested.

I hope you look back on your service to the Cuban teachers with satisfaction. You are surely entitled to do so.

The expedition as a whole was much more successful than anybody could possibly have anticipated. For me, it was the most interesting single piece of work that has ever come my way.

Jefferson returned to his teaching position at Brockton. On June 29, 1901, a letter was sent to him from Secretary Hurlburt of Harvard University that was to shape his career:[18]

A letter from C. T. McFarlane tells Professor Davis that he has resigned his position, the professorship of geography at the State Normal School, Ypsilanti, Michigan, to take a similar position at the State Normal School, Brockport, New York. Professor Davis and I are ready to back you for the position at Ypsilanti, if you want it.

Jefferson did apply for the post, received it, and settled down to live the most productive 48 years of his life.

CHAPTER FOUR

THE YPSILANTI YEARS

Jefferson arrived in southeastern Michigan's Ypsilanti late in September, 1901, direct from his post in the Brockton High School. His family and personal effects followed in a few days. Ypsilanti presented itself as a town not long since on the frontier, able to boast a population of over 5,000, the owner of the first Normal School established west of the Alleghenies which had only recently celebrated its 50th anniversary (an event feted by Putnam's *A History of the Michigan State Normal School at Ypsilanti, Michigan, 1849-1899*),[1] and a name borrowed from Demetrios Ypsilanti who had led the Greeks in their War of Independence against the Turks in 1823. Ypsilanti, clinging snugly to the banks of the ever-widening Huron River, rose on either side of the river's oft over-flowed banks to enjoy an invigorating air at elevations rising to over 800 feet. Meadows of grass, alternating with fields of corn, punctuated by knotted woodland, assured the Ypsilanti citizenry a certain rural charm. Situated on the Chicago Road, the main highway between Detroit and Chicago, which followed closely the old Sauk Indian Trail, Ypsilanti did not suffer isolation; she prospered in catering to travellers, and she learned the news from the big cities.

The people of the town were most friendly towards the newly arrived Jeffersons. The man of the house, Professor Jefferson, had already won the confidence and respect of the people by his very selection as a faculty member of the Normal. At the age of 38 Jefferson possessed in fair measure the attributes of all phases of academic success: a good physique, a yearning for knowledge, a passion for intellectual honesty, the habit of long hours, care and patience for all in need. And if there were any doubters in the community, some talks he gave from church and campus, open to students and public both, hastily reassured all that

Mark S. W. Jefferson was an erudite man indeed, versed thoroughly not only in land lore and earth lore, but also in philology and happenings during classical times. Faculty, in starched collar, cravat, hat in hand, came to his home, presented their cards and would wait to be introduced to Mr. Jefferson. If the manner were formal, it was also sincere and friendly. The natural science faculty members from the eight-mile distant University of Michigan, Ann Arbor, travelled to Ypsilanti on the inter-urban railway car and formally welcomed Mark Jefferson to the academic community. Mrs. Theodora Jefferson was made to feel comfortable in her new surroundings and in short time was active in civic affairs. Jefferson's wife, Theodora, was a tireless worker: meeting the needs of her family, maintaining her husband's affairs in his absences, investing thriftily the family savings, creatively experimenting with tree grafts, were all part of her daily round. Theodora was also the first woman in Ypsilanti to have a washing machine, to play tennis in public (though this was accomplished at sunrise), actively to support the movement for women's emancipation, crusade against the dreaded tuberculosis and check the cleanliness of the fresh milk being sold in Ypsilanti.[2] A Regency in the Daughters of the American Revolution meant several Colonial dress parties. "Wealthy Jackson," a huge negro lady from Ypsilanti's Hungry Hill, would arrange for helpers to aid Theodora and housekeeper-cook Mary Breen. When, in 1905, Theodora did not wish to continue renting from a neighbor, she designed a house with assistance from architect Gregory. A double lot was purchased on Normal Street, only yards distant from the College campus, and by 1906 the Jefferson family—mother, father, five children and housekeeper and cook, Mary Breen—had moved into the house of Mrs. Jefferson's design and in close proximity to a Mr. Sweet who would often take the children for a car ride around the block to their delight. Excerpts from a 4,000 word article written by Mrs. Jefferson, after the completion of the house, offer insight into the planning and care lavished upon the project by the mother and provide a notion of the type of house in which the Jefferson family lived:[3]

> *A house costing $6,933.64 (furniture estimated at $1,628.24) by Theodora A. B. Jefferson. E. W. Gregory of Detroit, Architect. Drawings by Geoffrey Jefferson (aged 13), photographs by the author. Building finished March, 1906.*
>
> *. . . in building this house the health, comfort and happiness of the children was considered paramount to all else . . . . In proposing the plans, the absolute essentials were a room for each member of the family, the best facilities for work and play, and the most sanitary construction . . . . The colonial style was our preference . . . Because*

it seemed more hygienic than paper, the walls are daintily tinted, and every effort is made to reduce dust-catchers, the door and window casing are as nearly flat as I could persuade the carpenter to make them. The doors have but two panels, which run up and down, the baseboards are perfectly flat with a simple ogee at the top . . . no draperies are allowed, except plain lawn sash curtains. All wood work except in ballroom is Georgia pine, the floors quarter sawed . . . . Metal work of the simplest, is all of old brass . . . we consider the bathroom eminently a successful room . . . shower and needle baths . . . . We feel the bannister and newel post are a distinct failure. In other parts of the house I persisted in my own ideas until I got the minimum of dust catching surface, but when it came to the bannisters I succumbed and let the carpenter have his own way, and I believe they will catch more dust than all the rest of the house together . . . . Oak and maple (not painted) . . . Oak book cases line the two blank walls of the study, a typewriter is by one of the windows, an oak cabinet stands between the two wide windows, to hold the unsightly necessaries of a study, such as letter files, paste pot, Kodak, etc.; plenty of light, good writing table and easy chairs make this the coziest room in the house . . .

. . . Our foundations were made of the beautiful field stones found about here: then all the joints were cemented over outside and in . . . On entering this house our friends exclaim "What a bright, cheerful house." And this is so all through, we tolerate no dark corners. Windows are large and numerous. The red oak and Georgia pine have not been stained. Dainty buffs, grays, grayish greens and light terra cotta colors are on the walls . . . When we bought our lot eighty-two by one hundred and fifty feet there was a disreputable old red barn on the northwest corner; we have not as yet accomplished the devised transformation with this. The back yard has been graded and seeded, but the children use it for a playground and we feel that is more essential than the grass which consequently has not thriven . . . yard provides tennis court, basketball and newcomb and space for a croquet set. An old wooden fence at the back is screened by white lilacs, old fashioned larkspur, golden glow and hop vines which run wild.

The father of the family insists on "plain, clean grass" in front of the house, so mother has only the south side of the house left for flowers, a space twenty-four by thirty-five feet . . . . She has a luxuriant growth and flowers at all seasons.

The house still stands at 205 North Normal Street, Ypsilanti.

The children had a spacious home, plenty of garden space in which to play, and Mary Breen who was always able to suggest a new game, a mother for whom nothing was too great a trouble, and a papa who would read them stories, let them hustle down to the ground floor living room at night time when it thundered, and would take them on summer holidays quite regularly. Cat "Penny Brown" and dog "Toby" completed the hearth. When Theodora died November 6, 1913, of a heart condition at the age of fifty the family suffered a tragedy, and Ypsilanti lost one of its foremost citizens.[4] In the summer of 1915 Jefferson remarried to Clara Frances Hopkins, a lady from Holland, Michigan. They had become acquainted on the campus of the Normal College. Clara raised three children by Jefferson, was a good mother and a faithful wife.

This was the domestic hearth to Jefferson's geographic accomplishment. It was here that his life as a devoted geographile began. On campus his task was to teach geography; off campus his self-imposed task was that of further geographic study. He ensconced himself in his study, began a contribution which was to effect a shift in the direction of American geographic thought in the first half of the twentieth century.

In these same years, 1901-1949, he proved to be a diligent worker in the cause of civic improvement. He helped found the Twenty Club (1905), instituted a discussion group in the Congregational Church (1906), encouraged the establishment of a Board of Commerce (1920), invested funds in the construction of a community hotel (1920), gave freely of his time to Harvey Colburn who wrote the history of Ypsilanti in book form to celebrate the centennial of the town in 1923,[5] and for many years constituted a one man city planning commission before being appointed chairman to the Ypsilanti City Planning Commission (1939). When the fifteenth Kiwanis Club of Michigan was founded in Ypsilanti, April 1921, Jefferson became a charter member. Rarely did he absent himself from a meeting. Frequently he attended the Kiwanis National Convention. He found the Kiwanis Club to be an instrument for civic improvement through which he could function efficiently. Whenever he wished to effect civic change he had himself appointed chairman of a Kiwanis committee. Noteworthy improvements accomplished included the installation of a softwater plant in Ypsilanti, school consolidation which eliminated the one-room schoolhouse, campaigns to have honest officials elected to office. His Kiwanis activity was to intensify in his retirement years.[6]

He often spoke to the townspeople through the medium of groups as the Congregational Church, the Ladies Literary Society, the Ladies Library Association, the Ypsilanti Study Club, the Ypsilanti Woman's Club, and meetings of the Civic Improvement Association. He explained star clusters to them; he lectured on the weather; compared parts of Norway to northern Michigan; unfolded his South American experiences; offered commentary on the Russo-Japanese War in the local newspaper; reported on the difficulties Amundsen faced in his journey to the South Pole; made comment on Ypsilanti rainfall and the level of Lake Huron. During both World Wars he gave numerous illustrated talks on the progress of the allies. Following both World Wars he lectured frequently on the peace treaties.[7] These talks to the townsfolk coupled with his Kiwanian work constituted a large part of the meagre time Jefferson allowed himself for social intercourse. The Twenty Club, Edwin Atson Strong, and visiting geographers virtually accounted for the remainder of Jefferson's social activity. The functioning of the Twenty Club, however, was one social activity very dear to Jefferson. Rarely in the next 44 years did he miss a meeting. The Club, which may well have owed to a Jefferson suggestion,[8] emerged during 1905 after four or five of the Normal faculty had dined one evening at the home of Clyde Ford, Head of the Language Department at the College (and the only person besides Ellsworth Huntington that Jefferson was to term "a gracious pen"). The largely built, amiable Ford, faintly coppered by the presence of Indian blood, had addressed his company after the meal. The occasion was a success and similar evenings followed. Attendance at these gatherings steadily increased. When the number reached twenty, the men present agreed not to increase membership in order that the group might preserve its social character. The Twenty Club had been born. Once each month a member would host the Club in his home and present a guest speaker for the evening. The after-meal presentations were of a high caliber. Jefferson arranged to have some of his geographer friends address the Twenty Club, including M. Aurousseau, H. H. Barrows, I. Bowman, C. Colby, D. Davis, W. M. Davis, E. Huntington, Clifton Johnson, R. Light, A. E. Parkins, V. Stefansson, G. Taylor. At other times Jefferson would invite a friend to be his guest at a Twenty Club meeting. One such guest was his friend J. Allende Posse (Argentine Republic) who, impressed with Jefferson's studies, wrote of the Ypsilanti Normal School and the Twenty Club in *Las Universidades En America Del Norte*.[9] Jefferson attempted to carry the idea of the Twenty Club into the Congregational Church by establishing a six o'clock Sunday tea followed by a talk and discussion of liberal leaning. Each of these meetings attracted twenty to thirty students from the Normal, but they seem not to have been continued after World War I.

Edwin Strong and Jefferson became firm friends. Strong, astrologer and Normal College professor of physical sciences, lived only yards distant from Jefferson. They visited each other frequently, talked much of scientific advance, played chess, and watched the stars from an apparatus that Strong had designed and installed in his own home. If Jefferson were ill and unable to hold class, Strong would frequently hold geography class for Jefferson. Similarly, Strong could and did teach literature, language and history. After the death of Strong in 1920 Jefferson never did find another such intellect with whom he could companion.[10] Visitation by geographer friends also constituted a part of Jefferson's social life. When he learned that one of his geographer friends was travelling between Harvard and Chicago, two of the most active centers of geography in early twentieth-century U.S.A., he would be sure to invite him to break his rail journey at Ypsilanti. Fortunately, Ypsilanti lay on the main east-west rail track from New York to Chicago, and his house was only a ten-minute walk from the railroad station. This encouraged a steady stream of geographers to visit Jefferson through the years, which intrusion upon his sequestered but not restful existence was a revel to his mind. On more than one occasion when W. M. Davis passed through Ypsilanti by train, yet could not break his journey, Jefferson took his children to greet Davis at the railway station. There, Davis, hanging from a train window, exchanged his bags of candy for home-made pastries baked by little Jefferson girls.

The absence of serious association was as unfortunate to Jefferson as an over-abundance of social visitors. How he enjoyed kindred geographic spirits! His children too enjoyed Papa's visitors who sent toys, or brought candy with them, even gave them time in play. Ellsworth Huntington was a constant source of delight to the young children; Isaiah Bowman who would take them on his knee was at ease in their presence, though W. M. Davis never seemed totally able to unbend and relax with them.[11] Huntington and Bowman were two of the most frequent visitors to the Jefferson home. Papa would soon take the new plaything from the children's grasp, then would follow in the study exchange of ideas, meditations, and undigested thoughts. At such times as those, the elusive gentle values and full meaning of scholarship would present itself to the two men in concert. This was American geography in the making.

Jefferson quite came to be regarded as the community geographer. He had made the subject well respected on the campus, was training teachers of geography and finding them school positions, was generous with his time and would offer an address free of charge to any citizens group, and was constantly winning mention from some other part of the state which would faithfully be reported in the Ypsilanti daily paper. Frequently Jefferson's studies would attract the attention of the commu-

nity. The community learned of Jefferson's river researches, his study of
the meander belts of rivers from Harvard's map collection, and his
observation that the limiting width of a meander belt seemed to be
eighteen times the mean width of the stream at any one given place.
The resultant publication entitled, "Limiting Width of Meander Belts,"
published in the *National Geographic Magazine,* 1902, had attracted
the attention of Ypsilanti's citizenry.[12] Later Baron Sten de Geer and
Vujevic confirmed Jefferson's findings from their respective works on
the Swedish Klarelv and the Hungarian Theiss.[13] Jefferson made a map
and Davisian "mud-pie" model of the town and its environs, vertical
scale exaggerated to show the town's proximity to the Huron River. He
claimed that the river used a meandering process to move, that housing
should not be permitted in the river meander belt, and suggested that
Ypsilanti should build away from the river and toward the 800' contour
some quarter of a mile from the tumbling stream that once was fording
place to Indians and fur trappers. The community listened to Jefferson's
river geography with surprise and concern and later decided his watch-
ful eye could well service Ypsilanti. He was appointed a one man City
Planning Authority.

When it was supposed (1904) that there might be a goodly supply of
oil south of Ypsilanti, both the geologist, William H. Sherzer, and
Jefferson became the center of much attention.[14] A company was at
once organized which drilled a well on the Martin Cremer farm, on the
flats skirting the town. Both Jefferson and campus geologist W. H.
Sherzer doubted the presence of a considerable quantity of oil, but
seized the opportunity to demand better mapping of the State of Michigan. State geologists Lane and Leverett of the U.S. Survey (the latter
stationed at Ann Arbor while making a study of pleistocene geology
with special reference to Michigan) were agreed on the need for a more
thorough cartographic state coverage and inventory.

If the citizenry were to excite over abnormal weather conditions, he
would address them on the matter or put an article in the daily. Jefferson arranged gatherings on the campus of the Michigan State Normal
College which the citizenry might attend. To these gatherings he would
occasionally bring his geographer friends, as he would to College functions. In 1923 Jefferson arranged for Stefansson to address a college
group and then build an ice house on the campus (Ypsilanti's senior
citizens still talk of "that man who built the ice house."). Four years
later Jefferson arranged for Huntington to address the Normal College
on the occasion of its 75th anniversary—"How Environment Strength-
ens its Chain."[15] Frequently on Saturdays he, together with Sherzer,
would take a group of Michigan school teachers, students, and inter-

ested citizens through glaciated southeastern Michigan. It was exciting to the citizenry to learn that students as Bowman, Colby, Davis, Parkins, and Stratton had all secured significant college appointments. Ypsilanti was proud of its Normal College. The good work of the Normal geography department, frequently evidenced, was again noticed in 1918 when five geographers who had studied at the Normal were engaged in the peace negotiations. Jefferson was appointed Chief Cartographer for the American Delegation to negotiate peace at Paris, Charles Stratton was first cartographic assistant, Isaiah Bowman was Chief Territorial Adviser to President Wilson. Harlan Barrows and Charles Colby worked with the U.S. War Trade Board in Washington, also as part of the war effort.[16] Barrows had graduated from the Normal under Jefferson's predecessor, C. T. McFarlane. The other three geographers had been Jefferson's students and one-time departmental assistants. Additionally, Frank Cobb, a graduate (history) of the Normal (1890) travelled to Paris as first secretary to Colonel House.

Jefferson was certainly one of the best known of Ypsilanti's citizens. If he had an article published, delivered a paper, were elected to an office, even if he took a vacation, the daily reported the matter. The town quite respected Jefferson as a geographer, as did the Normal College faculty and administration. He valued the collective town-gown unwritten expression of endorsement and proceeded to develop the geography department as he wished without bothersome restriction from administration. In his 39 years of service at the Normal College Jefferson experienced the administration of four presidents: Elmer A. Lyman, 1899-1902, Lewis H. Jones, 1902-1912, Charles McKenny, 1912-1933, and John Munson, 1933-1948. (In retirement he also came to know a fifth President, Eugene Elliott 1948-1965.) Fortunately Jefferson enjoyed good relations with all four presidents. Roles were well defined, responsibilities were assumed, and just enough administration was introduced to get the job done with no loss of time or energy. The number of administrative tasks for which he assumed responsibility was very limited . . . Chairman of the Honorary Degree Committee, member of President McKenny's (1912-33) five-man Executive Committee of the College Faculty (the Cabinet), and occasional member of a committee to report on departmental library needs. Jefferson was geography department head, spent his budget as he elected, hired his staff, decided what courses should be listed in the catalogue and how often they should be offered. A secretary assumed responsibility for routine detail: Jefferson did not allow himself to fall victim to the wasteful practice of investing intellectual capacity upon petty detail. A fundamental prerequisite to the Jefferson accomplishment was his ability to husband his own strengths and invest just enough time on the mechanics of life as was necessary. He spent his energy wisely. He would not engage in the great game of bunk versus debunk, did not waste time on his discreditors, allowed himself to be only a little peeved at academic piracies of his work. If a few minutes only were available, there would be a letter to type or a map to finish. Map-making on drawing boards which were kept both at his home and in his office could be undertaken when he felt ready. Larger periods of time were spent in his study where he could further the work he was currently engaged upon. He led a full life centered on his work at the College—"I have so much time on my hands that I have to sit up nights to use it all up."

Between the years 1901 and 1933 Jefferson placed much of geographic interest into the Normal College publication, whose circulation was not confined to Ypsilanti, but was national. Included were excerpts from geographic works as Hanns' *Meteorology,* Marsh's *Man and Nature,* Scott Keltie's report of 1885 to the Royal Geographical Society in Britain, Davis' *Physiography of the Lands.* If an issue of geographic import arose, Jefferson would write an opinion for the *News,* or, on occasion, submit opinion from several of his geographer friends together with his own; for example, the *News* of April 20, 1906, devoted two full columns of its front page to printing the opinions of I. C. Russell (University of Michigan), J. Paul Goode (University of Chicago), R. S. Tarr (Cornell University), W. H. Sherzer and M. Jefferson (Michigan State Normal College) concerning the extent of the upheaval that caused the San Francisco earthquake. Articles published in the College News included "Geography in the Grades," "The Educational Value of Geography," "Geography Work in the Grades," "The State Normal College as a Land Owner," and a series of six articles entitled "Material for Geography of Michigan."[17] *The Normal College News,* Magazine Number of October 20, 1905, gave a detailed account of this Michigan study, under the heading, "On the Geography of Michigan."[18] The same six articles were republished as a book in Ypsilanti, 1906,[19] which was later revised and rewritten as the Michigan State supplement to Dodge's Geography of the United States.[20]

The magazine edition of *The Normal College News* was replaced in October 1906 by *The Western Journal of Education,* and with the first edition of this publication in January 1913 came a new name—*The American Schoolmaster.* This publication continued as a regular feature of the Normal program until June of 1933. In the latter year, a depression year, the budget of Ypsilanti's Normal was pared drastically and the 27 years continuum of the publication was halted, never to be revived. Largely stemming from Jefferson's correspondence and requests, the editors of the Normal publication received manuscripts from many geographers including: H. H. Barrows (University of Chicago), L. Blakenship (Norton, Virginia), M. Bransom (Harris Teachers College, St. Louis, Missouri), A. P. Brigham (Colgate University), J. W. Brouilette (Principal, Port Barre School, Louisiana), R. M. Brown (Rhode Island College of Education, Providence), A. Farnham, J. Paul Goode (University of Chicago), Ellsworth Huntington (Yale University), A. E. Parkins (Peabody College, Nashville, Tennessee), D. Ridgley (Illinois State Normal University), Julia Shipman (State Normal School, New Britain, Connecticut), M. Sill (Michigan State Normal College, Ypsilanti), G. Taylor (University of Chicago), R. H. Whitbeck (University of Wisconsin), Ella Wilson (Michigan State Normal College). Jefferson himself was a frequent contributor of articles, notices, and book reviews to this publication.

For each of the courses Jefferson taught at the Normal College he developed written notes. Each course was planned in a separate notebook written in Jefferson's study.[21] Masses of information were accumulated in these notebooks. As the notebooks filled, a second and sometimes third notebook was added. This task of maintaining his notebooks became a hobby with him. Sometimes just for his own pleasure he would draw the most meticulous of maps in his notebook, otherwise surrounded by a sea of scribbled notes. They became, in fact, Jefferson's course books, and repositories of material from which he developed his textbooks. *Teachers Geography* published in 1906 was the first such text to emerge. These notebooks received addition throughout Jefferson's life, even into the retirement years. He had hoped to convert his notebooks on South America, Iberia, and Switzerland into texts, but never did.

His notebooks became more than collections of class notes and texts in embryo. In his 39 years at the Normal, Jefferson presented a total of over 600 courses to students. Teaching in so large an amount breeds its own essential extension, and concepts developed in the classroom became foci around which much of Jefferson's reading and thinking revolved. Frequently, the information he amassed in this way, and which he had been offering to his classes, became the subject matter of a paper which might be delivered before the Michigan Academy of Science, but after 1907 more probably would be presented before the Association of American Geographers. In written form prior to 1908 the essay might have been published in the *Journal of Geology,* the *Journal of School Geography,* the *Journal of Geography, Monthly Weather Review, Michigan Academy of Science Bulletin, Normal College News,* or *Science,* but after 1908 publication was very frequently with the *Geographical Review*. He was both a concerned teacher and a concerned geographer.

The teacher in him was largely responsible for his association with the *Journal of School Geography*. During his first year in Ypsilanti Jefferson became an associate editor for that publication at the invitation of the editor, R. E. Dodge.[22] Jefferson retained the position when, in the following year, 1902, the *Journal* changed its name to the *Journal of Geography* and increased its scope and circulation. He continued to contribute notes and articles to the *Journal* in his Ypsilanti years although after 1908 his more substantial contributions found their way to the pages of the *Geographical Review*. Jefferson did continue to review books for the *Journal of Geography* and had his own texts reviewed in the *Journal*. He gave much time and energy to encouraging the growth of the National Council of Geography Teachers founded in 1916 by G. J. Miller who worked through the offices of the *Journal*[23] (Miller had taken his first geography course under Jefferson 13 years earlier). Jefferson very frequently addressed the members of the National Council of Geography Teachers at their annual meetings in the years that followed. Since the National Council of Geography Teachers coupled its meetings with those of the Association of American Geographers at the same venue in the Christmas vacation for many years, Jefferson would address one or the other group and sometimes both groups. Complete record of his addresses to the National Council of Geography Teachers does not exist;[24] only partial record is available from the pages of the *Journal*. He did encourage the Michigan chapter of the National Council of Geography Teachers. When it lagged in the early 1920's, he took charge without taking office, had the names and addresses of the Michigan membership listed, sent letters to G. J. Miller insisting he must offer geography teachers something for their money and invited the Michigan chapter to a day's geography if they would come to Ypsilanti.[25]

The geographile in him was responsible for his enthusiasm for the Association of American Geographers. He was one of the forty-six Charter Members who gathered at Philadelphia in 1904 to give birth to the Association which W. M. Davis had suggested at St. Louis in 1903. At the outset the Association of American Geographers was little more than a program and a promise. It had no central office but it had strong officials. The Association met annually, usually during the Christmas Vacation (although between 1914 and 1922 an annual joint spring meeting of the Association and the American Geographical Society was held in the Society's rooms in New York). Jefferson spent the days following Christmas attending the annual meeting of the Association, frequently presenting a paper himself, listening attentively to the papers of others, and talking with correspondents of past months. Between the years 1904 and 1939 it is doubtful that he missed more than two meetings. In these same years he presented 33 papers before the Association,[26] a larger number than any other geographer in Association history. He was elected Second Vice President in 1910, First Vice President in 1915, President in 1916, and Councilor 1929-1931. In retirement he held office and attempted his annual paper, but age, winter ailments, and expense conspired against his attendance. Then, he sadly wrote "I am losing an old friend." He was much in favor of the annual meetings of the Association of American Geographers. He felt that a true association between geographers was being effected. Many geographers did not see each other from one year's end to the next excepting at the annual meeting. As J. Russell Smith wrote in 1962: "my sole relationship with him [Mark Jefferson] has been as a fellow member of the Association of American Geographers, and in this relation I met him a number of times from 1905 on."[27] He would arrange to dine with geographers at the meeting and discuss geographic matters of mutual interest. Occasionally if one of the better read geographers had absented himself from an association meeting, Jefferson would correspond with him and urge his attendance at the next meeting. Geographers who had presented thoughts which interested Jefferson would receive a letter from him on the subject and usually encouragement to continue in that line of work. If Jefferson felt a geographer should contribute a paper to the annual meeting he would insist this be accomplished. When in 1925, he felt that the work of his colleague, Ella Wilson, on the potato industry of Maine would interest the membership of the Association he insisted she present the essence of her study.[28] He encouraged and aided her with papers delivered at Association meetings in Philadelphia, 1926, Washington, 1932, and Evanston, 1932.[29] If a geographic matter were of interest to a group of geographers, Jefferson would write to the current president and urge a round-table conference on the matter. He felt that the role of the Association of American Geographers was to inspire, to bring geographers together annually, to serve as a clearing house of ideas. He felt the Association of American Geographers was a device, an instrument, and to that end on more than one occasion proposed that each member of the Association attach his specialty to his name on the annual roster of membership and a scheme be arranged whereby each geographer give a certain number of hours from his specialty to other geographer members requiring such. This notion probably developed from Jefferson's own experiences; he had exchanged thoughts which proved most fruitful to him, especially with

G. K. Gilbert on rivers, F. Matthes on glaciers, J. P. Goode on cartography, Barrows on human ecology, and all of these at Association meetings. But Jefferson did not believe in crusading for his notions regarding the Association. One letter sent was sufficient, and quite frequently his suggestions passed unheeded. He was not sympathetic toward the publication of the *Annals*. From his study in Ypsilanti he would prepare his paper for the next Association meeting quite as though this was the most important activity in his life. If he were particularly pleased with his work, he might venture to mention in correspondence to daughter Phoebe, "I have an idea that will tell well next Christmas," and to Bowman, "I shall bring a paper to——." Always he typed a copy of the paper he wished to present, but frequently, in the telling, the typed statement was discarded and he would talk impromptu. Frequently his paper won special mention in the *Geographical Review*. Always his talks were illustrated, and always they won interest from the membership:[30]

> He [*Jefferson*] will be remembered best, possibly, for his talks at the annual geographic conferences. All geographers know that when a speaker is announced, many people who have been listening to previous speakers head for the exit. I never saw this happen to Mark Jefferson. Every time he appeared on the program there was a rush to get into the conference room, not to get out of it.

His orally presented paper would be re-written, in greater detail, and then published, usually in the *Bulletin of the American Geographical Society* and after 1915 in the *Geographical Review*. He mentioned in correspondence that although he thought the *Review* was "the best thing of its kind in the English language," he published there in order to secure much needed additional income which such writing afforded. "Since 1908 when the American Geographical Society invited me to be a contributing editor I have not cared to publish in the Annals (A.A.G.). Everything in the Review is PAID. A writer finds that very desirable."[31]

Jefferson developed a close relationship with the American Geographical Society commencing in 1908, initially through the person of Cyrus Adams, and later through the persons of Isaiah Bowman, and Gladys Wrigley. Jefferson was impressed with the accomplishments of the Society. Additionally, the American Geographical Society paid Jefferson promptly for all he sent them. Such income was much appreciated by Jefferson, whose carefully maintained ledgers indicate that his savings were never able to withstand extravagance. Between the years 1909 and 1941 he published 31 papers in the American Geographical Society publication, a number unequaled by any geographer, and is awarded the appellation "seraph of the tried and true" by J. K. Wright in *Geography in the Making*.[32] The American Geographical Society provided Jefferson with 25 or 50 reprints of each of his articles and many of his reviews. Jefferson sent these to his geographer friends especially in the United States and Europe, who in turn, sent Jefferson reprints of many of their studies. In this way Jefferson developed a collection of many hundreds of reprints.

In these same Ypsilanti years Jefferson augmented his knowledge, supplemented his income, and enlarged his personal library by reviewing books which he was frequently invited to retain. Most of these reviews were written for the *Geographical Review*,[33] but other of his reviews appeared irregularly in other magazines and newspapers. He gave much time and thought to the reading of a book before he wrote a word of review. He insisted on the necessity of adequate book reviews as an aid to scientific advance and had published a note on the subject in the *Bulletin of the American Geographical Society*.[34] Jefferson's reviews were much sought by the American Geographical Society, and between the years 1910 and 1942 Jefferson reviewed 146 books for that Society. His reviews varied in length from 100 to 2,000 words, gave to many readers of the *Review* an intimate account of author accomplishment, rendered reviews in the English language of German, French, Spanish, and Swedish books which were otherwise inaccessible to American geographers. Several of his reviews have been cited and quoted as authoritative themselves. Occasionally he would reveal his own point of view in a review if he felt the author had become improbable, but usually an air of objective authority characterized his comment. He acquired a wonderful collection of geographic literature, certainly not equalled by the Normal School library. He collected atlases with the same zeal as he collected postage stamps. Geographical periodicals which he could not well afford, he ordered for the library, then insisted the periodicals be bound and shelved in his office, which caused many a tussle with librarian Genevieve Walton. Jefferson won out and held the periodicals. If his own library did not contain a book or article he needed, he would request the item or the information from the American Geographical Society rather than travel to eight-mile distant Ann Arbor and consult the library of the University of Michigan. If the American Geographical Society did not possess the item they would seek to purchase it at once, then forward it to Jefferson.

Publication of Jefferson's work in the *Geographical Review* meant a certain and substantial circulation for him. Summaries and notes of his *Geographical Review* articles were published in many geographical journals including: *Annales de Géographie, Geografiska Annaler,* the

Geographical Journal, the *Geographical Teacher, Geographisches Jahrbuch,* the *Scottish Geographical Magazine, Pettermanns Mitteilungen, Ymer,* and *Zeitschrift fur Geopolitik.*

Frequently his articles from the *Geographical Review* would be summarized in the pages of the New York *Times.* This was largely due to the influence of John H. Finley, President of the American Geographical Society, 1925-1934 (later Honorary President), and Editor for the New York *Times* (later editor emeritus).[35] In consequence, many geographers came to know of Jefferson's interests, which brought him into contact with men interested in matters similar to himself. It also increased his set of correspondents and was, in part, responsible for the honorifics bestowed upon the man.

Jefferson's services were sought by publishing companies who requested him to critique manuscripts of a geographic nature for a much needed $25 fee (one such manuscript was *Asia,* by Ellsworth Huntington).[36] In 1913 the Hanson Bellows Company wished to add a geography section to their encyclopedia which had already passed through several successful editions. The company invited Jefferson to assume the role of editor to this large undertaking. Owing to the pressure of classroom work, his own writing program, and the extended sickness of his wife which resulted in her death later that same year, Jefferson declined the invitation, at the same time recommending Ellsworth Huntington most strongly for the position. Huntington was duly offered the position of Encyclopedia editor which he accepted: Jefferson did contribute some dozen articles to the Encyclopedia at Huntington's request.[37] Map publishing companies hired his services as a cartographic editor; Jefferson was a member of the Editorial Board for A. J. Nystrom and Company for many years. Other companies requested his services. In order that he might give more of his time to thinking and writing geography and less to teaching, Jefferson had tried to secure as permanent teachers in his department Ellsworth Huntington, George McBride, and George T. Renner, but lack of funds had prevented on each occasion. Once he invited Miss G. Wrigley to teach summer school in 1924, but as Editor of the *Review,* Miss Wrigley was otherwise occupied. In the summer of 1925, Jefferson did employ a Miss Gorrie from Scotland, recommended by his friend George Chisholm, but that did not release him from a weekly classroom responsibility approximating twenty hours.

Frequently in the 1920's Jefferson was given to extended writing and map-making sessions. At these times his classes would have to wait. With two capable colleagues (Miss Sill and Miss Wilson) to attend his classes and give him time in library research, an admonition from President McKenny "to take time when he needed it," and a jolting note from Bowman in 1921 making reference to his advancing years, Jefferson's classroom absences were frequent and pronounced. Perhaps he felt he was writing in the sound of Time's hurrying chariot. His health was poorer in the 1920's than at any other time in his life. But the 1920's constituted Jefferson's most prolific decade as a glance at the bibliography indicates. In addition to the publication of ideas which had been with him for a long time he became involved in the making of maps not for companies or his own publications so much as for his own delight. "Nothing is so geographic as a map," he would declare. By the end of the 1920's Jefferson had produced and copyrighted approximately 18 base maps, of countries, continents, states, and the world, that were selling throughout the U.S.A. This map making spree culminated with the "6:6 World Map" in 1930.[38]

Many geographers and other academics came to wonder at the unusual spectacle of a normal school professor who was also one of the leading scholars in his field.[39] Many wondered why he never sought a chair of geography in one of the country's better known universities. Several of his critics advanced the notion that he had not acquired a doctor of philosophy degree and had best therefore remain as a Normal school teacher of teachers. His friends offered the apocryphal story that when asked why he had no doctoral degree, Jefferson had queried, "who would examine me?" Certainly little known is the fact that he had declined the opportunity of an honorary doctorate from Harvard University in the fall of 1922 when that University informally extended the offer to him.[40] He was writing "Peopling the Argentine Pampa" and stated simply he could not well afford the time or the money involved in its collection. Honorifics were an effort for the man. The honorifics that did come his way were strictly the product of his geographic ideas, industry, and contribution, and were in no way the product of a winning smile.

It was a little concealed honorific, when, in the December of 1931 the Association of American Geographers held their 28th annual meeting at Ypsilanti's Normal College. (The only occasion in the history of the Association when a Normal College was so honored.) The Charles McKenny Union Building had been recently completed and named in honor of the retiring Normal College President. Isaiah Bowman, President of the Association for that year, and former student of Jefferson, brought with him to Ypsilanti the Cullum Gold Medal from the American Geographical Society which was then presented to Jefferson at the banquet. In presenting the medal, Isaiah Bowman said:[41]

> To point the way of my remarks I choose an ancient and familiar text: "A man's gift maketh room for him and bringeth him unto the company of great men." Upon the walls of the Central Hall of the Ameri-

can *Geographical Society are the names of representative men of that company in the field of geography. First I mention Professor William Morris Davis, who needs no characterization; Stefansson, the Arctic explorer; Sir John Murray and the Prince of Monaco, oceanographers and many others.*

To win this judgment Professor Jefferson would not lift a finger. In an age of unblushing self-praise he stands out by contrast with the multitude.

The Cullum Medal is a work of art as well as a form of recognition. On one side it portrays a man in a boat. He searches eagerly the unknown shore before him to find a landing place and a way toward the unexplored interior. On the other side is a figure standing beside a globe on which Jefferson's friends will observe with approval a network of meridians and parallels! Beside the figure is a panel and into it Dr. Wrigley, the editor of the Geographical Review, has condensed an inscription far more expressive than the words I have used in this citation:

To
Professor Mark Jefferson
For The
Savor of True Geography
In His Ingenious And
Fruitful Inquiries
Into Man's Distribution
On the Earth
1931.

Jefferson's recorded final words of reply were, "I thank you, Dr. Bowman, for the honor of this medal and I will try to be worthy of it."

Hardly had Jefferson had time to recover from the Cullum Gold Medal shock when another former student of Jefferson's, Charles Colby, arose and announced that The Geographical Society of Chicago had presented the Helen Culver Medal, founded 1907, to Jefferson. The heavy gold medal carried the inscription: "Awarded to Mark Jefferson, pioneer in the development of scientific geography in America, inspiring teacher, distinguished contributor. December 21, 1931." Jefferson later remarked that two gold medals and a banquet were too much for the digestive system at a single sitting. This latter medal Jefferson collected from the Chicago Geographical Society in October of 1932. He wrote briefly of the occasion to his daughter, Phoebe:[42]

Saturday had to go to Chicago, the presentation-luncheon of the Chicago Geographic Society. Rather resplendent affair at Stevens Hotel in the Grand Ball Room. "The Greatest Hotel in the World." They admit it. There were 350 at table, largely Society people, the Society

having become fashionable. Seven newspaper shootings and a micro-
phone in front of each speaker, though I did not know it and no one
in Ypsilanti heard the talks. In all getting the medal cost me $20 which
I cannot well spare. The medals repose in my drawer at the bank. The
A.G.S. has given me a replica of their's in bronze which is gilded over
and looks like the original.

Soon he had sold both the gold medals to a jeweller in Ypsilanti to
help finance another printing of *Man in Europe*. The Cullum Medal
fetched $75. He later wrote "that much gold made me feel nervous."
He was, nevertheless, deeply moved by the double occasion as some
scribbled autobiographical notes show.

Honors bestowed upon the man include Corresponding Memberships
to the Belgrade Geographical Society, 1920; the American Geographical
Society, 1922; the Society of Anthropology and Geography, Stockholm,
1925; the University of Belgrade Geographical Society, 1932. He was
elected to several offices including the Presidency of the Michigan
Academy of Sciences, Arts and Letters, 1907, and the Presidency of the
Association of American Geographers 1916. He was listed in the first
eight editions of American Men of Science . . . 1906, 1910, 1921,
1927, 1933, 1938, 1944, 1949; *Who's Who in America,* 1906 to 1941
in sixteen biennial editions (volumes 4-21); the official *Who's Who in
Michigan* (1936), *Leaders in Education* (1941). And as he entered
retirement, in the December of 1939 on the occasion of the Association
of American Geographers—National Council of Geography Teachers
meeting at Chicago, the National Council of Geography Teachers presented Jefferson with their Annual Distinguished Service Award, "in
recognition of outstanding Contributions to Educational Geography."[43]

CHAPTER FIVE

TEACHING AT YPSILANTI'S NORMAL COLLEGE

The abundant campus of the Normal College which sprawled carelessly over ten acres of hillslope to the west of the Huron River, was an important part of the town. To insure the selection of Ypsilanti as the site of the State Normal, the citizenry of the 1840's, had guaranteed $13,500, temporary rooms, and the salary of the principal teacher of the model school for five years.[1] Ypsilanti was thus chosen in 1849 as the site of the State Normal notwithstanding requests from the towns of Jackson, Marshall, Gull Prairie, and Niles. Sixth of its kind established in the United States and first normal to open its doors west of the Allegheny Mountains,[2] the school published its earliest catalogue in 1853. Desire to emulate European normal school example probably provided the initial impetus for the appearance of geography in the Michigan Normal curriculum. Students entering the two year English course were required to "review Mitchell's Geography" over a seventeen week term in the first year, and "St. John's Geology" in the second year and geology in the third year. It is not known who taught the geography courses from 1853 to 1860 but in the latter year John Goodison commenced the teaching of three geography courses and some drawing, a position[3] he held from 1860-1861, 1862-1869 and 1885 until his death in October 1892.

Goodison's sudden death in 1892 led to the hiring of the twenty one year old Charles T. McFarlane, recently graduated from New York State Normal College. McFarlane rapidly won for himself a name in geography throughout the state; in *Educators of Michigan* one may read:[4]

> *Although among the youngest members of the Normal faculty he has already proven himself to be one of the most efficient before classes.*

As presented in this department Geography takes on a wholly new dress. Its effects are educative as they were not once, and are not in places supposed to be. The training partakes of the close observation and abundant inference of the sciences; of much of the close reasoning of physics and mathematics; and the rich insights into the ground of history and the social life. Geography with Professor McFarlane is among the popular subjects of the school, large classes electing them beyond all requirements.

Indeed, Isaiah Bowman who had commenced teaching in 1896 in the rural schools of St. Clair County, Michigan, attended teachers' institutes where he heard McFarlane "giving his enthusiastic speeches on geography." John Munson, President of the Normal 1933-1948 and one-time student roommate of Bowman, claims that Bowman derived his initial inspiration for geography from McFarlane.[5] Indeed, under McFarlane's guidance several students became very interested in geography: three such pupils were H. H. Barrows, R. D. Calkins, and D. H. Davis, later respectively geography department heads at the University of Chicago, Central Michigan College, and the University of Minnesota. McFarlane gave heavily of his time to geography, followed closely the recommendations of the Committee of Ten, 1892, and selected his geography assistants with care—Miss Averett, H. Barrows, R. Calkins, and Miss Lodeman.

In 1897, at a time when no other state-supported institution of higher learning in Michigan was offering geography and when only eight universities in the country were offering any geography,[6] Ypsilanti's Normal was one of several such schools assuming a very responsible charge in behalf of the development of geography in America. Empowered to award the bachelor's degree—the first teachers college in the United States to receive this authority—the pedagogical influence of the Normal College was unequalled in the State of Michigan. In 1898 McFarlane availed himself of a sabbatical leave, traveled to Europe and studied under Penck at the University of Vienna for one year. He returned in 1899 to experience the fiftieth anniversary of the founding of the State Normal School, was elected to the Faculty Council, and witnessed the graduation of the 3,347th student who had studied geography at the Normal. The Normal library under McFarlane's insistence was by 1900 subscribing to the *Geographical Journal, Journal of School Geography, National Geographic Magazine, Petermann's Mitteilungen,* and the *Scottish Geographical Journal.* McFarlane had brought youth, vigor, and administrative ability to the service of geography at the Normal.

The following year McFarlane left Ypsilanti to assume the principalship of the New York State Normal School, Brockport; by this time he had managed with his assistants to offer eight courses in geography: Elementary Geography, Physical Geography, Teachers Geography, Geographic Material, Physiography I, Physiography II, Geography of the U.S., Geography of Europe. In the same year, 1901, the Michigan State Board of Education awarded McFarlane an honorary Master of Pedagogics degree, and he was appointed associate editor of *The Bulletin of the American Bureau of Geography*. Later, McFarlane was awarded a Doctor of Pedagogics degree from his alma mater (1903) and his name became associated with Teachers College, Columbia, and the Brigham-McFarlane "Essentials of Geography" series. Shortly before McFarlane left Ypsilanti, the student newspaper proclaimed, "The Normal is again to lose one of its best teachers, this time from the geographical department. Prof. McFarlane has been called to Brockport. . . ."[7]

W. M. Davis at Harvard was quite aware that geography was being fostered and nurtured by the normal schools of the country. Guyot had lectured geography at Princeton (1854-1880) and Gilman at Yale (1863-1872), but as Dryer has observed "not incident to any general growth, but as local and personal sports."[8] It was with patience that American geographers had to await the founding of the first university department of geography in the country at the University of Chicago, 1903. In the following decades a large number of the country's universities created departments of geography. But the movement was slow, and the normal school continued to remain responsible to the teaching of geography.[9] The contribution of the normal school in helping geography win acceptance as a subject worthy of a place in higher education remains unwritten. The work of many normal school geographers in the early years of this century has remained a matter of local lore, but a few dedicated spirits necessarily win mention: R. M. Brown (Worcester, Massachusetts); R. D. Calkins (Mt. Pleasant, Michigan); J. F. Chamberlain (Los Angeles, California); E. Van Cleef (Duluth, Minnesota); S. W. Cushing (Salem, Massachusetts); C. R. Dryer (Terre Haute, Indiana); W. M. Gregory (Cleveland, Ohio); G. J. Miller (Mankato, Minnesota); W. J. Sutherland (Platteville, Wisconsin); R. H. Whitbeck (supervising state normal schools in New Jersey).

Davis did not wish to see geography decline in Ypsilanti with the departure of McFarlane.[10] He requested Harvard secretary Hurlburt to inform Jefferson immediately of the vacated position. Jefferson advanced his candidacy at once, and with Harvard support, was awarded the post.

By 1901, the Normal, an appellation that was understood throughout the state, had enrolled over 1,300 students, boasted twelve departments, a library of 22,000 volumes, and a faculty of 53 members. Only three years previously the institution had awarded its first bachelor's degree, and assumed the name, Michigan State Normal College.[11] It was in the classrooms of the Normal between the years 1901 and 1939, that Jefferson was to leave such an impress in the matter of teaching geography.

Soon after his arrival, Jefferson was introduced to the President of the Normal, a former professor of mathematics, Elmer Lyman. Extending his hand, the President announced he was glad to shake the hand of the new drawing and geography department head, but Jefferson would not respond to the toast. Eventually President Lyman shook hands with the Head of the Department of Geography. Drawing had become a separate department.

There were few schools in the U.S.A. of 1901 that could boast an autonomous department of geography and fewer that grew with the firmness and rapidity of the department at Ypsilanti. Jefferson's longevity as department head at Ypsilanti's "nursery of geographers" augured well for a continuity in growth and philosophy that was not unfulfilled. In 1902, Jefferson was offering a variety of eight courses in geography during the year different in content from those offered by McFarlane; by 1912, he offered twelve courses in the catalogue, by 1925, an expanded staff consisting of three full-time members jointly offered 25 courses, an offering that may be recognized as one of the largest in the United States at that time. Between 1901 and 1939 the Department offered 65 different courses; Jefferson, sooner or later, personally taught over 60 of these.[12] Geography was offered at extension centers as far north in the state of Michigan as Traverse City, Cheboygan, and Bad Axe by Margaret Sill and Ella Wilson. Between the years 1901 and 1939 it is probable that Jefferson personally addressed himself to the task of teaching 15,000 different students at the Normal. His colleagues, Margaret Sill and Ella Wilson, together with other assistants, probably addressed a further 7-8,000 different students. It is conservatively estimated that 80 per cent of the Normal's graduates entered the teaching field, that Jefferson directly influenced 12,000 teachers, and that the Jefferson department influenced 18,000 teachers. In turn, Jefferson and geography were passed on to another generation of students through the influence of these teachers, many of whom used Jefferson's text books and notes taken in his classes.

In the fall of 1901 Jefferson commenced to teach geography at the Normal College. He had read much of Mackinder, Mill, Partsch, Penck, Ratzel, Vidal de la Blache, Von Humboldt; received regularly the *Geographical Journal* from Britain, the *Annales de Géographie* from France, *Erdkunde* and *Petermann's Mitteilungen* from Germany; engaged in correspondence with travelers, observers, savants in three continents. Fascinated by the work of the early European geographical societies at Paris, Berlin, and London, eager to follow the work of the International Geographical Congresses, his inclination was to seek knowledge of "man in geography" wherever it might be found. At Harvard, with Davis through the years 1896-1898, man had been noticeably absent from Jefferson's study, but it was man on the land, not merely man and the land, that seemed to interest Jefferson. Jefferson was bent on teaching his experiences: experiences that this crowd-detesting wanderer, who had already trod the earth shell of three continents and the margins of a fourth, had gained in his voyages on land and at sea. He wanted to recount the beauties of Rio de Janeiro, the squalor of the Caribbean islands, the charm of society in the Argentine's Cordoba, to relate his observations that man's dwellings varied in size and structure, that in one region man lived in abundance and in another in poverty. And if this was not geography in the pedogogical sense it was what most interested Jefferson. In the Argentine Jefferson had studied the heavens, with Davis he studied the earth; at the Normal he gave himself to studying man on the earth. The human element of his geography was inserted in classroom presentations, and more vigorously so as the years passed and Jefferson freed himself from the great influence of Davis and Davisian physiography. Initially, in 1902 Jefferson's course offerings in the catalogue read:[13]

GEOGRAPHY

Elementary Geography.
The course will take up the distribution of physical, climatic and industrial regions of the earth. Class exercises and Tarr and McMurry's third Book.
Physical Geography.
An introductory course with Dryer's Physical Geography as text-book, maps, models, pictures and reading.
Teachers' Geography.
It is the object of this course to give thorough training in those fundamentals on which all good geographic teaching depends, as the earth as a planet, seasons, latitude, longitude, climate, and weathering and erosional processes. Lectures and laboratory work.
Field Geography.
This course offers training in the use of the local "out-of-doors" as matter of regular instruction in geography. The exercises will be conducted mostly in the open air.

Commercial Geography.

The object will be to treat of the geographic control on the production and exchange of such commodities as cotton, wheat, iron, copper, wool and manufactured articles, to develop the principles, underlying and guiding commercial activities. Adams's Commercial Geography and reading.

Physiography of the Lands

Text-book, Davis's Physical Geography. Lectures, models, maps, and reading.

Geography of the United States

(Not given in 1902, 1903)

Geography of Europe.

(Not given in 1902, 1903)

It was not until the publication of the 1906-1907 catalogue that one reads of "man" in Jefferson's geography:[14] "Course 4. General Geography, 12 weeks. This course is designed to extend the preparation offered by *Teachers Geography* to the distribution of Man and institutions in the principal countries of the world." Nevertheless, much of his teaching prior to this time had constituted a variety of human geography, though this had escaped mention in the college catalogues.[15] Geography at Michigan State Normal College began to flourish when it was realized that it no longer constituted a set of formulae, the rote memorization of names, sailor geography, or physiography. His inclination was to gather facts that brought man into geography, partly attributable no doubt to his reading of the works of European geographers and partly to his own interests. Although he had been steeped in Davisian physiography at Harvard for two years (1896-1898) and although he admired Davis' work more than that of any other geographer he was to discover during his life time, Jefferson committed himself to the study and teaching of man as a vital part of geography. For Jefferson, the study of the earth devoid of the study of human life was not geography. Man living on the earth, and not man and the earth, was the essence of his conception of geography. When he offered geography at the Normal in 1901, he insisted on the study of the human element, and so brought himself into opposition with the geographic tradition of that time. He lectured upon the theme to students and teachers in the State of Michigan and he published his thoughts which ran counter to the recommendations of the Committee of Ten.[16] His effort to reshape geography and claim for it a human field in addition to explanatory landform study in the decade 1902-1912 was bold. For here was a normal school man, responsible to the teaching of teaching, who was attacking the very program which had been erected to consolidate and enhance the academic position of geography.

More than the content of his courses won large classes for Jefferson. He possessed those hard-to-define qualities that distinguish great teaching, which established him as an intellectual ancestor to so many. A. C. Krey in attempting to grasp the essence of such greatness in the classroom essayed the following in 1936:[17]

> . . . There was a time which the new generation of teachers never knew, but the older cannot forget, when teaching was generally referred to as an art. There seemed no other way to define what good teachers did or how they did it. Under this caption, Mark Hopkins and his legendary log have long occupied a niche of fame. David Starr Jordan in biology, David Eugene Smith in mathematics, Frederick Jackson Turner and Henry Johnson in History, Mark Jefferson in geography, and William Rainey Harper in Semitics are among the great teachers most often characterized as artists. It is true that attempted description of their methods by their former students has nearly always proved inadequate. There is usually a margin, covered by a wide gesture, that marks the decisive element in their teaching as their students recall it. Only the word "art" can be used to describe skill of the order possessed by these great teachers.

Jefferson was a healthy man—he had numerous ideas. Largely self-tutored, his Greek clarity and largeness of manner, his copiousness of humanity and sympathy with the human undertaking enabled him to awake in many thousands of undergraduates their first appreciation of the world in which they lived. Students taking the courses were working with an interested and interesting geographer on the frontier of the unexplored. In gathering ideas and work from many parts of the world, and putting them together, putting flesh upon ideas, in sorting out the gathered impressions of his travels, Jefferson presented the spectacle of a living scholar to his classes. He well remembered that presence in the classroom was not attributable to a borrowed methodological system, although he had once asked Davis whether he thought his deductive system would work well with young minds. The inimitable Jefferson who claimed, "I don't know how to teach, . . . just go into the classroom and tell the story the best I know how," presented a bundle of human exuberance whose personal and academic classroom peculiarities lived on in the minds of generations of students. He did not particularly concern himself whether a student in class absorbed what he said or not, though he was insistent that his own presentation be intelligible for the student of serious intent. His ideas were put simply, he offered what he wanted, developed his own thinking as his classes progressed. Jefferson would deliver his lecture and the student would be left with the impression that he was being personally addressed. The classroom period never seemed over-prepared, but rather well thought about, as though the presentation were the result of works going on and never finished.

The class talk was an interruption to his scour for understanding and new ideas, during which time students would come to see what he was doing and to realize that geography was not simply place-name or commodity study. There was always something personal in his point of view, in his interpretation, as if the subject were being looked at differently from ever before, the product of a lively and irrepressible intellectual curiosity. Contagious enthusiasm and the power to carry students beyond the mere curriculum were his vital strengths.

He enjoyed sharing his scholarship with students who were challenge and stimulation for him. Anxious to draw from students the best that was in them, eager to equip each mind with an insatiable appetite for knowledge for its own sake, Jefferson did not seek to entertain, amuse, or train his students, but to educate them. Vigorously he would dismiss classroom apathy, lethargy and ignorance. Making available geographic knowledge to future teachers was one way to reveal "God's truths:"[18]

> *I understand the Westminster catechism suggests as the chief end of man to praise God and enjoy him forever. But how enjoy God if you go around blind to his works which encompass you on every hand. To think that millions find the world dull!*

He steadfastly maintained that initially education was a painful process, but if it could be made less painful by tactical demonstration—that was progress, but such efforts must never degenerate into license.

Interesting and typical of the man's philosophy is the observation he makes in the preface to his book, *Man in Europe*.[19]

> *The little book is for use in classes. It aims to tell not what the reader can make out for himself.*
>
> *When it comes to teaching—I told my wife she could lead a horse to water but not make him drink. She replied, "I'm not so sure. I can give him salt can't I?" We shall try to give them salt.*

Jefferson readily held the attention of his class from the moment of his entry into the classroom to the time of his departure. The class might construct model native dwellings of authentic design and proportion, dress in the indigenous costume of the Caribbean or Central Europe, practice caliper head measuring exercise to find cephalic indexes, or taste a national dish of another country; he would try to bring alive people from other lands in the classroom. To aid this study and appreciation of differentness, he would illustrate his discourse with slides made from pictures that he had taken on his travels. The student became an armchair traveler who was taught to see and think geographically. Jefferson, a rare artist with the camera, had been taking photographs since 1884. Many of these he had converted into slides so that by the time of his retirement in 1939, he had amassed a personal collection of 7,500 slides.[20] Frequently throughout his life Jefferson received letters from educators requesting copies of his slides.

In 1906 Jefferson began to experiment with stereoscopes. In the *Journal of Geography*, 1907, he published an article[21] favoring their use in the classroom, which brought correspondence and visits from representatives of other visual aid companies. He received complimentary copies of "views" which helped swell his collection of stereoscopic pictures for class use. Several of his own slides taken with a stereoscopic camera were adopted by the Keystone View Company and converted into commercial views.

Students had to work hard in Jefferson's classes. He used the question and answer method frequently and expected accurate and ready answers if his questions were drawn from prescribed work. He felt the student in the classroom should be made to participate and not merely listen. This principle reveals itself clearly in the books Jefferson wrote for his classes, which very frequently contain exercises to be completed by the students. These books include: *Material for Geography of Michigan*, 1906;[22] *Teachers Geography; A Note Book and Syllabus*, 1906;[23] *28 Exercises on Topographic Maps*, 1906;[24] *World Diagrams of Population, Temperatures, Rainfall and Plant Distribution; A Supplement to Teachers Geography*, 1908;[25] *Commercial Values, An Atlas of Raw Materials of Commerce and Commercial Interchanges*, 1912;[26] *Notes on the Geography of Europe*, 1917;[27] *Man in Europe: Here and There*, 1924;[28] *Atlas of Plates to Man in the United States*, 1926;[29] *Principles of Geography*, 1926;[30] *Exercises in Human Geography*, 1930;[31] *Man in the United States*, 1933.[32] Most editions of these several books were published in Ypsilanti and in limited numbers. Several of the books underwent numerous revisions, and on each occasion there was a new printing frequently undertaken by Fred Buytendorp of the Ypsilanti Press. Jefferson realized that his books would reach a larger market if he gave them to a nationally recognized publishing house, but he complained that he could not manipulate the revision of detail in his book at a distance. Furthermore, by publishing locally and less elaborately, Jefferson reduced costs, which allowed him to revise editions quite regularly. Notwithstanding the fact that his family was entirely dependent upon his salary, Jefferson did not concern himself with the making of profit on sales of his books. On more than one occasion he supplied his books to the students minus the covers. Collections of printed sheets were cheaper than hard cover books. In importing atlases for his classes from the George Philip Company of England, paying the duty, and correspondence fees, it seems probably that he lost money in rendering service to his students.

He wrote books for his classes that students would have a text. The text was the product of the man's experience and geographic understanding that had been tried with other classes and found acceptable. He gave the simplest expression to his feelings, using the encounters chance threw in his way, effecting a book in simple non-technical terms and in such a style that the layman might read and understand. A teacher by sympathy and with an instinctive interest in people, Jefferson's writing never approached dogma: his pen discussed rather than accepted, it guided, it chided, it suggested. Arising perpetually, with slow irresistible force, was a point of view: his books were never an abstention but were always inquisition. In the preface to *Man in Europe,* Jefferson wrote; "I have no mandate to define geography, but I have a point of view." His books were a perennial attempt to share with his students the joy of real thinking. His books were not text to a completed science, rather were they the program of his travel, correspondence, reading and thought, accompanied by a constant invitation to reflection and work. The books, meant for his classes, bore a legitimate and restrained ambition: never would Jefferson allow ambition to outrun capacity. One is almost drawn to the conclusion in reading Jefferson's classroom material, that his literary style is at root of a self-imposed act of humility; fluent and personal, it is the antithesis of an overwriting. Jefferson acquired an ease in prose that came with constant use. Taking rhetoric, he wrung its neck, incurring the wrath of Brigham,[33] yet insuring for his writing a triumph of sense over style. His writing was terse, blunt, meaningful, relevant. He wrote to be understood. Frequently in a haste to capture his thought on paper he became at times delightfully and democratically indifferent to delicacy of style. His writing—never a nest of singing birds—had about it the promise of permanence.[34]

> *Style has always seemed to me a stupid thing to dwell on. My problem is to think clearly and state clearly. The heaping up of phrases so traditional that we can tell at any moment what the next three words are going to be is abhorrent. People who tell their stories confusedly are not so much lacking in style as in clear view of their subject.*

His readiness and ability to commit pen to paper and complete a book in a few weeks, was unusual. Jefferson commenced *Man In Europe* after the summer school of 1924 had been completed. Before the fall semester had commenced, *Man In Europe* was between hard covers and Jefferson was at work on *Principles of Geography*.[35]

His books have to be read, for they are at once inimitable and unique in the literature of American geography. They were classroom equipment, and yet these books, by exerting a persistent if quiet authority, also were helping to build the discipline. Davisian physiography was losing popularity in U.S. schools after the turn of the century, notwithstanding the recommendations of the Committee of Ten, 1894. "Man" was now entering American geography and Jefferson's texts encouraged teachers and students to adopt this new direction. While teaching geography at Yale University in 1908, Isaiah Bowman wrote to his former teacher, Jefferson:[36]

> I have tried the "man-first" idea in my course in South America, starting with your population map, and the fellows were extremely interested in the map, and the lessons to be drawn from it. A corresponding change has been made in the presentation of the geography of North America, whereby the man element is first introduced and then the physical conditions brought in, in explanation of man's distribution and activities. The change has proved agreeable not only to the men but to myself, and I think this plan will remain fixed—or until some better plan presents itself.

Teachers Geography experienced 10 known editions and 18 printings between 1906 and 1923 and probably sold over 15,000 copies; *Man In Europe,* 1924 experienced minimally 3 printings between 1924 and 1936, *Principles of Geography,* 1926, 2 printings, *Exercises in Human Geography,* 1930, 3 printings. The exact number of book reprints and number of copies distributed is unknown since the records of the local Ypsilanti Press have been discarded. Frequently a book would be reprinted from previously established type-set with no notation of the reprinting.[37] He wrote to his daughter in 1923:[38]

> My 10th edition of Teachers Geography *all in type; printing the first form of sixteen pages now . . . beside the call for about 200, we have an order of 35 from Minnesota, and for 3 from a southern school. Single copies go every month or two all over—even to Japan and China. I am going to send copies to 20 or 30 Normal schools now. Hitherto I have never advertised at all.*

These textbooks, reviewed and adopted throughout the country, revealed Jefferson's geographic point of view to large numbers of teachers and students. His texts attracted inquiries from geography instructors and several normal school presidents, especially during the first quarter of the century. Many normal school faculty purchased Jefferson's texts, particularly *Teachers Geography,* as a ready made syllabus for a classroom course in geography. The point of view these texts contributed toward geographic education in the United States in the context of their time can be derived, in part, from encouraging and sometimes exciting reviews which his texts usually received in the *Bulletin of the American Geographical Society,* the *Geographical Review,* and the *Journal of Geography.*

Reviewing the 1911 Edition of *Teachers Geography* in the *Bulletin of the American Geographical Society,* C. W. Hotchkiss wrote:[39]

> This book embodies some of the results of a teacher's long experience with students in Normal Schools and Colleges. It cannot be denied that the majority of these students came to their professional training victims of the sins of omission and commission of Elementary and Secondary Schools, and as the case now stands, so far as geography is concerned, Normal Training Schools are called upon to supply the defects of early instruction and to prepare the student to teach . . .
>
> In the twelve weeks' course here outlined Mr. Jefferson devotes his instruction to the Distribution of Man upon the earth, and to Climate, one of the controlling factors of that distribution. Hand in hand with class instruction are daily exercises planned to make the student familiar with the weather elements, to test and strengthen his judgment concerning their effect upon his life, and to clarify the relation of his individual experience with the general laws whose effect on the earth at large he is studying. There are probably no phenomena about which young teachers show more ignorance than those connected with the general subject of climate. For this reason such a definite treatment, embodying a close study of maps as well as of daily weather happenings is destined to be of distinct service. The author has shown admirable restraint in confining this brief course to a definite topic and its applications. A teacher thus carefully trained in the use of maps and alert in his observation has the best possible foundation for the future culture his experience will bring him. If all teachers of geography could become familiar with the subject as presented in this admirable book the teaching of elementary geography would be on a distinctly higher plane.

Reviewing *Man in Europe: Here and There,* (1924 edition), Isaiah Bowman wrote in the *Geographical Review:*[40]

> Jefferson has worked some ripe philosophy into this book. It barely exceeds two hundred pages in a rather drab binding (but such as Ypsilanti, a town of 8,000 need not be ashamed of). The Sunday literary supplements will not notice it, but as an intellectual lever it should tilt the geographical world a little. There is no appendix of unvitalized statistics, no mere paraphernalia of scholarship, no gaudy illustrations, no waste of words. There are a goodly number of really geographical photographs with telling one-line captions, several original city maps loaded with geographical significances, outline maps in an unfinished state with directions for completing, so that you as reader

have work to do before you reap the otherwise too easy reward of Jefferson's thought, penetrating comments and questions, critically selected quotations from great literature. You have a growing sense of accomplishment as you advance from chapter to chapter to the end. One critic has well described the book as a grateful breeze blowing through an open window (this reader of course has his window open most of the time); another critic has equally well described the author as a man with no echoes in his mind.

It is a great thing to have done a little book like Jefferson's "Man in Europe." It is the issuance after toil. He has lived in France, Italy, Norway, and England. He speaks French and Spanish, not only as the result of book knowledge but also and particularly as a man who has lived a language with its people. Beside his condensed and thoughtful paragraphs, how barren seem so many other descriptions of European geography! The tyranny of that which has been still exercises its strange power over each successive writer. Jefferson's book is no "mine of information"; it is cut glass and hammered gold. Though intended for normal-school classes it should be used in every university course on the geography of Europe. It will teach the most mature student how to think more effectively in geographical terms. In it are no winds of current opinion, only basic things that influence and grow out of that solid folk life that survives dynasties and wars and gives geography its substantial content as a science. The list of chapters gives you no indication of the tone of the book, but for those who want headings here they are: Europe the Leading Continent; Distribution of Population; The Cities; Wealth; Some Pictures; What the European is Like; Climate; The Contest for the Northern Plains.

Reviewing *Principles of Geography* (1926), John Orchard wrote in the *Geographical Review:*[41]

"The power of the understanding is very great, that of the misunderstanding knows no limit." With this sentence of Bordon Parker Bowne, Professor Jefferson opens his "Principles of Geography," and in the spirit of the quotation the text has been written. The book is a challenge to misunderstanding, particularly misunderstanding arising through the acceptance by teachers and students of whatever may be taught without any critical examination in the light of common sense and common experience. It is a challenge to the persistence of error and of the geographic myths that have appeared in our text through so many generations. It is a text calculated to stimulate in the minds of teachers and students a healthy skepticism. And since it is a text for teachers of teachers, it should have a decided influence on the quality and accuracy of geographical instruction.

Professor Jefferson presents and discredits a number of statements regarding the earth and man's activities still current in geographical teaching, particularly the myths descriptive of the lands of the high and low latitudes and of their inhabitants. His own statements of geographical principles are carefully reasoned . . .

After a brief chapter on maps, which should better have been incorporated in some of the later chapters, there is a discussion of "Where the People Are" followed by a chapter on "Why the People are There". It is a method of treatment decidedly unusual in these days of regional geography; but it is a method nevertheless, that may be thoroughly geographic. It provides the opportunity for setting sharply the limits of the field of geography. In view of the author's studies of population it should be a particularly satisfactory method . . .

The style of the book might be termed Jeffersonian, for the wit of the author and a keen sense of humor serve to enliven and make interesting even the discussion of the most difficult subjects.

Man in the United States received notice in the Geographical Record section of the October, 1933, *Geographical Review:*[42]

THIS UNITED STATES. The United States of the moment is a very different thing from its predecessors, above all, says Professor Jefferson, from the United States of free homesteads for pioneer men and women. "Man in the United States" (1933) is Professor Jefferson's latest book of exercises, stimulating and provocative as usual. There is vitality in the text and in the sixty and more figures illustrating the population, their work, and the conditions under which they work. "A country is not merely a nation on territory, but in active relation to it, living from it." Activity means change: the "new" America is especially characterized by its urbanism.

A. E. Parkins reviewed the third edition of Jefferson's *Man in Europe* (1936), in the *Journal of Geography:*[43]

This book (a revision) is a brief geography of Europe in which a workbook has been incorporated.

There is much informality about the book. The style is chatty, thought stimulating, pithy, just what we have come to expect from "the Bernard Shaw of American geographers." The students and teacher are made to feel at home with each other.

It is a book to be studied, not merely read. In the preface the author tells us the book is prepared for use in the preparation of teachers. "It aims not to tell what the reader can work out for himself." This is a Mark Jeffersonian principle of teaching thoroughly in line with the best in present-day philosophy of education.

Jefferson seems to be firmly of the belief that pictures in books are there for edification, not for mere illustration. He presents sixty pic-

tures, halftones from his own negatives. These are carefully selected to illustrate some features of geography from the "top of Norway" to the Mediterranean and even beyond into Algeria. Each is an intimate presentation of the behavior of the people.

The author does not set up some hypothetical definition of geography which he strains to follow and bedevils all those who fail to agree with this particular definition. In his preface he says, "I have no mandate to define geography; but I want children to know where some of the more important people of the world are and what they are like, and I first want the teachers to know these things themselves." This is the keynote of his presentation.

One will find in the book several things that are new as one always expects in any product from the pen of Professor Jefferson.

After receiving a copy of *Man in Europe* (1936), Bowman wrote from his vacation home in East Wolfeboro, New Hampshire:[44]

The office has forwarded your Man in Europe to me up here knowing that I would want it at once (they have lived with me now for a year and more and have acquired perspicacity) and that there will be little time for reading after my return. Its arrival paralyzed my program yesterday morning and bids fair to do the same today. I like the swing, snap, punch, drive, vigor, originality, hang and set of the thing! There are no imitators. I never read your stuff without recalling A. P. Brigham's remark one time that your English was a disgrace to scholarship. Brigham had a smooth and slick style that sprang from his temperament I suppose and also no doubt from his pulpit experience. To me it lacked salt and it also lacked any least depth of thought or conviction. (You see I make no customary apologies for speaking de mortuis). No Emersonian stuff for him! Your style and your stuff will live. It is not meant for morons. Only thoughtful readers need apply. You do not ask as . . . "Is this just pure geography or am I spilling over into Sociology or History?" every time he comes on a paragraph that is unlabelled and unconventional. Damn these boundary fellows who think the Lord created "subjects". A man wrote me the other day about Davis—had him all sized up from his writings. I told him it was sawdust—that to separate a man's work from his setting was a crime, and that professional appraisal apart from biography was lop-sided. It is the same with "problems". Simon-pure geography is a blind man feeling the elephant's tail.

Maps also were drawn and reproduced in large numbers. These were distributed to his classes and were purchased at cost by schools and colleges across the nation in numbers reaching into the thousands. They include:[45]

United States; Multiple United States; United States (no cities); United States (cities, 1920); North America—Railroads; Temperature graphs (Chicago, St. Louis, Denver, etc.); Michigan cities and counties map; Average afternoon temperatures (Michigan); Michigan cities; Temperature Graph—Detroit; Ypsilanti; North & South America (7 x 7); South America (1° mesh); South America (outline); Latin America (outline); Latin America (10 on a sheet); Rain—South America, January—July; South America Railroads; Africa; Asia—Railroads; China Population; Australia; Australia (Large mesh); Australia (without mesh); Australia (9 to a sheet); Europe (blank); Europe (multiple); Europe (Railroads); Great Britain (cities, 1911); Scandinavia (in 1920); Switzerland (outline); World (6-6); Elliptical World Outlines.

Students were attracted to a geography course owing in part to the unusual appearance of course offerings in the Normal College catalogue. Courses in geography were there often described in detail, the descriptions occasionally occupying 300 words. Not infrequently the Geography section of the catalogue would contain a map, coupled with an essay presenting an idea that usually Jefferson had been recently developing: for example in 1931, there appeared the following statement accompanied by a Jefferson railway map of Europe, originally published in *Economic Geography* 1928, as "The Civilizing Rails":[46]

Geography is much concerned with every major fact of modern life that lends itself easily to mapping. As an example take the twenty-mile-wide white bands along every railway in Europe as if everyone within ten miles of the line was in the light of civilization, and so he is. In Western Europe the bands of white overlap in one great fabric of transportation, the RAILWEB of western Europe—England, France, Germany, Belgium, Holland, Denmark, Southern Sweden, with most of Switzerland and old Austria—Hungary. They are the nations of culture.

How sharp the edge of the railweb at Spain and Russia! Nations that build their railways of broader gauge than France and Germany to keep out armies. But they shut out light and progress, too. Spain and Russia have only a railnet between whose strands are broad backwoods of ignorance and peasantry.

Obviously distributions that concern men, as these do, are of high importance and attention is directed to such matters in our geographic study.

During the 38 years that Jefferson was head of the Department 65 different courses were offered to students:

Advanced Field work

Advanced Geography of: Europe

                           Latin America

                           Mediterranean lands.

                           Northern Europe

                           Switzerland

Advanced Principles of Geography

Applied Geography

Climatology

Commercial Geography

Economic Geography I

Economic Geography II

Elementary Geography

Field Geography

Field Geography (Teachers' Course)

General Geography

General Geography of the Continents

Geographic Conference

Geographic Excursions

Geographic Lesson Plans

Geographic Material

Geography (a preliminary course to prepare students to meet demands of a new certification law)

Geography of: American History

                   Cities

                   Commerce

                   Culture

                   Railroads

                   Africa

                   America

                   Asia

                   Asia, Australia and Africa

                   Australia

                   The Balkans

                   Caribbean Lands

                   Egypt

                   Europe

                   Europe and Asia

                   Far East

                   France

Great Britain
Latin America
Mediterranean Countries
Michigan
New England and New York
North America
Norway
Scandinavia
Scotland
South Atlantic Coast
The Old South
U.S.A.
U.S. and Canada
Geography Teachers' Course
Intensive Study of Geography of France
Illustrative Lessons in Geography
Map Drawing
Meteorology
Methods and Material in Geography Teaching
The New World
Physical Geography
Physiography of the Lands
Physiography of the dry lands
Physiography of the humid lands
Principles of Human Geography
Teachers' Geography

Jefferson introduced nearly all of these courses himself, and personally offered 62 of them. These courses often were inspired by field trips he had made or ideas which he had developed and invariably presented before gatherings of geographers, and later published. Such courses included, "The Geography of the New World," which followed his experience with the Inquiry and the Paris Peace Conference; "The Geography of Railways," which followed his 1927 paper on railways at the Nashville, Tennessee, meeting of the Association of American Geographers; "The Geography of the Old South" followed the sabbatical leave he spent at McClellanville, South Carolina, 1926; "Commercial Geography" was the product of his extended 1911 meeting with Edinburgh's George Chisholm; the "Geography of Scandinavia" was the product of a one-man summer field trip in the Loenfjord of Norway and extended correspondence and personal intercourse with Baron Sten de Geer of Sweden and his elected membership to the Swedish Geographical and Anthropological Society in 1925; two courses in the Geography of

The Department of Geography, 1930, *Left to right:* Ella Wilson, Margaret Sill, Mark Jefferson, and Secretary, Ida Brown.

France were largely the product of his Peace Conference experience; the "Geography of Culture" was the product of his own mind leavened by personal intercourse and correspondence with Ellsworth Huntington and Marcel Aurousseau. But the extent of Jefferson's achievement was made possible only with the help of a steady stream of departmental co-workers including: Isaiah Bowman (1903-4), Margaret Lockwood (1904-5), Darrell H. Davis (1905-08), Charles Colby (1906-8), A. E. Parkins (1908-11), Genevieve Clark (1911-18), Inez Bayes (1911-12), Elmer Clark (1914-15), Mary Cawood (1915-16), (1918-19), Mabel Weddel (1916-17), Ruth Hansen (1917-18), Ora Wilcox (1919-22), Margaret Sill (1921-present), Ella Wilson (1923-39). Furthermore, Jefferson frequently made heavy demands upon his associates, requiring them perhaps to arise at an early hour to record a temperature at a given point locally, to sacrifice a short vacation by gathering requested information from the library or to teach his own classes if he wished to be left alone for a few days. Jefferson was an indefatigable worker, and he expected his associates to demonstrate similar zeal and work habits. Without this cooperation his productivity would have suffered considerably.

Jefferson had developed by the end of the first decade of the twentieth century a philosophy concerning the values and merits of education and the teaching of geography—a philosophy which he was to emphasize frequently some of which he published in an article, "The Value of Geography as a school subject."[47]

He maintained that there are only two good reasons why a student should obtain geographic facts: firstly, such facts will increase his enjoyment of life, and, secondly, they will increase his ability to serve as a citizen. By showing phenomena in their associations geography increases our enjoyment of life, maintained Jefferson; for example, all are enchanted by the blueness of the Mediterranean, but he suggests there is an added charm in recognizing a part of this color splendor in the intense saltness of the water; the blacker waters of the Equator, under frequent rains that keep their surface almost fresh, acquire new interest. Travel, too, takes on added interest if we are able to recognize phenomena that are to be observed on our own doorsteps. He wrote that a knowledge of geography enabled one to view distant parts of the earth as the environment of long lost friends, or the hearth of an oft-read literary creation. Yet most firmly did he believe that the greatest value the discipline geography could offer resided in its ability to afford an honest intellectual endeavor for the student. This characteristic, he insisted, was shared alike by all disciplines and was not peculiar to geography. Serious study of a discipline cultivated the mind and brought with it intellectual and moral qualities: "give a young man good instruction in any object of his interest and moral good will come of it." Instruction in a discipline also satisfied a thirst for knowledge, a thirst which Jefferson declared to be "as divine as anything in the world save sympathy and kindliness." As a geographer Jefferson offered the students geographical facts, yet maintained steadfastly that the higher good resulting from this process was not the student's greater understanding of geography, but the moral betterment of his soul. Thus for Jefferson a student's choice of discipline became immaterial, as the highest end of education, enrichment of the mind, would be affected.

> *I conclude then that geography has not some special ethical and moral quality of its own to impart to its students, something that they cannot get from music or botany or philosophy, but it has an appeal to some people that none of these may have, and to whom it appeals it offers everything. It is a question through which of its appeals we shall have the world revealed to us. Not diversity of values in school subjects, but diversity in the student individual is the justification for the coexistence of the varied subjects of the curriculum. If geography interests a student and literature does not, literature will do him less good.*[48]

This liberal Jefferson philosophy bespoke interests which were not wholly confined to the Department of Geography at the Normal. Wherever the mind was being bettered, there lay Jefferson's interest. No one could accuse Jefferson of ethnocentric pedagogy, for his very philosophy had been formed from his findings in three continents. Jefferson had been able to borrow ideas and fragments of philosophies from the more sophisticated systems which Europe had been able to establish over many centuries, and thus brought to the Normal ideas and approaches that may well not have been so readily found in midwestern society. In so doing he complemented and strengthened Ypsilanti's fund of educational thought. In this way Jefferson helped develop the Normal philosophy and functions, helped the institution establish its direction and find its values in a world that was undergoing rapid change.

This man of many talents, 5'8" in height, weighing about 125 pounds, of firm stride, steel gray hair, bifocal rimless glasses, frequently sporting a goatee beard, invariably dressed in a gray or blue suit unless it be a Panama summer suit day, was known the length and breadth of the campus. Students recognized Jefferson as a hard grader, they also recognized him as an extremely erudite man. His personality was blunt, abrupt, much like his writing. He was always anxious to arrive at the heart of the matter without being in a haste. There was little time for trivia. If he were sick on occasion, the students would take class around Jefferson's bed. People as people were anathema to Jefferson; they were worth the ideas and thought they propounded. Jefferson was not haunted by a sense of the shortness of life, yet he fervently desired to uncover as many truths as possible. Each truth was to be savored and enjoyed; time should be taken in digesting each truth. He amplified his own truth in papers that were read or published. The truths of other geographers he broadcast in the classroom that his students might share. He would never tolerate pomposity, meretricious display, or human exhibition. His circle of faculty friendships was limited to the older faculty members on campus who were extremely competent in their respective fields; Strong (physics), Sherzer (geology), Ford (languages), "if only I had enough data I would write a book" Barbour (English), Pray (history). A belief that the cultured man should read widely in the classics and the history of the classical world permeated the man, yet he was able to converse easily with students. Jefferson was not born a teacher. He taught because it was a job affording the opportunity to read, write, and think, "Thinking is still the best thing I do." The product of his efforts he offered to his classes, sensing audience reaction and polishing his own presentation in performing his teaching duties. Frequently he wrote that if he had sufficient income he would have devoted his full time to geography devoid of the classroom. And he could still have been a very great teacher. Ellsworth Huntington in his capacity as research associate at Yale University did not teach in the classroom, though his teaching influence through the books and articles he published was very great. That was the strength of Jefferson in the classroom; he knew his subject and presented it in easily understandable terms to his students. No I. Q. or aptitude tests, no prerequisites would hamper a student in his classes provided he was prepared to work. Jefferson was greater than the sum of his parts. He left students feuding with him, with themselves, and with life, after one semester of his geography. He showed the student what was unattainable, then insisted the student reach for it.

His classroom manner was seemingly a natural and unstudied gift, but his ability to know exactly where to begin, to make his scenes spring alive, to develop in the student a wider range of interest, and to make "Teachers' Geography" a course that became an institution in North American geography, occasioned even the most plangent of the levellers to agree that Jefferson was a force in the teaching of things geographic. Teachers' Geography . . . the course at the Michigan State Normal College that became an institution. Its success was an admixture of numerous ingredients: care, learning, wide reading, and an abundance of new ideas (many embodied in papers delivered before the Association of American Geographers), thinking on the nature of geography, watching its evolution in many countries including the U.S.A. By selling *Teachers Geography, Principles of Geography, Exercises in Human Geography,* over a period extending from 1906 to 1939, to high schools, normal schools, and universities, the course, "Teacher's Geography," became widely known. For this textbook, continually under revision both of content and title, was really the Teachers' Geography course set down on paper. Course No. 1, "Teachers' Geography," began in 1901 as a study of the size and shape of the earth, a study in Greek cosmological speculation, latitude, longitude, the barometer. By the 1930's the same course, now entitled Principles of Geography (101-102), concerned itself with the distribution of man on the earth's surface, weather and climate, culture and civilization. Yet it was what was taught beyond the curriculum that was exciting; to wander through poetry, explorations, to hear of the doings of men as Stefansson, vagabonding with Harry Frank round the world, to drink yerba mate from a gourd, to see slides of the world taken from any one of Jefferson's numerous field excursions, were just some of the reasons why this course transcended the usual meaning of a regular classroom offering. In Jefferson's later years the course offered hardly less than a life time's findings. Students were left with an understanding of some geographical principles when they had experienced this grounding, on which they were thoroughly examined. The course was like a sponge that was large enough to absorb all the ideas that became available in this area of study. Several members of the department over the years taught the course, which was of departmental concern, but it was the man, Jefferson, offering the course rather than the curriculum that made the course an institution.

First offered in 1901, the course retired with Jefferson in 1939. The course, required of all students studying geography, was offered several times a year, to a classroom full of undergraduate students, many of whom used their lecture notes in later years for developing their own courses in school or colleges. Below is the course description of Teachers Geography reproduced by pentad from the Normal School Catalogue. It is suggestive of the evolution of Geography in twentieth century U.S.A.

1902: I. TEACHERS' GEOGRAPHY. Required of all students.

> *It is the object of this course to give thorough training in those fundamentals on which all good geographic teaching depends, as the earth as a planet, seasons, latitude, longitude, climate, and weathering and erosional processes. Lectures and Laboratory work.*[49]

1907: I. TEACHERS' GEOGRAPHY. 12 weeks. Two recitations a day.

> *This course is designed to prepare students for teaching geography*

in the public schools, as far as its subject matter is concerned. It deals with the nature and use of maps, and the study and teaching of weather and climate.[50]

1912: I. TEACHERS' GEOGRAPHY. 12 weeks.

This course is designed to prepare students for teaching geography in the public schools as far as its subject matter is concerned. It deals with the study of weather and climate, the making and reading of maps and the distribution of man over the earth with its broad grounds in the distribution of plants and in climatic features.[51]

1917: GEOGRAPHY I. TEACHERS' COURSE. 1 Unit.

Countries are regarded as groups of men under one government together with the portion of the earth they have in actual use. The distribution of men over the earth is regarded as the most important item of geography, and modern conceptions of such things as cities and countries are here explained. Climate figures a good deal in the course, especially in so far as the explanation of rainfall is concerned, for the distribution of rainfall over the earth enables man to live and thrive best in favored localities. The old-time teaching about the climates of the earth, for instance, has the merit of simplicity, but it is often the simplicity of ignorance, teaching what simply is not so, as that the equatorial regions are excessively hot, that Europe is given a mild climate by the Gulf Stream and that winds are cooled by snow-capped mountains. Of recent years abundant measurements and careful observations enable us to describe climates with some accuracy, and illustrate the chief principles that control them. Enough exercises in simple, but scientific map-drawing to enable the students to use maps better.

It is believed this course gives a sound foundation both for elementary teaching and for further study of geography.[52]

1922:1. TEACHERS' COURSE. 1 Unit.

Countries are regarded as groups of men under one government together with the portion of the earth they have in actual use. The distribution of men over the earth is regarded as the most important item of geography, and modern conceptions of such things as cities and countries are here explained. Climate figures a good deal in the course, especially in so far as the explanation of rainfall is concerned, for the distribution over the earth enables man to live and thrive best in favored localities. The old-time teaching about the climates of the earth, for instance, has the merit of simplicity but it is often the simplicity of ignorance, teaching what simply is not so, as that the equatorial regions are excessively hot, that Europe is given a mild climate by the Gulf Stream, and that winds are cooled by snow-

*capped mountains. Of recent years abundant measurements and care-
ful observations enable us to describe climates with some accuracy,
and illustrate the chief principles that control them. Enough exercises
are given in simple map drawing to enable the students to use maps
better. It is believed this course gives a sound foundation both for
elementary teaching and for further study of geography.*[53]

1927: 101. PRINCIPLES OF GEOGRAPHY 1. 4 term hours.

*It is about peoples and countries—The Peoples in their World—to
be put deliberately and intentionally in place of the customary world
and its people. New York, Philadelphia, Boston, Chicago, Detroit and
the hundred million dwellers in eastern United States are the great
features of North America not the Rocky Mountain nor the Great
Lakes. Countries are regarded as groups of people living each under
one government, each with a definite inheritance from its ancestors
and somewhat conditioned by the part of the world where they live,
and on which they impress something of their culture.*

*A nation—apart from any territory, or a territory apart from in-
habitants, has no interest here, only the actualities, countries.*

*There are exercises on maps and diagrams, the language in which
geography is expressed. There are exercises on the distribution of men
in the world, where swarming in multitudes, where few and far scattered. There are exercises on the great climatic element Rainfall, its
distribution and its utilization by men, for the distribution of rain
over the earth enables men to live best in favored localities. All
through the course there is observation and study of the passing
weather, essentially foundation for any understanding of climate.*

*This is no review of school geography but solid preparation for any
study that concerns itself with mankind.*[54]

*1932: 101. PRINCIPLES OF GEOGRAPHY. (Identical with course de-
scription of 1927)*[55]

1937: 101. PRINCIPLES OF GEOGRAPHY. 4 term hours.

*Geography 101 is required of all students who take more than one
course in Geography. There are exercises on maps and diagrams, the
language in which geography is expressed. There are exercises on the
distribution of men in the world, where swarming in multitudes,
where few and far scattered. There are exercises on the great climatic
element Rainfall, its distribution and its utilization by men. All
through the course there is observation and study of the passing
weather.*[56]

Examination of the text book used for the course reveals a marked
shift in content over the years, also apparent in the course description.

Teachers Geography 1903[57]

1. *The earth as a ball (taken from several sources in French, German and Greek)*
2. *Weather record (questions about)*
   Read in Davis why earth is thought round
   Doctrine of the Vertical
3. *Earth measures (Greeks on). Proof of roundness by:*
   a. *Eudoxus*
   b. *Aristotle BC 384-322*
   c. *Ships hull disappearance (Strabo)*
4. *The magnitude of the Earth. How to appreciate the size of the earth*
   The vastness of our planet.
5. *The problem of Eratosthenes (earth measurement)*
   Geometry.
6. *Post Greek (Grecian) views of earth shape.*
   a. *Childrey*
   b. *Other Paris academicians*
   c. *Colbert*
   d. *Expeditions of Louis XV*
7. *Simple Latitude Measurements.*
   a. *Sun angles*
   b. *Latitude itself*
8. *Longitude.*
9. *Date Line.*
10. *The map: Ptolemy's map appreciated in the Renaissance—not a map at all. (On map nets and their value).*
Pages missing 85-114
11. *On the barometer.*

Teachers Geography 1912 (4th edition)[58]
Paragraphs
   1-16: Study in population distribution.
   17- 28: Exercises—questions regarding population distribution and rainfall; also some population distribution maps.
   29- 32: Climate
   33- 91: Exercises concerning temperature, pressure, wind motions, presence and conditions of water.
   92- 94: Maps
   95-126: Exercises concerning Latitudes and Longitudes, map nets, rains, temperatures, plant regions.

In August, 1925, Jefferson resolved to retitle *Teachers Geography,* as this book had enjoyed such revision over the past nineteen years that it no longer resembled the original work of 1906. In 1925 he wrote to Gladys Wrigley:[59]

> . . . *The* Principles *is going to be greatly improved over the old* Teachers Geography. *That was the dry stuff, the requirements to take home and get a lesson with all the liver (live-er!) part reserved for class and I have been putting some of that in with good result. It is going to be better and easier to teach with.*
>
> *But my illustration programme will fall down. I cannot in the time get what I want. There will be few pictures only.*

Gladys Wrigley provided Jefferson with some illustrations and then proceeded to help with the editorial work, which he appreciated:[60]

> *I think I shall get much help from your subdivisions. The stuff is not orderly, I admit, yet there is a very fair, general sequence. Fortunately order is only order! A thing said backward may be very well said.*

And then on September 19, 1925 he wrote to editor Wrigley:[61]

> *I have finished the text of the* Principles *yesterday. It is not good; disorderly and incomplete; the name bigger than the book. What do you think of*
>
> ### SOME PRINCIPLES OF GEOGRAPHY
>
> *Anyway it is a lot better than any previous edition and some of it makes real reading.*
>
> *In my meager list of illustrations are 5 of yours. Please let me know how to acknowledge the loans.*

Exercises in Human Geography 1930[62]

EXERCISES

1. *Can you Read?*
2. *Great unoccupied spaces.*
3. *Migrations.*
4. *Very dense populations.*
5. *Dense and moderate population grades.*
6. *Extensive farming.*
7. *Thin and scanty population.*
8. *What the sun does to the ground.*
9. *Hot and cold regions.*
10. *The days of hot months and cold: where it gets hottest.*
11. *Air warmed in Flasks.*
12. *Balancing columns.*
13. *Spells of weather.*
14. *World Winds.*
15. *Monsoons of India.*

Some of the situations arising from his daily scheme of pedagogics warrant review, not that they might be emulated, but as a recording of an historicity that won for the man a success in the classroom that was recognized internationally.

On at least one occasion, Jefferson's students, who were studying the geography of Europe entered his classroom to find cutlery hanging from the ceiling. The more enterprising students of the group clambered on chairs to reach this odd assemblage and were rewarded by their labors with the knowledge that the cutlery had been made in Sheffield, England, and so was commenced a lesson concerning the economy of Britain.

His "mots" became a tradition, and a source of gentle amusement to his classes. All had heard the mots before, and all would hear them several times again. From Borden P. Bowne, a Boston University lecturer and author, Jefferson borrowed the mot, "The power of the understanding is great, the power of the misunderstanding knows no limits." From Shaler, his one time mentor, Jefferson borrowed, "The notebook is a tomb of ideas, in which many are buried and very few ever live to be resurrected"; from Davis he borrowed, "With us every season is exceptional, either the hottest, the coldest, the wettest or driest in the history of man"; and from his father he borrowed "There are milestones on the Dover Road." To these Jefferson added his own mots:

"The utter depravity of inanimate things," and, "Teachers know a lot of things which are just not so."

Jefferson adopted novel ways to test student alertness. On one occasion Jefferson sat reading at his cherry wood desk, while the class assembled. Minutes passed. Jefferson requested student papers. None were forthcoming. Some questions gazing chalkily from the blackboard coupled with Jefferson's silence had constituted a quiz. All students were awarded a zero mark. But under this gruff exterior lay a warm heart and an enormous store of patience; Jefferson always had time to explain once more to a student who had tried but not quite understood . . . he was a concerned pedagogue. To quote Marcel Aurousseau who knew Jefferson well, "he must have been a most stimulating teacher, if an inborn technique of putting people on their mettle through provocative comment be teaching."

Raye Platt has written:[63]

> *Jefferson always tried to make every class an exciting experience for his students and to open every class with something that put them on the alert. However, of all his dramatic class entrancings (he never appeared until the class was all seated), the only one I recall was one morning when he came in walking backwards and chanting "Backwards and forwards" and proceeded with a brief lecture on semantics. I am afraid, though, that only a few appreciated his brilliance. After all, he always treated everybody as adults, whereas, of course most of his students were just out of high school. Also he was a past master at illustration, his projector was always at the ready and there was rarely a class hour during which he did not interrupt his lecturing and quizzing by throwing on the screen slides from his voluminous collection.*

> *Again I must say that I am sure that he was very frequently over the heads of his students—which I am also sure was in general much to the good. There must have been only a few who did not come to appreciate his scholarship and even the dullest must have gotten some inkling of what it takes to make teaching inspirational.*

Occasionally Jefferson would show part of his superb slide collection for an entire class period without comment: at the next lesson he would ask the student what he had seen. If the course were "Field Geography," students would be mindful not to schedule another class later that day for the field geographers were warned in the catalogue that they might not return from the early afternoon class before 6 p.m. Students invariably returned at an hour later than the suggested 6 p.m. The course gained a measure of notoriety. Misses in his class, travelling on foot, were occasionally exhausted and prostrated from heat fatigue, while others, their ankle length skirts mud-caked and water-laden, had been known to break down and weep. But no one was hungry. Over an open fire Jefferson would bake the potatoes that he carried in a sack, break two raw eggs into a coffee pot that magically appeared from his person, while he would make certain that everyone was supplied with salt pills on warmer days.

Jefferson was a geographer and a writer of geography who made the classroom part of his way of life. His was the sensitivity of the poet, the erudition and spirit of inquiry of a scholar not seceded from the humanities, the vigor of a man of action. His teaching, the product of meditation and learning, offered student minds a series of opportunities. His one time student, Isaiah Bowman, who probably knew Jefferson more intimately than any other geographer with the exception of his departmental colleagues, Margaret Sill and Ella Wilson, later wrote of his teacher:[64]

> In his classes one did not "learn about map projections" but made them after calculating the elements. One did not "learn" merely how to read a map on a desk but went into the field and made a map. The diagram in the book was not enough for understanding geysers—the student had to set up a laboratory geyser and make it work. The Foucault pendulum demonstration of the earth's rotation and a dozen other exercises taught the student things and processes firsthand and led him to acquire the habit of using his hands and eyes and brain and creating a substantial part of his knowledge of geography as he went along.
>
> With small facilities Jefferson trained a host to teach geography with spirit and an understanding of basic facts and principles. And he kept his eye always open for the man or woman who had unusual abilities and after a year or two passed along his more talented students to the universities. Whoever their master might then be, they never forgot Jefferson, the cultured schoolmaster and thinker who considered himself well placed where he was and never sought a university chair. Part of this contentment, it is true, was due to self-depreciation. He often said of himself that he was too sharp and did not get along with people easily . . .
>
> Jefferson had no use for stock material in teaching and threw away his own old maps and plates as fast as new ideas arrived. His "Teachers' Geography" went through many private printings before he could be persuaded to put it in the hands of a commercial publisher, with "all its ideas, originality, and crankiness," as that publisher said when "Principles of Geography" made its appearance in 1926. It has not been surpassed as a generator of basic mental activity. Man in Europe, a book that should be used in every university, shows him at his best

in the use of maps, photographs, and ideas in the interpretation of a continent. In all his material for teaching, his skill with the pencil, his sense of line and letter, was evident. He made maps for his own pleasure as well as for teaching and publication. If Antarctic exploration was in the air, for example he compiled a new map from good sources and incorporated the new findings to see what they meant. If a thing was important and mappable, he had to try his hand at putting it on paper. Color and form engaged his interest on field trips. He had learned from Davis the dangers of "The petrographic habit" as Davis termed it—kneeling on the ground and looking at a rock specimen through a microscope to the exclusion of a broad view of the relations of the field. Beside that phrase he put another: "Look up once in a while, man; the sky is also a part of the picture . . . ."

Thoroughness marked all his work. The highest principle he recognized was that if you are to explain a matter you must know it through and through. As he kept his feet on the ground, so he put the feet of others on the ground. It was the ground first, then climate, and after that he was always ready to interpret while always on the lookout for the inexplicable and the capricious in his own culture as well as in another's. Physical geography, as all his students will remember, had to begin with physical principles. Never, never, would he let words take the place of understanding. You had to know why the wind blew and the rain fell! His writings show that he could grasp and handle competently the largest concepts and forces of culture and life, but he approached them through experience, facts, realities. Social forces detached from the earth he left to other disciplines. For himself he tried to find out what rooted men. Perhaps this was partly the result from his old-fashioned classical training; perhaps it was due to the rigours of mathematics that he loved. Whatever the cause, it made his work enduring.

Jefferson would not make any concession to teaching form. He would not tolerate the professionalization of teaching method and opposed the spread of the education department at the Normal School. He was swift to point out that the training of teachers did not necessitate the presence of an education department, merely a good library, a faculty endowed with scholarship and enthusiasm, and students.

Jefferson bitterly opposed the spread of the teaching of teaching and crusaded in all opportune moments for its eradication. In retirement he was to state his position succinctly, if bluntly, to his one time student classmate at Boston University, Caroline Atherton (née Stone):[65]

Here I have always been at war with the Normal School idea that a master of method can teach everything or anything, without knowing

> *it. Apparently one result of election of subjects is to omit all serious intellectual studies and get . . . educators. You can rely on them to know nothing. We have tried to get them into debate here. They claim the first chance, refuse to let us raise objections, put us off for a later day, and then have no later day. At most they make out that it is possible to know a lot without being a good teacher, which may be conceded easily but is not the point. Indeed I would rather have a teacher in any subject who knew it well, even if a wretched teacher than one ignorant of his subject. I shall undertake to get something out of him if he knows it. What hope if he doesn't?*

And again:[66]

> *The classes do take a lot of time, and somebody is always cropping up who demonstrates to me that I do not know how to teach! . . . However, I keep trying. These fellows who know how to teach, however, have the great advantage of not wasting any time trying. They just know how and they go ahead.*

For many years, however, Jefferson had supervised student teachers of geography. Always he insisted that they speak clearly, that they apply the principles of geography to the facts of environment. From Davis he had learned "to laugh with them and not at them." If his vocabulary of pedagogical technical skills was not well furbished, he had faith that native sense would be an adequate substitute. He sought simply to communicate his thoughts to his students, using language that was simple, punctuating his remarks with relevant slides drawn from his fine collection, and giving them a taste of reality with his regular field excursions. Typical of the man both inside and outside the classroom was his desire to bring about improvement.[67]

> *I like Henry Ford's motto about his factory. Nothing is done right here! The idea, of course, "Do Better." Nobody can teach well, not even you or I, but anyone if he watches his step can teach better. The grammar class that taught us to compare good, better, best, was stupid. It should be better, best, (of the group), good. Good or well is the unattainable superlative.*

Always then Jefferson strove to be simple, to teach truths and not opinion. In the preface to his book *Principles of Geography* 1926, he wrote:[68]

> *When Stefansson learned from African hunters that ostriches do not hide their heads in the sand when you chase them it seemed to him astonishing at first that he had never heard the truth about ostriches before, but later he saw that it was more astonishing that he had ever believed the foolish story. How could there be any ostriches today if their enemies found them so easy to catch? There is nothing to prevent*

an animal from committing suicide if it wants to, but if all the animals of a species take to suicide, that kind of animal must soon disappear.

To what degree have we been taught to think over in any way what we were taught in school? Have we been encouraged to test the things taught us in the light of such common sense and experience as we may have had? Evidently we ought not to have accepted everything from our teachers on faith, for they gave us this ostrich fable as true. They had not thought it through themselves. Evidently too when we teach things to others we ought to turn over in our minds the things we teach. We cannot always be sure that what we teach is true, but at least we can make sure it is not false on the face of it.

The world that science is always revealing to us is not merely an interesting one. Our explanations of the features and events of this world must make sense.

And again, in 1931, at the Ohio State Educational Conference, Jefferson was to take up the matter of teaching falsehoods:[69]

We have many things . . . which should be eliminated from our fund of knowledge. We need to find out more of these things that are not so, and eliminate them from our teaching of geography. It is singular how false doctrine spreads. The teachers teach so well that it is impossible to forget what they teach.

We have a notion—I believe it is in our dictionaries—that the French phrase for the author of a book, when he has not used his real one, is nom de plume. *Those of you speak French know that this is unknown in France. I was one time near Paris talking with the late George Chisholm and several professors from French universities. We had raised the question of this French phrase and agreed to leave it to the professors of the University of Paris, who were right there. We put the matter to them: "Suppose I write a book but do not want to put my own name on the title page, but use another name, what do you call that name? They gave us* pseudonym *and* nom de guerre, *but could mention no other. We finally suggested* nom de plume, *but none of them had ever heard of it!*

The same thing is true of our word sombrero. *Everybody, of course, knows that a sombrero is supposed to be a wide-brimmed Mexican hat. This is supposed to be a Spanish word, but as you are well aware* sombrero *in Spanish does not mean that kind of hat at all, but any kind of hat. Derby is* sombrero de copa; *lady's hat is* sombrero de paja.

Whenever we teach what is untrue, however widely believed, time is not merely wasted, but damage is done. I wonder if it is not true that in less well-prepared classrooms than yours we have the good old story about the warm winds from the Pacific Ocean that sweep against snow-

clad mountains, and are cooled by the snow on the summits, so that the winds throw down their water vapor in the form of rain and snow. Of course, if anybody thought of it, he could realize that in a few years, to say nothing of the centuries that have passed, it would be necessary for the iceman to come and put some more snow on those mountains. The only thing wrong with the explanation is that it is ridiculous and will not work. We should understand such things, we we should have long ago substituted something else for that story.

Well, geography is about countries, and its problem is to know what a country is. You know that hymn we sing, which the little boy said was "My Country Teazle-ee." If you look into that hymn you find out something about our country. It is made of rocks, rills, woods, and mountains. That is not my country at all. There are just as good rocks in Europe as there are in the United States. I have seen some rocks around Rio De Janeiro that are just as good as they are here. The thing that makes our country a thing to be fought for, to be admired, to be loved, is the people in it, past and present. And the people do not get any mention in those verses. I think some geographer who has the gift of verse should write a new anthem with our countrymen in it.

The eradication of these falsehoods was a favorite preoccupation with Jefferson, who frequently spoke on this theme at Teachers' Institutes, visits to schools, and to men's business clubs. In 1904 on the occasion of the Michigan State Teachers Association meeting, Jefferson presented a paper entitled, "Current Errors in Geography Teaching" in which he vigorously denounced the inaccuracies of much classroom teaching. Frequently he held up to ridicule the theses, "Hot air rises, causing wind," and "Mountains produce rain by chilling the moist air that blows against them." Occasionally Jefferson's students would find teachings in geographic literature which disagreed with explanations given by him in the classroom. In these cases all the literature available on the subject would be assembled and the conflict of belief would become a project lasting perhaps several weeks. Sometimes Jefferson would publish a note, or deliver a paper which covered the dispute in question. Often, too, he would write to an author requesting explanation. Typically on January 2, 1932, Jefferson wrote to George Philip and Son, Ltd., London:[70]

My students complain that your little "Political Europe" at page 7 shows German Territory on the West on the Rhine in Alsace and that you still show the rains of Chile in the old inaccurate way, corrected by my "Rainfall in Chile" Research Series No. 7 American Geographical Society of New York in 1921 and now adopted by all modern map makers both for annual and semiannual maps. In the middle 30's of

South Latitude central Chile is dry (and irrigated) between wet moun-
tains both east and west. The facts are notorious to anyone who has
traveled in Chile and the isohyetals have plenty of observations for
better drawing.

Another of Jefferson's favorite theses which he emphasized repeatedly in the classroom was the value of using anglicized place names. He
addressed several groups on this matter, including the meeting of the
National Council of Geography Teachers, Nashville, Tennessee, Christmas 1927:[71]

Went to Nashville, Tenn., Christmas meeting advising Anglicising all
geographic names (Lyons, France like lions and not as the school
recommend, lee-ong). Teachers fifteen years ago hooted at my sugges-
tion, but this time they liked it. Everybody but the school teacher, I
think, says Lyons and Marseilles (mar sales) and I think it absurd,
with the result that young people will not even try to name any foreign
place, at all. What I think is absurd is that teachers should hold out
for foreign pronunciations. Nobody dares say Rheims nowadays, but in
the Ingolsby Legends it rhymed with dreams—the Jackdaw of Rheims.
I am going to make as much of that in my new books as the publishers
will allow. School people claim to know better than the writers of
books you know what is good English, for instance. I met that years
ago with the phrase two hundred and fifty, the form affected by all
writers of good literature, old or new, but the school marms teach two
hundred fifty, as if they could improve on the language.

There were few students who did not see and hear Jefferson while he
was at the Normal, for attendance of students at the General Assembly
was compulsory. Both Faculty and students would gather together on
these occasions. Raye Platt has observed:[72]

Time and time again at these assemblies the college President would
announce (no matter what the planned program might be) that "Pro-
fessor Jefferson has something to say to us" and Jefferson would leap
to the front of the platform for a brief and always emphatically voiced
and gestured discourse on some current event to which the only impact
on most of the students must have been that "this must be important
since so important a man feels that he must bring it to our attention."
(I rather thought that Jefferson's object was really to get something off
his always indignant chest and also perhaps to try to bring a little light
to other members of the faculty of most of whom he had a rather poor
opinion.) By the way, Jefferson's work on the Inquiry had given him a
luster among his colleagues that had practically erased their previous
general disapproval and even fear of him because of the never-failing
acidity of his tongue. I recall particularly one of these assemblies. It
was in 1920 when Hiram Johnson was working for the Republican

nomination for President. The dean of Women was an enthusiastic
Republican (a member of the National Committee and a supporter of
Johnson). She asked me to attend with her (in W. W. I uniform!) a
dinner for Johnson in Ann Arbor. In the course of his discourse
Johnson was ranting about some possibility that troops were to be sent
to some foreign country. (I have forgotten what it was all about) and
shouted in his pompous way "If I am elected President I shall see to it
that our boys will never fight under a foreign flag." And then, noting a
good many W. W. I veterans in his audience and suspecting, I suppose,
that they might be a little proud of their overseas experience, he added
parenthetically "I shall see to it that they fight under the same flag that
they fought under at Soissons and Chateau Thierry." Well that was
enough for me, since in both engagements our troops were under the
French flag. So I got up and left as did a number of others in uniform.
I never knew how Johnson handled the situation, but the next morning
I met Jefferson on the street and reported Johnson's promise to him,
more as a joke that he would appreciate than anything else. But it was
no joke to Jefferson. That happened to be Assembly morning and there
was Jefferson on the platform denouncing a man so ignorant who
would presume to run for President and taking the occasion to put in a
good word for Wilson and the League of Nations.

On a number of other occasions newspaper criticism of one or
another of the Peace Conference decisions brought Jefferson to the
platform to set the matter right."

The students appreciated Jefferson, though more than a few over the
years grew to dislike his biting sense of humor and subtly used sarcasm.
The college Yearbook, *Aurora,* published annually a photographic por-
trait and brief biographical sketch of the faculty at the Normal College:
Jefferson's photograph and biographical sketch thus appeared regularly
over the years. Occasionally the Aurora staff would subject the character of faculty to verse. In 1906, the Aurora felt it appropriate to write
of Jefferson:[73]

What cares he for printed pages, with their dusty lore?
To his mind, there is a volume which contains much more;
'Tis the book great Nature opens in this world of ours;
With all her wondrous lessons in hills and streams and flowers.

In 1909 the *Aurora* saw fit to observe of Jefferson: "The earth is
to him a never ending number of wonderful roads which all lead to
God."

In 1910 Jefferson's picture in the *Aurora* was adorned by a quote
from Shakespeare: "Thy wit is a very bitter sweeting; it is a most sharp
sauce."

One year later the same publication observed of Jefferson:

The outward shows of sky and earth of hill and valley he has viewed
And impulses of deeper birth
Have come to him in solitude.

In 1917 the Yearbook remarked of Jefferson: ". . . Happy are those who call him teacher; happier those who call him friend."

Numerous other references were made in the College Yearbook to this geographic spirit that roamed the campus. Noteworthy is the dedication of the 1922 *Aurora* to Jefferson. On the title page of that yearbook may be read the inscription: "To Professor Mark Jefferson, student, scholar, teacher, who exemplifies in his classroom that fine definition of a teacher,—'one who invigorates life through learning,' the *Aurora* of 1922 is dedicated."

His strength as a teacher rendered his services continually in demand elsewhere in the State of Michigan and in the nation's universities. At the request of State Superintendent of Public Instruction, P. H. Kelley, Jefferson frequently visited teacher's institutes, a practice established by C. T. McFarlane in the 1890's. Usually he lectured on one of his trips abroad, using illustrations from his excellent collection. Prior to 1921 he lectured to any group that wanted him, for a fee, though the topic was of Jefferson's choosing. In 1921 an "Extension Department" under the direction of Horace Z. Wilber was established at the Normal to cater to the growing demand for education throughout the state. Jefferson would not teach regular extension courses; it was fatiguing and time consuming. Faculty colleagues, Margaret Sill and Ella Wilson, who joined him in 1921 and 1923 respectively, did undertake such work in the Normal's "invisible-campus." Jefferson was invited frequently by the President of the Normal, working through the Division of Field Services, to travel parts of the State of Michigan visiting high schools, spending a day with each. These invitations Jefferson accepted. Occasionally he would visit two or three high schools in as many days at which time he would listen to teachers teach language, social studies, history or geography; watch students' reactions; inspect equipment; and address individual classes and the school assembly. A report of his findings, usually compiled on the train journey home, typically included recommendations, which would then be sent to the high school principal and a copy to the Normal President. These same principals and teachers wrote frequently to Jefferson at Ypsilanti, before or after such visits, requesting advice.

Jefferson taught in summer schools at Harvard University 1898 and 1900, the University of Michigan 1903, Yale University 1907, the University of Chicago 1917, the University of California 1920, and Columbia University 1932. He was obliged to decline written invitations to teach summer school at Harvard University 1903, the University of Michigan 1905 and 1906, the University of Tennessee 1908, Columbia University 1917, Columbia University 1931, and the Ohio State University 1931. Probably more invitations would have come to Jefferson but he made it known that only every third summer was he free to entertain invitations for work away from Ypsilanti's Normal College; every third summer a faculty member was obliged to refrain from teaching at Ypsilanti's Normal in order to share employment with other faculty members and partly to give themselves a rest or change of environment.

No account of Jefferson the pedagogue would be complete without mention of his disciple record, a term coined by S. S. Visher who has described Jefferson's remarkable classroom success in the following words:[74]

> During his earlier years at Ypsilanti he started on their geographic careers three men who later became presidents of the Association of American Geographers and two others who have risen high in the Association: Isaiah Bowman, Charles C. Colby, A. E. Parkins, D. H. Davis, R. R. Platt; George J. Miller had his first course in geography as a student of Jefferson's at the University of Michigan in the summer of 1903. Three have received the Distinguished Service to Geography Award of the National Council of Geography Teachers. This disciple record is better than that of any other college. Indeed, few major universities with departments of geography and with large numbers of students, fine equipment, and graduate school opportunities have approached that record, of starting in geography as many men who subsequently rose high in the profession.

To this list might be added in particular the names of C. E. Cooper, F. W. Frostic, J. F. McBain, C. Stratton, Margaret Sill, Richard Mahard, all students of Jefferson who taught for many years in the classroom.

It is evident from a glance at the record that Jefferson's most accomplished students emerged under his tutelage in his early years at Ypsilanti's Normal: I. Bowman (Life Certificate 1904), Guy C. Smith (Life Certificate 1906), C. Colby (B. Pd 1909), F. Frostic (Life Certificate 1910), A. Parkins (A. B. 1911), W. Gregory (1911), C. Stratton (1914), R. Platt (1920), M. Sill (1921). Stephen Visher, following his findings in *Scientists Starred,* 1903-1943, in *American Men of Science* has observed that notable success has come to American pedagogues while they were in their younger years and closer to their students. Visher suggests that Jefferson was no exception to this pattern. Certainly Jefferson cared for those students who showed promise. Such

Jefferson with former students. The Association of American Geographers Annual Meeting, Ypsilanti, 1931. *Front row, left to right:* I. Bowman, C. Colby, M. Jefferson, A. Parkins, G. Miller. *Back row, left to right:* W. Gregory, D. Davis, R. Platt, R. Calkins.

students would be invited to take supper with Jefferson's family in his home, at which time he would recommend certain books that should be read and propose local field work that the student should undertake independently. If the student showed willingness and pursued Jefferson's suggestions, another supper would follow, and the student's future would be discussed. In the early 1900's Jefferson recommended Harvard to such students, where Davis was busy in an undertaking hardly less in scope than the reorganization of a discipline. Later, when Davis ceased teaching in the Harvard classroom, Jefferson referred his students to the University of Chicago and H. Barrows, J. Paul Goode, and R. D. Salisbury. From approximately 1925 until 1940 Jefferson recommended Columbia University for his advanced students, where the minds of Douglas Johnson, Lobeck, and Orchard stimulated thought while the American Geographical Society was within walking distance. Jefferson employed his promising students in the geography department at the Normal, giving them a valuable academic and teaching experience, which also provided them with money to offset the expenses of later graduate studies. Thus he employed Isaiah Bowman, Darrell Davis, Charles Colby, Almon Parkins, Charles Stratton. Raye Platt and Richard Mahard were granted this opportunity at a later date. Margaret Sill, employed in 1921 in the Normal geography department, continues her service to the present. To these students Jefferson would lend books from his own collection; he would encourage them to write and rewrite results of local field work that he had suggested, which occasionally meant publication; and when the students left Ypsilanti for Harvard, Chicago, or Columbia, he would maintain a steady correspondence with them. Perhaps just as satisfying to Jefferson was the enthusiasm which he had managed to instill into his "working men and housewife students," many of whom wrote to him in later years expressing their appreciation:[75]

> Tonight's "Enterprise" contained an item telling of the award of the Cullum Geographical Medal to you. Congratulations!
>
> Probably you do not remember little Edith Lovell graduating from Brockton High in 1899. You were one of those among the faculty who urged me to go to college instead of the Normal as I had planned, I went to Boston University, and graduated in 1903 . . . . Taken at least one course of study every year since graduating. Now 51 years old, I have still the zest for learning in order that I may grow and teach (not in public school.)
>
> No! I am not looking for a job.
>
> I want you to realize what you helped to start. I recognize in you a teacher who taught creative thinking, You taught by the "project

method" before that phrase was coined! I shall never forget how you rode around to my house on your bicycle (hammer sticking out of your pocket) to tell me that you were obliged to flunk me on the examination in Geology because you had warned me that I should be marked on the full number of questions, but that my answer to the first question showed so superior an understanding of the geological formation underlying this city that you considered it only just that I be marked highest in the class for the term's work! The cleverness and fairness you disclosed in handling the situation made a great impression upon me and your thoughtfulness in explaining it to me in advance and away from my classmates was greatly appreciated. I treasure that paper and the class notebook to this day . . . .

Geology has not been my speciality. I "took one course" afterwards. That is just what I did. What those ten out-of-door lessons did for me was to make me love the great out-of-doors, to observe more closely and to associate separate facts. The graded deposits of departed rain streams, sand pits, drumlins, Moraine street, often remind me of that high school class and its teacher and my growing appreciation is summed up in

I THANK YOU

Edith Lovell Stevens
(Mrs. B. Strout Stevens)

[76]*I tried to get in touch with you last year when you were in Boston, but reached your hotel just after you had left for the train.*

John Rose, geographer, of Washington D.C. has written me about you and I am bold enough to address you as an admiring student of yours in the Lexington High School in the nineties. You showed us how to pole vault, and beat us all at it. You took us on geology walks, showed us a hill of trap in Somerville which has since been entirely removed, several glacier scratches, etc.

You have become a geographer. I have become an architect, and have worked in Boston except for one year in Tweedo Park, New York . . . I recall the happy days of the L.H.S. class of 1898 with (!) the greatest clearness. Your face, the cut of your beard, and your extremely energetic manner stay in my mind's eye. Especially do I recall your enthusiasm in learning and teaching.

And so, forty five years later, I salute you and wish you well!

Sincerely,
William Roger Greeley

Interesting are excerpts from letters written by people who knew Jefferson's work as a pedagogue:[77]

> It was my privilege to have Mark Jefferson for all of my undergraduate work in geography. After being graduated in August, I came back in September 1921 to teach under him until his retirement in 1939.
>
> He was a most dynamic and forceful teacher. He did not tell you anything you could work out for yourself. His classes were so interesting that you were never aware of being in class fifty minutes.
>
> Perhaps I can illustrate his teaching best by saying that you did at least four different things during the class period. If after a few good thought questions, he discovered that the class had studied the lesson, he would not take time for a recitation, but would move on to something new. This might mean make a map, a graph, a chart, construct a Brazilian, French, or Dutch home. He would give exact measurements, students reduced the scale, and each student would make one. Lantern slides would be used anytime to clear an idea. Yerba mate would be served to show how it differed from green and black tea. A map would tear, and he would show you then and there how to mount it on cheese cloth with flour to starch paste. If you were studying Italy, you read Browning, if Britain, Grey's Elegy of the Country Churchyard; Canada, Evangeline was read; and so on.
>
> Mark Jefferson did not teach geography as straight facts. He knew literature, art, music, science, math, and the social sciences, and his courses were truly integrated and fused courses.
>
> He was not interested in quantitative learning. He was interested in quality. He was always eager to stimulate students to want to know where people live; what they are like! How they make a living; and why they work, play, worship, and govern themselves as they do.
>
> Statistics meant much to him. He read much into them, and used them for their story over and over again in his classes.

> [78]I believe that Jefferson was certainly the greatest teacher I ever had when it came to the business of teaching people to think. His own mind flashed and darted like a hummingbird exploring a trumpet vine. Thinking the way an expert comedian, master of repartee, deals with witticism. It seems to me that he was always asking "why!" He was a very skilled observer but once he had observed, he would try to "have a thought" about what he had observed. A student well acquainted with him learned to "Think before he spoke." I remember that he was delighted with the phrase, "What's worse than finding a worm in an apple?" He asked me that question one day out in the field. I thought before I spoke but the best I could come up with was to reply "to find two worms!" But he chuckled heartily and said, "to find half a worm."

[79]*Father's idea always was that if you were interested enough in a subject to be teaching it, you should be enthusiastic enough about it to find out for yourself how best to teach it. And his idea of teaching, was not just to impart knowledge. It was to make the subject so interesting that the students became enthusiastic about it too . . . . While none of us children took any of his classes, I recall at least two occasions when I spent a morning in the back of his classroom. I have no idea why. I've been trying repeatedly to recall the reasons. While the subject was not of interest to me, I was nevertheless impressed with the constant activity and the complete interest of the entire class. Something I never experienced in any other class that I recall.*

In the summer of 1937 Jefferson, at the age of 76, was retired from the classroom against his will. The Michigan State Board of Education had at that time recently passed a law decreeing that teachers over the age of 70 should be retired from the classroom. Jefferson was deeply offended by the letter that President Munson sent to him requesting a letter of resignation in compliance with the ruling of the State Board. He was offended that Munson had not written him a note of thanks for his 39 years of service to the Normal, and he was offended that his retirement salary was to be $1,200 instead of a sum, half of his regular salary at the time of retirement, which he had been promised by President McKenny (1912-1932). He wrote a letter to Mr. Munson tendering his resignation:[80]

Your suggestion that I write you a letter asking to be retired at the end of the current year is embarrassing. I do not wish to retire. My retirement will be a loss to the state of Michigan. I am a better teacher today than I ever was. I am doing right now my best work in original geography. Moreover my teaching and my original work are exceptionally good.

That is of course an immodest statement. It is, however, easily verifiable. I was President of the Association of American Geographers in 1917. The following persons will, I am sure endorse the statement:

"Michigan will find it very difficult to obtain anyone who can adequately replace Mark Jefferson as head of the department of geography in the state Normal College."

They are heads of departments of geography in the leading universities of the country.

Harvard, Derwent S. Whittlesey—Yale, Ellsworth Huntington—Columbia, J. Russell Smith, A. K. Lobeck—Chicago, Harlan H. Barrows, Charles C. Colby, Robert S. Platt—University of Pennsylvania, Frank E. Williams—Indiana University, Stephen S. Visher—Ohio State University, George D. Hubbard, Guy-Harold Smith, Eugene Van Cleef

—University of Wisconsin, V. C. Finch, this year President A.A.G., Glenn T. Trewartha—University of Minnesota, Darrell H. Davis, Richard Hartshorne—University of Michigan, Preston E. James, Sec. A. A. G.—University of Toronto, Griffith Taylor—George Peabody College, Nashville, Almon E. Parkins—Col. Claude H. Birdseye, President elect. A.A.G., 22 Grafton Street Chevy Chase, Maryland, and President Isaiah Bowman, Johns Hopkins University.

I have not written these men. Almost all of them have heard me present a paper December 28, 1938.

A few years ago President Roosevelt caused consternation in Washington in the U.S. Geological Survey by announcing that members of the corps over 70 must retire—on a pension that amounted I think to 60 per cent of their pay. Men already 70 and others nearing 70 were doing work that would simply have to be stopped if they were removed. Director Walter C. Mendenhall of the Geological Survey saw the President and the outcome was that Dr. Mendenhall was allowed to make appointments for one year at a time of 70-year old men whom he could assert were "indispendable." A number of men have been named to me and I can ascertain their names easily, although I have forgotten them at the moment.

What does it mean to be indispensable? One man can always go through another man's motions. Is it so very important that teaching be of a high grade? Schools do get along as a matter of fact with quite mediocre teaching.

The output of the Geological Survey is more concrete and tangible than that of school. It falls into the hands of very competent and critical men as soon as issued, men whose earnings and profits depend on good work being put before them. The output of the classroom is a much less tangible and examinable thing—will often take years to judge.

Two years ago I would have supposed that you would have been willing to go to the State Board of Education with such a plea to retain my services as too valuable for the state to give up. Probably you value them at less than I supposed. Perhaps you do not make suggestions to the Board of Education.

Of course, if such a one year's appointment were made, the next head of the department to reach retiring age would ask for the same reappointment. Well, if you have any head of department who has been president of the National Society of his branch of study or teaching, if he has received the only two gold medals offered in his subject in the country, and been made corresponding member of foreign societies concerned with his topic, if he is declared to be desirable to keep, even at his age by heads of his department in the great universities of this country, well perhaps—if he is obviously well, strong and young looking, why not! Is the good of the school as a teaching institution not of any account?

But perhaps you would not have many such.

I do not wish to apply to you for permission to retire. I do not wish to retire. This serves to acknowledge that I had from you in September, 1937, notification that I was automatically retired on July 1, if I had been passed my 70th birthday. As I have filed with the office a number of times the statement that I was born March 1, 1863, my last teaching should be concluded with that date. I have no defense. I must consider myself retired with the conclusion of the current year.

Jefferson had been upset. It was not a matter of pride, but of faith: faith that the institution would give him a respect after service, and faith that all promises would be fulfilled. Emeritus rank was not conferred upon him. Jefferson entered his retirement in bitterness. For the next three years immediately following his retirement Jefferson felt obliged to recount his victimization frequently in his correspondence, little matter to whom he wrote. This experience did much to drive Jefferson away from classroom matters and geography and into civic work in the ten years of his retirement. Several months before Jefferson retired, his two departmental colleagues, Ella Wilson and Margaret Sill, undertook to establish a Mark Jefferson Scholarship Fund, the income from which was to be awarded each year to an able junior who had shown unusual interest in geography. Letters were sent to many of the students that had sat in Jefferson's classes unfolding the plan of the Jefferson Scholarship Fund. Several hundred dollars were swiftly donated, many letters accompanied the contributions, expressing gratitude for Mr. Jefferson's work. Doubtless many, many more contributions would have been forthcoming, but the Normal never did organize its alumni group effectively. Students left the institution, and scattered themselves the world over, so that in 1939 the Normal administration probably had no more than 20% of the addresses of living alumni. The Misses Wilson and Sill in the June of 1939 carried the leather bound sheaf of acclaiming plaudits to the house of Mr. Jefferson. But he was unhappy: the fact of a broken promise and a curt demand for a self written letter of resignation would not be forgotten. His acceptance of the scholarship scheme on the very steps of his home was terse and brusque. His personal dislike of display and personal prominence were also doubtless contributing factors to his lack of enthusiasm for the scholarship. However, in 1947, in autobiographical notes he was preparing for the 50th anniversary of the Harvard Class of 1897, he found room for a little sentiment regarding this and other honorifics.

Plunder of the Scholarship Fund Letters seems a peculiarly fitting way to appreciate the man's pedagogic contribution in the context of his time. There follows a selection of the letters that were not lost to record:

From A. K. Lobeck[81]

I beg that you will accept from me this brief message of good wishes that I send in all sincerity. I have read almost all that you have written and have heard much that you have said and have always been charmed with the pungency of your expressions and the unusual point of view which you have introduced into the geographical world.

From Fred Mackay[82]

. . . We think that you have done a good job, given our round old earth more dignity, made us ashamed of short journeying. Is not that the essence of great living?

I am glad to have known you, too, in other relations than those of the classroom and the campus. I have learned that intellectual aristocracy can be delightfully democratic. You are the geographer par excellence, but you are also the Kiwanian Mark. That warms the cockles of the heart and prompts me to stretch up an inch higher.

As you retire from active work with us, do not think that we will allow you to break away from the circle of friendship; that cannot be. So for the present, I join in a hearty expression of personal good wishes and God-speed.

From Anna Field[83]

. . . And so to you, now, Mr. Jefferson, let us say that we highly respect your scholarship. We delight in the wit of your repartee, we appreciate the generosity of your immediate response whenever we turn to you for help, and we need the intellectual stimulus of your vigorous mind. We do not see why our professional and personal friendship need suffer because you now cease to meet your classes daily, and we wish that it might be possible for you to continue to live in the collegetown community that has been your home for so many years.

In whatever you do however, and wherever you go you have our gratitude and our friendship.

From Helen Strong[84]

I wish that I could be present on this memorable convocation. I owe much to you in many ways. You trained many of the men who inspired me to go on with my professional work in geography. When I began my work in geography, you discussed various questions with me on different occasions, always presenting new ideas. The meetings of the Association of American Geographers, to which you have contributed, and to which you will continue to contribute, have opened up horizons of understanding and research. The books you have published and the papers you have written have given us both the needed facts and the philosophy for thinking.

To me personally, your friendship and professional leadership has continually pointed the way to broader understanding of the service which a geographer may render, and has stimulated the desire for better and clearer thinking. I shall continue to look toward that leadership now that you are freed from the demands of the classroom and can devote your full time to research, study, writing, and travel.

May you continue to live richly.

From the University of Michigan[85]

The members of the Department of Geography at the University of Michigan wish to express their appreciation of your important services to the profession. For the many leading personalities who have entered the field through the inspiration of your teaching, and for the dominant position in research activities which you have long held, you deserve the highest honors. You are in that happy situation where recorded achievement makes words unnecessary. Please accept our best wishes for many more years of active scholarship.

Raye Platt, who Jefferson had placed at the American Geographical Society, wrote of his former tutor:[86]

In sending you my contribution to the fund for the scholarship in honor of Professor Jefferson (a contribution by no means commensurate with my regard for him), I want to try to express something of my appreciation of him.

I think, and I say it with all sincerity, that he is one of the great teachers of our time. The fact that so many of his students have become specialists in geography is evidence of his ability to inspire undergraduates, most of whom, when they entered his classes, never dreamed of making geography their life work, or, indeed had any idea that there was a life work in the subject. One scarcely expects to find really brilliant teaching in a freshman class in college. He must be a superior teacher indeed who can maintain a high level of brilliant, inspirational presentation of a subject even when dealing with immature minds. The teacher in such circumstances has to do all the work. Yet in his beginning class in Teachers' Geography as in all other classes that I had with Prof. Jefferson, I cannot recall a single dull moment or even a moment of let-down. One came to wait for his entry into the classroom much as one waits for the rise of a curtain at the performance of a new play by a great playwright and, when the class ended, to have the same feeling of regret that one has when the final curtain comes down. I do not mean that Prof. Jefferson was a show-man in his classes. I mean that each of his class presentations was a gem brought to the class exquisitely cut and carefully polished.

Quite as impressive to undergraduates was Prof. Jefferson's wide culture, especially since most of them, if not all of them, myself included, had been previously quite unaware that there were men whose knowledge was so wide and deep. His grounding in the classics, his facility with many modern languages, his wide reading (I remember that he read and discussed Main Street *when it was hot off the press and my awe when I saw French mystery stories on his table) must have inspired many of his students with a desire for the satisfaction that knowledge purely for the sake of knowledge affords.*

I can't say that Professor Jefferson was a gentle spirit. If one couldn't take it, he was often, very severe and sarcastic to the point of cruelty; but we need more, not less, of such cruelty in college teachers —provided always that the teacher has the scholarship to back it up and is not using cruelty as a screen for his own deficiencies.

For me to say anything about Prof. Jefferson's contribution to geo-graphical science would seem superflous, since many more worthy than I will be evaluating his work as a researcher and writer at this time. The inscription written by Miss Wrigley for the Cullum Geographical Medal awarded him by this Society in 1931 expresses well what geog-raphers think of his work: "For the savor of true geography in his ingenious and fruitful inquiries into man's distribution on the earth." I might add here parenthetically that Bob Speer and I had his course in the geography of Europe the winter that he was working out his Man in Europe. *That was a memorable experience of which we often speak now, although it was twenty years ago. Certainly his brilliant ideas, his qualities as a researcher, his intellectual integrity, his ability as a writer, and the high standards of his criticism of the work of his contemporaries have done much to elevate the level of geographical research and the presentation of the results of geographical research in this country.*

I sincerely hope that Prof. Jefferson's retirement from the Normal College will not mean his retirement from the teaching profession. I am sure that it will not mean his retirement from geographical re-search and writing.

Frank Hamilton expressed his gratitude to Jefferson with the follow-ing remarks in a letter dated June 11, 1939:[87]

. . . Since my first course in United States Geography, when I accompanied you from Martha's Vineyard to the breakwater at Galveston via McClellanville at Cape Romain in South Carolina, until the present Geography of Europe with her million cities, your teaching has been so interesting and different. I shall never forget Cordoba or Puerto Montt and while my work in Map Drawing and Physiography was anything but spectacular I'm sure I gained a lot. Finally the Field Work with its interesting terrace studies, river captures, beaches and shore lines, and contour intervals,—These six courses have gone far toward adding to my geographical happiness—They were not obligations but opportunities I assure you.

The task of expressing my gratitude for all you have done for me is a great one, indeed, but I feel sure it may be simplified by reminding you of how you once expressed your feelings toward Professor Davis. May I hold you in the same esteem.

And from Isaiah Bowman, while President of the Johns Hopkins University, in a letter dated June 7, 1939:[88]

It is a privilege to be invited to join other students of Professor Mark Jefferson in expressing appreciation of his many years of work at the Michigan State Normal College. When I entered the State Normal College and presented myself to Professor Jefferson as a special student in Geography, he gazed down at me from the upper levels of the platform with immediate interest and geniality. He at once gave me special work to do, in addition to the regular work in his courses. Within a few months he invited me to return as instructor in Geography after a year of study at Harvard under Professor W. M. Davis. I still remember the form of that invitation, which was that the year of study could be taken at Harvard, Yale, Princeton, or Johns Hopkins, but that he preferred that I go to Harvard. It was a wise choice. Professor Davis was at the top of his intellectual power at that time and an exceedingly rare and critical person. He was just the kind of person required by a student bent on specialization. Upon my return to Ypsilanti, Professor Jefferson was of inestimable help to me as a young teacher of advanced students. I may add that during my period of teaching at Ypsilanti and during ten years of teaching at Yale, my work was colored by Professor Jefferson's point of view, by his wide culture, and by his personal example as a scholar of unlimited curiosity. I still think that parts of his teaching were better than most of the teaching that I had in a number of schools. And some of it was unsurpassed in clarity and stimulating power.

As director of the American Geographical Society, I had the privilege of dealing with Professor Jefferson in the publication of several monographs and a number of articles. It was a day on which to hang out the flag when we received a manuscript from him. Everything he writes has a distinctive Jeffersonian touch. Every item that he has published is marked by new ideas and a fresh approach. These are qualities that few men are able to contribute to the culture of their times. They endure because they are backed up by other men and passed along to their friends and students in turn. I salute him as one of the most important geographers of the past forty years and as one whose contributions will live as long as science and Western civilization endure.

CHAPTER SIX

O'ER HILL AND DALE

Jefferson enjoyed travel. It constituted a vital part of his geography. W. M. Davis had once admonished him to "go and see—and see and understand." In his years at the Normal College he did go and see. Frequently he understood. His major sorties, usually undertaken in the summer vacation months, took him through three continents. On some of these trips he was to make lasting acquaintances with geographers and, occasionally, a resident of another land. He made his conversation engaging and learned from his traveling companions—this much he had made a practiced art. He sought out people's experiences seemingly aware of the fine line that separates personal experience from personal values and by diligent practice and careful management encouraged his conversant to tell where he had been and what he had seen. He carried a camera, notebook, and pencil on his trips. His notebooks always became repositories of the most detailed observation, and were invariably accompanied by diagrams and reference to slides he had taken. Usually a straw hat purposively covered his head. He would stump along at his own pace, his legs strong by usage, covering often twenty miles in a day. Experiences and knowledge gained from these travels came to form a significant part of the geography he taught and wrote. There were many other field excursions which he undertook in the midwest, usually of two or three days generation. Frequently his findings from a trip would find their way into a paper he wrote, and very frequently into his textbooks. He preferred to illustrate his own texts with photographs which he had taken, just as he preferred to write of matters which he had personally observed. He was always just a little suspicious of the printed word and much preferred to see phenomena for himself. He was a great believer in the process of observation and so followed in the wake of many nineteenth century thinkers whose work he quite respected.

The outings provided him with recreation which was a valuable alternate to his life in the classroom and the study. A recounting of the essentials of his more meaningful trips is a vital part of recounting Jefferson's life as a geographer. The more meaningful trips referred to include: Cuba, 1903; Norway, 1904; Colorado, 1910; Liverpool-Rome, 1911; the American Geographical Society Transcontinental Excursion, 1912; the ABC Expedition of the American Geographical Society, 1918; Arkansas, 1921; Panama, 1926; Iberia, 1935.

Jefferson's trip to Cuba in 1903 was in large part a response to numerous invitations from Cuban school teachers he had taught at Harvard in the summer of 1900. The Cuban schoolteachers escorted Jefferson the length and breadth of their island. He took many photographs, later converted into slides for classroom use, improved his Spanish, and was shown every social consideration. However he was not given much opportunity to prowl on his own and see what nature had to offer, then stare at it, and most likely convert his vision into a sketch. While on the island he began to develop an interest in the effects wind exerted on trees, an interest which revealed itself a few months later in "Wind Effects," an article published in the *Journal of Geography*.[1]

His visit to Norway, and more especially the Jostedalsbrae, was of a much more purposive nature. It was his first independent field work, undertaken entirely for reasons of personal satisfaction and at personal expense. It seems probable that Jefferson had set his mind on a visit to Norway prior to his departure for Cuba in the summer of 1903. Evidence suggests that he had commenced a refurbishing of his knowledge of the Scandinavian languages which he had acquired during his South American years. He had purchased a *Baedeker* of Norway and was planning his journey. The College at Ypsilanti was not able to offer him any financial support for field study. Neither was the Jefferson family monied, but both husband and wife considered the outlay of such money a happy investment. Jefferson had become a family man of modest taste. He had learned to gauge carefully each expenditure before his money was committed. The maintenance of daily expense accounts doubtless encouraged his frugality in addition to adding precision to a life which he seemed anxious to frequently weigh, assay, and measure.

This was the first intense and extended geographic field work Jefferson undertook alone and for his own satisfaction. His destination was the ice sheet, the Jostedalsbrae, of West Norway. As he later wrote:[2]

> *I went to Norway in the summer of 1904 to familiarize myself with the work in modifying topographic forms that the largest ice sheet in*

Europe is doing. This is the Jostedalsbrae, the word brae meaning any permanent sheet of snow or ice, moving or stagnant, level or inclined. It has an area of 360 square miles, and lies between the heads of Northfiord and Sognefiord, distant from the Atlantic 60 and 90 miles respectively by those fiords, at an elevation of about one mile above them. I visited this ice sheet by the Northfiord because the Olden and Loen lakes at its head lie close under the edge of the ice, though themselves only 150 feet above the sea, amid scenery that Richter has called the most characteristic in Norway.

It is likely that Jefferson's inspiration for this journey was derived partly from a course, *G*7 Physical Geography of Europe, taken under Davis at Harvard in 1898. In the notes Jefferson made from Davis' lectures, there is ample reference to the views of Richter, Playfair, Russell, Tarr, and Davis himself, concerning the mode of origin of certain types of Norwegian valleys, later known as hanging valleys.[3] It was at that time that Davis was changing his views on glaciation, using his classes and pupils as part correctives to his thinking out loud on the subject. Davis announced his new position concerning the work of ice when he published "Glacial Erosion in France, Switzerland and Norway," in *The Proceedings of the Boston Society of Natural History*.[4] Doubtless a ten-day excursion across Norway with the Director of the Norwegian Geological Survey, Dr. Reusch, was in part responsible for changing Davis' views concerning the work of ice. He reinterpreted the creation of the fjord and sent Jefferson postcards filled with scribbles and diagrams that bore witness to the man's excitement. Much of Davis' enthusiasm rubbed off onto Jefferson whether it was at Davis' tea parlor, in the university classrooms, through correspondence, or wherever else chance threw the two men together.

The ex-Kentucky cavalry man, and "Poet-Scientist", Shaler, of Harvard, also exercised an influence on Jefferson. Shaler's book *Glaciers,* with W. M. Davis as collaborator, had appeared in 1881 and had been read and annotated in the margins by Jefferson. William H. Sherzer of the Ypsilanti Normal Geology Department also possessed a marked interest in glaciers and the work of ice. Sherzer had already planned a trip to the Canadian Rockies and Selkirks for the summer of 1904 which was sponsored by the Smithsonian Institution. The two men frequently broke bread with each other and organized local Michigan field trips, and it is not unreasonable to suppose that Sherzer's trip design and preparatory readings aroused the curiosity of Jefferson.

The vessel, *United States,* took ten days to sight the Norwegian coast after making stops at Iceland and Scotland. Jefferson describes his impressions on seeing Norway for the first time:[5]

We soon made out a "fiord shoulder" as Suess calls the abrupt descent from the fjeld surface. The shoulder on either side was individually like enough to a Scotch cliff. The sky line however was at once distinct in its ruggedness from the Scotch shore. Smooth contours seemed quite lacking, and as the clouds rolled back the nakedness of the rock and its brownness, not in cliffs merely but everywhere was strikingly novel . . . not 5% of the surface green. Smoothing everywhere showed glaciation. I spoke of smooth contours in Scotland. The smoothness here was different. Scotch landscape lines were in mile long curves, these lines curved strongly in a hundred feet but sharp jagged points were not typical. Lee and sloss forms abound. What a hungry soil! There was no earth on it! All the earth had gone to Denmark and Germany across the Baltic as I have so liked to say of Ontario's loss to Illinois, Michigan, Indiana and Ohio. The thought is at once how can people live here?

The 10,000 ton, *United States,* dropped anchor in the roads of Christiansand on July 16. Jefferson learned that his boat for Bergen, the *Arendal,* did not leave until the following evening. He wished to rest a few hours at the *Baedeker* recommended Hotel Ernsts, but instead he recommended the hotel to some of his traveling companions, "I am not sure I ought not to have gone myself to learn about books and maps and things but I thought of expense." He read from the local Norwegian newspaper that little had happened in Manchuria since his departure from Ypsilanti, "beyond the taking of 3 forts about Port Arthur by the Japanese." Then he sought a berth on the steamer, *Arendal,* rested on the boat in place of the hotel, and awaited the departure for Bergen. On Sunday morning Jefferson wakened to find himself in Flekkefjord, his first fjord. Immediately he scribbled notes of what he saw and felt, which were later transcribed into his field notebook:[6]

The fjord waters are so smooth that anyone dwelling by them would inevitably be tempted to sail them, had he no better ship than a raft. How different the experience of the dwellers on Argentine coast or Vera Cruz coast! Not boldness of Norwegians gave them command of the sea but tameness of their extensive inshore waters coaxed them to sail. Sailing once, they ventured sooner or later out on the Atlantic. Were they not even helped by the certainty of escape in storms to secure refuge in shore in inlets.

As he traveled through other fjords, anchored a while at Egersund, then Stavanger, before reaching Bergen, Jefferson wrote extensive notes concerning the size and shape of fjords, their beauty, the houses he saw on fjord ledges, the evidences he surmised in support of glacial origin, and wind effects on trees. Before reaching Egersund he wrote:[7]

Norway in these regions is a land of naked rock. No one looking at it would hesitate to believe the world the ball of rock it essentially is. How would it strike my students who have to go 60 miles to see a ledge! New England has a good many patches, little patches, of bare rock: this part of Norway has rare patches of soil. There is no comparison possible between the two regions. New England may be rocky but Norway is rock! I never saw so much rock in my life.

In Bergen Jefferson registered at the *Baedeker* hotel and promptly set off to have both his spectacles and his aneroid barometer mended. Both had broken during his first day on board the *United States*. Then he visited a bookstore, purchased, for one kroner each, four sheets of the *Nordre Bergenhus Auit* which adequately mapped Jostedalsbrae. He wanted more data, more maps, more literature concerning West Norway and the Jostedalsbrae. Disappointed to learn that the 70,000 volume city library was closed until mid August, he consulted the Bergen museum library with more pleasing result:[8]

Went up to Museum and met Director Bronckhorst former botanist now occupied with administration and even gone into politics so he spends his winters in Christiansand. He speaks English and he put in two hours telling me where books were. We got a list together with some difficulty since the system used by the librarian was somewhat singular and Docent Kolderup had all the geological works in his office, which did not occur to us at first. He took me over to see the meteorologist, with whom I tried to converse in German and who was agreeable but said there was no map of isotherms, isobars or rainfall for Norway. Seemed not to want me to ask about some weather maps I saw he was preparing. Could not tell me the local variation of compass. Had never seen a rainfall map of Norway. Showed me a lot of data by Mohn of Christiansand, a famous meteorologist.

He stayed in Bergen for several days, promenaded in the city, read the newspapers, enjoyed the fruit and the fish markets, took brisk walks into the hinterland, observed hay drying, berry gathering, and house types. He marveled at the freshness of water "that comes leaping over the rocks in the good Norse way," the views "which at one hundred feet are unsurpassed," and he delighted in "being off all day and returning clean and cool, there being no dust." While in the environs of Bergen he wrote:[9]

Davis' Hanging Valleys are not satisfactory in explanation. Here they are to be seen close to Bergen and no glacier ever dug out the main valley. It is too short, too winding. Another explanation will win acceptance. I thought I had WMD's paper on the Hanging Valleys and glacial excavation in my trunk but do not find it. Still his main point is surely that when a side valley comes in high above the level of the main valley, the only adequate explanation is that the main valley has contained so much greater a glacier than the little one that the greater weight of ice has dug it out much deeper. Here however we have these hanging valleys opening into valleys not ever the abode of considerable glaciers.

On leaving Bergen, the *Alden* soon found passage into the 60 mile long North Fjord. The journey to Loen at the fjord head was not a direct one. The *Alden* stopped at Davik, then entered a branch of the fjord calling at Nordfjordeid, before proceeding to Loen, where Jefferson witnessed only three hours of twilight each night as the sun sank only a little more than 10° below the horizon. On either side of the fjord and high on the vidde, Pre-Cambrian rock bespoke an inhospitality.

Jefferson stayed for the next several weeks at Loen, a village then of 19 families and 118 people. A hotel of true West Norwegian character, within walking distance of the Jostedalsbrae, provided honest fare at a price convenient to Jefferson's pocket. He wrote of his journey along the North fjord:[10]

This fiord is some sixty miles in length to hardly three in width. It is enclosed in strong slopes descending from snow-spotted uplands two or three thousand feet above. In the sunlight it is grand but gloomy more often when roofed over tunnel-like by clouds that hang below the summit of the walls on either hand. At the fiord head is a mile-square patch of land that has inhabitants. It was anciently a delta of mountain streams built into the head of the arm of the sea when the land stood a hundred and fifty feet lower. Looking back over the fiord from this terrace, the scene is one of greater promise for men. Here on the terrace and about the lake above 368 people dwelled in 1904. The valley has been settled a thousand years. The land under such circumstances is very precious. It has no ascertainable price. It is not bought or sold. Each point has its own name and the people all have that name too. Thus the main settlement Loen has thirteen peasant proprietors and "always has had." Each of these families is named Loen, the individuals being distinguished by their christian names commonly with the addition of their father's name, as Marcus Andersen Loen, Rasmus Johansen Loen, Anders Marcussen Loen and so on. Infrequently individuals are found with the name of a neighbor settlement, but the rarity of this denotes fixity of residence through the generations.

Jefferson mapped the area as a first task, and was fascinated by the human distribution he found. Clinging to a thin layer of soil around the lake or on the lower fjord terrace only a little west of the largest ice sheet in Europe were eleven settlements, each very nearly self-sufficient.

Jefferson was especially interested to meet the people of these settlements. He was not able to communicate with the children whom he saw frequently gathering berries, but with the adults he had success in both Norwegian and Danish. He occasionally hired a Loen, Bodal, or Helset to act as his guide, or to row him across one of the larger lakes. He came to know some of the people well and corresponded with one of them for several years after 1904. It was from this source that he learned with sorrow that the two settlements of Bodal and Naesdal near the lakehead later perished to, "a great wave from the lake, caused by the fall of an enormous mass of rock from the cliff above." Already Jefferson's interest in man on the land was making itself clearly apparent. He studied carefully the type of dwelling standing in this part of Norway, sketching it, writing of it, photographing it. The better houses were made of wood planks, four inches thick, planed, tongued and grooved, the walls being held together entirely by the dovetailing at the corners and partition ends, the roof frequently consisting of birch bark and sod. This study in composition and form of the house as a response to local environment was one of Jefferson's major interests. A large percentage of his slide collection comprises pictures of "house types" and ranks him one of the first American geographers to treat the inquiry seriously.

Staying at the Hotel Alexandra in Loen, at the head of the fjord below the lake, which in turn was situated below the glacier, Jefferson journeyed daily to different parts of the ice sheet, taking pictures, making notes, always pondering what he saw. It excited him to think that the route by which he approached the Jostedalsbrae from Loen was hardly known in geographic literature of the time. The focal point of his interest concerned the tongues of the Jostedalsbrae:[11]

> *The ice accumulations of the Jostedal plateau are disposed of by melting and plunging over the cliffs in numerous streams, by falling bodily over the cliffs at more than a hundred points—the so-called glaciers of the second class—and in more than twenty great tongues of ice that cascade into the chasms at the fiord head. Two of these enter the Olden and Loen Lakes.*

He wrote extensively of the Kjendals Glacier, the Brixdals Glacier, and the Saeter Glacier, also on several hanging valleys which he observed. The conclusions he reached were summarized and published:[12]

> *I saw in the Northfjord moderate evidence of a glacier's power to grind its bed of rock with rock fragments for tools, some hanging valleys that may be the work of tributary valleys, as in the current explanation; more that seemed due to the enormous headward erosion of botner glaciers near the snowline; great activity of frost at all levels*

away from the coast and of running water below four or five thousand feet above the sea, operating to carry rock waste seaward so rapidly that it had little chance to weather during the trip.

The fjord farmer fascinated him quite as much as the ice sheet, which man-land relationship seen first hand further encouraged his departure from the physiography of W. M. Davis. His notes and approximately 250 slides taken during the summer served him well on his return to Ypsilanti when he gave numerous lectures before a variety of groups concerning life in West Norway. This theme did not escape an edition of his *Man in Europe, Teachers Geography* and *Principles of Geography,* or *Exercises in Human Geography.*

Jefferson's return journey to New York proved eventful. The boat returned via Scotland and Iceland collecting passengers at both ports of call. It was with one of the passengers who came aboard at Reykjavik, Iceland, that Jefferson fell to talking. The stranger told Jefferson of his Icelandic parentage and his desire to speak Icelandic fluently. Jefferson in turn told his companion of the height of storm waves in the Antarctic Ocean, this while the pair stood to the fore of the boat, pitching violently in mid-Atlantic. The passenger from Iceland was Vilhjalmur Stefansson. Stefansson and Jefferson were to become firm friends, growing to respect each other's work deeply. The following year Jefferson helped Church minister turned geographer, Albert Perry Brigham, compose and illustrate a paper—"Lake Loen (Norway) Landslip of January 1905"—which Brigham delivered to the Association of American Geographers' meeting, New York, 1905. Several years later, Jefferson presented a paper to the 1914 Chicago meeting of the Association, entitled "The Gulf Stream." The abstract reveals one of the ways Jefferson built his formal contributions around his personal observations:[13]

Considers the problem of the portion of the Atlantic to which this name is to be applied, the nature of the Gulf Stream, and its effect on the climate of Europe, with personal observation from Cuba to Norway.

The summer of 1910 saw Jefferson, together with W. M. Gregory (graduate of the M.S.N.C., 1894, and Head of the Geography Department, Teachers College, Cleveland, Ohio, 1909-1928) and W. E. Shuler (Fort Worth, Texas), studying the Rocky Mountains of Colorado under the guidance of W. M. Davis. Previously in Harvard's classrooms, Jefferson had studied the Colorado River of the West, writing a paper of that title for a W. M. Davis course early in 1897. In 1910 the work constituted part of a field course in advanced physiography, sponsored by the Harvard Summer School[14] and proved to be the first of three summer field excursions which Jefferson experienced in three consecutive summers under the leadership of W. M. Davis. Davis proved to be a most competent and thorough guide; he had either seen or walked the Rockies in 1869, 1877, 1883, 1891, 1897, 1900, 1901, 1902, 1904, 1909. Jefferson made ample notes in the field in four small notebooks, made sketches, took photographs, listened intently to Davis' exposition for more than three weeks in July. Following the departure of Davis, Jefferson spent a further few days with Gregory in the region before composing a 31 page paper entitled "The Rocky Mountains of Colorado," which paper was later submitted to Davis for the latter's approval.[15] The paper commenced with a statement of purpose:

> It was proposed to exemplify the method of description by structure, process and stage by applying it to a number of points in the Rocky Mountains of Colorado visited this summer. The general method has been to note salient items in the topography from the point of view of origin, with these to frame a theory of the genesis of the land forms of today, and then, turning the attention away from the present details, to deduce the logical consequences of the theory adopted, and finally to confront these deductions with the facts of nature. The last two items amount to prediction from theory of forms not observed and then looking for them.

For a thorough account of the physiography of the party's mountain study one may read "The Colorado Front Range" by W. M. Davis published in 1911.[16] Probably this sixty-two page statement accounts for the reason why Jefferson never published his own writing in whole or in part. More important than an account of the itinerary was the confrontation of Davis by a Jefferson thinking, teaching, and writing a variety of human geography. The letters Jefferson sent to his wife illustrate very clearly his great regard for Davis' powers of observation and interpretation and reveal his almost fiercely held belief that human geography had a greater appeal than physiography and would one day win for itself total respect from geographers. Excerpts from the correspondence provide:

> The rocks were splendid and the weather all right. W. M. Davis showed us many points I should not have seen . . .[17]
>
> Davis made us see Pene-plains and cycles that I should never have seen without him . . .[18]
>
> You would laugh to see our strenuous endeavors to draw and suit our leader . . .[19]
>
> He (Davis) seems disappointed at the prospects at Harvard. Jackson has retired, there is no instruction in palaeontology, and he has "no students", only two or three, he says, come to take his courses. We

chaff him some about the earth having been made on his plans but he takes it very well. As work this is interesting, but nothing like so much so as my human geography studies. Of course many of these are great earth features and of interest themselves for those who can get at them . . . it is not practical to make studies of the human features much, for W. M. Davis will not be turned aside for them. That must come later. It looks as if he had not been successful.[20]

I believe I think less and less of the purely physiographic work Davis advocates and does, the more I see of it, much as I must admire his insight, keenness, and amazing power with his pencil. My people idea is a better idea and will tell better.[21]

Davis is perpetually hammering at us to describe, to make a theory of origin, to deduce all imaginable consequences of this theory and then to compare these consequences with the facts; also to draw and I think we are making progress.[22]

To finish the work that he [Davis] urges, I have to spend one week in field work and one in writing up report which I will then send to him. We have to see pene plains everywhere! After that Gregory and I who are to work together, will spend a week or two out here seeing some of the more human interest . . . But the slopes of the Spanish peaks are well watered and wooded and the form studies that W. M. Davis desires us to make are illustrated there too. I have talked with him about my work etc. I think he has absolutely no interest in "Human" geography, though he tries to speak of it with respect. He thinks I ought to write an elementary book with man first not merely because it would pay, but it would be he says, a good thing to do. He says in connection with the scholarships for a study by Harvard men out of the country that he would like to see me attempting the Mexican plateau some winter, if I could get away. Probably a good report on the lines he has set out for us will be as helpful as anything I can do. We have learned a great deal from Professor Davis though not things in my own school line.[23]

The trip was rewarding to Jefferson who wrote, "I believe I have the 'recent' history of the mountains clear . . ."[24] The open air hiking was beneficial and he was excited to find a splendid specimen of a dead mountain sheep, whose skull and horns he won by petitioning the local authorities for its retention.

The following year, 1911, Jefferson took a boat to Dublin, Ireland, and thence journeyed for 66 days, June 1-August 5, through Ireland, England, Wales, France, Switzerland, into Italy in company with a selected group of geographers under the leadership of W. M. Davis. Jefferson and W. M. Davis were the only Americans present. The excursion has variously passed under titles as "The Dublin-Rome Excursion" or "Liverpool-Rome Excursion." W. M. Davis referred to the journey as "a Geographical Pilgrimage from Ireland to Italy,"[25] and explained his reference to pilgrims and pilgrimage in the opening paragraph of his article . . . "It took the name of 'Pilgrimage' because we visited many localities made famous in the history of physical geography by the work of masters in an earlier generation." Although the pilgrims totalled 32 in number and were drawn from fourteen different countries, rarely did the party number more than a dozen at any one time. Geographers usually with a fund of knowledge concerning the local area would join the excursion at prearranged locations and accompany the caravan for a few days before departing. Much of the journey was undertaken on foot. It was perhaps the jolliest of the field trips Jefferson was ever to experience. Waldbauer told funny stories never ceasing, Davis made famous the thing called "the skiou,"[26] Vacher coached Jefferson on the word "thingemebob," and Jefferson contributed to the fun—"'D'ou est Monsieur Briquet!', I asked, 'Il est de Douay', they answer laughing."[27] Jefferson's observations as recorded in his diary were particularly acute and indicate personal excitement. Later in life Jefferson frequently made mention of this trip in his correspondence with memories of satisfaction and enjoyment. Perhaps his enjoyment stemmed from his appreciation of the French regionalists who knew their "pays" with such intimacy. He was a great admirer of Paul Vidal de la Blache and the school of geographers that gathered around him. The 23 volume *Géographie Universelle* was to become one of his most prized possessions in later years. Jefferson maintained daily notes totaling approximately 20,000 words, which have been preserved,[28] and took over 600 photographs during this field trip. He later made frequent use of slides made from them in his Europe class and reproduced some of these photographs in his text *Man in Europe*. The field notes indicate the route followed, companions who joined or departed the group, members with whom Jefferson became closely acquainted, and above all what he saw. A comparison of Davis' physiographic account already mentioned, and the humanistic account produced by Jefferson in his notes are indicative of their respective points of view. Later Jefferson explained this in a letter:[29] "When I spent a few weeks in England in 1911, with Professor Davis and his party . . . Davis' interests were wholly in the hills and valleys—inhuman I called them and I took three days off to look at English country life."

Jefferson was sorry to learn that Jean Brunhes was not taking the trip. He had previously exchanged correspondence with Brunhes and had only recently published a review of the gold medal winning *La*

Géographie Humaine in the *Bulletin of the American Geographical Society*.[30] Jefferson was particularly interested in Brunhes' "facts of unproductive occupation of the soil—houses and roads". During the trip Jefferson devoted much of his attention to house plan and building materials. Much of his diary, and a large number of the photographs he took, were of houses—and frequently of house roofs. Later that year he presented a paper before the Association of American Geographers at Washington, D.C., entitled "Houses and House Materials in West Europe." Much of the paper was taken directly from his diary notes. The abstract was published in the *Annals of the Association of American Geographers:*[31]

> *The house, especially of the poor man, is made of the materials nearest at hand: if among abundant forest, of wood; where the forest is lacking, of stone or brick. Roofs are especially sensitive to the influence of local building materials, from their exposure to the weather and consequent need of repairs. Where some fissile rock abounds, they are of slate like slabs; where the rock is claying, of tiles; in the forest, of shingles; the poorest house often having thatch in any country where neither shingles nor slates are to be had.*
>
> *Inheritance, however, is also to be reckoned with.*

It was on this trip that Jefferson developed a particularly close friendship with George Chisholm (University of Edinburgh), J. Cvijic (University of Belgrade), Albert Demangeon (University of Lille), Pierre Denis and Lucien Gallois (University of Paris), Alfred Ruhl (University of Marburg), and Naomasa Yamasaki (University of Tokyo). Many letters, photographs, and publications were later exchanged as a result of these friendships.

The excursion, which assumed the form of a travelling international seminar was scheduled to terminate in Rome, venue of the 1911 International Geographical Congress. When the party reached Luzerne on September 27, the King of Italy sent a message indicating the Congress had been postponed.[32] Italy was at war with Turkey. Both Jefferson and Davis travelled as far as Milan in order to view the North Italian plain, although officially the trip disbanded at Lugano. Jefferson returned via Paris to Brittany where he took a boat for the United States. Davis remained in Paris as a visiting professor from Harvard, from which vantage point he could organize European membership to the 1912 American Geographical Society Transcontinental Excursion.

In 1912 for the third consecutive summer, Jefferson entered the field under the guidance of Davis. The Excursion (which celebrated the 60th anniversary of the American Geographical Society and the occupation by the Society of a new building), lasted 57 days, covered over 13,000 miles, and brought into daily contact 43 European geographers representing 14 countries and approximately 70 American geographers who joined and departed the Excursion, dependent upon their availability. The history of this undertaking has been well recorded in the *Memorial Volume of the Transcontinental Excursion*,[33] the first book published by the American Geographical Society. Davis appointed Jefferson First Marshal of the Excursion. Jefferson spoke several languages, could be relied upon to see the Excursion to a close, and was one of the people with whom Davis could work well. This was the last time that Davis and Jefferson were to share company on an extended field excursion; they had shared company in 1910 (Colorado), 1911 (Western Europe), and 1912 (Transcontinental Excursion). The confrontation provided by Davis' physiographic interests and abilities in the field were an important part of Jefferson's geographic education. Jefferson recognized this when he elected W. M. Davis his intellectual father.[34] R. Dodge and I. Bowman were appointed Second and Third Excursion Marshal respectively. Jefferson reported his duties were minimal, amounting to nominal leadership of the Excursion for one day in Yellowstone National Park when W. M. Davis was resting. During the Excursion Jefferson wrote frequently to his wife. Thirty-three of these letters have been preserved and afford personal insights of the Excursion experienced by him. He reported the splendor of Pullman accommodation, described the lavish hospitality provided by people and institutions enroute, detailed many of the sights seen that escaped the itinerary, mentioned the number of his own students of previous years who greeted him, and tended to confirm the suspicion that in undertaking so much travel, fatigue impaired the value of so many sights seen in so short a time. But he did take more than a thousand photographs which were to become the basis of his U.S. slide collection, and he did develop numerous friendships. He became well acquainted with some of the French geographers whom he had not met in 1911. Included were Baulig, E. de Margerie, E. de Martonne, and Herbette. He became well acquainted also with Emile Chaix (University of Geneva), Gunnar Andersson (University of Stockholm), Eduard Bruckner (University of Vienna), Alan Ogilvie (University of Oxford). He renewed friendships with Demangeon, Gallois, Vacher, Chisholm, Nussbaum, and Ruhl. Jefferson was not swift to make a person's acquaintance, and, without the close proximity fostered by the 1911 and 1912 Excursions, it is certain that he would not have come to know many of the geographers of these trips. En route many of the geographers gave informal addresses to the group, usually in the evening hours. Sometimes discussions of the most lively sort would ensue. Occasionally Jefferson would make reference to these informal discussions, or to the foreign geographers, in letters to his wife:[35]

> . . . *meeting with Professor Davis now in Lounge—later. A very lively discussion it was that ended in Dr. Niermeyer telling Davis that he was no geographer but a geomorphologist.*
>
> *The lobby, the dining room, and the lounge, which must have room and chairs for hundreds of people are all furnished in veneer of red birch which seems to cover acres of pseudo-square timbers, for the scheme of architecture is endless combinations of straight squared beams, even to the length of conventionalized cobwebs of straight squared rods, set with lights for transoms above dining room windows. All this is a direct response to two geographic factors; the prosperity and culture stand of the eastern humid United States and the color splendor of the young canon of the yellowstone. That seems to me geography. Davis gave a talk last night on the physical features of the Park and then another on "method of geographic description." As usual he spoke only of* physical *geography. He is too fair to deny this when accused of it and admits that he is really a physical geographer, but when Dr. Niermeyer of Utrecht rose and called attention to the point, everyone got excited and seemed to feel that Niermeyer was out of order. It is said that Niermeyer's contribution to geography is an admirable revision of an old work on Java where he lived for six months. I get the impression that he was longer than six months there from the way he speaks of his knowledge of the island. They say he contributed admirable description of scenery and made the work a son of Baedeker. He is called an anthropologist. It is odd how little open to new impressions our friends are, even to new points of view; very likely they feel the same way about me! Ruskin in Modern Painters has two chapters on "Mountain Splendor" and "The Mountain Gloom" and I made reference to the theme he then develops that man may lead a life of mean and sordid range of thought and feeling in the presence of the scenery that would ordinarily be called most inspiring. The traditional view is, of course, the opposite one, beauty of environment is supposed to have inspired Greek appreciation of scenery in general, despite the fact that five centuries of the same environment have not seemed to make any impression on the Turks.*
>
> *Finally after much useless discussion I bethought me to ask them the name of some Spanish "master" (offhand of course), then a Dutch, a French, an Italian and then, wickedly, a Swiss "master," who should have been inspired by the most beautiful scenery in Europe! Then I had the prudence to change the subject . . . The geographic point of view still has much way to make. I am pleased to have been*

useful to our European friends quite beyond my habits and many of them seem grateful.

And in another letter to his wife:[36]

. . . We have curious lights on foreign science. Have I mentioned De Margerie? His knowledge of American geology simply amazing for breadth and depth. Not all are like him. Cholnoky calls glacial striae marks of wind blown sand. Merzbacher does not believe Rocky Mountains wind effected and so on . . .

Jefferson delivered formal unpublished addresses to the gathering at Detroit and Chattanooga and was to have made a third presentation by popular request at the University of Virginia, Charlottesville, but time crowded him out of the program. His address entitled, "Geographic Instruction in America," later published in *The Proceedings of the Philosophical Society of the University of Virginia,* attracted the attention of a Mr. Philander Claxton, United States Commissioner of Education, who rode to Washington with Jefferson and tried to persuade the latter he should write "a 100 page booklet on geography teaching in normal schools."[37]

Perhaps Jefferson did not wander from the train as much as he would have liked owing in part to a strict itinerary and in part to a nasty fall he incurred on the steps of the Agricultural College, Madison, Wisconsin on August 28. Dr. Churchill, the Excursion physician, who called Davis "Uncle Will," examined and then bandaged Jefferson who soon recovered from the mishap. Almost certainly Jefferson would have preferred to have travelled fewer miles by train and more on foot, but he was totally agreed that the Excursion was a major success. Throughout the trip Jefferson shared sleeping quarters with his one-time student, Isaiah Bowman. The closeness encouraged Bowman to reveal to Jefferson that he, and some geographer friends, would like to see him write to President Lowell of Harvard and offer geography in the wake of the recently retired Davis. Relating this matter to his wife in a letter written while on the trip, Jefferson wrote . . . "Friends East of the Alleghenies are plotting to make Ypsilanti the home of the President of the Association of American Geographers as a step."[38] Jefferson had been appointed second vice president in 1910, but it was not until 1916 that he was appointed president. The transfer from Ypsilanti to Cambridge did not materialize. Wallace Atwood succeeded to the position occupied by Davis. Jefferson's wife was anxious to return to the East and especially to Boston, but Jefferson was not nearly so concerned to depart Ypsilanti. He frequently wrote that he was accomplishing much with his Normal College students and was well satisfied where he was. Theodora died the following year. This, coupled with the advent of the First

World War, interrupted Jefferson's habit of summer field work.

Jefferson was called out of field work retirement in 1918 by the American Geographical Society to make a study of colonization in Argentina, Brazil, and Chile. This has been written of elsewhere;[39] suffice it to say that Jefferson had all the freedoms a worker in the field could desire, and concomitantly he satisfied his own inclinations and appetites . . . and his studies could be human!

Two years later, in August 1920, Jefferson put his knowledge of river behavior to good use in the field when lawyers Davis, Costen, and Harrison representing Lee Wilson and other riparian owners in Southern Mississippi County, Arkansas, and on the advice of Isaiah Bowman employed Jefferson at $50 per day to demonstrate to the Government in court that the Golden Lake was in fact an oxbow lake. The suit for the old bed of Golden Lake had been pending in court for several months, as had other "sunken land" cases in the same country. The essential question involved in all of the sunken land cases of Mississippi County (and there had been several) had been a controversy of fact as to whether the disputed lands were really part of old lakes or merely lowlands. If it could be proved that the lands were not a part of the original lake beds, title would rest in the Government. Otherwise the disputed territory was the property of riparian owners in proportion to their interest in the meandering line of the lake. The court was apparently satisfied with Jefferson's testimony during an eight-hour examination in March, 1921,[40] and decided to restore 4,000 acres of valuable land to the riparian owners.

The raising of a family by Clara, his second wife, necessarily curtailed further field trips. It was not until the Christmas vacation of 1926, when he was advanced money by D. C. Heath Company against a series of high school geographies, that he took a trip to make photographs for his texts.[41] In the later part of December he travelled through Havana, Panama, and Jamaica sketching, taking photographs and doubtless taking notes, but the latter are not available. It was this journey to Panama which later provided Jefferson with a lecture in the Haas series which he gave at Northwestern University in 1940. Otherwise very little data exists on the journey which was undertaken in strict secrecy, a condition imposed by D. C. Heath Company. The Panama excursion was completed at the age of 63, and he was to make only one more extended field trip in his life . . . his long cherished dream of a stay in Iberia.

Jefferson wrote to Isaiah Bowman in September 1928 asking if the American Geographical Society would be able to finance a summer field trip for him in Iberia, the results either in the form of articles or a book, to be given to the American Geographical Society for publication either in the *Geographical Review* or in the Research Series.

> *The result planned is a little book—or several Review Articles, ready to print when I go aboard steamer facing west! Title, "Why Portugal?" meaning why not one Iberia or four—Gallegos, Castilians, Catalans, and Portuguese?*
>
> *The rather novel element in my plan is a three week sojourn in some coolish Portuguese coast town writing up the results, followed by a ten day moving toward Cherbourg or Southampton, picking up some dropped threads that may have developed.*[42]

Jefferson wished to travel the valley of the Tagus in Spain and Portugal, from its sources to the sea, with particular attention to the varying reaction of men to the arid Spanish and humid Portuguese climate.[43] Bowman encouraged Jefferson to proceed with the plan of Iberian field work in the summer of 1929 and offered to provide $250 as an advance payment for resultant articles, even though this practice had not previously been adopted by the American Geographical Society.[44] Unfortunately, Jefferson was taken ill in the spring of 1929 and was obliged to postpone his trip. The matter of the Iberian field work persisted with Jefferson, who mentioned it frequently in his correspondence to an interested Bowman. He seriously entertained the idea of the trip in 1930, 1931, and again in 1932, but the stringency of the depression years, a reduction in faculty salaries, and a governor's threat to close the Normal School discouraged his expenditure of money on such a venture. Eventually in 1935, armed with a supply of oranges enough for two a day on board boat, Jefferson, accompanied by his daughter, Phoebe, left New York for Antwerp. Once on the European continent the couple travelled through Paris, Bordeaux via the Ebro, to Madrid, and thence using the Tagus Valley, to Lisbon, making stops at Miranda de Ebro, Logrono, Zaragoza, Guadalajara, Madrid, Abrantes, Santarem, and Lisbon. The return journey was more swiftly accomplished also via Madrid and Paris to New York. The journeying delighted Jefferson who wrote of his joy to J. K. Wright:[45]

> *My summer in Iberia included five full days in Portugal. Portugal is a very lovely land! They are a people who have a rare knack of adorning their landscape. I like the Spaniards better, but Castile is not lovely at all, only the people very likeable. I like their cool interiors in summer, the tremendous breeziness of their houses and cafes. I had a great time and now must go again. I wondered in planning if I was not too old for a trip overseas, now I am planning on going again in 1938, and try mule-backs to places I didn't reach! 450 pictures!*
>
> *P.S. I shall bring a Tagus paper to St. Louis.*

Notes in a notebook, many photographs and sketches, and an ambition accomplished were the results. At the 1935 meeting of the Association of American Geographers in St. Louis Jefferson spoke on, "Motors as Criteria of Wealth in Europe, 1934," a presentation which contrasted the poverty of Iberia with the superior wealth of other European nations.[46] The following year, 1936, Jefferson delivered more of his Iberia findings at the Syracuse meeting of the Association, "Is the Iberian Plateau a Plain of Marine Denudation?"[47] A further Iberia talk at the Normal School founded a campus geography club.

CHAPTER SEVEN

THE AMERICAN GEOGRAPHICAL SOCIETY
AND THE ABC EXPEDITION

As Director of the American Geographical Society, Bowman had a pronounced interest in Latin America. This interest stemmed at least in part from his close association with Jefferson, both as a student and as an assistant in the years 1901-1904. While studying at Harvard, and teaching at Yale, Bowman maintained an interest in South America and a close relationship with his former teacher.[1] On each of his three trips to South America, 1907, 1911 and 1913, Bowman continued to correspond with Jefferson, asking questions, observing, describing hitherto little known facts. In 1907 on the occasion of Bowman's first visit to South America Jefferson taught in his place on the faculty of Yale University for the summer session.

In 1915 Bowman was elected Director of the American Geographical Society.[2] He hoped the Society would specialize in Latin American researches and received encouragement when, in 1916, the Society published his book, *The Andes of Southern Peru*. It was the Inquiry, however, which provided Bowman with the opportunity to informally commence such researches. By April 1918, a master plan containing nineteen research categories in the Latin American area had been established.[3] The sixth category was entitled, "European Colonies and Settlement." Prior knowledge of this Inquiry research may have been responsible for a letter Bowman wrote to Jefferson in October 1917:[4]

In considering the problem suppose we look at a few chapter titles in the proposed book, everything to be regarded as absolutely tentative so that I need nowhere add question marks:

The Colonies of Temperate South America

1. *The People and the Land (Jefferson)*
2. *The historical background of South American Colonization (Mc-Bride)*
3. *Contrasts between the later and earlier colonists (Jefferson et al)*
   a. *In Mode of life*
   b. *In state of civilization*
   c. *In political and social customs*
   d. *In racial mixture*
4. *The colony in the ultimate development of South American government policy. Here we talk of scattering the foreigner. There they hold up colonial provincialism as an attraction to the social and physiographic organization of the two sections?*
5. *Modern colonies (racial study chiefly)*
   Italian
   German
   Russian, etc., etc.
   Descriptive treatment with extreme care in literary style marked by brilliancy and broadness of thought so that the result will be the most-quoted and best work of its kind in any language.
6. *The modern colony in the economic organization of the South American state*
7. *Colonist and native in their political relations*
8. *Cultural relationships*

I set these down just as they came to mind. My oral sketch that got the funds was meager and dealt with the peaks only.

By peaks I mean this. No study of this sort has been made in South America. Now, and still more after the war, the South American colonist will be a big factor in the fresh advances of the merchant. The colonist will be appealed to by political parties who seek to adjust the development schemes, that bring revenue, to the extremely hard conditions that will then confront the nations. Will new settlers come? A man on the ground will get incalculable benefit from a study of the spirit of the colonist there now. Is he disgruntled? Was he before the war? Has he plans? Has he ideas?

A final chapter might well be prognostical and deal with our national, political, economic, and social relations with the temperate zone peoples of South America. The very spirit of modern geography should permeate the plan and the book. Map representation and especially the technique of it should show the highest skill. Every photograph should mean something. We now get no photographs at all to show the colonist and the characteristics of his life.

Finally, we speak of Argentina and Brazil as definite political and social entities. They are really a group of unlike sections and to the unlikeness and nature and race (as between Indian and Spaniard or Portuguese, from section to section) there is added the unlikeness of the relatively pure-blooded and provincial colonist set down into an inferior culture that certainly encourages him not to imitate the new, but to conserve and follow the old. What is his way out? When will the Italian cease going to Italy in droves each year? Will it be when Buenos Aires becomes as cultured as New York? The low-born foreigner who comes here sees an industrial organization superior to his own, and is in the way to acquire at least some of our so-called American characteristics. He begins to live up to the new people.

Here is a great field for much geographical philosophy based on accurate statistics and maps.

Can we get the Argentine government to cooperate? Will they make some local up-to-date censuses for our particular benefit? Will they loan assistants at their expense to an even more comprehensive plan? They have unpublished statistics bearing on the problem. Can we get them? Bailey Willis can steer us.

At the time of the Christmas meeting in Chicago we must get together for several days and work out details. You appeal to me as just the man for the work because your thinking begins where mine leaves off. This is no job for an untried man. You will develop it into a fine big thing. While some publishable results will be looked for by 1919 and a book by 1920, the last of the results of the study may occupy you back home for a much longer period.

A few weeks later Bowman wrote a confidential note to Jefferson, suggesting that he take an assistant and study colonization in Argentine, Brazil, and Chile, the venture to be financed to the extent of $6,000 and to be known as the American Geographical Society ABC Expedition. The essentials of the contract were agreed upon at the Christmas meeting of the Association of American Geographers in Chicago, 1917. A "Memorandum of an Understanding and Agreement between the American Geographical Society and Mark Jefferson . . . in respect to European Colonies in Temperate South America" for a sum of $6,000 was concluded on March 14, 1918.[5]

Chile had remained neutral throughout the war despite the violation of her neutrality by German and British warships, even prospering as a result of the large amount of nitrate she sold to the Allied powers.

Argentine, under the premiership of Hipolito Irigoyen, refused to give up neutrality during the war although German submarines sank Argentine ships. Of the three "ABC" powers only Brazil declared war on Germany. Brazil had severed relations with Germany on April 11, 1917, and declared war on October 26, 1917. A tardy Brazilian entry into the war and neutrality from Argentine and Chile were perhaps factors contributing to a desire to analyze the strength of German feeling and power in Argentine, Brazil, and Chile.

Charles Colby insists that the ABC Expedition was a part of the war effort and of the Inquiry program.[6] It is significant at least that the following statement by Colby in a book review published in the *Journal of Geography* went unchallenged:[7]

> In the spring of 1918, the American Geographical Society sent Professor Jefferson to the Argentine Republic, Brazil and Chile to study recent European colonization in those countries. At that time much concern was expressed over the German and other European influence in those Southern American republics and apparently this expedition was dispatched to ascertain the facts in the case.

Certainly it would seem unlikely that the Society would involve itself in theory rather than policy oriented research in South America at such a time and when Bowman could write to Jefferson,[8] "I am engaged in some extra war work and so extremely busy that it is hard to find time for any but the briefest letters." Preparations for the expedition were time-consuming at the American Geographical Society headquarters and Jefferson did not leave for South America until April of 1918, by which time the Inquiry work was proceeding swiftly. Strangely, Jefferson did not learn of the Inquiry or its work until his return from the ABC Expedition in September of 1918. Never, seemingly, did he recognize or contemplate his 1918 South American researches as a part of the Inquiry or war work.

Numerous letters from Jefferson to his wife and also to his daughter, Phoebe, posted while on the expedition, support the thesis that Jefferson had no idea his researches might be used to influence national policy. In any event, Bowman did not expect manuscripts for publication from Jefferson until 1920; that, too, was part of the ABC understanding. Yet when Jefferson returned from South America and reported to the American Geographical Society headquarters in New York, Bowman immediately expressed a desire to see Jefferson's notes. Bowman knew that Jefferson would have extensive notes of his work, as that was part of the ABC expedition agreement.

While in the field in 1918 Jefferson made many notes which were later welded together to form publications in the American Geographical Society Research Series. Among these notes may be found the following explanation of his understanding of the reason for the project:[9]

South America may be said to have been discovered three times, once by the Conquistadores, who got an amazing amount of it in their hands by 1550; again by the people of the United States along the beginning of the present century, efficiently helped by visits of Roosevelt and Root, at which time the ABC countries were perceived to have a certain prominence, hitherto unsuspected among us but well known in the Old World. A third discovery was that by German, Portuguese, Spanish and Italian families from the middle of the last century to the present time, families of Germans unhappy at the abuse of government in Germany about 1848 and south Europeans at a later date in economic distress at home—temperate South America offered them a sure refuge from their troubles.

It was the object of the Mission of the American Geographical Society of 1918 to ascertain the present condition of these new colonists of America, their relation to the older inhabitants and the parts they are now playing and are destined yet to play in the national life of the countries where they had made their homes.

The fact that the leader of the party had lived six years (1883-1889) among typical old time people of the Argentine Republic, where this new colonization has had most development, led naturally to emphasis on that country. The fact that he is a teacher limited the time available for the visit to the (northern) spring and summer of 1918.

It is very probable that the American Geographical Society wished to preserve anonymity in the matter of war work. Bowman was anxious not to associate the name of the Society publicly with war work. He wished the Society to remain objective, scientific, committed to furthering the cause of geographic science. But peace negotiations were being carried out under the appellation, "Inquiry," at the American Geographical Society to maintain secrecy. Bowman also recognized that the ABC Expedition, in attempting to define the attitude and measure the distribution of German-speaking peoples living in Argentine, Brazil, and Chile would serve the cause of geography well: he realized that the Expedition and resultant publications could be acknowledged as the beginning of the Latin American Research Program which he desired.

Lawrence Gelfand has suggested that Bowman used Inquiry funds to further his Society's researches in Latin America.[10] Bowman offers a different explanation in a letter to Jefferson dated October 8, 1917:[11]

Let me now relate details so that the whole plan will be before you.

This Society should have several men in the field all the time. This policy would contribute a steady stream of big constructive articles and *books. It requires the income of a quarter of a million capital. I did not get the quarter million but only the income on it for 1918, i.e. $12,500.*

This I propose to use on four plans of which three relate to South America. The first South American plan is yours, the second is more specific and physiographic in nature and also less expensive, the third is almost negligible as to expense.

Your problem would be the critical one. I want to justify the expense and so encourage the continuance of the plan during 1919 and for that matter indefinitely.

Jefferson did not start out on the Expedition until April 2, 1918. His preparations, which were rapid and comprehensive, comprised the hiring of an assistant, correspondence with men familiar with travel in the ABC countries, the acquisition of much literature—especially concerning South American trade, numerous photostated maps, the overhaul of his trusty typewriter which serviced him for nearly half a century, the borrowing of a set of cameras, including a stereo camera, enough Kodak film for a thousand pictures, a developing tank, the purchase of a lightweight panama suit, and his typical straw hat. Three days at the American Geographical Society discussing the Expedition with Bowman and reading in the library were followed by one day in Washington. Jefferson was given letters of introduction to numerous officials in South America which later proved useful.

Jefferson's first choice of assistant was Clifton Johnson of "Highways and Byways" fame. He felt Johnson was a skilled observer, artistic with a camera, accurate and deft with a pen. But Johnson was busily at work on two more travel books and could not accept. Jefferson then invited Wellington Jones of Chicago to accompany him on the Expedition, but the latter had already planned a trip to Asia after June of 1918 when the Jones' anticipated an addition to their family. Tower was Jefferson's third choice, but he was involved in war work.[12] On the suggestion of W. M. Davis, Arthur Colton was considered for the position of assistant, and although he, too, did not find it possible to make the journey, the correspondence between them produced an interesting letter—especially interesting since it was written on March 2, 1918, less than a month before the date of departure, at which time Jefferson's intended plan of field work was well established:[13]

The opportunity to see the best regions of Latin-America will be a fine one, I estimate the necessary cost of $1200 up, which in itself amounts to $200 a month. While I shall not linger at all in Valparaiso, Santiago, Buenos Aires, or Rio de Janeiro, we shall have to see most of those capitals, which are really of some great interest, Rio for instance, *being one of the scenic wonders of the earth. Our problem too is extremely interesting. For the last 50 or 60 years colonies of Germans have existed in southern Chile and southern Brazil and odd Italians in southern Brazil and along the Parana in the Argentine Republic which with other less important ones make count in the Argentine case as much as a quarter of all the people of the country. These Italians of the Argentine have created the great wheat production of that country. There is something quite analogous in their possibilities to the phenomena of our own population in the United States, in contrast to the mixed Indian blood of the older nationals of South America. Mitre wrote that pure Spanish descent in the Argentine meant descent from a Spaniard and an Indian woman, as Spanish women did not come over in the early days.*

Now I am to try to ascertain the present facts of these colonies, how they are prospering, comparing always with their country of origin and the creole population of their adopted country. I want to make many photographs, gather all sorts of concrete cases, individual histories, lists of public officers, wholesale and retail merchants, lawyers, doctors, school teachers in type localities, to learn what social activities, and what commercial and political activities these colonists enter on in the old established prosperous settlements. I want to learn what we can about criminal offenders. We shall have generalizations to establish, but I want to gather a vast amount of particular illustration.

It will mean incessant interviewing. I mean to employ local people, sons of colonists as "drivers" when we need a rig and find talkative men, as guides or "secretaries" on occasion to give us what information that they have and point out those who have more and put us in touch with them. I shall have to pay them, but there is no costly transportation in their case, and if we pick them well they should be of very great help.

My assistant should work with me just long enough to get the idea, and then by himself. If he develops special aptitude for some part of the work it will be assigned more and more to him. I plan to take a folding typewriter along and write up results almost incessantly while the details are fresh and full in mind. Although other experiences will modify much so written it is important to expand to the greatest fulness right at the moment of gathering observations. Later recollections are bound to be somewhat confused by the number and variety of impressions. Commercial information too must be gathered, what they buy of their home country, in how far they have changed their needs in their new environment, and not least, what market they may afford for American hardware, tools, and machinery. Methods of land purchase, and transfer, and record, and prices with actual cases as often as may be are also in the scheme. A general view of the wider facts and a very particular study of what appears to be type localities are the keynote to my plan.

The Society expects a volume of results from me in 1919. I have no contract or even statement about it but in general I know that they publish and allow the writer a generous royalty. They will gladly publish interesting fragments from our work in their Review when they pay $10. per thousand words. If you can do acceptable work they will certainly be glad to do the same for you. No pay or support during writing up is contemplated, but I shall endeavor to reserve funds for dictation work from my general allowance. If you can take upon yourself some part, some chapters or sections of the results I shall be only too glad to assign you your share in clerical provision and in royalty. Though I have not personally thought of that at all. We can promise you opportunity, all you can take, and meanwhile we are able to spend substantial sums in giving you a superb view of Latin America. I can hardly imagine a finer chance.

I believe from your letter and from what Professor Davis writes that you could give me assistance enough to make it worthwhile and even advantageous to take you if you care to go. I should expect much hard work and all of your time, the same zeal in short, that I expect to show myself. I expect to sail from New York, April 1 for Valparaiso, via Panama, spend two weeks in southern Chile, cross the Andes, Santiago to Mendoza by train, to Buenos Aires, most of May, June, July among the Italians of Argentine, and August in southern Brazil, coming home direct from Rio. I must be here October 1. Should you conclude to come a more comfortable steamer berth will be obtained by early action. I, of course, attend to that.

Jefferson eventually arranged to take an assistant named Alfred Coester, who spoke excellent Spanish, typed well and had an alert mind. Prior to sailing Jefferson had not been feeling well, "I am feeling very wretched. Strongly tempted to write Bowman I shall have to give up the trip, but I suppose the sea voyage may set me up."[14] The Expedition fascinated Jefferson. Consequently the two sailed from New York on April 2, on board the *S.S. Santa Ana,* United States and Pacific Line. The journey south served as a period during which time Jefferson and Coester became better acquainted.

The little vessel reached Valparaiso, Chile, on April 21, after several ports of call and passage through the Panama Canal. The bracing salt air and the ease of social life aboard the boat prepared and strengthened both men for the strenuous weeks of work ahead. Already at this time in his life Jefferson was beginning to show signs of increasing deafness but in later years claimed that the sea dispelled the ailment. On April 5, as the *Santa Ana* approached the tropics, Jefferson wrote:[15]

Such a balmy air, such an even sea, now beginning to take that indescribable deep liquid transparent blue of the tropic ocean . . . . We work a good many hours a day. Have the Argentine, Chile, Brazil trade items typewritten neatly for the years 1912-1917, accounts all up to date and Coester has typewritten about a third of my Temperature paper which I revise a few pages in advance of him. We have a folding table in the stateroom, which is large and airy. Ship is new, good, sweet smelling, as ships go. Smooth seas all the way from New York, amazing. Steadily warmer. This morning I have negligee shirt and Palm Beach suit. Bath in salt water at six—coffee and hot water for shaving at 6:30 . . . We have wireless but only messages from navy allowed so we have no idea how the battle of Picardy is going. I hope we learn at Colon of growing Allied successes.

Jefferson and Coester became acquainted with several of the fifty passengers on board the ship and took the opportunity to learn as much as possible of contemporary life and settlement in Chile. The pair, whose native tongue was English, spoke Spanish with ease, carried cameras, made frequent notes in diaries, typed in the stateroom, and asked many questions. They were soon met with suspicion by the passengers. Indeed, the ship's doctor became uneasy of Coester:[16]

The ship's doctor, a very curious sort of person who declines to give him (Coester) the typhoid treatment, asks authorization by Dr. Harris at Colon. I understand that Dr. Harris is the Health Officer of the Canal Zone. He regards me, the ship doctor does, as a suspicious person. Asked Coester if I was a German! He vaccinated Coester after a good deal of urging, but thinks the whole business queer. We are going to the healthiest place in the world, he says, what are we afraid of? I think I shall have to take the matter up with the captain before we get into Colon.

In occupying a table next to the Captain in the dining room, Jefferson soon made a friendship that was to prove rewarding. Jefferson and Captain Crossley exchanged information concerning the oceans, rainfall, salinity, storm paths, shipping routes, fueling stations, dangers to shipping in the War, views obtainable from the boat's rail, the wonder of the Panama Canal. The Captain, gruff in manner and exterior, made it known on board that Jefferson and his companion were to be treated well, and, as if to emphasize the point, the Captain took Jefferson ashore in his personal launch at all points of call and gave him glimpses of his charts and data from the log book. Jefferson was also given access to the Chief Engineer, who gave him water temperatures and boat speed every fourth hour throughout the journey.

At Lima Jefferson and Coester went ashore, again with the Captain, Jefferson to post his paper to Bowman, "The Real Temperatures Throughout North and South America,"[17] to look for wind effects in the trees, "I found them, and the winds are from the south," and to visit the meteorological office for data. Of the paper Jefferson had previously written to daughter Phoebe:[18]

> . . . I have a splendid new paper for Mr. Bowman nearly written. It has been going on really for 14 years, but he doesn't know it and it is new stuff. It is the greatest fun I know, to get out a new paper!

One day ashore and the *Santa Ana* continued south to Antofogasta where another day was passed on shore.[19]

> Called on U. S. Vice-Consul McGurk. Told him plans. He said perfectly safe to travel in south, but that if we travelled round asking questions the Germans would become suspicious. He wanted me to drop him a line if I learned anything of interest. There has been no disorder among the Germans of South Chile. Government is strong and no evidence exists that they desire disorders. I found an admirable little book on the southern part of Chile, Touring in Llanquihue, across the Argentine and Chilian Switzerland. A lot of material that I wanted. I saw it at a little picture store where we bought some photographs this morning. I asked the price, Coester and I had been talking in English—the young German who kept the store answered five pesos. I handed him a ten peso bill, and he stared at me as if he didn't want to wait on me. I didn't realize that he was German at first. He did not want to sell it to me, but it was exposed for sale, and I had simply helped myself so he could do nothing about it.

While in Antofogasta Jefferson made inquiries concerning a Professor Espinoza of Santiago, author of *Nueva Geografia de Chile*. He wanted to employ Espinoza temporarily in his inquiries, but could not find him. The coast was not unfamiliar to a Jefferson who had made the journey from Cordoba to Lima in 1886, but he was delighted to revisit the area and share its beauty in a letter to his wife:[20]

> We have had some tantalizing sights of land, beautiful forested mountains in Ecuador, bare desolate slopes in Peru and quantities of huge pelicans, several hundreds passed us today, once a flock of 150 all together. Then there have been a lot of seals playing in the water and porpoises, sometimes a hundred in school.

The work of the Expedition began earnestly soon after the boat landed in Valparaiso, on April 21. Coester and Jefferson gleaned all the literature available concerning Chile, its inhabitants, trade, history, potential. Then the pair travelled the interior valley from Santiago to Puerto Montt, either singly or together, gathering maps, literature, climatological data, questioning the inhabitants, photographing settlements, parsing attitudes, assaying the German-ness of southern Chile, always observing and taking notes. Jefferson took letters of introduction from Santiago to a Mr. and Mrs. Glass in Temuco. The couple were missionaries from London who knew parts of Chile intimately. They showed Jefferson a most unusual collection of Mapuche Indian artifacts and were otherwise very useful, "they helped me more than anyone in Chile." The rainy Mediterranean winter of southern Chile hindered Jefferson more than he had anticipated. It left him cold and damp, obliged him to travel much by carriage whereas he preferred to walk, and forced him to take photographs from the carriage instead of from the field. The photographs taken on the Expedition, however, did not seem to suffer in consequence.[21]

At the end of each day Jefferson would enter the expenses of the pair into a book so that he would be able to account the expenditure of American Geographical Society money. Then the pair would rewrite and type their field notes. Information-packed paragraphs were composed around sketches or paragraphs made during the day. A manuscript of sorts began to emerge from Jefferson's notes which were arranged under the headings: Landscape; Streets and Houses; Fauna, Flora and Products; Weather and Climate; People, Class, Dress; Transportation and Railway. Occasionally additional information was contained in the letters Jefferson sent to his wife, Clara. Usually however these letters were fundamentally rough drafts of his more carefully composed and typed field notes. The letters continued until early in May, at which time the correspondence ceased or has subsequently been lost. The letters contain occasional references to his concern for South American German attitude towards his work:

> He [Coester] is beginning to be scared of what the Germans in southern Chile will do to us and what they will suspect. But I do not see any reason to anticipate more than in Brazil, and I propose to have good advice about reasonably safe ways of going about it. He says he is told on board that the common people of Chile side strongly with the Germans in the present political troubles . . . I shall certainly be glad when this job is over.[22]

> Just had supper in this "Palace Hotel" and really there was nothing to eat. Usually I fare pretty well, had an excellent breakfast on the train, but I came here to avoid the Germans, who keep the best hotel, to this, which is kept by a Spaniard and it was the limit . . . The other day at Temuco, some four hours north of here by train, I sent Coester

back to Santiago and went on down to Puerto Montt alone. I can't think things out very well with him along, and there were a number of things he could be doing in Santiago, and it would be pleasanter there—the rain here is so depressing and he will talk English, which attracts attention of the Germans.[23]

The pair then journeyed north again from Puerto Montt, through Santiago and the Cumbre Pass to Cordoba, Rosario, Buenos Aires, then north through Uruguay to southern Brazil and Porto Alegre, São Paulo, and Rio before returning to New York. They stopped at numerous colonies en route, Polish, Jewish, Italian, Confederate, but their main concern was German settlement—its limits, type, contribution, growth, and German-ness. Additionally Jefferson visited numerous meteorological stations and gathered quantities of climatological statistics and information especially from his old friend, W. G. Davis, meteorologist from the Cordoban Observatory, from Frank Wiggin of the Meteorological Office, Buenos Aires, and from a correspondent, Henrique Morize of the Observatory at Rio. In the Argentine Jefferson renewed his acquaintance with some of the families he had known from his 1883-1889 residence; one of these families provided an escort, Justiniano Allende Posse—an engineer, author, and one-time President of the Argentine National Highway Commission—who guided Jefferson and Coester through parts of the Argentine and introduced them especially to areas of German settlement. Jefferson's work in the Argentine and southern Brazil was undoubtedly made less pleasant by the unusually cold winter of 1918; Mendoza had its first snow since 1886. This proved a hindrance to Jefferson who felt the cold bitterly. A further annoyance to the pair lay in timing their departure. Only one boat left Rio in the summer of 1918 for the U.S.A.; its date of departure was kept secret. Jefferson and Coester were obliged to spend two weeks waiting in Rio for a possible departure when they might have been studying Brazilian colonization.

Throughout the Expedition Jefferson maintained an objective attitude towards German immigrants and colonies. He had not forgotten the willingness of Germans to teach him their language in the Foreigners Club at Cordoba, 1883-1886, or the encouragement he had received from Argentine Germans to attend Heidelberg University. Furthermore, he had a preconceived notion of the German peasant as a diligent, hardworking, thrifty human, seeking an honest livelihood from the soil. Jefferson admired honest work and honest initiative beyond all else, and this is largely what he saw in German colonization in South America in 1918. Jefferson did not blame German peasantry in South America for calculated German governmental aggression. He was swift to recognize and emphasize in several of his writings that the United States was an extension of Europe and that it was the European who came to North America bringing with him his European culture that had made the U.S.A. He recognized that many of these Europeans were of German nationality, and they had helped settle and develop prosperous communities as Cincinnati and Milwaukee. These hard workers were repeating a pioneering process which they had successfully demonstrated in previous years over the face of East Europe. Jefferson's notes included the following quotation on the worth of the German migrant farmer in East Europe:[24]

> The Germans colonized all the Slavic countries to the east of the Reich, made settlements among the Slavs as civilizers of the region, exactly as New Englanders and New York people settled among the Indians of the Midwest. The Slavs were and are now much below the German standards in the common arts of civilized life. In every branch of industry the Germans "were incontestably superior, excelling in agriculture as well as in manufacturing and mining, in commerce as well as in seamanship. The Slavonic rulers saw with pleasure great tracts of worthless virgin forest turned into productive land around German towns, while little towns with free German institutions arose among them as centers of trade and communication. They felt their own power increased by the addition of actively producing and taxable subjects, and were anxious to lead German settlers into those parts of their countries which were still but imperfectly opened up," wrote Professor Joseph Partsch of Breslau, conservative and painstaking geographer, in 1903. He was a patriotic German but there can be no doubt of the soundness of his estimate of the culture of the German colonies.

Jefferson's mind was not biased. He opened his eyes, travelled much and noted his observations. It was with this perspective that he diligently worked in South America. It seems probably that Jefferson envisaged a single volume book concerning the peopling of South America as a result of the ABC Expedition. To this end he typed a delightful but unfinished forty-page study of Creole Chile under the title: "Chapter I. South America Re-Colonized: Chile, Argentine Republic, Brazil." This piece of work was advantaged over the others that resulted from the ABC Expedition, since he was able to assemble and compose much of it on the boat journey home and in Ypsilanti with South America fresh in his mind, prior to his ten-month involvement with the Inquiry in New York and the American Commission to Negotiate Peace in Paris. Perhaps Bowman's anxiety and persuasion to have something briefer and sooner, which might be shown to the American Geographical Society

Council as "results," encouraged Jefferson to publish the findings of the Expedition in numerous separates:[25] *Recent Colonization in Chile,*[26] *The Rainfall of Chile,*[27] "Pictures from Southern Brazil,"[28] and *Peopling the Argentine Pampa.*[29] Briefer publications resulting from ABC field work, include: "New Rainfall Maps of Brazil,"[30] "A New Map of World Rainfall,"[31] "Actual Temperatures of South America,"[32] and "An American Colony in Brazil."[33] These publications were noted as a very welcome addition to the geographical literature of South America. Reviews of the three books were extremely favorable in newspapers and geographical magazines on both sides of the Atlantic: more than 1,300 copies of each of the Chilean studies were sold, and approximately 2,000 copies of *Peopling the Argentine Pampa.*[34]

Recent Colonization in Chile, a pioneer study, was published by the American Geographical Society in its newly created Research Series. In 21,000 words the study revealed Jefferson at his best, relating what he had seen and learned of colonization in Chile. The study sketched the history and social condition of Chile, the feudalism of Creole Society, Governmental attempts to attract skilled European labor, and resultant colonization. Continued attention to the German-ness of the German immigrant and his colonization characterized the publication. In the literature to that date it had been supposed that southern Chile was strongly Germanic. Indeed, Jefferson noted[35] that in the February 1920 issue of the *Journal of Geography* E. Walther had written, "The temperate portions of southern Brazil and Chile are dotted with German villages, in which the majority of the people are Germans and the German language is spoken."[36] This notion Jefferson attempted to dispell. In the southern provinces of Cautin, Valdivia, and Llanquihue, Jefferson and Coester had visited several German colonies and found singularly little evidence of the supposed Germanization. Under a subheading, "The Germanization of Southern Chile a Myth," he wrote:[37]

> *Puerto Montt was said to speak German and read German newspapers. I was even told I should find people there who were born in the country but could speak no Spanish. All this is exaggeration of the grossest sort. Of certain places, like the German Hotel Hein, such a statement may be true; but apart from that I heard Spanish everywhere. Two newspapers in Spanish, La Alianza Liberal and El Llanquihue, were offered for sale everywhere, but I could not get any German paper. The directory of the telephone company, Sociedad Progreso de Llanquihue, lists as newspapers (diarios), the two mentioned above and no others, I found two persons who spoke no Spanish, but both were German-born. No street in the city has a German name, nor is German used on signs. Even German business houses*

give their names in the Spanish form—Casa Carsten, Hermanos Schmidt . . .

One hears much of the Germans at Temuco, capital of province Cautin. I was even told it was a German town. It is not at all . . .

The Chilean Germans are always surrounded by an overwhelming majority of Chileans.

He was particularly impressed with German peasant achievement in the southern part of the country, the *frontera,* rendered relatively inaccessible by heavy rains and humid forests. German influence in southern Chile meant agriculture and prosperous handicrafts to an hitherto marginal section of that country. Jefferson contended that the Chilean government program for colonization was not in the best interests of that country. He insisted that German and other foreign settlements were created only by the eviction of peon squatters who had perilously settled the land. German settlement, he perceived, was encouraged by land speculators who recognized that the value of the land marginal to the settlements would be enhanced. He emphasized the previously known but little appreciated fact that only eight per cent of Chile was productive and that the productive area of Chile had a density of population of 160 people per square mile for the entire country. Jefferson then made the case that it was folly to introduce additional laborers into such a country. The colonization study was read by Chilean statesmen and theorists and exerted considerable influence upon government policy and especially towards immigration policy.

His findings concerning the distribution of population in Chile were offered to the Association of American Geographers at Chicago in 1920 in the form of a paper entitled, "Chile: A Land Where Immigrants Need not Apply." The abstract was published in the *Annals of the Association of American Geographers:*[38]

Much of Chile's 290,000 square miles is little available for homes for men. The arid deserts of the north, the rain-soaked forests of the south, and the rough Andine slopes which fill the eastern half of the country for the whole three thousand miles of its length subtract so much from the total area of the country that its 13 people per square mile becomes 156 people to the square mile of usable territory. That is why Chilean agriculture is intensive, with yields per acre greater than elsewhere in America; why the peasant is ill paid, ill fed, landless and wretched; why immigrants are placed on the land only by ejecting the people of the country, and why fifty years of government-fostered immigration have not brought fifty thousand people to Chile.

Of the paper the *Geographical Review* commented:[39]

Professor Mark Jefferson's paper, "Chile: A Land Where Immigrants

Need not Apply", was undoubtedly the most brilliant paper of the session. With keen insight into the human conditions and reactions, and with rare judgment in the handling of the facts, Professor Jefferson traced in a masterly way the geographical conditions of German settlement in Chile. In preparation for his main point he emphasized particularly the high density of population and high productivity per unit of area of cereals, potatoes, etc., as compared with the Argentine, the United States, and France of that part of Chile where most of the people actually live, which is a very tiny section lying principally between Concepcion and Valparaiso.

In 1921 the work constituted the most recent source on Chilean colonization, and presented itself as an important contribution to the geographic literature on Chile available in the English language. C. Colby observed the geographic qualities of the study:[40]

The survey is written in a pleasingly virile, pungent style and throughout reflects the hand of a skilled geographer. In fact, Professor Jefferson presents this social problem with such skill that, in effect, he introduces his reader to the geography of Chile.

Thirty-seven years later, Colby wrote:[41]

I consider his (Jefferson's) monograph on German Settlement in Chile to be one of his finest publications. In fact, the early pages of that report constitute one of the best bits of writing in the geographic publications of the first half of the century.

In similar vein, Bowman wrote to Jefferson:[42]

Your manuscript on Chile has just arrived, together with the maps. Mr. Archer Huntington was in to see me directly after the manuscript came, and turning to the introduction read the first paragraph. His comment was, "That man can write. Look at the way in which he has woven statistics into a strong English sentence in the last few lines of that paragraph." Then he turned to later pages and from time to time exclaimed. "This is bully!—this is great stuff!—fine!—We must print this in the monograph series!"

I know from experience that you are not susceptible to flattery, and I am not telling you this for any such purpose; but at the same time you are human and cannot fail to appreciate the comments of our mutual friend, who doesn't make such comments unless he means them.

The reviewers of the publication were swift to note Jefferson's denial of the Germanization of the ABC countries. Charles Colby, reviewing the book in the *Journal of Geography*, wrote:[43]

In his bulletin on "Recent Colonization in Chile," Professor Jefferson states that the German element does not predominate in any part of

Chile. He found that, even in the southern part of the country, there are from ten to twenty times more Chileans than Germans and concludes that the "Germanization of Southern Chile is simply a myth."

A review in the official organ of the Royal Geographical Society, the *Geographical Journal,* by an unidentified author, states:[44]

As is well known, much of the modern colonization has been done by Germans, and it is a common idea that a large part of southern Chile has already become Germanized. This Professor Jefferson shows, is simply a myth, for even where Germans are most in evidence they form but a small fraction of the total population, and are surrounded by an overwhelming majority of Chileans.

An unknown reviewer writes in the *Geographical Teacher:*[45]

. . . The monograph gives very valuable facts about immigration into Chile in the nineteenth century, and shows that the supposed Germanization of southern Chile is a myth.

Theodore W. H. Irion, editor of *The American Schoolmaster,* wrote:[46]

Other notions which one acquires through general reading which this investigation dispells have to do with the German element as a factor in Chile. Occasionally one hears of the German settlements in Chile and begins to wonder if a new Germany is growing up in Chile. Jefferson definitely points out that the stories about German settlements and towns in which German is the spoken language and in which the papers are all printed in German, in which in fact everything is German, are almost complete myths.

The German magazines shunned the publication; *Petermann's Mitteilungen* reviewed the study in less than thirty words. Jefferson received several requests for the study from German geographers. These requests he forwarded to Bowman, refraining from correspondence with men who, he claimed, were German geographers rather than German and geographers. The propagandistic writing by German geographers in the war had offended Jefferson. He felt that their work had become characterized by an aggressive and pronounced German nationalism. Jefferson terminated his correspondence with German geographers at this time. Later when Gladys Wrigley requested Jefferson to review Hettner's works in January 1930[47] on the occasion of the award of the Cullum Medal by the American Geographical Society, Jefferson wrote in a letter to Bowman,[48] "Please tell Miss Wrigley that I cannot find time to examine the Hettner books," and to Miss Wrigley,[49] "Sorry to balk at Hettner, but he no longer interests me."

The Rainfall of Chile, also published in 1921, was a companion study to that on colonization. This bulletin contains probably the first accurate mean annual rainfall map of Chile. H. A. Matthews, writing in the *Scottish Geographical Magazine* for 1924, notes, "The rainfall map of Chile published with the [Jefferson] pamphlet is invaluable, as it is the only reasonable rainfall map of Chile in existence."[50] The map, colored and on scale of 1:10,000,000 was compiled from data for the years 1900 to 1919 collected from 167 stations. It replaced Voss's rainfall map of Chile (1907), showing the earlier map to have been constructed with insufficient data, especially in interior Chile. Jefferson placed the rainfall map of Chile alongside a map showing the distribution of forests, irrigated lands, and dry farms in central Chile. The relevance of rainfall to land use rendered more meaningful the history of colonization in Chile.

Bowman arranged for Jefferson to use some of the unspent ABC Expedition money to invest parts of two summers at the American Geographical Society, in order that the South American studies might be completed more swiftly than would otherwise be possible.[51] At the Society Jefferson would have access to a good collection of South American maps and literature. He was promised a desk and all the stenographic and typographical help he would need.

In the cool rooms of the American Geographical Society, August 1921, Jefferson worked intensively on "Unveiling of the Pampa,"[52] later published under the title, *Peopling the Argentine Pampa,* which was to become one of the standard works concerning the Argentine. Simultaneously he was able to renew an old established friendship with Vilhjalmur Stefansson.

While at the Society's rooms Bowman tried hard to harness Jefferson to his Latin American Research Program, which had been formalized by the Council on April 20 of that year.[53] The American Geographical Society had made overtures to Jefferson on several previous occasions dating from 1909 when the Society had inquired if the position of Librarian to the Society would interest him.[54] In the 1920's Bowman again bombarded Jefferson with letters of invitation to join him at the American Geographical Society. The first of these letters was written on March 24, 1920:[55]

> *I am writing about a matter that is to be kept strictly confidential until we make some public announcement of it in the near future. We have initiated a plan for Latin America research which will extend over a period of years. One of the aspects of the plan will be the compilation of a map of Latin America on the scale of 1:1,000,000 so far as the data exist for the preparation of a map on this scale. Of course there are many other aspects of the plan, which will involve the creation of a research file and the publication of a series of "Geographical Notes*

and Monographs" into which, by the way, your present book will fall.

I hope that we may talk over the various aspects of the plan in some detail in the not too distant future. It was for that reason particularly that I was anxious to get the early completion of your book, if possible by having you work here during the coming summer, though up to the present moment I have not been able to write you anything about the general basis of my wish.

My present suggestion is that you consider carefully the possibility of securing leave of absence for one of the quarters next year, to include if possible the summer also, thus enabling you to give us six months out of the coming year for the completion of your book and the supervision of a portion of our map program. If it were at all possible to get you this coming summer we should like to do it. It seems to me that the plan ought to attract you in many ways. Here is the beginning of a program that will last for some years to come, we hope for many years to come. If you could get part time off at Ypsilanti, I think you would enjoy the change and it would also increase your salary. Our idea would be to pay you proportionally for your services, taking into account the extra cost of living in New York.

Won't you give this matter very careful consideration and let me know to what extent you feel you could assist in the carrying out of such a program? I suppose that you would not feel willing to give us all of your time, coming to the Geographical Society on a regular appointment for the year or for a period of years. Why don't you think over these matters and let me hear from you?

On June 19, 1920, Bowman wrote to Jefferson:[56]

I would like to have you keep in mind the matter of giving us time for research during the summer months hereafter. Possibly you could give us even more than this by some special arrangement with the Normal College administrative officers. You would enjoy the association, especially at this time when we are building up a strong staff. Teggart of the University of California is with us and will give us half his time from his university duties "and then some." Alan Ogilvie is resigning his position at the University of Manchester to join us in October, and he and Teggart will be a sort of right and left bower. McBride will return to work on land tenure, Marbut will do soils, and I am now thinking of getting Griffith Taylor for the climate of Latin America, sending him there from Australia to gather all the existing data. There are four or five other assistants, but more of these later.

Teggart by the way, has worked out the history of the Philippine galleon, including the subsidiary galleons at the Manila end of the route and also the subsidiary galleon that ran from Acapulco to Callas.

One month later, on July 19, 1920, Bowman wrote:[57]

. . . Is it within your power to say that if the salary were adequate you would be willing to agree to a five-year term of employment?

Again, on February 4, 1921, Bowman to Jefferson:[58]

As part of our program of research in the field of Hispanic America we shall want to undertake work in city geography. Don't you want to be associated with us in the task? If you could give the matter a little consideration from the standpoint of your part in the job and what books and other material we could get to start the work under your direction something might come of it . . .

And again, March 28, 1921:[59]

When would you be free for work here, and what salary would you require? Would it be possible for you during the three summer months to finish up your South American work for publication this year, supervising the drafting of such maps as you wish to include reading proof, etc? Could you in addition to this push forward some of the city studies perceptibly? These questions need not be answered now. You can answer them in conversation in April, unless you prefer a definite arrangement now in order to present to your people . . . .

Bowman urgently wanted Jefferson to be associated with his Latin American Research Program but Jefferson was not to be lured away from Ypsilanti. He did, however, write to Bowman of a talented student in one of his classes—a Raye Platt. On Jefferson's word alone Bowman promised to hire Platt at the American Geographical Society if Jefferson would give him one year of geography and all the Spanish possible in that time. Jefferson encouraged Platt to concentrate his studies on geography and the Spanish language and sent him to Bowman and the American Geographical Society.[60] When A. Ogilvie returned to the University of Edinburgh in 1923 to succeed the recently retired G. G. Chisholm, Platt was put in charge of the 1:1,000,000 map of South America.

Jefferson completed work on the Argentine manuscript in March 1924, then tussled with W. L. G. Joerg for two years on editorial matters before the book, *Peopling the Argentine Pampa,* was published in November 1926.

Peopling the Argentine Pampa was a carefully written account describing the processes through which the pastoral and agricultural peoples of the Pampa had passed. Jefferson's work traced the origin and history of neighboring provinces, singling out after careful and planned field work the original Swiss colonies of Esperanza and San Geronimo and other settlements along the San Javier River to the north of Santa Fe and the colonies of Entre Rios to the south. The historical and geographical influences contributing to the peopling of the Pampa were traced, the necessity of the railroad to commercial agriculture emphasized, and an analysis of immigration statistics comprised a concluding chapter—immigration being the vital force behind late nineteenth-century Argentine expansion. The book, in its completed form, was much more nearly a product of Jefferson's reflections on his experiences and recollections between the years 1883-1889 and his work in 1918 than his original notes, centering heavily on everything German, would suggest. The study was leavened with much contemplation and reading and benefitted from Inquiry researches undertaken by other men in 1918.[61] The benefit of his earlier acquaintance with Creole life in the Argentine was emphasized by Jefferson:[62]

> The background of the Argentine study is some familiarity with the Creole life of the interior acquired during a residence there before the immigrants reached Cordoba or Tucuman cities in any numbers, from January 1884, to November 1889, the first three years in Cordoba as computer, third and second astronomer in the National Observatory, and the last three as assistant manager and treasurer of the sugar ingenio La Providencia near the city of Tucuman. Whatever changes the Argentine interior had at that time experienced from the old Creole-ways had come, not from foreigners immigrant to America, but from the impressions made on Creoles in their visits to Europe.
>
> I had a certain intimacy with two or three delightful Creole families and some familiarity with the language and customs of the country. I have spoken in the text of the contrasts of those times and the present. Whatever characterization I have been able to make of the aspects and effects of newer immigration must rest mainly on that earlier acquaintance with the country; and it is a characterization, a picture that I have tried to draw—a picture of a vigorous infant agricultural society born in the midst of an ancient cattle culture.

Peopling the Argentine Pampa has been regarded by many as the finest book Jefferson ever wrote. Resultant from ABC Expedition field work in Brazil were the Jefferson written articles: "New Rainfall Maps of Brazil," "A New Map of World Rainfall," "Actual Temperatures of South America," "Pictures from Southern Brazil," and "An American Colony in Brazil." Jefferson was impressed with the industry, the thrift, and zeal of south Brazilian German colonists. He was quite convinced that Portuguese southern Brazil had absorbed the German colonies, and rendered them Brazilian rather than German. In his article, "Pictures from Southern Brazil," Jefferson wrote strongly of German accomplishment and order, denying the presence of Pan German sentiment by Brazilian Germans when he wrote:[63]

> *There have been reports in American newspapers about insurrections of Germans against the Brazilian government in Porto Alegre, but I can say with confidence that nothing of the sort ever happened.*

The New York *Times* noticed the article in a five-hundred-word editorial, "Brazil's Melting Pot," which emphasized Jefferson's belief in the Brazilianization of colonizing Germans in that country.[64]

The three climatological studies were largely the product of data he collected from Henrique Morize. Morize had constructed a map of Brazilian rainfall based on data from 349 stations. Jefferson had the map redrawn (using American Geographical Society cartographic staff) and compared the new product with Voss' map of 1907, which was the product of data from only 74 stations.[65] The map comparison, together with some discussion concerning reasons for aridity in northeastern Brazil, comprised the essence of "New Rainfall Maps of Brazil," which article was noticed in the *Scottish Geographical Magazine*.[66]

Jefferson's "An American Colony in Brazil," constructed from the notes and observations of Coester, was a very brief study of Villa Americana—"a bit of the southern Confederacy set down in Brazil." In the following years the article brought Jefferson correspondence from several historians who were studying post-civil war Southern attempts to recreate "Dixie" colonies in Brazil where slavery was not abolished until 1888.

The notes and studies resulting from the ABC Expedition were of value to the Inquiry, were of help in the Million map project,[67] strengthened Bowman's Latin America Program while in its infancy, provided good geographic reading in the English language for a sparsely literatured Argentine, Brazil, and Chile, and via the number of readers consulting the studies—or reviews of the studies—must have been influential in reshaping the prevalent image of the dominance of Empire Germans in South America.

CHAPTER EIGHT

MAP MAKING: THE INQUIRY AND PARIS
PEACE CONFERENCE

Early in August, 1918, Jefferson and Coester boarded a craft at Rio de Janeiro bound for New York. They were bringing home to the United States a rich South American experience, Jefferson's assurance that the German populations of Argentine, Brazil, and Chile felt no special sympathy for the German cause, and a wealth of materials from which later emerged *The Rainfall of Chile*,[1] *Recent Colonization in Chile*,[2] "Actual Temperatures of South America,"[3] "Pictures from Southern Brazil,"[4] *Peopling the Argentine Pampa*,[5] "An American Colony in Brazil,"[6] and "Real Temperatures Throughout North and South America."[7]

The passage from Rio to New York was not pleasant. Germany was at war with the United States and the world. Jefferson and Coester found themselves traveling north from Brazil on board a steamer carrying frozen beef to the British Army in France. The boat put in at Charleston for orders and was sent to New York via shallow water to avoid German submarines. Crossing Chesapeake and Delaware Bay entrances in deep water, the beef steamer was obliged frequently to change its course to avoid the dangers of an encounter with any lurking German submarines. Jefferson reports passing close to one burning tanker in Chesapeake entrance which had been torpedoed the previous night. The unusual circumstances had obliged the steamer to pass close off Palm Beach and Atlantic City, far inside the usual ocean routes, which pleased Jefferson, who took more than fifty photographs of the Florida and Georgia littoral.

On landing at New York, Jefferson hurriedly took himself to the American Geographical Society building to report the successful completion of the "ABC Expedition." On arriving at the Society's House, however, Jefferson was not to report to Bowman his activities of the last several months, rather was Bowman to report to Jefferson on his and the American Geographical Society's activity of the recently passed months. The Society was a hive of industry. It was serving as headquarters to the Inquiry, a body of experts, gathered together by Colonel House on the advice of President Wilson, to collect data that might be needed at the settlement of the World War after the cessation of hostilities. A traditional policy of isolation from the Old World coupled with no immediate experience of European peacemakers and war settlements left the United States without direction yet with a disinterested outlook through the Inquiry years of 1917 and 1918. This disinterested attitude toward Europe was the very potential of the American contribution to an enduring peace. The challenge of individual wants and national interests would surely be present; non-German Europe wanted its pound of flesh, wanted to "bleed the boche" while he was weak, wanted to humiliate the military machine as a salve to decades of suffering at the hands of German military arrogance. The European victors were not ready to forgive or forget the butchering of ten million bodies on European soil, nor the anguish, grief, and sorrow of four years war. Chateau-Thierry and Belleau Wood were still close, the possession of land had become a passion of European peoples all heady with national interest, who remembered countless billions of property damaged. Hunger was constantly present while peace raced with anarchy. Land laid waste by the war had to be restored, normal commercial and industrial life of warring countries had to be re-established, aggressors were to be punished, idealists dreamed of the New Jerusalem, and 27 different states were represented besides the five British Dominions. An impoverished and an impatient Europe, hungry for a "to the Victors belong the spoils" settlement, was being represented in the Council of the Big Four by a Lloyd George who was obliged by pledge to the English electorate to "hang the Kaiser," by a Clemenceau encouraged by a Foch anxious to extend French territory to the left bank of the Rhine, and by an Orlando, so intent on satisfying an Italian national interest that his delegation retired from the Paris Peace Conference when Italian claims to Fiume met with determined opposition.

These interests, whims, displays of strength were recognized; that was one of the tasks of the Inquiry. President Wilson, originator of the Inquiry and later self-appointed leader of the American Commission to Negotiate Peace in Paris, envisaged an enduring peace hammered out on the anvil of abstract justice which would make the world safe . . . . But a lasting peace could be wrought from the dismembered scene only if the issues were laid bare before the assemblage of European delegates. The President's faith in human nature encouraged him to believe that, confronted with fact and truth welded into a reasoned instrument of recommendation, the leaders and people of Europe would forego a settlement that catered to her immediate individual and national interests. Colonel House's Commission, the Inquiry, was just that body established to search for fact and truth. The Paris variety of Wilsonian idealism was born with the Inquiry: democracy, self determination, accommodation, justice became guide lines to Inquiry endeavors.

Following a brief residence in the New York City Public Library, the Inquiry was relocated in a suite of rooms on the third floor of the American Geographical Society in New York, November 10, 1917. Soon the Inquiry had expanded its operation to dominate the building whose resources included 50,000 books, over 47,000 maps, and an unknown number of periodicals. From November, 1917, until early in December, 1918, the Inquiry, one hundred and fifty workers strong, labored at the Society's house under guard. This was the scene a surprised Jefferson encountered on his return from South America. Traveling through Chilean desert, Andean pass, Argentine Pampa, and Brazilian plateau from the early days of 1918, he had received no news of this development from Bowman, owing in part to Bowman's preoccupation with the task in hand yet more probably to the desire for secrecy. Yet another surprise was due Jefferson—Bowman, who had recently assumed acting directorship of the Inquiry from an ineffective Mezes, proposed to Jefferson that he direct the map making program for the Inquiry. Jefferson, married to his second wife Clara only two years previously, had spent already some nine months away from home and family life in Ypsilanti. He had firmly resolved to stay home for a while and devote time to the family; thus he had written in letters home from South America, thus he spoke to Bowman. But above all else was Isaiah Bowman quietly persistent and determined. A few hours after Jefferson had reached Ypsilanti a letter arrived:[8]

Dear Professor Jefferson:

The so-called Inquiry, which is working under the auspices of the Department of State in gathering material for an eventual peace conference is in great need of a cartographer. The number of people in the United States who can handle a large cartographic program in a scholarly way is so small that I scarcely know where to turn for assistance. I have been waiting for your return from South America in the hope that you could give all your time to this work. After talking with you,

I recognize your obligations to the college and to your family and do not wish to urge the matter too strongly. Nevertheless if you could spend the coming month, or practically all of September in New York working upon the map program, I am sure your ideas and work would give us a great start in the right direction.

I hope you will consider the matter very seriously, both from the professional standpoint of the work itself, and from the standpoint of national service, and come for at least a month if it is possible to arrange it.

Sincerely yours,
Isaiah Bowman

Bowman certainly knew how to win Jefferson to his cause. The lure of an opportunity to dissect Europe at the American Geographical Society surrounded by maps and thinking men was too much of a temptation. Bowman had reasoned that much. He recognized Jefferson as one of the most competent cartographers of his day and one well versed in European lore. Also of great significance to Jefferson in his moment of decision were, "the pathetic letters I have received from Gallois and Chisholm." One such letter from Gallois, Jefferson had retained in a privileged file:[9]

. . . I know that the Germans pretend now that their troops had been the target of some shooting. In the region where I was, I can assure you that no one shot outside of the regular troops. And with what could the peasants have shot? With hunting rifles and revolvers against men whose gun range is 1000 meters or more? When you have seen, as I did, the unhappy people running ahead of the enemy with all they could carry, in cars, in carts, often in baby carriages you realize that the horde did not think about resisting, and still less at provoking retaliation.

What is the strangest thing in this war is the German mentality. It looks as though a crazy wind has blown on this country. Nobody thinks any more, everything that the Government says is believed word for word. It is with great stupor that I read in the Zeitschrift of the Berlin Geographic Society, an article called "Belgium" by our friend Partsch where he affirms that the whole responsibility falls on the King of the Belgians who entered, said he in the conjuration planned by the Occidental nations against Germany, and on the advice of his advisers for resistance contrary to the right of the people, and suggested it to the population.

They have shown, adds-he, cruelty and dissimulated savagery that before was believed to characterize only the low plebs of the big towns and Partsch is certainly honest. He believes naively that Belgian women blinded the poor German soldiers not capable of the least cruelty and other similar stories. It is despairing. One should not be amazed if there cannot be anything in common any more between a nation with such a mentality and the nations that force themselves to see clearly in everything and put good faith above everything.

I apologize for allowing myself to be so involved. I did not expect to write to you at such a length, but how to restrain one's heart from talking? What I also want to tell you is that we are all just as resolute as on the first day and that we all feel that the future of our country is at stake. We will not fail. Our troops behaved admirably; our young men are and still will be heroic and how many fell and walked to their death without regret. It is a destroyed generation. Of all the ones you knew the youngest are in the army: Herbette, Baulig and the others. Demangeon and de Martonne are with me at the Geographical Service, Vacher who before the war had a very serious surgical operation is not in shape to walk. Maybe you remember a young student called Brienne who was with us at Brive. He was killed in the Argonne and how many more with him among our best students. Denis has had one brother killed but fortunately nothing has happened to him yet. There is no family that does not have its victims. I have a son who was severely wounded and whose right hand is still paralyzed and he thinks only about returning to the front. It is a beautiful youth and everywhere the spirit of the public is excellent. There will not be any faltering and since the war is a war of harassment we will see who will hold the longest. Neither the English nor we will give in. The Russians can move back but their army is always solid and their reserves in men inexhaustible.

Believe me your devoted,

Gallois

Bowman's selection of Jefferson as Chief Cartographer to the Inquiry was one of the most vital decisions made by any one man which affected the composition and performance of the American Commission which was destined to negotiate Peace at Paris. A concise, rapid, and initiate cartographic team was pivotal to the entire work of the Inquiry. Bowman was undoubtedly imbued with a realization of the importance of the chief cartographer's post, for he kept this position open for ten months after the formation of the Inquiry, permitting Cyrus Adams and John Storck to give their part-time help to the acquisition and drafting of maps that were thought needed. Early in June, 1918, a "Guide of the Map Program"[10] by John Storck was released, which contained a vague statement concerning the assets of the cartographic program, its wants, some recommendations and a miscellany of mechanical problems as that of the spelling of place names. It is clear from this account that the Inquiry map program was little advanced at that time.

Jefferson soon caught the spirit of Inquiry fever and began to gather together maps already in the American Geographical Society collection and the State Department, ordering those that were needed, and compiling those that would be needed. He selected as his first assistant Charles Stratton, a student who had graduated from the Michigan State Normal College in 1914. Stratton had pursued geography as his major area of study, excelling in map making under Jefferson. Stratton was always willing to learn, eager to please, precise in form, and the possessor of an approach and personality that complemented well that of Jefferson. Other members of the Inquiry associated with its mapping and cartographic section include:[11] C. Besswerger, W. J. Blank, J. W. Braback, W. Breisemeister, M. Cawood, S. Davis, D. Johnson, D. Krisch, A. K. Lobeck, W. F. Mathews, H. Nagel, H. D. Ralphs, Ellen Semple, E. Taidor, R. Wiget, and C. Wittenberg. The work of the cartographers, who by late October numerically comprised the largest section of the Inquiry, proceeded smoothly, and by mid-November the equipment of the cartographic section included: 100 copies each of 60 base maps of problem areas; approximately 1,000 maps from collections of the American Geographical Society; 5,000 books in diplomatic history, colonial history, geography, economic resources and ethnography; "present archives" consisting of reports and manuscripts and correspondence files.

On November 30, 1918, Jefferson received a letter from Secretary of State Lansing confirming Bowman's recommendation:[12]

> *You are hereby appointed to the staff of the American Commission to Negotiate Peace as Chief Cartographer, your salary to be at the rate of $550.00 a month, to begin on December first.*
>
> *The actual and necessary expenses of transportation and subsistence will also be allowed.*
>
> R. *Lansing*

Jefferson was Chief Cartographer of the American Commission to Negotiate Peace in Paris and significantly at a salary only inferior to those of Director Mezes ($825 per month) and I. Bowman, A. Young, and C. H. Haskins ($600 each per month). His qualifications which were responsible for his appointment to this position warrant attention.

It was clear that by 1918 Jefferson was a champion of the cartographic cause. He had been drawing maps since his days with the Argentine Geographical Society, had continued this habit through his high school teaching years, under Davis at Harvard and at the Michigan State Normal College where he had introduced courses in mapwork.

Bowman well knew of Jefferson's enthusiasm for "putting it on a map," for he had studied under Jefferson, 1901-1902, had been his assistant at Ypsilanti's Normal, was aware that Jefferson collected atlases with the same zeal that he collected books, had traveled to Davis and Harvard at the suggestion of Jefferson, and later used Jefferson's map outlines when he taught at Yale from 1905-1915. Following Bowman's departure from the Normal, he and Jefferson maintained a steady correspondence with each other that kept them both informed of the other's works and thoughts; in these letters Jefferson frequently described maps planned and accomplished. The impress of Jefferson's conception of geography on Bowman was profound and maps were a vital part of Jefferson's geography. After Bowman had been elected Director of the American Geographical Society in 1915, Jefferson took the opportunity to be firm with his former pupil and insist that bigger and better maps should be an important part of the Society's new leadership. "I am contending for recognition of the map as the geographer's language. If you do not join me in this I shall feel that you are no credit to your teachers."[13] In the same vein Jefferson insisted that the American Geographical Society should prepare a good base map of North America. "Everybody needs a good base. The A. G. S. will get it all back in sales if it will let us have them! Make one at 1:7,000,000 another about 1:30,000,000. There must be an immense demand, for in my dark corner, all unknown and unadvertised as I am, come in to me orders enough for my little base maps to make quite a little income. You ought to make the best base possible and advertise it earnestly."[14] Jefferson's cartographic influence was further felt at the Society when it prepared city maps of the United Kingdom, Europe, North America and Japan for his Presidential address to the Association of American Geographers in December, 1916. When Bowman wrote Jefferson, "A recent ruling of the Council makes it possible for me to allot space rates to maps which in my judgment are contributions of equal or greater importance than the text,"[15] he was meeting a Jefferson request. Later in the month the Council of the Society encouraged this cartographic trend by appropriating more money for such work after viewing Jefferson's 1916 Presidential address "city maps."

In July 1917 Jefferson's *Notes on the Geography of Europe*[16] was published, essentially for the use of his classroom students. Of the book, Bowman commented,[17] "I am delighted with your Geography of Europe . . . . I know of no one in this country who is doing such good work in map reproduction and certainly no one else is publishing such stimulating comment." The twenty-nine maps of the book bear witness to Jefferson's continued interest in cartography, while the work itself provided an indication of Jefferson's continuing interest in Europe. Prior to publication of his *Notes on the Geography of Europe* he had published several articles concerning Europe—"Caesar and the Central Plateau of France,"[18] "Man in West Norway,"[19] "The Culture of the Nations,"[20] "New Density of Population Map, Europe,"[21] "The Distribution of British Cities and the Empire,"[22] and several more concerning or involving cartography, "Note on the Expansion of Michigan,"[23] *Twenty-Eight Exercises on Topographic Maps,*[24] *About Nets for Map Drawing,*[25] *On Drawing Michigan,*[26] *World Diagrams—A Supplement to Teachers Geography,*[27] *Commercial Values—An Atlas of Raw Materials of Commerce and Commercial Interchanges.*[28] By 1918 Jefferson was competent in the use of several European languages—French, Spanish, Portuguese, German, Italian, Norwegian, Danish, Greek and Latin—a significant and meaningful accomplishment both for his European studies and for work with the Inquiry, since representatives of many foreign powers visited the Society's rooms in New York to express their hopes, their country's national interests, their anxieties. Jefferson had visited Europe twice in the year 1889, again in the years 1904 and 1911. A vigorous and extensive correspondence with many of Europe's leading geographers, some of whom he encountered personally on the occasion of the 1911 geographer's trip through Wales, England, and France for the scheduled 1911 International Geographical Union Congress, Rome, and again during the 1912 W. M. Davis Transcontinental 13,000 mile Excursion of the U.S.A., helped develop Jefferson's appreciation for Europe and Europeans. He was well read in European history, ethnography, economics, soil patterns, and land forms, but above all was he aware of man in Europe. *Man in Europe*[29] was indeed the title of the next geography book he wrote concerning Europe, published in 1924. Jefferson intended to extend his population studies and attempt to make the war intelligible to the world. He wrote Bowman a brief outline of his ideas which received further elaboration in *Notes on the Geography of Europe*—[30]

> *Cities, towns, and villages and their relations to the tilled land, the great plains inevitably the basis of all strong peoples and vigorous civilizations, the present war merely the most violent stage in the struggle for the hegemony of the great plains of northern Europe, where Germany felt hemmed in between Russia on the East and France on the West, while the plain of England was envied her safe aloofness across the channels silver strand . . . .*

Bowman, whose geographic interest was centered in South America, knew little of Europe; Bowman through the experience of association, also knew how to work with Jefferson. The arrangement proved admirable.

Interestingly, Charles Seymour has written of the functioning of the Inquiry:[31]

> My impression is that in the earlier stages of the Inquiry Bowman turned constantly to Jefferson for advice and that the latter exercised strong influence on the studies made during the autumn of 1918. In fact I should say that three men ran the Inquiry: Bowman, as virtual executive officer and in his organization of research actual chief of the organization; Lippmann with the clarity of his journalistic sense as organizer in the presentation of materials and conclusions of research; and Jefferson, as director of techniques. His influence with Bowman certainly continued at Paris.

Very early in December, 1918, the material that the Inquiry had assembled was loaded into three army trucks, carried to the *U.S.S. George Washington,* and deposited on board. On the morning of December 4, the Inquiry specialists,[32] their assistants, clerical personnel, the French Ambassador, Italian Ambassador, American Ambassador to England, Commissioner Plenipotentiary Henry White, together with the President, Mr. Wilson, assembled for departure to Paris. The *George Washington* left that same day bound for Brest; hence it was arranged that the American Delegation to Negotiate Peace would continue their journey to Paris by train. For ten days the American argosy of peace pitched and lurched its erudite way across a winterous Atlantic. "On board, fourteen of these men, the Inquiry specialists, were called in to Mr. Wilson's office on the George Washington on the voyage to Europe and told that he relied on them to keep him informed at every point of the discussion of matter that he should have in mind—they had access to him he added at any moment for this purpose." At this time the President inspired the scholars of the Inquiry in proclaiming,[33] "Tell me what's right and I'll fight for it. Give me a guaranteed position;" the President impressed the same group with his sincerity when he insisted that if the forth-coming conference failed "he would be ashamed to return to America, would look around for an out-of-the-way spot, Guam perhaps, to retire to . . . the world is faced by a task of terrible proportions and only the adoption of a cleansing process can recreate or regenerate the world."[34] These and other Wilsonianisms did much to develop in the American Delegation a community of purpose together with a sense of obligation above and beyond the mere selection of facts and figures. It was on board the *George Washington* and more especially while Wilson was blessing some food before an evening meal, that the President's simplicity and reverence for life moved Jefferson to rethink his obligations with the delegation which he now more clearly recognized as a moral force. No longer did Jefferson consider the making and supervising of maps to be his only concern; he would lend his energies to the conference whenever they were needed.

The ten-day voyage of the *George Washington* gave all members of the Peace delegation time to think, time to digest their statistical work in New York, and time to recognize the responsibilities and obligations which the Paris conference would confer upon them. Jefferson reports, the promenading on deck, the salt of the sea singing in the air around their persons, did them all good.

The entry of the *George Washington* into France was imposing. Jefferson wrote:[35]

> *Yesterday was most moving when we came into Brest. The night before we were accompanied by five destroyers and a battleship, the* Pennsylvania, *which led us across the Atlantic. This morning nine other dreadnoughts joined us and twenty four destroyers from the British station. The day was bright, with mists ahead, on the land. The escorting warships drew in close and formed an imposing picture with bright sunlight on their clean grey sides. Only the two destroyers that had come across the ocean with us were streaked with gaudy camouflage. Near noon nearly a dozen French warships came out on the right of our line each firing the Presidential salute of 21 guns as they came abreast, a fearful din. We did not answer. As we drew close to the anchorage the dreadnoughts formed two lines down which we passed very slowly. The crews of all the ships stood at attention along their sides and the band on each struck up the Star Spangled Banner as we came opposite, closing with a cheer as the next ship began. Then we dropped anchor at the end of the line and our guns fired the President's salute of 21 guns. Followed a long series of receptions by French officials who came out on a tender with military and naval notables, among them Admiral Sims and General Pershing. Rather a feature of the ceremonies was Sim's gruff inquiry of Pershing, how in Hell he did it, which made a foreign statesman's lady ejaculate. Then a tedious preparation of landing and the landing, more speeches and receptions ashore and the President's train is off. Ours started two hours later, most luxuriously supplied with food and even drinks. However we soon passed the President as we could arrive in Paris at 7:30 but he must not reach Paris before the time for official reception at 10!*
>
> *I am quite content not to be President . . .*

The American Delegation to Negotiate Peace was housed in the Hotel Crillon, fronting the Place de la Concorde, close by the Champs Élysées and the Tuileries, not far from the Seine. Jefferson reports "we have beautiful quarters in a heated, luxurious hotel with white bread, butter and sugar, all we want," and from this vantage point wrote on his first day in Paris, while standing on a table:[36]

Paris is tremendous. It is making a holiday of the reception to Mr. Wilson, and all the world is on the street. Such crowds! Soldiers everywhere, not so trim looking as at home. So many uniforms soiled and stained and rained on, so many shoes sodden with water. They are terribly earnest-looking and business-like, these French soldiers. Not so fine-looking, nor so young as our boys, middle-aged men innumerable. There is much variety in their uniforms too, and many English and Americans, but the horizon blue tinges the crowd. It was fine when the President drove down the Rue Royale in an open carriage, a little body of cuirassiers accompanying, but the blue ranks edging the front of the crowd along the whole immense distance in sight. The Place de la Concorde fronts our hotel. It is immense and wide open. In groups about it are almost endless parks of captured German cannon. Yet space remained for thousands and thousands of spectators. But the roadway was wide open between the blue borders on either side. The crowd was not noisy. There was some cheering of course, some firing of guns, and the surface of the crowd alive and amove with waving hats. Some noise of trumpets, and the oddest scurrying of people across open backgrounds to get to viewpoints. One girl is hustling along a hand cart, on which she means to stand. Two others are running with a step ladder they mean to set up behind the soldiers. Come to think of it I am standing on a table back of a second story window myself like many others. But somehow it was wonderful. It seemed as if France, all the French people were here.

It is astonishing how little of fine clothing is in sight too, here in Paris, the beautiful, the lovely city. Are all the fine-clothed people that thronged these streets foreign visitors now barred from the scene? Or have the French exhausted themselves in more vital things? I do not know the answer, but I am immensely impressed by the crowd. Mostly the soldiers, except American ones, have mother, wife, or sweetheart on their arms.

Another strange thing about the Parade was its brevity. No national hymns were played, only some bugle calls. I have come to feel an almost veneration for the President as I have learned to know him and listen to him explaining his hopes and aims. But I seemed to see him fall into insignificance beside the great people assembled here to welcome him. Not that he is less the great ideal statesman beside them, but France is so impressive.

A room in the Hotel Crillon became his home for the next six months. He came to know it well. He ate at the Hotel Crillon, slept at the Hotel Crillon, met friends and geographers at the Hotel Crillon, and made maps at the Hotel Crillon. The purpose of the arrangement was doubtless to save time, to keep the men of the American delegation constantly at work, but this result was unkind on a Jefferson who worked so intensely and whose body would have appreciated an enforced walk to the Crillon from another place of habitation. His room and its four walls became a bother to him: he knew its size, shape, the color and design of its wallpaper, the iron bed that was his sleeping place, the view of the Champs Élysées and the Square before the Seine. He knew the flaws of the ceiling, the plumbing, the way his clothes hung in a closet, the creak of the floor boards, and the habits of the hotel attendants. Alone with his work, he knew he had to be alone, no one could help him with it even if they wished, he yet had a faithful and reliable second in command in Charles Stratton. Further, Jefferson's group of draftsmen proved one of the most efficient at the Paris conference. Jefferson was a man alone at Paris . . . alone in middle age, alone without his Clara and children, without his home, his books, his correspondence, deepest friends of the Normal, and also his students. He had come to Paris directly from the Inquiry work, and he had been urged to New York, place of work of the Inquiry, by Isaiah Bowman barely a few days after completing a tiring and unsettling A.B.C. excursion. Never sustained by the delightful illusion of success, Jefferson committed his life and integrity irrevocably to the struggle, seemingly never to tire. Sustained by ideas, and the quietly exuberant, and of course, inner optimism of his understanding, he found time to explore the material domain of his resources as a man and a writer. This latter exploration was probably brought on by the mood of Paris. A man had to look to himself for hope and encouragement, not to a society harassed and badly frightened after more than four years of war. Jefferson began to maintain a diary. It was his talisman. The diary did not become a formal log of events in the world peace headquarters, but a simple sketch of happenings to which he had been witness during the course of each day. The scenes he depicted on sheets of "American Commission to Negotiate Peace" letterhead paper, held together by a shoelace through holes made by a knitting needle or some similarly crude device, are above all, realistic. Jefferson was not writing for posterity. He could hardly have envisioned his rudely scrawled and tersely compiled thoughts being included one day in archival deposits as a vital part of the recorded history of the Peace Conference. The diary was maintained for the period, January 17, 1919 to May 13, 1919.[37] Entries convey the tone of Conference work; its earnestness, hard pace, the mingling of scholarly minds, a sense of social exchange, the clash of national interest, the leavening force of idealism. The diary, hitherto unknown, leaves one a little breathless from a first reading, but the writer had the ability to single out meaningfully from the fabric of the days' events those issues and circumstances that warranted record, then to paint them with large Jeffersonian sweeps of the pen. Personal irritations, too, were recorded. Of much concern to Jefferson was the inability of the hotel to satisfy his breakfast habit—continental style, and in his room at 8:00 a.m. For Monday, January 27, the entry in his diary reads:

> *Breakfast in room at 8. How unFrench. Coffee with milk, American preserved cherries, prunes, pineapple and peach and two fried eggs and two slices of cold toast. Well served, but the toast hard, cold, and unbuttered. Hot toast cannot be had. The coffee is usually quite* warm. *There are no croissants so the old time petit dejeuner is out of the question. But I think the whole hotel is demoralized by our unsuccessful attempt to serve American food in France.*

Numerous other references in his diary to breakfast inadequacy doubtless contributed to his lack of happiness while at Paris. Jefferson was quite particular about what he ate and when he ate it. (During his work with the Inquiry in New York, his wife had regularly sent him loaves of home baked bread.) His attempts to have legitimate French bread smuggled into the hotel were thwarted. What may have seemed trivial to officials of the moment may well have conspired with other personal irritations to encourage his departure from Paris at an earlier date than might otherwise have been.

The American delegation, accommodated in the Hotel Crillon, converted that same hotel into delegation headquarters. Jefferson, his assistants, (Stratton and Lobeck) and draftsmen, were given two rooms in which to continue the cartographic program commenced in New York. The personnel of the cartographic section from Inquiry days had been changed. A new group of men fluctuating in number from 5 to 25 now constituted Jefferson's draftsmen, the number of draftsmen depending on the map needs of the Delegation and the availability of men. The men, borrowed from the American armed services, frequently had no knowledge of cartography, and had to be taught on the job. Among the more regular of the draftsmen were Stubbs, Blank, Morgan, Young, Maher, Deitch, Harp, White, VanTrees, Fryer, Carrier, Wheat, and Wittenberg. Jefferson had power to have slackers and inefficient men court marshalled, though he never did use it. However, he frequently sought replacement for incompetents. The draftsmen's living conditions were frequently not good and began to irritate a Jefferson overburdened with numerous trivial yet time-demanding matters in addition to his direction, supervision, and participation in the map-making program. On January 4, 1919, he sent the following memorandum to Bowman concerning a 24 year old junior partner in a New York law firm who was responsible for all photostat work.[38]

> *Memorandum . . . to improve conditions of Corporal Huber. Stratton*

got facts from Huber who is an unwilling informant. Huber is in charge of the photostat room. He sleeps with 8 soldiers—overcrowded, food is unsatisfactory, impairing his health. Room is not heated at all. He has two machines. Soldier help is not enthusiastic at all. He even lacks a table.

Reactions were slow to come from higher-ups. Jefferson became more irritated and more burdened as the winter wore on, as adequate accommodation was not secured for his made-over soldiers who wished to return to their homeland and as personnel were taken from him after he had trained them. As a product of these discontents he early desired to leave Paris and return to Ypsilanti. Hardships he would overcome but continued affronts to his opinion of what was reasonable drove him from Paris. On January 25th he sent a communication to Bowman announcing that his cartographic section was hopelessly overworked, and that his own son, Theodore Jefferson, was in France, available and a conscientious worker with experience in map making who could help the section. Bowman relayed the information and on January 28, Mezes sent a memorandum to Secretary Grew:[39]

Mr. Stratton, Assistant to the Cartographer, is quite overwhelmed by the work that falls to him. He is making every effort to keep up, but the task demands further assistance than is available. During the past week this Division has produced over 300 maps for the Commission. I recommend that if it be practicable the detail of Lieut. T. Jefferson of the Air Service be obtained from the military authorities for this purpose. He has had training in map work, and in kindred subjects that would make him to serve here admirably. Prompt action would be greatly appreciated.

Lieut. Jefferson's address is: Air Service, U.S. A.A.P.O. 724 (Issoudun).

The matter was dealt with by the Commissioners Plenipotentiary Friday, 31 January. The minutes of that meeting include the following:[40]

Herbert read to Lansing, White, Bliss, House . . . a memorandum prepared by the Secretariat, regarding a desire expressed by Dr. Mezes, to have Lieut. Jefferson of the Aerial Service in France assigned to the Commission as an assistant to the cartographer. General Bliss stated that he had received a confidential letter from Secretary Baker assigned to the Commission. General Bliss believed that too many assignments had already been made through personal friends and that the question of further assignments should not be considered until a study could be made of the present personnel on the Commission.

On February 3, 1919:[41]

> *Mr. Herter again brought up Memorandum No. 10 in regard to the assignment of Lieut. Jefferson to assist Mr. Stratton, assistant to the cartographer, and again the Commissioners requested that this question be postponed until the investigation of the Committee upon which Mr. White and General Bliss were both serving, had been completed.*

Jefferson's request had been an honest one and he felt abused by the manner of his rejection. He felt abused when other of the "experts" ordered maps from his office at a moment's notice, then criticized them freely and liberally after their completion without an awareness of inherent difficulties associated with the making of that specific map.

Early in February, the space allotted the cartographic program was increased to five rooms and an engraving apparatus was made available. Armed soldiers were posted outside the map rooms from morning till dusk and only the correct pass would gain admittance. Jefferson worked long hours with his map-making group, counselling, advising, suggesting, but always himself working on the maps. Bowman, concerned for Jefferson's health, mentioned time and again that his former teacher should try to delegate more work and responsibility. But that was not the Jefferson habit. He was regularly first to work in the morning, after breakfast in bed—a little indulgence that helped overcome the "invariably cold toast so unpalatable"—and last to leave the map rooms in the evening. His strength as leader of the map program derived from his own productive hand and from his personal example, which served as a model to the draftsmen. Jefferson was very happy in the knowledge that his maps were appreciated; enthusiasm in the delegation for his maps temporarily concealed his fatigue. "Am I busy? Rather! And they like my maps." He did not attend the receptions given for Colonel House or Secretary of State Lansing, did not have time to see the King of Italy who passed outside his map rooms December 18, 1918. His work was with the map, improving it, trying to make it speak. Determination, concentration and perseverance were his strengths. "It is a little touch of artistic sense, I think, that makes my work acceptable in maps. Surely I have a divine discontent with most of those I make."[42] Late in January he wrote,[43]

> *I do not study at all, apart from devising ways of showing up ideas on maps, which seems to go pretty well but is exhausting, especially overcoming the opposition of those who don't see what I am driving at. I have authority to have my own way, but always try to win them over, rather useless. The maps do it pretty often, my words rarely. I think I must be a very poor persuader.*

Jefferson, now 56 years of age, was severely taxing his strength, taking too little exercise and not sufficient rest: on Sunday, February

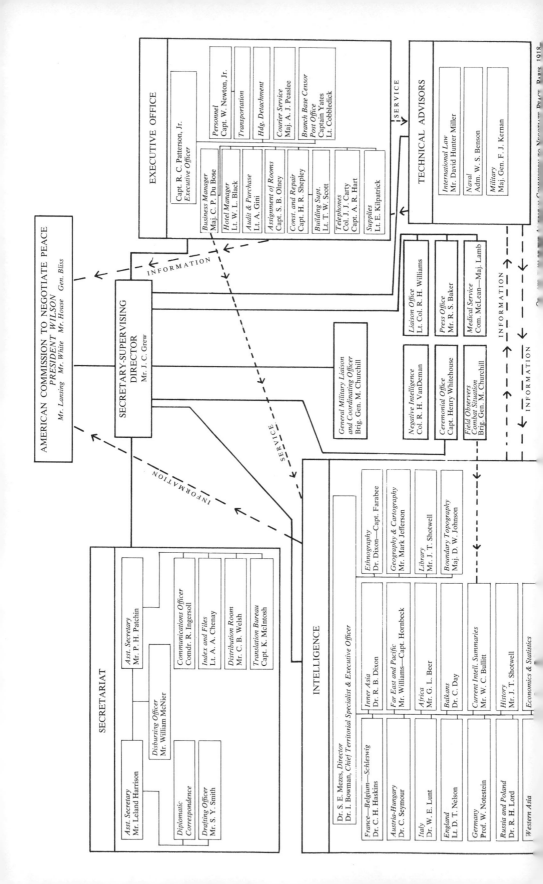

AMERICAN COMMISSION TO NEGOTIATE PEACE
PRESIDENT WILSON
Mr. Lansing   Mr. White   Mr. House   Gen. Bliss

SECRETARY-SUPERVISING DIRECTOR
Mr. J. C. Grew

EXECUTIVE OFFICE

Capt. R. C. Patterson, Jr.
Executive Officer

Business Manager
Maj. C. P. Du Bose

Hotel Manager
Lt. W. L. Black

Audit & Purchase
Lt. A. Gini

Assignment of Rooms
Capt. S. B. Olney

Const. and Repair
Capt. H. R. Shepley

Building Supt.
Lt. T. W. Scott

Telephones
Col. J. J. Carty
Capt. A. R. Hart

Supplies
Lt. E. Kilpatrick

Personnel
Capt. W. Newton, Jr.

Transportation

Hdg. Detachment

Courier Service
Maj. A. J. Peaslee

Branch Base Censor

Post Office
Captain Yates
Lt. Cobbledick

TECHNICAL ADVISORS

International Law
Mr. David Hunter Miller

Naval
Adm. W. S. Benson

Military
Maj. Gen. F. J. Kernan

SERVICE
INFORMATION

SECRETARIAT

Asst. Secretary
Mr. Leland Harrison

Asst. Secretary
Mr. P. H. Patchin

Diplomatic Correspondence

Drafting Officer
Mr. S. Y. Smith

Disbursing Officer
Mr. William McNier

Communications Officer
Comdr. R. Ingersoll

Index and Files
Lt. A. A. Chenay

Distribution Room
Mr. C. B. Welsh

Translation Bureau
Capt. K. McIntosh

General Military Liaison and Coordinating Officer
Brig. Gen. M. Churchill

Liaison Office
Lt. Col. R. H. Williams

Press Office
Mr. R. S. Baker

Medical Service
Com. McLean—Maj. Lamb

Negative Intelligence
Col. R. H. VanDeman

Ceremonial Office
Capt. Henry Whitehouse

Field Observers Combat Situation
Brig. Gen. M. Churchill

SERVICE
INFORMATION
INFORMATION
INFORMATION

INTELLIGENCE

Dr. S. E. Mezes, Director
Dr. I. Bowman, Chief Territorial Specialist & Executive Officer

France—Belgium—Schleswig
Dr. C. H. Haskins

Austria-Hungary
Dr. C. Seymour

Italy
Dr. W. E. Lunt

England
Lt. D. T. Nelson

Germany
Prof. W. Notestein

Russia and Poland
Dr. R. H. Lord

Western Asia

Inner Asia
Dr. R. B. Dixon

Far East and Pacific
Mr. Williams—Capt. Hornbeck

Africa
Mr. G. L. Beer

Balkans
Dr. C. Day

Current Intell. Summaries
Mr. W. C. Bullitt

History
Mr. J. T. Shotwell

Economics & Statistics

Ethnography
Dr. Dixon—Capt. Farabee

Geography & Cartography
Mr. Mark Jefferson

Library
Mr. J. T. Shotwell

Boundary Topography
Maj. D. W. Johnson

23, 1919, he fainted while bathing in his room and found himself the following week with a heavy cold, probably influenza. This merely confined him to bed for two days. Then he was back at work, motivated by will power and the spring warmth of Paris, to the consternation of Dr. Lamb, Delegation physician. Later, when Jefferson requested permission to leave the conference early in June, his task completed, Bowman wrote Secretary-General Grew:[44]

> *Professor Jefferson has devoted himself to the work of the Peace Conference in such a manner that I have been anxious about his health a number of times; in fact, he has actually been ill for several days at a time. All of the map work of the Commission centered in his office, and it was a case of working half way through the night to keep the wheels going, especially as he was undermanned during the first half of the work, just when the pressure was greatest . . .*

The value of the map had long been recognized prior to the Paris Peace Conference of 1919. Invariably, throughout the history of European peace negotiation, the map had been an integral part of settlement equipment; yet at Paris the map suddenly became everything. Never before had an American collection of maps been so carefully scrutinized, so accurate, so purposive in their numbers, so effective an instrument in negotiating peace. The ability of the map to show meaningful relations, to infuse life into columns of meaningless statistics, had not changed through the years beyond the increment contingent upon the advance of cartographic technique, but new objectives were in evidence at Paris. A just peace was sought by the Wilson-led American delegation; a peace that would not bow to the heady desires of European national interests, but a peace sought which would enable Europeans to live amicably together. But what was justice in the aftermath of the World War—the American delegation sought the answer in the map. Maps 6' x 4', 3' x 2', 11" x 8", 6" x 3", language maps, boundary maps, port maps, ethnographic maps, religion maps, city maps, coal maps, cereal maps, relief maps, political maps, outline maps were only some of the several hundred compiled, catalogued, and filed by Jefferson and his team.[45] Territorial decisions would at least be taken in a minimum of ignorance. Men's similarities and differences—the very stuff of war—would be noted. If justice were not meted out, it was not for lack of cartographic data, but from a lack of ability to define justice.[46]

> *Did the principle of justice permit the separation of East Prussia from Germany by the Polish Corridor, or did it demand that Poland be excluded from access to the sea and Polish populations be left under German rule? The principle of viability pointed toward the decision*

*that Czechoslovakia be allowed to maintain the historic Bohemian
frontier; the principle of self determination demanded with equal force
that the frontier be altered, so as to throw the German-speaking Bohemian group into the Reich.*

With the map and the abstract principle of Wilsonian justice, ill-
defined as it was, some three thousand miles of new boundaries were
created about the former states of central Europe: Bowman was later
able to write of this arrangement, "At no time in the history of Europe
have political boundaries more closely expressed the lines of ethnic
division or political sentiment."[47]

The map won acceptance as the most convenient method of carrying
information in a workable and readily usable form. It reduced 10,000
words to a concise expression. The map, with no word wastage, began
to replace the memorandum. The map became the universal language
of the American delegation at Paris and the international language of
the conference: a cartographic precedent. Copies of the original maps
compiled by Jefferson and his team were collected, reduced, and entered in the Black Book (European matters) or Red Book (Colonial
matters) of the American Delegation, which were constantly being consulted by the diplomats. In his diary for Friday, March 21, Jefferson
entered:

*Yesterday Warrin told me that over at a meeting at the English Com-
mission quarters the other day Lloyd George wanted to see the [Alsa-
tion] boundary of 1814. They could not show him any. Finally, someone remembered the American Black Book. There was one there, and
they pulled out our map for him!*

Nearly thirty years later he was to recall the matter in a letter to
Alfred Meyer:[48]

*Picture the Big 4 at Paris lying prone in Mr. Wilson's parlor on a 2
millionth of Europe till Mr. Lloyd George jumped up and asked for the
little black bible of the Americans containing the same things on the
scale allowing each map to be reproduced as a 7" x 11" sheet. The
large map is too unmanageable.*

The American delegation was not the sole possessor of maps at Paris.
Especially noteworthy was the mapwork and collections of maps rendered available by the Royal Geographical Society of Britain and the
Service Géographique of France, though all delegations had their own
maps. Bowman has suggested that some delegations used the map as an
instrument for the advancement of national interest:[49]

*Each one of the central European nationalities had its own bagful of
statistical and cartographic tricks. When statistics failed, use was made
of maps in color. It would take a huge monograph to contain an*

analysis of all the types of map forgeries that the War and the Peace Conference called forth. A new instrument was discovered—the map language. A map was as good as a brilliant poster, and just being a map made it respectable, authentic. A perverted map was a lifebelt to many a foundering argument. It was in the Balkans that the use of this process reached its most brilliant climax.

It is not known how many maps the section produced while in Paris. Frequently a map was made in a great hurry for one of the other sections of the American Delegation to illustrate relations that could hardly be expressed otherwise. Record was not always kept of such swiftly made, hand-drawn maps and duplicate copies were not made of them. Seymour and Day, with their requests for maps of Austria-Hungary and the Balkans respectively, probably made the largest individual demands on the cartographers. Maps needed by the other divisions of the American Delegation were noted by Jefferson. He would type a work order sheet for each map that was needed and assign the work to a draftsman. Many of these orders have been saved and sheets 1-64, 100-102, 486-792 are currently with the National Archives, in Washington D.C. Examples of the plan of these work orders made in New York and Paris by Jefferson are reproduced:

No. 534   Boundary of Ukraine
Base *Tracing from Stieler's Handatlas.*   *(Size 5.5 x*
For State Dept. Treaty Illustrations   *8.8 to be re-*
Date *Nov 12*   *duced to 4.4"*
Treatment   *in width.)*
Tracingcloth outline of boundary between Poland and Ukraine with the cities mentioned in the treaty lettered in and boundaries of the countries included in the single page area. To measure 4⁴⁄10 by 7²⁄10". Germany, Austria-Hungary, Poland, and Ukraine to be lettered on. And any rivers put in all detail that come close to the boundary of the Ukraine. From this drawing a zinc etching is to be made.
Draughtsman *Besswanger, 5 hrs.*
Material
Article II Treaty of Peace between Germany, Austria-Hungary, Bulgaria and Turkey and the Republic of Ukraine of Feb. 9, 1918, at Brest Litovsk.
Delivery
Completed Nov. 13. Sent to Electro Light Engraving Co. Nov. 19 for engraving.
Plates received and forwarded to Miss Bache-Wiig, 2 Jackson Place, Washington, D.C., November 25.

12 prints received Nov. 25.

No. 694a   Chantong Province, Railroads (694 corrected)

Base, *Section of International Corporation Map of China*

Date *Feb. 26, 1919*

For *Capt. Hornbeck*

Treatment

A corrected copy of 694

30 copies ordered 1:3,000,000

35 photostats received March 1, 1919

25 photostats received March 12

Material

Corrected copy of 694 with Typewritten instructions by Capt. Hornbeck.

Draftsman   *Blank*

Delivery

31 to Capt. Hornbeck March 1, 1919

1 to Dr. Bowman, March 1, 1919

28 to Mr. Wei, March 14

In Paris maps were not made only for specialists of the American delegation; Bowman requested Jefferson maps on orders from higher officials on numerous occasions and for other delegations . . . for example:

a) map 519 (National Archives). Rumania Language map. For professor De Martonne. Draftsman—Winget; 85 hours.

b) *Mark Jefferson, Paris Peace Conference diary* page 32. Entry for January 31, Friday, 1919.

> *Bowman told me China needed maps—30 copies to defend herself against Japan which was well prepared. I agreed to push it. Supper with Profs. Leith, Tower, and then Bowman joined us. Told him his map was being photostated, ready with one negative at eight. I worked on instructions to treat negatives in white to paint the thirty positives tomorrow. . . . Saturday morning, February 1, white work was finished before noon and photostats ready early p.m. at 3, I had colored one copy. Bowman came over to see. Approved but wanted more Japan added on map and a larger Shantung province. Designed that on our big China Base and sent up to photostat at 6 p.m. All first photostats done in color. Thirty-one copies at 7 p.m., Feb. 1.*

c) *Mark Jefferson, Paris Peace Conference diary* page 66, Tuesday, February 11, 1919. ". . . Seymour asked me to mount four Rumanian sheets, 1 millionth map for an English specialist. We buy the sheets from the English Government. We did it. Sent up two drawings to engrave . . . ."

And as Bowman has written:[50]

All delegations at the Peace Conference of Paris made wise use of the American maps and of the so-called Black Book and Red Book of the American delegation. These "books" were assemblies of proposed solutions of conference problems, the former of European problems mainly, the latter of colonial problems . . .

Unique in peace conference history was the map equipment of the American delegation. A full series of base maps of the problem areas of the world. This permitted (with the help of a photostat camera and a trained staff of draftsmen directed by Mark Jefferson) the daily preparation of maps in duplicate for all allied commissions that required them. An erroneous and misleading statement of the map program of the Inquiry and of the use of American maps at Paris appears in Mezes chapter in "What really happened at Paris."

Always there were maps waiting to be made: the demand was seemingly insatiable. On completion of a map Jefferson would scrutinize it. If the map were not satisfactory it would be redrawn. Usually Jefferson would consult his draftsmen while they were constructing the map, and so few maps were rejected. Some months after the American Delegation returned home Jefferson suggested to Bowman that Charles Stratton should compile a list of all the maps prepared by the American Delegation, both in New York and at Paris. Bowman thought the idea a good one, for Stratton had been curator of the map collection both at the Inquiry and Paris Peace Conference Headquarters, but the work was never undertaken. Currently these maps remain scattered in various archival deposits and are not to be found in one convenient collection. Jefferson did manage to collect copies of the maps that left his offices, and occasionally managed to retain a hand produced map, when no other copy had been made, by inquiring after it. In this way he brought back a fine collection of Peace Conference maps to Ypsilanti in the June of 1919. Later at the request of Bowman, Jefferson donated the larger part (329 maps) of his collection to the American Geographical Society, where scholars would have easier access to them. These maps have since been transferred to the Seymour Peace Collection, Yale University. A complete inventory of all the maps produced was never accomplished although Jefferson presented the matter as one of significance to Bowman:[51]

I have just received the letter and circular of the National Research Council, division of geology and geography. My capitalisation. Someday it will be division of Geography and Geology, with the wide-content subject first and the narrow one last!

It gives me an idea, a desire to write, to the chairman, to you, to

Stratton, to the librarian of Congress. As I have no stenographer, I am going to pass the idea to you. I cannot write so many letters. I shall have no objection at all to your adopting the idea if you like it.

It is the deliberate organization of a subject-list of important maps, classified by countries and subject matter. Such a working list as we had there in Paris with the gaps (i.e. Cable maps) filled. Besides a brief description of the map with statement of publisher and price, a statement of the libraries where the map was to be found and an arrangement by which photostat copies could be reproduced by those libraries on application, if the map was not obtainable in the market. A committee definitely organized to campaign for difficult maps, like those of administrative subdivisions, mineral deposits, and asking people like the Inquiry members to name desideratum.

Only modern maps, say since 1875 or latest map before that, if none after. Only best maps, accepting badly someones judgment. Stratton could comment on the maps he has a list of admirably, for a starter. I think he has an amazing fund of critical knowledge of the list at present, but of course it will fade with time and soon go.

In fact all the Inquiry members could be useful and I am sure they would be glad to, in view of the great service opened to them. I am not sure whether the Library of Congress or the AGS would be fitter patron.

Why not?

Bowman's reply was favourable to Jefferson's suggestion:[52]

Thanks, too, for your suggestion of a subject list of important maps, classified by countries and subject matter. An excellent idea. Let us set Stratton to work upon it at once. Nothing that he could do would be more valuable at this time and it would help him in his work . . . It is as precisely as you say! Why not?

But the maps were not assembled in one collection nor has a complete inventory of these maps ever been made. Original maps, photostat maps, and other types of map reproduction rendered more confusing the task of inventory, as did four cataloguing systems which have been applied to this one body of maps. The only readily available inventory, which is of a provisional nature, and which is admittedly incomplete, has been compiled by James B. Rhoads.[53]

The little known Geographers Commission of the Conference was born on February 2, 1919, when Mr. Dutasta, Secretary General of the Peace Conference, wrote to Secretary Grew of the American Delegation:[54]

. . . Concerning another matter, it appears as though there is interest in bringing together in a Commission as soon as possible the represent-

atives of the Geographical Services of the Great Powers taking part in
the Peace Conference, to study certain cartographic questions relative
to the maps furnished to this Conference.

Consequently, I shall be obliged if you will request Mr. Mark Jeffer-
son to assist at the first session of the Geographers Commission which
will take place under the presidency of Divisional General Bourgeois,
member of the Institute. Director of the Army Geographic Service,
140, rue de Grenelle . . . .

Grew requested Jefferson to attend the first session to be held, February 6, 1919, and informed Mr. Dutasta that he had so directed Jefferson. The Geographers Commission had been brought into existence. It
was not a direct creation of the Supreme Council, but was self-consti-
tuted upon the motion of Colonel Hedley, Director of the British Geographical Service of the Army, for the purpose of studying, together
with representatives of other Governments, "the proposition that the
International 1-1 Million Map be accepted as the official map of the
Conference."

Members of the Commission initially included Captain Maury—
Belgium; Colonel Hedley and Captain Ogilvie—Britain; General Bourgeois, Colonel Bellot, and Captain Pepin—France; Captain Romagnoli
—Italy; Colonel Nagai—Japan; and Mark Jefferson—U.S.A. Jefferson
was the only civilian on the Commission, neither West Point nor Annapolis recognizing the subject of geography at that time. The group
functioned well and the civilian felt quite at ease:[55]

I sit at General Bourgeois' left, Colonel Hedley (U.K.) at his right. At
first I spoke in English letting my old friend Major Ogilvie translate for
me but very soon I took to French too and get along better. I lack
vocabulary somewhat, but find myself appealed to quite naturally to
translate when French is needed. I have to laugh to find myself making
suggestions to a French General as to the correction of phrases in our
procès-verbal or report of meetings! But they are polite and take it
admirably.

The first two sessions were held on February 6 and February 10
respectively. At the latter meeting it was agreed that General Bourgeois
should send a report of accomplishment to Mr. Dutasta, Secretary General of the Peace Conference, and await his pleasure. Their good work
and potential use in helping define and delimit boundaries encouraged a
closer attention from the General Secretariat, who on March 28, 1919,
announced an official Geographical Commission of the Conference, and
that its powers were defined as follows:[56]

Coordination of the cartographic work concerning frontiers;
Selection of the best maps;

Tracing frontier lines;

Preparation of instructions for boundary Commissions.

Initially the geographers had been assembled to discuss the scale of maps to be used in the Conference. Extension of the geographers' meetings and the birth of the group as an official commission of the Conference may have been attributable in part to a Jefferson suggestion:[57]

> *Having learned that a commission of lawyers of the allied powers was going over the language of the Treaty as it left the hands of the Big Five to make sure that it would be able to meet legal assaults of later days, it occurred to Jefferson that there was an equally important chance here for geographers. The treaties were constructing new boundaries many miles long. Boundaries always offer the best possible grounds of quarrel, if men are inclined to quarrel. The descriptions of these boundaries by men neither acquainted with the ground traversed nor able to read the nature of the ground from maps, would be full of opportunity for real misunderstanding.*
>
> *What could be more useful than that men who were in the habit of reading maps and could study the ground in our chairs of the French War Offices, should go over the lines as delineated and where the delineations ordered would be impracticable on the ground, or would involve consequences unexpected by their authors, we should make suggestions leading to realization of results intended.*
>
> *They had been empowered by their several nations to select the maps on which the boundaries proposed should be marked out and to which the treaties might refer, but had no mandate from their governments to study the technical details of boundary description. Jefferson suggested that Captain Pepin, who was present in behalf of Marshal Foch to observe at the meetings, might intimate that if Marshal Foch should ask them to undertake such a study they were sure they could offer useful hints.*
>
> *At our next session Marshal Foch sent just such a request and they proceeded to comply with it.*
>
> *Governments must pretend to an infallibility quite beyond their capacities.*

The third meeting of the geographers which constituted the first meeting of the official Commission was held on April 5, 1919. Other meetings were held at frequent intervals until October 8th, by which time it had convened on 26 occasions. Jefferson participated vigorously in the first 12 sessions of this Commission prior to his departure from Paris on June 1. The personnel of the group remained little changed through those weeks; Major Wynne was immediately added to the British Delegation, and at the ninth Session of the Commission, May 13, Captain

Stoyanovitch representing Serbia was added. Whereas the meeting of February 6 concerned itself with the selection of a Conference map, and the second meeting of February 10 had been a request for direction from the General Secretariat, the meetings from April 5 forward concerned themselves essentially with the study of state boundaries. The subject matter of discussion included: Sessions III-IV—procedure; Session V—Examination of the frontiers of Czecho-slovakia; Sessions VI, VII, VIII—Examination of the frontiers of Germany; Session IX—Examination of the frontiers of Austria; Session X—Examination of the frontiers of Hungary; Sessions XI-XII—Study of instructional procedures to be given to the "Commissions of Delimitation."

Jefferson participated vigorously in these sessions, which were recorded in a little known but significant Parisian publication of 1932— *Recueil Des Actes de la Conference; Partie IV Commissions de la Conference; 9, Commission de Géographie.*[58] His contribution included: insistence on the worth of a map 1:200,000 rather than 1:1,000,000 for mapping the new state frontiers; demonstration that the word, *"Thalweg,"* was the source of much misunderstanding; a written note concerning the effect that river behaviour might exert on international frontiers; presentation of a study concerning Rumanian boundaries.

It was on April 11 that the Secretary General of the American Delegation received the following letter from the General Secretariat of the Peace Conference:[59]

Quai d'Orsay
Paris, 11 April 1919

Dear Sir:

The Secretary-General of the Peace Conference has the honor to inform the American Delegation that, with a view to studying from a technical point of view the tracing of the new frontiers proposed, a Commission of geographical experts comprising principally the representatives of the Geographical Services of the Great Powers; the United States of America, the British Empire, France, Italy, and Japan, and assisted if necessary by representatives of the Geographical Services of the other Powers, has been formed under the presidency of General Bourgeois, director of the Geographical Service of the (French) Army.

The duties of this Commission are:

a) At present:

  1. To choose the best map of large scale for the tracing of frontiers;

2. To transfer to these large-scale maps the frontiers proposed and at present drawn upon 1:1,000,000 maps in conformity with the request of the Central Committee of Territorial Affairs;

3. To study these tracings from a technical point of view, particularly from the point of view of future difficulties of delimitation.

These large-scale maps, as well as the technical observations which the Commission may express, will be communicated to the respective territorial Commissions.

b) In future:

1. To study the definitive tracings adopted by the Supreme Council of the Allies;

2. To prepare the instructions to be given to the Commissions for the delimitation of the new frontiers.

Seal: Peace Conference
General Secretariat

The Delegation gradually came to the realization that no American had ever been appointed to that Commission. Lansing tersely investigated the matter, sending memoranda to Jefferson through both Secretary Grew and Isaiah Bowman inquiring "if an appointment was ever made or whether he [Jefferson] was taking part in these meetings informally."

To Jefferson these terse inquiries bordered on the insolent; they were suggestive of personal advancement on his own initiative without official sanction. On May 12, Grew sent a memorandum to Herter that read:[60]

I have explained fully to Mr. Lansing Professor Jefferson's status on the Commission of Expert Georgraphers. Mr. Lansing agrees that Professor Jefferson is the proper official to represent the U.S. on that Commission and authorizes his appointment.

Too late. Almost at once Jefferson began to negotiate for his departure from Paris. He sought a replacement for himself on the Commission of Geographers and a skeleton staff for the maintenance of the mapping offices. Charles Stratton and Armin Lobeck wished to leave Paris with him. The cartographers had been seriously overworked and lack of consideration extended them contributed further to their unhappiness. Additionally, the essential work of the cartographic section had been completed. A skeleton staff of Corporal J. T. Deitch and Privates J. E. Van Trees and G. W. Wheat remained in the mapping offices as draftsmen, and Captain Scovell remained in charge of the photostat room.

On June 1, 1919, Jefferson left Paris. It was at this time that nine other members of the American Delegation to negotiate Peace also left

Paris, though their reason for departure was due to marked ideological conflict with the direction of the Peace Conference.

Colonel Theodore Dillon replaced Jefferson on the Central Geographical Committee and promptly informed Grew that "the work of the Geographical Committee does not seem to be important." After absenting himself from some meetings of the Geographical Committee, Colonel Dillon of the U.S. Engineers withdrew from the Peace Conference on August 1 and was replaced on the Commission of Geographers by Colonel D. C. Jones. Whereas Jefferson had played a major role in the work of the first 12 meetings of the Geographical Committee neither Dillon nor Jones attended or contributed much in the latter 14 meetings.

There were moments during Jefferson's five months stay in Paris when he was not in the map room, or sitting with the geographer's commission; in these moments he would "go out into France," perhaps to stroll along the Champs Élysées with Warrin, his favorite walking companion, "who had such a keen power of observation," visit a postage stamp fair with Leon Dominian, enjoy local theater, visit Jean Brunhes, receive Professor Romer or Paul Teleki, or talk geology with E. de Margerie. Yet it was a twelve-mile Sunday stroll alone through Melun, a quaint village with crooked streets, or through the forest of Fontainebleu, that Jefferson considered his pleasantest diversions. These walks enabled him to think. At table in the Crillon he listened much to Lord, Lunt, Dixon, Haskins, Putnam, but conversation did not allow him to think. On his walks he began to collect his thoughts concerning the vandal nation Germany, the Conference, the future. He was agreed with Wilson that the world should seek justice, but Jefferson felt that two Paris Peace Conferences were needed; the first conference to define the nature of the just,—the second conference to apply this truth to the problems of the world. He believed that there was a just solution to territorial adjustment in Europe. The just solution was that which was better than any other. To comprehend the just solution would require thorough understanding of Europe and an infinite amount of thought. He continued to think on this matter until his death in 1949; many scattered pages of handwritten and typed notes bear witness to the bothersome nature of this insoluble for him.

Jefferson had taken a very great interest in the proceedings of the Peace Conference. He had interrupted the write-up of his South American colonization studies (and that was part of the contract with the American Geographical Society), had invested much effort himself on the maps at the conference, had left his recently married second wife alone with the family, while in any case three of his sons had been directly involved in the war. He collected maps from as many delegations as possible, received aerial photographs of the war on the ground and the maps constructed from these—a new phase of military geography—carefully collected the literature which was being distributed by numerous delegations working in their own national interest. He made notes in the margins of works which had special interest for him and which included, "The Psychology of an Upstart Nation, The Bulgars," "The Dodecanese," "The Czecho-Slovaks," "La Question de L'Adriatique," "The Question of Scutari," "The Question of Istria," to "Pan Germanism," "Who Wanted War?," "The Violation by Germany of the Neutrality of Belgium and Luxembourg," "How Germany Seeks to Justify her Atrocities," "Conquest and Culture." Yet Jefferson was unhappy . . . dissatisfied.

Jefferson was not satisfied with the territorial settlement of Europe, his anxiety for the "Russian lost lands" could not be stemmed, neither was he happy that "the United States shamelessly allowed the scholars to whisper in the ears of the men with privilege of speech," at meetings of the Big Four ". . . Mr. Lansing appears quite reckless and cynical of an ignorance he does not acknowledge . . . He does not come informed. Would a lawyer dare to come to court with so little information about his client's case?"[61] He felt the specialists of the American Delegation were being abused when higher-ups began to make their own decisions without concern for the findings of the specialists, and he began to feel his labors were being wasted, witness the entry in his diary:[62]

> . . . they are surely finishing up fast. The Big Four has taken matters out of expert's hands much to the disgust of the experts, who thought their work was going to stand. On German-Bohemian frontier for instance Big Four disregarded a lot of little givings and takings along the frontier and said, "take the old line." In other words the experts did not exercise the sort of wisdom that was wanted. They mistook their role.

Jefferson did not feel the job was being done well and so wished to leave Paris. This desire to return to the United States was made known in several of the letters he sent to his daughter, Phoebe, in New York. Never could he express himself frankly concerning the "lost lands" in a letter, since this correspondence was invariably censored. In reply to his daughter's inquiry, "why do you wish to come home?" Jefferson once replied, "Ah, it is hard questions that my children ask me," but he did author some of the frustration that had been accumulating in him for several weeks.[63]

> I am a very impractical, foolish person, I admit, but you have no idea how useful to me and others too are the things I learned in my school

and college days and since. I know a lot of things about the geography of Europe that would save heaps of trouble that the Peace Treaty is pretty sure to arrange for as definitely as if the various Peace Commissions were planning it, if it were the common possession of the men who are going to close the affair! and they have listened to no end of tedious information too. They have had a hard time, I fear. Nothing is such a bore especially for statesmen, as to be handed out information.

Seymour has written of Jefferson's irritation and exasperation at the inefficiencies and inadequacies of some personnel:[64]

Jefferson was reserved in manner, rather brusque, direct and uncompromising in expression. He was critical of the memoranda handed him which he was to illustrate with his maps, and reasonably so, for the earlier studies of the so-called "experts" were often "amateurish," and still more often not applicable to the essential point. This was not surprising since we were given very little guidance in the preparation of memoranda. The "Men higher up" did not really know what they wanted. These uncertainties irritated Jefferson, although I rarely heard him complain of them. He liked his job to be clearcut and definite. He was careful never to complain of a colleague, although there were many occasions when I knew that he was exasperated by a sloppy report.

Jefferson was also quite distressed by the attitude of a new post-war France. In his diary for Monday, March 19, he wrote:

France is excessively selfish. She did not and could not win the war. She was saved by England, by Russia and by the United States. But she wants and is ready to cry for an old fashioned (1870) type of victory.

Twelve years later he wrote:[65]

In 1918 I went to Paris with Pres. Wilson in the George Washington as chief of the Division, and was there six months, getting an interesting view of the province of Oran, Algeria on the return. I did not find this visit to Paris pleasant. I had a number of friends in the University, geographers with whom I had tramped and driven across France and Switzerland in 1911 and travelled in our Transcontinental excursion across the U.S. the whole months of August and Sept. 1912. But all these friends—indeed all the Frenchmen I met after the war—were so transformed by the War experience, so insistent in pushing French plans and French ambition, regardless of the effect on other nations that I took no pleasure. I went to France pretty well aware of the details of that country's sufferings and of her immediate innocence of offence, and feeling for her a sympathy that I now feel considerably diminished. When we were discussing the details of certain proposed boundaries in the Teschen, our French chairman allowed himself to remark—"I don't see why a man should care whether he was a Pole or a Czech." Typical!

On May 31, 1919, after considerable negotiation Jefferson received a letter which read:[66]

Dear Professor Jefferson,

With the completion of your work with the American Commission to Negotiate Peace, we, the commissioners desire to extend to you, on behalf of the government which we represent, as well as personally, our warm thanks for the important services which you have rendered your country while on service here. The task of making peace has been great and arduous, and our country is indebted to those who, like you, have rendered such valuable service to the government.

You take with you the sincere wishes of the Commission for the future.

—Sad, for the signatures are but four, Robert Lansing, Henry White, Edward House, Tasker Bliss. Woodrow Wilson was already too ill to sign.

Permission to leave Paris by June 1 had been granted to Jefferson. Five days prior to his departure he attended the ceremony involving the presentation of the Cullum Geographical Medal to his friend and geographical acquaintance, Emmanuel de Margerie, by U.S. Ambassador Hugh Campbell Wallace at the United States Embassy in Paris. This was one of the rare occasions in Paris when Jefferson ventured into society, but he thought very highly of the work of E. de Margerie:[67]

This afternoon my phone was used by a young lady to call me and ask me to hold the line a moment. Then the secretary of Mr. Wallace, US. Ambassador to France called me. Mr. Wallace was to confer a gold medal on de Margerie tomorrow at 4, for the geographic society, not the National, *but the other, the American and would I be good enough to come? Surely, I knew M. de Margerie, and admired him. I would be very glad to and then I got particulars about the house and so on. Mr. Wallace will be very glad. It will only take you about twenty minutes.*

Now my heart doesn't beat any faster when magnates invite me, usually I shudder! Some weeks ago I had a card from Mrs. Lansing to attend her reception to meet the new American Ambassador, Mr. and Mrs. Wallace! I didn't want to go in the least and I didn't. I suppose they like a crowd at those things and I was to be part of the crowd. If you go in the crowd and attract attention *somehow you may be presently invited as yourself. This attracting attention is an odd stunt. You might do it probably by standing on your head, but I have a notion it*

*is better to only do it figuratively. I do not attract attention very well,
and do not make a good piece of the scenery so I mostly stay away.
Tomorrow, however, I shall not, for here M. Emmanuel de Margerie
comes into the story. He is a most charming French gentleman and
scholar. I met him first in 1912—Transcontinental Excursion. Man of
property, about my age, distinguished French geologist, speaks English
very well and knows more American geology than any one I know.*

*. . . I am glad to go and do de Margerie what honor I may, even if
I do have to go the the American Ambassador's house to do it!*

Jefferson and Stratton left Paris on June 1 and travelled south to
Carcasonne, where they enjoyed six days of sunshine. Two days were
spent visiting ancient buildings in Carcasonne and Nimes and two days
in Marseilles. Jefferson bought a vest pocket camera at an "absurd
price," but he simply had to take pictures after his stay of privation in
Paris. Some of them are reproduced in *Man in Europe,* 1924. Then
aboard the *Patria,* a steamer of the Fabre line, from Marseilles via
Straits of Gibraltar, Lisbon, and the Azores, the two men reached New
York 19 June.

During the following months in Ypsilanti he taught a course at the
Michigan State Normal College entitled "The New World." He also
presented an evening series of lectures to faculty and townsfolk concerning the war and the Peace Conference and gave many addresses in
the local community in praise of the League of Nations. He insisted the
boundary lines of Europe had been drawn in blood. In 1947, two years
prior to his death, he confirmed his gloomy prognostication in an embittered note to himself, "A Song of Victory":[68]

*. . . the blood of the First World War was not well shed, the treasure
was not well spent, men paid the price but did not get what they paid
for . . . an end of war and an advance of civilization.*

Jefferson had been convinced "the world was not safe" when he had
prepared maps detailing the accomplishment of the Brest-Litovsk
Treaty, and skillfully put the Treaty into approximately 750 words, in a
document which details national boundaries in the medium of description.[69] He did not consider the Treaty just. Its infamy haunted him until
his death. Perhaps the clearest expression of his discontent with the
"Russian lost lands" may be found in the first chapter of an unpublished manuscript, commenced in retirement, which he wanted to entitle, "A Geography for Grownups":[70]

*Germany lost World War I in 1918 and was penalized by the loss of
28 thousand square miles of territory—a little less than Belgium and
Holland together. The Russians counted it an almost unbearable grievance that they, who were first of all the Allies to go to the help of the*

invaded Serbians, who were the only Allies to advance promptly and deeply into Austrian and German territory, and who lost far more men in battle than any other of the Allies, should have a quarter million square miles wrested from them in the end! . . . The Soviet leaders pointed to their loss as an expression of the hatred of capitalistic nations for the Bolsheviks in the period from 1918 on, when they—as they saw it—were trying to realize a new experiment in human liberty . . .

BETWEEN WARS THE LOST LANDS DOMINATED SOVIET MINDS.

Through this period nothing was more in the minds of the Soviet leaders than this lost border land. What they believed was for them the truth. What the Allies believed was true for them equally. Perhaps God's truth did not exactly coincide with either view. Just such differences have led to war in the past and may again unless enough men and women take more thought than in the past. The Bolsheviks regarded the six nations created from the lost lands as a belt of enemy nations set up to oppose Socialism. The mass of the American people were unaware of the Soviet grievance or that the Soviets regarded themselves as crusaders in a holy war against the Profit-Motive in industry . . .

CHAPTER NINE

SOUTH CAROLINA INTERLUDE

Jefferson was granted a leave from the Michigan State Normal College from September, 1925, until June, 1926. The year was to be financed in part by sabbatical funds from the Normal College and in part by the D. C. Heath Company, which had entered a contract with Jefferson who was to write for them a world series of geographies. The challenge of the world geography series, with "man" to be very much included, decided Jefferson. He enjoyed putting his thoughts on paper, and he had already determined to write a "Man in the U.S.A." and a "Man in South America," following the style of his already published *Man in Europe*. Jefferson recognized that the books would receive wide circulation, which meant that "man in geography" would be currency wherever D. C. Heath Company plied their trade. Bowman, then Director of the American Geographical Society, had recommended Jefferson to the Heath Company as their author. After reading *Man in Europe* Heath agreed. Bowman was instrumental in helping persuade Jefferson that he should leave the Normal for one year in which to write. He wrote to Jefferson early in 1925:[1]

> *Lincoln's Birthday is a moment of leisure in which to pen a message respecting a project that will interest you.* Please treat it as confidential in the highest degree and address your reply to my house—*and likewise any subsequent correspondence in relation hereto.*
>
> *You have referred in times past to an elementary series of geographies. Recently D. C. Heath & Co., a first class house, and one of the four largest in the textbook business, have investigated the field, after years of more general interest, and have decided to go into it. They have asked me to undertake it* but this I cannot do for various reasons which I shall not attempt to detail here. *They mean business. It must*

be a thorough job. Five years will be required to complete the series. It is to be a flexible series, i.e., like Barrows and Parker of which the first work has been published (Silver, Burdette & Co.). In reality four little books but bound up as two if necessary. They intend to put into it the best that money will buy. I have conferred with them at their request —a half day session. They are eager and willing to make it the best —to sell on merit.

I believe they will be a success of the first order—"they" meaning both books and publisher—if the right authors can be brought together. I believe they (publishers) would be willing to allow the author's salary for extra time off to do it—up to a year or more. Though we haven't talked business details (except in the large) I believe they would not charge such compensation to royalties but rather to their own capital account. It seems to me the chance of a lifetime for you. *My suggestions are as follows:*

1) That you should be one of two (or possibly three) authors.

2) That there should be associated with you another man, preferably an able and known man in education, as from the Harvard or some Western school of education.

3) That your associate would be selected to give elementary style to the whole and if he could not do this at least he can take care of the pedagogical problems and school curriculum problems. These are very complex and bedeviling and require as much work as the scientific matter and just as much following up in later years.

4) If your associate cannot achieve the requisite simplicity and ease and grace of style, that a third person be employed to work upon it and paid outright, leaving the royalties to be divided equally between you and your associate.

5) It would be your series and named after you and your associate. The associate should be included because, as a younger man, he would probably outlive you; and in principle it is not good to have the author underground. Your heirs will appreciate this.

6) Will you write me at length respecting all phases of the matter— very frankly. Your summers, plus a half year off, and possibly a whole year, pay sufficient to see your family through, ought to put the project on its feet. Is there a first-class-work-school teacher or assistant of yours, whom you could employ (at publisher's expense) for five summers, and extra time between, to whip the stuff into shape?

7) Maps original!

Everything about them should be CLASS. Photographs gathered from original sources not Underwood and Underwood. Maps and

*photographs should be studied as much or more than text. Pub-
lisher will pay for all compilation of data, drafting under your
direction, assistants' time for experimentation, etc., etc. This the
publisher has not yet agreed to do: it has been presented to him:
but he will do it, I am sure.*

8) *If I have any relation to it, it will be as adviser only, and I am
not sure that I shall have anything to do with the development of
the plan. Very limited relation at best and only subsidiary mention (if at all).*

9) *The thing now is, what will you do? The old companies are all
tied up. The best men are tied up. Heath wants to move; he is
successful; he wants to be in the crowd that revolutionizes geography—in face he wants to be the crowd.*
Irrelevant detail left out
Modern stuff only
*The best there is in the subject developed in the right way and
fight competition on merit and the modern way not on bunk and
hot air.*

10) *Write fully. I want to see you do it.*

Yours

Jefferson was won over. He was swift to recognize that the texts
would teach hundreds of thousands of pupils, while at the Normal he
would address but a few hundred students in the course of one year.
President Pulsifer of the Heath Company, Bowman, and Jefferson conferred upon the series, and agreement was reached concerning the desired nature of the coming books. Furthermore Jefferson hoped that the
books would bring him a substantial royalty that he might be freed, for
a while at least, from the classroom. He wanted to spend six months in
Spain-Portugal and another six months in Switzerland that he might
write his intended "Man in Iberia" and "Man in Switzerland." He also
wanted to attend the International Geographical Congress to be held in
London and Cambridge, 1928, at which time he could again meet many
of his friends and correspondents and submit propositions concerning a
map of world precipitation. He was well aware that there was much to
do, and at the age of 63 he wanted to achieve before it was too late.
Jefferson passed the fall months in Ypsilanti preparing maps of the
U.S.A. for use in his classroom, maps published as an *Atlas of Plates
to Man in the U.S.A.* During that same fall he prepared to take his
second wife, Clara, and their three children, Sally, Mary, and Thomas,
to Charleston, South Carolina. Midway through December, the Jefferson family travelled south to McClellanville in South Carolina. A
change of environment had been recommended for Mrs. Jefferson, who

was suffering from a nervous condition and the Carolinas seemed suitably quiet to Jefferson, who wanted to be away from noise, hustle and bustle. Advertisements in a Carolina newspaper, *The News and Courier,* Charleston, South Carolina, had yielded a house for rent at McClellanville, a village 36 miles from the principal railway and on the coast north and east of Charleston. The village was all that the Jeffersons wanted. Jefferson later wrote of McClellanville:[2]

> *At high tide the Atlantic waters come up to the streets of that village and at low tide there are five miles of grassy marshes between it and Cape Romain, marshes resorted to by numerous wild ducks and herons and flamingoes. The village sits amid palmettoes and live oaks with a continuous forest of longleaf pines behind with thick carpet below of gallberries, much like our huckle-berries except for keeping green all winter long. On this feed the deer that were killed all around us and the bears that we did not see. The afternoon we reached the village they brought a deer by the house that they had just shot within five miles, and ducks were repeatedly shot from the front yard. The village is isolated. Inland lie broad swamps crossed by corduroy roads that are crossed by bold people who do not mind risking their springs. An excellent sand gravel road leads to the Cooper River opposite Charleston and there a steam ferry takes you across for fifty cents to a dollar each way according to your number of passengers. The ferries across the Santee in the other direction are free cable ferries and not without the attraction of adventure. Effectively the village is on an island: there is a freight boat once a week each way which brings the five or six stores their supplies, and taking away the products of the village, which are early potatoes in May, canned oysters in the winter and canned beans in spring, rosin and turpentine from the woods and some cotton.*

Jefferson remained with his family in McClellanville until May, 1926, thus escaping the cold of the Michigan winter. Five months in McClellanville also spared him numerous time consuming tasks which would have confronted him in Ypsilanti. The house rented at McClellanville was large and rambling in the planter mansion style. The interior was sparsely furnished but Mrs. Jefferson and family swiftly made the gaunt house into a home. A study containing father and typewriter swiftly emerged as the purpose of ensconcement some 750 miles distant from Ypsilanti, away from his friends and colleagues, and removed from his amassed collection of books, notes, and correspondence. But alone he could think, and frequently he had remarked thinking was the best thing he did.

The mid 1920's were the most prolific years of Jefferson's life: the envious spoke of literary industrialism, others asked, "but is it geography?" Jefferson did not linger over his work to find whether geography wanted it, he simply gave. He put his own thoughts into prose for himself. If these thoughts were not geographic, Jefferson assumed that either geography would change its course or he would not be regarded as a geographer. In the year 1926 alone, three of his books rolled off the printing press, though this is not to suggest that they were all written during this leave of absence from the Normal: the works were, *Atlas of Plates to Man in the United States* (Ypsilanti, 1926), *Principles of Geography* (Harcourt, Brace and Co. New York, 1926), *Peopling the Argentine Pampa* (American Geographical Society, Research Series No. 16, American Geographical Society, New York, 1926). A new and revised edition of his *Man in Europe* was published also in 1926 by the Harcourt Brace Company of New York. Other of his published work in 1926 included three articles for the *Geographical Review:* "A New Map of World Rainfall," "Actual Temperatures of South America," and "Pictures from Southern Brazil," together with an article published in *The American Schoolmaster* entitled "Scandinavia Steps Forward in Rainfall Studies." In this same year of 1926 he found time to review several books for the *Geographical Review,* take 300 selected photographs—most of them stereoscopic—largely in the environs of McClellanville, write an unpublished essay entitled "Down South," pry deep into the history of ante-bellum plantation life on the banks of the Santee, send letters to Clyde Ford, his language-professor friend at Ypsilanti's Normal, concerning word usage and place names of the Carolinas, and develop his civilizing-rails concept, which, after publication in the magazine, *Economic Geography* (1928), was to become one of the most extensively pirated articles in American geography.[3] He was at his best, for he was full to overbrimming with geographic ideas. Perhaps it was a loss to geography when he returned to the classroom in the fall of 1926. He had so much to say that much of it was never published. Long hours in the classroom, increasing civic responsibilities, advancing age, and continually new ideas all conspired to present him from completing his rough drafts of "Man in South America," "Man in Michigan," "Man in Iberia," and "Man in Switzerland." Although in McClellanville for the purpose of writing the world geography series, for D. C. Heath, Jefferson could not prevent ideas from sweeping over him, inundating him, demanding his time and demanding expression. Perhaps he felt spurred on by the continual encroachment of social studies upon geography: certainly he was vexed at the thought of social studies teachers offering erroneous geographic ideas in the schools. And perhaps he received stimulus from the knowledge that he only had this one year's respite from the classroom. One idea that held his attention while in the South concerned an accurate map of world rainfall. Jefferson wished to see such a map and hoped that the 1928 meeting of the International Geographical Congress (Cambridge, England) might be used to prosecute this vision. The proposal, which he later submitted to Isaiah Bowman (April 29, 1928), in his capacity as corresponding member of the American Geographical Society, was developed and written in note form at McClellanville:[4]

> *Dear Dr. Bowman:*
>
> *There follow some propositions on a map of World precipitation, International Plan.*
>
> *It is agreed that maps showing average or normal annual rainfall should be based on 25 or 30 years of simultaneous record.*
>
> *LENGTH OF PERIOD. At least 25 years because rainfall varies so much from year to year. Usually there are 2 to 7 years of less than average precipitation followed by 2 to 7 of more than average amount, several dry years followed by several wet years. 90 or 100 years would doubtless be better. The few places with long records do not show the same averages for successive periods of 30 years. Boston for instance showed one 30-year-average of 41.1 inches, the next 51.7, and the last 32.4, but records of that length will not be available for a very long time to come. The Boston record shows that a 30-year record may be within five or six inches of a true normal value. Shorter records may be in very large error indeed.*
>
> *SIMULTANEITY OF EPOCH. The same period of 25 to 30 years should be used for all places because otherwise we shall be comparing unlike periods of precipitation. The 30 years following 1870 for Boston should not be compared with the 30 years following 1880 for Worcester, as the years 1870 to 1880 might be unusually wet ones and the years 1900 to 1910 unusually dry ones with the result that we must make out Boston to be wetter than Worcester because of the date rather than the amount of rainfall measures. In practice if we had observations at the two places as suggested, and no others, we should do better to compare their records for the simultaneous years 1880 to 1900, which occur in both records, although we reduced the length of the series to 20 instead of 30 years.*
>
> *In most countries where meteorology is actively studied, new rain gauge stations are being set up all the time. These must necessarily have shorter series of observations than the older stations. Also at a good many stations a month or two of record is lost every now and then so that whenever an attempt is made to draw a rainfall map for any country it is necessary to interpolate values for missing years,*

making corrections to the records of observation in order that all may be brought up as near as the facts admit to a common epoch of observation. Unfortunately the corrections used are not always stated.

In this way it came about that Hellmann's great rainfall map of Germany (1906) makes use only of the years 1893-1902, ten years, although quite a number of German stations have records of over fifty. Further of the 3000 stations used for the map only half had a record for every one of the ten years. By comparison with the fewer 50-year series Hellmann showed that the east and northeast of Germany was 4-9 percent wetter and the north and northwest 2 to 7 percent drier than the average of the 50 years. It is more difficult to make a map for a whole continent than for a country since the observations are necessarily made and collected by several different meteorological services. If we combine the latest maps for continents into a map for the world we are combining data of different epochs and part of the differences shown on the map are not differences for places, but differences for epoch.

On most world maps of rainfall the arithmetical work in taking averages and the technical work in drawing lines is carried to a degree of refinement not justified by the records, especially because of the lack of simultaneity of the observations.

It would be highly desirable for the nations of the world to cooperate in preparing a simultaneous record for some future period of ten years, during which a great effort was made to attain completeness for all stations and simultaneity at the same time.

It might be possible for an international committee to indicate a number of extra stations which might be equipped at international expense in spots where a gauge is very much needed and where existing services do not feel able to establish them.

The study of the international observations and map should be made by a committee of Geographical Societies and meteorological services, inviting suggestions from all living authors of regional maps of rainfall. The observations would naturally be made by the respective meteorological services of the countries.

It would be desirable that Committees should consider the use of long period gauges on mountain tops, the simultaneous measurement of evaporation, river run-off, plant transpiration, tree growth and ring forming, and change of volume of glaciers.

The identity of the months and years used for all stations could be secured by making an extra observation on the last day of each calendar month at 2 p. m. Greenwich time, an hour that has the convenience of falling in daylight in most parts of the world, in early morning

> *in California to late at night in New Zealand. It would then be possible to get out the rainfall of months and years that shall be identical for all stations.*
>
> *It might be possible to plan the record for the 10 years beginning 1930.*
>
> *The important preliminary is the publication of a map locating existing stations already equipped for the work which can be counted on to cooperate for the ten years.*
>
> *After the preparation of a map indicating the locations at which new internationally supported stations are most needed with an estimate of the cost of equipping and operating them.*
>
> *Respectfully submitted in response to your suggestion that I prepare a proposition.*

Jefferson had already written in a letter to Bowman, March 11, 1928,[5] "You have already printed my scheme, *Geographical Review,* April 1926, pp. 289-290." He referred to his article "A New Map of World Rainfall," which concluded with a paragraph under the heading, "An Adequate Rainfall Map of the World."

> *An adequate rainfall map of the world calls for the cooperation of all meteorological services in the world. Observations should be contemporaneous. Ten years would give an excellent idea of distribution of the rain in space. If the years 1930 to 1939 could be used for the observation there would be time for an international committee headed by a man like Dr. Hellman to study the problem and make arrangements for observers in critical regions. Even without additional expense for extra stations such a cooperation might accomplish more than all the work of the last century.*

Jefferson's interest in an accurate map of world rainfall dated back at least to 1898, when Herbertson had published the first reliable map of world rainfall. Since that time Jefferson had been gathering data, maintaining correspondence, collecting maps and atlases with a special regard for rainfall studies. Yet it was at McClellanville that he conceived the idea of an International Geographical Union commission on world rainfall. And what of the fate of this proposal? Bowman deliberately let Jefferson's letter on this matter of March 7, 1928, litter his desk for several weeks at the American Geographical Society headquarters, in order to attract the attention of geographers that visited him.[6] In a postscript to one of his letters to Jefferson, March 9, 1928, Bowman wrote,[7] "I spilled your idea of world rainfall records by preconcerted plan to Wright, Wrigley, Platt, Joerg and they said Hurray!" Bowman wished Jefferson to develop the idea and present it personally at the International Geographical Congress. Although Jefferson had developed the idea, he now wished to leave the mechanics of manipulation to Bowman. Jefferson wished to see that accurate rainfall map of the world, but he had no desire to have his name attached to the project. Indeed, in his letter to Bowman of March 11, 1928, Jefferson wrote:

> No: I think as "Jefferson's" scheme it would be stillborn. It must be international. The great national meteorological services would have the bulk of the work to do and must be invited to take the lion's share in its direction. Yet I do not think it should be exclusively meteorological, as there are geographic elements such as the growth of trees in regions of interest where it is not possible to maintain rain gauges.
>
> I see you consulting Marvin early. I see Marvin asking the American Geographical Society to undertake correspondence. I see lists of all national meteorological services formed in libraries with addresses of chiefs, other lists of all living authors of rainfall maps, made by librarians. I see the American Geographical Society writing to the individuals of these lists, that it conceived the idea of a great rain-fall record and map for 1930 to 1940, first for all America and better for all the world—and invited ideas and interest in such a scheme for presentation to the coming Congress in London, looking to the formation of an international committee to prepare a detailed plan.

The idea emerged from his stay at McClellanville. So, too, did his "civilizing-rails" concept.

Jefferson perceived that the hand of economic and cultural stagnation had been laid on McClellanville because of the absence of a railroad or other compensating means of transportation. In his unpublished article, "Down South," Jefferson proclaimed McClellanville to be 750 miles distant from Ypsilanti and 75 years in time. He recognized that history played an important role in shaping the people's attitude and began to study the South statistically. He observed the Negro in McClellanville against the setting of the history of McClellanville and became much interested in the "Peculiar Institution." He wrote frequently to librarian Genevieve Walton of Ypsilanti's Normal, requesting that she immediately purchase this or that book relating to the South. He looked at McClellanville and recognized that its best days were gone. He studied the history of some of the plantations, met and became friendly with Uncle Jimmy, one of the oldest planters of McClellanville, who had driven food supply trains for the South during the Civil War. With emancipation came the death of the plantation, deer, bear, ducks, and sweet potatoes. At McClellanville there was no demand for a railroad, consequently no railroad was built joining McClellanville to nodal points of the South and East. Few people ever travelled to McClellanville, and few people left McClellanville. Jefferson calculated that in

1925, 94% of the people living in the Carolinas were born in the Carolinas compared to 90% for Georgia, 62% for Michigan, 59% for Massachusetts, and 38% of the people in the Far West.[8] People did not travel as much in the South as elsewhere, neither did ideas travel as much. Tide water plantations of decades gone by could sleep peaceably tucked away between the weathered Appalachians and the shore of the Atlantic. And where men and ideas failed to penetrate, there civilization would not advance, and a culture from an earlier time would survive and prevail. Jefferson had already perceived that an advance in culture was not possible apart from an increase in the paraphernalia of civilization—schools, art galleries, pieces of mail carried per capita, motor vehicles per thousand population, and libraries. Using these phenomena as indices, he had been busy measuring and then plotting the distribution of culture throughout the world during the two previous decades. Jefferson wrote on the matter of culture indices in the *Geographical Review*,[9] *Man in Europe, Exercises in Human Geography* and presented the matter in papers delivered before the Association of American Geographers,[10] The Michigan Academy of Sciences, Arts and Letters, and the National Council of Geography Teachers; Ellsworth Huntington had published some of Jefferson's world culture studies in *Civilization and Climate,* 1915.[11] McClellanville's distance from the railroad and Jefferson's perception that this had stemmed and halted cultural advance provided inspiration for his "civilizing-rails" notion. The essential work of the next paper he presented to the Association of American Geographers, "The Geography of Railway Transportation in 1920-1927," and his article, "The Civilizing Rails," later published in *Economic Geography* was completed in McClellanville. Working on a large scale map of each continent, he plotted the distribution of railways and zones of culture influence extending for ten miles on either side of the railroad throughout the world. Arbitrarily he decided that in the mid-twenties the civilizing influence of the locomotive and the iron rails extended approximately ten miles on either side of the track, "as if railway service was useful for ten miles each side of the tracks." Arbitrary though the ten-mile limit was, the suggestion was at least based on Jefferson's experiences in field-work in four continents. On completion of the world map of railways, Jefferson superimposed his map of national culture ratings upon it. He observed that areas of sparse railway density (rail tentacles) were frequently areas of low culture and that areas of heavy railway density (rail web) were areas of high culture. "The rails civilize," proclaimed Jefferson in an article entitled, "The Civilizing Rails." This article was frequently reproduced and referred to in geographic and railway literature of the years that followed.

Jefferson came to know the geography of the South. He did much walking, much note-taking, much photographing. He would stop the nearest passer-by if a question were even forming itself in his mind. Clad in a panama-suit, he spent many a day in the open air, walking and observing. At the end of the day he would repair to bed, bring his correspondence and diary to date, plan his activities for the coming day, think a little, then settle to reading usually a French detective story. Jules Verne in French became popular with him. Jefferson was encouraged to reread much of the history of the South: the environment stimulated him to this. The culture scape all around McClellanville spoke to him of another way, of another period now passed. Jefferson was anxious to comprehend man's life in the deep South. He travelled several plantations, surveyed the planter's home, observed the slave hovels, spoke with several of the older inhabitants.

> Yesterday we visited the finest Great House I have yet seen—a former rice planter's place. Such a fine place, having slavery written all over it just as the Tuileries and Louvre palaces have serfdom inscribed in their every line. A very poor man lives there now amid the splendor, for rice growing departed from the Santee delta with the passing of slavery. All the rice slaves came over to McClellanville and bought land which was sold them cheaply here—and not on sale over there at all. It is impressive to see the floodplain of Collins Creek still in rice—straw alongside the house 10 feet below. That is a tributary of the "mighty" Santee, the greatest rice river that they are to bridge near here this year. South Carolina is a land of unbridged rivers.[12]

Occasionally he would send a crate of kumquats or citrus fruits to his closest associates in Ypsilanti, though more frequently he would write of his new experiences:[13]

> The other day I got a picture of a bed of live oysters, the jolliest sight you ever saw. It is at low tide of course, and the oysters are all up on end as if standing up in a crowd. I never saw a picture of growing oysters before. You can imagine them shouting and waving their hands!

Jefferson became interested in the migratory movement of the black mallard, and while still at McClellanville, had prepared a class exercise for his intended course on the South East of the U.S.—a class exercise drawn directly from the field.[14]

To Roland Harper he wrote:[15]

> The vegetation keeps me minded of you. What can I lay hands on that will describe these trees and plants? And is there description of the geology and physiography of the coast country? Our woods are of course, nearly solid pine, mostly between 15 and 40 years of age . . .

> *They assert that the present growth, though yielding much turpentine*
> *—20,000 boxes were landed from the boat yesterday for local use—*
> *will never produce any lightwood. Is that so? Does Pinus Palustris*
> *occur here still? . . . Lots of Cassina everywhere, Christmas berry: Is*
> *that the plant you told me of, used in Georgia as tea and relative of*
> *Paraguayan Mate?*

And to Richard Clyde Ford, language professor at the Michigan State Normal School, Jefferson wrote:[16]

> *What can you make of pettiaugers, the combination sail and row boats*
> *the rice planters on the Santee used to send their crop to Charleston*
> *in? Professor U. B. Phillips of Ann Arbor is responsible for the word,*
> *History of Transportation in the Eastern Cotton Belt, p. 25, but he*
> *does not explain it. The word is not known even to old folks here,*
> *though we drive to the Santee in 30 minutes. Uncle Jimmy never heard*
> *the word.*

Jefferson was excited by the Southern Atlantic Coastal Plain, and so wrote to colleague Ella Wilson, Acting Head of the Department in his absence:[17]

> *You have no idea of the fascinating things I am getting hold of down*
> *here. I hardly expected to find so much geography in it. My pictures*
> *are coming out well. I have now 80 good stereoscopic and 40 odd*
> *printed and mounted for study and shall take a lot more . . . . . There*
> *are lovely spots to discover every day and revelations in people and*
> *ways. They have the plowing done now for the early Irish potatoes and*
> *the boats are busy bringing fertilizer. All the sunny days, about one-*
> *third of all days are delightful.*

He sent boxes of pine cones and varieties of grass to geographer Roland Harper for identification; received agricultural yearbooks, *Porgie,* and Clifton Johnson's, *Highways and By-ways of the South,* from the Ypsilanti Normal library, wrote a biographical account of Richard Tillia Morrison who had been a vital part of McClellanville for ninety-four years. The American Geographical Society sent him maps, loaned him a typewriter when his own broke down, shipped him books any or all of which he had been invited to review (with pay) for the *Geographical Review,* and kept him informed on the progress of the 1:1 million map of Hispanic America.

Busied by these varied activities, and exasperated by publishers requesting confirmation of a myriad details, Jefferson did not lose sight of the fact that he was at McClellanville to write the world geography books for D. C. Heath. He swiftly developed an outline for the books. Ella Wilson, one of his two faculty women colleagues in the Normal Geography Department, accepted his invitation to be associate editor for the series. She was to make sure that the writing would be easily comprehended by children, that the books would meet curriculum requirements, were adequately illustrated, and that there was just enough pedagogic gadgetry therein to please superintendents, principals, and all those in positions to purchase the series. The Heath Company had anticipated a five-year plan for the series, but Jefferson insisted on a two-year plan. He was able to write incisively, knowing precisely what he wanted to say, and saying it in a fashion that was readily understood. That is why in reviewing Jefferson's *Man in Europe* in the *Journal of Geography* (1924-25), A. E. Parkins referred to Jefferson as the George Bernard Shaw of American geographers. Writing for grade school students was a challenge to Jefferson. To be sure, Ella Wilson was to edit the written form of the work, but it was not intended that she re-write the whole work in grade school language. Jefferson had written numerous books specifically for his Normal College classes and had, to that extent, previously encountered the task of writing for a given audience. At all times Jefferson strove for simplicity of style, and this augured well for the success of the books planned. Frequently he used his own children as guinea pigs on the text and illustrations of the geographies. He was especially interested to see the manner in which nine-year-old Sally delighted to make houses following a suggested design and instructions: houses typifying the region were to be a feature of his books. Jefferson asked several European geographers to take specific photographs for him to illustrate his work. He frequently exchanged his own photographs of the United States for photographs of Europe taken by European geographers. To study more carefully "Denmark—the model dairy" and land reclamation in the Netherlands, he requested Marcel Aurousseau, a young Australian geographer, to undertake field work for him in these two areas. Aurousseau, temporarily living in Paris, knew Jefferson personally, for the two had met on several occasions in the early 1920's at the American Geographical Society. Indeed, in 1922, on the occasion of the meeting of the Association of American Geographers in Ann Arbor, Aurousseau had stayed with the Jefferson family eight miles away in Ypsilanti. Jefferson and Aurousseau were both vigorous geographers, and both were particularly interested in population distribution and the geography of cities. Aurousseau, wounded in the First World War, had recently completed a 947 mile walk from Paris to Madrid with an American friend, and was now resident in Paris and preparing to write a book of his journey. This work was later published as *Highway into Spain*.[18] Jefferson sent Aurousseau $280 from the D. C. Heath Company expense account. Aurousseau proceeded to Denmark and thence to the Netherlands.

Perhaps significantly Aurousseau was the only man Jefferson ever hired to undertake field work for him. Aurousseau's task commenced July 24 and was completed September 22, at which time he returned to Paris. Aurousseau remained in Denmark until September 8th, when he left for the Netherlands. Some detail of the Jefferson-Aurousseau arrangement seems worthy of recapitulation as an example of successfully accomplished field work by proxy. During this time Aurousseau sent his findings to Jefferson in the form of reports. Six of these neatly typed reports, accompanied by photographs, occupied 104 pages.[19] Specifically Jefferson had requested of Aurousseau information concerning the emergence of cooperatives in Denmark and dyking, reclamation, and irrigation in the Netherlands. No trouble was too great for the D. C. Heath geography texts. Aurousseau proceeded to Denmark and found the British Vice-Consul, a Mr. Godbey, in Aalborg. Mr. Godbey was immediately of help to an Aurousseau who could see but who could not speak the language of Denmark. Mr. Godbey, well versed in the Scandinavian languages and in the Danish pig industry, investigated the possibility of placing Aurousseau on a farm as the latter wished and as Jefferson had suggested. It was not possible to place Aurousseau on a farm since the local farmers were too busy harvesting, neither were they prepared to accept a paying boarder: either he must be a guest or a worker. Aurousseau sought employment as a farm hand, but could not find work because of his lack of familiarity with both the language and the work. Within a very short time, however, Mr. Godbey had selected Baelum, near Aalborg in Northern Jutland, as thoroughly representative of the small Danish community. Aurousseau took a room in a small hotel there and soon met a successful farmer, Mr. Hans Andersen, who had recently returned from an eleven-year stay in Portland, Oregon, U.S.A. Both Mr. and Mrs. Andersen spoke very good English, as did their children. Aurousseau was privileged to be given so intimate a view of Danish life. He later wrote to Jefferson . . .[20]

> *I have to thank you for sending me on this journey. Parts of the world I had never seen, unlike any I have seen. It has been absorbing. How different are our philosophical points of view. You are a real geographer; I am a spurious one, a generalizer, a facile observer, superficial. I am lost in economic considerations because I know how inadequate is my equipment to wrestle with them and I mistrust some of my deductions. I am deeply interested in life and people, and what the animals do to places; what the place does to them. But it is the beauty of it that I am really after, a kind of enjoyment. My pleasure in Baelum centered around the Christian Jensens and young Berting Hansens, and the forest, the mill, the barrows, the blueness of the flowers. May I*

admit that I have had to make myself write these reports? It is things of another nature that I want to write.

Aurousseau learned a lot of geography from his Danish sojourn and was inspired to see new patterns of meaning in facts he already knew. In his first report to Jefferson, August 7, 1926, Aurousseau wrote:

The geography of Denmark was a bugbear at school. I could never get the hang of Seeland, Fyen, Lolland, Moen, Falster and Jutland, with the Great Belt and the Little Belt, and the Skagerak and the Kattegat. One forgets which is which. I think, however, that for the outside world, Denmark can be made to live, through cows, pigs, eggs, motor ships, and porcelain. But above all, by an account of its peculiar communications! The great international rail routes that cross Denmark are so odd, with their train ferries, that they must stick in the mind. London, Esbjerg, Fredericia (ferry), Middelfart, Odense, Nyborg (ferry), Halskov, Copenhagen (ferry), Malmo, Stockholm! What an unconventional journey! Or, Paris, Hamburg, Warnemunde (ferry), Gjedser, Orehoved (ferry), Masnedsund, Copenhagen, Helsingor (ferry), Helsingborg, Oslo, Bergen! How can it fail to stick? Then, the position of Copenhagen, with reference to the lands around the Baltic, with the real gates to the Baltic not on Ore Sund, but way out, the Orkney-Shetland-Norway gap, and the Straits of Dover! But with Copenhagen in the "passing on" position for Denmark, Norway, Sweden, North Germany, Poland, Latvia, Esthonia, Russia, and Finland! The routes, that try to beat Copenhagen—the Kiel Canal, the Bergen-Oslo-Stockholm route; the Berlin-Sassnitz-Tralleborg-Stockholm route; the Narvik-Stockholm route.

Cooperatives, cows, pigs, storks, shipbuilding, intensive agriculture, transportation, towns, social customs, the people, were all reported upon by Aurousseau who travelled Denmark extensively before leaving the country for the Netherlands. In the Netherlands, Aurousseau visited his friend, Van der Klaauw, Professor of Zoology at the University of Leyden. Once again Aurousseau gleaned all the information he could and sent an extended report with special reference to the water problem to Jefferson, who, prior to 1926, had not visited the Netherlands. Jefferson sent letters to Aurousseau containing questions and ideas around which Aurousseau should work. One of these requested Aurousseau to study irrigation in the Netherlands, and so Aurousseau pursued the matter. In his report he wrote:[21]

Klaauw took me over to the Geology School in the afternoon, to Professor Escher, the likeliest man to know what I wanted. To know about it, I mean. There is no chair of Geography in Holland at any of the four universities (Amsterdam, Leyden, Utrecht, and Groningen) nor at the Delft Polytechnic. The next day I met Klaauw and his father-in-law, Mr. Bruins, at the station, and we went to a place called Warmonde by train where Bruins has a sumptuous motor boat. The whole day was spent along the canals and lakes, lunching at the club house of the Motor Boat Club. What I tell you is from these three, Klaauw, Escher, and Bruins. To begin with, they doubted the idea of a summer drought in Holland, and laughed inordinately at the idea of the ditches of fresh water being an irrigation resource in summer. "Why," they said, "Our problem is to get water off the land, not to put it on it." What about eastern Holland? "Eastern Holland is forest and farm, with an adequate rainfall all the year". And crops? "This is not a crop country, except in the southern province of Zealand, where there is also no question of drought." I asked for a source of data, and was referred to the Statistiek Jaarcijfeir *and* Statistisch Jaarboekje *(if that's the right spelling from pencil notes) obtainable at the Hague.*

Jefferson was amused to think that the Dutch people, themselves well versed in the peculiarities of their water problem, failed to realize that they irrigated, a fact Jefferson checked with the Dutch government. Later Jefferson frequently referred to this episode as an example of one of those geographic bubbles of ignorance that he had managed to burst.

By the middle of May, 1926, McClellanville was becoming too warm and humid for the comfort of the Jefferson family which now journeyed north to the large home on the Belknap's at Gilmanton, New Hampshire, ancestral to the family of Theodora Bohnstedt, Jefferson's first wife. Here in a bracing air and familiar environment, work on the geography series continued until the fall of 1926. In the September, October, November, and December of that year, Jefferson and his co-author Ella Wilson, proceeded to outline in great detail the overall plan of four books. That Christmas vacation Jefferson travelled to Panama, studied the meeting place of the Americas, recorded extensive notes on the building and success of the Panama Canal, returning home via the Caribbean. The trip was financed by the Heath Company.

The books began to emerge. It would be more correct to say, one long—indefinitely long—book, began to emerge, but this could be appropriately divided into four sections, thus creating four books. During this sabbatical year, Jefferson's mind was full of geographic thoughts, full of all the ideas he had successfully propounded in class. He wanted to write all his geography tersely and yet simply, so that other minds might share with him the joys of thinking geographically. The books were a synopsis of his geographic understandings at the time of his writing. It was a geography of farms, barns, people, transportation, diseases, soils, weather, politics, government, and distributions: it was a geography of common sense, an interpretation of the world about, an analysis of happenings and history, which Jefferson hoped would make the world a more intelligible place to live in. At McClellanville Jefferson mulled over the happenings of the Paris Peace Conference. The "Russian lost lands" continued to plague and bother him—he sensed the Soviets would never rest until they had regained their land—and he wished to make the issue widely known. The issue of the war, the "lost lands," behavior of the Powers, and the Peace Conference, became a part of his work for Heath. He also included ideas concerning the growth of cities, the industrialization of countries, the emergence and meaning of transportation facilities, the meaning and measurement of culture, and world distribution of population with special reference to the ecumenes of the larger world states. And just when it seemed as though younger minds would surely be tiring, Jefferson would come back to the delightful intimacy of the seashore, with its myriad fascinations for children, its rounded boulders, sandy, pebbled, or rocky beaches, green seaweeds of many varieties, the crabs and other organisms left stranded high on the beach when the tide recedes, the shells that bring the music of the sea to the human ear when far in land. And from the seashore Jefferson would proceed to the oceans, to their immensity, to the geographical bases of Atlantis and Mu, to man's conquest of nature's highways, to the idea of commerce and colonialism. Above all, this was a geography with man very much in the fore. Maps and illustrative diagrams were numerous. This geography was radically different from much of the Davisian physiography that still passed for geography in the school systems.

In the midst of what promised to be a successful school text venture, D. C. Heath, suddenly, and without notice, called Jefferson to their New York head office to discuss the matter. One day in the August of 1928, Jefferson was busy planning a trip to the Iberian Peninsula to study "Spain, dry Iberia, and Portugal, wet Iberia," with a view to making this a chapter in his texts, and the next day Jefferson was informed by Winfield Smyth, the recently appointed President of the D. C. Heath Company that the contract between himself and the Heath Company could not be fulfilled.[22] The Company anticipated a cost of $200,000 to place the Jefferson texts on the market, a sum which could only be recouped over a period of years. But the Company, advised by selected specialists, feared that a set of geography texts would not compete favorably with social studies texts. Geography at that time was not strongly established in the schools of the U.S.A., but the Heath Company thought they had espied a coming discipline with the upsurge of interest in peoples and places following the First World War and abandonment of the nation's century-long isolation. Now Heath Company had its doubts concerning grade school acceptance of geography. When the Company sought the opinion of grade school teachers of geography, they were surprised to find that few existed. Unfortunately, it was at this time that President Pulsifer of the Company had retired, owing to failing health, and he had withdrawn his personal investment of one-and-a-half million dollars from the Company. This, together with the approaching recession whose cold front was already being felt in certain sectors of the economy, further discouraged the Heath Company from a project of the proposed magnitude. The Company apologized to Jefferson, severed the contract by allowing him to retain his manuscripts and all expense monies allowed him to that date (August 1928), remunerated Miss Ella Wilson for her collaboration on the work, and granted Jefferson an additional lump sum of some $1300. The texts were never published. Jefferson's already established preference for Fred Buytendorp's local press in Ypsilanti over the large national publishing companies, was heightened considerably by this experience. Very soon his "Exercises in Human Geography" was published in Ypsilanti, and this did incorporate some of his work originally intended for the Heath Company, but most of his ideas for the geographic public, died with Heath's decision. Jefferson unreasonably assumed that his geographic thoughts would not be new or particularly worthwhile to practicing geographers, and he had no cause to enter a contract with another company for geography in the grades. His life's work was geography and not making money. At times Jefferson showed a disdain of money only possible on the part of the disinterested and detached scholar. Some of the thoughts suggested in the unpublished geographies were subtly scattered before members of the Association of American Geographers at their annual meetings through the years, but these papers were never published as read and only occasionally published with modification.

CHAPTER TEN

PEOPLE AND THEIR DISTRIBUTION

It was several years after meeting W. M. Davis, and while Head of the Geography Department at the Michigan State Normal College, Ypsilanti, that Jefferson began to realize that there was more to geography than the *ge*. He began to notice people, dwellings, and culture, began to realize that human beings created patterns on the face of the earth. He remembered the words Davis had once spoken to him, many years previously: "What is a city? Nobody knows what a city is." He promptly commenced study of the distribution of population, a matter which fascinated him to the end of his days.

Jefferson published his first essay concerning the distribution of population in the *Bulletin of the Geographical Society of Philadelphia,* July 1907. The article, entitled, "The Distribution of People in South America,"[1] was abstracted in the following words for *The International Catalogue of Scientific Literature:*[2]

> *Points out that the people live in the highlands in the Tropics, not far from the sea, while beyond the Tropics they are found on the plains. Cities of more than 5,000 people are grouped in the same way. Further confirmation is found in the size of provinces, small in the well settled regions and large where men are rare. A word is given to the use of such maps in schools.*

Five maps illustrated the article: the distribution of population in South America; the high cities of South America; size of all cities with over 5,000 people; people per square mile in each province; the distribution of population according to *Berghaus' Physical Atlas,* 1884. The first four of these Jefferson believed to be an advance upon any maps then known and stated so in his text. Intelligent observation and reasoning concerning population distribution dominate the article, which was certainly a departure from the tradition of geography in North America. Interestingly, Jefferson stated in his concluding paragraph:

> The result of such studies, a fairly correct view of the distribution of people in a continent, is entitled to prominence in teaching geography. Formerly, such maps were not possible. A statement in words of the facts of such a map leads to many questions of cause that introduce relief, temperature, rainfall, and commerce in a very natural way.

Less than six months later, Jefferson presented a paper entitled "The Distribution of Population Over the Earth" before the fourth annual meeting of the Association of American Geographers, Chicago, December 30, 1907-January 2, 1908. It was the first population distribution study to be read before the Association, and it aroused interest.[3] He received several requests by correspondents for copies of the population maps which illustrated his presentation. Almost certainly Jefferson spoke from notes rather than from a completed text, as was his habit at Association meetings. Unfortunately, only the title, not accompanied by an abstract, was listed in the 1907 program, published in the *Annals of the Association of American Geographers*. The population density maps of North America, Europe, and the World, which had been shown at Chicago, were, however, reproduced in his book, *Teachers' Geography*.[4]

Barely one month later, in the February of 1908, "Where Men Live in North America," appeared in the *Western Journal of Education*.[5] He abstracted his article for *The International Catalogue of Scientific Literature*:[6]

> Men live where there is more than twenty inches of rain in the year, which is in general east of the 100th meridian, on the south side of the 50th parallel. Exceptional parts of this last area are the tip of Florida and the Caribbean shores of Central America, where the rains are excessive and the vegetation almost untamable. The plant and climatic associations are pointed out that divide the continent between Latin and English races (Diagrams).

The *Western Journal of Education* published by the Michigan State Normal College at Ypsilanti, carried the article into many of the educational systems of the United States. There followed "Man in West Norway," an address Jefferson gave as President of the Michigan Academy of Sciences, Arts and Letters, at its annual meeting in Ann Arbor, March 1908. The address, later published in *The Tenth Annual Report of the Michigan Academy* and reproduced by the *Journal of Geography*, had been inspired by Jefferson's excursion to West Norway in the summer of 1904.[7] Jefferson summarized the essay:[8]

The Norsemen for all their large part in history, the widest, scattered folk in Europe. This due perhaps to their intimacy with the sea from early days. This intimacy like the sparseness of the peopling of the land, results from Norway's dearth of soil. The people cling only to the border of an empty land of rock.

The thesis of a near empty Norway peopled at its margins was one subject Jefferson used in his class texts until retirement.[9] Numerous slides of his own Norway population maps accompanied by slides of the West Norwegian culture-scape were visual aids used both in his classes and public addresses. The study of early Norwegian migration and Viking raids led Jefferson to a study of Viking plunder paths and European population distribution through the centuries. From this informal study carried on in his notebooks, there emerged his thesis of the plains as an invitation to militarism, which he wrote up immediately as "Man's Distribution Over the Earth,"[10] and which thesis was further developed in the *Hanson Bellows Encyclopedia*[11] and *Man in Europe*.[12]

During the summer and fall months of 1908 Jefferson gathered data and ideas for a paper which he delivered to the Association of American Geographers, Baltimore, December, 1908. "The Anthropography of Great Cities" was abstracted in the *Annals* of the A.A.G. as follows:[13]

The distribution of population density within great cities is under geographic control. The greatest density encompasses the business center where are many more residential buildings. Beyond this, population becomes less dense to a grade of ten thousand to the square mile, which is taken as suburban. The anthropographic city thus includes all adjacent territory populated more densely than this, regardless of political boundaries. There result anthropographic values of the population of great cities that are comparable. Geographic limits to a city's expansion immensely add to the maximum density within it, as shown by New York and Chicago with higher and lower densities than London, Paris, Berlin or Vienna. Attention was given to the causes and epoch of great cities, with a glance at the population of imperial Rome.

The paper was a great success and brought recognition to Jefferson, who recalled this circumstance many times in autobiographical notes he composed during his retirement years in the 1940's and in several letters, typical of which is the following:[14]

. . . by 1909 [I had] published the "Anthropography" from the Baltimore meeting of the A.A.G. Like all my previous papers before the Association, it was received rather contemptuously, Goode and Tower complaining that I put them out of Chicago and Philadelphia where they lived, because I claimed that the essence of a city was not a

*charter and charter limits—except for lawyers—but people living to-
gether in a huddle indicated, I suggested, by a continuous population
density of say 10,000 per square mile or more. They lived in the less
populous residential parts that characterize even large American cities,
which I call suburban.*

*Professor Albrecht Penck of Berlin (possibly Vienna at that date)
rose and commended the paper warmly, pointed out that Charlotten-
burg was one city with Berlin, opposite sides of the street being in the
two cities.*

*That made a great impression. My work was thereafter worth atten-
tion because one of those Germans that knew things approved of it!
The American Geographical Society of New York asked for the article, paid for it—which had never happened to me before,—and asked
me to become one of their contributing editors to write what occurred
to me at a fixed price. I have done so ever since.*

*That one should only be recognized when accepted authority ap-
proves, regardless of the content of one's contributions, would not
seem to make for scientific progress, but it is useful for a young
worker to bear in mind.*

Barely a week after the completion of the meeting Huntington wrote
to Jefferson:[15]

*. . . I wonder if you realize how much interest your paper at Balti-
more excited. It made everyone sit up and listen intently. I wish we
had dozens of such papers. They make geography extremely interesting
and valuable. Give us some more.*

The following day the Secretary of the American Geographical Society, Cyrus C. Adams, invited Jefferson to publish his paper in the
Bulletin of the Society:[16]

*We shall be glad to publish in the "Bulletin" of this Society the paper
which you recently read before the Association of American Geographers if you are able to send it to us for that purpose. From what we
have heard we believe the paper is just such a contribution as is desired
for our pages. The Society pays for the articles it prints at the rate of
$8.00 a thousand words. Hoping that you can oblige us in this matter.*

Jefferson replied to this letter:[17]

*The "Paper" on the Anthropography of some great cities only exists in
the form of notes at present, though a few days would probably suffice
to put it in shape for the printer and I should be very glad to have it
appear in the Bulletin . . . .*

The resultant publication appeared in the September issue of the
Bulletin of the American Geographical Society.[18] "The Anthropography
of Some Great Cities: A Study in Distribution of Population," was

8,686 words in length and provided Jefferson with a check for $69.48
. . . "My first invitation offering cash for a really scientific article!"
The idea of city anthropography was original. The article, "The Anthropography of Some Great Cities," a tour de force of powerful writing
and thought, became important to the entire literature of urban geography. It had been composed only after many letters had been sent to
friends, postmasters, Chambers of Commerce, police departments in
numerous U.S. cities, and the letters and replies filed, and the results
compiled in a notebook. This was a typical Jefferson procedure; gathering the facts, mounting them in meaningful arrangements, then, after
much study, breathing a new life into statistics remote of meaning.

Numerous ideas abound in the paper. Essentially concerned with city
population densities the paper examined the meaning attaching to real
and supposed density figures and began with a rejection of traditional
population estimates for imperial Rome. Bounded by the Aurelian wall
and enclosing an area of 4.47 square miles of land, estimates for the
Roman population had been calculated variously between one and two
million. Yet Jefferson noted that "the first census count seems to have
been made in Sweden, 1750," and that no accurate figures exist for
Rome. He proceeded to explain that the "million cities" of the Nineteenth Century were a product of the industrial revolution, and the
plains which constituted their sustenance space. Taking Million Cities
of the world and using figures for 1900-1905, Jefferson listed their
population, area, and population density per square mile. Paris, with all
her modern paraphernalia, boasted a density figure of only 88,000 people to the square mile in 1901. If the Rome of the Aurelian Wall had a
total population of 2 million her density would approximate 447,000 to
the square mile. If the Romans numbered 1 million, the density of the
imperial city would have approximated 223,500 people to the square
mile. Jefferson recognized that Bombay in 1901, with 35,000 people to
the square mile was the most densely populated city of the East then
counted, yet if Rome enjoyed a similar density her total population
would have numbered approximately 156,000 plus suburbs. After concluding, "that the old population was less than 500,000 will be confirmed by a study of the grading of population within the cities of
today," Jefferson continued the task of elaborating on the question,
"what is a city." He amassed data concerning the population density in
contemporary cities and arrived to the belief that the city could be best
defined and delimited only in these terms. This gave rise to his notion of
the anthropographic city:

> *A continuous area having everywhere ten thousand or more people to*
> *the square mile is a city . . . For distinction from the political city,*

> *this may be called the anthropographic one or city according to the distribution of people, just as lines indicating grades of population density may be called isanthropic lines and the maps isanthropic maps.*
>
> *. . . As for the method of drawing the isanthropic line of 10,000, it is a makeshift, perhaps the best thing that can be done to remedy the existing lack of uniformity in the meaning given to the name "city".*

Boundaries to the anthropographic city were draughted for St. Louis, Chicago, New York, Vienna, Berlin, Paris, London. The article was briefly summarized (120 words) by Baulig in the *Annales de Géographie* and by Otto Most in *Petermann's Mitteilungen Literaturbericht* (700 words), and also by Griffith Taylor in his chapter "Urban Geography," of the book *Geography in the Twentieth Century*[19] . . . "In America Mark Jefferson was the pioneer, with such papers as that of 1909 which dealt with the anthropogeography [sic] of some Great Cities." Taylor also referred to this article in his book, *Urban Geography,* in the following words:[20]

> *Perhaps we owe more to the veteran geographer, Mark Jefferson, than to any other in this field. As long ago as 1909 he wrote a brochure on the anthropogeography [sic] of some great cities, which was a pioneer among general urban studies. It dealt largely with variations in the densities of the wards of the great cities. Many great cities show a relatively empty nucleus surrounded by a zone of wards of high density (Fig. 78). Outside this again is a zone of larger wards with much lower densities. Various great American and European cities were charted by him to show this feature . . .*

Numerous American geographers wrote and thanked Jefferson for the Anthropography paper, including A. P. Brigham:[21]

> *. . . I am particularly glad to have the Baltimore paper in full. It will be very useful to every geographer who studies our cities and I for one appreciate the great amount of work and research which you put into it.*

The city anthropography article of 1909 was followed in the *Bulletin* by "New York and the four next largest American cities in 1910," a note in *Geographical Record.*[22] Jefferson applied his anthropographic city definition to New York, Chicago, Philadelphia, Boston, St. Louis, gave their respective anthropographic city populations and annual population growths. He wrote on the anthropography of New York:[23]

> *The city at the Hudson mouth has now over 5,000,000 inhabitants in the four municipalities, New York, Jersey City, Hoboken and Newark. Furthermore, it has gained over 1,500,000 since 1900. The city is still smaller than London, but its growth is over twice as rapid and it will probably outgrow London in the next decade.*

The concept, anthropography, next appeared at the eighth annual meeting of the Association of American Geographers in Washington, D.C. December, 1911. The paper, "The Anthropography of North America," was abstracted in the *Annals of the Association of American Geographers:*[24]

> The map—interpretation of the map—the point of view geographic, i.e. that there is a human response to environment which may be made out on such a map, the grades of density, their selection and history. The U.S. Census grades, influence of the point of view, treatment of cities, treatment of forests, isanthropic lines, the data and their treatment.

A brusque, coarse writing, which did not allow style to challenge content for attention, characterized many of Jefferson's abstracts, but perhaps this abstract was so coarsely composed that it lost some meaning. The North American Anthropography paper was reproduced in the *Bulletin of the American Geographical Society* in March, 1913.[25] The population density maps accompanying the article were among the most adequate of their kind produced to that date. As the abstract suggested, population distribution and reasons for it were the essential concern of the paper.

The *Bulletin of the American Geographical Society* of September, 1913, further advanced his published observation concerning population studies with "A New Density of Population Map of Europe."[26] This article offered the readers of the *Bulletin* analysis of a map and accompanying statement by L. Weise published in the January, 1913 issue of *Petermann's Mitteilungen.*[27] Of this work Jefferson wrote:[28] "Dr. Weise publishes a painstaking and extremely interesting new map of the distribution of population densities in Europe. Despite his modest disclaimer it must certainly be regarded as the map for its continent." Weise's map, which incorporated information from the censuses of 1910-1911 and which indicated twelve densities of population by color shade was simplified and redrawn by Jefferson (five density levels and black and white shading). This map was later reproduced in his texts, *Teachers Geography, Notes on the Geography of Europe,* and *Man in Europe.*

In September of that same year, 1913, *The Atlantic Monthly* published Jefferson's article originally entitled "The Birth of the Cities," but edited to read, "A Hopeful View of the Urban Problem."[29] Summarized for *The International Catalogue of Scientific Literature,* the abstract reads:[30]

> People are not leaving the country as often stated. Five million more country people in 1910 than 1900 in U.S. People are leaving

some country places and going to others. Rural population in the United States growing almost as fast as total population of Germany. Cities being taken as smaller and smaller by census. Really cities are springing up wonderfully as a result of country growth. It is normal that country population should remain thin, that cities should take up part of natural growth of country. Country, isolated houses, village neighbour houses, city defense against neighbors, at less than 300 per square mile, 300 to 10,000 and over 10,000.

Jefferson very positively developed the notion of an intimate relationship between urban and rural areas:[31]

With us, cities are as sure to spring up with the increase of country population as the forests to disappear. City and country are organically related. Crops cannot be grown without fields, nor exchanged and manufactured under the modern system of division of labor, without cities. Only in the rudest pioneer settlements do men dispense with this division of labor by doing everything painfully and badly on the farm. Such settlements are retarded and hampered until they have towns for the city part of the work. When we estimate that the average inhabitant of New York may have but a few score square feet for his own use, we are apt to forget that he can only exist on them because somewhere in the country there are acres of ground producing for him, as really and definitely for him as if he owned them and hired the labor on them—what Professor Penck has called his "sustenance space".

The article was widely read, fetched Jefferson a much-needed $60 check and occasioned comment in *Outlook Magazine,* September, 1913.[32]

It is a severe indictment of the city that Mr. G. S. Dickerman presents in the September number of the Atlantic Monthly. From him one would get the impression that the city is a leech that is sucking the blood of the country, a siren that lures the young to destruction, a monster which enslaves the growing child to arbitrary convention and robs him of self-reliance. Yet if, at its worst, the city is an evil, it is a necessary evil. And at its best it is something more. In the same number of the Atlantic in which Mr. Dickerman's article appears there is an article by Professor Mark Jefferson, who occupies the chair of Geography in the State Normal College at Ypsilanti, Michigan. Professor Jefferson shows the other side, the more promising, more constructive side of city life. He presents the cities as creatures of the country "that supplement and crown the life of the land." To the city, "with banks and high schools and theaters and factories, and stores with costlier grades of furniture and clothing and objects of luxury," the farmer goes to sell his crops; to it he looks "for the culture he wants in

the form of religion, of education for his family, or of social inter-
course and entertainment;" in it "he and his wife hope to spend their
last days." In this way the city, at its best, represents the ideals, or at
least many of the highest ideals, toward which modern civilization
moves.

At the annual meeting of the Association of American Geographers
at Princeton, December, 1913, Jefferson offered a paper entitled "The
Growth of American Cities,"[33] which paper was an extension of his
thinking concerning "A Hopeful View of the Urban Problem."

In 1914 another Jefferson population article appeared in the *Bulletin
of the American Geographical Society:* "Population estimates for the
countries of the world from 1914 to 1920."[34] Abstracted in deceptively
simple form for *The International Catalogue of Scientific Literature* one
reads:[35]

> *By plotting the population estimates of the last four decades, a curve is*
> *obtained and projected to 1920. From this is read off the values for the*
> *given years for 116 countries or groups of countries, the populations*
> *they will have if no catastrophe intervenes.*

Curves were plotted in Jefferson's City Notebook for 116 countries of
the world, several of which were reproduced in his *Bulletin* article, and
their respective populations were calculated for each year between 1914
and 1920. Five tables of statistics were compiled: population of the
countries of America, Europe, Australia, Asia, and Africa. The reliability and recentness of census reports and other sources of data used were
written into the text, and the 1914 population of the world calculated to
be 1,669 million.

In the June, 1914, *Bulletin of the American Geographical Society,*
Jefferson published "The Revolution and the Mexican Plateau."[36] The
inevitable distribution of population map accompanied the article which
Jefferson abstracted as follows:[37]

> *Shows how the populous part of Mexico, which includes its large cities*
> *was more than five thousand feet above the sea and that at that time*
> *(June 1914) the revolution had barely got up to that level from the*
> *fringe of lower levels where it began.*

Later, in the January volume, 1917, of the *Geographical Review* this
article and map were reprinted with only a slight modification in an
article entitled "The Frontier Region of Mexico: Notes to Accompany a
Map of the Frontier." At the request of the American Geographical
Society in December 1916, Jefferson wrote a supplemental note for this
article.[38] The two printings of Jefferson's Mexican study focused attention on the value of studying the distribution of people, at a time when
the U.S. national interest was involved.

Meanwhile Jefferson's prolificity with regard to distribution and density studies continued unabated. At the eleventh annual meeting of the Association of American Geographers at Chicago in December 1914, he presented, "Regional Characters in the Growth of American Cities," published the following year in the *Bulletin of the American Geographical Society* under the title "How American Cities Grow."[39] Bowman reproduced Jefferson's map and ideas concerning types of city growth in North America in the *Supplement to The New World,* 1923.[40] The paper, "Regional Characters in the Growth of American Cities," was abstracted in the *Annals of the Association of American Geographers:*[41]

> The details in the growth of our cities reveal an intimate relation to their environment. Thirty-four cities of the Humid East show vigorous growth adding larger numbers to their population with each decade. Cleveland and Columbus are fine types. Their platted curves are concave upwards. The river cities of the Humid East after early vigor show halting growth, as the railroads superseded river transportation. Cincinnati is the type, with curve distinctly convex upward. There are six such and the Great Lake cities show symptoms of the same disease since 1880.
>
> When the transcontinental railways opened up the Pacific Coast to the American people, who were adventurous and well equipped with material resources, there resulted an exuberant growth of the cities of the New West, doubling their population for two decades running. In this group are eight cities.
>
> How little the political function helps a city is seen by the sorry figure cut by Albany as a growing organism. Every city of 100,000 in the country has long outstripped it. Washington though earlier vigorous shows distinct signs of atrophy since its disfranchisement.

Lecture notes and numerous slides suggest that the notion of vigorous, halting, and exuberant city growth was a favorite theme with Jefferson in the classroom. Later Jefferson repeated his thesis of growth types in *Man in the United States,* 1933.[42]

In the November issue of the *Geographical Review,* 1916, Jefferson published "The Distribution of People in Japan in 1913,"[43] which was later rendered more accurate by a note in the French publication, *Annales de Géographie.*[44] Jefferson acknowledged and reduced the note to English in the *Geographical Review.*[45] The text, map, and district population figures used, were the result of an extended correspondence between Jefferson and Naomasa Yamasaki (the two geographers had met each other on the Liverpool-Rome excursion of 1911). Jefferson laboriously traced and plotted, retraced and replotted population maps of Japan, sending them to Yamasaki—first incumbent in the chair of geography established at Tokyo Imperial University in 1911—for improvement, always with queries and usually with some postage stamps for Yamasaki's philatelist children. After several months of collaboration, he sent his Japanese density of population maps, 100,000 city map of Japan and Korea, accompanied by a text, to Isaiah Bowman, the recently appointed Director of the American Geographic Society. Bowman had proofs made of the article which was returned to Jefferson for approval. Bowman's editing of the text produced an interesting written statement from Jefferson concerning his notion of anthropography:[46]

> In the text I have restored Anthropography (the distribution of man) for anthropogeography (the interaction between earth and man). The difference one of principle with me. I want to study the facts of distribution just as objectively as if they were quite matter of chance and then point out other facts to say it looks as if, as Davis says. That is why I closed my paper—at the end—by calling attention to regions of falling population or smaller growth and then writing "it is a very rugged mountainous region". I do not at all like your changing this, and making me say this is attributable to the mountainous character of the region.

And if this letter encouraged him to distinguish anthropography and anthropogeography, Jefferson lent definition to the term, only three months later, in his Presidential address to the Association of American Geographers entitled "Some Considerations on the Geographical Provinces of the United States":[47]

> Anthropogeography—A second sort of human geography is usually called anthropogeography. It attempts to explain the character and habits of a people by their environment. This field has special perils. A great part of what has been written is vague and fanciful rather than cautious and well-based. If no other explanation of qualities is available one may always refer to the "climate".
>
> Anthropography—The third field has been less cultivated, but is fundamental. It studies the distribution of men over the earth as a static fact, regardless of their movements or occupation, but paying much attention to the closeness with which they occupy their region, or the density of population from place to place. The full topical name, distribution of population-densities, is somewhat cumbrous. As an arbitrary name Anthropography would have advantages, and its etymology is quite as good as that of many accepted names. The questions, Where are men and How many of them are there must be answered with some care before we attempt to explain the reactions of men and inanimate nature.

In the same address Jefferson states:

> Yet it is curious that less attention has been paid to the facts of

anthropography than to the causes that ought to guide and control them. The geographic provinces of this viewpoint would be the actual groupings of men on the earth quite irrespective of any climatic or physiographic boundaries that should hypothetically control them.

It was anthropography, the study of population distribution, which was so central to Jefferson's conception of the spirit and purpose of geography in his post-Davisian days. The 9,000-word, 1916 Presidential address was a summary of Jefferson's anthropographic thought and research to that year. He advocated the anthropographic cause and insisted on the need for a world map showing settlements of more than 10,000 inhabitants. Three such maps, "Cities of the United States, India and the British Isles," were presented with the address.

The term anthropography was not adopted by American geographers, but at the 1914 Chicago meeting of the Association of American Geographers, Ellsworth Huntington delivered a paper entitled "The Anthropography of Guatemala."[48] It is interesting to find references to Jefferson's anthropography mistakenly assuming the form of the word anthropogeography, as in Griffith Taylor's *Geography in the Twentieth Century*[49] and *Urban Geography*,[50] and Stephen Visher's obituary, "Mark Jefferson," in the *Annals of the Association of American Geographers*.[51] The cover of the *Bulletin of the American Geographical Society* for 1909 refers to Jefferson's article as "The Anthropology of Some Great Cities."[52] In 1915 Jefferson expressed his interest in matters relating to population study in a letter to Bowman:[53]

I want to make a book on distribution of population that shall contain a lot of material that I have already gathered, without waiting to exhaust the subject or complete all the lines I have started. I think there is quite a lot of it. This has been on my mind a good deal lately, and today I find Huntington minded to make use of a number of ideas of mine that I would rather keep a claim to. But who would publish? There ought to be some color used as well as much black and white work. What can you suggest? I have thought of Wiley. Who would buy such a work? I fancy I hear him say. Who indeed? The little things I am working up here make good enough impression when I present them to make me feel that quite a little might come from these population studies were they fairly set out. Cities, towns and villages, and their relation to the tilled land, the great plains inevitably the basis of all strong peoples and all vigorous civilizations, the present war merely the most violent stage in the struggle for the hegemony of the great plains of northern Europe, where Germany felt hemmed in between Russia on the east and France on the west, while the plain of England was envied, her safe aloofness across the Channels silver strand—those are the chapters in the story. The city map and the town map are the quickest road to insight.

Jefferson did not write the book he had proposed to Bowman, but he incorporated much of his thought concerning population distribution in *Notes on the Geography of Europe* published in July, 1917, by an Ypsilanti printer. This book of modest title was much revised and reprinted in 1924, 1926, and 1936 as *Man in Europe*. Jefferson's "Notes" occupied twenty-nine chapters, each consisting of a series of penetrating questions, occasional thoughtful excursuses and a map. His interest in population distribution is markedly reflected in the first eight chapter headings of the text:

1. Distribution of population—densities;
2. The Million Cities and Half-Million Cities;
3. The Great Cities, those that have over a hundred thousand people;
4. The Great cities and coalfields of Great Britain;
5. The cities of Great Britain and Ireland of over 10,000 people;
6. Millions of people in 1917, using the boundaries of 1913 and making no allowance for losses by war;
7. Thousands of square miles in 1913;
8. Number of people per square mile;

These chapters reflect the content of Jefferson's earlier population studies. Frequently he referred to his own published work in footnotes, but the early chapters of the "Notes" were not solely a summary of his previous thought. He managed to go beyond himself by the use of exercises—questions which bred further questions and which were suggestive of thought which lay beyond articulation. This Europe text, adopted by several universities, colleges, and normal schools, was one of the first human geographies of Europe written by an American. In 1916 there had been a correspondence between Huntington and Jefferson concerning the possibility of joint authorship of a Europe text, Huntington even visiting Jefferson in Ypsilanti to talk over the matter in detail, but the task was not jointly undertaken. Both men, independently of the other, published European Geographies in 1917.

Jefferson's book included the essentials of an article published in November of that same year, 1917, in the *Geographical Review*, entitled "The Distribution of British Cities, and the Empire."[54] With this essay Jefferson became the first American geographer to demonstrate by text and map the location of swarms of British cities on the coalfields. He enumerated the swarms of South Wales, the Clyde, Newcastle, the Midlands and wrote that the intensity of the "city swarm" on British coalfields was not equalled by the U.S.A. or Germany. Many of the cities created, he noted, had for a sustenance space not merely the

British Isles but the British Empire. This notion of a city acquiring a trans-oceanic sustenance space was fresh to the thought of the time. Isaiah Bowman later reproduced Jefferson's "City and Coalfield" map in his book *The New World: Problems in Political Geography.*[55]

From April to September, 1918, Jefferson led the American Geographical Society "ABC" Excursion. The several months field work involved much study of settlement geography. Certainly the literature concerning people and their distribution was enhanced by two books and an article, products of the "ABC" Excursion: *Recent Colonization of Chile, Peopling the Argentine Pampa,* and "Pictures From Southern Brazil."

In the latter part of 1918 and early 1919 Jefferson worked with the Inquiry and then for the American Commission to negotiate peace at Paris. His interest in population distribution reveals itself in the maps he chose to draw, rather than to delegate while at Paris. Those he drew are to be distinguished by his signature in the bottom right-hand corner, or on the back of the map;[56] frequently his self-drawn maps concerned the distribution of population. Several of these maps were retained by Jefferson in a private collection of original maps he kept in his home following the Paris conference. The following maps are some of those that Jefferson chose to draw himself:

> 554 —*Russia—Cities.*
> *unnumbered —Cities of Europe in 1910. Scale 1-6,000,000.*
> 570 —*France—Cities.*
> *unnumbered —Cities and Coalfields of Germany. Scale 1-7,500,000.*
> 571 —*German Cities. Scale 1-3,000,000.*
> *unnumbered —Hotel Beds in Switzerland.*
> 573 —*Austria Hungary—Cities. Scale 1-3,000,000.*
> *unnumbered —The British Isles—Cities. Scale 1-4,300,000.*
> *unnumbered —Cities of Europe 1911.*
> 584a —*Areas of Population of Dalmation Islands in 1900.*

In 1922 the Swedish geographer, Sten de Geer, journeyed from Stockholm to teach at the University of Chicago. He took the opportunity to seek out Jefferson to discuss population distributions.[57] (Dating from 1905 Jefferson and De Geer had engaged in correspondence, initially concerning river meanderings, later concerning glaciation and the mapping of population.) De Geer stayed at the Jefferson home in Ypsilanti in the later part of August 1922. The pair then motored through Ohio into Pennsylvania. The journey and discussion constituted a significant part of the field work De Geer invested in his study of the geography of the United States manufacturing belt, later published in *Geografiska Annaler* as "The American Manufacturing Belt"[58] and reviewed in the *Geographical Review* by Jefferson.[59] On his return to Stockholm De Geer wrote Jefferson a note of appreciation:[60]

> *I am now since a few days in my home at Stockholm, and have just begun my courses here. I remember now my most interesting journey from Michigan past Ohio and into Pennsylvania, with large manufacturing districts and cities, many small American towns and the rural tracts passed, all showing many special American features. I will soon send a copy of Klaralfven. I hope you have reached Ypsilanti with your family after so many long Ford days. Please remember me to Mrs. Jefferson.*

Commencing in 1921 Jefferson published in the *Geographical Review*, four decennial studies of population growth or change in the United States; "Great Cities of the United States 1920,"[61] "The Distribution of People in the United States in 1910—As indicated by the distribution of the cities,"[62] "Great Cities of 1930 in the United States with a comparison of New York and London."[63] "The Great Cities of the United States, 1940."[64] Evidence suggests that Jefferson was preparing another Great Cities paper for 1950, but death intervened.

The Great Cities paper of 1920 listed in descending order of size the 64 cities which the U.S. census of 1920 claimed had exceeded a population of 100,000. Whereas the census recognised group cities only after they had been politically united, Jefferson recognised non-politically unified group cities as anthropographic cities. For these anthropographic cities he computed total populations:[65]

> *The criterion used in selecting the adjacent towns to be included with a city is continuity of close, city-like occupation of the ground on land areas, which includes park spaces, properly a part of a city to maintain the health of its citizens, but does not include farm lands and meadows that may be included within the political city area, as in Queens Borough, New York. The group city so conceived is a more real city than the Metropolitan Districts of the Census Bureau, which include all population centers of 5,000 people within 10 miles of the city limits.*

Jefferson was again asserting the merits of the anthropographic city over the political city when he listed the components of group cities in a separate table, these cities including: New York, Philadelphia, Detroit, Boston, St. Louis, Pittsburgh, Buffalo, Cincinnati, Kansas City, Oakland, Louisville, Omaha, Norfolk, Duluth.

Encouraged by the success of this article, and in 1924, he essayed, "The Distribution of People in the United States in 1910," whose main feature was three population maps on the scale of 1:9½ million: "Cities of the North," "Cities of the South," "Cities of the West." The text which accompanied the maps offered brief explanation concerning city distribution. Concluding, Jefferson wrote:[66]

> On all the maps we notice that the rivers are rarely strung with towns the way the railroads are. The railroads are now our principal means of transportation and the roads are beginning to rival them in the parts of the country where they are well built. Rivers with us, generally speaking, have long ceased to be of any great importance for transportation.
>
> Everywhere the larger towns occur only where there are a number of smaller ones. Wherever there is but one town in hundreds of miles it is sure to be a little one. A town of ten thousand among towns of ten, and so on to the largest cities. A city of a million usually has others of a hundred thousand or more around it.
>
> Our largest city, New York, has long been called the front office of the United States since large enterprises in all parts of the country find it to their advantage to have offices or agencies there.
>
> These cities are the essential United States. Their distribution shows how the American people are rooted in their soil. Transportation has now become so vital that it will be hard if not impossible to find a town of ten thousand people that is not on a railroad.

Of this paper J. Russell Smith wrote to Jefferson:[67]

> . . . Referring again to some of your map prowess. I have in hand, with a great deal of appreciation that map of yours showing distribution of people in the U.S. in 1910 as indicated by the distribution of cities . . . it is a corking thing.

The third of the decennial studies concerning Great Cities in the U.S.A., 1930, again returned to the question of city boundaries. Jefferson adhered to his notion that the real city, the anthropographic city, enjoyed a population density of 10,000 to the square mile, and then demonstrated with maps and text that the Detroit of the census was not anthropographic Detroit, the city he knew well, and which he had lived near for thirty years. Using anthropographic definitions and jousting for a wider acceptance of his anthropographic notion, he estimated that there were 87 great cities of more than 100,000 in the U.S., while the census listed ninety-six 100,000 metropolitan districts. Significantly he observed that, "for the first time in the history of the United States the decade 1920-1930 has seen great cities lose population," and he cited the cases of Lowell, New Bedford, Fall River, and Wilmington, commenting "that such a thing never happened before, that every city to attain hundred-thousand size in the 128 years since New York first reached it, has continued increasing in size until the decade 1920-1930 . . . . . a remarkable record."

Jefferson noted that the increment of population growth in 1920-1930 was 16.1%, a much lower percentage than earlier decennial figures. He also observed that the 1920-1930 decade was the first in the history of the U.S.A. when emmigration exceeded immigration, and he related the meaning of this loss to the cities. He analyzed the matter of potential population loss in the U.S. in an article, "Is the population of the United States now decreasing," published in the *Geographical Review,* October, 1934.[68] The matter was revisited again by Jefferson in a note entitled "Our Potential Parents and Potential Population," published in the *Geographical Review.*[69] Meanwhile a 500-word article entitled "City Growth," summarizing the Great Cities paper, appeared in the New York *Times* for January 16, 1933, barely days after the *Geographical Review* had been released.[70]

Jefferson's fourth, the 1940 Great City paper, written when he was 78, indicated that the great cities of the U.S. had enjoyed a smaller percentage growth than in any previous decade, and that the percentage growth in U.S. population was larger than the percentage population growth of the great cities. The great cities, their total population, and decennial increase were the subject of study. The remainder of the paper was a continued elaboration distinguishing the political city from the "actual" or "anthropographic" city.

These four decennial great city studies of the U.S.A., published in the *Geographical Review,* found no imitators among the geographers. They were regarded as sound pieces of scholarship, have frequently been referred to by scholars, and bore constant testimony to his interest in the concept of the anthropographic city. Later, in 1952 the American Geographical Society reprinted "Great Cities of 1930 in the U.S. with a Comparison of New York and London," in *Readings in the Geography of North America: A selection of articles from the Geographical Review.*

Jefferson's interest in the U.S. census and its figures had stemmed from the time of his earliest interest in city geography. In the early 1920's Jefferson had strongly recommended to Bowman that key census workers should be made familiar with geographical studies concerning matters of population. By May of 1924 a Mr. Batschelet of the Census Bureau was sent to the American Geographical Society at Bowman's request and under Bowman's direction, though it was with Marcel Aurousseau that Batschelet did much of his reading and thinking. Four letters indicate Jefferson as a prime mover in this venture and one who insisted on the worth of distinguishing (his) geographic from (Fenneman's) physiographic provinces.

Jefferson to Bowman, May 9, 1924:[71]

The Census Bureau has been reasonably responsive to my suggestions, in the few cases I have made any.

I have an objection to sending Sloan [a man from Census Bureau] to Fenneman, or to anyone who thinks geography the same thing as physiography. If one may judge by the last three school geographies published, his excellent revision of Physical Provinces has been an injury to school geography already.

Bowman to Jefferson, May 14, 1924:[72]

Mr. C. E. Batschelet, who has been appointed the Geographer of the Census, his appointment to run from August 1, when he finishes his work at the Society, has now arrived and begun reading in conferences under instructions of various members of the staff who can give him time. He spent a part of the morning with me out at my house discussing his plans and loading up on suggestions of various sorts. He is just an average bureau man, but he is most willing to receive sugges-tions and he is eager to have the support of the geographers of the country in working into his new position. We owe the suggestion of his coming to you, for Dr. Hill, whose letter you enclose and which I now return, sent me not only a copy of this letter but in addition a copy of your reply. As a result of further negotiation with him and of repeated agitation of the subject with my Board of Trustees I secured an appro-priation of $500 to cover the man's expenses for three months while working here in New York.

It seemed to me, however, that we could greatly broaden the value of the experiment if we operated through the Division of Geology and Geography of the National Research Council and had appointed a committee which was national in membership. Above all, the commit-tee was to include every geographer who had definite ideas as to the improvement of the census schedules or technique, or cartographic or other graphic methods. It seemed to me that Fenneman ought to be chairman of that committee because he had been serving as chairman of an earlier committee and had shown great skill in dealing with the Census representatives and with the members of his physiographic committee at an earlier time when he was completing his map. He was present at the Washington meeting of the Division of Geology and Geography of the National Research Council and that was also a reason, because it gave me a chance to talk over the matter with him in some detail. It is not my thought that members of the committee should deal with Fenneman hereafter when they want to convey a suggestion to the Census. The sole idea is that we should all pull together in getting the present Geographer equipped with some sort of training before he faces his new job. I suggested that you and Baker and a number of others should go on the committee because in your case particularly there was evidence of more interest and intelligence with reference to the Census than anyone else in the country had exhibited. I told this to Mr. Batschelet this morning and asked him to write you at once and especially to acknowledge his gratitude to you for having made the original suggestion that he come here to study. It is Aurousseau principally who has him in charge at the present time and the thing that he is pumping into him to the greatest extent is city geography. So I asked Batschelet if he would not read your various papers on city geography and write you at once about the whole question of the lower limit of city size as represented upon the statistical schedules of the Census. I hope he opens up the matter thoroughly and that you will let him have every suggestion that occurs to you.

I represented both to the National Research Council and to Stewart and Hill of the Census that we had two main objects in view in inviting him to come up here: 1. To become actually acquainted through personal conference and through correspondence with American Geographers interested in his work. 2. To gather together suggestions of all kinds pertinent to the population volume of the Census and to some degree other volumes so that he would go back loaded with ideas from the start. It is these two objects rather than any broad program of instruction that we have chiefly in mind. I spent a good deal of time in telling him about the trend of your studies and about the importance of them and he is prepared to receive all your suggestions in the best possible spirit. You can write to him directly at the Society's address.

Jefferson to Fenneman, May 16, 1924:[73]

I have your letters referring to Mr. Batschelet's work at New York and one from Dr. Lawson announcing the appointment of the committee of the National Research Council—Fenneman chairman, myself among members—"to cooperate with the Bureau of the Census as regards those features of its work which concern the subject of geography and graphics". He enclosed a copy of Director Stewart's letter of April 29.

I am glad this committee has been formed and that you are Chairman. I have been in touch with the situation for some months and think it highly important that Batschelet have all the contact with Dr. Bowman possible. The census needs more geography and if anyone can awaken a Bureau man to the fact it is Bowman.

Within the next two weeks I hope to submit for the consideration of the committee some suggestions of mine, and speaking of physiographic divisions I wish you would make a statement of just what use of them the Census ought to make . . . .

My general feeling is that very sharp distinction must be made between physiographic regions and geographic ones, but I have been surprised to note how well your major Physiographic divisions fall into the groups of the cities of my 1910 map which I have just issued in form convenient for use. I send you a copy under another cover with the boundaries pencilled in on the "North map."

Jefferson to Bowman, May 16, 1924:[74]

. . . I do not think you need to stress my work so very much to Batschelet, but he is in good hands with you and Aurousseau. I should not have wished to tie any strings to my suggestion that he come to you. You can make a man over in three months.

I thought first of asking to have him sent here, but that would have been useless. The very idea of a man from Washington regarding himself very likely as a high official coming to a fresh water Normal School! Nothing doing!

It is a matter of impressing that man with the dignity and importance of geography. You and your Environment (capital E) are needed. I think you will send him back impressed.

Bowman to Jefferson, May 20, 1924:[75]

. . . The cities map marked physiographically . . . .

In the meantime I am having Aurousseau study it and comment upon it to Batschelet. I am glad you found the physiographic boundaries useful. I see your point very clearly about the geographical provinces and of course the physiographic province map is not final . . . The real thing is the geographical province and I suppose we shall be discussing that for some years until we agree even tentatively upon the boundaries of such.

. . . He is already working most enthusiastically. If the plan succeeds we shall owe it all to your original suggestion. I shall not forget this.

A continuing interest and concern for population census figures inspired Jefferson to check Malthus' contention against available statistics. The resultant, "Looking Back at Malthus," published in the *Geographical Review,* April, 1925,[76] commanded the attention of many geographers. A Bowman-authored telegram was sent to Jefferson from the American Geographical Society by editor Gladys Wrigley: "Great stuff. Leading article for April."[77] In the *Annual Report of the Council of the American Geographical Society* delivered January 21, 1926 one may read:[78]

To the Fellows of the Society:

Among the papers in the Geographical Review that have stimulated discussion and represent new field work and new ideas the following may be mentioned as especially noteworthy:

"Looking Back at Malthus", by Professor Mark Jefferson, discusses
the trends of population growth and their relation to food supply.

A. W. Pezet of *The Forum* wrote to Jefferson requesting an article of 3,000-4,000 words in the vein of his Malthus paper to be used in a series of articles concerning war and peace,[79] and Professor Wilson Wallis wrote to Jefferson:[80]

Professor Malcom M. Willey and I are preparing a resource book in Sociology, to be published by Knopf in 1929, and we should like to include in it your article "Looking Back at Malthus" which appeared in the Geographical Review, 1925.

A New York *Times* editorial for Sunday, April 25, 1925, entitled "Malthus Cross-Examined," summarized Jefferson's article in less than 600 words and in so doing advertised the *Geographical Review* and Mark Jefferson. (The latter was often to find his name mentioned in the pages of the New York *Times* in the years to come.)

Jefferson had presented his views concerning Malthus, albeit briefly, at the annual meeting of the Association of American Geographers, Washington, 1924, in a paper entitled "Malthus in the Light of Subsequent Events." The published abstract of this paper reads:[81]

Malthus, living on the eve of the age of steam, feared that men would multiply so fast on the earth that some day they would be brought into terrible distress by hunger.

Abundant statistics of the hundred and twenty years that followed have not justified his fears. Food has become over abundant and populations shows distinct signs of being checked by another agency that operates independently of food supply. There is little likelihood that the world will ever be really crowded.

The Presidential address of that same meeting was given by President Marbut and was entitled "The Promulgation, Decline and Renaissance of Malthusianism and its relation to the character and Geographic Distribution of the soil"!

In his *Geographical Review* article Jefferson found fault with Malthus who had claimed that a doubling of the U.S. population within 25 years, lent substance to the doctrine that population, when unchecked, increases in a geometrical ratio. Jefferson indicated that Malthus' claim for a doubling of the U.S. population in the *Essay on the Principle of Population* published in 1798, came only eight years after the first census was taken in the U.S.A. Jefferson wrote that the population increase of the U.S. was in large part due not to biological increase but to unusually large numbers of immigrants arriving from Europe. From census study Jefferson noted:[82]

Measured periods of doubling now known but none of them made in

Malthus' day, are for Finland, 49 years to 1800, 58 years to 1858, and something like 62 years the third time; for the United Kingdom 70 years; for England, 45 years the first and 55 years the second time; for Sweden, 105; for Spain 131; for Denmark 91. France gives no sign of ever doubling.

Jefferson quoted Darwin in writing that the suggested Malthusian idea of the food supply increasing in arithmetic ratio has no foundation even in theory and that "the distinction between rates of increase of man and his food is not sound. Both are organic, and both show the same tendencies." He insisted that in the century and a quarter that followed Malthus and in those countries which had a population census, the food supply had increased more swiftly than the population.

Regardless of the validity of conclusion written into the Malthus paper, Jefferson signified his ingenuity of thought and kept the matter of population very much before an audience of American geographers.

The following year, 1926, saw the publication of *Atlas of Plates to Man in the United States* and *Principles of Geography*. The *Atlas of Plates* offered a foreword which began:

A text is in preparation with the title Man in the United States, which is in large part built around the study of such facts as are here set out in diagrams. The plates are published in advance merely for class use while the text is being prepared. It will be enough to note here that two useful features of the diagrams are quite new. The expression of all material quantities in dollars, and the use of figures the material size of which on the diagram corresponds somewhat to the value they indicate.

The first map of the *Atlas,* "1920. Hundreds of Thousands in each state," was reproduced in the Swedish geographical magazine, *Globen,* in 1927 and an interest expressed in Jefferson's novel method of indicating population distribution. The same issue of *Globen* also reviewed his *Atlas of Plates to Man in the U.S.A.*[83]

Man in the United States eventually appeared in 1933 and was printed by the Ypsilanti Publishing Company. The earlier *Atlas* maps however were not reproduced; Jefferson had made new and different maps.

Later in 1926, in the eleven-chaptered, 131 page *Principles of Geography* (another revision of *Teachers Geography* with the title changed), Jefferson devoted two chapters and 36 pages to the questions, "Where the People are" and "Why the People are there." In brief statements and exercises for students, these chapters summarized his population thought to that time, presenting his population studies in the form of a simplified but easily digestible continuum rather than as numerous diverse separates which had already become a fugitive litera-ture. In 1931, *Exercises in Human Geography,* published by the Ann Arbor Press, Michigan, appeared and replaced *Principles of Geography; The Exercises* was reprinted in 1936. Exercises in population study graced the opening pages of both editions of the book. The title page of both editions carried the inscription, "Our Geography is mainly con-cerned with Men—where they are and what they are like."

In the summer school of 1931 Jefferson offered his first course con-cerning itself solely with the distribution of population. Geography 420, "Geography of Cities," was offered at the Michigan State Normal Col-lege summer session, and was one of the earliest courses in urban geography offered on a U.S. university campus. The course centered around numerous of the articles previously published by Jefferson. Re-prints were circulated to the class, and questions and exercises were woven around this matter. The idea of the anthropographic city was amply in evidence. The course description read:[84] "Deals with nuclea-tion of population into villages, cities and towns, the nature of the Great Cities, their distribution and function in the life of modern coun-tries." While the course was in progress, the *Geographical Review* published Jefferson's, "Distribution of the World's City Folks: A study in comparative civilization." In this stimulating and original piece of work which became one of his most often quoted articles, Jefferson wrote, "Cities do not grow up of themselves, countrysides set them up to do tasks that must be performed in central places." And so was born the term "central place."[85] He insisted that "urban and rural, city and country are one thing, not two entities. Rural folk are only distinct from city folk in their sleep," and that in the numerous world censuses, no arbitrary ruling has been made or accepted distinguishing the rural from the urban. He insisted on the need for censuses of people awake, claim-ing that the city of New York at 2 a.m. was a very different entity from the New York of 2 p.m., a thesis to which he returned in the *Geograph-ical Review* of 1933 with a note concerning day and night population densities in the city of Tokyo. A map, "Distribution of Great City Life, 1927," drawn on Jefferson's own six-six projection[86] showed the percen-tage of population in cities of 100,000 throughout the world.

He produced statistics for each of the continents, showing the per-centage of people living in the great cities of 100,000 or more popula-tion. Similar percentages were derived and listed for each of the coun-tries of the world, and text was written concerning four world regions of "great-city" urbanization. A diagram illustrating the growing percentage of population in great cities by decades from 1870-1920 explained growth rates for eleven chosen countries. A fascinating diagram, charting the dates of attainment of U.S. and European cities to great city (100,000) size, was accompanied by the motive which inspired them to this accomplishment; "ocean," "river," "lake," "railway," or "other." In writing of the function of the super city, Jefferson was already conceiving his notion of the primate city. The essence of the paper had been delivered before the Association of American Geographers at Worcester in 1930, under the title "The Distribution of Urbanization." Of this paper the *Geographical Review* comments:[87]

> Mark Jefferson, in "The Geographical Distribution of Great Cities", presented a masterly analysis of the distribution of the larger cities throughout the world and their significance. This paper will be printed in the July number of the Geographical Review.

Abstracted in Jefferson's words the paper reads:[88]

> A percentage of urban population has been computed for many countries but on a variety of city bases, the city being taken at 500 people in Ukraine, 11,000 in Egypt, and 24,000 in Japan, and many values in between. These percentages are not comparable and cannot be used except to compare countries that use the same definition of city.
>
> This paper selects the Great City (100,000) as the standard of urban life, for several reasons. Life in them is really urban, which life in towns from one to five thousand is certainly not. The data for these cities are readily obtained in all parts of the world, and the growth of cities that has characterized the last century was mainly in cities of considerable size. With urban thus defined we find that nearly half of the Australians and English (not British) live in such cities, a third of the New Zealanders and Australians and more than a quarter of the people of the United States, Netherlands, Germany, Canada, Argentine and Uruguay; of the Japanese 14%, of the Chinese and Indians about 2%.
>
> These cities are modern. Their number has been doubled four times over in the last 125 years. The origin of such cities is European but they are not more numerous out of Europe than in that continent. In the United States the last century saw a regular succession of cities come to 100,000 size, first five ocean ports, then four river ports, five lake ports and lastly, from 1850 on, almost a new railway city every year. Europe had no such succession. She had all the great cities that were known in 1800, some of them ocean ports, some river ports and two grew to great cities by reason of their position at the crossing of land ways. In the second half of the century railways took up the transportation called for by great city life but the rivers and highways have already been of much use in Europe and continue so at the present time.

In studying the results we come on the regrettable fact that the census numbers for great cities are only for their sleeping moments, and at time omit large numbers who yet spend in them all their waking, working moments. The city in which we are interested is awake and at work. We need to know how many go in cities daily for their active avocations.

Following publication in the *Review,* Bowman wrote to Jefferson:[89]

Your stuff in the Geographical Review is crowding out editorial comment on the moratorium, baseball, Al Capone, "Legs" Diamond, Will Rogers, and the economic depression. I like the title of the second editorial, "More About Cities".

Believing that you will wish to keep Dr. Finley's letter as a souvenir I enclose it herewith. There are many others in our file, so we shall not miss this one.

It must be a great satisfaction to you to see the effects of a piece of work so widely distributed. An editorial also appeared in the New York Evening Sun, which I understand has already been forwarded to you by Miss Wrigley.

The enclosed letter from Dr. Finley of the New York *Times* reads:[90]

Dear Dr. Bowman,

There was so much interest in this article of Mr. Jefferson's that more than one editor wished to write about it. The President of the American Geographical Society could not have done as well as one of his associates has done.

The day following Finley's letter, two editorials summarizing Jefferson's article appeared in the New York *Times,* under the titles "Counting Noses at Night" and "By Daytime Count."

Later that same year, the American Geographical Society awarded the Cullum Gold Medal to Jefferson for "his ingenious and fruitful inquiries into man's distribution on the earth."[91]

Jefferson's concern for city anthropography was part of a larger interest in national anthropography: an inquiry into the distribution of population for a country.[92]

For several years I have realized that political maps are grievous sinners against sense in spreading their color evenly over the whole territory of countries, as if the Sahara were just as French as Algeria (if Algeria is French). I enclose a little map of South America, giving the national color to something like an ecumene or inhabited area and using only a very faint tint for the rest. With my craze for novelty of expression this appeals to me. One part of Brazil is not as Brazilian as another. The difficulty of course is to delineate the Ecumene, the outline on the South America being very crude. Emboldened by Mr.

> *Raye Platt's delineation of the inhabited valleys of the eastern Andes I*
> *attempted in August 1932 to make a delineation of the ecumene of all*
> *Latin America on his large base map (1:6 million?) by simply sketch-*
> *ing lines around the towns on that map (and some larger in Peru). It*
> *is venturesome but certainly gives a picture that corresponds much*
> *better to the truth than the usual flat tint which implies equal occupa-*
> *tion of the whole area. I am meaning some day to reproduce this on a*
> *small scale.*

Jefferson attempted to define the extent of an ecumene in an article, "The Problem of the Ecumene: The Case of Canada," which he sent to Gladys Wrigley, editor of the *Geographical Review*. This was the first Jefferson paper Miss Wrigley refused to accept in its then current form. The following letter Jefferson sent to editor Wrigley warrants reproduction since it reveals in part a program of work which he had established for himself.[93]

> *Your letter of yesterday upset me completely. Probably you did not*
> *mean to ask me to put, I should say, 30 solid hours more work on the*
> *little paper to make it "lively". I have written the National Resources*
> *Service, Department of the Interior of Canada for later maps, if he has*
> *them. To reproduce these maps by my method is excessively laborious.*
> *I personally trace all the detail from the 1:2¼ million map, including*
> *the one degree mesh. Some of the maps used have a two degree mesh.*
> *I bisect it. I make a similar small map with same net and draw down*
> *the detail degree by degree. I have been since June laboring on these*
> *maps. No one but myself I think would be willing to put so much*
> *labor into a job as I do. You have appliances for doing it both better*
> *and more quickly and cheaply. If you have a later map of either will*
> *you have a photostat made of say scale 1:ten million or so, precision*
> *of course does not matter? (I meant precise scale.)*
>
> *I cannot put any considerable further time on the matter and would*
> *much rather print it elsewhere if you feel the 1934 date of data*
> *important. If you are right about that, the matter is one we could not*
> *possibly agree on and the only thing to do is to send me back the*
> *article. I want it published and as early as possible. It is a part of a*
> *whole. I am working toward the case of the United States. Toward*
> *that I have already*
>
> > *A. Cities and towns in U.S. down to size 100 (one hundred people),*
> > *scale about 1:6 million, about half done.*
> > *B. Idem Canada all done, dates 1930 and 1931.*
> > *C. A rough list of the Ecumenes for all the countries of the world;*
> > *very bad values but a beginning, something to correct.*
>
> *A reason for my wishing this published promptly—by April cer-*

tainly—even if it is not by my preferred publishers, the American Geographical Society—is that Soderlund is just producing a remarkable use of the same essential conception, which I feel is quite new and epoch-making, very lively indeed and extremely appropriate for so progressive a journal as the Geographical Review to be associated with, in his

Folkskolans Kartbok, Stockholm July, 1933

of which I will send you an account as soon as I unravel his explanation in Globen for September 1933 . . . .

Jefferson sent the paper to the Swedish magazine, *Geografiska Annaler,* which published the article in November 1934.[94] He stressed the value of the concept of the ecumene, distinguishing the ecumene from the territory of Canada, deftly stating his problem: "How do we estimate the amount of Ecumene? Where draw its boundaries? That is the problem of the ecumene." Jefferson indicated two methods by which the ecumene might be delimited:[95]

An easy first approximation may be made with the help of the best population-density map available, by rejecting its scantily settled areas. The choice of the critical density is important and arbitrary, but if the criterion is stated, corrections to taste may be supplied by readers. The writer would select 2 or 2½ people per square mile, and call any population-density less than that negligible. Actually that will always involve large areas of no people at all.

Using this criterion we may throw out as unused territory two-thirds of Brazil, half of the Argentine Republic, five-sixths of Chile, a fifth of the United Kingdom and an eleventh of France. The population densities then go up, for Brazil from 13 to 40, for the Argentine from 11 to 22, for Chile from 14 to 84, for the United Kingdom from 495 to 602, and for France from 197 to 216.

A better way of ascertaining the outline of the ecumene, it seems to the writer, is to locate on a large map all population nuclei down to groups of only 100 people, marking each with a symbol that expresses number by its shape as well as its size.

Jefferson's other concern was to define a country as a nation on its ecumene, devoid of territory owned by the state. The *Geographical Review* noted Jefferson's article in the Swedish magazine in a four hundred word summary.[96]

As was Jefferson's habit, he had tried the idea before the Association of American Geographers, at its annual meeting at Evanston, Illinois, December 1932. His abstracted paper reads:[97]

The essential part of a country—its people—is often intimately associated with only a part of the national territories, the ecumene, which excludes all waste, unused and unoccupied spaces. These may vary from 18 percent for the United Kingdom to 31 for Switzerland or Japan, to 33 for the United States and 90 percent for Canada.

The ecumene is the house that enshrines the nation, the developed land owned by the nation and also lived on and used by it. All the cities are on it and the towns, even most of the villages. Almost the totality of the farmlands and forest clearing are on ecumene as well as the roads and railways. Isolated villages or isolated homes in the wilderness are bits of the country, their sites bits of the ecumene, but the wastes themselves are not parts of the country. They are merely national territory.

To determine the exact area and outline of the ecumene is very difficult. The railway map is a great help. Networks of roads of railways are always within the ecumene, though single tentacle lines may extend across the wastes. The completely drawn cities map, when it is possible to make one, is the best means of approach to an accurate delineation.

But, however difficult it may be to draw the outline of the ecumene, its entire omission leaves the map of any country unfinished.

In 1936 Jefferson produced the third revision of his text, *Man in Europe*. In the second chapter, entitled "Distribution of Population," he used the most recent census figures to determine the annual increment of population for each European country in 1936, based on the annual rate of increase for the last ten years. This part of the chapter he rewrote for "Geographical Record" in the *Geographical Review,* under the title, "The Growth of Europe's Population and an Estimate for 1936."[98] Jefferson indicated that the annual growth rate of population had political and military implication: with the map he showed total populations and annual population increase for each of the European states. The 1936 edition of *Man in Europe* also gave ample references to great cities and super cities. City size and reasons for a cities rise to eminence in population had fascinated him for many years. He was particularly interested in city growths and for several years had arranged the cities of various countries in descending order of size to emerge eventually with his concept of city primacy. "The Law of Primate Cities" was delivered before the Association of American Geographers at Cambridge in December, 1938. The Law was abstracted in the *Annals of the Association of American Geographers* as follows:[99]

In most important countries the largest city is two or more times as large as the next largest city, and other cities differ in size by much smaller numbers.

All great cities have, as important factors in their growth, the pro-

ductivity of their region and its extent, as well as their situation with regard to the chief lines of movement of internal and external commerce.

Cities generously endowed with these two elements of growth are likely to be very great cities. New development of resources or acquisition of new productive areas, or new development of transportation lines that favor them more than other cities are likely to cause them a sudden increment of population.

Another very important factor in a great cities growth is its primacy among the great cities of the land—its attainment of distinctly greater number of inhabitants. The moment that happens the force of primacy, which it alone possesses, causes it to take on a rate of growth so much larger than that of any other city in the region that it shoots up to a magnitude out of the class of any rival city. e.g., at no time in the past eighty years has any city in the United States had more than half as large a population as the City of New York.

The paper was noticed immediately after its delivery on the front page of the New York *Times,* under the column heading, "Links New Yorker and London Cockney; Geographer calls them 'True Provincials.' "[100] Insistence upon the cockney being England's true provincial encouraged *The Times* to come to the defense of cockneys and cockneyism with two articles, "Cockney Born"[101] and "True Provincials: Cockneys and New Yorkers."[102] In this latter column *The Times* amusingly confused the primate city with primitive city. The local paper of his own town, *The Ypsilanti Press,* and *The Detroit Free Press* made mention of the fact that Professor Jefferson's concept had been noticed in the metropolitan dailies, but it was *The Normal College News* that kept the student body and local citizenry awake to Jefferson's primate city with a reproduction of the December 30, New York *Times* editorial[103] followed by discussion of the London *Times* articles[104] which brought an invitation to Jefferson to address the Normal College General Assembly on the issue of the primate city.[105] A review of this address appeared soon after it was given.[106] So much publicity resulted in numerous groups and institutions sending requests to Jefferson for a talk on that subject. The *Geographical Review* noticed the paper in its summary of the 35th Annual Meeting of the Association of American Geographers:[107]

Besides the studies on Boston, four other papers dealt with cities, either collectively or individually. Of these, perhaps the most original and imaginative was by Mark Jefferson on "The Law of Primate Cities". Professor Jefferson aimed to demonstrate the reasons why one city in each country tends far to surpass any other in size and influence.

Meanwhile, Jefferson penned the article "The Law of the Primate City," which was published in the *Geographical Review*. It was Jefferson's last article while at normal.[108] Certainly it was one of his finest pieces. Of the article *Review* editor Gladys Wrigley wrote:[109]

> *You have put me in a quandary. My mind was firmly made up to accept NO MORE articles until I saw the glimmerings of daylight ahead—we have at least a year's supply. If "The Law of the Primate City" were not so concise I could cheerfully say "No"; if it did not fit in so well with Professor Mear's article "Postwar Locational Changes of British Industry", which goes in the April number, I might perhaps be firm, at least as regards time; but as it is, I must say "Yes" and squeeze the April Review some more.*

Jefferson wrote of the concept of primacy:[110]

> *Metropolitan London is not merely the largest city in the world; it is more than seven times as large as Britain's second city, Liverpool, and thereby stands out alone in a different order of magnitude and significance from that of all other cities in the country.*
>
> *The finest wares are always to be found there, the rarest articles, the greatest talents, the most skilled workers in every science and art. Thither flows an unending stream of the young and ambitious in search of fame and fortune, and there fame and fortune are found. London is the kingdom's market for all that is superlative in intellectual and material productions. Its supereminence as a market runs parallel to its supereminence in size. It is the primate city of the United Kingdom.*
>
> *In Denmark the less-than-a-million capital, Copenhagen, has won greater relative primacy. It is nine times as large as Denmark's second town.*

Jefferson collected statistics of city populations for the forty-four most advanced countries of the world and compared the population size of the first city with that of the second city. For Jefferson the 44 most advanced countries of the world were those that had attained the highest cultural achievement. Country selection presented no special problem to him, as he had been measuring and mapping the culture of states since 1911.[111] In 18 of the 44 cases selected in 1938 he found examples of triple primacy: the first city was numerically at least three times greater than the second city. In ten cases he found examples of double primacy: the first city was numerically twice as large as the second city. In six cases the first city was half as large again as the second city.

The only real exceptions to Jefferson's concept of primacy were the British Dominions, Spain, Italy, and Russia. Furthermore, Jefferson could explain the exceptions: the British Dominions were "able to look 'home' to London as their primate city"; Spain had divided itself into Castilians and Catalans—two capital cities emerged; Italy had not had enough time to grow since the time of her unification; while the USSR had not been able to develop a capital representative of her people in the absence of a good communications network.

Jefferson further developed the concept of primacy by insisting that the first city draws its inhabitants from all other cities and parts of the country, thus in character as well as in size expressing the national disposition more completely than any other city. It is the indigene of the city, stated Jefferson, who is narrow and limited—the nation's true provincial.

Since 1911, Jefferson had been mapping culture for the countries of the world, using such criteria as schools, patents, cities, communications, railroad freight, foreign commerce, pieces of mail delivered per capita, telegraph, telephones, automobiles, art galleries, societies for the prevention of cruelty to animals. Each country was given a culture index that was presumed to indicate the degree of cultural attainment which that country had achieved. Satisfied with his measuring device, Jefferson proceeded to group these countries into four categories on the basis of cultural attainment: a Teutonic group, Mediterranean group, Levantine group, and an Oriental group. These culture indices enjoyed considerable popularity in the early part of the century and encouraged Jefferson to calculate the culture of cities. His investigation showed that cities enjoying a high culture index invariably had a substantial population. Thus another dimension had been added to Jefferson's concept of primacy: the city was prime in culture and prime in number of population. This led Jefferson to state that, "A country's leading city is always disproportionately large and exceptionally expressive of national capacity and feeling." This was the law of primate cities, a law Jefferson asserted, by virtue of its constant recurrence the world over in "countries of age." Perhaps it was a little unfortunate that Jefferson, in his enthusiasm for the concept of primacy, should have adopted the term law—a term which the social scientist has concisely defined today as a statement of a relation or sequence of phenomena, invariable under the same conditions. But the enunciation of the concept was new to urban theory and has been frequently noted in the years that followed. "The Law of the Primate City," the product of many years thought, was not the last of his population studies. In 1941 for the annual meeting of the Association of American Geographers, Jefferson wrote a paper entitled, "The Rift in Our Population," abstracted, but probably never sent to program officials:[112]

In 1930 for the first time in the history of the United States a group of

*our people—those under three years of age—was found to be 207,000
smaller than the same group of ten years earlier. In 1940 this rift in
the population between a small diminishing and a large increasing part
had advanced to include all under age thirteen. There were about three
million fewer individuals under thirteen in 1940 than in 1930 and now
more than a fifth of the population was affected. There were 28 million
individuals under thirteen and 103 million thirteen or more years old.
The younger 28 million were 3 million fewer than in 1930 and the 103
million older people twelve million more numerous, masking the loss
of children in the net gain of 9 million for the whole population.*

*These 13-year-olds of 1940 were three years old in 1930 and will be
23 years old in 1950. Unless there is a new influx from Europe in the
present decade we may expect those under 23 in 1950 to be fewer than
in 1940. They number about 51 million now, say 39 percent of the
population. They may diminish as much as the remaining 80 million
increase and bring us near a stagnant population.*

*A population that was increasing (1920-1930) by 17 million in a
decade should produce many more children in 1930 than in 1920, but
about 1927 the fall in the birth-rate caused a greater defect of births
than the increased number of parents could match. As this was not
true in 1926 and earlier, the number of those 14 or more years old in
1940, is greater than in 1930. If the process goes on as now and the
total population has begun to decline, in 1950 or 1960 we may say
that the decline began to begin in 1927-28!*

*A practical subdivision of the population by age at any date is into
five groups—*

children	*(under age 5)*
young in training	*(5 to 19)*
adventurers	*(20 to 39)*
prime of lifers	*(40-69)*
pensioners	*(over 70)*

*At present more than half the people are adventurers or primers and
they are still increasing in number. They do the country's work.*

The paper had been composed and typed, but was not read, owing to
a bout of influenza which Jefferson contracted and his concern for the
journey to New York. At this meeting Griffith Taylor delivered his
Presidential Address, "Environment, Village and City: A Genetic approach to Urban Geography";[113] Jefferson as chairman of the Nominating Committee of the Association of American Geographers had proposed Taylor's name for the presidency.

This chapter has in no way attempted to portray the larger influence
of Jefferson's population studies; it is a summary of the more tangible

evidences he left behind of his thought concerning people and their distribution. The description of his thought is recorded chronologically so that the reader might parallel Jefferson's achievement with ideas and thoughts of the geographic and other disciplines. Jefferson's population studies are best understood in this manner. He followed no preconceived program of thought, but progressed from one idea to the next, not duplicating the work of others, but sometimes supplementing it, sometimes modifying it, sometimes directing it. His perpetual concern was not to insist on a relationship but to persist with the possibility of a relationship. He lent his work to a subject matter which later came to be known as urban geography, without his name being essentially attached to most of the ideas he contributed. Thus his visible accomplishment in population studies extends over a period of forty years and from the Normal School classroom to the front page of the New York *Times,* from an obscure book review in the pages of *The American Schoolmaster* or a fugitive collector's item such as "The Distribution of People in the United States in 1910—As Indicated by the Distribution of the Cities," to the easily available pages of the *Geographical Review.*

CHAPTER ELEVEN

CORRESPONDENTS AND CORRESPONDENCE

Letter writing was important in the life of Jefferson. He wrote because he wanted to, because he could express his thoughts at his own pace and in his own inimitable way, free of the social hindrances—gesticulation, reaction, surprise, and agreement—which frequently harass conversation. And he wrote many letters, perhaps averaging more than two a day for the greater part of his life span. Necessarily some letters were of a business character, others were of a social nature and written to friends and members of the family, but many reveal his thought and academic needs.

A marked break in the style of letter Jefferson wrote occurred in the 1890's. Prior to that time his letters were models of composition, rich in vocabulary, poetic in their graciousness, exquisite of penmanship, and invariably not less that 5,000 words in length. These were not sent solely to his Theodora, but also to his parents, classmates, and friends of the family. Ninety of these letters, which were written by Jefferson while he was residing in the Argentine in the years 1883-1889, have been preserved. Perhaps his style was attributable to his youth, South American living, or his interest in the balance and rhythm of language. He was a lover of language and believed that regular composition of a gracious letter was part of the life of an educated man. In these letters he would frequently translate poetry from Spanish, French, or Greek, or write of an idiomatic expression that he had recently discovered, then dwell on its meaning, quite as if he were sharing with his correspondent something rather wonderful.

After two years of Harvard, where he came strongly under the influence of W. M. Davis, Jefferson's style of writing changed, whether that style be observed in the diaries he frequently kept or the articles or letters he frequently wrote. His writing became abrupt, unclothed of composition, everything had to be told, nothing implied. If Jefferson were unfolding a notion, or an article he had recently read, he would tell the story in the fewest possible words, as though playing a game with himself and his typewriter with its slipping "e." If he were seeking information or challenging a point of view, his approach was so direct, blunt, and frequently personal, that it is not surprising to learn that his circle of regular correspondents was limited to a group of thinkers for whom meaning was a commodity to be exchanged free of any hindrance literary etiquette might properly impose. Jefferson's most stalwart correspondents included: Daniel Jefferson (1883-1889); Theodora Bohnstedt (1889-1891); Isaiah Bowman (1901-1949); George Chisholm (1911-1929); Gladys Wrigley (1915-1949); Caroline Atherton (1934-1946). Unfortunately correspondences enjoyed with W. M. Davis and E. Huntington are very incomplete. Selections from the correspondence Jefferson maintained with I. Bowman, G. Chisholm, G. Wrigley, and C. Atherton have been made. The letters are quoted in order to bring the reader closer to the thought of a geographer's life.[1]

Jefferson exchanged letters with many other people, be they geographers, thinkers, scientists from the ranks of other disciplines, civic officials, politicians and administrators. A large correspondence testifies to his letter writing habit, but the enumerated stalwarts are to be distinguished by the amount of correspondence which Jefferson exchanged with them and also by the ease which characterized this correspondence. Jefferson clearly felt that he needed no immediate reason to correspond with his stalwarts: therefore he frequently did not question, but merely stated or observed. Perhaps he would share with his correspondent an exciting moment he had experienced, reference to an interesting or stimulating study, or snippets of his own social philosophy. Usually these letters contained some reference to what seems geographical, but they were confined in no way by traditional disciplinal boundaries. The correspondence provided a medium in which he could begin to shape his ideas, structure his thoughts, and then commit them to paper with no essential loss of meaning. This was a habit which he developed over the years and which enabled him to say more nearly what he meant. Loose talking, loose writing, and loose thinking were not Jefferson traits, and when he recognized these traits in others he could be, and was frequently, ruthless in his condemnation of that practice. He had learned to say and write what he thought. Inevitably his correspondence kept him informed on a variety of national viewpoints, rewarded him with a variety of bibliographical sources and references, brought him a large number of reprints, together with critiques and suggestions for his work both published and unpublished. The letters are reproduced to show a Jefferson for whom correspondence was a road to freedom, a cleanser of human thought, an emancipation from the provincialism of Ypsilanti. He would not write a letter before knowing exactly what he wanted to say. Then, impatient to cast his finished thought into type he would hammer on his typewriter taking literary liberties which suggest that he did not believe in words, but in a language beyond words, and which was in fact, a letter-writing language. Words divorced from language are dead things, and Jefferson wrote in his own language of fleeting moods, profound philosophies, engaging subtleties—and is most intimately revealed in his style. Terse and direct, he wrote simply and to the point.

Jefferson and Bowman commenced correspondence after the latter had left the Michigan State Normal College in 1902 for graduate study at Harvard University. In the following 47 years many hundreds of letters were exchanged between the two men. It is possible that Jefferson and Bowman exchanged more letters between themselves than any two American geographers before or since.

This exchange may be best appreciated by recognizing three distinct phases in Bowman's career: 1902-1915, typified by Bowman emerging as the scholarly assistant professor of Yale, particularly interested in South America and much influenced by his former teacher, Mark Jefferson;[2] 1915-1935, Bowman as Director of the American Geographical Society in New York, borrowing ideas from Jefferson for the American Geographical Society research and publication program, and trying to bring this hard worker from Ypsilanti to his Society in New York; 1935-1949, Bowman as President of Johns Hopkins University and in retirement, at which time correspondence between the two men dwindled to meager proportions. It was in the 1915-1935 period that Jefferson and Bowman exchanged most of their correspondence on matters including the significance of good book reviews, Bowman's plans for the Society, pedagogy, the nature of Jefferson's researches, World War I, recently published books and articles of merit. There was time also for Jefferson to send Bowman postage stamps and toys for his children and for Bowman to send Jefferson yerba maté tea, bombilla and gourd, and books from his personal library.

Isaiah Bowman to Mark Jefferson, May 29, 1908:
What is this latest map flirtation that requires the Calcutta data? You are the most irrepressible map maker I ever saw, and long may you live and prosper! I am going to make map work the "piece de resistance" in the regional courses next year. That is the way to teach geography. The seed you have scattered has borne fruit you see. A great many of the maps I

shall use will be from government reports, and they will be printed up so that each man will have a map in front of him while the dear teacher is trying to help him see the point . . . I thank you heartily for those stereoscopic views. It was certainly thoughtful of you to send them. Do you not wish them returned? The N.A. maps are great. I want to order a million of them next year for the class. Why didn't you put your name on the small one? The class gets tired of hearing me say "Jefferson of Ypsi—he made 'em."

Isaiah Bowman to Mark Jefferson, November 27, 1908:

We had a great time during Professor Penck's stay and just to show what sort of a send-off we gave him I am sending you under separate cover a copy of the menu card that indicated the order in which certain immortal sayings were introduced. To understand it you must remember that there were ten lectures in all and that this 11th one was for the purpose of telling Penck what he would see when he took the journey around the world after his lecture engagements here and at Columbia are met. Each talk was illustrated by a funny map drawn for the occasion. The places were all disarranged with Yale and everything connected with it very conspicuous and a lot of references to the Fatherland and the short distance between it and Yale. It was a very jolly evening and we have had no end of congratulations on having arranged so novel a program. You see these affairs have become historic or traditional or whatever you call it and each department with which the lectures are associated lays itself out to do it better than ever before.

The lectures, I mean the serious ones Penck gave, were well attended and were for the most part very interesting although at the start he rather underestimated his audience. The one on "Man and the Ice Age" was a model scientific lecture. Most of the ideas he had already presented in his book on the glaciation of the Alps. The lectures will be printed by the University during the year.

Mark Jefferson to Isaiah Bowman, November 12, 1915:

(Enclosed "Utah the Oasis at the foot of the Wasatch")

I have not drawn any picture of the Mormon community, only justified the conception of it as an oasis—a hole in the ground in the desert. Davis howled with derision at the thought in New York and I really think this will help him . . .

Funny days those mate days, but a great comfort after a long ride in the sun and drought. I remember especially one trip for a fortnight west across the Sierra to Cordoba into San Juan, myself, Kentuckyan Alexander and a party of native friends who invited us along to visit lands of theirs. Good fellows in their way. I remember so well on the return a horserace we ran into at Las Plumerias to spend the night, where much drinking was going on with ginebra de Holanda, Marca LLave, how the kind natives sought to get North America drunk and were put to bed by the N.A. who ate their supper beside their cots and held their basins! Ay de mi!

Mark Jefferson to Isaiah Bowman, February 17, 1917:

Thanks for Southern Peru. Have been hoping to finish, have done first part. Helps the needed picture of Andine anthropography, am getting it clearer in mind. January check seemed large! though fearfully needed. Hoping daily a chance to write up United Kingdom map. Shall send *my* coal map which can be made at my expense, as I need it. Hope to write again soon. Good for Wilson! Now let the Ford factory turn out half a million "Sic 'em Henry's" for submarines and Billy can turn his mustache down and his toes up. Got to hustle over and hear a teacher (?) teach. In all the haste there is.

Isaiah Bowman to Mark Jefferson, August 1, 1917:

I am delighted with your "Geography in Europe." If I hadn't already said all the good things I could about yourself and your work I should attempt to characterise it in this letter. I appreciate particularly the trouble you have taken to mark important paragraphs on the margin and to color a large number of the maps. I know of no-one in this country who is doing such good work in map reproduction and certainly no-one else is publishing such stimulating comment.

I think so much of the hand-colored copy that I am turning this one over to the library with the inscription that it was colored in hand by the author. This sort of thing increases its value in future years.

Mark Jefferson to Isaiah Bowman, September 22, 1917:

I think the whole matter of reviewing scientific books or better geographic ones, the only ones that I have any right to speak of at all—needs a shaking up. I have long since printed my ideal of a review and it seems to me that to print casual comment and hasty impressions under the name of Reviews is to hinder the progress of science . . .

Mark Jefferson to Isaiah Bowman, August 28, 1920:

At the moment I am fearfully sluggish, I think softening of the brain or something of the sort, so be surprised at nothing! My table is heaped and I am afraid to tackle the mess. I have put an hour supervising Geography in the Training School down on my fall program here, which means attention to detailed lesson plans, for grade work, and that looks to a *good* geography! Glance at Atwood's (Ginn-Frye Book One) account of Chile and the humble Chilean. Truly something better is a crying want.

Isaiah Bowman to Mark Jefferson, September 15, 1920:

Don't ask me ever to look at Atwood's "Elementary Geography" again! I am sick of it. Look at the section on Iceland! He apparently has never heard of the big interior lava plateau of that island which is in large part responsible for the uninhabited character of it. His attention is all fastened on the idea that Iceland is chiefly covered with ice, and isn't it a sensible idea when you come to think of it! I haven't looked up Tierra del Fuego in his book but I'll bet he says it's a hot place because it is the "land of fire." This is at least rational geography. Also, it should please Davis because it is a deduction. Also what difference if it is wrong. The kids won't know any better and they will forget it by the time they have grown up. You speak of something better as a "crying want." The want is yelling now, not crying!

Mark Jefferson to Isaiah Bowman, February 2, 1921:

Taylor's article sounds attractive. How delightful to perceive what has been going on among men these last 800,000 years. I should like to meet him and look on the body containing so bold a spirit!

I'll be bound you never thought of the reader's problem in your resolve to hand him three months in one.

Mark Jefferson to Isaiah Bowman, February 5, 1921:

Miss Alice Sarles, freshman in the MSNC and person of very moderate training writes in an examination:

As man becomes accustomed to a country, he learns where the best soil, the best climates, and the best rainfall conditions are found. When a new country is discovered man rarely settles at first upon the best place in the country for his home. But this is found out through his experience with the country.

Isaiah Bowman to Mark Jefferson, February 8, 1921:

Taylor is creating quite a stir.

Don't believe it, says the reader.

Can you disprove it? says the editor.

Nope, invariably says the reader.

Of course, there are lots of fool things which one can't disprove, there's Atlantis for example.

Yes, we had thought of the reader's problem—his problem is to keep the magazine on the table for three months till he has read it and by that time he likes it so well that he binds it. Thus we achieve immortality!

Isaiah Bowman to Mark Jefferson, March 11, 1921:

Program—There will be an afternoon on Latin America. It has been left to me to arrange the meeting for that afternoon. We shall have three papers, by Ogilvie, McBride, and Aurousseau. We need someone to pitch into the discussion in a lively manner. Will you come on for that purpose at the expense of the Society? We should be able to kill two birds with one stone. Either come a day early or remain a day late, and let's talk city geography.

Isaiah Bowman to Mark Jefferson, January 31, 1922:

I wonder if I have written to you about a little book by Alfredo Niceforo, entitled "Les indices numériques de la Civilisation et du Progrès"? It appears to be an enquiry that runs parallel to your own of some years ago, concerning the distribution of culture. He is concerned with the mode of measurement of culture, and I should think that his little book of 200 odd pages ought to have a very careful reading at your hands . . .

Mark Jefferson to Isaiah Bowman, February 11, 1922:

Of my sort of meat there is none in the volume, but I kept thinking for sometime that at some page soon he was going to say something!

Mark Jefferson to Isaiah Bowman, January 11, 1924:

Your supplement to the New World has set me back terribly. Here I have been sitting at the typewriter pretending to be pushing for dear life at PEOPLING THE ARGENTINE PAMPA and really I have been simply reading your fascinating stuff ever since Tom handed me the mail, hardly daring to come in. Papa has told everyone so savagely to keep out and let him alone. I don't know how much time I have lost!

Mark Jefferson to Isaiah Bowman, January 21, 1924:

Irion our magazine editor, same who reviewed my Chile papers so appreciatively asked me to speak at his 20 Club night. I did on Argentine Farming, the paper our secretary of Agriculture was to hear, but could not. Highly appreciated, but Irion, getting me alone to thank me—effusively a bit—asks "What's the good of learning all this if you don't make it known? I look in all the geographies for Chile and they don't know anything of what you say. How are the teachers to know? I think it ought to be made known. I think they would be glad to use such matter. I find it fascinating. I had no notion of such things and neither have they."

Mark Jefferson to Isaiah Bowman, March 29, 1924:

The Walk Book is admirable. All hail a book that tempts one to such fine time-spending in a city that so abounds in temptation to inane spending of time and life!

I am glad to see Platt's name there in honor, though the reading public has little idea what an editor's part is . . . Had a strong temptation to grab it for my class in Geography of the United States.

Isaiah Bowman to Mark Jefferson, April 1, 1924:

You will know best if it is useful to you in your geography of the United States. The price of the book is $2.00. If your class wants it to the extent of ten copies it will cost them $1.15 each. There's reduction for you!

Mark Jefferson to Isaiah Bowman, June 29, 1924:

I am well and happier. Read a lot, teach some, do much public speaking and still think a lot, the best thing I do. We have growing numbers of students and shall have a large summer school. There are five teachers of geography this summer.

. . . . .

I have just received and thank you for the Research Series No. 4A and have run through it rather carefully. My, what a great man de Martonne is! He admits it. Look for Denis, and try to find what Vidal de la Blache stood for—not in the book! But it is a bit of a scandal to have no praise for Brunhes except "Jean Brunhes has the reputation of being a writer and an orator." Even Blanchard, who gets almost generous treatment is really explained p. 43 by the fact that he began "his work just at the time when Emannuel de Martonne left the University of Lyons for Paris."

Mark Jefferson to Isaiah Bowman, September 22, 1924:

I am sending you by American Railway Express a box of South American books, some loaned by the Society and some of them those that I bought for the Society or acquired by gift in South America.

The day after summer school ended I began a new book on Man in Europe and the last forms are now running through the press. A copy will reach you shortly. It runs to 211 pages and is a good deal better!

Mark Jefferson to Isaiah Bowman, December 25, 1925:

A Snapshot

Sally, two days B.C. (Before Christmas) to Tom, Santa Claus must be way up north now. Tom, Why? Sally, Oh it takes time to get here. It's Christmas everywhere the same day. Sally, thinking that over, Thomas, did you know they have night in Japan when we have day? Thomas, Why? Sally, Oh, that's the way the world's arranged. Thomas, offhand, Don't see much sense in fixing it like that!

Isaiah Bowman to Mark Jefferson, December 30, 1925:

I am having your so called Snapshot, the conversation between Tom and Sally, separately typed to circulate among a half dozen of the staff and to take home with me. That's good stuff. Better than anything in the Principles or the Andes of Southern Peru!

. . . . .

We are constantly in your debt for your help.

Mark Jefferson to Isaiah Bowman, March 23, 1926 (McClellanville):

Huguenots here give a singular accent to place names: *Porcher,* pronounced P'shea, and written Pshea in Holland, Michigan where the Huguenots also got in along with the Dutch, as in South Africa and Australia—witness Aurousseau! *Horry* County, S. C. pronounced Oree, accent on the ee. *Legare* St., in Charleston, and family name pron. Legree. *Vanderhorst,* place and family name S.C. pr. Vandrost. *Sabine* pronounced Sabeen.

Dr. R. Clyde Ford, of Ypsilanti, and I are to look the country over for what geography there is in the pronunciation of place names. Ford has a paper in next Atlantic: a graceful pen! He knows much of old French Michigan. The Review will be offered results if any.

This place most fascinating for geography. It has put clarity where was obscurity in my notions of Sea-island cotton, River-delta rice planting, southern mansions, slavery, the negro, and naval stores, to say nothing of lovely green winter scenery. I have made over 200 pictures, 100 of them certainly remarkable—all stereoscopic.

Isaiah Bowman to Mark Jefferson, September 18, 1926:

Is the present rate to be maintained—one book a week? Last week "Man in Europe" in its new dress, and now Atlas of Plates for "Man in the United States." Both excellent, like "Pictures from Southern Brazil" in October G.R. and the praise of Nash "Conquest of Brazil." Allah Ho Akbar!

Isaiah Bowman to Mark Jefferson, January 11, 1927:

A few readers have already commented on the excellence of the text of your book. I am sure that it is going to make a permanent impression upon scholarly-minded folks interested in Argentina. I repeat that it is the best thing you have ever written: and you may recall that I have already said some very emphatic things about other publications by M.J.

Mark Jefferson to Isaiah Bowman, January 19, 1927:

I think the book reads well and I take this occasion to thank you for offering the incentive and providing the means to make the rather closer acquaintance with events that have passed in the Argentine, than I should ever have had without your intervention. The labor that it has cost is of no moment if we have all helped to shed a little of the light of understanding on events.

Clarity is I think more important than soundness even, for if I set forth very clearly some view that is erroneous, it will not long remain unchallenged, and correction will ensue.

Mark Jefferson to Isaiah Bowman, March 7, 1928:

I wish you would stir up a campaign for a world rain map at the London meeting. Chisholm writes me you are going—a rain map based on universal observations 1930-1940, allowing regional committees by continents and countries, quite numerous, including all meteorological heads and special students with smaller and smaller directive committees above, to study the spots needed for special observation, raising funds perhaps for station placing at critical points in thinly settled countries, at any rate preparing maps showing the localities of greatest present ignorance of rainfall, which could be used—with proper text—to put the need before national governments and scientific bodies, before exploiting corporations and engineers to secure the widest possible cooperation, so that by 1930 a general plan should be in operation, with some uniformity. Each continent has a different need. The League of Nations might take some interest. Today a world map 1:10,000,000 with a dot for every point where there are five continuous years of observation of rain—nothing like enough—would be most instructive. Are you interested?

P.S. Why?

Because it is so splendid a thing to do! You do not have to study between my lines to find my "scheme." Being simple minded I haven't any. It is a glorious thing to advance science though—just like that!

Isaiah Bowman to Mark Jefferson, March 9, 1928:

Your paper is the first in the file marked "London." I like your idea and if you will permit me to put your name upon it as a label I shall be glad to see what I can do. Have you written to anyone else about it? Why don't you draft your plan in some detail and present it yourself and then let me boost it in whatever way I can

P.S. I spilled your idea of world rainfall records by preconcerted plan to Wright, Wrigley, Platt, Joerg and they said Hurray!

Mark Jefferson to Isaiah Bowman, April 20, 1929:

Your recommendation of Haut-Barsac—1920 is a bit tantalizing. A bottle would have been appreciated.

I brought a pint of St. Thomas Bay Rum up in 1927 from Jamaica, knowing its fine quality for *hair!* I did not have in mind at the time it was 50% alcohol. Of course I declared it in N.Y. and offered to spill it on the dock. But inspector said I'll fix it, and took the papers—not the bottle— away with him to bring back marked denatured and passed me! Rather clever chemistry, I thought, but it was really fine bay rum and I never drank a drop of it.

Mark Jefferson to Isaiah Bowman, June 7, 1930:

Thank you for your very kind appreciation of my map [6-6 World Map]. Your comments show that I did not make my aim evident to you—namely to produce a map that does show the world "as a whole" on flat paper— and at that without any great distortion of either shapes or relative proportions. My first series of world maps—rain, temperature, people, vegetation —was published on a world-in-hemispheres base. You used my map in your translation of Brunhes' Geographie Humaine. Later I tried mapping the world on the homolographic base—Atlas of Commercial values. These were not simply made and put out, but used with my classes day after day, about six hundred students a year. These students are of not high average mentality or perception. For twenty five years we have been meeting these reactions. I doubt if anyone in the world has paid more attention to the way a map strikes untechnical minds.

The new map is my answer to much consideration of these effects. The homolographic map is quite unusable for such people. It distorts shapes so severely, to the common mind grotesquely. The untechnical person has an imperfect conception of many geographic shapes, and therefore clings the more strongly to those he knows. North America he knows best with us, and North America is so badly twisted even if put on the midmeridian of a homolographic map that it annoys him. The shape we must have is the shape on the globe and the proportions must not greatly vary in different parts of the map. The world in hemispheres is nothing like so bad. Mercator's is intolerable, so is Goode's and the six maps described by Reeds. They cannot meet acceptance by any but the cartographically sophisticated. *I* am all that. *I* like Reeds Fig. 7 but for the general public it must not be used. None of these is really a projection, no continuous map of the whole world can be that. I take it projections result from connecting intersections of projection lines through actual points with some kind of a surface—not necessarily plane. A hemisphere is the limiting maximum and must be very liberally pared toward the margins to be usable.

My argument—which Goode calls logical—is:

1. The globe map is alone good.
2. The eye can only grasp a part of the globe in one glimpse (coup d'oeuil).
3. That part is about a sixth of the whole.
4. A sixth may be projected accurately enough.
5. Six sixths grouped with their latitudes corresponding allow exactly the same study that a globe would and the same unity just as certainly as still pictures moved rapidly before the eye give the complete effect of moving pictures, though *we* wish study and comparison, not motion.

It is interesting that Antevs gets his facts for the world only *partly* before his reader on three full page maps.

p. 636 N. America, Europe, Asia	1:100 million
p. 691 South America	1: 45 million
p. 695 New Zealand	1: 10 million
No mapping for Africa.	
none for Australia	

I give *all the world* on *two pages*. one map. That is Unity!

Mark Jefferson to Isaiah Bowman, December 1, 1930:

I was interested by your booklet—Reading with a purpose. It is clever of the publishers to insist on the author's including a book of his own, and incidentally obligating themselves to get writers who have contributed something worth while to the story. I shall have to read Shotwell's book some day, but a lot of common human nature must be changed before wars will be avoided. I have a better suggestion than Kellog's (?)

1. Two disagreeing nations debate the matter before judges, broadcasting everything *in English*.
2. Then the whole Diplomatic corps of each country and its upper house of parliament shall be stripped and weighed. The party having greatest weight shall have enough of its youngest, lowest ranking diplomats removed to balance the enemy in weight.

   Then after 30 days of whatever training they like the two bodies fight it out barehanded, till one party gives in. No time out, No rest. Fight to a finish. Both nations agree to abide by the result and sign in advance the concessions to be made if they lose.

I am willing to allow reasonable modifications of my plan! Also people are so slow to adopt really good ideas that I think they may never adopt it at all.

Isaiah Bowman to Mark Jefferson, December 8, 1930:

Miss Wrigley and I are both tremendously interested in your Worcester address. I thought both of us had conveyed that interest in the warmest terms. And yet, why should we, when one comes to think of it? You know perfectly well by this time that we are interested in everything that you write, and the only pain that you engender is when you publish somewhere else without giving us first chance. Or doesn't one "engender" a pain? The Oxford Dictionary is too far away. I shall let you struggle with it.

Mark Jefferson to Isaiah Bowman, July 17, 1931:

Thank you very much for Dr. Finleys holograph, which I shall prize. The attention of the Times is very flattering—and agreeable.

I fancy few of my readers have any idea of the enormous labor that goes into my papers. There is enough in my "Cities box", which covers the present job, to make a whole book.

As an item the whole treatment of comparative urbanization was written out to a finish on the basis of numbers of Great Cities per Hundred Million Inhabitants to each country in the spring of 1931, when I came to the conclusion that it too much neglected the superior civilizing powers of the Super-Cities (ie. those of half a million up) over the merely great ones. Switzerland came out far ahead of France for instance since it has a relatively large *number* of Great Cities, but these are for the most part barely up to "greatness"! The relatively few French Great Cities on the other hand were of far greater average size and, especially in the case of Paris, capable of drawing men of real talent away from the Little-City-Lands around, like Belgium, Holland and Switzerland.

The only remedy to that one sided view was to rewrite the whole thing basing on the percentage of total population living in great cities. This corrects the defect alluded to but you would be surprised to see how similar the results are for large spaces. Putting both series on scale of 100—

	No. Am.	Eur.	Asia	So. Am.	Afr.	Austral.
Percent	48	42	8	21	6	100
No. Great Cities	48	43	10	26	8	100

U.S. Austral. U.K. Jap. Germ. France Arg. all run very similarly.

The actual comment editorial is a bit odd as if *I were divorcing* families and not the habits of forty years past. A couple is divorced when they become persuaded they cannot get on together—not when the judge signs the papers. New York annexed Brooklyn half a century or more before the Legislature and the City Council discovered it and confirmed it by paper enactment!

Mrs. Jefferson is visiting her folks in England. In Scotland she is I suspect asking questions about her grandfather John Beck who graduated at Edinburgh and came, she writes me, of some wild Highland clan whose plaid she is probably donning for all time. I foresee trouble deeper than a daughtership of the Revolution.

I am minded now to adventure into Spain into 1932. Your offer still stands. (M.J. refers to $250 from G.R. articles I.B. promised him earlier). I wish I could see an extra $500 to secure motor transportation.

Isaiah Bowman to Mark Jefferson, October 19, 1931:

Remembering the pleasure I had years ago in meeting the Twenty Club at your house, I heartily accept your invitation to speak to them again. The subject "Looking Down on the Earth". A few weeks ago I flew from Geneva to Basle to Mannheim to Frankfort to Halle to Berlin—in one day. It has spoiled me for all other forms of travel. Twenty pictures can be passed around the company—not mine but Luft Hansa's. They are fairly large photographs that show some of the things I would talk about . . . . .

*　　*　　*

Jefferson travelled with George G. Chisholm of the University of Edinburgh, on the 1911 Liverpool-Rome pilgrimage, and again on the 1912 U.S. Transcontinental Excursion. Thence forth, until Chisholm's death in 1930, the pair corresponded but did not meet again. Jefferson respected Chisholm: most men he simply tolerated. He respected Chisholm's independence of thought, his wide reading and ability to converse intelligently quite readily on most matters. He enjoyed Chisholm the thinker, social reformer and commodity statistician, who trespassed in the field of geography at leisure. The two men passed much time together on the 1911 and 1912 geographic excursions, but it was the ensuing correspondence which shaped thoughts and fashioned feelings. While Chisholm corresponded with O. E. Baker on matters relating to agricultural economics, Malthus, and the need for world cooperation, with A. P. Brigham on the morality and ethics of World War I, Jefferson was busy submitting the fruit of his correspondence with Chisholm to any person with whom he was corresponding at the time; responses, further ideas, and suggestions were usually incorporated in his next letter to Chisholm. Unfortunately much of Chisholm's correspondence has been lost to record; since he invariably wrote with the pen, copies of his letters may only be retrieved from the archival deposits of his contemporaries, which may have been lost. Mr. Robinson of the University of Edinburgh writes that no deposit of G. Chisholm's works or papers is known to exist.[3] Jefferson saved Chisholm's letters with care, but since Jefferson's death in 1949, many of the Scot's letters have been destroyed. Similarly many of Jefferson's early letters to Chisholm are not available. This decimation of sources has encouraged selection of letters from the years 1927-1930.

Chisholm and Jefferson corresponded on all manner of issues which included: automobiles in the U.S.A., racial inheritance, difficulties of restricting size of Hindu families, European conservatism, William James' book, *The Moral Equivalent of War,* rights of tenants in the Irish Free State, the economy of high wages, the Malthusian idea and the need for world cooperation, social reform, spelling reform, the 1914-1918 War, the idea of the League of Nations, culture and civilization.

George Chisholm to Mark Jefferson, October 18, 1927:
Your letter of the 3rd inst. has reached me here. It is a letter that I will keep, most of all perhaps on account of the striking statement in it, "Build a new house in Ypsilanti and you assemble as many motor cars every day as there are workmen, and not all of the cheap kind that I drive." It is certainly a significant sentence and one that I want to ponder with the view of making up my mind as to the exact nature of that significance.

And now I take up a few of your points in order. I do not question the importance of racial inheritance, have I trust no disposition to belittle that importance. Yet that is not everything. Where in the United States have you purer representatives of the British stock than in those mountain valleys for the inhabitants of which Walter Hines Page invented the name of our Contemporary Ancestors?

You think that Ford could get our coal into commerce and pay the miners a living wage but perhaps at the cost of doing rude things to landowners. But can you give any good reasons for making an attack on wealth in land as distinguished from, say, wealth in bank credits? I don't put that as a question that cannot be answered, but I do think it is one not easy to answer, and one that I don't pretend to be able to answer.

I do not (see my article) question the enormous difficulty of getting Hindus to restrict their families. But that does not prove its impossibility. I am a great believer in the ultimate efficacy of self-interest when people acquire a proper sense of what is their interest. Who a few years ago would have been prepared for the announcement in yesterday's *Times* that the Maharajah of Mysore (not, as you know, a British state) had removed the sex disqualification for the membership of the Legislative Assembly?

"The Argentine is rich but has preserved old world greed. They have peasants there, we have none." I lately read with great interest a book by one Ruth Suckow entitled "Country People" seeming to give a very faithful account of what we would call peasants. I do not question that the picture is very different from what could be taken as typical in Argentina. But among other differences you have to consider that Argentina lacks the stimulus of a severe winter.

You are sorry that your Malthus paper makes no hit with me. I am sorry that I gave you that impression. I do not think there is anything in it that I would deny. I never supposed for a moment that you were thinking of me in writing it. The only thing in it to which I take exception is the implicit if not express denial of the significance of Malthus's warnings. M. expressed himself unfortunately. I attach no importance to his ratios (as I stated in my Malthus paper). As stated by one well-known English economist, Cannan, the essential significance of M's doctrine is that so far population has been kept within limits by disagreeable methods, and it is highly desirable to alter that if it can be done. Your method, of the multiplication of motor cars, is, I believe, good so far as it goes, but it does not go the whole way. I wish it had been possible to apply the nearest possible equivalent to that method in this country a hundred years ago. The equivalent I have in mind is legislation forbidding any approach to overcrowding in the building of factories or houses for factory employees. That would have prevented the too rapid and unbalanced development of manufactures in this country. We should now have been poorer but better off in any sane sense. I am glad that there are important thinkers in your country—Warren Thompson, Reuter, O. E. Baker, Raymond Pearl and others who see, I hope in good time, the importance of taking warning from us.

I have omitted, I see, to take note of two things in your letter which I intended to remark on. You ask, cannot Europe try new things? Well we are doing our best. Here also there are believers in high wages. In to-day's *Times* I find one of our leading industrialists, Sir Alfred Mond, who is able to say that in the company to which he belongs there has been no labour dispute in 53 years, reported as saying that "low wages and long hours as a remedy for industrial depression was a retrograde step. He wanted high production, cheap costs and high wages." For all that I have never heard high wages recommended as a remedy for the depression in our greatest industry, agriculture.

The other point on which I meant to say something is what I should have begun with, your opening statement that you do not make out very well the trend of my paper. My answer to that is that the trend is given in the first of the two quotations with which I close my article, in effect, that as the world now is and is tending more and more to become no country can permanently raise its standard of living without bringing up the standard in other countries too. The only way for any one country to make itself independent of the reactions of other countries is for it to prohibit the export of a single ounce.

Finally, I have written to the Manager of the Manchester Ship Canal asking for a copy of their last report. I will send it to you when it comes, and when I get home (end of next week) I will send other references on Canals. Meantime I remain with many thanks for your letter.

Mark Jefferson to George Chisholm, November 2, 1927:

A good letter and I thank you for the report on the Manchester Ship Canal for 1926, which has already come to hand.

You raise so many interesting points that I wish I had time to write you in more fullness. I am trying to write a book and find it time consuming.

Mr. Ford has certainly made the people of this country over. Getting a motor car in itself had no particular point. Nor the ability to live ten or fifteen miles from your work or your play, but the opening up of this possibility as not merely desirable but practicable to great numbers of people who never dreamed of such a thing, stationary people so to say, like so many cabbages, fixed to their stalks by a mental resignation to their immobility, are suddenly stirred into life, released mentally to a new lot of possibilities, stirred to effort to acquire and pay for a car, representing sums of money which they did not conceive themselves able to spend, an effort often accompanied by indebtedness but along with the debt, a keenness for earning, an alertness for opportunity, that seems more than adequate to carry the load, and all the world moves in wider orbits. It is not the wider material circles of personal daily travel, a citizen commonly moving slowly about many thousands of miles where he formerly used to travel but hundreds, but the enterprise and eagerness that makes new men of them.

Mr. Ford is admittedly a very ignorant man—of many things. Very likely he knows nothing of Indian Institutions and as little of the part England has played for over a century now in that country. Possibly on that very account I see him if he were set down in India, at once stirring the people of that most vegetative country, into general aspiration for a motor car—a thing I suppose quite out of their horizons. Once conceiving themselves as possible car owners I begin to see them planning how to earn, conceiving themselves able to earn. This ferment of desire of struggle to have, to acquire would ill brook resistances of Indian or British Institutions. This arousing the poverty stricken to wants that they are shown they can satisfy will be very effective in overthrowing taboos.

I am of course judging from people very far above Indian status, yet the difference is really one of degree. Attack of institutions you say! If I accepted your framing of the question I should make the answer you wish, but suppose we frame the question another way. A competent manager and willing workmen propose to deliver coal to the consumer in Britain and abroad at prices that favor movement of coal and other goods. Shall we allow individuals to say no, don't do that, it isn't profitable to me?

I enclose a pencil sketch of a house in Santa Fe, Argentine Republic, which projects eleven feet beyond the general house line into a narrow street—a picture in my Peopling the Argentine Pampa. A well dressed citizen saw me pacing in the street, making the sketch and we got conversing. The house interests me, I said. Why doesn't the city make him take it down and cease obstructing the public way? But he OWNS it said the Santafecino, he bought it and it is his. He can't have his private rights interfered with! I shouldn't have believed any people could accept such an attack by a private citizen on the common convenience! No less than six houses in that block project onto a three foot sidewalk, one completely closing it, and compelling all passers to step into the street.

Such an assertion of private vested rights seems to me to amount to a continuing attack by an individual on the community of which he ought to consider himself a part.

I would give those owners sixty days to remove their obstruction to traffic and if they did not I would bring a gang of workmen and remove it at their expense. I should not attempt to defend my right to attack them but should deny their right to oppose the public welfare.

When the United States in 1858 (more or less) refused to pay Sound Dues to Denmark, she refused to join Britain and Prussia in discussing with Denmark the sums to be paid the latter, for abandoning her claim, she may have showed ignorance of precedent and possibly international bad manners but unquestionably it makes for the well being of the world to question vested rights to obstruct useful activities most vigorously. It is natural that a new people in a new land should be impatient of asserted "rights" to a degree less easy to appreciate for Europeans or Asiatics whose environment is full of them. The wonder to me is that South America should be so illiberal.

Is Miss Ruth Suckow's book "Country People" about North Americans?

My test of the peasant is his belief about himself. He accepts an inferior position as properly and permanently his.

Your point about Argentine winter is also one I have to comment on. I incline to think winter is severe in proportion as it interferes with life's activities. I note in the warmer countries, where life may be lived in a house without artificial heating, except for cooking, a lowering of effectivity more than compensating for the effort that a colder climate compels you to apply to merely keep alive.

If I do not heat my house in winter the water pipes freeze and burst. To go away in winter means the plumber must come, cut off the water, draw all the water out of taps, and again in spring he must come and go over everything to make sure the system is all right. But, my heating system, and better still that of my neighbors, using oil, which kindles a fire automatically when cold enough and feeds more or less oil according to the weather, extinguishing it when warm, regulating everything with a thermostat, allows life to be lived in that house more effectively than winter is ever lived down South by people who shiver through a succession of cold spells.

Effectively I wonder if some of the countries of "mild" winter, may not in slowing and hindering human activity be more "severe" than distinctly "cold" climates. I fancy if I had a winter's writing to do in Europe I would do it better in Sweden than in England, though of course my habituation to a heated room enters here.

Opportunities for comfort in life seem to cure the large family evil. My wish for industrial England is that she might have shared more of the product of agriculture and industry with the laborer. The desire for comforts and luxuries is spreading everywhere and will keep the population down. Luxuries for all have many advantages over luxury for FEW.

Mark Jefferson to George Chisholm, December 19, 1927:

I have just read Ruth Suckow's "Country Folks." You wrote answering my assertion that we had no peasants in the United States—that her characters seemed to be peasants. Of course they are, but we regard them as *German* peasants, European peasants. There were many millions of them and there are a lot still. I fancy August's sister Mary, who wanted to go away to school is something like Miss Suckow herself. She did go away to school and got American contacts, ceased to be a peasant. Dr. Bowman's father— Baumann he called himself—was a German peasant. Isaiah was not allowed to go to school after reaching fourteen. The law compelled his father to send him till that age and then the father "demanded his time," as these Germans say. That is he made him work on the farm for him without pay till he was 21. Then, when he was free from parental authority Bowman went to "Ferris Institute" a famous private school here, which means one run for profit, and not maintained by public authorities of any sort. There he rapidly carried through the studies of later years corresponding to our High Schools and then came here to this Normal College, older than he would have been had his father followed the "American" plan of allowing his son to go to school as long as he wanted while his father supported him. But, although older, he had gained in power by his work on the farm. Power to carry through things that are not easily done. He does not readily admit that anything is impossible. I look on Bowman's father as a peasant, but not American. Herbert Quick's Hawkeye, Vandemark's Folly and a third—in trilogy—describe something similar from the early days in Iowa even better than Miss Suckow, for he shows the contacts with other American pioneers and the working out of the peasant feeling more plainly, going more into the complexities of nature. Perhaps I am merely argumentative in calling these German peasants. Perhaps I ought to admit that we have millions of peasants in the United States. I have just such people all around me here, our Michigan towns know the retired farmers just as well as Iowa ever did. We have quite a group of them here in Ypsilanti. They held German services in the Lutheran Church here since I came here, but now that is mostly given up. The children no longer speak any German and they would have gone into other churches had they not introduced English services to save them to the Lutheran community. I think when something of peasant ways crop out we say "German" which is rather begging the question, I admit. But the younger men at least are just as American as I am. There are no peasants among *them*.

I should have made a better statement had I said we have no peasant class. You have reminded that we have had many, probably still have many peasant communities, all however dissolving steadily. The melting pot is entirely real. South America however has, and so have our Southern States —the negroes. Bowman is not a peasant. Doubtless by peasant origin so am I. My Grandfather, a gardener near London, could not read. Father clerked for John Green in London and so brought into chance contact with Ralph Waldo Emerson was advised to come to this country where he was presently called to Boston to import English books for Little, Brown and Co., becoming extremely familiar with English literature by incessant reading, though little schooled. Quite English, but no peasant.

George Chisholm to Mark Jefferson, January 3, 1928:

I answer your last letter, December 19, first. I was much interested in the personal particulars you give both about yourself and Bowman. I hear that Bowman is coming over to the International Geographical Congress to be held at Cambridge, England, at the end of July (I hope you are too), and I am looking forward to meeting him there. I should like to know if what you tell me about his farm life is to be treated as confidential. If not, I should like to ask him about his experience. I have long felt that I have suffered from never having been taught to do something with my hands. I am inclined to look upon that as an essential part of education. I continue to be much impressed by William James's ideas set forth in his essay on *The Moral Equivalent of War*.

Many thanks also for sending me the American paper containing Mr. Garrett's article, and in return I send you today's *Scotsman* from which you will see one use of it I have made. I did not want to make my letter to the Sc. too long, otherwise I would have referred in it also to the amount of agricultural employment in your country for those displaced in other industries.

Lastly, with reference to your latest missives we want to thank you and Mrs. Jefferson for your Christmas and New Year card. In return we send two cards showing two of the latest additions to the sights of Edinburgh, the Scottish National War Memorial, and the American Scottish monument commemorating the same disastrous years.

And now I return to your letter of December 3. My last letter, called forth by the *Nation* article on the American coal war was only a partial answer to it, and there were some points to which I always meant to return.

First as to the *right* of a tenant in the Irish Free State to rent his land and sell that right. That is nothing new in Ireland. It is what is known as the Ulster tenant right, long a traditional custom in that province, and made legal and compulsory by Gladstone in that province in the early 70's and afterwards extended to the rest of Ireland, with the result of introducing such anomolies as to compel this country to pass a law to facilitate the purchase of their holdings by the tenants, and providing funds for the purpose to be repaid by annual installments including rent. It is very doubtful whether we have heard the last of that, for there is a party in the Free State in favour of repudiating those bargains.

As to oppressive interest and profits made by cutting down the rate of wages, what have you to say about the case recorded in the cutting which I attach below.

"WOMAN MONEYLENDER
INTEREST AT 520 PER CENT

An old woman wearing a shawl, who applied for a moneylender's certificate at Liverpool yesterday, said she could neither read nor write. She kept business in her brain. She said she lent dock labourers £1 on Mondays for their rent, and received £1. 2s. back on Saturdays.

The Magistrate pointed out that this interest worked out at 520 per cent per annum.

The woman said her clients were willing to pay, and she was willing to pay the necessary 25s. for a certificate.

Neighbours gave the woman a good character, and the certificate was granted."

We have a saying here (it probably runs also in America), "Hard cases make bad law." Would you suggest that the jute manufacturers of Bengal should be compelled to pay their employees a living wage according to the standard of England or America or even the very low standard of Dundee which they help to depress? I ask those questions with no desire to give an implied answer. Though I may add that I believe the employers ought to find it worth while to make the conditions of employment at the mills so attractive as to make homes for them and their families beside the works so that they might in time become more efficient and able to tend more complicated machinery, instead of wavering from mill to country village and back again, when the miseries at either end become intolerable. But then what would become of Dundee? Would it add another large contingent to our million of unemployed? And so we are carried from puzzlement to puzzlement. An English publicist has suggested that we should have in our country a standing body of specialists in government to spend their time in studying government problems to advise the responsible government of the day. I hope that (tho' long after I am in my grave) we may advance even further, when to use the words of one of your own economists (Taussig) we have escaped from "that low state of civilization under which millions of people fly at each other's throats," and when we may have a body of specialists (perhaps self chosen by mutually recognised fitness) to study world problems and advise the governments of the world.

But to return to the suggestion that has given rise to these remarks, I cannot recognise that giving a higher wage than seems necessary is an American idea. Read any good account of New Lanark by Robert Owen. How much older than he the idea may be I cannot say.

With unqualified approval I accept your remark on human nature, pretty much the same the world over you say. "I like my comfort and hate to have anyone interfere with it, but as soon as I make those around me comfortable too, I fancy my comfort increases more than it cost me to think of them." This last thought may carry us far.

Finally I want to say that our white collar class have suffered by the War in the same way as yours. Before the war we kept two maids, now only one domestic and we are peculiarly fortunate in having our domestic a married woman, the husband living in our house but not working for us, both however very efficient and devoted to us. But that is only our luck—not guaranteed tho' it has already lasted more than four years.

George Chisholm to Mark Jefferson, August 31, 1928:

I have not yet acknowledged receipt of the reprint of your article on the "Civilising Rails" which you were kind enough to send me some time ago. I read it with great interest and enjoyment. I greatly admire the ingenuity both of your maps and your expository terms, which latter I think, are well worthy of taking a place in geographical terminology.

Moreover, I have no exception to take to your thesis. Rails (with motor roads and steamships) are in fact the most efficient means of spreading that form of civilization which began with the invention of money and whose evolution has been going on ever since in somewhat diverse ways owing to differences in secondary influences.

For all that it is a civilization with which I cannot feel satisfied, and all the less the more nearly it approaches its apparent ideals. I find myself constantly but helplessly pondering the idea of a possible civilization at least in part independent of the money mechanism, marvellously efficient as that is. "The provision of subsistence and the necessaries of life ranks," says R. G. Hawtrey in "The Economic Problem", "or ought to rank, as the first charge upon economic activity." I have no reason to believe that Mr. Hawtrey would accept my definition of "necessaries of life," but whatever definition he adopted, I don't see how, on the one hand, this "first charge" can be met on a money basis if it is left to the "entire population" individually to do so, or, on the other hand, to relieve multitudes of the burden of that charge without demoralizing them to such an extent as to threaten to put an end to all economic activity.

Perhaps we may have to face more abrupt economic changes than we have had to face hitherto. This morning's paper gives a hint of an economic revolution contemplated by some in your country that goes beyond anything I had ever dreamt of at least in the near future. It is reported that a Mr. Robinson, one of your candidates for the Vice-Presidency, is accusing Mr. Hoover of urging on American farmers a policy that would have the effect of limiting their production to what can be consumed in the U.S.!

Mark Jefferson to George Chisholm, September 9, 1928:

Your comment on the Civilizing Rails almost coincides with that expressed just a month earlier by M. Aurousseau, an Australian geographer now resident in London. I presume you have met him.

"In the sense that (civilization) is being so diffused, and by the rails, the title is just . . . My mind opposes that spread of mechanical civilization. This increasing uniformity in everything, and finds it hateful. I am not so simple as to believe that such an attitude, assumed by a minority, can prevent what is going on, but I do not believe in what is going on. We have come to think that civilization and culture are the same thing. The latter is by far the more precious, insofar as it is culture which makes life a fuller experience, not civilization. From this point of view, the Spaniards seem to me to be the finest people I have met in Western Europe. Culture it seems to me, is a way of looking at life, a mental attitude of living, whereas civilization is an external manner of living. I haven't yet thought through these things, and will come out with an essay on the matter some time, but at least, I would say, that culture may be very high where civilization is relatively low, and that culture is the more valuable."

I do not know whether you know my Culture of the Nations, published in the Bulletin of the American Geographical Society in April 1911, in which I put numerical values on "culture" of countries on the strength of their general schooling of all the young, development of foreign commerce, and railways and use of the mails like this:

Switzerland	85	United States	67
Belgium	84	Denmark	65
United Kingdom	83	Newfoundland	57
Netherlands	77	France	56
Australia	75	Sweden	52
New Zealand	70	Norway	51
Canada	68	Spain	28
German Empire	68		

Which shows no bias of patriotism. All sorts of allowances are necessary, even on the scanty grounds used, canals supplementing RR in Norway, internal commerce in the US being as huge as external is limited. Belgium and Holland undoubtedly claiming more foreign commerce in statistics than is real.

But what is this culture so estimated? Distinctly Western, distinctly not Oriental. An Oriental grade under nine points exists in the study.

I called attention to the mapmaker's use of culture on his maps (black on U.S. brown relief—defined as "what Man has made"). With culture so conceived cultured man is the maker, the doer. Taking thought about doing is not inhibited but implied, for Western machines are thoughtful machines. Machines are thought given reality. Western man has made vastly more things than Oriental man.

This is again the civilization that you and Aurousseau do not like. The West excels in human sympathy. Whether Hospitals are an expression of western culture or of Christianity I do not know but they are distinctly western, belong with the railway, with commerce and with schools. Our little city spends $11,000 a year making up the deficit of our little hospital, which amounts to a dollar a head and would make London supply seven million dollars a year. I suppose Tokyo spends something too, but only because she has taken on something of western culture. What does Pekin spend or Angora?

Our luncheon clubs have taken up the cause here in America of the Underprivileged child, cripples and all such. Such work and all kinds of sanitation and relief of suffering are fine flowers of civilization, the very civilization that you are not satisfied with.

I wish I could get you and Aurousseau to make out the charges of the indictment rather definitely, just what are the bad things our civilization does?

I should like to try to point out the good ones.

Last year I made a new attempt to rank countries in civilization, to get in the new countries of Europe and the post-war conditions. I counted more data—schooling, RR freight and RR mileage, mail, commerce, number of Great Cities per million people, numbers of autos, telephones and patents issued, in all nine topics, all put on a scale of 100 for the leading country, with the result: [Europe only].

Denmark	79	Norway, Sweden	52
Switzerland	75	Austria	51
Belgium	70	France	45
United Kingdom	68	Czechoslovakia	34
Holland	63	Finland	31
Germany	54	Hungary	30
Irish F.S.	53	Spain	29

That seems to show agreement to me. Obviously such gradings are rude, and yet here is an objective grading of countries in this west-type of civilization which has value.

I find inventiveness worth attention. First I counted patents issued in any country 1871 to 1922 per thousand population 1922 and multiplied by 3 to make the leading country have index 100. Remarkable result Belgium 100, France 40, Germany 18, United Kingdom 36, Canada 75, U.S. 36.

Then I found Canada issued five patents to a "resident of the U.S.," to one to a resident of Canada, so I took patents issued to residents of the issuing country per thousand people (1925). This had involved correspondence with U.S. consuls over the world and shows in part U.S. 36, Canada 14, Sweden 32, Norway 18, Denmark 23, United Kingdom 19, Holland 5, Austria 18, Czechoslovakia 5, Japan 6, New Zealand 28.

But I learn that a good patent must be covered by claims in many countries and that I should count the patents taken out in any country and all countries by residents of U.S., of United Kingdom, of Belgium or of Holland, etc. This puts a very different complexion on the matter, for often countries with complete reports, 16 residents of Holland, 13 of Germany, 11 of U.S., 9 of Belgium, 7 of France and 6 of United Kingdom in each hundred thousand inhabitants (1925) take out patents in some foreign country. Reports in this case wholly by OTHER COUNTRIES! "Who Invents?" at Christmas.

George Chisholm to Mark Jefferson, September 21, 1928:

I write at once to thank you for the prompt reply to my comment on your article on The Civilizing Rails. My comment, I know, was written in haste, and I am sorry I have no recollection of what I said. I regret accordingly that the letter, hasty, and, no doubt, brief as it was, was not among those which I dictated to a typist.

I am sorry that I do not know Mr. Aurousseau, though I have been most interested in articles he has written, and I am glad to learn that his thoughts seem to some extent in the same direction as mine. I had guessed that from what I had read of his, and now that I know that he is resident in London I will take means to put myself in communication with him, if for nothing else, to ask him to let me know when and where his meditated essay on civilization and culture appears.

You are good enough to say that you would like me (and Aurousseau) to make out the charges of the indictment against civilization rather definitely. I think my best reply is to recommend you to read a small book (147 small pages) entitled "The Triumphant Machine" by R. M. Fox (for many years apprentice and journey man in an engineering workshop) published by Leonard and Virginia Woolf at the Hogarth Press, London, Tavistock Square, W.C. 1. I accept every item in his indictment, but, like the author of the preface (H.N. Brailsford) I do not think the remedies he proposes at all adequate. I have indeed in typed form two things that might contribute to make my ideas of reform clearer, but as they are confessedly not thought out I do not think it fair to trouble busy people with them. One is a development of the ideas expressed on p. 298 of my article on World Unity. The other is an article entitled, "Obscurities of the Population Problem," which I wrote for the Economic Journal but which the editor rejected. I have given my sole reason for not sending them to you, but if you would like to see them I shall be glad to send them.

George Chisholm to Mark Jefferson, December 27, 1928:
We have quite given up sending Christmas cards, but we are very glad to exchange greetings at this season, and though the year will have ceased to be new by the time this reaches you, you may be assured that it carries with it our best wishes for the year that is still in the future.

I am sending with it a little book which, I think, you will read with interest, although it expresses rather my than your view of the present trend of civilization. I had not read it when I last wrote in answer to your question as to what objections I had to make to prevalent ideas of civilization, but now I think it expresses my ideas on the subject even more precisely than Fox's The Triumphant Machine. Since you last wrote I have been trying to get into touch with Aurousseau, but hitherto without success. Yesterday morning I had the pleasure of receiving a very cordial letter from Prof. Warren L. Thompson of Scripps Foundation, Miami University, Oxford, Ohio, whom I have never met, but who seems to think very much as I do.

F. Chisholm (wife of George Chisholm) to Mark Jefferson, March 11, 1930:
Your letter of the 16th February reached here after G. Chisholm's death on the 9th February. He died suddenly in the tram car coming home from church. I was not with him, not being well enough to go out in cold weather. He was so happy that morning and felt, he said, so well. He wrote a long letter to an old school and college friend, to whom he wrote regularly every fortnight, before going.

I never saw him alive again. He passed away in a minute. He had been talking to a gentleman he knew a few minutes before when he fell forward dead. He had not a moment's suffering. You may before this have heard of his death. I should have written to you sooner, but I have been very ill.

I've been married 45 years, and we have been great friends and companions. Looking back on our long life together, I feel I've many memories. He never said a mean or uncharitable thing, and he was reverenced and loved by many of his students.

He always read me your letters, and got me interested in his work, his students and his friends. As you seem out of the way, I enclose a few reviews. The one from the London Times is not quite correct, as you will see from the back. There was a far better notice in the "Scotsman" of the 17th. That old one from the Boston paper was copied by someone from an article in the Scotsman and appeared in America eleven days after.

You write in such a friendly way, I think I'm not boring you.

Yours sincerely,
F. Chisholm

*   *   *

Jefferson's correspondence with Gladys Wrigley began after September 1920, when she was appointed editor of the *Geographical Review*. Between the years 1921 and 1949 the two exchanged over 600 letters. Most of the correspondence concerned articles or book reviews Jefferson was submitting to the *Geographical Review,* or articles or book reviews that Jefferson wished other geographers to undertake. It is hard to overestimate the significance of Jefferson's contribution to the emergence of the *Geographical Review,* through his alert and suggestive correspondence with both Gladys Wrigley and Isaiah Bowman. Jefferson and editor Wrigley would dash notes off to each other when one found an interesting reference or a fine piece of work, and they had so much fun doing it. Especially amusing is the humor and good taste with which Miss Wrigley replied to Jefferson's many requests and exhortations to render the quarterly *Review* a monthly.

Miss Wrigley expressed her appreciation of Jefferson in an article fittingly published in the *Geographical Review,* the centennial year of the Society's existence. An excerpt is culled from the article:[4]

Two of the Review's outstanding reviewers were Professor Jefferson himself and W. M. Davis. The former's frank appraisals were a delight but not always "fit to print".

I am glad to have seen the . . . Atlas. I think he must be a pompous army man with pull and little brains. He may very likely be pot bellied.

I don't like that man . . . he beats his wife.

Please excuse me from the . . . I do not want to become a common scold.

. . . is a terrible book. It adds about as near nothing to what I knew or wanted to know as any book well could . . . Long winded, wordy, preferring Latin words to Saxon ones always, certainly unable to write Latin, but wanting to use a lingo of their own like a child making up a dog Latin.

To one editorial revision he refused to have his name attached, but on another occasion he remarked:

Why yes: it seems very good indeed; but I would say I never wrote certain parts of it! If you say I did however there is no argument, you have us well trained.

Mark Jefferson to Gladys Wrigley, December 18, 1921:

Please ask Mr. Joerg to improve on the "Economics of Argentine Cultural Exports" as translating "Die Agrarische Exportwirtschaft Argentinens." I never know what to say for Wirtschaft anyway. I wish all the Germans would learn to speak English and write it. However, I suppose they would lose a good part of their intelligence and industry if deprived of the long training of trying to convey ideas through the medium of the most stupid of languages.

Gladys Wrigley to Mark Jefferson, September 26, 1922:

There is an article that I wish to have written—on the distribution of population in Europe according to the last censuses. We can pay $100 for such an article. We should wish to have it by the end of the year.

We could be of some assistance in getting together material . . . Surely you cannot resist so much population!

Mark Jefferson to Gladys Wrigley, October 2, 1922:

Perhaps I was hasty in agreeing to tackle the Population of Europe. I am actually at work putting the Argentine "Unveiling of the Pampa" into form, having a number of the first pages finished and pushing it forward. Not very important, perhaps to get it printed to store in the cellar, but I have had the thing on my mind so long that I want to get it out of the way so that I can do things I ought to have been at long ago . . .

There is another thing I have need of doing that would use up your $100 a deal better, and then some I fancy, namely the correspondence incidental to a study of the optimum season for travel all the world over . . . Best travel season Michigan May-June, best southern Chile January, best season Rome, about April. So the whole world. It is much needed. Baedeker affords a start in his prefaces. All on a map.

How does it sound Dr. Bowman? The questions are of course yours, but I am in haste—three classes to meet this morning.

Mark Jefferson to Gladys Wrigley, April 21, 1923:

I am volunteering herewith a note on the new Atlas of Sweden—which is warm but not half warm enough. The Atlas is a thing of beauty and a joy ever since it came. I carry it up to my bedside every night.

Gladys Wrigley to Mark Jefferson, June 28, 1923:

W. D. Durland, who prepared the article "Forests of the Dominican Republic," in the April 1922 number of the Review has just returned from the quebracho region of northern Argentina. He offers to prepare us an article thereon. I want to give him some points on the course of it. Can you give me any suggestions.

Mark Jefferson to Gladys Wrigley, September 11, 1923:

. . . I would rather do climate and weather stuff—most especially rainfall than anything I can imagine. Imagine the unused material at Washington!

If there were any chance of earning a living at that sort of thing I wouldn't school-teach!

Mark Jefferson to Gladys Wrigley, March 31, 1924:

Astonishing that we have only world maps for monthly pressures, and rainfall on scales so tiny and map net so coarse, as Herbertson and Bartholomew. These things are fundamental to all geography and yet the drawings representing existing knowledge are so tiny one can hardly see them.

There ought to be an international committee on the rainfall map with a subsection of each continent to keep a large scale map up to date in MS somewhere for year and months and supply at least photostats of it on demand.

Mark Jefferson to Gladys Wrigley, April 23, 1924:

I don't like that man Sutton. I think he beats his wife! or if he alibies "no wife" he certainly must have some of those British vices that we Americans want kept as tightly in the snug island as they keep rabies out.

I have been somewhat under the weather and overworked, and spring is slow, and students elect my work and I am foolish enough to give them always new stuff and civic things use so much time, all of today and all of next Monday for instance. Further a number of my things are not going, people lying down on them both here and elsewhere—to explain why I can't do anything more with Sutton. What I really want is summer and as long as there is ice in the Lakes we cannot have any hereabouts.

Mark Jefferson to Gladys Wrigley, October 5, 1924:

Two of my colleagues have just built houses side by side here on a hillside. One has made two steep terraces between his house and the street and three flights of steep steps to get to the front door. His wife's family from *Seattle* appear to provide the money for major expenses. The other, with the house floors level with his neighbor's, has graded to the gentlest possible slope and makes access to his front door by a winding path of very gentle grade. He and his wife are from New Orleans! Have you ever been on the Coast? Do you know their habit of building impossible streets and putting asphalt on the sidewalks for the feet to stick to and not slip to the bottom of the hill?

It is fascinating as the asphalt wears away and only patches remain to see folks going hop, skip and jump to keep on the asphalt!

Gladys Wrigley to Mark Jefferson, Telegram, February 11, 1925:

GREAT STUFF. LEADING ARTICLE FOR APRIL.

[Refers to article on Malthus]

Mark Jefferson to Gladys Wrigley, September 25, 1925.

We have 454 students in geography after disbanding a little class of 20 to make room for seven who wanted a course on Mediterranean geography with me after an average of six other courses . . .

In the Principles you and any reader will likely find the start with maps repellent. One can't read map construction directions with much interest. If I had had more time I would put that a little later in the book that a casual reader might not be turned away so abruptly. There are other parts of it that stand reading. I should always teach that first for the reason that motivates its existence is the fact that high school students do not of course, know how to read and these exercises really do help a little toward learning. For ten days they get their instructions by reading the book. When they ask help we try to help, but rather make a habit of pointing out a passage, "It tells you there. What does that say to do?" For teaching it will be much better than any book we have had, especially for my assistants.

Mark Jefferson to Gladys Wrigley, October 31, 1925:
Got a check today from Herald Tribune Books for my third review of Febvres' Geographical Introduction to History. Three reviews, three fees, a French copy and an English copy of the book which was worth reading. If I could work that right along I could afford to write reviews all the time.

Mark Jefferson to Gladys Wrigley, September 18, 1926:
Can an author expect to be satisfied with a review of his book? Brooks says not, in thanking me for my notice of his Why the Weather. They feel often an inclination to talk back, I fancy. Yet they get nowhere if they do, it seems. Mr. Orchard for instance as reviewer, attempting the rather impossible task of reviewing on galley sheets, thinks the map-work in Principles of Geography too hard. I think you had some similar reaction yourself, yet four times a year we take from 100 to 200 green high school graduates through it in ten days and they almost all really master it, and I have done it more than twenty years.

Mark Jefferson to Gladys Wrigley, July 13, 1927:
You admit that you lead a hectic life. I should call it four apoplexies a year. But I congratulate you on one more escape from peril.
The pictures are wonderful. Your Review is an indispensable part of the day's geography in every aspect. You may be very proud of it, though it is perhaps presumptuous for me to say so.

Mark Jefferson to Gladys Wrigley, October 23, 1928:
Aurousseau and Chisholm independently but coincidentally object to my Civilizing Rails—that there is—unfortunately—such a thing as Western Civilization in the world and they can't stop it but they don't like it!
Well all the more need to study it and know it when you see it. Aurousseau says I am a Progresista, by which I suppose he means I like bathtubs. I do! I wish I could have another, and have just spent $1,200 (and paid it) on a brand new heating plant, hot water, sixteen radiators, and of course an oil burner, which is magical. Starts up a fire any time the air chills off and keeps the climate civilized.
I should say so.

Mark Jefferson to Gladys Wrigley, November 14, 1929:

The Inventiveness paper has brought an unusual number of letters and requests for copies. One from a Swiss Doctor—exchange student Johns Hopkins to print in a Zurich newspaper, another from Committee before League of Nations, a surprising one from a southern professor of psychology.

Gladys Wrigley to Mark Jefferson, January 3, 1930:

I have an urgent request to make. The Council has awarded the Cullum Geographical Medal for 1929 to Alfred Hettner . . . I should like to publish a review of new editions of his work. This calls for a special kind of review by a "real" all round geographer and I don't know anyone who could do it half as well as you.

Mark Jefferson to Gladys Wrigley, January 17, 1930:

Tuesday night dinner—speech—Home Economics Club "Argentine Home Life" Wednesday night Dinner—talk. History Club Worlds Railways. Friday Luncheon Chairman, Natural Science and Geography Departments with addresses by a pupil friend, Professor of Farming.

Sorry to balk at Hettner, but he no longer interests me . . .

You have introduced me to so many charming books by sending them to me for reviewing that I have only reason for gratitude. I am grateful, but also old and short of time for the many fine things to do. I apologize for refusing.

Mark Jefferson to Gladys Wrigley, April 26, 1931:

Your April Review was remarkable —of course I have not read it all yet. I am forever indignant at the bulk of it. If I could give you orders you would have to bring it out weekly, an average of 15 pages, with numbers continuing!

Raisz' drawings are wonderful. He has gone far beyond Lobeck and someone will go yet beyond him.

But it is not for us common mortals. One must have the touch. I hope Raisz will go on. Of course he will.

Many thanks for the China cities article. I am not much impressed by these guesses but it will make the Sinologists happier to count 118 Chinese cities and I do not know the contrary.

Gladys Wrigley to Mark Jefferson, December 10, 1934:

Mr. Bowman has been chuckling over your note "More Potential Parents." It gives us a new slogan—Brighten the Review with Babies!

Mark Jefferson to Gladys Wrigley, January 21, 1939:

Thank you very much for the note from Tilby's Genius of Ireland. I wonder if he listed the men from Belfast "with a few additions suggested from other sources, and some omissions—" But I suppose he is not believing in genius in northern Ireland!

How very like the historian or Social Science writer! Everything special by itself. As if there were any *Irish* genius—only genius in Ireland, that is a mere case of humanity in one instance.

The Ann Arbor Rumanian Max Handman last June in Chicago declared confidently that excessive size of the chief city was a well-known characteristic of South America, was quite outraged when I told him not more than of Europe.

I am glad to see Tilby notes Rome an exception. How the glamor that was Rome blinds people. Mussolini means to use it to help unify his Italians until Rome is really the most Italian thing in Italy. Of course it isn't yet.

Smith raises a good question when he asks Primate of what? The little law is a part of a study—"What is a country?" Barcelona primate of Catalonia, Madrid of Spain, Lisbon of Portugal, for Iberia is not a country and Spain is not a country, Castile and Catalonia perhaps are.

When Lenin forbade the name Russia and substituted the Union of Soviet Socialist Republics did he not set out to destroy Russia and internationalize it?

Social laws appear to differ from material and atomic ones in that the elements subject to the law may become conscious of them and set out to defy them. The New Dealers defy Gresham's Law by calling in Gold—even paper stamped "gold"—and burying the gold in the ground, as the fairy tale princess tries to avoid the curse put on her by a wicked godmother.

As if water agreed to avoid slopes so as not to run downhill, and oxygen and hydrogen to stay away from each other to avoid consequences!

The Free Press wanted to interview me—Was Detroit a Primate City? I think it the only million-city in the world without a publishing house or a good bookstore. Of course Hudson's (Dry Goods) has a book counter.

Boston now, may be primate—But that's another story.

Yours in the usual haste,

＊　　　＊　　　＊

Jefferson and Caroline Stone were members of the '84 class, Boston University. They had been good friends and earnest students. When Jefferson departed New England for South America in the winter of 1883, he left behind a young lady with whom, at one time, he had kept company.

In 1934, on the occasion of the fiftieth anniversary of the class of '84, President Daniel Marsh of Boston University, invited all living members of that class to an Alumni Reunion.[5] Although Jefferson did not attend he learned that Caroline Stone had married, was now Caroline Atherton, and living at Jamaica Plain, Massachusetts. A vast correspondence ensued between the two classmates and was terminated only with the death of Mrs. Atherton in 1947.

Two minds quietly sat on the bye-lines of life and watched the world at work, at play, and at war. The two enjoyed the exchange of reminiscences relating to their student days, pondered all matter of personally significant issues and their careers—one had become a geography teacher, the other a high school teacher of Greek and Latin. In the 1930's Jefferson sent Mrs. Atherton copies of his books and reprints of his articles. In the 1940's he sent her regular letters which were rather in the nature of reports, containing commentary on the war, progress of his book and his latest civic undertakings. Her letters contained much encouragement for him to complete the book he was writing in those retirement years, summaries of her own reading, numerous references to articles or addresses which she thought might interest him, newspaper clippings, comments on some of Jefferson's books and articles which he sent her, and descriptions of her garden. Mrs. Atherton enjoyed her open rooms facing the fragrance of her carefully groomed garden at Jamaica Plain, where she passed her last years alone. Occasionally the garden would creep into her letters and shut the world away, so that she was alone with beauty, with quiet and with the past.

The exchange of correspondence was thoroughly enjoyed by both correspondents for whom it became a hobby. Jefferson was expressing a sentiment they both shared when he wrote to Mrs. Atherton on October 27, 1946, "There is no one I can write to in the same way as to you. Our generation has nearly gone by."

Caroline Atherton to Mark Jefferson, June 19, 1934:

It was good to have your greeting "after 50 years" and to read your pamphlet, The Civilizing Rails. You are still the thoughtful student as well as teacher, and on the lines you began so long ago to follow.

Have you ever seen Bishop McConnell's book on Borden P. Bowne? I think you would enjoy reading it, and it does bring back his courses, that were to me an undiscovered country.

Of course I married a teacher(!) and we read and study together. Latin and Greek and French and Italian occupy us a good deal. Mr. Atherton, Harvard '79, is now retired and we have visited the Pacific Coast four times, your railways have served us well.

We had the blessing of a visit to Italy and Greece, never to be forgotten. And we have found occasion to be of some slight service to our fellowmen, it has not all been pleasuring, you know that.

Forgive this bit of personal history, I thought you might like to know something of the doings of 50 years of your old class-mate.

Caroline Atherton to Mark Jefferson, September 4, 1936:
Your letter was forwarded to me in Maine, the book I have just brought back from the post-office here. It looks so interesting that I think I shall read every chapter. One thing I note from a cursory glance, and that is that the illustrations are where they belong, opposite the pages that deal with them . . .

Your trip [to Spain] with daughter Phoebe must have meant a lot to her and of course you got what you were after. You generally do, even if your Latin notes of the psychology course were not correct. Did you ever show them to anyone? . . .

Mr. Atherton left me very suddenly in August while we were in our summer home in Maine. A half-hour after he rose from the dinner table in good spirits and apparently quite himself, I found him, still, a happy, serene expression on his face. What a wonderful way to leave this life, no invalidism, no suffering . . .

I have just sold my cottage, where we spent thirty-five happy years, none happier than the last season we had together with our Greek, French, birds, for we did all our reading and studying together, a perfect comradeship for forty-three years. My trip to Maine was to dispose of my possessions there. Now that chapter is ended . . .

The days were lonely indeed at first and I joined a class that was reading Italian once a week, and have put quite a good deal of time into the study of verbs and composition. I should never qualify as a teacher, but it has been good fun.

Mark Jefferson to Caroline Atherton, January 21, 1940:
I write this for the carbon under it which stays with me. I may visit another church next Sunday, and write another but you won't get it unless you *ask!*
. . .

Sadly I have to sit very far front to hear. Out alone conspicuous! But not uncomfortable. Many changes in rostrum, Gilt cross, Choir of 14 in white smocks—What's the proper word—they come only to the waist. Purple collar band. Six men, Professor of gardening, a councilman I have quarrelled with, but mutual respect, a post office extra who is in Cooperative with me and asks explanations of things (They made me Vice President last Friday, me away and really unsuspecting. I had criticized strongly retention of dividends) and an unknown man. Girls, younger much, must be students. I do not know any of them except their leader who was 20 years ago a charming young girl with beautiful voice. Made hit here and stayed in our excellent conservatory.

Why is it easier to create a strong school of music than of other things? Or isn't it? Has the Boston University a strong school of music? I never hear of it. What did we hear of music in Boston University? South America was a burst into song and string for me. A gaucho who couldn't read music taught me the guitar. No began to teach me! Young men heard a new opera once and sang whole phrases of it. Little 60,000 Cordoba had its season of opera to which everyone bought season tickets to be there ON TIME, no affectation of late entrance which would have brought hisses. Easy for South America which had a handy July-August winter season to follow the January-February European one. We had whole companies come from Italy, Oh Yes Italians can sing. Patti sang there constantly and got there much money.

Minister in black surplice—new to me in Congregational Church. All he said was he wanted more evidence about something (Existence of a God?). Got on with faith and that Luke was a doctor, new to me. Also this I thought up when he mentioned God's anteroom and patients waiting that we are patients because we have to wait patiently for our turn with the doctor! . . .

I tried to find a message and didn't. He had a long printed program of many things to do. RISE. We used to know enough to rise without a printed programme. Congregation to sing. I had to look around to see if they were. Choir sang well 90 times the volume of Congregation. So responsive readings I guess I outread them all, shamelessly. I looked around. Yes—they were reading. Gordon—He is a Kiwanian and I am supposed to call him Gordon—ought to have said READ, BRETHERN READ. but he didn't (do much of anything he might have done).

Why go to church? Any Kiwanis meeting is more inspiring. Yes: of course I had my little reception afterward. All the programme stuff was meant to get up a religious spirit, but didn't. In this church is religion dead?

Over the Bright new Gilt Cross I noticed very dingy organ pipes. I wonder what a soft cloth full of hot soapsuds would have done to one. I want to break in some night and try it and leave that pipe all clean for an example. Has nobody noticed it? The front of the church is stained. Water has leaked in. Needs redecorating . . .

I thank Kiwanis Club more for godliness than the Congregational Church. We are all faiths there, Catholics, Lutherans, etc.

I must visit all the churches, but rapidly and write a little note to the Catholic priest—whom I know, asking if I may. Also I want to write a sermon Is There a God? I suspect this is the worst in town. Bill Shaw my Baptist friend I am sure does a lot better. He is really inspired, if he does find me embarrassing. Maybe when I have visited them all, a Salvation Army service too if they have them, I may give my friends my conclusions. How God is manifesting himself in Ypsilanti.

Next Sunday's report only on REQUEST!

Mark Jefferson to Caroline Atherton, April 27, 1940:

I received your letter as I was stepping into the car to go down to Tom's funeral. He died in my arms last Thursday. The poor lad never had a chance. The malignant tumor grew again and crowded his skull till it was visibly thrusting out the skull and at last it killed him. His mother was beside me, and the doctor at hand, but the end was inevitable.

It was to his mother he went back in January when he had no notion other than that he was suffering from sinus trouble and the treatment was for that, his head aching intolerably so that he could not sleep and everything he ate made him retch and vomit violently. She alone could soothe him by stroking his temples as he crept beside her. Nothing could have been gained had we known earlier except to save him those weeks of suffering. I may have mentioned my surmise that Dr. Peet severed important nerves when he operated that spared him pain. Thomas never came back from the operation table. The changeling that came back to us after ten days of unconsciousness was not Thomas. We learned to be fonder of him even than we had been of Thomas, as he lay there a helpless cripple. Mercifully he slept much even up to the end . . .

I have thought of the inhibition to study by his tumor that made school work difficult and finally intolerable to him, a rebellion at what he thought was his evident uselessness. I did not often reproach him, I think, but he knew his various school failings disappointed me. When I had no inkling of his frightful handicap I thought I had done better in my youth. I have a picture of myself at nearly his age and you have only to glance at the admirable, if somewhat puckish expression on his face at graduation from High School here two years ago to see how far he was from a failure to those who came in contact with him. We have been overwhelmed in flowers, pies, fruits and cakes and even steaks that friends have brought in! I am frightfully tired and so is Clara. All the sons and daughters have gone but Phoebe, who stays till tomorrow—Sunday—night. She and Clara are now in the kitchen busy with ironing. All have been busy all day.

I think you will agree with me that Tom's picture shows plainly enough that a contempt for Latin and Letters may coexist with real social gifts. Tom was a person of character, even if his disease drove him away from table every time outsiders were at table. You will please return the picture but I am sure you will concur with my thought. I am more and more persuaded that my education is properly reflected in the dull, self-satisfied face I wore at Tom's age. I have been apt to think poorly of Michigan school education. When I see their product in Tom, frightfully handicapped as he was, I have to admit that it is fine to shape folks to congenial neighborliness. I had to wait till I was sixty to learn to be a congenial neighbor.

Thomas was distinctly worthwhile!

Caroline Atherton to Mark Jefferson, July 21, 1940:

. . . You would like the color in my garden, hollyhocks many and varied, the best showing I ever had. It has been a good year for blossoming shrubs and plants, my roses were very lovely, a few stragglers still are. And I have been visiting a friend in Rockport on Cape Ann who has a beautiful garden, fine trees, birds nesting, a grand place. And while there I read Louis Adamic's "Laughing in the Jungle", his early years in America, his own experiences and those of other immigrants, try it.

Mark Jefferson to Caroline Atherton, August 31, 1940:

Your handwriting has not changed lately, but since 1893 it has taken on what they call character. I saw tonight in my scrapbook the earliest note of yours forwarding the good wishes of Class '84 when I left Boston University. It was very much the work of copy book writing class, lacking individuality.

Your present writing I like very much indeed. The odd thing is that you seem to me to have had more individuality then than now. I was, of course, very impressionable and admired you too much to make a judgment. Who, indeed, was I to judge? And what do I know about you now, how much you affect life in the circle of your contacts? But I do suspect you have done a lot of conforming to the ideas of those about. I should be a more agreeable person had I too learned to do more.

It has only come to me in the last 30 or 40 years that we can change people's views, if we are right and persist. I am still inclined to be too impatient. Almost no one can adopt a new idea on a single presentation of it. There is need of a lot of repetition, pleasant, friendly repetition.

Maurois says Churchill told him in 1935 that he ought to stop writing biographies and write only one article over and over again in as many different phrases as he could find, namely that France from the first air-power was becoming 5th or 6th, while Hitler was becoming first, and France was going to be destroyed if something was not done about it. He had not been able to see the need and how he regretted it bitterly!

Mark Jefferson to Caroline Atherton, January 18, 1941:

The week before had been a bad one. I confidently bought "woolen" socks of a dealer friend and put them on. Kept them on a cold, cold week before it dawned on me that they were mostly cotton and I was having chill after chill. Cold feet are my bane. The same week I met breast of guinea hen at 20 Club dinner and conclude that guineas would do better to stay in the barn yard and squawk at hawks. The same week I laid aside my habituated Sanka substitute for coffee and brewed again Mocha and Java mixed. Some or all of these experiments put me to bed for a pair of days.

Mark Jefferson to Caroline Atherton, March 2, 1941:

The English are amazing. The world's worst blunderers. They wouldn't let the French attack the Germans when they went into the Rhine country (with instructions to withdraw at once if resisted, we were told later) etc. etc. Yet now they are doing things fairly heroic. In this Hitler quite falls down. In real war he would meet four or five million English? As he wages it he has the whole population to fight and they fairly enjoy it. I think generalizations about the sexes are unsafe usually but I do believe women are more heedless of painful personal consequences than men are . . . They say on the great Spanish estates that once bred savage bulls for the Ring, that the cows of the race were terrible. No bull-fighter would tackle them.

Isn't this nice "The Geological Society of America takes note of the passing of another year, which, it appears from our records, brings you to the honored age of seventy-eight. We hope that the day may be full of pleasant recollections and the satisfaction that belongs to a long and busy life. The Society sends greetings and best wishes for other years to come.

Cordially yours,

Charles R. Berkey, President"

No abbreviations in the original costly paper and heavy . . . Every year since age seventy a letter. How Human BUT I am not a geologist, a life fellow of the Society yes, these 40 years. Only gave one paper before them and only published three papers in their memoirs. The Association of American Geographers of which I am charter member, past president and constant paper reader—sends no such note. How nice to have Berkey's though! and Carrie Stones!

Mark Jefferson to Caroline Atherton, May 30, 1941:

Don't worry about Athens—The Germans are crafty enough to demonstrate their "essential" kindness in Greece. They have too much conquered territory, the general hatred they engender is beginning to have an unsatisfactory taste.

Poor France that is the sad country. The Fleet and the colonies should have instantly taken up the fight French labor defaulted in at home. Of course Vichy is nothing but relayed Hitler.

As a geographer I am immensely interested. Germans know the geography of Greece and Crete better than the Greeks or Cretans. They advise the Nazis. Germans know better the military geography of the United States and Martinique than our army and Navy which has no "geographic branch." Neither at West Point or Annapolis is geography taught.

I represented the United States at Paris on one little commission on the language used to describe boundaries in the Peace Treaty, in order that bad description should not make future misunderstanding inevitable, like our old southern boundary of Michigan a line due east from the south point of Lake Michigan which put Toledo in Michigan and caused the "Toledo War". I was the only civilian on the commission . . . The American army had and has no geographic service . . .

I never was in Finland, but I know the Atlas de Finlande very well, a work that we can't match for the U.S. in spite of all our wealth. I think them marvellous. The world's heroes of the day. What they have done sounds incredible. I admire almost more its spiritual side more than its material one? They have punctured the Great Russian Boast! and shown its nothingness. How can they have resisted? How can Sweden and Norway not help them now while their help is needed. But alas it does not seem possible that they continue to keep off such hordes as Russia's.

Scandinavia now fears Germany and knows they cannot trust any promise Germans make.

The essence of the matter is that the German rulers are not Gentlemen! and that is a thing appalling! When realized.

Publishers do not refuse my stuff, but they keep too much of the profits! Harcourt Brace and Co. published—their request—two of my books but when a new edition was needed they wanted to reprint without changes that five years had made necessary . . . Most authors are so flattered to get into print that they let publishers take all the proceeds. Some men I know pay a good part of the publication expense. Every few months I get invitations from publishers that I disattend completely.

I write you always badly. I have no time and I condense all the time and do not get anything said. Davis once told me something I condensed for him was not elliptical but triangular.

Mark Jefferson to Caroline Atherton, October 7, 1941:

Just back from the annual Kiwanis Convention at Grand Rapids where I went to give two little speeches, cutting out the banquet and general sociabilities. I was touched—how much kindness and friendliness was shown me. Driving there Monday morning and back Tuesday afternoon and cutting out everything of fellowship so much is made of, merely going into a room at 2 Monday and again 9:30 Tuesday to speak as assigned. I have to charge all my expense to the Kiwanis treasury, as I couldn't go otherwise, but kept my expense down, was distinctly mean about spending—yet the great, unexpected cordiality, Hullo Mark from a dozen men I didn't even know by name and of course the tried friends of a number of campaigns.

My position in the club is very exceptional, not a past or present officer, merely given charge of a committee because I demand it. Generally no one else does and always asking to have new committees named, not on the Club list but aimed at accomplishments I personally have at heart.

The point must be that many men are moved by my appeals.

I wrote out last night at Grand Rapids the speech I had to make as I expected to be strictly limited to ten minutes, a difficult little fragment of time in which to get up enthusiasm. However it made a great hit and held them.

The 300 miles drive was beautiful. The roads good, tempting me up to 70 miles when I meant to travel but 50. The country here is just at the end of its best, grass still brilliantly green but color entering all the tree foliage masses, where there is no clear mass of green: only an occasional single tree.

Enormous activities here these two months. First my study came down again from 25 years on the second floor as designed when I built the house in 1905. Such an accumulation of books and papers, and files to clean and rearrange.

Caroline Atherton to Mark Jefferson, December 20, 1941:

What a grand correspondent you are! If you do not give a full consideration to any least question of mine, you send a second letter after the first, and I feel as if I had had a talk with you, I can visualize you . . .

I am reading Peattie, I like his English, his philosophy, his love of birds and flowers and Nature, "The Road of a Naturalist", it thrills me page after page . . .

Mark Jefferson to Caroline Atherton, March 30, 1945:

. . . As for the bits of us that fall off in the long life, they don't matter so much.

Take our teeth. *I still have them in the plural,* but oh so few. Oddly everyone of them is a gold-capped affair, put on so long ago that I do not recall when or where, but apparently much more than decoration.

You may have heard that the husky Ike Eisenhower has all 32 of his. Doesn't he come from the Texas town with the marvellous water? Happy Ike.

I am having a comical time with my eyes. Or rather my nose. I wear spectacles. The temples were thin and cut into me back of the ears. They gave me rubber and then celluloid tubes for the temples and that made the bridge cut into the top of my nose, which interfered with the circulation in small blood vessels in my upper nose that results in a very undesirable "Bloom," Happily this does not descend to the point of my nose but the bloom is there. I have had a new bridge made which seems to lessen the color, possibly it may remove it. You see I have something to wake for tomorrow, though it be nothing more than another glimpse of my own nose! The bridge is so new I cannot yet be sure of the outcome.

Mark Jefferson to Caroline Atherton, December 15, 1946:

I have just countermanded a hotel room Columbus Ohio, for the Christmas meeting of the Association of American Geographers, after sending in an abstract of Chapter VI *How Europe ran the world in 1914*. The job is to get at least one hour a day of real work.

Memory fails of course for little things, my friends' names for instance and yet on my feet speaking to people who are an audience I seem to recall all I know. Odd! . . .

Of course we all have our afflictions . . . We have J.L. and the Russians have democracy that kills off objectors by the million and puts other millions in labor camps because they want to own the products of their own labor. Now the Jugoslavs have formally voted the confiscation of everybody's property. The Argentines are admiring Hitler, The Chileans and we are so terribly wrong—toward the negro.

Once in Cuba, running for a train out of Habana I got on the last car— third class—for negroes, sat down beside a young negro who deliberately crowded me against the end of the seat so hard that I had to get up and move forward . . .

It would make an interesting geography that collected Ten GOOD POINTS FOR EVERY COUNTRY. We might advertize for others by local patriots. Mention of faults of course prohibited.

In retirement at the Jefferson home, Ypsilanti.

CHAPTER TWELVE

IN RETIREMENT

In June, 1939, and at the age of 76 Jefferson entered retirement. Not heavy and bowed with the weight of years, he wished to continue his employ and keep himself busy, "to have work to do and reasons to live for." The man did busy himself for the next ten years, though he was obliged to shift the locus of his commitment from the classroom to matters beyond. Perhaps it was a wishful thinking that made Jefferson insist he had good classroom years still before him: at this age he readily admitted he fell asleep with light provocation, needed a nap after lunch, had taken lip reading lessons as a one-man class from the Normal's Miss Bunger as early as 1937, and by 1939 found a hearing aid desirable. Nevertheless he continued his daily constitutional—one mile a day on foot—until the year of his death, 1949. Annually between 1942 and 1946 he painted parts of his spacious home and otherwise cared for the establishment: twice he turned his car over on the nearby Jackson road, escaping injury and refusing medical attention. Certainly age had not incapacitated him, though he was obliged to temper his more robust inclinations. In place of manually shovelling the snow from his sidewalks and house paths he employed a snow scooter on wheels. In place of the winter daily mile before breakfast, he would wait until a later hour when it was warmer. Further, a heavy blue serge suit and Alaska seal hat, gifts from two of his children, Geoffrey and Phoebe, and halibut liver oil capsules taken daily were pieces of an armory he employed against the winters of the forties, which he had not adopted previously. He never had taken kindly to cold winters and had frequently said that if he could avoid them he would live a long life. He would tend to doze during the day if bored, though this may also have been attributable to little sleep at night. Frequently he reported not falling asleep until three in the morning, employed till that hour by reading hosts of detective stories in French, on coverless, much-folded sheets in need of separation with a paper knife.

Now retired, he sought a position with a geography department in a warmer part of North America. His attentions were given to universities in Mexico and Arizona where he noted his annual $300 fuel bill would be much diminished, but it was with Syracuse University that a correspondence of serious nature concerning his employment ensued. Department members headed by George Cressey voted unanimously to receive Jefferson into their department in 1941, but the Syracuse University administration rejected the plan owing to Jefferson's age.[1] Reconciled to the fact of his retirement from geographic instruction, Jefferson sought to supplement his much reduced income in various ways; by writing geographic articles for the more popular magazines, talking publicly for fees, and renting rooms in his home to war workers. It is rather sad to note that he felt impelled to write the following note to Bowman:[2] ". . . if you hear of any hack-work of the kind that I can do please keep me in mind." Concern for income encouraged him to write to a New York literary agency which advertised an ability to sell articles and manuscripts for a percentage of the price so obtained. To this agency Jefferson sent two articles he composed, one concerning "the real coming of spring," and a second questioning the thesis that Germany was a country. Not written in the popular vein both failed to find a market. This rejection caused Jefferson to write Mrs. Atherton, "that perhaps I am getting old." He was delighted to find his occasional articles or book review accepted:[3]

> Hooray. Editor Gladys writes, 'Dear Professor Jefferson: We are happy to have another decade of the great cities. The July number was full, but I shall try to squeeze it in, so you will probably see proof before long. Sincerely yours, Gladys W. Wrigley.' That should mean $50 unless the squeeze means cutting. And that should mean some new clothes. In my situation earning is not easy but dress money must come from outside.

Nevertheless his geographic interests and appetites had not waned. He made numerous presentations of his geographic ideas in Michigan; especially numerous were his talks concerning the geographic factors of significance in the war and his cartographic illustration of the events of the war, many of them untidily inked but each the bearer of an individuality equalled only by the fingerprint. He followed the war closely. Each day he made notes of its progress from the radio, gathered newspaper and magazine clippings and pasted them in scrapbooks, and sent letters to his friends concerning the fortunes of the allies. He continued his life-time habit of patiently accumulating data, occasionally pausing to locate moral ideas in the penumbra of his work. But his creative reaching, itself derived from the process of patient accumulation, was interrupted frequently by demands upon which he lavished disproportionately large amounts of time and nervous energy, detracting from the growth of a book he set out to write in retirement. Invitation to receive the Distinguished Service Award of the National Council of Geographic Teachers 1939, to address local church groups, civic organizations, the Michigan Foreign Language Association, the Michigan Social Studies group, school groups, the Harris Lectures at Chicago, to give the Haas Lectures at Northwestern University, December 1940, were only some of the requests to which he hardly found it possible to say no. Washington requested his assistance in some war work, 1942; he wrote to daughter Phoebe, "I do not know whether I told you that I am asked to offer my services as a geographer at Washington but have not answered them yet." Jefferson frequently mentioned in his correspondence that such invitations and work restored much of his confidence, diminished by brusque treatment in his retirement year. Further, it provided him with opportunity to try out ideas and give them form prior to their incorporation into his book. But perpetual recommencement on a book incorporating his life's ideas was the price paid.

Of the Haas Lecture visit he wrote to his daughter:[4]

> I was put up at the magnificent University Club at Evanston, a building of vast spaces, heavy carpets and luxury of every kind, like other U. Clubs and unions. Their enormous reading rooms have vast electric lights everywhere, all too low in power, so that dim religious light prevails everywhere, about the quantity of light ladies like for a dinner table. I wanted to suggest a lighting engineer to study lights in that room. Of course I didn't. I am entitled by my age and a certain reputation as suggester of new things in geography to be venturesome there, but novel views are disturbing to most people. My treatment at Evanston was so flattering that I couldn't help having a good time. I dined and lunched with a new group of University men each day. I was constantly consulted as to my wishes. I was given most comfortable quarters, and two hours of conference each morning with advanced students who came to tell me their geographic hopes and aspirations. I had to work hard over five hours a day preparing my three lectures which went off successively better and better. Lantern broke down in the first. I had been warned students would begin to leave after 50 minutes so I stopped after 50 minutes. But I saw no leaving. Next days I gave them 70 and 75 minutes and they all stayed and still came up!
>
> I am tired, but happy.

In a letter to S.S. Visher, Jefferson, fresh from the triumph of his Haas lectures, wrote of his personal resources:[5]

> *Energy and enthusiasm I have unabated, perhaps rather increased. Boring tasks I have become quite feeble at. I am apt to fall asleep adding a column of figures if it is long and a wordy speech does for me every time. I have to beg a neighbor to nudge me if I snore! I am well and very active in my service . . . .*

While the war still raged several book companies requested of him a manuscript that would describe the new world after the devastation was finished, a request which meshed thoroughly with Jefferson's design. The Farrar and Rinehart Publishing Company sent him the following letter dated April 7, 1943:[6]

> *Major Preston James of the OSS has given me your name as a geographer who might be interested in doing a book for us which would fit into the group of books outlined in the enclosed memorandum.*
>
> *Our first quick thoughts on such a book would center it around such titles as GLOBAL GEOGRAPHY, or WORLD GEOGRAPHY or THE WORLD IS ROUND. It would be a book which would try to explain to the average layman the new concepts of and understanding of geography which he should and must know if the world is really going to have a sound basis for a permanent peace.*
>
> *If this project interests you, I would appreciate your thoughts on it and any suggestions you might have.*
>
> Sincerely yours,
> Theodore S. Amussen
> Assistant Editor

Evidence suggests that Jefferson had already undertaken work on a book of his own choosing. Indeed, a hurried red ink postscript attached to the above mentioned letter reads,[7] "A real compliment to you. Is this the Book referred to as being written by you in your letter of the 27th." Further attached to this communication from Farrar and Rinehart is an undated and unsent inked note in Jefferson's handwriting.

> *No: I don't like Farrar and Rinehart's plan but it and similar propositions from others set me to writing what I want to say. I shall perhaps submit it to Little, Brown Co. or Harcourt Brace who have published two books of mine. Possibly to Rinehart.*

It is probable that Jefferson formally commenced his manuscript in the latter part of 1942. He wanted to call it "A Geography for Grown-Ups" but feared lack of publisher and reader interest under such a title. Thus he chose to entitle his book "A Geographer Looks at War," but the book was never completed. Probably several are the reasons for his attempting the book as an octogenarian: he lived in order to keep busy, feared growing old in spirit, enjoyed thinking and putting his thoughts into words, was extremely concerned for his income and the future security of his wife and children, and had been attracted by Huntington's *Mainsprings of Civilization,* a work completed shortly before the latter's death and summarizing and elaborating the more important of his life's findings. Especially was he concerned for the future income of his wife, then recently entered on her fifties. He collected rents from war workers but realized this income was temporary. Rent prices had been frozen by the Ypsilanti council at the most modest of rates, and savings were hindered from this source by frequent short term occupancies of rooms, coupled with a larger maintenance bill that fuller usage of the house necessitated. Furthermore, Jefferson and his wife had housed and supported Henry, an elderly destitute brother of his who had not been able to secure income for himself since 1933. Henry, known in the family as Harry, had passed away on April 5, 1941, but his longevity had been an expense and concern to Jefferson since his retirement lest he die and leave Harry dependent on his own Clara. In order to raise money later in the forties, Jefferson sold numerous books from his collection to a dealer in New York who had been recommended by J. Russell Smith.

The scope of Jefferson's book was distinctly unusual and embodied much of his life's work. He made use of ideas borrowed from nearly all that he had written in his "post-physiographic" days, dating from his presentation of "The Anthropography of Some Great Cities" at Baltimore before the Association of American Geographers, 1908.

For his own convenience Jefferson listed the sub-headings under which he had been writing and which indicate the course of his labor:[8]

Chapter I: The Maritime Era Ends—The Airway Era Begins
The Maritime British Empire, The Story of Middlesborough, Coal and the British Empire, Home Islands Uninvaded Since 1066, Britain's Cities Stand on her Coal, Railways in World Commerce, The Railwebs, The Railnets, Transport-less Interiors, The Rise of Russia, The Victorious Soviets, British and Soviet Imports, The Airway Age, Air-routes Frequent Uninhabited Interiors, Advantages of Air Travel, Air Sovereignty and Air Freedom, Panamerican Airways, What Motor Transport has done to the Railroads, Politics of the Maritime Age
Chapter II: The Big Five and Nationality
The Paris Conference, The United Kingdom in World War I, The United States in World War I, France in World War I, Italy in World War I, How Italy Won Fiume, Japan in World War I, Russia in World War I, Russia in East Prussia, Limited Area of French Front, What is a Country?, Tribes and Races, Africa Home of Races, not Countries,

Raiders, The Balkans Tribal
Chapter III: Collaboration
Resisters and Collaborators, Soldiers as Bandits, Resisters Inimical to Nationalism
Chapter IV: Regrouping after World War II
Isolationism, A Shrunken World, War has become too Expensive, Big Five at San Francisco, Union of Soviet Socialist Republics, Soviet Union a new Nation, Spare time on a Farm, Great Cities Industrial, Great Cities Win Wars, United Kingdom in World War II, United States in World War II, France in World War II, China in World War II, China needs More Railroads
Chapter V: Soviet Union Begins National Life
New born Nations of 1919, Czechoslovakia, Yugoslavia, Yugoslavia Under Hitler, Tito Broz Russian, Who Shall Rule Yugoslavia?, Meeting of the Land and Sea Empires, The Army of the United States in Victory, The Red Army, Boring from Within, Trieste, What Does Russia Want?

His concern with war had a marked effect upon the book. It was fundamentally concerned with the life, being, and death of states between the two world wars. Since early in the century, as we have seen, Jefferson had been thinking, teaching, and writing about man on the land. Now he wrote about man on the land with special reference to the peace settlements following each of the Wars. Jefferson had never published anything on the Paris Peace Conference, though in his diary he had written ill of some of its events, and had spoken harshly of its boundary-line arrangements—"they are drawn in blood." Frequently in his later years he reminisced of the Paris Conference in his correspondence and seemingly needed to state his feelings concerning the lands lost by Russia. In his study he would pore over many of the maps he had made at Paris and recall the passage of events. He felt strongly that the Russians had been badly treated at the Conference and interpreted later Soviet actions in that context. In a letter to Caroline Atherton written in February, 1944, Jefferson outlined his feelings concerning Russia and her lands:[9]

> *Not writing but talking a good deal, and I fancy I put in more than ten hours preparing for a half hour talk. At present I have much in mind, an "It is only fair to Russia!"—I have given it twice already— growing each time. Again the 23rd of this month and probably more after that.*
>
> *The map enclosed gives the idea. Making the overwhelming feature Russia, the Russia of 1914 that went so heroically to the rescue of stricken Serbia in 1914.*

Note the dates July 28 Austria attacks Serbia. July 29 Russia demobilizes against Austria. August 3 Russia attacks East Prussia, the land of superman Junkers and so seriously that she has overrun all the provinces and besieges Konigsberg by August 28, a threat so serious, that Germany has to drop her plan of an overwhelming rush on Paris to send Hindenburg with great armies to ward off the attack. This completely changed the course of the war. Hindenburg crushed the Russian armies in the lakes of Masuria. Then the Russians changed to Galicia, having Hindenburg completely held at the Niemen on the east of East Prussia.

Now a look at the map—the Russia as all Russians see it still today, the Russia that was for it exists no more. The notable bulge at the west of the Russian frontier is the Jewish pale!, Russian but with a majority of Polish inhabitants looth [sic] the line so as to leave out the bulge and you have cut out the Poles. The Curzon line does that very thing smoothes out the line on the west. Now for the red outlined Poland, red denoting the states carved out of Russian Territory by the Allies at Paris. From north to south see them Finland, Estonia, Latvia, Lithuania, Poland and the Bessarabian part of Rumania. No Russian thinks of the present advance of Russian armies as "into Old Poland." That begs the question entirely. They have advanced into the former Jewish Pale. It had been Russian since 1795.

The part of red-outlined Poland on my map east of the Curzon line was inhabited by White Russians. Together with half as much more territory further east it makes up the home of the White Russians, where White Russian is today the dominating language.

This was not given to the Poles at Paris but was taken by Polish and French armies from the Bolsheviks in 1922. Now it is only fair to point out that the Russians, instant to help Serbia at the start, able to help in the war so effectively that the Germans never reached Paris at all, lost in battle 1,700,000 killed, more than any other belligerent, and collapsed as an Empire because the Czar's incompetent government could not supply them in July 1917, was not in existence at the peace conference date, was not represented at the peace table and her reward was to have the six states named carved in whole or part from her territories. At the time of the Peace Conference we had American soldiers—the Polar Bears—fighting the Bolsheviks about Arkhangel because we did not like their scheme of government.

Our accomplishment looks very small beside that of Russia. We declared war April 6, 1917, not like Russia when little Serbia was attacked but nearly three years later when we were being hit at the fight at Vantigny March 28, 1918, more than a year after declaring war. We lost, killed in battle, 66,000 men. We were in the fighting six days less than eight months to Russia's three years.

The Russian Empire gave its life for the defense of freedom-loving Serbia. Serbia was saved, enlarged (and has been a hotbed of internal strife ever since).

We only entered on war when our ships at sea were intolerably mistreated by the Germans, we dealt decisive blows but only after a long year's delay during which the war weary French and English were left to face the Foe, we had small losses and took a very decisive part in rearranging the map of Europe, in large part at the expense of the Russia that had so well deserved of liberty-loving nations, and left conditions ripe for the new Second World War to ensue.

Today the despised Bolsheviks of 1919 have made themselves into a mighty nation, the only one on European soil that has as yet been able to withstand the Nazi Blitzkrieg and is now driving the Nazis back.

It is only fair to Russia to say that she perished in a great cause after an heroic fight in defense of freedom as against oppression, and has been succeeded by a mighty nation of home and country-loving men and women, the Union of Soviet Socialist Republics.

This all leads to the newest map of the Soviet Union and the 16 Soviet Republics who are free now to discuss foreign relations with the world.

Does not this make clear why Russia occupied Poland east of the Curzon line when the Nazis invaded Poland from the west? Why she occupied the Baltic states and went to war with Poland. Why she thinks of her future western boundary in terms of the Russian bounds of 1914 and not those imposed without Russian participation or consent by the Peace of Versailles or later on the field of battle with Poles and Frenchmen against Bolsheviks.

We have been too aware of Bolshevik faults. Some of them the Soviets have already amended in the light of experience. They are now compelling attention to their merits as a nation.

I have faults. My enemies know them all—and perhaps some that I do not have. My friends know that I have merits too, perhaps again they impute to me some that I do not have.

The only real thing about me for the rest of the world is my merits. As for my faults why not assume that all the world has them.

We shall be weighed, as we say by the sums of the weight and importance of our merits, which really means only our merits matter and the merits of the Union of Soviet Socialistic Republics as a nation are proving to be very great.

All this takes time to put in shape and has kept me very busy.

Perhaps I gain points of view for the book in it. A singular problem. What is a nation? a country? Is France a country today, or Denmark, or Norway, or Germany or even Sweden?

The manuscript grew, parts of it were rewritten, chapter titles were changed. Jefferson admits to finding only an hour or two a day for the work in his retirement. The manuscript was not completed before his death in 1949 and it is unclear how much more writing was intended. In 1946, December 24, he wrote to daughter Barbara:[10]

I am very busy writing a book A Geographer looks at War. *Of course, they have to be satisfied with what I can hand them finished. Six chapters, about two thirds of it already done and clear typed, but I find it hard to get the time to write and do not really average two hours a day.*

Age, sleep, lectures, house painting, made their demands upon him as did personal sorrows, domestic duties, house management, and even the inability to purchase his favored Wo-hop tea. His youngest son, Thomas, died of a brain tumour in 1940 at age twenty, his wife spent much of her time working as a matron at the local Ypsilanti State Hospital (1942-45), his grandchild Linda frequently kept him out of his study, meal preparation became a task not previously undertaken and Jefferson himself entered hospital for a prostate gland operation of which he later wrote to his daughter Phoebe in his own humorous vein:[11]

I shall miss the girls that came in to take my temperature and pulse, five centimeters of blood first from left arm and then from the right arm and some medicine and something to drink. Rather entertaining. Now I think I go to bed.

Jefferson's geographic writing also had to compete during his retirement years with numerous other of his activities. In 1940 he was made chairman of a rapidly constructed city planning commission to cope with accomplished and anticipated change in Ypsilanti, resulting largely from acceleration in employment attributable to war work and proximity to Detroit. As a member of the Board of Commerce Public Affairs Committee he was often obliged to furnish information to townspeople and entrepreneurs, both established and prospective. Regular attendance and continuing activity with the Ypsilanti Kiwanis Club since its inauguration in 1923 led to his chairing a committee to discontinue 65 tax collecting agencies in the state of Michigan, and centralize their function in one agency in Lansing, the state capitol. Following the success of this mission, in 1943 Jefferson chaired another Kiwanis committee to advise and advertise Home Rule for nearby Wayne County, becoming a member of the larger executive committee—Citizens Committee on Home Rule for Wayne County. This activity involved Jefferson in a study of the history of Wayne County and the growth of Detroit. He offered the Detroit press an article he had written on County Government in Michigan, arranged public discussion on the issue, commanded the cooperation of 56 Michigan Kiwanis Presidents, cooperated closely with the Detroit newspaper through Frank Woodford and secured hundreds of names on numerous petitions to secure the issue on the ballot of November 2, 1944. During 1940 he continued in the capacity of Vice-President for the Ypsilanti Consumers Cooperative, and successfully attempted the extension of College Credit Union facilities to educators in nearby towns. He began to concern himself with the threat of inflation in the U.S.A., wrote to his friends that he wished Lindbergh would be quiet, wanted to see a total integration of the three branches of the armed forces, and wrote to his daughter Phoebe that she should visit New York's Mayor LaGuardia and suggest to him that all oil tanks around the country be camouflaged to avoid fifth-column sabotage. His concern was deep and human. He would anticipate allied or enemy moves, predict successes or failures, insist and believe that the allies would triumph. Late in 1940 the Council for Democracy asked Jefferson if he would allow his name to be placed in a register of scholars in various fields, who would write articles when needed in a readily comprehendable style on matters unclear to the American public. In the following typically pointed letter Jefferson offered his services to Carl Friedrich, Chairman of the Committee of Correspondence of the Council, a professor of government at Harvard University. It is reproduced here for its terseness and style, which rather defeated its own purpose with people who did not know Jefferson:[12]

> *I should be very glad to do anything I could for democracy, though I do not get a very clear idea from your letter of what might be wanted of me.*
>
> *I am a geographer, my special interest is in problems*
> *What is a country?*
> *What is a city?*
>
> *I have arrived at certain dogmas-things I teach wherever I can— Countries are made of people not dirt (territory) Quick and cheap transportation is the Greatest agent of civilization (See my Civilizing Rails)*
>
> *If the North could have provided the South with such a railweb as it already possessed in 1861 there would have been no civil war to fight.*
>
> *As I look at the list SOME PRESENT ISSUES I note only one— (5) which interests me. I lived for six years in the Argentine Republic, 1883-1889.*

Dec. 11, 12, 13, I give three lectures at Northwestern University Evanston, Illinois. Where the Americas meet, the Germans and other gringos in Latin America, and the Rails Civilized Latin America too.

The first is very important pointing out that North American rudeness as the Latins see it—prevents any cooperation.

(7) interests me I have just gotten myself made Chairman of a District Committee of Kiwanis International for the Michigan District ON TAXATION. We Kiwanians number 4000. I and my colleagues mean to have all 73 clubs hear at least one talk on Taxation in Michigan and what should be done about it.

I can't help pecuniarily. I am a retired teacher on very small pension. Even letters should be accompanied by postage if replies are wanted.

How German are you Mr. Friedrich? Are we to assume that you are no fifth column?

My mother's maiden name was Mantz. No doubt her schoolmates in London called her German. My first wife Theodora Augusta Bohnstedt was the daughter of a Prussian officer. Hitler is an anathema to me.

There is no record of Jefferson's being asked to contribute to the Council for Democracy. Yet Jefferson was immensely willing to help . . . to help the world and make it a better place. That accounts for the numerous civic responsibilities he assumed during retirement. Further, his work had been greatly slowed between 1946 and 1948 by three other ventures upon which he embarked and which undoubtedly in part prevented completion of the book. The first of these involved entanglement with the Ypsilanti police, the second was the writing of an autobiographical essay for the Harvard University Alumni handbook for the Class of 1897 on the occasion of its fiftieth anniversary, and the third was a mounting curiosity and concern for American war activities. A disturbing circumstance confronted him in 1946 when a police car ran into the side of his Ford in Ypsilanti. The officer claimed that the incident was Jefferson's fault. The geographer had his license suspended following a road test, and his insurance company was asked to pay for the damages. Convinced that the fault lay with the police Jefferson appealed to his friends with power in the Kiwanis, was given another road test, was granted a drivers license again, and the insurance company was not bothered further. But the method of redress, the weeks of waiting and the letters and diagrams Jefferson composed and sent to numerous personages to secure vindication were vexatiously enervating to the man. Nevertheless, he did not allow the matter to deter him from completing his autobiographical essay, which task became of ever increasing concern to himself and a detriment to the completion of his book as he typed, retyped, cut and pasted paragraphs, in an attempt to write meaningfully yet briefly of such a full life. The resultant essay of 31 pages, that cost 80 pages of attempted essay, was halved before submission to the office of Alumni Secretary and subsequently further reduced by the editor before being published in the Handbook.[13] This autobiographical sally represented a marked departure from earlier days when he shunned the opportunity to be listed with other men of science. His correspondence of this period also reflects a concern for what had been, not with a sense of remorse, but with the air of someone who has been aware of an issue for a life time, but who had only recently come to comprehend it. In the essay he reaffirmed his very great interest in things geographic, God's Truths as he called them, and announced yet again that his two greatest teachers were "the Darwin of Beagle fame" and his Harvard mentor W. M. Davis. "Surely," wrote Jefferson, "Davis read God's thoughts." Jefferson also announced that he liked a babe in the house and the happy qualities of vacations spent with the family, which matters he wrote of in his essay in the following words:[14]

> But a large part of life is a family. "A babe in the house is a wellspring of pleasure" wrote the Proverbial Philosopher. I believe it though some appear to prefer life dry. I have seven living children and some grands and we have had lots of fun. For many years we enjoyed an ancestral house built in 1814 at Gilmanton, N.H. in summer. It is occupied by my youngest son Hilary in his vacations from work in Yonkers. Gilmanton is a thousand feet above the sea, is overhung by a peaked Hill that attains 1400! Air good, food excellent, scenery admirable.
>
> In 1901 we camped on the seashore in tents so near the south shore of Martha's Vineyard that salt sprays would encrust the driven well that gave us cool fresh water on the hottest day. Nothing but a beach of sand for twenty miles. What could you do? Actually reading-matter taken was never unpacked. In three tents five children and three adults.
>
> In the Mid-West the Canadian shore opposite Michigan's Thumb attracted me. It was Crown land four rods from the Lake, but Kincardine wanted summerers and undertook the care of any house or goods I put there; even dragged away some fishermen's huts that pre-empted a choice spot. I built a very practical house. Several years it served us through the hot season. The out was transportation. Traffic on the lakes was just going out when I went to Ypsilanti in 1901. At first it so dominated that it stopped the N.Y.C. trains at the Detroit River, made them spend a half hour crossing on train ferries. By 1910 a tunnel let us cut across the river and streamers that used to take you everywhere along the Lakes have disappeared one by one. At first we went to Kincardine by boat or tried to, but the boat stuck in the mud

at Toledo and after five hot summer hours of waiting on a fare wharf in Detroit, five children, father, mother and maid had enough and a way was found by train. But that meant two junction waits and arrival at midnight. Once a boat did take us to Bay City for train transfer to Higgins Lake in Mid Lower Peninsula for one pleasant summer. Now all of those boats are gone. Investigating the Lake shores, which bristle with abandoned wharves, father found an admirable spot on the east side of a lake that opened into Lake Michigan 18 westering miles away.

Mother had knowledge of real estate and bought from the Lumber company 17 acres of cut-over land with 600 feet of sandy shore, a spring of our own which poured a stream of clear water by our kitchen door, and a cottage built for the lumbermen. For one or two years we made Charlevoix by rail, Horton Bay by lake steamer, and rowed a mile to our cottage. We had a lot of fun there. Roads began to be built and soon brought numbers to our shores. Finally when they offered me seven times as much as we paid we sold. We still had Gilmanton, and now we had a Ford. When I taught at Lexington, Mass., in 1890 Gilmanton was but 100 miles away. We had a horse and surrey then. It took me three days to drive the horse up every summer. The family went by train, the journey by horse being too arduous. With the Ford, though Gilmanton was now 750 miles away, we could all go by car very comfortably in the same three days.

Two years we tried camping in Farmer Fancis' woods at the south end of Lake Huron. The Canadian Grand Trunk conductor obligingly stopped his train in the woods for us. That was in tents.

His concern with the war, and his total resolve that the allies had to put down "nazi evil," absorbed him during the war years. Most of the letters that he wrote in those years indulged commentary of the war. Frequently his letters to Mrs. Atherton dealt with nothing but war. Once he offered the scheme to Gladys Wrigley that government officials and Parliamentarians should fight each other until one side surrendered, leaving the people out of the brawl! On another occasion he wrote to Miss Wrigley:[15]

Can your library lend me anything enlightening on the—say 1936-38—state of the agriculturists exchanged between Turkey and Greece after World War I—How are they getting along in their new homes?

You see I plan to take 10 to 20 thousand square miles somewhere in the most prosperous part of Germany—agricultural—give the total inhabitants 20 minutes to take their possessions that they can carry in two suitcases each—supervised in size—seal their doors and off with them by freight train to the Ukraine—some devasted part, putting the same number of dispossessed Ukrainians in their homes in Germany at once, Allied troops arranging simultaniety—Don't look in the Dictionary, you know what I mean. Then the reasonable taxes paid by the Ex-Ukrainers from their crops go the Ex-Germans in Ukraine to enable them to restore the country to its former status, Russian surveyors reporting and after twenty years allowing them to go back and exchange what they have wrought for an approximate equivalent in the old home. Perhaps ten years would be better. They might work harder for a ten year prospect?

Don't give it away. It's a secret yet, but the Greek-Turkish experience may help. You see?

In the months that followed the war, he investigated U.S. military efficiency during the war; the nation's tactical and strategic campaign strength, ability to cooperate with the allies, and blunders; the costs to the taxpayer and the inefficiency of men in high positions. He pieced together information from various sources, wrote to persons in authority for further information or explanation, and, if dissatisfied, he would send a letter to the Secretary of Defense or the local senator. His motive was to avoid future repetition of waste, inefficiency, and the horror of allies shooting allies. Two of the letters Jefferson wrote in this connection follow:[16]

I wish you would demand an accounting from our Secretary of Defense of the cost incurred by the absurd race for the rescue simultaneously by two uncoordinated branches of our defense service, of the men marooned and rescued in Greenland.

He has demonstrated his unfitness by allowing two men to act who are legally his subordinates. A man like Eisenhower, or our ailing secretary of state would have made the decision of how the rescue should be planned and executed, and ordered it done.

A civilian is no judge of the proper method that should have been used but he can see that the highly efficient operation of the Air Forces does not mask the fact that its work, was lawless, if it acted without orders from the defense secretary, and for all we know without his knowledge.

We shall be given the political answer—the rescue of those 19 American service men was worth any cost! But that is an evasion. Every American taxpayer is pleased that the men were saved. They and the Air Force generally have been so highly efficient in their operations that the 19 men have not apparently been allowed to be too uncomfortable. We are apt to judge the naval attempt a foolish one, but that no civilian is competent to judge.

The cost of sending the naval carrier and its helicopters on their wild goose chase must have been huge and we need an official at the head of defense policy who makes decisions and sees that his subordinates execute them.

What has this cost us? Haven't we a right to know? And again:[17]

Let a mere citizen express the hearty approval that I am sure many feel of your action in stopping the (secret?) construction work begun last week on the 65,000-ton airplane carrier, started by the Navy department at an estimated cost of 188 million dollars, expected to expand quickly to 250 million, and sure to involve over a billion through the accompanying vessels in any actual operation.

I believe all Americans are proud of you.

Odd how we agree in some things. What American does not trust and admire Eisenhower and Marshall? What American was not ashamed of the incompetence of our Army and Navy at Pearl Harbor to let the Japs slap us in the face?

When Army and Navy last December raced to rescue airmen marooned in Greenland, I took the liberty of asking our Senator Ferguson to call Sec. Forrestal to account for not being on the job of heading our Defenses. I enclose my letter to Senator Ferguson of Dec. 28, 1948 and the response that resulted from Secretary Forrestal Feb. 8, 1949. I had of course no way of knowing that he was on his way out of a job that he was physically, mentally and morally unable to handle. We are bothered by our agencies of Defense—Army, Navy Airplanes with their inner friction and complete inability to do anything for our present day need of defense against the penetrating propaganda of the cold war.

Your stopping work on the wasteful carrier deserves well of your countrymen.

Jefferson felt alone in retirement. His close friends of the Normal College faculty were largely no more, the Ypsilantian charm of earlier decades had been transformed by the creation of a Henry Ford eleven million dollar bomber plant to the east of town, which had encouraged an influx of 40,000 workers from the South, hungry for war wages and lacking the feeling of civic responsibililty that was second nature to the older inhabitants. New-born bombers roared low overhead every hour, and Jefferson found a source of income by renting rooms to war workers, of whom at one time there were eleven in his house, occasionally spilling onto his porch, there to spend the night. But Jefferson had lost his local academic contemporaries, many of his correspondents throughout the world, and his Ypsilanti. He was beginning to lose his long-time friend, the Association of American Geographers, of which he had been a founding father. He found it increasingly difficult to attend their annual meetings and was alarmed to note that several of the more competent American geographers no longer attended the meetings, that there was division imminent within the Association itself which division assumed form in 1943 when the American Society for Professional Geographers was formed, and that professionalisation was making itself a force within Association ranks. On the former matter Jefferson wrote to George Cressey:[18]

> I am disturbed by the number of good men who have withdrawn from our list. Matthes was about to withdraw, but I have persuaded him not to. Goldthwait has withdrawn, Douglas Johnson practically never comes, Bowman does not come, how long since Shantz has been there?
>
> Davis strongly desired to bring together workers in marginal and allied aspects of Geography. It just dawns on me that our Programs, by segregating papers of separate aspects, causes more Dissociation than Association. A good session would have grouped together papers of distinctly different instead of similar classification. How can we have effect on each other if we do not meet? As if a Jones family reunion separated off into separate rooms, the Jones by blood and those who had married into the tribe! I believe this is important.

Jefferson had been disturbed to witness the breaking away of a group of geographers from the main body of the Association in 1943. These geographic workers, largely employed at Washington, wanted association, but their work frequently remained classified (for example, geographers employed on the M project) and so they remained ineligible for membership in the Association. Jefferson was loathe to see formal publication a qualification, rather was he interested in capacity and enthusiasm. The A.S.P.G. remained outside the Association until 1948 when unnecessary duplication was recognized. Professionalisation offered itself as an integrative idea that would unite the two geographical societies, yet an idea to which Jefferson was opposed. The very word bothered him. It meant nothing to him, and was a step away from wholesome legitimate endeavor, and did little more than create distance between it and the laity. Jefferson had been active in the Association during his life and remained so during the 1940's. He was elected Chairman of the Nominating Committee, 1940-1941, evaluated several manuscripts submitted to Editor Derwent Whittlesey for publication in the *Annals,* and prepared three papers for the A.A.G. meetings between 1940 and 1949, but had not found attendance possible. Jefferson recognized professionalisation as an invidious force in the Association and wrote vigorously against the idea to President Charles Brooks in 1947, though it had been a matter of distaste with him for some time:[19]

I congratulate the AAG on your accession to the post of President. You are a worthy representative.

The proposition of uniting us into "a single Professional organization" does not interest me.

The adding "Professional" to the names of scientific societies has little to commend it as if there were a Professional geological society or an American Society of Professional Mathematicians. What is a Professional Geographer? Was our founder [of the AAG] a professional geographer? Are you? Am I? Is Bowman?—a good inquiry now that he is a mere University President, not chiefly interested in Geography.

I met first the word profession applied to geographers from young men who complained that the Standard requirement of original publication for election to membership in our AAG disbarred them from joining. We have I believe always encouraged men interested to attend our meetings and it has not been difficult for many of them to present papers if they could satisfy a member that it was of enough geographic interest.

When they formed the American Society of Professional Geographers it looked a bit as if they meant government job-holder geographers. Why the professional?

The little group of men—mostly members of the U.S. Geological Survey who formed the National Geographic Society about 1889— Gilbert, Powell, McGee and others and ran it until Alexander Graham Bell suggested to his son-in-law Grosvenor the admirable idea of a geographic picture book, rather than a journal of the work of Americans in original geography, were professional but also had something to say.

I am sorry I have not been able to attend meetings lately, Winter train travel is difficult for me but last year I thought to be at Columbus —until I saw the program! It did not look substantial and men who attended wrote me that it was somewhat dreary especially that men who were poorly prepared to present their ideas wasted time and habitually ran over the time allotted them, the officers being unable to prevent. I am sorry. I find geography most interesting. I should like to know what interesting things Blue Hill has learned lately and Chicago and Minnesota. But let's not professionalise.

Jefferson was concerned for the direction and future of the Association as it entered the forties. He perceived that physiographers seemed no longer welcome at the meetings and that there was less feeling for the geographic idea. He had been aggravated in 1939 when the Reading Committee of the *Annals of the Association of American Geographers* had found not suitable for publication his essay entitled "Is Germany a Country?", a matter about which he had been thinking since the first World War. He felt that office holding seemed to be emerging as a habit of some geographers as a substitute for geographic thinking. He did not see men emerging the equivalent of his own early halcyon Association Days . . . days of Davis, Tower, Huntington, Bowman, J. R. Smith, Matthes. Yet he did not forsake the Association. In 1940, elected chairman of the Nominating Committee, he was largely responsible for the selection of Griffith Taylor as President. He continued interest in Association undertakings, avidly read its publications, was consulted by Alfred Meyer concerning valuable research directions which the Association might assume, facilitated by the then recent Fulbright Act.[20]

> *At the Charlottesville's meetings of the AAG, the ASPG, and the NCGT, attention was directed to the opportunities for foreign geographic research under the provisions of the Fulbright Act. As a result, it was resolved to appoint a committee to further investigate the possibilities of promoting geographic research under this Act. A progress report of the committee by Lloyd D. Black appeared in the September issue of the Joint Newsletter of the AAG-ASPG.*
>
> *One of the chief functions of the committee would seem to be to propose specific projects or programs which geographers or geography organizations would like to see pursued in specific foreign areas. Because of your recognized leadership in geographic research, we are writing to you for specific suggestions along this line.*
>
> *I would deeply appreciate any suggestion you would like to make at your earliest convenience so we might benefit from it in time for our final report. For your convenience you may simply pen your note on the bottom or reverse of this letter, if you prefer.*

Jefferson's reply indicates that his earlier geographic interests in anthropography and climate had not been eradicated by his exceeding concern with war and peace conference settlements[21]

> *Yes, I can suggest a lot if you have workers willing to work, and money to pay costs. For instance, where are the people of the world? My Presidential address published in the Annals of the Association in 1917, with included maps for U.S., India and British Isles with cities of 10,000 inhabitants up, for elements, and the main map of the United States with 1000 up. The map is generous. Most of Canada is included. Griffith Taylor could quickly complete it for Canada on the same scale and the Canadian Census date 1911 is near enough to 1910.*
>
> *Mexico would be another story. One or more men would have to go there. They should know or learn Spanish. The Church was not sepa-*

rated from the state till 1917. For our date, 1910, the church records are invaluable and the cooperation of the church should be sought. Country by country the same work should be attempted all over the world. You should read my article for the argument. Raye Platt made an attempt for Peru in the Geographical Review but some years ago without precise differentiation by size. Supposing the world covered with this basal map made by workers on the ground—say in 50 years we can look at the relief map. The 1:7 million Relief map made by our Geological Survey in 1911 put alongside my City map will be most instructive. So will Kincer's rainfall map.

We need a world rain cooperation for ten years simultaneously. Ten years is a short time but simultaneity matters immensely and we have no right to assume that a 40, 60, or 80 year record is immutable. There may be progressive changes or fluctuations. I believe that to be a large piece of research by a great body of men, urging foreign coopera- tion because so much of the earth is alien. If this was followed or accompanied by similar preparation of presentations of the earth's physiography, at least its relief and precipitation, and the scale kept small enough to allow the map to lie on an ordinary desk or table, the maps will be much more studied.

I made a three part division of the United States, scale 9:million, for my students with the help of the American Geographical Society staff in 1917, and have copies which can be combined into a small U.S. sheet. I enclose one to you for which you can remit 50 cents if you like.

I can no longer distribute such material at my own expense as I have in the past. The covers contain explanatory comment.

The annual meeting of the Association of American Geographers, December 1938, held at the University of Chicago, had proved to be his last association meeting. Jefferson was treated handsomely. Accomo- dated in a sitting room, bath and bedroom with twin beds in the same building with the dining room he enjoyed the meeting greatly. The Association voted to "extend Jefferson's membership" so that he need pay no more annual dues since he was shortly to be retired. Jefferson composed papers for the 1941 New York meeting *(The Rift in Our Population)* and the 1946 Columbus meeting *(Europe's Control of the World in 1914),* but he attended neither. He enjoyed the task of think- ing about his annual paper, the anticipation of a geographical meeting, but the apprehension of winter travel and concern with expense com- bined to prevent his appearance. In the months of January and Febru- ary he would wistfully look back upon the meeting he had not attended and feel a little sad. Late in 1948 and at the age of 85 Jefferson began to doubt that he "could hold on for another year." The grand old man of U.S. geography attempted to write a paper for the Association meeting at Madison, Wisconsin. He wrote to Chauncey Harris, one of the program officers who had offered to help him reproduce ten copies of his paper:[22]

> Thank you for your kind offer to have the ten copies made of my paper. I will try to be there and to send MS on to you early in November, as suggested.
>
> I do not know why you offer to do me this service. Such things have happened to me in three continents, kind attention from people on whom I have no claim and would probably happen in the other three if I went there. It's a good world!
>
> Here's hoping we meet at Madison.

A severe winter coupled with a head cold prevented Jefferson's attendance.

The last of Jefferson's written work surviving to geographic record is a response to a Normal College Committee's request for his reflections as Head of the Department on the occasion of the Normal College Centennial in 1949. In his response Jefferson allowed himself and his Department just a little praise, a commodity of which he had been suspicious for a life time:[23]

> To the committee in charge of the May Centennial
>
> The last 40-year incumbent of the geography headship at Ypsilanti has been invited to report on the relations of the Michigan State Normal College to Geography.—in his day, he supposes.
>
> He hopes the College has given Michigan boys and girls a closer touch with the world about them than was had by Horace Mann's famous boy who, when asked by his teacher how he knew the world was round, rattled off "Because-brave-and-daring-men-have-sailed-around-it. But when Mr. Mann asked him whether he had ever seen this round world confessed that he had not.
>
> The task of the Normal, I take it, is to train the several hundred students who leave it each year to be good teachers—of Geography among other things—in our common schools.
>
> In higher institutions of instruction, however, in supplying colleges and universities with distinguished teachers of geography the Michigan State Normal College has made a better record than any other teacher training school, for supplying leaders in Geography and presidents and other high officers of the Association of American Geographers.
>
> We may well be proud of the university chairs of Geography that have been capably filled, like that at University of Chicago, where the head of the Department of Geography who is retiring this June, was a

student in our classes from 1904 to 1909, assistant on our Geography faculty here in 1907, for long years Professor of Geography in the University of Chicago, president of the Association of American Geographers at St. Louis in 1935, and coming to Ypsilanti in 1931, the year in which Ypsilanti entertained the Association here, under the presidency of Dr. Isaiah Bowman, announced at that meeting the presentation to the head of the Ypsilanti Department of Geography the Helen Culver gold medal of the Chicago Geographic Society, as Bowman brought the actual Cullum Geographical medal of the New York Society.

Their one-time teacher well recalls the two boys as students, both contributing acceptable novelties of viewpoint in some of the teacher's own work in the field, the one contributing most appreciated suggestions for saving the time of his fellow students which resulted in the birth of our class textbook, a valuable tool of instruction, the other contributing points of difference of opinion that were worth publishing.

Now that Bowman has retired from the presidency of the Johns Hopkins University, it is a pleasure to learn that that institution is gratefully setting up the Isaiah Bowman School of Geography and declaring him the greatest living geographer.

It is a pleasure to see our old student and assistant Darrel H. Davis now Professor of Geography at the University of Minnesota this many a year, and secretary of the Association of American Geographers in 1929, 1930 and 1931.

It was a pleasure to observe the zeal and success up to his death of A. E. Parkins, Professor of Geography at the George Peabody School for Teachers, president of the Association in 1930, student here in 1901 and assistant on our faculty here in 1906 and 1907.

The Normal College has always been interested in modern Geography.

Note to the Committee   *May 3, 1949*
Gentlemen:

Will you kindly substitute the above for the MS submitted yesterday and destroy that. Neither is adequate and if the attempt is not in line with the Committee's ideas, it's suppression will be understood.

Yours cordially,
Mark Jefferson
Professor of Geography
1901 to 1939

If this does not serve your purpose put it in the waste basket.

And before death on August 6, 1949, he managed to sign himself to one letter that he penned . . . Mark Jefferson: Geographer.

CHAPTER THIRTEEN

THE GEOGRAPHY OF MARK JEFFERSON: SOME THOUGHTS AND REFLECTIONS

Charles Colby, who virtually grew up as fellow geographer with Jefferson, has written:[1]

> *In his published work Jefferson was creative and in many cases brilliant, but seldom systematic and logical. Perhaps it is more accurate to state that he was systematic in his distributions and not in his explanations . . . Viewing the course of geographic thought in the first half of the Twentieth Century, I conclude that Jefferson created a one-man school of geography.*

Geographers have perhaps been rather pre-occupied by the visible part of Jefferson's geography—the novelty of idea suggested by Colby and numerous other geographers. His point of view and method have remained little known. But it is just such a study of method and point of view transcending time and place that provides the scientist of any age with excitement and wonder. Too frequently the geographer has confused the method of the individual geographer with disciplinal methodology. Rarely has the soul of a geographer been bared, his humanity and competence ordered and subjected to scrutiny, his intellectual apparatus and scientific system sought. The geographer may be guilty of not learning the lessons offered by a study of intellectual history. A dualism presents itself. Geography is not essentially a study of geographers' mind systems and thoughts; this may be the realm of the philosopher. Yet the discipline needs to associate itself intimately with the personalities, systems, philosophies of its forebears in addition to their works, if it is to grow strong and healthy, more nearly complete. It is difficult to understand the work of the intellectual of a bygone age unless one understands his approach and point of view which are method for the individual.

In attempting to unravel the mind system of a thinker who contributed much to geography one must not necessarily seek an ordered methodology: if one reveals a method that is as large as a personality, a method whose values and direction are an emotional response to experience in the latter part of the nineteenth century when historical positivism was sponsoring fact collection in social science, when social Darwinism was permeating every nook and cranny of inquiry and at a time when descriptive appreciation was legitimately science, if a method so characterized is revealed, it requires no reasoned explanation or justification.

Jefferson's supreme disregard of the question "what is geography" stemmed from his feeling that there might be no geography, only geographers. He refused to erect a schema, a position, and thus become prisoner to his own pronouncements. Believing that the subject was not yet ready to search for a discipline, he busied himself calling roll on the social and physical sciences, collecting, collocating, and synthesizing data that it might be made subject to scrutiny by the geographic fraternity.

Jefferson believed that the geographer who wished to observe, collect facts, witness truths, to develop thoughts, need have no more philosophy than a point of view. He believed that truths, once recognized, should be published and thus shared. He frequently remarked that the offering of a work was more vital than its correctness, for the work would serve as a basis for revision and improvement. His task was to explain, not to justify. He offered no glittering world system. No naive finalism controlled his study. Thought and yet more thought was the essence of his geography. Implicitly he believed an approach would come with the years of toil. Jefferson, inspired by Davis, and convinced by empiricism, had learned to say "it looks as if." Caution and prudence, patient unambitious analysis, was his way. The fact had, necessarily, to be studied in itself, carefully verified by observation and experiment. He applied sound judgement, was a constructive thinker, had read Newton and agreed that "the essential of discovery is patient thought," recognized that the scientific man does not stumble upon new facts or conclusions by accident, but finds what he looks for. His fertile imagination, though kept in firm check, nevertheless managed to leaven his notable powers of observation and leave behind the impression that this balance of imagination and observation was the very essence of discovery.

Jefferson presented the spectacle of a thinker, armed with his own chosen intellectual apparatus, a living exemplar of the process of self improvement, choosing to think of matters personally interesting and significant to himself, who only incidentally wondered at the structure of the discipline. Frequently he assumed the role of universalist trespassing in the field of geography. Only rarely did he peer at the structure that housed the subject matter of his interest. His enthusiasm was engendered not by earthly aspiration but by a compulsion to understand and to enjoy the life of an educated mind. Fortunately Jefferson's immediate environment was large enough to accommodate men of science wishing to find a new direction for their thoughts. The exuberant confidence of a United States, whose exhausting westward marathon was well-nigh run, encouraged a release of creative energies, significant since the social thought and clime of time and place inevitably form the environment to which intellectuals are bound. This milieu was responsible for, although not responsible to, scientific attitudes and appreciation by men of letters. America in mid-passage displayed fidelity to esthetic affirmation. Thought was uninhibited: no dogma biased constructive social thought; the field of research was essentially limitless; men were inspired by the aftermath power of the industrial revolution which encouraged the analytical quest, which affirmed the necessity of the freedom of inquiry and produced a large number of thinkers who focused their efforts on posited problems and thereby distinguished themselves, by their very attempt at use of a scientific method, from men of *belles lettres* with whom they coexisted. This larger milieu encouraged academics to feel free and think freely. No coercive group unanimity exercising cultural authority influenced Jefferson. And so his work was able to have about it the air of scientific neutrality; it was uncommitted to any metaphysical or theological interpretation of its findings, and it was free from all forms of control that those authorities can impose in the attempt to reconcile scientific findings with orthodoxy. He had no compulsive, automatic reactions, but simple loves of country, home, and soil.

Disciplinal boundary lines had not been established; inter-disciplinary academic piracies and jealousies did not sap energies which were set to the tasks of inquiry, fact gathering, and ordering. A long tradition in physiography, involving the names of Dutton, Powell, Gilbert, and Davis which dominated, was authoritative but not authoritarian as deviants from that tradition began to demonstrate early in the 1900's. Earnest and careful scholarship rather than attempted geographic science won acceptance in American geographic circles. This freedom was further advanced by universities, colleges, normal schools and high schools where faculty were thrown back upon their own resources to develop geography courses and fashion them from their own interests.

Jefferson's earliest courses at the Michigan State Normal College were such an amalgam, being a product of his personal travel experiences combined with the physiography he had learned from Davis at Harvard. Knowledge and understanding, and the inculcation of such in the classroom, seemed more important to Jefferson than geography. He had the freedom to study and teach what interested him most. His classroom teachings would very frequently parallel his own studies, his classroom elaboration helping his independent thought. At times one feels the chalk and the talk of the classroom in his writing. Jefferson's personal interests largely determined the nature of what he would next talk or write of as geographic. He worked in areas where others frequently had not trod, in what seemed geographic, always with the desire to bring an informed intelligence to bear on the matter and to encourage others to think on the finished results that they might better them. Especially did inaccurate pieces of work attract Jefferson's attention that they might be improved and made correct. Otherwise Jefferson had a no more sophisticate working definition of geography for his own purposes than the way people lived on the land.

Jefferson did have a geographical "point of view." It was subject to his evolution in thought and may be gleaned from a study of his course offerings, articles, books, slides, photographs, book reviews, autobiographical notes, and correspondence. Jefferson's geographical viewpoint did change. Initially he was steeped in Davisian physiography, but this gave way early in the century to a most loosely conceptualized interest in man on the land and especially in the factors which promote the full expression of a people's genius. This shift finds expression in Jefferson's interests as published in *American Men of Science:*[2] Edition I, 1906— tides, river meanders, beach cusps; Edition II, 1910—geography of tides, river meanders, beach cusps and rainfall of great lakes, distribution of man, distribution of temperatures; Edition III, 1921—same as Edition II; Edition IV, 1927—distribution of man, distribution of temperatures, population growth, geography of cities; Edition V, 1933 and Edition VI, 1938—distribution of man, distribution of climates and of culture, population growth, geography of cities.

Jefferson's only published physiographic and geologic articles, ten in number, found print in the decade 1897-1907. In that latter year he commenced publication of articles more interesting to the human geographer. Jefferson's post-Davisian geographic point of view is partly revealed in the following statements. On the occasion of the Roorbach questionnaire Symposium of 1914, Jefferson expressed his geographical point of view, paragraphs of which were later published in the *Bulletin of the American Geographical Society:*[3]

Mark Jefferson thinks "There is most need of investigation of the distribution of man over the earth and the explanation of the facts observed." This leads immediately, he says, "into the explanation of the facts observed."

Mark Jefferson says, "In general the greatest tasks of all are still the ascertainment of all possible facts of geography," and the putting of them "into groups and relationships admitting simple statements qualified by statement of the width of applicability to which they are entitled."

In the introduction to *Man in Europe,* 1924, Jefferson wrote:

I have no mandate to define geography but of course I have a point of view, which is colored by my occupation of teaching teachers of geography. I want children to know where some of the most important peoples of the world are and what they are like, so first I want the teachers to know these things themselves.

In 1930, and in the introduction to his book, *Exercises in Human Geography,* Jefferson wrote—"Our geography is mainly concerned with men—where they are and what they are like." In seeking the "where" of man, he studied the distribution and characteristics of houses in many parts of the world, plotted man's distribution and resultant settlement patterns, and concentrated especially upon the geography of cities. An integral part of Jefferson's "where" was a concealed "why." He never observed a distribution without asking "why?" This obliged him to rediscover the physical environment as the home of man. This is not to suggest that Jefferson ever neglected the physical environment, for his studies of climate had been numerous throughout his career, but as man consumed more of his time, correspondingly less was accorded study of the physical environment.

One year later, Jefferson essayed a longer statement concerning his point of view. In 1931 A. E. Parkins circulated a questionnaire concerning "The Nature of Geography" to approximately twenty leading geographers of the U.S.A. Parkins' collection of replies to the questionnaires has been destroyed, but a duplicate copy of Jefferson's response, drawn from his own personal papers, is reproduced here to depict his geographic point of view in 1931:[4]

Many people—even educated people—use the word geography in a merely locational or distributional sense. The geography of sardines, they would say, must deal with the distribution of sardines, either before or after catching and canning. The geography of whales would surely tell where to look for whales. What could the geography of wooden shoes mean but their distribution in space? If you could put all the wooden shoes in the world down on a map in the places where they are at the present moment, with some indication of their numbers at every point where they occur, that would certainly show the geography of wooden shoes.

Someone has said that anything that you can put on a map is subject matter of geography. That is what I call locational or distribution geography. Many would prefer to call the study of the features of the moon's visible face lunar geography. Anyone would understand that the geography of my study-furniture meant the placing of the chairs and tables about the room.

But geographers are contemplative persons who cannot be satisfied with so meagre an account of the subject. We contemplate the things and their distribution. If asked why, we can only say that we take pleasure in it. We like to. But no one can contemplate the distributions of the major features of the earth and its inhabitants without fancying that he perceives causes and relations behind and among distributions. No distribution on earth is fortuitous. One thing is not independent of another. Some sort of order is usually perceived in any distribution, even though not understood in all its details. Wooden shoes are at once seen to be the work of tool-using men who have risen at least to an iron-using culture. Also they occur only in lands with readily worked woods. Also they are a response to rainy and muddy weather. The maps of iron-using men, of forests and of rainy weather enable us to foretell where we shall find the wooden shoes. Then come the exceptions, like the United States, where we think we have found something better in rubber footwear. Their use in parts of France, and the presence of a compact body of people of French origin in Quebec province who are known to cling strongly to old ways, would make it reasonable to look for some use of wooden shoes among the Canadian French.

Geographers like to think of these contemplations and reasonings on the facts of distribution of geography. The nature of geography is the fact that there are discoverable causes of distributions and relations between distributions. We study geography when we seek to discover them.

The mere distributed facts are no more geography to us than a fossil is geology to the geologist. If to the heedless they are all of geography, geography means nothing much to them of necessity. The heedless do not even perceive any distribution or grouping at all. For them a map is as meaningless as a table of statistics to those who do not understand statistics. They are folks who see with the eye only and not with the mind. It appears to us that they do not see at all. For them there is neither art nor science.

But there is an art of geography—the delineation of the earth's features and inhabitants on maps—cartography, and a science of geography, which contemplates the fact delineated and seeks out causes of the form taken by each distribution and its relationship to others.

Jefferson's study of human distribution did not eliminate his interest in physiography. In 1935, at the age of 73, accompanied by his daughter Phoebe, Jefferson travelled the length of the Tagus Valley, taking numerous photographs of its physiographic and human features. Resultant from this excursion was a physiographic study presented to the Association of American Geographers in 1936, "Is the Iberian Plateau a Plain of Marine Denudation." His "man in geography" Jefferson recognized as a logical extension of the work of those geographers that had gone before him. He was building on an established geographical foundation; he was not beginning anew. He accepted, and was proud to claim intellectual descent from men who had centered their endeavors in the physical environment:[5]

> *You cannot pick your father. Fathers cannot always pick their sons. Your father had to take you a good deal as you happened. Your intellectual father, however, you are free to pick.*
>
> *The head of the school of geography at Ypsilanti picked William Morris Davis as his geographic father in 1897, when he recognized Davis' extraordinary powers of observation, analysis and reasoning applied to the forms of the Earth's surface. Happily this involved Professor Davis in no responsibility. Just as a physical father cannot always transmit his powers to his son, a self-elected intellectual son need not expect to attain the powers of the parent he desires, but he may hope to grow in the admired direction.*
>
> *Nor need one bother father in selecting remoter forebears. For scientific grandparent we select Jean Louis Rodolphe Agassiz. When he settled in America in 1848 he brought inspiration to a whole generation of American naturalists to pay more and more attention to Nature herself and give less slavish attention to words of print. There was opportunity of descent, for Davis came to Harvard in 1866 and entered classes where Agassiz and his teachings dominated. That influence we elect for grandparental.*

This fragment was written in 1924.

It was the ability of Jefferson to have his own "notion" that seemingly emancipated him from the bondage of Davis and physiography. After self-scrutiny and self-criticism, patient thought about acquired facts led him to develop his "Jeffersonian notions." Now these notions are not necessarily truths or laws, though he might refer to a notion as a law. He was not attempting immediately to propound causalities; the enunciated notion would be made public and rendered subject to further scrutiny. His notion would cause and encourage the further search for truth. His comprehension was the product of the submission of facts to close scrutiny over a period of time. It was the method of the man's mind, not a method developed for or derived from, an accepted discipline. He wanted more and more honest study, believing that system would inevitably evolve to manage the acquired facts. There was no orderly subjection of an idea to a hierarchy of preconceived questions, rather was his method a flow of an involved self over an idea or observation. Care, patience, thoroughness, even duplication and irrelevance characterized this method. Facts which Jefferson had long appreciated suddenly merged together, forming a new pattern: a notion had been born. This was the fruit of Jefferson's labor, and seemingly enabled him to wean himself from W. M. Davis, whose "notions" Jefferson had previously enjoyed. Jefferson felt his notions were assertions concerning God's truths. They were what won for him his refreshing and Jeffersonian point of view, his originality, his individuality. In 1940 Jefferson wrote in a casual letter:[6]

> All my work is animated, I like to think, by a desire to get at the meanings behind well-assured material data. I do not regard much that is imagined as standing on facts at all, except that facts are culled which seem to favor a "Notion" which is the writer's motive power.

The frequency with which Jefferson used the term "God's Truth" in his personal notes and correspondence warrants attention. His notions were "God's Truths" recognized. Jefferson's discovery of Darwin at the age of 23 and W. M. Davis at the age of 33 had confirmed his belief that strict biblical interpretation did not provide a rational explanation of the phenomenal world. He emerged with his own understanding of the meaning and role of religion which had vast implications for his life's work. He recognized religion as offering a set of values, a method of comprehending life, an attempt at interpretation of arrival to the present. As science and understanding progressed, he could substitute knowledge for religious interpretation. Jefferson did not doubt the existence of a "God of things as they are," an unknown force, which was for him the supreme challenge in comprehension; science and knowledge, Jefferson believed, would help the individual more nearly understand "the God of things as they are." The Bible was well written, it stretched man's imagination to compose it, but it was incomplete. It had to be added to. Darwin added to it. Aggassiz added to it. Davis added to it. The Bible was a beginning. It attempted to comprehend creation and the unfolding drama of man and animal on the earth. One could not expect it to be truth, but it was a position from which to work. It would cause controversy and thought. Truth would come with time. Thus Jefferson had a God, recognized a value in the Bible, and was able to write:[7]

> *I have never understood Easter as a matter of religion. I have never understood the role of the Cross in religion. Santa Cruz! Why Holy? Why not Infamous?*
>
> *I have never understood why his disciples turned against Jesus? Or didn't they? I find no inspiration in that. Seems as if Jesus failed in his most intimate associates.*
>
> *But he spoke fine words many of which are and will be an inspiration forever. The Cross has no value for me.*

In a sense understanding and rewriting religion became Jefferson's career. Ultimately for Jefferson, the world would be left with one religion, truth, as science was substituted for sentiment in the religions of the world.

Wanting to understand more about the world in which we live was the essence of his geography. Yet in offering provocations instead of panaceas; in thinking, criticizing, discussing, suggesting without end; in urgently seeking God's truths wherever they were to be found without a more accurately defined and sophisticated method than "go and see, then see and write;" in refusing to recognize barriers to the discipline which he made his, the Jefferson contribution remained largely scattered, inchoate, a series of truths, and penetrating insights, ideas, singly comprehended but not jointly appreciated. In retirement Jefferson attempted to synthesize the more fundamental of his findings in the style of a book, in which the pattern of his searchings was revealed. Death intervened before the work—*A Geographer Looks at War*—was published. As a document the work has great value for the comprehension of Jefferson's thought, but it does little for the progress of the discipline. The unfinished manuscript indicates that two World Wars, two peace conferences, history of the lives of states, and the depression greatly influenced his thinking. Jefferson learned to despise war. He regarded the destruction of property and the ill-utilization of resources as a sin. This thought led him to think of the issue, war and peace, at great length. He recognized international understanding as necessary to prevent war against man and wage successful war against poverty, disease and illiteracy. His thinking on this subject was influenced by the learned Scot, George Chisholm, for whom Jefferson had great respect. Jefferson recognized the worth of organized opinion. This was a large part of his enthusiasm for the League of Nations and the United Nations. He wanted to see the peoples of the world brought together in their common business of living on earth. He urged that people, stripped of rank and position, had a common desire everywhere to live well, to enjoy a prosperous happiness. Jefferson had a love of peace and a taste for its works—science, letters, and art. His academic work was undertaken in this context. It was an attempt to cast light on the human enterprise. Jefferson's geography reveals itself as a history of consecutive discoveries.

An enumeration of some Jeffersonian notions, coupled with mention of their first appearance in print, provides an orderly means of access to a vital part of his thought: river meanders and behavior, "Limiting Width of Meander Belts," 1902;[8] the anthropographic city, "The Anthropography of Some Great Cities," 1909;[9] anglicization of place-names, "A Plea for Anglicized Place-Names," 1910;[10] the quantitative measurement of culture and the establishment of grades of civilization, "The Culture of the Nations," 1911;[11] application of the annotation of value to the materials of commerce and commercial interchanges, *Commercial Values,* 1912;[12] the north European plain as an invitation to militarism, *Notes on the Geography of Europe,* 1917;[13] the rail tentacles, rail nets, rail webs, as creators of civilization, "The Civilizing Rails," 1928;[14] a map projection of six equal-area projections of sixths of the earth's surface, "The Six-Six World Map Giving Larger, Better Continents," 1930;[15] the ecumene measurement and the concept of a country as a nation on its ecumene, "The Problem of the Ecumene: The case of Canada," 1934;[16] the concept of developed societies evolving primate cities, "The Law of the Primate City," 1939.[17]

In other ways Jefferson helped advance geographic knowledge. His linguistic abilities enabled him to review numerous studies of a geographic nature from (especially) the work of French, German, Spanish, and Swedish authors for the *Geographical Review.* In this way he was instrumental in making European geographic thought more readily available to American geographers. He also frequently reviewed the works of American geographers, and ranks as one of the "Big Four" (reviewers) in J. K. Wrights's *Geography in the Making.*[18] His objectivity was a vital strength which enabled him to enjoy Huntington and Ratzel yet not embrace any form of Influence or Determinism and to embrace French regionalist literature without embracing Possibilism. This ability to step dispassionately between the schools was a fundamental prerequisite to the Jefferson act of creation. His ability to stand aside from personal issues and conflicts conserved his time and maintained him free of all political entanglement. He despised German geographers who wrote "German geography," but was able to admire sound scholarship which geographers from Germany had produced. His attitude freed him to appreciate a piece of work strictly on its merits, without feeling compromised by personal friendship with the author. The friendships that he enjoyed with his contemporaries were also of an objective nature. In all the personal papers of the man there is no evidence that he used a first name for anyone beyond his own family. In the Jefferson—Bowman correspondence, which exchange probably totaled 2,000 pieces, Isaiah Bowman was always Bowman! which encouraged the latter to write:[19] "I have never known a first class man who is also a jolly good chap." He was consulted on numerous occasions for his opinion, as though he were some kind of intellectually acceptable arbiter, on matters including the spelling and pronunciation of place names,[20] map form and expression,[21] the delimitation of the Western Hemisphere,[22] the origins of geologic terms including beach cusp, meander scar, and tarn.[23]

His work—spoken at meetings, written in correspondence, or published—helped advance the thought of innumerable individual geographers. Ellsworth Huntington, for example, drew worths and understanding from Jefferson's conception of the North European Plain as an invitation to militarism, from his attempted measurement of the culture of nations, from Jefferson's geographic point of view and quoted Jefferson's "Observations on the Terraces of Peru."[24] Jefferson's system of culture measurement wins extended use and acknowledgment in *Civilization and Climate.*[25] In the preface to *The Environmental Basis of Social Geography,* by C. C. Huntington and Carlson, 1929, one reads:[26]

Modern geography considers man the central theme of its study of the earth. However, as Professor Mark Jefferson says: "Geography is not to be regarded in its human aspects as the story of Earth and Man, but as the study of Man using and living on the Earth."

Jean Brunhes made frequent use of Jefferson's studies in the distribution of population in his lectures at the University of Paris. Numerous references to Jefferson's population studies may be found in *Human Geography* together with a reproduction of the map, "Distribution of population by hemispheres," from Jefferson's *Teachers' Geography.*[27] The same population map was reproduced in *La Géographie de l'Histoire* by Brunhes and Vallaux.[28]

Sten de Geer gained inspiration and information concerning river meanders, the mapping of population distribution and categorizing the culture of nations;[29] the Yugoslavs, Cvijic and Vukovic, were helped by Jefferson's river meander studies and fellow Yugoslav, Ivo Rubic, followed Jefferson's urban researches closely.[30] Chisholm received the Jefferson notion of the distinction between civilization and culture; little that Bowman wrote did not contain references to Jefferson's work, but special note might be made of his debt to Jefferson for the first two published articles of his career which concerned river behavior,[31] for his interest in South America, and for "Railways as Pioneers," a chapter in *The Pioneer Fringe* of 1931.[32]

Reproduction of Jefferson's articles or maps in American college textbook literature was commonplace for nearly half a century. Typical of this practice are some Jefferson maps reproduced in J. R. Smith's *Commerce and Industry,*[33] and in *Introductory Economic Geography* by Klimm, Starkey and Hall.[34] Reference to Jefferson's published work scattered legion through the pages of periodicals and books in footnotes and bibliographies, indicate that many other geographers found Jefferson's studies useful. D. H. Davis acknowledged Jefferson's earlier teaching as a source of numerous facts and ideas in the preface to his book, *The Earth and Man.*[35] It is not possible to know how many more geographers were influenced by Jefferson's point of view or his specific ideas. His work had soul, not the product of an occasion, but of heart, head, and vocation. Many have benefitted from it; relatively few have had occasion to acknowledge a geographic contribution which has become public domain.

Jefferson's geography would have been infinitely less rich and scientifically less productive if he had allowed a series of measurements to have been substituted for his flow of thought about man on the land. The apparatus of his life's concern was a home, a library, paper, pen and ink, the mail system, and access to the facilities of the American Geographical Society. With this apparatus and the feeling of a poet, he reached out accurately to understand what he saw, took hold of science, and became a powerful moving force while geography in North America was in the making.

APPENDIX A
Published Works of Mark Jefferson

"The Antecedent Colorado," *Science*. New Series VI, No. 138, August 20, 1897, pp. 293-295.

"Mean Sea Level," *The Journal of School Geography*. II, No. 3, March, 1898, pp. 113-114.

"Cotidal Lines," *The Journal of School Geography*. II, No. 4, April, 1898, pp. 149-150.

"The Postglacial Connecticut at Turners Falls, Mass." *The Journal of Geology*. VI, No. 5, July-August, 1898, pp. 463-472.

"Atlantic Estuarine Tides," *National Geographic Magazine*. IX, No. 9, September, 1898, pp. 400-409.

"What is the Tide of the Open Atlantic?" *National Geographic Magazine*, IX, No. 11, November, 1898, pp. 465-475.

"Atlantic Coast Tides," *National Geographic Magazine*. IX, No. 12, December, 1898, pp. 497-509.

"Caesar and the Central Plateau of France," *Journal of School Geography*, III, No. 3, March, 1899, pp. 84-89.

"Earth's Rotational Deflective-Force," *Journal of School Geography*, III, No. 10, December, 1899, p. 394.

"The Value of Winter," *Journal of School Geography*, III, No. 10, December, 1899, pp. 394-395.

"Beach Cusps," *Journal of Geology*, VII, No. 3, April-May, 1899, pp. 237-246.

The Fields of Brockton. Notes for Field Study in Geography and Geology. Brockton Public Schools, Brockton, 1900, 24 pages.

Harvard University Cuban Summer School 1900. Course in Geography, Field Excursions, Guide to 12 Excursions. Harvard University, Cambridge, 1900. 29 pages.

Harvard University Cuban Summer School 1900. Course in Geography, Outline of Lectures. Part 1, Lectures I-VI, 7 pages; Part II, Lectures VII-XVII, 15 pages. Harvard University, Cambridge, 1900.

"Weather Map Exercises for a Fall Course in Meteorology for High School Pupils 12 to 14 Years Old," *Journal of School Geography*. V, No. 2, February, 1901, pp. 51-59.

"The Rainfall of the Leeward and Windward Islands," *Monthly Weather Review*, XXIX, Part 1, February, 1901, pp. 56-57.

"Reversed Falls," *Journal of School Geography*, V, No. 6, June, 1901, pp. 236-238.

"The Reduction of Records of Rain Gages," *Monthly Weather Review*. XXIX, Part 2, November, 1901, pp. 499-500.

"Limiting Width of Meander Belts," *National Geographic Magazine*, XIII. No. 10, October, 1902, pp. 373-384.

"The Influence of Ponds and Rivers on Atmospheric Temperatures," *Journal of Geography*. I, No. 9, November, 1902, pp. 400-407.

"Flood Studies on the Matfield River," *Journal of Geography*. I, No. 9, November, 1902, pp. 403-407.

"Winter Aridity Indoors," *Journal of Geography*. I, No. 10, December, 1902, pp. 444-447.

"The Geography of Lake Huron at Kincardine, Ontario," *Journal of Geography*. II, No. 3, March, 1903, pp. 144-155.

"Geography in the Grades," *Normal College News*. XXII, No. 7, April, 1903, pp. 184-187.

"Note on the Expansion of Michigan," *Michigan Academy of Science.* Fourth Report, 1904, pp. 88-91.

"Current Errors in Geography Teaching," *Michigan State Teacher's Association,* General Session, 1904, pp. 40-42.

"Wind Effects," *Journal of Geography,* III, No. 1, January, 1904, pp. 128-129.

"Scaurs on the River Rouge," *Science.* New Series XIX, January 22, 1904, pp. 150-151.

"The Educational Value of Geography," *Normal College News.* I, No. 17, April 9, 1904, pp. 233-234 and I, No. 18, April 16, 1904, pp. 245-247.

"What Has Geology Done for Michigan," *The M.A.S. Bulletin* (Official Organ of the Michigan Academy of Science), I, No. 2, October, 1904, pp. 4-5.

"Geography Work in the Grades," Preliminary Report of a Committee of the State Teachers' Association on an Outline of Geography Work in the Grades, by Martha A. Sherwood, H. M. Slauson, O. G. Frederick, Mark S. W. Jefferson. *Normal College News.* II, No. 9, November 26, 1904, pp. 134-147.

"The State Normal College as a Land Owner," *Normal College News.* II, No. 12, December 17, 1904, pp. 210-211.

"Out of Door Work in Geography," *Journal of Geography.* IV, No. 2, February, 1905, pp. 49-57.

"Aims and Methods of Physiographic Work in Secondary Schools," *Proceedings of the Michigan Schoolmasters Club.* XL, March, 1905, pp. 74-75.

"Results to be Expected from a School Course in Geography," *Journal of Geography,* IV, No. 4, April, 1905, pp. 160-163.

"On the Lake Shore," *Normal College News,* Magazine Edition, III, No. 4, October 20, 1905, pp. 36-37.

Material for Geography of Michigan, *Normal College News,* Magazine Edition, III, No. 9, November 24, 1905, pp. 60-74.

Material for Geography of Michigan, "Old Beaches and Moraines," *Normal College News,* Magazine Edition, III, No. 13, December 22, 1905, pp. 116-126.

Material for Geography of Michigan, "Climate," *Normal College News,* Magazine Edition, III, No. 18, February 2, 1906, pp. 159-170.

Material for Geography of Michigan, "The Fruit Belt," *Normal College News,* Magazine Edition, III, No. 22, March 9, 1906, pp. 223-234.

Material for Geography of Michigan, "Forests," *Normal College News,* Magazine Edition, III, No. 28, April 27, 1906, pp. 260-273.

Material for Geography of Michigan, "Commerce of the Great Lakes," *The Western Journal of Education,* I, No. 1, pp. 31-54.

Material for Geography of Michigan, Ypsilanti, Press of the Scharf Tag, Label and Box Co., 1906, 90 pages.

Teachers Geography: A Notebook and Syllabus, Ypsilanti, 1906, 55 pages. Second Edition: Ypsilanti, 1909, 76 pages.

Teachers Geography: Man and Climate with Practical Exercises, 1911, 79 pages, Ypsilanti, Third Edition.

Fourth Edition, Ypsilanti, 1912, 78 pages.

Fifth Edition, Ypsilanti, 1913, 78 pages.

Sixth Edition, Date unknown.

Seventh Edition, Ypsilanti, 1916, 77 pages.

Eighth Edition, Ypsilanti, 1917, 77 pages.

Ninth Edition, Ypsilanti, 1921, 76 pages.

Tenth Edition, Ypsilanti, 1923, 96 pages.

Twenty-eight Exercises on Topographic Maps. Ypsilanti, 1906, 30 pages.

"Rainfall of the Lake Country for the Last 25 Years," *Michigan Academy of Science.* Eighth Annual Report, September, 1906, pp. 78-97.

"Uplift Increases Rainfall, Denudation Diminishes It," *Science.* New Series XXV, No. 649, June 7, 1907, pp. 909-910.

"The Distribution of People in South America," *Bulletin of the Geographical Society of Philadelphia.* July, 1907, pp. 1-11.

"Lateral Erosion on Some Michigan Rivers," *Bulletin of the Geological Society of America.* XVIII, November, 1907, pp. 413-426.

"Glacial Erosion in the Northfiord," *Bulletin of the Geological Society of America.* XVIII, November, 1907, pp. 413-426.

"Stereoscopes in School," *Journal of Geography.* VI, No. 5, December, 1907, pp. 151-156.

World Diagrams of Population, Temperatures, Rainfall and Plant Distribution; A Supplement to Teachers' Geography. Ypsilanti, 1908.

"Where Men Live in North America," *Western Journal of Education.* February, 1908, pp. 78-85.

"On Drawing Michigan," *Western Journal of Education.* I, No. 3, March, 1908, pp. 117-120.

"Man in West Norway," Michigan Academy of Science, Arts and Letters, *Tenth Annual Report.* April, 1908, pp. 23-29. (Reprinted *Journal of Geography,* VII, No. 4, December, 1908, pp. 86-96.)

"Some Remarks about the Meteorology to be Taught in a High School Course in Physiography," *School Science and Mathematics.* IX, No. 1, January, 1909, pp. 41-44.

"Man's Distribution Over the Earth," *The Educational Bi-Monthly.* III, No. 5, June, 1909, pp. 364-372.

"The Anthropography of Some Great Cities; A Study in Distribution of Population," *Bulletin of the American Geographical Society.* XLI, No. 9, September, 1909, pp. 537-566.

"New York and the Four Next Largest American Cities in 1910," *Bulletin of the American Geographical Society.* XLII, No. 10, October, 1910, pp. 778-779.

"A Plea for Anglicised Place-Names," *Journal of Geography.* IX, No. 2, October, 1910, pp. 43-45.

Michigan: State Supplement to Dodge's Geography. Rand McNally & Co., Chicago, 1910, 48 pages.

"The Value of Geography as a School Subject," *Western Journal of Education.* IV, No. 3, March, 1911, pp. 97-105

"The Culture of the Nations," *Bulletin of the American Geographical Society.* XLIII, No. 4, April, 1911, pp. 241-265.

"The Real New York in 1910," *Bulletin of the American Geographical Society.* XLIII, No. 10, October, 1911, pp. 737-740.

"Geographic Instruction in America," *Proceedings of the Philosophical Society.* University of Virginia Publications, 1911-1912, pp. 130-134.

"The Needs of Elementary Geography," *Journal of Geography.* X, No. 8, April, 1912, p. 256.

"The Winds in 'Robinson Crusoe'," *Journal of Geography.* XI, No. 1, September, 1912, pp. 23-25.

Commercial Values; An Atlas of Raw Materials of Commerce and Commercial Interchanges. Ginn and Company, Boston, 1912, 64 pages.

Key to Commercial Values, An Atlas of Raw Materials of Commerce and Commercial Interchanges. Boston: Ginn and Company, 1912, 10 pages.

"Distribution of Schooling in the United States," *American Schoolmaster*. VI, No. 6, June, 1912, pp. 255-263.

"The Anthropography of North America," *Bulletin of the American Geographical Society*. XLV, No. 3, March, 1913, pp. 161-180.

"A New Density of Population Map of Europe," *Bulletin of the American Geographical Society*. XLV, No. 9, September, 1913, pp. 667-670.

"A Hopeful View of the Urban Problem," *Atlantic Monthly*. CXII, No. 3, September, 1913, pp. 353-358.

"The Great Lakes in a Cold Wave," *Journal of Geography*. XII, No. 7, March, 1914, pp. 221-223.

"Population Estimates for the Countries of the World from 1914 to 1920," *Bulletin of the American Geographical Society*. XLVI, No. 6, June, 1914, pp. 401-413.

"The Revolution and the Mexican Plateau," *Bulletin of the American Geographical Society*. XLVI, No. 6, June, 1914, pp. 436-437.

"How American Cities Grow," *Bulletin of the American Geographical Society*. XLVII, No. 1, January, 1915, pp. 19-37.

"Book Reviews," *Bulletin of the American Geographical Society*. XLVII, No. 2, February, 1915, p. 129.

"Cape Verde Islands; A Visit to San Vicente in 1890," *Journal of Geography*. XIII, No. 7, March, 1915, pp. 224-226.

"Steady Warmth of the Tropics," *Bulletin of the American Geographical Society*. XLVII, No. 5, May 1915, pp. 346-348.

"Slight Effect of War on U.S. Total Commerce," *Bulletin of the American Geographical Society*. XLVII, No. 9, September, 1915, pp. 650-651.

"The Range and Township Plan of Roads," *Journal of Geography*. XIV, No. 3, November 1915, pp. 80-81.

"Aridity and Humidity Maps of the United States," *Geographical Review*. I, No. 3, March, 1916, pp. 203-208.

"Utah, the Oasis at the Foot of the Wasatch," *Geographical Review*. I, No. 5, May 1916, pp. 346-358.

"The Distribution of People in Japan in 1913," *Geographical Review*, II, No. 5, November, 1916, pp. 368-372.

"Some Considerations on the Geographical Provinces of the United States, Presidential Address, The Association of American Geographers, New York, December, 1916, *Annals of the Association of American Geographers*. VII, 1917, pp. 3-15.

"Our Trade in the Great War," *Geographical Review*. III, No. 6, June, 1917, pp. 474-480.

Notes on the Geography of Europe. Ypsilanti, 1917, 55 pages.

"Additional Notes on the Population Density of Japan," *Geographical Review*, IV, No. 4, October, 1917, p. 320.

"The Distribution of British Cities, and the Empire," *Geographical Review*. IV, No. 5, November, 1917, pp. 387-394.

"Pronouncing List of Place Names on the War Fronts," *American Schoolmaster*. XI, No. 1, January, 1918, pp. 28-29.

"The Rainfall of Java," *Geographical Review*. V, No. 6, June, 1918, pp. 492-495.

"The Real Temperatures Throughout North and South America," *Geographical Review*. VI, No. 3, September, 1918, pp. 240-267.

Texts of the Russian "Peace" (with maps). Washington—Government
printing office, 1918, IV, 233 pages including tables. pp. 221-222 "Memorandum on the Russian German Boundary as established by the Treaty
of Brest-Litovsk," by Mark Jefferson.

"Flying Fish," *Journal of Geography*. XVIII, No. 6, September, 1919, pp.
239-242.

Recent Colonization of Chile. (American Geographical Society Research
Series No. 6, American Geographical Society Expedition to the ABC
Countries 1918 pamphlet, No. 1). Oxford University Press, New York,
1921, 52 pp.

The Rainfall of Chile. (American Geographical Society Research Series No.
7, American Geographical Society Expedition to the ABC Countries,
1918 pamphlet, No. 2). Oxford University Press, New York, 1921, 32 pp.

"Great Cities of the United States, 1920," *Geographical Review*. XI, No. 3,
July, 1921, pp. 437-441.

"On Population Estimates and the Case of Constantinople in Byzantine
Days," *Geographical Review*, XI, No. 4, October, 1921, pp. 616-618.

"The Maps in the School Geographies," *Journal of Geography*. XXI, No. 1,
January, 1922, pp. 23-28.

"The Geographical Factor in Spanish Civilization," *Geographical Review*,
XII, No. 4, October, 1922, pp. 648-649.

"The Site of Toledo, Spain," *Geographical Review*, XIII, No. 3, July, 1923,
p. 469.

Man in Europe: Here and There, Ypsilanti, 1924, 211 pp. Man in Europe
(Revised Edition) New York: Harcourt Brace and Co. 1926, 215 pp.
Man in Europe (Revised edition) Ypsilanti: Evans-Starr Printing Co.
1936, 259 pp.

"Distribution of Population in Norway," XIV, No. 4, *Geographical Review*.
October, 1924, pp. 646-647.

"Mediterranean Climates of Eurasia and the Americas," *Geographical Review*, XIV, No. 4, October, 1924, p. 659.

"New Rainfall Maps of Brazil," *Geographical Review*. XIV, No. 1, January, 1924, pp. 127-135.

"The Distribution of People in the United States in 1910," Ypsilanti,
Spring, 1924. 6 pages.

"Listening or Looking?" *American Schoolmaster*. XVII, No. 9, November
15, 1924, pp. 341-343.

"Looking Back at Malthus," *Geographical Review*. XV, No. 2, April, 1925,
pp. 177-189.

"Old Ports of Andalusia," *Geographical Review*, XV, No. 2, April, 1925.

Atlas of Plates to Man in the United States. Ypsilanti, 1926, 47 pp.

Principles of Geography. Harcourt Brace and Co., New York, 1926, 135
pp.

Peopling the Argentine Pampa. (American Geographical Society Research
Series No. 16). American Geographical Society, New York, 211 pp.
1926. (Reprinted, 1930.)

"A New Map of World Rainfall," *Geographical Review*. XVI, No. 2, April,
1926, pp. 285-290.

"Limiting Values of Temperature and Rainfall Over the World," *Geographical Review*, XVI, No. 2, April, 1926, pp. 324-326.

"European Migratory Movements," *Geographical Review*, XVI, No. 2,
April, 1926, pp. 327-328.

"Actual Temperatures of South America," *Geographical Review*. XVI, No. 3, July 1926, pp. 443-466.

"A Rainfall Map of the Scandinavian Peninsula," *Geographical Review*, XVI, No. 3, July, 1926, pp. 495-497.

"Pictures from Southern Brazil," *Geographical Review*, XVI, No. 4, October, 1926, pp. 521-547.

"Scandinavia Steps Forward in Rainfall Studies," *American Schoolmaster*, XIX, No. 8, November 15, 1926, pp. 341-344.

"A Remarkable Population Forecast in the Argentine," *Geographical Review*, XVII, No. 1, January, 1927, p. 152.

"A New Rainfall Map of the Iberian Peninsula," *Geographical Review*, XVII, No. 1, January, 1927, pp. 153-154.

"A New Delimitation of the Arid Regions," *Geographical Review*, XVII, No. 2, April, 1927, pp. 335-338.

"Recent Advances in Geography," *American Schoolmaster*, XX, No. 5, May 15, 1927, pp. 195-199.

"International Friendship," in "Faculty Symposium," *American Schoolmaster*, XX, No. 9, December 15, 1927, pp. 363-364.

"An American Colony in Brazil," *Geographical Review*, XVIII, No. 2, April, 1928, pp. 226-231.

"Have You Flown Yet," *American Schoolmaster*, XXII, No. 5, May 15, 1929, pp. 184-185.

"The Source of the Anti-Evolution Laws," *American Schoolmaster*, XXI, No. 6, June 15, 1928, pp. 201-203.

"The Civilizing Rails," *Economic Geography*, IV, No. 3, July, 1928, pp. 217-231. (Reprinted, *Journal Michigan Schoolmasters Club*, XXX, No. 22, December, 1928, pp. 119-132.) (Reprinted, *Outside Readings in Geography*, F. E. Dohrs, L. M. Sommers, D. R. Petterson. New York: Thomas Y. Crowell Co., 1955, pp. 612-628.)

"The Geographic Distribution of Inventiveness," *Geographical Review*, XIX, No. 4, October, 1929, pp. 649-661.

"Swiss Colonization in Depopulated France," *Geographical Review*, XIX, No. 4, October, 1929, pp. 675-677.

Exercises in Human Geography. Ann Arbor Press, 1930, 124 pp. (Reprinted, Ypsilanti, 1931, 124 pp.) (Revised Edition, Ypsilanti Evans-Starr Printing Co. 1936, 149 pp.)

"Variation in Lake Huron Levels and the Chicago Drainage Canal," *Geographical Review*, XX, No. 1, January, 1930, pp. 133-137.

"The Six-Six World Map; Giving Larger, Better, Continents," *Annals of the Association of American Geographers* XX, No. 1, March, 1930, pp. 1-7.

"An Adventure in Cartography," *American Schoolmaster*, XXIII, No. 8, November 15, 1930, pp. 274-277. (Reprinted, Journal of Geography, XXX, No. 5, May, 1931, pp. 201-204.)

"Distribution of the World's City Folks; A Study in Comparative Civilization," *Geographical Review*, XXI, No. 3, July 1931, pp. 446-465. (Reprinted, *American Schoolmaster*, XXV, No. 7, October 15, 1931, pp. 239-257.)

"La Mancha and the Cantabrian Mountains and the North Spanish Riviera," *Geographical Review*, XXI, No. 3, July, 1931, pp. 491-492.

"Some Great Geographical Problems," *Proceedings of the Ohio State Educational Conference*, (Reprinted in The Ohio State University Bulletin, XXXVI, No. 3, September 15, 1931, pp. 213-223.)

"A Rainfall Map of the Iberian Peninsula," *Geographical Review,* XXII, No. 4. October, 1932. pp. 678-680.

"Great Cities of 1930 in the United States with a Comparison of New York and London," *Geographical Review,* XXIII, No. I, January, 1933, pp. 90-100.

"A Daytime Census in Tokyo and the Center of Population in Hokkaido," *Geographical Review,* XXIII, No. 2, April, 1933, pp. 333-334.

"Legal Fiction," *The Michigan Builder,* XIII, No. 6, June, 1933, p. 3.

"Wandering Lakes of Dry Regions: The Mar Chiquita," *Geographical Review,* XXIII, No. 4, October, 1933, p. 670.

"The Railway Geography of Switzerland," *Geographical Review,* XXIII, No. 4, October, 1933, pp. 673-674.

Man in the United States. Ypsilanti, 1933, 72 pp.

"The Problem of the Ecumene; The Case of Canada," *Geografiska Annaler* 1934, pp. 146-158.

"Is the Population of the United States Now Decreasing?" *Geographical Review,* XXIV, No. 4, October, 1934, pp. 634-637.

"Our Potential Parents and Potential Population," *Geographical Review,* XXV, No. 2, April, 1935, pp. 332-333.

"The Growth of Europe's Population and an Estimate for 1936," *Geographical Review,* XXVI, No. 1, January, 1936, pp. 148-149.

"Manioc," *Geographical Review,* XXVI, No. 3, July, 1936, p. 512.

"Human Progress as a Geographer Sees It," *Human Progress,* Pamphlet of Round Table Discussion at Michigan State Normal College, July 21, 1937.

"Bordeaux's Access to the Sea," *Geographical Review,* XXIX, No. 1, January, 1938, pp. 151-152.

"Standard Seasons," *Annals of the Association of American Geographers.* XXVIII, No. 1, March, 1938, pp. 1-12.

"Regional Geography of Portugal," *Geographical Review,* XXVIII, No. 2, April, 1938, pp. 325-326.

"The Law of the Primate City," *Geographical Review,* XXIX, No. 2, April, 1939, pp. 226-232.

"The Great Cities of the United States, 1940," *Geographical Review,* XXXI, No. 3, July 1941, pp. 479-487.

Mark Jefferson and Carl Pray. "Argentina". Historical section of an article. *Encyclopedia Britannica, Volume II, 1929.*

APPENDIX B

Book reviews by Mark Jefferson, published in the *Bulletin of the American Geographical Society*, and the *Geographical Review*.

Bulletin of the American Geographical Society

Ein unerschlossenes Kulturland, by W. Vallentin, XLII, No. 4, April 1910, pp. 296-7.

Ferdinand von Richthofens Vorlesungen und Allgemeine Siedlungs—und Verkehrsgeographie by O. Schlüter, XLII, No. 6, June 1910, pp. 463-5.

Maps and Map-Making by E. A. Reeves, XLIII, No. 3, March 1911, pp. 213-4.

Studies in the American Race Problem by Alfred H. Stone, XLIII, No. 4, April 1911, pp. 298-9.

Great Cities in America by D. F. Wilcox, XLIII, No. 4, April 1911, pp. 299-300.

Canada. The Land of Hope by E. W. Elkington, XLIII, No. 4, April 1911, p. 300.

Through the Wildernesses of Brazil by W. A. Cook, XLIII, No. 4, April, 1911, p. 302.

The High Roads of the Alps by C. L. Freeston, XLIII, No. 5, May 1911, pp. 381-2.

An Unknown People in an Unknown Land by W. B. Grubb, XLIII, No. 6, June 1911, p. 458.

Palestine and Its Transformation by E. Huntington, XLIII, No. 6, June 1911, pp. 461-2.

La Géographie Humaine. Essai de Classification. Positive Principes et Examples. by Jean Brunhes, XLIII, No. 6, June 1911, pp. 467-9.

Nautical Science in its Relation to Practical Navigation, together with a Study of the Tides and Tidal Currents by Charles Lane Poor, XLIII, No. 6, June 1911, pp. 469-470.

Argentina and Her People of Today by N. O. Winter, XLIII, No. 8, August, 1911, pp. 625-6.

Across South America by Hiram Bingham, XLIII, No. 9, September 1911, pp. 694-5.

Islam in China by M. Broomhall, XLIII, No. 10, October 1911, pp. 782-3.

Brazil by Pierre Denis, XLIII, No. 12, December 1911, pp. 924-5.

Characteristics of Existing Glaciers by W. H. Hobbs, XLIII, No. 12, December 1911, pp. 934-5.

Elements of Geology by E. Blackwelder and H. H. Barrows, XLIII, No. 12, December 1911, pp. 939-40.

Forest Physiography by Isaiah Bowman, XLIV, No. 2, February 1912, pp. 127-8.

Le Ciel et l'Atmosphère by Louis Houillevigue, XLIV, No. 2, February 1912, pp. 140-1.

South America To-Day by Georges Clemenceau, XLIV, No. 6, June 1912, p. 455.

Salvador of the Twentieth Century by Percy F. Martin, XLIV, No. 6, June 1912, pp. 455-6.

Annals of the Association of American Geographers I, 1911, Ed. R. E. Dodge, XLIV, No. 7, July 1912, p. 531.

Reisen in Bolivien und Peru by Rudolf Hauthal, XLIV, No. 8, August 1912, pp. 614-5.

Die Kabel des Weltverkehrs, hauptsächlich in Volkswirtschaftlicher Hinsicht by Max Roscher, XLIV, No. 8, August 1912, p. 619.

Anleitung zum Kartenzeichnen by Konrad Kretschmer, XLIV, No. 8, August 1912, p. 622.
South American Problems by Robert E. Speer, XLIV, No. 9, September 1912, pp. 694-5.
Mathematische Geographie by H. J. Klein, XLIV, No. 11, November 1912, p. 864.
The Association of History and Geography by A. J. Berry, XLIV, No. 11, pp. 864-5.
The Outlines of Military Geography by A. C. McDonnell, XLIV, No. 11, November 1912, p. 865.
Checking the Waste by Mary H. Gregory, XLIV, No. 12, December 1912, p. 924.
Chubut by W. Vallentin, XLV, No. 1, January 1913, pp. 55-6.
Le Sol et l'État by Camille Vallaux, XLV, No. 3, March 1913, p. 216.
Das Kartenlesen by Gabriel Fambri, XLV, No. 3, March 1913, pp. 222-3.
Le Brésil Méridional by C. M. Delgado de Carvalho, XLV, No. 4, April 1913, p. 295.
Pflanzengeographische Wandlungen der deutschen Landschaft, by Hans Hausrath, XLV, No. 4, April 1913, pp. 301-2.
Geographie des Atlantischen Ozeans by Gerhard Schott, XLV, No. 5, May 1913, pp. 378-9.
Modern Argentina by W. H. Koebel, XLV, No. 10, October 1913, pp. 770-1.
Nachrichten über den Aral See und den unteren Lauf des Amudarja von den ältesten Zeiten bis zum XVII. Jahrhundert by W. Barthold, XLV, No. 10, October 1913, p. 777.
Einwanderung und Einwanderungspolitik in Argentinien by Georg Hiller, XLV, No. 12, December 1913, p. 934.
Monograph on the Sub-Oceanic Physiography of the North Atlantic Ocean. by Edward Hull, XLV, No. 12, December 1913, pp. 938-9.
Scientific Papers by J. Y. Buchanan, XLV, No. 12, December 1913, p. 939.
Grundzüge der Physiogeographie by W. M. Davis and G. Braun, XLV, No. 12, December 1913, p. 940.
Through Our Unknown Southwest by Agnes C. Laut, XLVI, No. 4, April 1914, p. 296.
European Cities at Work by F. C. Howe, XLVI, No. 6, June 1914, p. 446.
Die Berner Alpenbahn (Lötschbergbahn) Dargestellt von Dr. Ed Platzhoff-Lejeune, XLVI, No. 6, June 1914, pp. 447-8.
The Depths of the Ocean by Sir John Murray and Johan Hjort, XLVI, No. 6, June 1914, p. 453.
La Vie dans les Océans by L. Joubin, XLVI, No. 6, June, 1914, pp. 453-4.
Argentinien, ein Land der Zukunft by A. Arent, XLVI, No. 7, July 1914, p. 537.
En Argentine by Jules Huret, XLVI, No. 7, July 1914, pp. 537-8.
Süd-und Mittel-Amerika by O. Preusse-Sperber, XLVI, No. 9, September, 1914, p. 688.
Geschichte Südamerikas by Hermann Lufft, XLVI, No. 11, November 1914, pp. 845-6.
Illustrated South America by W. D. Boyce, XLVI, No. 11, November 1914, p. 846.
The Ocean by Sir John Murray, XLVI, No. 11, November 1914, pp. 853-4.
Erdkunde für höhere Schulen by Heinrich Fischer, XLVI, No. 11, November 1914, p. 863.

The Teaching of Modern Subjects: Geography by James Welton and W. P. Welpton, XLVI, No. 11, November 1914, p. 864.

Die Entwickelung der Kartographie Südbadens im 16 und 17 Jahrhundert by Johannes Werner, XLVII, No. 2, February 1915, pp. 134-5.

Die Austiefung des Rheindurchbruchtals während der Eiszeit by C. Mordziol, XLVII, No. 2, February 1915, pp. 137-138.

The Waters of the Northeastern North Atlantic by Fridtjof Nansen, XLVII, No. 2, February 1915, p. 141.

In Deutschland und Brasilien by Gustav Stutzer, XLVII, No. 4, April 1915, p. 293.

The Volcanoes of Kilauea and Mauna Loa by William T. Brigham, XLVII, No. 5, May 1915, p. 381.

Geological and Topographical Maps by Arthur R. Dwerry-house, XLVII, No. 5, May 1915, pp. 466-7.

Contours and Maps: Explained and Illustrated by Frederick Morrow, XLVII, No. 5, May 1915, p. 467.

Economic Geography by John McFarlane, XLVII, No. 8, August 1915, p. 624.

American History and its Geographic Conditions by Ellen Churchill Semple, XLVII, No. 9, September 1915, pp. 699-700.

Rouen: Etude d'une agglomeration urbaine, by J. Levainville, XLVII, No. 9, September 1915, p. 714.

Die Marschbildungen an den deutschen Nordseeküsten by H. Gruner, XLVII, No. 9, September 1915, p. 715.

Argentina, Past and Present by W. H. Koebel, XLVII, No. 10, October 1915, p. 783-4.

The Plateau Peoples of South America by A. A. Adams, XLVII, No. 10, October 1915, p. 784.

Höhlen im Dachstein und ihre Bedeutung für die Geologie, Karst-hydrographie und die Theorien über die Entstehung des Höhleneises by Friedrich Simonys, XLVII, No. 10, October 1915, p. 787.

Die Schwarzerde by P. Kossowitsch, XLVII, No. 10, October 1915, p. 788.

The Scandinavian Element in the United States by K. C. Babcock, XLVII, No. 11, November 1915, p. 883.

The Salton Sea by D. T. MacDougal, XLVII, No. 11, November 1915, pp. 885-6.

Der Victoria-Njansa by Joachim Perthes, XLVII, No. 11, November 1915, p. 889.

Das deutsche Helgoland by E. Lindemann, XLVII, No. 12, December 1915, p. 968.

America, including Canada, Newfoundland, the British West Indies, and the Falkland Islands and Dependencies, Editors, A. J. Herbertson and O. J. R. Howarth. XLVII, No. 12, December 1915, pp. 971-2.

Geographical Review

The South Americans by W. H. Koebel, I, No. 1, January 1916, p. 66.

The Oxford Survey of the British Empire: Africa by A. J. Herbertson and J. R. Howarth, I, No. 1, January, 1916, p. 70.

Asia: A Geography Reader by E. Huntington, I, No. 1, January 1916, p. 72.

Geografía de América, adaptada a los nuevos programas de los colegios nacionales y escuelas normales, by J. A. Boero, I, No. 1, January 1916, p. 78.

Der Schwarzwald by E. Scheu, I, No. 2, February, 1916, p. 157.

Nature Notes for Ocean Voyagers by A. Carpenter and D. Wilson-Barker, I, No. 2, February, 1916, p. 166.

Hydrographique, Bulletin, pour l'Année Juillet 1913-Juin 1914 by Le Bureau du Conseil, Permanent International pour l'Exploration de la Mer, I, No. 3, March 1916, p. 242.

Neue Anschauungen über das nordatlantische Stromsystem by A. Merz, I, No. 3, March 1916, p. 242.

Guidebook of the Western United States. Part C: The Santa Fe Route, with a Side Trip to the Grand Canyon of the Colorado, by N. H. Darton and others, I, No. 4, April 1916, p. 312.

South America: A Geography Reader by I. Bowman, I, No. 4, April 1916, p. 314.

New York City, Development and Present Status of City Planning in: Being the Report of the Committee on the City Plan, I, No. 5, May 1916, p. 383.

Beiträge zur Kenntnis der Kapverdischen Inseln: Die Ergebnisse einer Studienreise im Sommer by I. Friedlaender, II, No. 3, September 1916, pp. 239-40.

Illustrierte Länderkunde by E. Banse, III, No. 1, Jan. 1917, pp. 84-5.

Volumetria della Sardegna by G. Anfossi, III, February 1917, No. 2, pp. 162-3.

Argentinien im zwangstigsten Jahrhundert by A. B. Martinez and M. Lewandowski, IV, No. 3, September 1917, p. 227.

Cities in evolution: An introduction to the town planning movement and to the study of civics by Patrick Geddes, IV, No. 3, September 1917, pp. 236-7.

Europa (ohne Deutschland und Alpenländer) by E. Oppermann, IV, No. 4, October 1917, p. 326.

South of Panama by E. A. Ross, V. No. 4, April 1918, pp. 337-8.

Grande Géographie Bong illustrée: Les pays et les peuples, I and II, Editor Onésime Reclus, VI, No. 4, October 1918, p. 378.

Compendio de la historia general de América by Carlos Navarro y Lamarca, VI, No. 5, November, 1918, p. 463.

Census of India 1911 by E. A. Gait, VII, No. 3, March 1919, p. 196.

Handbuch von Polen (Kongress-Polen): Beiträge zu einer allgemeinen Landeskunde, by E. Wunderlich, IX, No. 3, March 1920, pp. 215-6.

Polacy na Kresach pomorskich i pojeziernych by Eugeniusy Romer, X, No. 2, August 1920, pp. 115-6.

The Population Problem in India: A Census Study by P. K. Wattal XI, No. 3, July 1921, pp. 458-9

Town Planning in Ancient Dekkan by C. P. Venkatarama Ayyar, XI, No. 3, July, 1921, p. 459.

Die agrarische Exportwirtschaft Argentiniens by E. W. Schmidt, XII, No. 2, April 1922, pp. 317-8.

La Terre et l'évolution humaine: Introduction géographique à l'histoire by Lucien Febvre, XIII, No. 1, January 1923, pp. 147-8.

Die Wirtschaftspsychologie des Spaniers by Alfred Rühl, XIII, No. 1, January 1923, pp. 150-1.

The Swedish Touring Club's Atlas of Sweden by Cartographic Institute, Stockholm, XIII, No. 4, October 1923, p. 638.

Atlas of the economic geography of Norway with a survey of cultural and economic conditions, especially with regard to commerce by Nissen, XIII, No. 4, October 1923, pp. 638-9.

Goode's School Atlas, Physical, Political, and Economic for American Schools and Colleges, XV, No. 1, January 1925, pp. 168-9.
Die nordischen Staaten: Norwegen, Schweden, Finnland: Eine soziologische Länderkunde, by Gustav Braun, XV, No. 2, April 1925, pp. 333-4.
Svensk Skolatlas 1: För Folkskolan, Editor Alfred Söderlund, XV, No. 2, April 1925, p. 334.
Why the Weather by C. F. Brooks, XV, No. 2, April 1925, pp. 337-338.
Atlas of American Agriculture by O. E. Baker, XVI, No. 1, January 1926, pp. 160-1.
Geographie Dictionary of the Virgin Islands of the United States by J. W. McGuire, XVI, No. 2, April 1926, pp. 337-8.
Kleine Pflanzengeographie der Schweiz by Ernst Furrer, XVI, No. 3, July 1926, pp. 506-7.
Causas provaveis das seccas do nordeste brasileiro by J. de Sampaio Ferraz, XVI, No. 3, July 1926, pp. 510-11.
The Conquest of Brazil by Roy Nash, XVI, No. 4, October 1926, pp. 678-80.
Europa: Befolkningskarta, Editor A Söderlund, XVII, No. 3, July 1927, pp. 508-9.
Kommersiell Världskarta 1926, Editor A. Söderlund and G. Törnblom, XVII, No. 3, July 1927, pp. 508-9.
Nordamerika: Natur, bygd och svenskbygd Vol. I & II by Helge Nelson, XVII, No. 4, October 1927, pp. 692-3.
The American Manufacturing Belt by Sten de Geer, XVIII, No. 4, October 1928, p. 690.
Die Ostalpen und das Heutige Österreich: Eine Länderkunde by Norbert Krebs, XIX, No. 1, January 1929, p. 169.
Wald und offenes Land in Süd-Chile seit der spanischen Eroberung by Otto Berninger, XX, No. 1, January 1930, pp. 174-5.
Jahres-, Januar-und Juli-Niederschlagskarte der Republik Chile, by W. Knoche, XX, No. 1, January 1930, pp. 174-5.
Klimakunde von Südamerika by K. Knoch, XXI, No. 3, July 1931, pp. 527-8.
Svensk Världsatlas by Generalstabens Litografiska Anstalt, XXI, No. 4, October 1931, pp. 692-3.
The French Colonial Venture by Constant Southworth, XXII, No. 2, April 1932, pp. 339-40.
Portugal: Auf Grund eigener Reisen und der Literatur Part I. Das Land als Ganzes by H. Lautensach, XXIII, No. 2, April 1933, pp. 343-45.
Human Geography of the South: A Study in Regional Resources and Human Adequacy, XXIII, No. 3, July 1933, pp. 518-9, by Rupert Vance.
Canada by Alexander Brady, XXIII, No. 4, October 1933, pp. 688-690.
Aspects of Rainfall in the Western Cape Province: A Basis for Geographical and Agricultural Study by F. E. Plummer, XXIV, No. 1, January 1934, p. 161.
Die Bevölkerung der Philippinen: Eine anthropogeographische Untersuchung, by Siegfried Lenk, XXIV, No. 2, April 1934, pp. 348-349.
Eine neue Niederschlagskarte der Erde by Wilhelm Meinardus, XXIV, No. 3, July 1934, pp. 520-521.
Folkskolans Kartbok by Alfred Söderlund, XXIV, No. 3, July, 1934, p. 524.

Die wirtschaftliche Bedeutung von Barcelona by Julius O. Reichenheim, XXIV, No. 4, October 1934, p. 685.

Arctic Village by Robert Marshall, XXIV, No. 4, October 1934, p. 696.

Reconnaissance of the Northern Koyukuk Valley, Alaska (map) by Robert Marshall, XXIV, No. 4, October 1934, p. 696.

World Resources and Industries: A Functional Appraisal of the Availability of Agricultural and Industrial Resources by Erich W. Zimmermann, XXV, No. 1, January 1935, pp. 167-8.

Sky Determines: An Interpretation of the Southwest by Ross Calvin, XXV, No. 1, January, pp. 168-9.

Language and Race Problems in South Africa by Adriaan J. Barnouw, XXV, No. 3, July 1935, pp. 513-4.

Memoria, Dirección Nacional de Vialidad, República Argentina by Highway Department of the Argentina Government, XXV, No. 3, July 1935, pp. 520-1.

Méditerranée, Peninsules méditerraneennes by Max Sorre, Jules Sion, and Y. Chataigneau, XXV, No. 4, October 1935, pp. 694-6.

El régimen pluviométrico de la Republica Argentina, by Argentine Government, Ministry of Agriculture, XXVI, No. 2, April, 1936, pp. 345-6.

Norway Today: Glimpses of Modern Norway: Its Culture, Scenery and People, Science, Literature and Art, Travel, Sport and Exploration; Natural Resources, Trade and Industries Editor Karl Fischer, XXVII, No. 1, January 1937, pp. 168-9.

The South: Its Economic-Geographic Development by A. E. Parkins, XXVIII, No. 4, October, 1938, pp. 693-5.

Die Trockenseen der Erde: Eine vergleichend-geographische Untersuchung zur Gewässerkunde der Trockengebiete by Fritz Jaeger, XXX, No. 2, April 1940, pp. 349-50.

The Earth and Man: A Human Geography by Darrell H. Davis, XXXII, No. 4, October 1942, p. 698.

APPENDIX C

Papers presented by Mark Jefferson to the Association of American Geographers. All abstract references are to the *Annals of the Association of American Geographers*.

Abstract omission, or abstract published by title in the *Annals of the Association of American Geographers* are irregularities of form only. All of the papers listed below were presented by Jefferson to the Association of American Geographers.

Chicago, 1907	"The Distribution of Population," title listed, I, 1911, p. 108.
Baltimore, 1908	"The Anthropography of Great Cities," I, 1911, p. 114.
Boston-Cambridge, 1909	"The Dominant Factors in the Geography of America," I, 1911, pp. 116-7; and "Temperature Representation," I, 1911, p. 120.
Pittsburgh, 1910	"The Culture of the Nations," I, 1911, p. 147.
Washington, 1911	"Houses and House Materials in West Europe," II, 1912, p. 106.; "The Anthropography of North America," II, 1912, p. 107.
New Haven, 1912	"The Geographic Distribution of Culture in The United States," title listed, III, 1913, p. 118.
Princeton, 1913	"The Growth of American Cities," IV, 1914, p. 141.
Chicago, 1914	"The Gulf Stream," title listed V, 1915, p. 139; "Regional Characters in the Growth of American Cities," V, 1915, p. 140.
New York, 1915	"Utah, the Oasis at the Foot of the Wasatch," title listed V, 1915, p. 148.
Washington, 1915	"The Plains of Europe," title listed VI, 1916, p. 127.
New York, 1916	Presidential Address—"Some Considerations on the Geographical Provinces of the United States," VII, 1917, pp. 3-15.
Chicago, 1920	"Chile: A Land Where Immigrants Need Not Apply," XI, 1921, p. 126.
Cincinnati, 1923	"The Passing of the Waterways," XIV, 1924, p. 41; "The Rainfall Map of South America," XIV, 1924, p. 41; "The Size and Shape of Sheets of an Atlas of the U.S.A.," XIV, 1924, p. 41.
Washington, 1924	"Malthus in the Light of Subsequent Events," XV, No. 1, 1925, p. 39.
Philadelphia, 1926	"The Sea Island Coast," XXII, No. 1, 1927, pp. 31-32.
Nashville, 1927	"The Geography of Railway Transportation in 1920-27," XVIII, No. 1, 1928, pp. 64-65.
New York, 1928	"The Panamanians," XIX, No. 1, 1929, p. 34; "The Regional Culture and the Geography of Patent Grants," XIX, No. 1, 1929, pp. 35-36.

Columbus, 1929	"Lake Huron Exceptionally High," XX, No. 1, 1930, p. 35; "The Six-Six World Map Giving Larger, Better Continents," paper published in full XX, No. 1, 1930, pp. 1-6.
Worcester, 1930	"The Distribution of Urbanisation," XXI, No. 2, 1931, pp. 126-127.
Washington, 1932	"Communications and Civilization," XXIII, No. 1, 1932, pp. 47-48.
Evanston, 1932	"The Problem of the Ecumene: The Case of Canada," XXIV, No. 1, p. 57.
St. Louis, 1935	"Motors as Criteria of Wealth in Europe, 1934," XXVI, No. 1, 1936, p. 61.
Syracuse, 1936	"Is the Iberian Plateau a Plain of Marine Denudation?" (not mentioned in *Annals*).
Ann Arbor, 1937	"Standard Seasons," XXVII, No. 1, 1938, paper published in full, pp. 1-12.
Cambridge, Massachusetts, 1938	"The Law of Primate Cities," XXIX, No. 1, 1939, pp. 78-79.
Chicago, 1939	"Is Germany a Country? What is the Test?" XXX, No. 1, 1940, pp. 60-61.

APPENDIX D
Memberships, Offices, Honors

1885 Argentine Geographical Society
1897 Elected member—National Geographic Society
1900 Invitation to teach—Harvard Cuban Summer School
1901 Associate Editor—Journal of School Geography
1902 Associate Editor—Journal of Geography
1904 Elected member—The Geological Society of America
1904 Founding member—Association of American Geographers
1904 Vice-President—Geography and Geology Section, Michigan Academy of Science
1906 Elected fellow—American Association for the Advancement of Science
1907 President—Michigan Academy of Science
1910 Contributing Editor—Bulletin of the American Geographical Society
1910 Second Vice-President—Association of American Geographers
1912 First Marshall of the A.G.S Transcontinental Excursion
1915 First Vice-President—Association of American Geographers
1916 President—Association of American Geographers
1916 Election to membership of the Phi Beta Kappa Society of Massachusetts
1916 Elected to the Board of Directors—The National Council of Geography Teachers
1918 Appointed Chief Cartographer of the Inquiry
1918 Appointed Chief Cartographer of the American Commission to Negotiate Peace at Paris
1919 Appointed U.S. Representative to the Geographical Commission of the Paris Peace Conference
1920 Elected corresponding member of the Belgrade Geographical Society
1922 Elected corresponding member of the American Geographical Society
1922 Dedication of The Aurora—Yearbook of the Michigan State Normal College
1925 Elected a corresponding member of the Anthropology and Geography Society, Stockholm (Svenska Sallskapet for Antropologi och Geografi)
1929 Elected—Councilor of the Association of American Geographers for three years
1931 Awarded the Cullum Medal of the American Geographical Society
1931 Awarded the Helen Culver Medal of the Chicago Geographical Society
1932 Elected a corresponding member of the University of Belgrade Geographical Society
1932 Elected—member at large of the National Research Council for three years
1939 The Mark Jefferson Scholarship Fund, established—Michigan State Normal College
1939 The Distinguished Service Award—National Council of Geography Teachers
1940 Chairman—Nominating Committee, Association of American Geographers
1940 Gave the Haas Lectures in Geography—First Series, Northwestern University
1962—(Posthumously)—Eastern Michigan University Library named The Mark Jefferson Library.

APPENDIX E

Jefferson wrote in indirect opposition to the Report of the Committee of Ten in *The Normal College News* ("Geography in the Grades", XXII, No 7, April 1903, pp. 185-186):

> *Some countries are so paramount by their civilization, their history and their commercial relations that we must become familiar with them. To know England should mean to have live, vivid ideas of what England is, what her landscapes, what her shores, what her people, her cities, her villages, and above all, how she lives and what she stands for. How in English history is to be found that idea of representative government which was the germ of our form of government, and has served Europe in the present century as the model on which she has shaped her moderate infusion of constitutionalism.*
>
> *To know Germany should mean to have some image in the mind of German landscapes and German life and industry, and above all to have a notion of what German patience and thoroughness mean to modern science, and how Germany owes her modern place in the world as distinctly to the strength of union—one great state from many little ones—even as our American republic. To know the Germany of today, one needs must know something of Bismarck, something of the rise of Prussia.*
>
> *So in studying France we must not allow the pupil to be ignorant of that French pre-eminence in matters of taste that impresses itself on French relations with all the world.*
>
> *A few countries, made real in landscape, life and institutions, and those countries of greatest importance—that is my ideal of the geographic attainment in point of facts for the eight years of the grades.*

And again . . . in "Out of Door Work in Geography," (a paper he presented to the National Education Association, and later published in the *Journal of Geography*, IV, No. 2, February 1905, pp. 49-57):

> *The sub-committee on geography of the Committee of Ten, including Americans distinguished for their geographical attainments the world over, admitted that results now attained are not proportionate to the time they cost. They suggested observational geography from the start and went into valuable details in describing what they meant. They emphasized above all the need of teaching more geography to the teachers . . . The Committee urged in 1893 that an elementary course in physical geography be put in the last year of the grammar school, while physiography should be taught in the last year of the high school as soon as properly trained teachers could be obtained. This physiography I take it would differ from physical geography by using the strict logical arguments of geometry, physics and chemistry in the treatment of causes and effects. While such teachers could not be obtained, a course in geology might take its place. Either of these courses to be given as advanced work with field work and laboratory work. They declared that without such courses as these "a serious danger threatens the whole line of geographic study in the schools, for the great mass of teachers of geography have not taken courses beyond the high school —and if they are not taught the elementary processes and principles of these sciences there, they will have little strength as teachers of geography. They cannot go much beyond mere facts and formalities." The committee thought in this way to utilize the time given to geography. This programme has been in print now for ten years. What has been accomplished? A year ago I made an investigation into the status of geography in the high schools of Michigan. While that state may not*

accurately reproduce the conditions of the country at large, it may fairly be called a representative state. One hundred and twenty-nine of the largest high schools of the state reported and the general conclusion I draw is that not a dozen schools in that great state are doing what was advised. The last year in the high school has physiography in but two schools and geology in only six. Only a third of the schools reporting did any out of door work and a quarter of them any laboratory work. Add to this that physical geography is not generally taught in our grammar schools and we have the net result that the course in physiography or geology is simply omitted and the grammar school physical geography pushed up into the first year of the high school. The mass of the teachers are still receiving no preparation for good work in geography.

An unusual opportunity for him to speak on behalf of his geographic viewpoint presented itself when a "Commission on Secondary School Geography" was appointed to present a report concerning the status and needs of geography in United States secondary schools, to the National Education Association in 1909. This Committee, chaired by J. Chamberlain (Los Angeles, Cal.), included W. Field (Milton, Mass.), M. Genthe (Hartford, Conn.), M. Jefferson, W. Moore (South Hadley, Mass.), W. Snyder (Hollywood, Cal.), and R. Whitbeck (Trenton, N.J.). The group never met, owing to the amount of travel that would have been involved. Members corresponded one with the other, writing a report by concensus of opinion through the mail. The committee was soon dominated by Chamberlain, Whitbeck, and Jefferson, and by chance circumstances Jefferson's views were to be given preferential treatment. Whitbeck had sent his report to Chamberlain stating Jefferson was in agreement with the text of his message. Whitbeck had exchanged correspondence with Jefferson and came to believe that Jefferson and he were agreed on certain matters relating to secondary school education in the United States. Jefferson learned from Chamberlain of Whitbeck's unfortunate dispatch and at once expressed concern at the manner in which the report was being compiled. (See the letter: Mark Jefferson to Ray Whitbeck, February 18, 1909, p.p. M.J.). Chamberlain and Whitbeck, assuming apologetic roles, allowed Jefferson to incorporate many of his ideas into the report of this Committee on Secondary School Geography which was read before the science section of the National Education Association, Denver Convention, on Friday, July 9, 1909 (Report of the Committee on Secondary School Geography, *Journal of Proceedings and Addresses of the National Education Association,* Denver 1909, pp. 820-828). The Committee was favorably disposed towards the finished report, which had significant impact on geography in the secondary schools.

Later, on the occasion of The Transcontinental United States Geographical Excursion, one of Jefferson's evening addresses provides ("Geographic Instruction in America," *Proceedings of the Philosophical Society,* University of Virginia, 1911-1912, pp. 131-134):

The influence of the universities on the schools has been to encourage purely physiographic and geomorphologic work. In 1892 this encouragement took the form of the geographic part of the report of the famous Committee of Ten. It was characteristic that the committee thought physiography essential in the high schools if elementary school instruction in geography was to be saved from perishing. It thought something might be done towards this end by introducing courses in geology into the high school until teachers could be trained in the new physical geography. The Geography Conference of that Committee did recognize other aspects of geography than the rational explanation of land forms—calling them applied geography—but thought they ought to be taught in connection with the sciences to which they were most intimately related—as botany or zoology or history. It is plain that this university conception of geography is less broad than that prevalent in Europe, as represented by our distinguished visitors and also less broad than that which prevails in our elementary schools in which man and the relations of man to the Earth are regarded as essentials. We are more narrowly trained as individuals than our colleagues from across the sea. This excursion has shown us that every day. As a whole our European friends have more collateral training, in languages, ancient and modern, in botany and drawing, without appearing to lose anything from their geological preparation. It is likely that the elective system in America has brought it about that an American scientist of the present generation may have a range of training much more limited than would be possible for a European. That this narrow range of the American geographer usually lies within geomorphological lines is due to the fact that geography in higher instruction is wholly indebted for what place is granted it to a group of talented men whose work has been in the study of the forms of the Earth's surface.

Of human relations there was no note in the report of the Committee of Ten, but when the attempt was made to put physiography into the schools, the publishers, closely in touch with the schools, at once insisted on bringing "man" in to an extent that grew from year to year as the schools were heard from. For the American publisher is a close student of his market. He manufactures books to sell them and is keenly alive to the importance of satisfying the demands of "school men," a body of men who are not usually specially trained, but have a broad general education and are applying excellent judgment and common sense to school problems. . . .

Commercial geography has a place now in the universities and regional courses are beginning to be more numerous but probably a larger percentage of city high schools offer commercial geography than of colleges. The public school demand is that geography shall explain not so much the forms of the earth as the activities of man upon the earth. I believe that it is this demand of the public schools that is now meeting recognition in the universities too. A very useful and influential agency in discussing and shaping geographic adventures in high and normal schools in the last fifteen years has been the Journal of School Geography, later the Journal of Geography, under the able editorship of Professor Dodge, of Teachers College, Columbia University. . . .

The teachers in the elementary schools and in the smaller high schools are trained in the normal schools and colleges. Of these, between public and private, we have nearly three hundred. In all of these geography is taught, and there are about fifty professors of geography, rather more than half of them men, who give their whole time to the work. Some of these have one or more assistants. In a good many cases they have had some special training, but in the university it could only be in physical geography. Their own acquaintance with the schools has shown them their needs though they have little help in satisfying it and less leisure for the task. They have not generally taken an active part in offering new conceptions of geographic instruction but have faithfully reflected and supported the resistance of the schools to efforts at sidetracking "life" and "man".

BIBLIOGRAPHIC NOTE

The most important source for this study has been the collection of "Jeffersonia" located in Ypsilanti. Included are several thousand pieces of correspondence, lecture notes (1901-39), field notebooks, diaries, a slide collection, photograph albums, part of Jefferson's personal library, and numerous artifacts. Phoebe Jefferson (Manhattan, New York) has several pieces of correspondence from her father while he was in attendance at the Paris Peace Conference, 1918-1919. Barbara Jefferson (Oakland, California) and Hilary Jefferson (Gilmanton, New Hampshire) have a miscellany of artifacts relating to Jefferson's early life. The American Geographical Society files of correspondence between Jefferson and I. Bowman, W. Joerg, and G. Wrigley contain copies of letters lost to the Ypsilanti Jefferson collection.

In addition to the above, Jefferson's own published work completes the primary sources used in this study. Brief obituaries by Isaiah Bowman *(Geographical Review)* and Stephen S. Visher *(Annals of the Association of American Geographers, 1949, Proceedings of the Geological Society of America, 1950, and The Professional Geographer, May, 1965)* constitute the only previously published writing on Jefferson's life or thought.

Manuscript Collections and Archives

American Geographical Society Archives
Bowman (Isaiah) papers. Robert Bowman, Lincoln, Nebraska
Eastern Michigan University Archives
Harvard University Archives
Mahard (Richard). Denison University, Dept. of Geography and Geology.
National Archives, Washington, D.C.
Seymour Collection, Yale University
Stratton (C.G.) papers. Wisconsin State University, River Falls, Wisconsin
Ypsilanti Historical Society

Newspapers

Ann Arbor Daily News
Ann Arbor News
Boston Transcript
Brockton Enterprise
Detroit News
New York Times
The Times
Ypsilanti Daily News

Geographical Periodicals

The following Geographical Serials have provided summaries, notes, records, and correspondence concerning the work of Mark Jefferson: also articles in these publications contain many references to Jefferson's work.

Annales de Géographie
Association of American Geographers, Annals
Economic Geography
Erdkunde
Geografiska Annaler
Geographical Journal

Geographical Review
Geographische Zeitschrift
Journal of Geography
Petermanns Geographische Mitteilungen
Scottish Geographical Magazine
Zeitschrift fur Geopolitik
Ymer

SELECTED UNPUBLISHED WORKS BY MARK JEFFERSON

The name Argentine (c. 1884)
Final and Medial English Sonants (c. 1884)
The Correlation of Ideas (c. 1884)
Terry (c. 1884)
The Uranography of the Southern Hemisphere (c. 1889)
What is New England (c. 1891)
South America (c. 1898)
Remnants of Old Boston Geography (c. 1898)
Figure of Earth (c. 1902)
The Rocky Mountains of Colorado (1910)
Culture Within the U.S. (1911)
A Song of Victory (c. 1919)
The League of Nations (c. 1919)
Richard Tillia Morrison (1926)
Climates and Men (c. 1930)
Wind Effects (1937)
Is Germany a Country (1941)
The Coming of Spring (1941)
The Rift in Our Population (1941)
Russia and the Next Peace Conference (1943)
A Geographer Looks at War (unfinished book, 1941-1949)

NOTES

CHAPTER ONE

1. "Why My Parents Came to America," circa 1,000 words by Mark Jefferson (p.p. M.J.) (N.B. . . . p.p. M.J.—personal papers of Mark Jefferson) Also: Daniel Jefferson, Diary of the Voyage, 1849 (p.p. M.J.).
2. Letter, Mark Jefferson to himself, September 18, 1875 (p.p. M.J.).
3. "My Life," autobiographical notes by Mark Jefferson c. 1945 (p.p. M.J.).
4. Mark Jefferson studied the following courses while attending Boston University, 1880-1883: Latin, Greek, German, French, Italian, Spanish, Rhetoric, English Literature, Elocution, Ethics, Psychology, History, Mathematics, Calculus, Physics, Astronomy, Mechanics, Theory of Equations.
   Letter, Franklin C. Erickson (Boston University) to G. J. Martin, May 17, 1960.
5. "My Life," autobiographical notes by Mark Jefferson c. 1945 (p.p. M.J.).
6. Personal notes written by Theodora Bohnstedt, dated 1883 (p.p. M.J.).
7. Letter, The class of '84 to Mark Jefferson, November 20, 1883 (p.p. M.J.).
8. Letter, Mark Jefferson to Daniel Jefferson, December 3, 1883 (p.p. M.J.).
9. Letter, Mark Jefferson to Daniel Jefferson, April 20, 1883 (p.p. M.J.).
10. Mark Jefferson, "Flying Fish," *Journal of Geography,* XVIII, No. 6, September 1919, p. 239.
11. Letter, Mark Jefferson to Mary Mantz Jefferson, December 3, 1883 (p.p. M.J.).
12. Letter, Mark Jefferson to Daniel Jefferson, January 7, 1884 (p.p. M.J.).
13. Letter, Mark Jefferson to Daniel Jefferson, April 20, 1884 (p.p. M.J.).
14. Letter, Mark Jefferson to Daniel Jefferson, April 20, 1884 (p.p. M.J.).
15. Mark Jefferson Diary, Rio 1883 (p.p. M.J.).
16. Letter, Mark Jefferson to Daniel Jefferson, January 7, 1884 (p.p. M.J.).
17. Letter, Mark Jefferson to Daniel Jefferson, February 26, 1884 (p.p. M.J.).
18. Letter, Mark Jefferson to Daniel Jefferson, January 7, 1884 (p.p. M.J.).
19. Letter, Mark Jefferson to Christopher Jefferson, January 25, 1884 (p.p. M.J.).
20. Letter, Mark Jefferson to Christopher Jefferson, June 8, 1884 (p.p. M.J.).
21. Letter, Mark Jefferson to Daniel Jefferson, February 26, 1884 (p.p. M.J.).
22. "My Life," autobiographical notes by Mark Jefferson, c. 1947 (p.p. M.J.).
23. Letter, Mark Jefferson to Daniel Jefferson, April 20, 1884 (p.p. M.J.).
24. Letter, Mark Jefferson to Daniel Jefferson, May 8, 1886 (p.p. M.J.).
25. Letter, Mark Jefferson to Daniel Jefferson, May 8, 1886 (p.p. M.J.).
26. Letter, Mark Jefferson to Daniel Jefferson, May 8, 1886 (p.p. M.J.).
27. A contemporary term for Argentine wilderness.
28. Letter, Mark Jefferson to Daniel Jefferson, February 26, 1884 (p.p. M.J.).
29. Manuscript version of statement by Mark Jefferson used in *Harvard College Class of 1897—50th Anniversary Report 1897-1947* (Cambridge, 1947), p. 345 (p.p. M.J.).
30. Letter, Mark Jefferson to Daniel Jefferson, August 7, 1884 (p.p. M.J.).
31. Letter, Mark Jefferson to Daniel Jefferson, February 7, 1884 (p.p. M.J.).
32. Letter, Mark Jefferson to Ida Jefferson, August 30, 1885 (p.p. M.J.).
33. Letter, Mark Jefferson to Ida Jefferson, August 30, 1885 (p.p. M.J.).
34. Unaddressed and undated portion of a letter, written by Mark Jefferson while in South America (p.p. M.J.).
35. Letter, Mark Jefferson to Daniel Jefferson, October 6, 1888 (p.p. M.J.).
36. Mark Jefferson notebook, 504 pages, c. 1883—c. 1912. (p.p. M.J.).
37. Mark Jefferson notebook, pp. 35-36 (p.p. M.J.).
38. Handwritten essays among p.p. M.J.
39. Mark Jefferson notebook, pp. 131, 134-135, 160, etc.
40. Letters, Bernhard Berenson to Mark Jefferson, July 24, 1884. Bernhard Berenson to Mark Jefferson, December 23, 1884.
41. Letter, Mark Jefferson to Daniel Jefferson, August 16, 1887 (p.p. M.J.).

42. Letter, Mark Jefferson to Daniel Jefferson, April 20, 1884 (p.p. M.J.).
43. Letter, Mark Jefferson to Mary Mantz Jefferson, October 28, 1884 (p.p. M.J.).
44. Mark Jefferson notes on recollections of his life, written c. 1947 (p.p. M.J.).
45. Letter, Mark Jefferson to Daniel Jefferson, October 6, 1888 (p.p. M.J.).
46. Letter, Mark Jefferson to Daniel Jefferson, November 3, 1887 (p.p. M.J.).
47. Letter, Mark Jefferson to Mary Jefferson Smith, January 8, 1888 (p.p. M.J.).
48. Letter, Mark Jefferson to Daniel Jefferson, November 3, 1887 (p.p. M.J.).
49. Letter, Mark Jefferson to Daniel Jefferson, November 3, 1887 (p.p. M.J.).
50. Letter, Mark Jefferson to Daniel Jefferson, October 6, 1888 (p.p. M.J.).
51. Letter, Mark Jefferson to Mary Mantz Jefferson, September 29, 1887 (p.p. M.J.).
52. Letter, Mark Jefferson to Mary Mantz Jefferson, September 29, 1887 (p.p. M.J.).
53. Letter, Mark Jefferson to Mary Jefferson Smith, January 8, 1888 (p.p. M.J.).
54. Letter, Mark Jefferson to Helen Lovejoy, August 28, 1888 (p.p. M.J.).
55. Letter, Franklin Erickson, College of Liberal Arts, Boston University to Geoffrey J. Martin, May 17, 1960.
56. Letter, Mark Jefferson to Mary Jefferson Smith, March 25, 1888 (p.p. M.J.).
57. An account of this journey is to be found in Jefferson's Cordoba-Oroya diary (p.p. M.J.).
58. Mark Jefferson, notes on recollections of his life, written c. 1947 (p.p. M.J.).
59. Mark Jefferson, notes on recollections of his life, written c. 1947 (p.p. M.J.).
60. *Harvard College Class of 1897—50th Anniversary Report 1897-1947*, p. 347.
61. John Fiske, *Excursions of an Evolutionist,* The Riverside Press, Cambridge, 1883.
62. Letter, Mark Jefferson to Daniel Jefferson, January 16, 1886 (p.p. M.J.).
63. Letter, Mark Jefferson to Helen Lovejoy, August 28, 1888 (p.p. M.J.).
64. Letter, Mark Jefferson to Helen Lovejoy, August 28, 1888 (p.p. M.J.).
65. Letter, Mark Jefferson to Daniel Jefferson, undated (p.p. M.J.).
66. Letter, Daniel Jefferson to Mark Jefferson, May 26, 1889 (p.p. M.J.).
67. Letter, Mark Jefferson to Daniel Jefferson, July 26, 1889 (p.p. M.J.).
68. A handwritten copy of The Uranography of the Southern Heavens (in Spanish) is with the personal papers of Mark Jefferson.
69. Letter, Mark Jefferson to Daniel Jefferson, October 10, 1889 (p.p. M.J.).

CHAPTER TWO

1. Letter, Mark Jefferson to Daniel Jefferson, October 10, 1889 (p.p. M.J.). M.J.).
2. Letter, Mark Jefferson to Theodora Bohnstedt, November 18, 1890 (p.p. M.J.).
3. Undated, unsorted autobiographical notes by Mark Jefferson (p.p. M.J.).
4. Letter, Mark Jefferson to Daniel Jefferson, November 8, 1889 (p.p. M.J.).
5. Letter, Mark Jefferson to Daniel Jefferson, November 20, 1889 (p.p. M.J.).
6. Letter, Mark Jefferson to Daniel Jefferson, November 20, 1889 (p.p. M.J.).
7. Letter, Mark Jefferson to Theodora Bohnstedt, August 29, 1890 (p.p. M.J.).
8. Letter, Mark Jefferson to Theodora Bohnstedt, November 8, 1890 (p.p. M.J.).
9. Letter, Mark Jefferson to Theodora Bohnstedt, October 22, 1890 (p.p. M.J.).
10. Letter, Mark Jefferson to Theodora Bohnstedt, November 11, 1890 (p.p. M.J.).
11. Letter, Mark Jefferson to Theodora Bohnstedt, November 11, 1890 (p.p. M.J.).
12. Letter, Mark Jefferson to Theodora Bohnstedt, November 4, 1890 (p.p. M.J.).
13. Letter, Mark Jefferson to Theodora Bohnstedt, November 11, 1890 (p.p. M.J.).
14. Letter, Mark Jefferson to Theodora Bohnstedt, November 20, 1890 (p.p. M.J.).
15. Letter, Mark Jefferson to Theodora Bohnstedt, January 23, 1891 (p.p. M.J.).
16. Letter, Mark Jefferson to Theodora Bohnstedt, January 23, 1891 (p.p. M.J.).
17. Letter, Mark Jefferson to Theodora Bohnstedt, May 29, 1891 (p.p. M.J.).
18. Letter, Mark Jefferson to Theodora Bohnstedt, June 3, 1891 (p.p. M.J.).
19. Letter, Mark Jefferson to Theodora Bohnstedt, October 17, 1891 (p.p. M.J.).
20. Letter, Mark Jefferson to Theodora Bohnstedt, November 4, 1890 (translated from French by the author).

21. From unpublished autobiographical notes, 1947 (p.p. M.J.).
22. Undated notes written by Mark Jefferson (p.p. M.J.).
23. From unpublished autobiographical notes, 1947 (p.p. M.J.). The Director of the Graduate School, 1895-1908, was one-time professor of Greek, John Henry Wright, father of John Kirtland Wright.
24. From unpublished autobiographical notes, 1947 (p.p. M.J.).
25. From unpublished autobiographical notes, 1947 (p.p. M.J.).
26. Letter, John Hyde to Mark Jefferson, July 26, 1898 (p.p. M.J.).
27. W J McGee should be so written. W J are not initials, but are complete in themselves.
28. Letter, W J McGee to Mark Jefferson, September 1, 1898 (p.p. M.J.).
29. "Atlantic Estuarine Tides," *National Geographic Magazine,* IX, No. 9, September 1898, pp. 400-409.
30. "What is the Tide of the Open Atlantic?" *National Geographic Magazine,* IX, No. 11, November 1898, pp. 465-475.
31. "Atlantic Coast Tides," *National Geographic Magazine,* IX, No. 12, December 1898, pp. 497-509.
32. Post card, W. M. Davis to Mark Jefferson (p.p. M.J.).
33. From unpublished autobiographical notes, 1947 (p.p. M.J.).
34. *Journal of School Geography,* III, March 1899, p. 84.
35. From unpublished autobiographical notes, 1947 (p.p. M.J.).
36. The Fields of Brockton; Notes for Field Study in Geography and Geology. Brockton Public Schools, Brockton, 1900.
37. Herbertson submitted a thesis on monthly rainfall over the globe to the University of Freiburg—summer 1898; he also published "Professor Supan on the rainfall of the globe," *Geographical Journal,* XIII, pp. 61-64. *Geography,* A. J. Herbertson Centenary, Special Issue, Vol. L, Part 4, No. 229, November 1965.
38. Post card, W. M. Davis to Mark Jefferson, March 11, 1899 (p.p. M.J.).

CHAPTER THREE

1. Letter, Ernest Lee Conant and Alexis Everett Frye, to record activity and preparation of the Cuban Summer School, Havana, Cuba, June 22, 1900. See Page 2. *Album de la Expedicion de los Maestros Cubanos a la universidad de Harvard,* 1900, (Edited and copyrighted by Geo. C. Griffith, Cambridge, Mass., 1900).
2. "Extracts from original letter sent to President Eliot," by A. E. Frye, Havana, February 6, 1900, and President Eliot's Cablegram to Superintendent Frye, Cambridge, February 15, 1900. See Pages 2 and 3, Album de la Expedicion, Maestros Cubanos a la universidad de Harvard.
3. For example, "The Outlook," LXV, May—August, 1900, p. 780.
4. Letter, President Eliot (Harvard) to Mark Jefferson, April 2, 1900 (p.p. M.J.).
5. Harvard University. Cuban Summer School 1900. Course in Geography. Outline of first six lectures (I-VI); Course in Geography. Outline of lectures (VII-XVIII); Course in Geography. Campus Excursions (I-XII).
6. The *Educational Review,* XX, June—December, 1900, pp. 234-235.
7. "Summer School for Cubans and the work it has done: Instructor Mark S. W. Jefferson writes his views on the subject." *The Enterprise,* Saturday, August 18, 1900.
8. Letter, Mark Jefferson to Theodora Jefferson, July 1, 1900 (p.p. M.J.).
9. Letter, Mark Jefferson to Theodora Jefferson, June 18, 1900 (p.p. M.J.).
10. Letter, Mark Jefferson to Theodora Jefferson, July 10, 1900 (p.p. M.J.).
11. Letter, Mark Jefferson to Theodora Jefferson, July 5, 1900 (p.p. M.J.).
12. Letter, Mark Jefferson to Theodora Jefferson, July 6, 1900 (p.p. M.J.).
13. *The Educational Review,* XX, June—December, 1900, p. 235.
14. Major A. W. Lowe, "Excursions to Hobbs Brook, Kendal Green, and Squantum," *Lynn Newspaper,* August 3, 1900.

15. Letter, Mark Jefferson to Theodora Jefferson, July 27, 1900 (p.p. M.J.).
16. Letter, President Eliot to Mark Jefferson, August 4, 1900 (p.p. M.J.).
17. Letter, President Eliot to Mark Jefferson, August 21, 1900 (p.p. M.J.).
18. Letter, B. S. Hurlburt to Mark Jefferson, June 29, 1901 (p.p. M.J.).

CHAPTER FOUR

1. D. Putnam, *A History of the Michigan State Normal School at Ypsilanti, Michigan, 1849-1899,* Ypsilanti, Michigan, 1899, p. 14.
2. Letter, Barbara Eastman to G. J. Martin, June 22, 1962, p. 5.
3. Theodora A. B. Jefferson, *A house costing $6,933.64,* typed manuscript, Barbara Eastman Archives, Oakland, California.
4. Cora L. Rouillard, "Theodora Bohnstedt Jefferson," *Bostonia,* Vol. 14, No. 4, January, 1914, pp. 170-171.
5. Harvey C. Colburn, *The Story of Ypsilanti, written for the centennial celebration of the founding of the city in cooperation with the Committee on History,* Ypsilanti 1923.
6. Clarence M. Loesell, *A History of Kiwanis in Michigan,* McGrath—DeFoe Company, Charlotte, 1956, 218 pp.
7. See *The Ypsilanti Daily Press* (from June, 1913 to October, 1927 the paper experienced a name change to *Daily Ypsilantian Press).*
8. Barbara Eastman suggests that inspiration for the Twenty Club may have derived from Theodora's membership in a Women's Collegiate Alumni Association, Ann Arbor, and Mark's membership in the Entertainment Committee of the Harvard Club in Michigan. Interview, Barbara Eastman and G. J. Martin, September 1962.
9. J. Allende Posse, *Las Universidades En America Del Norte—Elementales Sobre Organizacion Universitaria.* Cordoba 1922, See especially Chapter 5, pp. 55-61.
10. *In Memoriam: Edwin Atson Strong,* 38 page booklet authored by a committee of the faculty for the Michigan State Normal College 1921: B. Dooge, M. Jefferson, F. Barbour, F. Alexander, F. Gorton, M. Putnam, J. Phelps.
11. Letter, Barbara Eastman to G. J. Martin, February 2, 1962, p. 7.
12. "Limiting Width of Meander Belts," *National Geographic Magazine,* XIII, No. 10, October 1902, pp. 373-384.
13. *Harvard College Class of 1897, Fiftieth Anniversary Report,* Harvard University Press, Cambridge, 1947, pp. 351-352.
14. *Op. cit.,* Colburn, pp. 281-282.
15. *Seventy-Fifth Anniversary of the Michigan State Normal College 1852-1927,* A Souvenir History published by the College, Ypsilanti, Michigan 1928, see p. 38.
16. Letter, Charles C. Colby to G. J. Martin, May 5, 1961.
17. "Material for Geography of Michigan," *Normal College News,* Magazine Edition, III, No. 9, November 24, 1905, pp. 60-74.
    "Material for Geography of Michigan, Old Beaches and Moraines," *Normal College News,* Magazine Edition, III, No. 13, December 22, 1905, pp. 116-126.
    "Material for Geography of Michigan, Climate," *Normal College News,* Magazine Edition, III, No. 18, February 2, 1906, pp. 159-170.
    "Material for Geography of Michigan, The Fruit Belt," *Normal College News,* Magazine Edition, III, No. 22, March 9, 1906, pp. 223-234.
    "Material for Geography of Michigan, Forests," *Normal College News,* Magazine Edition, III, No. 28, April 27, 1906, pp. 260-273.
    "Material for Geography of Michigan, Commerce of the Great Lakes," *The Western Journal of Education,* I, No. 1, pp. 31-54.
18. *Normal College News,* Magazine Edition, October 20, 1905.
19. *Material for Geography of Michigan,* Ypsilanti, Press of the Scharf tag, label and box Company, 1906, 90 pages.

20. *Michigan: State Supplement to Dodge's Geography,* Rand McNally & Company, Chicago, 1910, 48 pages.
21. These notebooks are with the pp M.J.
22. A little known doctoral dissertation concerning the career and contribution of R. E. Dodge is: "The Contribution of Richard Elwood Dodge to Educational Geography" by Paul Francis Griffin, Columbia University, 1952.
23. For a brief history of the National Council of Geography Teachers see: T. Barton, "Leadership in the Early Years of the National Council of Geography Teachers, 1916-1935." *Journal of Geography,* LXIII, No. 8, November 1964, pp. 354-355.
24. No record has been kept of the papers delivered at the National Council of Geography Teachers meetings since 1916 (correspondence T. Barton and G. Martin, 1965)
25. For the membership book and two undated carbon copies of letters to G. J. Miller see: p.p. M.J.
26. Appendix C.—Papers presented by Mark Jefferson to the Association of American Geographers.
27. Letter, J. Russell Smith to G. J. Martin, undated, c. June 1962.
28. Ella M. Wilson "Aroostook County Potatoe Culture," abstract published in *The Annals of the A.A.G.,* XVI, No. 1, March, 1926, pp. 38-39.
29. Ella Wilson, "Farmers and Farming in Cambridgeshire," Philadelphia, 1926. Abstract published in *The Annals of the Association of American Geographers,* XVI, No. 1, March, 1927, pp. 37-38.
    —————————, "National Population Figures Reduced to Standard Dates," Washington, 1932, Abstract published in *The Annals of the Association of American Geographers,* XXIII, No. 1, March, 1933, p. 56.
    —————————, "Zagazig—A cotton market," Evanston, 1932. Abstract published in *The Annals of the Association of American Geographers,* XXIV, No. 1, March 1934, p. 74.
30. Earl B. Shaw, "Forces Contributing to Changes in Geographic Education," *Journal of Geography,* LVII, No. 2, February, 1958, pp. 59-60.
31. Letter, Mark Jefferson to Ralph H. Brown, January 14, 1946 (p.p. M.J.).
32. J. K. Wright, *Geography in the Making,* pp. 294-295.
33. Appendix B.—Book reviews by Mark Jefferson published in *The Bulletin of the American Geographical Society* and the *Geographical Review.*
34. "Book Reviews," *Bulletin of the American Geographical Society* XLVII, No. 2, February, 1915, p. 129.
35. Isaiah Bowman, "John Huston Finley, 1863-1940," *Geographical Review,* XXX, No. 3, July 1940, pp. 355-357.
36. The manuscript was published as *Asia: A Geography Reader,* Rand McNally and Company, Chicago, New York, 1912.
37. *The New Practical Reference Library,* Ed. Charles Herbert Sylvester, 6 volumes, Hanson-Bellows Company, 1914.
    Argentina; Brazil; Colorado; Cuba; Massachusetts; Michigan; Desert; Great Lakes; Atlantic Ocean; Alps; Gulf Stream; Gaul; America.
38. "The Six-Six World Map; Giving Larger, Better Continents," *Annals of the Association of American Geographers,* XX, No. 1, March 1930, pp. 1-7.
39. Appendix D—Memberships, Offices, Honors.
40. Interview with Margaret Sill, March, 1960: interview with Anna Field, October, 1960.
41. *The Normal College News,* XXIX, No. 12, January 7, 1932, p. 1. A second account is given in *The Geographical Review,* 1932, p. 305.
42. Letter, Mark Jefferson to Phoebe Jefferson, October 29, 1932 (p.p. M.J.).
43. The *Journal of Geography,* XXXIX, No. 3, March, 1940, p. 124.

CHAPTER FIVE

1. D. Putnam, *A History of the Michigan State Normal School at Ypsilanti, Michigan, 1840-1899,* Ypsilanti, Michigan, 1899, p. 14.

2. The first five Normal Schools founded in the U.S.A. were: Lexington, Massachusetts, 1839; Barre, Massachusetts, 1839; Bridgewater, Massachusetts, 1840; Albany, New York, 1844; New Britain, Connecticut, 1849.

3. In this position Goodison initially taught also an occasional course in Latin and Greek.

4. *Educators of Michigan: A Choice Collection of Biographical Sketches and Portraits of the Teaching Profession* (Detroit: Wilton Smith Co., 1894), pp. 85-86.

5. John Munson, "Isaiah Bowman: Obituary," *Eastern Michigan State College Newsletter,* February 1950, p. 2.
   Mr. Bowman at 18 began teaching in the rural schools of St. Clair County. In attending teachers' institutes there he heard Charles T. McFarlane, head of the geography department at the Normal giving his enthusiastic speeches on geography. He then decided geography would be his career. Lacking high school preparation he entered Ferris Institute and did there his college preparatory work and incidentally came under the instruction of H. H. Barrows (recently retired as head of the geography department at the University of Chicago), a graduate of the Normal College who got his start under McFarlane. Mr. Bowman entered the Normal College in 1901. On arriving he was greatly disappointed to learn McFarlane had left to become head of the Normal School at Brockport, New York. It developed that Professor Mark Jefferson had come to take his place. After a few days Mr. Bowman said to his roommate, "I believe this new man is going to be all right. He seems to know his onions."

6. In these universities geography was offered as a supplement to geology or physiography. See: Charles R. Dryer, "A Century of Geographic Education in the United States," *Annals of the Association of American Geographers,* Vol. XIV, No. 3, (September, 1924), pp. 144-146.

7. *The Normal College News,* October 1901, pp. 29-30.

8. Dryer, p. 143.

9. Edna Arundel "The Evolution of Human Geography in Teacher Education," Ph.D. dissertation, 1942, Yale University.

10. See: G. J. Martin, "Geography, Geographers, and the Michigan State Normal School, 1853-1939," a paper presented before the Miami Meeting of the Association of American Geographers, 1962, abstract published in the *Annals of the Association of American Geographers,* III, No. 3, September 1962, p. 348.

11. Egbert Isbell, "A History of the Michigan State Normal," written but as yet unpublished.

12. See: *Michigan State Normal College Catalogues,* 1901-1939 (E.M.U. Archives).

13. *Michigan State Normal College Catalogue,* 1902-1909, pp. 57-58 (E.M.U. Archives).

14. *Michigan State Normal College Catalogue,* 1906-1907, pp. 77-78 (E.M.U. Archives).

15. See: Class examinations set for students, 1902-1906 (p.p. M.J.).

16. *Appendix E*—Jefferson in opposition to the Report of the Committee of Ten. Ten.

17. A. C. Krey, "Art Returns to Education," *Journal of Higher Education,* VII, No. 7, October 1936, pp. 345-355.

18. Manuscript prepared and submitted for Harvard College Class of 1897: *Fiftieth Anniversary Report, 1897-1947* (p.p. M.J.).

19. *Man in Europe, Here and There,* Ypsilanti, 1924.

20. The collection was broken after 1939, but much of it has been recollected by the author, 1959-1963.

21. See: Class examinations set for students, 1902-1906 (p.p. M.J.).

21. "Stereoscopes in School," *Journal of Geography,* VI, No. 5, December 1907, pp. 151-156.

22. *Material for Geography of Michigan,* Ypsilanti, 1906.

23. *Teachers Geography: A Notebook and Syllabus,* Ypsilanti, 1906.

24. *Twenty-Eight Exercises on Topographic Maps,* Ypsilanti, 1906.
25. *World Diagrams of Population, Temperatures, Rainfall and Plant Distribution; A Supplement to Teachers Geography,* Ypsilanti, 1908.
26. *Commercial Values, An Atlas of Raw Materials of Commerce and Commercial Interchanges,* Boston, Ginn and Company, 1912.
27. *Notes on the Geography of Europe,* Ypsilanti, 1917.
28. *Man in Europe Here and There,* Ypsilanti, 1924.
29. *Atlas of Plates to Man in the United States,* Ypsilanti, 1926.
30. *Principles of Geography,* New York, Harcourt Brace and Company, 1926.
31. *Exercises in Human Geography,* Ann Arbor, 1930.
32. *Man in the United States,* Ypsilanti, 1933.
33. Letter, Isaiah Bowman to Mark Jefferson, September 6, 1936 (p.p. M.J.).
34. Letter, Mark Jefferson to Caroline Atherton, April 7, 1941 (p.p. M.J.).
35. Letter, Mark Jefferson to Isaiah Bowman, September 22, 1924 (p.p. M.J.). M.J.).
36. Letter, Isaiah Bowman to Mark Jefferson, February 28, 1908 p.p. M.J.).
37. Evidence from Jefferson's family budget ledger, 1912-1921 (p.p. M.J.).
38. Letter, Mark Jefferson to Phoebe Jefferson, March 3, 1923 (p.p. M.J.).
39. *Bulletin of the American Geographical Society,* XLIV, No. 8, August 1912, pp. 622-623.
40. *Geographical Review,* XV, January 1925, p. 155.
41. *Geographical Review,* XVI, No. 1, January 1926, pp. 175-176.
42. *Geographical Review,* XXIII, No. 4, October 1933, pp. 664-665.
43. *Journal of Geography,* XXXVI, No. 2, February 1937, p. 76.
44. Letter, Isaiah Bowman to Mark Jefferson, September 6, 1936 (p.p. M.J.).
45. A typed list of maps drawn by Mark Jefferson, 1933 (p.p. M.J.).
46. *Michigan State Normal College Catalogue,* 1931 (E.M.U. Archives).
47. "The Value of Geography as a School Subject," *The Western Journal of Education,* IV, No. 3, March 1911, pp. 97-105.
48. "The Value of Geography as a School Subject," *The Western Journal of Education,* IV, No. 3, March 1911, p. 105.
49. *Michigan State Normal College Catalogue,* 1902, p. 57.
50. *Michigan State Normal College Catalogue,* 1907, p. 155.
51. *Michigan State Normal College Catalogue,* 1912, p. 89.
52. *Michigan State Normal College Catalogue,* 1917, p. 100.
53. *Michigan State Normal College Catalogue,* 1922, pp. 120-121.
54. *Michigan State Normal College Catalogue,* 1927, pp. 149-150.
55. *Michigan State Normal College Catalogue,* 1932, p. 150.
56. *Michigan State Normal College Catalogue,* 1937, p. 101.
57. One-hundred-twenty pages of hand-written lecture notes, pp. 85-114 are missing (p.p. M.J.).
58. *Teachers Geography,* 4th Edition, Ypsilanti, 1912.
59. Letter, Mark Jefferson to Gladys Wrigley, August 30, 1925 (p.p. M.J.).
60. Letter, Mark Jefferson to Gladys Wrigley, October 2, 1925 (p.p. M.J.).
61. Letter, Mark Jefferson to Gladys Wrigley, September 19, 1925 (p.p. M.J.).
62. *Exercises in Human Geography,* Ann Arbor, 1930.
63. Letter, Raye Platt to J. K. Wright, October 26, 1961.
64. Isaiah Bowman, "Mark Jefferson," *Geographical Review,* January 1950, XL, No. 1, pp. 134-137.
65. Letter, Mark Jefferson to Mrs. Atherton, July 13, 1941 (p.p. M.J.).
66. Letter, Mark Jefferson to Phoebe Jefferson, January 23, 1936 (p.p. M.J.).
67. Letter, Mark Jefferson to Phoebe Jefferson, February 7, 1933 (p.p. M.J.).
68. Preface to *Principles of Geography,* New York, Harcourt, Brace and Company, 1926.
69. "Some Great Geographical Problems," Proceedings of the Ohio Educational Conference, Eleventh Annual Session, *The Ohio State University Bulletin,* XXXVI, No. 3, September 15, 1931, pp. 213-223.
70. Letter, Mark Jefferson to George Philip and Son Publishing Company, January 2, 1932 (p.p. M.J.).

71. Letter, Mark Jefferson to Phoebe Jefferson, February 11, 1928 (p.p. M.J.).
72. Letter, Raye Platt to J. K. Wright, October 26, 1961 (p.p. M.J.).
73. A complete set of the college yearbook, *Aurora,* may be found in the E.M.U. Archives; pages are frequently unnumbered.
74. *Annals of the Association of American Geographers,* XXXIX, No. 4, December 1949, p. 307.
75. Letter, Edith Lovell Stevens to Mark Jefferson, September 21, 1932 (p.p. M.J.).
76. Letter, William Roger Greeley to Mark Jefferson, January 1, 1941 (p.p. M.J.).
77. Letter, Margaret Sill to Lester C. Oakes, April 16, 1958.
78. Letter, Richard Mahard to Lester C. Oakes, June 6, 1958.
79. Letter, Barbara Eastman to G. J. Martin, June 22, 1962.
80. Letter, Mark Jefferson to President John Munson, February 15, 1939 (p.p. M.J.).
81. Letter, A. K. Lobeck to Mark Jefferson, June 13, 1939 (p.p. M.J.).
82. Letter, Fred MacKay to Mark Jefferson, June 9, 1939 (p.p. M.J.).
83. Letter, Anna Field for the Faculty Women's Club of the Michigan State Normal College, undated (p.p. M.J.).
84. Letter, Helen Strong to Mark Jefferson, June 12, 1939 (p.p. M.J.).
85. Letter, Department of Geography, University of Michigan to Mark Jefferson, June 6, 1939 (p.p. M.J.).
86. Letter, Raye Platt to Ella Wilson, June 20, 1939 (p.p. M.J.).
87. Letter, Frank Hamilton to Mark Jefferson, June 11, 1939 (p.p. M.J.).
88. Letter, Isaiah Bowman to Ella Wilson, June 7, 1939 (p.p. M.J.).

CHAPTER SIX

1. "Wind Effects," *Journal of Geography,* III, No. 1, January, 1904, pp. 128-129.
2. "Glacial Erosion in the North Fiord," *Bulletin of the Geological Society of America,* XVIII, November 22, 1896, pp. 413-426.
3. G7. Physical Geography of Europe, Notes taken by Mark Jefferson, Course given by W. M. Davis, Harvard 1898, pp. 30-31 (p.p. M.J.).
4. W. M. Davis, "Glacial Erosion in France, Switzerland and Norway," *Proceedings of the Boston Society of Natural History,* XXIX, No. 14, pp. 273-322.
5. Norway I—Field Notes, pp. 3-5 (pp. M.J.).
6. Norway I—Field Notes, pp. 19-21 (pp. M.J.).
7. Norway I—Field Notes, pp. 22-23 (pp. M.J.).
8. Norway I—Field Notes, pp. 42-43 (pp. M.J.).
9. Norway I—Field Notes, pp. 53-54 (pp. M.J.).
10. "Man in West Norway," *10th Annual Report of the Michigan Academy of Science,* p. 27. Address of the President of the Michigan Academy of Science delivered at Ann Arbor, April 3, 1908.
11. "Glacial Erosion in the North Fiord," *Bulletin of the Geological Society of America,* XVIII, November 22, 1907, pp. 414-415.
12. "Glacial Erosion in the North Fiord," p. 426.
13. *Annals of the Association of American Geographers,* V, 1915, p. 137.
14. Jefferson did not seek or receive formal "credit hours" for this study.
15. "The Rocky Mountains of Colorado," 31 pages of double-spaced type (p.p. M.J.).
16. W. M. Davis, "The Colorado Front Range: A Study in Physiographic Presentation," *Annals of the Association of American Geographers,* I, 1911, pp. 21-83.
17. Letter, Mark Jefferson to Theodora Jefferson, July 10, 1910 (p.p. M.J.).
18. Letter, Mark Jefferson to Theodora Jefferson, July 12, 1910 (p.p. M.J.).
19. Letter, Mark Jefferson to Theodora Jefferson, July 13, 1910 (p.p. M.J.).
20. Letter, Mark Jefferson to Theodora Jefferson, July 19, 1910 (p.p. M.J.).
21. Letter, Mark Jefferson to Theodora Jefferson, July 20, 1910 (p.p. M.J.).
22. Letter, Mark Jefferson to Theodora Jefferson, July 21, 1910 (p.p. M.J.).

23. Letter, Mark Jefferson to Theodora Jefferson, July 28, 1910 (p.p. M.J.).
24. Letter, Mark Jefferson to Theodora Jefferson, August 14, 1910 (p.p. M.J.).
25. W. M. Davis, "A Geographical Pilgrimage from Ireland to Italy," *Annals of the Association of American Geographers,* II, 1912, pp. 73-100.
26. Vera E. Rigdon, "Physiographic Nomenclature a la William Morris Davis," *Annals of the Association of American Geographers,* XXV, No. 1, March 1935, pp. 52-53.
27. The G. J. Martin edited version of the Mark Jefferson Liverpool-Rome Diary, p. 7.
28. Four notebooks from this trip have been transcribed by G. J. Martin. The 55 page edited account is available from the Library Archives, Eastern Michigan University.
29. Letter, Mark Jefferson to Caroline Atherton, June 3, 1941 (p.p. M.J.).
30. *Bulletin of the American Geographical Society,* XLIII, No. 6, June 1911, pp. 467-9.
31. *Annals of the Association of American Geographers,* II, 1912, p. 106.
32. See: The G. J. Martin edited version of the Mark Jefferson Liverpool-Rome Diary, p. 42.
   Jefferson never did properly attend an International Geographical Congress, (Although he paid registration fees for the 1904 Washington meeting, it seems probable that he attended only one of its excursions, and not the bulk of the meeting, for this was the year of his field trip to the Jostedalsbrae of Norway).
33. *Memorial Volume of The Transcontinental Excursion of 1912,* published by the American Geographical Society, New York, 1915.
34. *The Aurora,* Michigan State Normal College Yearbook, 1924, p. 47 (E.M.U. Archives).
35. Letter, Mark Jefferson to Theodora Jefferson, September 5, 1912 (p.p. M.J.).
36. Letter, Mark Jefferson to Theodora Jefferson, September 30, 1912 (p.p. M.J.).
37. Letter, Mark Jefferson to Theodora Jefferson, October 13, 1913 (p.p. M.J.).
38. Letter, Mark Jefferson to Theodora Jefferson, September 4, 1912 (p.p. M.J.).
39. See: Chapter VII, "The American Geographical Society and the ABC Expedition."
40. Letter, Mark Jefferson to Barbara Jefferson, April 4, 1921 (p.p. M.J.).
41. See: Chapter IX, "South Carolina Interlude."
42. Letter, Mark Jefferson to Isaiah Bowman, September 17, 1928 (p.p. M.J.).
43. Letter, Mark Jefferson to Roger L. Scaife, April 7, 1931 (p.p. M.J.).
44. Letter, Isaiah Bowman to Mark Jefferson, September 24, 1928 (p.p. M.J.).
45. Letter, Mark Jefferson to J. K. Wright, undated but by context probably mid-November 1935 (p.p. M.J.).
46. Abstract published, *Annals of the Association of American Geographers,* XXVI, No. 1, 1936, p. 61.
47. The paper is neither mentioned by title nor abstracted in the *Annals of the Association of American Geographers.* See pp. M.J. for unpublished abstract.

CHAPTER SEVEN

1. The following letters (previously unknown) are vital to an understanding of the influence Jefferson exerted on Bowman prior to 1915 (p.p. M.J.).
   Letters, Isaiah Bowman to Mark Jefferson:
   1902—July 17; November 9.
   1903—January 2; March 6; May 13; June 13; July 6; July 20; August 6.
   1904—January 1; August 21; October 16; November 30.
   1905—April 20; May 28; July 5; October 6.
   1906—January 12; February 2; April 3; April 6; August 1; October 1.
   1907—January 5; January 8; January 31; February 19; March 13; March 22; June 9; December 10.
   1911—June 22.

1912—March 19.
1913—May 29.
Nine more Bowman letters are undated. It is not known how many more were written and have been lost. Jefferson's letters to Bowman are not available.

2. George A. Knadler, *Isaiah Bowman: Background of his Contribution to Thought*, Ed.D., dissertation, 1958, Indiana University (Geography).
3. Lawrence E. Gelfand, *The Inquiry*, New Haven and London, Yale University Press, 1963, p. 285.
4. Letter, Isaiah Bowman to Mark Jefferson, October 8, 1917 (p.p. M.J.).
5. A contract between the American Geographical Society and Mark Jefferson, March 14, 1918 (A.G.S. Archives).
6. Personal interviews, C. Colby and G. Martin, August 1960, August 1962.
7. *Journal of Geography*, XXII, No. 6, September 1923, p. 242.
8. Letter, Isaiah Bowman to Mark Jefferson, December 4, 1917 (p.p. M.J.).
9. Notes of the ABC Expedition—Introduction to Chapter I, "South America Re-Colonized." (p.p. M.J.).
10. Lawrence E. Gelfand, *The Inquiry*, Chapter 9, "Cartography and Latin America".
11. Letter, Isaiah Bowman to Mark Jefferson, October 8, 1917 (p.p. M.J.).
12. Letter, Mark Jefferson to W. S. Tower, January 6, 1918 (p.p. M.J.).
13. Letter, Mark Jefferson to Arthur Colton, March 2, 1918 (p.p. M.J.).
14. Letter, Mark Jefferson to Phoebe Jefferson, February 19, 1918 (p.p. M.J.).
15. Letter, Mark Jefferson to Clara Jefferson, April 5, 1918 (p.p. M.J.).
16. Letter, Mark Jefferson to Clara Jefferson, April 7, 1918 (p.p. M.J.).
17. "The Real Temperatures Throughout North and South America," *Geographical Review*, VI, No. 3, September 1918, pp. 240-267.
18. Letter, Mark Jefferson to Clara Jefferson, April 7, 1918 (p.p. M.J.).
19. Notes of the ABC Expedition, typed April 22, 1918, Santiago (p.p. M.J.).
20. Letter, Mark Jefferson to Clara Jefferson, April 22, 1918 (p.p. M.J.).
21. Two photograph albums and numerous slides made from other ABC Expedition photographs exist (p.p. M.J.).
22. Letter, Mark Jefferson to Clara Jefferson, April 8, 1918 (p.p. M.J.).
23. Letter, Mark Jefferson to Clara Jefferson, May 1, 1918 (p.p. M.J.).
24. Notes of the ABC Expedition (p.p. M.J.).
25. Letters, Isaiah Bowman to Mark Jefferson: August 9, 1919; March 24, 1920; June 2, 1921.
26. *Research Series*, No. 6, American Geographical Society, New York 1921.
27. *Research Series*, No. 7, American Geographical Society, New York 1921.
28. *The Geographical Review*, XVI, No. 4, October 1926, pp. 521-547.
29. *Research Series*, No. 16, American Geographical Society, New York 1926. (reprinted 1930).
30. *Geographical Review*, XIV, No. 1, January 24, pp. 127-135. Also noted: *Scottish Geographical Magazine*, XL, 1924, pp. 105-106.
31. *Geographical Review*, XVI, No. 2, April 1926, pp. 285-290.
32. *Geographical Review*, XVI, No. 3, July 1926, pp. 443-466.
33. *Geographical Review*, XVIII, No. 2, April 1928, pp. 226-231.
34. Letter, Wilma B. Fairchild to G. J. Martin, February 27, 1963.
35. *Recent Colonization in Chile*, p. 8.
36. "Suggestions for a Study of Latin America Based upon our Trade Relations," E. C. Walther, *Journal of Geography*, XIX, No. 2, February 1920, p. 47.
37. *Recent Colonization in Chile*, pp. 9-10.
38. *Annals of the Association of American Geographers*, XI, 1921, p. 126.
39. *Geographical Review*, XI, No. 1, January 1921, pp. 136-137.
40. C. C. Colby, *Journal of Geography*, XXII. No. 6, September 1923.
41. Letter, C. C. Colby to G. J. Martin, May 5, 1960.
42. Letter, Isaiah Bowman to Mark Jefferson, June 19, 1920 (p.p. M.J.).
43. *Journal of Geography*, XXII, No. 6, September 1923, pp. 242-243.
44. *The Geographical Journal*, LIX, No. 5, May 1922, pp. 396-397.
45. *The Geographical Teacher*, XI, No. 62, Part 4, Spring 1922, p. 273.

46. *The American Schoolmaster,* February 1922, p. 78.
47. Letter, Gladys Wrigley to Mark Jefferson, January 3, 1930 (A.G.S. Archives).
48. Letter, Mark Jefferson to Isaiah Bowman, January 6, 1930 (A.G.S. Archives).
49. Letter, Mark Jefferson to Gladys Wrigley, January 7, 1930 (A.G.S. Archives).
50. H. A. Matthews, "A Comparison between the Mediterranean Climates of Eurasia and the Americas," *Scottish Geographic Magazine,* XL, 1924, p. 155.
51. Letter, Isaiah Bowman to Mark Jefferson, May 9, 1921 (p.p. M.J.).
52. Letter, Mark Jefferson to Gladys Wrigley, October 2, 1922 (A.G.S. Archives).
53. J. K. Wright, *Geography in the Making; The American Geographical Society, 1851-1951,* New York, Published by the Society, 1952, p. 207.
54. Letters from Chandler Robbins to Mark Jefferson: September 19, 1910; September 28, 1910; October 15, 1910 (p.p. M.J.).
55. Letter, Isaiah Bowman to Mark Jefferson, March 24, 1920 (p.p. M.J.).
56. Letter, Isaiah Bowman to Mark Jefferson, June 19, 1920 (p.p. M.J.).
57. Letter, Isaiah Bowman to Mark Jefferson, July 19, 1920 (p.p. M.J.).
58. Letter, Isaiah Bowman to Mark Jefferson, February 4, 1921 (p.p. M.J.).
59. Letter, Isaiah Bowman to Mark Jefferson, March 28, 1921 (p.p. M.J.).
60. Letters, Mark Jefferson to Isaiah Bowman, May 12 and May 24, 1920 (p.p. M.J.).
    Letters, Isaiah Bowman to Mark Jefferson, June 14, 1920, August 24, 1920, September 24, 1920 (p.p. M.J.).
61. See: Letter, Isaiah Bowman to Mark Jefferson, October 5, 1921 (p.p. M.J.).
62. Mark Jefferson, *Peopling the Argentine Pampa,* p. vii (preface). See also: Isaiah Bowman, "Mark Jefferson," *Geographical Review,* XL, No. I, January 1950, pp. 134-137.
63. "Pictures from Southern Brazil," *Geographical Review,* XVI, No. 4, October 1926, p. 534.
64. *New York Times,* October 22, 20:2, 1926.
65. Letter, Mark Jefferson to Gladys Wrigley, April 7, 1923 (p.p. M.J.).
66. *Scottish Geographical Magazine,* 1924, Vol. 40, p. 105-106.
67. Letter, R. R. Platt to Mark Jefferson, November 4, 1921 (p.p. M.J.).

CHAPTER EIGHT

1. American Geographical Society Research Series No. 7, Oxford University Press, New York, 1921.
2. American Geographical Society Research Series No. 6, Oxford University Press, New York, 1921.
3. *Geographical Review,* XVI, No. 3, July 1926, pp. 443-446.
4. *Geographical Review,* XVI, No. 4, October 1926, pp. 521-547.
5. American Geographical Society Research Series No. 16, New York, 1926.
6. *Geographical Review,* XVIII, No. 2, April 1928, pp. 226-231.
7. *Geographical Review,* VI, No. 3, September 1918, pp. 240-267.
8. Letter, Isaiah Bowman to Mark Jefferson, August 23, 1918 (p.p. M.J.).
9. Letter, Lucien Gallois to Mark Jefferson, undated fragment (p.p. M.J.).
10. *Guide of the Map Program* by John Storck, Inquiry Document, No. 786, National Archives, Washington, D.C.
11. Lawrence Gelfand, *The Inquiry,* Appendix II, Yale University Press, 1963, pp. 341-342.
12. Letter, R. Lansing to Mark Jefferson, November 30, 1918 (p.p. M.J.).
13. Letter, Mark Jefferson to Isaiah Bowman, February 14, 1916 (p.p. M.J.).
14. Letter, Mark Jefferson to Isaiah Bowman, February 14, 1916 (p.p. M.J.).
15. Letter, Isaiah Bowman to Mark Jefferson, February 7, 1916 (p.p. M.J.).
16. *Notes on the Geography of Europe,* Ypsilanti, July 1917.
17. Letter, Isaiah Bowman to Mark Jefferson, August 1, 1917 (p.p. M.J.).
18. *Journal of School Geography,* III, No. 3, March 1899, pp. 85-89. Reprinted in *Journal of Geography,* VI, No. 4, November 1907, pp. 113-117.
19. Presidential Address, Michigan Academy of Science, Ann Arbor, April 3, 1908, *Tenth Annual Report of the Michigan Academy of Science.*

20. *Bulletin of the American Geographical Society,* XLIII, No. 4, 1911, pp. 241-265.
21. *Bulletin of the American Geographical Society,* LV, No. 9, September 1913, pp. 667-670.
22. *Geographical Review,* IV, No. 5, November 1917, pp. 387-394.
23. *Fourth Report of the Michigan Academy of Science,* 1904.
24. *Twenty-Eight Exercises on Topographic Maps,* Ypsilanti, 1906.
25. *Journal of Geography,* V, No. 4, April 1906, pp. 161-175.
26. *Western Journal of Education,* March 1908, published by Michigan State Normal College, pp. 117-120.
27. *World Diagrams—A Supplement to Teachers' Geography,* Ypsilanti, 1908.
28. *Commercial Values—An Atlas of Raw Materials of Commerce and Commercial Values,* New York, Ginn and Co., 1912.
29. *Man in Europe, Here and There,* Ypsilanti, 1924.
30. Letter, Mark Jefferson to Isaiah Bowman, November 3, 1915 (p.p. M.J.).
31. Letter, Charles Seymour to Geoffrey Martin, November 14, 1961.
32. The Inquiry specialists included:
    Director, S. E. Mezes, College of the City of New York
    Chief Territorial Specialist, Isaiah Bowman, American Geographical Society
    Regional Specialists:
        For the northwestern frontiers—Charles H. Haskins, Harvard University
        For Poland and Russia—R. H. Lord, Harvard University
        For Austria-Hungary—Charles Seymour, Yale University
        For Italian Boundaries—W. E. Lunt, Haverford College
        For the Balkans—Clive Day, Yale University
        For Western Asia—W. L. Westermann, University of Wisconsin
        For the Far East—Captain S. K. Hornbeck, U.S.A.
        For Colonial Problems—George L. Beer, formerly of Columbia University
    Economic Specialist—A. A. Young, Cornell University
    Librarian and Specialist in History—James T. Shotwell, Columbia University
    Chief Cartographer—Mark Jefferson, State Normal College, Ypsilanti, Michigan.
33. Charles Seymour, *Geography, Justice, and Politics at the Paris Peace Conference of 1919,* Bowman Memorial Lectures, American Geographical Society, New York, 1951, p. 17.
34. Charles Seymour, *Geography, Justice, and Politics at the Paris Peace Conference of 1919,* p. 13.
35. Letter, Mark Jefferson to Phoebe Jefferson, December 14, 1918 (p.p. M.J.).
36. Letter, Mark Jefferson to Phoebe Jefferson, December 14, 1918 (p.p. M.J.).
37. Mark Jefferson, *Paris Peace Conference Diary* (p.p. M.J.). Edited by G. J. Martin, Ann Arbor, University Microfilms, 1966, (OP 24,995).
38. A. E. Huber, Inquiry Document 184.1, January 4, 1919, National Archives, Washington, D.C., Mark Jefferson to Isaiah Bowman.
39. Memorandum, Mezes to Grew, subject: T. Jefferson, Inquiry Document 184.1, January 28, 1919, National Archives.
40. Minutes of the Daily Meetings of the Commissioners Plenipotentiary, Inquiry Document No. 184.00101/1, Friday, January 31, 1919, National Archives, p. 4.
41. Minutes of the Daily Meetings of the Commissioners Plenipotentiary, Inquiry Document No. 184.00101/3, paragraph 14, page VII, February 3, 1919, National Archives.
42. Letter, Mark Jefferson to Phoebe Jefferson, March 30, 1919 (p.p. M.J.).
43. Letter, Mark Jefferson to Phoebe Jefferson, January 25, 1919 (p.p. M.J.).
44. Memorandum, Isaiah Bowman to Mr. Grew regarding release of Mr. Jefferson April 15, 1919 (p.p. M.J.).
45. Copies of these maps are deposited at:
    1. Seymour Collection, Yale University Library
    2. State Department Archives, Washington, D.C.
    3. Archives, River Falls College, Wisconsin
    4. Archives of Mark Jefferson, Ypsilanti, Michigan

46. Charles Seymour, *Geography, Justice, and Politics at the Paris Peace Conference of 1919,* p. 13.
47. Isaiah Bowman, *The New World; Problems in Political Geography,* Fourth Edition, World Book Company, Yonkers-on-Hudson, 1928, p. 32.
48. Letter, Mark Jefferson to Alfred Meyer, November 26, 1948 (p.p. M.J.).
49. *What Really Happened at Paris; The Story of the Peace Conference, 1918-1919,* Chapter VII, Eds. Edward M. House and Charles Seymour. *Constantinople and the Balkans,* by Isaiah Bowman, p. 142.
50. Isaiah Bowman, unpublished notes addressed to James Truslow Adams at the latter's request for inclusion in the *Dictionary of American History,* notes entitled "The Inquiry" and dated March 8, 1939.
51. Letter, Mark Jefferson to Isaiah Bowman, July 5, 1919 (p.p. M.J.).
52. Letter, Isaiah Bowman to Mark Jefferson, July 24, 1919 (p.p. M.J.).
53. James Berton Rhoads, "Preliminary Inventories," *Cartographic Records of the American Commission to Negotiate Peace,* No. 68, National Archives, 1954.
54. Letter, Secretary of French Delegation to J. C. Grew, American Delegation, February 2, 1919 (in French-American Delegation Bureau translation) (p.p. M.J.).
55. Letter, Mark Jefferson to Phoebe Jefferson, February 25, 1919 (p.p. M.J.).
56. Typed notes: "Geography Commission," Inquiry Document No. 181-1901/1, National Archives.
57. "Mark Jefferson '84 since leaving Boston University," pp. 7-8, of unpublished manuscript of nine pages.
58. *Recueil Des Actes De La Conference,* Partie IV, Commissions de la Conference, B Questions Generales, 9 Commission de Geographie, Paris Imprimerie Nationale, 1932, pp. 1-86.
59. See: The personal papers of Mark Jefferson.
60. Memorandum, Grew to Herter, Inquiry Document No. 181.19/15, May 12, 1919, National Archives.
61. Mark Jefferson, *Paris Peace Conference Diary,* Thursday, May 8, pp. 96 and 98 (p.p. M.J.).
62. Mark Jefferson, *Paris Peace Conference Diary,* entry for Saturday, April 5, 1919, pp. 196-197 (p.p. M.J.).
63. Letter, Mark Jefferson to Phoebe Jefferson, March 30, 1919 (p.p. P.J.).
64. Letter, Charles Seymour to G. J. Martin, November 14, 1961.
65. Letter, Mark Jefferson to "Will," April 7, 1931 (p.p. M.J.).
66. Letter, The Commissioners of the American Commission to Negotiate Peace to Mark Jefferson, May 31, 1919 (p.p. M.J.).
67. Letter, Mark Jefferson to Phoebe Jefferson, May 26, 1919 (p.p. P.J.).
68. "A Song of Victory," pp. 1-2 (p.p. M.J.).
69. Memorandum on the Russian German Boundary as established by the Treaty of Brest-Litovsk, pp. 221-222. *Texts of the Russian "Peace" 1918.*
70. Unpublished manuscript, revision of sections of "Geography for Grownups," pp. 1, 2, 3 and 7. (p.p. M.J.).

CHAPTER NINE

1. Letter, Isaiah Bowman to Mark Jefferson, February 12, 1925 (p.p. M.J.).
2. Unpublished notes by Mark Jefferson (p.p. M.J.).
3. "The Civilizing Rails," *Economic Geography,* IV, No. 3, July 1928, pp. 217-231.
4. Letter, Mark Jefferson to Isaiah Bowman, April 29, 1928 (p.p. M.J.).
5. Letter, Mark Jefferson to Isaiah Bowman, March 11, 1928 (p.p. M.J.).
6. Letter, Mark Jefferson to Isaiah Bowman, March 7, 1928 (p.p. M.J.).
7. Letter, Isaiah Bowman to Mark Jefferson, March 9, 1928 (A.G.S. archives).
8. Mark Jefferson, Notebook, "South Atlantic Coastal Plain" (p.p. M.J.).
9. "The Culture of the Nations," *Bulletin of the A.G.S.,* XLIII, No. 4, April, 1911, pp. 241-265.

10. "The Culture of the Nations," Annual Meeting of the A.A.G., Pittsburgh, 1910. "The Geographic Distribution of Culture in the U.S.A.," Annual Meeting of the A.A.G., New Haven, 1912.
11. E. Huntington, *Civilization and Climate,* Yale University Press, 1915, p. 188, p. 192.
12. Letter, Mark Jefferson to Ella Wilson, February 15, 1926 (p.p. M.J.).
13. Letter, Mark Jefferson to Ella Wilson, March 7, 1926 (p.p. M.J.).
14. Exercise from notebook "South Atlantic Coastal Plain." (p.p. M.J.).
15. Letter, Mark Jefferson to R. Harper, February 25, 1926 (p.p. M.J.).
16. Letter, Mark Jefferson to R. Clyde Ford, March 7, 1926 (p.p. M.J.).
17. Letter, Mark Jefferson to Ella Wilson, February 5, 1926 (p.p. M.J.).
18. M. Aurousseau, *Highway into Spain,* Peter Davies Ltd., London, 1930.
19. These reports are with the personal papers of Mark Jefferson.
20. Letter, M. Aurousseau to Mark Jefferson, September 15, 1926, p. 16 (p.p. M.J.).
21. Letter, M. Aurousseau to Mark Jefferson, September 15, 1926, p. 6 (p.p. M.J.).
22. Letter, W. S. Smyth to Mark Jefferson, September 7, 1928 (p.p. M.J.).

CHAPTER TEN

1. "The Distribution of People in South America," *Bulletin of the Geographical Society of Philadelphia,* July 1907, pp. 1-11.
2. The abstract was not published in *The International Catalogue of Scientific Literature.* An extended note on the article appeared in the *Geographical Journal,* XXXI, No. 2, February 1908, pp. 220-221.
3. *Annals of the Association of American Geographers,* I, 1911, pp. 101-111.
4. *Teachers Geography,* 3rd edition, 1911, pp. 7-8, 10-11.
5. "Where Men Live in North America," *Western Journal of Education,* I, No. 2, February 1908, pp. 78-85.
6. The abstract was unpublished (p.p. M.J.).
7. "Man in West Norway," Presidential Address, Michigan Academy of Science, *Tenth Annual Report,* April 1908, pp. 23-29; also *Journal of Geography,* VII, No. 4, December 1908, pp. 86-96.
8. Unpublished manuscript (p.p. M.J.).
9. *Teachers Geography; Man in Europe; Principles of Geography; Exercises in Human Geography.*
10. "Man's Distribution Over the Earth," *The Educational Bi-Monthly,* June 1909, (pages unnumbered).
11. "Plains," *The New Practical Reference Library,* Ed. Charles Herbert Sylvester, 6 vols. (5 vols. A-Z and Educator Vol.); Hanson Bellows Co., 1914.
12. *Man in Europe,* 1924, 1926, 1936.
13. Abstract, "The Anthropography of Great Cities," *Annals of the Association of American Geographers,* I, (Baltimore, 1908), 1911, p. 114.
14. Letter, Mark Jefferson to Chauncy Harris, April 17, 1940 (p.p. M.J.).
15. Letter, Ellsworth Huntington to Mark Jefferson, January 7, 1909 (p.p. M.J.).
16. Letter, Cyrus C. Adams to Mark Jefferson, January 8, 1909 (p.p. M.J.).
17. Letter, Mark Jefferson to Cyrus C. Adams, January 11, 1909 (p.p. M.J.).
18. "The Anthropography of Some Great Cities. A Study in Distribution of Population," *Bulletin of the American Geographical Society,* XLI, No. 9, 1909, pp. 537-566.
19. *Geography in the Twentieth Century,* Ed Griffith Taylor, Philosophical Library, New York, 1953.
20. Griffith Taylor, *Urban Geography,* E. P. Dutton & Co., 1946, p. 173.
21. Letter, A. P. Brigham to Mark Jefferson, October 9, 1909 (p.p. M.J.).
22. *Bulletin of the American Geographical Society,* XLII, No. 10, October 1910, pp. 778-779.
23. "New York and the Four Next Largest American Cities in 1910," *Bulletin of the American Geographical Society,* XLII, No. 10, October 1910, p. 778.

24. *Annals of the Association of American Geographers*, II, 1912, p. 107.
25. "The Anthropography of North America," *Bulletin of the American Geographical Society*, XLV, No. 3, March 1913, pp. 161-180.
26. "A New Density of Population Map of Europe," *Bulletin of the American Geographical Society*, XLV, No. 9, September 1913, pp. 667-670.
27. *Petermann's Mitteilungen*, LIX, No. 1, 1913, pp. 7-11 with two plates.
28. "A New Density of Population Map of Europe," *Bulletin of the American Geographical Society*, XLV, No. 9, September 1913, p. 667.
29. "A Hopeful View of the Urban Problem," *Atlantic Monthly*, 112, No. 3, September 1913, pp. 353-358.
30. Unpublished abstract (p.p. M.J.).
31. "A Hopeful View of the Urban Problem," *Atlantic Monthly*, 112, No. 3, September 1913, pp. 354-355.
32. "The Lyons Exhibit," *The Outlook Magazine*, September 27, 1913, p. 160.
33. Abstract, "The Growth of American Cities," *Annals of the Association of American Geographers*, IV, 1914, p. 141.
34. *Bulletin of the American Geographical Society*, XLVI, No. 6, 1914, pp. 401-413.
35. Unpublished abstract (p.p. M.J.).
36. "The Revolution and the Mexican Plateau," *Bulletin of the American Geographical Society*, XLVI, No. 6, June 1914, pp. 436-437.
37. Unpublished abstract (p.p. M.J.).
38. Anonymous—written by staff member of the American Geographical Society, *Geographical Review*, III, January 1917, pp. 16-27.
39. *Bulletin of the American Geographical Society*, XLVII, 1915, pp. 19-37.
40. Isaiah Bowman, *Supplement to the New World: Problems in Political Geography*, Yonkers-on-Hudson, New York: World Book Company, 1923, p. 29.
41. *Annals of the Association of American Geographers*, V, 1915, p. 140.
42. *Man in the United States*, Ann Arbor, Michigan: Edwards Bros., 1933, p. 20.
43. *Geographical Review*, II, No. 5, November 1916, pp. 368-372.
44. *Annales de Geographie*, XXVI, No. 140, March 15, 1917, pp. 151-152.
45. *Geographical Review*, IV, No. 4, October 1917, p. 320.
46. Letter, Mark Jefferson to Isaiah Bowman, October 17, 1916 (p.p. M.J.).
47. "Some Considerations on the Geographical Provinces of the U.S.A. 1916," *Annals of the Association of American Geographers*, VII, 1917, pp. 3-15, plates I & II.
48. Ellsworth Huntington, Abstract, *Annals of the Association of American Geographers*, IV, 1914, p. 139.
49. *Geography in the Twentieth Century*, Ed. Griffith Taylor, 1951, p. 501.
50. Griffith Taylor, *Urban Geography*, p. 173.
51. "Mark Jefferson 1863-1949," *Annals of the Association of American Geographers*, XXXIX, No. 4, December 1949, p. 310.
52. *Bulletin of the American Geographical Society*, XLI, No. 9, September 1909.
53. Letter, Mark Jefferson to Isaiah Bowman, November 3, 1915 (p.p. M.J.).
54. *The Geographical Review*, IV, No. 5, November 1917, pp. 387-394.
55. See: Isaiah Bowman, *The New World*, 1924, Chapter II, Problems of Imperial Britain, p. 18.
56. Many of these original maps are with the personal papers of Mark Jefferson. Others of these are deposited with the National Archives, Washington, D.C., and the Seymour Peace Collection, Yale University.
57. Letter, Sten de Geer to Mark Jefferson, June 8, 1922 and August 16, 1922 (p.p. M.J.).
58. *Geografiska Annaler*, IX, 1927, pp. 233-359.
59. *Geographical Review*, XVIII, No. 4, October 1928, p. 690.
60. Letter, Sten de Geer to Mark Jefferson, October 7, 1922 (p.p. M.J.).
61. *Geographical Review*, XI, No. 3, July 1921, pp. 437-441.
62. The Ypsilanti Publishing Co., 1924. A printed folder enclosing three maps.
63. *Geographical Review*, XXIII, No. 1, January 1933, pp. 90-100.
64. *Geographical Review*, XXXI, No. 3, July 1941, pp. 479-487.

65. "Great Cities of the United States, 1920," *Geographical Review*, XI, No. 3, July 1921, pp. 437-441.
66. *The Distribution of People in the U.S. in 1910—As Indicated by the Distribution of the Cities*, pages unnumbered, Ypsilanti Publishing Co., 1924.
67. Letter, J. Russell Smith to Mark Jefferson, October 2, 1928 (p.p. M.J.).
68. *Geographical Review*, XXIV, No. 4, October 1934, pp. 634-637.
69. *Geographical Review*, XXV, No. 2, April 1935, pp. 332-333.
70. *New York Times*, January 16, 1933, p. 14, col. 2.
71. Letter, Mark Jefferson to Isaiah Bowman, May 9, 1924 (p.p. M.J.). *N.B.* In a letter, C. E. Batschelet to G. J. Martin, October 19, 1962, Batschelet wrote, "I regret to state that the files (of the Bureau of the Census) covering the period in question, that is, the twenties, have been destroyed . . ."
72. Letter, Isaiah Bowman to Mark Jefferson, May 14, 1924 (p.p. M.J.).
73. Letter, Mark Jefferson to Nevin Fenneman, May 16, 1924 (p.p. M.J.).
74. Letter, Mark Jefferson to Isaiah Bowman, May 16, 1924 (p.p. M.J.).
75. Letter, Isaiah Bowman to Mark Jefferson, May 20, 1924 (p.p. M.J.).
76. *Geographical Review*, XV, No. 2, April 1925, pp. 177-189.
77. Telegram, Gladys Wrigley to Mark Jefferson, February 11, 1925 (p.p. M.J.).
78. *Geographical Review*, XVI, No. 2, April 1926, p. 300.
79. Letter, A. W. Pezet to Mark Jefferson, April 30, 1925 (p.p. M.J.).
80. Quoted in a letter, Mark Jefferson to Isaiah Bowman, September 4, 1928 (p.p. M.J.).
81. *Annals of the Association of American Geographers*, XV, 1925, p. 39.
82. "Looking Back at Malthus," *Geographical Review*, XV, No. 2, April 1925, p. 182.
83. *Globen*, No. 3, March 1927, pp. 23-24.
84. *The Michigan State Normal College Catalogue*, 1931, p. 41. (E.M.U. Archives).
85. *Geographical Review*, XXI, No. 3, July 1931, pp. 446-465. See particularly p. 453. For independent confirmation see: Robert E. Dickinson, *City and Region*, Routledge and Kegan Paul, 1964, p. 49.
86. For the map (six-six projection) see: "The Six-Six World Map; Giving Larger, Better Continents," *Annals of the Association of American Geographers*, XX, No. 1, March 1930, pp. 1-6, April 1931, No. 2.
87. *Geographical Review*, XXI, No. 2, April 1931, p. 306.
88. "The Distribution of Urbanization," *Annals of the Association of American Geographers*, XXI, June 1931, p. 126.
89. Letter, Mark Jefferson to Isaiah Bowman, July 15, 1931 (p.p. M.J.).
90. Letter, John Finley to Isaiah Bowman, July 11, 1931 (p.p. M.J.).
91. *Geographical Review*, XXII, 1932, p. 305.
92. Letter, Mark Jefferson to Gladys Wrigley, January 27, 1934 (p.p. M.J.).
93. Letter, Mark Jefferson to Gladys Wrigley, January 29, 1934 (p.p. M.J.).
94. "The Problem of the Ecumene: The Case of Canada," *Geografiska Annaler*, November 1934, pp. 146-158.
95. "The Problem of the Ecumene: The Case of Canada," *Geografiska Annaler*, November 1934, p. 148.
96. *Geographical Review*, XXVI, No. 1, January 1936, p. 151.
97. *Annals of the Association of American Geographers*, XXIV, 1934, p. 57.
98. *Geographical Review*, XXVI, No. 1, January 1936, pp. 148-149.
99. *Annals of the Association of American Geographers*, XXIX, No. 1, March 1939, pp. 78-79.
100. *New York Times*, December 30, 1938, p. 1, col. 2.
101. *The Times*, January 11, 1939, p. 13, col. 4.
102. *The Times*, January 11, 1939, p. 11, col. 4.
103. *Normal College News*, XXXVI, No. 12, January 5, 1939, p. 1.
104. *Normal College News*, XXXVI, No. 18, February 16, 1939, p. 4.
105. *Normal College News*, XXXVI, No. 19, February 23, 1939, p. 1.
106. *Normal College News*, XXXVI, No. 20, March 2, 1939, p. 2.
107. *Geographical Review*, XXIX, No. 2, April 1939, p. 315.

108. *Geographical Review,* XXIX, No. 2, April 1939, pp. 226-232.
109. Gladys Wrigley, "Adventures in Serendipity," *Geographical Review,* XLII, No. 4, October 1952, pp. 527-528.
110. "The Law of the Primate City," *Geographical Review,* XXIX, No. 2, April 1939, p. 226.
111. "The Culture of the Nations," *Bulletin of the American Geographical Society,* XLIII, No. 4, April 1911, pp. 241-265.
112. p.p. M.J., Ypsilanti.
113. *Annals of the Association of American Geographers,* XXXII, March 1942, No. 1, pp. 1-67.

CHAPTER ELEVEN

1. All the letters quoted in this chapter are from the personal papers of Mark Jefferson.
2. For this period several letters from Bowman to Jefferson exist. Those from Jefferson to Bowman have not been found.
3. Letter, C. J. Robertson to G. J. Martin, March 23, 1963.
4. *Geographical Review,* XLII, No. 4, October, 1952, p. 534.
5. Letter, Daniel Marsh to Mark Jefferson, May 16, 1934 (p.p. M.J.).

CHAPTER TWELVE

1. Letter, George Cressey to Mark Jefferson, April 10, 1941 (p.p. M.J.).
2. Letter, Mark Jefferson to Isaiah Bowman, October 2, 1937 (Robert Bowman Archives).
3. Letter, Mark Jefferson to Mrs. Caroline Atherton, March 25, 1941 (p.p. M.J.).
4. Letter, Mark Jefferson to Phoebe Jefferson, December 15, 1940 (p.p. M.J.).
5. Letter, Mark Jefferson to S. S. Visher, December 18, 1940 (p.p. M.J.).
6. Letter, Farrer and Rinehart Publishing Company to Mark Jefferson, April 7, 1943 (p.p. M.J.).
7. Note attached to letter, Farrer and Rinehart Publishing Company to Mark Jefferson, April 7, 1943 (p.p. M.J.).
8. Untitled Manuscript of 112 pages (p.p. M.J.).
9. Letter, Mark Jefferson to Caroline Atherton, February 18, 1944 (p.p. M.J.).
10. Letter, Mark Jefferson to Barbara Jefferson, December 24, 1946 (p.p. M.J.).
11. Letter, Mark Jefferson to Phoebe Jefferson, May 7, 1944 (p.p. M.J.).
12. Letter, Mark Jefferson to Carl Friedrich, November 21, 1940 (p.p. M.J.).
13. *Harvard College Class of Ninety-Seven Fiftieth Anniversary Report,* Cambridge, 1947, pp. 345-353.
14. Autobiographical essay, pp. 13-14 (p.p. M.J.).
15. Letter, Mark Jefferson to Gladys Wrigley, November 14, 1943 (A.G.S. archives).
16. Letter, Mark Jefferson to Senator Ferguson, December 28, 1948 (p.p. M.J.).
17. Letter, Mark Jefferson to Hon. Secretary of Defense, April 26, 1949 (p.p. M.J.).
18. Letter, Mark Jefferson to George Cressey, February 19, 1940 (p.p. M.J.).
19. Letter, Mark Jefferson to Charles Brooks, November 30, 1947 (p.p. M.J.).
20. Letter, Alfred Meyer to Mark Jefferson, November 19, 1948 (p.p. M.J.).
21. Letter, Mark Jefferson to Alfred Meyer, November 26, 1948 (p.p. M.J.).
22. Letter, Mark Jefferson to Chauncy Harris, July 14, 1948 (p.p. M.J.).
23. Notes by Mark Jefferson entitled, "To the Committee in charge of the May Centennial, May 3, 1949." (E.M.U. Archives).

CHAPTER THIRTEEN

1. Charles Colby, "Mark Jefferson as a Geographer," 550 word statement to G. J. Martin, April 11, 1960.
2. *American Men of Science, A Biographical Directory,* The Science Press, Ed., J. McKeen Cattell, New York, 1906, p. 364.
3. G. B. Roorbach, "The Trend of Modern Geography; A Symposium," *Bulletin of the American Geographical Society,* XLVI, No. 2, November 1914, pp. 801-817.
4. "The Nature of Geography," March 1931, Mark Jefferson's reply to a questionnaire by A. E. Parkins requesting geographers' definitions of the nature of geography.
5. *The Aurora,* Michigan State Normal College Yearbook, 1924, p. 47 (E.M.U. archives).
6. Letter, Mark Jefferson to Roger Greeley, undated circa 1940.
7. Letter, Mark Jefferson to Caroline Atherton, May 30, 1941 (p.p. M.J.).
8. "Limiting Width of Meander Belts," *National Geographic Magazine,* XIII, No. 10, October 1902, pp. 373-384.
9. "The Anthropography of Some Great Cities; A Study in Distribution of Population," *Bulletin of the American Geographical Society,* XLI, No. 9, September 1909, pp. 537-566.
10. "A Plea for Anglicized Place-Names," *Journal of Geography,* IX, No. 2, October 1910, pp. 43-45.
11. "The Culture of the Nations," *Bulletin of the American Geographical Society,* XLIII, No. 4, April 1911, pp. 241-265.
12. *Commercial Values; An Atlas of Raw Materials of Commerce and Commercial Interchanges,* Ginn and Company, Boston 1912, p. 64.
13. *Notes on the Geography of Europe,* Ypsilanti, 1917, p. 55.
14. "The Civilizing Rails," *Economic Geography,* IV, No. 3, July 1928, pp. 217-231. Reprinted *Journal of the Michigan Schoolmasters Club,* XXX, No. 22, December 1928, pp. 119-132.
15. "The Six-Six World Map; Giving Larger, Better Continents," *Annals of the Association of American Geographers,* XX, No. 1, March 1930, pp. 274-277.
16. "The Problem of the Ecumene; The Case of Canada," *Geografiska Annaler,* 1934, pp. 146-158.
17. "The Law of the Primate City," *Geographical Review,* XXIX, No. 2, April 1939, pp. 226-232.
18. "Among the reviewers the 'big four' were Bowman, Jefferson, Davis and Ward." J. K. Wright, *Geography in the Making: The American Geographical Society, 1851-1951,* p. 295.
19. See: The personal papers of Isaiah Bowman (archives of Robert Bowman, Lincoln, Nebraska).
20. Letter, S. W. Boggs to Mark Jefferson, June 10, 1929 (p.p. M.J.).
21. Letter, C. C. Burkhard to Mark Jefferson, December 9, 1927 (p.p. M.J.).
22. Letter, Helen Strong to Mark Jefferson, August 31, 1926 (p.p. M.J.).
23. Letter, M. R. Campbell to Mark Jefferson, undated but early March 1926 (p.p. M.J.).
24. Ellsworth Huntington, "The Climate of the Historic Past. Part II. The New World.", *Monthly Weather Review,* Annual Summary 1908, XXXVI, No. 13, pp. 446-450.
25. Ellsworth Huntington, *Civilization and Climate,* Yale University Press, New Haven, 1915, pp. 188-189.
26. C. C. Huntington and F. Carlson, *Environmental Basis of Social Geography,* Preface vii, New York, Prentice-Hall, Inc., 1929.
27. Jean Brunhes, *Human Geography,* Translated by T. C. Le Compte, Eds.

Isaiah Bowman and R. Dodge, Rand McNally, New York, 1920, pp. 72-73, 178, 196, 389, 401. Also confirmed by G. J. Martin in an interview with Madame Jean-Brunhes Delamarre, (daughter of Jean Brunhes) Paris, France, August 1964.

28. Jean Brunhes and Camille Vallaux, *La Géographie de l'Histoire,* Librairie Felix Alcan, Paris, 1921, pp. 264-265.

29. Sten de Geer. *Manniskans och Naringslivets Geografi,* Stockholm, 1928, pp. 101-103.

30. Letter, Ivo Rubic to Mark Jefferson, June 20, 1947 (p.p. M.J.).

31. Isaiah Bowman, "A Typical Case of Stream Capture in Michigan," *Journal of Geology,* XII, May-June 1904, pp. 326-334. Isaiah Bowman, "Deflection of the Mississippi," *Science,* XX(N.S.), 1904, pp. 273-274.

32. Isaiah Bowman, *The Pioneer Fringe,* The American Geographical Society, Special Publication No. 13, 1931, Chapter 6, "Railways as Pioneers", pp. 64-75.

33. J. R. Smith, *Commerce and Industry,* Henry Holt and Company, New York, 1925, pp. 8-11, 32.

34. L. E. Klimm, O. P. Starkey, M. F. Hall, *Introductory Economic Geography,* Harcourt, Brace and Company, New York, 1937, pp. 284-285, p. 291.

35. D. H. Davis, *The Earth and Man,* Preface viii, The Macmillan Company, New York, 1942.

INDEX